LET'S GO:

CENTRAL AMERICA

is the best book for anyone traveling on a budget. Here's why:

■ No other guidebook has as many budget listings.

In Central America we list over 5,000 budget travel bargains. We tell you the cheapest way to get around, and where to get an inexpensive and satisfying meal once you've arrived. We give hundreds of money-saving tips that anyone can use, plus invaluable advice on discounts and deals for students, children, families, and senior travelers.

■ Let's Go researchers have to make it on their own.

Our Harvard-Radcliffe researcher-writers travel on budgets as tight as your own—no expense accounts, no free hotel rooms.

■ Let's Go is completely revised each year.

We don't just update the prices, we go back to the place. If a charming café has become an overpriced tourist trap, we'll replace the listing with a new and better one.

■ No other guidebook includes all this:

Honest, engaging coverage of both the cities and the countryside; up-to-the-minute prices, directions, addresses, phone numbers, and opening hours; in-depth essays on local culture, history, and politics; comprehensive listings on transportation between and within regions and cities; straight advice on work and study, budget accommodations, sights, nightlife, and food; detailed city and regional maps; and much more.

■ Let's Go is for anyone who wants to see Central America on a budget.

LET'S GO PUBLICATIONS

Let's Go: Alaska & The Pacific Northwest
Let's Go: Britain & Ireland
Let's Go: California
Let's Go: Central America
Let's Go: Eastern Europe
Let's Go: Europe
Let's Go: France
Let's Go: Germany
Let's Go: Greece & Turkey
Let's Go: Ireland
Let's Go: Israel & Egypt
Let's Go: Italy
Let's Go: London
Let's Go: Mexico
Let's Go: New York City
Let's Go: Paris
Let's Go: Rome
Let's Go: Southeast Asia
Let's Go: Spain & Portugal
Let's Go: Switzerland & Austria
Let's Go: USA
Let's Go: Washington, D.C.

Map Guides (coming March 1996)

Let's Go: Boston
Let's Go: London
Let's Go: New York City
Let's Go: Paris
Let's Go: San Francisco
Let's Go: Washington, D.C.

LET'S GO

The Budget Guide to

CENTRAL AMERICA 1996

Charles R. Kapelke
Editor

Alexander Travelli
Associate Editor

MACMILLAN

HELPING LET'S GO

If you want to share your discoveries, suggestions, or corrections, please drop us a line. We read every piece of correspondence, whether a postcard, a 10-page e-mail, or a coconut. All suggestions are passed along to our researcher-writers. Please note that mail received after May 1996 may be too late for the 1997 book, but will be retained for the following edition.

Address mail to:

Let's Go: Central America
Let's Go, Inc.
One Story Street
Cambridge, MA 02138
USA

Send e-mail to:

fanmail@letsgo.com
Subject: "Let's Go: Central America"

Visit Let's Go at:

http://www.letsgo.com/

In addition to the invaluable travel advice our readers share with us, many are kind enough to offer their services as researchers or editors. Unfortunately, the charter of Let's Go, Inc. enables us to employ only currently enrolled Harvard-Radcliffe students.

Published in Great Britain 1996 by Macmillan Reference Books, a division of Macmillan Publishers Limited, 25 Eccleston Place, London SW1W 9NF and Basingstoke

10 9 8 7 6 5 4 3 2 1

Map revisions pp. 55, 201, 257, 267, 316-317, 331 by Let's Go, Inc.

Published in the United States of America by St. Martin's Press, Inc.

ISBN: 0 333 65291 6

Let's Go: Central America is written by Let's Go Publications, 1 Story Street, Cambridge, MA 02138, USA.

Contents

Maps

About Let's Go

THIRTY-SIX YEARS OF WISDOM

Back in 1960, a few students at Harvard University banded together to produce a 20-page pamphlet offering a collection of tips on budget travel in Europe. This modest, mimeographed packet was offered to passengers as an extra on their student charter flights to Europe. The following year, students traveling to Europe researched the first full-fledged edition of *Let's Go: Europe*, a pocket-sized book featuring irreverent write-ups of sights and a decidedly youthful slant. Throughout the 60s, our guides reflected the times; one section of the 1968 *Let's Go: Europe* discussed "Street Singing in Europe on No Dollars a Day," which we said "has very little to do with music." The 1969 guide to America led off with sound advice on San Francisco's Haight-Ashbury ("dig the scene"). During the 70s and 80s, we gradually added regional and city guides, and expanded coverage into the Middle East, Central America, and Asia.

We've seen a lot in 36 years. *Let's Go: Europe* is now the world's best-selling international guide, translated into seven languages. And our guides are still researched, written, and produced entirely by students who know first-hand how to see the world on the cheap. As the budget travel world expands, so does Let's Go. The first editions of *Let's Go: Central America* and *Let's Go: Southeast Asia* hit the shelves this year, and *Let's Go: India & Nepal* is right on their heels. Our useful new series of map guides combine concise city coverage with vivid fold-out maps. Our new guides bring our total number of titles, with their spirit of adventure and their honesty, accuracy, and editorial integrity, to 28.

HOW WE DO IT

Each guide is completely revised and updated every year by a well-traveled set of 200 students, who work on all aspects of each guide's development. Every winter, we recruit over 110 researchers and 50 editors to write our books anew. After several months of training, Researcher-Writers hit the road for seven weeks of exploration, from Anchorage to Ankara, Estonia to El Salvador, Iceland to Indonesia. Those hired possess a rare combination of budget travel sense, writing ability, stamina, and courage. Train strikes, stolen luggage, food poisoning, and irate tourist officials are all part of a day's work. Editors work from spring to fall, massaging copy written on Himalayan bus rides into witty yet informative prose. A student staff of typesetters, cartographers, publicists, and managers keeps our lively and sophisticated team together. In September, the collected efforts of the summer are delivered to our printer, who turns them into books in record time. And even as you read this, work on next year's editions is well underway.

WHY WE DO IT

At Let's Go, our goal is to give you a great vacation. We don't think of budget travel as the last recourse of the destitute; we believe that it's the only way to travel. Living cheaply and simply brings you closer to the real people and places you've been saving up to visit. Our book will ease your anxieties and answer your questions about the basics—to help you get off the beaten track and explore. Once you learn the ropes, we encourage you to put Let's Go away now and then to strike out on your own. As any seasoned traveler will tell you, the best discoveries are often those you make yourself. When you find something worth sharing, drop us a line. We're Let's Go Publications, One Story Street, Cambridge, MA 02138, USA (e-mail: LetsGoşdelphi.com).

HAPPY TRAVELS!

Acknowledgments

Persistently psyched, delightfully deadpan, and constantly composed, T-bone Tim P. proffered body and soul every stage along the way. Ultra-special thanks to Jay R. for busting his guts, and to Fabian and Chris for a primo, pithy peninsula. "Hyper Type" Hannah B. ruled, as did Sam the Mapster. Thanks to Mike F. and R.I. Wilson for inspiration and aid, and to Cindy S., James B., Katie G., Lisa H., Nadim S., Nat R., Steve J., Timur H., ABBA, and Camel Joe for last-second marvels. Gracias to Joy Somberg and Karlene Rosera, interns extraordinaire, and to all others who helped—**C&A**

Summer's highlight was getting to know Aloysius TRAVELli, whose halcyon, hilarious company and sapid work found and changed me (cannot be undone). Thanks forever to all in the office, especially Dan O' Doom, Veranda Haneen and Krzysz, Jolly James, and Merry Michelle; to Tadd, Zac(h)s, and the Hehh guys; the posse in the Library Suite; Lisa D. and her flicks; The Paschotta Twins; the Cedar St. Boyz; and Tara and Mr. P, for love, laughs, and happy (To)days. Most of all, thanks to Mom, Dad, Grammy, Grandpa, Peter, Randy, Rita, Ian, and summer's joy, Anabel—**CRK**

Thanks above and beyond all reasoning to Chacapelci, the oft-depicted Maya god of editorial power and verbal verve; Chuck made more than one staffer's summer indoors an infinitely sunnier experience. Tristanne especially, Katie, James, and the Hot Room all glowed along sweetly. And to the Broadway-Dana Rose contingent, old, new, and honorary: Dave, Chicu, Cesca, Alp, T. again, D, Erik, Ben, Priya. And to our Ithaca hosts Ravi, Rich, Jimmy, and hell, to LL Nunn and other friends, hiding behind haybales. To Mom and Dad, Cam and Andrew, whom I've missed—**AHT**

Researcher-Writers

Samuel Brown *Belize, Honduras*

Each day of Sam's itinerary brought fresh growth to his beard, as well as to his collection of outstanding adventures. When he wasn't swinging bridges in Belize, sighin' for Mayan ruins, contemplating the sunburn on his kneecaps, staring at cool trees, snorkelling his way to boundless psychedelia, or charming the many *quates* (friends) he made along the way, Super Sam was a man on a mission. His excellent research paid off in subtle, quirky humor and mind-bendingly thorough copy, work that left him just enough spunk to bound off to Russia right after getting home!

Judith E. Dutton *Guatemala*

Gushing with gleeful gusto and gutsy to the extreme, Judy blew through Guatemala completely undaunted. A keen eye for detail and vibrant, vivid writing helped her to completely capture every place she visited; her unique flair and adulturated *Judyness* left us in constant awe. We relished hearing from her—that is, when she wasn't too busy hunting giant rodents, running cost-benefit analyses on her dredlocks, or nursing a sore behind after the hellish "joyride" to Tikal—a trip so unbearable that only our Ms. Dutton could have opted for a repeat after the job had ended.

Thomas Locke Hobbs *Western Guatemala, El Salvador*

By offering a whole pack of cigs to the shrine of Maximón, the Guatemalan god of good-times, Thomas guaranteed that his pioneering research in El Salvador would be simple-*Simón.* Neither whipping around hairpins on the tops of buses, nor standing face to face with a corpse, nor a severe dearth of Salvadoran podiatrists, nor even the country's street-layouts (whew!) managed to faze him in the end. With a shiny FMLN t-shirt in hand, T.L.'s solid fact-finding and valiant yen to explore sent the series' coverage of El Salvador off to a flying leap in the right direction.

Paul "Pogen" MacNeilage *Nicaragua, Northwest Costa Rica*

Pogen was a little bummed not to have met Rufino, ruler of Nicaragua's Rama tribe, but we think the Chief missed out on something, too. Moving from Nica to Tico, Pablo showed clarity, diligence, and out-of-control, hilariously bone-dry jokes that could only have come from a man drinking as much kick-ass coffee as he was. After handling a hostile hold-up with characteristic grace ("It was sort of annoying"), Pogen proved his skills as Viewmaster (3-D) of Nicaragua before finally "settling in" on a bungee-cord and surf-board on Costa Rica's Nicoya Peninsula. Wazoo, Pogio.

Orit Alcalay Sarfaty *Southwest Costa Rica, Panama*

Orit's kind demeanor, ever-attentive ears, and one swift karate-kick were just enough for her to master Panama in a single, first-time wallop (though only after waiting around in Costa Rica for a *lot* of buses, which probably still haven't arrived). Meanwhile, keeping kosher was never easier than in Bocas del Toro, where magical mango trees, melty sun, and a few frothy brews transported Orit beyond paradise. Her *chutzpah*-packed copy and insightful observations kept us thoroughly entertained, almost as much as did the rad *mola* oven-mits she brought home afterward.

Katherine Unterman *Costa Rica*

Katie loved Costa Rica, and Costa Rica loved Katie; we couldn't have asked anything more from the fruit of the happy couple's union. During her itinerary, Unterman the Überwoman truly did garner a sizeable fan-club of travelers and *ticos,* most of whom marvelled at her proclivity for starting raucous, mutinous, *guaro*-heavy parties (with plenty of *pitufos* to go around); others were partial to her exploits with cow's tongue and snake farms. We might just be Katie's biggest devotees, for her 110% effort, rock-solid research, and most of all, for her cheerful spirit.

Chris Baker *Yucatán Peninsula*

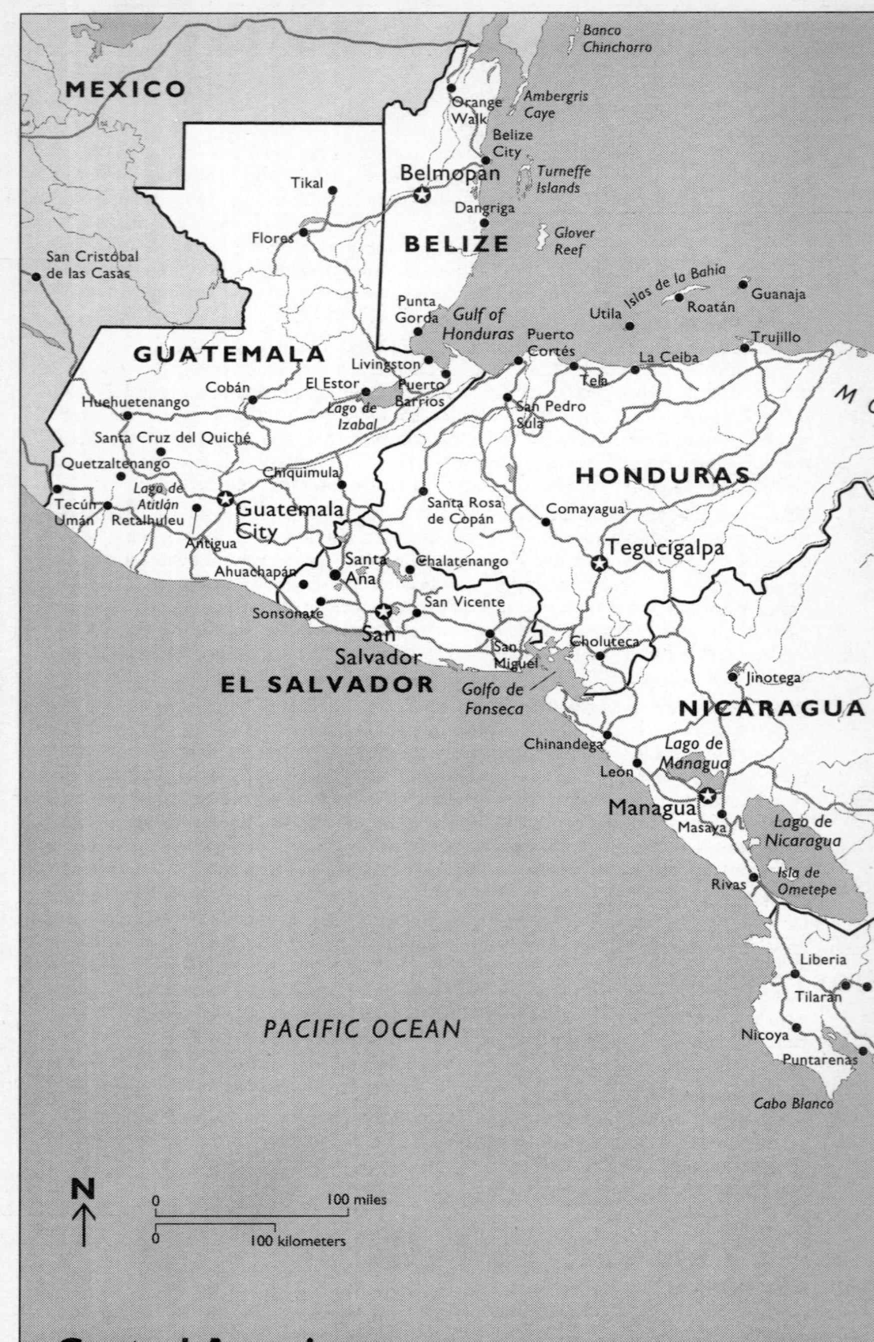
Banco Chinchorro
MEXICO
Orange Walk
Ambergris Caye
Belize City
Belmopan
Turneffe Islands
Tikal
Dangriga
Flores
BELIZE
Glover Reef
San Cristóbal de las Casas
Islas de la Bahía
Guanaja
Roatán
Utila
Punta Gorda
Gulf of Honduras
Puerto Cortés
Trujillo
GUATEMALA
Livingston
La Ceiba
Tela
Cobán
El Estor
Puerto Barrios
Lago de Izabal
San Pedro Sula
Huehuetenango
Santa Cruz del Quiché
Quetzaltenango
Chiquimula
HONDURAS
Lago de Atitlán
Tecún Umán
Retalhuleu
Guatemala City
Santa Rosa de Copán
Comayagua
Antigua
Tegucigalpa
Ahuachapán
Santa Ana
Chalatenango
San Vicente
Sonsonate
San Salvador
San Miguel
Choluteca
EL SALVADOR
Golfo de Fonseca
Jinotega
NICARAGUA
Chinandega
Lago de Managua
León
Managua
Masaya
Lago de Nicaragua
Isla de Ometepe
Rivas
Liberia
Tilarán
Nicoya
Puntarenas
Cabo Blanco
PACIFIC OCEAN
N
0
100 miles
0
100 kilometers
Central America

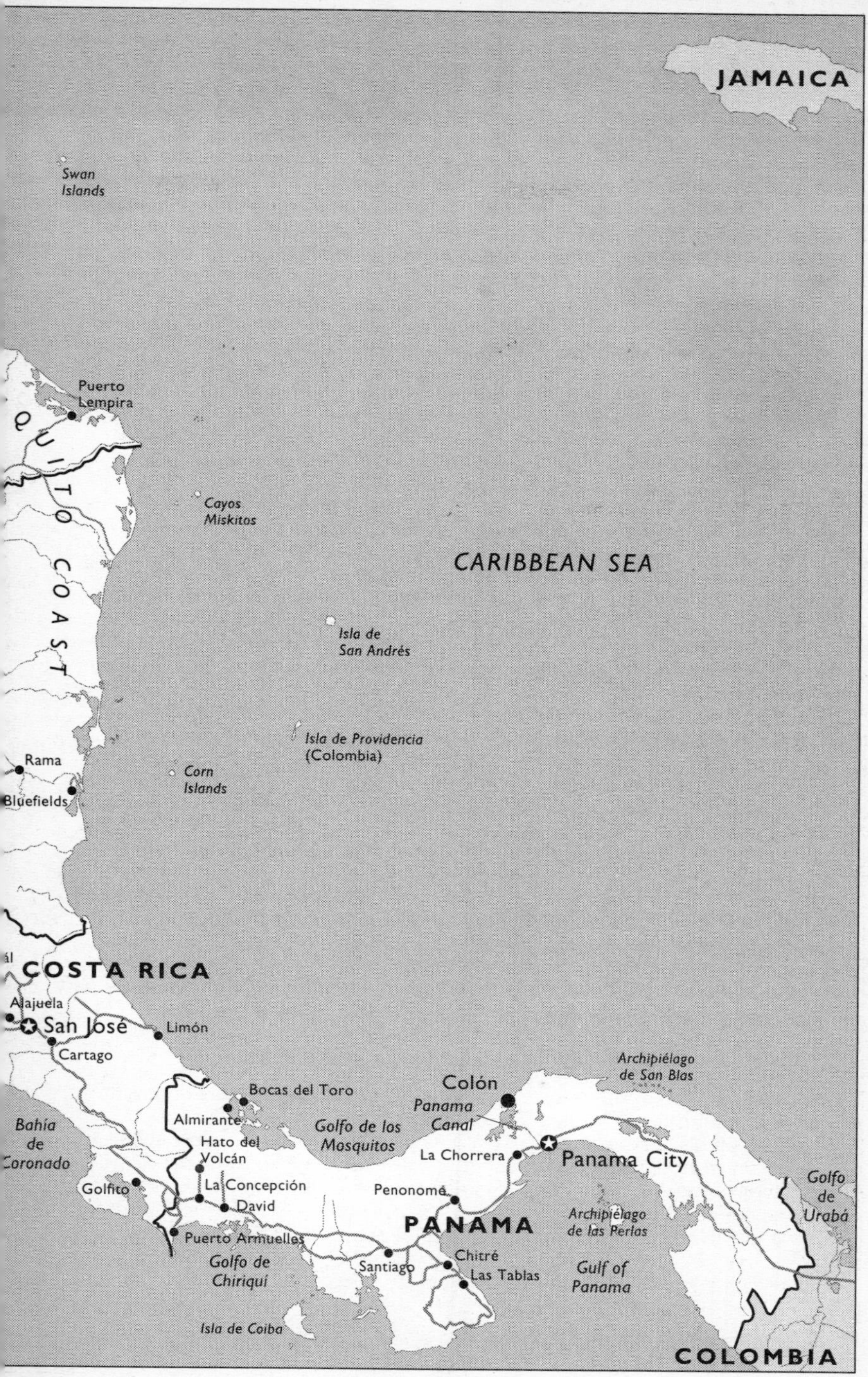

JAMAICA
Swan Islands
Puerto Lempira
MOSQUITO COAST
Cayos Miskitos
CARIBBEAN SEA
Isla de San Andrés
Isla de Providencia (Colombia)
Rama
Corn Islands
Bluefields
COSTA RICA
Alajuela
San José
Limón
Cartago
Archipiélago de San Blas
Colón
Bocas del Toro
Panama Canal
Almirante
Golfo de los Mosquitos
Bahía de Coronado
Hato del Volcán
La Chorrera
Panama City
Golfito
La Concepción
Penonomé
Golfo de Urabá
David
Archipiélago de las Perlas
PANAMA
Puerto Armuelles
Golfo de Chiriquí
Chitré
Santiago
Las Tablas
Gulf of Panama
Isla de Coiba
COLOMBIA

How To Use This Book

Let's Go: Central America 1996 is sparkling and spanking new, and we're proud to present one *very* cool place to *Let's Go* readers new and old. Whether you're down for a weekend jaunt to that butterfly farm you've heard so much about, or on a soul-searching exploration of the world (perhaps repeatedly hitting a giant snooze button on life), Central America promises adventure to the extreme. The region's seven countries are small, but each packs a mighty punch. This is a part of the world in which fuming volcanoes dribble lava into steaming hot springs, which percolate through misty rainforests, which enshroud Ancient Mayan ruins, which shelter exotic birds, which congregate on idyllic, post-cardian beaches, which offer plenty of shootable curl for surfers, who hang out with Caribbean Rastafari, whose banks are guarded by indigenous soldiers who wear traditional embroidered clothing while toting AK-47s. It's silly to encourage you to break away from the often-trod path, since in Central America, crowded tourist meccas are rare. Still, please remember that a travel guide is meant to provide happy tips, but doesn't guarantee the trip of a lifetime on its own; an open mind is more important than an open book, and a little initiative and creativity go a long way.

Fortune cookies aside, we have attempted to compile the efforts of our seven fine researchers into a book deeply infused with a sense of the distinctive cultures of each country; it's a collection of helpful advice presented with a zesty *picante* kick. The first chapter, the **Essentials** section, provides general listings of information services, volunteer organizations, disease prevention, and everything else. When in doubt (and certainly before leaving), check here. In addition, each country's introduction contains country-specific essentials and **histories.** Embassy listings can be found here, or in the practical information sections of capital cities. Masters of our mystical **black tabs** will note that countries are arranged west to east, north to south, as if you were reading the map like a book (and what a book that would be!).

Each city or town is sub-divided into a neat little care-package: introductions focus on culture and history, and try to answer a simple question: why should I go there? Then comes the **Orientation,** which describes the layout of the city, and **Practical Information,** which includes vital schedules, addresses, and numbers. **Accommodations, Food, Sights,** and **Entertainment** are pretty self-explanatory. Note that listings of hotels and restaurants are generally listed in descending order of preference; wherever possible, a wide range of budgets are considered.

The exception to the book's form, Mexico's **Yucatán Peninsula** is included after Panama, and is intended for travelers with an interest in exploring the rest of **La Ruta Maya.** For delicious and infinitely more thorough coverage of Yucatán and beyond, check out *Let's Go: Mexico 1996.* During your trip and forever thereafter, have fun, be safe, and if you have time, drop us a postcard to say how things went. Until then, may Central America fulfill all your dandiest, randiest fantasies.

A NOTE TO OUR READERS

The information for this book is gathered by Let's Go researchers during the summer months. Each listing is derived from the assigned researcher's opinion based upon his or her visit at a particular time. The opinions are expressed in a candid and forthright manner. Other travelers might disagree. Those traveling at a different time may have different experiences since prices, dates, hours, and conditions are always subject to change. You are urged to check beforehand to avoid inconvenience and surprises. Travel always involves a certain degree of risk, especially in low-cost areas. When traveling, especially on a budget, you should always take particular care to ensure your safety.

ESSENTIALS

PLANNING YOUR TRIP

Travelers to Central America necessarily thrive on adventure, but few anticipate the challenging labyrinth sometimes posed by the region's sluggish bureaucracies. Expect long waits for processing of visas, get used to delays on buses and airplanes, don't be surprised when the bank you've been desperately searching for shuts down early for a local festival, and never expect to be able to talk to someone by telephone. In short, the only recourse is to sit back and summon oodles of patience. For more information on individual countries, see each chapter's Essentials section.

■■■ WHEN TO GO

The weather in Central America varies wildly from region to region, but altitude, rather than latitude, is the climate's main determinant. In the lowlands (from sea level to 3,000 ft.), the daytime temperatures average about 90°F, but head up a few thousand feet, and both days and nights can get downright chilly, nighttime temperatures falling to 50°F. The coastal areas tend to be more humid, but are sometimes cooled by breezes. Overall, the humidity can be fierce, and travelers not used to the tropics should expect to sweat as never before.

The rainy season falls between May and November, with higher probability of hurricanes between August and October. (Note that this season is often called *invierno*, winter, which is the opposite of what a traveler from the northern hemisphere would expect.) Expect the rain to be more intense and longer-lasting in the highlands, and keep in mind that the Caribbean side of the isthmus gets twice as much rain as the Pacific side. Otherwise, things are sunny and dry; only about 15 percent of the rain on the Pacific Coast falls between November and April. Even during the rainy season, though, the sun usually rears its happy head for part of the day, with the majority of rainstorms occurring in the afternoon. Unless your sole objective is getting that deep, dark tan, the rainy season can be perfectly pleasant; temperatures never reach withering extremes, and showers render only a few dirt roads entirely inaccessible.

Still, it's not surprising that the touristic "high season" in Central America coincides with the dryer weather, since a good tan is pretty high on most people's lists. Along with better weather, expect the high season to bring larger crowds and boosted prices, particularly around Christmas vacation. *Semana Santa,* the festival associated with Easter Week in March or April, marks the most happening party in the region; Central Americans and tourists alike flock to popular tourist destinations. If traveling during this time of year, make an effort to book a room in advance.

■■■ FEED YOUR HEAD

HELPFUL PUBLICATIONS AND ORGANIZATIONS

The travel publishers and mail-oder bookstores listed below offer more detailed maps and information on everything from restaurants to festivals. Most of these books can be ordered directly from the publisher. For official **United States Department of State travel advisories,** including crime and security information, call the 24-hour hotline at 202-647-5225.

Another way to obtain information is via the **Internet.** The easiest Internet protocol to master is the **World Wide Web.** Point your browser to http://

www.yahoo.com/ to perform comprehensive keyword searches. Ask a systems administrator or a friendly net-surfer for more info.

Adventurous Traveler Bookstore, P.O. Box 577, Hinesburg, VT 05461 (tel. and fax (800) 282-3963, (802) 482-3546). Outdoor adventure travel books and maps.
Bon Voyage!, 2069 W. Bullard Ave., Fresno, CA 93711-1200 (tel. (800) 995-9716, (209) 447-8441). Mail order catalog offers books, travel goods, maps, and more.
Central American Information Center, P.O. Box 50211, San Diego, CA 92105 (tel. (619) 583-2925). Publishes *Travel Programs in Central America* (US$5); the staff doesn't work full-time, so write a letter.
Forsyth Travel Library, P.O. Box 2975, Shawnee Mission, KS 66201 (tel. (800) 367-7984). A mail-order service, wide range of maps. Write for a free catalog.
Latin American Travel Consultants, P.O. Box 17-17-908, Quito, Ecuador (fax (593) 2-562-566). Publishes the 15-page quarterly *Latin American Travel Advisor,* about safety and politics in Central America. US$39 for 1 year subscription.
South American Fiesta, 910 W. Mercury Blvd., Hampton, VA 23666 (tel. (800) 334-3782; fax (804) 826-1747). Tours and stays in Belize and Costa Rica.
Specialty Travel Index, 305 San Anselmo Avenue, Suite 313, San Anselmo, CA 94960 (tel. (415) 459-4900; fax 459-4974). Bi-yearly listing of "off the beaten track" and specialty tour operators (1copy US$6; 2 copies US$10).
Superintendent of Documents, U.S. Government Printing Office, P.O. Box 371954, Pittsburgh, PA 15250-7954 (tel. (202) 512-1800; fax 512-2250). Publishes *Your Trip Abroad* (US$1.25), *Health Information for International Travel* (US$7), and "Background Notes" on all countries (US$1 each), including *Tips for Travelers to Central and South America*. Postage is included in the prices. Open Mon.-Fri. 8am-4pm.

■■■ DOCUMENTS AND FORMALITIES

■ PASSPORTS

Before leaving, photocopy the page of your passport that contains your photograph and identifying information, especially your passport number. Carry this photocopy in a safe place apart from your passport, and leave another copy at home. These measures help prove your citizenship and facilitate the issuing of a new passport if you lose the original. Consulates also recommend carrying an expired passport or an official copy of your birth certificate. You can request a duplicate birth certificate from the **Bureau of Vital Records and Statistics** in your state or province of birth.

It may take weeks to process a replacement for a lost passport, and your new one may be valid only for a limited time. In addition, any visas stamped in your old passport will be irretrievably lost. If this happens, immediately notify the local police and the nearest embassy or consulate of your home government. To expedite its replacement, you will need to know all information previously recorded and show identification and proof of citizenship. Some consulates can issue new passports within two days if you can give them proof of citizenship. In an emergency, ask for immediate temporary traveling papers to reenter your home country. Your passport is a public document that belongs to your nation's government. You may have to surrender it to a foreign government official; however, if you don't get it back in a reasonable amount of time, inform the nearest mission of your home country.

U.S. citizens may apply for a passport, valid for 10 years (five years if under 18) at any clerk of court or post office authorized to accept passport applications or at a U.S. Passport Agency, located in several major cities. Refer to the "U.S. Government, State Department" or "Passport Services" section of the telephone directory, or call your local post office for addresses. U.S. embassies or consulates can usually issue new passports, given proof of citizenship. Contact the U.S. Passport Information's 24-hr. recorded message at (202) 647-0518 for general information. If your passport is lost or stolen in the U.S., report it in writing to Passport Services, U.S. Department of State, 1111 19th St., NW, Washington DC, 20522-1705 or to the nearest passport agency. For info. about the processing of your passport write to: National Passport Center, 31 Rochester Avenue, Portsmouth, NH, 03801 or call (603) 334-0500.

Canadian application forms in English and French are available at all passport offices, post offices, and most travel agencies. Citizens may apply in person at any one of 28 regional Passport Offices across Canada. If a passport is lost abroad, Canadians must be able to prove citizenship with another document. Apply by mail by sending a completed application form with appropriate documentation and the CDN$35 fee to Passport Office, Foreign Affairs, Ottawa, Ont., K1A OG3. For additional info., call (800) 567-6868 (24 hrs.; from Canada only). In Toronto call 973-3251. In Montreal, dial 283-2152. Refer to the booklet *Bon Voyage, But...* for help and a list of Canadian embassies and consulates, available for free from any passport office or from Info-Export (BPTE), External Affairs, Ottawa, Ont., K1A OG2.

British citizens, British Dependent Territories citizens, and British Overseas citizens may apply for a full passport. For a full passport, valid for 10 years (five years if under 16), apply in person or by mail to a passport office. Application forms are also available from main post offices (in Northern Ireland from any local office of the DSS). The fee is UK£18. The London office offers same-day walk-in rush service.

Irish citizens can apply for a passport by mail to either the Department of Foreign Affairs, Passport Office, Setanta Centre, Molesworth St., Dublin 2 (tel. (01) 671 16 33), or the Passport Office, 1A South Mall, Cork (tel. (021) 27 25 25). You can obtain an application form at a local Garda station or request one from a passport office.

Australian citizens must apply for a passport in person at a Post Office, a Passport Office, or an Australian diplomatic mission overseas. Contact your local passport office or post office for more information. Send cash, certified check, or money order made to: Australian Government Imprest Account. Personal checks are not accepted. For more info., call toll free (in Australia) 131 232.

New Zealand citizens must contact their local Link Centre, travel agent, or New Zealand Representative for an application form, which they must complete and mail to the New Zealand Passport Office, Documents of National Identity Division, Department of Internal Affairs, Box 10-526, Wellington (tel. (04) 474 81 00). The application fee is NZ$80.

South African citizens can apply for a passport at any Home Affairs Office. Two photos, either a birth certificate or an identity book, and the SAR38 fee must accompany a completed application.

VISAS

A visa is an endorsement that a foreign government stamps into a passport; it allows the bearer to stay in that country for a specified purpose and period of time. Most visas cost US$10-70 and allow you to spend about a month in a country, within six months to a year from the date of issue. Specific visa requirements are listed in the Getting There section of each country's Essentials section. Check the country's visa requirements and restrictions as close to your departure date as possible.

For more information, send for *Foreign Visa Requirements* (US$0.50) from Consumer Information Center, Pueblo, CO 81009 (tel. (719) 948-3334), or contact the Center for International Business and Travel (CIBT), 25 West 43rd St. #1420, New York, NY 10036 (tel. (800) 925-2428 or (212) 575-2811 from NYC), which secures visas for travel to and from all countries for an average cost of US$50 per visa.

CUSTOMS: COMING HOME

U.S. citizens may return with up to US$400 gifts, purchases, duty-free articles, and purchases for others. You must be more than 21 years old to bring in alcoholic beverages. For more information, get a copy of *Know Before You Go* from the U.S. Customs Service, Box 7407, Washington, D.C. 20044, or call (202) 927-6724. Foreign nationals living in the U.S. should get a copy of *Customs Hints for Visitors (Nonresidents)* by writing or calling the same address/phone number above.

Canadian citizens out of the country for more than a week may bring back up to CDN$300 worth of goods duty-free once every calendar year. For more information, including restrictions on tobacco and alcohol, write to Canadian Customs, 2265 St. Laurent Blvd., Ottawa, Ontario, K1G 4K3 (tel. (613) 993-0534). Or, from within Canada, call (800) 461-9999.

British citizens or visitors arriving in the U.K. from Central America are subject to duties on tobacco, alcohol, toilet water, and up to £165 of other goods. Contact Her Majesty's Customs and Excise, Custom House, Nettleton Road, Heathrow Airport, Hounslow, Middlesex, TW6 2LA (tel. (0181) 910-3744, fax (0181) 910-3765).

Irish citizens can contact The Revenue Commissioners, Dublin Castle (tel. (01) 679-2777; fax (01) 671-2021) or The Collector of Customs and Excise, The Custom House, Dublin 1 for more information about what duties to expect upon returning.

Australian travelers over age 18 may bring into Australia a duty/tax free allowance or A$400 (under 18, A$200) worth of goods intended as gifts. For further information contact the Australian Customs Service, 5 Constitution Ave., Canberra, ACT 2601 (tel. (011) 61 6 2756255; fax (011) 61 6 2756989).

New Zealand citizens may bring home up to NZ$700 worth of goods intended for personal use or as unsolicited gifts. For more info., consult *New Zealand Customs Guide for Travelers,* available from customs offices, or contact New Zealand Customs, 50 Anzac Avenue, Box 29, Aukland (tel. (09) 377 35 20; fax 309 29 78).

South African citizens can take their customs inquiries to: The Commissioner for Customs and Excise, Private Bag X47, Pretoria 0001, which distributes *South African Customs Information*. South Africans in the U.S. should contact: South African Mission to the IMF/World Bank, 3201 New Mexico Ave. #380 NW, Washington, DC 20016 (tel. (202) 364-8320; fax 364-6008).

IDENTIFICATION

Always carry on your person two or more forms of identification, including at least one photo ID. A passport combined with a driver's license or birth certificate usually serves as adequate proof of your identity and citizenship. Many establishments, especially banks, require several IDs before cashing traveler's checks. Never carry all your forms of ID together, however; you risk being left entirely without ID or funds in case of theft or loss. Also, carry half a dozen extra passport-size photos just in case. If you plan an extended stay, register your passport with the nearest embassy or consulate.

ENTRANCE REQUIREMENTS AND BORDER CROSSINGS

Check each chapter's Essentials sections for country-specific entrance requirements. In general, when you enter a country, dress neatly and carry **proof of your financial independence,** such as a visa to the next country on your itinerary, an airplane ticket to depart, or enough money to cover the cost of your living expenses. Admission as a visitor does not include the right to work, which is authorized only by a work permit (see Alternatives to Tourism, page 17). Entering certain countries to study requires a special visa, and immigration officers may also ask for proof of acceptance from a school and that the course of study will take up most of your time in the country.

■■■ MONEY MATTERS

CURRENCY AND EXCHANGE

Individual currencies' values are listed in each country's Essentials section. Expect to spend anywhere between US$5-50 per person per day, depending on the local cost of living and your needs. Don't sacrifice your health or safety for a cheaper tab. No matter how low your budget, you'll need to keep handy a larger amount of cash than usual. Personal checks from home will probably not be accepted no matter how many forms of identification you have.

The instability of Central American economies usually makes it impossible to exchange the currencies of one country in the banks of another; such transactions must be made at the border. **U.S. dollars** are as good as gold in almost all of Central America, maybe even better, except perhaps in the remotest jungles, where the national cash is preferred. In some places, U.S. currency may be preferred to local money. However, avoid using Western money when you can. Throwing dollars around to gain preferential treatment is offensive, and attracts theft. Also, it labels you as a foreigner and invites many locals to jack prices up as much as possible.

Other currencies may be more difficult to exchange, so even travelers from outside the U.S. should bring US$. Converting some money before departure allows smart travelers to zip through the airport while others languish in exchange lines and prevents the problem of getting stuck with no money after banking hours or on a holiday. **Black-market exchange** is a popular option in Latin America, since money can be exchanged during banks' closing hours. The traders aren't hard to find; they're the guys with huge wads of cash in one hand and a calculator in the other. While convenient, these transactions are riskier than exchange at banks.

Since every exchange transaction means losing some money, convert in large sums (unless the currency is depreciating rapidly). Travelers shouldn't change more than they will need for the country they're in, and only as much as they feel safe carrying on their person. When using traveler's checks or bills, carry some in small denominations (US$50 or less), especially for times when exchange must be made at disadvantageous rates.

TRAVELER'S CHECKS

Traveler's checks are one of the safest and least troublesome means of carrying funds. Several agencies and many banks sell them, usually for face value plus a 1% commission. In small towns, traveler's checks are less readily accepted than in cities with large tourist industries. Nonetheless, at least one place in every town should be willing to exchange them for local currency. In Central America, businesses rarely exchange traveler's checks, but nearly all banks perform the service for a small fee.

Each agency provides refunds if your checks are lost or stolen, and many provide additional services. You may need a police report verifying the loss or theft. Inquire about country-specific toll-free refund hotlines, emergency message relay services, and stolen credit card assistance. Expect a fair amount of red tape and delay in the event of theft or loss of traveler's checks. To expedite the refund process, keep your check receipts separate from your checks and store them in a safe place or with a traveling companion; record check numbers when you cash them and leave a list of check numbers with someone at home; ask for a list of refund centers when you buy your checks. Keep a separate supply of cash or traveler's checks for emergencies. Be sure never to countersign a check until you're prepared to cash it, and always bring your passport when you plan to use the checks.

American Express: Call (800) 221-7282 in the U.S. and Canada; in the U.K. (0800) 52 13 13; in New Zealand (0800) 44 10 68; in Australia (008) 25 19 02. Elsewhere, call U.S. collect (801) 964-6665. American Express traveler's checks are widely recognized in Central America. Purchase checks for a small fee at American Express Travel Service Offices, banks, and American Automobile Association offices (AAA members can buy the checks commission-free). Cardmembers can order via phone (tel. (800) 673-3782). American Express offices cash checks commission-free, although they often offer slightly worse rates than banks. Cheques for Two can be signed by either of two people traveling together.

Barclay's Bank: Call (800) 221-2426 in the U.S. and Canada. Sells Visa traveler's checks at a 1-3% commission depending on the bank. Branches throughout Britain, and are common in Belize. Barclay's banks cash any Visa checks for free.

Citicorp: Call (800) 645-6556 in the U.S. and Canada; in the U.K. (0171) 982 40 40; from elsewhere call U.S. collect (813) 623-1709. Commission is 1-2% on check purchases. Checkholders are automatically enrolled for 45 days in Travel Assist Hotline (tel. (800) 523-1199) which provides travelers with an English speaking

doctor, lawyer, or interpreter as well as check refund assistance. Citicorp's World Courier Service guarantees hand-delivery of checks anywhere in the world.

Visa: Call (800) 227-6811 in the U.S.; in the U.K. (0171) 937 8091; from elsewhere call the U.S. collect at (212) 858-8500. Sells its checks by mail; call (800) 235-7366. Any kind of Visa traveler's checks can be reported lost at the Visa number.

CREDIT CARDS AND CASH CARDS

More and more, businesses in Central America are willing to accept credit cards as a direct form of payment, although the overwhelming majority still demand cash. Credit cards are invaluable in any emergency which leaves you temporarily without other resources. Credit cards also offer an array of other services, from insurance to emergency assistance. Automatic teller machines (ATMs) are rare, but many banks give cash advances in local currency on major credit cards—**MasterCard** and **Visa** are the most welcomed. ATMs require a **Personal Identification Number (PIN),** which credit cards in the United States do not usually carry. You must ask American Express, MasterCard, or Visa to assign you one before you leave. Automatic teller machines are far too rare to be relied upon as a sole source of funds, but if you are planning on ever using this service, find out how much money can be withdrawn per day. Be sure to memorize your PIN code in numeral form since machines abroad often don't have letters on the keys. Also, if your PIN is longer than four digits, be sure to ask your bank whether the first four digits will work, or whether you need a new number. A great many ATMs are outdoors; don't let anyone distract you while at the machine and use discretion as you walk away from the machine.

American Express (tel. (800) CASH-NOW (528-4800)) hefty annual fee (US$55) but offers a number of services, such as Global Assist, a 24-hr. hotline offering information and legal assistance in emergencies (call U.S. collect (301) 214-8228). Other services include assistance in changing airline reservations, sending mailgrams and international cables, and holding your mail at an AmEx office.

MasterCard (tel. (800) 999-0454) and **Visa** (tel. (800) 336-8472) are issued in cooperation with individual banks and some other organizations, such as **Thomas Cook MasterCard** (tel. (800) 223-9920 in the U.S. and Canada; or call U.S. collect (609) 987-7300; from the U.K. call (0800) 622 101 free or (1733) 502 995 collect), offering emergency card replacement, communications, cash advances, airline ticket revalidation, re-routing, reservations, and travel planning.

GETTING MONEY FROM HOME

Money can be wired to every Central American country (within a few hours) through **Western Union.** In the U.S., call Western Union any time at (800) 325-6000 to cable money with your Visa or MasterCard. Rates are US$29 to send US$250, US$40 to send US$500, and US$50 to send US$1000. In emergencies, U.S. citizens can have money sent via the State Department's **Citizens Emergency Center,** Department of State, 2201 C St. NW, Washington, DC 20520 (tel. (202) 647-5225); at night and on Sundays and holidays (202) 647-4000). For a fee of US$15, the State Department will forward money within hours to the nearest consular office, which will then disburse it according to instructions. The center only serves Americans in the direst of straits and prefers not to send sums greater than US$500.

BARGAINING AND TIPPING

In some places it's okay to bargain, and a little practice at playing the "game" can make it well worth the effort. Bargaining for rooms works best in the low season, and it's not hard to get prices lowered at markets or from street vendors. The basic bargaining technique is to expect the first offered price to be higher than what the seller actually wants; pick a lower price, and marvel at the magic of compromise.

While many locals do not tip for food and other services, a little something extra is often expected from foreigners, who are assumed to be relatively affluent. There are no set values for gratuities as in the U.S., but 10-15% should be fine; leaving too small a tip is worse than leaving no tip. Even if you're not used to tipping for services, such as guided tours or maid-service, be aware that these people count on a small bonus.

Bargaining Basics

Part of the allure of traveling to Central America is that it's possible to get by on next to nothing. For some travelers, living on a microscopic budget becomes a sort of competition, and they seek boasting rights to having gone two months on US$10 a day or less. Too often, though, this strategy interferes with enjoyment of the region. Many scrimp and save until they get home, when they regret not having lived like royalty with their ultra-powerful currency. There are also those who incessantly try to bargain down prices in places where haggling isn't custom; shouting at an old, poor farmer that he should sell you some bananas for $.07 instead of $.10 is not only insulting, it's akin to robbery, especially since many assume that foreigners must have a decent amount of money to be traveling in the first place. It's easy to lose perspective on prices, so appreciate the low costs, bring enough money to pay normal prices, and don't push a good thing unless you know that bargaining is acceptable or that a price is too high.

■■■ INSURANCE

Beware of buying unnecessary travel coverage; your regular policies may well extend to many travel-related accidents. **Medical insurance** (especially university policies) often covers costs incurred abroad. Homeowners' insurance often covers theft during travel; insurance companies usually require a copy of police reports or receipts from medical expenses before they honor a claim; there may also be time limits on filing for reimbursement. Carry policy numbers and proof of insurance.

ISIC and **ITIC** provide US$3000 worth of accident and illness insurance and US$100 per day up to 60 days of hospitalization. The cards also give access to a toll-free Traveler's Assistance hotline (call collect to the U.S. (713) 267-2525); the multilingual staff can provide help in emergencies overseas. **Council** offers the inexpensive Trip-Safe plan with options covering medical treatment and hospitalization, accidents, baggage loss, and even charter flights missed due to illness; **STA** offers a more expensive, more comprehensive plan. (See Getting There: Travel Agencies, page 23, for these listings.)

ARM Coverage, Inc./Carefree Travel Insurance, 100 Garden City Plaza, P.O. Box 9366, Garden City, NY, 11530-9366 (tel. (800) 323-3149 or (516) 294-0220; fax (516) 294-1821). Coverage for trip delay, accident and sickness, medical, baggage loss, bag delay, accidental death and dismemberment, and travel supplier insolvency. Trip cancellation/interruption coverage may be purchased separately.

Globalcare Travel Insurance, 220 Broadway, Lynnfield MA, 01940 (tel. (800) 821-2488; fax (617) 592-7720). Complete services. On-the-spot payments and special student programs, including benefits for trip cancellation and interruption.

Travel Assistance International, by Worldwide Assistance Services, Inc., 1133 15th St. NW, Suite 400, Washington, DC 20005-2710 (tel. (800) 821-2828, (202) 828-5894; fax (202) 331-1530). 24-hr. hotline for emergencies and referrals.

■■■ PACKING

Pack lightly...that means you.

If you don't pack lightly, you will pay with either back problems or in the postage to mail stuff home. The more you have, the more you have to lose, and the more cumbersome it is to store stuff safely. Before you leave, pack your bag, strap it on, and imagine yourself walking uphill on hot asphalt for the next three hours. At the slightest sign of heaviness, unpack something.

Almost all travelers to Central America end up riding a lot of buses and covering a lot of ground by foot, for which the tried-and-true baggage is a sturdy **backpack**. In general, internal-frame packs are easier to carry and more efficient for general traveling purposes, though for extensive camping or hiking an external-frame pack works well. In any case, get a pack with a strong, padded hip belt to transfer weight from your shoulders to your legs. Quality packs cost between US$125 to US$400. Bring a **suitcase** or other heavy luggage only if you plan to live in one city and explore from there. An additional smaller bag allows you to leave your big bag in the hotel while you go sight-seeing.

Footwear is not the place to cut costs. Comfortable walking (or running) shoes are essential; save your sandals for short walks and evenings out. If you plan to hike, bring a pair of sturdy hiking shoes. Make sure they have good ventilation. Talcum powder in your shoes and on your feet can prevent sores, and moleskin is great for blisters. *Break in your shoes before you leave home.*

Many Central American cities have no public places to do **laundry.** One solution is to give your clothes to the hotel cleaning person. Make sure that whoever you approach is a permanent employee of the hotel, and establish a price in advance. Another possibility is to carry laundry soap and wash by hand in hotel sinks. A soft squash ball magically serves as a plug where there is usually none.

Natural fibers and lightweight cottons are the best clothing materials for hot weather, and some parts of Central America get downright smokin'. Pack a rain poncho to cover both you and your bag if you're traveling between May and October, and bring a sweatshirt or jacket for chilly nights if headed for the mountains. Don't forget a swimsuit. **Toiletries** such as aspirin and razor blades are available in Central American pharmacies, but some items—tampons, prescription drugs, saline solution, and contraceptives—are best brought from home. Over-the-counter items' ingredients may differ from the same-named product in the U.S. See Health: Before You Go, page 11, for other packing tips.

Custom should also be important in dictating your dress. Remember that clothing can make you stand out as a tourist, either because it is too flashy or just culturally inappropriate and even offensive, particularly in rural areas. Travelers are advised not to wear clothing specific to a culture of Central America; stash it in your bag until you're out of the country, as some people are offended when foreigners "buy" their cultural traditions, and others may get confused about your ethnicity. Similarly, do not wear camouflage clothing, or anything else that might cause others to associate you with the military. Sentiment toward U.S. soldiers runs strong, and innocent tourists in army clothes are putting themselves in danger.

Most Latin American **men** do not wear short pants, and instead don slacks or trousers on even the hottest days. Loose khaki pants and short-sleeve dress shirts do not look out of place, nor do shorts if worn with a nice shirt. Mostly, though, common budget-traveler attire is acceptable in Central America, even if it means getting some odd stares. The essential wardrobe might consist of several t-shirts, a sweatshirt, a few pairs of shorts, one pair of slacks or jeans, underwear, and socks.

Women should avoid dressing scantily; shorts, short skirts, or anything that shows too much skin might be interpreted in the wrong way, especially since foreigners are already commonly perceived to be "loose." Long skirts with t-shirts is an ideal combination, and definitely wear a bra at all times. Wearing appropriate clothing can improve your general safety and also earn you more respect from locals.

■■■ SAFETY AND SECURITY

Tourists are particularly vulnerable to crime because they often carry large amounts of cash and are not as savvy as locals. To avoid unwanted attention, try to blend in as much as possible. The gawking camera-toter is a more obvious target than the casual local look-alike. Walking into a cafe or shop to check your map is better than checking it on a street corner; act as if you know exactly where you're going.

Don't put money in a wallet in your back pocket. Never count money in public and carry as little as possible. A purse must be sturdy and have a secure clasp; carry it crosswise on the side, away from the street with the clasp against you. Buy some small combination padlocks to secure your pack shut. A **money belt** is the best way to carry cash; get them at most camping supply stores or through a travel organization. A **neck pouch,** although less accessible, is equally safe. Don't keep anything precious in a fanny-pack: your valuables will be highly visible and easy to steal. In city crowds and especially on public transportation, pick-pockets are amazingly deft at their craft. Hold your bags tightly. Keep some money separate from the rest to use in an emergency or in case of theft. Label every piece of luggage inside and out.

Many Central American cities and towns have more than their share of hustlers, particularly in those regions where English is spoken regularly. Fast-talking men frequently confront tourists, strike up a conversation, and soon begin demanding money; you should give strangers the cold shoulder if they seem overly effusive or if they offer to accompany you. It's not unusual for tourists to be called "racist" if they refuse to give money, or if they are cool to advances. Ignore the claims, and head into a bank or restaurant for safety. In these situations, do not respond or make eye contact, walk quickly away, and keep a solid grip on your belongings. Contact the police if a hustler is particularly insistent or aggressive.

When exploring a new city, extra vigilance may be wise, but no city should force you to panic. Find out about a town's unsafe areas from the police, from the manager of your hotel or hostel, or from a local whom you trust. Jot down the number of the police if you'll be in town for a couple days; someone at home should know your itinerary, as well. Never say that you're traveling alone. Both men and women may want to carry a small **whistle** to scare off attackers or attract attention. At night, stay near crowded and well-lit areas. Whenever possible, *Let's Go* warns of unsafe neighborhoods, but only your eyes can tell you for sure if you've wandered into one; buildings in disrepair, vacant lots, and general desertedness are all bad signs, whereas good signs include children playing, women walking in the open, and other signs of an active community. If you feel uncomfortable, leave quickly and directly. Careful, persistent exploration will build confidence and make your stay in an area that much more rewarding.

Never leave your belongings unattended; don't trust anyone to "watch your bag for a second." Even the most demure-looking hotel may be a den of thieves. If you feel unsafe, look for places with either a curfew or a night attendant. Keep your valuables on your person in low-budget hotels, and always in dormitories.

Before you go, a good self-defense course provides more concrete ways to react to different types of aggression, but it might cost you more money than your trip. **Model Mugging** (East Coast tel. (617) 232-7900; Midwest (312) 338-4545; West Coast (415) 592-7300), a national organization with offices in several major cities, teaches a very effective, comprehensive course on self-defense. (Course prices vary from US$400-500; women's and men's courses offered.) Community colleges frequently offer self-defense courses at more affordable prices. Complete information on safety while traveling may be found in *Travel Safety: Security and Safeguards at Home and Abroad,* from Hippocrene Books, Inc. (see Feed Your Head, page 1).

■■■ DRUGS AND ALCOHOL

Drinking in any part of Latin America is not for amateurs; bars are strongholds of *machismo*. When someone calls you *amigo* and orders you a beer, bow out quickly unless you want to match him glass for glass in a challenge lasting several days.

Drugs and traveling are not a good combination. If you carry **prescription drugs** while you travel, have a copy of the prescriptions themselves readily accessible at country borders. As far as **illegal drugs** are concerned, the specific laws in each Central American country are different, but don't risk having to learn them the hard way. Drug users and handlers are never treated leniently, so expect the worst. Similarly, don't bring drugs back into the U.S.; customs agents and their perceptive K-9s are not to be taken lightly. For the free pamphlet *Travel Warning on Drugs Abroad,* send a self-addressed, stamped envelope to the Bureau of Consular Affairs, Public Affairs #5807, Dept. of State, Washington, DC 20520 (tel. (202) 647-1488).

■■■ HEALTH

Before you can say "pass the *jalapeños,*" a long-anticipated vacation can turn into an unpleasant study of the wonders (and failings) of some Central American country's health care system. Local pharmacists can give shots and dispense other remedies for mild illnesses; a sterile, disposable needle is crucial. Wherever possible, *Let's Go* lists a pharmacy open for extended hours. If not listed, ask a policeman or cab driver where the pharmacy is. If you have an emergency and the door is locked, knock loudly; someone is probably sleeping inside.

Allergy sufferers should find out if their conditions are likely to be aggravated in the regions they plan to visit. Obtain a full supply of any necessary medication before your trip, since matching your prescription to a foreign equivalent is not always easy, safe, or possible. Carry up-to-date, legible prescriptions or a statement from your doctor, especially if you use insulin, a syringe, or a narcotic. Those with medical conditions that cannot be immediately recognized (e.g. diabetes, allergies to antibiotics, epilepsy, heart conditions) should obtain a steel **Medic Alert** identification tag (US$35), which identifies the disease and gives a toll-free number to call for information. Contact Medic Alert Foundation International's 24-hour hotline at (800) 432-5378. *Staying Healthy in Asia, Africa, and Latin America* by Dirk G. Schroeder, published by Moon Publications, is available in major bookstores, and offers sound health advice. Consult your local bookstore for other books on staying healthy or write to the **Superintendent of Documents** (see Feed Your Head, page 1) for their pamphlet *Health Information for International Travelers* (US$6.50) detailing immunization requirements and other health precautions for travelers.

BEFORE YOU GO

Bring a compact first-aid kit for minor health problems, including bandages, aspirin or other pain killer, antibiotic cream, a thermometer, a Swiss Army knife with tweezers, moleskin, a decongestant for colds, motion sickness remedy, medicine for diarrhea or stomach problems, sunscreen, insect repellent, and burn ointment.

In your passport, write the names of any people you wish to be contacted in case of a medical emergency, and also list any allergies or medical conditions you would want doctors to be aware of. If you wear glasses or contact lenses, carry an extra prescription and pair of glasses or arrange to have your doctor or a family member send a replacement pair in an emergency.

Global Emergency Medical Services (GEMS) provides 24 hr. immediate access to an emergency room registered nurse who has on-line access to your medical information, your primary physician, and a worldwide network of English-speaking medical providers. Subscribers also receive a pocket-sized, personal, portable medical record that contains important medical information. For more information call (800) 860-1111, or write: 2001 Westside Drive, Suite 120, Alpharetta, GA 30201. The **American Red Cross'** *First-Aid and Safety Handbook* (US$14.95) is purchasable by calling or writing to the American Red Cross, 61 Medford St., Somerville, MA 02143 (tel. (800) 564-1234). In the U.S., the American Red Cross also offers many first-aid and CPR courses, which are well-taught and relatively inexpensive.

The **United States Centers for Disease Control** (based in Atlanta, Georgia) is an excellent source of general information on health for travelers around the world, and maintains an international travelers hotline (tel. and fax 404-332-4559; (404) 639-3311 for public inquiries). Or write directly to the Centers for Disease Control and Prevention, 1600 Clifton Rd. NE, Atlanta, GA 30333. The CDC publishes the booklet *Health Information for International Travelers* (US$6.00), an annual global rundown of disease, immunization, and general health advice, including risks in particular countries. Request the booklet by calling the CDC's hotline, or writing the Superintendent of Documents (see Feed Your Head, page 1).

Also useful is the **International Association for Medical Assistance to Travelers.** Membership is free, and IAMAT offers a membership ID card, a directory of English-speaking doctors around the world who treat members for a set fee schedule, and detailed charts on immunization requirements, various tropical diseases, climate, and sanitation. Contact chapters in the **U.S.,** 417 Center St., Lewiston, NY 14092 (tel. (716) 754-4883), **Canada,** 40 Regal Road, Guelph, Ontario, N1K 1B5 (tel. (519) 836-0102) or 1287 St. Clair Avenue West, Toronto, M6E 1B8 (tel. (416) 652-0137; fax (519) 836-3412), or **New Zealand,** P.O. Box 5049, Christchurch 5.

The **United States State Department** compiles Consular Information Sheets on health, entry requirements, and other issues for all countries of the world. Call the Overseas Citizens' Services (tel. (202) 647-5225), get the info. by fax by dialing (202) 647-3000 from the fax and following the recorded instructions. The State Department's regional passport agencies in the U.S., field offices of the U.S. Chamber of Commerce, and U.S. embassies and consulates abroad provide the same data, or send a self-addressed, stamped envelope to the Overseas Citizens' Services, Bureau of Consular Affairs, Room 4811, U.S. Department of State, Washington, DC 20520.

Travelers' very specific questions are probably best answered by calling the **U.S. Public Health Quarantine Station:** Chicago: (312) 894-2961 or 894-2968; Hawaii: (808) 861-8531; Los Angeles: (310) 215-2365/6; Miami: (305) 526-2910; New York: (718) 553-1685; San Francisco: (415) 876-2872; or Seattle: (206) 553-4519; or try the fax service in Atlanta (404) 332-4565.

PREVENTING DISEASE

Take a look at your **immunization records** before you go. Visitors to the region do not need to carry vaccination certificates (though anyone entering Central America from South America or Africa may be asked to show proof of vaccination for **yellow fever**). However, a few medical precautions can make your trip safer.

Never touch animals in Central America. Unlike elsewhere, few dogs are given shots, and that random pooch at your feet is probably disease-ridden. Avoid animals with open wounds. Be concerned about **rabies** if you ever get bitten by an animal; be sure to clean your wound thoroughly and seek medical help immediately to determine whether you need treatment. Rabies is a particular risk in rural areas.

A good many diseases are transmitted by insects—mainly mosquitoes, fleas, ticks, and lice. Insect bites are always annoying, but they can be dangerous and even life-threatening. Be aware of insects in wet or forested areas, while hiking, and especially while camping. Mosquitoes are most active from dusk to dawn. Wear long pants and long sleeves (fabric need not be thick or warm; tropic-weight cottons can keep you comfortable in the heat) and buy a bednet for camping. Wear shoes and socks, and tuck long pants into socks. Use insect repellents; DEET can be bought in spray or liquid form, but use it sparingly, especially on children. Soak or spray your gear with permethrin, which is licensed in the U.S. for use on clothing. Natural repellents can also be useful: taking vitamin B-12 pills regularly can eventually make you smelly to insects, as can garlic pills. Still, be sure to supplement your vitamins with repellent. Calamine lotion or topical cortisones (like Cortaid©) may stop insect bites from itching, as can a bath with a half-cup of baking soda or oatmeal.

Malaria is transmitted by mosquitoes, and there are different strains of the protozoa which are resistant to different drugs. Preliminary symptoms include fever, flu symptoms, chills, aches, and fatigue. Treatment drugs are available, but left untreated, malaria can cause anemia, kidney failure, coma, and death. Risk is greatest in rural areas. If hiking or staying overnight in certain areas (whether camping or not), you may want to take weekly anti-malarial drugs. Contact your doctor for a prescription. Risk occurs in Belize, except in the central coastal District, Costa Rica, except in Cartago and San Jose provinces, in the rural areas of Guatemala, Honduras, Nicaragua, and Panama, and in many rural areas of Mexico; chloroquine is effective for almost all areas of Central America, except for eastern Panama, where mefloquine should be taken.

Dengue Fever is an "urban viral infection" that you get from mosquito bites. Dengue has flu-like symptoms and is often indicated by a rash 3-4 days after the onset of fever. There is no vaccine and no treatment; the only prevention is to avoid mosquito bites. Dengue mosquitoes bite during the day, rather than in the evening like their blood-sucking colleagues. Recent Dengue epidemics have been found in Belize, El Salvador, Guatemala, Honduras, Mexico, and Nicaragua

Filariasis is a round worm, transmitted by mosquitoes, which gives you elephantitis of extremities; there is no vaccine. **Leishmaniasis**, a parasite, is transmitted by sand flies. Common symptoms are fever, weakness, and a swollen spleen. There is a treatment, but no vaccine. **American Trypanomiasis/CHAGAS Disease** is another relatively common parasite. Transmitted by the reduviid bug a.k.a. cone nose or kissing bug, which infests mud, adobe, and thatch, the symptoms are fever, heart disease and later on, enlarged intestine. Avoid overnights in infested buildings. There is no vaccine and limited treatment.

FOOD- AND WATER-BORNE DISEASES

To ensure that your food is safe, make sure that everything is cooked properly (deep-fried is good, for once), and be positive the water you drink is clean. Don't order meat "rare," and eggs should be thoroughly cooked, not served sunny-side up.

Cholera is an intestinal disease caused by a bacteria, which is found in contaminated food; the disease has recently reached epidemic stages in Central and South America. The first severe symptoms of cholera are lots of watery diarrhea, dehydration, vomiting, and muscle cramps. Untreated, cholera can cause death very quickly. Antibiotics are available, but the most important treatment is rehydration. Consider getting a (50% effective) vaccine if you have stomach problems (e.g. ulcers), or if you will be camping a good deal or living where water is not always reliable. In Central America, the highest risk is mostly in Guatemala, Mexico, and El Salvador, but Belize, Costa Rica, Honduras, and Nicaragua also report cases.

Typhoid Fever is common in Central America, particularly in villages and rural areas. While mostly transmitted through contaminated food and water, it may also be acquired by direct contact with another person. Symptoms include fever, headaches, fatigue, loss of appetite, and constipation; antibiotics treat typhoid fever. The CDC recommends (70-90% effective) vaccinations if you will be going off the "usual tourist itineraries," that is, hiking, camping, and staying in small cities or rural areas.

Parasites (tapeworms, etc.) also hide in unsafe water and food. Giardia, for example, is acquired by drinking untreated water from streams or lakes; it can stay with you for years. Symptoms of parasitic infections in general include swollen glands or lymph nodes, fever, rashes or itchiness, digestive problems, eye problems, and anemia. Boil your water, wear shoes, avoid bugs, and eat cooked food.

Hepatitis A (distinct from B and C) is also a risk in Central America. Hep. A is a viral infection of the liver acquired primarily through contaminated water, ice, shellfish, or unpeeled fruits and vegetables (as well as from sexual contact). Symptoms include fatigue, fever, loss of appetite, nausea, dark urine, jaundice, vomiting, aches and pains, and light stools. Ask your doctor about a new vaccine called "Harvix," or ask to get an injection of immune globulin (IG; formerly called Gamma Globulin). Risk is highest in rural areas and the countryside, but is also present in urban areas.

Hepatitis B is a viral infection of the liver transmitted by sharing needles, having unprotected sex, or coming into direct contact with an infected person's lesioned skin. The risk of Hepatitis B virus infection is moderate for Central America. If you think you may be sexually active while travelling or if you are working or living in rural areas, you are typically advised to get the vaccination for Hepatitis B. Vaccination should begin six months before traveling.

Hepatitis C is like Hepatitis B, but the methods of transmission are different. At risk are intravenous drug users, those with occupational exposure to blood, hemodialysis patients, or recipients of a blood transfusion; doctors aren't sure if you can get it through sexual contact.

TRAVELER'S DIARRHEA

One of the biggest health threats in Central America is the water. **Traveler's diarrhea,** known as *turista,* is the dastardly consequence of ignoring this threat. *Turista* often lasts two or three days; symptoms include cramps, nausea, vomiting, chills, and a fever as high as 103°F (39°C). If the nasties hit you, have quick-energy, non-sugary foods with protein and carbohydrates to keep your strength up. Over-the-counter remedies (such as Pepto-Bismol© or Immodium©) may counteract the problems, but they can complicate serious infections; avoid anti-diarrheals if you suspect you have been exposed to contaminated food or water, which puts you at risk for other diseases. The most dangerous side effect of diarrhea is dehydration; the simplest and most effective anti-dehydration formula is eight oz. of (clean) water with a ½ tsp. of sugar or honey and a pinch of salt. Down several of these mixtures a day, rest, and wait for the disease to run its course. If you develop a fever or your symptoms don't go away after four or five days, consult a doctor.

To avoid *turista,* never drink unbottled water; ask for *agua purificada* in restaurants and hotels. To purify your own water, bring it to a rolling boil (simmering isn't enough), or treat it with iodine drops or tablets. Don't brush your teeth with tap water, and don't even rinse your toothbrush under the faucet. Keep your mouth closed in the shower. Don't be fooled by the clever disguise of impure water—the ice-cube. Stay away from salads: uncooked vegetables (including lettuce and coleslaw) are a great way to get *turista.* Other culprits are raw shellfish, unpasteurized milk and sauces containing raw eggs. Peel all fruits and vegetables, and beware of watermelon, which is often injected with impure water. Watch out for food from markets or street vendors that may have been washed in dirty water or fried in rancid cooking oil, such as juices, peeled fruits, and exposed coconut slices. Always wash your hands before eating. A golden rule in most of Latin America: boil it, peel it, cook it, or forget it, but don't get so paranoid about the water that you end up getting dehydrated.

HOT AND COLD

Common sense goes a long way toward preventing **heat exhaustion:** relax in hot weather, drink lots of non-alcoholic fluids, and lie down inside if you feel awful. Continuous heat stress can eventually lead to **heatstroke,** characterized by rising body temperature, severe headache, and cessation of sweating. Wear a hat, sunglasses, and a lightweight longsleeve shirt to avoid heatstroke. Victims must be cooled off with wet towels and taken to a doctor as soon as possible.

Always drink enough liquids to keep your urine clear. Alcoholic beverages are dehydrating, as are coffee, strong tea, and caffeinated sodas. You'll be sweating a lot, so be sure to eat enough salty food to prevent electrolyte depletion, which causes severe headaches. Less debilitating, but still dangerous, is **sunburn.** If you're prone to sunburn, bring sunscreen with you (it's often more expensive and hard to find), and apply it liberally and often to avoid burns and risk of skin cancer. If you get sunburned, drink more fluids than usual.

Surprisingly, it's possible to get excessively cold in Central America; a little rain, and nightfall at high altitudes could easily lead to **hypothermia.** The signs are easy to detect: body temperature drops rapidly, resulting in the failure to produce body heat; you may shiver, have poor coordination, feel exhausted, or have slurred speech, feel sleepy, hallucinate, or suffer amnesia. *Do not let hypothermia victims fall asleep* if they are in the advanced stages – their body temperature will drop more and if they lose consciousness they may die. Seek medical help as soon as possible. To avoid hypothermia, keep dry and stay out of the wind.

Travelers to **high altitudes** must allow their bodies a couple of days to adjust to lower oxygen levels in the air before exerting themselves. Also be careful about alcohol, especially if you're used to U.S. standards for beer – many foreign brews and liquors pack more punch, and at high altitudes where the air has less oxygen, any alcohol will do you in quickly.

WOMEN'S HEALTH

Women traveling in unsanitary conditions are vulnerable to urinary tract and bladder infections, common and severely uncomfortable bacterial diseases which cause a burning sensation and painful and sometimes frequent urination. Drink tons of vitamin-C-rich juice, plenty of clean water, and urinate frequently, especially right after intercourse. Untreated, these infections can lead to kidney infections, sterility, and even death. If symptoms persist, see a doctor. If you often develop vaginal yeast infections, take along an over-the-counter medicine, as treatments may not be readily available in Central America. Women may also be more susceptible to vaginal thrush and cystitis, two treatable but uncomfortable illnesses. Tampons and pads are sometimes hard to find in Central America; certainly your preferred brands may not be available, so it may be advisable to take supplies along. Some women also use diaphragms or cervical caps to temporarily trap menstrual flow. Refer to the *Handbook for Women Travellers* by Maggie and Gemma Moss (published by Piatkus Books) or to the women's health guide *Our Bodies, Our Selves* (published by the Boston Women's Health Collective) for more extensive information specific to women's health on the road.

BIRTH CONTROL

Reliable contraceptive devices may be difficult to find while traveling. Women on the pill should bring enough to allow for possible loss or extended stays and should bring a prescription, since forms of the pill vary a good deal. The sponge is probably too bulky to be worthwhile on the road; if you use a diaphragm, be sure that you have enough contraceptive jelly on hand. Though condoms are increasingly available, you might want to bring your favorite national brand before you go; availability and quality vary.

Abortion is completely illegal in all of Central America, except in Belize, Costa Rica, Honduras, and Panama, where it is only legal in cases in which a woman's physical health is threatened by the pregnancy or if she has been raped.

AIDS, HIV, STD'S

One of the leading causes of death world-wide, **Acquired Immune Deficiency Syndrome** (AIDS) is a growing problem in Central America. The World Health Organization estimates that there are 4.5 million people worldwide living with AIDS, and around 13 million people are HIV+; 8,000 of the reported cases come from Central America. Well over 90% of adults newly infected with HIV acquired their infection through heterosexual sex; women now represent 50% of all new HIV infections.

The easiest mode of HIV transmission is through direct blood to blood contact with an HIV+ person; *never* share intravenous drug, tattooing, or other needles. The most common mode is intercourse. Health professionals recommend the use of latex condoms; follow the instructions on the packet. Since it isn't always easy to buy condoms in Central America, take a supply with you before you depart for your trip. Casual contact (including drinking from the same glass or using the same eating utensils as an infected person) is believed to pose no risk.

For more information on AIDS, call the **U.S.Center for Disease Control's** 24-hour Hotline at (800)-342-2437 (Mon-Fri 10am-10pm; Spanish 800-344-7332, daily 8am-2am). The **World Health Organization** (tel. 202-861-3200) provides statistical material on AIDS internationally. Or write to the **Bureau of Consular Affairs,** #6831, Dept. of State, Washington, D.C. 20520.

Sexually transmitted diseases, or STDs, are very common, can be just as deadly, and a lot easier to catch than HIV. It's a wise idea to actually *look* at your partner's genitals before you have sex. If anything looks amiss, that should be your signal not to have sex with that person. When having sex, condoms may protect you from certain STDs, but oral or even tactile contact can lead to transmission.

ESSENTIALS

100%

■■■ ALTERNATIVES TO TOURISM

VOLUNTEER AND WORK

Volunteering is an excellent way to immerse yourself in Central American culture and Spanish language while improving the lives of others. The good news is that it's very easy to find volunteer positions; the bad news is that paid work can be exceedingly difficult to find. The leaders of developing nations aren't about to give up precious jobs to traveling *gringos* when many of their own people are unemployed. It's not impossible, as some businesses are eager to hire English-speaking personnel for prestige and the convenience of their patrons, but attitudes are in flux, and you might still be unwelcome even as an English teacher. Your employer must acquire a work permit if you do land a job; working without one is grounds for deportation.

The Archaeological Institute of America, 656 Beacon Street, Boston, MA 02215-2010 (tel. (617) 353-9361; fax (617) 353-6550) puts out the *Archaeological Fieldwork Opportunities Bulletin* (US$11.00 non-members) which lists over 250 field sites throughout the world. Contact Kendall/Hunt Publishing, 4050 Westmark Drive, Dubuque, Iowa 52002 (tel. (800) 228-0810).

Conservation International, Att. Abbe Reis, 1015 18th St. NW, Suite 1000, Washington DC, 20036 (tel. (202) 429-5660; fax (202) 887-5188). Offers information on environmental volunteer opportunities throughout Central America.

Council on International Educational Exchange (Council) publishes *Volunteer! the Comprehensive Guide to Voluntary Service in the U.S. and Abroad* (US$13, US$1.50 postage); *Work, Study, Travel Abroad;* and *The Whole World Handbook* (US$13.95). Write to CIEE-Pubs. Dept., 205 E. 42nd St., New York, NY 10017-5706.

Office of Overseas Schools, A/OS Room 245, SA-29, Dept. of State, Washington, DC 20522-2902 (tel. (703) 875-7800). Teaching jobs available in every Central American country but Panama.

Peace Brigades International, 2642 College Ave., Berkeley, CA 94704 (tel. (510) 540-0749). Unarmed peace teams providing protective accompaniment for threatened human rights leaders and peasant organizations. Volunteers must be at least 25 years old, fluent in Spanish, and willing to make a 7 month commitment.

Peace Corps, 1990 K St. NW, Washington, DC 20526 (tel. (800) 424-8580). Volunteers must be U.S. citizens willing to make a two-year commitment.

Transitions Abroad Publishing, Inc., 18 Hulst Rd., P.O. Box 1300, Amherst, MA 01004 (tel. and fax (800) 293-0373); publishes a bimonthly magazine listing opportunities and printed resources for those seeking to study, work, or travel abroad. They also publish an *Alternative Travel Planner,* a truly exhaustive listing of information for the "active international traveler." For subscriptions (USA US$19.95 for 6 issues, Canada US$26, other countries US$38), contact *Transitions Abroad,* Dept. TRA, Box 3000, Denville, NJ 07834.

Voluntarios Solidarios, 515 Broadway, Santa Cruz, CA 95060 (tel. (408) 423-1626; fax (408) 423-8716). Work with grassroots peace and justice organizations in Latin America. Volunteers commit to working for several months.

Volunteers for Peace, 43 Tiffany Rd., Belmont, VT 05730 (tel. (802) 259-2759; fax (802) 259-2922). A non-profit organization that arranges placement in small workcamps in Costa Rica, Guatemala, and Nicaragua. Get up-to-date listings in the annual *International Workcamp Directory* (US$12). Registration fee US$150. Some workcamps are open to 16 and 17 year olds for US$175. Free newsletter.

YMCA International Camp Counselor Abroad Program, 71 West 23rd St., Suite 1904, New York, NY 10010 (tel. (212) 727-8800; fax (212) 727-8814). Sometimes offers camp-counseling opportunities in Central America. Applicants must be U.S. citizens, aged 21-30, with previous experience working in a YMCA camp. Applications available for the following summer beginning in September.

STUDY

Foreign study programs vary tremendously in expense, academic quality, living conditions, degree of contact with local students, and exposure to the local culture and language. Most American undergraduates enroll in programs sponsored by U.S. universities, and many colleges give advice on international study. Take advantage of these counselors and put in some hours in their libraries. Also ask for the names of (and get in touch with) recent participants in the programs.

American Field Service (AFS), 3rd Floor, 220 E. 42nd St., New York, NY 10017 (tel. (212) 949-4242). Summer, semester, and year-long homestay high school exchange programs in Costa Rica and Honduras. Short-term service projects for adults also offered. Financial aid available.

Amerispan, P.O Box 40513, Philadelphia, PA, 19106-0513 (tel. (800) 879-6640; worldwide (215) 985-4522; fax (215) 985-4524). 2-4 week Spanish immersion programs in Costa Rica, El Salvador, Guatemala, Honduras, and Panama. Classes 1 to 1 or in small groups; homestay, travel insurance, and meals included. US$325-1,890. Send away for their fancy brochure.

Central Bureau for Educational Visits and Exchanges, Seymour Mews House, Seymour Mews, London W1H 9PE (tel. (0171) 486 51 01; fax (0171) 935 5741). Publishes *Working Holidays 1995, Volunteer Work, Teach Abroad,* and *Home from Home*. All books are UK£8.99. Distributed in North America by IIE Books.

Institute for Central American Development Studies (ICADS), Dept. 826, P.O. Box 025216, Miami, FL 33102-5216 or **Instituto de Estudios de Desarrollo Centroamericano,** Apdo. 3-2070, San José, Costa Rica (tel. (506) 225-0508; fax (506) 234-1337). Semester abroad programs in Costa Rica, Nicaragua, and Belize aimed at students who wish to work for social justice in Central America. Areas of study include women's studies, environmental/ecological studies, public health, and agriculture. 30-day intensive Spanish program US$1000, including classes, homestay, breakfast and lunch, field trips, and afternoon volunteer opportunities.

Institute of International Education (IIE), 809 United Nations Plaza, New York, NY 10017-3580 (tel. (212) 984-5413; fax (212) 984-5358). A nonprofit, international exchange agency. Publishes *Academic Year Abroad* (US$42 plus US$4 shipping) detailing over 2200 semester and year-long programs worldwide and

Vacation Study Abroad (US$37 plus US$4 shipping) which lists over 1600 short-term, summer, and language school programs.

U.S. Servas Committee, 11 John Street, Suite #407, New York, NY 10038-4009 (tel. (212) 267-0252; fax (212) 267-0292; contact Nori Jaffer-Touré) An international cooperative system devoted to promoting peace and understanding through contact among cultures. Travelers spend 2-day homestays in host's homes in over 100 countries. Contact hosts in advance and be prepared to follow the household routine. Prospective travelers must submit an application with references, have an interview, and pay a membership fee of US$55, plus a US$25 deposit. Servas is non-profit and no money passes between traveler and host.

World Learning, Inc., Summer Abroad, P.O. Box 676, Battleboro, VT 05302 (tel. (800) 345-2929 or (802) 257-7751). Founded in 1932 as The U.S. Experiment in International Living, the organization offers high school programs in Belize, Costa Rica, and Mexico as well as language-training programs with elective homestays.

■■■ GAY AND LESBIAN TRAVELERS

Until recently, the strength of the Catholic church in Central America hindered the gay rights movement; today the region's countries accept homosexuality to varying degrees. In general, Central Americans disapprove of public displays of homosexual affection, and discretion is advised. People in cities are bound to be more tolerant than in rural areas. Honduras has been cited as the most liberal country in Central America for gays, although Costa Rica has recently developed a more supportive community. Homosexuality is legal (or not mentioned in the laws) in Belize, Costa Rica (at 17 years), El Salvador, Guatemala (at 18 years), Honduras, and Panama. In Nicaragua, "sodomy" is illegal and punishable with hefty prison sentences, particularly for those who work with children on a daily basis. For more information, consult the following sources:

Ferrari Publications, Inc., P.O. Box 37887, Phoenix, AZ 85069 (tel. (602) 863-2408). Publishers of *Ferrari's Places of Interest* (US$16), *Ferrari's Places for Men* (US$15), *Ferrari's Places for Women* (US$13), and *Inn Places: US and Worldwide Gay Accommodations* (US$16). Available in bookstores, or by mail order (postage US$4.50 for the first item, US$1.00 for each additional item).

Giovanni's Room, 345 S. 12th St. Philadelphia, PA 19107 (tel. (215) 923-2960; fax (215) 923-0813). An international feminist, lesbian, and gay bookstore with mail-order service. Call or write for a free mail-order catalogue.

Inland Book Company, P.O. Box 120261, East Haven, CT 06512 (tel. (203) 467-4257). Publishers of *Women Going Places* (US$14), an international women's travel and resource guide emphasizing women-owned enterprises, geared toward lesbians, but offering advice appropriate for all women.

Spartacus International Gay Guides, published by Bruno Gmunder, Postfach 110729, D-10837 Berlin, Germany (tel. (49) 30 615 00 30). Lists of bars, restaurants, hotels, and bookstores around the world catering to gay men. Also lists hotlines for gay men. Spartacus provides homosexuality laws for each country it covers. However, laws sometimes change faster than the book. Available in the US by mail order from Giovanni's Room as well as in bookstores (US$29.95).

■■■ TRAVELERS WITH DISABILITIES

Central America is not tremendously amenable for disabled travelers. Rainforests, volcanoes, and beaches rarely have smooth paths, and wheelchair accessible buildings are rare. Still, there are exceptions, and the region is not off-limits to disabled tourists. Those with disabilities should inform airlines and hotels of their disabilities when making arrangements for travel; some time may be needed to prepare special accommodations. Travelers with seeing eye dogs need to inquire as to the specific quarantine policies of the destination country. At the very least, they will need a certificate of immunization against rabies. The following organizations provide helpful information and publications, or help to organize trips for the disabled:

American Foundation for the Blind, 11 Penn Plaza, New York, NY 10011 (tel. (212) 502-7600). Provides information and services for the visually impaired. For a catalogue of products, contact Lighthouse Low-Vision Products at (800) 829-0500. Open Mon.-Fri. 8:30am-4:30pm.

Directions Unlimited, 720 North Bedford Rd., Bedford Hills, NY 10507 (tel. (800) 533-5343, (914) 241-1700; fax (914) 241-0243). Specializes in arranging individual and group vacations, tours, and cruises for those with physical disabilities.

Facts on File, 460 Park Ave., New York, NY 10016 (tel. (212) 683-2244). Publishers of *Access to the World* (US$16.95), a guide to handicap-accessible accommodations and sights. Available in bookstores or by mail order.

Flying Wheels Travel Service, P.O. Box 382, 143 W. Bridge St., Owatonna, MN 55060, (tel. (800) 535-6790; fax (507) 451-1685). Arranges international trips for groups or individuals in wheelchairs or with other sorts of limited mobility.

Mobility International, USA (MIUSA), P.O. Box 10767, Eugene, OR 97440 (tel. (503) 343-1284; fax (503) 343-6812). International headquarters in Britain, 228 Borough High St., London SE1 1JX (tel. 44 (071) 403 56 88). Information on travel programs, strategy courses, international work camps, accommodations, access guides, and organized tours for those with physical disabilities. Membership costs US$20 per year, newsletter US$10. Also publishes *A World of Options: A Guide to International Educational Exchange, Community Service, and Travel for Persons with Disabilities* (US$14, nonmembers US$16, postpaid).

Society for the Advancement of Travel for the Handicapped, 347 Fifth Ave., Suite 610, New York, NY 10016 (tel. (212) 447-7284; fax (212) 725-8253). Publishes quarterly travel newsletter, information sheets, and booklets (free for members, US$3 each for nonmembers), which contain advice on trip planning for people with disabilities. Annual membership is US$45, students and seniors US$25, agents and corporations US$100.

■■■ KOSHER AND VEGETARIAN TRAVELERS

San José, Costa Rica, Tegucigalpa, Honduras, and Panama City, Panama all have sizeable Jewish communities. For lists of kosher restaurants around the world, plus synagogues and Jewish institutions, consult **Ballantine-Mitchell Publishers** (Newbury House 890-900, Eastern Ave., Newbury Park, Ilford, Essex IG2 7HH, U.K. (tel. 44 (181) 599 8866; fax (181) 599 0984), publishers of *The Jewish Travel Guide*, which lists synagogues, kosher restaurants, and Jewish institutions in over 80 countries.

Vegetarians are often frustrated by the heavy emphasis on chicken in Latin American cuisine, but rice and beans and a variety of fresh fruits and vegetables offer other options. For more tips, check out the publications of the **Vegetarian Society of the UK,** from Ballantine-Mitchell, Parkdale, Dunham Rd., Altringham, Cheshire WA14 4QG (tel. 44 (61) 928 07 93). The *International Vegetarian Travel Guide* was last published in 1991, but copies are still available for £1.99 from VSUK.

■■■ WOMEN TRAVELERS

Women travelers to Central America are often surprised by the unwanted attention they receive. If you look like an *extranjera* (foreigner), you will find it difficult to remain alone except when locked in your hotel room. Persistent men commonly insist on joining women, who should also expect to hear whistles and propositions while walking down the street. Offer no response and make no eye contact; any kind of answer could be interpreted as a come-on. Should a situation become threatening, however, do not hesitate to lash out with a scream or even physical force. Creating a loud fuss is often publicly humiliating for the menace, who may shrink back in defeat. In real emergencies, scream for help. Don't consider yourself safe because people in uniform are around or because you are in your hotel.

Awareness of Latin American social standards can also prevent unpleasant and dangerous confrontations. Bars are all-male institutions; the only women who ever enter are working, either as servers or as prostitutes.

If you are traveling with a male friend, it may help to pose as a couple. This will assuage any misgivings hotel proprietors have about letting you share rooms and may serve to chill the blood of your Central American admirer. Women traveling alone should consider preparing a story of an "uncle," or another male who is "supposed to show up any minute." Some women wear a "wedding ring" on their left hand to discourage unwanted attention.

To additionally ensure your safety, stay in well lit places. Memorize the emergency numbers of the countries or states you are visiting, and prepare yourself with a self-defense course before leaving. Generally trust your instincts; unsafe parts of town usually *feel* unsafe. Don't travel at night, and remember that hitchhiking is never safe. Carry a little extra stashed money for an emergency phone call. See Before You Go: Packing, page 8, for hints about what clothes are appropriate. For additional tips and general reference, consult the following sources:

National Organization for Women, branches across the country, can refer you to rape crisis centers, counselling services, and provide lists of feminist events in the area. Main offices include 22 W 21st, 7th floor, New York, NY 10010 (tel. (212) 807-0721); 1000 16th St. NW, Suite 700, Washington DC 20036 (tel. (202) 331-0066); 3543 18th St., San Francisco, CA 94110 (tel. (415) 861-8880).

Directory of Women's Media is available from the National Council for Research on Women, 530 Broadway, 10th Floor, New York, NY 10012 (tel. (212) 274-0730; fax 274-0821). Lists of women's publishers, bookstores, and news organizations.

Handbook For Women Travelers, by Maggie and Gemma Moss. Encyclopedic and well-written. Order from Piaktus Books, 5 Windmill St., London W1P 1HF (tel. (171) 631-0710). (£8.99).

Women Travel: Adventures, Advice & Experience, by Miranda Davies and Natania Jansz (Penguin US$13). Has info on specific foreign countries plus a decent bibliography and resource index.

■■■ SENIOR CITIZENS

Senior travelers should bring a medical record that includes an update on conditions and prescriptions; the name, phone number, and address of a regular doctor; and a summary of recent medical history.

Travel Tips for Older Americans (US$1) provides information on passports, health, and currency for those traveling abroad; contact the Superintendent of Documents (see Feed Your Head, page 1). The *International Health Guide for Senior Travelers* (US$4.95 plus US$1 postage) is available from Pilot Books, 103 Cooper St., Babylon, NY 11702 (tel. (516) 422-2225).

For more information, write to the tourism offices of the countries you plan to visit. The following organizations and publications can also be helpful:

Elderhostel, 75 Federal St., 3rd floor, Boston, MA 02110-1941 (tel. (617) 426-7788; fax (617) 426-8351). You must be 55 or over and may bring a spouse of any age. Programs at colleges and universities in Belize, Costa Rica, and Panama focus on varied subjects (but include field-trips), and generally last one to four weeks.

National Council of Senior Citizens, 1331 F St. NW, Washington, DC 20004 (202)-347-8800. Memberships are US$12 a year, US$30 for three years, or US$150 for a lifetime. Individuals or couples can receive hotel and auto rental discounts, a senior citizen newspaper, and use of a discount travel agency.

Pilot Books, 103 Cooper St., Babylon, NY 11702 (tel. (516) 422-2225). Publishes a large number of helpful guides including *The International Health Guide for Senior Citizens* (US$4.95, postage US$1). Call or write for a complete list of titles.

TRAVEL IN THE REGION

■■■ GETTING THERE

BY PLANE

Getting to Central America is not always easy, although flights are becoming more and more frequent as tourism to the region increases. Finding a cheap **airfare** in airlines' computerized jungle will be easier if you understand the system. Have a knowledgeable travel agent guide you; students and "youth" (people under 25) should never have to pay full price for a ticket. Seniors can also get great deals. Sunday newspapers often have travel sections which list bargain fares from the local airport. *The Airline Passenger's Guerrilla Handbook* (US$15; last published in 1990) is a renegade resource for finding the best fares.

Most airfares peak between mid-June and early September. Midweek (Mon.-Thurs. morning) flights run about US$30-40 cheaper than on weekends. Traveling from hub cities wins a more competitive fare than from smaller cities. **Miami** and **Houston** are popular points of departure for flights to Central America. Return-date flexibility is usually not an option for the budget traveler; traveling with an "open return" ticket can be pricier than fixing a return date and paying to change it. When flying internationally, confirm reservations 72 hours before your departure and arrive at the airport at least two hours before your flight.

Even paying the lowest published fare of a **commercial airline** may be a waste of hundreds of dollars. The airlines' lowest regular offer is the **APEX** (Advance Purchase Excursion Fare); specials advertised in newspapers may be cheaper, but have more restrictions and fewer available seats. APEX fares confirm reservations and allow "open-jaw" tickets (landing in and returning from different cities). Generally, reservations must be made seven to 21 days in advance with 7- to 14-day minimum and up to 90-day maximum stay limits; to cancel or change a flight can be costly.

STUDENT TRAVEL AGENCIES

Students and people under 26 with proper ID qualify for enticing reduced airfares. These are rarely available from airlines or regular travel agents, but instead from student travel agencies like those listed below. These agencies negotiate special reduced-rate bulk purchases with the airlines, then resell them to the youth market. Return-date change fees also tend to be low (around US$25 per segment through Council or Let's Go Travel). Most of their flights are on major airlines, though in peak season some seats may be on less reliable chartered aircraft. Student travel agencies can also help non-students and people over 26, but probably won't be able to get the same low fares. Call around for the best prices.

Campus Travel, 52 Grosvenor Gardens, London SW1W OAG. Campus Travel is a large supplier of student travel products in the U.K., with 37 branches throughout the country. They supply student cards, flights, trains, boats, and a full range of related products and services. In London, for telesales and bookings for Europe call (0171) 730 3402; for North America (0171) 730 2101; worldwide (0171) 730 811). In Manchester((0161) 273 1721. In Scotland (0131) 668 3303.

Council Travel, the travel division of Council, is a full-service travel agency specializing in student, youth, and budget travel with over 50 offices worldwide. They offer discount airfares on scheduled airlines, low-cost accommodations, budget tours, travel gear, and international identity cards. 41 offices in the U.S., call 800-2-COUNCIL (800-226-8624) for the closest one. **U.K.:** 28A Poland St., Oxford Circus, London W1V 3DB (tel. (0171) 437 7767).

STA Travel, 6560 North Scottsdale Rd. #F100, Scottsdale, AZ 85253 (tel. (800) 777-0112 nationwide; in London (0171) 938 4711); in Australia (03) 347 6911)). A student and youth travel organization with over 100 offices around the world

ESSENTIALS

and 14 U.S. locations offering discount airfares (for travelers under 26 and full-time students under 32), accommodations, tours, and insurance.

Journeys, 4011 Jackson Rd., Ann Arbor, MI 48103 (tel. (800) 255-8735). Offers small-group, 1-2 week guided explorations of 32 different countries, including Belize, Costa Rica, and Panama. Prices range from US$1000-2500. Free newsletter for prospective travelers.

Let's Go Travel, Harvard Student Agencies, 53A Church St., Cambridge, MA 02138 (800-5-LETS GO(800-553-8746), or 617-495-9649). Let's Go offers International ID cards, guidebooks, maps, bargain flights, and budget travel gear. All items available by mail; call for a catalog.

Travel CUTS (Canadian University Travel Services, Ltd.), 187 College St., Toronto, Ont. M5T 1P7 (tel. (416) 798-CUTS (798-2887); fax 979-8167). Offices across Canada. Also, in the **U.K.,** 295-A Regent St., London W1R 7YA (tel. (0171) 637 31 61). Discounted flights and other services. Special fares with valid ISIC or FIYTO cards. Offers free *Student Traveller* magazine, and info on Student Work Abroad.

Usit, 19-21 Aston Quay, O'Connell Bridge, Dublin 2 (tel. (01) 679 88 33; fax 677 88 43). Sells ISIC and *Let's Go*, in addition to discounted student fares on scheduled flights. Usit books its own charter flights for some of the best flight deals going.

CONSOLIDATORS AND COURIER FLIGHTS

Ticket consolidators, also known as "bucket shops," resell unsold tickets on commercial and charter airlines. Look for their tiny ads in weekend papers (in the U.S., the *Sunday New York Times* is best). In London, the Air Travel Advisory Bureau (tel. (0171) 636 50 00) provides a list of consolidators. There is rarely a maximum age or stay limits; tickets are also heavily discounted, and may offer extra flexibility or bypass advance purchase requirements. You won't be able to use your tickets on another flight if you miss yours, and you'll have to go back to the consolidator to get a refund, rather than the airline; get the refund policy in writing, along with a receipt. Consult Kelly Monaghan's *Consolidators: Air Travel's Bargain Basement* (US$5 plus US$3.50 shipping) from the Intrepid Traveler, P.O. Box 438, New York, NY 10034, for more information and a list of consolidators.

Me Again Travel, 66 Court St., Brooklyn, NY (tel. (718) 852-9410), specializes in travel to Latin America, and has special fares to Central American cities. **Generic Air Travels,** a sister-service of **Airhitch,** 2472 Broadway, Suite 200, New York, NY 10025 (tel. (800) 326-2009 or (212) 864-2000) and Santa Monica, CA (tel. (310) 394-0550), offers fares to San José, Costa Rica (US$460-500) and most other large Central American cities, with possible limitations to length of stay.

Those who travel light should consider flying as a **courier.** The company hiring you will use your checked luggage space for freight; you're only allowed to bring carry-ons. Restrictions to watch for: you must be over 18 and have a valid passport, most flights are round-trip only with short fixed-length stays (usually one week); you may not be able to travel with a companion (single tickets only); and most flights are from New York. **NOW Voyager,** 74 Varick St. #307, New York, NY 10013 (tel. (212) 431-1616), acts as an agent for many courier flights worldwide primarily from New York. They occasionally offer special last-minute deals to South American and Central American cities. You can also go directly through courier companies in New York, or check your bookstore or library for handbooks such as *The Courier Air Travel Handbook* (US$10 plus US$3.50 shipping), which explains how to travel as an air courier and contains names, phone numbers, and contact points of courier companies. It can be ordered directly from Bookmasters, Inc., P.O. Box 2039, Mansfield, OH 44905 (tel. (800) 507-2665).

If you really have travel time to spare, **Ford's Travel Guides,** 19448 Londelius St., Northridge, CA 91324 (tel. (818) 701-7414) lists **freighter companies** that will take passengers worldwide. Ask for their *Freighter Travel Guide and Waterways of the World* (US$15, plus US$2.50 postage if mailed outside the U.S.

BY BUS OR TRAIN

All overland routes to Central America from the U.S. necessarily go through Mexico. Greyhound serves many U.S.-Mexico border towns, including El Paso and Brownsville. It is also possible to travel by Amtrak to San Antonio (US$279 round-trip from New York) and take a bus from there to the border towns. More directly, you can take Amtrak to El Paso (US$254-494 round-trip from New York), walk across the border to Ciudad Juárez and from there use other forms of transportation to travel on to Central America. Buses tend not to cross the border, but at each of these stops you can pick up Mexican bus lines on the other side. **Tres Estrellas de Oro**, **Estrella Blanca**, and **Transportes Del Norte** provide service from the border.

Follow whatever bus route suits your fancy to get through Mexico (see *Let's Go: Mexico* for detailed information). A possible trip down to Central America (at the Guatemalan border) would bring you through Chihuahua, Torreón, Zacatecas, Aguas Calientes, Ciudad de México, Oaxaca, Tehuantapec, and Tapachula. **Omnibus de México** (tel. (5)567-67-56 or (5)567-72-86) buses run to and from most major destinations, through their hub in Mexico City. **Cristobál Colón** (tel. 916-2-61-22) is the major bus line in Chiapas, and goes right up to the Guatemalan border. The **Batty Brothers** line goes from Chetumal, Mexico to Belize, if that's you're preferred entry point. For wild adventures of another kind, and for the most free-spirited, flexible travelers, **Green Tortoise Adventure Travel,** 494 Broadway, San Francisco, CA 94133 (tel. (800) 867-8647 or (415) 956-7500; fax (415) 956-4900, maintains a fleet of old diesel coaches, dubbed "hostels on wheels," complete with foam mattresses, sofa seats, and dinettes. Travelers can expect communal cooking and frequent jaunts off the road for hikes, swims, and local explorations. "The Southern Migration" runs from San Francisco, California to Antigua, Guatemala for US$649 plus US$151 for food. Book ahead, as trips fill up fast. Call or write for a brochure.

Traveling through Mexico by train takes longer, but is considerably less expensive than the commonly preferred bus journey. The government-run Mexican railroads operate under the name of **Ferrocarriles Nacionales de Mexico** (National Railways of Mexico). Trains run from the border at Nogales, Piedras Negras, Nuevo Laredo, Matamoros, and Mexicali.

BY CAR

Cruising to Central America from the U.S. with a car can be a fantastically boundless and inexpensive way to get through Mexico, but it could easily turn into a nightmarish episode of pure traveling mayhem. Be prepared for the worst, make sure your shock-absorbers are primed, and come up with several ways to ensure your car's security; someone will likely try to break into it. In the United States, the **American Automobile Association (AAA)** offers emergency road services, travel services, and auto insurance (free for members, for a small fee if not). For emergency road services, call (800) 222-4357; to become a member, call (800) 926-4222 for the nearest office. Once in Mexico, the AAA-affiliated **Asociación Mexicana Automovilística, A.C. (AMA),** Av. Orizaba 7, Mexico, D.F. 06700 (tel. (5) 208-88-69; fax 511-62-85) provides information about car travel in Mexico, up-to-date road maps, emergency road assistance, and other services, including maps.

All non-Mexican **car insurance** is invalid in Mexico, no matter what your policy says. You will probably be able to buy insurance at the border at one of many small insurance offices located next door to immigration offices. **Sanborn's,** Home Office, P.O. Box 310, McAllen, TX 78505-0310 (tel. (210) 686-0711; fax 686-0732) offers Mexican and Central American insurance with all the trimmings, including road maps, newsletters, a ride board, a mile-by-mile guide to Mexico and Central America, and "Mexico Mike" in Dept. N at the McAllen address (write him for up-to-date information on driving in Mexico). Remember that if you are in an accident, the police might hold you in jail until everything is sorted out and all claims are settled. If you can prove your ability to pay, they will release you.

INTERNATIONAL DRIVER'S PERMIT

Acquiring an international driver's permit is recommended for travelers to Central America, although it is not mandatory. In Panama, Nicaragua, and Guatemala, your foreign license is valid for 30 days, but the international license is preferred in the other countries. Carry your registration papers and proof of ownership at all times. Contact the American Automobile Association (above), or a similar organization in your home country, to acquire an international permit. In Mexico, an international driver's permit is not required, but a **vehicle permit** is. For this document, be prepared with two proofs of ownership of your car and a credit card or cash to pay a financial guarantee for temporary importation.

■■■ ONCE THERE

BY PLANE

Flights between Central American cities are usually pretty cheap (compared to domestic fares in the U.S.), and are considerably more time-efficient than long, winding bus routes. Single- and twin-engine planes travel within countries and to islands and offer a unique flying experience; some planes are so small that one lucky passenger actually sits up front with the pilot. Make sure a line is reputably safe before boarding; most are, despite the ominous "In God We Trust" signs hanging over the doors of some planes; most passengers like to put trust in the pilot, too.

BY BOAT

The recent creation of **Ultimate Adventures Tours and Transport** has opened a new door for travelers working their way between countries. For US$250, you can purchase a ticket good for two years to board a ship traveling between Cancún, Mexico; Belize City, Belize, La Ceiba, Honduras; Bluefields, Nicaragua; Puerto Limon, Costa Rica; Colón, Panama; Cartagena, Colombia; Amuay, Venezuela; Santo Domingo, Dominican Republic; Port Antonio Jamaica; and Cienfuegos, Cuba. The ship comes to each port every two weeks, so you are free to dock wherever they want before hopping back on weeks later. There are hammock hooks on the ship's deck, or you can pay US$30 a night for a bunk. For more information, contact Third World Travel, 56088 1st. Ave. Marketplace, Vancouver, B.C., V5M 4S9, Canada, or call (604) 877-1692 or fax (604) 876-6194.

Bus a Move

While cruising between volcanoes and rainforests, take the time to avert your glance from landscapes to absorb the wild adventures offered by the buses, themselves. Every visitor to the region comes home with at least one story of drivers drag-racing over windy roads, con-men eloquently peddling "miracle pills" between stops, massive *bandido* hold-ups, or women clinging to unruly baskets of live poultry, all while some strange mélange of music wails through decrepid speakers in a second-hand school bus from the United States. Don't worry about getting hungry; at nearly every stop, villagers march through the aisle shoving juice and fried mystery-morsels in passengers' faces. Others conveniently dangle their wares through the windows from the outside by holding cleverly constructed poles with goodie-laden trays. Expect the alimentary onslaught moments after hearing the juice vendors' roaring war-cry: "*Jugojugos! Jugojugos!*" Meanwhile, the bus drivers or *ayudantes* (helpers) carry a mystique of their own. With shirts unbuttoned to the navel, the drivers valiantly load packages, babies, and elderly passengers with confident authority—but not without the inspirational icons on the dashboard. And after a while, most travelers long to be part of the universal brotherhood of drivers who salute each other along the road with honks, waves, secret handshakes, and burly shouts.

BY BUS

Most budget visitors to Central America get from place to place by bus. Direct, first-class trips are often available between major cities, but otherwise, expect at least a few harrowing and excellent adventures on the legendary Central American chicken buses. Don't expect to get to your destination on time. The vehicles' worn shocks often allow passengers to feel every bump in the rough roads, and drivers have few qualms about putting it into high gear on windy downhills. It's usually best to snag a window seat (unless you're tall) to enjoy the view and for cool, fresh air. Getting the shadier side is an even better bonus. Traveling by bus at night is often unsafe; check with authorities before doing so. Be particularly careful about your luggage; only put it you where you can see it.

BY CAR

If driving in a **taxi,** be sure to tell the driver where you want to go before you get in. If he agrees to take you, *always ask how the driver much the trip will cost.* If you think he's asking too much, you can either bite the bullet, try to bargain him down, or simply find another cab. Many drivers ask a higher-than-normal *gringo* rate, so beware. Taxi drivers don't like it when pedestrians or other drivers ask them for directions, and have often have no problems leading someone astray. Women are advised to always sit in the back of a taxi to avoid unwanted physical attention.

If you have your own **car,** the durability and security of your car are of unspeakable importance for successful travel through Central America. Parts, gas, and trustworthy service stations are all hard to come by, so be prepared for every possible occurrence. Come equipped with spare gas, tires, spare oil, spark plugs, fan belts, air, fuel filters, and most of all, thorough know-how. Try not to leave valuable possessions in the car while you're off rambling. If your tape deck or radio is removable, hide it in the trunk or take it with you; if it isn't, at least conceal it under a lot of junk. Similarly, hide baggage in the trunk, although savvy thieves can tell if a car is heavily loaded by the way it is settled on its tires. Park your vehicle in a garage or well-traveled area. If you must sleep in your car, do so as close to a police station or a 24-hr.service station as possible. Unleaded gas is no longer as hard to get as in years past. But even if you do find an unleaded pump, it may be filled with regular gasoline. Mechanically inclined drivers might want to order a "test" pipe from a specialty parts house to replace the catalytic converter so the car can process regular upon its arrival in the region.

Central American drivers have their own codes of right-of-way, and it takes time to get used to the street signs while traveling from country to country. In general, take it easy until you master the sign language of a country's roads.

Be especially careful driving during the rainy season (May-Oct.), when roads are often in poor condition, potholes become craters, and landslides are common. At night, pedestrians and livestock pop up on the roadway at the darndest times. This doesn't seem to bother the locals, many of whom drive without headlights. If you can help it, don't drive at night. When approaching a one-lane bridge, labeled *puente angosto* or *solo carril,* the first driver to flash headlights has the right of way. Lanes are narrow, so if a truck tries to pass your car on a two-lane road, you might need to pull off onto the gravel or dirt in order to give the vehicle enough room.

Highway drivers have become increasingly frequent victims of assaults and robberies. Be especially careful when traveling alone, and always check with local authorities or the nearest U.S. consulate to identify areas of potential danger. See country-specific Essentials sections for more information.

While on the road, you might be stopped by agents or the police for a search of your car and its contents. To avoid being detained or arrested, be as cooperative as possible. Do *not* carry drugs or firearms in your car.

If you get into a car accident realize that as soon as the police arrive, they will detain everybody until they have figured out what happened, no matter who's to blame. An insurance policy will usually spring you from jail.

BY THUMB

> *Let's Go* urges you to use common sense if you decide to hitch, and to seriously consider all possible risks before you make that decision. The information listed below and throughout the book is not intended to recommend hitchhiking; *Let's Go* does not recommend hitchhiking as a means of transportation.

The Central Americans who pick up tourists are commonly friendly, offering meals, tours, or other extras, but suspicion is often warranted. Those who hitch should find out where the driver is going before they get in, and think twice if he or she opens the door quickly and offers to drive anywhere. Do not accept a ride if any cause for concern arises; make an excuse and wait for another car to come along. Women should never hitchhike alone. Never accept a ride without sizing up the driver. On many highways, *bandidos* are common.

Before getting in, make sure the passenger window or door opens from inside. If there are several people in the car, do not sit in the middle. Assume a quick-exit position, which rules out the back seat of a two-door car. Keep backpacks and other baggage where they are easily accessible—don't let the driver store them in the trunk. If you have trouble getting out for any reason, affecting the pose of someone about to vomit works wonders.

Every city and every road has a best and worst spot for hitchhiking. Hitchers recommend gas stations and stretches near a major intersection where many cars converge. Hitchers should be cautious when standing on the shoulders of highways, since they are not considered off-limits to drivers, and they should bring along something to drink and some sort of protection from the sun and rain. Furthermore, it's said that those who appear neat and travel light have a better chance of getting a ride. Some drivers may ask for payment for the ride, especially in areas where no alternative form of public transportation exists. Truck drivers often earn extra revenue by taking on passengers. As with a taxi, riders should always ask what a ride in a truck will cost before getting in; it may seem expensive, it is usually based on expenses. Those in the know say that cargo trucks are easy to hitch with.

■■■ ACCOMMODATIONS

For information on homestays in Central America, see Alternatives to Tourism, page 17, and for camping tips, see Camping and Hiking, page 33.

Every large city in Central America offers a wide range of hotels, from the dirt-cheap (where the dirt comes cheaply) to the ultra-ritzy. The smaller the town, the narrower the selection. Usually located within a block or two of the main town square, the cheapest hotels rarely provide private bathrooms or other amenities. Slightly higher-priced hotels usually reside in the same district but are much better equipped, including rooms with private bathrooms. Before accepting any room, ask to see it, and always ask if the price includes any meals. Also don't forget to consider whether there are fans or air-conditioning, and beware the potential for nerve-wracking noise (usually based on the room's proximity to the street or bus station). If the hotel looks like it hasn't seen a customer in several days, a little bargaining may work wonders, especially if you offer to stay a number of days. For a room with one bed, request *un cuarto con una cama*. If bedding down with a fellow wayfarer, ask for one *con dos camas* (with two beds). Some proprietors might not allow unmarried mixed-sex couples to share a bed, so be prepared to settle for separation or to pose as glee-struck newlyweds.

If the hotels listed in *Let's Go* are full or don't appeal to you, ask cab drivers or vendors in the market for a good recommendation. Also, hotel people in one town are often a good source for hotel leads in the next town on your itinerary. For the bare-bones budget traveler, it's not a bad idea to get a hammock.

Hotels in Central America often lock their doors at night, and small-town establishments may do so surprisingly early. A locked door doesn't necessarily mean "closed for the night," as someone usually is on duty. By arriving early in small towns or calling ahead if you can't avoid arriving late, and by checking with the hotel desk before going out for a late night on the town, you'll save yourself some anxiety and the proprietor some sleep.

Reservations are not absolutely necessary (except during Christmas, *Semana Santa,* and other festivals), but if you're exhausted upon arrival, they make life much easier, assuming the hotel has a telephone. You can just about always find a bed somewhere, but without reservations you may waste money and time.

Prepare yourself for those toilets which don't have flush mechanisms; before using the john, look for a bucket and fill it with water. When you're done, quickly pour the water in the bowl and watch in amazement as the laws of lavatory gravity do their magical stuff (and successfully wash away your magical stuff)

■■■ KEEPING IN TOUCH

MAIL

Central American mail service ranges from slow and erratic to speedy and reliable, depending on the country and fate's whims. (See country-specific Keeping in Touch sections for more information.) Airmail often reaches the U.S. in as few as six days, but can just as easily take a month or more. It takes even longer (at least two weeks) to Europe and other destinations, since mail is usually routed through U.S. surface mail. Official estimates average 40 days by boat, but in reality may take months. Anything important should be sent registered mail, or else duplicates should be sent. Never deposit anything important in the black holes known euphemistically as mailboxes. *La estampilla* or *el timbre* is "the stamp" in Spanish, and *la carta* is "the letter."

You can have letters sent to you in Central America through **Lista de Correos,** a letter-holding service similar to General Delivery (*Entrega General*, or *Poste Restante*) in the U.S. When picking up mail sent to you via *Lista de Correos,* look for a list posted in the post office. Check it carefully for any possible misspellings or confusions. If there is no list posted, ask the attendant, "*¿Está la lista de hoy?*" (Is today's list here?). If it is, give your name. Letters and packages will be held for varying lengths of time, but count on two weeks. If you have friends or family in the area, using their address may be preferable. Hotels where you have reserved a room will usually hold mail for you. **American Express offices** will also hold mail for 30 days before returning it; just write "Client's Mail" on the envelope. You don't need to be a cardholder to receive this service as long as you purchase traveler's checks from AmEx. Call American Express customer service at (800) 528-4800 for more information and ask for the free *Directory of Traveler Service Offices*.

Mail sent to *Lista de Correos* should be addressed to a first and last name only, capitalizing and underlining the name under which the item should be filed alphabetically. Keep names as simple as possible. Because Latin American *apellidos* (paternal last names) fall in the middle of the written name, confusion arises for foreigners with more than a simple first and last name, or in the case of mail addressed to more than one person. A letter could be filed under any misspelled permutation of the recipient's names. If possible, go through the *Lista de Correos* yourself. If not, watch the person who does and ask for the mail under both your first and your last name, just to make sure. The letter should also be marked *Favor de retener hasta la llegada* ("Please hold until arrival"). Bring a passport or other ID to pick up General Delivery mail.

It's wise to use the Spanish abbreviations or names for countries (EEUU or EUA for the U.S.). Write *Por Avión* on all postcards and letters not otherwise marked, unless you don't mind it arriving sometime in the next millennium. Regulations for mailing parcels may vary from country to country. While it is often possible to send packages from smaller towns, post offices in large cities provide more reliable service. In order to send packages you must provide a list of contents including estimated value and nature of the package ("Gift" works best), address, and return address. In a trade office, you may need to show receipts for each item purchased.

TELEPHONES, FAXES, AND TELEGRAMS

Country-specific **telephone codes** are listed in each chapter's Essentials section. In some cases, **city codes** are listed under Telephones in the practical information sections. When trying to place telephone calls to Central America from another country, or even from town to town within a country, patience is the key to success. If you're calling information, don't be surprised if the phone is not answered right away. Many public phones are out of service, and the other half take rare low-denomination coins.

Getting lines to foreign countries is very difficult. Many public phones don't have access to international lines. If you speak Spanish fluently and can't reach the international operator, call the national operator, who will connect you (sometimes even a local operator can help). The term for a collect call is a *llamada por cobrar* or *llamada con cobro revertido*. Calling from hotels is usually faster. Fortunately, service from AT&T and other companies is improving, and collect calls with English-speaking operators is available from more and more central telephone offices.

Long-distance charges vary from place to place. Call collect to avoid the enormous surcharges that hotel switchboards impose if you call direct. Using a U.S. operator to call collect or with a calling card will let you pay U.S. rates (around US$5-6 per min. depending on distance between cities). After finding a new way to minimize the cost of calls from Central America, two cousins recently founded **The Budget Traveler,** a system of offices specializing in international telecommunications. They charge a blanket rate for calls: US$1.75 per minute to the U.S., US$2.50 to Canada, and US$3.50 per minute to Europe and Australia. They have thus far established offices in Guatemala, Belize, Honduras, and Costa Rica. Fax service is also available at most branches, as well as fact-sheets listing international news and travelers' tips. Affiliate offices are listed in city's practical information sections when applicable. For more information about the service, call (212) 826-5883 or fax (212) 758-6865.

You can place **international calls** from most telephones and from all telephone offices. To call Central America from the United States, dial the universal international access code (011) followed the country code, the city code, and the local number. Country codes and city codes may sometimes be listed with a zero in front (e.g. 502-09), but when using 011, drop successive zeros (e.g., dial 011-502-9). In some areas you will have to get an operator to place the call.

You may want to consider getting a **calling card** if you plan to make a lot of international calls; the cost is significantly lower. Your local long-distance phone company will have a number for you to dial while in a foreign country (either toll-free or charged as a local call) to connect instantly to an operator in your home country. Some companies will be able to connect you to numbers only in your home country; others will be able to provide other worldwide connections. For more information, call **AT&T** about its **USADirect** and **World Connect** services (tel. (800) 331-1140, from abroad (412) 553-7458); **Sprint** (tel. (800) 877-4646); or **MCI World Phone** and **World Reach** (tel. (800) 996-7535). If you are not an American, call your phone company in your home country; they offer similar services: in Canada contact Bell Canada **Canada Direct** (tel. (800) 561-8868), in Australia Telsta **Australia Direct** (tel. 13 22 00), in Ireland Telecom Eireann **Ireland Direct** (tel. (800) 25 25 25), in New Zealand Telecom New Zealand (tel. 123), in South Africa **Telkom South Africa** (tel. 0903), and in the U.K. British Telecom **BT Direct** (tel. (800) 34 51 44). Phone rates tend to be highest in the morning, low in the evening, and lowest on Sunday and at night (AT&T's and MCI's phone rates remain constant).

A surprisingly large number of Central American businesses have fax machines; even enterprises that couldn't possibly need instant communications (e.g. laundromats) have been convinced that capitalistic legitimacy means owning a fax machine. As a result, it's often easier to reach some people by fax than by telephone. Public faxes are often available at telephone offices, for both sending and receiving. International telegrams can also be faster and cheaper than using the phone. Fill out a form at most post or telephone offices.

■■■ CAMPING AND HIKING

If you have a tent to pitch, be sure to *always* ask local authorities first before camping anywhere. Sleeping out near a town poses risks of thieves and hostile property owners; heading into the wild to camp is dangerous for multiple other reasons. Regardless of whether you're venturing out on a day trip to some ruins or a full-fledged camping expedition in a rainforest, be aware of your safety at all times.

The three most important things to remember when hiking: stay warm, stay dry, stay hydrated. Don't underestimate how cold it can get at night in Central America, especially in the highlands. If you are going on any hike, pack raingear, warm layers (not cotton!), first-aid kit, high energy food, as much water as you can carry, and water purification tablets. Many rivers and lakes are contaminated with *giardia*; be sure to purify any water you take from a natural source. Always be aware of snakes and other dangerous animals in the wild. A more common problem in forested areas is insects. Many (notably mosquitoes) are most active at night, and many also carry dangerous diseases (see Health: Preventing Disease, page 12).

Always check weather forecasts and pay attention to the skies when hiking, as blue skies can turn to pouring rain before you can say "hypothermia." To avoid a twisted ankle, the most frequent outdoor injury, be sure to wear hiking boots appropriate for the terrain. Always try to go hiking with somebody, for fun and safety reasons; otherwise, let someone know exactly where you are headed, either a friend, your hotel, or a local outdoor organization. In Central America, criminals often take advantage of tourists in popular natural attractions; check with locals about the safety of your planned trip. Do not attempt a hike beyond your ability.

Future tourists should be allowed to appreciate Central America's natural wonders, too, so be careful to leave the nature exactly as you find it. Don't cut vegetation, don't clear campsites, and stay on marked trails. Make sure camping is permitted and that your campsite is at least 150ft. from water supplies or bodies of water. Always pack your trash in a plastic bag and carry it with you until you reach the next trash can; burning and burying pollutes the environment.

Central America: An Introduction

■■■ HISTORY

Like misfit pieces of an unsolvable jigsaw puzzle, the countries of Central America seem to have been doomed to permanent political fragmentation. Bound together by geography and language, the modern Central American nations also share many cultural and historical features, but despite these links have never successfully attained the isthmian unity for which many leaders have struggled. The political turbulence of the last few decades has received unprecedented attention from the international press, but the conflicts really just mark another bump in the region's long history of division and turmoil. Modern visitors who enjoy Central America for its unique heterogeneity (as well as those who thrive on the adventure of traveling across political land-mines) often aren't aware that the region's current status is the result of a historical roller-coaster with more downs than ups.

Some archaeologists speculate that humans inhabited the area as many as 40,000 years ago, but evidence points to the actual development of civilization around 3,000 years ago, when Mesoamerican, South American, and Caribbean populations spread over the area and began to exchange ideas. Though the Maya maintained the most developed **Pre-Columbian civilization** in Central America (See Mayan Marvels, page 35), they were by no means the area's only natives when Columbus arrived. The Chibcha inhabited Panama and Costa Rica after migrating from the South, modern day El Salvador and Nicaragua served as home to the Pipil and Nicarao groups, and the **Mosquitia** coast of Honduras and Nicaragua received the Miskito, Sumo, and Rama tribes, many of which exist still today. The Indians' continued presence is particularly impressive given the brute swiftness with which the Spanish conquered (and absorbed) many other indigenous groups after 1500.

The first Europeans to come to Central America, **Rodrigo de Bastidas** and **Christopher Columbus,** were merely interested in exploration; they bypassed settlement of the area, perhaps not recognizing the region's economic potential. The value of the area's riches was not lost on **Vasco Núñez de Balboa,** however, who not only settled in Panama, but fostered relations with the Indians and found his way through to the Pacific. Until 1517, the harsh treatment of the Indians by the Spanish was limited to the suffering caused by diseases the Europeans brought with them, but following the execution of Balboa and the ascension of **General Pedrarias Dávila,** the more familiar period of enslavement and genocide began. In a few years, Pedrarias had all but conquered the southern part of Central America; meanwhile, Cortés' forces headed south from Mexico, spreading the Spanish brutality to the rest of the land bridge. Relatively few Spanish forces annihilated millions of Indians and captured equal numbers as slaves (under the **Spanish New Laws** of 1542); they simultaneously established a tradition of oppressing the *indígenas* that to a lesser extent continues still today.

Using the wealth of precious metals taken from the region, strong Spanish leaders such as Pedro de Alvarado helped to form the **Kingdom of Guatemala** (between Chiapas, Mexico and Costa Rica) by 1530. When mineral deposits thinned out, cacao became Spain's principal export (though Panama grew steadily as the trans-isthmian crossing point for riches stripped from the Peruvian Incas.) As wealth increased, so did the strength of divisions within the class system, in which Creole landholders and Spanish administrators ruled Indian workers. Still, greed got the best of the Spanish, who were unable to successfully unify the area's various regions because of competition between haughty municipal councils. Through the next centuries, as wealth through exports increased, so did regionalistic sentiment; no ruler was willing to let wealth slip into his neighbors' coffers. By the 19th century, European wars had weakened Spain's hold on the isthmus; the Spanish allowed the installation of the **Cadíz Constitution** of 1812, which increased the colonies' representation in the national Parliament. Soon thereafter, the constitution was annulled, a royal act which divided Conservatives from Liberals.

Spain's Liberal Revolution of 1820 dealt the final blow to the European nation's grasp and set the stage for Central America's most successful attempt at union. In 1823, an assembly officially decreed the independence of the **United Province of Central America,** which included Guatemala, El Salvador, Honduras, Nicaragua, and Costa Rica (at the time, Belize was under British control and Panama was a part of Colombia). Despite relative autonomy granted to the states, leaders were unable to adhere to the federation's constitutional laws; jealousies and self-interest again led to unity's demise. Conservatives (royalists), pushing for the centralization of power, fought the reforming ideals of Liberal (republican) leaders such as Honduras' **Francisco Morazan,** and the organization again decayed into fragmented states by 1840.

The year 1847 marked the start of the formation of the Central American nations as we know them today. The four recently divided republics joined forces briefly against Nicaragua's (American) president **William Walker** (see page 264), but his defeat did not lead to renewed unity as many liberals had hoped. Walker's bizarre reign in Nicaragua was an ominous hint of what the countries could expect from the next 150 years, namely strong U.S. intervention in Central American affairs, first to satiate economic interests, and later for political reasons. After defeating Walker, the other four states instituted liberal policies like those the American had implemented; only in Nicaragua did liberalism take longer to initiate. Simultaneously, leaders such as **Justo Rufino Barrios** of Guatemala made countless efforts to reinstall the federation, but could not overcome the lack of unity and infrastructure within the individual countries themselves, nor did unity appeal to populations in which localism was becoming more deeply entrenched. For the next 80 years, "liberals" throughout Central America tried to hammer their nations into shape, supporting the development of staple export crops such as coffee and bananas, but also found that the U.S. was having more and more influence on their policies. **Teddy Roosevelt** sent down a warship to settle disputes between El Salvador and Guatemala, Nicaragua and Panama competed to be the site of the U.S. trans-continental bridge, and most importantly, American fruit producers such as the **United Fruit Company** (known as *El Pulpo*, or "the Octopus") became increasingly formidable influences and exacerbated the class division between land owners and laborers.

This lengthy period of inequality and injustice to workers reached its pinnacle during the Great Depression in 1929, after which unrest and revolution were inevitable. Most of the nations resorted to harsh dictatorial rule throughout the Second World War, when all five countries joined the side of the Allies. Following the War, Central America became intricately involved in **Cold War** politics and ideological conflict. Class division made the region prime for Marxists, and U.S. proximity and direct interests furthered the Capitalist cause. Today, following a century of bloody revolt, stern governmental rule and constant upheaval, Central American unity seems unimaginable. But despite strict borders between the countries, all share the heavy burdens common to developing nations, including increased poverty, illiteracy, and inequality. Some idealists seek another attempt at unification (the formation of the **Organization of Central American States** in 1951 was a step in this direction, as is the **Central American Common Market**); they theorize that the combined economies of Central America could surely rise above the desperate situation in which the countries independently find themselves. Others worry that such a move will only compound an already severe problem. Either way, the nations of Central America have developed distinct personalities and are unlikely to try to eradicate their borders anytime soon.

■■■ MAYAN MARVELS

Mesoamerica has long provided anthropologists and archaeologists, amateur and professional, with some of the greatest excuses in the world to travel. The **Aztecs** of Mexico, **Incas** of Peru, and other ancient civilizations indigenous to modern-day Latin America left behind intriguing remnants, but the civilization that developed in what is now Central America is the most incredible of all: that of the **Ancient Maya.**

'Incredible' can be taken literally, in the case of early European explorers' interpretation of the ruins they discovered. Stumbling upon the towering remains of temples, structures covered with alien and complex hieroglyphics, the first wave of *conquistadores* found it impossible to imagine that these monumental artifacts could have sprung fresh from the hands and minds of the region's natives. Even as they were laying waste to the postclassic outposts of the high Maya civilization, Cortés and his soldiers undermined the Mayan's greatest achievements by assuming that it was the result of some previous Old World expedition to the Americas. Today, archaeological evidence shows soundly that the indigenous inhabitants of the Americas, including the Maya, were profoundly original.

Of all the related New World cultures, the Maya were the most artistically and intellectually developed, although neither their political nor their economic unity ever matched that attained by the Aztecs or the Incans. Still, the binding cultural unity expressed by the various Maya city-states outlasted that of either of the other best-known American civilizations, surviving until 1697, when the Guatemalan city of **Tayasal** fell to siege. Some Maya, the **Lacandón,** were able to resist subjugation during the entire colonial period, waging something of a guerilla war from jungled highlands throughout the imperial rule.

If it weren't for the Mayas' distinctive cultural legacy, we would probably perceive the ruins as coming from several competing tribes and not from one vast, varying civilization. The diversity and originality that boggles the minds of anthropologists is even more astounding considering just how disjointed the civilization actually was. At different times, the ancient Mayans are thought to have covered Chiapas and **Yucatán,** the southernmost parts of Mexico, as well as all of Guatemala and Belize, most of El Salvador and Honduras, and even parts of Nicaragua, and that's not to mention the area populated by related groups such as the **Olmec** and central Mexican **Nahautl.** Still, the civilization never covered the whole region at one time. In fact, just as culture set the Maya apart from other New World Civilizations, so did it define different periods in Mayan history, commonly divided into three eras: the preclassic, the classic, and the postclassic periods.

The onset of the preclassic period is difficult to determine, but is generally thought to coincide with the development of several highland cities near the Pacific coast of the isthmus around 500 BC. The center of these highland centers was the city of **Kaminaljuyú,** in southern Guatemala; other remains, such as Tazumal and San Andrés, stand in modern El Salvador. The preclassic Maya of the north experimented with agriculture, but not until the classic period, in the first millennium AD, did scientific and cultural centers begin to descend into the hotter and more humid land of northern Guatemala, Belize, the Atlantic coast of Honduras, and the Yucatán Peninsula. By then, the Maya had already started to come up with their system of writing and time-keeping, as well as their mastery of math. The highland regions remained populated, but the truly cutting-edge Mayan culture pressed on toward Atlantic jungles, where archaeologists have found the richest and most famous ruins. The most famous Maya architecture dates back to this period, and it's for the their majestic temples and **stelae,** or carved and marked altars, that colossal cities such as Tikal and Copán are so popular as tourist sites. Nearby, less spectacular remains hint that suburban-sprawl is hardly a new trend; thousands of inhabitants were connected to the larger cities by extensive "suburban" networks and miles of paved highway. Meanwhile, the elite removed themselves more and more, keeping their heads in the stars and gaining insight into **astronomy** that was leaps and bounds ahead of their Old World contemporaries.

Over the next several hundred years, Mayan civilization fell into decline. Residents of the great focal points of the classical culture mysteriously ebbed off into the outlying jungle and into what is now Mexico, where they constructed the cities of the postclassic period. The most visible of these, **Chichén Itzá,** Mayapán, Tulum, and Uxmal, are all quite popular among ruin-seeking travelers, but less so among archaeologists, since most other aspects of the postclassic culture had diminished since the heyday of the big lowland cities.

Whatever drove the Maya from their strongest settlements to these newer locations also made them more susceptible to outside influence. Whereas previous generations of Maya had traded ideas and inventions among themselves, the postclassic inhabitants fell prey to the expanding Toltec culture of central Mexico; their eventual defeat at the hands of the unified Aztecs punctuated the decline of their culture. As to the mystery of why the classic age of Maya civilization ever came to an end in the first place, theories abound; none of them is especially satisfying. Perhaps drawing from our own environmental woes, some suggest that ecological abuses caused the lowlanders to flee; others suggest overpopulation, unbridled social stratification, or even extraterrestrial intervention as the reason for the Mayas' end.

Along with the question of decline linger other rich riddles. Perhaps most interesting were the unusual directions in which the culture's technology advanced. We remember the Maya best for their amazingly precise artistic and scientific practices, many of which matched those of Europe and the Far East. Their well-known arched and columned buildings are just a few of the traditional visual forms of art which had lasted at least as long as the first highland cities were established, as we can tell from dated remnants of their painting, ceramics, weaving, and sculpture. In the sciences, Mayan scholars are renowned for the complex arithmetical, algebraic, and geometrical calculations and records. The mathematics employed a **'zero'-character** of the sort that Europeans adopted from the Hindu mathematicians hundreds of years earlier. Mayan math was also tightly related to the calendrical system, which played a fundamental role in shaping the culture's agricultural cycle as well as many of their religious beliefs. And yet again, the indigenous Americans had beaten their invaders to the development of a working **sidereal calendar** (a calendar that measures years by gauging the earth's revolution relative to stars other than the Sun), a method much closer to the modern calendar than was Europe's at the time.

Given this sophistication, the Mayas' technological limitations are remarkable, and help to understand the civilization's inability to impress upon the *conquistadores* the stature and subtlety of their society. Literate Mayans were without exception remarkable stonecarvers, and used tools of flint, obsidian, and fire-hardened wood to carve dates and pictures into solid blocks of stone. They also were able to transport these enormous monoliths across hundreds of miles of hilly jungle. But astonishingly, the Maya never employed the **wheel** in any practical contexts (it had been used in children's games, however). They never domesticated animals, yet nonetheless managed to develop an extremely efficient system for irrigating and cultivating crops. Mayan social structure was sophisticated, but the pyramidal division of labor left small groups of elite men of science and religion to delegate responsibilities to their inferiors within a city government, and for these delegates to further pass the buck until the bottom- and most populous rung bent over to pull up the corn, beans, or **manioc** (cassava melon).

By the time Cortés came dancing across the water, the real damage to the ancient Mayan civilization had already been wrought by a combination of enigmatic internal corrosion and external pressure from trading with non-Mayan populations. Still, the decentralized city-states, usually buried deep within humid and insect-infested jungles, were able to resist European subjugation for much longer than were the more militaristic Aztecs and Incas. As the binding cultural ties faded, though, so too did any sense of a "Maya nation." Following rampant disease and economic exploitation, only a fragmented jumble of cultural odds and ends and an equally crumbled string of ruined temples were left to remember the great people. Today, even those ruins are in danger of irrevocable damage and dispersal. Visitors to the ruins can sense the structures' intrinsic worth, but only by looking deep into the perplexing and fascinating lives behind their construction can one grasp the culture's full value.

Head's up: Pok-ta-pok, anyone?

Depictions from other sites reveal that a challenging game was played at the courts: players had to keep a hefty rubber ball aloft without using their hands or feet. Perhaps this team sport resembled basketball more closely than the Hot Potato than this fact suggests; bouncing the ball from body to body, gleeful pok-ta-pokkers did their damnedest to pop the puck into one of the two circular stone goals that were mounted at either end of the enclosed court. Macaw-shaped markers were used for keeping score. Actually, the Roman gladiatorial arena might make an even better model (anthropologists still debate the details); hieroglyphic records indicate that the captains of a winning team won a robe from each spectator in the audience, right off their backs, while the losing captain—ouch—was ceremonially beheaded upon the game's conclusion!

■■■ ECOTOURISM

As recently as a decade ago, Central American tourism, as much as any other industry, led to destruction and exploitation of natural resources. Cruiseships brought littering foreigners to beaches, who then bought ornaments made from endangered tortoises' shells, roads were paved through jungles, and scuba resorts catered to customers' yen to feed fish and fondle coral. Since then, countries around the world, and particularly Central American nations, have faced increased demand for responsible, sustainable tourism, or as it is more popularly known, "ecotourism." The fastest growing sector of the tourist industry, ecotourism is intended to be environmentally friendly, to encourage enjoyment and appreciation of nature while at the same time contributing to its continued existence. With more than 500 million people traveling as tourists throughout the world each year, increased respect for the environment is clearly a refreshing trend. Still, although ecotourism has been predominantly praised in the past, the movement has also raised its share of criticism. Some say "eco" has come to mean economics rather than ecology, pointing to greedy entrepreneurs who lead ecotours but have little or no concern for nature; others warn that increased traffic in natural settings, no matter how **"low-impact"** it is, can only harm the ecology in the long run.

Central America is packed with natural wonders, and has been a favorite destination among ecotourists from the movement's beginning. The average number of international tourists to Belize has increased 250% since the 1960's, and the industry now brings in nearly 30% of the country's gross national product. Costa Rica, perhaps the world's model for successful ecotourism, has 20% of its land dedicated to the national park system; in 1994, tourists pumped US$650 million into Costa Rica's economy, the greater part of which came from ecotourists. Twenty years ago, the nation's **Monteverde Cloudforest Reserve** saw a few hundred human visitors each year; in the last few years there have been more than 50,000. Such numbers tantalize entrepreneurs and experienced tour leaders alike, who readily grasp that tagging their services as "eco" could yield huge profits. No certification is required to be an environmental tour guide, nor do foreign owners have to pay for the right to use the natural areas, which are often harmed by such eco-impostors. The most concerned tour leaders encourage limiting the number of visitors to popular destinations, even at the cost of losing money. Travelers are urged to go with those organizations which strive to have a minimum impact on the environment and which economically support conservation efforts.

Some other ill-effects of ecotourism are not as apparent. Increased migrations of Costa Ricans to popular (and profitable) regions such as Monteverde, for example, has imposed a strain on the local community. Locals who don't immediately jump on the tourist bandwagon face higher costs of living, lose the potential to farm land set aside as national parks, and often have to leave their land altogether. Many environmentalists worry about the state of indigenous cultures as well as prospering biodiversity, and thus urge that the communities be paid directly for use of their land for tourist purposes. Recent expansion of ecotourism to foster interest in native cultures has led to such stellar organizations as Belize's **Mayan Village Guesthouse Program,** which, like a true ecotour, allows visitors close-up observation and enjoyment, but which also benefits the local community directly.

Meanwhile, many nations have not yet figured out how to install a proper infrastructure for ecotourism's development. In an attempt to match Costa Rica's success, Honduras has more than doubled the amount of money it spends on marketing tourism per year. But along with proposed plans to develop nature trails through national parks are ideas for the construction of 1500 luxury rooms near Tela, an idea which seems to miss the point of low-impact tourism. Still, efforts of the **Bay Islands Conservation Association,** of which many scuba school owners are members, shed light on another benefit of increased environmental awareness. More and more, companies are realizing that they can actually increase profits in the long run by minimizing visitation now and by supporting efforts to conserve nature. Such businesses benefit not only because of improved reputation among travelers, but also because "unspoiled nature" continues to be a selling point to tourists. Overall, the new wave of environmentally conscious tourism has been an immensely rewarding, to the countries' economies, to tourists with a thirst for adventure and immersion in nature, and most importantly, to the environment itself, which will only continue to serve visitors if the pure notion of minimum impact ecotourism is upheld.

■■■ THE ENVIRONMENT OR FLORA AND FAUNA

The isthmus of Central America flourishes with an unbelievably diverse range of plants and animals, especially given the region's relatively compact size. In some places, such as the rainforests, this variety is packed into a hundred square miles. In the past few years, activists around the world have fought to protect the biodiversity of the rainforests, which in Central America are found mostly along the eastern half of the lowlands. Rainforests are host to tall, enveloping trees which form a several story high canopy, under which smaller ferns, palms, and other plants grow. The list of animals numbers that thrive within the confines of the forest numbers into the thousands; it includes the familiar, from deer, squirrels, and bats, to the comically (and poetically) exotic: kinkajous, and capybaras, plus coatimundis. Also there are peccaries, and even jaguarundis. The coasts, meanwhile, characterized by woodlands, savanna, and of course, palm-lined beaches, are a fisherperson's or diver's wildest dream come true, and bird-watchers, too, will delight at the huge number of tropical species. The Quetzal, for example, was worshipped by the Maya for the its brilliant plumage; members of the endangered species can be occasionally spotted today in cloud forests. Cloud forests are found in high-altitude regions, and are remarkable for their strange combination of cool, moist air and fairy-tale like flora. Wizened trees are covered in bright moss and colorful mushrooms, and one suspects the area must be home to at least a few gnomes or pixies.

■■■ FESTIVALS AND HOLIDAYS

By far the biggest parties of the year take place around **Semana Santa,** Holy Week, which is the week before Easter. Most countries have special party-meccas for the occasion (such as Chitré in Panama or Antigua in Guatemala), and you should plan well in advance for accommodations in more popular destinations. The festivities aren't isolated to the hotspots, though; you're bound to find something going on during this week wherever you are. Along with **Carnaval** ("Mardi Gras"), cities also sometimes seem to celebrate just for the hell of it during other times of the year.

Keep your eyes and ears peeled for local *fiestas* wherever you are, as they can be fascinating and exceptionally fun. Spend enough time in El Salvador, for example, and you might get to witness the Indians' unusual celebration of the **Historia de Moros y Cristianos,** a party carried over from Spanish lore and involving elaborate dances and costumes. Even familiar holidays are given a new twist; unlike the hyper-commercialized **Father's and Mother's Day** celebrations common to the United States, there is no gift-giving or flower-sending in Central America. Instead, mothers and fathers simply get to take the day off from work on their respective days to get together with other mothers or fathers to have a big party and relax. Regional festivals, such as those dedicated to patron saints of local communities, are another common reason to cut loose, and usually result in dancing, drinking to local music, and usually a beauty pageant or two. Don't necessarily worry if you think you hear some gun shots; *most* of the time, it's just some celebratory firecrackers.

See country-specific When To Go sections for more information.

■■■ THE PEOPLE

Most modern Central Americans are *mestizos,* people of mixed Indian and Spanish ancestry. The rest are predominantly *indígenas*, native Indians, although each country has its own distinct composition and the groups are not evenly distributed throughout the isthmus. An overwhelming majority of the extant Indian population lives in Guatemala, from where it is thought most other tribes migrated outward within the last millennium. More than 40% of Belize's population is of African descent (compared to 6% for the rest of the region), and the majority of Costa Ricans are of direct European descent. Within this isthmus-wide melting pot, traditions have meshed and created an overwhelming spectrum of cultural diversity. Still, one common link wherever you go is the ubiquity of U.S. culture: American fast food, clothes, and movies often seem to be inescapable while traveling. North American producers have not held back, reaping profits from the phenomenon that for many Central Americans, U.S. products are often associated with high status.

The cult of commercialism is still nothing compared to the deeply felt religiosity of almost all Central Americans. Probably the most lasting influence of the Spanish conquest was the conversion of the natives to Roman Catholicism. Those Indians who didn't fully convert still combined aspects of the European religion with their own. Today, one out of seven Central Americans *isn't* Catholic, and those in the minority are usually Protestant, converted by the more recent arrival of evangelical sects. While the Catholic Church has lost much of the political strength it once clenched, the Pope's decisions are immensely influential in how people live their lives, and thousands of Central Americans make devotional pilgrimages to various sacred shrines each year.

■■■ LANGUAGE

Central America is situated in the heart of Latin America, and not surprisingly, Spanish is the official language of six of the seven Central American countries. Brushing up on your *Me gusta*'s and other *vocabularios* before arriving will make things considerably easier (see Spanish Appendix, page 458). Still, in many places the romance language comes secondary. The official language of Belize is English, which is frequently spoken in many other Caribbean coastal towns throughout the region. In some places, English has blended with mixed African languages in the development of a funky-sounding creole that's just barely intelligible to native English speakers. Fun phrases include "Weh path yu gwine?" (Where are you going?) and "Weh de gwane?" (What's going on?). Elsewhere, particularly in Guatemala, Indian languages continue to thrive, although diffusion between groups and with Spanish speakers has created some frustrating combinations.

Even primed Spanish speakers get shocked when they hear the Central American dialects. "S" is often left off the end of words, or omitted from words completely (although it is still implied). To add to the confusion, different dialects (with occasional different vocabulary words) are spoken from country to country, so keep an open ear. In Honduras, for example, *pisto* means money (not *dinero,* as elsewhere), and *polo* isn't a cologne; it means drunk, pissed, wasted, *bebido.* Knowing how to say this particular phrase from country to country is bound to come in handy.

Also be aware that each country has its own terms for the citizens of other countries. To a Honduran, for example, a Guatemalan is a *Chapine,* a Nicaraguan is a *Muco,* a Salvadoran is a *Guanaco,* a Costa Rican is a *Tico,* a Panamanian is a *Canalero,* and a Honduran is a *Catracho.* These little names vary from country to country, and may be interpreted as insulting, so use tact.

■■■ SPORTS

There's no question about which sport dominates the isthmus in terms of popularity: fútbol! Few Latin Americans would dare to admit to *not* being a soccer fan, and although the nations of Central America are too small to consistently compete on an international level, the people are still unabashedly devoted. When, as in the recent World Cup in 1994, no Central American countries were competing, Argentina, Colombia, Mexico, and Brazil became the teams of choice (or whichever Latin American team happens to be advancing). Honduras was especially proud to be home to one of the tournament's *referees.* From the smallest children to the elderly, watching (or playing) the world's sport is a daily source of distraction and pleasure.

Contrary to popular belief, however, soccer is not the *only* sport in the world, nor is it the only game with which Central Americans concern themselves. Baseball is actually the national sport of Nicaragua, Belizeans enjoy a good game of cricket, and boxing, softball, basketball, and basketball are becoming more popular every year. To satisfy more bestial urges, cockfights and bullfights are also popular, particularly in rural areas.

■■■ CUSTOMS AND MANNERS

As a traveler, it doesn't take long to figure out that local customs and manners aren't always what you're used to. No one bats an eye when an elderly woman hawks a loogie on a public bus, but a traveler might be frowned upon for having a stubbly beard. To be fully respected by the people you encounter, it helps to be familiar with their social norms.

Foreign visitors are often shocked by the overwhelming *machismo* in some (especially rural) parts of Central America. Women hanging around in bars are often believed to be lascivious, a prejudice sometimes cast upon foreign women in general. Men who believe women should be quiet and meek are often shocked when a woman expresses her opinions, much less drinks and becomes raucous. Both men and women should be sensitive to rising testosterone levels, since often, *mucho macho* makes *mucho* "oucho!" Never, ever say anything about another man's mother, sister, grandma, aunt, daughter, wife, or girlfriend. Never.

Personal hygiene and appearance are often difficult to maintain while traveling, but how you look will correlate directly with how you are treated. Clean-shaven men with short hair and women who don't show much skin are most likely to be well received than scruffies and smellies or women without a bra. Men should remove any headgear when entering a building.

Punctuality isn't as important as it is in Europe and the United States (as you'll quickly confirm after riding the buses enough), but there are limits, of course. A different scope on time is also apparent during meals, which are rarely hurried in Central America. Similarly, every country enjoys the ingenious tradition of *siesta,* a time in the afternoon when it's just too hot to do anything but relax, have a drink, and maybe sleep a little. Don't expect much to happen during the mid-afternoon, as banks and businesses often shut their doors. While eating at a table with Central Americans, keep your hands on the tables and not in your lap, where manual activity could easily become an issue of concern for others at the table.

When meeting someone for the first time, shake hands firmly, look the person in the eye, and say "*Mucho gusto de conocerle,*" (pleased to meet you). Females often greet each other with a peck on the cheek or a quick hug. Most vulgar gestures elsewhere in the world are either rude or meaningless in Central America; there are few unfamiliar Central American gestures. Just don't make a fist with your thumb between the index and middle fingers. In private, have a glance at what this little posture looks like; it doesn't take much imagination to imagine why it's vulgar.

Lastly, be sensitive when taking photographs. Devotees at a shrine might be interesting to look at, but their religiosity is no novelty. Either don't take pictures of people, or ask very graciously first if they mind. Indigenous peoples object most strongly to being photographed, so just preserve the moment mentally.

GUATEMALA

GUATEMALA

Through the spring and summer of 1995, the U.S. State Department warned travelers to exercise extreme caution when traveling in Guatemala. Crime and terrorism in many parts of the country have made inter-city travel hazardous, especially after dark. Several tourists were attacked and even killed as a result of rumors about foreigners abducting Guatemalan children. And though this violence has not occurred in the more heavily touristed parts of the country, U.S citizens are encouraged to register with the U.S. Embassy, and all travelers, especially women, are advised to avoid contact with Guatemalan children.

More than any other Central American nation, Guatemala struggles to withstand the strains that plague the postcolonial world as a whole—the cultural, political, and economic divisions between the native and the imported. For visitors, the contrasts can be overwhelming; a few hours in a bus can feel like a journey through time, as they move between the massive, menacing frenzy of Guatemala City, with its theaters, orchestra, and ritzy *salsa* discos, to the rolling western highlands, where indigenous Maya Indians fire tortillas in thatched homes, weave complicated *huipiles*, their native dress, and live village life on the volcanic shores of Lake Atitlán just as their ancestors did 500 years ago. Revolt and war have left the country's infrastructure the least developed in the region—and thereby ensure adventure-hungry budget travelers a wealth of stories to tell back home. As a further bonus, travel in this country is often the least expensive in Central America, and visitors can find excellent meals for about US$2.25. The markets are filled with spectacular local clothing, leather, pottery, and woven blankets and rugs, all sold for a ridiculous fraction of what they would be elsewhere. Guatemala abounds with excellent places to live and shop in high comfort on a microscopic budget.

Guatemala's past has been difficult, but the country manages to maintain a veneer of stability and is a pleasant place to visit. Tourism is the second-largest source of foreign exchange behind coffee, so *gringos* are eagerly courted. Beyond the cities and mountains, the ruins of the Mayan city of Tikal are among the most compelling archaeological sites in the Americas, and the surrounding jungle can be parted to reveal peacocks, wild parrots, lizards, and the occasional sacred jaguar. The opportunities to relax on picturesque beaches, to climb steaming volcanoes, and to become one of many devotees of San Simón, the patron saint of partying, only rarely fall together between one nation's borders, and Guatemala's intriguing combination has been luring increasing numbers of tourists for years.

ESSENTIALS

■■■ WHEN TO GO

CLIMATE

Average temperature varies widely in Guatemala. In the coastal regions it can get as hot as 100°F, while in the highlands it gets down to freezing. In arid areas, the nights can be cool any time of the year. The rainy season lasts from May to October and is characterized by clear morning skies and afternoon or early-evening showers. The middle of the Motagua River valley is dominated by near-desert conditions, while the volcanoes facing the Pacific get pummeled by as much as 4m of rain each year. In other words, come prepared for everything.

FESTIVALS AND HOLIDAYS

Guatemalans are hard-core about their festivals; Patron Saints' festivals include ear-drum-pounding firecrackers and wacky parades, and while Indian influence on Christian traditions is discouraged by the church, these festivals sport the traits of several cultures' customs. **Antigua** hoots it up particularly loud for **Semana Santa,** when billowing trains of floats (carried by men, not cars) fill the streets. **Christmas** celebrations actually begin Dec. 7 with **The Burning of the Devil;** every household sets a heap of trash on fire in front of their house to purge evil vibes and clear the way for processions during the rest of the month. The closer it gets to Christmas in Quetzaltenango, for instance, the harder it is to see and breathe, as the entire Central Park area becomes enshrouded in smoke. And on the Thursday after Easter in Panajachel, all hell breaks loose during the celebration of the festival of **Corpus Cristi,** a Catholic holiday which nominally commemorates the Eucharist, but which has been infused heavily with Indian tradition. Snag a seat early on as the moving theater works its way through the town streets: men in elaborate masks whale on each other with huge bags of soccer balls while women dance around cawing out bird sounds.

For the most comprehensive and up-to-date listing of the village parties in each region, pick up a copy of the *Directorio de Fiestas,* which is available at INGUAT offices, and which also includes the schedules of Market Days across the country.

Expect banks and post offices to close down on national holidays, which include: **January 1** (New Year's Day); **March 31-April 7** (Easter Week, 1996); **May 1** (Labor Day); **June 30** (Army Day); **August 15** (Our Lady of the Assumption); **September 15** (Independence Day); **October 20** (Revolution Day); **November 1** (All Saints' Day); **December 24-25** (Christmas Eve/Christmas); and **December 31** (New Year's Eve).

■■■ FEED YOUR HEAD

For publications and travel organizations of general interest, see Feed Your Head in the Central America General Introduction, page 1.

Embassy of Guatemala, U.S. 2220 R St. NW, Washington, DC 20008 (tel. (202) 745-4952; fax (202) 745-1908). Open to the public Mon.-Fri. 9am-12:30pm. **U.K.** 13 Fawcett St., London, SW 10 9HN (tel. (0171) 351-3042; fax 376-5708).

Consulate of Guatemala, 57 Park Ave., New York, NY 10016 (tel. (212) 686-3837; fax (212) 447-6947). Open Mon.-Fri. 9:30am-12:30pm for document processing. Guatemala also maintains consulates in Washington, Los Angeles, San Francisco, Miami, New Orleans, Houston, and Chicago.

U.S. Consulate in Guatemala, Av. La Reforma 7-01, Zona 10 (tel. (2) 311-541; fax 310-564) publishes the invaluable *Helpful Hints for Americans in Guatemala,* which includes safety and practical information for travelers of all nationalities.

Guatemala Tourist Commission, 299 Alhambra Circle, Suite 510, Coral Gables, FL 33134 (tel. (800) 742-4529; fax (305) 442-1013). Write for loads of glossy brochures and maps, posters, information on Spanish schools and on the Mundo Maya project, plus a list of rates charged by all major hotels in the country.

■■■ DOCUMENTS AND FORMALITIES

All visitors to Guatemala need a valid **passport** and either a **visa** or a **tourist card.** A tourist card can be purchased at the border or at the airport departure gate for US$5, but you can save the fiver by obtaining a free visa at a consulate instead. When your card is issued, Guatemalan officials will decide how long you may stay; authorized stays range from one to three months. An extension on your tourist card can some-

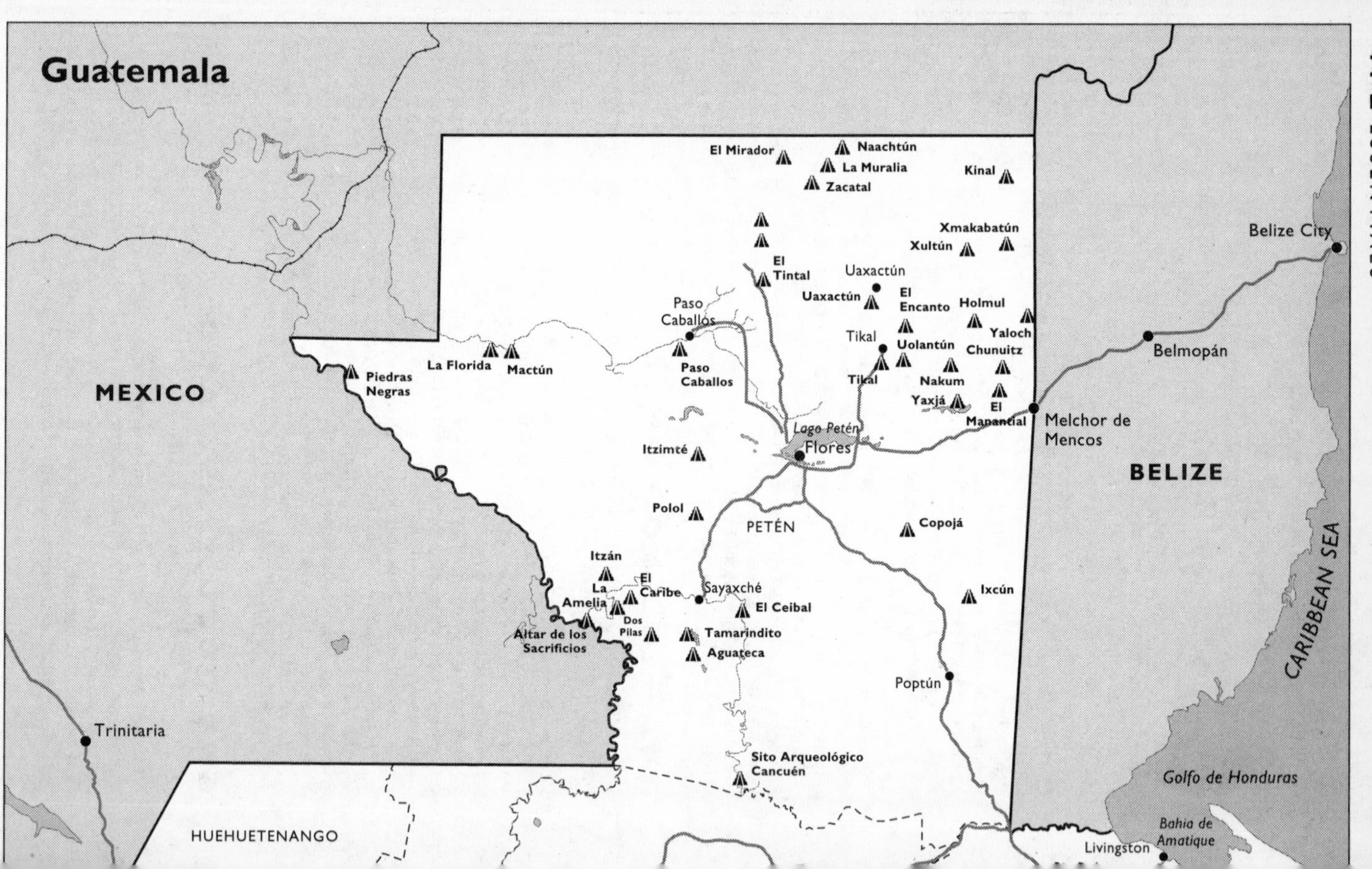
Guatemala
El Mirador
Naachtún
La Muralia
Zacatal
Kinal
Xmakabatún
Xultún
Belize City
El Tintal
Uaxactún
Uaxactún
El Encanto
Holmul
Paso Caballos
Yaloch
Tikal
Uolantún
Chunuitz
Belmopán
La Florida
Mactún
Paso Caballos
Tikal
Nakum
Piedras Negras
MEXICO
Yaxjá
El Manantial
Melchor de Mencos
Lago Petén
Flores
Itzimté
BELIZE
Polol
PETÉN
Copojá
CARIBBEAN SEA
Itzán
El Caribe
La Amelia
Sayaxché
Ixcún
El Ceibal
Dos Pilas
Altar de los Sacrificios
Tamarindito
Aguateca
Poptún
Trinitaria
Sito Arqueológico Cancuén
Golfo de Honduras
HUEHUETENANGO
Bahía de Amatique
Livingston

Todos Santos Cuchumatán
ALTA VERAPAZ
QUICHÉ
Cobán
Languín
Cuevas Semuc Champey
El Estor
IZABAL
Castillo de San Felipe
Puerto Barrios
Lago de Izabal
Mariscos
Río Motagua
Zaculeu
Huehuetenango
Quiriguá
Quiriguá
SAN MARCOS
TOTONI-CAPÁN
Santa Cruz del Quiché
Salamá
BAJA VERAPAZ
EL PROGRESO
ZACAPA
San Marcos
Totonicapán
Chichicastenango
El Progreso
Zacapa
Quetzaltenango
QUEZAL-TENANGO
SOLOLA
CHIMAL-TENANGO
GUATEMALA
Copán Ruins
V. Zunil
Solola
Iximché
Chiquimula
Santa Rosa de Copán
V. Santa María
V. Santo Tomás
V. San Pedro
Lago de Atitlán
Panajachel
Ciudad de Guatemala
Ciudad Tecún Umán
Santiago Atitlán
V. Tolimán
V. Atitlán
Chimaltenango
Jalapa
CHIQUIMULA
JALAPA
Esquipulas
HONDURAS
SACA-TEPÉQUEZ
Antigua Guatemala
Retalhuleu
Mazatenango
SUCHITEPÉQUEZ
RETALHULEU
Lago de Amatitlán
V. de Racaya
V. Jumaytepeque
Nueva Ocotepeque
Escuintla
Cuilapa
Jutiapa
Tulate
SANTA ROSA
JUTIAPA
ESCUINTLA
Valle Nuevo
Chalatenango
Puerto San José
Monterrico
Ahuachapán
Santa Ana
PACIFIC OCEAN
0
25 miles
0
25 kilometers
N
EL SALVADOR

times be obtained at the immigration office (see Guatemala City: Practical Information, page 56). Visas are free at Guatemalan consulates in Britain, Canada, and the U.S.; citizens of Southern Ireland, South Africa, and New Zealand must pay US$10. Obtain a visa several weeks before leaving home or at consulates in Comitán, Tapachula, or Chetumal (all in Mexico) if coming from the north. Citizens of most Western European nations need only a valid passport to enter the country. All visitors should carry identification at all times. Visitors departing from the Guatemala City airport must pay a small **exit tax.**

Drivers in Guatemala must carry a valid foreign driver's license, a title, and registration. When driving across the border, visitors receive a 30-90 day driving permit. After that, get a license at the Departamento de Tránsito, 6 Avenida and 14 Calle, Zona 1 (Q20). The whole process sounds innocuous enough, but actually amounts to a bureaucratic nightmare. Insurance is not required for driving in Guatemala.

■■■ MONEY MATTERS

US$1 = 5.71 quetzales	**Q1 = US$0.18**
CDN$1 = Q4.20	**Q1 = CDN$0.24**
UK£1 = Q8.88	**Q1 = UK£0.11**
IR£1 = Q9.05	**Q1 = IR£0.11**
AUS$1 = Q4.21	**Q1 = AUS$0.24**
NZ$1 = Q3.75	**Q1 = NZ$0.27**
SARand = Q1.56	**Q1 = SARand 0.64**

The Guatemalan unit of currency is the *quetzal*, named for the colorful bird and abbreviated with a 'Q' in place of the dollar's 'US$.' U.S. dollars are the only directly exchangeable currency. For other currencies use **Banco de Guatemala** or **Ban-Quetzal,** which has a branch at the airport in Guatemala City. They will first change your currency into U.S. dollars, then into quetzales. For **Western Union** money transfers, call (2) 344-326-8 or contact the Sociedad Internacional de Serviciones, S.A., 7a Avenida "A" 4-30, Zona 9.

There seems to be little rhyme and less reason to which banks accept which kinds of traveler's checks. American Express checks are more difficult to exchange in Guatemala than elsewhere. The **Thomas Cook MasterCard** home office in Guatemala is at Unitours S.A., 7A Avenida 7-91, Zona 4, Guatemala City 01004 (tel. 314-166; fax 342-001). There are **PLUS (ATM)** machines at the Camino Real and Villa Magna (Radisson) hotels in Guatemala City. **American Express** is located at Edificio Banco del Café, Ave. Reforma and 9a Calle, Zona 9 (tel. 340-040).

Bargaining is expected in markets and handicrafts shops, but not in urban shopping centers. When bargaining, aim for 20-30% off the original price. **Tipping** is not customary in *comedores*. Many restaurants will include a 10% tip in your bill.

■■■ SAFETY

Crime is a problem in many parts of Guatemala. Pickpockets and purse snatchers consitute a perennial hazard in Guatemala City, especially in the central market; protect yourself by keeping money in a moneybelt (*not* in a pocket or a fanny pack) and by holding on to your bags tightly. Antigua is considered to be one of the safest areas in the country. Rural areas are especially risky.

In the summer of 1995, travel between cities after sunset was considered very unsafe. **Armed bandits** stopped city buses and tour buses along highways at night, but their intended victims reportedly escaped injury by following their assailants' directions, exiting the bus in a calm fashion, and not attempting to flee. Many travelers and locals consider daylight bus rides to be relatively safe, however.

Those driving from Guatemala City to Lake Atitlán should take the Interamerican Hwy. (CA-1) through Chimaltenango and Tecpan to the crossroads at Los Encuentros, and then either CA-1 to Solola and Panajachel or CA-15 to Chichicastenango. Other routes to Lake Atitlán are more dangerous. Bandits are most active on the road between Tikal and the Guatemala-Belize border at Melchor de Mencos; tourists should only drive along this road if absolutely necessary, and at their own risk.

Climbing **volcanoes** in Guatemala is particularly risky. The volcanoes are prime spots for robberies and assaults; even travelers in groups have been pulled off the path to be robbed and raped. The U.S. Consulate in Guatemala recommends not only traveling with groups, but doing so in groups with *armed tour leaders*. Also, check up on the safety of an area before venturing out.

Do *not* carry drugs in Guatemala. Under a 1992 anti-narcotics law, anyone caught in the possession of even small amounts of illegal drugs can spend several months in jail—before their case is decided. Those convicted face serious jail sentences.

U.S. citizens should register with the Consular Section of the U.S. Embassy in Guatemala City upon arrival. This means filling out an application and providing two photos and proof of citizenship. Informal registration may be accomplished by mail or fax; include local address and telephone, planned itinerary, emergency contact in the U.S., and intended length of stay.

In case of emergencies, call the **police** (tel. 120) or **fire department** (122 or 123).

■■■ HEALTH

See Central America: Health (page 11) for more information.

Diarrhea strikes many foreigners traveling in Guatemala, and local amoebas love to induce cases of amoebic dysentery, generally transmitted by drinking or cleaning with impure water, by eating improperly cleaned foods, or simply by handling currency. Bottled water is a prudent investment in the cities and absolutely necessary in the smaller villages. It might be a good idea to carry a small bottle of iodine; add a few drops to your water and wait 15 minutes before drinking. Preventive pills are handy, but don't forget to let nature take its course. As always, avoid dehydration. **Cholera** was still a presence in Guatemala as of the summer of 1995, as was **malaria,** which is a risk in the rural areas of the country. Those venturing off the beaten trail should bring a supply of chloroquine tablets; take one tablet a week, starting before you leave home. **Dengue fever,** also big in Guatemala, is also transmitted by mosquitoes, so slap on that repellent. **Typhoid fever** is common, and vaccinations are recommended for campers and visitors to rural areas. **Hepatitis A** is another hazard common to rural areas, although it's also available in cities.

■■■ ALTERNATIVES TO TOURISM

If you somehow manage to land a **job** in Guatemala, contact the Ministerio de Trabajo, 14 Calle 5-49, Edificio Nasa, 4o. Nivel, Zona 1 (tel. 301-360-8) for a work permit. These are granted to resident foreigners who do not have a Guatemalan spouse or children but who do have a written offer of employment and other documents. Expect 15-20 days for processing.

Guatemala is full of **language institutes** where you can pick up or polish Spanish-speaking skills. Antigua in particular is full of schools. Indigenous languages are also taught at a number of institutions. Most schools offer individual instruction at flexible times (usually 4-7 hrs., 5 days per week). In a one-on-one situation, the skill of the individual teacher is the crucial factor. Weekly payment plans, where available, make it easy to switch instructors. Schools encourage potential students to make written reservations well in advance, but it is often possible and even advisable to arrive without arrangements and then to shop around. Tuition may be US$30 to US$70 for a week of instruction (five days, four hours per day). Some students have had success bargaining higher tuitions down to lower levels. You can avoid commissions and middlemen by arranging study directly through the schools.

Virtually all schools can arrange homestays with Guatemalan families. Room and board goes for about US$40 per week. Many schools will also help students find apartments for extended stays.

Keep in mind that speaking Spanish will only get you so far in Guatemala, especially as you travel farther off the *gringo*-beaten track into the smaller *pueblos*. Twenty-three Indian languages are spoken, the most complete and widespread of which is Quiché. To know it when you hear it, imagine a percussive stream of roof-of-the-mouth clicks and back-of-the-throat clucks, the exact opposite of a sonorous Italian opera. Those who study the language report having to chew lozenges while learning to speak Quiché, in order to numb their raw, tickled tonsils.

Antigua is the center of the language study universe, but schools are also located in Guatemala City, Petén, Huehuetenango, Quetzaltenango, and elsewhere. The following list includes some of the available schools, as well as local volunteer organizations. See Central America: Alternatives to Tourism (page 17) for more listings:

Amerispan, 6 Avenida Norte #34, Antigua, Guatemala (tel. and fax 323-343). 2-4-week language courses with homestay and meals. Offers information and services for pre-registered students and travelers just arriving.

Casa Guatemala, 14 Calle 10-63, Zona 1, Guatemala City (tel. 225-517; fax 319-408). A non-profit organization dedicated to helping neglected, abandoned, and displaced children. Volunteers and paid employees are needed to serve as medical personnel, lab technicians, baby-sitters, and maintenance staff in their medical clinic. Volunteers also help social workers distribute food to 1500 children and 500 pregnant women. Also administers a volunteer program at the Río Dulce Children's Community in the eastern rainforests.

Centro de Español Don Pedro de Alvarado, 1 Calle Pte. #24, Antigua, Guatemala (tel. 324-180; fax 320-602). The only school in Antigua authorized to give the ACTFL and FSI foreign proficiency exams, which may qualify students for college credit in the U.S. Rates as low as US$35 per week for 4 hrs. per day.

Centro de Estudios de Español Pop Wuj, Apdo. 68, Quetzaltenango, Guatemala (tel. and fax 618-286). This cooperatively-owned intensive Spanish school donates its profits to scholarships, community construction efforts, and health and nutritional programs. Students learn Spanish while participating in projects to help Guatemala's poor. US$100 per week includes homestay, meals, and all activities; fees slightly higher during the summer and in January. In the U.S. write to P.O. Box 43685, Washington, DC 20011-9685.

Conservation International, Attn: Abbe Reis, Program Assoc., 1015-18th St. NW, Suite 100, Washington, DC, 20036 (tel. (202) 429-5660; fax (202) 887-5188). Offers placement in a school in the Petén region combining language instruction and environmental work.

Desarrollo Del Pueblo Instituto de Español, Diagonal 12 6-28, Apdo. Postal 41, Quetzaltenango, Zona 1 (tel. and fax 614-624). One-on-one instruction 5 hrs. per day, US$115-125 per week, homestay and meals included. Students are encouraged to perform service work, assisting in vaccination drives, rural clinics, and local construction projects.

Guatemalensis Spanish School, 19 Av. 2-14, Apdo. Postal 53, Quetzaltenango, Zona 1 (fax 632-198). A non-profit program featuring 25 hrs. per week of one-on-one language instruction, weekend ecological excursions, cultural study, and the opportunity to participate in community development projects. About US$100 per week includes tuition, materials, activities, homestay, and meals. For information and an application, contact John Hauser, 358 Casanova Ave., Monterey, CA 93940-3850 (tel. (408) 375-2844).

Popol Vuh International Language School, 7 Avenida Sur #10, Antigua. Offers instruction in Mayan languages in addition to Spanish. 4-hr., one-on-one sessions, US$65 per day. Homestays available.

Proyecto Lingüístico Francisco Marroquín, Apdo. 237, Antigua 03901 (tel. (800) 552-205; fax (9) 322-886). The oldest and largest school in Antigua. A non-profit foundation whose revenue goes toward preserving Mayan languages. Also organizes regular *fiestas* for its students and excursions to many parts of Guatemala. 6 hrs. per day of one-on-one instruction US$125 per week, homestay US$50 per week. 2-week minimum stay during summer. Make reservations 8-10 weeks in advance.

■■■ GETTING THERE

La Aurora International Airport in Guatemala City is served by many major **airlines**. In the summer of 1995, round-trip tickets arranged for a four-week stay were as low as US$507 from both New York and Los Angeles. **Aeroquetzal, American, Aviateca, British Airways, Continental, Mexicana,** and **Tapsa** are among the carriers serving the city. (See Guatemala City, Practical Information, Airport, page 56.)

When entering Guatemala **by land,** it is advisable to arrive at the border as early in the day as possible, both to facilitate transportation connections and to avoid delay, should the border close at an unofficially early hour (as has been known to happen). Make sure you have enough time to reach a town from the border before sunset.

Overland **bus** service connects Guatemala City and the interior to all major border crossings from Mexico, El Salvador, and Honduras. See Guatemala City: Orientation: Transportation (page 54) for details.

BORDER CROSSINGS

Those entering Guatemala **by car** from **Mexico** usually cross the border at Tecún Umán (Highway CA-2) on the Pacific coast, or else at La Mesilla (Highway CA-1) in the highlands. The La Mesilla border crossing was closed during the January 1994 uprising in Chiapas, Mexico, and as of 1995 the U.S. State Department encourages travelers to postpone non-essential travel to Chiapas. Check with a consulate and the U.S. State Department before attempting to cross at La Mesilla. The border crossing between Las Chinamas, **El Salvador** and Valle Nuevo, Guatemala is preferred for connections between those two countries (open daily 8am-5pm; see El Salvador, Near Ahuachapán, page 182, for more information). When going to **Honduras**, go through El Florido or Agua Caliente, or take the Jungle Route (see page 104).

■■■ ONCE THERE

The government tourist bureau is the **Instituto Guatemalteco de Turismo** (INGUAT). There are INGUAT offices in Guatemala City, Antigua, Quetzaltenango, Panajachel, Tecún Umán, La Mesilla, Flores, and Totonicapán. For information about goings–on in Antigua and Guatemala City, check *The Revue,* an English-language publication. For the most current information on 24- hr. pharmacies, consult a local paper and look for the *Farmacias, servicio 24 horas* listing.

TRANSPORTATION

Travel **by air** within Guatemala is not particularly cheap, but it may be worth a premium in order to skip the hassles of bus travel during the rainy season. See Guatemala City: Practical Information (page 56) for details on flights. **Common buses,** cursed by some as "mobile chicken coops," are converted school buses that sit three to a bench. Many travelers have reported getting overcharged on Guatemalan buses and being told of a special "gringo rate." Inquire about authorized tariffs ahead of time, and whenever possible, pay in exact change so the drivers don't give themselves a little bonus. **Driving** your own vehicle in Guatemala can be a hazardous experience. Road conditions are generally poor. Those involved in accidents can be put in jail regardless of who is at fault, and armed car thefts are common. The safest strategy if cornered by armed bandits on the road is to surrender your car without resistance. See Safety (page 46) for more information.

ADDRESSES

Many streets in Guatemalan cities are numbered but not named. This can be confusing because addresses typically also include building-numbers. The name or number of the *avenida* or *calle* always comes first. For example, "6 Av. 25" refers to #25 on Sixth Avenue. You will also see "6a Av. 25," which means the same thing ("6a" short for *sexta*). In cities that are divided into zones, we designate the zone with "Zona #," e.g. 6 Av. 25 Zona 1. A building with the address 12 Calle 6-14, is on 12 Calle between 6 and 7 Avs. at #14.

Buildings can also be specified without any number; in this case, the two closest cross streets are used instead. For example, an address could be 6 Av., 1 Calle, meaning at the intersection of Sixth Avenue and First Street. In a further permutation, addresses can specify the street and the *two* cross streets. For example, 6 Av., 1/2 Calles, meaning on Sixth Avenue between First and Second Streets.

KEEPING IN TOUCH

Guatemala's **postal service** is plagued by strikes and poor management, but a letter only costs Q0.25. If necessary, packages can be sent to the U.S. using **UPS** or **DHL,** but it's very expensive (about US$20 per lb.). **First-class air mail** ought to take 10-14 days to reach the U.S., but it's not uncommon for a letter to take several months. You can receive mail general delivery at most post offices through the *lista de correos* (see Central America: Planning Your Trip: Keeping in Touch (page 31) for details). Mail should be addressed:

Tadd A. PIKE
a/c Lista de Correos
Antigua [city], Guatemala
Central America

Telephones are handled by **Guatel,** the national communications network. Service is erratic throughout the country. Phoning can be horribly difficult, even from Guatel *cabinas,* so try the more expensive hotels when placing international or domestic calls. Local calls cost Q0.86 for three minutes; inter-city, in-country calls cost Q1-3. Calling to the U.S. costs Q74 for three minutes; calls to the U.K. cost Q185. Collect calls and credit-card calls can be made from pay phones free of charge by dialing 190 for AT&T, 189 for MCI, 195 for a Sprint operator, or 171 for an international operator. Some cities (like Antigua, for example) have limited direct dial and international operator service, and many public phones do not offer long-distance service. Some phones require money to make a calling-card call; others do not. Listen for the amazing Guatemalan feedback effect; most conversations are spent listening to your own echo, and then awkwardly waiting for a response to "Hello? Can you hear me?" When dialing into Guatemala City from somewhere else in the country, dial 02; when dialing from the city to the outside it may be necessary to dial 0 first. Region-specific phone codes are erratic and ill-defined; try throwing a 9 in at the beginning if all else fails—and a 2, if the 9 doesn't work. Guatemala's **country code** is 502.

GUATEMALA: AN INTRODUCTION

■■■ HISTORY

Conquest and oppression of indigenous populations is a disturbing and familiar part of every Central American country's past, but in Guatemala it is an episode that continues even today. The Guatemalans write the annals of their difficult history in 23 *indígena* languages and dialects, as well as in Spanish. About half of Guatemala's nine million citizens are descended from the Quiché (Toltec) Maya Indians, who conquered the Guatemalan arm of the Mayan Empire in 1000 AD to become the dominant force in the land. In 1524, one of Cortés' lieutenants, **Pedro de Alvarado,** claimed the whole country with that uncanny ease characteristic of Spanish explorers—his army of 635 men and four cannons sustained only six casualties. The Spanish leader defeated the last king of the Quiché, **Tecún Umán,** in hand-to-hand combat, and to this day the highland Indians hold the legend that their fallen king will one day rise from the dead and rule his people justly. It is understandable that the Indians still look to such mythical sources for hope, as the Guatemalan government has given them little else to count on. Just as the Maya underclasses occasionally revolted against their leaders, even before the Spanish arrived, Guatemalan history since the Spanish conquest traces countless efforts by the Indians to protect their culture and free themselves from fierce governmental oppression.

Spanish rule, based in modern day Antigua until 1773, continued for three hundred years. Like many other Central American countries, Guatemala first gained independence from Spain on September 15, 1821, as a part of the Mexican Empire and then as the center of the **United Provinces of Central America,** which eventually collapsed in 1840. Guatemala was subsequently governed by a succession of military and civilian dictators, all members of the quasi-ethnic, quasi-socioeconomic group Guatemalans call **ladinos,** people of predominantly European descent. The first of these dictators, **Rafael Carrera,** implemented a nationalistic policy and declared Guatemala a sovereign nation in 1847; his Conservative successor was overthrown by Liberals, who ruled nearly continuously until 1944. Traditionally, the Liberals have tried to transform the country's socioeconomic situation through political progress, while the Conservatives have centralized power in the church and the government (and so the parties' names seem aptly chosen). The most notable Liberal leader, **Justo Rufino Barrios,** introduced sweeping reforms in 1872, creating a new constitution and laying out a solid infrastructure of roads and industrial base. The next few presidents enacted fewer reforms, and one of them was ousted when the assembly declared him insane. The last of the Conservative dictators, **General Jorge Ubico,** was the first to address the problems of the Indians directly, and for that they pledged their allegiance to him. However, his leadership was still too restrictive for many students and workers, who organized the **October Revolution** to overthrow his dictatorship in 1944.

Guatemala experimented with a socialistic government under President **Juan José Arévalo Bermejo,** who implemented liberal labor laws and governmental concern for the Indians' situation; and then with a fully communist regime, under **Jacobo Arbenz,** who in 1952 tried in vain to effect limited land reform. Arbenz's attempt unnerved many groups, including the United Fruit Company, which controlled the banana crop—the U.S. government helped to instigate a successful military coup in order to safeguard the economic well-being of the massive fruit exporting conglomerate. A procession of military dictators followed, each opposed by various marauding guerrilla rebel forces. A massive earthquake in 1976 caused widespread famine and disease, which in turn heightened Indian unrest, and by 1982 a series of Indian revolts seemed to have successfully secured a foothold for Guatemala's indigenous population. Soon thereafter, however, the government seized the reins again. The regime of **General Garcia** was characterized by repression by brutal death squads; such levels of institutionalized cruelty were tempered by his successor, **General Ríos Montt,** who nonetheless attempted to squelch Indian unrest by burning villages and "civilizing" the *indígenas* through an intense program of Christian evangelism. However horrible the means, the result of the Indians' continued plight has been the gradual and irrecoverable disappearance of much of their culture. Guatemalan political leaders have always heeded that sanguine maxim of the French Revolution: "Terror is the order of the day." In the past three decades it is estimated that the army has conducted 100,000 political *extrajudicia* killings. Guatemala has one of the worst human rights records in the world.

After effectively pardoning itself for the decade's earlier atrocities, the government has since made a nominal transition to democracy. The country became more stable after 1985, when civilian president **Vinicio Cerezo** was elected, but the situation has improved in only some respects. New and powerful civil rights groups formed, and the Marxist rebels were politically weakened to the extent that a sane process for selecting Cerezo's successor was possible. The constitution of 1986 paved the way for the election of a civilian, democratic government. The Guatemalan government has implemented economic reforms according to World Bank austerity policies in return for financial assistance, albeit often at the expense of more peripheral sectors of the economy, such as small-scale agricultural production. Still, the private watch-dog organization *Americas Watch* announced in 1990 that human rights abuses had returned to the levels of the old military regimes, and Cerezo's government acquired a reputation for corruption and indifference. In May of 1993, President Serrano suspended parts of the Constitution as civil unrest escalated, and the **Unidad Revolucionaria Nacional Guatemalteca (URNG),** the main guerrilla group, withdrew from peace negotiations in 1994, citing persistent human rights violations by the government. Serrano was ousted after trying to gather what little control he could through force, leaving his successor, **President De León Carpio,** to scramble in an attempt to rein in both the national army *and* the guerillas.

Despite these efforts, the government is still mired in problems. Eighty percent of Guatemalan children under five are malnourished, half the population is either unemployed or underemployed, and 20 families control 80% of the nation's land. Guatemala is posted on the U.S. State Department's "drug problem list" in honor of its work in the transportation of cocaine and the manufacture of opium. And the nation is still trying to reclaim Belize, which it says was unjustly granted independence by Great Britain. Meanwhile, the historical discrimination against the large *indígena* population continues today, but with heightened awareness on the part of outsiders and the Guatemalan government. Because of this troublesome history, Guatemala hosted the international conference of indigenous peoples: *Majawil Q'ij*: 500 Years of Indigenous and Popular Resistance. *Indígenas* gathered in October 1991 to commemorate the tragic significance of Columbus's discovery of the Americas, and to proclaim the "New Dawn" of an era to claim the social, economic, and political respect they deserve. Perhaps as a sign of change, exiled activist for indigenous peoples in Guatemala and Nobel Peace Prize laureate, **Rigoberta Menchú,** was allowed to return to participate in the conference. Her autobiography, *I, Rigoberta Menchú*, is a horrifying account of life on a small Guatemalan farm.

■■■ THE ARTS

Guatemala's literary tradition dates back to the roots of civilization: the *Popol Vuh*, or Mayan Bible, an ancient document whose existence was first recorded by the Spanish in Chichicastenango in 1701. Since then, Guatemalan writers have continuously forged the gap between Indian myth and the European literary form; magic and the fantastic recur as frequent elements, and authors have tended to take the psychological turn, in order explore their protagonists' interiors, as well as their public actions. The country has produced few playwrights, but one of the few was a woman, Vicenta Laparra de La Cerda (1834-1905). Guatemala is most proud of the work of Miguel Angel Asturias (1899-1974), who won the Nobel Prize for his work in 1967, and whose novels penetrate deep political realities of this century. Most notable among his writings are *El señor Presidente* (1946), *Maladrón* (1969), and the more highly charged *Banana Trilogy* from the 1950s. Similarly critical of the sociopolitical conditions of the Indians are the novels of Mario Monteforte Toledo, who was forced into exile in Mexico for his work. Rigoberta Menchú (see history) was treated similarly by the government for her frank portrayal, written in cooperation with a French anthropologist.

Traveling around, you're likely to hear the *marimba,* which could easily be considered the national instrument of Guatemala. Something of a large, mellow-toned xylophone, the marimba's players often band together in orchestras to create haunting (or happy) melodies to the accompaniment of dancing.

Fruit Loops of the Loom

Famous the world over, authentic Guatemalan indigenous clothing is a rich tapestry of colors fit for a toucan's beak and intricate woven patterns, each piece of which can take up to six months to make. The natural dyes are fashioned from *clavel* and heraño flowers, and mixed with the crushed bodies of mosquitoes to keep the dye from running. The bugs themselves are often depicted in the resulting patterns, which are woven on to huge, unwieldy looms, and which are specific to each village, although such subtleties are difficult to detect with the untrained eye. The clothing is nearly always produced and worn by women.

Travelers in search of genuine hand-made clothing will be courted in the tourist-saturated markets with machine-made replicas; shop carefully. An easy way to tell a fake is by gold or silver synthetic fibers woven into the fabric, or if the stitching on the back is suspiciously neat. Or just look for prices that are too good to be true. Q50 will not buy you six months' labor. Skirt the over-hustled markets at Panajachel and Chichicastenango and shop in the smaller villages. And remember to be cautious about wearing the clothing in Guatemala; to some Indians, a foreigner in native dress reeks of blasphemy (it's especially insulting when women tourists wear traditionally male garments—like a hat for elderly men to wear at festivals), even though most are happy to share a good thing.

■■■ FOOD AND DRINK

Chicken rules supreme in Central American *típico* fare; don't be surprised if chicken is occasionally served with the feet still attached. But as the meat's the treat, meals are weighed down with rice, beans, eggs, and stick-to-your-ribs (and anything else) tortillas. There is good reason why tortillas in Guatemala are all made out of corn: according to Quiché traditional myths, humans *came* from the corn, and the grain is our essence.

Along the coasts, seafood is more common, usually peppered with Creole flare as it appears on the Caribbean coast. Despite the fruit's menacing, thorny, green exterior, the *sandía's* juicy, deep magenta core is definitely worth trying. If restaurant grub isn't your thing, have no fear: nearly every town has its own tent-strewn market, stocked with tons of fruits, vegetables, and other food, as well as clothes and other goods at bargain prices (that can often be bargained even lower). Caution, though: the fruit is often not washed in *agua purificada,* so munching can be risky.

■■■ MEDIA

In both circulation and sheer mass, *Prensa Libre* is the biggest Guatemalan daily newspaper, followed by *Siglo XXI.* The bi-weekly news journal *Crónica* is like the U.S. magazine *Time* in name as well as in format; the Guatemalan journal provides in-depth analysis of national and international events. *Crítica* comes out once a month, and provides a tempestuous forum for Guatemalan intellectuals.

Guatemala is hardly a 3.2 televisions-per-household country, and TV-watching is a deeply communal activity. Locals join family and friends in bars and restaurants to watch their favorite shows on cable. The cathode-hungry crowds often clog the doorways, especially during soccer games.

■■■ RECENT NEWS

The Guatemalan government and left-wing URNG guerrilas are currently in a state of cease fire, and both sides are prepared for peace talks; the guerrillas have wanted to move the talks from August until after the November presidential elections. The major issues at hand are the guerrilas' demands for a reduction in the size in the national army and an abolition of obligatory military service, as well as the return of communal lands which were taken from them decades ago. President Ramiro de León Carpio was not allowed to run for re-election, an issue with which he intentionally complied in order to block any presidential hopes for General Ríos Montt, who also has already served. Meanwhile, the U.S. continues to suspend military assistance to Guatemala because of persistent human rights violations, especially following allegations that some deaths might have been ordered by the CIA. The family of murdered author Myrna Mack, as well as other families, have been bolstering support for these protests.

On the tourism front, INGUAT is planning to market heavily in Europe to recoup losses from the fall in tourism resulting from the U.S. State Department's travel advisory. Last year, hostile confrontations between villagers and travelers were caused by rumors that U.S. citizens were snatching Guatemalan children to harvest their organs in the States. Incidents have been isolated, and the problem has waned, but crime continues to plague visitors to Guatemala. In July 1995, an Aviateca airliner full of passengers crashed into a Salvadoran volcano, en route to San Salvador; everyone aboard was killed.

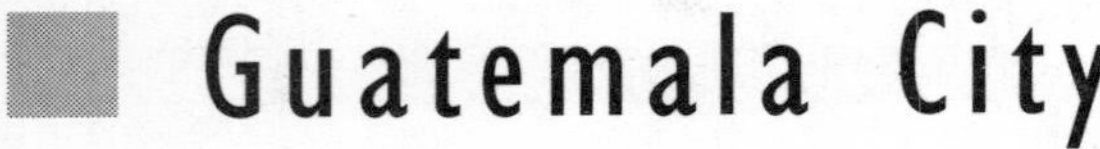

Guatemala City

Guate (GUAH-tuh), as Guatemalans affectionately (or not so affectionately) call it, is where the tensions plaguing the Republic reach their highest pitch. Political activists cry out for indigenous rights in the Parque Central, and rebellious students and gangs lash out at the prevailing law and order. Elsewhere in the country, tin-roofed shacks and grubby, sprawling markets attain a certain rustic romanticism amid the jungles and adjoining farmlands of the Pueblos; in Guatemala City however, poverty is stripped of charm, and instead festers in particularly harsh contrast to the antiseptic shopping malls and guard-patrolled, fortress-like mansions of the nation's wealthiest neighborhoods. The city teems gracelessly with vendors, business people, and beggars. Most tourists don't spend much time here, opting to quickly flee the smog-belching buses of the city for the verdant volcanoes of the western highlands.

Nevertheless, Guatemala City (pop. 3 million) is a force to be reckoned with at some time or another. Its museums provide a good introduction to indigenous history and culture, and an electric night life keeps the city convulsing long after sunset. Shaking and rocking is nothing new to Guatemala City, which was dubbed the new capital in 1775 after an earthquake in Antigua left the government scrambling for a safer haven. Although city leaders' sense of security was dashed by quakes in 1917, 1918, and 1976, Guatemala City has swollen ceaselessly, spreading into the surrounding valleys to become the largest urban amalgamation in Central America.

■■■ ORIENTATION

The enormous capital is divided into 21 zones, but nearly all sights and services of interest are in Zonas 1, 4, 9, 10, and 13. A line drawn from the airport (in Zona 13) to the Plaza Mayor (in Zona 1) would pass first along Av. de la Reforma (the border between Zonas 9 and 10), then through Zona 4, and finally through Zona 1. Walking at night is not recommended anywhere in the city. Taxi cabs should be hired only from clearly marked stands at the airport, at major hotels, at major intersections, and at certain parks. Make sure that your cab has a number painted on its side and a license plate that begins with "A."

Zona 1, the city's downtown, is its oldest section, housing all the budget hotels and restaurants. It is considered unsafe for after-dark perambulation. Be on guard during daylight hours, as well. *Calles* run east-west, with street numbers increasing as you move southward. *Avenidas* run north-south, with numbers increasing as you

Guatemala City Center

Bus Station, **10**
Cathedral, **2**
Central Market, **3**
Cultural Canter Miguel Angel Asturias, **8**
Iglesia Santa Clara, **6**
La Merced, **4**
Main Post Office, **5**
National Palace, **1**
Tourist Office, **9**
Train Station, **7**

A
B
C
D
1
2
3
4
5
6
7
N
3a Calle
4a Calle
Parque del Centenario
5a Calle
6a Calle
7a Calle
8a Calle
Plaza de las Armas (Plaza Mayor)
9a Calle
10a Calle
11 Calle
12 Calle
13 Calle
14 Calle
15 Calle
16 Calle
17 Calle
18 Calle
19 Calle
20 Calle
21 Calle
22 Calle
24 Calle
25 Calle
26 Calle
29 Calle
31 Calle
32 Calle
1 Calle
4 Calle
Calle Marsical Cruz
Avenida Elena
1a Avenida
2a Avenida
3a Avenida
4a Avenida
5a Avenida
6a Avenida
7a Avenida
8a Avenida
9a Avenida
10a Avenida
10a Avenida A
11 Avenida
12 Avenida
13 Avenida
15 Avenida
5 Avenida
8 Avenida
10 Avenida
Avenida Bolivar
Diagonal 4
Diagonal 7
Diagonal
Ruta 1
Ruta 2
Ruta 3
Ruta 4
Ruta 5
Ruta 6
Ruta 7
Ruta 8
Via 1
Via 2
Via 3
Via 4
Via 5
ZONA 1
ZONA 4
ZONA 5
Puerto Barrios
Train Station
Antigua, Mexico
Airport, Museums
0
500 yards
0
500 meters

GUATEMALA

move eastward. The major thoroughfare is **6 Avenida,** which passes the **Plaza Mayor** (the city's main plaza) in the northern part of Zona 1 and continues south through Zonas 4 and 9.

Zona 4 lies immediately to the south of Zona 1. An industrial area, Zona 4 boasts few tourist attractions. A series of northeast-to-southwest *vías* and northwest-to-southeast *rutas* (with numbers increasing north to south) complicate the street pattern established in Zona 1. Fortunately, Zona 4 is too small to deprive you of your bearings.

Zonas 9 and **10** are realms unto themselves—expect to see exclusive boutiques, fancy restaurants, five-star hotels, and homes of the elite. The southern portion of Zona 10 is the **Zona Viva** (Lively Zone), where the bulk of the city's most happening (and expensive) nightclubs and discos provide entertainment into the wee hours. These two *zonas* are both relatively pickpocket-free and generally safe. They are divided by the north-south **Avenida de la Reforma;** Zona 9 is to the west and Zona 10 to the east. *Avenidas* run parallel to La Reforma and increase eastward, starting at 1 Av. in each *zona*. *Calles* run perpendicular to them and increase southward.

Zona 13 is south of Zona 9 and contains museums, parks, and the international airport. Lucky 13 is removed from the hubbub of the center, and is generally safe.

Dilapidated, crowded *camionetas* (buses) go almost anywhere in the city for Q0.90. Bus #82 follows perhaps the most useful route, from 10 Av. in Zona 1, through Zona 4, and down Av. Reforma between Zonas 9 and 10. Returning, it travels north on Av. Reforma, through Zona 4, and up 9 Av. in Zona 1. Bus #83 goes from 10 Av. in Zona 1 to the airport and the Zona 13 attractions and returns to 9 Av. in Zona 1. *Micros* (vans or smaller buses) charge Q0.90 and course the same routes as *camionetas,* plus many additional ones. Destinations are posted on the windshields. Wave to the driver to get on; otherwise, the buses might just puff on by.

Guatemala City has no central **bus terminal;** instead, dozens of bus companies maintain separate offices throughout the city. Many buses leave from 19 Calle between 7 and 10 Avs. (near the train station in Zona 1). Several others leave from the huge combined terminal/market in Zona 4, between 1 and 4 Avs. and 1 and 7 Calles. Few companies have offices in these areas; buses simply idle in one of the two enormous parking lots while crews call out their destinations.

■■■ PRACTICAL INFORMATION

Tourist Office: Instituto Guatemalteco de Turismo (INGUAT), 7 Av. 1-17, Zona 4 (tel. 311-333), in the Centro Cívico just south of the Zona 1 border. Helpful, knowledgeable, and fluent in English. Maps (Q3) of the city and surrounding areas and invaluable free lists of bus destinations, terminals, and schedules. Open Mon.-Fri. 8am-4pm, Sat. 8am-1pm. **Airport branch** (tel. 314-256), before passport control as you exit the plane. Open daily 6am-9pm.

Police: 6 Av. 13-71, Zona 1 (tel. 120).

Central Post Office: 7 Av. 11-67, Zona 1 (tel. 26-101), in the enormous pink building. Open Mon.-Sat. 7:30am-6:30pm. *Lista de correos* in Room 110 (ext. 106). Open Mon.-Fri. 8am-4:30pm. **Postal code:** 01001. **United Parcel Service,** 2 Calle 6-40, Zona 9 (tel. 312-094). Open Mon.-Sat. 8am-8pm.

Embassies: U.S., Av. Reforma 7-01, Zona 10 (tel. 311-541). Open Mon.-Fri. 8am-noon and 1-3pm. Emergency assistance after hours (tel. 323-347) at the embassy Marine Guard. **Canada,** 13 Calle 8-44, Zona 10, Edyma Plaza Niv. 8 (tel. 336-102). Open Mon.-Thurs. 8am-4:30pm, Fri. 8am-3:30pm. **U.K.,** 7 Av. 5-10, Zona 4 (tel. 341-984), 7th floor of the Centro Financiero Torre II. Open Mon.-Thurs. 9am-noon and 2-4pm, Fri. 2-4pm. **Mexico,** 15 Calle 3-20, Zona 10 (tel. 337-258), on the 7th floor of the Edifico Centro. **Belize** is represented by the U.K. embassy. **Costa Rica,** Av. Reforma 8-60, Zona 9 (tel. 319-604), #320 in Edificio Galerías Reforma. Open Mon.-Fri. 9am-3pm. **Honduras,** 15 Calle 3-20, Zona 10 (tel. 374-344). Open Mon.-Fri. 8:30am-1:30pm. **Nicaragua,** 10 Av. 14-72, Zona 10 (tel. 680-785). Open Mon.-Fri. 9am-1pm. **El Salvador,** 12 Calle 5-43, Zona 9 (tel. 325-848). Open Mon.-Fri 8am-2pm. **Panama,** 5 Av. 15-45, Zona 10 (tel. 337-182). Open Mon.-Fri. 8:30am-1pm. Consult the phone book for other embassies.

Telephones: Guatel, main office at 12 Calle 8-42, Zona 1 (tel. 531-399). Open 24 hrs. **Phone, fax,** and **radiogram** service. Long-distance calls also from any of the Guatel branches located throughout the city, including 7 Av. 3-34, Zona 4 and 8 Av., 12 Calle, Zona 1. Open daily 7am-midnight. **Telephone code:** 2.

Telegrams: At the main post office (see above).

Consulate: Mexico, 13 Calle 7-30, Zona 9 (tel. 318-165), ½ block from Av. Reforma. Get your **Mexican tourist card** here. Open Mon.-Fri. 8:30am-2:30pm, Sat. 9-11am. Arrive as early as possible. **U.S.,** Av. La Reforma 7-01, Zona 10 (tel. 311-541). **Canada,** 13 Calle 8-44, Zona 10 (tel. 336-102). **U.K.,** 7 Av. 5-10, Zona 4 (tel. 321-601). Open Mon.-Thurs. 9am-noon and 2-4pm, Sat. 1:30pm-5pm. Consult the blue section of the phone book for the other consulates.

Immigration Office: 41 Calle 17-36, Zona 8 (tel. 714-670). Open Mon.-Fri. 8am-3pm. Catch bus #71 from 10 Av. (Q0.90).

Currency Exchange: The daily newspaper *Siglo XXI* publishes a list of the previous day's exchange rates. There is a **BanQuetzal** at the airport, open Mon.-Fri. 7am-8pm, Sat.-Sun. 8am-6pm. **Banco Agro,** 9 Calle 5-39, Zona 1 (tel. 514-026), is open Mon.-Fri. 9am-7pm, Sat. 10am-2pm. **Lloyd's Bank International,** 11 Calle 8-20, Zona 1 (tel. 532-250), and 6 Av. 9-51, Zona 9 (tel. 327-580), and **Banco Internacional,** 7 Av. 11-20, Zona 1 (tel. 518-066), are all open Mon.-Fri. 9am-3pm.

American Express: Av. La Reforma 9-00, Zona 9 (tel. 340-040), in the Banco del Café building. Will hold mail for card holders for traveler's check holders. Will also issue traveler's checks in exchange for personal checks to card holders. Open Mon.-Fri. 8:30am-4:30pm.

Airport: La Aurora International Airport (tel. 318-392), about 7km south of downtown, in Zona 13. Served by **American** (tel. 347-379), **British Airways** (tel. 327-402), **Continental** (tel. 353-341), **Mexicana** (tel. 312-697), and other domestic and international carriers. **Aeroquetzal** (tel. 373-467), **Tapsa** (tel. 314-860), and **Aviateca** (tel. 318-222) fly to **Flores** (near Tikal) for Q750 round-trip, **San José** for Q299. Check at hotels and INGUAT offices for special rates. Bus #83 shuttles passengers between Zona 1 and the airport for Q0.90. Taxis charge Q40 for the same route.

Buses: A morass of different terminals and lines, with each destination served by its own company. Consult the tourist office for their free list. Buses to **Antigua** depart from 15 Calle, between 3 and 4 Av., Zona 1 (every 30min., 7am-6pm, 1 hr., Q2.50); to **Chichicastenengo** from 9 Calle, 4 Av., Zona 1 (every 30min, 5am-6pm, 3 hrs., Q8); to **Cobán** from 8 Av. 15-16, Zona 1 (every hr., 4am-5pm, 4 hrs., Q12.10); to **Talisman,** and the frontier to Mexico, leave from 7 Av. 19-44, Zona 1 (6 daily, 6am-5:30pm, 5 hrs., Q24.15); to **Copán** from 19 Calle 8-18, Zona 1 (every 30min., 5am-6pm, 3½ hrs., Q13.50); to **Esquipulas** from 19 Calle 8-18, Zona 1 (every 30min., 4am-6pm, 4 hrs., Q17.50); to **Huehuetenango** from 7 Av. 15-27, Zona 1 (7am, 2pm; 5 hrs., Q19); to **La Democracia** from Muelle Central, Zona 4 (every 30min., 6am-4:30pm, 2 hrs., Q6); to **La Mesilla,** and the frontier to Mexico, from 20 Calle, 2 Av, Zona 1 (every hr., 8:30am-4pm, 7 hrs.); to the **Pacific Coast (Monterrico Reserve)** from Muelle Central, Zona 4 (at 10:30am, 12:30, and 2:30pm, 4½ hrs., Q7); to **Panajachel** from 21 Calle 1-34, Zona 1 (every hr., 6:30am-4pm, 3 hrs., Q10); to **Puerto Barrios** from 15 Calle 10-42, Zona 1 (8 per day, 7am-3pm, 5 hrs., Q32); to **Puerto de San Jose** from Frebol, Zona 12 (every 10min., 5am-5pm, 1 hr., Q3); to **Quetzaltenango** from 7 Av. 19-44, Zona 1 (7 per day, 5:30am-7pm, 4 hrs., Q16.50); to **Río Dulce** from 17 Calle 8-46, Zona 1 (7 per day, 7:30am-9pm, 5 hrs., Q25); to **Tikal** from 17 Calle 9-36, Zona 1 (at 4, 6, and 8pm, 12 hrs., Q50); to **San Salvador** from 3 Av. 1-38, Zona 9 (every hr., 5:30am-4:30pm, 5 hrs., Q32.10); to **Tecpan,** near Iximché, leaves from 20 Calle, Av. Bolívar, Zona 1 (every 20min., 5:30am-7pm, 2 hrs., Q4.50); to **Tecún Umán** from 19 Calle 8-70, Zona 1 (at 1:30, 3, 3:30, and 5:30pm, 5 hrs., Q20); to **Amatitlan** from 20 Calle, 2 Av., Zona 1 (every 30min, 7am-7pm, 30min., Q1.60).

Taxis: Always be sure that the car is marked as a taxi and that the license begins with an "A." 24- hr. service. **Biltmore y Camino Real,** Zona 10 (tel. 335-613). **Reforma,** Zona 10 (tel. 681-354). **Infantil Colón,** Zona 1 (tel. 539-304). Many

GUATEMALA

hotels work with cab drivers who have documented and reliable track-records. Fare between Zona 1 and Zona Viva Q35.

Car Rental: Tally, 7 Av. 14-60, Zona 1 (tel. 514-113), open Mon.-Sat. 7am-8pm, Sun. 8am-6pm; at the airport (tel. 345-925), open daily 6am-9pm. Small cars Q166 per day, including taxes, insurance, and 100km free, Q0.30 each additional km. **Dollar,** at Av. La Reforma 6-14, Zona 9 (tel. 348-285), open Mon.-Fri. 8am-5pm; at Av. Reforma 6-14, Zona 9 (tel. 341-541), open daily 6am-9pm; and at the airport (tel. 317-185), open Mon.-Sat. 6am-9pm, Sun. 7am-8pm. Small cars, including taxes, insurance, and unlimited mileage, US$41 per day.

Market: Central Market, 6/8 Calles, 8/9 Avs. Open Mon.-Sat. 6am-6pm, Sun. 7am-noon. Virtually ignored by tourists, the whole market's in a big, cement, underground garage, but boasts a good selection of indigenous wares at more sensible prices than Chichi or Panajachel. There is also a big **food market** around the bus terminal in Zona 4, open daily 7am-6pm. **Supermarket: Paiz,** 18 Calle 6-85, Zona 1 (tel. 535-674). Open Mon.-Sat. 9am-8pm, Sun. 9am-6pm.

Laundry: El Siglo, 4 Av. 13-09 (tel. 21-469). Q7 per wash, Q7 per dry. Other locations around the city. Open Mon.-Sat. 8am-6pm.

English Bookstores: Arnel, 9 Calle, 7 Av. (tel. 24-631), Edificio el Centro 108. Large selection of books. Hours unreliable. Try your luck Mon.-Fri. 11am-12:30pm and 3:30-7pm, Sat. 11am-12:30pm. Best selection of U.S. magazines is at **Book Nook** in the Camino Real Hotel, Av. Reforma 14-30, Zona 9 (tel. 334-633). The latest bestsellers Q20-35. Open daily 7am-9pm.

Pharmacy: Farmacia Sinai Centro, 4 Av. 12-74, Zona 1 (tel. 515-276). Open 24 hrs.

Crisis Hotline: INGUAT, the tourist office, has a 24- hr. information and crisis hotline (tel. 333-075). English spoken.

Ambulance: (tel. 128) 24- hr. service.

Red Cross: 3 Calle 8-40, Zona 1 (tel. 125). 24- hr. emergency service.

■■■ ACCOMMODATIONS

Budget accommodations are concentrated in Zona 1, the city's aging downtown area. Like most of Guatemala City, Zona 1 is plagued by muggings and robberies. Even if it costs a bit extra, make safety a top consideration in choosing a hotel—windows should be barred, balconies secure, locks functional, and management conscientious. Call hotels ahead of time—this ain't a great town in which to wander around at night.

Pensión Meza, 10 Calle 10-17, Zona 1 (tel. 23-177). Your happy hippie hangout in Guate, perhaps the best place for travel tips. Chill in the shady courtyard or play ping-pong. Rooms and common bathrooms are dark and a bit dilapidated, but creative graffiti livens them up. Warm, friendly service and a gregarious atmosphere. The management here is super nice, speaks English, and has a phone. Open 24 hrs. Singles Q33; doubles Q38; triples with private bath Q55.

Lessing House, 12 Calle 4-35, Zona 1 (tel. 513-891). Bathrooms could be cleaner, but they're all private, and some of the Art Deco nightstands could fetch a pretty penny in a U.S. antique shop. Big wooden doors out front are locked at night. Refrigerator, shared TV. Singles Q47; doubles Q82; triples Q117, including taxes.

Hoteles Centroamérica, 9 Av. 16-38, Zona 1 (tel. 26-917). The bubbling fountain seems to mumble of happier times seen here. Echoed footsteps lead to smallish rooms; dirt lurks in the corners of the public facilities, toilet seats are mysteriously missing. Nevertheless, local calls are free, the television is color, foreign currency is exchanged, and restaurant, taxi, and fax services are all provided. Singles Q46, Q56 with bath; doubles Q46, Q83 with bath.

Hotel Colonial, 7 Av. 14-19, Zona 1 (tel. 26-722). Colonial Guatemala City was destroyed by earthquakes, but a bit of its flavor survives here. Dark, polished antique beds and heavy wardrobes and nightstands. Bathrooms are very clean, but the lack of hot water evokes the colonial past all too clearly. Most rooms have small sitting areas. Restaurant serves breakfast. *Agua purificada* on sale at the desk. Very friendly staff. Singles US$15, US$20 with bath; doubles US$20, US$27 with bath. Taxes (17%) not included.

Chalet Suizo, 14 Calle 6-82, Zona 1 (tel. 513-786; fax 772-134). A former budget hotel, now upgraded to the middle range, but still profoundly confused about its national loyalties. "Swiss Chalet" strives for a Zen atmosphere with Japanese-style details, but the paper-thin walls allow yodeling neighbors to disturb your meditation all too effortlessly. Plain but spacious rooms. Spotless bathrooms verge on the gleaming. Singles Q71, Q137 with bath; doubles Q91, Q160 with bath.

El Aeropuerto Guest House, 15 Calle "A" 7-32, Zona 13 (tel. 323-086). Location, location, location—only 150m from the airport. Immaculate rooms and bathrooms (mostly communal) in a homey, friendly atmosphere. Hot water, cable TV in the living room. Includes breakfast and free transportation to and from the airport (versus Q40 for a taxi or a 30-min. bus ride). Call when you arrive at the airport for a free pickup. Singles US$25, US$30 with private bath; doubles US$30, US$35 with private bath; triples US$35, US$40 with private bath.

Hotel Letona, 8 Av., 14 Calle 62 (tel. 513-252). A little dark and dingy, but high ceilings, stained glass windows, and cheery service raise it above other, seedier places. Eight rooms donut themselves around a cafeteria and lounge. If profane traffic-squawkings hurt your ears, ask for a back room. Singles Q27, Q45 with bath; doubles Q35, Q45 with bath; triples Q45, Q70 with bath.

GUATEMALA

■■■ FOOD

In Guatemala City, grub runs the gamut, but no establishment has asserted itself as *the* place to go. Indulge your taste for egg rolls, pizzas or *chiles rellenos.* At many moderately priced restaurants, dishes cost between four and five dollars.

Delicadezas Hamburgo, 15 Calle 5-34, Zona 1, at the south side of the Parque Centenario. A weekly rotating menu in a '50s-style lunch joint with Parque Centenario's street performers and political activists barking at your doorstep. Chicken sandwich Q7, spaghetti Q15.75. One-half roasted chicken with fries Q23, filet mignon with potatoes Q35.50. Open daily 7am-10pm.

Productos Integrales, 8 Calle 5-36, Zona 1, on the south side of Parque Central. The lunch crowd packs into this unconventional *comedor* for whole-grain cakes (Q7), fruit *licuados* made with soy milk (Q4), and vegetarian dishes that change every day (Q7). Stock up here on vitamins A through zinc. Burning incense smells better than the bus exhaust which dominates the air outside. Open Mon.-Sat. 7am-9pm.

Restaurant Los Tecomates, 6 Av. 15-69, Zona 1 (tel. 512-886). A bit of the sleepy western highlands in the heart of Zona 1. Pine needles blanket the floor and colored streamers hang from the ceiling, evoking the feel of many an *indígena* church. As always, real Quiché don't eat quiche—*carnes asadas* (Q18), tacos (Q2.75-Q3), and soups (Q3.50-8). Open daily noon-10pm.

Restaurant Fu Lu Sho, 6 Av. 12-09, Zona 1. The name means "Happiness, Prosperity, Longevity." One of the most popular middle-range Chinese restaurants in Zona 1, striving for Oriental flair with a jet-black ceiling and an elaborate staircase swooning to the second tier. Chicken in curry or pineapple, meat dishes with a variety of spicy vegetables. Open daily 9am-11pm.

La Spaghetteria, Av. Reforma, 11 Calle, across from the American Express office in Zona 10. Popular outdoor café serves great cappuccino, pizza (Q30), and ravioli (Q22). Extensive menu includes many toothsome desserts. Open daily, noon-1am.

Las Tertulias, Av. Reforma 10-31, Zona 10 (tel. 320-057). A large menu, but its main attraction is the super bargainous *super lunch ejecutivo,* with soup, an entree, salad, and dessert for Q17.50—it's not just for CEOs anymore. Live music after 5pm. Open daily 7am-11pm.

■■■ SIGHTS

Zona 1

La Plaza Mayor (also called *Parque Central*) consists of two large plazas—**Parque de Centenario** and **Plaza de las Armas,** bounded on the west and east by 6 and 7 Avs. and on the north and south by 6 and 8 Calles. Permanently animated by persistent *limpiabotas* (shoe-shine boys), and often beseiged by the political demonstrators who have set up office here, Plaza Mayor never bores. It's been called "the center of all Guatemala," and it is easiest to understand why on Sundays, when *indígenas* from all groups and regions come to sell their textiles or simply to take their afternoon strolls.

To the east of the plaza rises the beautiful, neoclassical **Catedral Metropolitana,** constructed between 1782 and 1868 (open Mon.-Sat. 7am-6pm, Sun. 7am-8pm). To the north, guarded by dozens of camouflaged and gun-toting soldiers, is the **Palacio Nacional, the** uncomfortable seat of the Republic's troubled government. It was built between 1938 and 1943 under the orders of president Jorge Ubico. The public is allowed in the two most impressive of the 350 rooms in the palace—**La Sala de Recepción** and **La Sala de Banquetes.** The Sala de Recepción awes visitors with its massive Bohemian crystal chandelier, decorated with graceful *quetzals* in brass and gold. The parquet floor was sliced from the tropical hardwoods of Petén and the elaborate reception table was carved in Spain from a single piece of wood. The Sala de Banquetes features another chandelier in Bohemian crystal and 18-karat gold. The stained-glass windows, shattered by a bomb 14 years ago, hint at the political turmoil that lurks behind the elegance (free tours in Spanish or English Mon.-Fri. 8am-4:30pm).

Behind the cathedral, between 8 and 9 Avs. and 6 and 8 Calles, is the underground **Mercado Central,** which boasts a fantastic selection of food, crafts, and flowers. With great deals offered in every stall, this market caters primarily to locals (open Mon.-Sat. 8am-6pm, Sun. 8am-noon).

The **Miguel Angel Asturias Cultural Center** is at the south end of Zona 1, located in the Civic Center. It houses the National Theater, a chamber theater, and an open-air theater. The oldest church in the Ermita Valley, **Cerrito del Carmen** (finished in 1620), rests peacefully at 12 Av., 2 Calle. The first public clock in the city ticks away in one of the two towers of the **Santo Domingo Church,** 12 Av., 10 Calle. But the church most often praised for its elaborate paintings, sculptures, woodcarvings, and mosaics is **La Merced,** which stands at 11 Av. and 5 Calle.

Zona 2

The **Mapa en Relieve,** an enormous horizontal relief map of Guatemala, puzzles and fascinates tourists and Guatemalans alike. The vertical scale of the map is twice the horizontal scale, contributing to an overwhelming sense of vertigo. Viewers mount towers on either side of the map, which was designed and built in the early 1900s, to look down upon a precise representation of the mountainous country. If you bring a microscope you can watch a tiny replica of yourself looking at the map.... The *mapa* is at the end of 6 Av., about 2km north of the plaza (take buses #1, 45, or 46 from 5 Av. in Zona 1).

Zonas 4, 9, and 10

The most architecturally playful chapel in the city, **Iglesia Yurrita,** is in Zona 4, on 6 Ruta 8-54; unfortunately, it's closed most of the time. The border between Zonas 4 and 9 is marked by a smaller version of the Eiffel Tower, known as **El Torre del Reformador** (in memory of Justo Rufino Barrio's attempt to unite Central America). Just a block west of it is the **Botanical Garden** (open Mon.-Fri. 8am-3:30pm, Sat.-Sun. 8am-noon).

Eight blocks down on Av. Reforma is Guatemala's most famous museum, **Popol-Vuh,** Av. Reforma 8-60, Zona 9 (tel. 347-121), on the sixth floor of Edificio Galerías Reforma. Named after the sacred Mayan book, a cyclical cosmological epic, the museum houses a large collection of pre-Columbian Mayan pottery. There are no signs in the museum, so you might consider buying a guide book (Q6 in English, Q5 in Spanish). Open Mon.-Sat. 9am-5pm. Admission Q5.

The very fabric of indigenous life is on display at the **Museo Ixchel del Traje Indígena,** in a new building on the campus of the Universidad Francisco Marroquín, 6 Calle Final, Zona 10 (tel. 313-739), scheduled to re-open in June 1995. The museum offers a richly textured introduction to the weaving and textile traditions of the Guatemalan highlands. A 20-minute video (in English and Spanish) spins the story of indigenous dress from pre-Hispanic times to the present. Interwoven with the weft of history and shot through with the threads of tradition, the galleries exhibit antique textiles and paintings of indigenous costumes (open Mon.-Fri. 8am-4:50pm, Sat. 9am-12:30pm, admission Q10).

Zona 13

Only a 20-minute walk from the airport, Zona 13 is full of tourist attractions and provides a great way to while away the hours until your flight. The **Mercado de Artesanías,** Blvd. Aeropuerto, 6 Calle, Zona 13, is your last chance to shop for traditional textiles, ceramics, and jewelry from each region of the country. Prices are high (open Mon.-Sat. 8am-6pm, Sun. 8am-noon). The zoo next door, also called **Parque Aurora,** offers a chance to stare long and hard at all those animals and birds of which you caught only fleeting glimpses in the jungle of Tikal or down the Río Dulce. If their small cement cells will turn your stomach, spare yourself the visit (open Tues.-Fri. 9am-5pm Sat.-Sun. 8am-5pm; admission Q1). Behind the market and the zoo is the **Museo de Arte Moderno** (tel. 720-467), a solid collection which features the works of contemporary Guatemalan artists such as Carlos Mérida and Humberto Garavito (open Tues.-Fri. 9am-4pm, Sat.-Sun. 9am-noon and 2-4pm; admission Q25). **Museo Nacional de Arqueología y Etnología** (tel. 720-489) primarily traces Mayan preclassic, classic, and postclassic history in a display of hundreds of Mayan artifacts from all over Guatemala; an excellent scale model of the ancient city at Tikal, an exhibit of regional apparel *típico*; and a large collection of ceremonial masks, both pre-Hispanic and modern. There is also the reconstruced grave site of a Mayan ruler (open Tues.-Fri. 9am-4pm, Sat.-Sun. 9am-noon and 2-4pm; admission Q1). **Museo de Historia Natural** (tel. 720-468) is home to a stuffed effigy of the sacred bird of the Mayas, the *quetzal* (open Tues.-Fri. 9am-4pm, Sat.-Sun. 9am-noon and 2-4pm; admission free). To get to any of these destinations catch bus #83 from 10 Av. or #63 and #85 (red) from 4 Av. (fare Q0.90).

■■■ ENTERTAINMENT

For a current listing of cultural events and movies, check **La Prensa Libre** (Q1.25) or any of the other local newspapers. Theater and opera performances in both English and Spanish are staged at **Teatro IGA,** 1 Ruta 4-05, Zona 4 (tel. 310-022), on Friday and Saturday nights at 8pm (tickets Q10). Sometimes there are free showings of movies at the theater; for information, call the office Monday through Friday from 8am-5pm. Theater performances in Spanish are also presented at the **Teatro Nacional,** 24 Calle 3-81, Zona 1 (tel. 531-743), **Teatro La Universidad Popular,** 10 Calle 10-32, Zona 1 (tel. 25-181), and in several other theaters throughout the city. (Universidad Popular performances Fri. 8:30pm, Sat. 4:30pm and 8:30pm, and Sun. 4pm and 6:30pm; tickets Q15). The **Conservatorio Nacional de Música,** 5 Calle, 3 Av., Zona 1 (tel. 28-726), organizes performances every other Thursday at 8pm (tickets Q30). **Alianza Francesa,** 4 Av. 12-39, Zona 1 (tel. 531-129), has free movie showings (in Spanish or French) Mondays at 6pm and Saturdays at 4pm.

Guatemala City's nightlife gets pretty active, particularly in the newly developed **Zona Viva** (Zona 9). It's best to bar-hop in cabs, since the city is unsafe at night. The pace picks up at 11pm and winds down around 3am. The **Tropical Room** (between the Sheraton and a strip joint on 6 Av., Zona 4) is the best place to practice your *salsa,* but there is no pressure to dance. All age groups hang out harmoniously.

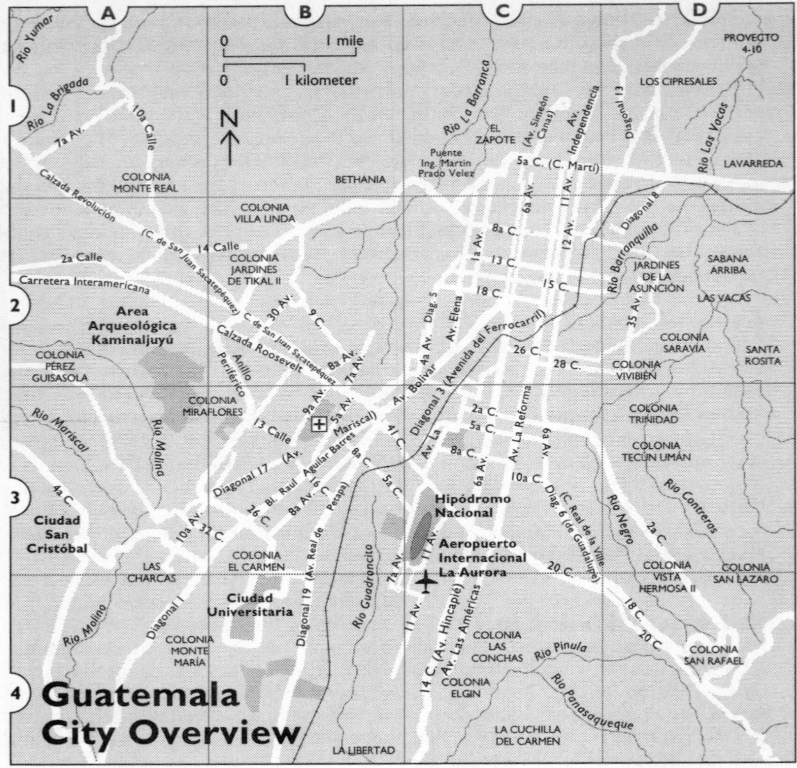

Guatemala City Overview

(open Mon.-Sat. 6:30pm-12:45am; cover Q15; beer Q8). The grown-up wanna-bes swarm to **Dash** (tel. 26-030), in the Geminis commercial complex on 10 Calle, Zona 10. It's a modern disco: Thursday nights feature *música en vivo* (open Mon.-Sat. 8pm-1am; cover Thurs.-Sat. Q15; beer Q12, vodka Q5). Next on the city's "hot spot" list comes **Le Pont,** 13 Calle 0-48, Zona 10, decorated in a French Caribbean theme (open Wed.-Sat. 7pm-1am; cover Q20; beer Q10). The newest nightlife mecca is **La Terraza,** on the fourth floor of the Centro Commercial Los Próceres. The elevator opens onto a security check-point, beyond which throb four discos and 10 bars—some of the hippest bars and nightclubs in Guatemala.

■ NEAR GUATEMALA CITY

VOLCÁN PACAYA

Guatemala's volcanoes have been plagued with robberies, rapes, and murders, and the Pacaya Volcano has been at the center of these troubles. In the summer of 1994, a group of sixteen Americans was assaulted by three armed men, who robbed them and raped one of the women in the group. In the summer of 1995, the volcano was considered safer than in the past, as guards have been stationed around the mountain, and it is possible to make the ascent in groups (often with an armed guide). Travel agencies in Guatemala City or Antigua will be able to procure guides for volcano-climbing. For updated information on the safety of traveling to the volcanoes, check with the INGUAT office in Guatemala City or Antigua and the U.S. embassy in Guatemala City (see Practical Information, above). Buses leave Guatemala City from the terminal in Zona 4 to San Viciente Pacaya, to El Cedro, and to San Francisco de Salle. Some climbers stay the night at one of these villages and start the two-hour ascent early the next morning, in order to catch the early afternoon bus back to Guatemala City. Climb at your own risk.

SAN JUAN DE COMALAPA

Comalapa is a small Cakchiquel village famed for its indigenous "primitivist" art. It is 40km from the capital, in the province of Chimaltenango. In fact, most of the works of indigenous art in the Museum of Modern Art in Guatemala City come from Comalapa; many more can be seen on a trip to the village. Seven art galleries line the **Calle Principal** and sell excellent pieces of art depicting the traditional folk rituals which are still a way of life in Comalapa.

Plan to visit Comalapa during the week of June 20-26, when the local *feria* in honor of the patron saint of the village, San Juan, takes place. Everyone turns out to strut their stuff in daily processions—*marimba* orchestras, masked dancers, hot air balloons, and a dancing, fireworks-spewing *torre*. **Buses** to Comalapa leave Guatemala City from the terminal at 20 Calle, 1 Av., Zona 1 (every hr., 7am-5:30pm, 2 hrs., Q4). It's also possible to take any bus that passes through Chimaltenango and change there for one of the buses that leaves hourly for San Juan. The last bus leaves San Juan around 3 or 4pm, so plan ahead; there are no hotels and few restaurants.

WESTERN HIGHLANDS

■■■ ANTIGUA

Antigua was improvidently built at the base of the magnificent Volcán de Agua in 1527. Within two decades, the volcano spewed forth enough lava to wipe the city off the map. Unfazed, the Spaniards re-built Antigua in the Valley of Panchoz; it soon became the political capital of the region. Alas, another natural disaster, this time a gargantuan earthquake, destroyed the city in the 1770s, and jostled it from its position as a center of political power in the process.

Set in rugged green mountains, today's Antigua is a tourist magnet. Restaurants and hotels catering to international travelers have cropped up everywhere and have lent the city a cosmopolitan air. Ironically, but not coincidentally, in a city famed for its Spanish-language schools, knowledge of Spanish is rather unnecessary—English is everywhere. At times, Antigua can feel a bit too cozy; some feel the narrow streets aren't meant to hold as many *gringos* as they do, especially as things have started to look a lot like home. Through it all, though, Antigua's colonial charm has not been obscured. The cobblestone streets are kept spotless, earthquakes have limited the construction of awkward, oversized buildings, and the hanging of signs and advertisements is forbidden, a rule which enhances the city's mystique, but which makes most everything damn hard to find. Year after year, Antigua continues to embrace the hearts of most visitors as it did that of Aldous Huxley, who deemed the town one of the most romantic in the world.

ORIENTATION

While Antigua is only 45km west-southwest of Guatemala City, the trip over winding mountain roads can consume an hour and a half. Frequent second-class, converted school buses connect the cities. **Transportes Unidos, América Preciosa,** and several other lines leave Guatemala City every half-hour (see Guatemala City: Practical Information: page 56) and arrive in Antigua at *el mercado* on Alameda Santa Lucía, three blocks west of the central plaza (Q2.35).

Though compact, Antigua can prove tricky to navigate. Very few of its *calles* and *avenidas* are marked, street numbers follow no obvious plan, and many streets look

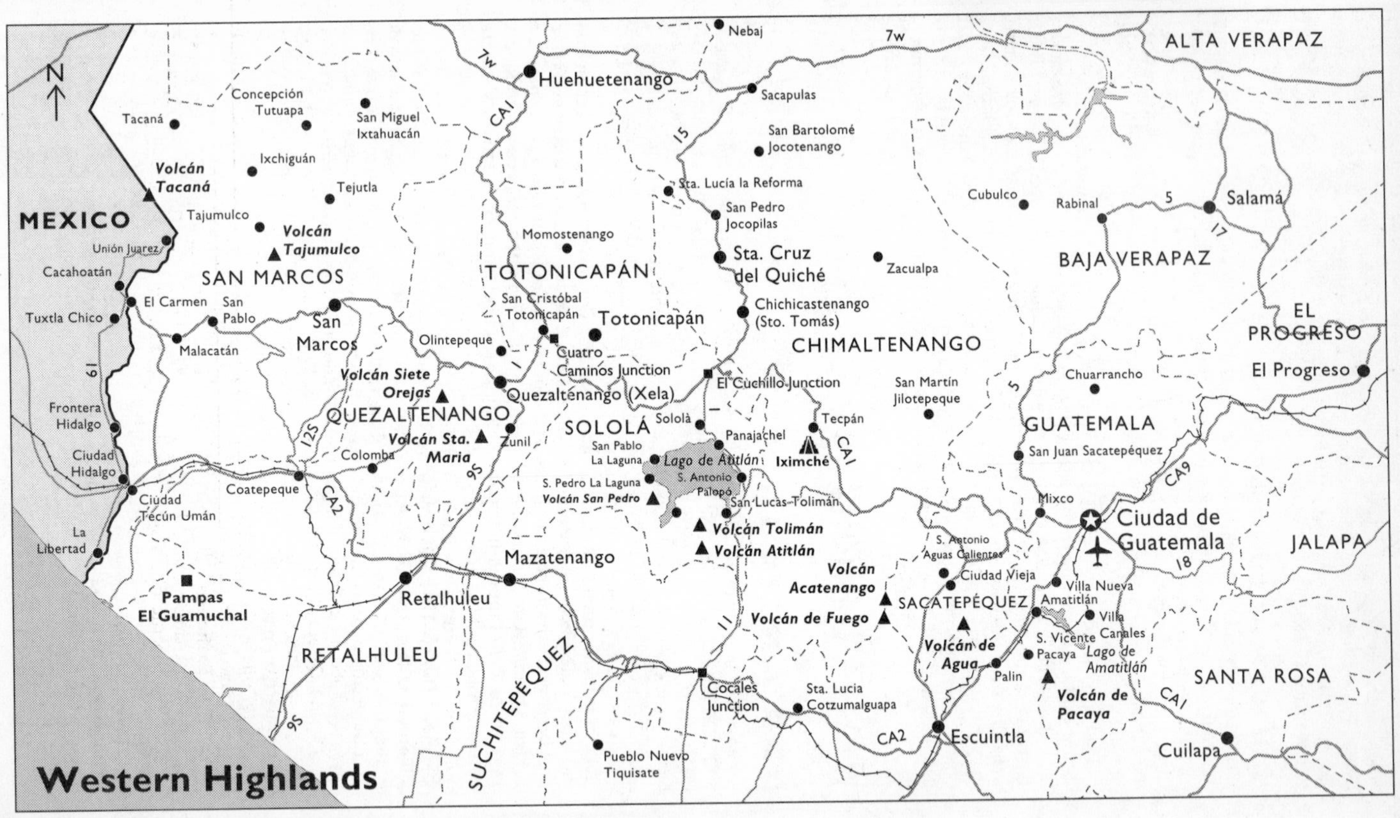
Western Highlands
N
MEXICO
ALTA VERAPAZ
BAJA VERAPAZ
EL PROGRESO
JALAPA
GUATEMALA
SANTA ROSA
CHIMALTENANGO
SACATEPÉQUEZ
SOLOLÁ
TOTONICAPÁN
QUEZALTENANGO
SAN MARCOS
RETALHULEU
SUCHITEPÉQUEZ
Ciudad de Guatemala
Huehuetenango
Nebaj
Sacapulas
San Bartolomé Jocotenango
Sta. Lucía la Reforma
San Pedro Jocopilas
Sta. Cruz del Quiché
Zacualpa
Chichicastenango (Sto. Tomás)
Cubulco
Rabinal
Salamá
El Progreso
Chuarrancho
San Martín Jilotepeque
San Juan Sacatepéquez
Mixco
Villa Nueva
Amatitlán
Villa Canales
S. Vicente Pacaya
Lago de Amatitlán
Volcán de Pacaya
Palin
Escuintla
Cuilapa
S. Antonio Aguas Calientes
Ciudad Vieja
Volcán de Agua
Volcán Acatenango
Volcán de Fuego
Sta. Lucia Cotzumalguapa
Cocales Junction
Pueblo Nuevo Tiquisate
Tecpán
Iximché
El Cuchillo Junction
Sololá
Panajachel
Lago de Atitlán
San Pablo La Laguna
S. Antonio Palopó
S. Pedro La Laguna
Volcán San Pedro
San Lucas Tolimán
Volcán Tolimán
Volcán Atitlán
Momostenango
San Cristóbal Totonicapán
Totonicapán
Cuatro Caminos Junction
Quezaltenango (Xela)
Olintepeque
Zunil
Volcán Siete Orejas
Volcán Sta. Maria
Colomba
Mazatenango
Retalhuleu
Coatepeque
Ciudad Tecún Umán
Pampas El Guamuchal
Concepción Tutuapa
San Miguel Ixtahuacán
Tacaná
Ixchiguán
Tejutla
Volcán Tacaná
Tajumulco
Volcán Tajumulco
Unión Juarez
Cacahoatán
El Carmen
San Pablo
San Marcos
Tuxtla Chico
Malacatán
Frontera Hidalgo
Ciudad Hidalgo
La Libertad
7w
CA1
CA2
CA9
15
5
17
18
11
19
9S
12S

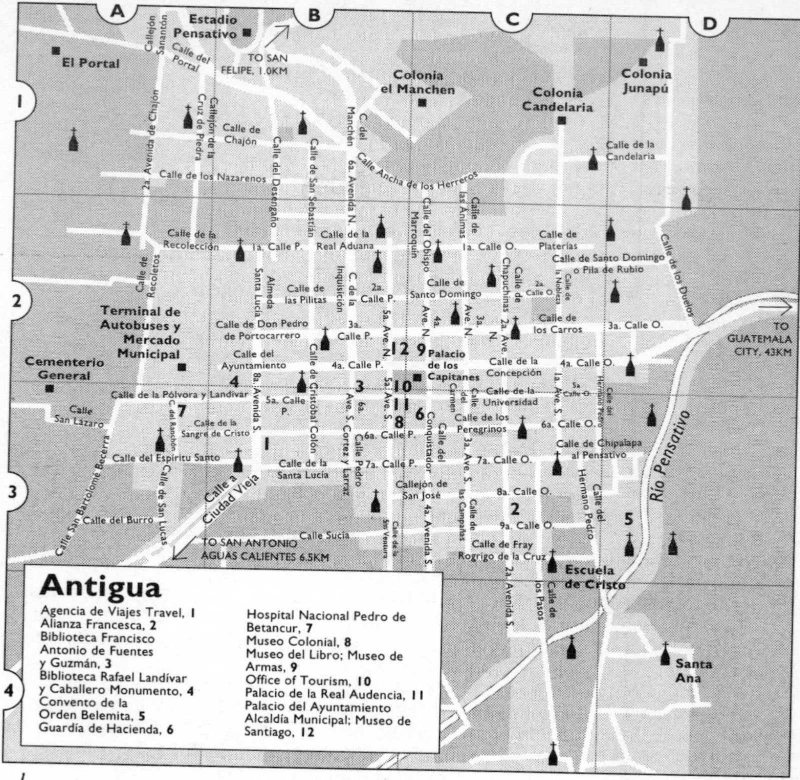

alike. *Avenidas* run north-south and are numbered 1 to 7 beginning in the east. North of 5 Calle, *avenidas* are all designated *Norte* (Nte.); south of it, *Sur*. *Calles* run east-west and are numbered 1 to 9 starting in the north. East of 4 Av., *calles* are named *Oriente* (Ote.); west of it, *Poniente* (Pte.). The **Parque Central** is bounded by 4 and 5 Calles on the north and south, respectively, and by 4 and 5 Av. on the east and west.

PRACTICAL INFORMATION

Tourist Office: INGUAT, 5 Calle Ote., 4 Av. Sur, (tel. 320-763), in the Palacio de los Capitanes Generales, on the southeast corner of the Parque Central. Brochures and an excellent map. English spoken. Open daily 8am-6pm. Other, less established information centers include **Viajes Tivoli** (tel. 322-728), 5a. Av. Nte. 15, and **Quetzal Expeditions,** Alameda Santa Lucía Sur. 6. Guides of all types roam the Parque Central looking to show tourists around for a hefty price (4 hrs. through Antigua and San Antonio Aguas Calientes, US$35).

Police: Policía Nacional (tel. 320-251), on the south side of the Parque Central in the Palacio de los Capitanes Generales. 24- hr. emergency service.

Currency Exchange: Might as well roll the dice to determine which of Antigua's 7 banks is exchanging traveler's checks the day you're there. **Banco del Agro** (tel. 320-793), on the north side of the Parque Central, always exchanges dollars. Open Mon.-Fri. 9am-8pm, Sat. 9am-6pm. **Banco Industrial,** 5 Av. Sur 4 (tel. 320-958), has a 24-hr. **ATM** which can give a cash advance on Visa cards (and only on Visa cards). Open Mon.-Fri. 8:30am-4pm, Sat. 8:30am-12:30pm.

Post Office: Alameda de Santa Lucía at 4 Calle Pte. (tel. 320-485), across the street from the market and the bus stop. **UPS,** 6 Calle Pte. 19. Packages going abroad must be under 2kg. Open Mon.-Fri. 8am-2:30pm. **Postal code:** 03.

Telephones: Use pay phones on the south and west sides of Parque Central for direct-dial international calls. **Guatel,** on 5 Av. Sur 2 (tel. 322-498), just south of the southwest corner of the park, will place both domestic and pricey international calls; often crowded. Open daily 7am-10pm. Private telecommunications services may offer better rates and advertise all over. **The Budget Traveler** (tel. 322-972) has an office in the Tecún Umán Spanish School. **Telephone code:** 0.

Telegrams: Alameda de Santa Lucía at 4 Calle Pte., (tel. 320-485) next door to the post office. Open daily 8am-7pm. **Western Union** at El Unicorno, 5 Calle Pte. 11B (tel. 323-316). Open Mon.-Fri. 9am-noon and 2-6pm, Sat. 9am-noon.

Bus Station: Behind the market on 5 Calle Pte. To find your bus, ask your way through the jungled parking lot; there is no main office. To **Guatemala City** (every 15min., 5am-7pm, 45min., Q2.50); to **Chimaltenango** (every 15min., 5am-7pm, Q1.25); to **San Antonio Aguas Calientes** (every 20min., 7am-7pm, 30min., Q0.75); to **Ciudad Vieja** (at 7, 8am, 1, 2, and 3pm, Q0.50); to **Santa María de Jesús** (every hr., 7am-7pm, 2 hrs., Q1.25); to **Puerto San José** (6, 7am, 1, 2pm, 1½ hrs., Q3). Hotels and travel agencies advertise various shuttles to the **airport** (US$7-10) and to **Panajachel** (US$12).

Taxis: (tel. 320-526), lined up along the east side of Parque Central. To Ciudad Vieja Q25-35. Negotiable.

Car Rental: Americar, 6 Av. Nte. 3 (tel. 320-794), rents 2-door Hyundais for Q223 per day. **Avis** (tel. 322-692), 5 Av. Nte 25, rents small Nissans for Q315 per day, including insurance and unlimited mileage. **Ahorent,** 4 Calle Ote. 14, rents cars for Q189 a day.

Motorcycle Rental: Jopa Motorcycle Rental, 6 Av. Nte. 3 (tel. 320-794), rents *motos* for Q85 per 4 hrs., including insurance, helmet, tools, and unlimited mileage. Better rates for longer rentals. Credit card or US$1000 deposit required. Open 8am-12:30pm and 2-5:30pm.

Bike Rental: Posada de Don Pedro de Alvarado, 4 Calle Pte. 27-D. Q15 per day and you can't keep it overnight. Open 8am-6:30pm. **Hotel San Vicente,** 6 Av. Sur between 5 and 6 Calle Pte. Q6 per hr. or Q35 per day. **Bike Center,** 6 Av. Nte. 12, charges Q60 per day for rentals. **Mayan Mountain Bike Tours,** 3 Av. Nte. 3, Q10 per day; organized bike tours for all levels. Open 8am-6pm.

Camping Equipment Rental: 4 Calle Ote. 5 (tel. 320-161), across from Doña Lucía. Tents Q10 per day. Sleeping bags Q10 per day. US$100 deposit per item. Open Mon.-Fri. 9am-6:50pm, Sat. 9am-7pm.

Travel Agency: Turansa, 5 Av. Norte 17 (tel. 322-664), ½ block north of Parque Central. Makes ticket reservations, organizes tours to Panajachel, Chichicastenango, Copán, Quiriguá, and Esquipulas. Open Mon.-Fri. 8am-1pm and 2-6pm, Sat. 8:30am-1pm. **Sensational Tours Quintanilla** (tel. and fax 722-304) and **Servicios Turisticos Atitlán,** 6 Av. 7 (tel. 320-648) also offer tours. Shop around for tour packages since prices vary widely and change frequently.

English Bookstore: Un Poco de Todo (tel. 320-892), on the west side of Parque Central. Paperbacks Q6-10. Open Mon.-Sat. 9am-7:30pm, Sun. 10am-6:30pm. **Libreria La Mariposa,** 5 Av. 1, stationary supplies and xerox copies.

Market: On the west side of Alameda de Sta. Lucía, 1/5 Calles Pte. Open daily 7am-6pm. Batteries, socks, and buckets of fruit all under labyrinthine tent.

Laundromat: Lavandería Summer, 5 Av. Sur 24A, 6 Calle Pte. 14A, or 7 Av. Nte. 78B. Will wash 7 items in cold water for Q7. Drop it off in the morning, pick it up in the afternoon. Open Mon.-Fri. 7:15am-6pm, Sat. 7:15am-3pm. Additionally, many hotels have their own washing machines.

Pharmacy: Farmacia Santa María, 5 Av. Nte. (tel. 320-572), on the west side of Parque Central. Open daily 8am-10pm. Rotating schedule for 24- hr. pharmacies; all are required to post the name of the *farmacia de turno* on their door.

Hospital: Hospital Pedro de Betancur, 6 Calle Ote. 20, 3/4 Avs. (tel. 320-883), in a big yellow building with few windows. English spoken. Open daily 7am-8pm.

Emergency: Los Bomberos (tel. 320-234), on the north side of the bus station.

ACCOMMODATIONS

In every crack of Antigua's cobblestone streets sprouts a budget hotel. Be careful of places that promise hot showers; many deliver shower spigots with electric heaters attached, so ask to test the hot water before paying. Many families provide room and board to Spanish-language students for about US$40 per week. Such homestays can be a great deal; your belongings are secure, the food is safer than street grub, and you can practice your Spanish over dinner. Contact one of the language schools in Antigua (see Guatemala: Planning Your Trip: Alternatives to Tourism, page 47, or inquire at travel agencies for willing families.). Prices quoted below do not include taxes (which can be 17% or more).

Hospedaje El Pasaje, Santa Lucía Sur 3, south of the bus stop. Big, white, basic rooms. Hot water is hot, and bathrooms simply *are.* Simple roof-top terrace bedecked with droopy horticulture. As conveniences, they change money, have a washing machine, and offer a shuttle service to the airport. Check-out 11am. Singles Q20; doubles Q35, with bath Q50.

Posada San Francisco, 3 Calle Ote. 19 (tel. 320-266), 1 block north and 2½ blocks east of the cathedral. A largish place that has its act together. Roomy rooms with big, windy windows open onto a courty courtyard populated by funny bunnies. Singles Q25, with bath Q40; doubles Q40, with bath Q60.

Posada Landívar, 5 Calle Pte. 23 (tel. 322-962), ½ block southeast of the *mercado.* Look for the sign visible from Alameda Santa Lucía. A four-story Bohemian delight; red tiling rules. Hot water flows freely in clean bathrooms. Jugs of *agua purificada* in the halls. Singles and doubles Q35, with bath Q50.

Posada la Quinta, 5 Calle Pte. 19, just a few doors down from Posada Landívar. Plants and kittens included; don't water the kittens. Bathrooms very clean. Spartan rooms overlook a florally effusive courtyard. Singles Q25, with bath Q35; doubles Q35, with bath Q45.

Villa San Francisco, 1 Av. Sur 15 (tel. and fax 323-383). The technological avant-garde of hotels—fax, long-distance phone service, and e-mail. Behind the big wooden colonial doors stretches a long, thin courtyard. Some rooms have tapestries and wrought-iron light fixtures. Clean bathrooms. Singles Q40, doubles Q50.

Posada Ruíz, 2 Calle Ote. 24. There's no sign, so look for the arched doorway. There also aren't exotic plants or peacocks in the courtyard, but the hotel's price and smiling service leave nothing to be desired. Rooms are adequate, campy, and quiet. Common bathroom and laundry machine. Singles Q16.50, doubles Q30.

FOOD

Some only half-jokingly call Antigua "the capital of international budget cuisine"—incredibly enough, there are more restaurants here than there are ruined churches. In Antigua, everything is possible and nothing is forbidden: chow down on burgers, *chiles rellenos,* fresh pasta, and all the culinary madness which lies between. Most meals please your papillae without breaking your budgetary back. Many eateries are cafés where *gringos* talk, and sometimes study, all afternoon.

Cafetería de Doña Luisa, 4 Calle Ote. 12, in 2 floors of a 17th-century house. *Everyone* goes here. Sit in the sunny courtyard with the *gringos,* or gawk at the floor-to-ceiling bulletin board for the latest traveler's info, including houses for rent and personals. Eggs with frijoles Q10, sandwiches Q14. Breaking Mesoamerican tradition, the second cup of coffee is *gratis.* Open daily 7am-9:30pm.

Quesos y Vino, 5 Av. Nte. 31A, just past the arch. The Beautiful People (and the regular folks) come here for fresh homemade pasta and wines from France, Italy, Chile, and Argentina. *Pasta con ricotta y tomate* Q21. Medium pizza Q26.25. Sandwiches Q16. Open Wed.-Mon. 8:30am-4 and 5:30-10pm.

Resaturante San Carlos, on the west side of the Parque Central. Watch TV with the locals in the back, or relish people-watching in the park out front. No-nonsense chow—*chiles rellenos* Q15, grilled steak Q25. Open daily 8am-10pm.

Sueños del Quetzal, 4 Calle Ote. 14. Three-page menu of vegetarian cuisine. Listen to the fountain gurgle in the courtyard. Tofu with pineapple Q20, falafel Q18. Potato latkes with applesauce (whooah, Nelly!) Q18. Open daily 8am-7pm.

Café El Jardín, 5 Av. Nte., on the west side of the Parque Central. Breakfast for the backpacker. Coffee, cornflakes, yogurt, and a big plate of fruit Q13.50. Waffles with honey and juice Q15. Open Mon.-Sat. 8:30am-8pm, Sat. 8:30am-9:30pm.

La Cenicienta, 5 Av. Nte. 7. Sip imported wine from long-stemmed glasses in a plush, polished café offering the most seductive desserts in town. Brownies Q2, chunks of choco-banana cake Q3.50, and cheese and fruit *postres* Q3.25 seduce passers-by with their siren song. Open daily 8:30am-8pm.

SIGHTS

Travelers come to Antigua not for any particular "sights" but for the combined effect of the city's broad, peaceful streets, melancholy colonial ruins, and green mountains. Antigua's charms are best absorbed on a leisurely, day-long walking tour.

The city's centerpiece is the **Parque Central,** now a tranquil park, but for most of its history a muddy hubbub of markets and public hangings. Today, foreigners practice their *español* with long-suffering locals around the 250-year-old central fountain, **La Llamada de las Sirenas** (the Siren's Call). On the north side of the plaza is the **Palacio del Noble Ayuntamiento,** built in 1743. Unlike most of Antigua's other buildings, the Palacio, well-braced by its meter-thick walls, survived the earthquakes of 1773 and 1776. Once a jail, the building now houses two museums. The small **Museo de Santiago** exhibits colonial furniture, art, and weapons aplenty (open Tues.-Fri. 9am-4pm, Sat.-Sun. 9am-noon and 2-4pm; admission Q0.25). Also in the *Ayuntamiento* (city hall) is the **Museo del Libro Antiguo** (Old Book Museum), which displays a reproduction of the first printing press in Central America, brought to Antigua in 1660. Some of the fruits of that old press are displayed nearby, including an 18th-century lexicon of Guatemala's indigenous languages (open Mon.-Fri. 9am-4pm, Sat.-Sun. 9am-noon and 2-4pm; admission Q0.25).

The main **cathedral** stands on the east side of the park. The structure visible today is but a shadow of its former self. Once the most spectacular of its kind in Spanish America, the cathedral was begun in 1670 and was renowned for its five naves, 18 chapels, towering dome, and silver-and-pearl inlaid altar. Unfortunately, the earthquake of 1773 leveled the awesome edifice, and only two partially restored and entirely unremarkable chapels remain. The rest of the old cathedral lies in ruins behind the modern church. A small crypt at the east end of the ruins houses a much venerated, completely charred, 313-year-old **black Christ** (site open daily 9am-4:30pm; admission Q1).

On the south side of the Parque Central is the **Palacio de los Capitanes Generales,** rebuilt after the 1773 earthquake. The Palacio was the political nerve center of colonial Guatemala, which included Chiapas and all of Central America, minus Panama. The most powerful men between Mexico and the Andes once ruled from this building, surrounded by bureaucrats, law courts, tax offices, and a mint. Today, the building's purpose is more prosaic—it houses the police and the tourist office.

Half a block east of Plaza Mayor on 5 Calle Ote. is the old building of the **University of San Carlos de Borromeo.** Founded in 1676, San Carlos was the third university in all of Spanish America. Today it houses the **Museo de Arte Colonial** and temporary exhibits of contemporary Guatemalan art. Especially impressive are the large canvasses by Thomas de Merlo, each depicting a scene from the life of Saint Francis. The university is among the fittest of colonial Antigua's architectural survivors—cast your eyes heavenward to see the graceful *mudéjar* arches of the central patio, or the colonial wooden ceilings and baroque mouldings of its large gallery (open Tues.-Fri. 9am-4pm, Sat.-Sun. 9am-noon and 2-4pm; admission Q0.25).

Just northwest of San Francisco are the ruins of **Santa Clara,** 2 Av. Sur 27, at 6 Calle Ote. The massive convent, founded in 1699, was a popular place for aristocratic women to take the veil. The ruins are among the most beautiful in the city. Overgrown with flowers, the convent's crumbling archways frame breathtaking vistas. Come in the early morning or in late evening, when the play of light and shadow dapples the courtyard (open Tues.-Sun. 9am-5pm; admission Q10).

Round out your tour of Antigua's churches with a visit to **La Merced,** on 1 Calle Nte. at the northern end of 5 Av. Originally built in 1548, the church survived the 1760 earthquake, only to collapse in the 1773 quake. Although the rebuilt interior is unspectacular, the yellow façade offers the best extant example of Antigua's baroque style (open daily 6am-noon and 3-7pm; admission Q0.50).

To the west of Santa Clara lies the **Parque de la Unión.** This sun-bleached, unkempt patch of palm trees has long served as the local laundromat. Although scrubbing clothes by hand has become a dwindling practice, the queued stone basins still get their fair share of use.

Farther north on 2 Av. is **Las Capuchinas,** 2 Calle Ote. and 2 Av. Nte., built in 1736, destroyed 37 years later. The **Torre de Retiro** (Tower of Retreat) towers on its north side; here nuns used to cloister themselves for months of meditation. To compensate for their deprivation, they had one luxury of the flesh—private baths with running water. Today, mannequin nuns pray in fiberglass eternity. As you wander through the complex you can still see the nuns' kitchen, chimneys, and food-storage areas. The chambers with dripping water were used for corporal and psychological punishment (open Tues.-Sun. 9am-5pm; admission Q10).

One of Antigua's most interesting attractions is **Casa K'ojom,** Recoletos 55 (tel. 323-087), a museum dedicated to the traditional song and dance of Guatemala's *indígenas*. To reach the Casa, follow 5 Calle Pte. west to the outskirts of town, turning right just before the road ends at the cemetery; it's the third entrance on the left. The director is concerned that western pop and the increasing popularity of Christian evangelical denominations are squelching *indígena* music and dance by prohibiting traditional dancing and singing among their converts. Casa K'ojom attempts to document these waning traditions. A program of slides and music is shown at 10, 11am, 2, 3, and 4pm, followed by a guided tour of the two exhibit halls. At other times, exhibits are still open and a less-than-spectacular videotape is available (open Mon.-Sat. 9:30am-12:30pm and 2-5pm; admission Q5).

For classical concerts and dramatic productions in both English and Spanish, head to the **Proyecto Cultural el Sitio,** at 5 Calle Pte. 15 (tel. 323-037), open Tues.-Sun. 11am-7pm. Ticket prices vary from Q10-25. **Los Naza Renos,** 6 Calle Pte, 3, exhibits paintings by local artists of local attractions, from lovely Parque Central to fuming volcanos. Prices range from Q150-1800. The synthesizers lying around are for music classes offered to children on Saturdays.

To shed Antigua's sultry air, a short jaunt by bus or by foot brings you to the perch of a volcano and to the largest two of the local *pueblos,* **Santa Monica** and **San Antonio Agua Caliente,** known for their regal churches and hand-made fabrics. A textile store halfway to San Antonio has an unbeatable selection at better prices than you see in Antigua. A room in back displays the village's finest ceremonial robes, which take over six months to complete, and which are unfortunately not for sale.

ENTERTAINMENT

For food, flicks, and fun, try **Cinemala,** 2 Calle Ote. 4, inside the Landívar Spanish Academy, which shows two different films a day at 3:30pm, 6pm, and 8:30pm on VCRs. Bring your own popcorn. Shows cost Q10. Antigua is as sleepy as it is distinguished; only on the weekends do the bars keep buzzing late at night. Check local papers for other movies in full-size theaters.

The tourist office tells visitors to go to bed early; they want to keep you off of Antigua's dark and empty nighttime streets, where muggings have been known to occur. If you go out in a group, though, you can enjoy a small but lively bar scene; just be careful. The haunt of choice for most is **La Chimenea,** 7 Av. Nte. 7, where foreigners aplenty chatter in several tongues, sip down brews, and lounge on sofas, caught in the sway of live music performances (open daily 10am-1am).

Macondo, 5 Calle Pte., 28, is a classy drinking establishment that somehow manages to keep its prices as low as other places. An architecturally gripping mahogany staircase leads to three spacious tiers, and rock and jazz bounce off lavender tiles and framed pictures of Charlie Chaplin and the Blues Brothers. This is serious pop culture—an oxymoron familiar to the bars of Antigua (beer Q6; open 6-12pm).

Come to **Rainbow Café,** at 7 Ave. Sur 8, to watch wanna-be intellectuals ruminate alone or with each other, borrow books from the library, and stare contemplatively into an open fire with beer, coffee, or a goblet of the Rainbow's specialty drinks. Poetry readings on Thursdays, local musicians on Fridays, deep thoughts and cosmopolitan chatter at all times. Crazy, baby, crazy. Inventive vegetarian fare available (open Thurs.-Tues. 9am-12am). There is a small group of bars on 7 Av. Nte., where the action starts to pick up around 10pm. **Latinos Bar,** 7 Av. Nte. 16, has live music most nights (open Mon.-Sat. 6pm-1am; happy hour 6-9pm; no cover). The **Abstracto Bar** next door is no philosopher's lair, but rather specializes in Metallica and Guns n' Roses (open Mon.-Sat. 7pm-1am). **Picasso's,** down the block a bit at 7 Av. Nte. 3, is always packed with travelers and students (open daily 6pm-1am). The dance scene is pretty much dead; schools occasionally sponsor rock/merengue hybrids, where dance-craving visitors and locals choke the entrance in a mad stampede to shake their booties.

■■■ LAGO ATITLÁN AND PANAJACHEL

According to Quiché belief, Lago Atitlán was one of the four lakes which demarcated the corners of the world. For tourists visiting Guatemala, magnificent Lago Atitlán is simply the center of the universe. Hugged on all sides by the green-checkered hillsides of farmland dotted with grazing cattle, the lake emanates endless natural beauty. In the late afternoon, rays of sun tango seductively in the sloping hills around the lake. When an electrical storm blows in and lingers, wet and heavy, the squall lights up the ridge in silhouette and illuminates the whole expanse of water, purging evening shadows. Atitlán is ringed by a coterie of 12 small villages inhabited mainly by *indígena* of Cakchiquel descent. Today, many villagers proudly wear the traditional dress that distinguishes each town from its neighbors.

Panajachel, the thirteenth town on Atitlán, is also a sort of rowdy ringleader for its 12 cousins, replete with beach-side belly dancers, mellow market-lovin' hippies, and a large number of retirees who peacefully while away the days in expensive hotels. Perhaps because of its eclectic spirit and individuality, *Pana,* as locals have affectionately dubbed it (they also not-so-affectionately call it *Gringotenango*), is the most touristed town in the area. While indigenous fishermen cast off from their villages in wooden skiffs, *gringos* set out in rented kayaks and launches to drink their fill of Atitlán's scenery. Though hardly the most authentic town on the lake, Panajachel is a convenient place to run errands, to savor waffles with fruit and honey, or just to take a hot shower. The town is home to an amiable group of international expatriates whose shops, restaurants, and bars line the streets. This *gringo* outpost and way-station has become increasingly popular with prosperous weekenders from Guatemala City who are eager to escape the congestion of the capital. Many Guatemalans have begun building vacation homes in town and along the lake, and their incoming capital supports a good selection of video salons and vegetarian restaurants. After a meal and a flick, however, consider ferrying across the lake to a less expensive village.

ORIENTATION AND PRACTICAL INFORMATION

Panajachel is small enough that addresses and street names are not often used, but many signs point the way to various accommodations off the main street. Buses pull into Panajachel along its **Calle Principal** (the "Main Street" on INGUAT's English-language map) and stop at or near its most important intersection, at **Calle Santander,** about 30m from the tourist office. Calle Santander begins here and stretches southward to the lakefront; **Calle Rancho Grande** runs parallel to it to the east. Going

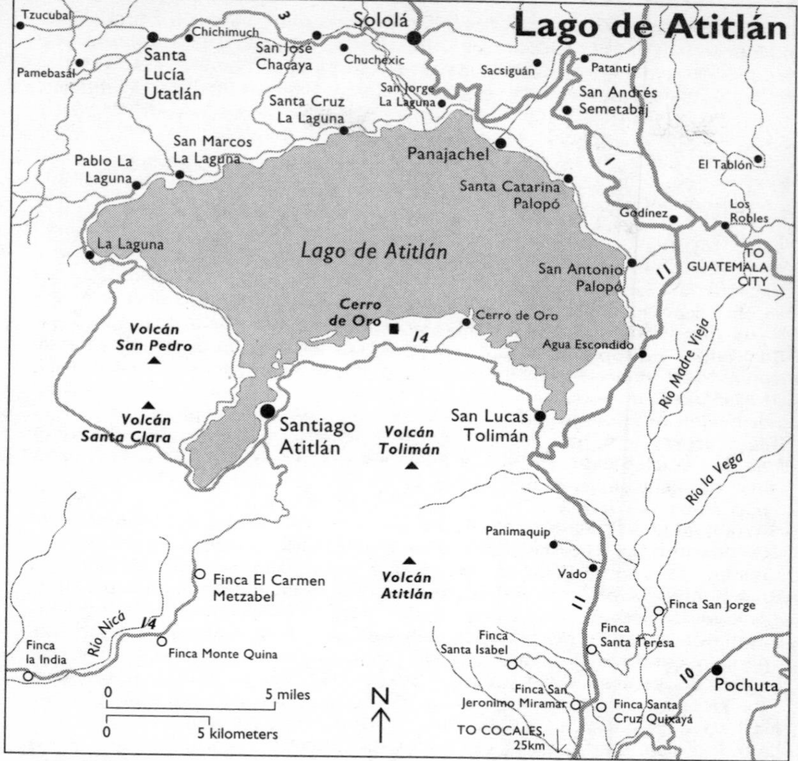

north from the main intersection, Calle Principal forks. Its name lives on to the right side of the fork, while **Av. Los Árboles** rises to the left. All services and most hotels are on Calle Principal, Calle Santander, and Av. Los Árboles. The public beach is at the end of Calle Santander and to the left.

Tourist Office: (tel. 622-337, 621-392), on Calle Santander, in the "Rincón Sai" building at the intersection with Calle Principal. Free maps of town and of the lake. Safety updates on volcanoes and countryside. English spoken. Very friendly. Open daily 8am-6pm. During the high season, a small beachfront extension office operates Wed., Fri., and Sat. 9am-5pm, Sun. 8am-3pm.

Police: (tel. 621-120), at the end of Calle Principal in the municipal building. No English spoken.

Currency Exchange: Banco Inmobilario (tel. 621-056), on Av. Los Árboles, 2 blocks from Calle Principal. Open for exchange Mon.-Fri. 9am-1pm and 3-6pm, Sat. 10am-1pm. **Banco Agrícola Mercantil** (tel. 621-145), on Calle Principal at Calle Santander. 24-hr. ATM. Open Mon.-Fri. 9am-4:30pm, Sat. 9am-12:30pm.

Post Office and Telegrams: Up Calle Principal and behind the Catholic church. Post office open Mon.-Fri. 8am-4:30pm, telegram office open 24 hrs. **Postal code:** 07010.

Phones: Guatel, halfway down Calle Santander. Long-distance calls. Open daily 7am-midnight. **The Budget Traveler** (tel. 622-046) has an office in Pana Tours on Calle Santander. **Telephone code:** 0.

Buses: Normally, buses arrive at and depart from Calle Principal, near the Banco Agrícola Mercantil, to **Guatemala City** (11 per day, 3½ hrs., Q10) and to **Chichicastenango** (6 per day, 1 hr., Q5). Take any bus to Guatemala City, disembark at

Los Encuentros, then board buses to **Quetzaltenango** (6 per day, 2 hrs., Q7) or to **Antigua** (10:45am, 2½ hrs., Q8.50). Alternatively, take any Guatemala City-bound bus to **Chimaltenango,** then change to an Antigua-bound bus to **Cocales** on the Pacific Highway (4 per day, 1½ hrs., Q6). To reach the **Mexican border,** take any Guatemala City bus to Los Encuentros, then change to a "Galgos" or "El Condor" bus to La Mesilla, El Carmen, or **Tecún Umán,** to San Antonio or Santa Catarina (5, 8:30, and 10:30am, 30min., Q2).

Ferries: Join commuters on the beautiful ferry rides around the lake; from the docks in front of Hotel del Lago to **Santiago** (3 per day, 1 hr., Q10) and to **San Pedro** (4 per day, 8:30am-5pm, 1½ hrs., Q10). All departures are in the morning and early afternoon. There is irregular ferry service to Santa Catarina, to San Antonio, and to San Lucas Tolimán. Some San Pedro ferries stop at Santa Clara, San Marcos, and Santa Cruz. **Tours** of the lake (Q40) leave the docks at 8:30am and stop at San Antonio, Santiago, and San Pedro, returning at 3:30pm.

Taxis: (tel. 622-028). Call, or look for one in front of Grapevine on Calle Santander.

Car Rental: Daiton Rent-a-Car, represented by BIGSA Moto Rent (tel. 621-253), on Av. Los Árboles, between Circus Bar and Restaurant El Chisme. Small Nissan US$45 per 24-hr. period, including unlimited mileage and insurance, with US$800 deductible to be covered with a credit card impression or a deposit.

Bike/Motorcycle Rental: Moto Servicio Quiché (tel. 622-089), at the corner of Av. Los Árboles and Calle Principal. For motorcycles, Q30 per hr. or Q85 per 8 hrs., including unlimited mileage and insurance. Q500 deposit and copy of passport required. For bikes, Q5 per hr. or Q30 per 8 hrs. Bikes can also be rented from a stand on Calle Rancho Grande, around the corner from the laundromat. Q5 per hr. or Q30 per day. **Panarenta,** Calle Santander, rents Yamahas for Q25 per hr., Q125 for the day, US$600 deposit. Open 8:30am-noon and 2-6:30pm.

Boat Rental: Diversiones Balam, on the beach inside the main lifeguard tower. Individual (Q10 per hr.) or double (Q20 per hr.) kayaks. Canoes Q20 per hr. Water bicycles Q20 per hr. Open daily 8am-5pm. Ferry and launch companies also hire out private launches (Q175 for 1-5 people).

English Bookstores: Gallery Bookstore (tel. 622-015), on Av. Los Árboles near the Restaurant El Chisme. Paperbacks Q5-17. Open Mon.-Sat. 9am-6pm.

Market: At the north end of Calle Principal. Open daily 7am-6pm.

Laundry: Lavandería, 1½ blocks from Calle Santander, down the street which branches off to the left (facing the lake) after Guatel, inside Sevananda Restaurant. 1-10 lbs. for Q20; add Q5 for same-day service. Open 9am-6pm.

Pharmacy: Farmacia La Unión (tel. 622-041), on Santander near Mario's Rooms. Home delivery daily 8am-11pm. Open 24 hrs. Ring bell if door is closed.

Medical Emergency: Drs. Eduardo Hernández and Francisco Ordoñez (tel. 621-068), on Calle Principal near the fire department, speak some English. Dr. Bracamonte (tel. 622-139), on Calle Principal 2 blocks from the market, can run basic laboratory tests.

ACCOMMODATIONS

Pana is more expensive than the surrounding villages. Practically none of the available budget rooms has much personality, and all are far from luxurious, but a few of the places make up for it with gorgeously tended gardens and courtyards. Consider renting a house if you're planning to stay a while; check the bulletin boards at Restaurante El Chisme, on Av. Los Árboles, or ask at the tourist office. Alternatively, stay in San Pedro for US$2 a night. There's a public campground at the east end of the public beach, on the other side of the Panajachel River, but it has no services or security. While many places promise hot water, few deliver.

Hotel Panajachel, on Calle Principal just south of the market. Clean, basic rooms around a courtyard brightened by ruby-red trim, Mayan-style paintings, and a snappy little restaurant. The service is very warm; the water sometimes isn't. Shared bathrooms are in good shape. Singles Q25, doubles Q50. Ask for a discount (Q5-10) if business is slow.

Hospedaje Pana Rooms, up Av. Los Árboles and left (west) at the dirt road just past the natural foods store. Small rooms with low ceilings. Clean shared bathrooms have 24-hr. hot water. Upstairs rooms line a balcony with a view of volcanoes. A wall around the courtyard and locked doors make the place relatively secure. Pump your way to the heavyweight championship with the exercise room's weights and boxing gloves; if pugilism isn't your speed, try fattening up on snacks from the adjoining store. Singles Q21, doubles Q26, triples Q31.

Hospedaje Eli, next door to Pana Rooms. One of the cleanest and comfiest for your money. Rugged wooden floors, a tiled balcony overlooks a grassy sunburned courtyard. When tourism picks up, the owner opens a restaurant downstairs. Cheap eats with a TV and a mural of the Last Supper to boot. Public bathrooms are clean. Laundry service available for Q2. Singles Q15 (+Q5 for hot shower); doubles Q27 (+Q7 for hot shower); triples Q26 (+Q10 for hot shower). Sandwich Q4, breakfast Q6.50.

Hospedaje Ramos, near the beach behind Bungalows El Rosario. Feels faintly like a chain hotel, which on the plus side means tidy rooms and immaculate, contemporary bathrooms. Marimba tones and the giggles of happy tourists float in from the beach. Singles Q40.95, doubles Q79, triples Q99.

Hospedaje Santa Elena, Calle Monterey. Baby turkeys skitter while parrots and doves eye you from the ubiquitous tangles of vines. The owners living on the first floor are friendly and resolutely vigilant. Public bathrooms have adequate, stone-built showers. Open 7am-3pm. Singles Q17.75, doubles Q23. For a hot water shower, add Q1.50.

Dos Mercedes, across from Hospedaje Eli. A tiny, six-room alternative to Eli and Hotel Pana. A cracked cement courtyard supports a few plants—nothing fancy, but service is friendly, and the dirt in the bathroom is as clean as dirt. Extra beds available. Singles Q15, doubles Q30, quads Q40.

Bungalows El Rosario (tel. 621-491), just off the lake behind the line of restaurants. Clean, spacious rooms have private bathrooms. Close to the lakefront, far from everything else. As with all beach-side bungalows, tourist-buzz and belly dancers are right at the doorstep. Singles Q43, doubles Q86, triples Q129.

FOOD

If *plátanos* and peanuts don't tempt your tastebuds, fear not: Panajachel's gourmet restaurants are sure to pleasure the palate. The large tourist population has made its influence felt, so the many foreign and ex-pat owners have gauged their menus for a healthier, more cosmopolitan milieu; most establishments serve granola, yogurt, corn flakes, tofu, and pancakes. Prices tend to be higher than in other parts of Guatemala, and in the lakeside restaurants they are out of control. Alimentary options are more limited but much less expensive the smaller towns. For a refresher, tropical milkshakes and *licuado* stands on Calle Principal placate the weary.

Deli Restaurant, on Calle Principal, above the Banco Agrícola Mercantil. Look for the small green sign. A second location on Calle Santander near the lakefront. Two of the best breakfast places in town. The first location makes homemade waffles with fruit and syrup or honey (Q8.50). Both serve oatmeal with raisins, nuts, and banana (Q8.50). Papaya *licuados* are thick and delicious, but they run up the tab. Complete breakfasts with pancakes, eggs, or omelettes (Q10-14). Homemade *fettucine alfredo* Q18. Bagels! Open daily 7:30am-5:45pm.

Restaurant Vegetariano Hsieh, on Calle Los Árboles, just after the intersection with Calle Principal. *Típico* atmosphere, health-conscious menu: crepes (Q8.50), granola (Q8), or the special of the day (lasagna, pizza, pasta, or *chile relleno* with soup, salad, and whole-wheat bread, Q13). Open Tues.-Sun. 9am-10pm.

Maria's Restaurant, on Calle Santander halfway between the intersection with Calle Principal and the lakefront. A cheap joint popular with the backpacker brigade. Cinderblock walls enlivened by windows and funky contemporary art. Slap your ham and cheese sandwich (Q4) up alongside it and see if anyone makes you an offer. Spaghetti Q10, omelettes Q7-8, chicken dinner with pasta, salad, and bread Q18. Open daily 8am-8:30pm.

Ranchón Típico, on Calle Santander. One of the only *típico* places in Panajachel. Check out the *currasco ranchón típico,* which entrains soup *du jour,* roasted meat, fried bananas with cream, beans with cheese, guacamole, fries, mixed vegetables, and tortillas—all for only Q30. Vendors wander from table to table and woo prospective customers. Open daily 9am-9pm.

Cafetería Panajachel, on Calle Principal near the center of town. A moodless little square of a restaurant which nevertheless serves cheap eats in big portions. The huge, whole fried fish with guacamole is brutally satisfying (Q25). Channel surf the cable television above the fridge or instead cast aspersions through the arches that open out onto the street.

Bombay Pub and Café, Calle de los Árboles under El Cine next to Ubu's. Trash novels galore and many English-language magazines, from *Vogue* to *Time* to *The New Yorker*. Watch out for slivers when you make your selection; the shelves are a carpenter's nightmare. Rest for hours tucked away from the streets in a verdant, shady courtyard. Burritos Q5, coffee Q3.

ENTERTAINMENT

Panajachel offers more amusements than do its cheaper neighbors on the lake. A popular pastime is to dodge the treacherous obstacle course of *artesanía* vendors between your hotel and the lakefront. Try saying "*no estoy de compras, gracias*" (I'm not shopping, thanks), which is stronger than a simple "*no, gracias*." For a bit of high culture before diving head-first into the bar scene, **The Art Gallery,** Calle Río Grande, displays the spiritual pastels of world-renowned artist Nan Cruz, as well as the work of other artists. Three video salons—the **Grapevine** and **El VideoClub** on Calle Santander, and **The Carrot Chic** on Av. Los Árboles—show a different film at each screening (3, 6, and 8pm at the latter two, and hourly from 1-10pm at Grapevine). All films cost Q10. **Ubu's Cosmic Café,** behind Restaurant Sevananda, occasionally shows free movies, though it's polite to have a drink or two.

Cowboys rearin' for a foot-stompin', heart-stoppin' good time can head over to **The Circus Bar and Pizzeria,** on Av. Los Árboles. Swing through the saloon doors as a clunky piano and dusty sound system boom flamenco and gypsy, blaring at 9pm nightly. Ceramic lights cast a wan light on circus posters, ghosts of the owner's crushed dream to start a three-ringer in Panajachel. Pick your poison: sit on the patio by the trees, in deep, wooden booths, squish into comfy cushions, or just hop onto the checker-cloth tables. Roll the dice and double your drink (Sun.-Thurs.). Have a beer (Q5.50) with your imported Italian pasta in an egg cream sauce (Q14). (Open daily 2pm-1am.) **Ubu's Cosmic Café,** behind Restaurant Sevenanda, opens when the owner gets there and closes when the guests go home (approximately noon-4am). The owner is gracefully ignorant of the clock but thorough with his entertainment, offering the best live rhythm and reggae Panajachel has to offer, as well as free flicks every night. Addicts rejoice: "The Simpsons" are shown religiously. Plump, well-loved couches and chairs beckon for intimacy as Christmas lights twinkle above among the flags and piñatas. English spoken. Beer Q7.

Flyin' Mayan Yacht Club, on Calle Principal, assaults its visitors with "carnivalization"; management vamps their establishment with the latest holiday paraphernalia while pumping rock and blues to a modest, family restaurant crowd. Eco-consciousness hits its high note as kids crayon dogmatic coloring book pictures and a sign declares that the kitchen uses gas stoves instead of wood. The owners care, and it shows: pizza for Q19, beer for Q6 (open noon-10pm).

■ AROUND LAGO ATITLÁN

The café-filled streets of *Gringotenango* can't compete with the necklace of *indígena* villages hung around Lake Atitlán. All the villages are accessible as daytrips from Panajachel, and it's possible to visit two or three in a single, leisurely day. Alternatively, you could work your way around the lake gradually, stopping to spend the night in whatever village seems most comfortable. The hyperadventurous skip the boat entirely and make the circuit on foot. There are several trails that wind around the water and over the volcanoes; the trip takes at least a week, so adequate preparation and a solid foundation of safety information are absolute prerequisites for this journey. The one place which is heartily *not* recommended is San Lucas Tolimán, on the southeastern shores of the lake, where there have been problems with crime and assault specifically. Check with the tourist office about safety at other destinations before hitting the trail, or jumping on a bus or boat.

SANTIAGO DE ATITLÁN

The largest and most touristed of the *pueblos* is Santiago de Atitlán, nestled between the San Pedro and Tolimán volcanoes. **Launches,** or *lanchas,* run from Panajachel to Santiago (5 per day, 8:30am-5pm, 1½ hrs., Q10). Santiago is home to the Tzutuhil people, who were Pedro de Alvarado's allies in subduing the Cakchiquel of Panajachel. Santiago was the most influential of the Atitlán villages until its former rival Panajachel took sweet revenge and reclaimed the title of largest Atitlán village.

In today's Santiago, indigenous cultural forms have become somewhat obscured. Few women still sport the *xocop,* the extraordinary, 10m-long red strap worn wrapped around the head. However, on July 25 (the feast of Santiago) or during Semana Santa, the *xocops* are out in full force. Even the men get funky during the feast, donning their multi-colored trousers and cowboy hats. Aside from colorful garb, Santiago is known for its paintings of the lake and its woodcarvings of St. James. If you're looking for relief from the *artesanía* of Panajachel, you've come to the wrong place.

Make sure to step into Santiago's **church,** where saints stand dressed in homemade scarves that look strangely like neckties. Some distance from the church, lost among the houses near the edge of town, hides a sacred, alternative center of worship, one of the more bizarre examples of religious syncretism in a country known for its folk-Catholicism. Local kids will show you the way for a few quetzals. The shrine is dedicated to **Maximón,** or San Simón in his Christian incarnation, a wooden figure dressed in European garb and associated with vices such as smoking and drinking. Maximón, ever a consummate enemy of the church, is quite popular in Santiago. According to the Popol Vuh, the statue is carved from the same wood from which the gods fashioned proto-humans. The incense-choked shrine is full of devotees praying, playing the guitar, and making offerings of liquor and cigarettes. The saint's specialty is casting curses, so beware. On the Wednesday of Semana Santa, Maximón' idol is paraded through the village, and worshipers stand chomping on unlit stogies as the procession passes. Newcomers can experience the ritual themselves. For Q10 the head counter will mummify you and solemnly spit alcohol in your face. Or just let him bum a cig or some of whatever else you have on you.

The **post office** is in front of the market, near the municipal building (open Mon.-Sat. 8am-2pm), and for **phone** calls, **Guatel** is on the main street, behind the church (open 7-8pm). **Buses** leave from one end of the market for Guatemala City every hour from 7:30-11:30am and for Esquintla via San Lucas at 1:30pm. **Launches** leave from Santiago to Panajachel (7 per day, 6am-5pm, 1 hr., Q7.50) and to towns along the lake's western edge. The **doctors** in town are Francisco Pulo and Juan Carlos Perez, both of whom have offices in the center of town. That huge, purple creature in the village center is the **cinema,** which plays fuzzy Hollywood hits at 6:30 and 8pm.

It's cheap and easy to spend the night in Santiago, and you'll get a glimpse of the town after the crowds of daytrippers have sailed back to Pana. As increasing tourism has driven up prices at some hotels near the lakefront, it's become worth hiking up the hill to the Catholic church, where the **Hospedaje Santa Rita** offers plain but pleasant quarters and communal bathrooms with working hot water, a real luxury (singles Q10, doubles Q20). The adjoining restaurant also is a good deal: eggs, beans, and cheese for Q8, fried chicken with french fries, or fish and rice with guacamole for Q10, sandwiches for Q5. If you don't want to lug your pack up the hill, you could stay at **Chi Nim Ya,** just above the dock, where the rooms are a bit brighter, and a bit more expensive. Laundry service available for guests. (Q20 per person, Q30 per person with private bath.)

SAN PEDRO LA LAGUNA

To escape the bustle of Pana, you might try joining the relaxed crowd at San Pedro La Laguna, which has become a popular destination for besandaled backpackers, particularly for its beautiful beaches. **Launches** from Pana to San Pedro leave from the docks in front of Pana's Hotel del Lago (5 per day, 2 hrs., Q10).

The font of all wisdom in San Pedro is an individual known variously as "Ken" and **"Dr. Sixteen,"** an expatriate who lived in Room 16 of the Hospedaje Ti'Kaaj for a little over a year. In the absence of an INGUAT office, Dr. Sixteen's house past the Lago Azul serves as *the* tourist resource. Everyone knows the good doctor, although no one ever knows quite where he is. San Pedro's **post office** is tucked behind the church (open Mon.-Fri. 8am-4pm, Sat. 8am-noon). **Guatel phones** are on the main street up from the dock (open daily 7am-10pm). **Launches** leave San Pedro for Pana (15 per day, 4:15am-5pm, 1¼ hrs., Q6) and for Santiago (8 per day, 6am-3pm, 45min., Q5). Some launches to Pana stop at the towns on the western shore of the lake and, though scenic, take considerably longer than an hour. Be aware that the last boat to Pana does not leave from the main dock in front of Villa Sol, but from the one in front of Restaurant Johana, about 1km away. The trail between the two docks winds through the village and branches several times, but one of the local kids can lead you through for a small tip.

Down a winding dirt road that veers off from the dock, relaxed folks hang out in the hammocks of the **Hospedaje Ti-Kaaj,** whose basic cement rooms surround a leafy garden. Communal bathrooms have dirt-strewn floors and water streaks in the showers. Wonder of wonders, the toilets lack toilet seats. Get an extra bed for Q8. Check-out's at noon, and quiet time begins at 10pm—shhhh (singles Q10, doubles Q18, triples Q26). Next door **Pensión Chausinahi** (also known, inexplicably, as Hotel Villa del Sol) closes in on larger, brighter, and cleaner rooms. The joint's owners run a tight ship, keeping written record of all customers and an office that's open 24 hours (doubles Q25, Q30 with private bath). **Hospedaje Balneario,** at the base of the street leading up to the village center, is an open mall of rugged-but-clean singles with communal bathrooms. The glassless windows have a panoramic view of the lake. Owner is friendly and will rap your window to give a "wakeup call." When tourism peaks, a patio café opens in the courtyard (singles Q8).

The **beach** here is much nicer than Pana's, and the town sits at the foot of the San Pedro volcano, making it a good jumping-off point for ascents. Locals rent **horses** (Q15 per hr.), which can take you part-way up the volcano and to other destinations. It's also possible to rent kayaks much more cheaply here than in Pana (1-person kayak Q2 per hr., 2-person kayak Q3 per hr.). Farther up on the hill is **Amigos Viajeros,** a front porch hangout where the local bigwigs clap you on the back in welcome and haggle you into renting kayaks or taking their horses in usufruct for the day. It's not a bad idea to fall to their mercy. Another local resident, Pedro, stops by El Fondeadero Restaurant for other horse trips. After hours, **Sheik Yerbouti** and friends hang out at **Restaurant Ti Kaaj,** where the rock is cranked to the bone. Look for the hotel with the huge, ugly mural of volcanoes, and follow the power chords emanating from there. More the metal to ya'.

SAN MARCOS

San Marcos la Laguna, on the western side of the lake, is famous for its fishing. For lusty lake crab, this is the place to come. **Hotel San Marcos** takes you away from it all. The tiny six-room establishment peeks out from an orchard of orange trees, but nonetheless offers the contemporary comfort of spanking new toilets. Big beds have an extra blanket laid thoughtfully at the end, and everything is clean. Showers are cold, but take it as part of the "roughing it" experience (singles Q20, doubles Q40). The lap of luxury sits at **La Paz,** where nature clamors at your window while electric stoves and televisions purr inside. Each four-person bungalow is an architectural wonder, with its own walk-in courtyard and richly furnished sitting room. As a finishing touch, a tree-branch ladder leads to the loft. Bathrooms are communal, but immaculate. The water is cold, so wait until the afternoon when the sun sears

(US$20 for 4 people). In front is the prestigious **La Paz** vegetarian cuisine, cooked with finesse and served generously for Q20. Also worth a visit is the neighboring **Manuela's,** where luscious loaves of Italian bread bake in clay ovens (Q4.75).

The dirt trails wind upward to the center of town, a sky-wide panorama of gardens, patios, and basketball courts. An **amphitheater** stages plays and musical concerts. Those tired of traveling through Central America can try a journey within themselves at **Las Piramides Centro de Meditación,** which paves the Way with fasting, silences, and secluded straw huts. Unfortunately, *Let's Go: You* isn't yet ready for publication. For another trip, trails along the coast offer breathtaking views of the azure Lake Atitlán. That's right, not blue: *azure.* And please, please **swim.** The lake is astonishingly deep right up to the shoreline, and the water on the other side of the docks wiggles with nary a ripple.

SAN ANTONIO PALOPÓ AND SANTA CRUZ

Two other lakeside towns are popular among visitors. **San Antonio Palopó,** on the eastern side of the lake, is a Cakchiquel town whose inhabitants make reed mats and maguey fiber products. It's often included in the three-town tour of the lake offered by the launch companies. **Santa Cruz La Laguna** boasts a 16th-century church surrounded by colonial homes. Its hotel, **El Arco de Noe,** is reputed to be more expensive than those in other villages, but the five-course meal it serves its guests is legendary. The Panajachel INGUAT office can offer further information on these and other villages on the lake.

■ HIKING AND VOLCANOES

Don't let the tranquil beauty of the lake lull you into complacency about safety. The region around Lake Atitlán has a history of muggings and assaults, so make sure to check with the INGUAT office in Panajachel before romping out in the wilderness.

Three volcanoes dominate the south shore of Lake Atitlán. **Volcán Atitlán,** at 3535m (11,604 ft.), is the tallest of the three, while **Volcán Tolimán,** standing at a height of 3158m (10,360 ft.), is the only active one. Ascending Tolimán and Atitlán are not recommended due to the high incidence of theft and violence. **Volcán San Pedro** (3020m, 9908ft.) is considered safer and easier to climb. It's usually necessary to spend the night prior to the climb in San Pedro, since the guides who take groups along the volcano's poorly marked trails set out around 6am, long before the first launch from Pana arrives. The group usually returns to San Pedro well before dinnertime. Guides can be found around town or at the Hospedaje Ti-Kaaj. Prices are never high, but exact amounts vary with demand.

The lake is perhaps most spectacular when seen from the heights that surround it, but it's not necessary to climb San Pedro to catch the view; many of the roads and trails around Atitlán climb into the hills above the towns. One easy but spectacular hike descends a trail from the hilltop town of **Godinez,** on the east side of the lake, to the lakeshore town of San Antonio. Godinez is accessible from Panajachel on a regular bus. Afterwards, hikers can return from San Antonio to Pana by launch, minibus, or on foot. Halfway along the 8km road from San Antonio to Pana, you'll pass the village of **Santa Catarina Palopó.**

Alternatively, hikers could follow the chain of towns on the western side of the lake, beginning in San Pedro and ending in Santa Cruz. The distance as a whole is no more than 20km on trails and dirt roads, and it can be traversed by mountain bike (see Panajachel: Practical Information, page 70) or on foot. There are seven indigenous towns along the way, with no more than 8km between any two villages.

■■■ IXIMCHÉ

Iximché is the ancient capital of the Cakchiquel people and the first capital of Guatemala. The city was founded in 1470 under governors **Juntoh, Vukubatz,** and **Ho Evets,** who eventually liberated the Cakchiquel from the Quiché, only to fall under the rule of the Spaniards in 1524. The city surrendered peacefully to Pedro de Alvarado, but abuses and the cruel extraction of tribute (in gold and services) caused two bloody rebellions in 1526 and 1532. That period of conflict concluded in 1535 with the death of Cakchiquel governors of the city.

Iximché is a naturally fortified city, surrounded on all sides by deep ravines. The present **archaeological site** encompasses the palaces and temples of the governors. The huge stone edifices rise out of the earth as if in a deep slumber, some fully uncovered, some still caked in grass and trees. The majority of Iximché's people lived in the surrounding countryside, in much the way that their descendents do today. The ruins' natural surroundings are tame, more like a picnic area than a site of sanguineous seizure (site open daily 8am-5pm; admission Q50, free Sun.). There is also a **museum** exhibiting pictures and objects from the excavation project (open daily 8am-noon and 1-4pm). There are no guides, but a small brochure (free, in Spanish) summarizes the significance of the artifacts on display in the museum.

Iximché is located about 5km from the village of **Tecpán,** which is only interesting as a pitstop. To get to Tecpán, catch a **bus** from the Panajachel bus terminal in Guatemala City on Calle 20, Zona 1 (every 30min., 2 hrs., Q4). If coming from elsewhere, take a Guatemala City-bound bus to Los Encuentros and there change to Tecpán (1 hr., Q2). From Tecpán to Iximché either walk the 5km or hire a taxi (Q20). If you plan to take a taxi, do so right where the bus drops you off, because it is hard to find one in town. Hitching here is frustrating, as few cars pass. The walk is beautiful, and you can mosey alongside the cattle, goats, and other domesticates.

■■■ CHICHICASTENANGO

The town of Chichicastenango is, without question, the most popular destination in the Department of El Quiché. Its Sunday and Thursday markets attract droves of tourists from Guatemala City, Panajachel, and Antigua. But there's more to the region than brightly colored tapestries, wooden figurines, and *rebajas* (bargains). The soot from charcoal cookfires, the lilt of spoken Maya-Quiché, and the haze of devotional incense remind visitors that Chichicastenango is still very much an authentic *indígena* town, despite its stature as a tourist mecca.

Chichicastenango was built by the Spaniards in the 16th century as a home for refugees from Utatlán, the Quiché capital they had brutally leveled. In the centuries following the Conquest, El Quiché has witnessed countless human rights abuses. During the 19th century, the Guatemalan government used forced-labor laws written during the colonial era to pull Quiché workers down from the mountains to work on coffee plantations. In the 1970s, Chichicastenango became a major center of guerrilla activity, but the guerrillas have since been driven into the rainforests to the north, far from town. Remarkably, the region's *indígena* strain of Catholicism survives here in an atmosphere of official tolerance, despite years of repression and persecution.

ORIENTATION

Chichicastenango is built on a hill 37km north of Panajachel. The town is laid out in a grid. *Avenidas* run north-south and are numbered from west to east. *Calles* run east-west and are numbered from north to south. Street addresses are not very useful, since most street signs display Maya-Quiché names and locals tend to speak in terms of place names and landmarks. The main street through town is **5 Av.,** which is where the buses stop. A large green arch with Mayan-style decoration marks the northern end of 5 Av. The main plaza, which doubles as the market square, is in the opposite direction from that in which the buses stop.

PRACTICAL INFORMATION

There is no **tourist office,** but registered guides loiter at the bus terminal. The **police station,** 8 Calle between 5 and 6 Avs., in a blue building to the left of the church, posts a map of town and answers questions cheerfully (open 24 hrs.). For **currency**

exchange, try **Banco del Ejército** (tel. 561-201), 6 Calle between 5 and 6 Avs. (open for exchange Mon.-Fri. 9am-noon and 2-4pm, Sat. 9am-2pm, Sun. 9am-1pm). The **post** and **telegraph** office, at 7 Av. 8-4, is open Mon.-Fri. 8am-4pm. **Phone** home from **Guatel** (tel. 561-398), 7 Av. 8-21, near the post office. There's also a public **fax** (open Mon.-Fri. 8:30am-noon and 3-7pm, Sat.-Sun. 8am-noon). **Buses** leave from 5 Av., between 2 and 3 Calles, to Guatemala City (30 per day, 3am-6pm, 3 hrs., Q8.50); Quetzaltenango (7 per day, 6am-3pm, 2½ hrs., Q8); and Panajachel (8 per day, 6am- 2:30 pm, 1 hr, Q2.50).

The famed **market** is on the plaza in front of the church. There's also an enclosed produce market in the building to the left of the plaza, facing the front of the church. **Farmacia Zapete,** on 5 Av. near the arch and the bus drop-off point, is open daily 7am-9pm, and **Farmacia Agnacio,** 4 Av. 6065, is open daily 8am-9pm. There is a rotating schedule for 24-hour pharmacies, but it is rarely observed here. The **Centro de Salud** (tel. 561-356) is at the edge of town on 2 Av. and 2 Calle. The **Clínica Médica Dr. Bonilla** (tel. 561-309) is a private institution on 5 Calle 6-30 (open Mon.-Fri. 8:30am-noon and 3-7pm, Sat.-Sun. 8am-noon). In an emergency, call **Los Bomberos** (tel. 561-066)—these folks have the only ambulance.

ACCOMMODATIONS

Like any self-respecting indigenous village, Chichicastenango has several luxury hotels, but a flock of recently built budget hotels tip the balance in frugality's favor. **Hotel Posada Belén,** 12 Calle 5-55, Zona 1 (tel. 561-244), is an excellent buy. Rooms come with two views: the *pueblos* on one side, the town on the other. Sprawl out to snooze on cushy beds. The private bathrooms are immaculate, the communal one not so good. Warm water is available 24 hours a day. Laundry service is available for Q1 per piece. (Singles Q20, Q35 with bath; doubles Q20, Q70 with bath; triples Q70, Q90 with bath.) **Coffee Shop New York** downstairs keeps Big Applers close to goings-on up in the Empire State. **Hospedaje El Salvador** coruscates on 5 Av., two blocks beyond the church. The street drops down a hill, then rises again; the hotel is on the right on the upward slope. Eccentric staircases lead to clean rooms arranged along balconies. Bougainvillea and hibiscus complement stucco walls, and the upper floors enjoy wonderful views of town. Private bathrooms are spotless, but communal facilities are more water-streaked and gritty in the corners. (Singles Q35, Q55 with bath; doubles Q35, Q55 with bath; triples Q45, Q90 with bath). **Hotel Giron,** 6 Calle 4-52 (tel. 561-156), just off 5 Av., between the bus stop and the church. Lusciously decorated rooms (with matching oak furniture) are arranged around a patio that doubles as a parking lot. Bathrooms are spotless and the beds are magnificently comfortable. Both private and communal bathrooms have hot water. The market couldn't be closer (singles Q35, Q45 with bath; doubles Q58, Q65 with bath). If you really want to conserve quetzales, try the **Posada Santa Marta,** 5 Av. 3-27, down the hill from the bus stop and past the arch. Nine small, dark rooms surround a patio that's locked 24 hours a day. (Knock to get in.) Communal bathrooms are not so clean and have only cold water (singles Q15, doubles Q25).

FOOD

For the cheapest fare, plunge into the heart of the market, where tent-swaddled *comedores* await. Tortillas sizzle on every grill, and dogs slither beneath your feet looking for scraps. Fight your way through the ring of *artesanía* stalls that surround them; on non-market days these *comedores* serve as the local hangouts. Otherwise, inexpensive restaurants surround the plaza. **Restaurante Tziguan Tinamit,** 5 Av. 5-67 (tel. 561-144), 1½ blocks from the plaza, lets you watch the telly while you enjoy what may be the best meal in town. The place is super-saturated with tourists on market days. Breakfasts cost Q8-11, lunches run Q12-30, and come complete with soup, salad, potatoes or rice, dessert, and coffee or tea. Sandwiches Q8-12.50. They serve pizza, too. All vegetables are rinsed in *agua purificada.* (Open daily 7am-9pm.) **Café-Restaurante La Villa de los Cofrades,** on the small arcade on the north side of the market. Turn right as you enter the plaza from 5 Av. The people-watching's better here than anywhere else in town, and breakfast is a bargain (Q6.50-13.50), as are the full meals. A lunch of *pollo asado* (roast chicken) with soup, salad, rice or potatoes, and vegetables goes for Q19. Soups Q5-6; sandwiches Q7. (Open daily 7am-about 10pm.) **Restaurante La Fonda del Tzijdaj** jactitates on the second floor of Centro Commercial Santo Tomás, on the north side of the market. Comfy booths and poppy music invoke the Happy Days set; the balcony offers a bird's eye view of the market below. (Tortilla with cheese Q5, *chiquitos* Q4, sandwiches Q5). Postcards for sale, too. **Las Brasas,** on the left side of the church Santo Tomás, on the second floor, in a quiet, brick-warm setting, provides escape from the maniacal shop-o-rama below. Known best for their beef steak and aspic (Q20), they also serve coffee, alcohol, and fruit juice (with milk, for the galactophagous).

SIGHTS

On Sundays and Thursdays, Chichicastenango is host to one of the most famous indigenous **handicraft markets** in Latin America. What is otherwise a quiet town swells with *artesanía* vendors from the nearby highlands and tourists from all over the world. Prices, however, are by no means the lowest in the country. To get real deals, some collectors venture out into the highlands where many items are made; as of the summer of 1995, the U.S. State Department strongly warned against such ventures. Check with the State Department before setting out on an outback shopping expedition. In Chichicastenango, your best bet is to buy on the afternoon before market day, or after 3pm on the day of the market, when the balance of bargaining power tips decisively in the buyer's favor; expect to get 30-50% off the asking price. If you don't get a little thorny about the initial price, the vendor will look at you funny; some bargaining is expected. Beware of "antique" wooden masks which have very often spent less time "aging" in a hole than you've spent in Guatemala. Authentic antique masks are available in the country, but they are much more expensive than those you see in the markets. Be sure to shop carefully; quality merchandise is sometimes lost among piles of more mediocre wares. Large, wooly blankets can cost Q200, hammocks generally sell at Q175, and wooden masks go for Q25-40. Most vendors don't speak English well, but they've learned to make do with what vocabulary they've got—all of them know how to deal with numbers.

The market is by no means Chichicastanango's only attraction. The **Iglesia de Santo Tomás** rises above the southeast corner of the central market plaza. On market days it is a scene of sacred ritual: an incense fire is kept burning at the base of the church's steps and brightly dressed indigenous women blanket one side of the stairs with hibiscus, lilies, roses, and gladiolas, selling the blooms as offerings to churchgoers. An extension of the chapel, the church steps are as sacred as the interior, especially when the fire is burning. This is not a place to sit and chat.

The structure of the church provides a fascinating glimpse into the hybrid folk Catholicism of the Maya-Quiché. The church is built on an ancient Maya-Quiché holy site, and has been sacred to local indigenous communities since Father Francisco Jiménez, an 18th-century parish priest, began re-copying the Popol Vuh, a cosmogony and collection of *indígena* legends. Jiménez's work introduced the outside world to the Popol Vuh, and his respect for indigenous beliefs drew many to worship once again at their ancient sacred site. *Indígenas* today make an elaborate ritual of ascending the steps, repeatedly kneeling, and waving incensiaries. Respectful visitors are welcome, but they should use the side entrance, to the right. Clouded by a haze of incense, the interior buzzes with mumbled prayers. Candles flicker on low platforms between the pews, reflecting off the glass cases which house statues of saints. The devout gather around the platforms, lighting candles, murmuring prayers, and strewing flower petals. Do *not* take photographs.

On the opposite side of the plaza stands the chapel of **El Calvario,** which reserved exclusively for *indígenas*. Along the south side is the small **Rossbach Museum,** containing a small collection of pre-Hispanic artifacts, most of them donated by local families (open Wed.-Mon. 8am-noon and 2-5pm; admission is free). Beyond the plaza, 9 Calle, the street lining the south side of the square, leads down the hill to the town's **cemetery,** where monuments cluster around another *indígena* shrine.

■■■ SANTA CRUZ DEL QUICHÉ

The village of Santa Cruz del Quiché is located about 30km north of Panajachel. Though small, unattractive, and offering virtually nothing to do, it serves as the primary launching point for tourists on their way to the undeveloped ruins of Utatlán.

ORIENTATION AND PRACTICAL INFORMATION

Santa Cruz del Quiché is built in the familiar grid of north-south *avenidas* and east-west *calles.* There are five *zonas,* but they do not disrupt the regularity of the grid. **Parque Central** is framed by 1 Avenida to the east, 2 Avenida to the west, 4 Calle to the north, and 5 Calle to the south. The church is on the east side of the park. The **police** make their nest at 0 Av., 3 Calle, Zona 1(tel. 120; open 24 hrs). Change **traveler's checks** at **Banco G & T,** 6 Calle and 3 Av., Zona 1 (tel. 551-650), at the northwest corner of the park (open Mon-Fri. 9am-5pm, Sat. 10am-2pm), or at **Banco Industrial,** 3 Calle, 2 Av. (tel. 551-079), which also changes U.S. dollars (open Mon.-Fri. 8:30am-5:30pm, Sat. 10am-2pm). The **post office** is hidden in a building with no sign, on 0/1 Avs., Zona 5 (tel. 551-085), and is open Mon.-Fri. 8am-4:30pm. The **postal code** is 14501. The **telegraph office** is next door to the post office and is open 24 hrs. Knock on the door if it appears locked. **Guatel,** 1 Av., 2 Calle, Zona 5, will make calls for you, open daily 7am-midnight. The **bus station,** 1 Av., 10 Calle has service to Guatemala City (every 15min. from 2:30am-5:30pm, 4 hrs., Q9.50); to Panajachel (every hour, 6am-2:30pm, 2 hrs., Q5); to Quetzaltenango (4 per day, 4am-8:30pm, 3 hrs., Q7.50), Tecún Umán (1:45pm, Q14) Navaj (9, 10am, 2pm, 4½ hrs., Q8) and Chicamán (5 per day, 2:30-6pm, Q12). **Farmacia Santa Cruz,** 7 Calle 0-15, Zona 1 (tel. 551-424), is officially open daily 7am-7pm, but will answer emergencies 24 hrs. The owner is a private doctor. For medical **emergencies** contact the Los Bomberos (tel. 551-122) on 2 Calle 0-11, Zona 1.

ACCOMMODATIONS

Santa Cruz lacks the well-oiled machinery needed to cater suitably to the needs of the occasional tourists who show up on the town's front step. The best place to spend the night is **Hotel San Pascual,** 7 Calle, ½ Avs. It's about as charming as a garage with some hanging plants, but rooms are huge and comfortable and the communal baths well-kept. Hot water runs from 6:30-7:30am only (singles Q23, with bath 25; doubles Q25, with bath Q38; triples Q47, with bath Q82). Somewhat darker and lacking showers, but nonetheless comfortable and immaculately clean, are the rooms in the **Posada Calle Real,** 2 Av. 7-36, Zona 1 (tel. 551-438), Q21 per person. If you just need a place to crash, then the **Hospedaje Tropicales,** 1 Av., 9 Calle 5, right up from the bus stop, definitely does the job. Communal bathrooms may give travelers pause. Bus stop clamor rings through the indoor courtyard (singles Q9, doubles Q14).

SIGHTS

K'umarkaaj, also known as Utatlán, was the capital of the Quiché Kingdom, which formed during the postclassic period (1000-1523AD) of Maya civilization and under the ruler Q'uk'ab extended from the Pacific almost to the Atlantic, encompassing nine different nations. Two of these, the Tzutuhil and Cakchiquel, are the two major indigenous groups around Lago Atitlán today. The name *K'umarkaaj* has been translated as "Houses of Old Reeds." The official **archaeological site** covers an area of 8km-square, but the few discernible structures are located around a single plaza. Most everything consists in mounds of grass, the regular shapes of which suggest underlying buildings. Perhaps the most interesting element in all of this is a **small cave,** only 100m from the plaza and along an indicated trail, where the past and the present come together in the living tradition of the *indígenas.* The cave is still used by local people for religious and healing ceremonies much as it was 500 years ago. If you smell incense and see smoke coming out of its entrance, don't hesitate to enter, just be considerate and keep your camera in your bag. You need a flashlight to enter the cave and if you have not brought your own, you can rent one at the museum for Q2. The **museum** itself has posters explaining the social and political structure of the Quiché Kingdom and the chronology of its history and its rulers (all signs are in Spanish). If interested in the history and legends of Quiché People, ask for Sr. Morales, who will gladly and proudly retell you what he heard from his father, who heard it from his father before him, who heard it from his father, who heard it from his father. Site open daily 8am-4:30pm; admission Q0.25.

To get to K'umarkaaj, either walk the 5km or hire a taxi from the bus station at 1 Av., 10 Calle, Zona 5, which takes you there, waits, and brings passengers back for Q40.

■■■ QUETZALTENANGO

Quetzaltenango is full of monuments to what might have been. In 1823, when the Central American Federation broke away from Mexico, Quetzaltenango boldly declared itself the capital of the independent state of Los Altos, which encompassed much of Guatemala's western highlands. Seventeen years later, dreams of independence were smothered by the emergence of Guatemalan dictator Rafael Carrera. With the coffee boom of the 19th century, though, Quetzaltenango again flourished, drawing boatloads of German capital and immigrants to its extraordinarily rich land. Bus alas, Quetzaltenango's aspirations crumbled again in 1902, when a devastating earthquake leveled the city. Somehow still full of ambition, the city leaders rebuilt the city, scattering numerous neo-classical buildings throughout the small metropolis. Unfortunately, the momentum had been spent, and by the 1930s Guatemala City had outpaced its one-time rival for the title of national capital. More recently, city leaders constructed the **Pasaje Enrique,** a glass-ceilinged, European-style concourse on the plaza intended to be a sophisticated shopping center. Instead, it sits nearly vacant; a sign posted on the outside warns visitors of falling glass. Quetzaltenango has forever been something of a provincial might-have-been.

Don't be surprised if you never hear the name "Quetzaltenango" mentioned in town. Locals are more likely to refer to their city as **Xela** (SHEH-lah), an abbreviation of the Quiché name Xelajú, which means "under the ten," a reference to the ten mountain-dwelling gods of the Quiché. Xela has long been a center of Quiché culture; its teeming market and busy Parque Central draw *indígenas* from all over the western highlands. Xela proper won't detain you for more than a day or two; though its markets are among the best in the country, most visitors come to commune with the surrounding countryside and to soak in the hot sulfuric springs in nearby Zunil and Fuentes Georgina.

ORIENTATION

Quetzaltenango's *avenidas* run north-south and the *calles* run east-west. *Avenida* numbers increase to the west, *calle* numbers to the south. The **Parque Centroamérica** is at the center of town in Zona 1 and is bordered by 11 Avenida on the east, 12 Avenida on the west, 4 Calle to the north, and 7 Calle to the south. Most services are located in Zona 1. The second-class bus station and the main market are in Zona 3, northwest of the city center. If you arrive at this station, the **Terminal La Minerva,** walk though the market to its south side. Any of the buses going left (east) on 4 Calle or 6 Calle will take you to the Parque (Q0.50). If you arrive on a first-class pullman, you can walk to the park in the time it would take to wait for a bus.

PRACTICAL INFORMATION

Tourist Office: INGUAT, 7 Calle, 12 Av. (tel. 614-931), at the south side of the park. Free city maps. Some English spoken. Open Mon.-Fri. 8am-1pm and 2-5pm.

Police: (tel. 630-202), 10 Calle 12-21, Zona 1. Open 24 hrs.

Currency Exchange: Banco Immobilario, 12 Av., 4 Calle (tel. 614-161), on the west side of the park (open Mon.-Sat. 9am-8pm). **Banco Industrial** (tel. 612-258), on the east side of the park. Home to a 24-hr., Visa-friendly **ATM.** Open Mon.-Fri. 10am-5pm, Sat. 10am-2pm.

Post Office: 4 Calle 15-07, Zona 1 (tel. 612-651). Open Mon.-Fri. 8am-4:30pm.

Telephones: Guatel, 4 Calle, 15 Av. (tel. 614-498). **Phone, fax,** and **telegram** service. Open daily 7am-midnight. **The Budget Traveler** (tel. 618-525) has an branch in Atitlán Shop. **Telephone code:** 0.

Buses: Most buses leave from **Terminal La Minerva** at the northwest end of Zona 3. To get to the terminal, take any city bus, since all routes eventually pass through the station; any buses on 14 Av. go directly there. The #6, from 8 Calle, 12 Av., Zona 1 (Q0.50), is particularly direct. Most buses from La Minerva pass though La Rotonda on Calzada Independencia in Zona 2, which is a 15-min. walk or a Q6 taxi ride away from Zona 1. From Terminal La Minerva, buses leave for Tecún Umán (3½ hrs., Q11). Buses also run to La Mesilla (6 per day, 6 hrs., Q12); to Guatemala City (every 15min., 5am-5:30pm and at 8pm, 4½ hrs., Q18); to Huehuetenango (every 30min., 5am-5pm, 2 hrs., Q8); to Panajachel (6 per day, 2½ hrs., Q10); and to Chichicastenango (5 per day, 2½ hrs., Q8). Since direct buses to Panajachel and Chichicastenango run infrequently, it's often easier to take a bus to Los Encuentros in Guatemala City instead; buses to Panajachel and Chichicastenango wait there. Buses to Retalhuleu leave every hour (7am-5pm, 2 hrs., Q5). **Galgos,** Calle Rodolfo Robles 17-43 (tel. 612-931), runs 1st-class pullmans to Guatemala City (7 per day, 4½ hrs., Q16).

Public Transportation: City buses run 6:30am-7pm (Q.50 per trip).

Taxis: (tel. 614-085), lined up along the east side of the Park. To Terminal La Minerva Q10, to La Rotonda Q6.
Library: In the Casa de la Cultura, 7 Calle 11-27, Zona 1. No English books. Open Mon.-Fri. 8am-noon and 2-6pm.
Market: At Terminal La Minerva, Zona 3. Open Mon.-Sat. 6am-5pm. To get there, catch bus #6 from 8 Calle, 12 Av., Zona 1, or any bus to the terminal.
Supermarket: La Selecta, 4 Calle 13-16, Zona 1 (tel. 612-004). Open Mon.-Sat. 9am-1pm and 3-7pm, Sun. 9am-1pm.
Laundromat: Lavandería Mini-max, 14 Av. C-47, Zona 1 (tel. 612-952). Wash and dry Q10 per load. Open Mon.-Sat. 7:30am-7:30pm.
Pharmacy: Farmacia Nueva, 10 Av., 6 Calle (tel. 614-531). Open Mon.-Fri. 8am-8pm. There is a rotating schedule for 24- hr. pharmacies; the name of the current *farmacia de turno* should be posted near the entrance of every pharmacy.
Red Cross: (tel. 125), 8 Av. 6-62, Zona 1. Open 24 hrs.
Medical Services: Hospital San Rafael, 9 Calle 10-41, Zona 1 (tel. 614-414), is the closest to downtown. English spoken. Open 24 hrs. The best hospital in town is said to be **Hospital Privado Quetzaltenango,** a bit farther from the city center at Calle Rodolfo Robles 23-51, Zona 1 (tel. 614-381). Both are private institutions.

ACCOMMODATIONS

Quetzaltenango is sprinkled with bargain hotels and guest houses, most of them within a few blocks of the Parque Central. The city's high altitude makes it quite cool (the average temperature is 65°F/18°C); it's worth the extra quetzales for a bathroom with hot water.

Casa Kaehler, 13 Av. 3-33, Zona 1 (tel. 612-091). Set in a refurbished colonial-style house with hardwood floors, most rooms are on the 2nd-floor balcony; from some of these, you can see gas-belching cars drive by. The 19th-century rockers and a working fireplace cozify chilly Xela nights. The front door is locked 24 hrs.; guests have keys. The communal bathrooms are perfectly adequate, and the management's very friendly. Singles Q41, Q47 with bath; doubles Q53, Q59 with bath. All taxes included, so it's not quite as pricey as it sounds.

Hotel Horiami, 2 Calle, 12 Av., Zona 1 (tel. 630-815). The tile floors are well-swept and the rooms brightly lit by a large window overlooking the smog-spewing cars on the street below. The communal bathrooms are irreproachable. Well worth the low price. Singles Q15, doubles Q22.

Hotel Río Azul, 2 Calle 12-15, Zona 1 (tel. 630-654). Large, immaculate rooms have spotless bathrooms and reliable hot water. Communal balconies overlook the exhaust-exhaling buses on the street. Trade words at the small book exchange. Singles Q50, doubles Q65.

Pensión Radar 99, 13 Av. 3-27, Zona 1. Rooms are small and dark, but the price is good—and you're none too far from the pollution-puking motorists. Bathrooms have hot water and are reasonably clean. Singles Q15, Q20 with bath; doubles Q20, Q25 with bath.

Pensión Altense, 9 Calle 8-48, Zona 1 (tel. 612-811). Spacious rooms around a courtyard bursting with bougainvillea. Large windows with bars for safety look out onto the fume-farting buses on the street (or the courtyard). Some rooms and bathrooms are cleaner than others; check first. Hot water flows in most bathrooms. Q15 per person, Q20 per person with bath.

FOOD

If you haven't tried *típico* cuisine, start here. It's affordable, it's delicious, and if your nerve (or stomach) fails, cheap *gringo* food abounds. Many restaurants are within blocks of the Parque Central.

Restaurant Utz-Hua, (Gesundheit), 12 Av. 3-02, Zona 1. Family-run place which serves mmm-good, mmm-cheap Guatemalan food. Try the *típico* platter with a steak and spicy sausage (Q16), or the *carne asada* in tangy tomato sauce (Q12). *Comida corridente* Q8, fresh fruit Q4. Relax and watch the latest installment of your favorite *telenovela* on the 19" TV. Bring your camera—otherwise, friends back home won't believe it when you tell them that the cat can open the restaurant door. Open Mon.-Sat. 7:30am-9:00pm.

Café Baviera, 5 Calle, 12-50, Zona 1. Popular hangout for the Spanish-school crowd, decorated with nostalgic pictures of Xela in the good old days. Pineapple pie (Q6) is superb. Sandwiches Q7.50 and quiche (not Quiché) Q5.50. Used books for sale. Open daily 8am-8pm.

La Polonesa, 14 Av. "A" 4-45, Zona 1. Small and friendly family place serving some of the cheapest meals in town. *Comida económica* Q5. Pancakes Q4.50. One-quarter chicken with french fries Q8. Make it a ½ chicken with potatoes, salad, soup, rice, and dessert for Q20. One whole chicken and a Coke Q25. Open Mon.-Sat. 7:30-9pm.

Pizza Ricca, 14 Av. 2-42, Zona 1 (tel. 618-162). Brick-oven pizzas freshly made in a fast-foody environment. Locals (even *indígenas*) dig into personal pizzas Q10-11. Spaghetti Q13. A vegetarian's best bet is their tasty cheese pizza. Delivery available. Open daily 11am-9:30pm.

Restaurante Deli-Crepe, 14 Av. 3-11, Zona 1. A small, tavern-like, crepe-like place, Deli-Crepe is probably the only crepe place in Xela where you'll find crepes; crepes with ham and cheese Q10, or crepes with your choice of dessert topping, including strawberries or crepes (Q10). They also serve other American food like crepes, hamburgers (Q3.50), and crepes (open daily 9am-9pm).

GUATEMALA

SIGHTS AND ENTERTAINMENT

Xela's biggest attraction is its vibrant produce **market,** which is one of the major commercial centers of the western highlands—you might be the only one there who doesn't speak Quiché. Large, wooly blankets go for Q200, hammocks for Q175, wooden masks conveying every expression and emotion for Q25-40. Bargaining is expected—most vendors don't speak English but they know the numbers well from having clashed wills with tourists for generations. Prices can drop 30% in the blink of an eye. Ask before taking any photographs, and beware of pickpockets. To reach the market, take any bus on 14 Av. (Q0.50).

Aside from the market, Xela offers few diversions. The **Casa de Cultura,** 7 Calle 11-27, Zona 1 (tel. 616-427), is next to the tourist office on the south side of Parque Centroamericano. The museum inside is a swirl of Mayan artifacts, taxidermy, old manuscripts, and local herbology (open Mon.-Fri. 8am-noon and 2-6pm, Sat. 8am-4pm; free). The Casa de Cultura is also an unparalleled source for information on current cultural events. On the first Sunday of each month, the Parque Centroamericano is host to an important handicrafts market, accompanied by outdoor concerts and performances of traditional music. The city's main **festival** takes place September 12-18. The **Municipal Theater,** 1 Calle, 14 Av., Zona 1 (tel. 612-218), houses ballet, *marimba,* orchestra, and theater performances (every other Fri. and Sat., Q3-25). There are also three movie theatres in town, which show a mix of dubbed and subtitled foreign films. **Café Qon,** 12 diagonal and 7 Calle, Zona 1, is a popular hangout for the ex-pat crowd.

■ NEAR QUETZALTENANGO

The town of **Zunil,** about 7 km from Xela toward the coast, is home to yet another shrine to the Mayan God *Maximón,* also known by his Christian name of **San Simón** (see Santiago de Atlitlán, page 75, for more information). Offerings of any kind may be made to San Simón; the seedier, the better (ask around for directions, admission for tourists is Q2). Also at the shrine is a **shaman,** who may be able to do something about those bunions. Buses leave the corner of 4 Calle and 10 Av. in Zona 1 (Via Almolanga) about every 20min. (Q1.50). Buses to Zunil also leave from Terminal Minerva.

About 9km from Zunil on a narrow dirt road bubble the hot springs of **Fuentes Georgina.** Set in a forested notch part of the way up a volcano, Fuentes Georgina is a peaceful place to come and purge the cool, wet weather of Quetzaltenango (admission Q5). Cabins with fireplaces for overnight stays are available for Q35 for one person and Q10 for each additional person. There is no bus to Fuente Georgina but trucks lined up in front of the church in Zunil will take you there for Q20. Unless you plan to walk back (a manageable & downhill 9km) or stay overnight, you'll have to pay the taxi an additional Q30 (Q20 for the trip back and Q10 for the hour the driver waits while you frolic in the springs).

If neither the shaman nor Fuentes Georgina cured your boils and blisters, head over to **El Recreo,** just after Almolonga, which is on the way to Zunil. Ask the bus driver to be let off at the hot springs. Other destinations for daytrips include a number of towns specializing in *artesanía*. **Salcajá** (9km from Xela, on the way to Cuatro Caminos), is known for its embroidered textiles and is home to (as some historians claim) the oldest church in Guatemala.

San Francisco El Alto (17km from Xela) sits atop a hill overlooking Quetzaltenango and Santa María Volcano. On Fridays, the central plaza bustles with vendors for the weekly market; other days it's a bit boring. If you decide to spend the night, **Hotel Vista Herma** (tel. 661-060) has single rooms for Q7, Q6 for each additional person. Some of the rooms have beautiful views of Xela. **Buses** for San Francisco leave from Terminal Minerva about every 30 minutes (Q1.50). Farther beyond San Francisco is the town of **Momostenango.** Centered in Guatemala's wool-growing region, Momostenango hosts a popular Sunday market. By bus it's about 1½ hrs. and buses leave every half hour from Terminal Minerva.

The nearby **Volcán Santa María** towers over Xela and is a popular destination for visitors to Quetzaltenango. The tourist office says that there have been no robberies or assaults on the volcano, and INGUAT considers Santa María to be one of the safest to climb in Guatemala. Buses to **Llanos de Pinal,** leaving from Terminal Minerva (7:30am-5:30pm, Q3), pass near the trailhead for the volcano. Ask the bus driver to let you off at the crossroads near the trailhead (*¿Podría dejarme cerca del camino que sube el volcán?*). Following the road toward the volcano about 200m on the left, you'll pass a plaque dedicated to the Guatemalan Mountaineering Club. From here the road veers to the right, while the trail continues straight. The first section of the trail is wide and strewn with many small boulders. Rising up through a small valley dotted with cornfields, the trail gently curves to the left of the cave (visible if it's not cloudy). **Black arrows** painted on boulders indicate the appropriate trail.

After an hour's hike, the trail arrives at a flat, **grassy area** about 50m in length. One trail skirts the edge of the meadow, but the trail up the volcano cuts directly through it. If the weather is clear, the top of the cone can be seen from here. It looks tantalizingly close, but don't be fooled; you're not even a third of the way up. From here, the trail becomes much narrower and steeper, leaving the farmland and proceeding up the mountain surrounded by pine trees and undergrowth. From the meadow, the climb is two to three hours of **misery.** The trail is steep, irregular, and poorly maintained—going down is almost as hard as going up. At this point, the trail is more diligently marked with frequent beer cans, graffiti, and many notches in the trees, but it's still not hard to get lost.

If you're lucky, the view at the summit is spectacular, with the Cuchumantanes to the north and volcanos to the east and west; then again, the view might be nothing at all, as the summit is frequently enshrouded by clouds, especially in the afternoon. The best way to catch a view is to head up at dawn; Xela is usually covered by an early morning layer of fog, but the summit is almost always clear. To accomplish this requires that you camp near the summit. There are a number of sites and **camping** is permitted, but only do so if you are adequately prepared with food, water, and especially warm clothing. Otherwise, the climb up Santa María can made into a daytrip. Hikers who attempt this climb should be in good shape and well-acclimated to the elevation. The round-trip takes between 5-7 hours of hiking. If you're hiking during the rainy season (May-Oct.), leave early in the day, as afternoon rains can make the trip down hellish.

■■■ HUEHUETENANGO

Huehuetenango has fewer than 40,000 inhabitants, but has somehow managed to embrace its own style of urban sprawl. It stretches four kilometers from end to end, and riding a bus through the town feels something like riding a giant pendulum, by the time relatively frenzied town activity has gradually given way to serene rolling hills and farms. Still, the town's center retains a distinctive and seemingly timeless charm. As local *indígenas* hustle and bustle in the marketplace, the predominantly *ladino* population scoots about on mopeds and little cars. The central plaza, replete with Neoclassical church and raging pink bandstand, manages to achieve some degree of serenity in the face of its gaudy accoutrements.

Just big enough to supply passers-through with necessities and a little taste of the good life, today's "Huehue" began its life as a suburb of **Zaculeu,** the nearby Mayan ruins. Over the course of centuries since the conquest, the area has borne witness to a couple of minor silver rushes and the region-wide coffee boom; the mineral has since petered out, but the beany-brew still runs strong. The Interamerican Highway doesn't go through here, but for its value as a prime pit stop on the way to Mexico, or simply as a headquarters for exploring nearby ruins, this amiable, traditional, and way, (way) cool town should not be overlooked.

ORIENTATION

Huehuetenango lies 226km northwest of the capital and about 90km north of Quetzaltenango. *Avenidas* run north-south, increasing in numbers as you go westward. East-west running *calles* increase from north to south. The **main square** is in Zona 1, bounded by 2 Calle and 4 Calle on the north and south, respectively, and by 4 Avenida and 5 Avenida on the east and west. The main market is just east of the central square.

First- and second-class buses pull into the terminal, which is about 1km west of El Centro. City buses leave for the center about every 15min. (Q0.50). Taxis run to the central square for about Q10. The main plaza and surrounding areas provide most practical essentials.

PRACTICAL INFORMATION

Police: Policía Nacional (emergency tel. 641-150), 5 Av. between 6 and 7 Calles. Ready to serve 24 hrs. a day.

Currency Exchange: Bancor, 2 Calle at 3 Av. (tel. 642-606; fax 641-487). Gives money, money, money in exchange for traveler's checks, Mastercard, and Visa. Open Mon.-Fri. 9am-4pm, Sat. 9am-1pm. **Bancafe,** 3 Calle at 6 Av. (tel. 641-112), also accepts traveler's checks. Open Mon.-Fri 8:30am-8pm, Sat. 10am-2pm.

Post Office: Mail away at 2 Calle between 4 and 3 Avs. Open Mon.-Fri 8am-4:30pm.

Telephones: Guatel, 2 Calle between 4 and 3 Avs, 1 block east of the square. Open daily 7am-midnight.

Buses: Buses arrive and depart from the terminal just off 6 Calle, about 1km west of the plaza. Most municipal buses pass through the terminal and there are stops along 5 Calle near the plaza. From the terminal, buses leave for **La Mesilla** (every 30min., 4am-7pm, 2 hrs., Q5); for **Quetzaltenango/Xela** (every 30-45min., 9am-6pm, 2 hrs., Q5); and for **Guatemala City** (every hour, 7am-4pm, 5½ hrs., Q15). For service to **Panajachel,** it's easiest to take a bus to Guatemala City and then transfer at Los Encuentros. Velasquez runs first-class pullmans from the terminal to **Guatemala City** (every 2 hrs. from 7:30am-5:30pm, Q22). To **Todos Santos Cuchumatán** (3am—yes, in the morning—and 11am, 3 hrs.).

Public Transportation: fares within town are Q0.50. Buses to the terminal run along 5 and 6 Calles. Buses to **Zaculeu** leave from 2 Calle and 7 Av. every hour; to **Chiantla**, they run every 20min. from 1 Calle and 1 Av.

Taxis: Line up along 5 Av. in front of the church. To the terminal Q10.

Market: Along 2 Av. between 2 and 3 Calles; sells some food and snappy souvenirs along with loads of practical stuff. Open daily 6am-6pm.

Supermarket: Casa Saenz, 4 Calle and 5 Av. Open Mon.-Sat. 8:30am-6:30pm.

Pharmacy: Farmacía Del Cid, 4 Calle and 5 Av. Open 8am-12:30pm, 2-8pm daily. Near the central square, you're never more than a block from a pharmacy. The rotating schedule of 24-hr. pharmacies is posted in front of every pharmacy.

Consulate: Get your tourist card in advance at the **Mexican Consulate**, on 5 Av., between 4 and 5 Calles. Open Mon.-Fri. 9am-noon and 2-5pm.

Medical Services: National Hospital (tel. 641-414 for **emergencies**), 6 Calle just west of 7 Av. Available 24 hrs. Very little English spoken.

ACCOMMODATIONS

Even though Huehuetenango is not a major tourist attraction, cheap (and not coincidentally, shoddy) hotels abound, concentrated mostly to the immediate north and west of the central square.

Hotel Mary 2 Calle 3-52 (tel. 641-618; fax 641-228), just across the street from the Guatel office. The rooms are narrow and small, but the pink-stuccoed walls and lacquered wooden doors, all centered around a well-lit, multi-story atrium, lend an air of sophistication to this inexpensive hotel. The collective baths are clean and odorless. Reservations welcome. Singles Q25; doubles Q35, with bath and cable TV Q70. There is also a cafeteria on the second floor that serves three meals a day. Dishes run about Q10.

Todos Santos Inn 2 Calle 6-64 (tel. 641-241), between 6a and 7a Avs. A peek through the whitewashed concrete entrance reveals polished tile floors and rich blue bedspreads, all in color-coordinated rooms. Situated on the quiet end of the square, some rooms have views of the beautiful surrounding countryside. Continental breakfast included. *Se hable inglés*. Singles are Q25, Q40 with bath, doubles Q45, Q70 with bath. An additional charge of Q12 is added for TV.

Hotel Viajero, 2 Calle 5-32, Zona 1., one block west of the central square. The ceilings are low, the mattresses stiff, and the single, nude lightbulb a sickly yellow. The difference between a room at Hotel Viajero and a refrigerator box is small, but don't all hotel rooms look the same once you turn off the light? At Q10 for singles and Q20 for doubles, the price is hard to beat.

FOOD

Huehue may not be the culinary capital of Guatemala, but the food comes cheap. There are a number of *comedores* just east of the church in and around the marketplace. Most mid-range hotels also have their own (mid-range) restaurants.

Villa Flor, 7 A. 3-41, Zona 1 (tel. and fax 642-586), located in Hotel Casa Blanca. The hotel devotes its entire Spanish courtyard to the restaurant, a placid oasis from polluted streets. For company, dine to the gentle gurgling of the fountain. All meals served at reasonable prices; hamburgers (Q9), omelette with ham Q14. Open daily 6am-10pm.

Pizza Hugareño, 2a Calle, just east of the square, across from Guatel. The colorblind may well love the interior; faux gold baroque mirrors, bright green drapes, and tangerine stucco surround the hungry-eño. The food is doubleplusgood, though, and vegetarians will do back flips over the large cheese pizza (Q18.50). Open Tues.-Sun. 9:30am-9pm.

Jardín Cafe Restaurante, on the corner of 6a Av. and 4a Calle. Feeling Grecian? Come for hanging ferns, industrious ceiling fans, and late-night Mediterranean dinners. Situated on a noisy street corner, the Jardín sports a large menu with both local and American-style food. *Chile relleno con sopa y ensalada* Q17, hamburgers Q8. Open daily 6am-11pm.

Restaurante Bougainvilia, 5 Av., facing the church. This four-story restaurant sticks out like a concrete thumb in this mostly one-story town; the kitchen is on street level as you walk in, and there are tables on the upper three floors with breezy views; the *comida típica* (Q13) changes from day to day, but generally runs heavy on the flesh: *carne asada, chorizo* (sausage), or some sort of chicken.

NEAR HUEHUETENANGO

About 4km west of Huehuetenango lies the ancient Mayan site of **Zaculeu,** the former capital and cultural center of the Mam tribe from 600AD. The Mam reached all the way to Todos Santos, and their language continues in the area today. Ruled by the Quiché until the 15th century, the tribe managed to escape oppression from the fellow Indians, but fell right out of the frying pan and into the Spanish fire. When an army led by Gonzalo de Alvarado met the Mam on a battlefield, the Indians took a look at the fearsome Iberians and retreated to their base at Zaculeu. Their home had been built to protect them; the temples, plaza, and ball court that comprise the present site were fortified on three sides. Instead, the Spanish simply waited a few months until hunger set in, and the weakened Mam were forced to surrender.

The United Fruit Company, already notorious for dipping its fingers in places it shouldn't (see Central America: History, page 33), sponsored an overzealous restoration of Zaculeu earlier this century. Today, few of the original stones aren't slathered in stucco, and Zaculeu is not what you'd expect from ancient ruins; no jungly vines envelop the area, and nary a temple is strewn with toppled towers or relics. The site exudes some of the sterility of a mini-golf course, but while perhaps not the best place to explore Mayan mysteries, Zaculeu does tell us plenty about another odd culture, that of imaginative and anal-compulsive archaeologists. Bus #2 leaves Huehuetenango from the mini-plaza at 2 Calle and 7 Av. every hour. The walk takes 30-45min. Head west on 2 Calle out of town, past the soccer stadium, and from there signs point the way to the ruins; look for the 17m temple (site open daily from 8am-4pm; admission Q1).

■■■ TODOS SANTOS CUCHUMATÁN

If you're lucky enough to get a window seat (or only to sit on top), the ride to Todos Santos is one of the most spectacular in Guatemala. Ascending skyward over 1000m from Huehuetenango, the road snakes around sharp ravines; with each turn, the road below looks smaller, narrower—and the low ground much more alluring than before. After a brief passage through a high plateau, the road nose dives into a valley at dizzying speeds before arriving safely (knock on wood) at Todos Santos. This trip is *not* for those prone to carsickness, but for others, it'll blow your freakin' mind.

The spectacular, if arduous, three-hour trek is well worth the prize waiting at the end. The small village of Todos Santos Cuchumatán, nestled between two towering bridges, evokes a lifestyle from pre-Columbian times. In fact, some of the folks here, men decked out in crazy red-striped, bell-bottom pants and tall cowboy hats, and women dressed in bright red *huipiles* and dark blue *cortes,* might very well have lost track of time as we know it, since Todos Santos is one of the few villages left that follows the 260-day Mayan calendar for religious events. Don't worry, though; nobody around here forgets when there's a holiday coming up, especially the **All Saint's Day** celebration from Oct. 31 to Nov. 5 (see the gray box in Sights, below); the party's unforgettable. While the core population of Todos Santos is composed of only about a thousand, thousands more depend on the town, particularly farmers who come down from their mountains for trade and services.

There are few services in Todos Santos, and there's no way to get really lost. It might be hard to get directions anywhere, though, since Mam (and not Spanish) is the native tongue of most locals. The **post office** is open Mon.-Fri. 8am-4:30pm. **Buses** back to Huehue leave at 4:30am and 5am (Q6; 3 hrs.). There is a **post office** in the center of town (open Mon.-Fri. 8am-4:30pm), and next to it a small (one-room) **museum** where you can ask for directions to the various villages.

Recent spurts of construction have markedly improved local lodgings. **Hospedaje Casa Familiar,** the nicest of the town's three hotels, is just up the street from the museum: signs point the way (singles Q15, doubles Q25, hot water costs an extra Q5). A block before the museum lurks **Hotel Tres Olguitas,** which has divided up a

GUATEMALA

whole floor into a dozen airplane-lavatory-sized rooms (singles only Q10). As a last resort, (without any other element of "resort" attached), there's **Hospedaje La Paz,** also a block before the museum. Rooms are dark, spartan, a bit creepy, but super cheapy (singles Q6, doubles Q12). After the bus ride makes you spill your guts, fill them up again at **Comedor Katy,** adjacent to Casa Familiar. They serve a fine chicken (Q8), but vegetarians will have to be content with eggs and beans *(*open 7am-9pm)..

Hold on to your horses!

Todos Santos' residents kick off their out-of-control, outrageously fun All Saint's Day revelry with one of the wildest customs around. For the cost of a few quetzales, locals rent horses and enter a no-holds-barred, last-one-standing-wins race through the village. There's no finish line to the course, though its length is finite. Whenever a rider makes it to either of the two ends, he has to take a shot of the specially prepared moonshine; each successful lap incurs another two shots. Thanks to the time-honored tradition of using chickens to whip the horses into gear, the race starts off at break-neck speeds—until riders start to break their own necks, which usually doesn't take very long. Even so, ardent contestants tie themselves onto their horses in order to keep from toppling, and the race's winner is anybody still mounted and conscious at the end. Afterwards, back in town, the marimbas belt out everyone's favorite hits while villagers hold a different "no-bars-barred" competition of a similar sort, *sin* chickens.

THE PACIFIC SLOPE

The Pacific coast offers something quite different from the striking Mayan temples, gorgeous mountain vistas, and ever-bright native costumes familiar to the nearby highland region—namely, a sweltering, generally unattractive plain of coffee and banana plantations and diesel trucks on their way to someplace else. Still, *La Costa Sur,* as Guatemalans call the area, is worth a gander, if only to check out the bracing contrasts between these black sand beaches and crashing coastal currents and those of stereotypical, postcard-worthy stretches of sand evident elsewhere in the world.

■■■ RETALHULEU

Reu (RAY-oo), as Retalhuleu is concisely nicknamed, has managed to carve itself a liveable, even likeable patch out of an area where swamps' stench and muggy, muddy muck usually ward off tourists like mosquitoes from the DEET you should wear here. Spared the pollution of trucks on the distant CA-2 Highway, the road into colonial Retalhuleu is lined with majestic royal palms and the homes of the town's rich. The central square testifies to the civilized plantain-plantation-pretensions; the appropriately banana-colored city hall is built in a stately neo-classical style, and the snowy-white colonial church is flanked by even *more* royal palms. There isn't exactly boundless potential for having fun here, but it's not a bad place to spend a day or so, perhaps simply by sipping cups of the unbeatable, locally produced coffee and sugar.

ORIENTATION AND PRACTICAL INFORMATION

Avenidas in Retalhuleu run north-south and *Calles* run east-west. The central square is bounded by 5 and 6 Calles on the north and south sides, respectively, and by 4 and 6 Avs. on the east and west. Retalhuleu's bus terminal is about seven blocks due north of the central square.

Banks line the central square, though only a few accept traveler's checks. **Banco Agricola Mercantile** (tel. 710-176), on the east end of the square, is one of these proud few (open Mon.-Fri. 8:30am-8pm, Sat. 9am-1pm). The **post office** is on the other end of the square (open Mon.-Fri. 8am-4:30pm), and **Guatel** roosts just around the corner, on 5 Calle (open daily from 7am-10pm).

Because the town's just off the CA-2 highway, **buses** traveling between the capital and the border crossing at Tecún Umán pull into the terminal all day long. Buses to Tecún Umán (2 hrs., Q6) leave via Coatepeque (1 hr., Q3) every thirty minutes. Buses to Guatemala City (4 hrs., Q20) via Esquintla (3 hrs., Q15) also leave every 30 minutes. Buses leave for Quetzaltenango every hour from 7am to 5pm (2 hrs., Q5). There are taxis lined up in front of the church that charge Q5 to the terminal, but the distance is definitely short enough to walk. Hanker for a hunk of cheese, or imported breakfast cereals and potato chips? Go to the small **supermarket, La Exclusiva,** 7 Calle 4-44 (tel. 710-373), which is open daily from 8:30am-12:30pm and 2:30-6:30pm. There are a number of **pharmacies** within a few blocks of the central square, including **Farmacia San Antonio** (tel 710-853), at 5 Av. just north of 6 Calle (open daily 7:30am-8pm).

ACCOMMODATIONS AND FOOD

Retalhuleu is not geared for tight budgets, and the choices are bleak for a place to stay. On the cheap side, there's **Hotel Pacífico** (tel. 711-178), on 7 Av. between 9 and 10 Calles, which charges Q12 per person for dim, scraggly, rooms and a needy communal bath. From there the prices jump significantly. **Hotel Modelo,** 5 Calle 4-53 (tel 710-256), isn't exactly model; dark but well-kept rooms have ceiling fans and private bath (Q41 for singles, Q59 for doubles). **Posada Don José** (tel. 710-851), on the corner of 5 Av. and 5 Calle, has a sterile personality, but the baths are super and all rooms have ceiling fans (singles Q51, doubles Q80).

Pack that grumbly stomach full at **Cafetería La Luna** or **Restaurante al Patio,** both located on 5 Calle in front of the church, each a typical *comedor* serving *carne asada* (Q15), *pollo frito* (Q15) and hamburgers (Q9); both open at 9am and close at 9pm. In fact, they seem to be the same restaurant entirely. A bit south of the square at 7 Calle 4-44 is **Pizza Rondinella,** serving small cheese pizza for Q14.50 in a restaurant that more resembles a *comedor* than a fast food joint.

■ NEAR RETALHULEU

Situated on a narrow black dune and separated from the mainland by a narrow channel, **Tulate** is home to one of the nicest beaches on Guatemala's Pacific Coast; the sand is black, of course, and it lacks the development, garbage, and pollution of other nearby coastal towns, which makes it the perfect daytrip from Retalhuleu or even Quetzaltenango. If one day isn't enough, Tulate is home to a lone *hospedaje*, **Rancho de Xelaju,** where Q20 buys one or two reed-stuffed cots under a thatched roof, replete with swirling bats and communal bath (with fresh water).

There are no direct **buses** from Retahuleu to Tulate; instead, take a bus headed to **Mazatenango** (they leave every 30 minutes), and transfer at **Cuyotenango** (1 hr. Q2). From there the ride is about 2 hrs. on a good day (Q5).

CROSSING THE BORDER TO MEXICO

Two hours west of Retahuleu is the border town of **Tecún Umán.** Like most border towns, Tecún Umán is rather unattractive, with the added disadvantage of being along the broiling Pacific Coast. As Guatemala's main entry point from Mexico, however, the crossing is busy 24 hrs. The spanning bridge symbolically links the two nations. **Tourist cards** from Guatemala can be had at the border for Q10. There are a number of cheap hotels in Tecún, but there is no reason to linger; **buses** for Guatemala city and other destinations in between leave every 30 minutes from 5am-10pm (see Yucatán, Tourist Cards, page 442, for more information on requirements for getting into Mexico).

■■■ MONTERRICO

So many beach paradises are spoiled with overpriced, high-rise hotels, and greenback-pushing tour groups, that it's often hard to imagine what it means when some salty ex-pat moans, "you should've seen this place ten years ago." In Monterrico, ten years ago is today. Situated on the finest stretch of black sand beach on Guatemala's Pacific Coast, Monterrico has somehow escaped the ravages of development, remaining an undiscovered jewel. Home to a surprising number of transplanted foreigners, Monterrico is like a lush roach motel, capturing tourists who say they'll spend a weekend and end up staying their whole lives. Sadly, though, developers are starting to pick at this gem-in-matrix with greater gusto than ever; the more they pick, the more it looks like Puerto San José. One small, 30-room upscale hotel has already been built 2km to the west of town, and bigger projects are in the works. Pretty soon, Monterrico's 10 years' tranquility will be up, so get there while it's not yet hot.

Monterrico's accommodations are very reasonable. **Turicentro Doble "L,"** located on the beach about 20m to the right of where the main street ends at the beach, is only one of a number of cheap *pensiones* with dark rooms and cockroach-infested public baths, but it is the only one to have mosquito nets for its guests, a must in the rainy season (Q15 per person). Run by a former Peace Corps volunteer, **Hotel Baule Beach** (tel. 736-196, call after 7:30pm), located on the beach about 100m to the left of the main street, is a significant notch up, offering private baths, comfortable beds, and mosquito netting (singles Q41, doubles Q58; prices go down for stays of longer than two nights). A bit newer and funkier, **Kaiman Inn,** adjacent to Baule Beach, offers similar amenities at Q50 per person, Q55 on weekends. For after-dark entertainment, **Pig Pen** is the place. Run by Miguel, a Canadian expatriate, Pig Pen serves up drinks to the sound of sultry tropical tunes. Located 10m to the right of main street and open nightly, from dusk "till you're done drinking."

Set up as a reserve for sea turtles to lay eggs, **Biotopo Monterrico** also preserves one of the last remaining mangrove swamps on Guatemala's Pacific coast, and is home to thousands of birds. Local fishermen give tours on their boats (Q10 an hour). The magnificent **sea turtles** can be seen coming ashore to lay their eggs in the early morning hours of the summer months, but it's not easy (to see them).

Situated on a narrow strip of land and separated from the mainland by 2km of mangrove swamp, Monterrico is accessible by two routes. The faster is to proceed by bus from Escuintla to Taxisco (every 30min., 1 hr., Q2). From there the buses leave hourly from 6am till 5pm for La Avellana (1 hr., Q2), whence goeth a quick ferry to Monterrico (Q2). All this takes about 3 hrs. from the capital. An alternate route is to take the bus due south to Iztapa, cross the channel, then to take a bus over a slow and bumpy dirt road the 15km to Monterrico. Four buses leave daily from Iztapa to Monterrico at 5am, 11am, noon, and 5pm.

ALTA Y BAJA VERAPAZ

For years the Kikché Indians of this area successfully resisted the Spanish conquest, which gave rise to the Kikché name of the region: *Tuzuntohil,* or "Land of War." Meanwhile Fray Bartolomé de las Casas and the Franciscan friars organized a powerful campaign in defense of the *indígenas.* The result was something the world had never seen before or after; the most powerful empire in the world halted its military conquest to consider questions of its own morality and justifiability. Las Casas was granted five military-free years for the peaceful and "humane" conversion of the Kikché. His success was spectacular. He and the friars learned Kikché and composed songs with the gospel in it. They passed the tunes on to a few merchants who frequently visited the warring areas, and the visitors sang the songs while showing mirrors, knives, and other objects from European civilization. The chiefs, assured that the friars were not interested in their gold and their land, finally let them in and conversion followed peacefully shortly thereafter. Thus the region obtained its present name, *Verapaz* or "true peace," which is unfortunately a misnomer; Verapaz is the base for many guerrilla troops, who were recently involved in violent action with local landowners.

■■■ SALAMÁ

The *pueblos* that speckle the mountains here funnel their political and commercial energies into Salamá, capital of Baja Verapaz. On Mondays and Fridays the small town's market overflows with produce from the surrounding countryside; on Sundays the cathedral-sized colonial church **San Mateo** draws a hefty congregation and is the site of renowned regional festivals on Sept. 15-17. The **San Jeronimo ruins** are the only other site of interest, but even these aren't all that interesting. Really, the town is only useful as a stop on the way to Cobán, and as a point of departure to the tiny handicraft centers of **San Miguel Chicaj** and **Rabinal,** nine and 18 kilometers west of Salamá, respectively.

The **police** hang out on 5 Calle 8-77, Zona 1 (tel. 400-050). Exchange traveler's checks at **Banco de Café,** 5 Av. 6-21, Zona 1 (open Mon-Fri. 9am-5pm, Sat. 10am-2pm). **Guatel** sits on 7 Av. near the central park (open 7am-9pm). For medical help call on **Dr. Eder Sandoval,** 4 Calle, 419, Zona 1 (tel. 400-035). **Farmacia San José,** on 4a Calle 1, Zona 1, is open 7am-7pm. Pickings are sparse for accommodations and food in Salamá. **Hospedaje Juarez,** behind the San Mateo church, lovingly tucks you into your hard little bed, which is tucked into a cubicle of a room. Public baths have that well-scrubbed look, and the service is friendly (singles Q10, doubles Q18). If you'd rather avoid doing penance, go to **Hotel Tozulutlán,** 7 Av, Zona 1 (tel. 400-141), where a lush courtyard hides talking parrots and a wildcat. Rooms are clean and spacious, and a pitcher of water is thoughtfully set on each dresser. The **restaurant** spoons out eats for cheap (breakfast Q5, lunch and dinner Q20).

■■■ COBÁN

Once the center of *Tuzuntobil,* Cobán was overrun by the Spanish conquistadors and later by German coffee plantation lords, who were driven out by American troops during WWII. Today the Land of War is on coffee break, catching a breath as a sultry tourist town with natural parks and scattered *balnerios,* scenic bathing pools, ideal for dawdling in the clean mountain air. Mother Nature is always nearby in Cobán, but paved roads and modern conveniences keep your feet firmly planted in civilization while some of the best coffee in the world keeps veins surging.

ORIENTATION AND PRACTICAL INFORMATION

Primera Avenida (north-south) and **I Calle** (east-west) divide the city into four quadrants. The northwest is labelled Zona 1, the southeast Zona 2, the southeast Zona 3 and the northeast Zona 4. The central park is framed by 1 and 2 Avs. and 1 and 2 Calles in Zona 2.

Tourist Office: Información Turística, 1 Calle 1-11, Zona 1 (tel. 511-305). Helpful information on sights in the region and crudely drawn but detailed city maps for Q.75. English spoken. Open Mon.-Sat. 9am-12:30pm, 2:30-6pm.

Police: 1 Calle 5-12, Zona 1 (tel. 511-225). Open 24 hrs.

Currency Exchange: Cobán may be your only chance to change money in this part of the country. **Banco del Café,** 1 Av. 2-66, Zona 2 (tel. 511-011), changes traveler's checks Mon.-Fri. 8:30am-8pm. **Occidente Banco,** 1 Calle, Zona 1 (tel. 513-651) does the same. Open Mon.-Fri. 8:30am-4pm, Sat. 9am-2pm. **Banco Industrial,** 1 Calle, 2 Av., Zona 1, has a 24-hr. ATM and exchanges traveler's checks.

Post and Telegraph Office: 3 Calle 2-00, Zona 3 (tel. 511-140). Post office open Mon.-Fri. 8am-4pm. Telegraphs 24 hrs. **Postal Code:** 17001.

Phones: Guatel, 1 Calle, 2 Av., Zona 1 (tel. 511-498). Open daily 7am-10pm.

Buses: Transportes Escobar y Monja Blanca, 2 Calle 3-77, Zona 4 (tel. 511-952). To Guatemala City (every hr., 2am-4pm, 4 hrs., Q18). All other buses leave from the bus terminal at the end of 2 Calle, Zona 4. To San Cristóbal (every 30min., 6am-6pm, 4 hrs., Q1.25); to Languín (5, 6, 10am, 3pm, 2½ hrs., Q5; the 5am and 6am buses leave from 1 Calle, 3 Av., Zona 4, in front of Cine Norte).

Taxis: (tel. 511-897), lined up on the north side of the central park.

Laundromat: Lavandería La Providencia, Diagonal 4, 2-43, Zona 2, on the south side of the central park. 7-lb. wash (Q4.30) and dry (Q4.25). Open Mon.-Sat. 8am-noon and 2-5pm.

Pharmacy: Farmacia Carvi, 1 Calle 4-53, Zona 3 (tel. 513-094). Open 24 hrs.

Medical Emergency: Los Bomberos (tel. 511-212), 3 Calle, 3 Av., Zona 4. Open 24 hrs.

Red Cross: "Cruz Roja" (tel. 125).

ACCOMMODATIONS AND FOOD

Accommodations in Cobán are chock-full of tourists year-round; finding a room may take a little wandering. Lucky cheapskates get into **Hospedaje Maya,** 1a Calle 2-33, Zona 4 (tel. 512-380). Basic, uneventful rooms have comfy beds. Public bathrooms smell like a leaky barn, but modern refurbishments (washer, dryer, and leather reclining chairs) make up for it (Q6 per person). For bright rooms with private bath, head to **Hotel la Providencia,** Diagonal 4, 2-43, Zona 2 (tel. 511-209), on the southwest corner of the central park (singles Q12, doubles Q20.50). **Pensión Familiar,** Diagonal 4, 2-49, Zona 2, awaits next door to Hotel La Providencia. Its larger rooms are brighter and smell nicer. Toucans and doves spruce up a drab garage-like lounge with their fruity-tropical colors and screeches. Follow your nose—it always knows. No hot water (Q15 per person). **Hotel Nuevo Monterrey,** 6 Av., 1 Calle, Zona 1 (tel. 511-131), is connected to the Hotel Cobán Imperial and has well-maintained rooms and decent communal baths with hot water (singles Q15 with bath; doubles Q25, with bath Q30.50; triples Q45, with bath Q38.60). **Hotel La Paz,** 6 Av. 2-19, Zona 1 (tel. 511-358), is a safe bet, with slightly worn but tidy rooms and baboon-statues shouldering potted plants. The cafeteria in front offers cheap chow and toiletries (dinner and breakfast Q10, lunch Q12).

Hard-rockin' action flicks distract both customers and employees at **Restaurant El Refugio,** 2 Calle 1-34, Zona 4. Privacy is no problem, as tables are spaced light-years apart. The service is exceptionally generous. *Refugio Special* Q12.50, *chile relleno* with rice and beans Q15.50, lasagna Q25. Open daily 11am-11pm. **Cafetería Ticos Pancakes,** 1 Calle, 4/5 Avs., Zona 3, hits all 3 Bs: *bueno, bonito, and barato* (good, nice, and cheap). Pancakes with banana, apple, strawberries, blueberries, or snozberries (Q6), cereal with fruit (Q5), sandwiches (Q6). (Open 24 hrs.) **Restaurant Kam-mun,** 1 Calle 8-12, Zona 1, serves traditional Chinese fare in traditional Chinese chintz. Fried rice with shrimp and eggs Q19, chicken chow mein Q17. Open daily noon-10pm. An enticing tunnel entrance leads to **Café El Tirol,** 1 Calle 3-13, Zona 1, offers a great place to bring a book—or borrow from the Café's baby library of paperbacks—and murmur sweet, intellectual nothings over a rich selection of even richer coffees, teas, and chocolate drinks, hot or cold (coffee Q2, sandwiches Q7.50-8).

SIGHTS AND ENTERTAINMENT

No matter how hot and hectic it gets among the gurgling cars and baking streets of Cobán, tranquility always awaits at **Parque Las Victorias,** seven blocks west and two blocks north of Parque Central. Puff alongside joggers through shady, fern-covered paths to the rhythmic trill of crickets. Definitely swing by the **Bajaritos,** a thatch-roofed village of swings, slides, and exercise equipment as innovative in its construction as to the residences on *Gilligan's Island.* Nearby, the foliage breaks into a sun-drenched clearing, where a garden coddles the region's native and endangered plants and flowers. And contrary to the decor that seems to mark the church as the proper place for parties, locals all come out here, to the woods, when they want to get wild. At the front of the park, **Iglesia Calbario** provides a wonderful view of Cobán from on high.

■ NEAR COBÁN

Cobán just can't seem to get enough **balnearios,** scenic swimming pools that are often built alongside rivers. The most lovely nearby is **Las Islas,** where water bounces through a rocky riverbed into a natural pool, surrounded along its length by picnic bungalows. To get there, take a bus to Carchá from the Cobán bus terminal (every 15min., 10min, Q1.50). From Carchá, take a taxi (Q5) or walk 20min.; admission is Q11. Or try **Hermanas del León,** 20min. down Diagonal 4 (free camping), or **La Colonia;** take a bus to Carchá, get off at the bridge, and walk for about 30min. east. If you somehow still haven't had enough swimming, **Balneario de Camché,** near Tactic, 31 km north of Cobán, is yet another local favorite. Three daily buses (6am, 1pm, and 3pm; 1 hr.) pass through Tactic on their way to Lanquín.

■■■ LANQUÍN

Seventy kilometers north of Cobán, the little village of Lanquín possesses two of the most spectacular jewels in the vast crown of Guatemala—the natural bridge and cascades of **Samuc Champey** and the enormous caves, **Grutas de Lanquín,** which are said to be Guatemala's most beautiful. The cave is 2km before the village, but first go into town and look for the policeman who can turn the electricity on for you (Q10 per person); he works in the big municipal building in the center of town. The policeman works until 5pm, but the cave is open 24 hrs.; get there at dusk to witness the soul-shaking flocks of bats. Bring a flashlight or two; getting caught in the caves without any light could lead to calamity.

Visiting Samuc Champey is more of a challenge. It's a long 2-½ hour, 10-km walk from Lanquín. **Hotel El Recreo,** 1.5km past the cave and ½km before town, organizes tours for Q20 per person during the high season, but it's much cheaper to ask around in the village and find out if there's a pick-up that will take you in that direction for a small fee (offer Q2-5).

Only three **buses** get to Lanquín (6am, 10am, and 3pm buses from Cobán; 3 hrs.; Q6.50) and only three go out (4am, 3pm, and 6pm buses to Cobán). Times are not exact, so be there at least half an hour early and be ready to wait as long as an hour. Limited transportation makes Lanquín difficult as a daytrip, so spend the night at **Pensión la Providencia,** on the main street, which claims exclusive boasting rights to hot water, and also to with spacious rooms and hammocks (Q7.20 per person). Nearby **Lugar el Turista** offers a more delapidated option, with springy beds stuffed into an airy loft. If the coils get to you, try the hammocks (Q7 per person). Both places have attached restaurants where beans, eggs, and steak go for about Q10. **Hotel El Recreo** (see above) glitters with its own pool and well-cultivated wildlife kingdom. Immaculate bungalow rooms for Q20 per person, and carpeted chambers for much more (singles Q93, doubles Q126, triples Q66). Lavish multi-course meals include soup, steak, *frijoles,* and tortillas (Q20).

■ BIOTOPO QUETZAL MARIO DARY

Some of the last remaining *quetzales,* the bright green-and-red bird emblematic to Guatemala, hang out at this reserve, 160km north of Guatemala City on the highway to Cobán. The reserve is in a cloud-strewn highland forest with trails twisting throughout. The free park is open from 6am to 4pm, but these regal and rare, long-plumed deities (whose tail feathers can reach a yard in length and were used to adorn the headdresses of Mayan royalty) only deign to appear between 5:30am and 7am. Bizarrely, the best place to view them is not the in *biotopo,* but rather from the

Hospedaje Ranchito del Quetzal, about 50m farther down the road to Cobán. Viewing them in a zoo is not an option, as these noble birds cannot survive in captivity. Bring binoculars or the super-zoom from your camera if you want to get an in-your-face view of these pompadoured *pájaros.* The **hospedaje** has basic dorms for Q9 per person and private rooms for Q20 per person. Tumble out of bed and see the birdies right outside your door. The attached restaurant serves eggs and beans for Q7 and coffee for Q2. (Open 7am-8pm.)

EASTERN GUATEMALA

Want to lose the crowds in *Gringotenango* and the western highlands? Go east, young person. The eastern *biotopos* (wildlife reserves), ruins, and *aguas bonitas* offer diversions unparalleled in the west, and everything's served in the sauce of a hang-loose, come-as-you-are atmosphere. The well-maintained Atlantic Highway offers access to some of the eastern hot spots; buses between Guatemala City and Puerto Barrios usually make stops along the way, at Quiriguá and near Lago Izabal; just ask beforehand to be let off at your destination. To head south to Chiquimula and Esquipulas, get off at Río Hondo or head toward Zacapa.

■■■ ESQUIPULAS

Sniff carefully: the crystal mountain air of Esquipulas does not smell of tourists, but of ardent religiosity. Ever since Spanish missionaries set a wood-carving of Christ's face in the town church in 1595, hordes of Guatemalans have come here on pilgrimages to worship and make offerings to the same mahogany miracle-worker which supposedly cured Archbishop Figueroa of his ailments in 1737. **El Cristo Negro** hovers in the cloud-white **Basílica de Esquipulas,** which itself towers majestically over the town's other buildings and vendors' tents as haze enshrouds the natural background of mountains. The church's interior shimmers with candles and the murmurs of half-sung hymns; some devotees crouch in pews, while others drop to their knees at the entrance or join the queue that stretches through the side entrance—all of its members come to pay homage to the statue in person. While local commercialism has become intimately entwined with the hanging shrine, it hasn't yet tainted the deep faith that draws the pilgrims, most of whom come around January 15 each year.

In front of the church, locals enjoy picnics in the **Parque Central** while surrounding vendors peddle a rainbow assortment of candles and religious paraphernalia: Mother Mary keychains go for Q2-3, and for Q15 you can sport a straw hat decked with ornaments and a Christ figurine sacrificially pinioned to the rim.

Banco G&T, across from the bus station, exchanges money. The **post office** is at Calle Principal, 3 Av. (open 8am-4pm) and its **postal code** is 9002. **Guatel** sits on 5 Av., 9 Calle, Zona 1 (tel. 431-098; open 8am-8pm). **Buses** leave for Guatemala City (every 30min., 2:30am-5:30pm, 4 hrs., Q21.50); for Chiquimula (every 30min., 5am-5pm, 1 hr., Q4); and for Quiriguá (6:15am, 2 hrs.). There's a **pharmacy** on 3 Av. 26, Zona 1. (Open 7am-10pm.)

Hotels and **restaurants** in Esquipulas rely on devout visitors' willingness to abstain from corporeal comforts; most establishments are of poor quality and *not* priced accordingly. **Hotel San Francisco,** 2 Av., 11-22, Zona 1 (tel. 431-402) provides rooms off long, dark hallways; the communal bathrooms could use some tender loving cleaning (Q15 per person, Q20 with bath). In **Hotel Paris,** 10 Calle, 2 Av. 1-99 (tel. 431-276), rooms are less homely and more homey, but also more expensive. Its entrance has stained glass windows, and second floor abodes overlook a parking court. Common bathrooms are clean (singles Q30, doubles Q30). **Hotel Zacapo,** 3 Av. 9-51, Zona 1 (tel. 431-151) provides a box of a room to sleep in and a toilet to squat on, and not much more (singles Q15, doubles Q30).

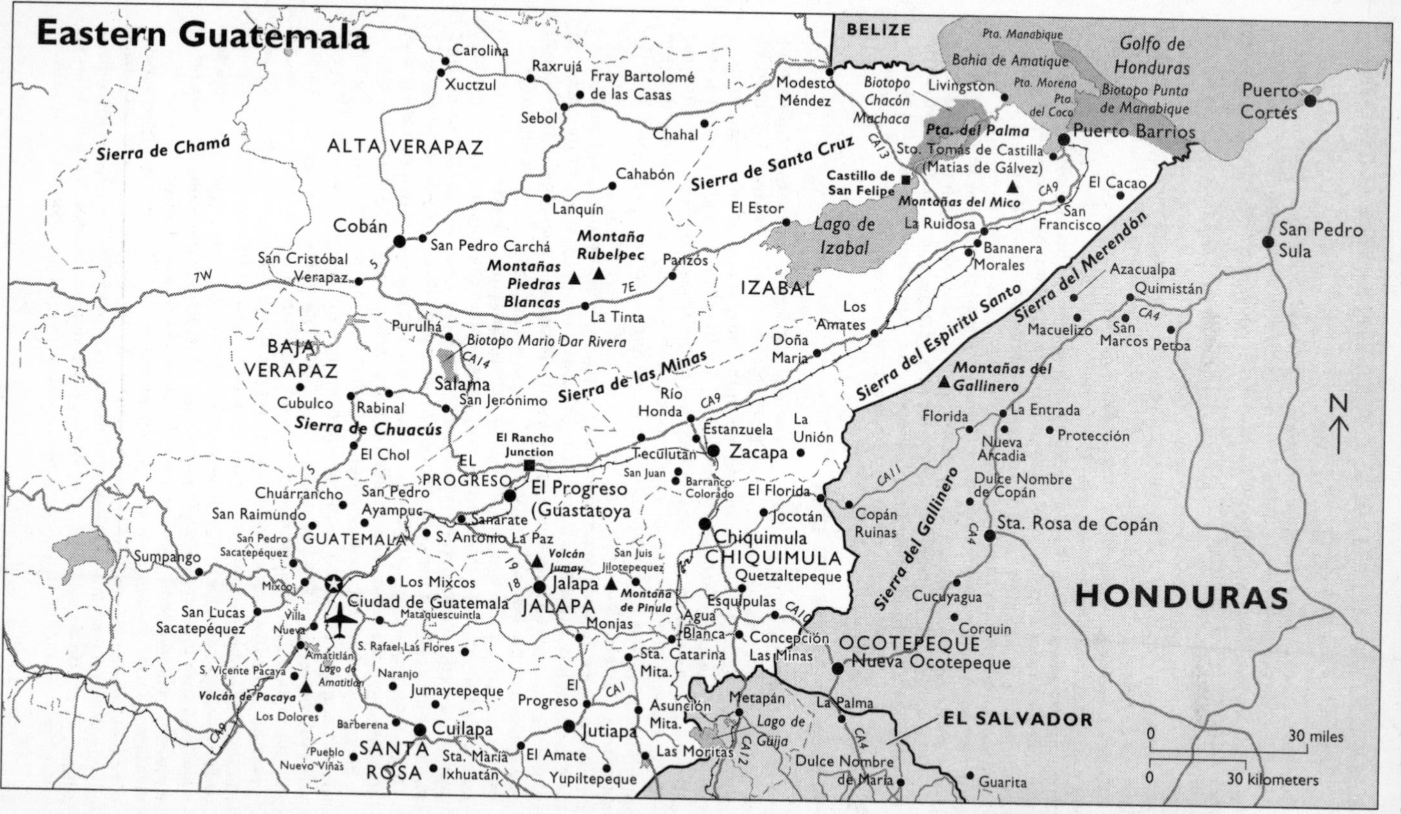
Eastern Guatemala
BELIZE
HONDURAS
EL SALVADOR
Golfo de Honduras
Bahia de Amatique
Biotopo Punta de Manabique
Puerto Cortés
San Pedro Sula
Puerto Barrios
Livingston
Modesto Méndez
Lago de Izabal
Castillo de San Felipe
IZABAL
ALTA VERAPAZ
BAJA VERAPAZ
EL PROGRESO
GUATEMALA
JALAPA
CHIQUIMULA
SANTA ROSA
OCOTEPEQUE
Cobán
Salama
Zacapa
Chiquimula
Esquipulas
Jalapa
Jutiapa
Cuilapa
Ciudad de Guatemala
El Progreso (Guastatoya)
Copán Ruinas
Sta. Rosa de Copán
Nueva Ocotepeque
Sierra del Merendón
Sierra del Espiritu Santo
Sierra de las Minas
Sierra de Santa Cruz
Sierra de Chuacús
Sierra de Chamá
Sierra del Gallinero
Montañas del Mico
Lago de Güija
Volcán de Pacaya
El Rancho Junction
30 miles
30 kilometers

■ NEAR ESQUIPULAS: CROSSING THE BORDER INTO HONDURAS

From the center of town, taxi and *colectivo* drivers can take you to **Agua Caliente,** the site of the border crossing. While both taxis and *colectivos* cost about Q4, taxis usually make it to the border more quickly. And though money can be exchanged in Esquipulas, better rates can be had at the border.

The immigration office at the border in Agua Caliente is open daily from 4am-9pm. Your passport will be marked with a free 30-day tourist stamp. Quetzales can be exchanged by any of the wad-flashing, calculator-toting money-changers; ask around to get the best rate. Dollars and traveler's checks can be changed at the **ACOSA Casa de Cambio** (open daily 6am-5pm). Remember to push your watch forward by an hour on your way into Honduras.

If you're driving across the border, go to the *tránsito* office around the corner from immigration. The form you fill out (and the fee you pay) depends on your plans. (See Honduras: Practical Information: Documents and Formalities, page 202, for information on paperwork and fees.)

Buses go to San Pedro Sula at 8am, 1pm, and 3pm daily; look for the yellow schoolbuses of the **Sonotran** line. These buses crawl as slowly as a slug over the misty hills; bring along something to read. These buses also hit **Santa Rosa de Copán** and **La Entrada,** from whence other buses run regularly to **Copán Ruínas.** Sometimes pick-ups run from the border directly to Copán, and some folks hitch.

■■■ QUIRIGUÁ

In the first century, Quiriguá broke away from the arm of the Maya empire headquartered in Copán and, under the indefatigable leadership of **Cavac Sky,** immediately began to carve out the enormous stone monuments that would bring it prestige long after the empire's demise. Work on the stelae continued under leader after leader, flourishing (along with the city) during the early classic period of the Maya (250-400 AD). In typically mysterious Mayan form, Quiriguá collapsed by the late classic period (600-900 AD). The ruins remained forgotten until John C. Stephens arrived in 1840.

Thatch roofs abate the wear and tear on the seven stelae (designated with letters of the alphabet). Stela E, relatively towering at a strapping 12m, is the tallest in Mesoamerica and is featured on the 10-centavo Guatemala coin. The archaeological site consists of the **Plaza Central,** where the stelae are located, the **stadium** for the Mayan ball game at the southwest end of the plaza, and the **Acropolis,** the residence quarters of the elite, to the south of the plaza. The surrounding forest provides a beautiful green backdrop, but try to go early in the day to avoid the heat and humidity, and lather up with mosquito repellent (open daily 8am-5:30pm; admission Q1). To get there, take one of the buses, which run from the highway down a dirt road and through 3.5km of banana plantation to the ruins (every 20min., 15min., Q1).

Pickin's are slim for food and hotels; Quiriguá is best made a daytrip from Río Hondo or a stop en route to somewhere else along the Atlantic Highway. The town of **Los Amates,** just a few kilometers down *Carretera al Atlántico,* 4km west of the turnoff to the ruins, is home to **Hotel Royal,** itself a great place to rest your inscription-filled head; the large, clean rooms pass the white-glove test (singles Q17, doubles Q27). The **restaurant** in front serves inexpensive, full-course meals, while a **billiard table** next door lets you ruin a rack or two. Also in Los Amates is **Hotel/Restaurant Santa Monica,** at the Texaco station. The yellow brick building has balconies, wrought iron, and fans (singles Q25, doubles Q50).

There is a **public phone** at the Texaco station and an administered phone half a block farther (open daily 7:30am-9pm). Along the single main street of Los Amates you'll also find a **post** and **telegram** office (open Mon.-Fri. 7am-6pm) and a pharmacy, **Farmacia Salud** (open daily 7am-7pm). From Los Amates, there are bus connections to Guatemala City (every 30min., 6am-6pm, 4 hrs., Q30); to Puerto Barrios (every 30min., 6am-9pm, 1½ hrs., Q6); and to Chiquimula (every 30min., 6am-6pm, 2 hrs., Q7).

LAGO IZABAL

Lago Izabal, the largest lake in Guatemala, empties out from Río Dulce and then into the Caribbean. These three bodies of water together make one of the most alluring and lusciously lush parts of the country. The lake is still home to the endangered manatee (sea cow), and while not the best place to swim (the water tends to be on the shallow and muddy side), there are no waves, and so it's ideal for water sports. Izabal isn't very much like Atitlán, and some say there's no comparison, but without good reason: the enormous variety of colorful birds and ultra-*tranquillo* Guatemalans who inhabit the lake's shore prosper in perfect harmony with the water's serenity and contribute to a combination that more than merits a visit.

■■■ MARISCOS

The quiet beat of Lago Izabal's waves and the gentle rock of ubiquitous hammocks are the only timekeepers in Mariscos, situated on the southern shore of the lake, 14km from Cruzero Trincheras. Uninhabited mountains melt into grazing fields dotted with horses and cattle, and these join the occasional thatch-roofed bamboo hut to set a scene of untamed beauty and happy oblivion.

Everything is located on one street in Mariscos. The **post office** sits immediately north of Distribuidora Marinela (open Mon.-Fri. 7:30am-noon and 2-6pm). **Guatel,** next door, is open daily from 8am-8pm. The **police** station is on a small plot which adjoins the main street opposite Comedor Los Pilotos (open 24 hrs.). The medical center, **Puesto de Salud,** is right next door (open Mon.-Fri. 8am-4pm). For all other services (banks, bookstores, etc.), go back to civilization.

One **bus** leaves for Guatemala City (daily at 8am, 5 hrs., Q14) and one for Puerto Barrios (8am, 3 hrs., Q6). Other than that, Mariscos's only connection with the outside world is a lone truck that shuttles back-and-forth at random intervals between the village and **Cruzero Trincheras** on the highway (1 hr., Q3). The bus going to Puerto Barrios can also drop you off at Cruzero Trincheras. The earliest bus out of Mariscos leaves at 8am and the last into the village is at 5pm. There is a **ferry** which runs to El Estor daily at 1pm (2 hrs., Q10) and returns the following day at 8am.

Three nearly identical **hotels** house the town's rare tourists. Rooms in all three are minimalist in design and communal facilities are reasonably clean. The cheapest is **Hospedaje Los Almendros** (tel. 487-104), on the curve of the road (Q15 per person; some rooms have fans). But if you want the lake to caress your feet while you drift asleep, go a little farther down the street to **Hotel Karinlinda** (singles Q15, Q35 with private bath; doubles Q40, Q60 with private bath), where the walls don't reach the roof, or **Hotel Marinita** (Q15 per person; no fans at all). These two have attached **restaurants** with gorgeous views of the lake (open daily 6am-9:30pm), where pancakes go for Q10, vegetable soup for Q15, and fried fish served with salad and fries for Q20.

For daytime **entertainment**—if swimming and contemplating the surrounding beauty aren't quite enough—hike to **Playa Dorada,** a golden beach 4km west along the shoreline, or rent a boat (Q60 per hour per boat, 10 person maximum) from what looks like a parking lot at the curve of the road. **Nightlife,** on the other hand, is a challenge, even for the most imaginative. Occasionally, someone whips out speakers for reggae and salsa dancing on the main launch. If you're completely stuck, though, try the U.S. **action movie** shown daily at 7:30pm on the VCR in **Cantina El Corazal** (Q1, films change daily).

■■■ EL ESTOR

Some of that relaxed Caribbean feel must have swum upstream to El Estor, a town where neighbors gather around to watch TV, where blackouts faze not a soul, and where the young crowd moves in slo-mo, and it moves until the rooster crows. In addition, El Estor is within a boat ride from the ravishing beauty of the **Boquerón Canyon** and a dive or a cannonball away from the lake's calm swimming waters. El Estor is located on the north side of Lago Izabal, at a distance of 262km from the capital and 128km from Puerto Barrios. The village is much larger than it may seem at first, and its broad streets form a regular grid of north-south *avenidas* and east-west *calles.* Calles start with 1 along the lake shore and increase heading north. *Avenidas* start at 1, also at the waterfront, and increase as you move east. The street that starts at the main dock is 5 Av.

The **post office,** 5 Av. 3-53, on the east side of the park, is open Mon.-Fri. 8am-4pm. **Guatel,** 8 Av., 5 Calle, has the only telephone in town (open Mon.-Fri. 7am-9pm, Sat.-Sun. 7am-7pm). The **market,** 7 Av., 3 Calle, is open daily 6am-6pm. **Farmacia Providencia,** 5 Av. 3-04, at the southeast corner of the park, is open daily from 6am-10pm. **Clínica Médica,** 4 Calle 4-80, a half block west of the park, responds to **emergencies** 24 hrs., and so do the **police,** 5 Av., 1 Calle, across from the dock. The only **buses** running from El Estor zoom directly to **Cobán;** they leave from 3 Calle (8 per day, 1am-3:30pm). By water, the connection is to **Mariscos** at 6am (2 hrs., Q7), whence buses take passengers on to Guatemala City or to Puerto Barrios (see Mariscos, page 99).

All accommodations in El Estor are inexpensive, but some more than others. The best value is **Hotel Hillela,** 6 Av. 2-06, which has immaculate rooms with private baths and fans and the added bonus of a marvelous, palm-tree lined inner courtyard (Q17 per person). **Hospedaje Santa Clara,** 5 Av. 2-11 (tel. 487-244), is a large, two-story establishment with an extremely cool balcony-lounge (singles Q17, Q20 with private bath; doubles Q26, Q34 with private bath). The cheapest is Pensión El Milagro, 2 Calle 4-63, where use of a bed and a remote bathroom and shower (all guarded by an intimidating barbed-wire fence) goes for Q10. The best place to make travel connections, overhear tips, or just have a good meal is **Hugo's Restaurant,** 5 Av., 3 Calle. While conquering the steak (Q20) or chicken (Q20), see if Señor Hugo is willing take you on a boat ride up the Boquerón River the next day (open daily 9am-9pm). For good salsa music and welcoming ambience, take refuge in the bamboo hut of **Ranchón y Disco Bambú,** 4 Av., 2 Calle. A variety of sandwiches go for Q3.50, and fresh fish for Q13.50 (open daily 11am-11pm).

At night, choose between **Disco Bambú** and the daily 7:30 showing of action movies in **Salón Alan,** 11 Calle, between 7 and 8 Calles (Q1, films change daily). In the daytime, an alternative to dipping your head into Lago Izabal is to tackle the mountain terrain at the **bike rental** (Q3 per hour), 6 Av., 4-26, Zona 1 (open 6am-6pm). Or take the exceptionally scenic boat ride to the **canyon** of the Boquerón River. The trip lasts three hours and includes a visit to a cluster of small caves as well as time for swimming up- and downstream (Q30 per person, 2 person minimum). A flashlight is helpful, but not vital, since the caves aren't that deep. Make arrangements with Hugo at his restaurant (see above).

RÍO DULCE

A conduit between Lago Izabal and Amatique Bay on the Caribbean, the Río Dulce offers some of the most scenic boat rides in the country, occasional manatee sightings, and the unique Caribbean culture of Livingston at its mouth. It also makes a marvelous diversion of a few hours' time, well worth inserting into the formidable capital-to-Tikal trek.

A bridge spans the Río Dulce where it begins at the northeastern end of Lago Izabal. To the south of the bridge sprawls the town **El Relleno;** to the north lies **Fronteras,** where you can spend the night. Four kilometers upstream on the Fronteras bank is the fortress/town of **Castillo San Felipe.** Two bus lines travel to Fronteras: **Fuente del Norte** buses run from Guatemala City to Flores or snag a **Litegua** bus to Puerto Barrrios and get off at **La Ruidosa,** the highway junction nearest the Río Dulce bridge. From there, take one of the infrequent local buses the remaining 34km to the Río Dulce bridge. Launches beneath the bridge will shuttle passengers to and from nearby sights (see Livingston, below, for details).

■■■ CASTILLO SAN FELIPE

A 17th century Spanish fortress built to stave off plundering pirates, the **Castillo de San Felipe** roosts in all its cannon-bristling splendor at the mouth of the Río Dulce, at one end of Lake Izabal. Bring a flashlight if you've got one—it'll help to spelunk the maze of tunnels leading through the dungeons. A cartoon history of the oft-plundered castle (in Spanish or in English) is free with the Q5 entrance fee. The Castillo grounds also include a creature-from-the-deep-colored pool (Q2), bathrooms, clocks, picnic facilities, and a **restaurant** (fried chicken Q15; burgers Q5.50; open daily 7am-6pm). Hordes of Guatemalan weekenders flock to the castle for family outings (open daily 8am-5pm). An alternative to swimming in the pool is swimming in the lake at **Playa La Cabaña,** 300m west. An alternative to swimming altogether is shimmying to the beat at the **Discoteque Conga** next door.

The budget option of the area is the **Hotel Don Humberto,** 300m west of the Castillo San Felipe. Small cement rooms have royal beds and private baths. The reign of tranquility is regularly shattered here by an early-morning radio show (singles Q35, doubles Q53, triples Q70). RV parking is available at the **Tienda Glendy** next to Don Humberto. If you really want reed-woven walls to whistle you to sleep, walk ½km back to Fronteras for **La Cabaña de Viajero,** on the beach. Communal facilities are campy but clean (singles Q20, Q25 with private bath; doubles Q35, Q40 with private bath). Downstairs the restaurant serves *mojarra* (a fish—Q20) and sandwiches for Q5 (open 7am-10pm).

San Felipe can be reached by private *lancha,* from the Río Dulce bridge (one way Q40). There is also a 4km-long road between Fronteras and San Felipe, but there is no regular transport, so either walk its distance, or hire a pick-up from Fronteras' main street (Q25). Some may find that passing vehicles give rides along this road.

■■■ LIVINGSTON

Where the Río Dulce tickles the waves of the Atlantic, life is oh-so-sweet. Livingston is Guatemala's riff on the laid-back Caribbean, mon, tracing its roots back to African slaves brought to the New World, who then joined sailors and indigenous Maya to form a distinct culture and language incorporating African, Mayan, and European elements. Once the largest port in Central America, Livingston now fritters away its hours with all-week partying and the shuttling of tourists to the wild array of nearby beautiful sites, from the cascades of the **Seven Altars** to the effervescent **aguas calientes.** In town, steady infusions of coconut bread, fresh fish, and steady, streaming reggae and punta rock refine *tranquillo* to unheard-of levels.

ORIENTATION AND PRACTICAL INFORMATION

Livingston really only has two main streets, and they run perpendicular to each other. Each is parallel to a different beach, however, because the town basks along a promontory. The largest street (known as the "principal street") leads directly up a hill from the main dock, and the other ("secondary street") branches left at the public school.

The **police** are on the main street leading up from the dock, right after the Guatel sign (open 24 hrs.; knock if the door is closed). Change **traveler's checks** at **Banco Commercial,** to the left of the launch (open Mon.-Fri. 8:30am-4pm). **Guatel** is on the hill leading up from the dock (open daily 7am-7pm). **The Budget Traveler** (tel. 48-1094) has an office right across from Guatel in Colibri. The **post office** is right behind it (open Mon.-Fri. 8am-4:30pm). (**Postal Code:** 18002.) **Farmacia Livingston** (open daily 8am-8:30pm) is also on the main drag. The **Centro de Salud** is above Playa la Capitanilla about 200m to the left of the Guatel sign on the main street (open 24 hrs.). Dr. Mario Serva Rossi works nearby, too (tel. 481-589), across from the Guatel sign (open Mon.-Fri. 8am-noon and 2-6pm).

Fire-breathing buses are nowhere to be found; Livingston is only accessible by water. Public **boats** leave for Puerto Barrios daily at 5am and 2pm (1½ hrs., Q2.40-3.50). Private *lanchas* leave from the same dock every hour or as soon as there are five or six people gathered (Q15 per person, 25min.). *Expressos* leave whenever you want them for Q150 per trip (6 person maximum). To the Río Dulce bridge and Fronteras (to connect with the road to Flores, Tikal, or Guatemala City), there is a direct service with the mail boat (daily at 8:30am, 2½ hrs., Q15). Otherwise, private *lanchas* make the trip for Q300 (Q50 per person minimum), stopping along the way at the **hot springs,** the **biotopo,** and **Castillo San Felipe** (4 hrs.). Add Q10 per person for the return leg of the trip. With a *cayuco,* a smaller and less stable boat, the same trip is Q40 per person, plus Q10 for the return. You can also hire boats to less common destinations, but then prices are set on a per-trip basis, and it's up to you to find people to share the cost; six to eight people fit in a boat. Watercraft goes to **Punta del Pirata,** the **Siete Altares** waterfalls, the biotopo, and the aguas calientes for Q100-250 round-trip. You can also hire a *lancha* to Punta Gorda, Belize, for Q500 per lancha (6-8 people). Get your exit stamp at the **immigration office** in Livingston, located 100m to the right of the main street at the Guatel sign (open daily 8am-6pm). For more information on entry requirements for Belize, see Belize: Documents and Formalities (page 116).

ACCOMMODATIONS

El Chiringuito, a 1-hr. walk (or hire a launch) from Livingston on the beach, and 15min. from the cascades. Beauty of a deserted beach, comfort of cane bungalow suites with sitting room and bedroom, and the owner's unparalleled friendliness conspire to make this ideal place for longer vacations (Q25 per night, Q75 per week, Q350 per month). Attached restaurant serves outstanding food (vegetarian spaghetti Q10, fresh fish Q15).

African Place, at the end of secondary street. More of a palace than a place, with drawbridge and untamed jungle licking its doormat, this hotel takes you beyond the Caribbean back to the regal roots of *Gariganu* culture. The rooms overwhelm—high ceilings, inlaid tile, and a leaf-crackling tropical breeze, wafting in the window while fans circle above. The owner sells English books (singles 23, Q35 with bath; doubles Q35, Q47 with bath; triples Q47, Q58.50 with bath.)

Hotel Caribe, 50m left from the dock, the first hotel you see. Many travelers never go farther. Rooms are basic but clean, and the sound of ocean waves lulls you to sleep. Private bathrooms sparkle, while the communal facilities are a bit grittier. If insects give you the willies, look elsewhere. The singles have no fans. Lockout at midnight (singles Q10; doubles Q17, Q24 with private bath).

FOOD

Livingston's two main streets are lined with inexpensive eateries of the Garifuna, who lavish their *plato típico* with all things exotic. *Tapato,* a local favorite consisting of seafood and plantains drenched in a spicy coconut broth, can be so complicated to make that it sometimes has to be ordered a day in advance (and it's worth the wait!). For dessert, the Caribbean *pan de coco* and *pie de pina* will leave you wobbling back to your hammock, woozy with ecstasy.

African Place, (see Accommodations, above). An architectural beacon amid the tin roof diners, with a menu that charms. Some tables overlook the jungle. Chicken *a la nigerianer* (Q20), crab soup (Q15), pancakes with honey (Q7). Open Mon.-Sat. 7am-9pm.

Restaurant El Tiburón, behind Hotel Tucán Dugú. The classiest straw hut around, with a gorgeous view of Río Dulce's surrender to the Caribbean. Prices reflect the *haute* hotel adjacent, but the seafood entrees are so fresh they can almost speak for themselves, if they weren't already dead. Whole fish (Q41), conch or shrimp (Q40), lobster (Q94). Open daily 7am-10pm.

Restaurant Margoth, 50m down the secondary street. The Margoth may not look like anything special, but locals revere its specialties. *Tapado* (without the wait) Q30, shrimp ceviche Q15. Ice made from boiled water makes drinking *licuados* and *refrescos* a cool, safe experience. Open 9-11am and 6:30-9:30pm.

Banana Republic, 50m to the right of the Guatel sign. A cozy and oddly named hut lined with shelves of the few books in town. Vegetarians will feel right at home with fruit plates (Q15) and vegetarian pasta (Q18), but Garifuna specialties such as *tapado* are also available. Bring two books, get one in exchange.

SIGHTS AND ENTERTAINMENT

Thirty minutes down the Río Dulce through the looming escarpments lie the **aguas calientes** (hot springs). Boat drivers can take you to them, but travelers with decent nasal skills may be able to sniff out these sulfur springs on their own. The piping-hot waters form a natural hot tub beneath the encroaching jungle. The Río Dulce boat ride is well worth the time and money it costs you, even if you only got its last half hour, when the river winds through a towering chasm.

Chug up the river another half hour to the **Biotopo Chocon Machacas,** which supposedly protects manatees (open daily 7am-4pm). Your 15-minute jaunt along the jungle path in the *biotopo* will only flush out a jaguar or a tapir when the moon is blue, and the shy sea cows do a great job of hiding in the river. Still, the *biotopo* is worthwhile—if not for the giant tree ferns and butterflies on the walk, then for the eclectic collection in the "museum" (donations accepted), from a manatee skeleton to "white tail deer legs donated by a hunter." The resident flat-footed monkey does passable Fred Astaire imitations. The aquatic part of the *biotopo* includes several scenic lagoons; ply your boat driver to take you through them. The *biotopo* has a free camping area with bathrooms, kitchen facilities, and well-trained mosquito squadrons. Some drivers will continue all the way in to **Castillo San Felipe.**

On the Caribbean side of Livingston cascade the cascades, **Siete Altares,** a 90-min. walk from town along the beach (or hire a launch). By boat, the waves make it a bucking-bronco boat trip, and the crisp, clear pools dribbling with sunlight are light-years better than Livingston's beaches. Climb and clamber up the rocks, as each pool of water is more refreshing than the last. If you're walking, you can stop for refreshments or a stay at **El Chiringuito Hotel** on the way.

Mellow village by day, Livingston pumps up the jam at night, in a clatter of live Garifuna music. Bongo drums, tortoise shells, and maracas pound out frenetic, hollow rhythms while couples do the vertical dirty on the floor after downing sweet rum punch. Bars and beachside discos, however, have a bad reputation for drug and alcohol problems, robberies, and fights; watch your step. The **Banana Republic** (see Restaurants, above) unwinds with a long, sun-weary **happy hour** during the day, only to rewind, happily, with staccato beats starting around 8pm every evening. Following the music trail, **Ubafu Life Music** is 50m down the secondary street. Painted to resemble a pack of Life-Savers on its exterior, painted on the inside to depict Bob Marley's inspirational visage, the live music here is truly *alive* (open daily until 1am). And after converting whole-heartedly to Rasta mode, there's the chance to make travels that much easier with some **dredlocks.** Get 'em at one of the two locations on the principal street (look for the sign depicting a person's head) and throw out that shampoo-conditioner (Q30; minimum braidable hair length required). Finally, after thumpin' to the beat all night long, head for the **massage parlor** (look for the sign on the principal street). The illustrious Robert Soriano can bring you to new heights of relaxation. When not he's not kneading your back, he also makes many of the drums and tortoise-shell percussion toys played in town. They're for sale for about Q400-900.

■■■ PUERTO BARRIOS

At the end of the highway from Guatemala to the Caribbean, Puerto Barrios was once the nation's most important port. Recently, however, the city's significance has faded as commerce has moved to Guatemala's Pacific ports. Still, garrulous sailors haunt the bars and stagger through the streets in a vigorous effort to keep the town rowdy. When it's hot, the streets of Puerto Barrios streets whirl with blinding dust clouds. Because it's not much more pleasant when the weather's bearable, most travelers use Puerto Barrios only as a stepping stone into Honduras or Belize.

Change currency at **Banco del Café,** 13 Calle, 7 Av. (tel. 480-995; open Mon.-Thurs. 8:30am-8pm, Fri. 8am-8pm, Sat. 10am-2pm), or at **Construbanco** (tel. 480-540), 7 Calle between 6 and 7 Avs. (open Mon.-Fri. 8:30am-7pm). The **post office,** 6 Av., 6 Calle (tel. 480-748), is open Monday through Friday from 8am to 4:30pm. The **postal code** is 18001. **Phones** and a **fax** are available at **Guatel,** 8 Av., 10 Calle (tel. 482-198; fax 480-89; open daily 7am-midnight). For late-night medicine, try **Farmacia Americana,** 9 Calle, 6/7 Avs. (tel. 480-842; open Mon.-Fri. 7am-9pm, Sat. 7am-8pm, Sun. 7am-noon). In a **medical emergency,** call on **Los Bomberos**—any time, day or night—at 5 Av., 5/6 Calles (tel. 122). The **police** are available around the clock at 6 Av., 5 Calle (tel. 480-730).

Litegua buses, 6 Av., 9/10 Calles (tel. 481-172), go to Guatemala City (12 per day, 5-6 hrs., Q35). To get to Tikal in the Petén, ask for the proper transfer: buses leave for the north from La Ruidosa, which is about 45 minutes from Puerto Barrios. Just hop on a (non-direct) bus headed for Guatemala City and ask for the transfer. **Ferries** dock at 1 Av., 12 Calle, and go to Livingston (every hr., 8am-5pm, 30min., Q15) and to Punta Gorda, Belize (Tues. and Fri. 7-8am, 1½ hrs., Q75). Buy tickets to Belize at least one day in advance from **Agencia Lineas Marítimas Empornac,** 1 Av., 11/12 Calles (open Mon.-Sat. 7am-noon and 2-5pm.)

If you decide to spend the night in Puerto Barrios, you'll probably feel safest at **Caribbean Hotel and Restaurant Calypso,** 7 Calle, 6/7 Avs. (tel. 480-494). Cable TV is an added perk (singles Q70, Q88 with A/C; doubles Q105, Q129 with A/C; triples Q158, Q178 with A/C). The 24-hour restaurant attached to the hotel features conch with coconut milk (Q46.50) and a seafood shishkebab (Q46.50). The **Hotel Caribeña** (tel. 480-860), is ready and waiting on 4 Av. between 10 and 11 Calles. Simple square rooms boast clean bathrooms, a lovely view of the parking lot, and fans so powerful they tend to suck in and shred up the curtains. Check-out is at 1pm (singles Q35, Q40 with private bath; doubles Q52; triples Q65; quads Q76). The attached restaurant has a *menú del día* for Q13.

■ NEAR PUERTO BARRIOS: CROSSING THE BORDER INTO HONDURAS

Citizens of certain countries need Honduran visas to cross the border (for more information, see Honduras: Planning your Trip: Documents and Formalities, page 202). If this applies to you, then visit the **Honduran Consulate** in Puerto Barrios (tel. 481-483), on Calzada between 16 and 17 Calle. Ask for Gilma Magali Nuñez. Visas cost Q15 (open Mon.-Fri. 8am-3pm). Visas may also be acquired at the more conveniently located **Libreria Norte,** 7 Calle, 6/7 Avs. (tel. 480-467), next to the Hotel Caribbean. Ask for David Vargas during the hours that the consulate is open.

If you're coming down from Belize and want to go to Copán or take a well-traveled route into Honduras, go to Chiquimula. Buses heading that way leave from 6 Av., 9 Calle. Catch the hourly bus to Chiquimula; from Chiquimula, a connecting bus runs to Esquipulas at the Honduran border. If you want a direct ride and are willing to get up godawful early, a **Carmencita** bus leaves daily at 4:40am and goes directly to Esquipulas (6 hrs., Q13). Keep in mind that the ride from the border to San Pedro Sula takes about six hours. A **taxi** to the border will set you back about Q300; split the price with some new "friends." If you can find a good number of these who have aquatic aspirations, some **boats** in Puerto Barrios will run to Puerto Cortés, but usually for a lot of money.

There is another, more adventurous way to get to Honduras. Allow some time for the journey, and definitely get your exit visa before you leave, then ask around in Puerto Cortés for more specific directions for this trip. (Here's a rough approximation:) at the bus terminal, snag a bus headed for **Río Motagua,** to the towns of **Entre Ríos, Chinok,** or **El Cinchado** (every hr., 9:45am-6pm, 2 hrs., Q6). The only legal way to cross the border is at El Cinchado, and though it's possible to get an exit stamp here, you shouldn't count on it. Launches will take you to the border (Q25). After what usually amounts to a few hours on boat, walk 15min. along the river where another launch on the Honduran side takes you on to **Cuyamel** for 10 lempiras. From there, buses run to **Puerto Cortés** (1½ hrs., 5 lempiras). Otherwise, ask directions for getting to Corinto, which also has runs buses to Puerto Cortés. Come adequately prepared for this journey (with food, water, cash, and adequate supplies, should you have to camp). Some advise that this trip should only be attempted during the dry season.

GUATEMALA

EL PETÉN

Anyone taking a glance at a map of Guatemala for the first time can't help but be puzzled by the immensely vast, intimidating, and seemingly deserted northern region known as El Petén. The bewilderment is justified, especially since the southern and western parts of the country are so densely populated in comparison to this northern monster. The looming Petén region has not been particularly welcoming to humans, ever since the Maya mysteriously abandoned their power center at Tikal. Early Spanish settlers quickly found the jungle too dense and the soil too poor for serious mining or farming, and despite a brief resurrection of *homo sapien* interest following the discovery of the masticatory potential of *chicle*, only a tough-as-nails group of Guatemalans known as Peteneros continues to live there, set in both geographical and cultural isolation from the rest of the country. Meanwhile, countless non-human species flourish in the thick jungles, from giant rodents to tiny butterflies and skulking jaguars. In fact, although virtually no travelers would ever make the journey to ominous El Petén were it not for the resplendence of Tikal and other nearby ruins, most visitors who've actually gotten there agree that the pure air, moist from the jungle, the rustic, underdeveloped setting, and tantalizing jungles provide more than enough reason to stick around.

■■■ POPTÚN

Though considerably less spectacular and less popular than the Tikal area, southern Petén is a vital part of Guatemala's archaeological record. Unfortunately, its numerous sites remain largely undeveloped and would hardly attract anyone beside certified archaeological fiends. The real reason to visit Poptún, the largest town in South Petén, is **Finca Ixobel,** a traveler's Eden within daytrip distance of fascinating caves and gorgeous rainforest.

ORIENTATION AND PRACTICAL INFORMATION

Poptún's muddy streets yearn in vain for names and numbers. Buses arrive and depart from the gas station on the main street, but services are dispersed throughout town. The **police** (tel. 507-315) have an office next to the municipal building two blocks west of the gas station, and are open 24 hrs. **Change money** at **Bandesa** (tel. 507-312), located three blocks west and four blocks south of the gas station (open Mon.-Fri. 8:30am-2:30pm). The **post** and **telegraph office** is in front of Salón de Usos Múltiples, 300m north of the gas station (open Mon.-Fri. 8am-4:30pm and 24 hrs., respectively). **Guatel** (tel. 507-298) is three blocks west and half a block south of the gas station (open daily 7am-9pm). The **market,** a block west of the gas station, is busy daily from 6am to 6pm. **Farmacia Hermano Pedro** (tel. 507-218), on the main drag and behind the gas station, is open daily 7am-9pm. The **Centro de Salud** (tel. 507-303), 150m north of the gas station, is open 24 hrs. for emergencies.

Maya Express (tel. 507-483), one block south of the gas station, runs first-class buses to Guatemala City (2 per day, 9 hrs., Q45) and to Flores (2 per day, 3 hrs., Q15). **Fuente del Norte** (tel. 507-290) operates more first-class buses to Guatemala City (4 per day, Q50) and to Flores (4 per day, Q15). A second-class bus goes to Guatemala City at 5am (Q35).

ACCOMMODATIONS AND FOOD

Consider spending a night and a day at **Finca Ixobel,** 3km south of Poptún, but if you are set on sleeping in town, there are several good places to do so. **Hospedaje Fonda Ixobel,** right where the bus drops you off, is run by the same people as the Finca and has big, clean rooms and big, but not-so-clean communal baths. Cold water only (singles Q9, doubles Q14, triples with bath Q20). For more comfort, try **Posada de los Castellanos** (tel. 507-222), in front of the market, one block west and half a block south of the bus drop-off point. Spotless rooms have neither hot water nor fans, but all have private baths (singles Q27.50, doubles Q33, triples Q38.50).

The best food around is waiting to be found at **Restaurante La Fonda Ixobel,** in front of the gas station. This place is also run by the same people as the Finca, so learn here what the Finca is all about and make your plans to visit the next day. All food (including bread, granola, yogurt, etc.) is home-made, deliciously. *Chimichangas* (big tortilla with meat, beans, cheese, and onions) go for Q11.50, granola with fruit for Q9. The banana bread of your dreams is Q2.25 (open daily 7am-midnight).

SIGHTS AND ENTERTAINMENT

Finca Ixobel, 3km south of Poptún, has become notorious for the spell it casts upon travelers, who come for a day, but end up staying for several days, several weeks, or even several months. Owner Carol Divine gained international attention recently after going on a hunger strike to motivate the U.S. government to investigate the murder of her husband, but her farm continues to delight throngs each year. The Finca offers thrilling one-day cave excursions—you'll swim parts, dive in deep, dark pools, and do a bit of rock-climbing, all the while balancing candles and flashlights (Q25; bring sturdy shoes and a flashlight, or buy one for Q12). For those who want either to conquer or commune with nature, a four-day trip plunges you into the spectacular jungle for four days, where you'll ride horses, sleep in a cave, swing in hammocks from the trees, and—if you're willing—hunt *tepeizcuinte,* ('cavy' in English; a rodent that gets bigger than as one meter in length). Do it all, including 2 days on horseback, for Q450. Also available are inner-tubing trips on the Machiquila River (Q60), horseback riding (Q40 for 2 hrs.), self-guided tours to two nearby caves (25min. and 45min. walks), swimming in a pond with an exceptionally scenic background, soccer, volleyball, ping-pong, frisbee, and the super-friendly company of other travelers. The resident spider monkey will try to suck up to you if you're eating, while the parrot retains a greater compusure and sense of self.

At night, sleep in a hammock or a sleeping bag (Q2.50, bag rental is free), a dorm bed (Q18), or an adult-size tree house (Q20 for a new model, or Q12 for an old one). You can also camp (Q10) or take a comfortable private room (singles Q36, doubles Q48). And watch your incredible expanding waist; the cook is a virtuoso and everything is homemade—from the bread and granola to the unforgettable family-style buffet dinners (Q27), enormous sandwiches (Q12-14), and five-star banana, apple, or carrot bread (Q2.50). The *tepeizcuinte* is only served on special occasions, as the rodent is dwindling in numbers.

To get there, ask the man who drives the bus out of town to drop you off at the big sign for Finca Ixobel and then walk the remaining 1.5km, or else borrow a bike from Fonda Ixobel in Poptún and bike the 3km south. Walking to the Finca at night is *not* advised.

The archaeological sights of **Poxté** (40km), **Ixtupu** (30km), and **Dolores** (28km), all north of Poptún, are all at least partially developed, though still very small. Dolores has the most to offer enthusiasts; the person to look for is Sr. Dacio Castellanos, an inspector of national monuments. (Ask local people for his whereabouts.) He will gladly take you for free to and through the ruins of **Ixcun,** 8km north of Dolores, or to **Ixtonton,** 1.5km northeast. Both sprout stelae and small temples and are accessible only by hoof (rent horses for Q10 per day). The tour and entrances are free. If you have a hammock or a sleeping bag, you can also stay at the guardian's house for free. All Flores-bound buses pass through Dolores (45min., Q3) from Poptún.

■■■ FLORES AND SANTA ELENA

Amid the dense wilderness and winding dirt roads of the Petén lie Santa Elena and the island city of Flores, an isolated enclave of civilization in relentless and grueling battle with the encroaching jungle. The two towns are connected by a causeway over **Lago Itzá,** which steadily threatens to engulf the fringes of the island while authorities work to siphon if off. Locals shuttle tourists to *biotopos* around the lake, which is sometimes scenic, but often so polluted that swimming is impossible.

Flores has been settled ever since the Maya reigned over the region, but the population remains tiny. There are very few cars on the island, and one could easily walk its confining perimeter in 15 minutes. Santa Elena, on the other hand, is an aggressive sprawl of shacks, banks, and streetside *comedores.* Despite the rigors of survival (and worries that new roads through the Petén will re-route travelers away from Flores completely), the towns vie to remain pleasant refueling stops for trips to Tikal and other, lesser-known ruins and attractions nearby.

ORIENTATION AND PRACTICAL INFORMATION

Flores' main street, Av. Central America, is round, like the island. Buses stop in Santa Elena's dusty market, just a few hundred meters across the causeway. Stock up for long hauls here, then head across the lake to Flores.

Tourist Office: INGUAT has an office in Santa Elena's airport and in Flores on Pasaje Progreso. Information is also available at Información Turística El Tucán, on Av. Central America (tel. 501-380), near the intersection with Calle 30 de Junio. Open Mon.-Sat. 8am-noon and 2-6pm.

Currency Exchange: Banco de Guatemala, at the end of Calle 30 de Junio in Flores (tel. 501-363), does the changin' thaaang. Open Mon.-Thurs. 8:30am-2pm, Friday 8:30am-2:30pm. **Bandesa,** 0 Av. and 2 Calle, is open Mon.-Fri. 8am-4pm. If you need cash after hours, several luxury hotels change money. Beyond the causeway, walk left on Central America and bear right at the end of the street. **Hotel Petén,** on the left, changes traveler's checks until 9pm, at a fair rate.

Post Office: In the center of Flores on Pasaje Progreso, just east of the central park. Open Mon.-Fri. 8am-4pm.

Telephones: Guatel (tel. 501-299), on the corner of 6 Av. and 5 Calle in Santa Elena. Open daily 7am-9pm. **Hotel Petén** in Flores makes international calls before 9pm; there's a Q5 fee on collect calls for non-guests. **The Budget Traveler** (tel. 500-527) has a branch in Tucán Viajes.

Airport: leave Santa Elena's airport for **Guatemala City** (4 per day, US$64-91); **Belize City** (2 per day, Mon. and Fri., US$63); and **Cancún, Mexico** (1 per day except Sunday, US$140). Make reservations at any travel agency. For the best deals, contact **Agencia de Viajes Arco Iris,** on Av. Central America in Flores (tel. 501-266). They will drive you to the airport for half the price of other hotels and taxis, and if you buy the tickets from them, for free. Open Mon.-Sat. 8am-noon and 2-6pm, Sun. 8am-noon.

Buses: Travelers intending to head to Belize from Santa Elena or Flores should read the **warning** on page 147. Second-class Fuente del Norte buses (tel. 500-517) leave Santa Elena from a yellow building on the right, three blocks through the market. Buy tickets in advance to Guatemala City (2 per day, 14 hrs., Q35) via **Río Dulce** (Q25). **First-class buses** leave daily (12 hrs., Q50) via Río Dulce (Q40). **Maya Express** (tel. 500-127) has a direct bus to Guatemala City (11am, 5 and 8pm, 12 hrs., Q50). One bus a day goes to Melchor de Mencos on the Belizean border (7am, 3 hrs., Q10). The office will store your luggage for the day (7am-10pm) for Q1 per piece. **Pinita** buses go to Melchor and the Belizean border (3 hrs., Q10); to El Naranjo (5 hrs., Q10); and to Sayaxché (2 hrs., Q5), departing from the Santa Elena market. Pinita buses also go to Tikal (6:30am and 1pm, 2½ hrs, Q10), as do numerous **express vans** (1 hr., one way Q20, round- trip Q30). Sign up for a van at any of the travel agencies and at most hotels in Flores and Santa Elena. **Travel Agency San Juan** (tel. 500-042), in Hotel San Juan, just off the causeway in Santa Elena, has special bus services to Belize, Chetumal, and Ceibal. **Rosita** serves Melchor and **Del Rocio** serves Sayaxché. Both leave from Santa Elena's market. To Poptún (3 hrs., Q6) and to Río Dulce (7½ hrs., Q50), take any of the Guatemala City-bound buses.

Taxis: (tel. 500-034), near the market in Santa Elena. From Flores to Santa Elena should cost Q10 or less, Q15 to the airport.

Laundromat: Lavanderia Petenchel, on Av. Central America in Flores, washes and dries in modern appliances for Q16 per load. Open daily 8am-8pm.

Pharmacy: Next to Las Puertas. Open daily 8:30am-1pm and 2-10pm.

ACCOMMODATIONS

Both cities offer an array of budget accommodations that may be preferable to shelling out the heavy cash at Tikal's resorts. Flores is the more expensive of the two towns, but it's also cleaner and nicer. **El Tucán** (tel. 500-577), Av. Central America, at the far end of the avenue on the water, has a gorgeous lake view; sunlight bounces off the spacious rooms and sparkling bathrooms are equipped with hot water (doubles Q50, triples Q75). **Doña Goya,** on the other side of the island, charges Q20 for clean, airy two-bed rooms (Q25 with private bath). It's a bird, it's a plane, it's **Hotel Itzá;** it's on Calle Principal along the lake shore. While the decor doesn't earn any super-rave reviews, the rooms do have private baths and fans (singles Q25, doubles Q30, triples Q45). In Santa Elena, the best-run place is **Hotel Alonzo,** across from the Guatel office. Bathrooms have an endless supply of hot water, and fans spin at hair-messing velocity. The Alonzo changes traveler's checks and stays open 24 hrs. A cheap *comedor* in front is open 6:30am-10pm. The Hotel San Juan, on 2a Calle, one block from the causeway, is where the 5am bus **to Naranjo** departs (singles Q25; doubles Q25, with bath Q50; triples Q60).

FOOD

In Santa Elena, cheapo (and sometimes unsanitary) *comedores* rule the day, offering standard fare of eggs and beans for Q10; chicken and meat generally go for Q15. In Flores, **Las Puertas,** with classical music by day and jazz by night, has pretty much cornered the health food market: Q16 gets you carrot juice, yogurt licuados, and a mountain of fresh fruit and natural yogurt over pancakes (open 8am-midnight). Serving the rest of the local vegetarian dishes is **Restaurant Lago Azul,** 2 Calle and 4 Av. Small portions of vegetable soup Q5, spaghetti Q7, chicken with fries and salad Q15. For a bit more culinary personality, cross the causeway and search Flores' nooks and crannies, where exotic specialties like *tepeizcuinte,* deer, and armadillo await in an overwrought jungle decor. **La Mesa de los Mayas,** on El Crucero off Av. Central America, serves atypical *típico* fare: grilled deer (Q35), armadillo (Q35), wild turkey (the beast, not the beverage: Q35), and tongue (not the beverage: Q15). They're open daily 8am-11pm. **El Koben,** near Hotel Tucán, serves up the standards: *nativo* includes cheese, rice, and fried plantains (Q20), "Maya" includes tacos and *frijoles,* and "Petenera" comes served with *tepeizcuinte* (Q32; open daily 7am-10pm). For the Italian-starved, **Pizzería Picasso** serves ravioli (Q22), antipasto (Q10.50), and of course, cubist pizza (Q28). Pop tunes added free of charge.

SIGHTS AND ENTERTAINMENT

Tikal overshadows any diversions Flores and Santa Elena have to offer; still, the lake's attractions manage to keep travelers busy. Near the park in Flores, an **art museum** displays a good selection of local artisan work. On the lake is the **Petencito,** a small zoo with dishearteningly small cages. Nearby, home-made **waterslides** whip the foolhardy around rickety corners at Mach speeds. Careful: some judge these dangerous. Launches leave any time for Q50 (up to 5 people) if you just want to **cruise** around the lake. Swimming in the lake is not recommended because of pollution. Instead, visit the **Actun Can Cave,** 2km south of Santa Elena. If Actun Can, anyone can. The cave has 300m (30min.) well-illuminated paths with signs pointing to imaginative natural shapes, and several kilometers of unilluminated pathways, which have outlets as far north as Santa Elena and on the south side of the mountain (bring your own flashlight). To get to the cave, follow the street which is a continuation of the causeway; bear left at its end and then turn right at the red arrow marked (shockingly), "Actun Can" (open daily 8am-6pm; admission Q7). The **nocturnal** crowd's only refuge is to hang at **Las Puertas** (see Food, above), which cranks live jazz, Latin, and Brazilian tunes most nights of the week.

■■■ TIKAL

Tikal is probably the most fascinating archaeological site in the Americas. Situated in the northern region of Petén, 670km north of Guatemala City, the ruins encompass over 3000 different Mayan stone constructions, including six towers, two of which are entirely excavated. While other ruins, such as those at Copán, Honduras, are in pristine condition and are often more useful to scholars of Mayan culture, most travelers agree that witnessing the awesome immensity of Tikal's towers jutting out of the merciless jungle is an experience that goes *right* to the gut. Those fortunate enough to witness a full moon rising over Temple IV and the endless expanse of forest behind it invariably cite is as one of the most memorable sights of their life. And as a special little bonus, the surrounding **Parque Nacional Tikal** (222 square mi.) is nearly as intriguing as the stone temples. Falling fruit is a tell-tale sign of spider monkeys overhead; remote paths hide wild parrots, peacocks, lizards, iguanas, and buzzcocks; and lucky early risers may spot a sacred jaguar slinking through the undergrowth.

GETTING THERE

Not all roads lead to Tikal; in fact, it's pretty hard to get there. Most bus connections are made through **Flores,** one hour outside Tikal. Overland routes connect Tikal with Tenosique (Mexico), Guatemala City, and Belize City. The Belize route is popular (the buses run daily, between Belize City and the Guatemalan border, via San Ignacio), but is considered unsafe (see Belize, San Ignacio, and accompanying **warning:** page 147). Buses to Flores leave the border between 5am and 4pm (3 hrs., Q10). Get off at the intersection two-thirds of the way to Flores at El Cruce (**Ixlu crossing**) and catch either of the Pinita buses which run to Tikal (6:30am and 1pm, 2½ hrs., Q10). Microbuses also make the trip (6 and 8am, 45min., Q20). Few cars go to Tikal, so hitching is virtually impossible and not recommended. Consult either the U.S. State Department or the U.S. Consulate in Guatemala City about the safety of overland routes to Tikal (see Guatemala: Safety, page 46).

Buses leave from Flores directly to Tikal (at 4, 6, 8, and 10am, 2½ hrs., Q35), from Hotel San Juan, near the causeway. Tikal-bound microbuses leave from most hotels at 6am and 8am (45min., Q20), returning at 2 and 4pm. Some bus companies have instituted a policy of charging non-Guatemalans double the price for the trip, so shop around first.

Four **airlines** shuttle daily between Guatemala City and Santa Elena, which is just across the lake from Flores, and which is served by the same buses and microbuses. Buy your ticket in the capital of Santa Elena and book at least one day in advance. The planes leave Guatemala City at 7am and 4pm, returning at 8am and 4pm (1 hr., US$64-91). Charter flights from Mexico and Belize also serve Santa Elena.

Not surprisingly, buses from Guatemala City are cheaper than planes, but by land you'll suffer through 280km of jarring dirt roads in the leg between Morales and Santa Elena (see gray box, below). Should you decide to brave the bus, take the first-class Pullman, which has shock absorbers and doesn't make rest stops to relieve the chickens (12 hrs., Q70). The regular bus takes at least 15 hours on a good day (Q35). The wisest bus to take is the 5pm Maya Express, which leaves the capital from 17a Calle 9-36, Zona 1, and arrives in Santa Elena at 6am, in time to catch some of the microbuses to Tikal.

To keep up with the Indiana Joneses, take the wildest and most cinematic alternative: a boat and bus odyssey from Tenosique, Mexico. This involves a four-hour cruise up the Río San Pedro to El Naranjo, Guatemala (expensive at Q75, but fun). From El Naranjo, you'll bounce five hours east over dirt roads to Santa Elena (Q12).

Passing into Tikal National Park, officials will relieve you of Q30 at a checkpoint, 17km from the site itself. Save the ticket; you'll need it to enter the ruins. If you plan to stay in the ruins past 5pm, for the sunset, have an inspector stamp it (good until 8pm; the stamp is free).

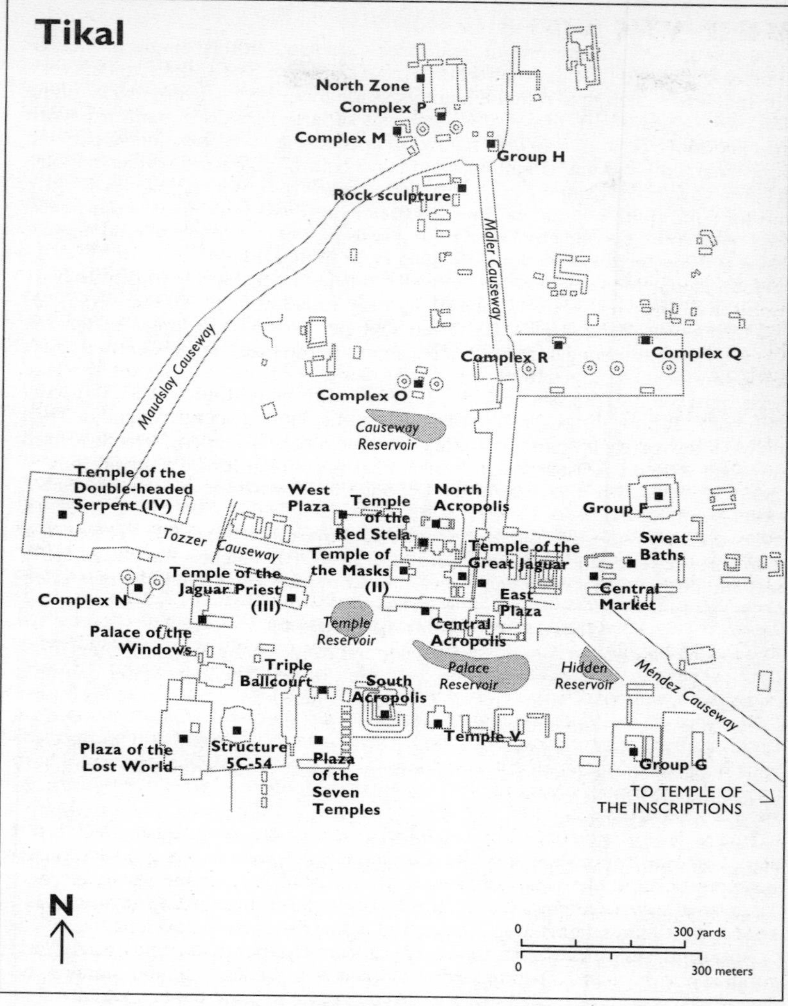

Because of its remoteness and the expense required to visit it, Tikal requires no special safety precautions. Camping, solo walks in the jungle, and sleeping in the ruins (though illegal) pose no unusual dangers (except possible arrest).

PRACTICAL INFORMATION

As befits a small jungle outpost, Tikal offers few services. There is a small **visitor's center** which has a scale model of the site and sells maps (Q2) and guidebooks (Q45). It's located in the large building on the left, next to the **Café Restaurant del Parque. Change money** before you get there; the exchange rate in hotels here is 10% worse than in banks and even hotels in Flores. The **post office** (open Mon.-Fri. 8am-noon and 2-4pm, **telegraph** 8am-noon and 2-6pm) is on the right as you enter the complex. There are **public bathrooms** in the visitor's center and throughout the archaeological site. For **medical emergencies,** go to Flores; the clinic at Tikal has minimal resources (open Mon.-Fri. 7am-noon and 2-5pm).

ACCOMMODATIONS AND FOOD

Tikal has one good campground and three expensive hotels. Single rooms are expensive, and it'd be wise to travel to Tikal in groups of two or three to cut costs. The hotels have started to rent out hammocks for about Q30. The popular camping complex, set in a vast, grassy field, consists of large, concrete platforms with thatched roofs. Less amiable than fellow backpackers are the mosquito squads and occasional scorpions and tarantulas. Communal bathrooms have showers, but lockers aren't available. Camping costs Q30 per person. To rent a hammock add Q10, and for a mosquito net add another Q5 (2-person tents Q20). Many a tourist has tried to sleep in the ruins by bribing the guards, but as one tour guide points out, this is as disrespectful as someone sleeping in the White House.

Hotel Jaguar Inn offers expensive, well-furnished bungalows with private bathrooms and three meals a day. Electricity only runs between 6-9:30pm (singles US$32, doubles US$52, triples US$72, tent Q60 per person). **The Jungle Lodge** (tel. 770-570) has basic bungalows with a restaurant in the main lodge. Electricity runs 4:30-9am (for those urges to blow-dry your hair at 4:45am), and current also connects between 5-11pm (singles US$15, US$47 with bath; doubles US$20, US$59 with bath). If bungalows drive you bonkers and splurging sounds splendid, **Tikal Inn** has a few pretty little rooms arranged around a palatial garden. Volts flow from 6pm-9am. The breakfast-and-dinner meal plan is optional (brace yourself: singles US$55, US$65 with meals; doubles US$55, US$75 with meals, triples US$82, US$112 with meals).

A couple of fly-infested *comedores* and a **mini-mart** face the visitor's center. The *comedores* have identical menus: eggs and beans (Q10), chicken and beans (Q15), beef and beans (Q15), open daily 6am-9pm. **Comedor Tikal** offers the best selec-

Riding on the Highway of Hell

Although many tourists get to Tikal quickly and painlessly by airplane, others opt for the 15-hour bus ride, a journey which has gained legendary status among travelers around the world. To help you decide, here's an hour-by-hour account of what you're getting into when you go with the bus:

Hour 1: Giddy with optimism, you take your seat, self-assuredly chuckling about the chickens in the overhead compartment and the "Jesus is my Pilot" stickers plastering the driver's window.

Hour 3: The driver's miraculous whipping by other vehicles on blind, uphill roads is convincing enough that yes, Jesus really must be on his side.

Hour 4: A bitter, fowl stench wafts from above, as chickens cease to seem cute.

Hour 5: At Río Dulce, more people get on, and now you're packed in three to a seat. Miserable souls in the aisle don't stand so much as they lean on each other. For lack of room, two *gringos* get tossed on the roof.

Hour 7: Bug-eyed and nauseous, you quickly learn to anticipate the biggest bumps by that extra split-second in which the bus hovers in mid-air before crashing down; that tickling in your tailbone bursts into raw pain.

Hour 9: The road narrows and the universe shakes. Your bus squeezes past another as grating metal shrieks and glass cracks. Acrobatically shifting your tailbone onto its least painful spot, you wonder if the guys on top have fallen off yet.

Hour 12: Just past Poptún, the bus slows and everyone peers out the window to gawk down the 150m cliff at The Bus Who Didn't Make It, overturned and half-concealed in the foliage. You gulp and murmur a quick prayer.

Hour 15: Your butt feels like it was brutally spanked by the Hand of God for all the sins you ever thought of committing, but the bus has pulled into Santa Elena—home free. A vendor at the terminal sells "I took the bus to Tikal and survived" t-shirts, and the frazzled couple from the top of the bus wave quetzales at him like born-again lunatics. As the sound of a jet shuttling in passengers overhead reminds you that the last fifteen hours were a self-induced hardship, granting you passage into that travel elite, you waddle toward that vendor, too.

tion for budget travelers (sandwiches for Q8-15, vegetarian dishes Q15, spaghetti Q10), open daily 7am-9pm. The **Restaurant Jaguar Inn** caters to the millionaire-at-eighteen crowd, with bean prices set accordingly. A full breakfast (pancake, eggs, fried bananas, homemade bread, and coffee) costs Q15. Complete lunches and dinners go for Q30 (open daily 7am-9pm).

SIGHTS

How cool is this place? George Lucas considered it worthy enough to be the setting for *Star Wars,* in which the ruins are shown to be part of the rebel base near the planet **Javin.** Ceramic shards reveal little about civilizations from a long, long ago in a galaxy far, far away, but they of manage to prove that the ancient Maya settled the site at Tikal at least as early as 600 BC. Seashells from the Pacific Coast and jade from the highlands testify to Tikal's extensive role in the Mesoamerican trade network. Architectural details and artifacts from several tombs suggest that Tikal was influenced by distant Teotihuacán, near modern Mexico City. Most of the temples and other constructions at Tikal date from the late classic period (550-900 AD), when Tikal may have had anywhere from 20,000 to 70,000 inhabitants. It thrived longer than any other ancient metropolis, but like Palenque and other important Mayan lowland centers, Tikal collapsed mysteriously at the end of the classic era. Competing theories as to the details of its downfall include descriptions of war with the Aztecs, a fast-spreading plague, or a catastrophic rebellion.

While postclassic descendants of the original population continued to live and worship at Tikal, they did little of much lasting significance other than pillage the tombs of the classical period. By 1000 AD, the jungle was the final usurper of Tikal's civilization. The modern world did not rediscover Tikal until a commercial expedition in search of chewing-gum stumbled across the site in 1848. Guatemalans **Medesto Mendez** and **Ambrosio Tut** organized an official excavation 58 years later to expose layer upon layer of platforms and monuments.

Begin your tour at the **Great Plaza,** Tikal's geographic and ceremonial heart, 2km west of the site entrance. The terraced **North Acropolis** lies ahead, facing north into the plaza. To its right and left are the symmetrical **Temples I** and **II.** The **Central Acropolis** is behind, exhibits the spiritual importance of the number nine—Mayans believed the a world beneath the earth to be ruled by the Nine Lords of the Night.

Temple I, a.k.a. the Temple of the Great Jaguar, towers 45m (145ft.) above the Grand Plaza. Built sometime around 700 AD, this structure, the modern-day symbol of Tikal, has nine sharply ascending terraces supporting a three-chambered temple on top. The first seven steps have been restored to their original state, but the stairs to the top are well-worn, and so climbing is extremely dangerous, and prohibited. Archaeologists suppose that the original builders of the temple could not have meant for anyone to simply walk up its steps, as on a casual stroll; rather, they climbed it, mumbling and grunting prayers between each massive stone level; the ascent to the top probably took several hours. Its uniquely westward orientation (toward the setting sun) and the fact that the other temples face it emphasize the temple's awesome importance among Tikal's constructions.

Across the plaza, **Temple II,** or the Temple of the Masks, is shorter and easy to scale. Excavations at the **North Acropolis,** a partially restored complex of temples, have revealed at least 10 levels of construction, all of which date back from progressively earlier eras, as well as several stelae and rich burial tombs. Descendants of the Mayans now leave their marks on the acropolis in brightly colored spray paint. The **ballcourt,** just south of Temple I, used to host wild games of *pok-ta-pok.* Rulers occupied the Great Plaza and buried their dead under great pyramids, while commoners lived in thatched huts and laid their dead to rest under kitchen floors.

One kilometer west of the Great Plaza on Tozzer Causeway, you see **Temple IV,** or the Temple of the Two-Headed Serpent (dating from 741 AD), the tallest construction in pre-Columbian America. Seventy meters (212ft.) from base to roof, the pyramid is almost totally cloaked by jungle growth. Clamber up the tangle of roots and ladders at the structure's northeast corner to the summit, where a satisfying view awaits. It takes walls 40 ft. thick to support the massive ornamental roof comb.

Temple V faces east, 500m south of the Great Plaza. The 57m (190ft.) temple has a small chamber at the top, accessible only by daring ascent up metal scaffolding. The subterranean **Palace of the Masks** has been buried for preservation, and is no longer accessible. Ornate hieroglyphs cover the looming roof comb of the **Temple of the Inscriptions,** 2km southeast of the Great Plaza. Most visible at dawn, the monumental symbols record the Mayan date 9.16.15.0.0 (766 AD). Ancient graffiti at **Maler's Place** tells of the Mayan practice of squeezing the head of a ruling class infant between two boards to create the high-status flattened skull. At **Group G,** the walls depict a human sacrifice in which the victim spread-eagled over an altar to facilitate the removal of his heart. The walls are channeled to allow orderly outflow of newly liberated blood. Unfortunately, the tunnel with the drawings has been closed to the public. Southwest of the Great Plaza is **Mundo Perdido** (Lost World). Rumor has it that the name derives from a depiction of two men making love, found in one of the tunnels in the complex. Teotihuacán's architectural influence shows through in hulking structures such as the **Temple of the Warriors.**

The small **Museum of Tikal,** at the entrance to the site, displays a collection of ceramics, stelae, jade offerings, and carved and painted bones. Richly detailed Stela 31 depicts Stormy Sky, a 5th-century AD governor of Tikal. Peer down at the reconstruction of Tomb 116, which contains a full skeleton accompanied by shells and ceramics, as well as 16 pounds of jade (admission Q10). The **Litico Museum of Stelae** at the visitor's center is free, and there you'll see stelae inscribed with legible, crudely deciphered hieroglyphics sit sheltered from wind and rain (both are open Mon.-Fri. 9am-5pm, Sat.-Sun. 9am-4pm).

Visit the ruins at dawn or dusk, when the air is cool and the animals most active. The tiny gray foxes living in Temple I gladly (and forcefully) share visitors' meals, as do the resident spider and howler monkeys, some of whom are bold enough to rifle through your backpack themselves. The poisonous, six-foot long fer-de-lance ("two-step snake," or *barba amarilla*), tarantulas, and scorpions lurk in the undergrowth, although sightings are so rare that visitors shouldn't be deterred.

Climb Temple IV at **sunrise** for a breath-taking view of the jungle coming alive and the ruins staying dead. Leave from the camping or the hotels by 5:30am to arrive on time. The Mundo Perdido pyramid is great for viewing the sunset. Bring mosquito repellent and a flashlight (for exploring dark corners and finding your way out at nightfall). The site is officially open daily from 6am-6pm (admission Q30), but you can stay until 8pm if you get the back of your ticket stamped in advance at the administration building (to your left, up a small slope at the site entrance). The ticket must be renewed each day. No food is available at the site, except as purchased from the occasional wandering vendor.

To view Tikal intelligently, invest in a handbook to the ruins or hire a guide; a quick study of the scale model by the museum provides a good introduction to Tikal, but it doesn't suffice. Tikal's major attractions are dispersed over a four square-km area, and few signs point the way. A useful map of the site (Q2) is available at hotels, as well as at the Visitors Center. Better yet, pick up William Coe's *Tikal,* the classic guide to the ruins, with a large pull-out map, beautiful illustrations, and a thorough, if often tiresome text (Q65). Tour guides are available at the hotels and at the entrance to the site (some of the most "studied" guides have merely memorized Coe's handbook). Tours that include the ruins, the flora, and the fauna last three hours and cost Q150-200.

BELIZE

Still in its late post-colonial development, peopled with a wildly heterogeneous population and graced with a nearly untouched natural beauty, the tiny nation of Belize fills a unique role in Central America. More Caribbean than Latin, this peaceful eye of the storm of Central American politics is anomalous in nearly every way. Apart from being somewhat more expensive than its neighbors, the country is otherwise extremely accessible to tourists. English is the official language, transportation is a relative piece of cake, and few other places in the world offer such mind-boggling diversity packed into such a small space (8,867 square miles, or about the size of Massachusetts). Ten years ago, many travelers viewed Belize as a stop-over between Mexico and Guatemala; the boom in ecotourism since then has increased the number of yearly visitors tenfold, and has made the tourist industry the nation's leading money-maker. Fortunately, though, development of the tourist industry has been kept far below the leviathan proportions of places like Cancún in Mexico, but the country's infrastructure is being pushed to its limits by the recent influx. Its most popular destinations are still the national parks, nearly 20 of which have been set aside for preservation.

There's an amazing array of things to do in Belize; in one day, a hyperactive traveler could snorkel at the largest barrier reef in the hemisphere, scale Mayan temples, and slide down waterfalls in a pine forest, along the way stopping in at a jaguar preserve or a baboon sanctuary. The country also offers plenty of opportunity to do nothing. Once they find themselves on one of Belize's countless idyllic beaches along the crystalline Caribbean, chomping inexpensive lobster and sipping smooth Belikin beers, many travelers don't want to budge an inch. It's hard not to fall in with this crowd, especially after meeting a few of the amiable, ultra-mellow Creoles along the coast. Regardless of their motivation, thousands more tourists arrive each year to explore the country's natural wonders and affirm the tourist bureau's catchy slogan, "You've got to see it to Belize it."

ESSENTIALS

■■■ WHEN TO GO

CLIMATE

A brisk prevailing wind from the Caribbean cools this sub-tropical climate. Hot and humid summer rarely sizzles at more than 95°F; winter cools rarely dip below 60°F. The rainy season extends from June through August.

FESTIVALS AND HOLIDAYS

Public holidays and local festivals are derived from both Catholic and traditional British sources; as a result, a party can pop up at any given moment. Some public holidays (when banks, post offices, etc. shut down) include: **January 1** (New Year's Day); **February 13-15** (San Pedro Carnival); **March 9** (Baron Bliss Day); **March or April** (Holy Week); **May 1** (Labor Day), **May 24** (Commonwealth Day); **September 10** (St. George's Caye Day); **September 21** (National Independence Day); **October 12** (Pan-American Day); **November 19** (Garifuna Settlement Day); **December 25** (Christmas Day); **December 26** (Boxing Day).

■■■ FEED YOUR HEAD

For publications and travel organizations of general interest, see Central America: An Introduction, page 1.

Embassy of Belize, 2535 Massachusetts Ave. NW, Washington, DC 20008 (tel. (202) 332-9636; fax 332-6888). Open daily to the public 9am-noon.

Consulate of Belize, 862 NE 2nd Ave., Miami, FL 33138 (tel. (305) 751-5655). Open 9am-noon. Belize also maintains consulates in New York (tel. (212) 599-0233), Washington DC, Chicago, New Orleans, San Francisco, Houston, and other cities.

Belize Tourist Board, 421 7th Ave., Suite 1110, New York, NY 10001 (tel. (800) 624-0686, (212) 563-6011; fax 563-6033). Exhaustive sheet of information available. In **Belize,** 83 N. Front St., P.O. Box 325, Belize City (tel. 02-772-13 or 732-55, fax 774-90). Detailed maps of Belize (BZ$5-6) and loads of loose info.

Belize Audobon Society, (tel. 234-987) 12 Fort St., Belize City. Information about all national parks and wildlife, as well as where to find the biggest bounty of beauteous birds in Belize. Sells a guide to Belize's wildlife (BZ$10).

Belize Center for Environmental Studies, Box 666, 55 Eve St., Belize City (tel. 02-455-45, 02-323-48; fax 02-32-347). Promotes sustainable management of Belize's natural resources; conducts research on social and environmental issues; disseminates information on both international and local conservation. Accepts volunteers/interns as positions become available.

Department of Archaeology, Independence Hill, Belmopan, Belize (tel. 822-106; fax 823-345). Provides information on ruins and archaeological sites.

School for International Training, College Semester Abroad Admissions, Kipling Rd., P.O. Box 676, Battleboro, VT 05302 (tel. (800) 336-1616 or (802) 258-3279). Runs semester-long programs featuring cultural orientation, intensive language study, homestudy, and field and independent study. Programs cost US$8200-10,300, all expenses included.

Jungle Drift Lodge and Tours, P.O. Box 1442, Belize City (tel. 232-842; fax 278-160). Canoe and kayak trips, high-canopy jungle walk, horseback riding and birding in Belize's Community Baboon Sanctuary. Lodging: double US$20, single US$15, camping US$5.

Laughing Heart Adventures, P.O. Box 669, Willow Creek, CA 95573 (tel. (800) 541-1256 or (916) 629-3516). Offers tours that include barrier-reef snorkeling, jungle canoeing, and exploration of Mayan ruins in Belize.

Glover's Atoll Resort and Marine Biology Station, P.O Box 563, Belize City (tel. 523-048). US$95 week packages include boat trip, snorkeling, fishing, and marine science lectures. Cabins have toilets and kitchens. Camping US$70 per week.

Triton Tours, 1111 Veterans Blvd., Ste. 5, Kenner, LA 70062 (tel. (504) 464-796; fax 464-7965). Airfare and accommodations organized for diving and ecotourism in Belize.

■■■ DOCUMENTS AND FORMALITIES

Passports are required of all visitors to Belize. Visits are limited to one month and travelers must demonstrate that they have sufficient funds for their visit and a ticket to their next destination. Extensions beyond 30 days (for up to 90 days) cost BZ$25 and are granted by the immigration office in Belize City.

Visas are not required for citizens of the U.S., Canada, the U.K. and Commonwealth countries, Australia, Ireland, New Zealand, or European Community countries. Other citizens, such as those of Israel and South Africa, may need visas; inquire at an embassy or consulate. A visa takes seven days to issue and costs US$25.

You will be charged a US$11.25 **airport departure and security tax** upon leaving Belize. **Third-party insurance,** required of everyone driving into Belize, can be purchased at the border from the Belize International Insurance Company (Belinsco) for around BZ$35. Be aware of potential limits on goods brought into and out of the

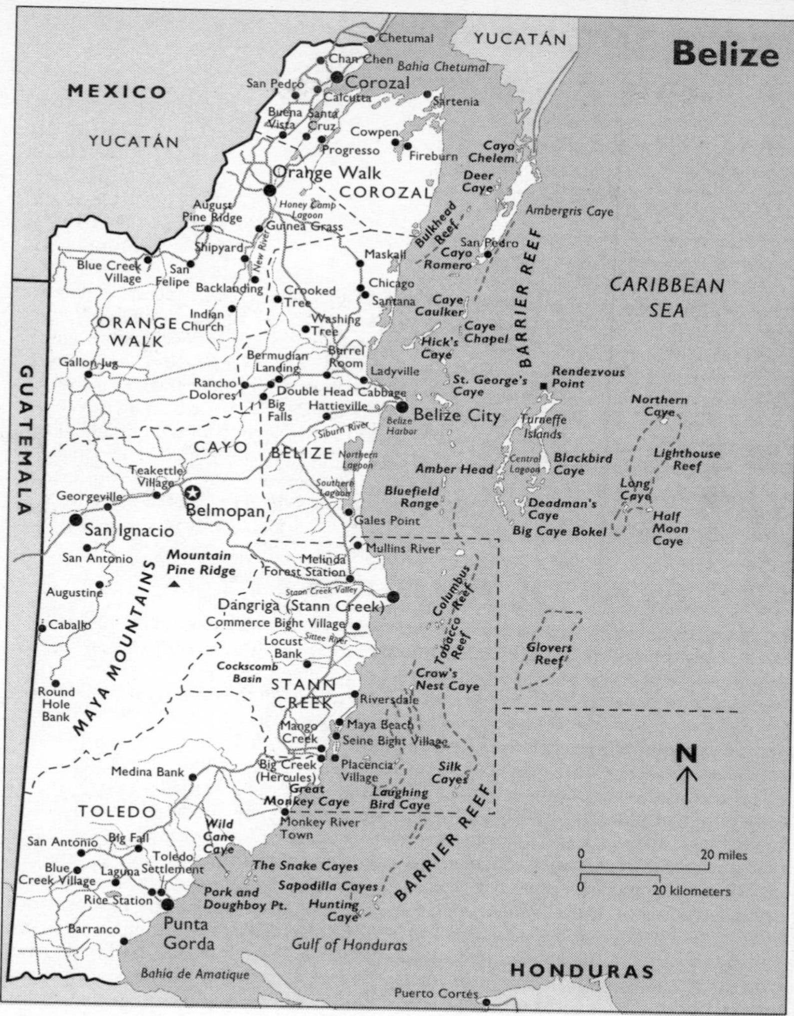

country. U.S. residents are permitted a duty-free tax exemption of US$400 per person, plus 200 cigarettes (or 250g tobacco, or 50 cigars) and one quart of alcohol for those 21 or over. Carrying certain goods will keep you out of the country; Belize will not let you in if an immigration officer suspects you of drug use. Attention, beachgoers: you may not leave Belize carrying fish, coral, or shells; and attempting to bring out certain marine species could land you in jail.

■■■ MONEY MATTERS

CURRENCY AND EXCHANGE

US$1 = BZ$2	**BZ$1 = US$0.5**
CDN$1 = BZ$1.47	**BZ$1 = CDN$0.68**
UK£1 = BZ$3.11	**BZ$1 = UK£0.32**
IR£1 = BZ$3.17	**BZ$1 = IR£0.32**
AUS$1 = BZ$1.47	**BZ$1 = AUS$0.68**
NZ$1 = BZ$1.31	**BZ$1 = NZ$0.76**
SARand = BZ$0.55	**BZ$1 = SARand 1.83**

The Belizean dollar is tied directly to the U.S. dollar, so exchange rates are guaranteed for Americans. The official rate is fixed at US$1=BZ$2 but actual currency exchange rates at banks are slightly below two for one. Most banks will only change pounds and U.S. and Canadian dollars, but many accept traveler's checks. You must show a passport and a return plane ticket out of Belize to change traveler's checks for more than US$250. Barclay's Bank is usually a better choice for cashing traveler's checks and getting cash advances, as they don't charge service fees. Strangely, businesses exchanging traveler's checks often do so at better rates than do the banks.

If you are coming from Mexico or Guatemala, it's best to exchange all your pesos for Belizean dollars at the border, since banks don't exchange unstable currencies.

The BZ$0.25 coin is known as a "shilling." U.S. coins are usually not accepted.

■■■ HEALTH AND SAFETY

See "Central America: An Introduction" for more specific information about disease risk and prevention in Belize. Don't bumble blithely into that great Belizean scuba vacation—prepare yourself, or you might find yourself in deep water, medically speaking. **Malaria** is a hazard everywhere in Belize except in the central coastal district. Recent epidemics of **dengue fever** have also been reported across the country, along with **typhoid fever, cholera,** and **hepatitis A**. Sunscreen is almost impossible to obtain in Belize, so stock up before you leave, in order to avoid a painful sunburn. As for water, "if it ain't bottled, you hadn't better," especially in rural areas.

The nonmedical hazards of Belize come in three flavors: the inebriated rowdy, the on-the-make male, and the anxious-to-sell-drugs heavy; a few Belizeans manage to wear several of these hats. Particularly in English-speaking areas (along the coast), expect hustlers and self-appointed "guides" to confront you at every step; firmly and immediately refuse their services, make it clear you won't give them money, but don't be rude (the problem could escalate). Public drunkenness is not infrequent in Belize, and women should take the usual precautions. The intensified drug trade has resulted in an infusion of U.S.-style gang violence into Belize. Visitors are often approached by dealers; to avoid a confrontation, some try explaining that they already got theirs elsewhere, thanks. Remember that the nearest **police** station can be reached anywhere in Belize by dialing 220-22.

■■■ ONCE THERE

TRANSPORTATION

The **international airport** is located 16km northwest of Belize City, on the northern highway. U.S. cash is accepted in Belize, so you need not change money at the airport. Try to share a cab, as the fare could run you BZ$30. There is also a shuttle bus that runs regularly into town (every 1½ hrs., BZ$2.50). It heads to town on Freetown Rd., passing Barrick Rd. and Hydes Ln., crossing the river over the Swing Bridge and down Albert St. (25min.). The **municipal airport** in Belize City offers flights to points within Belize, including Ambergris Caye and Caye Chapel (US$35), and other parts of Central America. Flying from the smaller airport is cheaper than from the international, enough so to cover the BZ$7.50 for the bus ride between them. (See Getting There: Documents and Formalities, page 116, for information on departure taxes.)

Travel is often over water, rather than over land—you'll find yourself hopping on launches and ferries instead of buses or trains. Water routes connect Belize City to Caye Caulker and Ambergris Caye; from Punta Gorda you can catch a ferry to Puerto Barrios, Guatemala. (For details, see the Practical Information sections of the corresponding areas.) Traditional overland routes are extensive, too, and Belizean **buses** are cheap (US$20 to cross the country the long way, north to south). Bus seats are often reserved, but just as often as not, someone will take your reserved seat. Be persistent about reclaiming it, and ask the driver for help, if necessary.

KEEPING IN TOUCH

The **mail** system is fairly reliable. It costs BZ$0.60 to mail a letter from Belize to the U.S., BZ$0.30 for a postcard. To Europe, letters are BZ$0.75 and postcards are BZ$0.40. First-class airmail takes about 10-15 days to travel between the U.S. and Belize. Pharmacies sell stamps and have mailboxes. You can have mail sent to you in Belize through general delivery. Address letters:

Tara Reddy
Poste Restante
Orange Walk (city), Belize
CENTRAL AMERICA

Belizean **telephone** offices generally provide cheap and reliable service. Calls to the U.S. cost BZ$9.60 for the first three minutes, and BZ$3.20 per minute after that. Calls to Europe cost BZ$6 per minute. Collect calls are free in Belize. **Direct-dial service** is available between Belize and the U.S. and Canada. To dial Belize from either country, dial 011-501, drop the first zero from the local number, then dial the remaining numbers. For example, to reach 02-12345, dial 011-501-2-12345. **Collect calls** and **AT&T credit card calls** can be made to the U.S. through an operator in Belize (dial 115). Belize operates on U.S. Central Standard Time, and daylight-saving time is not observed.

BELIZE: AN INTRODUCTION

■■■ HISTORY

Belize's unusual status in Central America partially stems from Spain's choice not to settle the area back in the 16th century. Frustrated by the area's lack of natural minerals and the Mayas' unwillingness to convert to Christianity, the Spanish moved on to greener pastures. Meanwhile, shipwrecked English sailors discovered another value for Belize; they settled the area (which was still under Spanish sovereignty) and took large quantities of precious mahogany and logwood (used for dyes) to finance their buccaneering ventures. After the 1655 capture of Jamaica from Spain, British soldiers (known as **"baymen"**) and their families joined the growing settlement. The white settlers imported slaves from Jamaica and other English territories, to log the wood. Meanwhile, British pirates frequently took booty from the Spanish Navy and hid among the Cayes, finding protection behind the shallow coral reef. After 200 years of uncertain legal status and skirmishes with Spain, England won decisive control over Belize at the **Battle of St. George's Caye** in 1798. British Honduras became an official colony in 1862, but by then the supply of wood was thinning out and thousands of Creole workers were left in poverty.

Belize's modern hodgepodge population results from the immigration of various groups in the late 19th century. Although Belize considers English its official language, only the most talented polyglots will feel fluent in all regions of the country. Refugees from the **Caste War** of 1847-48 and from more recent fighting in Guatemala, Nicaragua, Honduras, and El Salvador add a heavy infusion of Spanish, especially in the Cayo, Orange Walk, and Corozal districts. A Mayan people flourished here between 300 and 1000 AD, and then, for reasons unknown, abandoned their homesteads and migrated elsewhere. Their **Ketchi** and **Mopan-Maya** speaking descendants still dwell in Belize. In the Stann Creek and Toledo districts to the south live **Garifunas,** descendants of a race created when survivors of an African slave shipwreck intermixed with so-called Red Caribe natives, forming a new culture called Garifuna or Black Caribe, unique to Belize and the Bay Islands of Honduras. East Indian and Chinese laborers who came looking for work in the beginning of the century even out the cultural melange, along with a few expatriate Americans and several thousand German **Mennonite** farmers who escaped oppression before settling in the 19th century. Along with the Mennonites, nearly a third of Belizeans are Protestant, as evangelism was facilitated by the population's familiarity with English.

Recent Belizean politics have not been quite as heterogeneous. Since the 1950s, a two-party democratic system has gradually developed in the country characterized by the domination of the centrist **People's Unity Party** (PUP), which is headed by the cautious liberal George Price. On June 30, 1993, in an early election called by the PUP, the United Democratic Party (UDP), headed by **Manuél Esquivel,** broke the PUP rule for the second time in nearly 30 years in a fantastically close election. Still, Belize did not achieve full independence from Great Britain until September 21, 1981, and Guatemalans only recently relented on their long-standing claim that Belize actually belongs to them. The 2000-man British garrison, which had long guarded Belize against Guatemala's one-time onerous claims of sovereignty over the area, was scheduled to withdraw by September 1994 amid considerable controversy and debate.

Despite (or perhaps because of) efforts by the United States to transform Belize into a prosperous, fully democratic nation, the country is still struggling economically. Agriculture and tourism are the most important chunks of Belize's economy, although the timber industry has fallen drastically after wood was stripped by English colonists. Illiteracy is high, a hindrance unaided by the high tariffs on book imports that make bookstores nearly obsolete. **Slash-and-burn farmers** are starting to accept the role of ecotourism as an efficient source of income for them too, but in the short term feel hindered in their fight against poverty by the new restrictions on their land use. Still, despite a feeble economy, the people seem unfazed; national pride runs high. Most Belizeans cite their 53 stations of cable as proof that the country isn't underdeveloped, and residents live on happily, sporting t-shirts with the resounding phrase "Belize da fu we" ("Belize, there for us!").

■■■ THE ARTS

The artistic tradition of Belize reflects the nation's unique blend of cultures and the daily lives and struggles of its people. A growing body of Belizean **literature** includes Zee Edgell's *In Times Like These,* which explores one woman's struggle for self-definition and Zoila Elli's bright collection of short stories, *On Heroes, Lizards, and Passion*. Conducive to expression in all languages, poetry also has a strong tradition in Belize. James Martinez' departure from outmoded English into free-flowing Creole poems opened the way for folk literature and expression; Hugh F. Fuller's pieces elegantly depict the country's natural beauty, and the works of Evan X. Hyde, such as *North Amerikkan Blues,* are laced with biting political criticism. Unfortunately, these works are difficult to find in the country: the billboard just outside Belize City sums up the situation: "Be literate." While Belize waits for the epiphany that illiterates will need to read the sign, the country languishes in a meager supply of randomly selected books—mainly textbooks—and office supplies.

Internationally renowned artist **Benjamin Nicholas** is at the fore of Belizean painting; his colorful depictions of daily life among the Creoles and Garifuna hang all over the country, particularly in Dangriga, where he lives.

Shake your Soca! Pump your Punta!

Like that of other regions around the Caribbean, Belize's musical tradition resulted from the blending of Carib and African cultures. Some modern Belizeans (particularly a group in Punta Gorda) valiantly strive to maintain the markedly African dance and music of the Garifuna, notable for enchanting, triplet-based rhythms played out on large wooden drums. Infusions of reggae have led to the development of up-speed, backbeat-based *punta* and *soca* rock, which is popular at dance clubs. Soca music isn't as intimately entwined with body-shaking, but dance is crucial to Punta; to boogie with the best, try to stay stationary from the waist up, but below the belt let your legs flail like whirling dervishes.

■■■ FOOD AND DRINK

The types of food in Belize match the multi-ethnic composition of the population. Generally, the country's residents eat a lot of rice and beans, as well as beans and rice. Lest one protest this as tautology, note the difference: rice and beans is the two mixed and cooked together; beans and rice are separate, the beans soupier. Other commonly served local specialties are Garifuna and Creole dishes, which combine seafood with cassava, plantain, coconut, and green bananas, as well as a dash of the ubiquitous Melinda's hot sauce. **Escabeche** is a potent onion soup. A **garnache** is sort of like a Mexican *tostada*, a fried tortilla covered with beans, cheese, and vegetables, whereas the more distinctive **salbute** is a fried puff-tortilla covered with chicken, fish, tomatoes, or cabbage. A **panade** is a folded tortilla fried with fish (most often, shark) inside. For breakfast, **"fryjacks"** are similar to Mexican sopapillas (fried dough), and **"johnny cakes"** are closer to American pancakes. In addition, the nation supports a surprisingly large number of high-quality Chinese and Indian restaurants. Lobster is available in-season (June 15-March 15); restaurants ought to be (and usually are) strict about this policy. Until commercial chains over-fished and snapped them up at cheap prices, coastal waters were crawling with lobsters. Now our tasty little antennaed friends need some time for romance. A last resort for food in Belize is always **HL's Burger,** the self-proclaimed "Burger King of Belize." Along with the ever-present Coca-Cola, fruit juice competes with **Belikin Beer** as the most popular beverage in Belize; Belikin is light, smooth, and goes with just about everything. Lunch is the biggest meal of the day for most Belizeans, with dinner or supper sometimes referred to as "tea." Also important to know is the convention that "to have" means you'll eat in the restaurant, "to take" means you'll eat somewhere else.

■■■ MEDIA

Belizeans proudly enjoy one of the best-pirated cable TV systems in the world, though it's not clear if anybody's actually paying for it. International broadcasting is occasionally interrupted with congenial reminders like, "Brought to you by Social

Security." When not watching HBO, citizens keep themselves well abreast of international news with CNN. Cable also allows the Chinese- and Spanish-speaking members of the population to tap into programming in their own language. Unfortunately, Belizeans are not as on top of national news, although some read weekly papers such as *The Amandala*, which is helping to further a burgeoning African-Belizean movement. The government-operated Belize Radio broadcasts in both Spanish and English.

■■■ RECENT NEWS

Prime Minister Manuel Esquivel has encouraged a crackdown on the problem of illegal immigration to Belize; Asian immigrants were supposedly entering the country, from where they were eventually smuggled into the United States. The country's growth was down in 1994, but efforts to free up the economy (such as the privatization of Belize Telecommunications by MCI) are expected to boost the future fiscal situation. Meanwhile, Belizeans have been taking advantage of the fallen peso in Mexico, making jaunts across the border to purchase goods.

Belize City

Young Creole day-laborers wearing Chicago Bulls caps over their dreadlocks blast reggae music from shiny boom boxes while smoking joints the size of large cigars. The gospel yells of a Seventh-Day Adventist revival meeting mingle with the roar of buses arriving at the station. Unlike the rest of the country, Belize City (pop. 60,000) in many ways lives up to Aldous Huxley's bleak commentary: "If the world had any ends, British Honduras would surely be one of them." Streams of sewage flow in the canals that line the streets, buildings wobble on weak foundations, and the entire city needs a paint job. Belize City, it appears, is still reeling from 1961's Hurricane Hattie, which killed 300 people, prompted the government to move to Belmopan, and generally loosed anarchic and destructive energies on the metropolis. If you're psyched for adventure, the city admittedly pulses like no other place in the country; a vibrant (though rather hostile) personality oozes from every crumbling wall.

Be wary of criminals in Belize City. Don't show money on the street, and remove all jewelry; you'll look fine without it. Aggressive hustlers will walk beside and behind you, offering information you didn't ask for and demanding a cash payment in return (though some "guides" don't ask for money, they expect it). When a hustler approaches, be firm but not obnoxious, use all your common sense, and stay out of alleys. If you can, avoid the downtown/bus station part of town in favor of the relatively more peaceful neighborhoods to the northwest. Belize City is especially unsafe after dark—in the evening, walk with friends along a busy main street or take a taxi. Never park your car on the street in Belize City; if it is not spirited away altogether, it will almost certainly be broken into. If you must bring your car, try to find a private, guarded lot.

Still, every cloud has its silver lining (though Belize City is an awfully gray cloud). The city is definitely a morning person; the sun rises over cool, calm streets and the city's erstwhile colonial grandeur peers shyly through layers of peeling paint, even as the swing bridge's 6am rotation marks confusion's return. Most of the residents aren't out to get you, and are well worth stopping to talk to; many locals despise the roaming hustlers and crackheads as much as travelers do. And besides, rare is the city where so many characters are gathered. Most travelers are just passing through Belize City on their way to the Cayes or the interior. Those dead-set on spending the day here can enjoy a leisurely seafood fest in a good budget restaurant, and—armed

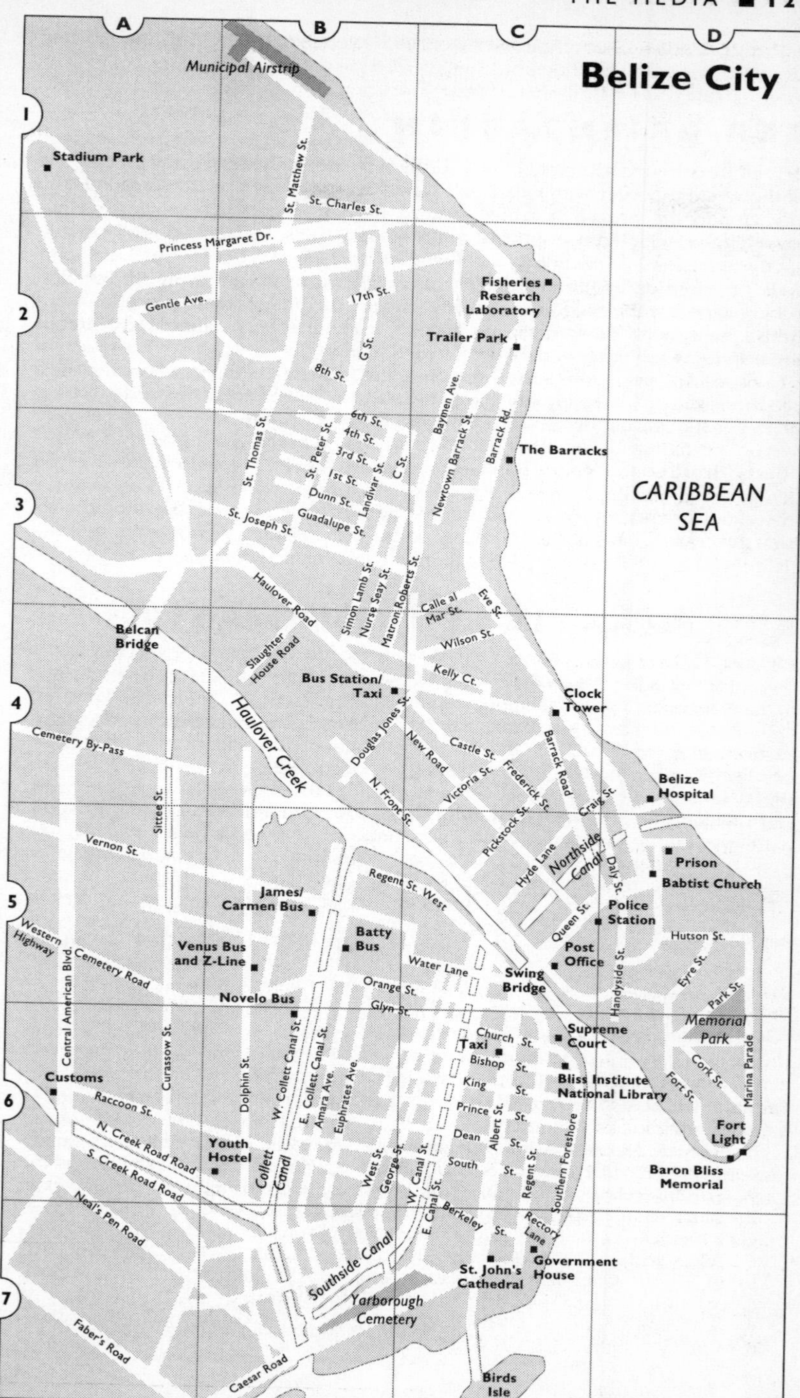
Belize City
A
B
C
D
1
2
3
4
5
6
7
Municipal Airstrip
Stadium Park
St. Matthew St.
St. Charles St.
Princess Margaret Dr.
Gentle Ave.
17th St.
G St.
8th St.
Fisheries Research Laboratory
Trailer Park
Baymen Ave.
Newtown Barrack St.
Barrack Rd.
The Barracks
6th St.
4th St.
3rd St.
1st St.
Dunn St.
Guadalupe St.
St. Joseph St.
St. Thomas St.
St. Peter St.
Landivar St.
C St.
CARIBBEAN SEA
Haulover Road
Simon Lamb St.
Nurse Seay St.
Matron Roberts St.
Calle al Mar St.
Eve St.
Wilson St.
Kelly Ct.
Belcan Bridge
Slaughter House Road
Bus Station/ Taxi
Clock Tower
Haulover Creek
Cemetery By-Pass
Douglas Jones St.
New Road
Castle St.
Barrack Road
Victoria St.
Frederick St.
N. Front St.
Belize Hospital
Craig St.
Pickstock St.
Sittee St.
Vernon St.
Hyde Lane
Northside Canal
Daly St.
Prison
Babtist Church
Regent St. West
James/ Carmen Bus
Queen St.
Police Station
Hutson St.
Batty Bus
Venus Bus and Z-Line
Western Highway
Cemetery Road
Post Office
Water Lane
Swing Bridge
Eyre St.
Handyside St.
Park St.
Novelo Bus
Orange St.
Glyn St.
Supreme Court
Memorial Park
Church St.
Taxi
Bishop St.
Bliss Institute National Library
Central American Blvd.
Curassow St.
Dolphin St.
W. Collett Canal St.
E. Collett Canal St.
Amara Ave.
Euphrates Ave.
King St.
Prince St.
Albert St.
Dean St.
South St.
Cork St.
Fort St.
Marina Parade
Customs
Raccoon St.
N. Creek Road Road
S. Creek Road Road
Youth Hostel
Collett Canal
West St.
George St.
W. Canal St.
E. Canal St.
Regent St.
Southern Foreshore
Fort Light
Baron Bliss Memorial
Neal's Pen Road
Berkeley St.
Rectory Lane
Southside Canal
St. John's Cathedral
Government House
Yarborough Cemetery
Faber's Road
Caesar Road
Birds Isle

BELIZE

with a thick skin—discover pleasant faces and voices behind the city's intimidating façade.

■■■ ORIENTATION

Belize City is 154km south of Belize's northern border with Mexico and 134km east of the western border with Guatemala. The Caribbean Sea virtually surrounds the city, lapping the virtually beachless eastern, northern, and southern shores. **Haulover Creek,** which runs southeast to the sea and splits the city into northern and southern sections, is spanned by the **Swing Bridge;** most services are within a short walk of the bridge. **Queen Street** runs northeast from the Swing Bridge, and **Albert Street** is the major thoroughfare south of the bridge (remember, this was a British possession). **Town Park,** at Church St. and Albert St., occupies the center of town and is two blocks south of the Swing Bridge.

Taxis, usually monstrous station wagons identifiable by their green license plates, can be flagged down on any street or at the stand in Town Park. The standard fare is BZ$5 per stop within Belize City, plus BZ$1 for each extra person. *Always* ask the fare before getting in, and never get into a car that lacks the green plates.

Batty Brother and **Venus** buses head north to Mexico, **Novelo's** goes west to Benque Viejo, and the **Z-line** takes the southern route to Dangriga and Punta Gorda. Bus stations are clustered around the pound yard on Orange St., six long blocks from the center of the city; it's probably best to take a cab where you're going, especially if you have a lot of gear. The stations are in a rough part of town—be alert.

BELIZE

■■■ PRACTICAL INFORMATION

Belize Tourist Board: 83 N. Front St. (tel. 772-13; fax 774-90). Cross the Swing Bridge to Albert St., turn right, 3rd building on the right. Offers cutting-edge maps of Belize (BZ$15) and heaping spoonfuls of information. Open Mon.-Fri. 8am-noon and 1-5pm. Closes 30min. early on Fri. **Belize Tourism Industry Association,** 99 Albert St. (tel. 757-17; fax 787-10), right on the road's fork.

Police: 9 Queen St. (tel. 722-22), at New Rd. Open 24 hrs.

Post Office: Queen St. and N. Front St. (tel. 722-01; fax 309-36), near the Swing Bridge. *Poste Restante*. Open Mon.-Thurs. 8am-5pm, Fri. 8am-4:30pm. Passport photos can be obtained at a small watchmaker's shop on Barrack Road (tel. 320-23). Take Queen St. about 3 blocks past Swing Bridge, turn left on Barrack, go ½ block down on right. Four photos for BZ$8. Open Mon.-Fri. 9am-4pm.

Telephones: There are public phones on both sides of the Swing Bridge. **Belize Telecommunications Limited,** 1 Church St. (tel. 770-85), off Albert St., has A/C and private booths. Direct and collect calls, no surcharge. To the U.S. or Canada, BZ$3.20 per minute, to Europe BZ$6.00 per minute. BZ$30 deposit required. Open Mon.-Sat. 8am-9pm (until 10pm for collect calls), Sun. 8am-10pm (collect calls only). **Faxes** sent at the same rate as international calls, plus a BZ$2.50 service charge. **Telephone code:** 02. **Telegram** service (tel. 771-79) is in the same office as the phones. To the U.S. or Canada BZ$0.32 per word, to Europe BZ$0.60 per word. Open Mon.-Sat. 8am-noon and 1-5pm.

Embassies: U.S., 20 Gabourel Ln. (tel. 771-61), at Hutson St. Take Queen St. northeast until it meets Gabourel and turn right—the embassy is the old white house on your left. Open Mon.-Fri. 8am-noon and 1-4pm. The entrance to the consulate is around the corner, about 15m back. **Mexico,** 20 N. Park St. (tel. 301-93), on the waterfront. Pass the U.S. Embassy on Hutson St. and turn right; it's at the end of the block. Don't make the trip from Belize to Chetumal twice in the same day—get a **Mexican tourist card** from the embassy's consular division before leaving. Travelers without cards have been turned back at the border. Open Mon.-Fri. 9am-12:30pm. **Canadian Consulate,** 83 N. Front St., above the Tourist Bureau. Open Mon.-Fri. 9am-1pm. The **British High Commission** is in Belmopan. If you're heading across the westward border, go to the **Guatemalan Consulate** for a free visa; otherwise, pay BZ$5 at the border. Take the shore road north until it swings west. At the bump sign, turn right. It's just over a block on the right; the trip takes 20min. by foot.

Currency Exchange: All of the commercial banks clustered around Town Park change money. The hard-to-miss **Barclay's Bank,** near Town Park at 21 Albert St., offers cash advances (with no service fee, unlike other banks) and exchanges all stable currencies. **Banco Serfín** (tel. 78-25), on the corner of Eyre and Hudson, changes dollars or Mexican pesos. Beware, banks close between 1 and 3pm. After hours, **Brodie's** (off Town Park) will let you buy a piece of candy with a traveler's check (with proper ID) and keep the change.

American Express: Global Travel Services, 41 Albert St. right next to HL's Burgers (tel. 771-85; fax 752-13). Will hold mail for cardholders, Box 244, Belize City. Other cardmember services upstairs, enter to the left of the Travel Service. 1% service fee. Open Mon.-Fri. 8am-noon and 1-5pm, Sat. 8am-noon.

Airports: Belize International Airport, 49 New Rd. (tel. 325-22), 16km northwest of Belize City. For an excellent guide to the numerous little airlines, check with Ernie at **Belize Air Travel Service,** 31 Regent; parallel to Albert—about 5 blocks south of Swing Bridge (tel. 731-74, 727-07). Fares vary by season. **Continental,** 32 Albert St. (tel. 778-27), serves Houston with 1 flight daily. **American Airlines** (tel. 325-22) serves Miami (4 times weekly). Miami, New Orleans, San Francisco, and central Mexico are serviced by **Taca Airlines,** 41 Albert St. (tel. 771-85, 773-63). **Aerovías,** 55 Regent St. (tel. 754-45, 754-46), flies to Guatemala City (BZ$187) via Flores (BZ$116). The **airport shuttle** runs 6 times per day and makes pick-ups throughout the city (BZ$2.50, call 739-77 or 778-11). Cheaper flights to the Cayes and the interior depart daily from the international airport and from the **Belize Municipal Airstrip,** on the waterfront north of town (BZ$5 for a cab ride). **Maya Airways,** 6 Fort St. (tel. 440-32), to San Pedro (every 2 hrs., 30min., BZ$35); to Dangriga (20min., BZ$50) and Placencia (1 hr., BZ$70) on the way to Punta Gorda (30min., BZ$84).

Bus Stations: Batty Brothers Bus Service, 15 Mosul St. (tel. 720-25), to Chetumal (every hr., 4-11am, 4 hrs., BZ$9; plus a 6am express, 3 hrs., BZ$10); to Belmopan (6 departures before 10am, 1½ hrs., BZ$3.50; continuing on to San Ignacio, 2½ hrs., BZ$5), and to Melchor de Mencos in Guatemala (5, 6, 7, 9, and 10am, BZ$6). To reach **Venus Bus Lines,** 2371 Magazine Rd. (tel. 733-54), take Orange St. 3 blocks west of Collet Canal, then make a right onto Magazine Rd. Afternoon trips to Chetumal (6 per day, 5 on Sun., 4 hrs., BZ$10); to Orange Walk (1½ hrs., BZ$4.50); to Corozal (2-3 hrs., BZ$7.50); and to Sarteneja (12:30pm, 3 hrs., BZ$9.50). **Z-line,** in the same building as Venus (tel. 739-37), services Dangriga (2-5 per day, 4 hrs., BZ$10) and Punta Gorda (2-5 per day, 7-9 hrs., BZ$22). From the pound yard across the bridge from Batty Bros., **Escalante** sends 3 yellow school buses to Orange Walk (Mon.-Fri. 4 per day, Sat. 12:30pm and 5pm, 1½ hrs., BZ$4.50). To reach **Novelo's,** 19 W. Canal (tel. 773-72), take Orange St. west, turn left immediately after the bridge and walk 1 block north. Service to San Ignacio (every hr., 11am-9pm, 2½ hrs., BZ$5) on the way to Benque Viejo (3 hrs., BZ$5.50) via and to Belmopan (1¼ hrs., BZ$3.50). Call the bus stations or contact the tourist bureau as schedules change often.

Supermarket: Brodie's (tel. 770-70), on Albert St. off Town Park. Bounty of food items, feminine hygiene, some books. They happily accept traveler's checks at weak rates. Open Mon.-Thurs. 8:30am-7pm, Fri. 8:30am-9pm, Sat. 8:30am-5pm, Sun. 9am-12:30pm.

Laundromat: Larry's Laundry, 33 Barracle Rd. (tel. 330-83). BZ$8 self-service or BZ$10 full-service. Open Mon.-Sat. 8am-5:30pm. **Stan's Laundry** is open Mon.-Sat. 8am-noon and 1-6pm and charges BZ$10 per load. Take Albert St. south. Turn right 1 block after community drug stores—it's down about a block on the left.

Bookstores: Stock up, as new books are hard to find in other parts of the country. **Brodie's** has some cheap novels. At **The Belize Book Shop,** on the corner of Regent and Rectory (tel. 720-54), a staff of helpful teenagers offer a motley mélange of travel books (around BZ$30) and English literature, as well as a history of Belize (BZ$25). Open Mon.-Tues., Thurs.-Fri. 8am-4pm, Wed. and Sat. 8am-noon. For those interested in **African-Belizean issues,** the store **Kremandala East,** 50 Regent St., (tel. 714-89), highlights African culture, crafts, and literature.

They host an annual African Liberation Day celebration every May 25 and sell groovy t-shirts. Open Mon.-Fri. 9am-5pm, Sat. 10am-3pm.

Pharmacy: Central Pharmacy, 1 Market Square (tel. 723-16), just south of Swing Bridge. Amply stocked. Open Mon.-Sat. 8am-9:30pm.

Hospital: Belize City Hospital (tel. 772-51), on Eve St., which intersects Queen St. about 5 blocks north of the Swing Bridge. Outpatient entrance (usually open until 10pm) on the corner of Eve and Craig St. For **ambulance,** call 327-23. Open Mon.-Fri. 8am-5pm. On weekends, go to the casualties entrance, 1 gate to the right. Open 24 hrs.

Emergency: Dial the **police emergency** number 722-43, or 911, or 90.

■■■ ACCOMMODATIONS

Budget hotels in Belize City consistently provide one indispensable service: heaps of good advice, both about further travel and staying safe in the city. Some places, sadly, are not safe. Check carefully the number of locks between you and a crafty burglar; although crime against tourists appears to be on the decline, safety is never in over-supply. Hustlers sometimes swarm to popular hotels, causing managers to lock their main entrances at regular hours each night. Be sure to find out about hotel curfew before going out at night, as some close as early as 10pm. Most importantly, be acutely aware of the type of neighborhood in which a hotel is located. However, once inside, groups of travelers often gather to gab and share travel stories—the camaraderie can be choice. Most places serve a breakfast of toast, eggs, and coffee for around BZ$6. There is a 6% (soon to be 7%) tax on all hotel rooms. Most hotels charge BZ$1 for phone calls.

Seaside Guest House, 3 Prince St. (tel. 783-39). Take Albert St. south, turn left at the community drug store, look for the last house on the left. Run by a couple of cool Quakers as a labor of love, the Seaside is mighty mellow, and has an ideal location right on the Belizean "beach." John, a garrulous teacher at the university, is chock full of insight and advice. Rooms upstairs have three locked doors to keep guests from ghouls. Common bathrooms with hot water. Checkout 11am. Dorms BZ$16, singles BZ$28, doubles BZ$40, triples BZ$50. BZ$10 key deposit. Serves beer (BZ$2.75) and breakfast (BZ$6). Will keep guests' bags overnight for BZ$1 per bag. Reservations taken, but must be pre-paid.

Isabel Guest House (tel. 731-39), hidden behind the Central Drugstore to the right, itself behind the Swing Bridge; head upstairs. Only 3 rooms for now, but each is large and pristine. Palatial common room with TV. Checkout 11am. Singles BZ$35, doubles BZ$40. Gigantic room with cute lamps, wooden floors, private bath, and 5 beds for rent: 1 person BZ$40, 2 people BZ$60, 3 people BZ$75—willing to rent one bed dormitory-style for BZ$25. Reservations taken.

Glenthorne Manor Bed and Breakfast, 27 Barrack Rd. Take Queen St. from Swing Bridge about 3 blocks, go left on Barrack; it's about 2 blocks down on the right. A welcome (albeit slightly more expensive), well-maintained retreat from the city. So hip the rooms don't even have numbers—they're color-coded. The owner is an interior decorator, and it shows; even the mosquito netting is placed just so. Kitchenette available, breakfast included. Summer singles BZ$45, doubles BZ$70, triples BZ$80. Winter rates about BZ$15 higher. A/C is an extra BZ$15; fans are free. Laundry: wash/dry BZ$5 each. Private parking BZ$5 per night.

Downtown Guest House (tel. 209-51), on Eve St. about 2 blocks west from Queen. Comes with the essentials for Belize City: cheap prices, locks, and a guard dog. Rooms share common bathrooms with hot water. Albatross ceiling fans flail and struggle to cool guests. Doors locked at 10pm. Singles BZ$15, with bath $25; doubles BZ$25, with bath $35. Slightly larger rooms BZ$20 and BZ$30.

Golden Dragon Hotel and Restaurant, 29 Queen St. (tel. 728-17). Staff speaks Chinese, Spanish, and good business; learn one of those languages or gesticulate like crazy. Kill two birds with one stone in the bathrooms; the toilet is in the shower. Rooms with private bath and fans are BZ$37 (pack in as many people as you want). Nicer rooms (the toilet isn't in the shower) with A/C BZ$80. Reputable restaurant below.

■■■ FOOD

Palate-tickling (and pocketbook-sparing) rice, beans, and pastries can be had at **Babb's,** Queen and Eve St., or **Gon's,** Barrack Rd. and Hyde's Ln. Meat pies and fruit tarts are available at a number of places around town, and are laced with Creole pizzazz. **HL's Burger** is on Albert St., near Town Park.

GiGi's Café and Patio, 2-B King St. (tel. 743-78). The friendly owner loves to show off his ancient Scottish real estate lease; afterwards, relax on the candlelit patio and enjoy wonderfully prepared food; burgers (BZ$7) and amply stewed chicken with beans and rice (BZ$6.75). Sinful rum raisin ice-cream BZ$3.50. Open Mon.-Thurs. 11:30am-2pm and 5:30-9pm, Fri.-Sat. 11:30am-2pm and 5:30-10pm. Closed holidays and first 2 weeks of July.

Macy's Café, 18 Bishop St. (tel. 734-19), 1 block southwest of Town Park, between Albert and S. Side Canal St. The interior's dark and hot; expect outstanding Belizean food cooked with coconut milk and fresh ingredients. If not for grub, at least admire the awning which a young River Phoenix liked to shimmy up while filming *Mosquito Coast.* Menu changes daily, but whole fish and rice and beans are always at hand with huge glasses of lime juice (BZ$2) to rinse it all down (with coleslaw and fried plantain, BZ$10). Open Mon.-Sat. 11:30am-9:30pm. Sunday by reservation.

El Centro, 4 Bishop St. (tel. 724-13), a couple doors down from Macy's. What this restaurant lacks in ambience it more than makes up for with cleanliness and *air-conditioning*(!). Their prices are pretty low, and the service is prompt and friendly. Beans, rice, and meat BZ$7. Turtle BZ$9. Club sandwich BZ$7. Open Mon.-Sat. 6:30am-2pm.

Dit's Restaurant, 50 King St. (tel. 733-30), between Albert and S. Side Canal St. A café/bakery, kept cool with funky rotating ceiling fans. Standard rice and bean dishes. Try the *garnaches* (3 for BZ$1). Known locally for great pastries, including coconut, custard, lemon, and raisin pies (BZ$1.50 per slice). Open Mon.-Sat. 7am-9pm, Sun. 8am-4pm.

Ark Restaurant and Community Center, 109 N. Front St., just past the Texaco Station. Bernie, the chef and owner, is a retired nutritionist from the U.S. Army who returned to his native Belize and found God on a late-night evangelical TV show. The Ark was closed while Bernie studied theology, he but plans to re-open with entrees from BZ$3-6. His grand scheme is to introduce Biblical dinner theater; meanwhile, the community center helps teens stay off the street. Bernard serves a great cow-foot soup (BZ$5), plus other regional specialties, and loves to talk politics and religion; it's worth stopping by just to get an earful. Open Mon.-Sat. 7am-midnight, Sun. 2pm-midnight.

■■■ SIGHTS AND ENTERTAINMENT

Belize City's attractions are unusual; there are no museums or cultural centers, but the few things worth seeing are still packed full of insight about the country. Travelers who want to become a part of history *and* show off their strength to the locals are in luck; tell Jim at the **Swing Bridge** how strong you are and he'll let you actually swing the bridge open to let ships pass. The manual bridge is unusual in the country and in the world. It swings at 6am and 5:30pm, when ships want passage. Be prepared for a workout.

One building well worth the 10-minute walk is **St. John's Cathedral,** at the southern end of Albert St. Dedicated in 1826, the structure was built with bricks originally used as ballast on English ships and stands as the oldest Anglican cathedral in Central

America. Today, it serves as a refreshingly idyllic edifice in unhappily urban Belize City. The caretaker sometimes sings spirituals and gives brief tours.

Just past St. John's (directly south) is **Bird's Isle,** which isn't even an island, but a private peninsula. Frequently rented for special events, the slightly run-down island offers a quiet setting for some impressive views and satisfying breezes. Locals mostly use the spot for swimming. A sign on the isle lists the types of people the management doesn't want hanging around: "God has no use for thieves, dungheads, and nasty people."

Go for a breezy waterfront stroll along **Marine Parade** or **Southern Fore Shore** road, where the city's poshest homes are isolated from the squalor. A few beaches outside of town offer some relief, but the walk back is quite a workout in the heat. It's best to stifle your urge to swim until you make it to the Cayes. Belizeans picnic on **Gillett Beach,** 7km out on Western Highway.

For those not yet exhausted by 10pm, Belize City offers some dance clubs which feature *punta, soca,* and reggae. Although crime levels have decreased slightly, tourists who check out the night scene should expect to be street-smart or endangered. Never go solo. Always have a reliable ride home. Keep all body parts inside the ride at all times. Hold on tight and have fun.

Locals swear by three dance clubs. The most notorious is **Pub Amnesia** (tel. 359-24) on Barrack Road, the first intersection past the Ramada on the left (open Thurs.-Sat. 10pm-2am or 3am, BZ$10 cover charge, women half-price on Sat.). Wednesday after 10pm is karaoke night. Just down the street at the Ramada is **Calypso** (tel. 326-70). According to visitors, it's worth the BZ$10 cover charge, as Calypso features The Messengers, a local band playing *punta* and reggae every weekend (open Thurs.-Sat. 10pm-2am, Sun. 10pm-midnight). For more penny-pinching party-seekers, the **Bellevue Hotel** (tel. 770-51) has a disco in the basement which operates Friday and Saturday from 10pm to 2am. To get there, take Albert St. south, turn left on King St., and then it's right at the ocean. It's usually free, but the disco charges BZ$10 admission if a live band is playing, which happens sporadically.

■ NEAR BELIZE CITY

ALTUN HA

50km north of Belize City near Rock Stone Pond Village, off of the old Northern Highway, stand the Mayan ruins of Altun Ha, the most thoroughly excavated site in all of Belize. During the Classical Period (250-900 AD), Altun Ha functioned as a major ceremonial center and as an important trading link between Caribbean shores and inland Mayan centers. The head of Kinisch Ahau was discovered here; weighing in at nearly 5kg (and making frequent appearances on Belizean bank notes), the piece is thought to be the largest existing Mayan jade carving. The site is comprised of two main plazas, plus 13 temples and residential structures; tourists find the ruins ideal for exploration because the temples are close together and don't demand heavy hiking.

Getting to Altun Ha has historically been a nightmare, but a new business offers hope. Some locals started a combination bus service/tour that leaves for the ruins at 8:30am, 11:30am, and 2:30pm from the depot at Mile 19, Midway Restaurant. To get to Mile 19, take any northbound bus from **Batty Brothers** or **Venus** (allow 45min. to get to Mile 19; ask the driver to stop). Homer Leslie, president of Belize Tour Guide Association, runs the show (tel. 758-19, 782-47; fax 740-07). Reservations are accepted. Call first to be sure things haven't changed. US$12.50 covers the ride and tour (site open daily 8am-4:30pm, BZ$3).

Otherwise, fend for yourself, by following the trail of past travelers heading to the ruins. Some have banded together and taken a taxi (US$25 per person if 4-5 people go, depending on the cabbie). Some hitch a ride back in the afternoon; *Let's Go* does not recommend hitchhiking. The only overnight accommodations are at the Maruba resort, which doesn't even list prices (US$119 per night) in its multi-page glossy brochure.

BERMUDIAN LANDING AND BABOON PRESERVE

So loud is the lion-like scream of the black howler monkey (called "baboon" in the local Creole) that it can be heard for 2km. In order to protect these playful, vocal primates, which are currently an endangered species, the **Community Baboon Sanctuary** was established in 1985. Farmers in the tiny village of **Bermudian Landing,** in seven other small communities, and on privately held land pledged to abide by certain conservation plans to protect the howlers' habitat. The 20 square miles of sanctuary protect approximately 1600 black howler monkeys. Visitors to the sanctuary can expect to hear the endangered monkey's loud, throaty howl, and will likely catch sight of the dark and gregarious vegetarians hanging out in the tree canopy. Local, knowledgeable guides ensure at least one sighting in each tour (BZ$10).

Bermudian Landing itself boasts Belize's only natural history museum. For overnighters, basic bed and breakfast accommodations are available (BZ$15). A bus leaves Belize City at 12:30pm and 5:30pm (BZ$3.50) from next to the bridge connecting Orange and Cemetery Roads, just past the Batty Brothers' Terminal, but does not return until the next morning at 5:30am. For more info, call Bermudian Landing (tel. 444-05).

THE BELIZE ZOO

U.S. naturalist Sharon Matola opened the Belize Zoo in 1983. Forty-six km west of Belize City on the Western Highway, the menagerie has expanded to house 70 of the species native to Belize. Jaguar, ocelot, monkey, tapir—the sublime, the bizarre, and the ugly—exist side by side for your pleasure and bewilderment.

The zoo is refreshingly unorthodox—there are no moats, concrete platforms, or cotton candy. The watchword here is symbiosis. Hand-painted, doggerel signs keep visitors on their toes. One line, for example, gloats about the digital superiority of spider monkeys: "When you're minus a thumb, brachiation is a breeze." Although some residents are elusive, most (including the jaguar) can be spotted 24 hrs. per day, seven days a week, with a minimum of effort. Tours available only with two weeks advance notice and cost BZ$20-50 depending on group size. Admission is BZ$10 for foreign adults, BZ$5 for foreign children, Peace Corps, and military. Help support the underfunded park with a purchase from the gift shop, perhaps some cool mugs (BZ$10-14) or a distinctive t-shirt (BZ$22-25). Traveler's checks accepted with passport. The zoo is open daily 9am-4pm.

Well worth a stop on the Tikal-Belize City trail, the zoo is easily accessible by car or bus. Eastbound and westbound **buses** on the Western Highway pass the 200m dirt access road approximately hourly. The fare from Belize City is BZ$3, return trip BZ$2 (45min.).

NORTHERN BELIZE

■■■ ORANGE WALK

When European settlers built a Catholic church where the town now stands, they planted orange trees along the path to the church's front door—hence the name. Today's Orange Walk (pop. 10,000) is a mellow collection of fading, pastel-painted homes mounted on stilts. Much friendlier than Belize City, Orange Walk even boasts a vigorous scout troop. Residents make their living growing sugarcane, and their biggest worry is the nefarious screwworm, an insect whose larva burrows into open sores and nostrils. The town is in fact home to a diverse range of nostrils, a microcosmic representation of Belize's heterogeneity: Dutch/German Mennonite, Chinese-Belizean, and *mestizo* schnozzles all inhale Orange Walk's hot air. Although at first glance a seemingly pointless pitstop on the path to some ruins or Mexico,

Orange Walk hides precious glimpses of local life, both from now and a few millennia ago. It also serves well as a departure point for the ruins at Lamanai.

ORIENTATION

Buses arriving from Mexico or Belize City deposit passengers on the town's principal north-south drag, **Belize-Corozal Rd.** It is sometimes called *the* main street, not to be confused with Main St. Once you hop off the bus, face the red-topped gazebo of the small city park; you're looking east. Between the park and the fire station three blocks south, Belize-Corozal Rd. becomes **Queen Victoria Rd.** The street east of the park is **Lover's Lane,** which used to be a favorite make-out spot for frisky couples who met in the park. Another block east is **Main St.,** a strip dominated by markets and butchers.

PRACTICAL INFORMATION

Tourist Office: The closest thing to a proper office is **Novelo's,** on the southeast corner of the park. Look inside **Lovers' Restaurant.** While most of their information concerns daytrips to the ruins, it's worth asking about goings-on in town.

Police: (tel. 220-22, 911), 4 blocks north of the park on Belize-Corozal Rd.

Post Office: (tel. 223-45), 3 blocks north of the park on Belize-Corozal Rd., in the same building as the treasury. The sign on the door says "Sub Treasury"—just walk in. *Poste Restante* available. Open Mon.-Thurs. 8am-noon and 1-4:30pm, Fri. 8am-4:30pm.

Telephones: Public phones are located at various points along Belize Corozol Rd., including by the park. Many are broken, but many restaurants allow calls for BZ$1 per min. **Telephone code:** 03.

Currency Exchange: Bank of Nova Scotia (tel. 221-94), the turquoise building on the northeast corner of the park. No cash advances. Only U.S., British, and Canadian currencies and traveler's checks will be cashed. Open Mon.-Thurs. 8am-1pm, Fri. 8am-1pm and 3-6pm.

Buses: Located ½ block north of the park, **Batty Brothers** (tel. 228-58) offers hourly service to Chetumal with a stop at Corozal (6am-1pm about every hr., 2 hrs., BZ$4.50) and Belize City (1:30pm-8:30pm, about every hr., 2 hrs., BZ$4.50).

Taxis: On the block-long strip 1 block north of the city park where the buses pull in. **Orange Walk Taxi Union** (tel. 220-50). **Taxi Association** (tel. 225-60).

Pharmacy: Delafuentes' Pharmacy, 16 Main St. (tel. 220-35). Open Mon.-Sat. 8am-noon, 1:30-5pm, and 7-9pm. Carries tampons, diapers, drugs, etc.

Market: The People's Store, 51 Main St. (tel. 220-03), is fully stocked with food, juice, etc. Open Mon.-Sat. 8am-noon, 1:30-5pm, 7-9pm.

Hospital: (tel. 220-72), several blocks north of the police station on Belize-Corozal Rd. Open 24 hrs.

ACCOMMODATIONS

Taisan Hotel, directly across from the southbound bus stop/taxi depot. Clean rooms, towering ceilings, and shared bathrooms. A good deal, although proximity to the bus station may drive you batty. Double beds (single or double) BZ$25, two double beds BZ$40. Beware: you're locked in until 7:30am, when the owner takes the padlocks off the main doors.

Mi Amor Hotel (tel. 220-31; fax 234-62), near the fire station. Clean, carpeted rooms. Private baths with hot water. Check-out 1pm. Traveler's checks accepted. Adjacent to noisy Mi Amor Lounge, which features nightly appearances by The Comets, who play synthesizers pre-programmed with sexy Latin ballads conducive to *amor.* Singles BZ$42.40 a night with or without A/C; doubles BZ$58.30, with A/C for BZ$74.20. Each extra person BZ$5.30. TV costs BZ$5 per night.

D'Victoria Hotel (tel. 225-18; fax 228-47). Sign advises guests to be "clean, careful, and educated"—no d'vulgarity or d'violence here. Spotless and spacious rooms boast A/C, private baths, and access to a vast balcony. Check-out 1pm. BZ$44.50 for 1 person (double bed, no A/C); BZ$50 for a room of similar size with 2 double beds. A/C costs about BZ$30 more per night. Reservations accepted.

FOOD

Orange Walk's array of restaurants is as Belizean as it gets, since every part of the population is represented; its finest restaurants are exclusively Chinese, a perfect antidote for the traveler whose very soul is becoming rice and beans. For those still eager for variations on the old R&B standard (or who are weary of MSG), great Mexican-style food is still cheap grub here.

Lover's Restaurant, southeast corner of the park. Named for the lane on which it sits, this restaurant is run by the notoriously loquacious Novelo brothers. While their grub isn't directly aphrodisiac, it sates another basic urge—dem food taste good! And the price is amazing: BZ$4 for almost every item on the menu. Open Sun.-Thurs. 6am-10pm; Fri.-Sat. 6am-midnight.

Juanita's, 8 Santa Ana St., ½ block west of the Shell station (2 blocks north of the firehouse). Named after the sister of Oscar, the ultra-friendly manager, this local favorite offers traditional Belizean fare. Breakfast served at 6am for early risers. Bacon with eggs and beans BZ$5, rice and beans with chicken BZ$4, and wicked-good cow-foot soup (BZ$4.50).

Lee's Restaurant (tel. 221-74), 1 block west of the firehouse. Pricey, but tops among Chinese places. Capacious and air-conditioned. Go for the "Special Chow Mein" (BZ$10) or Conch Fried Rice (BZ$8). Open daily 11am-midnight.

Hong Kong Restaurant (tel. 24-06), near firehouse, next to Mi Amor Hotel. Like the city it's named for, the Hong Kong is known for its syncretism; both Chinese and Belizean specialties are served. Sweet and sour pork with rice (BZ$10.50), fried lobster with fries and salad (BZ$11).

SIGHTS

Although Orange Walk itself has a few attractions, with its eponymous **Catholic church** at the south end of Main St. and an amazing **river bank** (well worth a picnic outfitted by **The People's Store**), its claim to tourist fame is its proximity to a multiplicity of Mayan ruins (see Near Orange Walk, below). For those yearnin' for night life, the two snazzy hotels, **Mi Amor** and **D'Victoria** have dance clubs which open at 10pm. For family entertainment, the **Escapade Cinema** is the building directly south of the Shell Station on Belize-Corozal Road. Painted rather garishly, the cinema features U.S.-made movies (with about a month delay) for BZ$4 for adults and BZ$2 for children. Showtime is 8pm Tues.-Thurs., and 5:30, 8, and 10pm Fri.-Sun. The theater (TEE-ter) is always open for snacks, even when a film isn't showing.

■ NEAR ORANGE WALK

LAMANAI

An important part of *el mundo Maya,* Lamanai represents well over two millennia of continuous inhabitation, ending only in the 17th century under the chilling impact of European diseases. Originally called *Lamanain* (submerged crocodile), a linguistic blooper blessed this city-state with its current name, which means "drowned insect." In either case, it's not hard to understand the water fixation, since the ruin is situated on the beautiful Mew River Lagoon. A visit to Lamanai includes not only three magnificent temples with sweet panoramic views, but also a 100-km round-trip river safari and arduous nature hike. To get the most bang for your Belizean buck, check out the view from the Main Temple, the impressive stela, the Mask Temple, and the howler monkeys, the arboreal caretakers of the region's jungle. Although the guides are quick to point out that the Mayans revered the disabled (and add to their own maudlin sermon on the subject), Lamanai remains utterly inaccessible to the disabled traveler.

Nearly every Orange Walk resident with a boat and a brain is prepared to move tourists to the ruin. The trips invariably start at 9am and end around 3:30-4pm. Most boats leave from the large hut with the thatched roof—from town, take a bus heading south and ask to be let off at the toll bridge (BZ$1); look for a hut to the left. The

BELIZE

Maruba Resort, normally far beyond the budget range, offers an excellent tour including lunch drinks for BZ$70. For lunch, a reservation must be made at least a day in advance (tel. 221-99). **Novelo's,** at the southeast corner of the park in Orange Walk (same building as Lover's Restaurant), is the base for **Jungle River Tours** (tel. 222-93; fax 237-49), an ecotourism group which leads treks to the ruins. They offer a tour for US$40. Otherwise, stop at the hotel/restaurant across from the hut, **New River Park, Ltd.** (tel. 239-87)—they know which boat is going and when. For budding botanists, **Carlos Godoy** (tel. 229-69) is the local expert on orchids. His tours to Lamanai, although more expensive, include a strong focus on New River flora. Tours (US$48) require at least two people and include lunch and entrance fees.

CUELLO

Orange Walk boasts at least two more ruins, less spectacular than Lamanai but rewarding nonetheless. The ruin at **Cuello** is definitely older than Lamanai, perhaps by more than 1000 years. (Two archaeologists have dated it; one says 2500BC, the other 1500BC). It's a single temple and the Mayan equivalent of a wine cellar, situated in the middle of soft, verdant fields. To get there, take a bus from Tillett's, which leaves from Sagú, the supermarket behind the fire station (BZ$1 each way). Ask the driver to stop at "qua-yo." Head toward the modern rum distillery, the only building visible from where the bus stops, and ask the manager for permission to view the site (it's on private land). Head through the gate around to the left of the distillery, and follow the trail to the ruin. Bring your own H2O, and beware the intoxicating influence of the sweet fumes.

NOH MUL

Another ruin is slightly less accessible. **Noh Mul** (Tall Hill) is about 2½km outside the village of **San Pablo,** which is about 13km north of Orange Walk Town. Only partially excavated, this ruin is for the truly adventurous: the hike is great, and the Mayan remains are enshrouded in dense jungle. The view from atop the second temple takes away what breath is left after climbing; look around to see both Mexico and Orange Walk Town. Enrique Bacab, a policeman in Orange Walk Town who hails from San Pablo, has agreed to take *Let's Go* readers to the site for a negotiable amount (shoot for BZ$5). Either call (tel. 350-75, 351-43) or stop by the police station. He gets off work at 4pm; the trip lasts about two and a half hours.

MENNONITES

If ruins and birds aren't your thing, several German Mennonite communities—**Little Belize, Blue Creek,** and **Shipyard**—are accessible from Orange Walk. The roads around these villages are traveled only by horses and buggies. Women wear full, restrictive dresses and men sport overalls and straw hats; if you can agree on language (Spanish works best), many of the Mennonite men are willing to chat. Of the settlements, Blue Creek is the most tourist-friendly and the most interesting—its Mayan ruins are currently being excavated. On the other hand, only the very curious should visit Shipyard, as its 200 residents are spread out over a vast area. Photography is prohibited in all three Mennonite communities. To reach the towns, look for the schoolbuses that leave from Sagú, the store half a block behind the fire station. They leave between 9am and noon—just follow the straw hats and overalls of the Mennonites (1 hr., BZ$2.50 each way). When you board, ask when buses head back to Orange Walk.

■■■ COROZAL

Affectionately called "Janet Town" in honor of the hurricane that forced a civil engineering renaissance of this erstwhile zoning nightmare, Corozal was initially settled in 1847. The first inhabitants, refugees from the massacres in Bacalav, Mexico, were advised by the owner of the property, Mr. Blake, to farm sugarcane. Both the immigration and the newfound vocation stuck. Named for its palm trees (Corozal means "*cohune* area"), the Corozal of today (pop. 8000) is actually still rooted in sugarcane production. The Mexican border runs a stone's throw from the town, and consequently Spanish is the preferred tongue among locals. Few tourists come to the little town, but even for those with no interest in the intricacies of 'cane-farming, Corozal offers some righteous views, pleasant swimming areas, inexpensive seaside respite, as well as easy access to two interesting **Mayan ruins,** Santa Rita and Cerros Maya.

Orientation and Practical Information Despite what is essentially a grid of streets, navigation in banana-shaped Corozal somehow manages to be confusing. Locals are familiar with what's where, but even they have to go out in search of their mail to determine their own addresses. Major landmarks include the sea, which runs along the eastern side of the city, the town square (home to **Town Hall**), and the town park ("Central Park"), next to the Catholic church in town. The avenues run parallel to the shore and are numbered starting from the bay.

Tourist information is hard to come by. The **public library,** on the south end of the town park, has some tourist information, and locals say there is a travel agent south of town, along the shore road. Also, Mark at **Nestor's Hotel** is a gold mine of information and contacts. The small, friendly **police** force has an office on the west side of Central Park (tel. 220-22), open 24 hrs. Many local businesses will **exchange** US$ without the service charge imposed by banks, but be sure to compare rates first. **Atlantic Bank,** 1 Park St. (tel. 234-74), near the park, offers cash advances on Visa (BZ$10 for authorization call) and cashes traveler's checks with a BZ$0.50 per check service charge (open Mon.-Fri. 8am-2pm). The **post office** skulks on the west side of the park, across from the taxi stand. *Poste restante.* Open Mon.-Thurs. 8:30am-noon and 1-4:30pm, Fri. 8:30am-noon and 1-4pm. **BTL** is right by the post office (open Mon.-Fri. 8am-noon, 1-4pm, Sat. 8am-noon). The **telephone code** is 04.

Batty Bus is located about 4 blocks north of the park. **Venus Bus** (tel. 221-32) is located on the south end of town, where 6th Ave. curves sharply. They send buses to Belize City (every hr., 4am-11:30am, 2½ hrs., BZ$7.50) with an express at 4:30am (2 hrs., BZ$7.50) and to Chetumal, Mexico (about every hr., 2:45-9:30pm, 30min., BZ$2.50). **Taxis** (tel. 220-35) huddle on the western edge of Central Park. One trip within the town costs BZ$4, to the Mexican border pay BZ$25. **Super Mirna's,** 4th Ave. and 2nd St. South (tel. 221-49), 2 blocks south of the park, has complete grocery-store fare. (Open Mon.-Thurs. 7:30am-7:30pm, Fri. 7:30am-8pm, Sat. 7:30am-9:30pm, Sun. 7:30am-12:30pm). The **General Discount Drugstore** (tel. 221-24), 5th Ave. just south of the park, offers feminine hygiene products and drugs (open Mon.-Fri. 8am-noon, 2-5:30pm, and 7-8:30pm, Sat. 8am-noon and 7-8:30pm). Head to the **Hospital** (tel. 220-76), 4-5 blocks from the police on the grassy knoll (open 24 hrs).

Accommodations and Food Because so few tourists come to Corozal, rooms are almost always available and are relatively cheap. Corozal is said to be fairly safe, but the big *S* should still be a primary consideration in choosing a hotel. The **Caribbean Village Restaurant and Motel** (tel. 220-45, 227-45), a few blocks south of town on the shore road, has cute *cabañas* just meters from the beautiful seashore; the convenient restaurant offers scrumptious meals. All have private bath (singles BZ$30, doubles BZ$40). **Nestor's,** 123 5th Ave. (tel. 223-54), 4 blocks south of Town Park on 5th Ave., is a good place to go to feel secure; massive owner Mark puts the fear of God into thieving locals, and says his place is the locus of tourist activity in the town. The hotel sports a great bar and restaurant, a multitude of cheap rooms with fans and hot water. Key deposit BZ$5. Checkout 11am. Wheelchair accessible rooms. Guard posted all night; you can get a room anytime. Mark is also willing to connect travelers, even those who don't stay at his hotel, with tour guides for exploring. His bar, which boasts 2 TVs, is the site of safe nightlife in Corozal (singles BZ$20, doubles BZ$25, two twin beds BZ$29, two double beds BZ$35). **Capri** (tel. 220-42), on the corner of 4th and 5th Ave., is on the shore, isn't luxurious, but it's *cheap!* Peek into a few rooms first to guarantee hot water and adequate locks (singles BZ$8.50, BZ$12.50 with private bath; doubles BZ$12.50, BZ$17.50 with private bath).

Corozal has a heapin' helping of Chinese restaurants, which all seem to provide the same fare, and too meager a handful of Belizean restaurants, such as **Lydia's** and **Blue Dahlia's,** which are in the same building one block south of the park. Two fine (but still inexpensive) restaurants are associated with hotels: **Nestor's** and **Caribbean Village. Crisis,** at 1 9th St. North, on the far north end of town, is pronounced CREE-sas, so beware when asking directions. It serves solid Belizean food at low prices in a comfortable setting. Big portion of T-bone with rice and beans (BZ$10). Live music Sat. night (open Sun.-Thurs. 11am-4pm, Fri. 11am-10pm, Sat. 11am-1am).

Sights If you can draw yourself away from the mesmerizing lilt of waves nudging the shore, take a gander at the historical **mural** in the Town Hall, at the south end of Central Park; locals are quite proud of it. Two ruins nearby are open for tourist perusal, **Santa Rita** and **Cerros Maya.** Santa Rita is a 20-minute walk from Central Park. Take the road past the police station for six or seven blocks; veer left at the hunched-shoulders statue, then take the second right at the Belize security-force station. The ruin sits on the left. Roy, the caretaker, gives a tour with the entrance fee (BZ$2). The ruins are nothing spectacular, but they evoke the tranquil and mysterious. It's not hard to imagine the high priest sipping a club soda on the veranda of this *cabaña antigua.*

Cerros Maya, the more spectacular ruin, is also the more expensive; one of the earliest settlements, it is also featured on several postcards. The ruin lies across the bay and requires a boat ride which costs about BZ$70. The caretaker, Tanis Range, is willing to take tourists, leaves sometime after 8am, and will charge BZ$20 per person for a group of seven or more. The other option is Richard, a local fisherman. Contact Mark at **Nestor's Hotel** to reach Richard, whose prices are negotiable.

THE CAYES

The Cayes (pronounced "keys"), Belize's 175 coastal mini-islands, are the late 20th century's service-enhanced version of the perfect tropical isle. Like pennies from heaven, world-class diving, snorkeling, and fishing opportunities await both experienced lovers of the deep and the newly converted. British pirates were some of the first to discover the Cayes' mystique; they used the Barrier Reef to hide from the Spanish navy, coming ashore afterward to stock up on provisions. Of late, investors have become hip to the isles' built-in tourist appeal, and the towns of **Caye Chapel** and **San Pedro** on Ambergris Caye boast landing strips and posh hotels. For the time being, activity remains concentrated on Ambergris Caye and, to a lesser extent, on nearby Caye Caulker; most of the islands are still uninhabited mangrove swamps.

The cayes right off Belize City are the most accessible. Flights from the municipal airport take vacationers to Ambergris Caye and Caye Chapel, and regularly scheduled launches zip travelers from Belize City to Caye Caulker. Charter a launch to reach the other cayes (ask at the Shell Station by the Swing Bridge in Belize City).

■■■ CAYE CAULKER

Caye Caulker (pop. 600) cools and calms the spirit after the dingy population density of Belize City. Geckos sun themselves, coconut trees sway in the afternoon breeze, and the pace of life is slow, slow, slow. Five *mestizo* families from the Yucatán settled here in 1850 to fish; their descendants now run modest seaside hotels where you can feast on lobster tails (in season June 15-Feb. 15) and beer. Even the most ambitious of travelers end up deciding to just sit back, nurse another rum punch, and forget what day it is.

The Cayes

Progresso
Progresso Lagoon
Fireburn
Condemned Pt.
Cayo Chelem
Laguna de Cantena
Freshwater Creek Forest Reserve
Doubloon Bank Lagoon
High Bluff
Deer Caye
Reef Pt.
Honey Camp Lagoon
Bulkhead Lagoon
Cayo Negro (Blackadore Caye)
Palmero Pt.
Ambergris Caye
Bennett's Lagoon
Spanish Pt.
Mosquito Caye
Northern Hwy.
Will Edward's Lagoon
Stone Crab Pt.
Entrada de Mato
Buena Vista Pt.
Bomba
Bulkhead Reef
Cayo Romero
San Pedro
Entrada de San Pedro
Jones Lagoon
Maskall
North River Lagoon
Corozalito
Laguna de San Pedro
Chicago
Santana
Cangrejo Cay
Cowhead Creek
Caye Caulker
BARRIER REEF
Midwinters Lagoon
Biscayne
Hick's Caye
Washing Tree
Salt Creek
Rocky Pt. Lagoon
Caye Chapel
Grace Bank
Little Rocky Pt.
Long Caye
Flowers Bank
Sand Hill
Hen and Chickens Cayes
Mauger Caye Lighthouse
Montego Caye
Frenchman's Caye
Crawl Caye
Burrell Boom
Ladyville
Rider's Caye
St. George's Cay
Rendezvous Pt.
Lord's Bank
Moho Caye
Three Corner Caye
Belize City
Drowned Cays
Northern Lagoon (Vincent's)
Hattieville
Belize Harbor
Swallow Caye
Spanish Lookout Caye
Freshwater Creek
Sandbore Caye
Northern Caye
Freetown
Sibun R.
Sibun
Snake Pt.
Pelican Caye
Ceder Bank
Crickozeen Creek
Ramsey's Caye
Water Caye
Turneffe Islands
Lighthouse Reef
Gracy Rock Bank
Northern Lagoon
Douglas Caye
Central Lagoon
Blackbird Caye
Harry Jones Point
Long Caye
Ambergris Creek
Amber Head
Middle Long Caye
Calabash Caye
Southern Lagoon
Cross Cay
Grand Bogoe
Bluefield Range
Joe's Hole
Deadman's Caye
Half Moon Caye
Gales Point
Alligator Caye
Blue Creek
Big Cay Bokel
Long Caye
Colson Cayes
Mullins River
Stann Creek Valley
Melinda Forest Station
Southern Long Cayes
Pemone
Blunt Pt.
Sandfly Cayes
Columbus Caye
Caribbean Sea
Sarawine
Alta Vista
Garbutts Caye
Cross Caye
Dangriga (Stann Creek)
New Town
Columbus Reef
Commerce Bight
Coco Plum Caye
Man of War Caye
Commerce Bight Village
Hopkins
False Sittee Pt.
Tobacco Reef
Sittee R.
Kendal
Middle Bank
Sittee Pt.
Twin Cayes
Glovers Reef
Locust Bank
All Pines
Sapodilla Lagoon
Stewart Caye
Southern Hwy.
Bread and Butter Caye
Crow's Nest Caye
Middle Caye
Northeast Caye
Long Caye
South Stann Cr.
Peter Douglas Caye
Placentia Lagoon
South Cut
Saddle Caye
Southwest Caye
Blair Atholl
Jonathan Pt.
Northeast Caye Range
Maya Beach
False Caye
Channel Caye
Seine Bight Village
Tarpum Caye
Alabama Wharf
False Pt.
Round Caye
Mango Creek
Wippari Caye
Crawl Caye
Gladden Caye
Independence
Rum Pt.
Baker's Rendezvous
Jack's Caye
Savannah Forest Station
Big Creek (Hercules)
Lark Caye
Spider Caye
Gladden Entrance
Bugle Cayes
Cary Caye
Hatchet Caye
Palmetto Caye
Harvest Caye
Scipio Caye
Long Coco Caye
Queen Caye Entrance
Rocky Pt.
Laughing Bird Caye
Silk Cayes

The local community is quiet, laid-back, and uniformly friendly, but they aren't receptive to loud North American tourists. Guest-house signs warn against raucous late-night behavior. Wind down and enjoy yourself—this isn't a place for partying hard. Don't be naïve, though. While the residents are generous, vagrants from the coast have discovered Caye Caulker's charm too, and crime, particularly hotel theft, is on the rise. Snorkeling and scuba trips to the reef offer an escape from the heat, the mosquitoes, and the raging lassitude of the shore. True, there's little sandy beach, but you won't find jet skis, T-shirt boutiques, or tequila-crazed teens on the rampage, either.

Zoom from Belize City to Caye Caulker by **high-speed launch** (1 hr., BZ$15). Several islanders make daily round trips from the caye at 6:45am; they head back between 10:30am and 11am from **A&R's Service Station** (a.k.a. the Texaco station), 73 N. Front St., two blocks west of the Swing Bridge. Ask inside for Chocolate, a reliable boatman who runs a mahogany skiff called *Soledad* that is the first to leave in the morning. Other boats leave whenever a group gathers. Generally, boats leave every half hour between 9am and 4pm. In the off-season, as few as two boats per day may go, at 11:30am and 4pm.

Inspect all craft before boarding; a charter ride on an overcrowded boat with a puny motor can easily become the Minnow's proverbial "three-hour tour." Any boat going to San Pedro will stop at Caye Caulker on request. To avoid the clamor of Belize City Harbor, fly to Caye Caulker from the municipal airport (15min., BZ$39 one way, BZ$70 round-trip) or the more expensive international airport.

Diving for Dollars

The barrier reef along Belize and Honduras is the largest in the hemisphere, and the Caribbean's crystalline waters provide excellent visibility for exploring the mind-bending shapes and colors below the surface. The many dive shops on the Cayes offer travelers the chance to get certified and explore the fantastic reefs, and in some cases, for considerably cheaper than in the U.S. Unfortunately, though, competition between shops has also caused some corner-cutting. Safety awareness and quality of instruction are exchanged for mass-output certification. Shop (and ask) around before settling on a dive center. Make sure the instructor is fully certified with NAUI or PADI, the biggest divers' organizations. Similarly, the dive master leading your trip must have more than a clue. If some shop's deals seem too good to be true, they probably are; bad air or poor instruction can lead to decompression sickness and death. Never dive or snorkel alone; the buddy system is fundamental to diving safety. Don't drink and dive, be aware of all the rules, and don't test the strength of the sea; it is bigger than you are.

While preserving your own safety, make an effort to protect the well-being of the coral and sea life, as well. Divers' early efforts to conserve precious coral and protect water organisms may in fact have been the start of the ecotourism movement. Still, some careless and greedy dive instructors still do not preach the importance of keeping your equipment near your body or of not touching or kicking your fins near the coral, and so coral-heads that took millions of years to develop are being lost in a matter of seconds. Have respect for the sea; look but don't touch, and convert "low-impact" into the eco-conscious diver's mantra, "Leave only bubbles."

ORIENTATION

Urban legend holds that Hurricane Hattie rent Caye Caulker in two, back in 1961. Actually, after a creek was broadened by Hattie, people finished the job, dredging the gap into what is now called "the split." In any event, Caye Caulker now has halves. The town stands at the northern tip of the southern portion. There are no street signs in Caye Caulker—indeed, there are no street names and no addresses. Two parallel dirt roads, known informally as "the front street" and "the back street," run north-south through town. A leisurely walk from end to end takes 15 minutes. A hand-drawn map, on display at most restaurants and guest houses, will help you get your bearings. Landmarks include the **police station,** on the front street at the center of town, and the **two largest piers** which jut out on the east and west sides of the island, a bit south of the police station. Most boats from Belize City leave passengers on the east side, but some stop on the west. Just ask which way is north upon disembarking and orientation will be fairly easy.

PRACTICAL INFORMATION

Tourist Information: Hicaco Tours (tel. 20-73, from Belize City tel. 758-19), Front St. just north of Rainbow dock. Ramón Rosado, although partisan, will help with information on tours, etc. There are cheaper tours, so push him for other operators' names. Open daily 6am-10pm, except when he's giving a tour.

Police: (tel. 21-20), in a green-and-cream house by the basketball half-court on the front road. 1-man squadron available (sort of) 24 hrs., inside or out, on the court.

Post Office: Celi's Mini-Supermarket (tel. 21-01), at the southern end of Back St. Mail picked up on Tues. and Fri. Poste Restante available. Open Mon.-Fri. 8am-noon and 3-6pm, Sat. 9am-noon. Mini-supermarket stays open until 7pm.

Telephones: Belize Telecommunications Limited. (tel. 21-68 or 21-69), on the 2nd floor of a building near the middle of Front St. Free international collect calls. **Fax service** available (fax 22-39). Open Mon.-Fri. 8am-noon and 1-4pm, Sat. 8am-noon. Deposit required. **Telegram** service available at the same office and hrs. as the phones, but Mon.-Fri. only. BZ$0.32 per word. **The Budget Traveler** (tel. 20-77) has an office in Tracis Island Shop. **Telephone code:** 022.

Currency Exchange: The spiffy new **Atlantic Bank** (tel. 22-07), on Back St. near the middle of town, offers cash advances on MC and Visa, and exchanges U.S. currency. Open Mon.-Fri. 8am-noon and 1-2pm, Sat. 9am-noon. **Celi's Mini-Supermarket** (see above) will change cash and traveler's checks during store hours. In general, it's cheaper to change U.S. currency (including traveler's checks) at stores since they don't charge a service fee. Always ask first, though.

Airstrip: In easy walking distance on the south side of town. Any San Pedro-Belize City flight will stop on request at Caye Caulker, simply mention it when buying your ticket (see listing in San Pedro, page 140).

Boats: Boats returning to Belize City leave at 6:30m, 7, 8am, and 3pm (BZ$15). At 10am a boat leaves Caye Caulker for San Pedro (30min., BZ$15). Other boats to San Pedro can be picked up as they stop on the west dock to drop off people from Belize City, often as late as 4pm. A fun, leisurely way to San Pedro is to go with **Hicaco Tours.** For BZ$10 more than the taxi, it's possible to stop at Hol Chan Marine Reserve (BZ$3) and there to snorkel (gear included) for 1-2 hrs., all the way to San Pedro. Ramón likes to leave around 10:30am and to arrive in San Pedro at about 12:30pm.

Market: Jan's Deli (tel. 21-88), at the north end of Front St. between Chocolate's and Cabana's. Open Mon.-Sat. 7am-1pm and 3-7pm, Sun. 8am-noon. **Chan's** (tel. 21-65), on Back St., is open Mon.-Sat. 7:30am-9pm, Sun. 7:30am-1pm.

Laundromat: Caye Caulker Laundromat, on Middle St., 1 block south of the soccer fields. BZ$10 per load, wash and dry. No self-service. Open daily 8am-noon, 1-6pm.

Pharmacy: Centers Store (tel. 21-46), across Back St. from Atlantic Bank, boasts Caye Caulker's best attempt at a pharmacy. It has no prescription drugs but it carries most over-the-counter (OTC) medications.

Medical Services: Caye Caulker Health Center (tel. 21-66), 2 blocks from the police station. Open Mon.-Thurs. 8am-5pm, Fri. 8am-4:30pm. Emergency only, after hours.

ACCOMMODATIONS

Simple hotels, communal showers, cold water, and fans keep the Cancún jet set away. Look for a place on the Caribbean side, right on the water; a steady breeze keeps things cool here while giving the cold shoulder to voracious mosquitoes and sand flies. Campers can wander to a desolate part of the isle or, preferably, ask around to see which hotels allow camping. To minimize attacks by kamikaze mosquitoes, burn mosquito coil (BZ$1.50) and keep the lights off. Many places have few rooms and fill them all between November and April; a reservation isn't a bad idea.

Castaway's Hotel (tel. 22-94). Owner Bob, an ex-Brit serviceman, helps travelers plan trips beyond Caye Caulker, and has a Scrabble™ board for rainy days. *Let's Go* recommends ZWIEBACK (243 points on a triple-word score). Simple rooms with unsullied, shared bathrooms. Check-out 11am. Singles BZ$14, doubles BZ$22—comes with coffee. The restaurant downstairs is quality.

Daisy's Hotel (tel. 21-50), very close to Celi's. Spacious blue rooms in excellent shape, if set a bit too far back from the breeze. Strong fans. Friendly management lives next door, past the contingent of canines. Check-out 10am. Send 50% deposit to reserve. Singles BZ$20, doubles BZ$26.50, triples BZ$35. Add BZ$10 during peak season.

Tom's Hotel (tel. 21-02). Arriving at the island from the east, it's on the far left (south), overlooking the Caribbean. Cut through the cemetery at Tropical Paradise Hotel and walk up the beach a bit. Unassuming, cozy rooms with feeble ceiling fans. Spiffy communal bathrooms. Young travelers read, rap, and drink rum on the breezy veranda. Check-out 10am. Singles BZ$20, doubles BZ$25, triples BZ$45. *Cabañas* with private bath and hot water BZ$45 for 2, BZ$55 for 3. Office open 6am-6pm.

Anchorage Hotel (tel. 20-02), southeastern beach, past Tropical Paradise Hotel. Adorable little *cabañas* with authentic thatched roofs dot the Anchorage's own patch of beach. Each has a double bed and private bath with unheated water. *Cabañas* BZ$30 plus tax. Don't bother the office after 7pm. Checkout 10am, but the owner will store luggage in her kitchen for free. Wheelchair accessible.

Barbara's Guest House (tel. 22-15), north end of island, 1 block south of the split. Run by a mellow, lovable Canadian, the House boasts low prices, clean rooms, and the latest in commode worship: the common toilet sits on an altar. The padlock is undernourished. Barbara allows the use of her phone without an extra service charge and seems to take everything in stride. Checkout 9am, but you can store stuff with Barbara. Laundry BZ$10. Singles BZ$20 nightly, $75 for the week.

Vega Inn and Garden (tel. 21-42), on Front St. across from BTL, the telephone office. Glamorous proprietor Tony had a bit part in the film *Mosquito Coast,* though sadly his part was bigger before the editors got to it. Summer-camp-like lodge with hammocks by the sea for all the lounging you can stand. Shared bathrooms with hot water and strong fans. Noon check-out. Singles BZ$3, doubles BZ$45, triples BZ$55. Camping BZ$14 per person. Send 50% deposit to reserve. Traveler's checks accepted.

Ignacio's Huts (tel. 22-12), southeastern end of island, south of Anchorage. Eccentric owner and rustic huts make this a backpacker's mecca. Each hut is clean and has a private bath. A great deal for small groups, since the cost is a flat rate. Ground hut BZ$20. Stilts BZ$30. High-season prices BZ$10-15 higher. *Toilet paper not included.* No visitors allowed, a rule which Ignacio strictly enforces.

FOOD

Caye Caulker's restaurants are legendary for cheap seafood and laid-back (i.e. slow) service. Lobster and eggs for breakfast cost just BZ$5.50, but the food may not arrive until lunchtime. To some, the wait is annoying; to others, it's simply an excuse to down a few more beers. Several homes, including **Claudette's Kitchen** (one block south of the split), post signs advertising daily specials, including some of the best pastries and conch fritters on the island. A few restaurants close for the off-season, and some hotel restaurants, e.g. **Castaway's,** offer excellent food, good prices, and long opening hours.

Sandbox (tel. 22-00), past the police station on the way to the cut. Eat mounded platefuls of local specialties under the cozy light shed by low-hanging lamps, each of the dishes prepared with a dash of international style. Homemade pasta and vegetarian dishes also served. The spinach-lobster lasagna was featured in *Gourmet* magazine—ooh la la. Fish filet with sweet pepper and onions, rice, and salad

(BZ$10), conch fritters (BZ$6), and mega-tasty coconut ice cream (BZ$3). Open Thurs.-Tues. noon-3pm and 6-10pm. Kitchen closes at 9pm.

Glenda's, on Back St. a few blocks south of the soccer field. *The* place for breakfast before 10am. Icy, fresh orange juice (BZ$4) per bottle. Coffee, eggs, bacon, fresh baked bread, and cinnamon rolls (BZ$5). Lobster burritos (BZ$3). Open Mon.-Sat. 7-10am for breakfast, noon-3pm for lunch.

Mad Annie's Restaurant and Bar, Front St. next to the police station. Friendly atmosphere and homestyle cooking. Spanish and Creole specialties; try the delicious conch fritters. Waffles with fruit BZ$5. Open daily 7am-midnight.

Syd's, on the back path by Glenda's. A great bet for lunch. Chicken tostadas BZ$1, a trio of *garnaches* BZ$1, burritos BZ$1.50. Catch the island-renowned BBQ on Sat. night. Open daily 11:30am-3pm and 6-9pm.

Marin's Restaurant and Bar (tel. 21-04), on the back path behind the church. Inside, lights pulse to a reggae beat, while cooler and quieter dining transpires on the back patio. Lobster, eggs, and hotcakes for BZ$6.50, and Marin's special, including lobster, fish, shrimp, and conch, for BZ$17. Espresso (a rarity in Belize) BZ$2. Open daily 8am-2pm and 5:30-10pm. Kitchen closes 9:30pm. Traveler's checks accepted.

BELIZE

SIGHTS AND ENTERTAINMENT

Faintly visible to the east of Caye Caulker lies a stretch of the 250-km **Barrier Reef,** the largest reef in this hemisphere and the second longest in the known universe. By launch, the reef is just minutes away. Popular half-day snorkeling trips to the reef's shallow coral gardens and deeper channels are an agreeable alternative to hallucinogens, in terms of sensory stimulation and hangover. Boats leave between 9am and 10:30am, stop at three snorkeling sites, and return by early afternoon (BZ$25 plus gear rental, no flashbacks). Rent fins, a mask, and a snorkel from the shop in the center of town (BZ$5 plus credit card deposit). Open daily 8am-5pm.

Captains hang out at the docks soliciting passengers. Before arriving at the docks, ask around for the name of a reliable operator. Be sure to leave your valuables ashore. Chocolate is a reliable informant; ask for him between November and August at **Chocolate's Gift Shop** (tel. 21-51). Another legendary local tour guide is **Juni,** who firmly believes in competition. He is cheaper than almost all other boats, and he refuses for ethical reasons to bother the manatees. Look for his house halfway up Front St. or call him (tel. 20-95). Full day of snorkeling at **Hol Chan,** with gear and entrance fee, BZ$20; book one day in advance. Also reliable is Ramón Rosado of **Hicaco Tours.** His shop is in the middle of the island, just south of Rainbow dock, and his prices are BZ$5-10 more expensive than Juni's. Most hotels arrange trips, too.

Frenchie's (tel. 22-34), past Chocolate's, caters to the scuba enthusiast with a PADI course (US$250). Two tank dives cost BZ$80, or BZ$105 with gear. Night diving costs BZ$55. **Belize Diving Services** (tel. 21-43), behind the soccer field, offers two tank dives for BZ$80, or BZ$117 with gear. A four-day NAUI or PADI certification course runs US$300. Open Mon.-Sat. 8am-6pm, Sun. 8am-5pm, 365 days a year. Ambergris Caye offers more extensive diving opportunities.

For sailing trips to the surrounding cayes and to San Pedro, find Gamuza at Annie's Restaurant or at the dock. Bring rum, and he'll supply the sailboat *Tina* for snorkeling on the high seas (BZ$20, snacks included). Camping trips to nearby deserted Goff's Caye may be available in the near future; ask for Harrison.

Caye Caulker's only strip of sandy beach lies to the north of the split. Although this is a good area for snorkeling when currents and wind are low, would-be tanners beware: insects are especially fierce here because of the heavy vegetation nearby. Opt instead for the piers on the Caribbean side of the island.

For entertainment, islanders and oven-toasted travelers tend to follow a two-stop circuit. **Mad Annie's Restaurant and Bar** serves rum and lime to a crowd that loves to tell outrageous fish stories. Afterwards, islanders drift down to the **Reef Bar** for the rum, the Coke, and the reggae.

While you're on Caye Caulker, find **Ellen McCrae,** a resident marine biologist and conservationist who wisely changed her research site from the Bering Sea to the Caribbean and moved to Belize for good. She conducts marine biology tours of the reef, as well as birdwatching expeditions. She can tell you everything you could possibly want to know about coral reefs and marine life.

■■■ AMBERGRIS CAYE AND SAN PEDRO

Belize's leading tourist destination, Ambergris Caye, lies 58km north of Belize City. Although fishing remains an important industry for many of the town's 2500 permanent residents, tourists are fast becoming the island's most lucrative catch. Indeed, the majority of those who come to the Caye are well-off, middle-aged Americans, puttering around the tiny isle on a US$50-per-day golf cart. While most natives watch TV in small shacks, the Belize Yacht Club offers the wealthy a place to relax during those otherwise unbearable days on shore. The Yacht Club aside, it's still possible to enjoy diving without pinching every last sand dollar.

The Caye's main attraction—the Barrier Reef—brings in hordes of scuba enthusiasts, and **San Pedro** attracts travelers who are willing to pay a bit more and to sacrifice some of Caye Caulker's Gilliganesque aura.

Ambergris Caye has a pleasant beach, and because the Barrier Reef runs right along the isle's eastern shores, diving is easier here than at Caye Caulker. The **Hol Chan Marine Reserve,** just south of Ambergris, attracts an assortment of pampered fishies who expect stale bread from divers (admission BZ$3).

Several flights depart daily for Ambergris Caye from the international and municipal airports in Belize City, and a number of boats link the island with the mainland. A high speed launch called **Thunderbolt** (charter tel. 22-17) leaves Cesario's dock at 7am Monday through Saturday, on the southwest side of the island (to Belize City, 1 hr.). The **Hustler** leaves from the Bellevue Hotel (Mon.-Fri. at 4pm, Sun. at 1pm, 1¼ hrs., BZ$40 round-trip). **Triple J** (tel. 02-443-75) leaves at 9am daily from the foot of the Swing Bridge, to return to Belize City at 3pm. For early birds trying to catch worms, **Andrea Lines** leaves from the north-end dock at 7am.

ORIENTATION

Boats from Belize City usually arrive at the Texaco dock on the eastern shore of the island, although some cruise around to the other side. A simple query will help you square your bearings. If you're coming from the east, the first sandy road you will hit is Front St. The three streets of San Pedro that run from north to south have official names, but few locals know them by anything other than **Front St. (Barrier Reef Road**), **Middle St. (Pescador Dr.**), and **Back St. (Coral St.**). The center of town is on Front St. at the Children's Park and the Barrier Reef Hotel. The northern and southern ends of the island cater to the jet set while the rest of the town offers attractions for every budget. Most hotels, shops, and restaurants are located along Front St. To avoid the heat of midday, don't wander far from there; the other streets have no breeze and are home to extended bug families.

PRACTICAL INFORMATION

Tourist Information: Belize Visitor and Tours (tel. 27-28; fax 24-02) on the south end of middle street, north of the airstrip. Impartial Terri is an expert on all price ranges, even budget. Open Mon.-Sat. 8am-noon, 1-6:30pm.

Police: (tel. 20-22.) On Front St. just north of Atlantic Bank; turn right before Central Park.

Post Office: (tel. 21-11), just off of Front St. near the banks. *Poste Restante* available. Open Mon.-Thurs. 8am-noon and 1-5pm, Fri. 8am-noon and 1-4:30pm.

Telephones: Belize Telecommunications Ltd. (tel. 21-99), at the north end of Middle St. next to the bellowing electric generator. Free collect and AT&T credit-card calls to the U.S.; otherwise, BZ$9.60 per 3min. Open Mon.-Fri. 8am-noon and

1-4pm, Sat. 8am-noon. **The Budget Traveler** (tel. 28-06) has an office in the Tortuga Dive Shop. **Telephone code** for San Pedro: 026.

Currency Exchange: Atlantic Bank Ltd. (tel. 21-95; fax 25-13), just south of the town center on Front St. Dollars and traveler's checks changed. Cash advances on Visa and MC. Open Mon., Tues., and Thurs. 8am-noon and 1-3pm, Wed. 8am-1pm, Fri. 8am-noon and 1-3pm, Sat. 8:30am-noon.

Airstrip: The **San Pedro airstrip** is located at the southwest end of town and can be reached by taxi or on foot. **Island Air** (tel. 24-35) sends hourly flights to Belize City Municipal Airport daily from 7am-5pm (15min., BZ$39 one-way), and also services Corozal (twice daily, 35min., one-way BZ$60). **Tropic Air** (tel. 20-12) flies to Belize City (every hour, on the hour, 7am-5pm, round-trip to municipal airport BZ$77, round-trip to international airport BZ$154). Any flight will stop on request at Caye Caulker (BZ$35). Reserve several days in advance during the high season (Nov.-May).

Market: Rock's Store (tel. 20-44), on Middle St., stocks everything from suntan lotion to fresh bread. Open daily 6am-10pm.

Laundry: J's Laundromat (tel. 23-73), on Middle St. near the center of town. Look for the dancing frog sign. Full service up to 5kg, BZ$10. Open Mon.-Sat. 8am-8pm (except Wed., closed at 6pm), Sun. 8am-2pm.

Pharmacy: San Carlos Pharmacy (tel. 29-18), on north end of Middle St. Open Mon.-Sat. 8am-noon and 2-9pm, Sun. 5-9pm. 24-hr. emergency service.

Medical Services: San Pedro Lion's Clinic (tel. 20-73), behind the airstrip. Open Mon.-Fri. 8am-4pm. Open for emergencies, 24 hrs. There is also a hyperbaric compression chamber for divers, 2 doors north of the clinic, called **Sub-Aquatic Safety Services of Belize, Ltd.** (tel. 28-51).

ACCOMMODATIONS

Inexpensive rooms are more scarce here than on Caye Caulker, especially during high season, but during low season many proprietors will negotiate their prices.

Hotel San Pedrano (tel. 20-54; fax 20-93), next to Tómas Hotel on Front St. The white walls with sea-colored trim make up for the lack of an ocean view. Classy *and* budgety. All rooms have private bath. Singles BZ$20, doubles BZ$2, triples BZ$30. Add about BZ$5 in high season, and BZ$10 for A/C. 8% service charge waived for walk-ins.

Milo's (tel. 20-33), at the north end of Front St. Beware: there are 3 places called Milo's. Office is in grocery store below. Exquisitely cheap for San Pedro. Decent rooms with shared bath. Toilet rejects paper. Singles BZ$21, doubles BZ$26.50, triples BZ$37.

Tómas Hotel (tel. 20-61), at the north side of Front St. Provided you don't rouse him from a *siesta,* Tómas, the endearing proprietor, will make you feel welcome. Clean rooms with newly tiled bathrooms. Strong ceiling fans, lumpy beds. Singles and doubles BZ$50, with A/C BZ$70. Traveler's checks accepted.

Rubie's Hotel, across from the school on Front St.'s south end (tel. 20-63; fax 24-34). Best bet for a seaview. Noon check-out. Doubles BZ$26.50, with bath (hot water) on 2nd floor BZ$53, on 3rd floor BZ$65, triples with bath BZ$75. To reserve, send 1 night's deposit. Personal checks and traveler's checks accepted.

FOOD

Before complaining at the lack of tasty food for your bored, hotel-fed palate, remember that Belizeans eat out only occasionally; they can't afford the insanely boosted prices you see at the resorts. Look hard and find several restaurants that serve big plates of seafood and local (i.e. Belizean and Mexican) cuisine at reasonable rates.

Elvi's Kitchen (tel. 21-76; fax 30-56), on Middle St. near the center of town. Built around a tree with sand on the floor, Elvi's will make you feel like you never left the beach. Not quite Graceland, but the locals still pronounce the name like the King's."Di place for seafood" offers a mix of seafood and Creole fare for BZ$5-20. Live music Thurs.-Fri. Open Mon.-Sat. 11am-2pm and 5:30-10pm.

Reef Restaurant, just north of the middle of Middle St. Reputed by locals to be the cheapest place in town, this place delivers with Latin gusto. Conch cerviche BZ$6, burritos BZ$1.50. Open Mon.-Sat. 11:30am-2pm and 6-9pm.

Luigi's (tel. 21-40), around the middle of Middle St. Bland atmosphere, but another local favorite for its Mexican and Belizean fare. Try to snag the cheery cook for a chat. *Salbutes* BZ$6. Accepts traveler's checks. Open Mon.-Sat. 11:30am-2pm and 6-9pm.

Fido's and the Pizza Place (tel. 24-44), at the north side of Front St. ("Fee-do's") Located on the water, "Fee-do's" thatched-roof bar-and-grill is esteemed for the live music on weekend nights, the TV with CNN most of the time, and its status as a swingin' pick-up spot. Large (16") single-item pizza BZ$24 (dig them fresh tomatoes). The pizza joint is open Thurs.-Tues. 7am-9pm.

SIGHTS AND ENTERTAINMENT

Dive-a-rama. Dives-R-Us. Diver-roni. *Ad nauseam*. This is some of the best diving in the world, and even experienced divers will be amazed by the colorful array of fish and coral around Ambergris Caye. Try to negotiate prices during the off-season, as many of the operators are willing to haggle. For non-certified scuba divers, snorkeling at the nearby **Hol Chan Marine Reserve** (BZ$3) affords an opportunity to swim amid barracudas, moray eels, lobsters, yellowtail snappers, parrotfish, eagle rays, and even the occasional benevolent shark.

For experienced divers, many dive shops regularly make trips to the **Blue Hole** at the Lighthouse Reef Atoll. Nearly 300m in diameter and 144m deep, the hole forms a nearly-perfect sapphire circle in the pale teal water. The hole was first explored in the late 1980s by Jacques Cousteau, who braved the depths in a miniature submarine; today, it's a world-famous site. Qualified divers can explore mind-blowing stalagmite and stalactite formations and swim below an undercut canyon believed to have been a land cave 10,000 years ago. A daytrip usually includes three meals, gear, and several stops (about US$165). Snorkelers can tag along for about US$110.

The *Southern Beauty,* a glass-bottomed boat, leaves from the **Tackle Box Bar** dock near the center of town, escorting snorkelers and anyone else to the Marine Reserve. It departs twice daily, at 9am and 2pm, for half-day excursions (BZ$20, with snorkel gear BZ$26).

Many shops on the island offer similar trips (at similar rates) to those offered at dive sites along the reef. The **Bottom Time Diveshop** (tel. 23-48; fax 27-66), at the Sun Breeze Resort on the south end of the isle, offers a free introductory scuba lesson. Twice daily (9am and 2pm), motorboats and certified instructors take divers to various dive sites around Ambergris (BZ$50 per tank dive, with all rental equipment BZ$70). Bottom Time also offers PADI certification (5-day course US$350). **Tortuga Dive Centre** (tel. 24-26; fax 28-06) offers two back-to-back dives in the morning for US$40, a single dive for US$28, and a night dive for US$30 (US$15 extra for diving equipment, US$6 for snorkeling equipment).

Stop at the **Tackle Box Bar** at the end of the pier on the southern side of town to peer at the sharks that they keep out back. Live music Fridays and Saturdays; open Mon.-Thurs. 9am-midnight, Fri.-Sat. 9am-2am. **Tarzan's Nite Club** (tel. 29-47), right in the middle of town, boasts a big dance floor complete with videos (Fri. and Sat.), Jane look-alike barmaids, and a waterfall (open Tues.-Thurs. and Sun. 9pm-midnight, Fri.-Sat. 9pm-3am; BZ$5 cover charge). **Big Daddy's** is just across the way. There's dancing and live music on weekends with cover charge (varies, but usually BZ$15).

WESTERN BELIZE

Belize's **Western Highway** runs 124km from Belize City to the frontier, spanning grassy savannas before winding into the Maya Mountains. Although it's possible to power from Belize City to Tikal in one exhausting day, a few hours of sight-seeing in western Belize will make the trip far more pleasant.

According to Belizean archaeologist Jaime Awe, there are more unexcavated Mayan sites in Belize than there are modern houses. Many of the small, grass-covered mounds visible from the roadside are, in fact, Mayan platforms, temples, and plazas that will remain untouched until the money can be found to begin excavating new sites. You can visit the Belize Zoo and tickle a jaguar (see Near Belize City, page 128), spend the night in **San Ignacio,** trek through the nearby ruins of **Xunantunich,** explore **Mountain Pine Ridge** national forest, or float down the nearby Macal River. From San Ignacio, the great ruins of **Tikal** in the Guatemalan Petén are a hop, skip, and a bumpy four-hour bus ride away.

■■■ BELMOPAN

Hurricane Hattie had it in for haggard Belize; the storm was the last straw for the country's government, which was tired of getting pummeled by storms along the coast. In hapless retreat from nature, leaders simply picked up and left Belize City to head west for Belmopan and create a new capital. Nowadays, the newly formed city is exactly what it feels like: a functional, bureaucratic, and bizarrely hollow remnant of the '70s. In general, there is little for tourists to do here; for most, it's a far from memorable stop on the way to San Ignacio. Still, some find in it a welcome rest from frenetic Belize City, and others, frustrated at the lack of artifacts at the Mayan ruins, are excited to find that they haven't all been lost by bungling bureaucrats: a large collection is maintained here by the department of archaeology.

Orientation The **Independence Plaza,** heart of the national government buildings, serves as the center of the town, which stretches off lazily in every direction. The highway runs to the west of the center of town; the **Ring Road,** where most of the cool stuff can be found, circumscribes the town. The Western portion of the Ring Road is called Constitution Drive. All buses stop at the market place, which is adjacent to Independence Plaza. Police warn that the south end of town can be dangerous at night.

Practical Information Belmopan has no tourist office. The **Police** (tel. 222-22) are located northeast of the market in Independence Plaza. 911 is still the **emergency number,** and they're open 24 hrs. The **Post Office,** on the north end of the market, is open Mon.-Thurs. 8am-noon and 1-4:30pm, Fri. 8-noon and 1-4pm. *Poste restante* available. **Telephones** and **telegrams** (as well as cheap **fax** service) are available at **BTL** (tel. 221-93; fax 223-66) located south of the market on the Ring Road. It's open Mon.-Fri. 8am-noon and 1-4pm. The **telephone code** is 08. **Barclay's Bank** (tel. 223-82; 235-79), visible just to the north of the market, exchanges U.S. dollars, pounds sterling, Canadian dollars, and traveler's checks (BZ$1 for amounts less than BZ$100) with a not-so-great exchange rate. They provide cash advances on MC, Visa, and Discover with no additional fee (open Mon.-Thurs. 8am-1pm, Fri. 8am-4:30pm). **Buses** leave from the market. **Novelo's** has a terminal on the west side of the market. They send buses to Belize City (every 30min., 6am-12:30pm, 1½ hrs., BZ$3.50) and to Benque Viejo (every 30min., 12:30-9pm, 70min., BZ$2.50). To San Ignacio, take the Benque Viejo bus (BZ$2.25). For any other service, stand in the middle of the market and gesticulate madly. **Brodie's** (tel. 230-78), a well-stocked **supermarket,** is a 10-minute walk from the market—take the concrete walkway heading east from Independence Plaza. Take the left fork, past the little school. Open Mon.-Thurs. 8am-noon and 2-7pm, Fri.-Sat. 8am-noon and 2-9pm. **Cardinal Pharmacy** (tel. 228-07) is located just south of Brodie's and has feminine hygiene products and OTC and prescription drugs (open Mon.-Thurs. 8:30-noon, 2:30-7pm, Fri.-Sat. 8:30-noon, 2:30-9pm). The **hospital** (emergency tel. 225-18) is located north of the market. Take the Ring Road on the west side of the market and go a couple of blocks due north. The office (tel. 222-64) is around back (open Mon.-Fri. 8am-5pm). Ambulance service is available.

Accommodations and Food Grab grub from one of the many vendors around the bus depot; if you can help it, hold back until San Ignacio. Unfortunately, the general absence of tourist-processing in other parts of town makes staying here difficult. There are three hotels in town, and two of them are *way* outside the budget range. **El Rey,** 23 Moho (tel. 234-38), lives up to its name by default. Go east from the hospital, take the third left from the main road, then the second right. The rates are reasonable, the rooms clean and spacious with private baths (no A/C, check-out 11am. Singles BZ$35, doubles BZ$45, tax included).The local favorite for food is **Caladium** (tel. 227-54), located at the north end of the market (open Mon.-Fri. 8am-8pm, Sat. 8am-7pm). They serve weight-watching portions of the standard fare: two eggs, bacon, and jacks for BZ$7. The cleverly named **Chinese Restaurant** (tel. 233-06) squats at Brodie's shopping center. Morose pictures of weeping children add to the strange ambience of this humble restaurant. Shrimp chow mein is BZ$10 (open daily 10am–10pm).

Sights Well worth negotiating the encompassing bureaucratic chaos is the collection of Mayan artifacts at the **Department of Archaeology** (tel. 221-06), the building on the west side of Independence Plaza. Enter and then head left. Tours are provided (donations are accepted with large smiles) on Mon., Wed., and Fri. afternoons, but only with advance appointment. This collection includes all the artifacts taken from the multiplicity of Mayan monuments across Belize. The inchoate National Museum currently stands at a majestic twenty centimeters in height and a resplendent half a meter in length. A scale model of the structure can be seen at the **department of museums,** the white building on the southeast side of the market.

■■■ SAN IGNACIO

The tightly packed thoroughfare of San Ignacio (pop. 8000) creates an impression of constant bustling and a spirit of spunkiness not merited by the town's size. The village boomed between 1920 and 1950 as a center for the vigorous exploitation of mahogany and chicle. Eventually the trees dwindled, Mr. Wrigley found cheap synthetic substances to placate gum-popping teenage mandibles, and the chicle industry fell into precipitous decline. Although livestock and agriculture account for much of present-day revenue, the Cayo district—of which San Ignacio is the capital—attracts increasing numbers of ecotourists who come to hike, canoe, and ride on horseback through the area's stunning parks and archaeological sites. The result is bittersweet, as it's sometimes hard to avoid seeing other travelers. San Ignacio's inexpensive food and lodging, as well as its bank and telephone office, make it a good base for exploring the bountiful Mountain Pine Ridge Forest Reserve or the Mayan ruins of Xunantunich. The San Ignacio region is also home to two Mennonite communities, which lie north of the Western Highway at Spanish Lookout.

Orientation Entering San Ignacio after passing through unexceptional next-door neighbor Santa Elena, you'll pass over the Macal River on Hawkesburg Bridge, Belize's only suspension bridge, built in 1949. Entering the bridge entrance requires passage through one of Belize's three traffic lights. When the light functions, locals rarely acknowledge it. To continue toward Benque Viejo del Carmen and Guatemala, make the first left on Old Benque Viejo Rd. and head uphill out of town. To reach the town center, take the first right onto **Burns Ave.** and walk two blocks to **Belize Bank.** Buses stop near here. Burns Av., running north-south, is San Ignacio's commercial strip.

Practical Information Fast becoming a legend, **Eva's Restaurant,** 22 Burns Ave., serves up as-official-as-it-gets **tourist information** to nearly every traveler who sets foot in San Ignacio. Ask here about arranging eco-trips and hiring ruins guides (open Sun.-Thurs. 7am-11pm, Fri.-Sat. 7am-midnight). The **police station** (tel. 20-22) is just west of the bridge at the town park (open 24 hrs.). The **post office** (tel. 20-

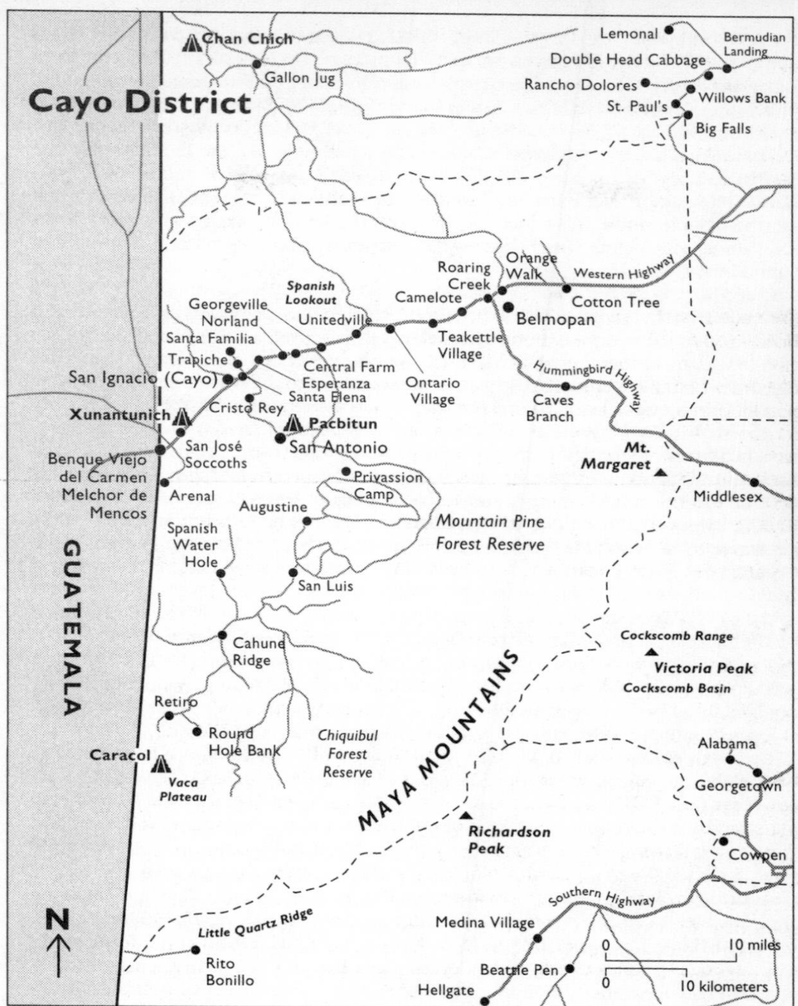

49) is located above the police station (stairs to the right, through the door labeled "district commissioner") near the bridge. *Poste Restante* is available. (Open Mon.-Thurs. 8am-noon and 1-4:30pm, Fri. 8am-noon and 1-4pm). For **telephones, telegrams,** and **fax** service, head for **BTL** (tel. 20-90), across from the Venus Hotel on Burns Ave. (open Mon.-Fri. 8am-noon and 1-4pm). After hours, use the public phones in the small park in front of the police station. The **telephone code** is 092. **Rent bikes** at **BĞM,** across Burns from Eva's. (BZ$5 per hr., BZ$20 per day, or BZ$50 for a weekend. Add BZ$10 during high season.) Exchange currency at most stores, hotels, restaurants, or at **Atlantic Bank** (tel. 23-47), one block south of Eva's on Burns Ave. Cash advances on credit cards (fee BZ$10; open Mon.-Tues. and Thurs.-Fri. 8am-noon and 1-3pm, Wed. 8am-1pm; Sat. 8:30am-noon). If all else fails, ask Bob at Eva's about changing currency. **Bus** fares and schedules change faster than traffic lights here. At least one line makes the 120km trip to Belize City every hour. **Shaw's** leaves for Belmopan (every hr. on the ½ hr., 7:30am-12:30pm, then

every 30min. from 1-4:45pm, 45min., BZ$2.25). After noon, it's **Batty Brothers** (2½ hrs., BZ$5). The **Z-Line** also goes to Belmopan (1½ hrs., BZ$2) and changes to Dangriga (4 hrs., BZ$10). **Taxis** take passengers from San Ignacio to Ciudad Melchor de Mencos at the Guatemalan border for BZ$20. **Shaw's** sends two buses to Melchor (Mon.-Sat. 7:30 and 8:30am, 45min., BZ$1.50), as do most of the carriers. Do not take a late bus to Guatemala; it's not safe at night. **Arfam Laundromat** (tel. 39-56) eagerly awaits dirty clothes at BZ$6 per load, full- or self-service, plus BZ$0.50 for soap. Take Burns Ave. south from Eva's, take first right, then turn left at Martha's Guest House; it's down the street on the left. The **drug store** is on Burns Ave. under the Venus Hotel (open Mon.-Sat. 8am-noon, 1-5pm, and 7-9pm, Sun. 9am-noon).

Accommodations Several hotels in San Ignacio provide comfortable and cheap places to spend the night. The stately **Hi-Et Hotel,** 12 West St. at Waight St., two blocks from the center, lacks Hyatt splendor but does offer clean rooms with balconies (and meager locks). Be sure to wear a towel to the bathroom; on your way you'll be passing the living room. The friendly owner lends out his canoe (check-out 11am, singles BZ$10, doubles BZ$20). **Central Hotel** (tel. 22-53), located on Burns Ave. next to Eva's building and upstairs, offers simple rooms with fans, coconut-shell ashtrays, and hot water for those oddballs who need a hot shower in the tropics. The balcony has a hammock for siestas (check-out 10am, singles BZ$19, doubles BZ$22, triples BZ$28; weekly rates available). Slightly pricier but luxurious by budget standards is **Hotel Maxima** (tel. 22-65) on Hudson St., 1½ blocks south of Eva's. Comfortable beds, cheap A/C, and cable TV make this a siren call for the weariest backpackers. (Check-out noon; singles BZ$25, with A/C BZ30; doubles BZ$30, with A/C BZ$35. Prices stay the same during high season). For those who feel restrained by the protection of an expensive roof and walls, **Mida's Eco-Resort** (tel. 31-72, 21-01), a 10-minute walk north of Eva's on Burns Ave., offers camping for BZ$7 per person. Free pick-up. Pricey rooms are also available (singles with private bath BZ$40; doubles BZ$45). Tourists deathly afraid of imminent homelessness can turn to Bob at Eva's Restaurant, who know almost every operator in Cayo District.

The jungle around San Ignacio hides retreats and lodges ranging from back-to-basics affairs to full-blown resorts. 5km out of San Ignacio, in Bullet Tree Falls, **Parrot Nest** (tel. 37-02) cozies right up to the Mopan River. Listen to the overwhelming sounds of the jungle from your treehouse or cabin. Owner Fred radiates good vibes and is starting a botanical garden near the treehouses. Bullet Tree is close to **El Pilar,** an extensive Mayan archaeological site still in the preliminary stages of excavation. Horseback riding (with or without guides, BZ$35 for a full day) and canoeing are available. A cab there runs BZ$6-10; just ask for Parrot Nest (BZ$40 for a cabin; breakfast BZ$4.50, dinner BZ$9). Even farther from civilization is the **Rancho de Los Amigos** (phones usually out of order; have Bob at Eva's radio them), a strenuous 2km hike from the turnoff into San José Succotz directly across from the Xunantunich ferry. An acupuncturist and nutritionist have cleared only enough trees to build two immaculately clean huts and a dining area where all the cooking is done over fires. Call ahead. (Two meals are included with a *casita,* for US$25 per person. Camping available.)

Food The cuisine here is cheap, delicious, and filling. **Eva's Restaurant,** 22 Burns Ave. (tel. 22-67), has traditionally been a home base for local tourism, and is crawling with sated, smoking, young-at-heart types. They also serve some beautiful burritos. The behemoth chicken burrito (BZ$5) is particularly tasty. A good place to hook up with other tourists (open Sun.-Thurs. 7am-11pm, Fri.-Sat. 7am-midnight). More recently, a rival to Eva's has arisen in the form of the **Sandcastle** restaurant, behind the Batty Brothers' bus terminal. Sand floor and open-air atmosphere provide a backdrop for great meals. Cheese and veggie omelette BZ$7. Try the pizza burrito for BZ$7; it's out-of-control good. (Open Mon.-Sat. 7am-11pm; Sunday hours planned for winter 1995.) Offering a refreshing change of style is **Roots,** which serves up hearty vegetarian dishes, Rasta-foods, and fresh, pulpy juices. Vegetable pizza with herbal crust is BZ$6, a "Roots" sandwich is BZ$6, and a glass of seaweed juice will set you back BZ$2. They also are willing to arrange for their buddies to come pierce belly-buttons for those with the urge. The place for breakfast is the **Maya Café** (tel. 36-25), a couple doors down from Eva's. They offer several flavors of yogurt with excellent granola and fruit for BZ$4. They'll also pack formidable lunches for day trips for BZ$9.50 (open Mon.-Tues. and Thurs.-Sun. 6:30am-9:30pm, Fri.-Sat. 6:30am-10:30pm).

SIGHTS

> WARNING: The U.S. State Department warns that highway bandits are particularly active between Melchor de Mencos at the Guatemala-Belize border and Tikal. If you must make the trip from San Ignacio (and are unable to travel to Tikal from the south), ONLY travel during the day.

San Ignacio can serve as a departure point for those wishing to catch the amazing ruins at **Tikal,** Guatemala (See Guatemala: Tikal, page 110). Catch an early Benque Viejo bus (also known as the Melchor bus) and take it to Succotz, the Xunantunich ferry—across the street is the Guatemalan consulate (open Mon.-Fri. 9am-1pm). Get a visa there, then catch the next bus to Melchor. Cross the border, paying about US$1 (don't let the immigration officers cheat; they've got a bad reputation). Right outside the doors are buses and minivans waiting to speed tourists over the back-breaking Guatemalan roads (5, 6, 7, 8,11am, 1, 4pm, 3½ hrs., Q10). The bus, a true dust-devil-generating Central American chicken bus, is dreaded among travelers. The safer and more comfortable route is by taxi. Beware hustlers. For four people, the standard price is US$10-15 per person. Just wait for more tourists to show up, then ride together. By car, the journey is said to take a mere two hours. Entrance to Guatemala costs 5 quetzales with the visa or US$5 without the visa. Although it is not usually considered one, Tikal could be shoehorned a daytrip. Local (San Ignacio) operators will go to Tikal for US$75 per person.

Only 800m from San Ignacio lie the lazy traveler's Mayan ruins; it's no trek at all to **Cahal Pech** (Place of the Ticks). Although Cahal Pech is only a medium-sized Mayan center, it has produced some of the earliest evidence of occupation in the area (from 1000 BC until 900 AD). Excavation at the site began only in 1988, and archaeologists are still at work on the site. As the researchers sift through buckets of dirt in search of stone tools and other artifacts, you'll be able to see the various layers of soil where different generations of Mayans spread new floors across the entire plaza. Current excavators and visiting archaeologists grumble about the overly imaginative restoration of the site; you should take the masks depicted on the temple and the main arch with, as they say, "a bucket of salt." Places where the crews didn't get carried away with cement can be found back behind the main "range structure" at the rear of the plaza, where one can follow narrow paths through the dark rooms of the royal chamber. Archaeologists are impressed with the remaining red dye on some ledges in these rooms. While work on the site is far from complete, the ruins are worth the hour or two it takes to see them (admission BZ$3). Take a cab from San Ignacio to avoid the uphill climb (BZ$5). Be sure to clarify that you're going to the Cahal Pech ruins. After checking out the ruins, reward yourself with a frothy, frosty beverage at the **Cahal Pech Bar and Grill,** the giant *palapa* on the hill.

There are a few possibilities for those who want to enjoy the local rivers without getting wet. Next to the bus terminal, the focal point of the canoe scene is **Sandcastle Restaurant,** from which proprietor "Remo" Dan runs **Float Belize** (tel. 32-13). Fully outfitted three-person canoes rent for about BZ$35, without a guide. The Macal is a mellow river, and the only real hazard to boaters is the shallows, where you may have to get out and push your boat upstream. Starting by the bridge, canoers can paddle upstream beyond the reach of the town's noise and into the lush, peaceful jungle nearby. Any place on the bank can serve as a refreshing swimming spot, and afterwards the downstream trip back to town is a piece of cake.

Guided tours are another alternative (BZ$25 per day). **"Remo" Dan's** experienced guides leave around 9am, take you 16km upstream with a vehicle, then drop you off for a day-long, down-river float. Dan guarantees you'll see parrots and iguanas. Tours usually stop for lunch at the Mayan village of **Cristo Rey,** so bring a little cash along. For more information, head to the Sandcastle, or ask around at Eva's. Also, "Remo" Dan is trying to break the time-worn mold for tours, and is developing night trips and variations on the winning theme.

Canoe tours are the best way to visit the **Panti Nature Trail** (or **Rainforest Medicine Trail,** tel. 38-70) at Ix Chel Farm, 10km west of San Ignacio near Chaa Creek, where you can learn about the astounding medicinal uses of the area's flora. At 103-years-old and counting (knock on wood), Panti is a renowned master of holistic medicine, and the ailing have come from all over the world to sample his herbal cures. The Panti trail snakes through **Healer's Hut**, a small house made entirely of earth and plants. Admission for self-guided tours with a pamphlet (BZ$10) is often a better deal than the guided tours (BZ$15-50), during which a guide essentially reads the pamphlet to you. The trail starts at the corner of Old Bengue and Chaa Creek Rd.

BELIZE

After day hikes and canoeing trips, you can drain the last of your sweat by dancing the night away. A group usually gathers at Eva's after dinner to chug some Belikins before heading over to their preferred hot spot. Most popular is the **Blue Angel** night club on Hudson St. Rumor has it that the fence on the second-floor balcony was constructed after rambunctious British soldiers nearly threw someone over. (Cover charge on weekends for live bands varies, but it's always BZ$5 more for men than women. Open Tues.-Thurs. and Sun. 7pm-midnight, Fri.-Sat. 7pm-3am.) A recently opened but increasingly popular choice is Santa Elena's **Snooty Fox** (tel. 21-50), which boasts a pool table, a great view, and that inscrutable name. The **Cahal Pech Tavern** sits on the hill and is open weekends after 9pm for dancing.

■ NEAR SAN IGNACIO

SAN ANTONIO

The origins of San Antonio (known locally as TaNah, Mayan for "Our Home"), are shrouded in myth. Some claim that the town's earliest settlers lived in nearby Mountain Pine Ridge but were brought down to TaNah while hunting a *wari.* When the *wari* magically disappeared, the hunters took it as a sign from the Mayan god Yum Kax-Ku to start a new settlement. Others tell a different story: some chickens and turkeys were missing from a nearby village; the two newest villagers were blamed and whipped. Upon leaving town, the two ominously warned, "You will pay for this deed." When villagers started dying inexplicably, the town was deemed cursed; its residents dispersed, heading to what is now San Antonio.

Free from evil spells of every kind, San Antonio (pop. 1500) has since become a living, breathing center of Mayan culture. Among the villagers are a snake doctor and an old master healer who supposedly was once sent to administer to the Queen of England. The Mayan García sisters, distantly related to the late, great Jerry, also live in town—their **museum** of Mayan art (admission BZ$6) is the town's tourist center. The sisters became interested in art when they discovered a slate stone in the fields and, intrigued with the stone as a medium, carved a whale from it. Paintings and sculpture by the García sisters, a Mayan ceremonial table, medicinal herbs, and other artifacts of Mayan culture are on display (open daily 7am-6pm).

Two trucks a day (10 and 10:30am) take villagers home to San Antonio and will let tourists ride along for BZ$2. They return the next day. The village offers only a few services. The only **BTL** phone (tel. 32-16, 32-66) is three blocks up from the police station at the crossroads, while the **mini-post office** is inside the Indita Maya Restaurant. The only **accommodation** in town is the **Chichan Ka Lodge,** a traditional Mayan building at the García's place (singles BZ$25, doubles BZ$30). **Hilltop camping** provides a plot of ground for BZ$5 per person. Some pass the night in San Antonio, but most are just stopping by on their way to Mountain Pine Ridge. If you do stay, be sure to look at the horses' manes in the morning. According to legend, perfectly trimmed manes indicate that dwarves from the hills rode them in the night and wrapped their feet in the horses' hair. What the nocturnal dwarves' feet will do to a 4x4 vehicle is still unclear.

MOUNTAIN PINE RIDGE RESERVE

Mountain Pine Ridge, just south of San Ignacio, is a great daytrip for civilization's discontented, especially if they have a car. Tall conifers, mountains, ancient caves, and clear streams grace the large forest reserve, accessible by a road branching off the Western Highway just east of San Ignacio at Georgeville. A list of guides willing to take you to the reserve is available at Eva's and at the Sandcastle; it's not difficult to assemble the required five-person group. Expect to pay BZ$35 per person. Without your own wheels or a guide, renting a car is the only way you'll make it to the reserve. The **Venus Hotel** (tel. 32-03) rents Suzuki Samurais for BZ$125 per 24 hrs., not including gas. Those depending on their own car should make sure it's sturdy and in good condition—the roads are brutal. Sadly, this has left many rental vehicles prone to breakdown; plan carefully for all contingencies. To reach the reserve, follow the road until you reach San Antonio and then turn left; a few miles later, turn right. Signs will guide you, and it's hard to get lost. You're in the reserve when the green jungle gives way to tall pines.

The turn-off for **Hidden Valley Falls** is about a 25 minutes drive past the main gate. A left turn here brings you a slow 16km down a steep hill (look for the sign); spectacular views of the pine-covered slopes, soaring birds, and a plummeting 300m waterfall will be your reward (open 8am-6pm; admission BZ$2). The trip in and back to the main road takes about an hour. Continuing on the main road, the most practical next stop is the town of **Augustine,** where you can find the only official camping spot in the park, the **Douglas D'Silva Forest Station** (to the left as you drive in). Many recommend staying overnight here to get the most out of the Reserve. Those continuing on to Caracol should acquire a permit at the station. Taking the road to the right through Augustine leads visitors to the caves at Río Frío. To the right of the road is a small nature trail where you can see *chicle*-producing sapodilla trees, along with some mahogany trees that the British seem to have missed. The most impressive site, however, is the cave at trail's end. A sign erected by Colorado State University students reads: "Tell me your secrets and I'll guard them too." Whether or not you choose to spill your guts, the massive main cave inspires respect. Openings on both ends shine light on stalactite formations, dark pools, and naturally eroded stone steps; the towering ceiling will take your damp breath away. Stones form an easily manageable path to the cave's heart, and there's a path the locals know to the left, if you're facing up the river. The ledges to the right, however, are quite dangerous. Bring a flashlight and hiking companions. If the path is negotiable, it leads through the cave to a pleasant nature walk. Scope out the spooky bats that snooze in the holes in the ceiling.

What the Río Frío takes out of you, the pools at Río On will put right back in. Ten minutes back on the road toward Cayo, on the left, rocks have trapped the descending river, forming several ideal swimming holes (don't dive in head first). Picnic tables which provide a great view of the tumbling waters are available a bit farther on. A little squirming and pushing on your part turn the smaller falls into a water slide. Beware unexpectedly slippery rocks. On the way back, a unique but expensive place to grab a beer (BZ$4) and enjoy the view is Francis Ford Coppola's **Blancaneaux Lodge** (tel. 38-78), a few kilometers away from the gate. This posh resort has its own hydroelectric plant. Coppola only flies down for special occasions. Though the resort would be a lovely setting in which to wile away the hours before the apocalypse, now it's fun just to visit.

CARACOL

A few years ago, the ruins at Caracol were accessible only to the mightiest of vehicles. Today the road has improved considerably, and Caracol is within striking distance of Augustine (one hour by car). Indeed, the most difficult part of getting to Caracol is obtaining a visitor's permit—stop at the Douglas D'Silva Forest Station in Augustin, and within minutes you can be back on the road to the ruins, permit in hand. Although only partially excavated, Caracol is thought by some to rival Tikal in importance. Led by Lord Water, Caracol defeated Tikal in a war in 562 AD. Since 1985, archaeologists have discovered over 4000 structures on the site's 88 acres, including a royal tomb, stelae depicting magical dwarves, and the 42m-high **Kanaa palace,** which offers a stunning view of the surrounding jungle-enshrouded hills. Caracol may only be viewed with a tour guide, and tours are conducted only a few times a day. Schedules vary. While the guides are under-informed, they manage to show you plenty. The tour is free, but tips are appreciated. Make sure you get to see the 700-year-old Ceiba tree. Take the time to absorb Caracol's beauty; the shrill insects above will hypnotize you whether you like it or not.

If renting a car is out of the question, getting a tour/taxi to Caracol is pretty expensive. The going rate is US$50 per person, although Hector, a local driver, will take his spacious and comfy station wagon to Caracol for US$150—in a group of five, each pays US$30 per person. Ask for Hector at the town park or at Eva's.

XUNANTUNICH

The ruins at **Xunantunich** stand shorter than Caracol, but they're much more convenient to San Ignacio. Coming from Cayo on the road to Guatemala, **El Castillo,** the main temple of Xunantunich, towers in the distance to the right. Xunantunich (Maiden of the Rock) was an important city in the late Classic period (700-900 AD) and either a rival or a satellite settlement of Tikal. Only partially excavated and studied, the ruins at Xunantunich include an impressive pyramid. Like many Mayan sites, the accessible ruins here are mostly former residences and temples. While workers lived down in the Mopan river-valley, where fertile soil made agriculture easier, the aristocracy resided here, where special paths connected their homes to other important structures.

The steps of **El Castillo** lead up to the top of the temple; looking down on the plaza, envisioning humbled crowds below, it's easy to wax megalomaniacal. El Castillo dwarfs the other temples and unexcavated mounds. Scamper up its lower portion, which is still engulfed by vegetation, to the partially restored stucco frieze on the eastern corner. On display here are masks devoted to Kinich Ahau, the sun deity, and Ixchel, the moon god. Swing around back, then up the not-so-obvious stairs in the center, all the way to the top. From El Castillo's reconstructed roof, the settlements of Succotz, Benque Viejo del Carmen, and Melchor de Mencos (in Guatemala) are visible from left to right, tucked into the green hills.

After investigating the tower (and turning your legs to lactic pudding in the process), examination of the enclosed stelae next to the offices offers a pleasant change of pace. Some of the stones seem blank or non-representational, but expert analysis has revealed hidden images of the god K'awil, a serpent-footed deity associated with ancestors. Xunantunich rests atop a hill, across the Mopan River and 1½km up a dirt road from the hamlet of **San José Succotz.** About 9km from San Ignacio, Succotz is accessible via a *colectivo* that shuttles between the Esso station in San Ignacio and the town of Benque Viejo del Carmen on the border (BZ$1). **Batty Bus Service** heads to Benque Viejo from San Ignacio (every hr. until noon, on the hr., BZ$1). From Succotz take the small cable-drawn **ferry** across the Mopan; for a real hoot, ask to operate the ferry yourself (operates daily 8am-4pm, free). The dirt road leading up to the ruins is rough and steep, making for a vigorous hike or a jangly drive (ruins open daily 8am-5pm, admission BZ$3).

SOUTHERN COAST

■■■ DANGRIGA

Crack open the bus or car window on your way southeast down **Hummingbird Highway** for an evolving olfactory journey. First you'll catch a whiff of fresh mist off the Cahune palm trees, which were sacred to the Mayans for their brilliant performances as food, roofing, and fuel. As the rolling hills flatten out, brace your nose—the bitter smoke is a result of the area's slash-and-burn farming. Soon the odor of smoke will give way to the smell of the sweet blossoms and endless citrus groves which support the local economy. Only when salty, fishy air wafts your way will you be near Dangriga (pop. 8100).

Once known as Stann Creek, this oceanfront community was established by Puritans from New Providence who farmed Tobacco Caye and the rich soil of the Coastal Belt and used the town as a trading post, or stand (thus, "stann"). Today, most of the town's residents are Garifunas—Black Caribs of mixed African and native Caribbean descent whose ancestors fled Honduras in 1823 in the wake of a failed rebellion. Dangriga (which means "standing water") has become a center for both Garifuna culture and, unfortunately, pesty hustlers, whose mischief occasionally rouses the city from its otherwise peaceful existence.

BELIZE

Orientation The ocean is to the east. One main road runs parallel to the coast and crosses the Stann Creek River, which flows into the sea; the road is called St. Vincent St. south of the bridge and Commerce St. north of it. Intensely aggressive hustlers tend to congregate near the bridge. Police warn that the "back of town" area, around the "Havanna" bridge ½km south of the main bridge, is not safe at night. Free-lance tour guides roaming about town will arrange boat trips; stick with reputable agents like Captain Buck or Shipmates Restaurant as hustlers often have boats up their sleeves.

PRACTICAL INFORMATION

Tourist office: The most helpful one is inside the Bonefish Hotel, 2 blocks south and 1 block east of the bridge.

Police: 107 Commerce St. (tel. 220-22), north of the river, open 24 hrs.

Currency Exchange: Barclay's Bank (tel. 222-40), 3 blocks north of the bridge on the east side of Commerce St., gives cash advances on credit cards and changes traveler's checks. Open Mon.-Thurs. 8am-1pm, Fri. 8am-4:30pm. The best place to change U.S. **traveler's checks** is **Kaylen Hardware** (tel. 222-35), 10m north of the main bridge. Open Mon.-Thurs. 7:30am-noon and 1:30-5pm, Fri. until 9pm, Sat. 7:30am-1pm.

Post office: 16 Caney St. (tel. 220-35), on the south side of the bridge; turn east off St. Vincent St. at the Dangriaga Photo Plus sign onto Mahogany St., then head to the sea. The post office is on the left. Open Mon.-Thurs. 8am-noon and 1-5pm, Fri. 8am-noon and 1-4:30pm.

Telephones and telegrams: Belize Telecommunications Ltd. (tel. and fax 220-38) across the street from the police. Make collect and credit-card calls for free; otherwise, phone the U.S. for 3min. for BZ$9.60 station-to-station. Open Mon.-Fri. 8am-noon and 1-4pm, Sat. 8am-noon. The **telephone code** is 05 (but may as well be 052). **Telegram** service (BZ$0.32 a word to the U.S.)

Buses: Z-line buses (tel. 221-60), next to the river on the south side, serve Punta Gorda (Mon.-Sat. noon and 7pm, Sun. 2pm and 7pm, 5 hrs., BZ$13), Belize City (5 morning runs, 3 hrs., BZ$10; one last run at 3:30pm, 4 hrs.), and Belmopan (BZ$6). Buy your ticket early, and watch your luggage during the trip. Z-Line also goes to Placencia daily at 1pm, 3 hrs., BZ$8. The Sun. bus stops in Hopkins). If you miss the connection to Placencia, catch a bus to Mango Creek or Punta Gorda.

Ferry: From Mango Creek, Placencia is just a short boat ride away (BZ$30 per person; call Gina in Mango Creek at **Café Hello,** tel. 06-224-28, to charter a boat).

Laundromat: on Commerce St., across from the statue of Christ, charges BZ$8.50 per load. Open Mon.-Sat. 9am-noon and 2-8pm.

Pharmacy: Young's Drug Store, on Commerce St. Alberto Paquiul, chemist and druggist, is "licensed to sell drugs and poison" as well as fresh popcorn. Open Mon.-Sat. 8am-noon, 2-4pm, and 7-9pm.

Hospital: (tel. 220-78) 2 blocks north and 1 block east of the bridge. Follow the frontage road to the east as it curves north. Ambulance available. Open 24 hrs.

Clinic: (tel. 221-38, emergency 227-00), on St. Vincent St., 1 block south of the bridge, run by Dr. Sangar. Open Mon.-Fri. 8am-noon and 2-5pm, Sat. 8:30am-noon.

ACCOMMODATIONS

Riverside Hotel (tel. 221-68) provides spotless rooms and comfy beds adjoining a large living room. Clean, shared bathrooms come with weak showerheads. Reservations and traveler's checks are accepted. BZ$20 per person plus tax.

Dangriga Central Hotel (tel. 220-08) 1 block north of the bridge, on the left. A bit cheaper and grungier than the Riverside. Sure, the mattresses are flimsy, but the furniture on the balcony is upholstered. BZ$10.50 per person.

The Hub Guest House, 573 S. Riverside (tel. 223-97), conveniently located just southwest of the bridge, features eight second-story rooms, circled around a lounge with a TV. Check-out 10am. Singles BZ$12, with bath BZ$25; doubles BZ$24, with bath BZ$40.

FOOD

Many local women sell baked goods right out of their homes. If you can't ingratiate yourself into any of these a few fancier options remain:

Pola's Kitchen, 25A Tubroos St. (tel. 226-75), take St. Vincent south 4 blocks, look on the left. A monument to Garifuna culture, Pola's serves great Garifuna cuisine like *hudut* (plantains in coconut gravy with steamed fish). Her display of Garifuna items also includes U.S. civil rights posters, including a tribute to a bold, young Rosa Parks. Open Wed.-Mon. 8am-2pm and 6-10pm. All items BZ$6.50-8.50.

Ritchie's Dinette Creole and Spanish Food (tel. 21-12), 1 block north of the phone office, dishes out the fryjacks and johnny cakes with eggs and a gargantuan orange juice: a great breakfast, at BZ$7. At lunch, scarf a magnificent chicken burrito for only BZ$2.50. Open Mon.-Thurs. 7am-10pm, Fri.-Sat. 7am-11pm.

Starlight Restaurant, on the north end of Commerce St., serves Chinese food and curry for about BZ$10 and has CNN on its TV. Open daily 8:30am-3:30pm and 7-11pm, until midnight on Sat.

Sights and Entertainment Dangriga is a fine place to see and hear and taste Garifuna culture. World-renowned artist Benjamin Nicholas, who lives and works just behind the post office, may let you come in and have a look at whatever he's working on. (If you don't get to Nicholas' house, fear not. His paintings, which depict Garifuna life, hang all over town, including on the wall of the Z-line bus station.) Those with a musical bent can go two blocks west and two blocks south of the post office to see Rodriguez, who makes drums in the traditional Garifuna style. Locals love to swim and play ball just east of the bridge, where the river meets the sea. And there's always wave watching and chatting with non-solicitous locals.

At night, head to the second-floor **Kennedy Club,** a few blocks north of the police station, which on Thursdays and Saturdays jams to *punta* rock. Alternatively, try the **Road House** (tel. 224-87), a reggae dance hall.

■ NEAR DANGRIGA

HOPKINS VILLAGE

The nearby mountains and ever-shimmering Caribbean offer a variety of options for daytrips out of Dangriga. Ten miles south of Dangriga, the inhabitants of the fishing community of Hopkins Village still pull wooden dugout canoes (called "dories") up onto the beach. Chickens, dogs, and children outnumber everything but coconuts in this old Garifuna village. Electricity came to Hopkins two years ago, but the village remains unscathed. For those who are interested in nearly untouched Garifuna culture, Hopkins's relative accessibility and basic services (not to mention its beautiful beaches) make it an ideal stop. What services exist can be accessed through one of the town's two telephones, at 220-33 or 228-03 (same code as Dangriga). The **Sandy Beach Resort** is a thatch-roof establishment located at the south end of the village and run by a local women's cooperative. (Check-out 11am. Singles BZ$15, with bath BZ$23; doubles BZ$18.50, with bath BZ$32. Bed in a 10-bed dorm BZ$15.) The new **Caribbean View Hotel,** located at the north end of town, offers simple rooms with fans; two rooms face the water. (Check-out 1pm. Singles BZ$18.50, BZ$5 per additional person.) Share a beer with fishermen at **Isabahari** or **Larubeya,** both of which are near the beach and open pretty much all day. Buses run from Dangriga to Hopkins Monday to Saturday at 12:30 pm (1 hr., BZ$3) and the Z-line leaves on Sunday at 1 pm.

BELIZE

COCKSCOMB BASIN WILDLIFE SANCTUARY

The Cockscomb Basin Wildlife Sanctuary, in the Maya Mountains about 32km south of Dangriga and 11km past the village of Maya, was established in 1984 as the world's only jaguar ('tiger') preserve. The jaguars aren't easy to see. Although they can grow up to 1.8m in length and 158kg (350lbs.) in weight, they are shy, nocturnal creatures. Keep your eyes peeled for tracks. Pumas are equally rare, but deer, lizards, tapirs, boas, and to-die-for tropical birds abound. **Victoria Peak,** Belize's highest point (1100m), rises from within the sanctuary, and a two-day hike will take prepared hikers to the summit. A visitors center, basic bunkhouse (BZ$12 for a bed), and campsites are available. Contact the **Belize Audobon Society** in Belize City (see Belize Essentials: Reading Up, page 116) for more information, or write Cockscomb Basin Wildlife Sanctuary, P.O. Box 90, Dangriga. Daytrips can be arranged through some of the better hotels in town, including the **Pelican Beach Resort** (tel. 220-44; fax 225-70), which brings you to the Sanctuary and stops at the Maya Centre and Hopkins Village on the way back. These trips can be costly (BZ$135 for 1-4 people), so try to get a group of four people together. If you're dead-set on seeing a jaguar, an overnight arrangement is best, since the carnivores are nocturnal; night-trips can be arranged on site. The cheapest way to the site is by bus. Take any southbound bus in the morning and ask to be let off at the Cockscomb entrance. The bus ride takes about 2 hours, and there's an 8km hike from the entrance. Buses head back to Dangriga as late as 3 or 4 pm; plan carefully if this is to be a day trip; campsites are available for a few Belizean bucks.

BLUE HOLE NATIONAL PARK

Those travelers tired of the salty sea can journey inland a bit to the Blue Hole National Park (not to be confused with Blue Hole, the mondo-good scuba spot). While the entire park encompasses a massive 575 acres, most points of interest are within hiking distance. The Blue Hole itself is the emerging subterranean Sibun River. Masquerading as a pool, the river is surrounded by an echo-cavern filled with water that's delicious for swimming. From the Blue Hole, a couple of miles of rugged trails lead to **St. Heiman's Cave,** which was used by the Maya and is still being excavated today. To get to the national park, catch an early bus from Belmopan or Dangriga and ask the driver to let you off at the main entrance to the south; the Park is conveniently located right on the Hummingbird Highway.

TOBACCO CAYE

Set squarely atop the reef, Tobacco Caye (pop. 18) provides wanna-be castaways with the ultimate in weekend adventure. Unlike Caye Caulker or Ambergris, this five-acre island has neither restaurants nor stores; content yourself with little hotels and *cabañas* run by islanders who will cook for you. Visitors to the Caye spend their time lying in the sand, enjoying terrific reef snorkeling, and ripping open heaping helpings of coconuts. Hammocks are everywhere, so bring a good book; as night falls, plan to watch the sun set over the sea and the Tobacco Caye Range to the west. To reach the Caye from Dangriga, ask around near the bridge (be alert—hustlers abound). Chartering a boat costs about BZ$30 each way. At the Caye, stay at a *cabaña,* the cheapest of which is **Fairweather and Friends.** (In Belize City, tel. 728-66; Singles BZ$25, doubles BZ$30 with shared bathrooms.) Since meals here must be paid for separately, the Fairweather is best-suited to the content-to-be-eatin'-coconuts crowd. Those who want three tasty meals a day can opt for the **Gaviota Resort** (in Belize City, tel. 220-85), which offers better rooms and clean bathrooms. (BZ$50 for 1 person, BZ$80 for 2 people.) Snorkel gear can be rented at any of the hotels, starting at BZ$10. **Shipmate's Restaurant** (tel. 221-71) sits right next to the bridge. They're willing to arrange reliable rides to the Cayes and radio the "resorts" for interested tourists (open Mon.-Thurs. 8am-6pm, Sat.-Sun. 8am-3pm and 7pm-midnight).

■■■ PLACENCIA

Only a skinny strip of land separates Placencia's lagoon from the ocean, and the water seems poised to swallow up the town at any moment. Not so. This resilient, peninsular community of old sea salts has a hardy staying power; many residents are descendents of French pirates who came ashore for scurvy-preventing lemons and limes. Mellow Placencia's **Main Street** is a meandering path just wide enough for two to walk hand-in-hand, and the sense of time is molasses-slow. For the still-satiable and curious, many fishermen are open to guests and are willing to show their trade. Coconut-denuding techniques are freely taught and well worth the time, especially since drinks (and everything else) are a bit more expensive in Placencia. Still most beloved, the town's beaches are among the finest in Belize, and after a day of tapping coconuts and pondering the light crashing of the waves, even high-stress sorts develop a relaxed I-am-a-palm-tree-and-I-will-take-root-in-the-sand feeling.

Practical Information Locals in the know comment that those who come to Placencia for easy access to marijuana are rarely disappointed, but they may well be bamboozled. Most cases of theft in Placencia are limited to incidents involving tourists getting high-jinxed. Boats and buses arrive near the gas dock at the southern tip of the 26km peninsula, more than 160km south of Belize City. The scintillating sea sits to the east; the lagoon lies to the west. The only artery through town, the narrow, main **sidewalk,** heads north along the beach. Facing the water, south of the dock, the **Paradise Vacation Hotel, Tentacles Restaurant and Bar,** and **Brenda's Restaurant** sun themselves 100m down the sandy path.

Call the **police** in the event of an emergency (tel. 911). The police station (tel. 231-29, 911) is on the beach between Sunny's Restaurant and the Trade Winds Hotel. The gas dock is the focal point of Placencia's service industry. Along one side of it is the **Belize Telecommunications Ltd.** office (tel. 231-01) in which Shelly Jackson, chairperson (mayor) of the village, toils. Shelly can answer most questions about the town. She has just started a tourist information bureau call **Déjà Vu Charters** (tel. 233-01, 233-02) right on the gas dock, which connects travelers with local guides for snorkeling, scuba, and ecotourist adventures. The BTL office is open for **fax service, telegrams,** and free international collect calls (Mon.-Fri. 8am-noon and 1-4pm, Sat. 8am-noon). The **telephone code** is 06. The **post office** (tel. 231-02), across the dock on the second floor of the white building, can be used for *Poste Restante* (open Mon.-Fri. 8am-noon and 1:30pm-4pm). For all your **currency exchange** and alimentary needs, head to **Wallen's Market,** down the dirt road from the post office. Fresh produce arrives on Sundays (open Mon.-Wed. and Fri.-Sat. 8am-noon and 3-6pm, Sun. 8am-noon). The nearest banks are in Big Creek and Mango Creek, and these are only open on Fridays. Two **buses** leave Placencia for Dangriga (Mon.-Sat. at 5:45 and 6am, BZ$7) where connections can be made on **Z-line** to Belize City. For a southern connection, catch a boat to Mango Creek or Big Creek; schedule a ride at the BTL office, or ask around by the dock (connections can be expensive; Mon.-Fri. at 6:30am, catch a ride with the schoolchildren from the pier next to the gas dock for about BZ$10. On Fridays, villagers go to the bank in the morning; tagging along generally costs BZ$10. Otherwise, a charter is the only option, which runs BZ$30-35); from there, catch the daily 2pm bus to Punta Gorda (BZ$9, 3 hrs.). The road the bus uses, the "back road" or "highway" runs north-south along the west side of the peninsula and starts at the gas dock. Placencia's **airstrip** is 3km from town; every day, six flights run to various points within Belize. **Maya Airways** flights can be booked at the BTL office, or by calling (02) 440-32. They offer service to Punta Gorda (BZ$63); to Dangriga (BZ$62); to San Pedro (Caye Caulker on same flight) (BZ$138); and to Belize City (BZ$97). **Tropic Air** (tel. (02) 456-71) tickets can be bought at the Orange Peel next to Wallen's Market. The Placencia **health center** (tel. 231-92, after-hours emergencies 231-70) is in the middle of the sidewalk (open Mon.-Fri. 8am-noon and 1-5pm). It's closed during the off-season.

Accommodations and Food There are a few budget hotels in Placencia, and some locals turn their homes into guest houses during busy times of year. Keep your eyes open for "Room for Rent" signs in the windows of private houses along the main walkway. Almost every hotel is within 25m of the sea; most have very simple (low-security) locks, but the locals seem to think that's okay.

Lydia's Rooms (tel. and fax 231-17) is a perennial favorite of the backpacking crowd and offers breakfast (BZ$6), a canoe free for guests' use, and an enveloping hammock on the upstairs porch. Take the sidewalk north 50m past The Flamboyant's, to the white house on the left. Lydia's husband Conrad runs a tour business out of their house. **Traveler's Inn** (tel. 231-90), right after the Driftwood Café, just off the sidewalk, offers rustic rooms with wooden floors and fans; some rooms boast private toilets and trickling showers (BZ$10.50 per person, some rooms BZ$12.50 per person). The primary attraction is owner Maurice, who can take you night fishing. The **Sea Spray Hotel** (tel. 231-48) sits on the north end of the main sidewalk across from Flamboyant's. If no one's in the office, see Gail at the house behind the hotel. Make a beeline for the cozy *palapa* on the beach—it's Edenic. Rooms can get a bit noisy. (Singles BZ$21.20, with bath BZ$26.50; doubles BZ$31.80, triples BZ$42.40. Nicer rooms with refrigerator, hot water, and coffee pot available too, singles BZ$53, doubles BZ$74.20. Reserve in advance. Off-season prices lower.

Food in Placencia is just like the rest of life: slow, enjoyable, and steeped deeply in everything marine. Michael at the **Driftwood Café** (tel. 232-48), midway up the sidewalk, serves his own brilliantly jammin' lobster jambalaya (BZ$15) and other seafood. Boycotting high lobster prices, he only serves the lobster he catches (open daily 8am-10pm, unless he's out fishing). Try **Brenda's,** halfway between Tentacles and the post office, for terrific multi-course meals for BZ$15-25. Mind-warpingly delicious lobster comes with a slurpy cocktail and sponge cake (BZ$25). **Flamboyant's,** situated across from the Sea Spray, dishes out conch (BZ$15), shrimp (BZ$18), and lobster (BZ$20). Sunday night is BBQ night (open Fri.-Wed. 7am-11pm. Kitchen closes at 10pm). Behind the soccer field, the **Galley Restaurant and Bar** (tel. 231-33) whips up tasty fruit shakes and seaweed punch (BZ$3); it tastes kind of like egg nog. Locals love the vegetable stir-fry (BZ$10, add different meats for a few Belizean bucks). They're quite proud of their new bar and warped, surreal paintings (open daily 7:30am-10pm, kitchen closed from 2:30-6:30pm). For amazing cheese (sweet) bread (BZ$3) or cinnamon buns (BZ$4.25 per ½ dozen), try **John the Baker Man** (tel. 233-12). Heading north on the sidewalk, turn left at the sign and go 200 ft. in the sand (open Mon.-Sat. 7am-7pm). The dock of **Tentacles**

Bar and Restaurant (tel. 231-56) is the best spot to meet local fishermen. Inquire here for the skinny on nearby cayes (happy hour Sat. evenings, open Thurs.-Tues. 7:30am-10pm).

Sights and Entertainment If you've been looking for a place to stash booty and settle down, Placencia will make you happy indeed—deserted island getaways don't get much better than this. The water is steely blue, the sand is grainy, and the cayes are downright drooly. Boaters will typically ferry tourists to the uninhabited isles around Placencia for fishing, snorkeling, and camping good times. The cayes are almost all privately owned, but many are provisioned by their owners with accommodations for tourists. Ask around to find out about those cayes where you can spend the night.

Nearly every building in town has a sign advertising the phone number of a guide or charter to the Cayes. To expedite your search, head to Tentacles or the Caribbean Club (directly adjacent to the gas dock) and ask for a reliable captain; one captain who can be counted on is Glen Eiley (tel. 231-18). Expect to pay a whopping BZ$250 per six-person boatload; the price usually covers a full-day trip with fishing and snorkeling. In high season, daily sailboat excursions may also be available for about BZ$50 per person. Another option is to contact **Déjà Vu Tours** or Shelly Jackson at BTL. Her finger is in every pie, and she can frequently get lower prices.

The most popular cayes are the most convenient ones—**Laughing Bird Caye** and **Ranguana Caye.** David Dial (tel. 222-67) of **Jojo's Charters** (tel. 231-68) will take you to Laughing Bird and provide a kitchen and accommodations for two nights and three full days for BZ$120; for BZ$10 per person you can camp and use the kitchen. 13km northeast of Placencia, camping (BZ$10 a night) and *cabañas* (BZ$50 a night) are available on **Wippari Caye,** noted for great fishing, which has no beach to speak of. Boats to Wippari can be chartered with George Cabral (tel. 231-30) for about BZ$100.

Locally recommended **Placencia Dive Shop,** located just north of the gas dock, takes eager scuba enthusiasts to the reef, to Laughing Bird Caye, and to other delightful destinations for US$65 per two-tank dive (lunch included). Snorkeling gear is BZ$10 a day (that's the standard price in Placencia), and a snorkeling trip is US$40 per day (bring a passport as a deposit). The cheaper option for snorkeling is with local fishermen. Conrad, Lydia's husband (see Accommodations, above) leads snorkeling trips to Laughing Bird Caye for BZ$50 per person, not including gear (four-person minimum).

Even the placid manatee has discovered Placencia's laid-back appeal; according to one report, approximately half of the sea cows that mumble "Belize da fu we" spend their lives basking in the lagoon near Placencia. For a tour to see them, and for other **sea-kayaking trips,** call Michael at the Driftwood Café (tel. 232-48; US$20 per day for a kayak, US$10 for a half-day).

Night life in Placencia starts out innocuously, but participants invariably end up swaggering home; get your disco shoes ready. Starting off at **Tentacles Dockside Bar, Mike's Caribbean Club** (just south of the gas dock), or **Flamboyant's,** which features Garifuna drums and dancing on Sunday nights, get yourself ready for the main disco in the village, **Cozy Corner** (halfway up the village from the sidewalk). Perform the ritual Tues.-Thurs. and Sun., 8 pm-midnight, and Fri.-Sat. 8 pm-2 am.

■■■ PUNTA GORDA

Pristine but definitely soggy, the rainforested **Toledo District** is a regular nirvana for the dashing adventure traveler (machete optional). Punta Gorda (pop. 3100), the center of activity in Toledo, was founded by Puritan traders in the 17th century and has at various times been used as an outpost both English pirates and by Spanish soldiers. After the U.S. Civil War, a group of Confederate veterans tried to establish plantations here similar to the ones they left behind in the South. Their genteel, pseudo-antebellum dreamland failed to materialize; ironically, by importing laborers from all over the globe, the settlers succeeded only in populating Punta Gorda with a variety of non-white skins and cultures—Garifuna, Mayan, Creole, and East Asian. Two distinguished older gentlemen, along with their families, are the last survivors on the colonizer-side of this bizarre enterprise. In addition to the rich diversity of Homo sapiens, Toledo is host to a panoply of exotic flora and fauna. Some predict that the region's "otherness" will soon make it a center of ecotourism, and the bureaucracy has already been developing in that direction.

ORIENTATION AND PRACTICAL INFORMATION

Punta Gorda hugs the coastline. **Front Street** runs along the sea, and **Main Street** runs parallel to it. Most activity is concentrated on these streets. The airstrip lies to the north, the hospital to the south (next to the Z-line bus terminal) and **Far West St**. traces, logically, the western boundary of P.G., as the city is most frequently called. If you're arriving on a Z-line bus, don't wait until the terminal to get off; it's a bit out of town. Instead, tell the driver where you want to go (often you can even mention the name of a particular hotel) and he or she will let you off at the nearest stop.

Tourist Information: Belize Hotel of Tourism Reservation Center, 11 Front. St. (tel. 228-34; fax 228-35), 1 block north of the post office on Front St., offers booking for tours and launches and lots of information. Open Mon.-Fri. 8am-noon, 2-6:30pm, Sat. 8am-noon. **Tourist Information Center** (tel. 224-70), on Front St. behind the customs office. Information on tours, flights, and things to do in Punta Gorda and the Toledo District. Up-to-date bus schedules and prices. Open Mon.-Wed. and Fri.-Sat. 7am-noon. Also, William Schmidt at **Nature's Way Guest House** (below) is a storehouse of information about all aspects of Toledo, particularly those off the beaten track.

Police: (tel. 20-22), next to the post office. Open 24 hrs.

Currency Exchange: Belize Bank (tel. 221-83, 223-23; fax 223-25), on Front St., near the town center. Changes pounds, U.S. and Canadian dollars, and traveler's checks. Cash advances on Visa and MC. Open Mon.-Thurs. 8am-1pm, Fri. 8am-4:30pm. In a bind, Mr. King at the Texaco exchanges travelers' checks for amounts more than US$100.

Post Office: on Front St. and King St., across from the customs office. Open Mon.-Fri. 8:30am-noon and 1-5pm, Fridays until 4:30pm.

Telephones: Belize Telecommunications Ltd. (tel. 20-48), on Main St., 1 block north of Central Park. Free international collect calls. Also available are **fax** and **telegram service.** Open Mon.-Fri. 8am-noon and 1-5pm, Sat. 8am-noon. **Telephone code:** 07.

Buses: Z-line, on Back St. south of town, goes to Dangriga (5 hrs., BZ$13) and to Belize City (5am and 11am, 8 hrs., BZ$22) daily. **James** buses head along the same route (Sun. 6am, Tues. noon, Fri. noon) for the same prices. They leave from the lot next to the police station.

Flights: Maya Airlines and **Tropic Air** go to Belize City from the airstrip on the west side of town (3 per day, 1 hr., BZ$125). Buy tickets at **Penell & Penell's Hardware Store** (tel. 220-14), on Front St. Open daily 8am-noon and 1:30-5pm.

Ferry: To Guatemala's Puerto Barrios leaves Tues. and Fri. at noon (4 hrs., BZ$14). Get your tickets well ahead of time at **Maya de Indita Tienda,** 24 Main Middle St. (tel. 22-265). Open Tues. and Fri. after 7am. You'll need to have your **passport** stamped at the police station by 1pm. If you can't wait for the ferry, a man named Paco, up the block from Honeycomb Club, runs charters to Livingston (1 hr., BZ$20) and to Puerto Barrios (1½ hrs., BZ$20). Memo (227-18) offers slightly cheaper rates for slightly slower engines. Ship captains are usually responsible for finding a customs official before departure, so relax and let them sweat about it.

Market: Vernon's Store, on Front St. by Sylvia's, offers a wide selection of snacks and dry goods. Open Mon.-Wed. and Fri.-Sat. 8am-noon and 2-5pm, Thurs. 8am-noon.

Pharmacy: Genus Pharmacy (tel. 221-07), on Main St. near the bank. Open Mon.-Sat. 8am-noon and 2-5pm.

Medical Services: Punta Gorda Hospital (tel. 20-26), at the end of Main St. near the bus station and the cemetery. Outpatient clinic and emergency room.

ACCOMMODATIONS

Guest houses in Punta Gorda provide plenty of bang for the Belizean buck. Both less-expensive and mid-priced hotel rooms provide clean and spacious rooms. Moreover, proprietors rarely inflate prices during the high season, so you don't generally find the Jekyll-and-Hyde seasonal rates common in other parts of the country.

Nature's Way Guest House and Restaurant (tel. 221-19), at the south end of Front St. Airy rooms, wooden floors, desks, and super-clean common bathrooms. You may be awakened "nature's way" at 5am by the roosters next door. Ultra-cool William "Chet" Schmidt is a great source of info on exploring the jungle, Mayan villages, and nearby cayes. Singles BZ$16, doubles BZ$26, triples BZ$40. Breakfast BZ$7.

The St. Charles, 23 King St. (tel. 221-49), take Main St. south to King, turn left. Worth the slightly extra cost. Spacious rooms with flowered curtains, big beds, and vintage televisions with cable. Rooms have extra locks, but not water. Check-out 1pm. Singles BZ$15, with bath BZ$25; doubles BZ$25, with bath BZ$35.

Pallavi's Hotel, 19 Main St. (tel. 224-14), just north of BTL. Clean, freshly painted white and gray rooms. The proprietor tends to hide out in the small store below the hotel. Singles BZ$16; doubles BZ$21, with bath BZ$32.

Rokagus Inn, 49 Main Middle St. (tel. 220-86; fax 224-69), conveniently located at the center of town near the clock tower. Solve the mystery of the hotel's name while dozing off in clean rooms with TV, hot water, and swell standing fans. Check-out noon. Singles with bath BZ$31.80, doubles (one bed) with bath BZ$37.10.

FOOD

Punta Gorda is a hotbed of Creole kitchens, and the hungry traveler is seldom more than 20 paces from a heaping plate of seafood, rice, and fried plantain. Generally, prices are low and restaurant proprietors are talkative. If you're lucky, you'll get an earful with your mouthful – take each with a little salt.

Vicky's Ice Cream Parlor (tel. 220-72), on Main St. 1½ blocks south of Nature's Way, not only serves up the only *helado* in town, she also cooks up great food cheap. Papaya shake BZ$1.50. Veggie cheeseburger (i.e. a cheese sandwich) BZ$2.75. Open Mon.-Sat. 10am-2pm and 4-10pm, Sun. 4pm-10pm.

Punta Caliente, 108 José Maria St. (tel. 225-61), just north of the bus terminal, is Punta Gorda's rising star. Also on the rise are diners' eyes—a hypnotic sky-and-cloud motif covers the ceiling. Stewed chicken with rice and beans is BZ$7; a hamburger goes for BZ$4. Open daily 7am-11pm.

Granny's, two blocks north of customs on Front St. (tel. 226-70), is the place for breakfast. Eggs, beans, and a drink, BZ$5. They will cook lunch and dinner if given advance notice. Granny's husband is one of the two remaining Confederate gentlemen.

Man Man's 5-Star Restaurant, on Far West St. at the northwest corner of town, is a little shanty with two groovy signs, one of which gave the restaurant the latter half of its present name. A delighted Duncan Hines employee sent his newfound cook kudos in the form of a sign. Man Man is a scream; he cooks quick, greasy, and utterly delicious creole dinners for BZ$9. They're eaten in his living room, to the music of Man Man's wild tales. Open daily, 5am 'till Man Man falls asleep.

Morning Glory (tel. 224-94), near the middle of Front St., is much more popular with locals and travelers than the plant, even though the former is more expensive. Belize's standard breakfast BZ$8. Open Mon.-Sat. 7am-3pm and 7-11pm.

SIGHTS AND ENTERTAINMENT

For sea-, and caye-farers, the nearest island is **Moho Caye.** Charters are available, and Memo (tel. 227-18) will take a boat out for snorkeling for US$100, including gear.

He's willing to sardine 15 passengers into his boat, but check the weather before heading out. Easy, good-time kayaking can be arranged through Nature's Way (above) for BZ$25 per day. A guide is required (BZ$25) to accompany the kayaks. The area around Punta Gorda is ripe in *avant-garde* nature-tourist appeal; the government is paving the mine-field currently called a "highway" so that travelers can better immerse themselves with both indigenous culture and in nature. What little nightlife there is can be found at the **Honeycomb Club,** on the north end of Front St., and at **Massive Rock Disco,** just north of the bus terminal; the image of elephants dancing *punta* is slightly misleading. Otherwise, talk to Memo at the disco, or stay tuned for local events, which often come in downpours.

Village Guest House Program

The brainchild of William Schmidt and villagers struggling to remain viable, this program is the *pièce de résistance* of Belizean ecotourism, an attempt to bring travelers and locals together without the exploitation and cultural decimation so prevalent elsewhere. The Toledo Ecotourism Association (TEA) has built several guest houses in Mayan and Garifuna villages that provide lodging (BZ$18.50 per person) for guests. Tourists are sent in bundles to each of the villages one-at-a-time, on a rotating basis (to ensure fairness to the villages), and there they spend at least 24 hrs. As a minimum, guests enjoy three authentic Mayan meals, much the same as those served in the ruins centuries ago (all three meals BZ$21), spend four-plus hours exploring the jungle and nearby ruins (BZ$28 per person), and have time left over to get acquainted with Mayan families in the village. Other options include canoeing, horseback riding, listening to storytellers, watching dancers, and learning crafts from artisans. But as enjoyable as the program is, its greatest virtue comes from the fact that 80% of all the money stays in the village. Rotation ensures that the special communal nature of Mayan villages is not seriously disrupted.

Separate sleeping quarters allow privacy—other programs that include actual home-stays have caused problems and have been banned by some villages, as tourists' and farmers' waking hours didn't quite coincide. Meanwhile, revenue from the program decreases the villagers' dependence on slash-and-burn farming. William Schmidt also invites travelers to visit a Garifuna village under similar circumstances, and is prepared to persuade anyone of the program's merits. The only serious problem is transportation; remain flexible. The regular bus leaves P.G. at 5am and at 11am and returns at 5pm. The cost of a chartered van is steep (BZ$75) and private or rented vehicles work just fine. Some walk out to the main highway to catch rides.

A market bus heads out of P.G. in the evening on Mondays, Wednesdays, and Saturdays and returns from the villages at 5 or 6 am on Mondays, Wednesdays, and Saturdays—William Schmidt will help arrange transportation. To join up, head to the TEA office at 65 Front St. (tel. 221-19; fax 221-99), which is adjoined to Nature's Way Guesthouse (above).

Ruins and Natural Projects

The area around Punta Gorda is dotted with ancient Mayan ruins, a few of which have intriguing histories. Probably the best know is **Lubaantun** ("place of the fallen stones"—boy, have they fallen) located about 5km from San Antonio and accessible through the Guesthouse program (above). It's technically possible to drive all the way, but only with the mightiest of vehicles, so most opt for the pleasant hike instead. The site is unrestored, the guides knowledgeable and free (although tips are appreciated). Lubaantun's structures also impress for their lack of over-imaginative restoration and mortar, which is refreshing for purists and which gives powerful testament to the skill of ancient Mayan stone masons; pieces were carefully sculpted to fit together seamlessly. Sadly, trees have recklessly toppled parts of the structures, and two other important pieces are missing: the mysterious **Crystal Skull** and the **ball court markers**. The first can be found in Canada, and is the subject of much raw, frenzied speculation; there are no tool marks on the crystal, and the jaw moves, making it unique among Mayan artifacts. The skull serves as some of the best "proof" offered by advocates of the U.F.O. theory of Mayan decline. The markers help to verify that the small patches of dirt were in fact ball courts; these remnants were spirited away long ago to Harvard's Peabody Museum. **Num Li Punit** is the next ruin south from Lubaantun and boasts an alarmingly long and stunning stela. While none of the Toledo ruins provide the easy thrills of more monumental temples, they are interesting and well-worth a visit for aficionados of antiquities.

Punta Gorda proffers sights natural as well as cultural, although delving into the nearby eco-projects can be hindered by a familiarly frustrating lack of transportation. Just 1.6km west of Punta Gorda, the **Habia Barra Garinago Cerro** is a 19-station botanical trail and educational center which displays examples of Garifuna sustainable farming practices; ask at Nature's Way (see above) for more information.

26km outside of town is the **Dem Dat's Doin** farm (tel. 224-70), where for BZ$10 you can tour a futuristic agricultural complex; check out its solar lighting system and smell-a-licious organic perfume production.

Just up the road from the farm is a **butterfly ranch**, full of fluttery friends. Once used for theme parks, the products of the ranch are now applied to ecological purposes, and eager "pupals" are taught the intricacies of butterfly wrangling. Both the farm and the ranch are pretty close to San Antonio, and both are worth a visit

EL SALVADOR

A few years ago, tourism was the last thing on the minds of El Salvador's nearly six million inhabitants. Barraged by bullets and enshrouded in a dark, sullen cloak of death and loss, Salvadorans worried instead about preserving their land, their political causes, and most of all, their lives. In a nation the size of Massachusetts, the chafe of social tensions and conflicting ideologies came to bear in an unbelieveably bloody, bitter civil war. Today, the government and the FMLN (Farabundo Martí National Liberation Front, the leftist guerrillas), in accord with their 1992 cease-fire pact, strive to settle their differences in the political arena; the Salvadoran people, meanwhile, reluctanctly return to life as they lived it before, and always with the painful realization of loss and of the new challenges looming ahead.

Since the war, few tourists have set El Salvador on their itineraries. While the political situation is relatively stable, the country's history remains only in crumbling fragments, much of the devastation due to years of carpet bombing, but other buildings and sites having been demolished during centuries of thunderous earthquakes. Still, while lacking in cathedrals or monuments, El Salvador does not want for natural splendor; its black-sand beaches, for example, offer the added bonus of abutting some of the best surf waves in Central America. Meanwhile, ecotourism will undoubtedly start to draw throngs to the country's smoking volcanoes and fairy-tale like Montecristo Cloud Forest, especially since visitors are practically guaranteed isolation in the more touristed sites. Finally, a smattering of travelers have come (and will most likely continue to come) to El Salvador to experience first-hand the intensely exciting atmosphere of a nation on the road to recovery.

ESSENTIALS

■■■ WHEN TO GO

CLIMATE

El Salvador's mountainous terrain generally keeps temperatures under relative control, with temperatures ranging between 60-75° in the highlands. The lower in altitude you are, the higher the temperatures; 80° is about average in the lowlands, and San Salvador can average about 90° in the summer (March). The rainy season, accompanied by the *temporales* (heavy downpours), lasts from May to October. The greatest numbers of tourists come during the dry season.

FESTIVALS AND HOLIDAYS

Check around for local festivals, usually dedicated to patron saints. **Santa Ana's** July Festival to the Virgin Mary is raucous, indeed, as is **Sonsonate's** party in February. **San Miguel** busts out on November 24. Nationally, banks and other public services are bound to be closed on the following days: **January 1** (New Year's); **May 1** (Labor Day); **May 10** (Mother's Day); **June 17** (Father's Day); **June 22** (Día del Maestro; Teacher's Day); **August 1-6** (Patron Saint Salvador's Festival); **Sept. 15** (Independence Day); **October 12** (Día de la Raza); **Nov. 2** (Día de los Santos Difuntos; All Saint's Day); **Nov. 5** (Primer Grito de Independencia; First Cry of Independence); **December 24-25** (Christmas Eve and Christmas); **Dec. 31** (New Year's Eve).

■■■ FEED YOUR HEAD

For publications and travel organizations of general interest, see Central America: An Introduction, page 33.

Embassy of El Salvador, U.S. 2308 California St. NW, Washington, DC 20008 (tel. (202) 265-9671; fax (202) 328-0563). **U.K.** Tennyson House 159, Great Portland St. 51, London W1N 5FD (tel. (44) 171-436-8282; fax 436-8181). **Canada,** 209 Kent St., Ottawa, Ontario K2P 1Z8 (tel. 613-238-2939; fax 238-6940).

Consulate of El Salvador, 1010 16th St. NW, 3rd Floor, Washington, DC 20036 (tel. (202) 331-4032; fax (202) 331-4036) There's also an office in New York City (tel. (212) 889-3608). Contact either branch for visa information.

Instituto Salvadoreño de Turismo, Calle Rubén Darío #619, San Salvador (tel. 222-8000, 222-0960; fax 222-1208). Send away for lively, turquoise brochures, maps, and general information about tourism. Open 8am-4pm.

CISPES (Committee in Solidarity with the People of El Salvador), 19 West 21st St., Room 502, New York, NY 10010 (tel. (212) 229-1290). A grass-roots organization working for justice, better working conditions, and civil liberties in El Salvador.

NEST (New El Salvador Today), PO Box 411436, San Francisco, CA 94141 (tel. (415) 864-7755). Offers work and volunteer opportunities in El Salvador.

■■■ DOCUMENTS AND FORMALITIES

Citizens of all countries need a valid passport to enter El Salvador. Residents of the United States and Canada additionally need either a **visa** or a **tourist card;** travelers from South Africa, Australia, and Ireland need to acquire a visa before arriving. A visa is free from the Consulate of El Salvador, and takes 3-4 days to process; have two passport-size photos available. For U.S. citizens, the visa is good for as long as the passport is valid, but the **tourist card** is good for one entry for as long as 30 days (with extensions up to 90 days). For citizens of other countries, a processed visa is good for 30 days, with extensions possible up to 60 days. In many cases, capricious immigration officials at the border have the authority to determine the length of time you may spend in El Salvador; they often act based on how you look or behave: the spiffier you appear, the longer you stay.

Drivers to El Salvador need only a car registration and valid driver's license, although an international driver's permit is recommended. You may have to purchase a permit for ¢100. The license is valid for 30 days. **Children** (under the age of 18) traveling to El Salvador need the written consent of both parents to enter. There is an **airport tax** of US$13 for all travelers flying to and from El Salvador.

■■■ MONEY MATTERS

CURRENCY AND EXCHANGE

US$1 = ¢8.71	**¢1 = US$0.12**
CDN$1 = ¢6.41	**¢1 = CDN$0.16**
UK£1 = ¢13.537	**¢1 = UK£0.07**
IRL£1 = ¢13.80	**¢1 = IRL£0.07**
AUS$1 = ¢6.42	**¢1 = AUS$0.16**
NZ$1 = ¢5.71	**¢1 = NZ$0.18**
SARand = ¢2.38	**¢1 = SARand0.42**

Columbus' legacy persists on Salvadoran cash; the national currency is the **colón,** denoted by a "¢." (The colón is sometimes called a *peso.*) As in Costa Rica, there are 100 centavos (like U.S. cents) to a single colón. Change any currency at the border when leaving, since colones are hard to get rid of once you've left. The two banks that regularly change traveler's checks are **Banco Salvadoreño** and **Banco Hipote-**

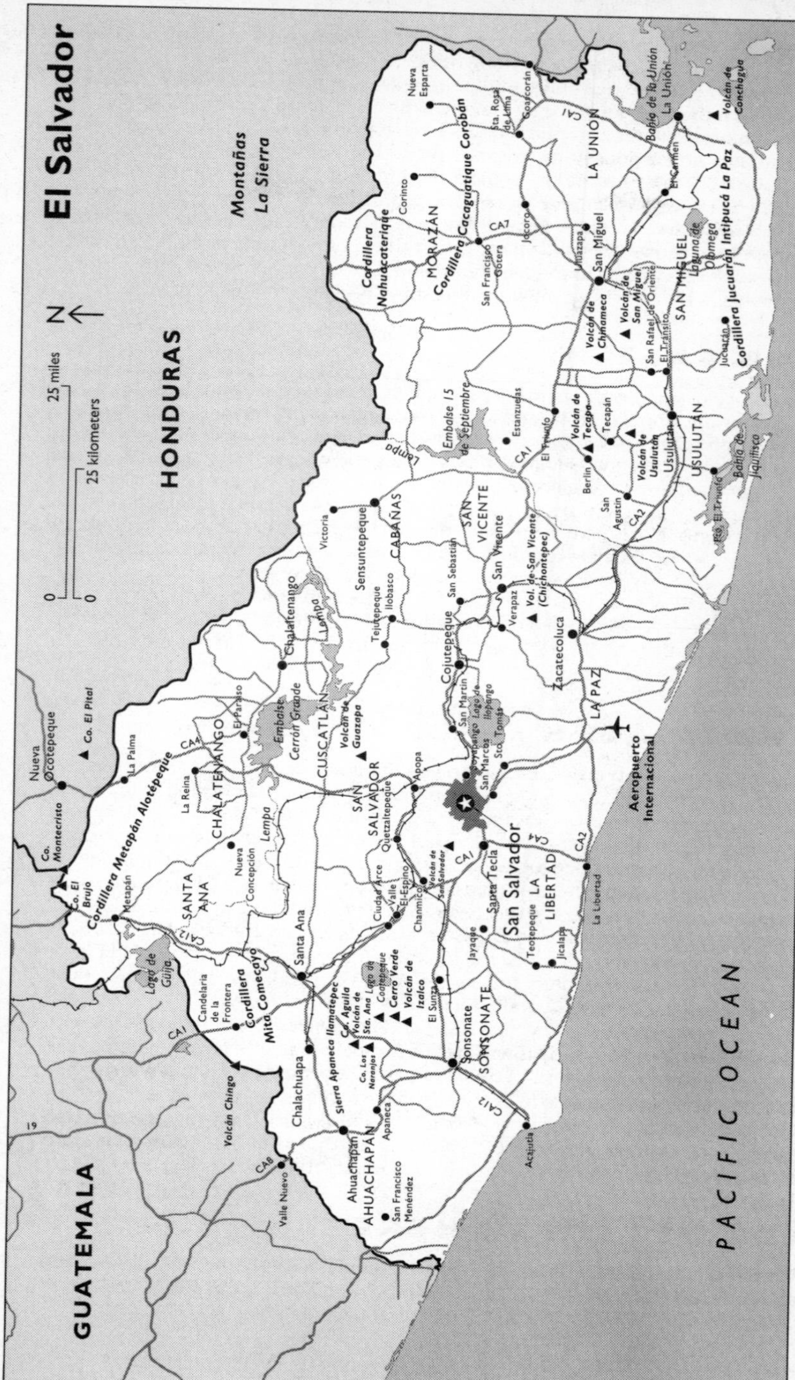

El Salvador

0 25 miles
0 25 kilometers
N

GUATEMALA
HONDURAS
PACIFIC OCEAN
Montañas La Sierra

AHUACHAPÁN
SANTA ANA
SONSONATE
CHALATENANGO
LA LIBERTAD
SAN SALVADOR
CUSCATLÁN
CABAÑAS
LA PAZ
SAN VICENTE
USULUTÁN
SAN MIGUEL
MORAZÁN
LA UNIÓN

Ahuachapán
Apaneca
San Francisco Menéndez
Valle Nuevo
Volcán Chingo
Chalachuapa
Candelaria de la Frontera
Cordillera Mita Comecayo
Lago de Güija
Metapán
Co. El Brujo
Co. Montecristo
Cordillera Metapán Alotépeque
Nueva Ocotepeque
Co. El Pital
La Palma
La Reina
Nueva Concepción
Santa Ana
Sierra Apaneca Ilamatepec
Co. Los Naranjos
Volcán de Sta. Ana
Co. Aguila
Lago de Coatepeque
Cerro Verde
Volcán de Izalco
Sonsonate
Acajutla
El Sunza
Ciudad Arce
Valle El Espino
Chanmico
Volcán de San Salvador
Quetzaltepeque
Apopa
Jayaque
Santa Tecla
San Salvador
Teotepeque
Jicalapa
La Libertad
Soyapango
San Marcos
Sto. Tomás
Lago de Ilopango
San Martín
Aeropuerto Internacional
Cojutepeque
Zacatecoluca
Volcán de Guazapa
Embalse Cerrón Grande
El Paraíso
Chalatenango
Tejutepeque
Ilobasco
Sensuntepeque
Victoria
Lempa
Verapaz
San Vicente
San Sebastián
Vol. de San Vicente (Chichontepec)
Embalse 15 de Septiembre
Estanzuelas
El Triunfo
Berlín
Volcán de Tecapa
Volcán de Usulután
Tecapán
San Agustín
Usulután
Bahía de Jiquilisco
Pto. El Triunfo
Volcán de Chinameca
Volcán de San Miguel
San Miguel
San Rafael de Oriente
El Tránsito
Jucuarán
Cordillera Jucuarán Intipucá La Paz
Laguna de Olomega
El Carmen
Uluazapa
San Francisco Gotera
Cordillera Cacaguatique Corobán
Cordillera Nahuacatarique
Corinto
Jocoro
Nueva Esparta
Sta. Rosa de Lima
Goascorán
La Unión
Bahía de la Unión
Volcán de Conchagua
CA1
CA2
CA4
CA7
CA8
CA12

EL SALVADOR

cario; a branch of either is in just about every medium-to large-sized town. At other banks, forget about changing anything but cold, hard cash. **ATMs** are prevalent in San Salvador, but the machines aren't linked to common networks like Cirrus or Plus; rather, they are hooked only into the bank, itself. **Credit cards** are accepted in many businesses in the capital, but elsewhere, only the poshest places accept Visa, MasterCard, or occasionally, American Express. There is an American Express office (tel. 223-0177) in San Salvador. Contact the office of Visa-MasterCard Credomatic (tel. 224-5155) for problems or for regular cash advances.

The **black market** is rarely a good deal in El Salvador, since rates are worse than those given in banks. They only trade cash, though often during hours when banks are closed. As elsewhere in the region, **tipping** is greatly appreciated, particularly at restaurants. A bonus is not mandatory though, especially not for cab drivers.

■■■ SAFETY

In the wake of war, crime is a major problem in El Salvador; a disturbingly large proportion of the population has firearms, and gang-related violence is on the rise. Whenever possible, stay indoors or in well-lit areas, and take care of business during the day. Salvadorans got used to curfews during the war, and so not a lot happens after 9pm even now. Travelers (especially women) are advised not go out alone at night. Visitors should always avoid carrying valuables in public places; San Salvador's crime problem is particularly bad. Women should be very cautious in northern El Salvador, where the men routinely whistle and hoot at local women. The country sees few tourists, so expect some stares of curiosity wherever you go.

Despite the Peace Accords of 1992, the U.S. State Department warns travelers not to travel after dark, and to avoid unpaved roads as much as possible. Campers in undesignated sites should never go far off the road, particularly in the northern regions of the country, as unexploded land mines pose a serious threat.

■■■ HEALTH

For in-depth descriptions of disease prevention and risk, see Central America: An Introduction, page 11. If arriving from an infected area, a vaccination certificate is required for **yellow fever** for everyone over 6 months old. **Malaria** is a risk in rural areas only; if planning on spending time out in the country, chloroquine is an effective treatment. A recent **dengue fever** epidemic makes it wise to avoid mosquitoes as much as possible. Insect-borne parasites are ever problematic. **Cholera** has swept through El Salvador, as has **typhoid fever.** Avoid unclean food and intimate contact to stay clear of **Hepatitis A and B.** Also on the rise in El Salvador is **HIV/AIDS,** so proper precautions should be taken. Applicants for permanent residence in El Salvador need to have an in-country test for the AIDS virus. Take precautions against all other diseases common to Central America.

Nearly every Salvadoran town has a slew of pharmacies; open hours usually span between 7am-6pm, but many towns have a **turno,** a rotating system which ensures that at least one pharmacy stays open 24 hrs. A schedule explaining which pharmacy is open when is posted in every pharmacy's window.

Locals swear the tap **water** in San Salvador is safe, but drink at your own risk; elsewhere in the country, never chance drinking anything but *agua cristal* or *agua purificada,* which are always safer than what comes from the tap.

■■■ GETTING THERE

Major international airlines such as United, Continental, and American all serve San Salvador's international airport, as does the native **Taca.** Taca, **Copa,** and **Lacsa** serve other Central American capitals and most major cities.

Tica Bus (tel. 222-4818) serves all Central American capitals; see individual cities' Practical Information sections for other buses to border areas.

The preferred border crossings from Guatemala are at **Las Chinamas** (in El Salvador; Valle Nuevo in Guatemala), on the Interamerican Highway leading to Ahuachapán, and at **La Hachadura** on the Pacific Highway over the Río Paz. Coming in from Las Chinamas, it's about half an hour to Ahuachapán. The border crossings to Honduras are at **El Amatillo** and **El Poy,** but this area has been plagued by bandits in the past. Arrive early in the day to avoid missing buses on to major cities.

■■■ ONCE THERE

TRANSPORTATION

El Salvador is small enough that there is no reason to get around by any means of transport other than bus or car. The country is so densely populated that buses move slower than elsewhere, since they constantly stop to pick people up. Domestic buses can get very crowded, but it's still usually possible to get a seat. Crowded buses run between popular routes (such as San Salvador-Chalatenango). Don't expect much pity if you have a big backpack; buses often don't even stop, but rather slow to a crawl, so that even elderly passengers have to sprint and jump on.

The roads in El Salvador are surprisingly well-maintained, despite the heavy traffic nearly everywhere. Buses pass far too frequently to make hitching a necessary option, and cars almost never stop. Pick-ups sometimes transport travelers, but the drivers expect payment for the trip. *Let's Go* does not recommend hitchhiking.

ACCOMMODATIONS

There are no organized campgrounds in El Salvador, even in the national parks; it's often dangerous if you're camping near a beach resort, urban an area, or area with lots of soldiers, which is pretty much everywhere (see Safety, above). It's possible, however, in the more sparsely populated northern and western areas, however. Strangely, many of El Salvador's hotels charge varying rates based on length of stay. Check in after 5pm and leave before 9am in some hotels, and you pay half what you would for staying 24 hrs. Another accommodations quirk in the country is the chance for travelers to stay at one of many **Centros de Los Obreros,** workers' residences that have spare rooms, often with running water and decent beds. The best thing about the Centros is that they're absolutely free for travelers; all you have to do is get a permit ahead of time in San Salvador (see San Salvador, Practical Information, page 172).

ADDRESSES

Streets in El Salvador appease that geometer lying latent in everybody's heart. Most cities are laid out according to a grid-like plan with numbering based on orientation with respect to an origin. In most cities, *avenidas* are streets that run north-south; *calles* run east-west. There are two keystone streets: a central *avenida* (the y-axis), and a central *calle* (the x-axis). Even-numbered streets and avenues are on one side of the axis, odd numbers on the other. In most cities (such as San Salvador), odd-numbered *avenidas* increase in number as you proceed west of the center; odd numbered *calles* increase to the north. Even-numbered *avenidas* and *calles* increase toward the east and south, respectively. Some cities employ variations on this numbering scheme, however. Occasionally, even numbers are to the northwest (as in Santa Ana, Ahuachapan, or San Sonate), northeast (as in San Miguel), or even to the south west. Be sure to note how a particular city handles its numbering.

KEEPING IN TOUCH

Mail sent to the U.S. or Europe from El Salvador is relatively reliable; normal letters take 1-2 weeks, and cost about US$0.40. Express mail services in San Salvador, such as **DHL** (tel. 279-0411; fax 223-2441) and **Urgent Express,** tap right into the U.S.

postal service, and so are reliable and fast, but at a price (usually about US$5 per package). If you want to send a letter to someone in El Salvador by general delivery, address it:

Jimmy Boynton DOWNING (name)
Lista de Correos
Sonsonate (city), República de El Salvador
Centroamérica

Letters sent to San Salvador's main post office should be addressed to "Centro de Gobierno, San Salvador", in the place of an ordinary city name.

The state telecommunications office, ANTEL, has offices throughout the country. Calls within the country only cost about ¢0.10 for a few minutes. Calls to the U.S. or Europe are expensive (about US US$5 per minute), so it's better to call collect or use a calling card. Dialing 119 gets you an operator for **international long distance,** 190 summons an **AT&T** operator, 191 gets you an operator for **Sprint,** and 195 brings you to an **MCI** operator. The **country code** for El Salvador is 503.

EL SALVADOR: AN INTRODUCTION

■■■ HISTORY

Ever since the *conquistadores'* first appearance, the mountainous and heavily populated strip of Pacific coast dubbed "The Savior" by the Spanish seems to have been aching for its namesake. The world has been interested in Salvadoran happenings since the outbreak of its latest and most protracted civil war in the early 1980s, but often fails to understand the larger movements out of which today's struggling factions arose.

Fresh from ploughing through the more expansive Maya settlements of northern Guatemala, colonists under the order of **Perdo de Alvarado** pushed south into the western territories modern El Salvador in 1524, bringing with them the domination and disease characteristic of the Conquest. The preclassic Mayan settlements of Tazumal and San Andrés had already dissipated, but the indigenous **Pipil** people remained to resist invasion. Relatives of the Nahuatl tribes of central Mexico, the Pipil were quickly routed to their capital city of Cuscatlán, driven from the west by the Spaniards' superior military technology. The Pipil made their last stand in the land they called "Izalcos," which later became part of the Sonsonate department — as well as the site of the *matanza,* one of the most notorious massacres in the post-colonial history of the Americas. In subsequent expeditions, Alvarado established nearby San Salvador as a base of operations, and organized the eastern three-quarters of present-day El Salvador around the fledgling city, which has stood as the region's capital ever since. At the time, all but the western territories of Sonsonate, Santa Ana, and Ahuachapán was called "San Salvador," which comprised a province under the larger "captaincy general" of the Kingdom of Guatemala.

El Salvador's arable regions furnished a lion's share of the captaincy's produce and livestock. Cocoa exports gave way to **indigo,** a tough legume used in the production of cool-hued dyes, which was of absolutely no use to the indigenous farmers; their labor's fruits were entirely inedible. The indigo boom cemented the relationship between the landed commercial class and the indigenous *campesinos,* a stand-offish relation that has since marked nearly every political and economic movement in the country. As the lands' original tenants were displaced from their traditional subsistence farming locales to make room for transiently profitable crops-for-export, they were traded food and shelter for work on the new agricultural tracts. The surplus afforded by the innovations of mass production were absorbed almost entirely by the landowners, and so any remainder translated into increased control over the tiring native population.

The first stirrings for independence along the Central American isthmus started among the indigo-growing people of El Salvador. Salvadorans unanimously detested the Guatemalan commercial clout and the captaincy general's bishop. A Salvadoran uprising in 1811, nominally directed against Spain, was gently suppressed by the Guatemalan regime. Discontent with Spain swelled on both sides of the common border, and so the two provinces of the Spanish empire found themselves in happy unity in 1821, when the Guatemalans were finally ready to join the Salvadorans in rejecting their status as mere colonists. They signed a joint declaration of independence, although for a brief period it seemed that each might be absorbed into new and separate empires; in response to a short-lived Guatemalan plan to accept incorporation into a pan-Mexican assemblage, the new state of San Salvador threatened to offer itself up to the United States as an annex. The Mexican government foundered, and the simultaneous flourishing of a Central American constitutional convention encouraged Guatemalan-Salvadoran unity under a new guise. When the presidency of the new coalition, the **Federal Republic of Central America,** fell into the hands of **Manuel Arce,** one of the leaders of the 1811 uprising, Salvadoran support for federation fell into place.

El Salvador soon lost its love for Arce and his Conservative compatriots in the federal legislature, but remained committed to the pan-American ideals he espoused. By 1827, Liberal usurpers had brought conflict to the point of civil war, and within two years they had toppled Arce's government, acting under the command of the Salvadoran hero **Francisco Morazán.** Raised and felled by Salvadorans, the federation moved its capital to San Salvador after Morazán's takeover, and then survived in name until 1841—by which point all four other states had already seceded!

The ensuing decades of independence in El Salvador were among its least stable. Generally, El Salvador engaged in small wars and border skirmishes with its neighbors and other foreign influences for the remainder of the nineteenth century, often resorting to the fascistic Guatemalan leader Rafael Carrera to resolve disputes. Its economy floundered over these decades, in reaction to the development of new, synthetic dyes that gradually extinguished Europe's dependence on the indigo harvest. The Salvadoran republic found the solution to political instability in a solution: **coffee.** Supplying Europe with caffeine transformed El Salvador's agricultural base and the entire economy.

A first important consequence of the move to a coffee industry was that more land needed to be cultivated; the government needed to waive all ownership and protection of federally owned land. El Salvador's native population was forced to relinquish its lands for a "public" cause. The sale of the indigenous peoples' lands engendered uprisings, which were ruthlessly suppressed; coffee money in El Salvador was an even tighter link between the ownership of land and political power. An extremely small, rich, and powerful group of the nation's elite, the "Fourteen Families," organized an effective stranglehold on almost all of the little country's land, its money, and its might. Their might has survived to the present, but it was most obvious in the period between 1913 and 1927, when the Salvadoran presidency was occupied by members of just two of the families, the Meléndez and the Quiñónez.

During the Great Depression, El Salvador's plutocracy degenerated as quickly as did profits of the coffee export, and the oligarchy turned into a brute dictatorship. The pressures of the Depression were first felt among the laboring coffee workers, who led a brief revolt that proved to be neither the country's first, nor its last, but without a doubt its bloodiest. Facing mounting tensions among the lower classes, the **General Maximilano Hernández Martínez** supplanted the (nominally) elected president in 1931. Under the direction of **Augustín Farabundo Martí,** the martyred founder of El Salvador's Communist Party, thousands of farm workers rebelled in 1932. In response, Martínez orchestrated the crushing massacre known as *la matanza:* the summary execution of over 10,000 Salvadoran citizens suspected of having been involved in the uprising. The execution marked a bloody, portentous turning point for internal affairs in El Salvador. Martínez, who sought to emulate the better-known fascists of the time and who entertained a lifelong fascination with the occult, was able to keep himself in power until a coup deposed him in 1948. Ensuing dictators, including his immediate successor, all played puppet to the paranoid landed elite while pursuing moderately successful programs for economic reform. Reforms successfully buttressed the position of a growing middle class's financial interests, but miserably to stem the steady flow of violent military coups.

By the mid-1960s, El Salvador had ascended to a level of relative economic comfort, several reform programs having resulted in new levels of diversification and international exchange. At the same time, the political front was loosening up a little, largely in response to the emergence of a middle class, which backed the **Christian Democratic Party (PDC)** and its leader, **José Napoleón Duarte.** Duarte actually won his first candidacy, for the mayor of San Salvador; but even as moderates were able to gain a foothold in El Salvador's polarized electoral arena, the federal government was organizing a large, right-wing KGB of sorts, ORDEN ("order" in Spanish), which came to play prominent, though silent role in the ongoing suppression of the Salvadoran left. Internal strife was put on hold for a period, however, with the outbreak of the "Soccer War" or *Guerra de Fútbol,* against longtime rival Honduras. The conflict was motivated by outstanding border disputes, economic issues, and the treatment of an immense congregation of Salvadoran refugees on Honduran soil. Begun on the heels of a tense World Cup play-off, the struggle cost each nation thousands of lives and was not fully resolved for 11 years.

EL SALVADOR

Meanwhile, **ORDEN** made its role in Salvadoran life more visible, in reaction to growing support for the middle-of-the-road PDC, by arranging to oversee the 1972 presidential elections. Whether they were more influential in scaring the voting populace or in the subsequent counting of ballots has always been unclear and irrelevant; despite obvious and nearly overwhelming support for Duarte's bid, the more conservative, actively anti-Communist candidate favored by the ORDEN troops registered victory in the end. And thus began the most recent form of the interminable struggle between the rich and the many in El Salvador. Violent passions surged periodically throughout the 1970s, when the Roman Catholic church joined the opposition and shifted the focus of its Salvadoran mission to "liberation theology," which fueled the fires of the popular mass movements that were already responsible for many public protests and strikes. The ruling regime was unable to respond other than by increasing the voltage of the already-brutal measures installed to quell the dissent. Aggression came to a memorable climax in 1975, when ORDEN troops gunned down students protesting the use of federal funds to secure El Salvador as the site of the annual Miss Universe pageant. The cycle escalated until another coup ensued in 1979, marking the beginning of the nation's world-infamous civil war.

Duarte, in Venezuelan exile since his presidential "defeat" of 1972, returned to a hero's welcome after the '79 coup to sit at the front of the popular and provisional interim government. The land-owning, wealthy fragment of the populace stood impervious in the face of the revolution that put Duarte into power, and so was able to regroup and to resume their hegemony. The answer lay in winning the political support of the middle-class and urban centers, and leaving the would-be revolutionaries in the rural north out in the cold. To this end, the families organized the Nationalist Republican Alliance, or **ARENA,** and used the party to apply monetary leverage against the unruly wing of the left. ARENA did not supplant the reigning junta at the time of its inception in 1981, but with the military on its side, it managed to pressure the would-be reformist regime of Duarte's tenure into a vicious struggle with the ever-expanding guerilla movement. A hopeless triangle formed between the rich, ARENA, and the military, on one point; Duarte, a majority of the enfranchised middle-class, and something like the old PDC on another; and the Catholic clergy and a rugged, diverse, and desperate opposition on the other side—this unhappy trinity oversaw a bloody civil war of epic proportions, one that was responsible for the loss of over 75,000 lives by the time of its tentative conclusion in 1992. Contributing critical firepower at a critical juncture was the United States government, under the big-stick direction of the Reagan administration, which donated over US$4 billion worth of military aid to the right over the course of the war.

The only member of the political triad that was not interested in annihilating its opponent(s) was Duarte's, and he was powerless to halt the flow of public funds to the murderous, rightist 'death squads' or into overt campaigns against the guerilla movements. The Reagan government's efforts, however, weren't totally humanitarian in aim; El Salvador had been singled out by the great superpower as an example of how the military might of the West could be used to suppress communist insurgencies. In 1981, at the same time that ARENA was first marshaling its forces, the guerilla armies unified into the **FMLN** (Farabundo Martí National Liberation Front). The rebels had finally gathered sufficient momentum to wage a full-fledged war against the established base of Salvadoran power when one of its Héroes, the **Archbishop Oscar Romero,** was assassinated at the hands of a right-wing death squad. The military establishment fired shots heard 'round the world in the middle of a Sunday Mass in March of 1980, gunning down the popular and strident critic of the Salvadoran peasants while he delivered his sermon. This killing was followed by the rape and murder of three American nuns and a lay volunteer who had also been working on missions of mercy in FMLN-supporting territories, despite the international furor that Romero's slaying had caused. The world was faced with the paradox of a government that seemed intent on making good its ill-fated proposals for agrarian reform, while at the same time pursuing a barbarous program of clandestine extermination of its enemies. In the end, the US found it easier to tolerate the death squads than the revolutionary and agitated rural poor.

The FMLN's first unified war efforts began with the mislabeled "final offensive," a fierce battle that broke out all over the capital and dragged on for months, tapering off into an endless series of smaller and more furtive assaults across the entire country. Fighting was always at its most pitched in the mountainous northwest, which has since been leveled under the weight of random, relentless bombings of peasant villages. Tens of thousands of innocent civilians were killed over the course of the war, most of them by U.S. arms in the hands of U.S.-trained soldiers.

Between the continuing war, an understandably shattered economy, and the failure of almost every social reform of Duarte's, no one was left happy with the moderate, limping government of the late 1980s. Coupled with allegations of rampant corruption in Duarte's administration, these disappointments resulted in 1989 in Duarte's presidential defeat to **Alfredo Cristiani,** ARENA's charismatic and highly westernized candidate. Cristiani punished public sedition more openly than had his allies, but at the same time he was able to maneuver with enough freedom as to start taking seriously the FMLN's demands for social justice. In 1992, under U.N. supervision, an historical accord was reached between the two dominant, and extreme factions, reminiscent of a similar, and failed effort in 1984; so far, this one has been effective, though in his first year in office, President Armando Calderón Sol did little to bolster his popularity; in fact, only 17% of surveyed Salvadorans were willing to call his work so far "good." Still, the three-year old cease-fire should be considered a fortunate respite for the battered combatants, and for every other Salvadoran. The conditions responsible for its declaration are more those of a deeply-felt weariness and frustration than of the kind of reconciliation of interests that might be expected to outlast El Salvador's attempts to nurse its most vital wounds.

■■■ THE ARTS

Rather than expressing the hardship of life in densely populated El Salvador, the country's literature generally offers a chance for the people to escape. Romantic poets include José Batres Montúfar and Arturo Ambrogi, who is also known for his short stories. Indeed, theater and short stories, more accessible media than hefty (and hard-to-publish) novels, have always been favored forms. Later writers continued to tap into popular dreams and sentiment; Carlos Bustamante's *Mi Caso* reflected on the most intimate human feelings with the aid of overtly psychological themes, as did the works of the first acclaimed Salvadoran writer, Claudia Lars (1899-1974). Literature has since come to strive for progress less by lambasting the current system than by evoking impressions of what might one day be.

Some of El Salvador's recent **artists** explore similar themes, tapping into common experience to evoke harmony and peace. Dorian Díaz's "El Pescado" and Gilberto Arriaza's "La Luna" are among the colorfully playful works recently to emerge from the country. Salvadoran traditional handicrafts are made from a number of natural materials; some of the most well-known pieces include the wicker furniture from Nahuizalco and the various ceramics and weavings from La Palma, Chalatenango.

Run Through the Jungle

Despite the fount of fine arts to be savored in the work of El Salvador's natives, U.S. pop has put a spell on Salvadoran youth culture, and Creedence Clearwater Revival reigns supreme. Never mind the Beatles or the Stones, if you've even heard of them; these kids want those fortunate *norteamericano* sons, and buy up their records like crazy. Expect to hear CCR's chart-bustin' singles played one after another at every hip bar in El Salvador's cities. U.S. rock critics have credited the "gutsiest, most joyous, tastiest, no bullshit, kick-ass rock and roll" of all time to this traveling band, but they owe the commotion they've caused in El Salvador, mirrored in many PacRim countries, to that pure "American" grit embodied in Fogarty's brassy vocals and the band's pounding rhythms. Born far from the bayou, CCR hails from El Cerrito, California, but this fine point is probably lost on the rockin' teens who've put them on the throne of Latin Pop.

■■■ FOOD AND DRINK

Often, waitresses claim to serve vegetarian fare, then bring out a plate full of little fleshy morsels. Vegetarians can find salvation in three herbivore-friendly establishments in the capital. *Pupusas* are tortillas stuffed with some sort of dairy, meat, or vegetable filling. *Comedores* tend to just have your average *"pollo* al whatever" and *"carne* fill-in-the-blank," which are often served buffet-style, pick-and-choose, or as Salvadorans call it, *a la vista.* Food stands also sell thin, odd little hamburgers and soggy french fries. Breakfast is eaten between 6am-7:30am, lunch between noon-2pm, and dinner between 6-8pm. A typical breakfast consists of eggs, beans, cheese, and milk, and for an occasional special treat, *pan dulce* (sweet bread, or cake with no frosting) and coffee. For beers, Pilsener and Suprema are made by the same brewery, and the two brands are everywhere, as are their phallic ads. Another popular beer is Regia. Harder drinkers go for a **Tic-Tack,** a ferocious rum-type concoction distilled from sugarcane.

■■■ MEDIA

La Prensa Gráfica and *Diario de Hoy* are the best Salvadoran daily newspapers, although both tend toward tabloid-type news now and then. *La Noticia* has gained popularity in the last few years. The paper allows you to learn about governmental intrigues and the Hugh Grant scandal in one solid read. In San Salvador, pick up the *El Salvador News Gazette* for bilingual tips and news. There are six TV stations, most of which serve up the usual soap operas, news programs, and soccer games. Of the many radio stations, a few are run by the FMLN.

■■■ RECENT NEWS

Political forecasters are not predicting sunny skies for President Armando Calderón Sol, whose popularity has sunk to its lowest since his election in 1994. Polls show that the majority of Salvadorans want the ill-favored *presidente* to generate jobs and crack down on organized crime. One step forward was Sol's dissolution of the

Policía Nacional (PN), a 127-year-old institution identified with terror, corruption, and repression. Political change is also underway in the founding of two new parties: the Consejo Superior del Trabajo (CST), a national labor council, and the left-wing Partido Demócrata, formed by the merging of three social democratic parties. In July 1995, an Aviateca airliner full of passengers crashed into a Salvadoran volcano, en route to San Salvador; everyone aboard was killed.

San Salvador

Incorrigibly resilient and steadfastly proud, the city of San Salvador has shaken off more than its share of devastating blows. Following *conquistador* Pedro de Alvarado's imprudent decision to build a city in this earthquake-prone valley ("Valley of the Hammocks," named for the seismic sway), nearly every generation of the city's inhabitants since 1525 has known suffering and loss followed by fragile recuperation. The city was levelled (or seriously damaged) by earthquakes in 1854, 1873, and most recently in 1986, when over 1000 people were killed; a few years later, the war shook down most of what buildings still stood. No colonial remnants exist to evoke the past, nor is there a middle line in San Salvador: buildings are either spanking new or on the verge of crumbling to dust.

True to character, modern residents of San Salvador are proud of their accomplishments of the past few years. Returning emigrés have supplied capital for a building boom, and poverty-stricken farmers are finally leaving the city and returning to their lands. The city's new look is eclectic and electric, but full of painful contrasts, between luxury and deprivation. Still, the capital seems united by something more basic. The link, whether merely the lung-graying layer of smog that envelops the city, or just a spirit of trust among sufferers, is unmistakably San Salvadoran.

Ignore the city's visual brutality, and San Salvador opens its arms in reception. The people are unusually friendly for a large city, and while there are admittedly few sights in the city and surrounding areas, many visitors find themselves here for a few days anyway, mostly to dive into the vast bureaucracy and copious tourist resources not to be found elsewhere in the country.

■■■ ORIENTATION

San Salvador's leaders have made a valiant effort to make the city's plan as logical as possible. The northwest corner of the **cathedral** is the city's Cartesian origin; it's here that the "zeroeth" streets intersect. **Calle Arce** to the west and **Calle Delgado** to the east form the horizontal axis; **Avenida España** to the north and **Avenida Cuscatlán** to the south form the vertical. All other streets in the vicinity of the center are numbered. The city's main east-west artery is undergoing quite an identity crisis. **2 Calles Oriente,** as it's known east of Avenida Cuscatlán, changes in name to **Calle Rubén Darío.** At 25 Av., the name changes to **Alameda Franklin Delano Roosevelt,** and at Plaza Las Américas, the name changes yet again to **Paseo General Escalon.** A couple of other important east-west arteries are **Boulevard Venezuela** to the south and **Alameda Juan Pablo III** (formerly 7 Calle, but changed in 1983 to honor the Pope, who'd walked along the street during a visit to El Salvador) to the north. Unfortunately, this logic is slowly losing out; the suburbs popping up around the city don't follow such a logical layout.

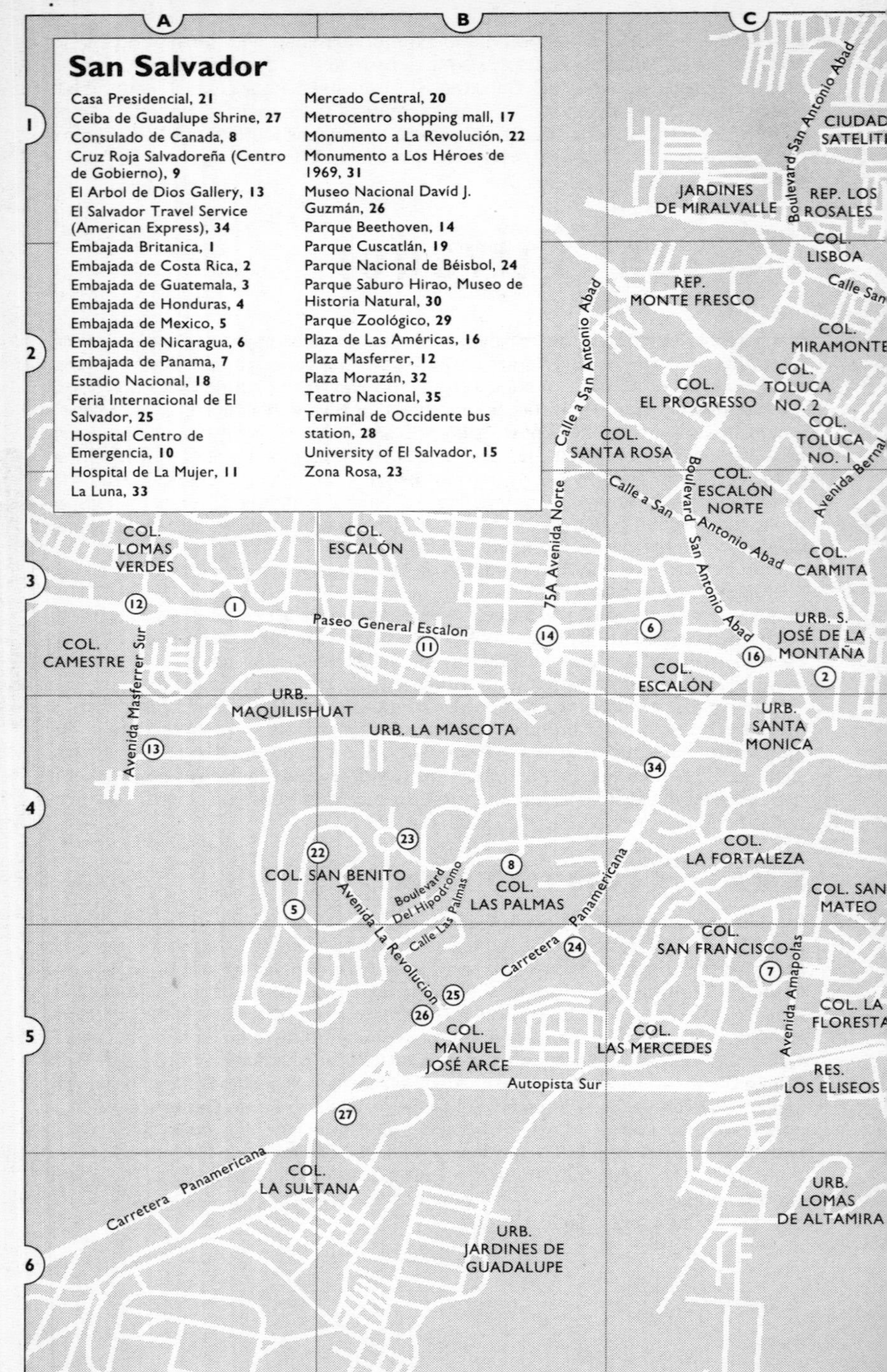
San Salvador
Casa Presidencial, 21
Ceiba de Guadalupe Shrine, 27
Consulado de Canada, 8
Cruz Roja Salvadoreña (Centro de Gobierno), 9
El Arbol de Dios Gallery, 13
El Salvador Travel Service (American Express), 34
Embajada Britanica, 1
Embajada de Costa Rica, 2
Embajada de Guatemala, 3
Embajada de Honduras, 4
Embajada de Mexico, 5
Embajada de Nicaragua, 6
Embajada de Panama, 7
Estadio Nacional, 18
Feria Internacional de El Salvador, 25
Hospital Centro de Emergencia, 10
Hospital de La Mujer, 11
La Luna, 33
Mercado Central, 20
Metrocentro shopping mall, 17
Monumento a La Revolución, 22
Monumento a Los Héroes de 1969, 31
Museo Nacional Davíd J. Guzmán, 26
Parque Beethoven, 14
Parque Cuscatlán, 19
Parque Nacional de Béisbol, 24
Parque Saburo Hirao, Museo de Historia Natural, 30
Parque Zoológico, 29
Plaza de Las Américas, 16
Plaza Masferrer, 12
Plaza Morazán, 32
Teatro Nacional, 35
Terminal de Occidente bus station, 28
University of El Salvador, 15
Zona Rosa, 23
A
B
C
1
2
3
4
5
6
Boulevard San Antonio Abad
CIUDAD SATELIT
JARDINES DE MIRALVALLE
REP. LOS ROSALES
COL. LISBOA
REP. MONTE FRESCO
Calle San
Calle a San Antonio Abad
COL. MIRAMONTE
COL. TOLUCA NO. 2
COL. EL PROGRESSO
COL. TOLUCA NO. 1
COL. SANTA ROSA
Avenida Bernal
Calle a San Antonio Abad
Boulevard San Antonio Abad
COL. ESCALÓN NORTE
75A Avenida Norte
COL. LOMAS VERDES
COL. ESCALÓN
COL. CARMITA
Paseo General Escalon
URB. S. JOSÉ DE LA MONTAÑA
COL. CAMESTRE
Avenida Masferrer Sur
COL. ESCALÓN
URB. MAQUILISHUAT
URB. LA MASCOTA
URB. SANTA MONICA
COL. LA FORTALEZA
COL. SAN BENITO
Boulevard Del Hipodromo
Calle Las Palmas
COL. LAS PALMAS
Carretera Panamericana
COL. SAN MATEO
Avenida La Revolucion
COL. SAN FRANCISCO
Avenida Amapolas
COL. LA FLORESTA
COL. MANUEL JOSÉ ARCE
COL. LAS MERCEDES
Autopista Sur
RES. LOS ELISEOS
Carretera Panamericana
COL. LA SULTANA
URB. LOMAS DE ALTAMIRA
URB. JARDINES DE GUADALUPE

D
E
F
RES. MONTE BELLO
Avenida Bernal
COLONIA FORTUNA
COLONIA LA FOSA
CIVIDAD UNIVERSITARIA
COL. EL REFUGIO
COL. JARIDINES DE MONPEGÓN
URB. SN CARLOS
COL. EL ENCANTO
COL. LAS ROSAS
COL. SAN JOSÉ
COL. EL ROBLE
Autopista Norte
URB. AIDA
REP. 2 DE ABRIL
COL. STA. ROSA
COL. SAN CARLOS
COL. EL PRADO
COL. 17 DE MAYO
URB. CALIFORNIA
COL. LARCO
COL. CENTRO AMERICA
COL. SANTA VICTORIA
REPARTO DON RUA
URB. PALOMO
COL. SAN JOSÉ
COL. RODEZNO
Boulevard de Los Héroes
COL. BUENOS AIRES
URB. S. ERNESTO
URB. LA ESPERANZA
COL. ISIDRO MENÉNDEZ
URB. STA. ADELA
CAMP. 3 DE MAYO
URB. LA FLORIDA
CENTRO DE GOBIERNO
COL. GUADALUPE
COL. STA. EUGENIA
Avenida España
COL. MIRAMONTE
COL. TUTUNICHAPA
Avenida Gustavo Guerrero
COL. LAS TERRAZAS
Tercera Séptima Calle Poniente
Alameda Juan Pablo
1a Calle Poniente
3a Calle Poniente
3a Calle Oriente
Alameda Franklin Delano Roosevelt
Calle Arce
Calle Rubén Darió
Calle Delgado
49A Avenida Norte
COL. FLOR BLANCA
Calle Gerardo Barrios
Avenida Cuscatlan
COL. CUCUMACAYAN
Boulevard Venezuela
COL. GUERRERO
COL. B. AIRES
25A Avenida Sur
COL. SANTA CRISTINA
COL. FERROCARRIL
COL. DAVIDSON
CENTRO URBANO I.V.U.
COL. SAN JUAN
COL. MALAGA
COL. STA CARLOTA
COL. LUZ
COL. DINA
COL. LA PROVIDENCIA
RES. MODELO
COL. B. AIRES
COL. NICARAGUA COSTA RICA
COL. MANZANO
COL. MENJIVAR
CENTRO URB. MONTSERRAT
COL. MINERVA
COL. BUENAVISTA
COL. MILITAR
N

■■■ PRACTICAL INFORMATION

Tourist Office: Instituto Salvadoreño de Turismo (ISTU) (tel. 222-8000), between 9 and 11 Calles on Calle Rubén Darío. The staff is a bit surprised when an authentic tourist walks in, but service is nevertheless helpful. Maps are free; pick up their great schedule of inter-city buses throughout El Salvador. Open Mon.-Fri. 8am-4pm, Sat. 8am-noon. There is also a branch at the **airport** (tel. 339-9464).

Special Permits: Obtain a permit to stay in the country's scattered **Centros de Los Obreros** at the Edificio Abrego Urrutia I, 15 Calle and 7 Av., just northeast of the Centro de Gobierno. Open Mon.-Fri. 8am-4pm.

Police: (tel. 121 or 123). The national police squad has its office here.

Currency Exchange: Changing traveler's checks should be no hassle in the capital. **Banco Hipotecario** (tel. 222-2122), on Av. Cuscatlán and 4 Calle, changes with little fuss. Open Mon.-Fri. 9am-4:30pm, Sat. 9am-noon. **Banco Salvadoreño,** in the center on Calle Ruben between 11 and 13 Av., also on in the Metrocentro, is another safe bet.

Post Office: (tel. 271-1922), in the Centro Gobierno on 11 Av. near 13 Calle. Open Mon.-Fri. 7am-5pm, Sat. 8am-4pm. **DHL** (tel. 279-0411; fax 223-2441), 43 Av. and Alemeda Juan Pablo II, just across from Metrosur, offers speedier service. Open Mon.-Fri. 8am-6pm, Sat. 8am-noon.

Telephones: The main branch of **Antel** is on Calle Rubén Darío and 5 Av., next to McDonald's. Open daily 6am-10pm. A smaller, less hectic **branch** offering all the same services stands at Torre Roble in the Metrocentro.

Embassies: U.S. (tel. 228-4444; fax 278-6011), Blvd. Santa Elena, Antiguo Cuscatlán. Open Mon.-Fri. 8am-4pm. **Canada,** Avenida Las Palmas #111, Col. San Benito (tel. 224-1648; fax 279-0765). Open Mon.-Fri. 8am-noon and 1:30-4:30pm. **U.K.,** Paseo General Escalon #4828 (tel. 298-2772; fax 298 3328). Open Mon.-Thurs. 8am-1pm and 2-4:30pm, Fri. 8am-1pm. **Mexico,** Pasaje 12 and Calle Circunvalación, Col. San Benito, across from Hotel Presidente (tel. 298-1079; fax 298-2651). Open Mon.-Fri. 8-11am. **Belize,** Condominio Médico "B", Local 5, 2nd floor, Blvd. Tutunichapa, Urb. La Esperanza (tel. 226-3588; fax 226-3682). Open Mon.-Fri. 8am-noon and 1-5pm, Sat. 8am-noon. **Costa Rica,** Edificio La Centroamericana, Avenida Roosevelt #3107 (tel. 279-0303; fax 223-7975). Open Mon.-Fri. 8am-1:30pm. **Guatemala** (tel. 222-2903; fax 221-3019), on 15 Av. between Calle Arce and 1 Calle. Open Mon.-Fri. 8am-noon. **Honduras,** 37 Av. Sur #530, Colonia Flor Blanca (tel. 271-2139; fax 221-2248). Open Mon.-Fri. 9am-noon and 1-3pm. **Nicaragua,** 71 Av. and 1 Calle, Colonia Escalón (tel. 223-7729; fax 224-0970). Open Mon.-Fri. 8am-1pm and 3-5pm. A booklet distributed by the tourist office contains a list of many more embassies and consulates. **Australia** and **New Zealand** have no embassies in El Salvador.

Immigration Office: located in the Centro de Gobierno (tel. 221-2111). Open Mon.-Fri. 8am-4pm and Sat. 8am-noon.

American Express: (tel. 223-0177), in Comercial la Mascota on the corner of Calle la Mascota and Interamerican Highway. Will hold mail for cardholders or check holders in addition to refunding your lost checks. Buses #34 and #101 both go here from the city center.

Airport: The **international airport** is 44km south of the city and is served by a number of airlines in addition to **Taca** (tel. 298-5055; fax 223-3757), the national airline which only flies internationally. El Salvador is served by **American** (tel. 298-0777; fax 298-0762); **British Airways** (tel. 224-4980); **Continental** (tel. 279-2233; fax 223-8968); **Mexicana** (tel. 279-3744; fax 279-4034); **United** (tel. 279-4469; fax 223-0097), and a number of other carriers. **Acaya** (tel. 271-4937), runs a microbus service to the airport several times daily. Their office is at 19 Av. and 3 Calle in San Salvador.

Intercity Buses: With a few exceptions, intercity buses all leave from either **Terminal Occidente** (reached by Bus #34 from *el centro*), serving destinations in the western half of the country, or Terminal Oriente, which serves the country's eastern half. Leaving from **Terminal Occidente** on Blvd. Venezuela near 49 Av.: buses to Santa Ana (#201; every 5min., 5am-6:40pm, 1 hr., ¢4.20); to Sonsonate

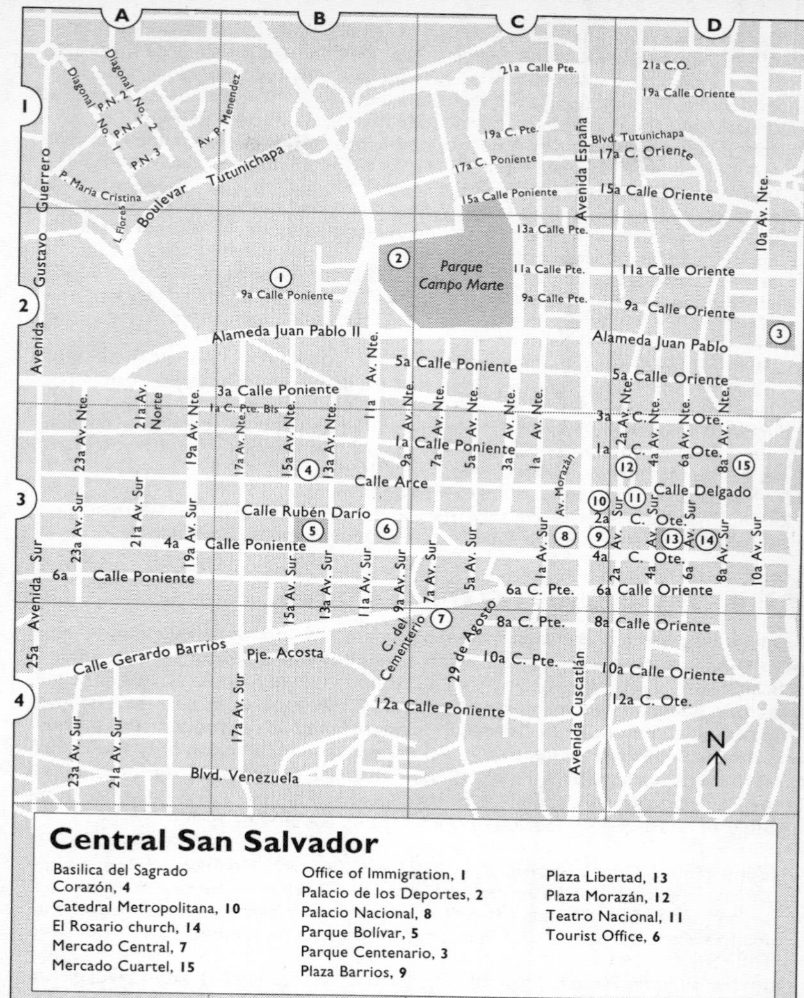

(#205; every 10min., 5am-6:40pm, 1½ hrs., ¢4.20); to Ahuachapán (#202; every 15min., 5am-6:40pm, 2 hrs., ¢4.50); the Guatemalan border at Las Chinamas (every hour, 6am-5pm, 3 hrs., ¢6); and at La Hechadura (2 per day, 7am and 2pm, 3½ hrs., ¢6.40). Leaving from **Terminal Oriente:** buses to Chalatenango (#125; every 10min., 4am-5pm, 2 hrs., ¢5); to the Honduran border at El Poy and passing through La Palma (#119; every 30min., 4:30am-4:30pm, 4 hrs., ¢8); to San Miguel (#301; every 10min., 4am-5:30pm, 3 hrs., ¢13.50); and to Usulatán (every 10min., 4am-4:30pm, 4 hrs., ¢12). Buses #7, 29 and 34 all go from the terminal to *el centro;* #29 continues on to the Metrocentro on Blvd. de los Héroes. Bus #102 for La Libertad leaves from *el centro* near the corner of 13 Av. and 4 Calle (1 hr., ¢5.50).

International Buses: International bus service is handled by a number of private companies. **Tica Bus** (tel. 222-4808) has one bus per day leaving at 5:30am in front of Hotel San Carlos at Calle Concepción #121 for Tegucigalpa (7 hrs., ¢260); for Managua (12 hrs., ¢608); for San José (2 days, ¢870); and for Panama City (3 days, ¢1304). Tica Bus also has a bus leaving at 6am for Guatemala City (5 hrs., ¢138). **Puerto Bus** (tel. 222-2158; fax 222-2138), located on Alemeda Juan Pablo II and 19 Av., also has bus service to Guatemala City (every hour, 3:30am-4pm, ¢45) and to Tegucigalpa (2 per day, 6am and 1pm, ¢130). Buses for La Libertad (#102) leave the capital every 15min.; the trip takes just over an hour.

Public Transportation: City buses are ubiquitous and serve destinations throughout the city. Service 6am-9:30pm, fares from ¢.60-1.25. Bus #34 runs between the two terminals and passes through the center.

Taxis: Marked by the familiar bright yellow and found throughout the city. Fares generally run ¢20-30; bargain if you think the price is too high. Prices generally go up after dark and near expensive hotels.

Car Rental: Budget (tel. 279-2811), **Avis** (224-2623), **Sure RentaCar** (225-1488).

Market: Central market, between Avs. 5 and 7 on 6 Calle. Open daily 6am-6pm. **Mercado Ex. Cuartel,** on 8 Av. and Calle Delgado, specializes in *artesanía.* Open daily 7:30am-5:30pm.

Laundry: Lavapronto on Calle Sisimiles #2924, 100m behind Hotel Camino Real, washes clothes with same-day service. Wash and dry ¢15 each per load. Open Mon.-Sat. 8am-5pm.

English Bookstores: Despite the presence of an Anglophonic expatriate community, the closest thing San Salvador has to an English bookstore is the newsstand in the **Hotel Camino Real** on Blvd. de Los Héroes.

Red Cross: (tel. 222-5155), in the Centro de Gobierno.

24-hr. Pharmacy: Farmacia Internacional, in the mini-mall (not Metrosur) on the corner of 49 Av. and Blvd. de los Héroes and Alemeda Juan Pablo II.

■■■ ACCOMMODATIONS

As might be expected, the capital is not a place to save money on ridiculously inexpensive accommodations. Cheap sleeps exist, but you'll pay for it with either a shocking lack of amenities or by being holed up in one of Salvador's seedier neighborhoods. Budget hotels are clustered around four separate areas, near the Terminal Oriente, the center, near the Terminal Occidente, and in the residential neighborhoods near Boulevard de los Héroes. In dangerous San Salvador, only the last of these four is actually viable for a stay of more than one or two days. The area around Terminal Occidente, for example, is relatively safe and almost walking distance from nightlife along Paseo Col. Escalon or Boulevard de Los Héroes.

Happy House Guest Home, 2951 Calle Sisimiles (tel. 226-6866), 200m behind the better-known Hotel Camino Real, and near Blvd. de los Héroes. Windows let in light, and cheery rooms have all the trimmings: clean, functional baths, firm mattresses, and a helpful and friendly staff. Singles ¢76; doubles ¢110, ¢180 with bath; triples ¢180.

Ximena's Guest House, 202 Calle San Salvador (tel. 226-9268). From Blvd. de los Héroes, turn west onto Calle Gabriela Mistral; the first left splits into three; take the middle one. Expatriates, Peace Corps volunteers, and other travelers in the know flock to this place for its homey atmosphere and cheap, modern rooms. Singles ¢50, ¢180 with bath; doubles ¢70, ¢160 with bath.

Hospedaje Clementina (tel. and fax 225-5962), on the corner of 39 Av. Norte (what Calle Gabriela Mistral becomes after Calle San Antonio) and Calle Washington, near Blvd. de los Héroes. Cool rooms with ceiling fans face a garden with hammocks and a restaurant. The lobby has an incredible book exchange, probably the highest concentration of English language books in the capital. Singles ¢100, doubles ¢170, quads ¢260.

American Guest House (tel. 271-0224; fax 271-3667), on 17 Av. between Calle Arce and 1 Calle. Much like San Salvador, this hotel has undergone countless renovations and add-ons. As a result, hallways zig-zag around and stairways pop up in odd places. The old rooms definitely have character, and public baths have hot water and are modern and clean. An attached restaurant serves food and little snacks. Singles ¢120, ¢150 with bath; doubles ¢120, ¢180 with bath.

Hotel Yucatán, 673 Calle Concepción (tel. 221-2585). Near Terminal Oriente. The concrete-slabs of rooms are dark and a bit dusty, but the beds are thick and comfortable. The bathroom is brighter than most, but this just highlights the funk in the tiles. Maybe it's the potted plants in the courtyard, but the management here seems to try harder than elsewhere. Rooms (singles or doubles) ¢20 per person, ¢25 with bath.

Hotel Roma, 3145 Blvd. Venezuela (tel. 224-0256), a block west of Terminal Occidente on the opposite side of the road. Painted an enticing combo of brown and yellow, Roma has musty, but surprisingly bright rooms with desk fans; the mattresses are firm but slightly odor-tainted. Ask for a room off the street if noise is a problem. Singles ¢50, ¢70 with bath; doubles ¢60.

■■■ FOOD

Food is definitely San Salvador's strong point. Restaurants abound, and cheap, tasty meals of every sort are not hard to come by. Small *puposa* and *tortilla* stands are absolutely everywhere throughout the city, even in some of the quieter residential neighborhoods. The area around **Boulevard de Los Héroes,** in addition to being one of Salvador's prime nightspots, is U.S. fast-food row. Weary travelers hankering for a Big Mac or pan pizza should hamburgle their ways here. **McDonald's, Burger King, Pollo Campero, Wendy's,** and two **Pizza Huts** line the boulevard. In addition, there are a number of upscale Mexican restaurants and steak houses. Given the nightlife-oriented nature of the area, most restaurants are open until at least 10pm, and some are open until midnight or later. **Metrosur,** Metrocentro's southern annex on Blvd. de Los Héroes and Alemeda Juan Pablo II. The open-air food court is home to a number of inexpensive fast-foody and local places serving up quick and cheap eats. Just behind Hotel Camino Real on **Calle Lamatepec** extends a row of about a dozen seafood places. As is typical of seafood, prices for dishes are a little pricey, but all the restaurants are in a row, so if you don't like the price in one, just walk next door.

Restaurante Karen (tel. 226-1552), just off Blvd. de Los Héroes between Bressler's and Wendy's, a block before Calle Gabriela Mistral. A classic and damn good little *comedor* for travelers seeking an authentic taste of Salvadoran cuisine. Typical plates run ¢15-20. Open daily 8am-10pm.

Restaurante Taiwan, on Calle San Antonio Abad #1437, a block west of the top of Blvd. de Los Héroes (tel. 226-0707). Given the genuine Chinese food, the restaurant's prices aren't through the roof. Can't complain about chow mein (¢25), *chorizo de Taiwan* (¢16), or *Won Ton Frito de Camara* (¢16). Open daily 11:30am-3pm and 5:30-10pm.

Restaurante Koradi (tel. 221-2545), on 9 Av. and 4 Calle. A small *comedor*-like restaurant abutting a health-food store in *el centro,* Koradi serves vegetarian food at a decent price, including fresh salad (¢8) and unbleached rice (¢6). Open Mon.-Fri. 7:30am-5:45pm, Sat. 7:30am-3pm.

Café Bella Napolés (tel. 222-6879), on 4 Av. between Calle Delgado and 2 Calle. Smack in the chaos of the center, Café Bella Napolés' air-conditioned environs make for sweet relief from the heat. A favorite coffeehouse with locals, who often pack the place. Eggs with bacon ¢8, spaghetti ¢15. Open daily 7:30am-8pm.

■■■ SIGHTS

The latest version of **Catedral Metropolitana's** tall gray dome looms over the center of San Salvador, serving as daily reminder of the city's capricious and disaster-prone fate. The original cathedral was begun in 1808 and completed a decade later, only to be completely destroyed by an earthquake in 1873. Subsequently rebuilt, the new church was brought down again in 1951, this time by fire. The present, structure is strictly functional and sturdy, built in simple Byzantine style with drab, unadorned concrete. It was here in 1980 that a lone gunman shot down **Oscar Romero** as he was giving Mass; the Archbishop's crypt is inside the cathedral. Yet another earthquake damaged the structure in 1986, and so the building remains closed.

The entrance to the cathedral is on 2 Calle, facing **Plaza Barrios,** Salvador's main square. On the west end of the plaza is the bright yellow, neo-classical **Palacio Nacional.** Once the seat of government, the building was also ravaged by the '86 'quake and remains closed to this day. Two blocks east of Plaza Barrios is **Plaza Libertad,** a less hectic counterpoint to the main *zócalo.* Facing this plaza is a rather bizarre church, **El Rosario.** The church's external, crumbling structure is like a half-cylinder turned on its side, but inside hide some very interesting modern sculptures, mostly made from steel rebars and other scraps, depicting religious scenes. The church is also home to the tomb of **Father Delgado,** an important figure in Central America's independence movement.

Continuing east from the center a few blocks is the **Mercado Ex-Cuartel.** Bounded by 8 and 10 Avs., Calle Delgado, and 1 Calle, the market specializes in *artesanía* from all over El Salvador. The huge pavilion is home to dozens of vendors hawking wares and eagerly waving tourists into their stalls (open daily 8am-6pm).

Southwest of the center, along the Interamerican Highway (the *carretera* out to Santa Tecla) lies **Museo Nacional David Gúzman,** located at the corner of the Interamerican Highway and Av. La Revolución. The museum is home to El Salvador's finest Mayan artifacts, including the intricate **Stela of Tazumal.** Unfortunately, the museum is temporarily closed, its artifacts locked away in storage while a new museum is built on the site. Construction is slated to be completed by late 1996. Just before the museum on the Carretera Panamericana, on the site of the international fairgrounds, is the **Mercado Nacional de Artesanías,** a scaled-down version of Mercado Ex-Cuartel (open daily 9am-6pm). Buses #34 and #101 from San Salvador pass by both places.

EL SALVADOR

At the end of Av. La Revolución is **Monumento a la Revolución,** a 60ft-tall modernist mosaic of a figure breaking free of its shackles and reaching for the sky. The monument is a tribute to the peoples of Central America; ironically, the mural is situated in the center of San Salvador's most exclusive neighborhood.

A little farther out in the same direction is **Jardín Botánico La Laguna,** a quiet botanical garden housing a variety of flora. Set in an extinct volcanic crater, La Laguna actually *was* a lake until 1873, when an earthquake opened a drain-like fissure below the water's surface. Today the crater is home to an odd and unfortunate mix of gardens and a contaminating industrial complex. Fortunately, several shady trails through the park are muffled from the loud factory booms. Bus #101C passes through Antiguo Cuscatlán from the center and #44 from Metrocentro. From Antiguo Cuscatlan, it's about a one-km walk to the gardens.

■■■ ENTERTAINMENT

San Salvador can get rough at night, so be on guard, particularly in the city center. City buses only run until about 9:30pm, so plan on taking a taxi for the return; fares tend to go up once the buses stop running. The capital is a great place to catch a **movie.** Theatres typically show sub-titled, two-month old Hollywood flicks (admission ¢15-20). **Caribe** (tel. 223-6968) at Plaza Las Américas, **Beethoven** (tel. 224-2084) at Parque Beethoven, and **Variedades** (tel. 225-1242) at Calle San Antonio Abad and Calle Gabriela Mistral (near Blvd. de Los Héroes) all show films in relatively safe neighborhoods. Check newspapers for local listings.

Boulevard de Los Héroes is one of the prime nightspots in San Salvador. *Mariachi* bands stroll around looking for customers, and the whirl and screams of fairground rides blare in the background while fire-spitters work the main intersections. Higher up along the boulevard, open-air restaurants boogie to live bands. **Las Antorchas** and the adjacent **El Coral Steakhouse,** located on the Blvd. two blocks north of Calle Gabriela Mistral, host live bands of all types (salsa, merengue, and rock); thump and jiggle nightly until 1am.

WEST OF SAN SALVADOR

■■■ LA LIBERTAD

What might have been a charming fishing village, La Libertad has the unfortunate luck of being the closest beach to the capital; San Salvadorans pack the town's seaside resorts on weekends, and bring with them hints of the capital's bedlam and babel. On weekdays, though, La Libertad winds down (and cleans up) as locals assume their rightful place as the town's owners. The beach's proximity to San Salvador doesn't translate into comfort, dishearteningly; the shore is rocky, and the strong current can be dangerous, flaws which are probably responsible for saving the town from gratuitous development. La Libertad is a nice place to stay, but realistically, it could easily be reached as a daytrip from the capital.

Orientation and Practical Information Set in a broad, curved bay, the beach is split in half by a long pier where fishermen dock and hawk the catch of the day. The town is several streets deep. **Calle Calvario,** the principal *calle,* is the main drag to the west, and a block south, **2 Calle** is the main street heading east. A block south of that, 4 Calle runs along the ocean. Walking the town's 10 blocks takes little more than five minutes.

There are no **banks** in town, so travelers should take care of their money-changing needs elsewhere. **Antel** is on the corner of 2 Calle and 2 Avenida (open daily 6am-10pm). The **post office** roosts just next door on 2 Av. (open Mon.-Fri. 8am-4pm, Sat. 8am-noon). For immediate **bus** destinations west along the coast, #80 runs to Zunzal (every 20min.) and bus #192 heads to La Perla. Traveling farther east along the Costa Balsamo is difficult by public transportation. **"El Pacífico"** goes all the way to Sonsonate (6am and 11am, 2½ hrs). To Zacatecoluca zoom eight buses daily (#540; 5:40, 8, 8:20, 9am, and 4 times between noon and 3pm, 2 hrs., ¢5.50). It's possible to transfer at La Flecha to go to Costa del Sol. Stalls of the **market** line the streets along 2 Av. and 1 Calle. **Farmacia Jerusalem** (tel. 335-3508) is between 1 Av. and Av. Bolívar on Calle Calvario (open 7am-6pm).

Accommodations and Food The best deal on the coast is the **Centro de Los Obreros,** about 1km west of town. Tourists are permitted to stay for free, providing that they first obtain permission in San Salvador (see San Salvador, Practical Information, page 172). The *centros* have large rooms with up to six cots with shared bath, but no bedding. There's a swimming pool on the grounds as well as a *cantina* that's occasionally open. The center is very crowded during the day, but at night it becomes The Shining By The Sea; just watch out for frustrated writers wielding axes.

In town, **Puerto Bello** (tel. 335-3013), on the corner of 1 Av. and 2 Calle, offers a great deal. Clean plaster-and-tile rooms face a bright courtyard. The mattresses are firm, and the shared bath, one of those open-air deals, is kept quite sanitary. Ask for the room up top: extending like a lighthouse two stories above the hotel, the room has a 360® view of the town. And it's the same price as all the other rooms (¢50 per person). **Hotel Amor y Paz** (tel. 335-3187), on 1 Av. and 4 Calle, is the cheapest place on the beach. Mattresses are thin reed mats and the heavy barred doors evoke Alcatraz. The public baths are wretched, but for the location and price, it's not a bad deal (singles ¢40, doubles ¢60). On the west end of town, the beach curves around to parallel 5 Av. Sur to the home of La Libertad's nicest hotels and restaurants; at the beginning at 5 Av. and 4 Calle lolls **Motel Rick** (tel. 335-3033). The paint is fresh and all rooms have desk fan and private baths separated by a half-wall (singles ¢85, doubles ¢150 for 24 hrs.).

La Libertad is sprinkled with cheap *comedores* serving the basics: beans and rice, *carne asada, pollo dorado,* and some seafood. The shoreline is packed with gorgeous restaurants perched over crashing waves. Prices tend to be inflated, but keep in mind that you're paying for the location as much as the food. **Rancho Mar El Delfín,** across the street from Posada Don Lito, is probably the slickest of these. Lobster with shrimp ¢100, *coctel de ceviche* ¢35. **Restaurante Punta Roca** (tel. 335-3261), next door, has a similar set-up, but it's a bit more homey. Prices are marginally lower. *Filete de marisco* ¢45, *carne asada* ¢38.

■■■ SONSONATE

This center of El Salvador's cattle-producing region is more than 450 years old, but you'd never guess it; any evidence of the town's history has been wiped out entirely. Even the cathedral and El Pilar church smack of the modern age, and the rest of the town (pop. 65,000) whirls and pulses with a vigor far beyond its size. The main drag has its share of wannabe ritzy shops, record stores thumping out the hits, and grumbling trucks passing through from the port of Acajutla on their way to the capital. After tapping into the amenities, travelers use Sonsonate as launching pad for pleasant daytrips to nearby villages and natural attractions.

Orientation and Practical Information Sonsonate is laid out in the standard grid pattern with Avenida Morazán and Paseo 15 de Septiembre as keystone streets. Even-numbered *avenidas* and *calles* extend to the north and west respectively, and odd numbers run to the south and east. Some of the numbered streets have been renamed in honor of various figures, but street names and addresses aren't commonly used anyway. Long and narrow, Sonsonate is sprawled out along Paseo 15 de Septiembre. The bus terminal is out in the 20's of *avenidas,* and the church and park stand next to the zeroeth intersection.

Change traveler's checks and take care of **currency exchange** at **Banco Agrícola Mercantil** (tel. 451-0008), located at the intersection of Paseo 15 de Septiembre and Av. Morazán, on the park (open Mon.-Fri. 8am-5pm, Sat. 9am-noon). A number of banks are scattered around the square and Paseo 15 de Septiembre, but few change traveler's checks. There's a **post office** in a non-descript building next to a gargantuan movie theater on 1 Av. between 3 and 5 Calles (open Mon.-Fri. 8am-noon and 2-5pm, Sat. 8am-noon). Call your significant other from **Antel,** just a block north of the square on Avenida Morazán and 2 Calle (open daily 6am-10pm).

Buses leave from the terminal on Paseo 15 de Septiembre, about 10 blocks west of the square. To San Salvador (every 10min., 4am-5pm, 1½ hrs., ¢4.20); to Santa Ana (every 20min., 4am-4pm, 2 hrs., ¢4.50); to the Guatemalan border at La Hechadura (every 15min., 4am-6pm, 1½ hrs., ¢4); to La Libertad (5:40am and 3:20pm, 2½ hrs., ¢5.30); to Acajutla (every 30min., 4am-4pm, 45min., ¢2); to Los Cobanos (every hr., 5am-6pm, 45min.,¢2.50); and to Ahuachapán (every hr., 5am-5pm, ¢5). Bright blue **local buses** are all #53 followed by some letter. They travel between the square and the terminal, and to surrounding villages. Bus #53D goes to Nabuizalco every 10min., #53A goes to Izalco every 5min. Both leave from the square and fares are ¢1 or less. The familiar bright yellow **taxis** line up on the east end of the park and charge a pricey ¢15 to the terminal. The **central markets,** on Paseo 15 de Septiembre just inside the railroad tracks, about three blocks from the square. Also, the streets to the immediate northeast of the park are lined with stalls. Both stay open while the sun shines (6am-6pm, roughly). **Farmacia Firenze** (tel. 451-1156) deals drugs on the town's medical row, 5 Av. between 1 and 3 Calles (open daily 8am-6:30pm). Pharmacies also dot the streets near the park. Have ingrown toenails removed at the **Hospital Municipal,** on 5 Av. between 1 and 3 Calles, which stands along with a slew of doctor's offices. Call 24 hrs. for an **emergency** (tel. 451-0200).

Accommodations and Food There are two clusters of hotels in *centro.* Sonsonate: near the bus terminal and in the center of town. Those near the bus terminal are uniformly rough and dirty, while those in the center are better, but inconvenient for travelers on a layover. **Hotel Florida,** on 18 Av., just half a block north of Paseo 15 de Septiembre and two blocks east of the terminal, combines cleanliness and value with dark rooms with working ceiling fans circled around a central courtyard. The public bath isn't above reproach, but does the trick (singles ¢30, doubles ¢40). Similar in style and price is **Hospedaje Brasil,** on 14 Av., half a block south of Paseo 15 de Septiembre. The beds aren't as comfy as those in Hotel Florida, nor do the rooms have ceiling fans, but it'll do if you're desperate (singles ¢30, doubles ¢50). **Hotel Orbe** (tel. 451-1416, 451-1517), 4 Calle and 2 Av., two blocks north of the square, offers sweet refuge for weary travelers. The poshest place in town is a miraculous value. Beds are snuggly-soft, the private baths pass the white glove test, and the fans will blow your freakin' mind (singles ¢60, doubles ¢92).

Sonsonate is probably not the place to try to experience Salvadoran cuisine in all its glory. Seized by the fast-food craze sweeping El Salvador, travelers would be hard-pressed to find a restaurant that doesn't serve hamburgers. There are two **Pizza Atto's** in town, one out by the bus terminal on Paseo 15 de Septiembre and the other near the square in a mini-mall on Paseo 15 de Septiembre and 1 Av. Both locations serve up mighty fine pizza with generous toppings and cheese sent straight from heaven; try a personal-size pepperoni pizza (¢24), or garlic bread with cheese (¢10; open daily 11am-8:30pm). **Sabor Club** (tel. 451-5401), on the north end of the square, specializes in all kinds of fruit shakes (¢8.50) and juices (¢7): pineapple, mango, papaya, and even plain vanilla. They also serve sandwiches (open daily 7am-7:30pm).

■ NEAR SONSONATE

Set on the gentle alluvial fan of Santa Ana Volcano and Cerro Verde, the scenic countryside surrounding Sonsonate is dotted with a number of interesting villages. **Nahuizalco,** 6km to the north, is a Pipil town specializing in basketry and furniture, and lo and behold, there are a few stores that sell nice hand-crafted furniture and baskets at low prices. The town has a *feria de artesanía* from June 18-25. Bus #53D leaves from the square in Sonsonate every 10 minutes.

Just outside of the nearby town of **Izalco** is the *turicentro* **Atecozol,** a serene, forested area with trails, a swimming pool, and basketball courts (open daily 7am-6pm; admission ¢7, *cabañas* available for ¢35). Bus #53A (from the central square in Sonsonate) zips to Izalco; from there, the *turicentro* is six blocks from the church. Facing the church, take the road to the right.

For dabbling in more dribbly natural wonders, **Salto Las Victorias** is a pleasant, if not terribly impressive waterfall. Set 2km outside of **Caluco,** the falls are an easy walk through beautiful farmland; in some ways, the journey, not the destination, is the attraction. To get to the falls, take the road out of Caluco to the left of the church, score a goal at the soccer field, and continue for about 1km. Turn right at a palm-tree-lined road paved with bright red volcanic gravel and scurry across the railroad tracks. From there it's a short distance through some small cornfields. A bus leaves hourly from Sonsonate and passes through Izalco along the way to Caluco. Pick-up trucks also leave from Izalco to Caluco about once every 30min.

■■■ AHUACHAPÁN

The departmental capital of Ahuachapán distinguishes itself neither for its beauty nor lack thereof, but instead jives on java, of which it produces enough to jump-start a nation. Surprisingly, the town gets its electricity not from their own, beany-brew infused veins, but from *ausoles,* boiling mud pits which can be tapped for electricity. Prospering and placid, Ahuachapán goes on its merry, fortunate way, especially after having been spared the violence of the civil war. What most distinguishes Ahuachapán from so many other towns are its *two* central plazas, **Parque Menéndez** to the north and **La Concordia** to the south. Most importantly, Ahuachapán is the first (or last) stop for travelers from (or going to) Guatemala.

Orientation and Practical Information Situated 23km from the Guatemalan border at Las Chinamas, Ahuachapán is the first sizable town on the road to the capital. **Calle Barrios** and **Avenida Menéndez** comprise the town's axes; their intersection is unremarkably marked by a bank and a fast-food restaurant. **Parque Menéndez** is bounded by Avenida Menéndez on the west and 6 Calle on the north. Buses run past here before pulling into the **terminal,** 2 blocks south on Menéndez. **La Concordia** is on 1 Av. and 3 Calle.

Banco Hipotecario has been known to accept American Express checks. Located on the corner of Av. Menéndez and 1 Calle (open Mon.-Fri. 9am-4:30pm, Sat. 9am-noon). If this doesn't work, Av. Menéndez is blessed with many more banks that, *ojalá,* will change your checks. The **post office** is on Calle Barrios between 1 and 3 Avs. (open Mon.-Fri. 8am-5pm, Sat. 8am-noon, Sun. 8-11am). **Antel** is on the south side of **La Concordia,** and pay phones are sprinkled liberally throughout the city, with concentrations in the two parks. **Buses** radiate out from the terminal in Ahuachapán in three directions. To the north is the border with Guatemala at Las Chinamas, (#263; every 15min., 6am-5pm, 45min., ¢2.50). Bus #249 runs south to Sonsonate (every hr., 6am-5pm, 2 hrs., ¢5); and to the east zoom buses to Santa Ana (#202; 1½ hrs., ¢2) that continue on to San Salvador (every 10min., 4am-4:30pm, 3 hrs., ¢4.50). Buy a cheap watch or leather purse among the thousands for sale at the municipal **market** on the west side of Parque Menéndez (open daily 6am-6pm). And for travelers who *must* have their corn flakes, there is a **supermarket** at the zeroeth intersection, next to Mister Pollo.

Accommodations and Food Hotels in Ahuachapán are uniformly clean and decent places to stay; the only downside is there are no dirt-cheap dives for the bankrupt. **Hospedaje Granada** (tel. 443-1074), located on 8 Calle between 4 and 6 Av., has spartan but well-kept rooms with hypnotic ceiling fan and firm mattresses. The sullied public bathroom shows where money you don't pay doesn't go (singles ¢40, doubles ¢60). With nearly same-quality rooms, **Hotel San José** (tel. 443-1820), on 6 Calle facing Parque Menéndez, might be worth extra for the clean private baths (¢50 per bed). Go whole-hog at **Boarding House Casa Blanca,** which has immaculate rooms with a ceiling fan or A/C (¢50 extra) and gorgeous baths with hot water. The hotel is set around a lush Spanish courtyard with large comfortable chairs and a 19-inch TV in one corner (¢100).

Perhaps the only other distinguishing characteristic of Ahuachapán is its utter lack of *comedores.* The closest thing is **Mister Pollo,** providently located at the town's center (Calle Barrios and Avenida Menéndez), serving four pieces of fast-food chicken (¢20) and fantastic American-style milkshakes (¢9). Barring Mister Pollo (which wouldn't be nice), there's always the market and street vendors.

■ NEAR AHUACHAPÁN: BORDER TO GUATEMALA

A 45-min. bus ride to the north leads to the border with Guatemala at **Las Chinamas,** one of four points of entry shared by El Salvador and Guatemala. The fairly quiet post is open daily from 8am-5pm. It is possible to cross later, though public transportation stops running about this time. There is no entrance fee and only a small exit fee of ¢5. **Buses** and pick-up trucks to Ahuachapán leave every 15 minutes and the fare is ¢5. Buses to Guatemala City leave roughly every hour. Finally, there is a **tourist office (ISTU)** at Las Chinamas, open same hours as the border, which hands out reams of photocopied sheets in English and Spanish about various sites in El Salvador. Especially helpful is the list of bus schedules they hand out.

■■■ SANTA ANA

Rather than huff and puff to catch up with San Salvador, Santa Ana's 210,000 residents have resigned themselves to living in the nation's *segunda ciudad,* thus sparing themselves the burdens of burdensome urban sprawl and decay. Instead, the city cranks forward with halcyon charm; the central square is predictably quiet, but even the market and bus terminal, normally nodes of chaos, are orderly and efficient. As the major transportation hub for western El Salvador, Santa Ana is an ideal base for a tour of some of the country's most fantastic attractions, including **Lago de Coatepeque, Parque Nacional Cerro Verde,** and the Mayan ruins at **Tazumál.**

ORIENTATION AND PRACTICAL INFORMATION

At the southwest corner of the *zócalo* is the intersection of Calle Libertad and Avenida Independencia. To the north and west, the streets and avenues increase in even integers, and to the south and east, they ascend in odd numbers. Most of the town lies just southwest of the square: the **bus terminal** stands at 10 Av. and 15 Calle, most of the budget hotels await a few blocks north along 10 Av., and several restaurants glut along Av. Independencia to the south of the square (3-11 Calles).

Police: Main station on 5 Av. and 4 Calle; 24-hr. **emergency** number is 440-0280.
Post Office: On 7 Calle, between 2 and 4 Avs. Open Mon.-Fri. 8am-noon and 2-5pm, Sat. 8am-noon.
Telephones: Antel, 2 blocks east of the square on 5 Av. and Calle Libertad. Open daily 6am-10pm. Pay phones are scattered sparsely throughout the city.
Currency Exchange: Banco Salvadoreño (tel. 441-0207) on 1 and 2 Avs., is one of the few banks that changes traveler's checks. Open Mon.-Fri. 9am-4pm.
Buses: Santa Ana is the transportation hub for western El Salvador, and you'll never have to wait long for a bus to any destination. To **San Salvador** (leaving frequently from 4am-5:30pm, 1½ hrs., ¢4.20); to **Ahuachapán** (every 15min., 4:15am-6pm, 1 hr., ¢2.50); to **Sonsonate** (every 20min., 4:40am-5pm, 2 hrs., ¢5); to **Metapán** (every 15min., 4:30am-6:20pm, 1½ hr., ¢4.50); to the Guatemalan border at **San Cristóbal** (every 15min., 5:45am-6:30pm, 1 hr., ¢2.50); to **Lago Coatepeque** (every 45min., 5:50am-4:40pm, 1 hr., ¢2.20); and to **Cerro Verde** (8:30am, 1:30pm, 10:30pm, 2 hrs., ¢6).
Local Buses: Route #51 is the local bus, serving various points within Santa Ana. Most eventually pass by the terminal; the fare is ¢1.
Taxis: An uncommon site in this compact city, taxis occasionally line up along the square and charge ¢10 to the terminal.
Market: The streets immediately to the north and west of the bus terminal are chock-full of market stalls. Open during daylight hours.
Pharmacy: Farmacia Fray Martín (tel. 441-2194) is conveniently located on 10 Av. between 7 and 9 Calles. Open daily 8:30am-6pm.
Medical Services: The central **Hospital** is a bit out of the way at 13 Av. and 1 Calle, 7 blocks east of the square. **Emergency** number: 441-1780.

ACCOMMODATIONS

Many hotels in Santa Ana are cut from the same mold, in which dark, windowless rooms open onto a courtyard. Some have private baths, and public baths are usually a row of stalls exposed to the open air, guarded only by a flimsy wooden door.

Hospedaje San Miguel (tel. 441-3465), Avenida Delgado (12 Av.) near 7 Calle. For the price, you'd expect the worst, but San Miguel's nice, so it's listed first. The whole place is well-swept and maintained, except for not-so-fresh public bathrooms. The rooms lack fans, but nights here are cool. Singles ¢20, doubles ¢30.
Hotel Livingston (tel. 441-1801), on 10 Av. between 9 and 7 Calles, about 5 blocks north of the bus terminal. The rooms are as clean as San Miguel's, but they have fans, the beds are more comfortable, and the public baths are in a better shape—all for double the price. Singles ¢40, ¢50 with bath; doubles ¢65, ¢80 with bath.
Hospedaje Tikal, on 10 Av. between 11 and 9 Calles, about 4 blocks north of the bus terminal. The management tries hard here, judging by the courtyard's cheerily-spruced appearance and abundance of potted plants. Otherwise, the rooms are clean enough (no fans) and the public bath passable. ¢30 per bed.

Internacional Inn, on 10 Av. and 25 Calle, five blocks south of the terminal. Santa Ana's splurge-central breaks the mold. Rooms all have windows, gorgeous private bath, and ceiling fans. The hotel is cluttered with eclectic knick-knacks, from odd pink lamps in every room to floral print bedspreads to ubiquitous pictures of Germany. Singles ¢100, doubles ¢180. Washer-dryer facilities available for a fee.

FOOD

Fast-food joints, pizzerias, and ubiquitous *comedores* clog Avenida Independencia, Santa Ana's restaurant row, between 3 and 9 Calles.

Pollo Campero, Av. Independencia and 7 Calle. Ubiquitous throughout El Salvador, this is the spot for middle-class hungroids to chow on fast-food fried chicken; the immense room is always packed. Dinner of 3 pieces with french fries and soft drink ¢25. One of the few places open for breakfast. Open daily 6:30am-9pm.

Toto's Pizza (tel. 441-0880), on Av. Independecia and 1 Calle. Just one of the pizzerias ubiquitous in Santa Ana, and Dorothy would be proud. Notable for its salad bar, vegetables washed in purified water, and vegetarian pizza, loaded with *verduras* and large enough for two (¢45). Open daily 11:30am-9:30pm.

Restaurante Ky Jua (tel. 447-7379), on Calle Libertad between 2 and 4 Av. A pleasant, upscale restaurant that serves authentic Chinese food. Quite a rarity in these parts. Soup Won Ton, pile it on; *pollo cantonesa,* shove it in your face-a (¢20-30). Open daily 11:30am-9pm.

SIGHTS

Santa Ana's Gothic-styled **cathedral,** built in 1905, is in a sad state of disrepair, making it seem much older than it actually is. That's plaster on the brick façade, not offerings from the pigeon population living above. Situated next door, the neo-classical, banana-yellow **Teatro de Santa Ana** is in excellent shape, given it's 85-year history as a theater for drama, movies, and decades of decay. The current restoration effort has been temporarily stymied due to lack of funds.

■ NEAR SANTA ANA

TAZUMAL

The area surrounding the Mayan ruins of **Tazumal** has been occupied for nearly 7000 years, but the 14-step pyramid dates back a "mere" 1200 years. Whether your interests lie in pre-Mayan or only in pre-Columbian ruins, Tazumal is worth a trip, more so than any other ruins to be found in El Salvador.

Situated on the outskirts of the town of **Chalchuapa,** 13km west of Santa Ana, the site covers an impressive patch of land. The main site consists of the pyramid, 180m wide at its base and 25m in height, an adjoining ballcourt, and an excavated tomb where sacrifical slaves were buried. Meanwhile, for fans of the *very* old, there's an on-site museum packed to the brim with intricately designed pottery and other artifacts from the original settlements. To get there from Santa Ana, bus #236 runs every 30min. to Chalchuapa from Santa Ana's terminal (20min., ¢2). The bus makes a circuit of the center and then stops a mere 100m from the ruins' entrance (open Tues.-Sun. 9am-noon and 1-5:30pm; admission free).

PARQUE NACIONAL CERRO VERDE

Perched atop a half million year-old extinct volcano, **Cerro Verde National Park** is home to some of El Salvador's most awe-inspiring scenery. The mountain (this is no mere *cerro,* or hill) teems with a fantastic assortment of wildlife, mostly of the flighty, hollow-boned variety. An easy, 30-minute loop encircles the peak and lets you soak in views of nearby Lago Coatepeque and Volcán Santa Ana. Additionally, veering from the road about 100m before the park entrance, an extremely well-marked and maintained trail leads to the summit of **Volcán Izalco.** The trail descends about 1200ft through the forest of Cerro Verde in staircase-fashion until reaching the base. From here the trail becomes rocky as you climb to the bare cone. The descent is especially tricky. From the base to the summit amounts to a 1000ft elevation gain; the round-trip hike takes about 3 hours. The air gets pretty chilly at 6500 feet, so be prepared with warm clothes and plenty of water (admission ¢7). To get there, bus #248 leaves from Santa Ana at 8:30 and 10:30am (2 hrs.). Returning buses leave Cerro Verde at 3:30 and 5:30pm. **Camping** is permitted in the park and spartan *cabañas* are available for a pricey ¢200.

Grab a beer and laugh at fate and the ironic misfortunes of the **Hotel de Montaña** (tel. 271-2434). The owners constructed the hotel back in the 50s for tourists interested in romantic, volcano-side getaways by Volcán Izalco. After all, back then, the volcano spewed fumes and spurted lava on a daily basis, scaring the heck out of locals and earning nicknames from sailors, who could see the glow from off the coast. Just as the hotel was completed in 1957, however, old Izalco petered out, and so the hotel now has nice views of a big, black pyramid. Stay here if you've got the wad: rooms are pricey but reasonable, at ¢260 per person. Mon.-Thurs., though the rate shoots up to ¢400-450 on the weekends.

Also accessible within the park are trails leading to neighboring **Volcán Santa Ana** (7800ft). The trail leaves from the loop trail; there's no sign, but the junction is about midway between the vista points for the lake and Volcán Santa Ana. The trail descends about 200m to the base and then begins the ascent. Getting to the crater takes about three hours.

LAGO DE COATEPEQUE

Down the eastern slope of Volcán Santa Ana lie the clear waters of **Lago de Coatepeque,** one of the hot spots where the rich from San Salvador come to spend their weekends. Set in a volcanic crater, the lake is surrounded by verdant slopes rising 500 meters above, as well as by the towering Cerro Verde and Santa Ana Volcano. The crystal waters of the lake offer swimming and even snorkeling.

There are a number of places to stay around the lake; the best deal is the **Balneario de Los Obreros.** A resort built for government workers, it is **free** for tourists who have written permission from the Edificio Abrego Urruti (see San Salvador, Practical Information, page 172). The rooms are pretty sparse but all have a private bath, and it's hard to beat the price. There are several other hotels around the lake if you don't have a permit.

As the bus descends down to the lake, the *balneario* sits just at the the road' s junction around the lake. Bus #220 leaves from Santa Ana every 40 minutes, circling a third of the way around the lake before turning back. From San Salvador take the bus to El Congo, 15km before Santa Ana and 5km from the lake, and change there.

NORTHWEST EL SALVADOR

■■■ METAPÁN

The Western Union office is one of the most prominent structures in the town of Metapán, a subtle hint of the city's immense dependence on dollars sent home by daughters and sons living in other parts of the world. Still, Metapán fares reasonably well; situated in the far northwest near the Guatemalan border, the town saw some intense action during the civil war, but still exudes an oddly prosperous sheen. The brand-new five-story hotel, ubiquitous restaurants, and the large number of *salvadoreños* recently returned from abroad suggest that life is getting back to normal. The town itself offers little to travelers, but rather acts as a soft, service-filled cushion for those lonely times between daytrips to Montecristo Preserve and Lago Güija.

Metapán is roughly 45km north of Santa Ana on an extremely well-maintained road. The highway passes to the east and then curves around to form the town's north end. The familiar odd and even *avenida* and *calle* system holds, with odd streets and avenues to the north and west. Street names are rarely used, but the town is small enough and you can always ask locals for directions.

Antel, 2 Av. and 2 Calle, just 2 blocks down the street to the left of the bus terminal, has phones and more (open 6am-10pm). One block north and east of Antel is a **bank** (tel. 442-0128), which, amazingly, accepts travelers checks (open Mon.-Fri. 8am-4pm, Sat. 8:30am-noon). **Buses** go to Santa Ana (#235; every 20min., 4am-6pm 1½ hr., ¢4.50) or head in the opposite direction to the Guatemalan border at Anguiató (20min.). Different buses leave twice daily to make the four-hour trip over agonizingly slow dirt roads to the Honduran border at El Poy (4 and 5am, ¢12).

For respectable accommodations, **Hospedaje Central,** on 2 Av. and Calle 15 de Septiembre, is not a bad deal for singles as clean as these are (¢25 per room, with bath ¢35), although the dark and not too comfortable rooms are about what you'd expect for the price. A nicer option is **Hotel California,** 200m north of the bus terminal on the left side of the highway. All rooms have fans and private baths, and the management is quite friendly; they won't stab you with their steely knives, but will let you leave (singles ¢50, doubles ¢75).

Chicken Bell, 2 Calle (about a block before Antel), is Metapán's attempt at fast food. Owned by a former manager of a Kentucky Fried Chicken in the U.S., the owner claims to have stolen the Colonel's secret recipe and brought it to northwest El Salvador. One whole chicken and a coke ¢18 (open 7am-9pm). About a block before that is **Multidelicas** (tel. 442-0226), which serves pizza (¢28), double hamburgers (¢13), "fresh salad" (¢9), all in a *comedor*-like environment.

■ NEAR METAPÁN

The **Montecristo Wilderness Preserve** contains some of the purest and most exotic wildlife in El Salvador. Established to promote friendship between El Salvador, Guatemala, and Honduras, whose borders converge at El Trifinio, Montecristo's 2418m summit, the reserve is home to agoutis, porcupines, anteaters, and similarly bizarre and rare creatures. The moist, cool cloud forest at 2100m contains trees with twisted, moss-covered trunks.

The park is located 14km northeast of Metapán along a rough road accessible only by 4x4's. There is no public transportation to the park, so the only option is to hike the distance or hire a private auto. **Hotel San José** (tel. 442-0556) organizes daytrips up to the park and will take a group of up to 12 people for a flat fee of ¢300. Also, asking around at the bus terminal might yield information on cheaper deals. Most of the park is closed April through September for the animals' breeding season, but some parts are open during the summer months (park admission ¢10).

To the south of Metapán lolls tranquil **Lago Güija,** one half of which lies in El Salvador, the other half of which lies in Guatemala. While not as scenic as some of El Salvador's other lakes, Güija is cradled by hills and volcanoes, and not by the homes of San Salvador's rich. Lago Güija's principal attractions are the Mayan hieroglyphics carved into some of the boulders along the lake shore, locally referred to as **Las Figuras.** It's possible to hire one of the fishing boats for a tour around the lake, but this really isn't necessary (unless you want to fish), as the lake can be seen by walking along the shore.

To get to the lake, take bus #235 south towards Santa Ana and get off at Desagüe, a small unmarked village along the road about 20 minutes south of Metapán. From the highway, a dirt road forks off to the right. Follow this about 100m until it merges with some railroad tracks, follow the tracks across the bridge and then continue along the trail as it slopes gently to the right. Continue through the village and the lake is just beyond it.

■ LA PALMA AND EL POY

In El Salvador, so many shelves in so many shops in so many cities are lined with so many craftworks, it's a wonder the source is so small. The tiny village of La Palma, situated on the highway to the Honduran border at El Poy, has grown famous around the country for its local *artesanía*—particularly brightly painted wooden figurines depicting religious and rural scenes. There's no shortage of shops here; La Palma is home to several galleries, including that of **Alfredo Linares,** a renowned painter of stylized rural scenes; his gallery is located a block uphill from **Antel.**

Travelers wishing to spend the night can hole up at **Hotel La Palma** (tel. 335-9012), which has charming rooms decorated with the work of local artists, though having the vivid little wooden people near the bed has been reported to induce strange dreams (singles ¢150, doubles ¢200). For a cheaper choice, hop on a bus going 20 minutes north along the highway to **Hotel Cayahuanca** (tel. 335-9464). Named after a nearby mountain, it's a friendly hotel with an attached restaurant. All rooms have two beds (¢50, ¢80 with bath).

Near La Palma at the border to Honduras spreads the town of **El Poy.** Buses go to San Salvador from El Poy (every 30min., until 4pm), or continue across the border. There is a ¢8 exit fee for leaving El Salvador; buses leave hourly to Nueva Ocotepeque in Honduras (6am-6pm).

■■■ CHALATENANGO

No city was untouched by the civil war in El Salvador, but as the years pass, blood and tear stains fade into the sad but healing scars of memories. In Chalatenango, however, war's wounds continue to fester as ever before. For a time, the town of 30,000 was one of the FMLN's strongholds, as evidenced by the red graffiti decorating the streets and walls. The uneasiness and awkwardness of peace is only barely palatable; the city's center is strictly divided between conspicuous army barracks on one side and the nearly deserted square and market pushed back several blocks on the other. As the economic center of the region, Chalatenango sees many people come and go; almost none of them are tourists. Expect some soul-penetrating stares if you visit the town—usually not looks of maliciousness, but rather of curiosity and disbelief that a traveler would want to come here.

Orientation and Practical Information Fifty-five kilometers northeast of the capital, Chalatenango is the largest city in and seat of the department of the same name. Like San Salvador, Chalatenango is laid out in the familiar *avenidas* and *calles* pattern. **Avenida Libertad** and **Calle José María San Martin** (say it ten times fast) form the principals; odd *calles* and *avenidas* ascend in number out from the center towards the north and west, respectively. Buses drive in along 3 Av. a few blocks south of the square. 3 Av. passes right through the center, with the church to the east and the military encampment to the north.

On 3 Av. between 4 and 6 Calles hide the vaults of **Banco Salvadoreño,** which changes traveler's checks (open Mon.-Fri. 8am-4pm, Sat. 8am-noon). Bus #125 makes the trip to and from Terminal de Oriente in San Salvador (every 10min., 4am-5pm, ¢5). At the Desvío El Mayo it is possible to change buses and head north to El Poy or west to Nueva Concepción. **Antel** is on the main *calle* three blocks west of the church (open 6am-10pm). The **Correo** is on 3 Calle between 6 and 4 Av. (open Mon.-Fri. 8am-noon and 2-5pm, Sat. 8am-noon, Sun. 8-11am). The town's **market** is also on the main *calle* at Avenida Libertad, with stalls spilling out onto the surrounding streets. As in most towns, pharmacies dot the center. **Farmacia Guadalupena,** on the corner of Avenida Libertad and 4 Calle, is but one of oh-so many (open Mon.-Fri. 8am-5pm).

Accommodations and Food Low demand has caused a downward shift of supply of accommodations in Chalatenango. **Hospedaje Nuevo Amenecer** is between Avenida Libertad and 2 Av. on 1 Calle. Customer service and diligence aren't top priorities here, but once you make yourself heard, the reward is, well, a dark room and a dank public bathroom. Better take it than leave it; you have no other option for lodging in town. An overnight stay from 5pm-7am (yessiree, that's

7am checkout; think of it as an excuse to get an early start) costs ¢25; 24-hr. service is double! All rooms have one bed and share a public bath. If you arrive early, they'll gladly guard your stuff until check-in time.

Thankfully, the eating situation isn't nearly as bad. **Comedor y Cafetín Portalito,** on 4 Calle just uphill from Avenida Libertad, is a breezy place on a terrace overlooking the street. All meals served, and the food here is plentiful and cheap. *Pollo con arroz* ¢14, *carne asada* ¢16 (open daily 7am-9pm). **Restaurant El Paraíso** (tel. 335-2356), on 2 Av. and 1 Calle doesn't live up to its name, but its wanna-be posh interior is pleasant enough. A meat-and-potatoes kind of place, their specialty is seafood. Try the *tiburón en salsa roja* (shark!) for ¢25 (open 11am-11pm). A couple of dingy *comedores* serve cheap food next to the *hospedaje.*

■ NEAR CHALATENANGO

Just to the northeast of town is the **Turicentro Aguas Frías.** Better maintained and busier than most *turicentros,* Aguas Frías' specialty is swimming pools. There are three pools here—one for *niños*, a larger pool for general merriment, and an Olympic-sized pool for serious swimmers. The *turicentro* is also a good place for a picnic, or just spend a few hours in the restaurant trying to take off your swim-cap (open daily 7am-6pm; admission ¢7).

Slightly farther afield is the town of **Concepción Quezaltepeque,** a 30-minute bus ride away (#300B, leaving from 3 Av. in Chalatenango every 45 minutes). A quiet village with cobbled stone streets, Concepción Quezaltepeque's specialty is hammocks. It seems that every house here is in on the racket and a random walk through town brings you by a dozen workshops. Travelers whose hammocks are their body and soul might be curious as to just how their stringy friends are made. Though most of the hammocks are shipped elsewhere, Concepción Quezaltepeque is a good place to pick up a few wholesale. Bargaining is expected.

EAST OF SAN SALVADOR

■■■ ZACATECOLUCA

Say this town's name enough times, and you might have more fun than Zacatecoluca has to offer otherwise. Zacatecoluca, or simply Zacate, as it's known locally (to foreigners' great relief), situated 55km southeast of San Salvador and nestled at the foot of Volcán de San Vicente, surveys some beautiful views of its surrounding countryside. The church in the Central Square impresses with its main spire, soaring up 150 feet and towering over the town. Zacatecoluca is also home to one of the larger *turicentros,* **Ichanmichen.** It's a cool place to unwind for the afternoon, but alone isn't enough of an incentive to venture to Zacate. The town's only real value to travelers is its proximity to **La Costa del Sol,** one of El Salvador's prime vacation spots. The utter lack of cheap accommodations along the coast makes Zacatecoluca an attractive place from which to launch salt-sun-sandy daytrips.

Zacate is a long and narrow town. Three *avenidas* run the length of town: **Avenida Villacorta,** on which the buses arrive, **Avenida Delgado,** its partner to the west and the street on which buses leave, and **Avenida Monterrey.** The meat of the town runs from 9 Calle to the south and 14 Calle to the north. **Banco Hipotecario** (tel. 334-0060), on Av. Delgado and 1 Calle, changes traveler's checks with minimal fuss (open Mon.-Fri. 8:30am-5pm, Sat. 9am-noon). The obligatory **Antel** office is on Calle Nicolas Pena and Av. Monterrey (open daily 6am-10pm). The **bus terminal** is on 7 Calle between Av. Villacorta and Av. Delgado. The bus leaves for San Salvador (#133, every 10min., 3:40am-6pm, 1½ hrs., ¢4.20); to San Vicente (#177, every 20min., 5am-6pm, 1 hr.); to La Libertad (hourly, 6am-4pm, 2 hrs., ¢5.50); to La Costa del Sol (#193; every 30min., 5am-5pm, 2 hrs., ¢6); and to Usulatán (#131; 5, 5:40, 11am, 1½ hrs.). Local bus #92 goes 15km to the *turicentro* at Ichanmichen.

Zacatecoluca has but one hotel, **Motel Brolin** (tel. 334-1084), between Av. Villacorta and Av. Monterrey on 7 Calle. The rooms have comfortable beds, private bath, ceiling fans, and hammocks. It's a decent hotel that's kept pretty clean; compared to the sticker shock at Costa del Sol, the price is right (singles ¢80, doubles ¢150).

Zacate's restaurants are all of the *comedor* variety; the *gringo* to native ratio is near to zero, so prices are reasonable. **Restaurante El Pescador,** on Av. Villacorta between 3 and 5 Calles, has a concrete floor, vinyl chairs, and the obligatory Wurlitzer. Chow down on *pollo dorado* (¢18) or some bodacious *bistec* (¢25), all the while wondering about the skinned racoons on the walls (open daily 10am-10pm).

■ LA COSTA DEL SOL

La Costa del Sol is the spot in the sun for El Salvador's well-to-do, and with good reason; a stroll along the ten-mile stretch of beach is an infinite journey through your gentlest beach-oriented fantasies—just as long as those dreams include mansions with barbed-wire-topped walls and shotgun toting guards off to the side. On la Costa del Sol, though, it's not just the rich who come to play; each weekend marks a new Exodus of *Capatalinos* of all stripes. Anti-social types should come on a weekday, when the pace slows down considerably.

The coast is a long, thin peninsula with the pounding waves to the north and to the south. A good paved road traverses the entire length of the coast going southeast until it reaches the estuary at the sea. There's a **bus** going up or down the coast at least every half hour. It there's no convenient bus leaving from Zacate or San Salvador, it's easy to catch bus #133 instead, the bus between Zacate and San Salvador, and get off at La Flecha, about 20km west of Zacate, where you can transfer. The last bus back to San Salvador leaves at 3pm, to Zacatecoluca at 4pm. The coastal stretch begins, more or less, at the new supermarket and the recently-built **Pops Ice Cream.** The bus proceeds southeast, passing the *turicentro* 5km later, and ending at the estuary another 10km down the road.

Cheap lodging of any kind is utterly lacking along the coast; the area is best enjoyed as a daytrip. At the end of the bus line at the estuary to the right, 50 meters from the shore, is an unnamed and inconspicuous restaurant that rents a few rooms in the back. The rooms aren't painted and the only real difference between this and camping is the flimsy and unattached roof. Even these rooms go for ¢125 (for two beds; try bargaining). A kilometer and a half up the estuary is the **Pacific Paradise Hotel** (tel. 887-0544). About as upscale as Salvadoreño hotels get, Pacific Paradise is a smallish, family-oriented place. The rooms have fantabulous private baths and air-conditioning as a matter of course. With two queen-size beds, each room can sleep up to four people. The price is—are you ready?—¢565. Luckily, **camping** is an option. The area around the estuary is said to be safe, but be sure your tent isn't on private property and that it stands above the tide line. The **turicentro** closes at 5:30pm and they kick everyone out, so it's not an option to sleep there.

The **food** situation isn't quite as bad; the estuary is lined with thatched huts offering mostly seafood. Don't be deceived by the bare-bones set-up; these places can be outrageously expensive. It's good to pin down a price beforehand and never let them quote you in dollars.

■■■ COJUTEPEQUE

Like so many towns in El Salvador, Cojutepeque hides its long history far too well. Modern as the town seems, the *encomienda* of Coxutepeq was founded in the 1530s at the site of an indigenous village; since then, the name has undergone a number of alterations, along the way substituting the x in Coxute with a "y," then later with a "j." Just out of the reach of the Interamerican Highway's din, the unassuming *pueblo's* cobblestone streets beam like rays of sunlight from the laid-back central square; luckily, the town's military complex is inconspicuous. Cojutepeque provides a relaxing outing from larger cities, especially if you visit the **Cerro de Las Pavas** (Hill of the Turkeys), or imbibe the holy vibes of the **Virgen of Fátima.**

Orientation and Practical Information Cojutepeque lies 32km east of San Salvador, just south of the Interamerican Highway. The town is set on a small plateau just to the south of Cerro de Las Pavas; uphill is south, downhill is north. **Calle Delgado, Avenida José María Rivas,** and **Avenida Raul Contreras** lie at the heart of the familiar grid. Odd-numbered *calles* and *avenidas* ascend from the origin to the north and west respectively; several of the streets have honorary names, as when 2 Av. becomes **Av. Santa Ana** south of Calle Delgado.

There is no place to change traveler's checks in Cojutepeque. The **post office** is on Av. Rivas, two blocks north of the church (open Mon.-Fri. 7am-5pm, Sat. 8am-noon, Sun. 8-11am). **Antel** has branch at Av. Contreras and 6 Calle, to the south of the church (open daily 6am-10pm). **Buses** are a cinch in Cojutepeque. The #113 zips directly to San Salvador from Av. Santa Ana and 5 Calle (every 10min., 4:20am-7:30pm; 1 hr.). Going east, any bus traveling along the Interamerican Highway will stop in Cojutepeque, including #111 to Ilobasco, #116 to San Vicente, #110 to San Sebastian, #306 to Santa Rosa de Lima, and #310 to San Miguel. Each of these passes through town every 10-20min. or so and fares are about ¢2 less than if you've started in San Salvador. The town's **market** lines Av. Contreras and 2 Av. south of the church all the way up to Cerro de Las Pavas. **Farmacia San Antonio** (tel. 332-0388) advertises service 25 hrs. a day, 8 days a week. Regular hours are 7am-9pm daily; after that, ring the bell. Look for it on 6 Calle between 1 and 3 Avs.

Accommodations and Food Cojutepeque is no bargain hunter's eden, but given the scarcity of lodging here, the prices are reasonable at least. **Hospedaje Cojutepecano,** on Av. Santa Ana (2 Av.) between Calle Delgado and 1 Calle, one block north of the church, has six underground rooms with a grotto-like feel. Beds are fairly comfortable; private baths are separated by a half-wall (singles ¢50). **Hospedaje Jovel,** on 1 Av. between 6 and 8 Calles, has above-ground rooms, but they're still dark; a single, nude lightbulb hangs over thin mattresses on shaky cots. All rooms are singles; service from 5pm-8am is ¢25, double for a whole day.

Expect to eat well in Cojutepeque. The highway passing through the north end of town is lined with good, inexpensive *comedores* and *pupuserias.* One of the stand-outs of these is **Licuados El Paso,** on the highway between Av. Rivas and Av. Santa Ana (2 Av.). You guessed it, the restaurant specializes in fresh fruit drinks. Set back from the highway just a bit, the restaurant is ideal for grabbing a small meal and watching humanity pass by (open 6am-6pm). The area around town is also sprinkled with good *comedores* and food stands. One of the nicer restaurants is **Restaurante Adentro Cojutepeque's** (tel. 332-0434) on the corner of 3 Calle and Av. Brioso (6 Av.). Situated on the third floor, the large, open restaurant has great views of nearby Cerro de Las Pavas and Volcán San Vicente. At night, there's live music at a bar overlooking the dance floor. Dishes run ¢40-50, about double the prices at the *comedores* (open Mon.-Thurs. 11am-11pm, Fri.-Sun. 11am-3am).

Sights Cojutepeque's primary (and only) attraction is **Cerro de Las Pavas.** The forested hill stands several hundred feet above the town to the south, and is home to the nationally beloved **Virgen de Fátima,** which is said to have performed countless miracles. Originally sighted in Fátima, Portugal on May 13, 1917, the statue was brought to El Salvador in 1949. Cerro de Las Pavas, which until then had only been a local landmark, became known throughout Central America as a holy site; thousands of pilgrims since then have come to pay homage, and they still do today. The virgin to this day attracts many pilgrims. The statue is nestled in a little cove and is surrounded by flowers, neon lights, and dozens of plaques, all left in thanks for miracles delivered. The hill also has some great views of **Lago de Ilopango,** Volcán San Vicente, and the coast beyond. The very top is a fenced-off communications complex patrolled by the army, but frequently the gate is left open and visitors are allowed to see the panoramic view. To get to the hill, follow Av. Contreras south to the edge of town, where a number of paths diverge; all lead to the top. The walk takes about 20min.

■ NEAR COJUTEPEQUE

Ilobasco stands as one of El Salvador's finest arts and crafts villages, second only to La Palma (see La Palma, page 186). Ilobasco's small, painted ceramics are well-known throughout the country. Shops selling the *artesanía* are scattered throughout the town, marked by a sign saying Venta de Jugetes (toy sale). **Taller Escuela de Ceramicas "Kiki"** (tel. 332-2324), on Av. Bonilla #61 (the route the bus takes into town), about 5 blocks south of the square, gives tours of the craft-making process. The small operation employs over 75 people and all stages of production, from the mixing of the clay to the final application of glaze, can be observed simultaneously. There's a store out front that sells the factory's wares.

While easily accessible from the capital, the cool air and quiet pace of Ilobasco makes it a great place to spend the night. **Hotel La Casona** (tel. 332-2388), on 3 Av. between 2 Calle and Calle Perdomo, two blocks west of the square, has modern rooms at old-fashioned prices. The rooms with two beds have private bath, large windows, and ceiling fans (one person ¢75, two people ¢90). The *cuarto sencillo* has no fan or bath, but costs less than ¢95, for one person anyway.

■■■ SAN VICENTE

The Interamerican Highway passes San Vicente from a ridge several kilometers to the north, but even from there, the town's soaring white clocktower and clustered, red-roofed buildings emanate something magical. Meanwhile, **Volcán Chichontepec** slowly curves up to the south, eventually giving way to seemingly endless waves of green forest. With such a spectacular approach, San Vicente promises much; fortunately, it delivers. The town is tranquil and scenic, home to one of the oldest churches in El Salvador, and is one of the best places to stay—San Vicente's hotels are all a great deal. Top it all off with the opportunity for exploration in the nearby natural splendor, and you've got yourself one darn fine little town.

Orientation and Practical Information San Vicente is laid out in the same old grid pattern: odd-numbered streets and avenues ascending to the north and west, respectively. **Av. José María Carnejo** is the primary north-south *avenida* and **Calle Quiñonez de Osorio** the main *calle.* The main square is bounded by Av. Cornejo and 1 Calle at its southwest corner. The bus station is two blocks south of the square at 2 Av. and 4 Calle. The intercity bus terminal is at the corner of 2 Av. and 4 Calle, two blocks south of the square.

Changing money is no trouble at all at **Banco Hipotecario** (tel. 333-0108), at the south end of the main square on 1 Calle, which accepts traveler's checks. The **post office** is on Calle Osorio between 2 Av. and Av. Cornejo (open Mon.-Fri. 8am-noon and 2-5pm, Sat. 8am-noon, Sun. 8-11am). **Antel's** branch is just around the corner at 2 Av. just south of 1 Calle and the church (open daily 6am-10pm). Only two **buses** leave from this terminal: to San Salvador (#116; every 10min., 3am-6:30pm, 2 hrs., ¢4.20) and to Zacatecoluca (#177; every 20min., 4:30am-6pm, 1 hr., ¢3). For service elsewhere to the east, take #116 to the Desuío about 2km from town and change there. Local buses line up and wait on 5 Av. between Calle Orsorio and 1 Calle. **Farmacia La Moderna** (tel. 333-0577), on Calle Orsorio between 1 and 3 Av., is open 7:30am-12:30pm and 2-6pm.

Accommodations and Food Relatively speaking, San Vicente bursts at the seams with inexpensive lodging. While a bit lacking in the dirt-cheap range, the towns' rooms are full of ammenities. **Casa de Huespedes El Turista,** on the corner of 1 Av. and 4 Calle, as if sent from heaven, is a weary traveler's paradise. The rooms all have a corpulent twin bed, private bath, hammocks, furnishings, and TV with cable—all for a pittance (¢65 a night). **Hotel Central Park** (tel. 333-0383), as the name might indicate, is on the west side of the main square on Av. Cornejo. The modestly dark, but well-cleaned rooms all come with private bath and fan. A nice lounge with comfy sofas overlooks the narrow courtyard, and guests have free use of the water cooler (singles ¢55, ¢100 with A/C; doubles ¢90, ¢125 with A/C; add ¢10 for television). **Hotel Rivoly** (tel. 333-0128), is on 7 Calle between Av. Cornejo and 1 Av. If it's Saturday night and you're really running low on colones, head here; otherwise steer clear. This hotel has been left behind by the competition for cleanliness. The rooms house a vile mattress and the ceilings (the underside of the roof) are a practical wildlife refuge. The shared bath is spider-web city. The only advantage is the price (singles ¢30, ¢25 after 5pm).

The shores of San Vicente have yet to be touched by the fast-food tsunami engulfing El Salvador. While this makes for a town without bright neon signs, it also means that *comida típica* is about all there is to eat. Most *comedores* only serve about five dishes, all centered around some combination of beef and chicken. **Casa de Comida "La Cabaña,"** on 3 Calle and Av. Cornejo, has ingeniously disquised its shoddy construction with bamboo panelling to style itself as a beachy restaurant. Meat dishes (*pollo o carne*) run ¢23 and come with rice, salad, and french fries (open 11am-2pm and 5-8pm). **Restaurante Pueblito Viejo,** at the northwest corner of the small *zócalo* formed by the old church, is mainly attractive for its live music on Saturday nights, when the place rocks past midnight. At other times, chow down on *carne asada* (¢22; open Mon.-Fri. 10am-10pm, later on weekends).

EL SALVADOR

Sights Aside from soaking up the general atmosphere, visitors should check out **El Pilar,** the old church constructed in the 1760s. With all the earthquakes in El Salvador, it's rare that a church this old still exists, so appreciate its stubbornness along with its small, subdued baroque form. The church opens onto a small square, bathed by shade from trees almost as old as the church itself. In the town's Central Square, the **clocktower** can't be missed from the outside, and, on the inside, the view from the top will stir the essence of your very soul (if you can get up there). The tower is usually locked, but it's not difficult for the park attendant to unlock it.

NEAR SAN VICENTE

About 10km northeast of San Vicente, on the other side of the Interamerican Highway, dawdles **Laguna de Apastepeque.** It's not obvious at first glance, but the *laguna* is at the bottom of an ancient volcanic crater. On the opposite side of the lake from the highway is a very small **turicentro;** the restaurant alone is reason to come in. Built under a beautiful gazebo, the restaurant overlooks the lake and serves yum-tummery food. On weekdays, the place is deserted; for ¢7 you can feel like you own the place. Bus #156 (from San Vicente to Santa Clara) leaves once an hour from 5 Av. between Calle Orsorio and 1 Calle. Buses going to the town of Apastepeque stop a few km short.

A couple of km to the south of San Vicente, at the base of Volcán Chichontepec, is another *turicentro,* **Amapulapa.** Much more like the standard *turicentro,* Amapulapa has swimming pools, *cabañas,* and restaurants. Outside the entrance is one of the trails leading to the summit of **Chichontepec.** Although the volcano isn't terribly high, the trail starts at a considerable distance from the base, and the hike is long; allow a full day. Bus #171 leaves San Vicente from the corner of 5 Av. and 1 Calle every 15min. until 2pm, and goes directly to the *turicentro.*

EASTERN EL SALVADOR

■■■ SANTIAGO DE MARÍA

Set along a plateau and surrounded on three sides by volcanoes, Santiago de María shimmers like a jewel nuzzled in a bed of gold. Not only is this one of the most beautiful regions in El Salvador, but the town's elevation makes it one of the coolest locales, as well; suck in as much sweet air as you can before returning to the sweltering coast or the smothering capital. Santiago de María is unpretentious, and few travelers have yet taken advantage of the area's potential for scenic hikes through vegetation, or simply vegetating, here or in nearby Berlín.

Orientation and Practical Information Santiago de María lies 12km south of the Interamerican Highway. The small town is laid out in the standard grid pattern. The main square is bounded by 2 Av. and 2 Calle. Believe it or not, it's actually possible to **change money** in Santiago; there's a branch of **Banco Salvadoreño** (tel. 663-0051) in town, on the square at the corner of 2 Av. and 2 Calle (open Mon.-Fri. 8am-4pm, Sat. 9am-noon). Just across the street is the town's **Antel** office (open daily 6am-10pm). One block south and three blocks west of Antel is the **post office,** on 4 Calle and 5 Av. (open Mon.-Fri. 8am-noon and 1-5pm, Sat. 9am-noon). The town's makeshift **bus terminal** is at the triangular park on 3 Av. and 4 Calle, one block south and one block west of the square. From here, catch direct buses to El Triunfo (every 10min., 4am-6pm, 20min., ¢1.50). From El Triunfo, it's possible to change to the #310 bus, going west to San Salvador (2 hrs., ¢12) or east to San Miguel (1 hr., ¢4). The local bus to Berlín leaves from 3 Av. and 1 Calle. The town's **market** is two blocks west of the square.

EL SALVADOR

Accommodations and Food For views aplenty, head over to **Hotel Villahermosa** (tel. 663-0146), on 3 Av. and 1 Calle. The balcony has hammocks to relax and overlook the courtyard and the countryside beyond. The rooms are a bit stale, but pass as pleasant (singles or doubles ¢40, ¢55 with private bath). Villahermosa's poorer cousin sits right next door at **Hospedaje El Quetzal.** Their courtyard is just as green, but rooms aren't as nice. Single rickety cots squat over dusty cement floors as a light bulb hangs corpse-like from the ceiling; pay ¢5 for an extra mattress! (Rooms ¢30).

Comedores and *pupuserías* line the central park in Santiago. **Comedor y Restaurante El Unico,** on the west end of the park at 2 Av., in this case means "the only," which it often is, since other *comedores* in town keep irregular hours. The owner is exceptionally conscientious, and works hard to see that his guests enjoy their meal. If nothing looks good (*a la vista*), he'll gladly whip together something fresh. Best of all, the prices won't bludgeon your billfold (chicken with rice and salad ¢15).

■ NEAR SANTIAGO DE MARÍA

Just outside of town, **Cerro de Tigre** offers oxygen-seizing views of nearby volcanoes. To get to the hill, follow 4 Calle east out of town. Turn right at 10 Av.; the street quickly fades, but the small trail continues right up the hill. About half way up the mountain, you'll come to a dirt road that switch-backs up the rest of the hill. Mark this spot ; on the way back down, it's tempting to follow the road all the way down, where it dead-ends. From the top of the hill, it's possible to see the town, south to Volcán Usulatan, and squint really hard to see the delta for the Río Lempa. The view is well worth the 40min. walk.

To the west of Santiago de María, the town of **Berlín** is also scenically located and offers exploratory opportunities in its own right; getting there is half the fun, as the entire route is filled with gorgeous views of the Río Lempa Valley and the mountains in Honduras to the north. A bus leaves from 3 Av. and 1 Calle in Santiago once an hour until 4pm; pick-up trucks also supplement the bus service, and views from the cab are more vivid and intense than through a smeared window in a bus. Should you decide to stay in Berlín, **Hospedaje Berlines** (tel. 663-2053), located on 4 Calle Oriente and 2 Av. Sur, southeast of Berlín's park, has quiet and clean rooms with a fan, TV, and private bath (singles ¢50, doubles ¢60).

■■■ SAN MIGUEL

The commercial hub of eastern El Salvador, San Miguel rushes headlong into the future without looking back. The countryside around the city of 200,000 is rapidly being consumed by complexes of townhouses and strip-malls, and on Avenida Roosevelt, the city's main drag, a new fast-food joint opens up every month. The symbol and centerpiece for the progress is the Metrocentro, replete with pink stucco and palm trees and right out of Suburbia, USA. Life in San Miguel isn't all pan pizzas and ice cream, though; the eastern part of the country is also the poorer part, as the throngs of beggars in front of the cathedral can testify. Travelers generally try to poke through the enshrouding fog of consumerism (or indulge themselves within it) to exploit the city's convenience as a base for jaunts to the sea and for resting after porking out on pizza.

ORIENTATION AND PRACTICAL INFORMATION

San Miguel is the capital of the department of the same name. Streets follow the grid system: *avenidas* run north-south and *calles* extend east-west. The central *avenida* is called **Avenida Geraldo Barrios,** north of the point where it intersects the central calle, and **Avenida José Simón Cañas** to the south of it. The central *calle* is called **Calle Sirama** in the eastern half and **Calle Chaparristique** to the west. San Miguel makes a perfect base for exploring the east; the bus terminal is four blocks east of the cathedral on 6 Calle.

Tourist Office: The nearest branch of ISTU is at the Honduran border at El Amatillo, but the information desk at **city hall,** on the south end of the park on 2 Calle, has very nice maps and a few good tips on visiting local sights (open Mon.-Fri. 8am-4pm).

Police: Policía Nacional Civil (tel. 661-0233).

Currency Exchange: The local branch of **Banco Hipotecario** (tel. 661-6203) is on the corner of Av. Barrios and 2 Calle. They change traveler's checks as usual. Open Mon.-Fri. 8:30am-4pm, Sat. 9am-2pm. Oddly, the **Banco Salvadoreño** in San Miguel doesn't accept traveler's checks.

Post Office: At 4 Av. and 3 Calle. Open Mon.-Fri. 7:30am-noon and 2-5pm, Sat. 8am-noon, Sun. 8-11am.

Telephones: Antel, 4 Av. and 2 Calle, just south of the park. Open daily 6am-9pm.

Buses: To **San Salvador** (#301; every 15min., 3:40am-4:15pm; 3 hrs.; ¢14). There's also *servicio especial,* which makes the trip direct (leaves at 8, 9am, and 1, 2, 3pm, ¢19); to **Santa Rosa de Lima** (#330; 1[hrs., ¢5) and the Honduran border at **El Amatillo** (every 15min., 3:40am-6pm, 1[-2 hrs., ¢6); to **Playa El Cuco** (#320; every 30min., 5:15am-5:45pm, 90min., ¢5); to **Usulután** (#373; every 10min., 4am-6pm, 90min., ¢5.50); to **San Francisco Gotera** (#328; every 20min., 4am-6pm, 80min., ¢5); and to Perquín (#334B; 3 hrs., ¢11) continuing to the Honduran border at **Sabanetas** (every hr., 6am-2pm, 5 hrs., ¢17).

Public transportation: City buses run from 6am-7pm; fare is ¢1. The main bus stops in the the center are at 2 Av. and 4 Calle (across from the Banco Salvadoreño) and at 2 Calle and 2 Av., a block to the south. Bus #88 goes out to the hospital, #94 goes past the turicentro at Altos de la Cueva, bus #90-F passes by the Metrocentro, and bus #90-G goes out to Quelepa.

Taxis: Lined up along the central park and at the bus terminal. A typical intra-city fare runs ¢15-20.

Car Rental: Uno Rent-a-car (tel. 661-7618), on Av. Roosevelt and Calle Chaparristique. Rents cars to adults 25 yrs. and older. Passport, international driver's license, and major credit card required. A 2-door subcompact without A/C, ¢220 a day; 4-door with A/C ¢365; monthly rates available.

Market: Central Market can be found along 1 Av. and Calle Chaparristique (open during daylight, but busiest in the morning). **Superselectos,** on Av. Roosevelt Sur and 11 Calle, is a supermarket. Open Mon.-Sat. 8am-8pm, Sun. 8am-6pm.

Pharmacy: Farmacia La Luz (tel. 661-0880), 4 Calle and 6 Av., is one of many pharmacies dotting the center. The pharmacy *al turno* is posted on the door. Open 6am-6pm daily.

Hospital: Hospital Nacional is out along the west edge of town. Take local bus #88 from the center. 24 hr. emergency number (tel. 661-0888, 661-2200).

Red Cross: (tel. 661-1771).

ACCOMMODATIONS

Apart from the roadside motels dotting the highway into town, nearly all of San Miguel's hotels are within a couple of blocks of the bus terminal. Prices correlate to what ammenities to expect; you get what you pay for. Most rooms come with fan and private bath. The real prized (and costly) commodity in San Miguel is air-conditioning; the city's low elevation makes for some very hot days and nights.

Hotel San Rafael (tel. 661-4113), on 10 Av. and 6 Calle, one block east of the bus terminal. The rooms here are standard enough: private bath, ceiling and desk fan, hammocks, and a big twin bed. The in-house restaurant serves cheap food and is a friendly place to hang out. The lounge upstairs has comfortable chairs and cable TV (singles ¢68, ¢150 with A/C; doubles ¢90, ¢150 with A/C).

Hotel Migueleño, between 8 and 10 Av. on 4 Calle, behind (south) of the bus station. Basic rooms and the private baths are a bit musty, but Hotel Migueleño has all the essentials for a good night's sleep: good mattresses, ceiling fan, and clean sheets (singles ¢40, doubles ¢60).

Hotel La Terminal (tel. 661-1086), on 6 Calle directly across from the bus terminal and the Shell station. The ugly parking lot is *nada que ver,* but the rooms are Abba-fabulous. A/C and a 17-inch cable TV are standard in every room. Private baths have showers with a showerhead. True, even their baths don't have hot water, but there's absolutely no need here (singles ¢113; doubles ¢180, with two twin beds ¢195).

Hotel Caleta, on the corner of 3 Av. Sur and 11 Calle Poniente (tel. 661-3233). From the inside, you'd never know that Hotel Caleta is in the center of a city. A wide dirt courtyard is planted with palms on the inside, and the low row of rooms with hammocks feels like a beach resort. Its primary disadvantage is its distance (15min. walking) from the bus terminal (singles ¢35, ¢50 with private bath, ¢100 with A/C; doubles ¢70, ¢82 with private bath, ¢142 with A/C).

FOOD

Avenida Roosevelt is fast filling in with mini-malls and fast-food burger joints. In the center, cheap *comedores* exist, but can be hard to find. Love it or hate it, Metrocentro is the place to pick up authentic, U.S.-style fast food. The shopping mall comes complete with a Pizza Hut, a *Pollo Campero,* and a food court with a number of smaller, similar places. Bus #90-F runs past here from the center until 7pm; after that, it'll cost ¢15 for a taxi.

Lorena's (tel. 661-7370), on 1 Av. between 2 and 4 Calles. The sign out front says "Un nuevo concepto en comida a la vista." (A new concept in food-by-viewing). What this really means is a *comedor* with fast-food sensibilities. Don your shades upon entering, which is *that* bright and clean. Their lunch special, which includes some kind of meat, salad, and rice, is only ¢12. Open daily 7am-4pm.

Baty Carnitas Restaurant (tel. 661-0606), on 4 Calle between Av. Barrios and 1 Av. Come here to drink from a wide selection of *licuados* (¢8-12) and *batidos,* like a licuado, only thicker (¢12-16), served in all kinds of batty flavors, or on the stiffer side, a huge selection of imported beers and hard liquors. Some people eat here, too: Pavo al horno (¢60), "bisteak" (¢38). Open Mon.-Sat. 8am-9pm.

Pastelería Rhinele's, on 6 Calle between 2 and 4 Av., heading west from the bus terminal, is lined with *pastelerías,* which are excellent places to grab a slice of *pan dulce* and coffee for a quick and cheap breakfast. Rhinele's is one of the nicest of these. Open daily 6am-6pm.

SIGHTS

Try as one might, it's really not possible to avoid the central **cathedral.** The tall, beige, Romanesque church with tall, red-capped spires, is, apart from seeming pretty un-Latin American, mighty tall. Around the corner from the cathedral is the Antiguo Teatro National, which isn't up to par with the theaters in bigger cities, but which is worth a peek inside, if only to see if there are plays going on.

One km north of town is the large *turicentro* at **Altos de la Cueva,** which wasn't built around any natural wonders, but which has refreshing swimming pools and cool trees to stare at for a pleasant diversion from the hectic pace of San Miguel (open daily 7:30am-5:30pm; admission ¢7). To get there, take Bus #94 from the north end of the central square.

Ruinas de Quelepa, San Miguel's entry into the pre-Columbian ruins sweepstakes, might win a booby-prize or two, but at least the ruins stand as proof of life in San Miguel before Pizza Hut. Bus #90-G runs out to Quelapa every 30min. from the central square. The bus lets off about a ten minute walk from the archaeological site.

■■■ EL CUCO

The residents of the relatively oppressive urbana of San Miguel aren't cuckoo for El Cuco for its proximity alone; the sands here are silky soft—just don't expect to see much of them, since the long stretch of beach is cluttered with row after row of thatched huts filled with vacationing Salvadoreños and drying fish. Should you manage to land a spot near the water, the waves along El Cuco are strong and currents can be a problem, but generally, the utter lack of stones makes swimming fairly safe.

The bus comes in and stops just before the **Antel** (open daily 6am-9pm). Straight ahead (to the south) is the street to the beach which is lined with *comedores* and seafood stands. To the left (east) is the road that parallels thebeach.

One thing that El Cuco doesn't have in common with Costa del Sol is that here there are actually places to stay. Just put on your beach-resort price-goggles and there won't be any problems. Were it anywhere but on a beach, **Hospedaje Buenos Aires** would not fare well. Guests get a tile floor (a concrete structure safe from high tide), a lightbulb, (sort of) running water, but *no mattresses.* The rooms have but one bed and the price fluctuates around ¢30 for 12 hrs. This place locks valuables during the day, and at ¢30 per day it costs less than a *cabaña* at a *turicentro.* To get here, take the gentle left from just before Antel. It's the street that approaches the beach at a diagonal; the hospedaje is on the right about 50m down the beach. A nicer option is **Hotel Los Leones Marinos** (tel. 619-9015), 100m down the road parallel to the beach (left at Antel). The rooms not only have secure locks, but also have an armed security guard. The rooms are clean enough and have illuminating windows. For ¢100 a night (4pm-8am; double the price for 24 hrs.), you get two canvas cots with sheets, a hammock, and a private bath.

The best bet for food is either the *pupusa* stands right along the beach or the line of *comedores* along the street to to the bus stop. Prices here are only slightly more expensive than in town. An interesting, (but potentially unsafe) treat is servings of fresh conch, scooped out of the shell before your eyes and served with salad (¢25).

NEAR EL CUCO: EL TAMARINDO

One of El Salvador's finest beaches can be found a quick bus ride south of La Unión at the small fishing village of **El Tamarindo,** which follows a broad, curving bay in sight of nearby volcanic islands, Honduras, and Nicaragua in the distance. Reasons to celebrate: the beach is covered with fine white sand, a rarity in this country; the bay is sheltered from the ocean, so the waves are gentle and perfect for swimming, and El Tamarindo is almost entirely undeveloped: an ideal combination. As a solitary drawback, the town's unemployment rate is very high, and there are a number of menacing characters around town and along the beach, so be careful.

The best, and pretty much only place to stay is the **Centro de Los Obreros,** about 500m before the village along the main road. Staying here is free, provided you have permission (see San Salvador, Practical Information, page 172). The rooms are pretty basic, but they're situated in pleasant bungalows with their own baths and running water. The Centro also provides a safe place to stash your stuff while you play in the water; the beach here is a bit safer than that closer to town. The only **bus** to El Tamarindo is #383 (every 20min., 4am-5:30pm, 90min., ¢5).

NORTHEAST EL SALVADOR

■■■ SANTA ROSA DE LIMA

The small, commercial town of Santa Rosa de Lima buzzes with a surprisingly spunky spirit of wheeling and dealing; Santa Rosa's proximity to the border with Honduras its prime asset for travelers, especially those who miss the last bus and need to spend the night. Santa Rosa de Lima lies 40km east of San Miguel and 18km west of the border at El Amatillo along La Ruta Militar, a well-paved highway that's the more direct route from San Miguel to the border. Santa Rosa's layout is the standard grid with **Calle Giron** and **Av. General Larios** as the central streets. Santa Rosa's **market** is much larger than a town of this size would normally warrant, and sprawls about the streets between the terminal and the square.

Banco Salvadoreño (tel. 664-2391), on the corner of Av. Larios and 4 Calle, is the only bank that changes traveler's checks, and the only American Express under close scrutiny. No banks or *casas de cambio* change Honduran lempiras, so you have to wait and change to with the guys at the border. The **post office** is on Av. Larios and 1 Calle, a block north of the main square (open Mon.-Fri. 8am-noon and 2-5pm, Sat. 8am-noon, Sun. 8-11am). **Antel's** office is at 4 Av. and Calle Giron, a block east of the square (open daily 6am-8pm). **Bus** #330 zips between San Miguel and El Amatillo, stopping in Santa Rosa in between. Buses leave in either direction every 10min. from 5am-5:30pm (6pm for San Miguel). It's 30 minutes to the border (¢3) and just over an hour to San Miguel (¢5). Bus #306 leaves for San Salvador (every 30min., 4am-2:20pm, 4 hrs., ¢18), or snag the non-stop wonder (5am and 10am, 3 hrs., ¢26). Finally, to **La Unión** (#342, every 15min., 4am-5:30pm, 90min., ¢5).

Hotel El Recreo (tel. 664-2126), on 4 Av. Nte. between Calle Giron and 1 Calle, is the first choice in town. This new hotel has shiny white rooms with hammocks, fat mattresses, and ceiling fans. The public baths are new, clean, and reassuringly smell of disinfectant. Curfew is at 10:30pm (¢40 per person). Around the corner on Calle Giron and 6 Av. is **Hotel El Tejano.** These rooms have all the same ammenities, including hammocks and ceiling fans, but the rooms are dark and dusty, the mattresses a pale shade of brown. Public baths have an impenetrable layer of scum built up in the corners (singles ¢30). It's 7pm on Saturday. The border's closed. Banks don't open until Monday, and you've got ¢28 to your name—**Hospedaje Mundial** is your only option. The bargain basement rooms have thin mattresses on sorry cots under an unattached roof to help you sing to the buggies (singles ¢20, doubles ¢28).

Comedor Nuevo serves cheap, decent, and rather uninspired food. Located on 6 Calle, two blocks west of the terminal, dishes run ¢10-15. **Pollo Campestre** is Santa Rosa's fast-food outpost. It wouldn't be worthy of mention, save that it's the only place in town, aside from banks, that's air-conditioned. Based in fried chicken, meals run ¢20-30 (open daily 8:30am-9pm).

CROSSING THE BORDER TO HONDURAS

The CA-1 crosses into Honduras a scant 18km east of Santa Rosa at the town of **El Amatillo.** Change cash here with one of the many lucripetous money changers hovering about. The Salvadoran side is open 5:30am-7pm, and there's a ¢5 exit fee on foot and ¢18 for a car. Also at the border is an ISTU **tourist office** (tel. 649-9607). One of three in the country (the other two are in San Salvador and at the Guatemalan border at Las Chinamas), the office is mostly good for the pile of photocopied sheets which include information about inter-city bus routes and popular beaches (open 5:30am-7pm). **Buses** to San Miguel leave every 10min. until 5:30pm, and buses on the Honduran side leave frequently for Tegucigalpa.

■■■ SAN FRANCISCO GOTERA

War's aftermath dies hard in San Francisco Gotera. The department of Morazán, of which San Francisco Gotera is the capital, was the primary base of support for the FMLN; the rebels' headquarters was just to the north in the village of Perquín. US$600 in U.S. military aid saw to it that San Francisco Gotera never fell into the hands of the FMLN's hands, however, and the tension still lingers heavy. The central square, normally the center of activity for a town, is nearly always deserted, the large plaza in front of the church having been converted into basketball courts for soldiers. A stop in San Francisco Gotera is worthwhile for a study in contrast, particularly with other, less war-torn cities or even the repopulated communities, cooperative communities to the north.

Orientation and Practical Information The city of 50,000 feels much smaller than it is; it's laid out in the standard grid pattern with a few interruptions due to steep hills. **Avenida Morazán** and **Calle Joaquin Rodezno** form the axes of the grid. The bus terminal is on Av. between 1 and 3 Calles. There's nothing to distinguish this corner from any other where buses stop; even the *despacho* lacks a desk. **Banco Salvadoreño,** at 1 Calle between 1 and 3 Avs. sometimes changes traveler's checks. (open Mon.-Fri. 8am-4pm, Sat. 8am-noon). The **post office** is at 3 Av. and 1 Calle (open Mon.-Fri. 8am-noon and 2-5pm, Sat. 8am-noon, Sun. 7-11am). Just across the street is the **Policía Nacional Civil** (tel. 664-0084). **Antel** is located at the *"origen,"* where Calle Rodezno and Avenida Morazán cross (open 6am-10pm). **Buses** run from the terminal to San Salvador (#305; 5am, 6am, noon, 4 hrs., ¢19); to San Miguel (#328; every 10min., 4:30am-6:15pm, 90min., ¢4), and to Perquín (#332; 4:30, 7, 7:30, 8am, noon, 1, 2, 3pm, 2 hrs., ¢6). San Francisco Gotera's **market** is quiet and subdued; stalls cluster around Av. Morazán and 1 Calle.

Accommodations and Food **Motel Arco Iris** (tel. 664-0183), on Av. Morazán between 3 and 5 Calles, looks like a big mechanic's shop. Rooms face a driveway covered by a canopy of corrugated metal and steel. Inside, the rooms aren't bad, with hammocks, ceiling fans, and private bath; the mattresses are rather thin, though. Curfew is at 10pm (singles ¢30, doubles ¢40). Just next door, **Hospedaje San Francisco** (tel. 664-0066) doesn't rate quite as high on the price/value scale. Rooms have a hammock and a good mattress, but are dark and lack bath (singles ¢30, doubles ¢50). The doubles in the two-story annex are much nicer, with ceiling fan and private bath (¢75).

A comedor with air-conditioning? **Comedor Melita,** on 3 Calle between Av. Morazán and 1 Av., has this and more. Cool off from the northeast's blazing heat while paying a visit to their *comida a la vista.* Chicken with rice and salad only ¢13 (open daily 6:30am-7:30pm). Across the street, **Restaurante Bonanza** has more upscale fare, but their ambience is that of an eatery. Their *pollo frito* is only ¢17, but after that prices go up. *Camarones* and *mariscos* ¢60 (open daily 9am-10pm).

■ NEAR SAN FRANCISCO GOTERA: PERQUÍN

Continuing north along the road from San Francisco Gotera, the road rises over a series of ridges before finally arriving at the mountain village of Perquín. During the Civil War, Perquin was the headquarters for the FMLN. Today, the village and surrounding country is still very much the rebels' territory. On a bright note, though, the locally organized cooperatives are developing in a different direction from the capital, where shopping malls and townhouses are the order of the day. The thing to see in Perquín is the **Museo a la Revolución.** The museum exhibits the history of armed struggle in El Salvador from the FMLN's standpoint. Particularly moving is a collection of testimonials from survivors of the **Mozote** massacre placed around a simple common grave. The museum also has pictures and propaganda from throughout the civil war, as well as a few exhibits on the FMLN's weapons of warfare. Not missing out on a chance to cash in on the revolution, there's a gift shop at the museum where tourists can purchase FMLN t-shirts and bandanas (open Tues.-Sun. 9am-5pm; admission ¢10). Just outside the museum is a small hill with a great view of the surrounding country. **Bus** #332 runs from San Miguel several times between 5 and 8pm and several more from noon-3pm (3 hrs., ¢8).

For overnight accommodations, **Casa de Huespedes El Gigante** is located about 100m before (south) of the village square on a small turnoff (to the west), about 20m below the village sign. The place is large barn with cement floor partitioned into about twenty cubicles, each of which has two bunk beds. The communal baths are well-cleaned, and the kitchen here serves good food—good in part because it's the only grub in Perquín (rooms ¢25 per person).

HONDURAS

Never quite autonomous, always slightly absurd, Honduras manages to present a friendly, relaxed face to visitors. Newcomers to the prototypical "banana republic" quickly learn to live with the quirks and deprivations of Honduran life—erratic running water, somewhat surreal politics, even the occasional tank wandering aimlessly through the streets—and promptly find their way to the country's relatively untouched and unseen natural splendor. Hondurans themselves are by no means passive, but they have come to accept a degree of disorder and unpredictability with a halcyon grace that soothes and welcomes foreign guests.

Still, it is more because of than in spite of Honduras's whims that an ever-increasing number of adventure-seeking tourists arrive each year. To accommodate, the government has been attempting to develop ecotourism à la Costa Rica, although efforts thus far have been aimed more at older, wealthier tourists than at shoestring travelers. While not every path has been paved, nor every trail marked, Mother Nature's kind donations to Honduras's geography cry out for discovery, from the irreproachable beaches and coral reefs of the Bay Islands to the fairy-tale cloud forests of Parque Nacional Celaque, and for some, the ominous and engulfing jungles of the Mosquito Coast to the east. Meanwhile, the people, too, are opening up to tourism, from the Moskito Indians in the East, to the Garifuna (see Belize: An Introduction, page 119) along the north coast, to the Maya in the East, and to the *mestizos* throughout the country. Despite recent isolated expressions of anti-U.S. sentiment, most Hondurans are remarkably friendly, always offering to lend a hand to the visiting *gringo.* Travelers will be pleasantly surprised as long as they accept Honduras on its own terms—as a warm, lovely, mildly schizophrenic nation striving to define its identity in an era of new alliances.

ESSENTIALS

■■■ WHEN TO GO

CLIMATE

Three-quarters of Honduras is mountainous; coastal plains, swamps, and riverbeds comprise the rest of the country. The northern lowlands, along the Caribbean shore, are uniformly hot and rainy; the average temperature is 27°C (82°F) and average rainfall can reach 2.5m. Intermontane valleys in the central regions are cooler, with an average temperature hovering at 21°C (70°F). Almost all regions receive more than 1m of rainfall annually.

FESTIVALS AND HOLIDAYS

The Instituto Hondureño de Turismo provides a general list of festivals, holidays, and other celebrations throughout the country. Some of the more widely celebrated holidays, other than the national holidays, include Patron Saint festivals around **January 15,** San Sebastián's Day on **January 20,** Virgen de Candelaria on **February 2,** San José on **March 19,** San Gaspar and Marcos on **April 25,** Día de La Cruz on **May 3,** San Isidro on **May 15,** Santa Rita de Casia on **May 22,** San Antonio on **June 13,** San Juan Bautista on **June 24,** Días de Santiago and Santa Ana on **July 25 and 26,** Virgen del Tránsito on **August 15,** Santa Rosa on **August 30,** San Miguel on **September 29,** San Francisco de Asis on **October 4,** and Virgen de Concepción on **December 8.**

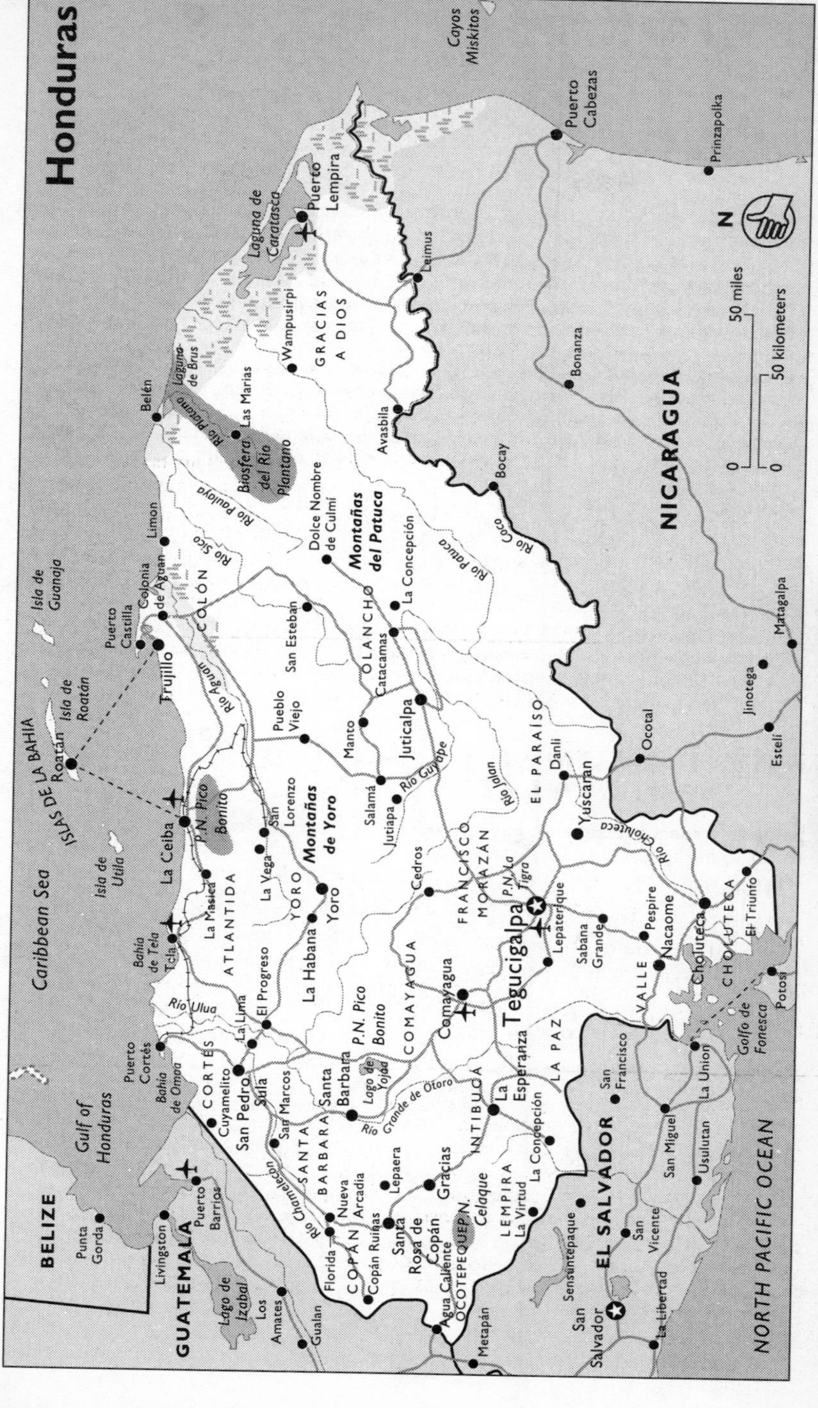
Honduras
Caribbean Sea
Gulf of Honduras
BELIZE
GUATEMALA
EL SALVADOR
NICARAGUA
NORTH PACIFIC OCEAN
Cayos Miskitos
ISLAS DE LA BAHIA
Isla de Utila
Isla de Roatán
Isla de Guanaja
Roatán
Punta Gorda
Livingston
Puerto Barrios
Lago de Izabal
Los Amates
Gualan
Puerto Cortés
Bahía de Omoa
Cuyamelito
San Pedro Sula
La Lima
El Progreso
Río Ulua
Bahía de Tela
Tela
La Masica
La Ceiba
P.N. Pico Bonito
Trujillo
Puerto Castilla
Colonia de Aguan
Limon
Río Aguan
Río Sico
Río Paulaya
Belén
Río Plátano
Laguna de Brus
Las Marias
Biosfera del Río Plátano
Wampusirpi
Laguna de Caratasca
Puerto Lempira
GRACIAS A DIOS
Leimus
Avasbila
Bocay
Puerto Cabezas
Prinzapolka
Bonanza
Matagalpa
Jinotega
Estelí
Ocotal
CORTÉS
ATLANTIDA
COLÓN
YORO
OLANCHO
EL PARAÍSO
FRANCISCO MORAZÁN
COMAYAGUA
SANTA BARBARA
COPÁN
OCOTEPEQUE
LEMPIRA
INTIBUCÁ
LA PAZ
VALLE
CHOLUTECA
La Vega
San Lorenzo
Montañas de Yoro
Yoro
La Habana
P.N. Pico Bonito
Pueblo Viejo
San Esteban
Dolce Nombre de Culmí
Montañas del Patuca
La Concepción
Catacamas
Juticalpa
Manto
Salamá
Jutiapa
Río Guayape
Río Patuca
Río Coco
Río Jalan
Cedros
P.N. La Tigra
Tegucigalpa
Lepaterique
Danli
Yuscaran
Río Choluteca
Sabana Grande
Pespire
Nacaome
Choluteca
El Triunfo
Potosi
Golfo de Fonesca
La Union
San Francisco
San Miguel
Usulutan
San Vicente
Sensuntepaque
San Salvador
La Libertad
Metapán
Comayagua
La Esperanza
La Paz
Río Grande de Otoro
Lago de Yojoa
Santa Barbara
San Marcos
Río Chamelecón
Nueva Arcadia
Florida
Copán Ruinas
Santa Rosa de Copán
Lepaera
Gracias
Celaque
La Virtud
La Concepción
Agua Caliente
N
0 50 miles
0 50 kilometers

HONDURAS

■■■ FEED YOUR HEAD

For publications and travel organizations of general interest, see Central America: Feed Your Head, page 1.

Embassy of Honduras, U.S. 3007 Tilden St. NW, Washington, DC 20008 (tel. (202) 966-7702; fax (202) 966-9751). **Canada** 151 Slater St., Suite 908, Ottawa, Ontario, K1P 5H3 (tel. (613) 233-8900; fax 232-0193). **U.K.** 115 Gloucester Pl., London, W1H 3PJ (fax (44) 171-486-4880).

Honduran Consulate, 1612 K St. NW, Suite 310, Washington, DC 20006 (tel. (202) 223-0185; fax (202) 223-0202). Honduras also has consulates in New York (tel. (212) 269-3612), Los Angeles, Miami, Chicago, New Orleans, and Houston.

CODA, Attn: Noemí D. Espanoza, Apdo 21, Colonia Kennedy, Tegucigalpa, Honduras (tel. 32-82-23). Offers volunteer opportunities in Honduras.

Peacework, 305 Washington St. SW, Blacksburg, VA 24060 (tel. (703) 552-2473). Promotes work programs in Honduras.

Escuela de Español Ixbalanque, Copán Ruinas, Honduras (tel. 98-3432). One-on-one instruction 4 hrs. a day, 5 days a week costs US$85, with homestay and full board US$125. Located just 1km from the ruins at Copán.

Centro Internacional de Idiomas, Attn: Belinda Linton, Apartado 71, Trujillo, Colón (fax 44-47-70). Offers week-long, one-on-one classes with certified Honduran instructors. Homestays possible.

Americas Tours and Travel, 1402 Third Ave., Suite 1019, Seattle, WA 98101-2110 (tel. (800) 553-2513 or (206) 623-885; fax (206) 467-0454. In San Pedro Sula, 57-40-6). Arranges travel to Honduras on Continental and American Airlines. Ask for Javier Pinel, a remarkably friendly guy with a bed and breakfast in San Pedro Sula. He can take you fishing on Lake Yojoa, and offers daytrips to Copán and Lancetilla botanical gardens.

Roatan Charter, Inc., P.O. Box 877, San Antonio, FL 33576 (tel. (800) 282-8932). Tour packages to the Bay Islands, ruins, jungles, large cities, and small villages. Copán ruins tour plus 3 nights and 6 meals US$245. 3-day tour of lagoon, marine park, and gardens, plus 3 nights and all meals US$560.

■■■ DOCUMENTS AND FORMALITIES

A valid **passport** is needed to enter Honduras. A **visa** is not required for citizens of the U.S., the U.K., Australia, New Zealand, and most European nations; citizens of Canada, Israel, and South Africa need to get visas (with same-day processing) for US$30-40. If you're unsure, contact an embassy or consulate before you leave home. When you enter Honduras, your passport will be marked with a 30-day tourist stamp. At the end of 30 days, you must visit the Immigration Office (see Tegucigalpa: Practical Information, page 210) in order to have it renewed; otherwise, you'll be fined. You can extend your permit twice, for a total stay of 90 days. After 90 days, you must leave the country for three days before you are able to re-enter.

You will be charged about 70 lempiras for **inspection and immigration charges** when you enter the country. If you're flying home, you'll pay about US$15 in **airport departure taxes.** There are no limits on bringing goods out of Honduras.

A valid foreign **driver's license** and **proof of registration** are needed to drive in Honduras. The paperwork and fees you'll face will depend on your plans. If you're staying a while, you'll need to fork over 20 lempiras for the 9A-1; if you're driving through Honduras to other countries, you'll pay five lempiras for the 9A-3. Vehicle permits last 30 days, and may be renewed for up to six months.

■■■ MONEY MATTERS

US$1 = 9.50 lempiras	**1 lempira = US$0.10**
CDN$1 = 6.99 lempiras	**1 lempira = CDN$0.14**
UK£1 = 14.76 lempiras	**1 lempira = UK£0.07**
IR£1 = 15.04 lempiras	**1 lempira = IR£0.07**
AUS$1 = 7.00 lempiras	**1 lempira = AUS$0.14**
NZ$1 = 6.23 lempiras	**1 lempira = NZ$0.16**
SARand = 2.60 lempiras	**1 lempira = SARand 0.39**

The Honduran unit of currency is the **lempira.** Bills come in denominations of one, two, five, 10, 20, 50, and 100 lempiras. The lempira is divided into 100 centavos. Coins are issued in values of one, two, five, 10, 20, and 50 centavos. The 10-centavo coin is sometimes called a *daime,* you'll occasionally hear a 20-centavo coin called a *búfalo,* and 50-centavo pieces are commonly called *tostónes.* Life will be made infinitely easier if you carry some currency in U.S. dollars. Personal checks are impossible to cash, and it's very difficult to get money transferred to Honduras, especially in the Bay Islands, where there are few banks.

Banks are generally easy to find in Honduras, and most are open Monday through Friday from 9am to 3pm, and half-days Saturdays. Most **ATM** machines accept only Honduran bank cards and aren't compatible with U.S. systems. Honduras doesn't have many *casas de cambio.* **Banco de Honduras** often only changes Citicorp traveler's checks, and **Creditlan** has an expensive surcharge. Larger cities have small **black markets** for currency exchange, but the marketeers offer the same rates as banks for cash exchange, and their rates for traveler's checks are often much worse. Banks commonly give *retiro de tarjeta de crédito,* cash advances on credit cards.

There are few hard-and-fast rules for **tipping** in Honduras. Leave a 10% tip at restaurants, and give a few lempiras to anyone who does you a favor.

■■■ SAFETY AND HEALTH

Travelers report that they feel relatively safe in Honduras. However, robberies and assaults are on the rise in both cities and rural areas. Hang on to your money and luggage, and watch out for pickpockets. Don't wear jewelry in public, and carry your valuables in a money belt. Remember that the money you're carrying in your wallet is probably more than some of these people make in a year. Male travelers will probably escape most hassling, but women will certainly receive unwelcome attention, especially on buses. If heckled, respond firmly: tell the offender to stop, and ask someone nearby to help, if necessary.

See Central America: Health, page 11, for general information about **disease prevention** and diseases in Honduras. Vaccinations aren't required to enter Honduras, but it would be wise to consult a doctor about getting a few preventative shots. **Cholera** has recently reached epidemic levels in parts of Honduras, as has **typhoid fever.** Also common in Honduras are **malaria** and **dengue fever;** as always, **Hepatitis A** is also a risk. **AIDS** is a particularly great danger in Honduras; more than 4,000 cases have been reported.

Don't drink tap water in Honduras—your bowels will never forgive you. Drink only *agua purificada,* and never eat ice unless you're sure it was made with purified water. Hondurans know this too, and everyone drinks the little sealed pouches of water sold in stores. *Never* drink from the plastic bags with straws that vendors peddle at bus stops and on the streets.

■■■ GETTING THERE

There are three international airports in Honduras: in Tegucigalpa, in San Pedro Sula, and in La Ceiba.

It's possible to journey from Guatemala to Honduras by **bus.** From Guatemala City, **Rutas Orientales** sends buses to Chiquimula, where you can transfer to a Buses Vilma vehicle, which will take you to El Florido on the Honduran border (the entire trip costs Q13.50). Make reservations one to two days in advance (see Guatemala City: Practical Information: Buses, page 56, for details). From El Florido, you can catch a bus to other points in Honduras. See Near Puerto Barrios: Crossing the Border into Honduras, page 104, for more information; a more adventurous option for crossing from Puerto Barrios to Puerto Cortés is also listed there.

The Nicaragua-Honduras **border crossings** at Las Manos and El Espino, and with the Guatemala-Honduras crossing at Agua Caliente, are open only during daylight hours, so plan ahead (see Guatemala: Esquipulas for more information). The Nicaragua-Honduras crossing at Guasaule is open daily from 8am-4pm. Use caution if you're traveling to border regions near Guatemala, El Salvador, and Nicaragua; contact the U.S. State Department's Emergency Hotline (tel. (202) 647-5225) for current information on safety in border regions.

■■■ ONCE THERE

TRANSPORTATION

The **bus** system in Honduras is excellent. Buses run on time and are operated by private companies. Unfortunately, it's often the case that each destination is served by a different company, and so several terminals are scattered throughout the city. **Road conditions** vary throughout the country. The government only recently decided to bring unleaded gasoline to the country (to stem pollution), so drivers should make sure that their vehicles are equipped with a proper catalytic convertor.

Taca (tel. 31-2-83; fax 31-15-17) and **Isleña** (tel. 33-7-64; fax 33-18-94) both operate domestic flights within Honduras.

Plus, if you act now...

Nobody ever said that Honduran buses lack for hearty entertainment, but once in a while, an extra bonus comes along. While cruising from town to town, keep an eye, ear, and throat peeled for the silky-smooth snake-oil salesmen, who often stand in the aisle to deliver eloquent spiels about cure-all medicine. Holding up jars of *stuff* (and often some 6-year-old's pop-up anatomy book), the "doctors" explain how the pills they're peddling can cure fatigue, impotence, cancer, *and* those nagging hemorrhoids. Afterwards, some passengers whip out wads of cash for the guy in return for vials of their own, but the pills usually turn out to be multi-vitamin tablets or skin lotion. Sadly, some of the con-artists claim their pills can cure AIDS, and that no other preventive measures are necessary. In any case, the pills are best avoided, lest you end up contracting some rare disease named for a long-deceased German physician.

ACCOMMODATIONS

The cheapest **hotels** in Honduras (10-20 lempiras per person) typically provide a cell-like room with a bed and a small window. Expect concrete floors and communal bathrooms without hot water. A little more money (25 lempiras) often buys you a simple private bath. The next step up (40-50 lempiras) provides a huge improvement in quality—maid service, clean bathrooms, comfy beds, and fans.

KEEPING IN TOUCH

A letter sent from Honduras can take as long as 12 or 14 days to reach the U.S.; allow a week at least. Sending a 10g letter anywhere in the Americas costs 5.40 lempiras, and letters weighing between 20 and 50 grams cost 7.15 lempiras to send to the U.S. There are several **express mail** services around (**EMS,** tel. 22-49-71 in Tegucigalpa, and **Urgente Express** offices are common), but they're generally pricier (94 lempi-

HONDURAS

ras for up to 250g). You can receive mail in Honduras though general delivery (*Lista de Correos*), typically paying a small fee (2.15 lempiras) when you pick up your letter. Address envelopes to general delivery as follows:

Diann MORRIS
a/c Lista de Correos
Tegucigalpa (town), Francisco Morazán (department)
República de Honduras, CENTRAL AMERICA

The Honduran **phone** company, **Hondutel,** provides efficient and convenient service. Every notable town has a Hondutel office that keeps long hours (some are open around the clock). Hondutel has a contract with AT&T, so simply dial 123 to be connected to an AT&T operator in the U.S. for calling-card or collect calls. It's almost impossible to use a non-AT&T phone card from a public phone in Honduras. From most phone offices, you can dial 121 for Sprint service, 122 for an MCI operator. **Faxes** (18 lempiras per page) and **telegrams** (0.75 lempiras per word) are generally available in Hondutel offices, too. Public phones generally cost 0.10 lempiras; the operator may choose to cut you off after a minute or two, so talk fast. The **country code** for Honduras is **504;** there are no city codes. Honduras operates on **Central Standard Time.**

HONDURAS: AN INTRODUCTION

■■■ HISTORY

The recent discovery of an ancient ceremonial burial site in the **Talgua Caves** in Olancho, Honduras has archaeologists in a hussy. Probably the most important Honduran find since Copán, the bones and buried goods at Talgua point to the existence of an advanced American civilization (perhaps ancestors of the Lenca) in the area as many as 3,000 years ago, a full millennium before evidence of Mayans in the area. Today, the direct descendants of pre-Columbian inhabitants thrive as members of the Lenca, Maya, and various tribes that survive scattered throughout the Eastern jungles of the country.

When Central America finally shook off its Spanish shackles, Honduras was even poorer and more isolated than its neighbors in the region. Steep mountains isolated each village from the next; floods and droughts frustrated farmers. Honduras briefly joined the **Federation of Central America,** sending liberal leader **Francisco Morazán** to head the alliance of nations, but the Federation dissolved in 1839. When a group of Hondurans traveled to Europe to commission a statue of Morazán, they found themselves without enough money to pay for the monument. Instead, they bought a second-hand statue of an obscure Napoleonic military leader and erected the hand-me-down in honor of Morazán; it still stands in Tegucigalpa.

Nominally ruled in the mid-19th century by a string of conservative governments, Honduras was actually controlled by its powerful **cattle barons.** Rivalries between ranchers often erupted in war, and bandits roamed the country. Honduras's difficult terrain prevented political and economic unification; the country desperately needed a transportation infrastructure. Successive governments sunk huge sums into building an interoceanic railway—but in the end, only 92km of track were laid, and the rails soon fell into disrepair.

Meanwhile, Guatemala and Nicaragua constantly dipped their fingers into Honduran politics, ruining all chances of internal stability. After the assassination of **president José Santos Guardiola** in 1862, Honduras was ruled by 20 leaders in just 10 years. Six different constitutions were drafted between 1865 and 1924. As various factions fought for control, the federal capital bounced back and forth between the liberal city of Tegucigalpa and conservative Comayagua. Soil erosion and fires in Comayagua eventually shifted the balance toward "Tegus," where the capital has remained, even as the nation's economic locus has moved on to San Pedro Sula.

In the late 1870s, **President Marco Aurelio Soto** pacified warring factions, undertook capital improvements, and expanded the education system. But no commercial bourgeoisie had emerged in Honduras by the turn of the century, and their absence left an economic and political vacuum. Into the void stepped a handful of foreign companies, most notably the **United Fruit Company (UFCO).** The UFCO bought huge tracts of land for its banana plantations, set up its own system of banks and railroads, and created an elaborate political machine. By 1918, the UFCO and two other large companies controlled 75% of the nation's banana-growing land. For the next four decades, "El Pulpo" (or "The Octopus," as the UFCO was known) held Honduras in the grip of its strong tentacles. The banana giant brought tens of thousands of jobs to Honduras, equipping the nation with schools, hospitals, electric plants, and plumbing systems. But democracy was effectively dead; El Pulpo called the shots, and ordinary citizens had little say in the political process.

Disease ravaged Honduras's banana plants in the 1940s, causing the UFCO to relax its grip on the nation as banana exports dropped. Since then, the government has worked on its own to build roads, improve public health, and implement an agrarian reform program. But fear and sporadic violence continue to plague Honduras. The nation has seen so many illegal seizures of power that Hondurans wryly refer to their capital as "Tegucigolpe," a pun on the Spanish word for "coup" (*golpe*). One post-war dictator was so paranoid that he outlawed baseball, fearing that his enemies would assault him with bats. Tensions with neighboring El Salvador ran high in the mid-1960s, and erupted after the two countries confronted each other in a 1969 World Cup qualifier match. The incident, known as **"The Soccer War,"** left 2000 Honduran civilians dead and sent 130,000 Salvadoran refugees fleeing back across the border.

Petty squabbling among Honduran leaders lends a strange twist to current politics. In 1985, neither of the two major parties could decide on a candidate; instead, a collection of candidates from both parties all ran at once, the winner-by-plurality garnering only 25% of the total vote. The situation reached uniquely bizarre levels in February of 1993, when residents of Tegucigalpa awoke to find tanks and camouflage-clad troops roaming their streets. The president and the military both claimed responsibility for the occupation, while many Hondurans suspected the influence of the opposition party leader. The reason for the deployment was vague; in any case, the siege ended within a few days.

The days of the banana bosses are gone, yet Honduras is far from autonomous. In the 1980s, the U.S. turned Honduras into a huge military base for the Nicaraguan *contras.* With massive amounts of military aid and generous civil loans, the U.S. bought the right to station thousands of troops along Honduras's southern border. The capital influx—amounting to at least US$190 million per year—helped to shore up the Honduran economy, but the nation remained the second poorest country in the western hemisphere, just behind Haiti. Furthermore, the U.S.-contra occupation shoved more than 2000 small farmers off their lands, creating a class of **desplazados** (displaced persons) living as refugees in their own country. With the end of the Nicaraguan civil war, foreign aid melted away and U.S. troops evaporated, only to be replaced by 11,000 armed and aimless contras seeking refuge in Honduras. Dependence on outside support has plagued Hondurans' nationalism; most attempts to isolate a sense of self-identity are stifled by a quick look around the average city street, where Dunkin' Donuts has replaced bakeries and children clamor for L.A. Gear shoes.

Somehow, time and again, Hondurans manage to make do with what little they have. In the summer of 1994, the flow of water over the nation's hydroelectric dam slowed to a trickle, causing periodic **blackouts** throughout the nation. Hondurans simply went about their business, getting by on short spurts of electricity. Newfangled innovation butts heads with the old ways in domestic affairs, as well: in a recent and internationally broadcast scandal, a woman sued her husband for slander after he claimed she was not a virgin at the time of their marriage. These tensions fatigue Honduras's resolve in a way that is all-too-familiar, all around the Third World. The **Chortis,** descendants of the Maya who created the structures at Copán, have marched to the capital twice in the last year in an effort to declare their rights, marching past American fast-food restaurants in a desperate attempt to be remembered as the government tries to push the nation forward.

■■■ THE ARTS

It took a while for Honduran **literature** to boom, especially after the short-lived 19th century Federation of Central America drew the center of intellectual activity to Guatemala. Out of the wave of liberalism that followed, the Romantic movement finally found its voice in the Honduran writers Marco Aurelio Soto (who served as president for a while) and Ramón Rosa. In this century, modernist poet Juan Ramón Molina's pained, expressive works set the course for more politically oriented writers like Marcos Carías Reyes, whose *Trópico* denounced the influence of the banana industry in his nation. Argentina Díaz Lozano applied the criticism of the intelligentsia to the vernacular style of the people in *Peregrinaje*, an autobiography, and *Mayapán.* Since then, poets, writers, and playwrights have continued to serve as representatives of the people through eloquent denunciation of their social and economic burdens.

Honduran **musical tastes** seem to be a conglomeration of styles that have trickled down from Mexico, Guatemala, and from Caribbean; the only music halfway native to the country is that of the Garifuna who live along the northern coast (See Belize: The Arts, page 52). Cruising around on buses or in taxis, you're most likely to hear Mexican cheese-pop and American Top 40 from about five years back. Popular rock bands include "Triángulo de Eva" and "Fusión."

Mayan ruins are scattered throughout Honduras, and the country proudly displays the **artifacts** of the mysterious civilization in a number of museums. Several Honduran painters try to capture their culture in color, among them Ana Isabel Acosta, Rosa María de Larios, Armando Lara, and Marco Rietti. Still, modern art hasn't consistently caught on. Three bronze statues recently erected in San Pedro Sula by artist Regina Aguilar were supposed to honor national hero José Cecilio del Valle, but instead launched a still-raging controversy; Valle is depicted in the nude, his genitals fully exposed.

■■■ FOOD AND DRINK

Honduran *típico* fare is usually a hodgepodge of rice and beans, tortillas, and fresh, delicate seafood, especially along the coasts. A little experimentation is in order, whether you like it or not, since Hondurans have their own word for just about every regional specialty. For starters, a **pupusa** is a tortilla with beans and pork rinds. A **baleada** is sort of like a burrito; most often, it's a tortilla smeared with fried beans and onions. Garifuna food usually includes **casabe** (cassava) and **tapado** (soup made of fish), both drenched in rich coconut milk. A favorite dish on the Bay Islands, rarely seen in their restaurants, is *tapado,* comprised of fish, potatoes, yucca, and other vegetables all cooked in diluted coconut milk and poured over rice into one big tasty stew. **Machuka** is another name for the soup, and some dip plantains into it for that sweet and salty sensation. Conch soup is also popular. Vegetarians and vegans will want to look for the long, slender green vegetable sold in markets: it's the high-protein **yucca,** which tastes like a flavorful potato when it's steamed.

To **drink, guanábana frescos** aren't to be missed. Hondurans tend to be partial to one of four beers: **Port Royal Export** is a *sapid* export which ought to be nursed on the ideal, long afternoon. **Salva Vida** is the most popular, has a bit less body, but goes down smoothly. The third, **Nacional,** is even more *suave;* though short on taste, it's refreshing and goes well with food. **Imperial** is a bit weaker, and can be found predominantly in the southwest of the country.

■■■ MEDIA

Particularly in the cities, Hondurans stay on top of the news through one of the country's six dailies. *La Prensa,* the oldest of the bunch, is still the most respectable, but demand for gore and gratuitous skin has made all six papers increasingly guilty of sensationalism over the last few decades. *El Periódico, El Heraldo,* and *El Tiempo* are some of the other papers around. Fewer Hondurans have TVs than read the papers, but crowds gather around electronics shops' windows when big stories break (or when there's a hot soccer game on). The weekly English-language "Honduras This Week" is a comprehensive and informative newspaper.

■■■ RECENT NEWS

Hondurans give mixed reviews to their current president, **Carlos Roberto Reina.** Reina replaced forced military service with voluntary conscription, which freed up some time for a lot of young men and only infuriated the army, which says it needs more money to be at all effective. On the other hand, Reina mysteriously dissolved the anti-corruption commission he himself instituted

Two members of Reina's own administration were charged with selling false diplomatic passports and U.S. entry visas during a recent investigation. The explosion of a grenade near President Reina while he was visiting a mall in San Pedro Sula may have been an assassination attempt, of which there have been many during his administration. Only 21% of Hondurans polled were willing to call Reina's work so far "very good," and the president of the National Congress, **Carlos Flores,** is gaining popularity. Perhaps out of fear of public uprisings, Reina reactivated the country's national defense and security council.

Tegucigalpa

What's in a name? In Tegucigalpa's case, so many clunky syllables that Hondurans simply refer to their capital as "Tegus." The tongue-twisting "Tegucigalpa" originally meant something like "boom town." After a vein of silver was discovered on the slopes of Picacho in September of 1578, a town sprang up rapidly—its name came from the Náhuatl words for "hill" (*teguz*) and "silver" (*galpa*). Throughout the colonial period, the town's economic and political importance grew, and in 1880 the government moved south to Tegus from Comayagua. At the time, the new capital wasn't linked to Comayagüela, the city across the river, but by the end of the century both were incorporated into a "central district." Even then, few bridges linked the areas, and people were taken across in a basket suspended from a cable.

Today's city stretches out in all directions, threatening to rip the cloth from which it was cut. Rows of houses run up and over hills and wind into valleys; Eastern-bloc style gray buildings are constantly being constructed; and the city, already home to 850,000 people, swells with new arrivals. But step back for a breather, away from the curtains of auto exhaust that shroud the Tegus part; the city reveals itself as something more than a fast-growing behemoth. Tegucigalpa is speckled with pleasant parks and is among the safest large cities in Latin America, at least for travelers. Malls and Burger Kings are everywhere, even as small-time entrepreneurs sell garlic door-to-door. Most travelers come to Tegus to take care of practical business, to meet up with Peace Corps pals returning from the Mosquito Coast, or to splurge on

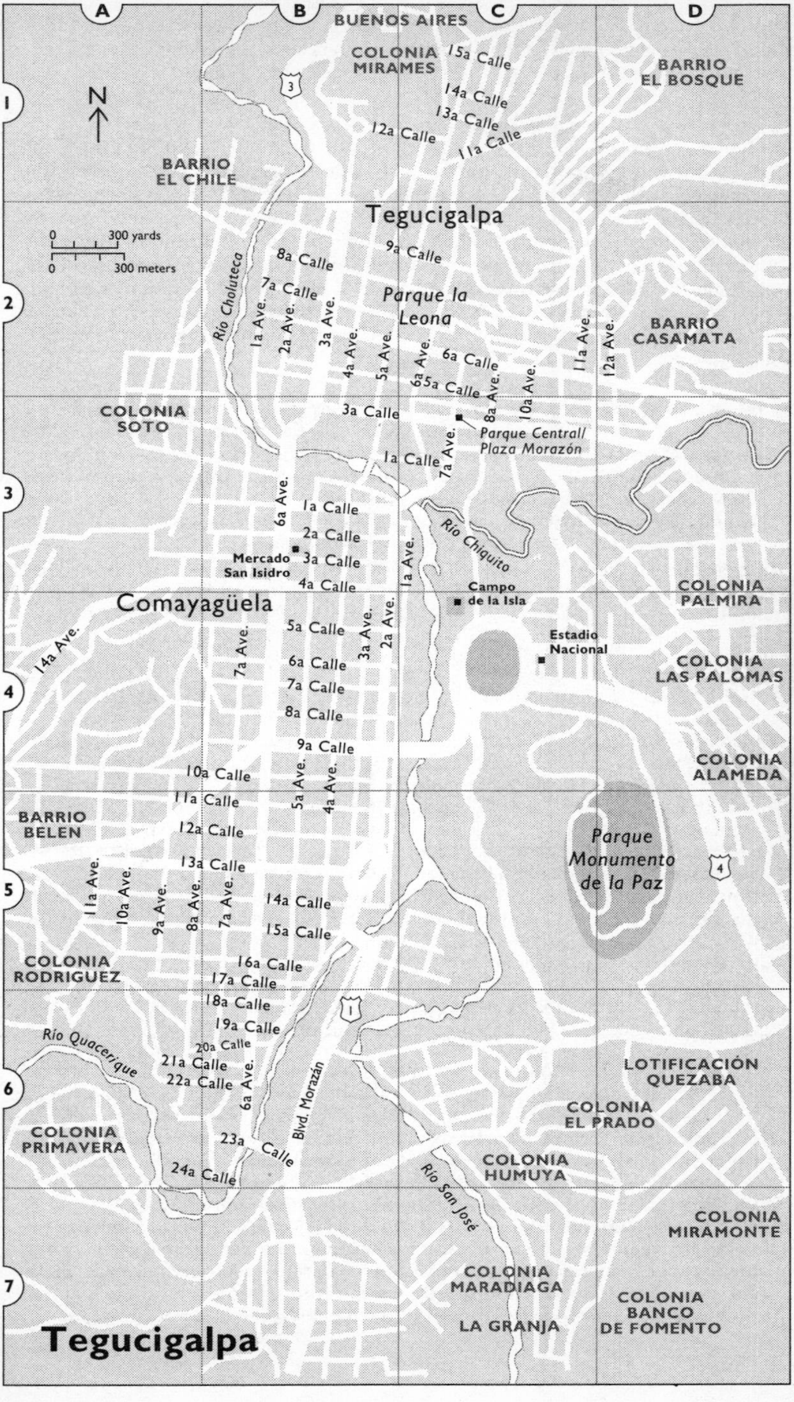

Tegucigalpa

A B C D

1 2 3 4 5 6 7

N

0 300 yards
0 300 meters

BUENOS AIRES
COLONIA MIRAMES
BARRIO EL BOSQUE
15a Calle
14a Calle
13a Calle
12a Calle
11a Calle
BARRIO EL CHILE
Tegucigalpa
9a Calle
8a Calle
7a Calle
Río Choluteca
Parque la Leona
1a Ave.
2a Ave.
3a Ave.
4a Ave.
5a Ave.
6a Ave.
6a Calle
5a Calle
8a Ave.
10a Ave.
11a Ave.
12a Ave.
BARRIO CASAMATA
COLONIA SOTO
3a Calle
Parque Central/ Plaza Morazón
1a Calle
7a Ave.
6a Ave.
1a Calle
2a Calle
Mercado San Isidro
3a Calle
4a Calle
Río Chiquito
1a Ave.
Campo de la Isla
COLONIA PALMIRA
Comayagüela
2a Ave.
3a Ave.
5a Calle
14a Ave.
7a Ave.
6a Calle
7a Calle
8a Calle
Estadio Nacional
COLONIA LAS PALOMAS
9a Calle
10a Calle
5a Ave.
4a Ave.
COLONIA ALAMEDA
11a Calle
BARRIO BELEN
12a Calle
13a Calle
Parque Monumento de la Paz
11a Ave.
10a Ave.
9a Ave.
8a Ave.
7a Ave.
14a Calle
15a Calle
4
COLONIA RODRIGUEZ
16a Calle
17a Calle
18a Calle
1
19a Calle
Río Quacerique
20a Calle
21a Calle
22a Calle
6a Ave.
Blvd. Morazán
LOTIFICACIÓN QUEZABA
COLONIA EL PRADO
COLONIA PRIMAVERA
23a Calle
24a Calle
COLONIA HUMUYA
Río San José
COLONIA MIRAMONTE
COLONIA MARADIAGA
LA GRANJA
COLONIA BANCO DE FOMENTO

Tegucigalpa

a hotel room equipped with hot water and cable TV. Other visitors come to Tegus simply to put a little urban spring in their step before heading off to the greener pastures of Copán or the sandier pastures of the Bay Islands.

■■■ ORIENTATION

Finding your way around Tegus can be quite difficult–directions are typically given in terms of vaguely-defined *barrios* rather than streets. Buses generally arrive in **Comayagüela,** which is west and south of the **Río Choluteca.** Its streets are numbered from a central point just south of **El Centro** in Tegus. In turn, this river splits the city in two. To the north of the river, orient yourself in terms of the **Parque Central.** From the park, the **cathedral** is to the east, and Iglesia los Dolores is three blocks west and one block north of it. **Barrio Guanacaste** is about a seven-minute walk from the Parque to the east. The colossal **Hotel Honduras Maya** is a 15-minute walk to the southeast, along Av. Cervantes.

■■■ PRACTICAL INFORMATION

Tourist Office: Instituto Hondureño de Turismo (tel./ fax 22-66-21), on the 3rd floor of the Edificio Europa at Calle Rep. de México and Av. Ramón Ernesto Cruz, a few blocks from the U.S. Embassy (around the corner from Lloyd's Bank). Maps and info for the entire country. Ask here about excursions to nearby areas. Open Mon.-Fri. 8:30am-4:30pm. Closed briefly around noon.

Police: FUSEP (tel. 22-87-36) is behind Iglesia los Dolores, a bit beyond the Hotel Imperial. Open 24 hrs. The **policía femenina** (tel. 37-21-84) is 1 block west of Parque Herrera; entirely comprised of women, this force deals primarily with children's and women's problems.

Immigration Office: (tel. 22-77-11), on Av. Jeréz next to Hotel La Ronda. Get a visa extension here for 10 lempiras. Leave it in the morning, pick it up the next day at 3pm (they'll give you a copy for the day). Australian citizens must pay 20 lempiras for an extension. Open Mon.-Fri. 8:30am-noon and 1-4:30pm.

Embassies: Belize (tel. 32-31-91, ex. 7770), in the basement of the Hotel Honduras Maya. Open Mon.-Fri. 8:30am-1pm and 2-5pm. **Costa Rica** (tel. 32-17-68; fax 32-18-76), Colonia El Triangulo, 1a Calle. **El Salvador** (tel. 36-73-44; fax 36-94-03), Colonia San Carlos, No. 205. **Guatemala** (tel. 32-97-04; fax 31-56-55), Colonia Las Minitas, 4a Calle Arturo López Rodezno, casa 2421. **Nicaragua** (tel. 32-42-90; fax 31-14-12), Colonia Las Lomas del Tepeyac, Bloque M-1. **United Kingdom** (tel. 32-54-29; fax 32-54-80), Edificio Palmira, 3rd floor, Colonia Palmira. Across from the Hotel Honduras Maya. **U.S.** (tel. 36-93-20, 36-31-20; fax 36-77-76), on Av. La Paz. It's big, and everyone knows where it is (just ask). The consulate is across the way. Open Mon.-Fri. 8am-noon and 1-5pm.

Currency Exchange: Banks are everywhere—most change only U.S. dollars, some exchange traveler's checks. Some larger stores have *casas de cambio*, but their schedules are erratic. **Bancahsa** (tel. 37-11-71; fax 38-49-91), at Av. Cristobal Colón and Calle los Dolores, one block south of Los Dolores church. Checks changed, cash advanced on Visa cards. Open Mon.-Fri. 9am-5pm, Sat. 9am-noon.

American Express: Mundirama Travel Service (tel. 32-39-43; fax 32-00-72), Col. Palmira, Edificio CIICSA, Paseo Rep. de Panamá at Av. Rep. de Chile, 1 block from the Hotel Honduras Maya. Mon.-Fri. 8am-noon and 1-5pm, Sat. 8am-noon.

Post Office: (tel. 37-88-30), Av. Paz Barahona and Calle Telégrafo. *Lista de correos.* Open Mon.-Fri. 7am-7pm, Sat. 8am-1pm. In Comayagüela, the office (tel. 37-84-48) is on Av. 6a near the Instituto Abelardo R. Fortin. Open Mon.-Fri. 7am-7pm, Sat. 8am-1pm. **Postal code:** Tegucigalpa 11101, Comayagüela 11103.

Telephones: Hondutel (tel. 37-79-00; fax 37-97-15), near the post office on Av. Colón between Calles Telégrafo and los Dolores (look for the orange-and-white tower). AT&T booths (3min. to the U.S. 65 lempiras). **Fax** service (20 lempiras per page to the U.S.). Open 24 hrs. For **telegrams,** open Mon.-Fri. 7am-7pm, Sat. 8am-noon. In Comayagüela, **Hondutel** (tel. 38-14-48) is next to the post office.

Airport: Toncontin International Airport is 7km from downtown. **American** (tel. 32-14-14) and **Continental** (tel. 33-76-76) fly to the U.S. **Taca** (tel. 33-35-65), to San Pedro Sula (9:30am, 30min., 193 lempiras). **Isleña** (tel. 37-33-62), to La Ceiba (9am and 3pm, 30min., 256 lempiras). Airlines have offices in the airport; to book tickets in advance, contact **Mundirama Travel Service** (see AmEx above).

Buses: Buses leave from Comayagüela, most near 12 Calle and 7 and 10 Avs. southeast. If you need other connections, ask around. **Saenz** (tel. 37-65-21), 12 Calle between Avs. 7a and 8a, goes to San Pedro (13 per day, 7am-5:30pm and at 2am and 5am, 4 hrs., 20 lempiras). **Traliasa** (tel. 37-75-38), 12 Calle between Avs. 8a and 9a, to Tela (6am and 9am, 4½ hrs., 35 lempiras); and La Ceiba (6am and 9am, 7 hrs., 40 lempiras). **Etrucsa** (tel. 43-27-15), across the street from Traliasa, to Tela (10am and 4pm, 5 hrs., 40 lempiras); and to La Ceiba (10am and 4pm, 7 hrs., 40 lempiras). **Transportes Sultana de Occidente** (tel. 37-81-01), 12 Calle and 8 Av., through La Entrada (6am, 6 hrs., 28 lempiras) to Santa Rosa de Copán (7 hrs., 30 lempiras). **Cotraipbal,** Av. 7a, 11a and 12a Calles, to Trujillo (5am, 9am, noon, 8 hrs. 50 lempiras).

Intra-city buses: Buses' signs usually indicate the *barrios* or *colonias* between which they are traveling; many stop on the north side of the Parque Central or coming across the bridge from Comayagüela. Fare is 70 centavos.

International buses: Tica Bus, at 17a Calle, 7a and 8a Av. Comayagüela (tel. 38-70-40), is air-conditioned, has a *baño,* and isn't crowded. It handles migration stuff and is more expensive, and only stops at major cities. Destinations from Tegus are: Guatemala City (US$23), San Salvador (US$15), San José (US$35), and Managua (US$20).

Taxis: Ubiquitous. Within the city, fares typically run 5-15 lempiras. Try declaring a (fair) price upon entering. Never wait until leaving the cab to set the price. Fare to the airport is 20-25 lempiras. From the airport, don't take the yellow cabs, which charge 50 lempiras; walk out to the street for fares of 25 lempiras.

Supermarket: Mas x Menos, Av. La Paz Colonia Palmira—2 blocks down from the U.S. embassy. Every imaginable item for sale. Open daily 7:30am-9pm.

Laundromat: Lavandería Maya (tel. 31-36-49), in Col. Palmira, at Calzada Maipu. Heading away from the center, on Blvd. Morazán, look left one block before Pizza Hut. 6 lempiras per pound. Open Mon.-Fri. 7am-6pm and Sat. 8am-4pm.

English Bookstore: Book Village (tel. 32-71-08), in the Centre Comercial Los Castaños, on Blvd. Morazán. Go through the arch just past the KOBS sign, heading away from the center. Open Mon.-Fri. 9am-noon and 2-6pm, Sat. 9am-noon.

Cultural Center: Ministerio de Cultura (tel. 36-97-57), on Av. La Paz, 2 blocks up from the U.S. Embassy. Information on concerts, theater, and other cultural happenings about town. Open Mon.-Fri. 8:30am-4:30pm.

Pharmacy: For a list of pharmacies open until 9pm and on weekends, call Hondutel's 192 information number, or look for the list posted during the day in pharmacy windows. **Farmacia Santa Teresa** (tel. 37-06-32), 1 block east of the southeast corner of the Parque Central, across from the Hotel Prado, has some English-speaking staffers. Open Mon.-Fri. 8am-noon and 2-6pm, Sat. 8am-noon.

Medical Services: Clínicas Viera (tel. 37-31-56), across from Hotel La Ronda on Av. Colon. Open 24 hrs. Dr. Plutarco Castellanos' English is fluent. Consultations 100 lempiras. He sees patients 3:30-7pm.

Emergency numbers: Red Cross (tel. 37-86-54) and **Bomberos** (firefighters) (tel. 32-54-74).

■■■ ACCOMMODATIONS

Fractured into different neighborhoods, Tegucigalpa boasts hotels which vary considerably according to their location. Situated in the center of it all, accommodations near the Parque Central feed off the city's energy; very cheap places to pass the night are located near the Iglesia Los Dolores. For mid-priced hotels blessed with clean bathrooms, head for the Barrio Guanacaste. Conveniently close to the bus station, though not very safe at night, Comayagüela boasts plenty of hotels. In order to avoid diesel-induced nightmares, try to get a back room, far away from the street.

Café Allegro (tel. 32-81-22; fax 32-81-22), Av. República de Chile in Colonia Palmira. Look for the small sign on the left, 1½ blocks beyond the Hotel Honduras Maya. Close to the Peace Corps office, Allegro is filled with international volunteers. Nay: rooms are hostel-like, and the walk to the center is a long one. Yay: excellent restaurant, beautiful bar, comfy TV room, a piano in case you're feeling rusty, and overall spotlessness. The yays have it. 45 lempiras per person.

Hotel Granada (tel. 37-23-81), Av. Gutemburg, Barrio Guanacaste. A block up from the big Hotel Nankin sign. Rooms are large and clean. If you wear yourself out trudging down the halls (there are 48 rooms), there's a TV for taking mind-numbing breaks. Check-out 1pm. Singles 35 lempiras, with bath 60 lempiras; doubles 45 lempiras, with bath 70 lempiras; 2 beds 60 lempiras, with bath 95 lempiras; 2 beds and 3 people 70 lempiras, with bath 105 lempiras.

Hotel Fortuna, facing Iglesia Los Dolores and 1 block back to the left. Ideal for minimalists, each of these stark rooms has only a single, tiny window. No street noise, but the employees jabber it up outside the window. There's *agua purificada* to make up for the collapsing roofs and cold, cement bathrooms. The price is right. Singles 25 lempiras, doubles 30 lempiras.

Hotelito Elvin, Av. Colón and Calle Morelos, 1 block north of the post office, 1 block east of Parque Herrera. The small, jungly courtyard provides a welcome respite from Tegus' urban madness. The bedrooms are big and the bathrooms are private, but neither earn brownie points for cleanliness. 1 bed 35 lempiras, 2 people 35 lempiras, 2 beds 50 lempiras.

Hotel Maria José (tel. 37-72-92), in Comayagüela, at 12 Calle between Avs. 7 and 8, a block from the bus station. Impeccably clean rooms with TVs and either fans or A/C—take your pick. Double bed with fan 65 lempiras, 70 lempiras with a bigger TV, and 95 lempiras for the biggest TV.

■■■ FOOD

Alimentación in Tegus is as wild and varied as the city itself. Restaurants of nearly every description and price range fight to win the stomachs of *gringos* and *catrachos* (Hondurans) alike. For bargain food, the market, just across the bridge in Comayagüela, is convenient, as are the *comedores* and *cafeterías* nearby. The *merenderos* tend to serve hearty portions at heartening prices.

Restaurante al Natural (tel. 38-34-22), on the little street behind the cathedral in the Parque Central. A toucan greets you at the door and parrots squawk and scream as they chew on their metal cages. Welcome to chow time, *al natural.* Omelettes, salads (13-29 lempiras), sandwiches, and great *licuados.* Suck on a fruit if you want fresher-tasting juices. Open Mon.-Fri. 8am-7pm, Sat. 8am-3pm.

Café Allegro (tel. 32-81-22), attached to the hotel of the same name (see above). If a diet of tortillas has sapped your *joie de vivre,* splurge here. Enticing, unusual offerings and way-fresh pasta. The epitome: Spaghetti al Whisky (with bacon, fresh tomato, garlic, and a splash of moonshine 38.50 lempiras). Import beers, specialty coffee, and lip-drippety ice cream with the melty liquor of your choice.

La Terraza de Don Pepe (tel. 37-10-84), on Av. Colón, 2 blocks west from the Parque Central. At exactly 7:30pm on Sept. 2, 1986, Don Pepe's men's room became famous throughout Honduras—the nationally sacred Virgen de Suyapa, which had been stolen a few weeks earlier, was discovered next to the toilet, wrapped in newspaper like a piece of fish. Now the old bathroom is a shrine; the walls are plastered with newspaper clippings featuring the tiny statue, the Pope with the statue, the toilet, various people pointing to the toilet, etc. Even if you don't eat here, stop in to check out the shrine; find salvation in a warm potty. Meanwhile, in the fine tradition of Latin American cuisine, the menu boasts Chinese food and a good selection of cigarettes. Fried rice with chop suey 19.50 lempiras. Chicken *cordon bleu* 26.50 lempiras. Open daily 8am-10pm.

Restaurante y Pizzeria Nino (tel. 22-33-15), on the little Paseo de los Dolores, off the southeast corner of the church. The owner is Italian; the food is both authentic and irresistible. The walls of this classy place are hung with amateur surrealist paintings; order the mushroom pizza at your own risk (large 55 lempiras). Small *pizza romana* 30 lempiras. Open Mon.-Sat. 8:30am-9pm.

■■■ SIGHTS

How much time you spend in Tegucigalpa depends on how excited you get about gazing at church altars—most folks spend a day, maybe two, sightseeing in Tegus. The city's attractions are all within walking distance of the Parque Central; some are so close that you could walk to them from the park on your hands.

The **Parque Central** (also called the Plaza Morazán) is a must-see—actually, if you don't see it, you're probably in the wrong town. A statue of the hero Morazán stands in the middle of the park, surrounded by relaxing locals enjoying the shady trees. The trees teem with birds; rather than try to spy a bird by looking up with a gaping mouth, look at the ground for a different sort of proof. The park is also a good place to get your sandals shined—the red-shirted guys have cornered the spiffying-up-of-footwear market. With your sandals newly snazzed-up, you might begin a walking tour of Tegus.

Though built in 1728, the **Catedral San Miguel,** on the east side of the park, appears as if it's been whitewashed every day for 267 years. At the heart of the cathedral's simple interior stands a striking gold Baroque altar. Two blocks east of the cathedral is the 16th-century **Iglesia San Francisco,** the oldest church in Tegus. Two blocks west and one block north of the park, **Iglesia Los Dolores** (built in 1732) fronts a plaza filled with beggars asking church-goers for a lempira or two. The church's inner chamber is adorned with gaily painted statues of the saints; the altar is notable for its neon lights and fake flowers.

Walk south to Av. Colón and then west to **Parque Herrera,** with its massive tree and fountain. Directly south of the park is the **Teatro Nacional Manuel Bonilla.** Completed in 1910, the theater occasionally hosts concerts, plays, and cultural events. If you're looking for one more reason to become President of Honduras, feast your eyes on the seats in the center balcony—they're reserved exclusively for *el presidente* and his guests (open Mon.-Fri. 8:30am-4:30pm). Just to the northwest sits a strange little church with neon lights, a macabre tomb, and a Christ in Mardi Gras regalia.

About four blocks north of the theater is the **Parque La Concordia,** a little old park which resembles a miniature golf course. Meandering paths, cuddly-cute high-school couples licking each other's lips, and carefully crafted, shrunk-to-size replicas of the ruins at Copán fill the park. Wonderfully gnarled trees shade the ground at the park's north end.

From the park, head one block back east and one long block north; the **Museo Nacional Villa Roy** is tucked in behind a hill. With artifacts and exhibits on history and anthropology, the museum emphasizes the importance of the indigenous peoples in the history of Honduras in pre-Conquest times. Pop music provides the perfect backdrop for intricate panoramic models and pedantic discourses on evolution (open Wed.-Sun. 8:30am-3:30pm; admission 10 lempiras).

Two blocks south of the Parque Central are the **Parque Merced,** with its own (relatively unimpressive) church, and the **Antiguo Paraninfo Universitaria** (Old University Auditorium), which is being transformed into an art museum, scheduled to open in early 1996. They promise to outdo any government museum, but haven't yet set hours or admission fees. A block west, the old Presidential Palace has now been converted into the **Museo Historico de la República** (tel. 37-02-68). Dedicated in 1993, the exhibit picks up where the Museo Nacional leaves off, presenting Honduras's political history from independence in 1821 to the present. (Open Tues.-Sat. 9am-noon and 1:30-4pm. Admission 15 lempiras, free last Thurs. of each month.)

The **San Isidro Market,** just across the bridge in Comayagüela, is both huge and inventoried to the gills. For a view of Tegus, head via taxi (establish the fare before hopping in) to **Cerro Juan A. Linaez,** the large hill in Comayagüela with a stone monument and flag on top. The air is as fresh, as are the couples who come here to smooch. It's also relatively easy to walk to the top—just walk 20 minutes up the hill behind the soccer stadium. The peak to the north, **El Picacho,** also offers a sweeping view. Unfortunately, however, the area is somewhat unsafe. Be sure to ask about safety at the tourist office before scampering up El Picacho.

(Paul and) Art Behind Bars

Well-meaning friends may have warned you about ending up in a Central American jail, but there's actually good reason to visit **La Penitenciaria Central** at Av. San Martín de Flores and Av. Molina, in southeast Tegus. To bide their time, the prison's inmates produce woodworks, hammocks, and musical instruments, which are cheap and definitely high quality, granted that the prisoners are not formally trained. Previously, tourists could enter the prison after emptying their pockets of potential valuables, and were given a small metal tag (accompanied by the ominous threat, "you lose this, you're not leaving"). To avoid the red-tape hassles, prison officials have opened a small shop outside, where a guard summons the peddling prisoners, who proffer toothy smiles and modest English ("You buy?") with their well-fashioned wares. More than 80 people visit the store every day. In general, the prisoners are friendly to potential customers, and are psyched to jam out their favorite Steely Dan or Simon and Garfunkel guitar licks while chatting with guests. Just stay away from "So, what are you in for?", a conversational theme that corks conversations with astonishing alacrity. Most like to bargain on prices; supposedly, all profits go to the crafts' producers. Hammocks are 180-200 lempiras, guitars are 180-300 lempiras (open daily 8am-2pm).

■■■ ENTERTAINMENT

Tegucigalpa has its fair share of dazzling *discotecas.* Some of the joints are on Av. Juan Pablo II, but most are on Blvd. Morazán. The area can get iffy after dark—when you're done clubbing, catch a cab home. Many discos are located near Burger King—you'll know 'em when you see 'em. **Tropical Port** is becoming increasingly popular with locals and foreigners. Cover is 10 lempiras per person (open from 8pm 'til late weekdays, until dawn on weekends). Mega-disco **Metropolis,** next to El Rodeo Steakhouse, has a central dance floor; show off your moves to the crowd seated at tables. Remember Saturday Night Fever? This disco ball is mighty indeed (open nightly 7pm-?; cover 10 lempiras). **Cocteles** wins the new-and-chic sweepstakes. Dress to impress. The three awesome pool tables are largely ignored by the youth of Tegus in favor of the dance floor and bar (open 10pm-?; cover 20 lempiras). Across the way, **Kloster** is a hip, pricey bar/restaurant serving imported beers; a Grölsch will set you back 14.50 lempiras (open Mon.-Thurs. 6pm-1am, Fri.-Sat. 4pm-3am). More sedate pleasures are to be found at the **movie theaters** sprinkled everywhere. The theater one block west of Pizza Hut shows fairly ancient flicks—nothing screened here was filmed before the Jurassic era. Papers have listings.

■ NEAR TEGUCIGALPA

VALLE DE ANGELES

Valle de Angeles certainly lives up to its name: the sign announcing the town is the herald of a heavenly hamlet in the mountains outside Tegus. The town is best known for its *artesanías* (handicrafts); local artisans sell woodcarvings, pottery, hammocks, etc., at kindly prices in a gorgeous setting. It's also a primo starting point for a daytrip to La Tigra (see below). Valle proper extends north and south from its central park, with a church on the north and the *Palacio Municipal* on the south end of the park. Angels don't lack for services. **FUSEP** (tel. 76-21-51), the police force, is on the north end of Calle Principal (open 5am to midnight). The *palacio* contains **Banco de Occidente** (open Mon.-Fri. 9am-noon and 2-5pm), the **post office** (with *lista de correos;* open Mon.-Fri. 8am-noon and 2-5pm, Sat. 8am-noon), and the **Hondutel** office (tel. 76-21-42; open daily 7am-noon and 2-5pm, weekends without the lunch break). They don't have a fax machine; would-be faxers resort to telepathy. The **Farmacia Karyfarm** is on the north end of Calle Principal (open Mon.-Fri. 9am-noon and 2-6pm, Sat. 9am-3pm).

For **accommodations,** the angels resort to yin and yang: there is one nice but expensive hotel and one cheap but dismal *hospedaje.* **La Posada del Angel** (tel. 76-22-33), on the north end of Av. 1a, offers attractive rooms with private baths and hot water around a beautiful park for 60 lempiras per person. A guard sticks around at night for security, insomniacs, and late-night arrivals. Pack your tummy at the **Posada del Angel's** attached restaurant; tasty *típico* treats are available daily 7am-6:30pm. Chicken in wine with rice and vegetables 25 lempiras, club sandwich with fries 12 lempiras. Check out the cool old instruments and ask to see a flick on their projection TV. For some serious Garifuna action, head to **El Buyei** on Calle Principal, just south of the park. The name is a mystery (i.e. it means "mystery" in Garifuna), but there's no enigma behind tasty eats, only about what became of the animals whose pelts adorn the walls. Seafood soup 30 lempiras. *Plato típico* 25 lempiras.

The reason most people come to Valle de Angeles is to go crazy getting goods, and to bask in the glory of undeniably magnificent handicrafts. The pieces are sold in the *salones,* which cluster on Av. 1a, especially at the extreme south end at the *mercado.* Half of the *mercado* is devoted to *artesanías,* and that section is open every day but Monday, while the light persists. The shops are generally open every day and accept Visa and Mastercard. The markets are painfully bloated with tourists on weekends, and the prices are not much lower in the *mercado,* although haggling is an option there, whereas it most certainly is not in the stores. A relatively cheap store is the second one on the right, walking away from the market. To get to Valle, take a bus from the terminal in Tegus (heading up Av. La Paz, there's a big statue of Simón Bolívar; turn right at the gas station, then take the first left). Buses leave every 45minutes from 6:15am to 5:30pm (30min., 2.50 lempiras).

PARQUE NACIONAL LA TIGRA

Parque Nacional La Tigra is only 21km northeast of Tegucigalpa, but the setting couldn't be more different. Covering some 238 square kilometers, the park includes a well-preserved cloud forest stocked with orchids, plus more than 200 species of birds, ocelots, monkeys, and pumas. There are gorgeous trails, but hikers should be forewarned that these trails are steep. Locals mumble with a sardonic smile *"hay que subir"* (you gotta climb), but this doesn't begin to describe it. Consider leaving heavier things in a hotel in Tegus, especially if you're not in great shape.

There are two ways to do the park, from the top down, and from the bottom up. The descent takes about four hours of hiking; the ascent could take twice as long. The descent starts from **Jutiapa** or **Las Limones,** accessible by buses that leave from Parque Herrera in Tegus (erratic schedules—usually 3 per day starting around 7am, 45min., 3 lempiras). From there, walk a couple kilometers to **Rancho Quemado** (the ranger station) and start the descent, which ultimately ends at **El Rosario,** the other ranger station. Magín, the extremely friendly ranger, lives at El Rosario, and services are centered there; ask him about trails. To make the ascent, take the frustratingly unreliable buses to the village of **San Juancito;** buses leave Tegus from Mercado San Pablo in Barrio El Manchen, in the northeast part of the capital (9am and 11am, 1½ hrs., 10 lempiras). The other option is to take a more reliable bus to Valle de Angeles, then walk north along Calle Principal, which becomes the road to San Juancito. The hike is a healthy 11km, but buses pass every couple hours during daylight hours and some travelers hitchhike with moderate success.

From San Juancito, and with your back to the FUSEP office, turn left and walk ½km up the hill. Following the sign, turn left again, and walk about 4-5km uphill.

Keep an eye out for the small house where world-famous **Amalia Elvir de Ramos** cooks up *típica* dishes for travelers for 10 lempiras. Continuing further up, the *Casa de Visitantes* becomes visible. Accommodations with small mattresses and blankets for three people are available for 20 lempiras per person; there's even a bathtub.

CROSSING THE BORDER INTO NICARAGUA

Tegus is often a stopping point for those headed farther south, and is conveniently close to Choluteca, the hub for all border crossings. To get to Choluteca, grab a bus from **Mi Esperanza,** Av. 6a., 23a and 24a Calles (tel. 38-28-63; every 1½ hrs., 4am-6:30pm, 3 hrs., 13.50 lempiras). From Choluteca, take a *colectivo* (10-15 lempiras) or a bus (6 lempiras) to Gausaule, the border crossing. The ride takes 30-60min., and drops you off at the immigration office. It costs five lempiras to leave Honduras, and the office is open daily 6am-noon and 1-5pm.

Cross the bridge and change currency (be careful not to get skunked by dishonest changers). Welcome to Nicaragua, whose doors are open 7am-5pm every day. The entrance costs US$2. Buses leave for the interior until 5pm. A direct bus leaves for Managua at 1:30pm. The ride to Managua generally takes 3-4 hours, so it's possible to get from Tegus to Managua in a day (see Nicaragua: Documents and Formalities, page 256, for more information).

WESTERN HONDURAS

■■■ COMAYAGUA

Heavily laden with churches, the town of Comayagua makes an interesting historical interlude on the road from Tegucigalpa to San Pedro Sula. Situated 80km north of Tegus, Comayagua was Honduras's first capital, until erosion, exhaustion of the natural environment, and fires debilitated the city in the late 1800s. Comayagua's 17th-century **cathedral** was one of the first churches built in Honduras, and the church is nationally known as a symbol of Hispanic-American Baroque art. Look for the ancient clock tower, which was supposedly given to the town as a gift from Phillip II, taken from Spain's Alhambra. Locals will swear to you that the clock still works, and it does—twice a day, every day. Three blocks south of the back of the cathedral sits **Iglesia la Merced,** the oldest (16th century) church in all of Honduras. Although it lacks the incredible altar-work of the cathedral, its statues are stunning.

Across the street to the south is the **Museo Colonial.** This three-room museum is stuffed with religious objects culled from churches in and around Comayagua, including crucifixes, silver statues, glimmering gold chalices, a letter of Francisco Morazán (a Honduran liberal leader who promulgated anti-clerical laws after Independence), and a chair used by Pope John Paul II during a visit to the region (open daily 10am-noon and 2-5pm; admission 5 lempiras). Also on the south end, San Sebastián Church is famed for its gold-and-silver altar, as well as for its status as the burial place of ex-president General José Trinidad Cabañas.

A block north of the plaza stands a museum of a different sort, the **Museo Regional de Arquelogía.** A part of the Instituto Hondureño de Antropología e Historia, the museum exhibits fossils, Honduras's first printing press, and a range of artifacts from the region's indigenous civilizations (open Wed.-Fri. 8am-noon and 1-4pm, Sat.-Sun. 9am-noon and 1-4pm; admission 10 lempiras).

To reach Comayagua from Tegus, take a second-class San Pedro-bound bus. Ask to be let off at Comayagua—you'll find yourself on the highway, 1km (or 4-lempira cab ride) from town. **Empresa de Transportes Catrachos** (tel. 72-02-60) goes directly to Comayagua (every 40min., 6am-7pm, 1½ hrs., 9 lempiras). Unfortunately, the company's terminal is a 15-minute cab ride outside Comayagua. Return buses leave

Comayagua every 40 minutes from 5:15am-6pm. Generally, all Tegus-San Pedro Sula buses stop here, except the ultra-expresses.

A full range of services are available to cushion your stay in Comayagua. **FUSEP** (tel. 72-00-80) is one block east of Hondutel (open 24 hrs.). **Banco Ficensa** (tel. and fax 72-00-75), on the west side of the park, does the traveler's check thing (open Mon.-Fri. 9am-3pm, Sat. 8:30-11:30am). **Hondutel** (tel. 72-00-03) is just east of the cathedral (open daily 7am-9pm, with 2 ½-hr. breaks for lunch and dinner). Next door is the **post office** (tel. 72-02-89; open Mon.-Fri. 8am-noon and 1-4pm, Sat. 8-noon). **Farmacia Pritania** is across from the Hotel America (open Mon.-Fri. 8am-12:30pm and 2-7:30pm). The **Red Cross** emergency number is 195.

For accommodations, **Hotel Maru** (tel. 72-13-11) is four blocks south of the *parque* and one block west of Av. 1a. Rooms are simple and kinda loud, but equipped with fans; some have private bathrooms (25 lempiras for one person with no bath, 35 lempiras for two beds and a private bath). Right on the *parque,* **Hotel Libertad** (tel. 92-00-91) has big-but-basic rooms. The enormous windows would serve perfectly as docking bays for alien aircraft. Fans 2 lempiras; check-out noon (singles 18 lempiras, doubles 30 lempiras, triples 36 lempiras).

For **food,** try the market a few blocks south of the *parque,* or **Ricos,** one block east of Calle Principal and just south of the park, where *típica* adventures eagerly await. *Desayuno* 12 lempiras, big chicken tacos 9 lempiras (open daily 7am-5:30pm). Another option is **Palmeras** (tel. 72-03-52), near the Hotel Libertad on the south side of the *parque.* The cool pictures of stelae evoke that "just like Grandma Maya used to make" ambience. Particularly good is the chicken with rice for only 25 lempiras (open daily 7am-8:30pm).

For **entertainment,** the ultra-cheap *cine* (5 lempiras) shows the hits of yester-month with Spanish subtitles. Go one block west of the park and two north at 7pm for cinematic pleasure. The Sunday matinee (1pm) is only 2 lempiras. Near Comayagua, there's the increasingly popular **Lago Yojoa** and **Cuevas de Taulabé,** both about an hour north along the highway. The lake is party to stellar fishing, snorkeling, swimming, and boating, and home to extensive archaeological finds in the nearby village of **Los Naranjos.** Specific arrangements should be made in the hotels surrounding the lake. Buses leave Comayagua (they're all San Pedro-bound; ask for *Yojoa* or *Las Cuevas*) about every 40 minutes, from just before dawn until sunset (1 hr., 5 lempiras). Entrance to the lake is free; the caves cost a couple lempiras.

■■■ SANTA ROSA DE COPÁN

Tucked tightly into the lulling hills of the Copán department, Santa Rosa sacrifices Mayan-seeking throngs of tourists for peaceful isolation; few would suspect the town's status as the political center of Western Honduras. In fact, Santa Rosa (formerly called "Los Llanos") has been capital of the department for more than a hundred years, but has carried itself with reserved dignity. Commonly used as a crossroads to Gracias and the Copán ruins, the village is ideal for a relaxing, low *gringo*-content introduction to Honduras (don't confuse the cruddy bus terminal with the town itself). Charming and comparatively cheap, it's almost redundant (but still worthwhile) to explore Santa Rosa's nearby *reserva* (forest preserve) and serene *laguna* (lake), which sleep only a 20-minute bus ride away.

Orientation and Practical Information The two parts of town, *el centro* and *el terminal,* are separated by a two-mile stretch of unrelated buildings. The former sees most of the action and is laid out like a Central American town should be—around the **Parque Central.** The main drag, called **Calle Centenario,** runs east-west along the south side of the park. No one really uses the street numbers or names, just directions from the park. A taxi from *el terminal* costs about 4 lempiras.

The closest thing to a **tourist office** is the lobby of **Hotel Elvir** (see Accommodations, below). They arrange trips and distribute maps of Santa Rosa and bus schedules (open 24 hrs.). The **police** (tel. 62-00-91, emergency 121) are available 24 hours a day, at the big building on the north end of the park labeled "Fuerza de Seguridad Publica." They feel that Santa Rosa is quite safe. Have some **currency exchanged** at **El Banco de Occidente** at the southeast side of the park (tel. 62-00-22; fax 62-00-26); they change traveler's checks and give credit card advances (open Mon.-Fri. 8am-noon and 2-5pm, Sat. 8-11:30am). The **post office** (tel. 62-00-30) awaits on the west side of the park and has *lista de correos* (open Mon.-Fri. 8am-noon, 2-5pm; Sat. 8am-noon). Speedier modes of communication are available next door at **Hondutel** (tel. 62-09-87, 62-09-89; open daily 7am-9pm). **Fax** and **telegrams** are also available. The **buses** run from La Terminal (look for the sign that says Bodeguita Terminal) to San Pedro Sula (every 30min., 4am-5:30pm, 3½ hrs., 13 lempiras); to Tegucigalpa (Mon.-Sat. 4am, Sun. 10:30am, 6½ hrs., 25 lempiras); to Copán Ruinas (actually buses go to La Entrada, then continue to the ruins: daily at noon, 3 hrs., 13 lempiras); to Ocotepeque at the border (every 3 hrs., 6am-3:30pm, 4 hrs., 8 lempiras); and to Gracias (every 1½ hrs., 7:15am-5:30pm, 2½ hrs., 8 lempiras). For **grocery** needs there are two options, *el mercado* and *el supermercado*—decide whether the distinction is valid. The *mercado* boasts the cool things tourists buy for friends, including machetes and other artisan products, as well as fresh fruit. Stand at the south side of the park, facing south; turn right, and go two blocks past the park. Turn left at the Banhcafe sign (open Mon.-Sat. 6am-5pm, Sun. 6am-3pm). The supermarket, **Supermercado Jaar** (tel. 62-01-88), offers standard supermarket fare. Same directions as *el mercado,* but go one block past the Banhcafe sign, turn right, and it's down one block on the left. The **pharmacy** is adjacent to the park and is called, not surprisingly, **Farmacia Central** (tel. 62-04-65; open Mon.-Fri. 8am-6pm, Sat. 8am-noon). The **Hospital de Occidente** (tel. 62-01-12) is west of the park (open 24 hrs). Take Calle Centenario five blocks west of the park; turn left at Hogar de Niñas. Wash dirt at **Super Lavandería Florencia.** Full service costs 23 lempiras per load (open Mon.-Sat. 8am-6:30pm).

Accommodations and Food The hotels are about standard for Honduras; 30-40 lempiras buys a cubicle with a bed and refreshingly cold shower, and 70-100 lempiras gets a palatial room loaded with perquisites. Both varieties are clustered around the city center and bus terminal. **Hotel Copán,** across the street from the *mercado* at 1a calle and Av. 3a (tel. 62-02-65), offers budget splendor. Small, decent rooms have private baths and hot water; there's a guarded parking lot for guests. Fans are 10 lempiras extra (singles 40 lempiras, doubles 70 lempiras, triples 105 lempiras). Make a break from common bathrooms to splurge at **Hotel Elvir,** on Calle Centenario (tel. and fax 62-01-03), a couple of blocks west of the park. Posh and very clean by budget standards, the rooms are often stuffed with *gringos* and vacationing Peace Corps volunteers, who feel at home with sports cable TV, hot water, and comfy beds (singles 118 lempiras, doubles 193 lempiras, triples 214 lempiras).

Down by the terminal stands a similarly posed pair of hotels: 200m down the Boulevard is **Hotel El Rey** (tel. 62-06-20), the budget option with small rooms and creaky beds, though all rooms have private baths. Check-out time is noon. (Singles 32 lempiras, with hot water 53.50 lempiras; doubles 64.20 lempiras, with hot water 107 lempiras; triples 96 lempiras, with hot water 160 lempiras.)

Avoid the hotels' costly restaurants; the food in Santa Rosa is plentiful and fairly cheap. Cookeries are clustered around the central park. **La Cafetería Danny,** right on the south side of the park, keeps 'em coming back for its *pollo frito* (18 lempiras) and banana splits (9 lempiras; open Mon.-Sat. 8:30am-7pm). **Hamburguesas Marbellas,** one block southeast of the park, slaps tasty flesh on warm buns. Their *especial,* with fries, is 12 lempiras (open daily 7:30am-10pm).

Sights and Entertainment Hustle and bustle wear thin; for a change from heavily touristed attractions, head out to the *laguna* at **La Montañita Preserve,** a few kilometers out of town, for picnic bliss. Take any bus to Gracias (2 lempiras) and ask the driver to stop at La Montañita. With your back to Santa Rosa, look for a little road to the left; follow the signs for the preserve. Follow the main path (3m across) for five minutes through pleasant, lush forest; the laguna spreads to the left. Locals swim and fish in this pond. For a picnic (*amor* not included), head to the table and firepit. Don't let pesties ruin a good moment; bring repellant, especially after a rain. For nightlife, domestics *and* imports rush to **Glamour** (call the contact guy at home, 62-04-45), a block from Hamburguesas Marbellas (see Food, above). They throw parties Friday (6 lempiras), Saturday (8 lempiras), and Sunday (5 lempiras), 8am to 2am. Current remodeling may increase cover charges in the future.

■■■ GRACIAS

Ever since Juan de Chavez, the first settler to the region, exclaimed, "*¡Gracias a Dios que hemos hallado tierra llana!*" (Thank God we finally found flat land!), Gracias has become, ironically, a comfortable base camp for travelers seeking far-from-flat terrain. Gracias was founded in 1536 as a garrison for Spanish soldiers intent on attacking indigenous communities to the east, and the valley seemed a secure headquarters. By the time the 17th century fizzled out, Gracias had served as both the capital of Honduras and as a seat of government for all of Spanish Central America. As the Honduran economy's center of gravity shifted north and east, Gracias's importance faded and the city mellowed—the peace here is disturbed only by the chiming of church bells and the clickety-click of running schoolchildren slapping the cobbled streets with their shoes. But ambitious visitors typically stop in Gracias *en route* to the breath-taking cloud forest in **Parque Nacional Celaque,** where they exhaust their bones before macerating in the **hot springs.**

Orientation and Practical Information Getting around Gracias is simple. Get off the bus and you'll be one block west and three blocks north of the park and the cathedral. The market is roughly three blocks west of the park, though it's tucked in behind some buildings and isn't too easy to spot.

While there is no **tourist office,** visitors can walk four blocks up and four blocks left from the park to get to the **COHDEFOR** office, which has helpful information about Mt. Celaque (open Mon.-Fri. 8am-4pm). The **police** (tel. 98-44-36) are next to the park (available 24 hrs). **Exchange currency** and traveler's checks at **Banco de Occidente** (tel. 98-40-17), across from the market (open Mon.-Fri. 8am-noon and 2-4:30pm, Sat. 8-11:30am). The **post office** (tel. 98-40-22) is a few blocks from the central park and posts a *lista de correos* (open Mon.-Fri. 8am-noon and 1-5pm, Sat. 8am-noon). The **postal code** is 42101. **Hondutel** (tel. 98-44-01, 98-44-02) is next door (open daily 7am-noon, 2-9pm). **Transportes Lempira buses** leave half a block from Hotel Erick and run to Santa Rosa de Copán (7 per day, 6:15am-5pm, 1¾ hrs., 8.50 lempiras). For pharmaceutical needs, **Venta de Medicinas Lempira** is two blocks from the market (open daily 8am-noon, 2-5pm, 7-9pm). The **doctor**'s office is in the same building (open Mon.-Fri. 4-9pm, Sat. 8am-4pm, Sun. 8am-noon). After-hours, head for the **hospital** (tel. 98-44-25).

Accommodations and Food Gracias's few hotels are located in the center of town between the market and the *parque central.* Backpackers flock to **Hotel Erick** (tel. 98-40-66), half a block east of the bus terminal. Outfitted with private bath, rooms are spacious and pretty. Beds are super-comfy. Guests going to Celaque can leave gear here. (1 person 21 lempiras; 2 people 32 lempiras, with fan, lamp, and hot water 70 lempiras, with TV 100 lempiras.) Another hunky-dory budget option is **Hotel Iris,** two blocks west and five blocks south of the park (remember to pronounce it with a Spanish accent: "Ee-rees"). Clean rooms with private bath, fan, and psychedelic blue walls right out of the movie *Brazil.* (25 lempiras per person, check-out noonish. Check in the adjacent restaurant if no one's in the office.) Just a half a block from the Banco de Occidente is **Anexo Hospedaje Corazón de Jesus.** Locks are small, mattresses nearly non-existent, and the ambience contemporary Chechnya, but it's a cheap sleep. (12 lempiras per person *sans* bath; with bath, singles 30 lempiras, doubles 50 lempiras.)

The culinary center of Gracias is **Restaurante Guancascos,** a.k.a. **Los Lencas** (tel. 98-45-16). Prices are reasonable, and travelers frequent the establishment to buy food and Lencan handicrafts, and to chug potable water. *Cena típica* 18 lempiras, *almuerzo vegetariano* 18 lempiras, banana split 12 lempiras (open Mon.-Sat. 7am-10pm, Sun. 8am-10pm). Other choices are **La Fonda**, next to Hondutel, and **Las Gemelas,** a couple blocks west. Both are frequented by locals.

Sights As for leisure, many locals head off to shoot some pool after work. If your eight-ball isn't up to snuff, take a walk up to the **Fort of San Cristobál.** They call it a castle (*castillo*), but that's a little too imaginative. The view of town through the watchtower's murder holes is excellent. Here you can visit the tomb of former Honduran President Juan Lindo (open daily 7am-noon and 1-5pm). The churches of Gracias are pretty unimpressive; if you feel compelled to visit a house of worship, though, **Las Mercedes,** two blocks from the park, is more interesting than the rest.

■ NEAR GRACIAS

HOT SPRINGS AND VILLAGES

For budget travelers left sore and stressed by the rigors of cranky beds, painful bus rides, and long hikes, salvation is only a hot, spring, and jump away. The **hot springs** (*aguas termales*) near Gracias are guaranteed to loosen even the most knotted of muscles. To reach relaxation, head out past Hondutel and La Fonda and turn left. After a block, walk to the right down the hill; follow the road to the left. Cross the bridge along the gravel road and walk for 15 minutes. You'll see a second (blue) bridge; about 150m before it, follow the road up the hill to the right. Almost a kilometer later, the road finally splits—turn left (there's a house at the corner). Continue past farmlands, along a footpath, to the river; there's a footbridge 20m upstream. Cross, and follow the path about 1km. The road forks at an old gate; keep straight (the right fork). You'll climb a hill on a path that looks like a dry stream bed. At the top, go straight down a wide dirt road. At the bottom you'll see a **turquoise shack**—that's the place! Admission is two lempiras. There is a small shack, changing rooms (with voyeuristic frogs), and toilets (squatting ones—if you're lazy, go before you leave). One pool (essentially just walls built around the stream) is warm; the one on the left is hotter and has a wide step for basking on your back. Thanks to dense water and wacky physics, it's possible to float securely in the hotter pool. Lie on the wide step, back down; inhale deeply, and enjoy your newly discovered pastime—this experience alone is well worth the two-hour round-trip hike.

Two words of caution about planning the hike back: the hill is tiring for newly jellied legs—you may give up halfway and decide to spend another hour in the pools; Also, before the river, there's a fork that isn't as clear on the way up—go right.

Two nearby villages, **La Campa** and **San Sebastián,** offer another option for a getaway from Gracias. La Campa is home to a stunningly beautiful colonial church with artwork from centuries ago, and San Sebastian is a wonderfully cheap village that is experimenting with sustainable farming practices under the aegis of the Peace Corps; check out the apple trees. Buses head in the general direction of these places; it's best to discuss with several locals how exactly to make the trip. Be careful, and plan carefully for the trip. Don't automatically extend village day-trips to other destinations, however. The police warn that two nearby villages, **La Unión** and **Lepaeta,** are dangerous for tourists.

PARQUE NACIONAL CELAQUE

Looming to the west of Gracias is the 66,000-acre **Parque Nacional Celaque;** inside the park stands **Mt. Celaque** (2489m), the tallest peak in the nation. From the base of the mountain to its summit rises a cloud forest so fantastic that it might be the setting for a fairy tale—avoid tripping over gnomes as you ascend the mountain. While the trail up Celaque is dense with foliage, the forest on top is relatively sparse and mossy. If you have the eyes of a hawk, you might be able to spot a *quetzal* or a toucan. Pumas, jaguars, and white-faced monkeys also live in the park.

Current information on both trail conditions and the logistics of getting to Celaque can be obtained at the **COHDEFOR** office (see Gracias, Practical Information, page 219). To reach the park from Gracias, walk toward the cemetery, which is behind the fort on the hill and in the direction of the mountain. Follow the road that runs to the left of the cemetery; at the fork veer to the right, and then veer right at the church with pink steeples. The walk from the church to the park is along a dirt road and should take three to four hours. Many ask around for someone who might be able to give them a ride down the road for a fee. As always, exercise good judgement. After entering the park (there's a sign), it's an hour to the **visitor's center.** There are about 10 bunks (with very limited bedding), a rustic kitchen, and friendly Miguel, who takes care of the place. If you haven't brought food, his mother cooks up mean *frijolitos* and electrifying coffee, served up in a warm little cooking hut. She asks five lempiras for your stay at the hut.

If you're not a triathlete and plan to go to the summit and back in a single day, leave the visitor's center at dawn. The hike to the first camp, **Don Tomás,** takes three to four hours. The camp is a small hut outfitted with mattress-less bunks, a latrine, and a firepit. Since the camp is locked, ask for a key at the visitor's center before setting out. The next camp, **Naranjo,** is two to three hours beyond Don Tomás. The camp is slightly off the path and can be hard to spot—look for the firewood stash, and keep your eyes open for an orange carrot; occasionally the visitor's center caretaker hangs one out as emergency food. Naranjo has only tent spots; there's no hut here.

It is at Naranjo that the cloud forest actually begins; the summit is two to three hours away. In the cloud forest, the path is marked by pink and yellow ribbons pinned to the trees. Be sure to keep the ribbons in sight and be suspicious if you find yourself in an area without them; one path leads down the far side of Celaque to Belén Gualche. The mountain's summit is a small area with a less-than-spectacular view—you should aim for the top only if you want to brag back in Gracias. As you get closer to the summit, the air becomes increasingly cool and damp; be sure to bring clothing that can keep you both warm and dry. The trail can be tricky to follow at night, and crossing the rivers that slice across the path can be difficult with only a flashlight. Being forced to camp on the path is not an unheard-of fate.

To make the hike both easier and more enjoyable, consider hiring Miguel to guide you. Miguel knows the cloud forest and the trail which runs through it exceptionally well; he charges about 100 lempiras for a round-trip and can be found at the visitor's center. Prepare for your trip by bringing water (or a means of treating water), warm clothes, rain gear, bedding (if you're overnighting), and a flashlight. Also be sure to bring a watch; the trail is often thick with trees, and it's difficult to tell what time it is. In general, the path is not especially difficult to find, but when the ground is wet things can get pretty hairy.

■■■ COPÁN

Copán wows. Visited by several thousands each year hailing from over 50 countries, Copán is by far Honduras's most famous and most impressive attraction; the ruins are a special link in the chain of Mayan remnants which sweeps south from the Yucatán into Belize, Guatemala, and Honduras. While some ruins, notably Guatemala's Tikal and Mexico's Chichén Itzá, are larger, no site can match Copán for magnificently detailed ornamentation, well-preserved artwork, long strings of hieroglyphics, and carefully wrought and terrifically intricate carvings. In 1980, the ruins were named a UNESCO World Heritage Site in recognition of their importance to global culture.

The town of Copán Ruinas (pop. 25,000), 1km west of the ruins, would be worth passing through even if it weren't the base of choice for exploring the ruins. After a day spent admiring etchings of awe-inspiring deities and power-hungry rulers, coming back to Copán Ruinas is a pleasure. Singing from the church often wafts into its Parque Central, saturating the air with soaring melodies as small boys ride horses up and down the town's few stone streets.

ORIENTATION AND PRACTICAL INFORMATION

Copán Ruinas is fairly easy to navigate. The bus terminal is at the bottom of a hill; one block uphill and to the left is the Parque Central. Services cluster within two or three blocks of the church, which is at the east end of the park. The ruins lie to the east of the town. Copán is typically cooler than the lowlands; bringing along a sweatshirt might not be a bad idea.

Tourist Office: Loads of friendly **local kids** roam the park and nearby areas, ready to help tourists work out their plans. The kids know everything and everyone, and the tips tourists give them (just a few lempiras) generally go to their mothers. Alternatively, the pamphlet **Honduras Tips** provides invaluable information about the ruins, nearby towns, and pretty much everything else in Honduras. Copies available at Tunkul (see Food below).

Police: FUSEP (tel. 98-30-60), across the bridge, 1½ blocks from the Hotel Marina Copán. Open 24 hrs.

Currency Exchange: Banco de Occidente (tel. 98-84-15), at the southeast corner of the park. Cashes traveler's checks. No cash advances on credit cards. Open Mon.-Fri. 8am-noon and 2-4:30pm, Sat. 8-11:30am. To get *quetzales,* check at local restaurants such as **Llama del Bosque;** you'll get more favorable rates at the border.

Post Office: (tel. 98-34-47), ½ block from the park on the side opposite the church. Posts a *lista de correos.* Open Mon.-Fri. 8am-noon and 2-5pm, Sat. 8am-noon. **Postal code:** 41209.

Telephones: Hondutel (tel. 98-30-11; fax 98-00-04), next to the post office. Open Mon.-Sat. 7am-8:30pm. The phone next to the booths is for AT&T direct calls. **The Budget Traveler** (tel. 98-3432) has a branch at Go Native Travel.

Buses: Empresa Etumi runs to San Pedro Sula (4am and 6am, 4-5 hrs., 18 lempiras) and **La Entrada** (every 45min., 5am-4:30pm, 2 hrs., 10 lempiras), where connections can be made to Santa Rosa de Copán and to San Pedro Sula. To get to the Guatemalan border, hang around the park and bus station in the morning and look for pick-ups as they drive by; the pick-ups make themselves conspicuous and charge a fee. Be clear about the price before boarding.

Laundromat: Justo a Tiempo, just west of the church. Washes and dries monopolistically at 9 lempiras per pound. Also sports a book exchange. Open Mon.-Sat. 7:30am-noon and 1-5:30pm.

Pharmacy: Farmacia Felix M. Jandal (tel. 98-30-51), a block up the hill from the Hotel Marina Copán. Open daily 7am-7pm; closed for lunch.

Medical Services: Dr. Luis Castro's office (tel. 98-35-04) is next to the bank, and he speaks English. Open Mon.-Sat. 8am-noon and 2-5pm.

ACCOMMODATIONS

There are several small, cheap hotels around town and a few budding resorts, although all seem to raise their prices with each passing day. For a luxury splurge (and to catch up on videos about Honduras), try **Casa de Café,** four blocks west of the central park. Hotels are generally within a couple blocks of the Parque Central; none has yet managed to establish itself as *the* place to go for budgeted backpackers. Ask about **camping** in the area around the ruins; get permission before pounding in any stakes. Fans aren't as crucial here as along the coast.

Los Gemelos (tel. 98-30-77), 1 block east of the park. The eponymous *twins* are grown and gone, but their delightful mother still runs things at the clean and carefully kept hotel. The courtyard, a botanical sedative, might be the perfect place to *finally* solve those lingering Mayan riddles. No hot water. Check-out 10am, but she'll store gear. Singles 30 lempiras, doubles 50 lempiras, triples 75 lempiras.

Hotel La Posada (tel. 98-30-70, shared with Hotel Marina Copán), across from the Marina Copán. The 22 rooms are well-kept and the owner ultra-mellow. The multiplicity of stalls in the common bathrooms prevent anxious waits, though anxious you'll be after conversing with the creaky beds. No fans, but who needs 'em? Singles 40 lempiras, doubles 60 lempiras.

Posada Honduras (tel. 98-30-82), south of the bus station. Rooms around the courtyard are simple and tidy, but the mattresses are a bit old, and the common bathrooms a tad dark. Next to a souvenir shop. Check-out 11am. Singles 25 lempiras, doubles 30 lempiras, triples 40 lempiras.

Hotel Paty (tel. 98-34-73), ½ block uphill from the bus station. Recently remodeled rooms are airy, clean, and come with hot water, but the price might be high if your lemp-level is limp. Singles 70 lempiras, doubles 80 lempiras. Prices rise during peak tourist season.

Hotel Brisas Copán (tel. 98-30-18), up the hill from the bus terminal. Rooms are impeccable, have private bathrooms, and are well worth the extra lempiras. 60 lempiras for one person, 100 lempiras for 2 people, 160 lempiras with hot water.

FOOD

Unfortunately, Copán has no culinary focal point—there's no centrally located spot crammed with *baleada* stands and fruit vendors, although there's usually something for sale at the park. The town's restaurants have been somewhat *gringo*-fied; menus indulge U.S. tastes, and prices are relatively high. However, there are still some *copaneco* restaurants with decent prices and authentic food, especially behind the church to the northeast.

Tunkul Restaurante and Bar (tel. 98-34-10), 2 blocks west of the southwest corner of the park. On the *Autobahn* to legendary status and motoring along at 100km per hr., Tunkul's friendly owners aren't leaving any tourists behind. The burritos are simply massive. Vegetarian plates are available, and veggie stuffings can be substituted for meat upon request. Come here to take part in the only real nightlife in town; a *tunkul* is a Mayan sacrificial drum, and this eatery doesn't miss a beat. Chicken or beef burritos 25 lempiras, with veggies instead of meat 20 lempiras. Open daily 7am-10pm, with happy hour from 8-9pm. Open for drinks until midnight.

El Jacal, next to Hotel Brisas (above), on the hill. They don't serve jackal here, nor is it necessary to compete with scavengers to delight in flavorful (and thoroughly cooked) meals. Meanwhile, laugh with joy, and the other desert dogs, at lower prices. Chicken tacos 6 lempiras. Open daily 6:30am-9pm.

Restaurante Llama del Bosque (tel. 98-34-31). Fellow travelers abound in this restaurant's pleasant, spacious patio-esque dining area. The menu is diverse (though a bit high-end, perhaps), but breakfast is cheap and deservedly popular. Chow mein 25 lempiras. Fried chicken 35 lempiras. Open daily 6:30am-10pm.

Restaurante El Sesteo (tel. 98-30-27), next to the Hotel Paty. With 67 items on the menu, it's hard to miss. They serve some of the foods you *do* miss: spaghetti with white sauce 20 lempiras. *Cena típica* 20 lempiras. Open daily 6am-9pm.

Bacab Restaurant, 1 block north and ½ block northwest of the Parque Central. A quiet restaurant, and a perfect place to catch up on postcard-writing—*bacab* is Mayan for "scribe." *Plato típico* 22 lempiras. Open daily 7am-9pm.

THE RUINS

William Blake believed he could see the universe in a grain of sand; likewise, if one meditates for long enough on Copán's hieroglyphics and ornate stelae, the mysteries which enshroud the Mayan universe may be drawn aside curtain-like.

Since the jungle began to reclaim it almost 800 years ago, Copán has been discovered and re-discovered several times over. When *conquistadores* invaded the area in the 15th century, they used Náhuatl-speaking *indígenas* as guides. Locals led the Spanish to what the Náhuatl called "Copantl," or "Place of the Wooden Bridge." Mrs. Malaprop intervened, and Copantl became Copán.

In 1839, John Lloyd Stephens became the next to stumble upon the ruins. The American liked what he found so much that he bought the ruins for the equivalent of US$50, and subsequently published *Incidents of Travel in Central America, Chiapas, and Yucatán,* which contains illustrations of Copán. Inspired by the site, Stephens waved away the bigoted theories popular in the 19th century. "America, say historians, was peopled by savages—but savages never reared these structures, savages never carved these stones," Stephens proclaimed. While Stephens's work sparked interest in the ruins, few scholars made the trip to Copán; only pillaging pot-poachers beat paths to the site.

Things began to change in 1952, when the Honduran Instituto Nacional Antropología e Historia took over the site. Scholars working under the Institute's auspices (and using UNESCO money) have radically changed the world's conceptualization of the Mayan world in general, and Copán in particular. It had previously been assumed that Mayan society was thoroughly theocratic, that Mayan culture and government revolved around priests and temples. Scholars believed Copán's functions were purely ceremonial—the structures still visible today were believed to be temples and the art which adorned the structures supposedly represented divine beings, while the hieroglyphics scrawled across them were thought to be no more than articulations of prophecies made using divination.

Over the last 25 years, Institute archaeologists have turned these tenets of conventional wisdom on their collective head. Scholars now believe that Mayan society, while deeply religious, was fundamentally secular. Copán wasn't merely a ceremonial center—perhaps as many as 15,000 ordinary Mayans lived and worked in the city. Its artwork is now thought to be of a political as well as of a religious nature, representing rulers and nobles, not just divine beings. Many hieroglyphics recorded not prophecies but historical events.

The city which the Maya called "Xukpi" for the ubiquitous black-crowned motmot bird was first settled nearly 2000 years ago. Situated in a fertile valley well suited to corn's cultivation, Copán grew slowly. The city's Golden Age occurred between 628 and 800; during those years, Copán was ruled by a series of strong leaders, all of whom had exceptionally cool names. Under Smoke Jaguar (628-695 AD), the 12th king of Copán, the city grew into a military powerhouse; by the time he died at age 82, Copán had swelled substantially. Next came 18 Rabbit (695-738 AD), who was captured and killed while battling his neighbors; 18 Rabbit was succeeded by Smoke Monkey, who ruled Copán for only 11 years (738-749 AD). The reign of Smoke Monkey's son, Smoke Shell (749-763 AD), was marked by unprecedented cultural flowering and academic learning. During his reign, Mayan astronomers met at Copán to pool their research on eclipses. Soon after Smoke Shell's death, things took a turn for the worse. For reasons not entirely clear to archaeologists, Copán ceased to be agriculturally self-sufficient. Forced to rely on foodstuffs shipped down the Copán River by satellite settlements, Copán's power waned, and by about 1100 AD, the lush vegetation of the jungle started to reclaim Copán. For the sake of modern tourists and scholars, the vines and trees have recently been swept aside, and Copán, obscured for so long, has been allowed to re-assert itself.

A trip to the ruins is best begun with a visit to the **Museo Copán** (tel. 98-34-37), in the town square; the 30-lempira ticket covers admission to the museum, the ruins themselves, and Las Sepulturas (see below) at any time during the next two days. The museum sketches the contours of Mayan history and displays some artifacts from the site, including several that have been brought inside for preservation. Be sure to slip in the room with "El Brujillo" written on the doorjamb, just before the exit. A relatively complete Mayan (*sans* soft tissue) lies entombed with his pet *tortugas* (turtles). (Open daily 8am-4pm.)

The **entrance** to the ruins is a 15-minute walk 1km east of town; southwest of the entrance, look for the **Museum of Mayan Sculpture,** scheduled to open in December 1995. The museum will include a life-sized model of **Rosalila,** a temple that was later enclosed entirely by Temple 16. For obvious reasons, the inner temple, with its preserved paint, can't be shown to the public, but this excellent replica should give

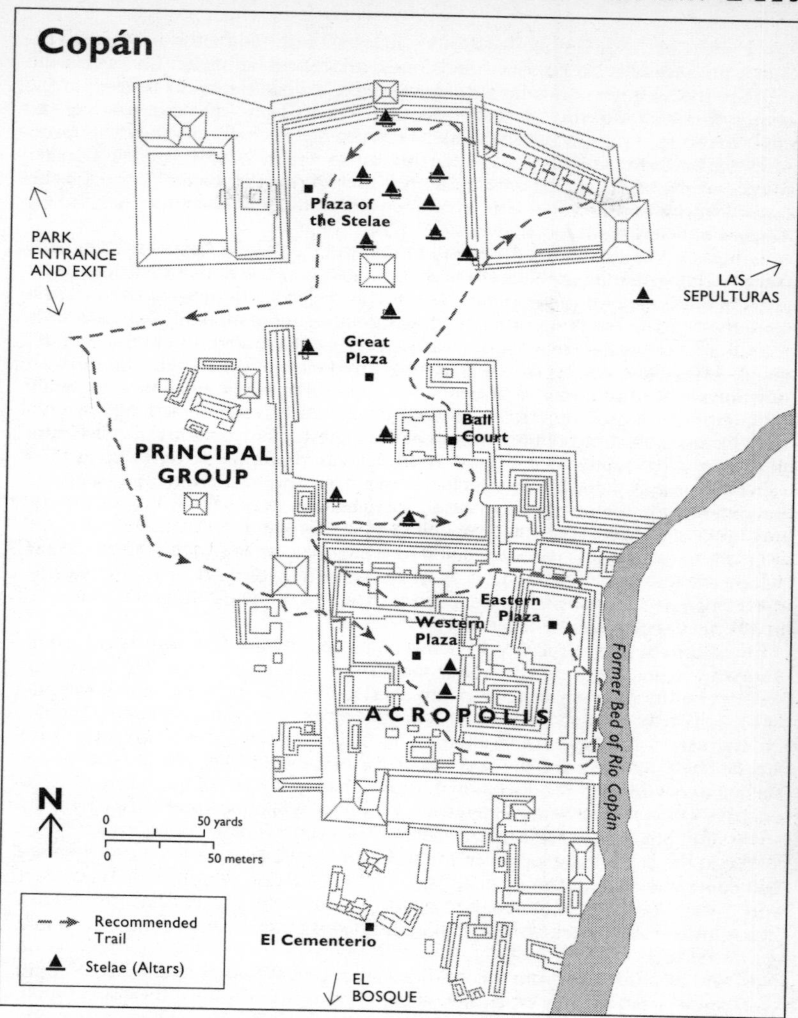

a feel for the brightness of Mayan architecture. In an attempt to mimic of the entrance atop the Plaza of Jaguars, admission to the museum will only be possible by walking through a serpent's mouth. Walk back toward the main ruins from the **visitor's center** (where you'll buy your ticket, if you haven't yet done so) and you'll pass a nature trail. The trail is short and essentially uninspiring, a pleasant time-killer but little more. If you walk the trail, avoid the thorny, rash-causing *chichicaste.*

The entrance to the ruins (where you present your ticket) is near the visitor's center. Collectively, the ruins are called the **Principal Group.** Keep in mind as you wander through them that the jungle is speckled with other stelae—rulers of Copán asserted their power by building monuments to themselves throughout the area. The suggested path through the main park takes you first to the elevated **Acropolis,** which is divided into the **west and east courts.** The west court includes **Temple 16,** where the ancient Rosalila was recently discovered, buried but entirely intact; needless to say, archaeologists are in a frenzy to uncover all they can. The famous **Altar**

Q is also at the site of Temple 16, its sides guarded by 16 elaborately costumed men sitting on piles of what appear to be stones. Recent research has shown that the men are the 16 governors who successively ruled Copán during its history. In the center, Yax-Kuk Mo, the city's first ruler, passes a baton—and control over the city—to the 16th ruler, Yax-Pac. Nestled between the rulers is a glyph which represents the long-ago date, July 2, 763 BC, the day on which Yax-Pac became Copán's ruler. **Temple 11,** also in the west court, was built during the reign of Yax-Pac as his door-to-worlds-beyond and boasts an ornately decorated staircase which leads to the **Temple of Inscriptions,** notable for its glyphs.

In the east court, diminutive **Temple 22** sits atop the **Plaza of Jaguars.** The importance of this structure, at the north end of the east court, is not immediately apparent. On either side of the entrance lie what look like small tusks of stone. These were the fangs of a serpent, through whose mouth entered thoughtful devotees. On the left is a fascinating **stela,** illustrating the cycles of life and death. In the center, a female leg leads to what is clearly an opening to the birth canal; to the left lurks the newborn baby. The upper right contains a representation of an adolescent, while the bottom right presents a full-grown man. Ominously, each depiction is perched atop a large skull, representing the end of the mortal sojourn. A similar stela (featuring a man's leg) stands to the right. Mortality is an omnipresent *leitmotif* at these ruins—the turtles depicted in the Great Plaza have two heads: one represents life, the other death. Invincible, eternally youthful backpackers will likely miss the majesty of the message—wise folks may well empathize with the Maya.

From the Acropolis, the path leads to the grassy, stela-studded **Great Plaza.** Adorned with the glyphs found at Tikal and Palenque, **Stela A** provides evidence that Copán had at least some contact with these distant cities. **Stela B** was erected in 695 AD to celebrate the ascension of 18 Rabbit.

The southern part of the Great Plaza is dominated by the 10m-high **Hieroglyphic Stairway,** which is covered by a large tarp. The stairway's 63 steps are carved with well over a thousand intricate inscriptions. Decoded, the steps become something of a history text, relating the story of Copán's battles with nearby Quirigua, and noting the dates of the ascension and death of all of Copán's rulers up to the 15th, Smoke Shell, who erected the stairway. Together, the 2500 glyphs are the longest single inscription ever produced by the Maya. Just to the left of the stairway, workers have excavated several hidden tombs; tourists willing to hear a sales pitch for some authentic artifact-replicas are generally allowed to enter.

Also in the Great Plaza, between the stelae and the stairway, is the well-preserved **ball court,** the second largest built by the Maya (see Central America: Mayan Marvels, page 37). The detailed carving and the excellent condition of the macaw heads, once used to keep score, distinguish Copán's ball courts from others in *el mundo maya.*

A 2-km hike due east from the visitor's center lie **Las Sepulturas,** ruins of upper-class residences currently under investigation by archaeologists. The striking sculpture known as El Brujo (The Witch), now on display in the Museo Copán, was originally found in this residential area of the ruins. Also worth a visit are **Los Sapos,** where the women of Copán were thought to have retreated to give birth. The structures you see are stoned frogs. Los Sapos are a 45-minute walk from the Principal Group, and the site is accessible by horseback.

The key to getting a free tour is to buy a couple bags of cookies from the market (no more than 10 lempiras) before heading out to the ruins. The place is swarming with caretakers and excavators who know more than most of the guides. In exchange for a few cookies (or lempiras), they'll give the full story of the ruins. Enough cookies may even buy entrance to the temples, although such access is officially prohibited. Tours are entirely in Spanish. Alternatively, the workers are also happy to introduce their friendly simian Pancho, a spider monkey who loves candy and doesn't mind human attention; his tours are a bit less informative, however.

Guides hired at the visitor's center are US$20 for two hours, but groups can pool together. For a trip to Los Sapos, **Go Native Tours** (tel. 98-34-32) offers English guided tours for US$25 per person, US$20 per person for groups of two, and US$15 per person for groups of three or more. Prices are cheaper if you take the tour in Spanish. Instead, you might choose to use their horses and forget about the guide; it'll cost you US$10 for four hours per horse, and Go Native can tell you how to get to Los Sapos. They also rent mountain bikes for 10 lempiras per hour or 50 lempiras per day, as well as inner tubes for 10 lempiras per day.

The mountains near Copán Ruinas are full of great places to ride, and the well-connected kids in the park can find good horses for neighry a lempira (unless you want to tip). Make sure to get a guide or detailed directions; spending a lonely night in a forest full of giant, ancient frogs could induce some most disturbing nightmares.

■■■ SAN PEDRO SULA

San Pedro has always stood in front of things. Geographically, the city of San Pedro Sula sprawls along La Cordillera del Merendón, the eminent mountains to the west. But like the "sula" (dove) in its name, the city also has a tradition of soaring ahead. Founded in 1536, the city grew only moderately at first, but by the end of the 19th century its banana boom had turned behemoth, a process facilitated by the development of railroads. The spirited commerce attracted Arab and European immigrants, vaulting San Pedro to the fore of Honduras's economy and industry. Today's San Pedro bristles with capitalism, commerce, and people, but seems in many ways to have gotten ahead of itself. The 800,000 residents and thousands of transient workers daily bump elbows and other body parts as the city is frenetically stretched to its limits. The urban-ness hasn't made things more urbane: while luxury hotels, fax machines, and a lone Burger King gild the city with a prosperous sheen, poverty lies just beneath the surface, and petty crime is on the rise. Meanwhile, high-energy San Pedro suffers from frequent power outages—in 1994, the nearby hydroelectric dam was periodically constipated by sediment washing down from deforested lands, and drought led officials to cut off the water supply entirely in the summer of 1995.

Of course, the advantageous result of all this commotion is a city full of action and intensity, a stark contrast to the sleepy regions nearby. Travelers desperate for a break from the rural and rustic can relish the diversity and further appreciate that uncanny Honduran ability to stand up to adversity with wit and savvy.

ORIENTATION AND PRACTICAL INFORMATION

San Pedro Sula's streets form a grid around the central train station. From the center, east-west *calles* and north-south *avenidas* extend outward into four quadrants—NO (northwest), NE (northeast), SO (southwest), and SE (southeast). Thus, 6a Calle and 4th Av. SO is six blocks west and four blocks south of the central point. The **Circunvalación** runs around the city, and 5a SO is sometimes called Av. Lempira. Notable landmarks are the **Parque Central** and the **plaza,** both between 1a and 3a Calles and 2a and 3a Avs. SO. Most hotels and the bus station are in the SO quadrant. The mountains, with their Big Brother-like Coke sign, lie to the west. If going past about 7a Calle, use street signs to count blocks: Intersections outside the central area tend to lack signs, an ulcer- and sweat-inducing omission. Locals warn that east of the railroad tracks and south of 7a Calle are the dangerous parts of town.

Tourist Office: Unofficially, Jorge Molanphy, at **Maya Tropic Tours** (tel. 52-24-05 and 52-54-01) in the lobby of the Gran Hotel Sula, will help budget travelers in need, even though his tours are a bit beyond budget bounds. He is bilingual and exceptionally cool; look for him Mon.-Fri. 7:30-11:30am and 1:30-5:30pm, Sat. 7:30-11:30am. Officially, there are two offices: **Instituto Hondureño de Turismo** (tel. 52-30-23; fax 57-60-01), 3rd floor of the **Edificio Inmosa,** 4a Calle between 3a and 4a Avs. NO; look for the DHL Courier sign. Maps of Honduras, bus schedules, and information on other parts of the country. Open Mon.-Fri. 8am-4pm. Next door, the **Oficina de Cultura** has information regarding cultural goings-on, although it's mainly for Hondurans. Open Mon.-Fri. 8am-4pm.

Police: Right next to the post office. Open 24 hrs.

Post Office: (tel. 52-31-83), 3a Av. between 9a and 10a Calles SO. Posts a *lista de correos.* Open Mon.-Fri. 7:30am-8pm, Sat. 8:30am-noon. **Express mail** service next door at **E.M.S. Honduras** (tel. 57-07-07). A 2kg package takes 3-4 days to the U.S. (230 lempiras). Open Mon.-Fri. 7am-5pm, Sat. 7am-2pm. The **postal code** for the city is by sector: **NE,** 21101; **NO,** 21102; **SE,** 21103; **SO,** 21104.

Telephones: Hondutel (tel. 57-22-22; fax 52-49-23), 4a Av. and 4a Calle. A separate room for AT&T Direct calling card and collect service to the U.S. Otherwise, prices to the U.S. vary by state. **Faxes** (17 lempiras per page to the U.S., 23.50 lempiras per page to Europe) and **telegrams** (.70 lempiras per word to the U.S.). Open 24 hrs., but you may have to bang on the door to wake up the guard. Fax and telegram services are open 7am-7pm and 7am-5pm respectively.

Consulates: There is no U.S. consulate in San Pedro Sula. **British Consulate** (tel. 53-26-00), 4a Calle between 4a and 5a Avs. NO, 2nd floor. Open Mon.-Fri. 7:30-11:30am and 1:30-5:30pm. **Guatemalan Consulate** (tel. 53-35-60), 8a Calle between 5a and 6a Avs. NO. Open Mon.-Fri. 8am-2pm.

Currency Exchange: It's easier to change cash than traveler's checks in the park with the people that yell *"dólares."* Be persistent, and compare rates. Almost every bank is open Mon.-Fri. 9am-3pm. **Banffaa,** next to American Express in the southern shadow of the cathedral, is open until 4pm, for the perpetually late. Plan ahead. **Creditlan** (tel. 53-48-00; fax 53-48-02), 3a Av. between 1a and 2a Calles NO. Cash advances on Visa credit cards. Open Mon.-Fri. 9am-3pm, Sat. 9am-noon.

American Express: Mundirama Travel Agency (tel. 53-01-92; fax 57-90-22), 2a Calle between 2a and 3a Avs. SO, on the south side of the cathedral. Same-day replacement of lost traveler's checks; they'll give up to US$1000 a month for personal checks. Card-holder's service. English spoken. Open for AmEx service Mon.-Fri. 8-11:30am and 1:30-2pm, and Sat. 8am-noon.

Airport: Villeda Morales sits about 15km out of town. The airport is accessible by cab for 50 lempiras (ask around), or by taking an "El Progreso"-bound bus to the airport exit, and hoping that a cab comes by to take you the last few kms. **Isleña Airlines** (tel. 52-83-22) flies to La Ceiba (twice daily Mon.-Sat., 1 hr., 164 lempiras), or to Roatán (twice daily, 1¼ hrs., 295 lempiras). **Taca** (tel. 53-26-49) flies to Tegucigalpa (daily at 5pm, 1 hr., 120 lempiras).

Buses: Most bus terminals are located in the SO sector, although discovering the exact location of each terminal can be hellish. **Saenz** (tel. 53-18-29), 9a Av. and 9a-10a Calles SO, to Tegucigalpa (15 a day, 2am-5:30pm, 4 hrs., 20 lempiras); their ultra-deluxe bus leaves from 8a Av. and 5a Calle (80 lempiras includes a meal, drinks, and TV). **Catisa,** from the parking lot at 2a Av. between 5a and 6a Calles SO, goes to La Lima (every 6min., 5am-10pm, 30min., 1.30 lempiras) and to El Progreso (every 20min., 30min., 2.70 lempiras). From El Progreso, you can snag a bus to Tela. **Etumi**, 6a Av. and 6a Calle SO, runs to Copán (11am and 1pm, 5 hrs., 20 lempiras). To get to the border at Agua Caliente, service rotates irregularly between 2 lines: **Sonotran,** 4a Calle, 2a Av. SE, and **Transporto Congolón,** 8a Av. between 9a and 10a Calle SO (6½ hrs., about 40 lempiras, schedule varies; ask the companies). **Toritos y Copanecos,** 6a Av., 8a and 9a Calles SO goes to Sta. Rosa de Copán (every 25min., 3:45am-5:15pm, 3 hrs., 13 lempiras) with 2 direct buses (8:30am and 2pm, 2 hrs., 20 lempiras). **CITUL,** 6a Av., 7a and 8a Calles SO, goes to Puerto Cortés (every 30min., 5:30am-7pm, 70min., 5 lempiras).

Taxis: They're everywhere. Rides within the city are 6-10 lempiras.

Laundromat: Lavandería Almich (tel. 53-16-87), 5a Calle between 9a and 10a Avs. SO. Open Mon.-Fri. 8-11:30am and 1-5pm, Sat. 8am-noon. Most hotels will clean your clothes for about 1 lempira per piece.

English Bookstore: Coello Bookstore, at the corner of 9a Av. and 4a Calle SO, has a tolerable English section (open Mon.-Fri. 8am-5:30pm, Sat. 8am-5pm).

English Library: Centro Cultural Sampedrano, 3a Calle between 3a and 4a Av. NO. Extensive collection includes books, mags, and those calculus textbooks you've been longing for. Open Mon.-Fri. 8am-noon and 1-6pm, Sat. 9am-noon.

Pharmacies: To find out which pharmacy is open late or on the weekend, go to any pharmacy, the tourist office, or the police station. Or, call Hondutel's 192

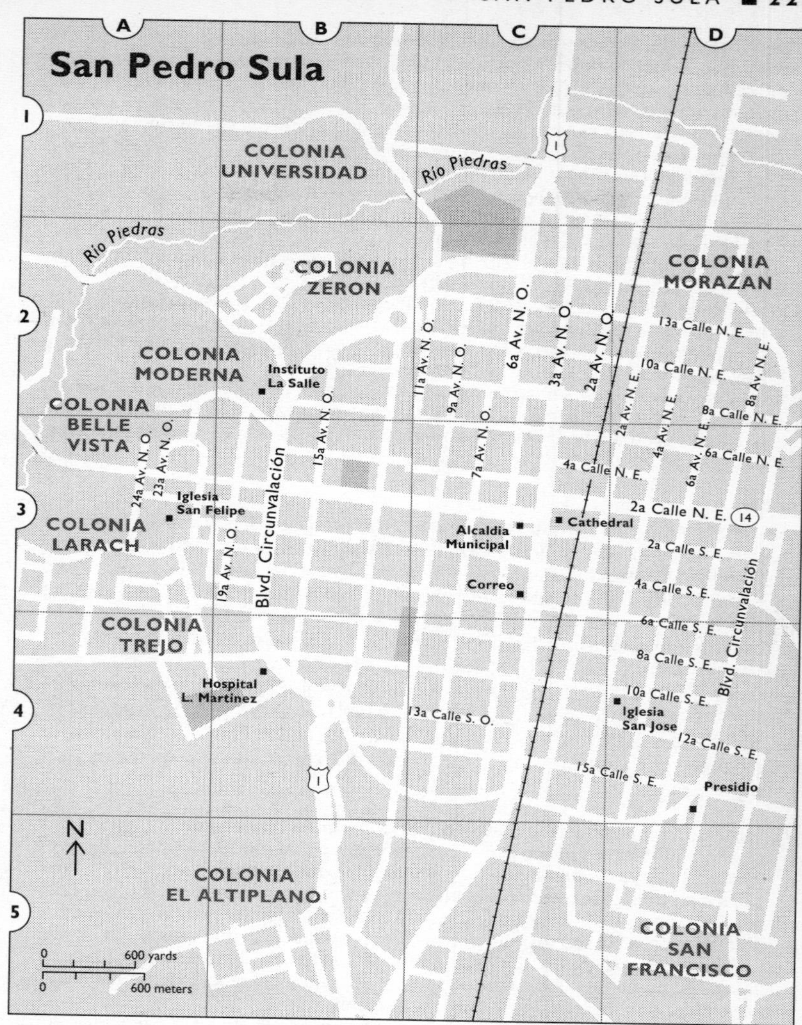

information number. Most pharmacies, like **Farmacía Siman** (tel. 52-06-24) next to the bookstore, take credit cards.

Hospital: Cemesa (tel. 52-74-01), Calle Altamira 21-22a, Blvd. del Sur. 24-hr. emergency service.

Emergency numbers: Dial 199; for firefighters, call 198.

ACCOMMODATIONS

San Pedro's hotel architects must have been a generous breed; it's hard to find a room that doesn't dwarf whatever little bed sits in it. Fans are a must. The SO quadrant is convenient to the bus terminals and bursts with cheap rooms. Unfortunately, many of these 25-lempira "bargains" are afflicted with lumpy beds and rank-smelling shared bathrooms. The hospedajes seem particularly risky.

HONDURAS

Hotel Brisas de Occidente (tel. 52-23-09), 5a Av. at 7a Calle SO. Massive rooms with pseudo-marble floors would be a great place to host a dance party for all the international backpackers who stay here; just slide your bed aside and push that cute, ornamental desk out of the way. Ask for one of the breezy top-floor rooms. Common bath. Luggage storage. Reservations accepted. Check-out noon. Singles 28 lempiras, doubles 35 lempiras, triples 50 lempiras.

Hotel San José (tel. 57-1208), 6a Av. between 5a and 6a Calles SO. A bit pricey, but large, super-clean rooms and comfy beds are well worth it. Look out for those teal bookshelves. TV and *agua purificada* in the lobby. Single with double bed 53.50 lempiras, with A/C 86 lempiras, doubles 64 lempiras, with A/C 96 lempiras, triples 86 lempiras, *con aire* 107 lempiras. Married couples pay only the single rate, so act fast and wed your travel partner.

Hotel Porto Alegre (tel. 57-21-88), 5a Calle at 2a Av. NE. Big, clean rooms with tidy bathrooms, private bath, and c-c-c-cold water. Pricey, but a decent deal for two willing to share a bed. Check-out noon. 1-bed doubles 60 lempiras, 2-bed doubles 100 lempiras, 3-bed room 140 lempiras.

Hotel Brisas de Copán, 6a Av. at 6a Calle SO. Incense-tainted office and smothering, infernally hot rooms make you wish there were a breeze. By all means, move that fan closer to the bed. Check-out noon. Singles 30 lempiras, doubles 35 lempiras, triples 50 lempiras.

FOOD

San Pedro is stuffed to the gills with restaurants, foodstands, and cafés; there's no reason not to go and get stuffed yourself. Although much of the food is expensive, careful *mochileros* (backpackers) can still squeak by eating local food, though some of the stuff peddled on the streets can wreak havoc on the bowels. When picking from the vendors' entrees, avoid the Winchester goose. Restaurants tend to be safer. For that fearsome American **fast-food** fix, head to the cluster (with Wendy's and Burger King) at 4a Av. and 3a Calle SO; the Pizza Hut (delivery tel. 57-83-83) next to the soccer stadium has a decent (and clean! Clean!) salad bar (all-you-can-eat for 24 lempiras), perhaps a welcome change for grease-laden palates. Fresh fruit can be purchased at the *mercado,* at 7a Calle and 4a Av. SE, and at **Mercado Guamilito** at 6a Calle between 8a and 9a Avs. On the weekends, food stands pop up throughout the Parque Central.

Cafetería Mayan Way (tel. 57-08-10), at 6a Av. between 4a and 5a Calles SO. A favorite with locals and travelers, this place serves up cheap, delicious plates of *típico* dishes. *Ranchero*-style eggs, beans, plantain, tortillas, 14 lempiras. Pork chops with fries, salad, beans, and plantain 18 lempiras. Open Mon.-Sat. 7am-1am.

Pizzería Italia (tel. 53-00-94), 1a Calle and 7a Av. NO. Elbow pads around the bar let you comfortably drown your sorrows in some delicious thin-crust pizza. While they don't have parmesan, the Satan's Salsa spices up any slice. Grubbin' ham and sausage pizza (enough for 1 or 2 people) 25 lempiras. Lasagna 25 lempiras. Vegetarian pizza 32 lempiras. Open daily 10am-11pm.

Café Skandia (tel. 52-99-99), in the lobby of the unavoidable Gran Hotel Sula. An eerie 50s soda-fountain feel, coupled with Western-style food and chilly A/C makes this a favorite with wealthy tourists. Icy fruit drinks (9 lempiras), ice cream (11 lempiras), and cheeseburgers (21 lempiras). Open 24 hrs., but at 3am the A/C isn't such a big deal.

Bigos, 1a Calle at 6a Av. More like a 50s burger hop than the tire shop it sounds like. A marvelous multiplicity of meaty burgers. They're not quite as good at marketing, however: their tasty *pollobigo* (chicken burger, 12.40 lempiras) isn't on the menu. Burgers 9-15 lempiras. Open Mon.-Thurs. 8am-1am, Fri.-Sun. 8am-4am.

SIGHTS AND ENTERTAINMENT

San Pedro Sula's pride and joy is the brand new **Museo de Antropologia e Historia** (tel. 57-14-96), at 3a Av. between 3a and 4a Calles NO. Dedicated in January, 1994, the museum is the city's first, and the whole nation is justifiably proud. The modern building is home to permanent and temporary exhibit space, a library, a lab for working archaeologists, and a massive theater which recently welcomed the Kiev ballet on its first visit to Honduras. The museum's top floor displays artifacts from the Paya and Jicaque, indigenous peoples who once dominated western Honduras. Ceramics, cooking tools, and other chronologically arranged pieces impart a sense of what life was like between the Archaic Period (circa 3500 BC) and the Conquest. Weapons and colorful paintings provide a window on the region's colonial era. Smaller exhibits on themes such as 19th-century cockfighting and the role of cacao in Honduran cuisine round out the picture. A final exhibit focuses on the imperialists and immigrants who had an important influence on San Pedro's development.

The whole exhibit is in Spanish, and none of the regular guides speak English. The director speaks English, though, and occasionally leads tours for large groups. Come to the museum in the afternoon; before lunch, the joint is packed with hordes of frenzied schoolchildren not yet learned in the fine art of museum etiquette (open Tues.-Sat. 10am-4pm, Sat. 10am-6pm; admission US$2 for foreigners).

Beyond the museum, San Pedro offers only a handful of attractions of interest to tourists. Though morbid, the town **cemetery,** at 5a Av. and 11a Calle SO, is a place where you can rest in peace between the large, intriguing tombs built for San Pedro's founding fathers and mothers.

The immense yet reserved **cathedral** squats solidly at the northeast end of the park, and is worth the time (10min.) and money (0 lempiras) required to tour it and see its remarkably modern iconography. The pew-fuls full of *sanpedranos* use the cathedral to escape two awful heats: hell-fire and the summer sun.

Apart from being a good source of chow, the Mercado Guamilito (see Food, above) plays host to the **Asociación Nacional de Artesanos de Honduras.** Go there to meander through rows and rows of *artesanía* goodies, including wood carvings, inexpensive bayonets, and carefully crafted ceramics.

Another easy hour-killer is to take a taxi to the **Mirador Bella Vista,** a point next to the Coca-Cola sign on the mountain that offers a prodigious view of the city and valley on clear days (round-trip 40 lempiras). Be sure to specify "Mirador" to the cabbie, since "Bella Vista" is also the name of a posh neighborhood only halfway there.

For evening entertainment, there are several movie theaters around town; check the paper for listings. Head to the **Teatro Colombia,** located on 5a Av. between 3a and 5a Calles, if you want to tell your grandkids you saw movies for less than a buck (6 lempiras). The theater is starting to lean toward porn, but sometimes shows classic martial arts movies by both Chuck Norris *and* Bruce Lee. Grab balcony seats (the pricier ones), as drunk locals sometimes throw **bags of urine** and other liquids on eager viewers below. For more current movies (also with Spanish subtitles), check the paper for theaters and showtimes. The **cines** cluster in the NO quadrant near the soccer stadium (admission 10-12 lempira).

Later at night, San Pedro's chic set heads out to any of the several **discotecas** scattered about town. All discos have a minimal dress code (no shorts, t-shirts, or sandals), and it's standard to be frisked upon entry. (Virtually all clubs are open Mon.-Sat. 6pm-4am.) The hippest spot in town is **Confetti's,** on the Circunvalación near the Puerto Cortés exit, where an I-just-turned-twenty crowd pays 30 lempiras to shake to modern disco hits on a petite dance floor (beer 13 lempiras). (Open Tues.-Sun. from 7pm on; Wed. is Ladies' Night.) **Henry's,** just up the street (about 2 blocks west on the Circunvalación), offers stiff competition—same action for the same prices. Bored economists may want to explore this phenomenon more carefully.

For a high concentration of bars and dance floors, head to the **Zona Viva,** centered at 10a Calle and 15a Av. Some start their evenings with cocktails at bars such as **Fantasy's** (1 block south and 1 west of the corner) or **Tom Collins,** where you can slurp down a you-know-who seated in relaxing wicker chairs. As far as discos go, **Bar Paradise** is the spot. A dressy crowd (some men wear ties) increasingly comprised of Pretty People sways to pop classics and the newest hits (cover 20 lempiras). Next door is the **Club Copacabana** (cover 30 lempiras; mixed drinks 12-15 lempiras), and around the corner is **Terraza's,** at the main Zona Viva intersection, where an older crowd dances to Latin ballads under a disco ball (cover 20 lempiras).

Women in particular should be warned that city bars are a potent breeding ground for *machismo.* Go with people you trust (not alone), keep your judgment clear, and dance defensively.

San Pedro Sula is nationally famous for its month-long **Feria Juniana** (Fair of June). Dating back to 1846, the festival used to include a tennis tournament, marathon, even a party in the city jail, sponsored by the "San Pedro Sula Ladies." During the week-long party these days, Garifuna dancers, drum corps, and pre-pubescent beauty queens (see gray box, below) parade down the street. Vendors and food booths stay open late as merry-makers enjoy themselves into the wee hours. Grab a silly cardboard mask and join the fun.

"Young and sweet, only 17"

Even after all the kegs of Salva Vida are kicked, the conch-shell bands have marched by, and the marimbas have chimed their last mellow tones, no Honduran party is deemed done until the proudest and most elite, the beauty queens, are finally allowed to strut their stuff. While the glory of beauty pageantry elsewhere in the world has waned, most Central Americans continue unabashedly to prize the prettiest and neg the most napiform of their women. Or should we say girls? Indeed, competitions are held for girls as young as eight years old. The children aren't subjected to the "Best Legs" bouts familiar to their older counterparts, but do occasionally participate in swimsuit competitions. Most beauty contests are fierce, since the winners earn instant status and advance from the local ("Miss Utila") up to the national and international levels. Commonly, local businessmen and politicians act as judges, giving marks in such categories as hairstyle, swimwear, and responses to questions about political and economic issues, all of which help to indicate the winning beauty's diplomatic virtues.

■ NEAR SAN PEDRO SULA

WATERFALLS

As soon as the urban urge begins to wane, it's probably time to wax waterfall-adventurous and head to the **Catarata Pulhapanzak.** (Hondurans have added lexical bang to the more moderate *cascada* and have come up with *catarata,* which is a wicked *big* waterfall—a "cataract.") Whatever you call it, Pulhapanzak's falls plummet from a 15m cliff, and the area's swimming spots make for a pleasant daytrip.

The best way to do the waterfall is to grab an over-eager *niñito* (wanna-be tour-guide) and head down the steep path. Note that part of the trail involves using tree roots as a ladder—it's not a trivial descent, but the reward is great. The spray is refreshing, and a small pool to the left (facing the waterfall) is popular for swimming. Oddly, children tend to swim in a section of the river directly upstream from the powerful crashing of the falls, but it's reportedly safe. Refreshing as the water is, you're unlikely to be the only visitor; the joint jumps with picnickers, particularly on hot weekends. There's a snack shop, but it's overpriced. They serve *tortillas con queso* for 7 lempiras, and hamburgers for 10 lempiras. The site also contains barbecue areas and bathrooms.

To reach the falls, board a bus in San Pedro at 1a Av. between 4a and 5a Calles SO, headed toward Río Lindo (every 40min., 7am-5pm, 1¾ hrs., 6.50 lempiras). These buses often go beyond the falls, so tell your driver in advance where you want to get off. Return buses to San Pedro Sula leave about every half-hour during daylight hours. Keep your eyes peeled for the sign on the left side of the road—the drivers often forget to stop, even when asked. Once out of the bus, take the main, concrete road through town. After just under 1km, the road forks. Go left, up the hill for several hundred more meters—the *balneario* (baths) is on the right.

Nearby signs lead to **Las Gradas** as well, but this *cascada* is measly in comparison; still, if the crowds at the main falls get your goat, there are picnic tables in minigazebos at Las Gradas that rent for 20 lempiras each. Otherwise, it's probably not worth the 5-10 minute walk (admission 5 lempiras).

LA LIMA

For those driven absolutely bananas by the overabundance of untamed wilderness, **La Lima,** 15km outside San Pedro, is a center of activity in that zany fruit's industry. La Lima is home to several *plantas* (processing plants) and *fincas* (banana plantations), including the **Chiquita plant,** which is open for visitors to observe the very intricate process of banana preparation. In a *planta,* someone cuts bananas off the stem, others stick thermometers into them to classify them, while others simply pack them together. A somewhat similar cutting, collecting, and covering ritual can be observed on the *fincas.* A visitor's pass is required for entrance to either, and these are obtainable at the **Tela Railroad Company** (tel. 68-28-07) and at **Compañería Agricola Río Tinto** (tel. 68-22-25), both in La Lima. There's only one problem: only the head honchos (*gerentes*) can sign the pass, and they're often gone in the afternoon. It's best to go in the morning and get a pass, which can be used all day. (Everything's open Mon.-Fri. 6am until about 5pm.)

To get there, take a La Lima or El Progreso bus from San Pedro, telling the driver, conductor, and all your neighbors on the bus that you want the *planta de Chiquita.* Watch for the watertower with the Chiquita seal; dismount once you get there.

THE CARIBBEAN COAST

■■■ PUERTO CORTÉS

In the 19th century, investors plunged millions into a plan to construct a railroad from the Caribbean through the isthmus to San Lorenzo on the Pacific; Puerto Cortés was to be the entry point on the Atlantic, and so reasonably expected to turn into a Honduran version of Panama City, rich in culture and bursting with trade. The railroad scheme failed, but Puerto Cortés wasn't left behind completely. These days, the city comes up short on the stunning-site tally, but it sees more than its share of imports and exports as the largest port in Honduras, and as one of the largest on the Atlantic coast of Central America. Still, most travelers spend much more time *near* the city than actually *in* it, mostly because of the fascinating, nearby **Fortaleza de Omoa** and the beaches at **Garifuna villages,** also nearby. Duty-free shops are nice, but the chance to live free of duties on the alluring beaches prompts classic action-flick advice: "There is nothing to see here; please disperse."

ORIENTATION AND PRACTICAL INFORMATION

The town bends around with the port. The *avenidas* run parallel to the coastline, and 1a Avenida (*la primera*) runs along the shore. The *calles* intersect them, starting with 1a calle at an arbitrary point at the northern tip of town. The **Parque Central** sits between 2a and 3a Avs. at 4a Calle. You're holding the closest thing to a **tourist office** in this town. The **police** (tel. 55-04-49, no English) are ready to serve 24 hours a day at 1a Av. and 9a Calle (stationed at the south end of town). **Currency and traveler's checks** can be exchanged at **Banco Atlantida,** 2a Av. between 3a and 4a Calle. They also give cash advances on Visa (open Mon.-Fri. 9am-4pm, Sat. 8am-11am). The **post office** (tel. 55-04-55) awaits at the corner of 1a Calle and 2a Av. (open Mon.-Fri. 8am-noon and 2-5pm, Sat. 8am-noon). As usual, they've got *lista de correos* and an **EMS** (tel. 55-04-54) next door. **Hondutel** (tel. 55-00-59; fax 55-00-44) reaches out and touches someone, namely the post office (open 24 hrs. for calls). **Fax** and **telegrams** are available there (Mon.-Fri. 7am-noon and 2-5pm, Sat. 7-11am). **Buses** cluster around the park and 3a Calle at 3a Av. Most go to San Pedro Sula (every 30min., 2am-7pm, 30-90min., 5 lempiras). They also head out to Omoa (every 30min., 6am-7:30pm, 30min., 2 lempiras) and to the Garifuna villages (about 2 buses per day, 30min.), though this takes some patience and asking around. **Boats** leave regularly from the port, to Belize City and to the Bay Islands; ask around for specific trips.

Taxis roam the streets, but aren't necessary within the city (4-5 lempira); a cab costs 60 lempiras to **Bajamar** and to 30 lempiras to **Travesia.** The **Farmacia Cruz Rojo** eagerly awaits nauseous *gringos* at 2a Av. and 4a Calle, at the southeast corner of the park (open Mon.-Fri. 8am-6pm, Sat. 8am-noon). The different pharmacies take turns being open on Sunday. **Supermercado Corea** (tel. 55-11-82) stands prepared to sate shopping needs on 2a Av. between 2a and 3a Calles (daily from 7am-8pm). If not cured by the pharmacist, there's the **Hospital Cemeco** (tel. 55-04-60) at 5a Av. and 8a Calle (open 24 hrs. for emergencies).

ACCOMMODATIONS AND FOOD

There are some okay places to snooze if caught in Puerto Cortés, though lodging is perhaps better sought elsewhere. Expect prices to go *way* up during *Semana Santa.* Unfortunately, even in the low-tourist season, shabbies can cost 25 lempiras, and a decent room runs over 40 lempiras. The **Formosa Hotel,** located up 3a Av. four blocks north of the park, stands a little more prominently than its namesake, thanks to the absence of the P.R.C. in Puerto Cortés. The rooms are large and decent, but don't quite warrant swooning with joy (singles with bath 40 lempiras, doubles 40 lempiras, with bath 60 lempiras, with bath and A/C 100 lempiras). **Hotel Zanzibar** awaits just down the street at 3a Av. and 2a Calle. The stairs and hallways are springy like a trampoline, but too much jumping might break through the crumbling boards. Cheap is as cheap does (singles 25 lempiras, doubles 35 lempiras).

HONDURAS

Food in Puerto Cortés is a happier story. There are several *típica* places, such as **Buffet Irma** at 3a Calle and 3a Av. (*plato típico* 20 lempiras), which has a nice TV and A/C. Or head to **El Merendero,** at 2a Av. and 1a and 2a Calles; enjoy some *cena típica* (11 lempiras) while the baby depicted on the wall attempts to do the same. On the slightly more expensive side, who knew the King was married? **Burger Queen** (tel. 55-13-26) lives at 2a Av. between 8a and 9a Calles, and offers the Dumbo Queen (not elephant, but rather jumbo beef) for 14 lempiras, as well as lots of seafood. Open daily 8am-midnight. Farther north on 2a Av. are the semi-elegant **Candiles** and the **Cabaña,** where entrees run 20-100 lempiras.

SIGHTS AND ENTERTAINMENT

Haunted by paranoid delusions of vicious pirates storming your very soul? The **Fortress** (*Fortaleza*) **of San Fernando of Omoa** might be just the thing to comfort the insecure. Renowned throughout Honduras, this imposing stronghold was built from 1759-1775 as a bastion in the defense against pirates and the English Navy. In the 20th century, the fortress has failed to withstand the foreign onslaught—a sizeable number of tourists visit each year, and most aren't worried about scurvy. The site was declared a national monument on its 200th birthday, and a museum/visitor's center has been built in honor of the occasion. Start a tour at the museum after getting a general admission ticket (10 lempiras). The museum houses some fascinating swords and guns, as well as a cooking cauldron big enough to bathe in.

From the museum, the fortress itself is a brief walk away. The beautiful courtyard at the entrance is bordered by two sets of stairs and about 15 doorways. The rooms are worth investigating: some roost bats, some wear an iridescent green mold, and others contain many of the over 4000 still-remaining cannon balls. Step quickly and consistently on the stone floor for an *exact* acoustic representation of a mob of pirates running on the roof.

After exhausting the ground floor's entertainment possibilities, the roof is a perfect spot for a smuggled picnic (the sign says no food or drink—*Let's Go* does not recommend getting caught). The view is spectacular, the grassy areas comfy, and the gunholes full of potential for creative kicks. On the way back down, notice the extensive coral interred in the stairs and walls.

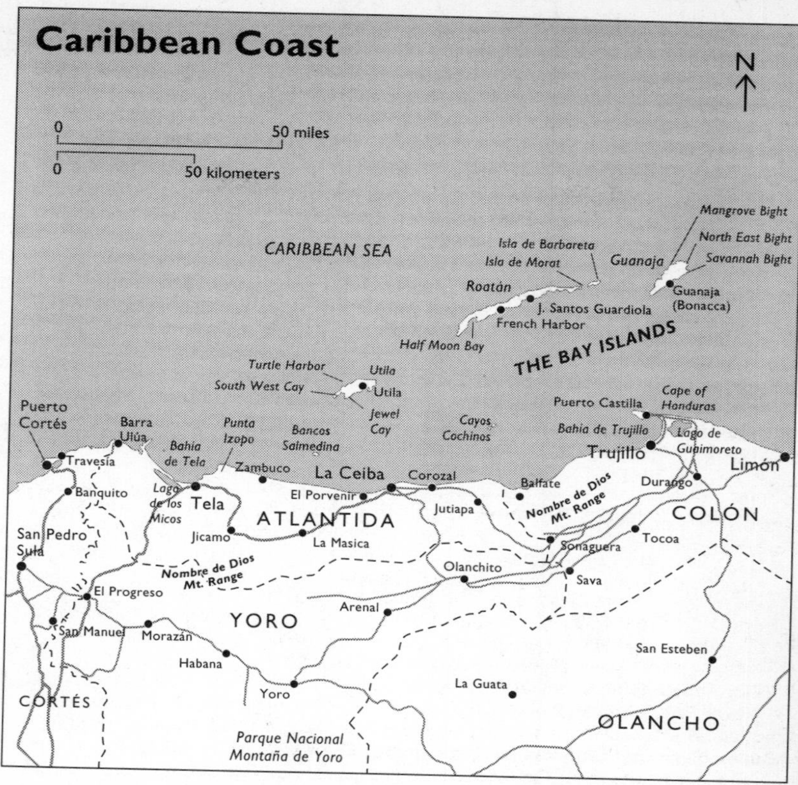

To get to the site, grab an Omoa bus from Puerto Cortés for two lempiras. Keep those eyes peeled for the Coca-Cola "Welcome to Omoa" sign; dismount about two blocks later. A paved road to the right runs about 1km to the site. If lost, just ask for the *Castillo* or the *Fortaleza.* The whole trip can be completed in 2½ hours.

Another option is to head for the Garifuna villages of **Travesia** and **Bajamar** to engage in time-honored relaxation rituals. Both sit along fine beaches and crystalline water; just grab a bus or a taxi in that direction and go. It's not easy to spend the night at either place, so make advance plans for returning on the same day.

In terms of in-town **nightlife,** Puerto Cortés's fun-lovers head to **Studio 54,** a disco, and to the good old **Cine.** Studio 54 is on the south end of 2a Ave, a few blocks past the Catholic school, and it's open Friday and Saturday from 9pm until everyone tires of twisting and turning. Cover is 20 lempiras, and a beer costs 7 lempiras. The *cine* is at the northeast corner of the park; relatively current films cost 10 lempiras.

■■■ TELA

Yes, we have no bananas, we have no bananas today.

—popular song of the 1920s

Tela has no bananas today—or at least a lot fewer than it used to. When the city was the principal port of the massive and powerful United Fruit Company, it exported tens of millions of sticky bunches each year. After a while, disease ravaged Tela's trees, but despite the banana's split, the city has hardly lost appeal. Tela (pop.

70,000) still exports more than its share of bananas, and city has cashed in on the tourist trade. Tela's choice beach-front location, the fresh seafood served in its restaurants, and its proximity to nature reserves and north coast Garifuna villages, now lure bands of backpackers with brain cells to kill and a suntan to snag.

ORIENTATION AND PRACTICAL INFORMATION

Tela is divided into two sections. West of the **Río Tela** is **Tela Nueva; Tela Vieja** is east of the river. Two bridges span the river. Services are concentrated in Tela Vieja, while quieter Tela Nueva contains the Hotel Villas Telamar, a luxury resort that used to provide residences for the United Fruit Company's employees.

Tela's *calles* run east-west; their numbers increase as you head north. Occasionally numbered but typically named, *avenidas* run north-south. The sea is to the north. The main drag is **9a Calle,** and the central park is on 9a Calle between 5a and 6a Avs. Many hotels are near the bus station or along the street next to the beach.

Tourist Office: PROLANSATE (tel. 48-20-42; fax 48-20-42), across from Bancahsa on 9a Calle. The closest thing to a tourist office in town. Focuses on ecotourism and preservation of the local environment. They sell maps (mostly photocopies) of the town and nearby nature preserves. They also offer guided tours. English spoken. Mon.-Fri. 8am-noon and 1-5pm, Sat. 8am-noon.

Police: FUSEP (tel. 48-20-79), atop the stairs at the end of 7a Av. No English.

Currency Exchange: Bancahsa (tel. 48-21-77; fax 48-27-79), on the main street. Changes traveler's checks and gives cash advances on Visa cards. Open Mon.-Fri. 8-11:30am and 1:30-4:30pm, Sat. 8am-11:30am. Alternatively, try Ferdinand, an English-speaking Garifuna guy who changes traveler's checks at a rate just below the bank's. During the day, look for him 1 block east of the bank on 9a Calle.

Post Office: (tel. 48-20-94), a white building 2 blocks inland from 9a Calle, northeast on Av. Guatemala (4a Av.). Posts a *lista de correos.* Open Mon.-Fri. 7:30am-3:30pm, Sat. 7:30am-11:30am. **Postal code:** 31301.

Telephones: Hondutel (tel. 48-20-03, 48-22-99; fax 48-29-42), just past the post office. **Fax, telegrams,** AT&T USA Direct collect/calling card calls from booths 6, 7, and 8. Open daily 7am-9pm. Telegrams open Mon.-Fri. 8am-4pm, Sat. 8-11am.

Buses: Terminal Empresa de Transportes CITY, LTDA, at 9a Av., on 9a Calle. Daily departures to La Ceiba (every 30min., 4am-6pm, 2 hrs., 6.50 lempiras) and El Progreso (every 30min., 4:30am-6pm, 2 hrs., 5 lempiras). Buses leave El Progreso for San Pedro Sula until 6pm. Buses for Triunfo depart irregularly (about 4 buses per day, 20min., 2 lempiras; ask around at 10a Av. and 7a Calle).

Taxis: Intra-city taxis 4-5 lempiras. A ride to Lancetilla 20-30 lempiras.

Bike Rentals: A great way to reach nearby sites and villages. **Garifuna Tours,** on the southwest corner of the park, rents decent mountain bikes at a rate of 9 lempiras per hr., 18 lempiras per ½ day, 30 lempiras per whole day. Also, the souvenir shop at the **Hotel Villas Telamar** rents bikes for 5-8 lempiras per hr. and 30-50 lempiras per day, depending on the size of the bike.

Laundry: Lavandería El Centro is just up the street from the post office. They'll wash up to 12lbs. for 20 lempiras. Open Mon.-Sat. 8am-5pm, Sun. 8am-noon.

Red Cross: tel. 48-21-21.

Pharmacy: Farmacía Escalante, on 9a Av. To find out who's open late this week (7am-10pm), check lists on pharmacy doors or the sign at the corner of the park.

Medical Services: Clínica de Emergencias (tel. 48-24-56), 7a Av. in Barrio Centro, 1 block up from 9a Av., by the bus station. Some of the doctors speak English. Open 24 hrs. Also, **Hospital Tela Integrado** (tel. 48-20-51).

Emergency: Fire Dept. (tel. 48-23-50).

ACCOMMODATIONS

The types of tourists titillated by Tela tend to tan their terrific torsos tirelessly. Proximity to the beach, where sun and the cooling sea breeze await, is supremely important in choosing a hotel. Cheap deals can be found throughout Tela Vieja. Some people string a hammock between two of the beach's many palm trees. You can rent hammocks at **Cesar Mariscos** for 10 lempiras per day. Keep a close eye on your

HONDURAS

stuff. Those who like hiking may want to check out **Paradise Hotel,** a 40-minute trek west of the bridge on the beach. The *cabañas* rent for 10 lempiras per night.

Boarding House Sara (tel. 48-23-80), 1 block from the beach on the far east end. Inhabited almost entirely by international backpackers. Noisy rooms *sans* fans with common bathrooms that could use help. Spacious *cabañas* with fans, private bathrooms, and maybe even a kitchen. Across the street, 3 bars compete to see who can be loudest; Sara's beds vibrate to a pumping bass until well past 5am on weekends. The owner loves to speak English and to curse the noise. Check-out noon. Rooms 25 lempiras for 1 person, 40 lempiras for 2 people. *Cabañas* 60-100 lempiras; give a go at bargaining.

Hotel Playa, on the west end of the beach (the door's on the first street in). Some of its 15 ample rooms come with exotic curtains, which aid philosophical contemplation of the aged beds. Relatively serene rooms. Check-out noon. 25 lempiras per person.

Gran Hotel Miramar, at the west end of 9a Av., near the bridge. Dress up as a rook and play human-scale chess on the tile floor. The disco has an odd habit of convulsing to music. Singles with outhouse-like common bathrooms, 30 lempiras, and two can use one bed for the same price.

Hotel Tela (tel. 48-21-50), on 9a Av. near the epicenter of town. Pricey, but the massive adjoining restaurant conjures up the groovy feel of a 40s-era retirement home. Big, beautiful rooms outfitted with lamps, closets, and tables. Some rooms have hot water. Check-out noon. Singles 50 lempiras, doubles 70 lempiras.

Hotel/Salon Villas del Mar, ½ block west of the bus terminal. Cheaper than lunch. Become acquainted with bedsprings as never before. Rudimentary rooms with basic common bathrooms. Singles 15-20 lempiras, 1-bed doubles 20 lempiras, 2-bed doubles 60 lempiras.

FOOD

Restaurante Luces del Norte, 2 blocks toward the beach from the central park. A Canadian-owned travelers' favorite, this comfortable joint serves up hearty, tasty dishes. Breakfast 17-20 lempiras. Peanut-butter-and-banana sandwich 7 lempiras. Astounding shrimp soup 25 lempiras. Open daily 7am-10pm.

Oso Costero, on the main drag, 4 blocks west of the bridge in Tela Nueva. For travelers as hungry as bears, this coastal kinsman is prepared to serve excellent Honduran food at respectable prices. Full lunch with a soft drink comes to 14 lempiras. Vegetarian offerings and tasty fruit *frescos* available. Open Mon.-Thurs. 8am-midnight, Fri.-Sun. 'til everyone's asleep or sated.

Cafetería Hotel Villas Telamar, a pleasant beach hike from Tela Vieja. Attached to the Villas Telamar resort, but not to be confused with the Delfin on the dock. Breezy, patio-esque dining area and a menu that aims to please. Spaghetti 20 lempiras. Ecumenical seafood-kebab dinner 55 lempiras. Open daily 7am-11pm.

Cesar Mariscos, in the middle of the beach in Tela Vieja. A step above other beach restaurants in both price and quality. Shrimp in a fine garlic sauce 60 lempiras. Seafood soup 30 lempiras. Chicken creole 33 lempiras. Open daily 9am-10pm.

SIGHTS AND ENTERTAINMENT

The beauty of the beaches in and around Tela is that they provide few temptations to move a muscle. Snorkeling isn't terrifically popular, and no one indulges in calorie-depleting water sports; slothful relaxation on miles of powdery sand is all that's expected of you. The beach and water along Tela Vieja are somewhat silty and litter-strewn, but stretches of sand to the west are so beautiful that they seem like a travel brochure come to life. Head in the direction of Villas Telamar. For those moderately motivated (but not enough to leave the beach), **Garifuna Tours** (see page 236) rents wind-surfing equipment for 30 lempiras per hr. and 80 lempiras per half-day.

For 20 lempiras per day, non-guests of the **Hotel Villas Telamar** (tel. 48-21-96; fax 48-29-84) get full use of the facilities, which include a pool, jacuzzi, sauna, tennis courts, and a nine-hole golf course. The hotel also offers horseback riding (20 lempiras per hr., contact ext. 605, or go directly to Oscar Reyez's cabaña, #605).

When it comes to nightlife, Tela refuses to miss a beat. All day long, pumping tunes can be heard on virtually every block; as night falls, the beach bars metamorphose into discos. For live music on Sundays and for a mixed crowd seven days a week, head for the **Multi-Disco Napoles,** at the west end of 9a Av., near the bridge, which charges a minimal cover.

■ NEAR TELA

LANCETILLA BOTANIC GARDENS

The Lancetilla Botanic Gardens make an easy and pleasant daytrip from Tela. The gardens were developed by the United Fruit Company in 1925 to determine which fruits would grow well in Honduras and to preserve the region's diverse flora and fauna. The project was the brainchild of Wilson Popenoe, whose very name has the ring of an exotic fruit; as a result of Popenoe's efforts, visitors can see a staggering amalgamation of plant species quicker than you can say *Musa paradisiaca sapientum.* There are tons of cool things to check out: a long tunnel formed out of towering clusters of bamboo trees, a fresh swimming hole at the end of the main road, and 200 species of soaring and singing birds. Even without considering the metaphysical implications of each plant you see, simply walking around and taking deep whiffs of the cool, sweet air cleanses the spirit.

While the park is most easily reached by car or bike, hiking from Tela is possible. The entrance is along the main road to La Ceiba. From town, walk or bike to Nueva Tela, beyond the Instituto San Antonio, and turn left on the dirt road behind the golf course. Follow this road until you hit the main road; the gate is just across the way. Alternatively, hop on any bus leaving Tela and get off at the gate (inform the driver of your plans in advance). A taxi from Tela to the gate costs about 25 lempiras.

While the gate is 1.5km from town, the park is another 3.5km along a dirt road. Once you see buildings, head for the small house on the right. It houses the Visitors Center, where you can snag a three-lempira map with information in Spanish; also on sale are T-shirts and seeds for at-home experimentation. Refreshment stands are nearby. Questions can be answered at the Administrative Center (beyond the bamboo tunnel), where you can get permission to camp in the park. There are dorms, but these are primarily for large groups; ask and they might loan you a bed. (Gardens open Tues.-Fri. 7:30am-3:30pm, Sat.-Sun. 8:30am-4pm. Admission US$5 for foreigners. For more information, call COHDEFOR at 48-21-65.)

CANOEING TO MIAMI

For an awesome daytrip, rent a canoe from Garifuna tours (see Practical Information, above) and paddle to Miami (no, not *that* Miami), a Garifuna village west of Tela. A one-person canoe costs 50 lempiras for a full day, and for an extra 10 lempiras, the owners will take you all the way to Miami and arrange a time to pick you up. Wedged onto a strip of land bordering the sulfuric **Laguna de los Micos,** Miami is pure rhapsody, notable for its outrageously clean beaches and water. Residents live in small huts made of mangrove branches or *jagua* (palm-wood boards) and earn their living fishing from dugout canoes. The village is entirely undeveloped—three saline wells provide water for cleaning, and fresh water must be hauled in from a neighboring village—but there are a few tiny shops, modest restaurants, and coconut-bread bakeries where you can catch a bite to eat. From Miami, you can maneuver your canoe through canals and mangroves back to the lagoon, inhaling the tangy sulfuric mist. Listen along the shore for the rustling of white-faced monkeys, or just silently paddle toward the trees and see what animals appear.

PARQUE NACIONAL PUNTA SAL

Miami serves as a convenient base camp for forays into the gorgeous Punta Sal National Park further to the northwest, which is pictured on the 1995 Honduras telephone book. Go on, reach out and touch this captivating nature preserve, which is chock full of floral bounty and abundant fauna. From Miami, it's a 3½-hr. hike along the beach to the neck of a peninsula which terminates in a mini-archipelago. Near the neck are paths and a *cabaña* from which locals present morsels to hungry hikers. Camping can also be arranged with these people, although it doesn't seem to be necessary to gain permission. The preserve is full of infrequently encountered species, and has the rare and sad distinction of having a martyr for a founder. Naturalist Jeanette Kawas, the most ardent and eloquent defender of the preserves, was murdered in the spring of 1995. The government investigation ended quickly, without convictions, and many think that the killing was related to profiteers interested in developing the land. There is no legal proof, but much attention has been focused on the park of late.

Some travelers canoe or sea-kayak all the way to the park; others take a bus to Tornobé from Tela and then a truck to Miami, walking the rest of the way. If you go this way, it's best to start early, as none of the transport works after dark. The lazier option (but not less spectacular) is to take a tour (see Practical Information, above). **PROLANSATE** offers a tour that leaves at 7:30am, including ride and lunch, for 100 lempiras. For 120 lempiras, **Garifuna Tours** offers a similar tour, but they include snorkeling with gear and exclude lunch (although they take people to a *cabaña* for 20-lempira chow). For both tours, it's best to make a reservation the day before. For brave souls hiking in, local children often offer their services as travel guides for a nominal fee. Ask to see **Puerto Escondido,** an erstwhile pirates' refuge across the peninsula from the *cabaña,* to search for hidden treasure.

PUNTA IZOPO RESERVE

Standing at Tela's beach and looking out to the right over the ocean, you'll see the Refugio de Vida Silvestre Punta Izopo (Punta Izopo Reserve) extending out into the sea. One of Honduras's 77 wildlife preserves, the 28,000-acre reserve is home to a prodigious number of plant and animal species. Tuck back your lids and search for sea tortoises, toucans, and other colorful birds. The reserve attracts few visitors, so you're likely to get all the solitude you wish. The easiest way to get there is to take a bus from Tela to **Triunfo de la Cruz.** Once in Triunfo, go to the beach, turn right, and walk for 1½ hrs. There's a mini-lighthouse with a pretty view near the shore. The trick is to be creative and wander, using a compass. There are few trails and few established sites, so wander until bored and then head back. On the way are two rivers, which generally stop 10m before the sea. In the rainy season, you may have to doff hiking boots and walk 10m in the surf on the oceanside. Don't swim; the water's full of *aguas malas* (stinging jellyfish). Questions can be directed to PROLANSATE or to Garifuna Tours (which offer tours for 70 lempiras). Just row up the coast from Tela to the opening of a river, though inexperienced naturalists may want a guide—these rivers are thick with mangrove patches and can be confusing.

■■■ LA CEIBA

Once upon a time, the feather in La Ceiba's cap was a tree—a whopping, umbrella-shaped *ceiba* (silk-cotton tree) stood near the coast, shading the merchants who gathered under it to peddle their wares. However, La Ceiba's claim to fame is no longer a tree but a banana—the Standard Fruit Company, better known as Dole, developed the hefty and disease-resistant Cavendish banana here. A major port for banana and pineapple exports, today's La Ceiba is all bustle and boom. Under its fruity head of steam, ambitious La Ceiba has become Honduras's third-largest city. And while it has swelled, La Ceiba retains the sensibility of an unpolished small town and is relatively easy to get to know.

Tourists typically visit La Ceiba to take care of their city business, to catch a plane to the Bay Islands or the Mosquito Coast, or to enjoy the city's famous *carnaval.* When it's *carnaval* time—and it's *carnaval* time every year during the third week of May—La Ceiba becomes a wild tangle of parades, costumes, and tributes to local patron San Isidro. The festivities end on the third Saturday in May, when La Ceiba earns its reputation: throughout the nation it is said, *"Tegucigalpa piensa, San*

Pedro Sula trabaja, y La Ceiba se divierte." (Roughly translated: Tegus does the thinking, San Pedro does the working, and La Ceiba does the rocking and rolling.)

ORIENTATION AND PRACTICAL INFORMATION

Orienting yourself in La Ceiba is pretty easy. Cabbies coming from the airport or bus terminal typically drop passengers off at the **Parque Central,** a pretty little square between 8a and 9a Calles, adorned with benches, paths, and statues of Latin American heroes. Try to identify whose bust is represented on the statue in the middle. Extending toward the water on the east side of the park is **Av. San Isidro,** the main drag. One block west is **Av. La República.** One block east is **Av. 14 de Julio.** The street that runs along the water is **1a Calle.** From 1a, *calle* numbers increase as you move south. A **canal** cuts through town to the sea; it starts about three blocks east of Av. San Isidro on 1a Calle.

Tourist Office: On the west side of the Parque Central, this small kiosk provides maps and information. Open (in theory) Mon.-Fri. 7:30-11:30am and 1:30-5:30pm, Sat. 7:30-11:30am. **Consejo Municipal de Turismo** (tel. 43-28-63), on the ground floor of the Edificio de la Gobernación Política, which is on 1a Calle, just west of Centro Médico. Provides *carnaval* information. Open Mon.-Fri. 7:30-11:30am and 1:30-5:30pm, Sat. 7:30-11:30am.

Travel Agency: Transmundo (tel. 43-28-20), on the north side of the Parque Central. Open Mon.-Fri. 7:30-11:30am and 1:30-5pm, Sat. 7:30-11:30am. They speak English.

Currency Exchange: Bancahsa (tel. 43-03-42), 2 blocks north of the park on Av. San Isidro. Look for the Carrion sign. Changes traveler's checks. Open Mon.-Fri. 8-11:30am and 1:30-2pm, Sat. 8-11:30am. Across the way, **Banco Atlantída** (tel. 43-24-22; fax 43-12-30) has a 24-hr. **ATM.** Changing checks here can be difficult. Open Mon.-Fri. 8-11:30am and 1:30-4:30pm, Sat. 8-11:30am.

Post Office: (tel. 42-00-30; fax 42-00-24), at the corner of 13a Calle and Av. Morazán (southwest part of town). *Lista de correos.* Open Mon.-Fri. 8am-5pm, Sat. 8am-noon. **EMS Express Mail** is housed in the same building. Open Mon.-Fri. 8am-noon and 2-5pm; Sat. 8am-noon.

Telephones: Hondutel (tel. 42-00-06; fax 43-07-00), 3 blocks east of Av. San Isidro between 5a and 6a Calles, under the huge red-and-white radio tower. **Fax** and AT&T USA Direct Services available 24 hrs. **Telegrams** available Mon.-Fri. 7am-noon and 2-5pm, Sat. 7-11am.

Airport: Aeropuerto Goloson, 6km from town on the road to Tela. Snag a bus for 60 centavos, and ask to be let off by the airport or else get a taxi from the *punto de taxis* at the corner of the park. For 4 lempiras they'll go to Confite, a point 2 blocks form the airport terminal. Taking a taxi "to the airport" costs 25-30 lempiras. Most of the airlines have offices around the Parque Central. **SOSA** (tel. 43-18-94) flies to Utila Mon.-Sat. at 6am, 11:30am, and 3:30pm (15min., 102 lempiras). **Isleña** (tel. 43-27-39) flies to Roatán (6 per day, Mon.-Sat. 6am-4pm, 15-30min., 133 lempiras); to San Pedro Sula (Mon.-Sat. 7:40am and 2pm, 30-45min., 164 lempiras); and to Tegucigalpa (Mon.-Sat. 8am, 10am, 2pm, and 8pm, 55min., 256 lempiras). Buy your ticket early, as planes are small and fill up quickly.

Buses: Intercity buses leave from the terminal on Blvd. 15, halfway to the airport and a 5-10-min. cab ride from town. To Tela (2 per hr., 5am-6pm, 2 hrs., 6.50 lempiras); to San Pedro Sula (1 per hr., 5:30am-6pm, 3 hrs., 20 lempiras); and to Tegucigalpa, 1st class with **Etrusca** (at 3am, 10am, and 3pm, 6½ hrs., 40 lempiras).

Boats: Nuevo Muelle de Cabotaje (Yacht Harbor) serves as a departure point for boats to the Bay Islands. If you have any tendency to get motion sickness, some form of medication or treatment ahead of time is a *great* idea. On windy days, nearly everybody going out to the islands ends up with a tasty little bag of vomit in hand. Godspeed. The harbor is 22km from La Ceiba; you'll need to take a cab (20min., about 15 lempiras for 1 person, 20 lempiras for 2 people). **M/V Tropical** leaves from the harbor for Utila (Tues.-Fri. 10am, 1¼ hrs., 50 lempiras) and Roatán (Mon. 5am, Tues.-Fri. 3:30pm, Sat.-Sun. 7am, 2¼ hrs., 65 lempiras). Other random boats leave throughout the week. Ask around at the water or at

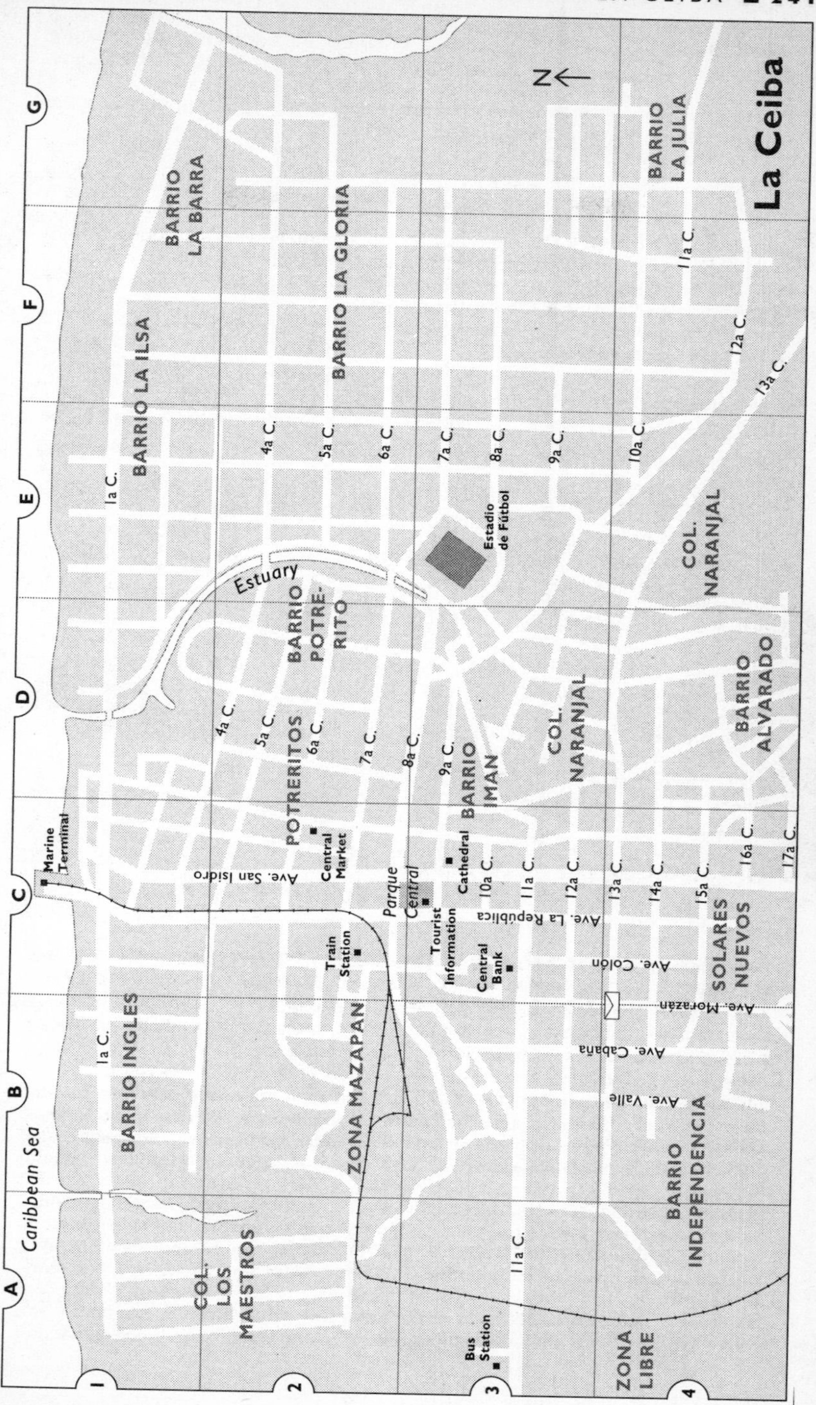

La Ceiba

Caribbean Sea
Estuary
Marine Terminal
Bus Station
Train Station
Central Market
Parque Central
Tourist Information
Central Bank
Cathedral
Estadio de Fútbol
COL. LOS MAESTROS
BARRIO INGLES
ZONA MAZAPAN
ZONA LIBRE
BARRIO INDEPENDENCIA
SOLARES NUEVOS
POTRERITOS
BARRIO POTRE-RITO
BARRIO IMAN
COL. NARANJAL
BARRIO ALVARADO
BARRIO LA ILSA
BARRIO LA BARRA
BARRIO LA GLORIA
BARRIO LA JULIA
Ave. San Isidro
Ave. La República
Ave. Colón
Ave. Morazán
Ave. Cabaña
Ave. Valle
1a C.
4a C.
5a C.
6a C.
7a C.
8a C.
9a C.
10a C.
11a C.
12a C.
13a C.
14a C.
15a C.
16a C.
17a C.
A B C D E F G
1 2 3 4
N

Capt. Renali's (tel. 43-04-72), on San Isidro. Also, the **Lady Michelle** leaves for Guanaja on Thursday at 8pm, returning Tues. at 7am every week. They'll let travelers join them on the eight-hour trip, one-way for 70 lempiras.

Taxis: Intra-city fare 3-5 lempiras. Cabs cruise everywhere, but they cluster at the southwest side of Parque Central. 5 lempiras to the bus terminal.

Market: Palmira (tel. 43-22-70), at 6a Calle, 2 blocks east of Av. San Isidro. One of the largest grocery stores in Central America—sort of a department store. Check out the live MC. Open Mon.-Sat. 7am-8pm, Sun. 7am-1pm. The un-super *mercado* is across from Palmira.

Laundromat: Next to Hotel Amsterdam 2001. The hotel owner's daughter washes and dries clothes for 5 lempiras per kilogram. Open daily 7am-9pm.

Free Air-Conditioning: Banks are good, but the guards are too heavily armed. Try Palmira's meat freezers in a sunstroke emergency.

ACCOMMODATIONS

The cheapest spots in town congregate on Av. San Isidro and 14 de Julio. Expect to pay no more than 30 lempiras for a fairly run-down room. La Ceiba is a densely packed city—no matter where you end up, getting around is a cinch, so don't be too concerned if your hotel isn't downtown or near the beach.

Hotel Royal, Av. 4 de Julio, 4a and 5a *calles* (tel. 43-28-38). Looks like a set from an old Western; the creaky boards provide for the thrilling stalking scene at the end. Decent rooms have double locks. No toilet seats; build muscles for horseback riding. Prices based on number of available beds only. 1 bed 20 lempiras, with bath 32 lempiras; 2 beds 30 lempiras, with bath 45 lempiras; 3 beds 45 lempiras, with bath 60 lempiras. Checkout at noon. Office open daily 6am-9pm.

Hotel Amsterdam 2001 (tel. 43-23-11), 7 blocks east of San Isidro on 1a Calle. A near-the-beach backpacker's fave. The savvy, chatty (in Dutch, English, and Spanish) owner grumbles about people who bargain; be wary of trying. Luggage storage, easy access to laundry. Some private rooms are wheelchair accessible; the dorms most certainly are not. The 6-bed dorm is the real deal (22 lempiras), with its own toilet-bath (no sink). Otherwise, the prices are getting high. Singles or doubles with bath are 60 lempiras, triples 75 lempiras.

Hotel Ligeros (tel. 43-01-81), between 4a and 5a Calles, 1 block east of San Isidro. Simple but clean rooms with fans and private baths. Smack dab between the beach and downtown, on a relatively tranquil street. Caution: if you stumble through the halls in an altered state, some of the zany wall art may induce seizures. Check-out noon. Singles 32 lempiras, with bath 42 lempiras; doubles 48 lempiras, with bath 53 lempiras; triples 64 lempiras, with bath 80 lempiras.

FOOD

La Ceiba boasts enough mid-priced *comedores* to keep the wise budget traveler healthy and wealthy. Seafood is usually the way to go. While considered something of a red-light district, Barrio La Barra, on the east end of 1a Calle along the beach, is home to a good number of *típico* places. The *mercado* is at 6a Calle, three blocks east of Av. San Isidro. *Platos típicos* and fruit are sold there.

Rincón de Don Felipe, on Av. San Isidro, 9 blocks south of the park. A relatively new Tex-Mex style restaurant. The English-speaking owner is friendly and knows that the *gringo* tourist army travels on its belly. Massive burrito 15 lempiras. Taco dinner 18 lempiras. Hulking *fajitas* 35 lempiras. Open Tues.-Sun. 11am-2pm and 4-11pm.

Masapan: Comida Rápida, 1 block off San Isidro on the street that's a block north of Pizza Hut. Look for the huge sign. Cafeteria line has special stations with sandwiches, beans, meats, fruits, and *frescos.* Prices depend number of items, not quantity—build your own adventure. Full meals from 8-40 lempiras. Open daily 6:30am-10pm.

Cafetería Cobel (tel. 42-21-92), north of Pizza Hut, 1 block on Av. San Isidro and look to your right for cheap Honduran fare in a comfortable, airy dining room; the restaurant's reputation is on the rise among locals. *Desayuno* and *almuerzo* 13 lempiras. Open Mon.-Sat. 7am-5:30pm, Sun. 7-11:30am.

La Carreta (tel. 43-01-11), 4a Calle, 2½ blocks east of San Isidro. A bit pricier. Comfy, plant-covered patio and an open grill—the superb atmosphere is enhanced by hanging ceramic plates inscribed by previous visitors. As you eat, consider words of wisdom such as "Clyde, Oct. '93," or "Greetings from Chicago." Grace posterity with your own ceramic epitaph. Lip-smacking barbecued *pinchos* 35 lempiras. Asian-style chicken 32 lempiras. Open daily 11am-11:30pm.

SIGHTS AND ENTERTAINMENT

If you somehow tire of the Pizza Hut playground near the Parque Central (as if that were possible), it's hard to keep busy in La Ceiba. The beach and pier are not the prettiest around, but they're a decent place for a sunset stroll or an afternoon nap. They're less safe after dark, and if you swim by day, don't leave your stuff lying around. For superior sands, walk a kilometer in either direction from La Ceiba. For more active fun, fork over 15 lempiras and use the pool and dehydrated water-slide at the Gran Hotel Paris by the Parque Central.

Most of La Ceiba's hip nightspots are near the beach along 1a Calle. On weekend nights, the thoroughfare throbs. Clubs rarely have dress codes, but few people wear sandals and shorts. Among the most popular discos is **D'Lido's,** near the estuary, which wears its disco balls and flashing lights with zip. Bop to a mix of Latin and U.S. top-40 hits; the music starts at 7pm (3-7 lempira cover on weekends; free otherwise). **Black and White,** one block west and two blocks south of Hotel Amsterdam 2001, sports a huge dance floor and sells some of the funkiest T-shirts on Earth (3 lempira cover). A new disco, **Buhos,** farther east down 1a Calle, caters to La Ceiba's chic upper crust, with Latin and U.S. dance hits (10 lempira cover).

■ NEAR LA CEIBA

La Ceiba makes a great base for expeditions into the wilderness or to the waterfalls. **Eurohonduras** (tel. and fax 43-09-33), next to the medical clinic on 1a Calle, arranges and guides trips to nearby areas; **La Ceiba Ecotours,** on San Isidro, offers similar packages.

The lush **Pico Bonito National Park,** to the south of La Ceiba, is accessible by guide or on your own, and well worth a day or two. Trails slither through the park's virtually untouched rainforest and into the realm of snakes, huge butterflies, lizards, spiders, and jaguars. Even though reaching the summit of Pico Bonito mountain (2435m) is out of the question for most (the final stretch requires heavy-duty, mondo-technical climbing), Pico Bonito is a blast. If you plan on heading into the park without a guide, pack fresh water or iodine tablets and bring a buddy in case of mishap. From La Ceiba, take the "1a de Mayo" bus (from the Parque Central or estuary, about every hour) to the small town of **Armenia Bonito.** Alternatively, snag a bus heading toward Tela and tell the driver to drop you off near Río Bonito or at the entrance of the road to Armenia. Look for the sign that reads "Taller de Soldadura." Taxis also go to Armenia (30 lempiras, from the airport 5-10 lempiras).

From Armenia, walk along the dirt road back toward the mountain. You'll need to cut through some gates and to cross over a few plantations, but owners just watch as you mosey on by. The road soon becomes a footpath, and if the water isn't too high it's possible to walk upstream along the river on huge, slippery boulders. If you can't follow the river, follow the trail along the bank until you reach the **Campamento del CURLA** (if you're on the river, keep your eye out for the stairs on the left). This deserted visitor's center still serves as a base for several trails that lead up the steep mountain. The trails are passed so infrequently that they're often blocked by spider webs. As there are few real destinations (6km up the river are waterfalls and caves, but it's a hard 6km), just turn around when you get tired. If you get lost, follow one of the rivers back down toward Armenia. Bring a compass. Don't stress if you can't find the *campamento*—the hike up the boulders is exhilarating, and if you get tired, go for a swim in one of the many pools. If you decide to go up the hill, wear repellant; the mosquitoes are vicious.

If mountains aren't as seductive as nearly deserted islands, relax, baby, there's always **Cayos Cochinos** (the hog cayes), not far off the coast from La Ceiba. Islanders provide lodging (20 lempiras per person) and food (20 lempiras per meal); guests supply their best Robinson Crusoe imitations, bottled water, and whatever else they might want to consume. The snorkeling's hog-heaven. Otherwise, there's nothing to do but relax, sunbathe, swim, meditate, smooch, read, chill, vegetate, dream, float, stare at cool trees, write poetry, build sandcastles, strum a sitar, pluck coconuts, digest, sleep, read the *Bhagavad Gita*... To get there, go to **Nueva Armenia** on the bus or taxi, then ask around about transport. Locals take tourists in canoes and agree on a time to pick them up from the Cayes. Waterproof your bags and bring puh-lenty of drinking water.

■■■ TRUJILLO

Nestled on the frontier between civilized Honduras and feral, unforgiving La Mosquitia to the east, Trujillo has passively and placidly served as a gateway since the late 15th century, when Christopher Columbus disembarked here and said his first mass in the Americas. Through it all, though, the comely city has worried little—nobody knows whether the citizens built the fort on the hill to resist pesky pirates, or simply to have a cool place with a view. Continuing its method of passive resistance, Trujillo has also been indifferent to tourists; its natural beauty is for the most part unmarred. And despite the invasion of a behemoth pleasure palace recently built outside the town, wise bets are that Trujillo will merrily ignore this development as well, and continue instead to kiss the ocean with its eternally sandy lips.

ORIENTATION AND PRACTICAL INFORMATION

Trujillo's main road (**Calle Principal**) runs three blocks off (and parallel to) the beach. Police warn that the beach areas outside of town are unsafe at night. The **Parque Central,** the principal landmark, is one block closer to the sea than Calle Principal. There's no tourist office, but the people at the bars on the beach know the nitty-gritty. The **police** (tel. 44-40-38) are on the north of the park, ready to serve 8766 hrs. a year. **Currency** can be exchanged, and credit cards converted to cash at **Banco de Occidente** (tel. and fax 44-49-91), on the Calle Principal (open Mon.-Fri. 8am-noon and 2-5pm, Sat. 8-11:30am). **Mail** can be obtained and dispatched (even through *lista de correos*) at the **Correo** (tel. 44-45-43), two blocks inland from the church on the road south of it (open Mon.-Fri. 8am-noon and 1:30-4:30pm, Sat. 8-11am). Zippier communications are available at **Hondutel** (tel. 44-41-12), right next to the post office (open daily 7am-9pm). Faxes and telegrams are also available (Mon.-Fri. 7am-noon and 2-5pm, Sat. 7-11am). Located on the Calle Principal a few blocks north of the park is **Lavandería Colón;** they'll wash and dry a bag of clothes for 20 lempiras (daily 8am to 5pm). A block or so south, **Farmacia Almim** (tel. 44-42-43) even has an **emergency number** (44-42-42) for those sudden, severe headaches. The **hospital** (tel. 44-40-93) is just south of the park (open daily 8am-4pm).

ACCOMMODATIONS AND FOOD

If the gargantuan Christopher Columbus Resort isn't your speed, fear not, there's a delightful set of cabins available for a fraction of the cost. **Hotel Catrachos** (tel. 44-44-32) offers a whole chorus line of cute little rooms with fans, lamps, and locks, designed to look like cabins. Heading south on *Calle Principal* from the park, turn right one block after the street the post office is on and follow that street west for one block. The cabins await on the corner (singles 35 lempiras, doubles 45 lempiras, two beds 75 lempiras). Another option is **Hotel Mar de Plata,** at the northern end of the main drag, four blocks north of the church. The acceptable rooms have locks (singles 30 lempiras, with bath 40 lempiras; doubles with bath 50 lempiras).

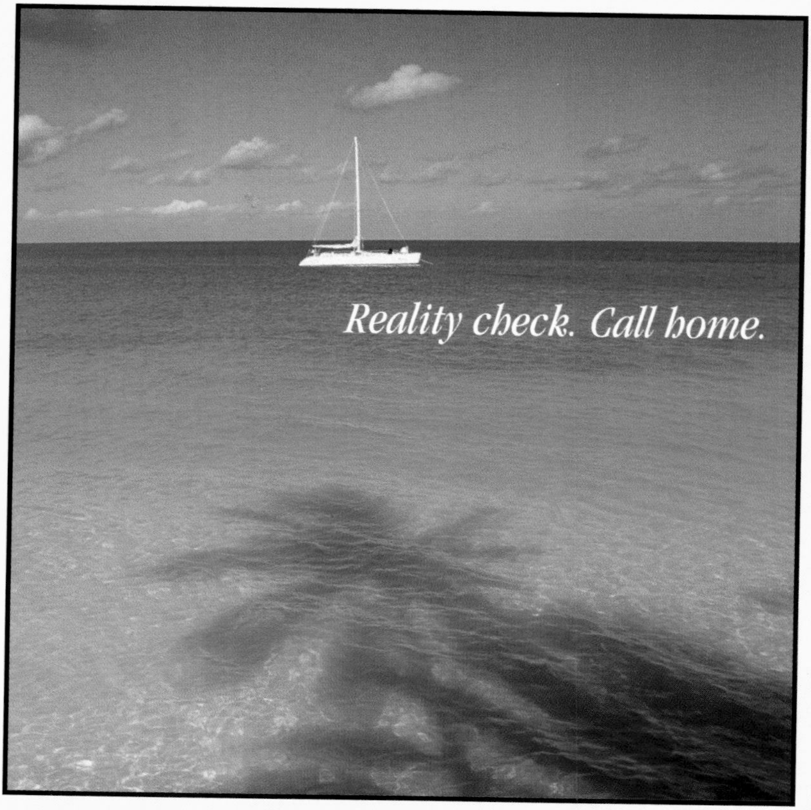

THUMBS UP FROM LET'S GO

With pen and notebook in hand, a change of underwear in our backpacks, and a budget as tight as your own, we spent the summer roaming the globe in search of travel bargains.

We've put the best of our discoveries into the book you're now holding. Our researchers hit the road for seven weeks of exploration, from Anchorage to Ankara, Estonia to El Salvador, Iceland to Indonesia. Editors work from spring to fall, massaging copy written on Himalayan bus rides into witty yet informative prose. A brand-new edition of each guide hits the shelves every year, only months after it is researched, so you know you're getting the most reliable, up-to-date, and comprehensive information available.

We're an indispensable companion, but the best discoveries are often those you make yourself. When you find something worth sharing, drop us a line. We're Let's Go Publications, One Story Street, Cambridge, MA 02138, USA (e-mail: LetsGo@delphi.com). Good luck, and happy travels!

Photo: R. Olken

Along the beach sit a squadron of splendid seafood restaurants. Catch the catch of the day at **Rincón de Los Amigos,** in the middle of it all. This is the place for *punta* as well, especially on Sunday nights. The English-speaking owner is eager to chat with *gringos* eating the special, a full fish and half a lobster with all the trimmings for 60 lempiras. **Horfez** (tel. 44-44-33; see Sights and Entertainment, below) serves up fish dinners for 35 lempiras. Otherwise, walk the shoreline and look for *comidas corrientes* and other listed specials.

SIGHTS AND ENTERTAINMENT

Believe it or not, Trujillo offers more than just mesmerizing beaches. Just outside town, an eclectic private museum (usually simply called **El Museo**) guarantees a strange and unforgettable experience. From the middle of town, walk along the main street with the sea to your right, all the way to the Hotel Mar de Plata. Take the next left, then the first right, and follow that road past two cemeteries. Eventually (5-10 minutes later), watch for the museum's creatively painted signs. The museum has been aptly described as "an old man getting paid to show off his junk," but the junk includes dozens of ancient guns and swords, antique phonographs, pre-Columbian figurines, parts of a crashed airplane, a conked-out Xerox machine, a dilapidated printing press, a battery of broken 10-key adding machines, and a freaky, space-trip of an organic ceiling. Out back he has some cute monkeys and *balnearios* (swimming holes). All the thrills of this modern Xanadu are included in the admission price (5 lempiras). The museum is open during daylight hours. On the way back, **William Walker** (see Nicaragua, page 264) devotees should check out his final resting place in the old cemetery, the one closer to town. For non-historic-obsessives, this gravesite is singularly unimpressive.

Context is everything during a visit to **La Fortaleza de Santa Barbara.** The caretakers love to show off their 10 (bowling-ball-esque) cannon balls in an old bowling-alley-like room, but the display lacks appeal. The reason to pay the 1 lempira admission fee is the sweeping, *amor*-inducing view, especially near sunrise and sunset. The fort is right next to the hospital and open from about 8am to about 5pm, depending on the mood of the caretakers.

If the beach overwhelms your senses and makes you want to break out the funkiness at night, check out **Horfez** (tel. 44-44-33) on the main drag next to the laundromat. On the weekends the place becomes a **disco** from 8pm-3am. The prices are a bit high, but so are a good number of the merry young dancers.

NEAR TRUJILLO

If you have the time for a sojourn away from Trujillo, several options await: Garifuna villages to the west, historic Puerto Castilla, hiking and ecotourism, and playing maritime Russian roulette by randomly hopping the commercial boats along the port. **Santa Fe** is the closest of the Garifuna villages (about 9km along the beach) and boasts a secret caye, **Cayo Blanco.** When U.S. forces were stationed in Honduras, they used the hapless caye for target practice, which eventually led to the Atlantis syndrome—the entire caye now rests beneath at least ½ meter of water, 1km off the coast; locals relish taking interested snorkelers out for a look-see. The marine life is reputed to be well worth the effort. **Puerto Castilla** is the point at which Columbus reached mainland Honduras, and there's a little monument commemorating his arrival, as well as a pretty little town. The three buses a day leave from next to the bank in Trujillo (7:30am, 8am, and 8:30am, 30min., 3 lempiras). A last bus returns from Puerto Castilla at 4pm.

For the latest on hiking trips to nearby **Guaimoreto lagoon,** as well as to Calentura and Capiro mountains. Contact **FUCAGUA** (tel. and fax 44-42-94), an organization which strives to protect and promote local Indian cultures as well as sustainable tourism and development. The trips range in difficulty, but even the most rugged paths are being made more accessible with time.

The last option is by far the most adventurous. An assortment of **commercial vessels** leave from the dock, headed for Guanaja (8 hrs., 40-50 lempira) and random points in La Mosquitia. Schedules vary, and travels can be wild and crazy, but they promise a cheap, rather eventful way to travel. Ask around at the dock or **Rincón de Los Amigos** (see Accommodations, page 244) for more information.

THE BAY ISLANDS

Scattered off Honduras' northern coast, the Bay Islands—Utila, Roatán, and Guanaja—are heirs to a colorful history that has rendered them ethnically and linguistically distinct from the mainland. Spain claimed the islands in 1502, sending indigenous islanders to work as slaves in Mexico and the West Indies. In 1638, Puritans from Maryland in the U.S. colonized Roatán but were summarily expelled. Spain had a harder time dealing with slippery pirates, who would hide in the reefs and harbors, coming ashore to hunt pigs and turtles. Two naval superpowers—Britain and Spain—fought over the islands throughout the late 1700s, but the real victims of the wars were the islands' black residents, many of whom were sold as slaves when the British were chased out. In 1852, residents joined Belize as a British possession, but the U.S. protested, frightened by the specter of creeping British imperialism. Under pressure from the north, the islands were returned to Honduras.

Although the islands were at one time solely populated by English-speaking descendants of African and British settlers, the situation has changed. Perhaps taking their cue from travelers, masses of "Hondureños" (the islanders don't usually consider themselves Hondurans) have moved from the mainland, yielding a change in the cultural feel of the islands and a bit of racial tension. Islanders argue that outsiders are despoiling the pristine islands. Whatever the cause, the idyllic, isolated isles are showing their first (unexpected) signs of urban decay.

However, the primary draw of the islands is not really the islands themselves; for most, they're just a place to breathe uncompressed air and to swap fins for Tevas in order to stroll to the restaurant. Those that come to the islands to dive do so for good reason—the reefs are a mind-melting marine menagerie, from the giant barracudas' mangling jaws to the angelfish's gracefully sloping face and the lobster's fluttering antennae. Most alluringly, these natural wonders are relatively cheap, especially on Utila, a veritable diving-certification assembly-line. Diving is inexpensive almost everywhere, and snorkeling is free and easy (excluding rental); the reef is almost always within 100m of the islands. (See Belize, page 136) for more info.

Wait! There's more! The islands, especially Guanaja, are possessed of a pristine beauty that deserves attention, and the islands' inhabitants are wonderfully easy-going. In fact, the only real drawback are the sand flies, which admittedly can be unbearable, but are manageable with a little coconut oil or other repellant.

■■■ UTILA

For well over a hundred years, residents of Utila (pop. 2000) have been drawing water from **La Cola de Mico** ("Monkey's Tail"), a freshwater well. According to legend, all those who drink from La Cola must someday return to Utila; grab the first bucket at hand when you get to the island—a return trip would be pure sweetness. Diving and snorkeling is superb here, but don't worry if you're a beginner—certification is cheap, cheap, cheap at a number of reputable diving schools on the island. Three tranquil cayes afford solitary dives, and non-divers can go canoeing, biking, or exploring.

PRACTICAL INFORMATION

The nameless main drag runs along the bay. A small park lies off of it. Unless otherwise indicated, everything listed below is on this main street.

Tourist Information: Try the shack next to Mermaid's Corner Restaurant, which also houses the Bay Islands Conservation Association. Maps, T-shirts, and guides to local reserves. Open Mon.-Fri. noon-7pm, Sat.-Sun. 7-8pm.

Police: (tel. 45-32-55), upstairs from the post office. English spoken. Open Mon.-Fri. 8-11am and 2-4pm. For off-hour emergencies, contact the Chief of Police (45-31-87) or **FUSEP** (tel. 45-31-45), which is next to the park and open 24 hrs.

Currency Exchange: Bancahsa (tel. and fax 45-31-57), halfway down the main street, at its only intersection. Traveler's checks cashed. Open Mon.-Fri. 8-11:30am and 1:30-4pm, Sat. 8-11:30pm. After hours, go to **Henderson's Store,** on the main drag; he gives the bank rate. Open Mon.-Sat. 6:30am-noon and 2-6pm.

Post Office: Next to the park down an alley. Posts a *lista de correos.* Open Mon.-Fri. 8am-noon and 2-5pm, Sat. 8-11am. **Postal code:** 34201.

Telephones: Hondutel (tel. 45-31-01; fax 45-31-06), left of the post office. Telephones open around the clock. Also send **faxes** and **telegrams.** Open Mon.-Fri. 7am-5pm, Sat. 7-11am. **The Budget Traveler** (tel. 45-3368; fax 45-3386) has a branch at Utila Tour and Travel.

Airport: At the far end of the road. Buy **SOSA** plane tickets at **Hunter and Morgan Store,** near the center of town. Service to La Ceiba (Mon.-Sat. 7am, 11am, and 3pm, 15min., 102 lempiras). To reach Roatán, you must first fly to La Ceiba.

Boats: Leave from the dock near the intersection; get to the dock at least 15min. before scheduled departure time. **M/V Tropical** goes to La Ceiba (Tues.-Fri. 11:30am, 1½ hrs., 50 lempiras). From La Ceiba, head for Roatán (82 lempiras); see La Ceiba, Practical Information, page 239. Alternatively, inquire about the schedules of **M/V Starfish** and **Tonia C. II,** or the **Utila Express.** For information on the Utila Express, contact the **Green Ribbon** store (tel. 45-31-97).

Medical Services: Community Clinic (tel. 45-31-37), across from the park. Open Mon.-Fri. 8am-noon; the doctor can be reached 24 hrs. on the yacht "Tabitha" (radio VHF CH-06).

ACCOMMODATIONS

It can be hard to find reasonable, decent residence, particularly in the high-season. Don't fret about finding a fan, since electricity is turned off nightly, anyway. Quintessentially cheap is the **Blue Room Store,** on the main road two blocks south of the dock. Each stall on the concrete floor costs 20 lempiras, irrespective of how many bodies are crammed inside. Bring mosquito coil—there are no screens. Another relatively cheap option is **Cooper's Inn,** farther down the main street. The rooms are a tad more exciting and a notch more expensive. The owner promises 24- hour electricity by 1996 (singles with fan 30 lempiras, doubles with fan 40 lempiras). Find your thrills at **Blue Berry Hill** (tel. 45-31-41), a few blocks up the hill from the bank. Rooms are small but cheap, and they come equipped with mosquito nets. The wall in the common bathroom has been vandalized by someone in an apocalyptic mood: "And after we die there will be cockroaches. Venerate decay." Rooms are 20 lempiras for one or two people. If available, the huts, which include bath and cooking facilities, are a great deal (1-2 people 40 lempiras, 3 people 60 lempiras, 4 people 80 lempiras). Near the airport, the **Bahía del Mar** offers hammock and tent spaces for 10 lempiras per night on a caye out back.

FOOD

Because most of the seafood caught near Utila is sent off for mastication by rich, foreign mandibles, you'll have to sweat to get tasty *mariscos.* There is, however, salvation; join the nightly pilgrimage to **Selly's** (the Ole-Ole). The going is rough and the rewards are absolutely mind-altering. Take the road at Bancahsa up hill until it forks. Follow the concrete footpath that continues straight, then turn right when it becomes dirt. Selly has made it her mission to provide the largest plates on the island, and she succeeds with gusto. A humongous plate of fish steaks, coleslaw, french fries, and gravy costs 30 lempiras (open daily 6-10pm).

Though not quite the revelation, **Myrtle's Restaurant,** half a block from the bank, serves large, tasty dishes of *comida corriente* for 18 lempiras. The local crowd can be overwhelming, but the food makes it worthwhile (open daily 8am-11:45pm). Two restaurants serve up yummy and affordable Italian food: **Delany's Island Kitchen,** under Cooper's Inn, dishes out delicious whole pizzas (40-55 lempiras) and plates of lasagna with salad or garlic bread (25 lempiras; open daily 10am-10:30pm). A few doors down, **Mermaid's Corner** offers whopping plates of lasagna (meat or vegetarian) for 25 lempiras (open Sun.-Fri. 7am-10:30pm). For breakfast, everyone heads up the hill from the bank to **Thompson's Bakery.** The walls are covered with wise adages, and the pancakes with banana are super tasty, priced to sell like hotcakes at 12 lempiras (open daily 6am-1pm).

SIGHTS AND ENTERTAINMENT

For certification-hungry prospective divers, Utila is utopia. Even though the mayor has stipulated a minimum price for an open water certification course (US$139), many still argue that Utila is the cheapest place in the world to certify. One advantage to the price-fixing is that now dive shops must compete in ways that really matter. Use this freedom to select a dive shop carefully. First and foremost, check safety: diving is the worst arena in which to follow a reckless pied-piper. Then check personality: you'll be spending hours listening to this person pontificate at close quarters. Don't be afraid to comparison shop. Most divscuba divinge shops offer four to six instruction dives, but they're not allowed to give free fun dives anymore. Also check for languages *spoken* (many dive shops say they're multi-lingual and all that means is they've got the PADI manual in a foreign language); several dive shops have divemasters who are native speakers of different languages. For those already certified, "fun dives" typically run US$10-20; especially popular are packages of 10 dives for US$100. All certification courses costs US$139 unless otherwise listed. **Parrots Dive Shop** (tel. 45-31-59) is relatively new; hence, so is their equipment. Colorado-native John, the instructor, is super-cool. **Utila Dive Centre** has confident, experienced instructors and sports divemasters conversant in six languages. They're halfway to the airport on the main drag (tel. 45-33-26; fax 45-33-27). **Paradise Divers** (tel. 45-33-87) is also excited to train at the going rate. They also offer 10 fun dives for US$100, which can be divided among friends. **Gunter's Dive Shop** has been around forever, and they know their stuff. Because a maximum of four people go in each class, personal attention is the rule of the day. While you're taking the course, you can use their snorkeling stuff for free. (If you want to snorkel but aren't taking their course, Gunter's will rent out equipment for 25 lempiras per day.)

HONDURAS

For those who haven't come to Utila to dive, there are plenty of ways to while away the hours. **Canoes** can be rented from the Blue Bayou Hotel, a 25-minute walk down the shore from town. For **bike riding,** head to Myrtle's Restaurant. (Bikes 20 lempira for 4 hrs., 30 lempira for 8 hrs.) To really get under Utila's skin, call up **Shelby McNab** (tel. 45-32-23), a life-long resident of the island who offers "Robinson Crusoe Tours" of Utila's "historical sites." Go **snorkeling** at **Blue Bayou,** a ways past Gunter's, for only five lempiras. Diehards can try the water near the airport runway.

By foot, bike, or horse, head straight up the road past Thompson's Bakery and the Bucket of Blood; the road forks three ways. Go left and up the hill to **Gunther's Gran View Gallery,** which is basically divemaster Gunther's art-laden living room (some of the pictures are for sale). Known as the "rat race escape artist," he does paintings, drawings, and carvings of life on an island (open Mon.-Sat. during the day). Try to catch Gunther here or downstairs pumping iron—he's fun to talk to.

Head straight down the footpath past Selly's restaurant for about 4.5km to reach **Pumpkin Hill Beach,** one of the few actual beaches on Utila and home to lots of insects. Along the path are some caves prime for exploration. Bring a flashlight and rope and hire one of the local kids as a guide to find the best spots—they often know the caves well. Another good hiking path is up **Stuart Hill,** which affords terrific views of Roatán; follow the path across from the post office up the water tank. On the road past the airport extends the **Iron Shore,** so-called because the volcanic rock here seems never to give an inch to the relentless pounding of the waves.

For relaxation on an even more deserted island or snorkeling good times, head for a nearby caye. Especially popular are **Water Caye, Jewel Caye,** and **Sandy Caye.** Talk to Jake Whitefield (tel. 45-33-08) about getting to the Cayes. He charges 150 lempiras for 1-3 people, US$5 per person for a group. Hammocks on the cayes typically rent for about US$1.

At night, Utila residents head to any number of discos and bars. For a good party, try the **Casino** disco, across from the bank (open weekends 8-11:30pm). During the week, head for **Salon 07,** a block closer to the airport. It's fast becoming the spot for partying, mainly because they offer free rum (poured verrry sloooowly) on Tuesday and Friday between 10 and 11pm. Almost a cult favorite is the recently instituted **Utila Film Club** (tel. and fax 45-31-03), between the airport and town center. Run by the guys at Underwater Vision, it's started a **movie night,** with lights out, popcorn, and a projector. The vintage flicks are 20 lempiras and start at 7pm in the building on the sidewalk to Cross Creek Dive Shop.

■■■ ROATÁN

The largest and most populous of the Bay Islands, Roatán is also the most beloved among travelers. Clear and warm, the waters around Roatán shroud an extension of Belize's barrier reef; the island boasts excellent diving. The island's beaches are covered with cloud-soft sand and studded with lanky coconut trees—Roatán is where they must film all of those happy-couple-strolling-on-a-perfect-beach commercials. While resortification is pushing up prices across the island, it's still possible to get by pretty cheaply, especially on the west end of the island.

Tourists don't visit most of the long, Cuba-shaped island, huddling instead in west end villages such as **Sandy Bay** and the indubitable village of **West End.** Boats typically land at **Coxen Hole,** a tiny town sometimes called "Roatán" which is home to the island's airport and most of its services.

COXEN HOLE

Coxen Hole (also known as Roatán) is the capital of the Bay Islands, but you wouldn't know it; it's just a small village veering slightly toward squalor. The pace of life is slightly faster here than elsewhere on the island; take care of your errands here, since most businesses and services not related to diving are concentrated in Coxen Hole. It's certainly not a bad place to spend time, but serious divers and beach-goers will want to relocate to other parts of the island. **Back St.** runs through Coxen Hole, along the water, while **Ticket Rd.** runs to the west end.

Practical Information The **tourist office, Columbia Tours** (tel. 45-17-47), is more of a tour agency, in the gift shop across from Bay Islands Tour and Travel Agency, near the banks and upstairs (open Mon.-Fri. 8am-noon and 1:30-5pm, Sat. 8am-noon). They sell expensive maps also available in gift shops across the island. For **police,** contact **FUSEP** (tel. 45-12-25), at the end of the dirt road, 100m back left of the hospital. The police speak some English. Change money and traveler's checks at **Bancahsa,** halfway down Back St. (open Mon.-Fri. 8-11:30am and 1:30-4pm, Sat. 8-11:30am). The **post office** (tel. 45-13-21), across from the bank, posts a *lista de correos* (open Mon.-Fri. 8am-noon and 2-5pm, Sat. 8am-noon). The **postal code** for Coxen Hole is 34101. Make AT&T **calls** and send **faxes** or **telegrams** at **Hondutel** (tel. 45-10-02), at the back of the path behind Bancahsa (open daily 7am-9pm; fax and telegram service are open Mon.-Fri. 8am-4pm). **The Budget Traveler** (tel. 45-11-67) has a branch at Joana's Gifts.

Isleña Airlines (tel. 45-10-88) flies to La Ceiba (7, 9am, 1, 3, and 5pm, 30min., 133 lempiras). **Taxis** (tel. 45-11-46) from Coxen Hole to West End (7 lempiras) and van-like buses (5 lempiras) leave throughout the day from **H.B. Warren's** supermarket on the main street. A taxi from the airport to West End costs 20 lempiras.

Drug Store Coral View (tel. 45-14-80) is fairly well-stocked pharmacy at the center of town (open Mon.-Fri. 8am-noon and 2-6pm, Sat. 8am-6pm). **Hospital Roatán** (tel. 45-12-25) is on Ticket Rd. a few blocks from Back St. (open 24 hrs.).

Accommodations and Food If you need a place to bed down in Coxen Hole, the **Hotel Coral** (tel. 45-10-80) is in the center of things and offers rooms with fans and communal bathrooms (50 lempiras per person). Set a bit farther back on Ticket Rd., behind the Shell gas station, **Hotel Allen** has 11 well-kept rooms. The owner is one of the nicest people in the hemisphere (check-out 11am; 50 lempiras per room).

If you're hungry and you like your fries on the soggy side, **Restaurante Golden Gate,** on the east end of Back St., is a good bet. The roof is thatched, and cute fake flowers adorn the tables. The special (spaghetti with beans and rice) is a deal at 20 lempiras (open daily). The biggest and cheapest supermarket on the island, **H.B. Warren** (tel. 45-12-08), has an attached diner-style café. Top off a three-piece chicken dinner (24 lempiras) with a rapidly-melting serving of ice cream for eight lempiras (open daily 7am-5:30pm).

Going Green If you're interested in environmental issues, check out the headquarters of the **Bay Islands Conservation Association** (tel. 45-14-24), upstairs in the Cooper Building and next to Bancahsa. This organization works for the preservation of the island and surrounding marine life. As a result of their eco-efforts, a long strip of water along the north side of the island has been declared a marine preserve—it can no longer be touched by human hands or industry. Together with some local dive shops, BICA is trying to transform all of the waters around Roatán into a similar reserve. The office offers information on the island and peddles t-shirts and an excellent book, *The Bay Islands: Nature and People,* worth the 40 lempiras if just for the cause (open Mon.-Fri. 8am-noon and 1:30-5pm).

Nightlife can be a hoot. Locals recommend going to French Harbor to **Bolongos** (20 lempiras cover). Closer and cheaper (5 lempiras on weekends) is **Harbor View** on Back St. (open from 9pm until people pass out).

SANDY BAY

A small outpost 5km away from West End on the road from Coxen Hole, Sandy Bay is chronically second-best—its beaches are more sludgy and less sandy than West End's, and its diving opportunities, while good, are more expensive than those farther west. The dolphins are the main draw for budget travelers.

Accommodations and Food If you're staying the night at Sandy Bay, try out **Beth's Hostel** (tel. 45-12-66), which is a bit off the beach. From Anthony's Key, head toward Coxen Hole along the beach. Turn right at the Bamboo Inn and head up the hill. The hostel is run by U.S.-born Beth, whose nervous system responds very badly to even a whiff of tobacco; smoking is strictly prohibited. The four rooms share bathroom facilities. Snorkeling gear is available, and it's just 90m to the beach. (US$10 per person, or US$60 for 7 nights). There are often rooms to rent along the beach, but most charge exorbitant rates.

For eats in Sandy Bay, head to **The Ceiba Tree,** across the road from Sun Rise Resort. Divemasters often come here for Nachos Supreme (28 lempiras), footlongs with chili (20 lempiras), and spaghetti dinners with garlic bread (20 lempiras). There's a different dessert treat each day (open daily 4pm-midnight).

Sights and Entertainment The two dive shops in town, **scuba divingSun Rise Divers** (tel. 45-12-65) and **Anthony's Key Resort,** are too expensive to consider (US$300 for PADI certification). They're both on the beach and charge about US$30 for a fun dive. It's probably best to head out from West End to the dive sites they cover. The reason to come to Sandy Bay for is the dolphins. Despite recent protests from animal-rights activists, including a threatened boycott of tourism to Honduras from Vogue supermodel Rosie Vela, the **Institute of Marine Sciences** still lets people snorkel among dolphins for the cost of a month's rent (US$75; open Tues.-Thurs. 8:45am, 10:30am, 2:30pm; make a reservation). Go to the Ocean Side Inn, the hotel-enclave in Anthony's Key. Once you're ready to snorkel, walk off their back dock and head for the cage; the dolphins will come to visit and serenade. Don't touch the fence—the dolphins nuzzle and hurt their noses. Beyond, the reef is impressive, stuffed with lobster, eels, barracuda, and parrot fish. Don't stay too close to the shore—the reef is too shallow and you can get trapped. Diving is also possible for US$100 (gear not included).

As a cheaper option, there's the dolphin show, which costs 20 lempiras and includes entrance to the museum as well. Some travelers who've claimed that they're guests say it's possible to get across to the resort island on the little ferry, ask to use one of the kayaks they have there, and float along for a free, water-level view of the entire show. Resist the urge to free Willy. The **museum** displays artifacts discovered on Roatán (open Thurs.-Tues. 9am-5pm).

Across the road from Anthony's, the nature trails of the **Carambola Botanical Gardens** snake through the jungle and rainforest (admission US$3 or 30 lempiras, with guide US$5 or 50 lempiras; open daily 7am-5pm; it's best to go in the morning).

WEST END

West End is a parent's worst nightmare come true, a place so beautiful and so serene that backpacking children who discover it may never want to click their heels together and return home. Many West-Enders follow a grueling daily regime of waking up, diving, sipping beers, playing volleyball on the warm afternoon sand, and feasting on delicious dinners. If you're looking for a place to crash for 30 years, come to West End. Just remember to call home every so often.

Practical Information **Telephone calls** can be made from the **Intertel** office in **Supertienda Chris** (tel. 45-11-71) toward the east side of town. International calls and **fax** service available (Mon.-Sat. 7am-7pm). **The Budget Traveler** (tel. 45-10-05) has a branch in the Sunset Inn. Supertienda is also well-stocked with food. **Cornerstone Emergency Medical Service** (tel. and fax 45-15-15; radio CH26) is equipped to treat diving emergencies around the clock. **Traveler's checks** can be cashed at Seagrape Plantation Dive Shop (see Sights and Entertainment, below). Ask for Ernie or Ray—they give the bank rate.

Accommodations and Food Keep your eyes peeled for "rooms for rent" signs along the village's single, sandy street. Prices may change by season. There are two budget hotels in the western part of town; both offer more or less spartan living conditions. **Jimmy's** has simple rooms for 48 lempiras. Guests can also sleep in a massive room outfitted with more than a dozen mattresses and mosquito nets. The big room is an ideal place to meet people as they tangle with their net, but look elsewhere for privacy (24 lempiras per person). **Sam's** has 10 rooms. Each room has at least one bed and nothing else. Common bathrooms have no doors on the stalls and *no water* (40 lempiras for 2 single beds, 50 lempiras for a single and a double bed). The **Seaview Hotel** (tel. 45-17-55), on the east side of the main street, boasts running water 'til well past lunch (7pm). Check-out is at noon (55 lempiras for a room with bed and basic common bathroom, 70 lempiras for a room with a "bigger bed," 90 lempiras for 2 beds). For tasty eats, head for **The Bite on the Beach,** about 100m down the beach from Sam's. Typically, the joint is packed. The menu prepared by the U.S.-born owner varies daily, but fish and meat dishes almost always make appearances. Meals come with vegetables, salad, and bread or potatoes; expect to pay 34-36 lempiras for dinner (open Tues.-Sat. 4-9pm, dinner from 6-9pm). For breakfast, almost everyone involved in the local diving scene heads for **Cabinas a Orillas del Mar** (tel. 45-12-05), toward the middle of the road. Whenever an order of flapjacks is ready, the owner proclaims "Best-in-the-West pancakes at the window!" Banana pancakes are 15 lempiras. Good omelets (open 6:30am-9pm).

Sights and Entertainment Particularly for beginners, Roatán's waters offer some spectacular diving opportunities. Experts, however, may find the water lacking an adequate number of diversions. Drift-diving entails starting at the point, and after flowing with the current, getting out somewhere else. A commonly frequented site is **Peter's Place,** at the end of Marine Park, where tons of big fish, deep canyons, and vertical walls wow divers. Also popular is **West End Wall,** which offers drift-diving along a wall densely packed with fishies. The famous **Hole in the Wall** is suited for advanced and very cautious divers; the hole is a good sand-chute that qualified swimmers can wriggle through. **Bear's Den,** which offers cave-like, enclosed canyons ready for exploration, is appropriate only for experienced and highly skilled divers.

If you're getting certified, make sure you get along with your divemaster and feel confident that he or she is concerned with safety. The folks at **Seagrape Plantation Dive Shop** (tel. 45-17-17) are friendly, experienced, and safety-conscious. Plus, they've got some of the nicest equipment around. Seagrape is at the extreme north end of the village, a 5-minute walk past the road to Coxen Hole. Just follow the signs to the Dive Shop, but not the resort of the same name. They charge Roatán's standard US$175 for a PADI certification and US$15-25 for fun dives, depending on the package. They also rent and sell snorkeling equipment (US$31 for used fins, mask, and snorkel). The people at **Ocean Divers** (fax 45-10-05, attn: Ocean Divers) are super-cool, reliable, and active in marine preservation. They do PADI certification courses for US$187, and charge US$20 per dive (US$25 with gear), equipment included. Five dives will run US$100. Snorkeling gear can be rented for US$5 per 24 hours, and a snorkeling trip on the boat costs US$10, drink included (open daily 8am-5pm). **West End Divers** (tel. 45-15-31) has good equipment and offers night dives for US$35 (open daily 8am-5pm). Talk to other travelers for recommendations, since diving with shops is often a matter of personal taste.

There are a couple of convenient (and free) snorkeling spots in West End. The easiest is **Half Moon Bay** at the north end of the village. Snork the perimeter then pop out 10m to the reef for the best views. Less accessible, but absolutely bodacious, is West Bay Beach, 30 minutes south of the village (or take a 7-lempira water taxi from **Foster's and Vivian's**). The reef is 20m from shore and is stuffed to the gills with schools of angelfish, needlefish, parrot fish, and even occasional rays. The closer to the point, the better.

If you're afraid of getting wet, **Far Tortuga Charters** (tel. 45-16-48) takes passengers around the island for half-day trips (9am-noon or 1-4pm, US$25) or full-day excursions (9am-4pm, US$50). If vacuum-packed romantic moments are your thing, fork over US$15 for a sunset-moonrise trip. Ask at the Coconut Tree Restaurant.

For a different sort of tour, **Island Adventures** takes a minimum of five people on five-hour tours of the whole island. For US$25, they'll take you to the Garifuna village of Punta Gorda for a dance performance, guide you through tropical gardens, and steer you on a boat trip through mangrove tunnels. For more information, ask at the **Librería Casi Todo** (tel. 45-11-71), which has almost everything a good West End slugabed could possibly want. Come here for English maps and books (open Mon.-Sat. 9am-5pm). To cruise around the island on your own power, **Joana's Gift Shop,** next to Ocean Divers, rents **bikes.** (10 lempiras for 1 hr., 60 lempiras for the 9am-5pm shift, 90 lempiras for 24 hrs. Open daily 9am-5pm.)

Getting to **beaches** is a piece of (sandfly) pie. Head to the village beach, or keep on hiking farther and farther from town, where the beaches get nicer. Slather your skin with oil to keep the flies away. Good luck.

As for **nightlife,** the beaches at West End would be a fantabulous place for a moondance. **Sam's** is a good place to kick back and ponder the stars above and your position in the universe. Beer-sipping and philosophizing are popular nocturnal pastimes. For more traditional fun, **The Bamboo Hut,** on the main road in about the middle of town, has started to show **free movies** to their guests with a projection-TV every night at 7:30pm. Buy a drink and settle in.

■■■ GUANAJA

The most remote of the Bay Islands, Guanaja baffles. Despite the main island's broad expanses of virgin forest and dazzling beaches, nearly the entire population is crammed onto squalid Bonacca, or Guanaja town, a tiny caye off the coast. The original settlers tenaciously dumped coral and rocks into the channels between the tiny isles, creating Honduras's own version of (similarly trashy) Venice, Italy, and leaving room for overzealous, overpriced diving resorts. Getting off of expensive Bonacca isn't easy, but a concerted effort yields spectacular rewards—if nothing else, a chance to enjoy abundant, untouched nature in solitude.

Orientation and Practical Information The airport is on the south side of the island, surrounded by "The Airport Hillton" (note the legally important extra L) and miles of nothing. Don't panic. Water taxis are eager to take visitors to **the caye** (sometimes called **low caye**, whenever a plane arrives, 10min., 10-12 lempiras). The Caye is a cluttered mess; someone could easily step from roof to roof. The "roads" are cement sidewalks just big enough for two strollers. The main road is called **Hog Cay** on the south end and **Fire Pit** on the north.

The closest thing to a **tourist office** is Hugo at the **SOSA office** (tel. 45-41-32), halfway up the main street. **FUSEP** (tel. 45-43-10) works around the clock on the pier behind **Depósito Millers** (look for the sign), with an imposing jail across the way. **Currency exchange** for traveler's checks takes place at **Bancahsa** (tel. 45-42-34), a couple blocks south of SOSA (open Mon.-Fri. 8-11:30am and 1:30-4pm, Sat. 8-11:30am). The **post office** hides behind the little door across from Bancahsa, ready to handle your parcels (open Mon.-Fri. 8am-noon and 2-5pm). Speedier communication awaits at **Hondutel** (tel. 45-42-01; fax 45-41-46), a bit farther south (open Mon.-Fri. 7am-9pm with 2½-hr. breaks for meals, Sat. 7am-11am and 12:30-4pm). There are some random tubes of **medication** at the supermarket, **Casa Sikaffy,** three-quarters of the way to the north tip of the caye (open Mon.-Sat. 8am-7pm, Sun. 8am-noon). The **Centro de Salud** isn't much; it's down the sidestreet from the supermarket (open 7am-noon and 12:30-3pm). In an **emergency,** call the doctor at home (tel. 45-42-33). The staff speaks English. **Airplanes** leave Guanaja for Roatán (10am, Mon.-Sat., 30min., 133 lempiras), with continuing service to La Ceiba (another 30min., 174 lempira). Buy tickets at the SOSA office—flights fill up quickly.

Accommodations and Food If you can get to the north end of the island, some *campesinos* will let you pitch a tent on their land; ask first, and bring your own food and water. Finding an inexpensive bed can be brutal. Resorts' prices are out of control, and there's little else. **Fifi Café,** across from the SOSA office, has two rooms, each with a double bed. The common bathroom is rustic, but the beds are functional. Most importantly, the owner doesn't care how many people sleep in the room. First night 60 lempiras, additional nights 50 lempiras. The other budget option is **Hugo** (fax 45-42-19), who has some rooms connected to the SOSA office that he rents for US$5 a night. The owner's store of knowledge adds a bonus, but the otherwise satisfactory rooms are often occupied. A more thrilling option is to head to **West Peak Inn,** on the north side of the island. The owner is building a resort but lets people stay in tents pitched on the site for US$10 a night. The primary draw is the gorgeous beach. The primary problem is getting there: a water taxi is 180 lempira each way. However, there are ways around this common problem (see Sights and Entertainment, below).

For chow, dig into standard fare in restaurants with that old-musty-walls ambience. Although the menu is occasionally limited to cheese sandwiches and French fries, the **Café Bonacco** provides gratifying grub. They're tucked into a corner of the Casa Sikaffy and are open daily 6am-noon and 6-9pm (sandwich and fries 14 lempira, *desayuno típico* 13 lempiras). **Joe's,** past the Centro de Salud at the first left, down about two blocks on the right, and across from the El Cubanito sign, is a favor-

HONDURAS

ite among frugal locals. A full fish dinner is 25 lempiras; Sundays bring no-holds-barred special dishes (open daily 10:30am-2pm and 6-11pm).

Sights and Entertainment Guanaja is all about paying homage to Mother Nature. Diving opportunities abound, and the north side of the island is teeming with beaches, mountains, and reefs. For some of that scuba sweetness, talk to Hugo at **Diving Freedom Dive Shop.** He charges a steep US$200 for PDIC certification and US$25 per tank for fun dives. One of the most popular sites is the **Wreck of the Jade Trader,** preserved at a cool 20-30m below the surface and waiting to be explored (again).

To add a little shape to your island wanderings, and for a splurge that's still below resort prices, head over to Bo Bush's **Island House** (fax 45-41-46, or call Hugo at SOSA), a new resort on the north side of the island. For US$35 per day you get a great room right off the beach and three big meals. For another US$35 per day, you get two boat dives and unlimited shore diving with Bo, who is a certified divemaster with his own compressor. If you stay several days, he'll take you back to the airport for free (saving you about 200 lempiras). The reef is a mere five-minute swim away, and the island's famous **waterfall** is just a 30-minute hike. Bo's also sits near the highest peak on the island, a great place to watch overwhelmingly romantic sunsets.

To get to the north side, some folks just ask around at all the docks on Bonacca for someone heading that way; they're often invited to ride along. It may take a day or two, but it's much cheaper and a little more exciting once you're there. Then you can just relax and disappear into dreamy Caribbean oblivion.

■■■ LA MOSQUITIA

Farther east still from Trujillo along the Caribbean Coast looms *La Mosquitia* (The Mosquito Coast), a stretch of seemingly impermeable jungle hundreds of miles wide and reaching as far south as Costa Rica. The eastern part of Honduras is perhaps the most amenable part of La Mosquitia for travelers, but that's not saying much; getting to remote Puerto Lempira, the point of departure for most tour groups, is costly, and guides should be hired out of La Ceiba, though some operators work out of Tegucigalpa or Trujillo. Regardless of difficulties, those who have visited the area claim that the adventure is worth every *centavo,* partly because so much can happen. A trip starting off in fast-water rapids slows first for sightings of exotic animals, and eventually for maddeningly limaceous floats into the heart of darkness, along the way stopping in the tiny villages of the indigenous **Pech, Tawahka,** and **Moskito** Indians; every minute of the trip sears the soul with indelible memories. A visit to the home of the Tawahka, along the confluence of the Patuca and Wampu rivers, might include feasting on soup made out of *tepescuintle* (cavy; a giant rodent) and cooked monkey, learning to create *mijao* carrying bags, or foot-stompin' romp with *Mayana Rikini,* a local roots dance group.

Currently the leader among trip-leaders to the Mosquitia, **La Mosquitia Ecoaventuras,** P.O. Box 3577, Tegucigalpa, Honduras (tel. and fax 37-93-98), specializes in river-rafting trips all along the Mosquito Coast. Many trips actually start in Tegucigalpa, but accommodations can be made for travelers in La Ceiba. Custom itineraries are available if you have special wishes, but book at least 1 month in advance. Prices range from US$200 to US$1200. Talk to the guys at **Go Native Tours** (see Copán, page 223), for info about other trips. Or do the whole darn thing yourself by flying from Ceiba to Palacios or Puerto Lempira and looking for a guide from there. If you make the trip on your own, adequate preparation (carrying enough food, water, lempiras, and camping supplies) is absolutely necessary.

NICARAGUA

Nicaragua is a small country, but its sizeable name is well-known around the globe. No news is not always good news, but big international news is one of the surest few signs of disastrous news familiar to the modern world. Nicaragua is larger than any of the other Central American countries in terms of sheer land mass, but it is also one of the most sparsely populated; over 90% of its citizens live in a region that amounts to less than 15% of its total area, and these few million have suffered tremendously during the course of the notorious internal strife that has plagued their nation in the past several decades. Of the thousands of beautiful and awe-inspiring sights that await travelers in Nicaragua's cities and countryside, all stand likely to be eclipsed in the eye of the visiting foreigner, eclipsed by knowledge of the land's infamous history and eclipsed by the evident toll that these conflicts have taken. Here, especially, every visitor is a student of the natives. Here you can come to know an idealistic people, always aspiring but sometimes weary. And you can draw your own conclusions about what went on here recently and what may yet come to pass.

Nicaragua is not a country that is going to embrace the tourism industry anytime soon. Much of the country simply isn't ready, and while many cities have tourism offices (Inturismo is the government tourism agency), the staff is often so surprised to see a real, live tourist walk through the door that they don't know quite what to do. Many Nicaraguans see tourism as a sell-out; they want an economic base, built to last. Ecotourism is in its infancy here. In terms of environmental policy, Nicaragua is far behind a country like Costa Rica. But Nicaragua is also the largest country in Central America. Its unprotected virgin forests, saved only by an economy that can't build roads, dwarf the ecologically progressive Costa Rican park system. The fate of these lands is sure to become a controversial and important issue in the future.

There is, about the country, an atmosphere of the could've been, the might've been, and the might-still-be. It is a wonderful place to travel, offering a cerebral as well as sensual adventure. One of the country's greatest treasures is its conversation; the dearth of foreign travelers offers a grand opportunity to get to know the Nicaraguans, who will most often gladly talk about what they've lived through, and pretty much everyone older than twenty has at least a few memories of the war. If you remain open-minded, you can easily hear all sides. Like an ornithologist trying to sight as many birds as possible, you can collect points of view, keeping an ear out for rare strains. Language may be an initial barrier to conversation, however. Nicaraguan Spanish is delicious, and that is why its native speakers swallow half of every word. The letter "s," perhaps because of its association with the Somoza family, has fled the country, and makes only occasional appearances in Nicaraguan Spanish.

The advantages to traveling in an untouristed country are obvious. While few travel experiences can put you in the shoes of a native, in Nicaragua, a traveler has the opportunity to gain a very real appreciation of the land. Awaiting each visitor are beautiful places, interesting people, and at least one once-in-a-lifetime experience.

ESSENTIALS

■■■ WHEN TO GO

CLIMATE

Nicaragua has three climatic zones: Atlantic, Central, and Pacific. All three have two seasons, rainy *(invierno),* and dry *(verano).* In the Pacific zone, nine months of the year is *invierno.* February-April is *verano.* Most of Nicaragua remains dry from

March to May, but even then intermittent rain is not unheard of. In Managua temperatures tend to range from 30°-38°C for most of the year. Masaya and Granada are comparable to Managua. In Granada, the lake has a moderating effect. Isla de Ometepe is perfect, a bit wet, but very pleasant. The east coast remains cooler than the west, but wetter. Nicaragua is one of the most humid nations in Central America.

FESTIVALS AND HOLIDAYS

Some of Nicaragua's many local festivals and holidays (i.e. times when services slow or shut down completely, and when you should get those dancin' shoes ready) are **January 1** (New Year's Day); **February 25** (Anniversary of Elections); **May 1** (Labor Day); **July 19** (Revolution's Anniversary); **September 14-15** (Independence Day); **October 12** (Columbus Day); **December 8** (Immaculate Conception Day); **December 25** (Christmas).

■■■ FEED YOUR HEAD

For publications and travel organizations of general interest, see Central America: An Introduction.

Embassy of Nicaragua, U.S. 1627 New Hampshire Ave. NW, Washington, DC 20009 (tel. (202) 939-6570; fax (202) 939-6574). **Canada** 130 Albert St., Suite 407, Ottawa, Ontario, K1P 5G4 (tel. (613) 234-9361; fax 238-7666). **U.K.** (tel. (44) 171-409-2536; 409-2593). The **consulates,** which provide visa information and informational packets, can be reached through the embassies.

Nicaraguan Institute of Tourism, Apartado 122, Cost. Hotel Intercontinental, 1 c. Abajo, 1 c. al Sur, Managua (tel. (505-2) 28-12-38; fax 28-11-87).

Centro Nicaragüense de Derechos Humanos (CENIDH), Apartado 4402, Managua, Nicaragua; their monthly bulletin provides statistical (and other) information about human rights in Nicaragua and Central America.

Council of Evangelical Churches of Nicaragua (CEPAD), Attn: Director of Communications, Apartado 3091, Managua, Nicaragua (tel. (505-2) 66-46-28; fax 66-42-36). Publishes a bimonthly bulletin with information about the struggle of the Nicaraguan people for justice and peace, as well as about the evangelical church in the country.

Nicaraguan Center for Community Action, 2140 Shattuck Ave., Box 2063, Berkeley, CA, 94704 (tel. (510) 832-4959, fax (510) 654-8635). Informative, comprehensive quarterly—subscribe for US$10 plus contributions.

■■■ DOCUMENTS AND FORMALITIES

All visitors entering Nicaragua must have a **passport** (valid for at least the next six months), an onward/return ticket, and sufficient funds (US$200 minimum). U.S. and U.K. citizens do not need **visas;** citizens of Australia, New Zealand, South Africa, and most western European nations do need visas, which can be obtained from a Nicaraguan embassy of consulate prior to arrival in Nicaragua. Make checks for US$25 payable to Consulate of Nicaragua/Washington; visas are issued within 10 to 15 working days of application. Nationals of other countries should check with a Nicaraguan consulate.

All visitors to Nicaragua are restricted to a stay of 30 days, but you can obtain up to two extensions on your passport (up to 90 days total) at the immigration office in Managua (Carretera Sur, tel. 66-60-10; fax 66-60-46). After that you must leave the country and re-enter. To drive a car you need only what is called a *"Provisional"* to be carried at all times and produced on demand. This can be obtained at the border; you'll need to show a valid passport and your title to the car. Insurance is optional in Nicaragua. There is an **airport tax** of US$12 upon arrival., and US$7 for departure. Visitors are allowed to bring one carton of cigarettes or 1-4 pounds of tobacco, as well as 3 liters of liquor into Nicaragua.

Electric current in Nicaragua is 110 volts, 60 cycles. The country is one hour behind U.S. Eastern Standard time, although this shifts to two hours when the U.S. is on daylight savings.

■■■ MONEY MATTERS

US$1= 7.70 córdobas	**1 córdoba=US$0.13**
CDN$1= 5.66 córdobas	**1 córdoba=CDN$0.18**
UK£1= 11.96 córdobas	**1 córdoba=UK£0.08**
IR£1= 12.19 córdobas	**1 córdoba=IR£0.08**
AUS$1= 5.68 córdobas	**1 córdoba=AUS$0.176**
NZ$1= 5.05 córdobas	**1 córdoba=NZ$0.198**
SARand 1 = 2.10 córdobas	**1 córdoba = SARand 0.48**

The Nicaraguan unit of currency is the **córdoba** (C$). There are 100 centavos to the córdoba. Colloquially, córdobas are sometimes referred to as pesos. 10 centavos may also be called a *real.* Córdoba notes appear in denominations up to 100 córdobas; large bills are hard to break. The only coins regularly used are 50 centavo pieces. There are also bills for one, 50 and 25 centavos. Most Nicaraguans (even hotel employees) have so little currency that they'll be hard pressed to break even a 50-córdoba bill. A cumbersome option is to carry lots of one-córdoba bills.

Dollars are widely accepted, especially by large hotels, airlines, and especially on the east coast. Changing dollars to córdobas is never a problem and most banks will exchange at the official rate. **Banco Nacional de Desarollo (BND)** and **Banco Nicaraguense de Industria y Comercios** are the two large banks with branches all over the country. Banks are often clustered together, for example along an Esquina de Bancos. Nicaragua's *coyotes,* found on streetcorners, will also safely change U.S. dollars at competitive rates. Make sure all the bills are genuine; counterfeit currency is rampant in Nicaragua. Also, avoid changing currency at night. While officially illegal, this black market is generally accepted.

Changing **traveler's checks** is more difficult in Nicaragua than elsewhere in Central America. Many *casas de cambio* in Managua will do this; León also has a *casa de cambio.* Most banks will not change traveler's checks, and those that do will usually make you pay a service charge. Most hotels and restaurants accept neither traveler's checks nor credit cards. *Coyotes* are less willing to change traveler's checks. All foreign currency other than U.S. dollars should be changed into dollars or córdobas in Managua. The American Express office in Managua (tel. 66-40-50, 66-40-55, or 66-87-20) is at Viajes Atlantida by El Ritiro. There are no ATMs in Nicaragua that accept North American bank cards. The best way to receive money abroad is through the Western Union office in Managua (see Managua: Practical Information).

Tipping is left to the discretion of the traveler; be kind if service is exceptional, but be aware that gratuity is often incorporated into the price of goods. Taxi drivers don't get tips unless they do something special (like wait, or give you a juicy tip).

■■■ SAFETY

By and large, Nicaragua is not a dangerous country for tourists. Managua, like any large Central American city, demands a certain degree of caution and common sense, but most of the country is sleepy, untouristed, and poor; people spend a lot of time simply watching TV. Avoid heading out into any city after dark unless you have to. Touristed areas are often hot-spots for crimes. Avoid as much as possible heading out into rural areas alone, and if someone asks for your money, give it to them without any trickery. Rare sporadic armed violence is reported throughout the country, and bandits have been known to operate on the roads after dark. Visitors should notify their respective embassies in Managua upon arrival to the county. The most dangerous areas in Nicaragua are in the north of the country, where land reform remains a major issue and violence is not uncommon. All that Nicaragua asks of its visitors is a sense of diplomacy. Call the U.S. State Department's Travel Advisories Hotline for information about safety in Nicaragua (tel. (202) 647-5225).

While women travelers should (as always) be particularly cautious, Nicaragua is blessed with a solid support organization for the country's women. **El Movimiento**

de Mujeres Nicaragüenses "Luisa Amanda Espinoza" (AMNLAE; tel. 75-9-11; fax 27-58-94), named after the first militant woman activist in the FSLN, has set up "Casas de la Mujer" in more than 50 towns throughout Nicaragua; while the "Casas" deal primarily with women's civil liberties, they are equipped to offer help to women travelers, as well. Write to AMNLAE, Aptdo. A-238, Managua, Nicaragua (see Managua, Practical Information, page 270, for more information).

■■■ HEALTH

Health concerns in Nicaragua are the same as in much of Central America; see Central America: Health (page 11) for more information. **Malaria** is a problem in rural areas and town outskirts; all visitors should take chloroquine tablets for malaria prevention (take one tablet a week before you leave). Since malaria and **dengue fever** are transmitted by mosquitoes, the wise traveler to Nicaragua will wear plenty of insect repellent DEET. **Cholera** has also been recently reported in Nicaragua, as has **Hepatitis A. Typhoid fever** is prevalent throughout Central America; vaccines are recommended for travel to infected areas. For reliable and current public health information contact the **Ministerio de Salud Publica** in Managua (tel. 94312, 97808, or 97395, fax 97997), located at Complejo Concepción Palacio, in Barrio Rubenia. Water in Managua is considered quite safe, but to be extra careful, purified water is readily available. Elsewhere, just ask for chlorinated water.

■■■ ALTERNATIVES TO TOURISM

STUDY

Short-term study opportunities for foreigners are somewhat more limited in Nicaragua than in other parts of Central America; try to make informal arrangements on your own. The **Universidad Centro Americana (UCA)** (tel. 70-58-7, 70-23-6, or 75-44-2), south of Managua proper in front of Radio Ja, offers eight-week intensive programs in Spanish language for US$200; food and lodging is left up to the student. **The Centro Nicaraguense de Aprendizaje Cultural (CENAC),** in Estelí teaches Spanish for US$120 per week. The price includes four hours of class per day, room and board with a local family, and weekend excursions. Or you can skip the classroom part; CENAC will place you with a local family for US$40 per week. The **University of Mobile** (that's Mobile, AL) recently opened a branch campus in San Marcos, a small town 20 minutes outside of Masaya. The University is primarily designed for full-time undergraduates, but may also be a good place to find out about other educational opportunities within Nicaragua. Intensive Spanish and English are taught to an international student body. In the U.S. call the University of Mobile at (334) 675-5990 and ask for the director of admissions, or write to P.O. Box 13220, Mobile, AL 36663-0220. In Nicaragua, contact Yadira Gonzalez, University of Mobile, Latin American Campus, Admissions Office, San Marcos, Carazo (tel. (505) 43-22-298). In addition, the university is affiliated with various international consortia thus enabling its students to study in 20 countries throughout the world.

VOLUNTEER

There are plenty of reasons to get involved in Nicaragua, and if you'll be there anyway, very few excuses not to. Volunteers in Nicaragua can get involved in reforestation, land management, public health, community organization, human rights, and education. Many organizations in the United States and elsewhere can provide information and direct individual initiative. **NICCA, CEPAD,** and **CENIDH** (see Useful Publications, page 256) offer the above volunteer opportunities and even more.

Fundación Nicaraguense por el Desarollo Comunitario Integral (FUNDECI), Casa Benjamin Linder, Aptdo postal 2694, Managua (tel. 66-43-73, fax 66-33-81). Informal clearing-house for volunteer opportunities in Nicaragua. Net-

NICARAGUA

work at the Thursday morning meetings at Casa Ben Linder (see Managua: Community Activities). FUNDECI's U.S. representative, and a good resource for researching volunteer opportunities from the U.S., is Rita Clark at the Nicaragua-U.S. Friendship Office APSNICA/FUNDECI, Technical Assistance Program, Church of the Brethren, 337 North Carolina Ave. SE, 20003 (tel. (202) 546-0915, fax 546-0935).

Nicaragua Network, 2025 I St. NW, Washington DC 20006 (tel. 202-223-2328); allows volunteers to work on summer reforestation and construction brigades in Nicaragua.

Nicaragua Exchange, 239 Centre St., NY, NY 10013 (tel. 212-219-8620). Allows volunteers to work on coffee and cotton harvest work brigades in Nicaragua.

■■■ GETTING THERE

Carriers such as **Air France, Iberia, SAHSA, TACA, Continental, American,** and **Aeroflot** airlines fly to Managua's Augusto C. Sandino International Airport from points in the U.S. and Europe. In the summer of 1995, low-end student/youth round-trip fares were US$560 from New York, US$580 from Chicago, and US$300 from Miami.

There are two international **bus** lines that run between Managua and nearby capitals. **Tica Bus** (tel. 22-60-94), is headquartered in the Barrio Marta Quezada, two blocks east of the Casino Pasapogo (cabbies might know it as the Cine Dorado). Tica runs buses to and from Tegucigalpa (US$20), San Salvador (US$35), Guatemala City (US$43), and San José, Costa Rica (US$15). **Sirca Bus** (tel. 67-38-33 or 75-7-26) services San José (180 cólones) from its station at Altamira de Este, two blocks south of Distribuidora Vicky.

Crossing the border by land can be tedious; bring U.S. dollars, or your life will be hell. You'll walk through customs of the country you're leaving (Honduras or Costa Rica), all the while warding off aggressive money changers. Better rates are available in Nicaragua, but even if you decide to exchange currency here, save a few greenbacks. Next, you may have to hike several kilometers across the border (pack light), or shag a bus. At Nicaraguan customs, you may (inexplicably) be asked to pay two entrance fees: a small tax of five córdobas (less than US$1), plus another fee (US$7) *payable only in U.S. dollars*—though it's clear to everyone that we're all in Nicaragua at this point. Finally, you'll board a bus to your destination of choice. Some bus lines actually cross the border and take passengers's passports inside to be stamped. Should you cross the border at any point other than a designated border crossing, find an immigration office immediately.

The suggested **border crossing** for entry to or from **Honduras** is Las Manos, El Espino, and Gausaule, which are only open during the day. The U.S. State Dept. reports that travelers have experienced harassment at border crossings while crossing the Gulf of Fonseca by ferry between Potosi, Nicaragua and La Union, El Salvador. To get to **Costa Rica,** the most traveled route is along the Inter-american Highway at Peñas Blancas. **Vehicles** may be driven in with driver's license and registration for US$20.

■■■ ONCE THERE

The government tourist office is the **Instituto Nicaragüense de Turismo (Inturismo)** (tel. (2) 22-74-23, 28-12-38, or 28-13-37, fax 28-11-87), one block south and one block west of the Intercontinental Hotel in Managua. The helpful staff provides maps and information. (Open Mon.-Fri. 8am-12:30pm and 1:30-5pm.) Another excellent source of information are the newspapers **La Prensa, El Nuevo Diario, La Tribuna,** and **Barricada,** the official Sandinista newspaper. **AMNLAE** offices, listed in the Practical Information for most cities, provides information and assistance for women, both national and travelers.

TRANSPORTATION

Buses are the primary mode of transport in Nicaragua. Most of Nicaragua's bus fleet is composed of sturdy-but-cramped yellow school buses retired from North America. Whenever possible, take an express bus to your destination; the few extra córdobas (usually) assure you of a seat and increase the likelihood of arriving before your passport expires. The Nicaraguan bus network leaves little danger of being stranded, and you can get to Managua quite easily from almost anywhere. If necessary, however, you can always take a taxi, as many trips involve short distances. The roads, if paved, are usually in decent condition, although buses' bad shocks pick up the potholes. Don't drive at night unless you absolutely have to.

Nica and La Costancia fly to Bluefields and Isla de Maiz Grande and other Atlantic Coast destinations. Flying to these destinations will save you a day of travel, and the fares are still quite cheap.

ADDRESSES

Nicaragua is funny this way. Addresses are almost always given in terms of their relation to a nebulous canon of landmarks within a given city: a museum is three blocks west and two blocks south of a gas station, a pharmacy is 1½ blocks north of a playground. The plot thickens, however, with the occasional substitution of *arriba* and *abajo* for east and west, respectively. Then again, if you happen to be in a city set on a hill, *arriba* and *abajo* may only refer to relative elevation. In Managua, north becomes *al lago* and some of the cardinal landmarks haven't existed for years. Another directional device is *al salida* or *al entrada,* as in *"al salida a Juigalpa."* Look for this address where the road for Juigalpa leaves town. Many streets are named, but the names are almost never used.

KEEPING IN TOUCH

Nicaraguan **mail** is comparable to other Central American postal systems, perhaps a bit slower. Allow a good 15 days for addresses within the U.S., 20 days for Europe. TELCOR also has its own courier service, E.M.S., slightly cheaper than private couriers. Post offices are generally open Mon.-Fri. 8am-noon and 2-5pm, Sat. 8am-noon. Towns with fax service are open during the same hours. You can receive *poste restante* mail at any TELCOR office in Nicaragua, in most cases, mail will be held for one month, though some offices will hold mail for only two weeks. Letters sent to small towns may take longer than those addressed to hub cities. Mail should be addressed as follows:

David "Juice" SPIEGEL (name)
Lista de Correos
TELCOR Estelí (town name), Estelí (department name)
Nicaragua, CENTRAL AMERICA

Many hotels and shops let patrons use their telephone for about 3 córdobas for 5 minutes. Generally, though, while in Nicaragua, your link with the rest of the world will be through **TELCOR** (Instituto Nicaraguense de Telecommunicaciones y Correos). Most every city, town, or hamlet in Nicaragua has a TELCOR, home to the postal and telephone office, and usually identifiable by a tall radio tower; offices are generally open daily 7am-9pm. TELCOR staffers will place your international call and direct you to a booth to take the call. If you're calling with AT&T USADirect, they will still ask you for the two names and a number; if you want to place a call with a credit card or phone card, simply explain that you must speak with the AT&T operator in person. **Collect calls** through the Nicaraguan phone system are harder (sometimes impossible) to make. To reach a U.S. AT&T operator, dial 164 or dial 9 to get the Nicaraguan operator and ask to be connected to an AT&T operator for a collect call. Dial 166 for MCI Call U.S.A., or 161 for Sprint Express. Other important phone numbers are: 112 for **information**, 114 for **international information**, 110 for a **national long-distance operator**. The Nicaragua **country code** is 505. See Practical Information sections for each city's local telephone code.

NICARAGUA: AN INTRODUCTION

■■■ HISTORY

In 1519, a Spanish expedition under **Gil González de Avila** (or "Dávila") encountered an indigenous settlement on the southern shores of what would later be known as Lago de Nicaragua. Dávila and his *conquistadores* returned as military entrepreneurs in 1522, only to be rebuffed by the fighting natives of the Caribbean coast, led by the famed **King Nicarao.** Dávila had made serious inroads into the region, prior to his rout, however, and set the stage for the pillage that was to accompany European immigration to Nicaragua as it had every previous venture into the New World: he hauled away the land's natural resources, starting with its gold, and then abducted thousands of its original residents to sell them as slaves. In 1524, **Francisco Hernández de Córdoba** brought the first wave of successful colonists to settle in the eastern lowlands. They named the new country Nicaragua, after Nicarao, the *indígena* chief who had welcomed their first advances, and much later their descendents would call the local coin "córdoba," in honor of his European guest. Direct confrontation between the invaders and the invaded was brief and relatively bloodless, compared to the conflicts seen during the disintegration of the Aztec and Maya empires. But the annihilation of Nicarao's people was no less complete for being indirect; Old World diseases, against which the indigenous had never developed immunity, killed hundreds of thousands in the first few decades of their introduction. The disease-driven depopulation was accelerated by the thriving slave trade practiced by the Spanish colonists, who captured and sold off a majority of the plague-resistant natives during the same period.

León was founded in 1524, only to be destroyed by an earthquake 86 years later. The city moved west and became both the colonial capital and the center of liberal politics in Nicaragua. Its rival settlement, Granada, lay on the northwest shore of the Lago de Nicaragua, and was able to exploit the commercial and military superiority of its location to great advantage during its early colonial period, and soon became a powerful, affluent, and conservative city. León and Granada remained ideological opponents, often feuding violently, until 1857, when the capital was moved to Managua as a compromise conceded to liberals on the part of ruling conservatives. Nicaragua gained its independence from Spain in 1821. For a while, the country was part of Mexico, and then part of the **Central American Federation,** before becoming completely independent in 1835. But with the withdrawal of the Spanish, British and North American influence grew, creeping west from the Caribbean. Cornelius Vanderbilt started the **Accessory Transit Company,** which transported thousands of forty-niners (among others) from the Caribbean, across Nicaragua by boat and stagecoach to the Pacific, and from there to California.

With León supporting him, **William Walker,** a renegade North American, attacked Granada in 1855 with 56 men, captured the city and declared himself president. After drawing Vanderbilt's ire by seizing his company, Walker was expelled from Nicaragua by the U.S. Navy, the transit company, and five other republics in 1857, only to make two subsequent unsuccessful attempts to recapture the country. (See the gray box below.)

Nicaragua's conservatives gained power and held it until 1893, when the left-leaning **José Santos Zelaya** overthrew the government and proclaimed himself dictator. Zelaya was not only leftist and autocratic; he was also Nicaragua's first effective nationalist, and his emergence marked the beginning of a long line of North American interventions—dictatorships, after all, were nothing new. He spoke of a renewed Central American unity, as had been partially attained several decades before, and of the importance of blocking the U.S. from securing trans-isthmian canal-building rights. In those days, Panama had not yet been explored as a possible location for an inter-oceanic canal, and so the U.S. State Department was especially alarmed to hear rumors that Zelaya might be planning to grant the same land to Japan. In 1889, the U.S. government, portending future foreign policy in Latin America, orchestrated Zelaya's overthrow along with his persisting conservative detractors, and sent in the Marine Corps, subsequently controlling the country through puppet governments for the next 16 years. During most this period of occupation *de facto* (which was strikingly parallel to the Nicaragua of the early 1990s), three liberal leaders maintained a steady resistance. The three, Sacasa, Moncada, and **Augusto César Sandino,** all led their troops into fiery rebellion in 1927, in response to a changing of the puppets and a further importation of U.S. Marines. Six months' fighting was enough for Sacasa and Moncada, who both settled peacefully with the U.S.-backed government, in exchange for an elected presidency for each. Sandino, on the other hand, continued to fight against the foreign influence and the dubious democracy that it supported; he would do so for as long as North American soldiers remained in Nicaragua.

The Marines left their replacements, the brutal Guardia Nacional, under the command of **Anastasio Somoza García,** later "Tacho," who used the hated unit to support the Somoza family dictatorship for 50 years. In 1934, Somoza assassinated Augusto Cesar Sandino, national hero and anti-American inspirational leader. The Somozas and their associates plundered the country, amassing huge fortunes and vast land holdings while Nicaragua wallowed in miserable poverty. Vicious repression, torture, and disappearances were commonplace. U.S. support for the regime was unfaltering. FDR once said of Anastasio Somoza, "He may be a son of a bitch, but he's ours." On September 21, 1956, **Rigoberto López Pérez** shot and killed Anastasio Somoza in León. Pérez, a liberal poet, was martyred immediately. Anastasio Somoza was succeeded by his son, Luis Somoza Debayle, who ruled until his death 11 years later. His younger brother, Anastasio Somoza Debayle, called "Tachito," assumed the presidency in 1967, and held onto the official position for the four years that the new constitution allowed.

Opposition grew as the Somoza dynasty endured. Carlos Fonseca Amador, born in Matagalpa in 1936, was a radical student leader and prominent Somoza opponent. In 1961, he and other radicals formed the **Frente Sandinista de Liberación Nacional (FSLN).** The name was meant to invoke the memory of Cesar Augusto Sandino. They were called **Sandinistas** and their movement was *Sandinismo.*

In 1972 a massive earthquake virtually leveled Managua, killing 6000 Nicaraguans and leaving over 300,000 others isolated from food and shelter. The momentarily dethroned Somoza exploited the opportunity to marshal the Guardia Nacional into a "National Emergency Committee," and himself the ruler, by martial law. Almost before the rubble from the quake had settled, he had re-installed himself as President. When international relief money went straight to Tachito Somoza's personal coffers, opposition to his regime solidified. By 1974, both the **Union Democracia de Liberación (UDEL)** and the FSLN were gaining ground. As opposition to the government increased, so did brutal repression by the Guardia Nacional. In January of 1978, Pedro Joaquín Chamorro, leader of the UDEL and publisher of the popular and respected newspaper *La Prensa,* was assassinated by the Guardia Nacional. The Revolution began in earnest. For a year and a half, the country was beset with general strikes and armed standoffs, with firefights and pitched battles. On July 17, 1979, President Somoza fled the country. Two days later, the Sandinistas marched as victors into Managua. (Today, many small towns all over Nicaragua are named "17 Julio", and others "19 Julio.") Somoza was assassinated a year later in Paraguay.

But that, of course, is not the end of the story. After the euphoria of victory had subsided, the victors set about resuscitating a country in sorry shape. Murals, no matter how uplifting or revolutionary, cannot feed children, clean streets, or plant crops. The Sandinistas, like any opposition movement *cum* governing party, immediately faced a new opposition movement, in this case, the Contras. Some Contras were ex-Guardia Nacional, others mercenaries, scared teenagers pressed into service by Contras, or ordinary Nicaraguans ideologically opposed to the Sandinistas.

Unfortunately for Sandinistas, they rose to power just as **Ronald Reagan** was assuming the U.S. presidency—only a year after they marched into Managua, he marched into Washington. A movie-star cowboy turned foreign-policy cowboy, Reagan was determined to halt the spread of Communism in Central America; halting the Soviet-backed Sandinistas was the linchpin of the Reagan Administration's policy, and the Contras were supplied with massive support.

Throughout the 1980s, Contra-Sandinista war ravaged Nicaragua. In 1984, **Daniel Ortega** of the FSLN won a popular presidential election neutrally monitored and generally accepted as honest. The U.S. mined Nicaraguan harbors and spearheaded an economic embargo of the country. Food and supplies ran short. Inflation spiraled to a staggering 30,000%. Revolutionary idealism began to wane, and as the war became a war of attrition, it became clear that if the Nicaraguans chose a new ruling party in the 1990 elections (something more amenable to U.S. interests), conditions would improve. Sure enough, under economic siege, the electorate went to the polls in 1990, and replaced the Sandinistas with **Violeta Chamorro** of the Unión Nacional Opposición (UNO), a coalition of fourteen smaller parties. Mrs. Chamorro, the widow of Pedro Joaquín Chamorro, carried 55% of the vote. When Chamorro took office, the Contras disarmed. Though some violence continues to this day, the war, for all intents and purposes, was over.

Today, Nicaragua is peaceful; travel is safe. It often seems hard to believe that violence reigned here so recently. Much of the country's infrastructure is in understandable disrepair. Nicaragua is a very poor country, and a few families control what little wealth there is. Official unemployment figures hover at around 70%. No longer burdened with an economic embargo, however, Nicaragua suffers no serious shortages. On the contrary, the UNO government is doing its best to promote market-driven capitalism, a trend opposed by the socialist Sandinistas. The result is a

William Walker, What a Killer

Webster's lists as its first definition of "filibuster" (from the Spanish, *filibustero*, or "freebooter"): "an irregular military adventurer; *specif:* an American engaged in fomenting insurrections in Latin America in the mid-19th century." This word's long-standing place in our language is due no doubt to the dastardly exploits of this man. Born in Nashville, Tennessee in 1824, Walker's gall and derring-do have gone unmatched in all the subsequent decades of *norteamericano* fiddling with Latin American affairs. After years spent studying to be a physician, at Pennsylvania and in Paris, he left medicine to practice law in New Orleans. Within a few years' time his overweening ambition had outgrown even the practice of litigation; he drifted out to California, one beat behind the Gold Rush, and ended up in command of a successful U.S. military expedition in the Baja region of the Mexican state. Walker set important personal precedent by declaring the land an independent state, and himself its president. Quickly chased out by Mexico and acquitted by a San Francisco judiciary, he next turned his rabid gaze to Nicaragua, and here he made his mark on history. Would-be canal-builders funded the renegade to land a small brigade on the shore of the fledgling nation. Unbelievably, Walker conquered Granada within days of arrival. Less believably, he established himself as the President of Nicaragua within the year and legalized slavery. Only when he announced his plans to forge out into the other four Central American states did Nicaraguans amass the support they needed to oust him. His regime regrouped in Alabama, and from there attempted two new invasions, equally bold, but less fruitful. His final foray ended in Trujillo, Honduras, where British troops captured him and surrendered him to the Honduran authorities—who promptly stood him up before the firing squad.

country in a kind of extended limbo: Nicaragua's elite (many wealthy Nicaraguans fled the country during the 1980s and returned only recently, encouraged by Violeta's victory) whisk themselves around in tint-windowed Land Cruisers. Hundreds of striking Revolutionary murals all over the country remind passers-by of the enormous popular victory that took place here, and of the angry idealism that lingers still today. Sandino's image is everywhere. As an outsized silhouette, a blurry, black and white poster, a stylized portrait, or stenciled vandalism, he is always surveying the country from beneath his wide-brimmed sombrero.

■■■ THE ARTS

Probably the greatest of all Central American literary figures was Nicaragua's own **Rubén Darío** (1867-1916); the government must have thought so, since just about every other park, street, or monument in the country was named after the leader of *Latino* **letters.** Darío's resonant, sensitive poems include "Sonatina," the politically edged "A Roosevelt," and his most praised "Cantos de vida y esperanza" (Songs of Life and Hope). His work "Azul" is thought to have started Modernism in Latin America, and the poet's death is considered by some to mark the movement's end.

Later Nicaraguan writers felt the need to distance themselves from Darío to express their own voice, and have concerned themselves less with the aesthetic than with the urgency of their country's sociopolitical condition. Vanguardist Pablo Antonio Cuadra and poet Ernesto Cardenal fall into this latter group.

Nicaragua's contribution to **music** has not been as significant. Native musicians of jam on a variety of instruments, including the *Chirimía*, a primitive clarinet, and the fearsome, thunderous *juco,* a bull-roarer played by pulling a string through a drum head. Lucky travelers might even get to see "El Güegünse," a farcical, musical street drama about an old man who repeatedly outwits authorities. Not all the music of the country is from *indígenas,* though. The most famous Nicaraguan composer is probably Luis A. Delgadillo, who wrote a **ballet** for children and has put some of Rubén Darío's texts to music.

■■■ FOOD AND DRINK

Most often served up at the *comida corrientes* (meal o' the day, or "running meal"), and favored among street buffet grills, are chicken, fruit, and tortillas, the staples of the Nicaraguan diet. Beyond that, live and learn and learn to love the other basics: *gallo pinto* is rice and beans; *platanos* (plantains) are served up *maduro* (fried, greasy, and sweet), or *verde* (crispy, like potato chips); cheese is usually squeaky and mild, or crumbly and very sharp; *Carne Asuda* is code for barbecued, marinated, yummy-to-the-tummy meat. And not to be left out, *mondongo* is tripe (stomach) cooked together with beef knuckles. Yes, beef knuckles. For vegetarians (who likely *won't* be going for the *mondongo*), *ensaladas* are usually comprised of cabbage with tomatoes and vinegary dressing. The *filete jalapeño* is usually beef smothered with a delicious, creamy onion and pepper sauce. The average mealtimes are 7-10am for breakfast, noon-3pm for lunch, and 6-8pm for dinner.

Scrumptious rums are produced locally, and not coincidentally, are drunk locally in huge quantities. *Flor de Caña,* produced in Chinandega, is the most popular brand, and is smooth and rich in flavor. *Victoria* and *Toña* are the national beers, and at the half the price of imports, are worth getting to like. For the most refreshing drinks after a hard day of rough-and-rugged traveling, dip into the *refrescos naturales,* fruit juice mixed down with a little water and sugar. As always, though, be damn sure the water and ice are clean, and use caution when eating and drinking any of Nicaragua's food. See Central America, Health, page 11, for more tips.

■■■ MEDIA

Nicaraguans stay abreast of national and international news through television programming from the United States; a steadily increasing number of TVs in Nicaragua are equipped with cable, including CNN, ESPN, MTV, as well as Univision for Spanish programming. For daily local news (and, of course, the latest baseball standings and statistics), the most popular newspapers are *La Prensa* (which leans to the right), *La Barricada* (published by the Sandinistas), and *La Nueva Día,* which walks the fence.

■■■ RECENT NEWS

Just when President Violeta Barrios de Chamorro thought she could fulfill her campaign promises of reducing debt and settling property disputes with the Sandinistas, she lost the support of the legislature because of a disagreement about to what extent the telephone and mail service, TELCOR, should be privatized. As a result, the legislature is working to limit the terms of presidents and prevent their relatives from running for office. The opposition Sandinista party (FSLN) was concurrently weakened, however, as a moderate sector of the party split off. Among the Nicaraguan people, primary and secondary school teachers went on strike to reap higher wages, and border tension continues with Costa Rica; arrests have been made on both sides because of arguments over property rights. Exports were up last year, but the country faces another drought because of the El Niño winds.

Managua

At first, Managua may strike you as a confusing city, scarred, scared, and guarded. After a few days of exploring and conversing, Managua will still be all of those things, but also exciting, noble, and sometimes even uplifting. Managua takes getting used to; this is not a city made for tourism—it's too real, and far too gritty. Only experienced travelers and Peace Corps travelers spend time here, and then only to see what the raw core of a country with a past as turbulent as Nicaragua's looks like.

In Náhuatl, "Managua" means "where there is an extension of water." Sure enough, there's water aplenty here: the city drinks at the edges of Lago de Managua, the second-largest lake in the nation. Managua was raised on the ashes of an ancient indigenous village, and the city's former residents have literally left their prints on the modern city—10,000 years ago, residents ran from an erupting volcano; the lava that pursued them preserved their fleeing footsteps, now on display in El Museo Huellas de Acahualinca. Since then, Managuans haven't run from much of anything.

Situated midway between liberal León and conservative Granada, politically as well as geographically, Managua was declared the capital of Nicaragua in 1857 in an attempt to quell feuding between the rival cities. Prematurely thrust into the limelight, the tiny city didn't mature until the turn of the century, when new railroads turned the infant capital into a center for the booming coffee export trade. Managua thrived until 1931, when it was suddenly razed by an earthquake. Five years later, a massive fire made cinders of the ruins. Surviving Managuans dug their heels in against elements and the city was rebuilt, soon to face new disasters. In December of 1972, Managua was leveled by another earthquake that killed 6,000 people. The city center was never reconstructed and Managua still sits low on its haunches; busy streets cross deserted meadows and lots, bustling markets abut gutted buildings.

Composed of distinct *barrios,* the city sprawls into a series of massive suburbs, each neighborhood's identity linked to ten years of revolutionary idealism. Strident public art decorates the city—revolutionary murals and radical graffiti, a huge sil-

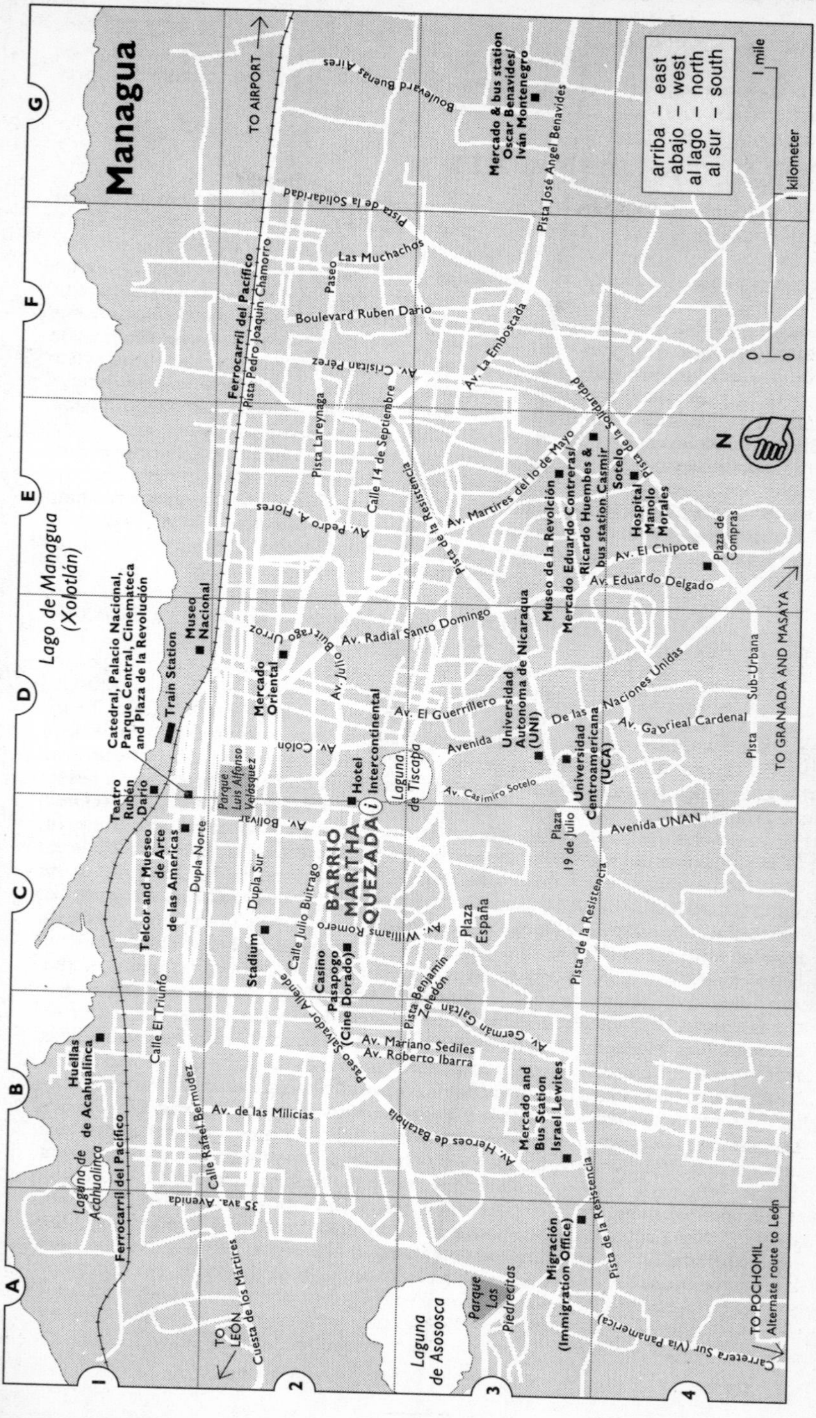

Managua

Lago de Managua (Xolotlán)

arriba – east
abajo – west
al lago – north
al sur – south

0 — 1 kilometer
0 — 1 mile

N

TO AIRPORT
TO LEÓN
TO GRANADA AND MASAYA
TO POCHOMIL Alternate route to León

Catedral, Palacio Nacional, Parque Central, Cinemateca and Plaza de la Revolución
Train Station
Museo Nacional
Teatro Rubén Darío
Telcor and Museo de Arte de las Americas
Huellas de Acahualinca
Laguna de Acahualinca
Ferrocarril del Pacífico
Stadium
Casino Pasapogo (Cine Dorado)
BARRIO MARTHA QUEZADA
Hotel Intercontinental
Laguna de Tiscapa
Parque Luis Alfonso Velásquez
Mercado Oriental
Universidad Autonoma de Nicaragua (UNI)
Universidad Centroamericana (UCA)
Museo de la Revolción
Mercado Eduardo Contreras/ Ricardo Huembes & bus station Casmir Sotelo
Hospital Manolo Morales
Plaza de Compras
Mercado & bus station Oscar Benavides/ Iván Montenegro
Plaza España
Plaza 19 de Julio
Mercado and Bus Station Israel Lewites
Migración (Immigration Office)
Laguna de Asososca
Parque Las Piedrecitas

Pista Pedro Joaquín Chamorro
Boulevard Buenas Aires
Pista de la Solidaridad
Pista José Angel Benavides
Paseo Las Muchachos
Boulevard Ruben Darío
Av. Cristian Pérez
Av. La Emboscada
Pista Lareynaga
Calle 14 de Septiembre
Av. Pedro A. Flores
Pista de la Resistencia
Av. Martires del lo de Mayo
Av. El Chipote
Av. Eduardo Delgado
Av. Radial Santo Domingo
Av. Julio Buitrago Urroz
Av. El Guerrillero
Av. Colón
Avenida De las Naciones Unidas
Av. Gabrieal Cardenal
Pista Sub-Urbana
Av. Casimiro Sotelo
Avenida UNAN
Av. Bolívar
Dupla Norte
Dupla Sur
Calle Julio Buitrago
Av. Williams Romero
Pista Benjamin Zeledón
Av. Germán Gaitán
Av. Mariano Sediles
Av. Roberto Ibarra
Paseo Salvador Allende
Calle El Triunfo
Av. de las Milicias
Calle Rafael Bermudez
Av. Heroes de Batahola
35 ava. Avenida
Cuesta de los Mártires
Carretera Sur (Via Panamerica)

A B C D E F G
1 2 3 4

NICARAGUA

houette of Sandino, and, perhaps most arresting, an outsized, wrought-iron *campesino* triumphantly lifting a machine gun in his left hand. Like the lava that cast the ancient footprints—the city's oldest "public art"—today's Managua is hot, riveting, and red.

■■■ ORIENTATION

This is tough. Managua has dispensed almost entirely with the unnecessary formality of naming its streets. A precious few *avenidas* and most of the *carreterras* have names (though these may be disputed), but most 'addresses' are given in terms of their proximity to recognized landmarks—a Texaco station, a university, a statue, where a cinema used to be, etc. What's more, even the cardinal points have Managuan pseudonyms: the direction 'south' remains *al sur*, but 'north' becomes *al lago*, 'east' is *arriba,* and 'west' is *abajo*. (*Arriba* designates the side of the horizon from which the sun rises, and *abajo* the side on which it descends.) Thus, when told that your destination is *"De Tica Bus una cuadra abajo y media cuadra al lago,"* you must first find the Tica Bus Station, then walk one block west and half a block north. It is not unlike chess.

Managua lies on the south shore of Lake Managua (locally, and more properly, called Lago Xolotlán), which sits 39m above sea level. From the old city center on the lake shore, Managua expands in all directions. The **Cesar Augusto Sandino International Airport** is 12km east of the city on the Carreterra Norte. Taxis from the airport to Marta Quezada (see Accommodations, below) cost an unreasonable US$10-12. But walk 100m in the direction of the Carreterra and the price suddenly drops to US$4-5; that's the easiest five bucks you'll ever save.

The plush **Hotel Intercontinental,** a valiant attempt at neo-Mayan architecture, was one of the few structures in downtown Managua to survive the 1972 earthquake. It is a major landmark, and can be considered the effective center of the city. The "Inter," as it is often called, sits just below the crest of a hill; the distinctive façade is on the north of the hotel. On the same hillside, just east of the Inter, looms Sandino's sombrero and silhouette. **Avenida Bolívar** runs north-south to the west of the hotel. From the Inter, Bolívar descends half a mile to meet the lake shore and the old city center, arriving promptly at the Teatro Rubén Darío. Along the way it passes the **Asamblea Nacional** and the Bank of America skyscraper, the **Palacio Nacional,** the tomb of Rubén Darío, the ruined **Santo Domingo Cathedral,** and the main **TELCOR office. Barrio Marta Quezada,** west of the Inter-Continental, is home to most of Managua's budget hotels and *hospedajes.* The western border of the Barrio Marta Quezada is Avenida Williams Roberto, on which sits the **Casino Pasapogo** (it used to be called the **Cine Dorado**). Eight blocks south of the Casino is the **Plaza de España,** where many banks, travel agencies, and a supermarket are located. From Barrio Marta Quezada, **Mercado Israel Lewites,** one of Managua's major market areas, lies to the southwest, as does the highway to León. **Mercado Oriental** is to the northeast of the Inter, and **Mercado Roberto Huembes** lies to the southeast. **Mercado Ivan Montenegro** is at the far east end of the city. Buses leave from all of these markets, bound for nearly every other part of Nicaragua.

Despite the fact that Managua is not an especially dangerous city, visitors will do all right if they keep their wits about them (see Nicaragua, Safety, page 258, for general advice). The greatest risk is undoubtedly the threat posed by pickpockets. Managuan buses are notorious for their deft-fingered pickpockets, so try to get a seat. When you have to remain standing, use one hand to steady yourself and keep the other one down around your pockets. When push comes to shove (literally), hold tight to your córdobas; they'll emerge a sweaty wad, but they'll emerge. The *camiones* (the truckish buses with boarded-up beds) are said to be safer, because they have an on-board conductor and only one door.

■■■ PRACTICAL INFORMATION

Tourist Office: Inturismo (tel. 22-66-52, 22-33-33, 22-24-98), 1 block south and 1 block west of the Hotel Intercontinental. Friendly, helpful staff. Office sells a helpful, bimonthly guide to Nicaragua called **Guía Fácil Nicaragua** (8 córdobas) and an invaluable, if cumbersome, map (15 córdobas). The guide is packed full of great information, including an exhaustive list bookstores, libraries, galleries, and museums. It also lists restaurants by food-type and features calendar listings of local events, concerts, etc., and a full list of travel agencies and embassies. Open Mon.-Fri. 8am-1pm and 2-5pm. Airport office (tel. 31-2-97) open daily from 9am until last flight gets in.

Police: (tel. 74-1-30), at the Plaza El Sol.

Post Office and Telephones: Each **TELCOR** office keeps its own hours, but the big TELCOR in the old downtown area is usually your best bet. Look for the biggest, baddest antenna in town, which can be spotted easily from the Inter. It stands in the north end of the city, just west of the Old Cathedral and the Palacio Nacional. **Postal services** (tel. 22-41-94) available Mon.-Fri. 8am-noon and 2-5pm, Sat. 8am-noon. **Telephone services,** local and long distance, available daily 7am-10:30pm. **Information:** (tel. 112). **Telephone code:** 02. **DHL** (tel. 28-40-81, 28-40-85), 1 block north of the Hotel Intercontinental, and **Trans-Express** (tel 26-3-52 or 22-2-70), 1 block west and 1½ blocks south of the Inter, both ship to Miami; from there, your package will travel though the U.S. postal service.

Western Union: (tel. 66-81-26, 66-81-29). Head north from the Inter to the military hospital, and take the right fork at the "Y" in the road. The office is 400m down the hill and around the bend on the right. Open Mon.-Fri. 8am-5pm, Sat. 8am-12:30pm.

Travel Agency: Senderos (tel. 68-18-93, 68-18-94), 200m before Western Union on the left. Open Mon.-Fri. 8am-3pm, Sat. 8am-12:30pm. A number of other agencies, such as **Viajes America** (tel. 66-11-30, 66-06-84), are located in the Plaza de España, in the big complex to the southeast of the rotary.

Embassies: U.S. (tel. 66-60-10, 66-60-12, or 66-60-13), 4½km down Carreterra Sur., in Barrio Botahola Norte, southwest of Barrio Marta Quezada. Open Mon.-Fri. 9am-1pm. **Canada** (tel. 28-75-74, 28-13-04, or 28-48-21; fax 28-48-21), on the north side of the big TELCOR office, next door to the Museo de Arte Contemporanea Julio Cortázar. Open Mon.-Thurs. 9am-noon. **U.K.** (tel. 78-00-14, 78-08-87; fax 78-40-85), on Reparto Los Robles, south of Av. Rubén Darío. Open Mon.-Fri. 9am-noon. Open Mon.-Tues. and Thurs.-Fri. 9am-noon, closed Wed. **Honduras,** Planes de Altamira #64 (tel. 67-01-84, 67-01-85; fax 67-01-83). Open Mon.-Fri. 8:30am-1:30pm. **Guatemala** (tel. 79-98-34; fax 79-96-10),km 11.5 down Carreterra Masaya, south of town. Open Mon.-Fri. 9am-1pm. **Costa Rica** (tel. 66-39-55), 3rd floor of the old IBM building, in Barrio Batahola Norte. Open Mon.-Fri. 9am-3pm. A complete list of Embassies and Consulates can be found in the Guía Fácil (see Tourist Office, above).

Currency Exchange: With U.S. dollars, this is a cinch. Try the **Buro Internacional de Cambio** (tel. 66-32-96), 2 blocks south of Plaza de España on the east side of the street, next to Viajes America travel agency. They change other Central American currencies, U.S. dollars, and traveler's checks, for a trifling US$2 charge. For more than US$100 in traveler's checks, they render half the amount in U.S. dollars and the other half in córdobas. For less than US$100, it's all córdobas. (Open Mon.-Fri. 8:30am-4:45pm, Sat. 8:30am-noon.) Another possibility in the Plaza de España is the **Banco de America Central** (tel. 66-70-61, 66-70-64), located in the complex to the southwest of the rotary next to La Colonia supermarket. They charge 6% on traveler's checks. Open Mon.-Fri. 8:30am-5:30pm, Sat. 8am-1pm. When the *casas de cambio* are out of dollars, as is often the case, try the big supermarkets (La Colonia in Plaza España, for example) or the banks. They will exchange traveler's checks at the same rates.If you're willing to go under the table, *coyotes* wait on many street corners (on Av. Bolívar, outside the

Inter, and in the Mercado Roberto Huembes, most reliably) to change your dollars into córdobas. Be careful; they didn't get their name for nothing.

City Buses: The #119 is useful; its stops include the Mercado Roberto Huembes, Carreterra Masaya, Universidad Centroamericana, Plaza España, and Iglesia Lezcano. The #118 serves the Mercado Ivan Montenegro, the Red Cross, the Hotel Intercontinental, Cine Pasapogo, and the Centro Civico. The #110 lumbers between 3 markets: Israel Lewites, Roberto Huembes, and Ivan Montenegro.

Regional Buses: At Mercado Roberto Huembes, buses leave from the west end of the market, beginning at about 5am and dwindling in frequency toward late afternoon. To **Masaya** (the direct every 30min., 3 córdobas; the indirect every 10min., 2½ córdobas); to **Granada** (every 20min., 1½ hrs., 4 córdobas); to **Rivas** (every 30min., 3 hrs., 10 córdobas); to **Matagalpa** (every 30min., 3 hrs., 10 córdobas); and to Estelí (every 30min., 3½ hrs., 10 córdobas). From Mercado Israel Lewites, to **Chinandega** (every 30min., 2 hrs., 14 córdobas); to **León,** express, (every 30min., 2½ hrs., 10 córdobas); to **Jinotepe** (every 30min., 1st bus at 5:30am, 1½ hrs., 4 córdobas); and to **Pochomil** (every 30min., 2 hrs., 7 córdobas). From Mercado Ivan Montenegro, to **Tititapa** (every 10min., 2 córdobas); and to **Rama** (every hr., from 4am to early afternoon).

Taxis: Taxis are all over Managua, and can deliver you just about anywhere in the city at a fair fare. A crosstown ride should *always* cost only 15 córdobas; to the airport costs more. Taxis will almost always ask a higher-than-average rate of their *gringo* fares, given the chance, so be sure to agree on a price before entering.

Car Rental: Hertz and **Budget** offices dwell in the Hotel Intercontinental (tel. 22-23-30). Budget rentals start at US$19 for 25yrs. and older. Add US$9 for ages 21-25. Hertz rentals start at US$25 for ages 23 and up. Budget is open daily 7am-6pm. Hertz is open daily 7am-8pm. Insurance is optional and costs an extra fee from either of the companies.

Bicycle Rental: Casa Shannon y Candy (tel. 49-50-27), at the traffic light on Av. Rubenia, 200m southwest and 1km east of Mercado Roberto Huembes. Sells and repairs, but also rents good-quality bikes for US$3 per day, US$15 per week. This can be a fun way to get around Managua, and also something of a headache. Open Mon.-Sat. 9am-7pm.

Supermarket: La Colonia (tel. 66-13-58, 66-70-67), in the Plaza España. Open Mon.-Sat. 8am-8pm. Huge, U.S.-style supermarket with 15 aisles. Complete pharmacy and good-sized book section, including English spy novels and Shakespeare-in-Spanish ("to be or not to be, that is the *pregunta*"). A/C makes every shopping experience that much more enjoyable.

Red Cross: (central tel. 65-20-83, 65-20-84, 65-11-97, 65-17-61, 51-5-92), in Belmonte. 24-hr. ambulance service.

Pharmacies: Super Farmacia Xolotlán (tel. 65-55-55), 3 blocks south (uphill) of the Intercontinental, on Av. Bolívar. Open Mon.-Fri. 8am-7pm, Sat. 8am-1pm. There is also a pharmacy located in La Colonia supermarket in the Plaza España (see Supermarket, above). **Farmacia Magaui** (tel. 22-29-80) is 1 block south and ½ block east of the casino in Barrio Marta Quezada.

AMNLAE: Casa Nora Astorga (tel. 71-6-61 or 73-5-98), 2½ blocks south of the Entrada Principal San Juan, #582, behind the UCA. Provides medical services and counseling to women. (See Nicaragua, Safety, page 258.)

Hospital: Hospital Manolo Morales (tel. 70-9-90, 70-9-91, 70-9-92, 70-9-93), near the intersection of Pista de la Solidaridad and Av. Martires del lo de Mayo.

■■■ ACCOMMODATIONS

All the hotels and *hospedajes* listed below are in the Barrio Marta Quezada, near the Casino Pasapogo, an amiable neighborhood comprised of comfortable homes, bohemian lodgings, and the occasional wandering pig. The *barrio* is about 10 blocks north of the Plaza España and lies between the Intercontinental to the east and the stadium to the northwest.

Managua Center

Airports
Hospitals
Tourist information

'al lago' (north: toward the lake)
'abajo' (west)
'arriba' (east)
'al sur' (south)

A B C D
1 2 3 4 5 6 7

Lago de Managua (Xolotlán)
Huellas de Acahualinca
Teatro de Rubén Darío
Bus Station
SAN SEBASTIAN
Calle el Triunfo
Ruinas de la Catedral
TELCOR Office
Avenida del Guerrillero
JULIO BUITRAGO
Dupla Norte
SAN ANTONIO
Parque Luis Alfonso Velásquez
Calle 15 de Septiembre
JAVIER CUADRA
Dupla Sur
Rincón Español
Avenida Bolívar
LOS ANGELES
19 DE JULIO
Avenida Colón
Paseo Salvador Allende
Calle Julio Buitrago
CIUDAD JARDIN
LAS PALMAS
MARTHA QUEZADA
BUENOS AIRES
Avenida Julio Buitrago Urroz
EL CARMEN
Williams Romero
Bus Station
Hotel Intercontinental
Avenida Mariano Sediles
Avenida de Radial
LARGA ESPADA
Laguna de Tiscapa
BOLONIA
BOSQUES DE BOLONIA
Calle Jose Martí
Pista Benjamín Zeledón
Avenida
SERRANO
Avenida Casimiro Sotelo
Avenida el Guerrillero
Santo Domingo
ALTAGRACIA
Plaza España
JORGE DIMITROV
Avenida Germán Gaitán
JONATHAN GONZALEZ
EL RECREO
14 DE JUNIO
Ministerio de Cultura
Plaza 19 de Julio
RENE CISNEROS
TISCAPA
PANCASAN
Pista de la Resistencia
Avenida de las Naciones Unidas
Avenida UNAN
SAN JUAN
ALTAMIRA
Bus Station
CASIMIRO SOTELO
LOS ROBLES
Pista Sub-Urbana
Avenida Gabriel Cardenal
MIGUEL BONILLA
Boulevar de los Martires
VILLA PANAMA

Guest House Santos (tel. 22-37-13), 1 block north and 1½ blocks east of Casino Pasapogo, 1 block west of Hospedaje Quintana, near Av. Williams Romero and Calle Julio Buitrago. No awards for architectural design, but it's a favorite with the budget travelers who congregate in the spacious covered courtyard. The Big Bad Wolf would kill the cardboard walls with a sigh, and the padlocks on the doors are of diary caliber, but the comradely atmosphere guarantee security. Spartan rooms, all with baths, are rendered habitable by a fleet of gasping fans. Singles and doubles 30 córdobas per person; triples 75 córdobas total.

Hospedaje Quintana, 1 block north and 1½ blocks east of the Casina Pasapogo (or "Cine Dorado"). Rows of simple, spotless rooms adjoin a bright red main hallway. Guests may command a broad vista of neighborhood activity from the elevated porch. The communal bathroom has shower and toilets with seats and paper included. Stay cool with cold drinks and fans. 25 córdobas per person.

Hospedaje El Dorado (tel. 22-60-12), ½ block east of Casino Pasapogo. *Hospedaje* or top-secret NASA bunker? The gates and long hallways that guard El Dorado's innards would seem to indicate the latter. However, a number of cozy rooms huddle around an intimate patio and shared baths. Rooms and bathrooms are clean. Cautious and friendly couple runs the place. 30 córdobas per person, with fan 35.

Hospedaje Meza (tel. 22-20-46), 1 block north, 2½ blocks east of the Casino. Same street as Santos and Quintana. The entryway houses a wash basin and barbwire clotheslines that threaten to decapitate anyone over 1½m tall. Simple, sometimes cramped rooms have walls that don't reach the ceiling, which gives the rooms a spacious, airy feel, but which makes every wheezy snore, tummy-grumbling, and sleep-babble from next door clearly audible. All rooms have toilet and shower spigots, but no toilet paper. 30 córdobas per person includes a fan.

Hotel Jardín D'Italia (tel. 22-79-67, 66-44-31), 3 blocks east and ½ block north of Casino Pasapogo, or 1 block east and ½ block north of Tica bus station. Look for the lime-green façade. Inside the courtyard, a clean niche in the building provides a pleasant place to lounge. Refreshments for sale and the *dueña* cooks meals when enough people are interested. Rooms all have good showers and toilet paper. US$7 (or equivalent in córdobas) per person, US$12 for rooms with A/C.

Hospedaje Pablo Megnio, 1 block south and 75m east of Casino Pasapogo. Management is friendly, but friendly doesn't clean the place. Rooms perhaps maintained by the shaggy, yawning dog. A cheap sleep. 20 córdobas per person.

■■■ FOOD

Good food is not hard to find in Managua; there's no reason to leave the city with *gallo pinto* spilling out of your ears. Perhaps Managua's greatest culinary asset is its abundance of *fritangas,* sidewalk *comedores* who offer a traditional deep-fried buffet. You point to it, they throw it into a pan of boiling oil (be careful what you point to). This is Nicaraguan *dim sum.* Bananas and cheese go especially well together. Listings below are all in Marta Quezada.

Comedor Sara, 1 door east of the Tica bus station. Corrugated roof lends this place the feel of an airplane hangar. Not your run-of-the-mill hangar—it's clean and serves heaping plates of excellent curry. Chicken 25 córdobas, vegetable 22 córdobas, shrimp 30 córdobas. A rightful *gringo* favorite. Open daily noon-11pm.

Mirna's Pancakes (tel. 22-79-13), 1 block east and 1 block south of Casino Pasapogo. Probably the best damn flapjacks in Managua. Mirna also serves up a rockin' *comida corriente* of eggs, potatoes, rice, and beans. Eggs, juice, and coffee 14 córdobas. Open daily 7am-3pm.

Comedor Doña Pilar, right across the street from Delicias del Mar in Barrio Marta Quezada (no sign). This joint rules; a *comedor* as authentic as they get. Doña Pilar herself takes the raw material down from the hooks and cooks it up before your very eyes. *Carne asada,* chicken, potatoes, *plátanos, enchiladas,* and more, priced to sell. Open regular dining hours (informally).

Delicias del Mar, 1 block east and ½ block north of Casino Pasapogo. Clean and colorful food and decor. Tasty seafood convenient to the lodger (in the Barrio

Marta Quezada). Mountainous portions will leave you happy, but *won't* leave you hankering for more. "Sailor's Rice" (25 córdobas) is an awful lot like *paella* (25 córdobas). Fish filet 25 córdobas. shrimp, breaded or garlicked, 40 córdobas. Open daily noon-11pm.

Tonalli (tel. 22-43-42), 5 blocks east and ½ block north of Casino Pasapogo in the heart of Marta Quezada. A collectivist bakery run by Nicaraguan women. Black bread, whole wheat bread, granola, yogurt, natural pastas. Open Mon.-Fri. 8am-5:30pm, Sat. 8am-3pm.

Tacos, 1 block south of Casino Pasapogo. Hmmm, let's see. Don't ask twice—they're tacos, chicken (12 córdobas) or cheese (10 córdobas). Wash 'em down with one of the *refrescos naturales* made of pulped carrot, mango, papaya, or other exotic fruits (3 córdobas—same as a Coke, but these are bigger and tastier). Tacos 12 córdobas. Open Mon.-Fri. 9am-3pm and 5:30-8pm, Sat.-Sun. 4-8pm.

Aladdin (tel. 67-00-15), located on the Carreterra Masuya next door to the King's Royal Palace Hotel. Specializes in Middle Eastern food. A nice alternative for vegetarians sick of beans, rice, and cheese, try falafel, baba ganoush, or hummus as dishes or in sandwiches. Sandwiches are about 15 córdobas and dinners about 30 córdobas. Open daily 11am-11pm.

Casa del Café (tel. 78-06-05): from Aladdin, 1½ blocks toward Managua on the *carreterra,* then right 1 block, then right ½ block; it's on your right. Nestled in a posh-looking neighborhood, a hangout for the local intelligentsia. Nicaraguan coffee in every variety (and by the 1-lb. bag), a wide selection of fancy desserts, and good old American apple pie (13 córdobas). Open Mon.-Sat. 9am-8:30pm.

■■■ SIGHTS & ENTERTAINMENT

For a city of its size, Managua offers surprisingly little in the way of standard amusements. **El Museo Nacional** (tel. 22-52-91) doesn't look like much of a National Museum, and it's not. Nevertheless, it has on display an assortment of the bizarre and beautiful creatures that inhabit Nicaragua's wilderness, including an impressive collection of stuffed agoutis and *perezosas* (sloths). The museum also has a number of archaeological artifacts from all over Nicaragua, some dating as far back as 400BC (open Mon.-Fri. 8am-4pm; admission 10 córdobas). **El Museo de Arte Contemporanea** (tel. 22-4-40), across from TELCOR, next to the Canadian Embassy, is a wonderful museum displaying contemporary artwork from all over Latin America, including pieces by Ernesto Cardenal and Alfredo Caballero. On sale at the museum is a small collection of cultural and historical books (open Wed. and Fri. 10:30am-5pm and Sat.-Sun. 2-5pm; admission 10 córdobas). **El Museo Huellas de Acahualinca** (tel. 66-57-74), on the western edge of the old city center, displays the 6000-year-old, lava-preserved footprints that were left by ancient inhabitants of the city while they fled a volcanic eruption. The museum is quite a trek from Managua proper, but the miles of the trip should be worthwhile for any visitor of even mild archaeological bent. Take bus #102, 112, or 159 (open Mon-Fri. 8am-4pm; admission 10 córdobas, but ask about a student rate). Two museums, **El Museo de la Revolución** and **El Museo de Alfabetazación** (telling the story of the highly successful Sandinista literacy campaign), have both been closed, political victims of budget cutbacks. But ask around; both are said to have been great museums, and rumors say that they will eventually reopen.

A slow stroll down Bolívar is the best way to see Managua's sights. Walking north (downhill) from the Inter, you'll pass the **Casa Presidencial** and the **Asamblea Nacional,** both on your right behind the blue brick wall. The Bank of America skyscraper rises behind both. When the Assembly is not in session, you can walk in and have a look around. (Assembly is open only on weekdays.) On the other side of Bolívar from the Asamblea Nacional sits a small orchard kept scruffy by a stand of eucalyptus whose toxic leaves oppress the struggling undergrowth beneath. If you walk west through the park you can visit an eerie, dilapidated cemetery sprouting tombstones that date back to the late nineteenth century. Looming over the graveyard are the pathetic, yet poetic, remains of the deserted **Instituto Nacional de Seguridad Social** (National Institute of Social Security). The irony is thick here.

Continuing north along Bolívar, you'll arrive in the **Plaza de la Revolución,** arranged around the tomb of Sandinista leader Carlos Fonseca and doing double duty as a monument to the Nicaraguan modernist poet Rubén Darío, the "Prince of Spanish-American literature." In the southeast corner of the Plaza stands the **Palacio Nacional,** a colonial building that survived the earthquake and was subsequently used to house government offices. In the summer of 1995, it was being converted into the Palacio Nacional de la Cultura. This will no doubt be a nice complement to the **Centro Cultural Managua** (tel. 28-40-45, 28-40-10, or 22-20-68), which was recently erected next door. It houses various art workshops and galleries, and hosts events of all kinds throughout the year, from plays and dance shows to music concerts and art exhibitions. The upstairs is mainly composed of administrative offices (including the main office of the Guía Fácil), and its corridors are lined with more photographs of the pre-quake downtown area. Call or drop by to pick up a calendar of local events (open daily 8am-8pm.) The Centro Cultural is also home to a snack shop, the **Sorbetería Arco Iris** (tel. 28-13-14), a quiet and spacious lilypad for a drink or even a meal (open Mon.-Sat. 9am-9pm). On the east side of the plaza, next to the Palacio Nacional, stands the ruined Cathedral Santo Domingo, a beautiful and eerie vision of elegance in repose. Also on the Plaza, near the lake, is the big and boxy **Teatro Rubén Darío,** which also houses the **Teatro Experimental.** Both theaters have good programs; check the schedule of events posted by the ticket booth.

Managua's *mercados* are a must-see. **Mercado Roberto Huembes,** east of the universities, is an enormous mega-market where you can find just about anything you're looking for and a whole lot more, from a Masayan hammock to a skinned pig's head. They also carve coiffures here, in any of the numerous "beauty salons." **Mercado Israel Lewites** offers a notable array of sizzling *comedores.* **Mercado Oriental,** a sprawling labyrinth, sells some good wooden products but is somewhat sordid. It is said that at the height of the U.S. embargo, it was possible to walk in here and buy a new Mercedes-Benz, if you had the proper billfold. **Mercado Ivan Montenegro** is notable primarily for its buses to Rama.

Managua has a few discos. **Lobo Jack** (tel. 67-01-23), near the intersection of Pista Portezuelo and Carreterra Masaya, is said to be the biggest disco in Central America (cover 30 córdobas for men, with expensive drinks; open Wed.-Sun. 8pm-4am). **Mansion Reggae** (tel. 94-8-04), 6km down Carreterra Norte, plays West Indian music from the Atlantic coast (open daily 7pm-3am).

There are quite a few **pool halls** in Managua and some of them are pretty tough. There is one in Barrio Marta Quezada, ½ block south of the Casino called **Mr. Pool,** with a taco stand abutting the street (closed Sun.). **Black Ball** (tel. 67-51-72), on the Camino de Oriente, has a bar and charges 39 córdobas per hour for pool (open daily 3pm-2am). **Baseball** is the national sport, and you can catch the fever by going to the stadium in Marta Quezada to watch a game between October and April—the Nicos *really* get into it. Championship games take place in early June. Don't worry if you hear the neighborhood cheer and then hear a bunch of loud bangs. It's not the start of another civil war; the home team just won.

The North American community in Managua holds a weekly seminar/discussion on Thursdays at 8:30am in the **Casa Benjamin Linder** (see Planning Your Trip, Volunteering, on page 259). Guest speakers discuss current Nicaraguan social and political issues. Interested guests are welcome (be sure to arrive on time). The discussions are a great way to find out what's going on in Managua and the rest of the country. Named after a North American *internacionalista* who was killed by the *contras* in 1987, the house functions as a community center of sorts.

■ NEAR MANAGUA

XILOA

Xiloa (hel-WA) is about 10km west of Managua. A volcanic lake with a lush backdrop of mountains, Xiloa has become quite developed; picnic tables and *refresco* stands line its shore. The lake is clean and popular with families. It costs 10 córdobas to use the lake facilities, 25 if you're driving. During *Semana Santa,* buses run frequently from Mercado Israel Lewites to the *centro turístico* at Xiloa. These buses also run on the weekends, though less frequently. At all other times—when the lake will probably be yours for the swimming—your best bet is to catch one of the buses plying the *carreterra* to León and ask to be let out at the *entrada principal a Xiloa.* Most of these buses leave from Israel Lewites bound for Mateare, Nagorote, and León; alternatively, you could catch a bus at the Parque Las Piedrecitas, just south of the Laguna de Asososca, in the southwest corner of the city. Once in Xiloa, people wait at the *entrada,* usually in groups, across from the 24-hour Texaco, until they manage to thumb down a pick-up truck. Caution should be exercised, especially by women and solo travelers. Xiloa is five minutes up the twisty road. Another potentially palatable option is to hoof the 5km yourself, which pays off with a breathtaking tour of the native terrain. To return, walk back to the *carreterra* and jump on a bus headed back to Managua. Rooms at the **Hotel Xiloa** start at 76 córdobas.

LEÓN VIEJO

León Viejo lies at the foot of **Volcán Momotombo,** northwest of the city, on the other side of Lago de Managua. Founded in 1524, León was the colonial capital of Nicaragua; in 1610, a volcano-induced earthquake destroyed the city. In the wake of the destruction, the city packed up its bags and moved 30km west, leaving its former self to be buried slowly by volcanic ash. León Viejo is now partially excavated, and along with the nearby **Museo Imabite,** promises a rewarding daytrip. Both the ruins and the *museo* (open daily 8am-5pm) are located in the village of **Momotombo** (pop. 1500) and both are stuffed with exuberant and friendly youths who strive to personally guide each and every visitor, glutting them on feasts of bite-sized factoids along the way. The view from the shore of Lake Xolotlán (a trickier way to say *Lago de Nicaragua*) may incite orgasmic writhing in the soft, volcanic mud below. The ramshackle shambles of José Santos Zelaya's own Victorian house are visible from the lakeshore, as are the posts from the dock from which all commercial traffic between Managua and León used to pass. The dock fell apart from disuse after the introduction of the railroad, and left the town of Momotombo to sink gently into obscurity. The tour of the ruins begins at the foundations of the cathedral, where the city's founder, Hernández de Córdoba, was beheaded. Some travelers climb Volcán Momotombo—before doing so, however, all of them need to get permission from the Instituto Nicaragüense de Energía.

Convenient to all the ruins, **Museo Imabite** offers the curious traveler finer inspection of regional relics. The entire collection fills only one room but definitely merits a close look. The many pre-Columbian artifacts are fully and precisely inventoried by the museum's guide. The museum also displays old, locally-found muskets, a pictorial depiction of what León Viejo might have looked like, and other snappy odds and ends. Both the ruins and the museum are open daily 8am-5pm.

To get to Momotombo and its plethora of exciting sights (both of them), you must first get to **La Paz Centro,** 56km from Managua and 31km from León. Buses leave frequently from both towns, from León's station and from Managua's Mercado Israel Lewites. You would also need to pass through La Paz were you on your way to León Viejo, 16km away. The hard part for the Momotombo-bound crowd consists in the La Paz-Momotombo leg. The bus makes the trip four or five times a day and departure times vary. The first bus leaves around 6am and they run about every one and a half hours until 3pm. Anticipate a similarly rough schedule for the return trip. To get better information, ask the locals who depend on the line's vicissitudes. When it comes, the Momotombo bus leaves you a few blocks from the museum, and about a five-minute walk (down the same road) from the ruins. To get to the lakeshore, walk straight in the direction that the bus was headed. If at any time you get lost, ask for directions; the *momotombitos* are usually more than happy to help out.

To get to León Viejo, first head to La Paz Centro, 40km from Managua along the Managua-León highway. Buses run hourly to La Paz Centro from Mercado Israel Lewites, but it's just as easy to take a bus bound for León and ask to be let off at La Paz Centro, whence León Viejo is 16km away. An occasional bus traverses this distance, and some travelers find hitching relatively easy here.

NEARBY BEACHES

Pochomil, Masachapa, and **Montelimar** are three adjacent beaches on the Pacific Coast about 60km from Managua. The bus to Pochomil leaves every 45 minutes from Mercado Israel Lewites and serves all three beaches. It takes the buses two hours to climb up into the mountains and cruise down across the coastal plain on the other side. It's easy to visit all three beaches, since it's only about a 30-minute stroll from southernmost Pochomil, past the lazy fishing village of Masachapa, to the ritzy resort of Montelimar. The beach at Pochomil is lined with hotels and restaurants. Accommodations range from the **Bajamar,** a reasonably fancy resort complex that offers rooms for one or two people (150 córdobas with fan, or 230 córdobas with A/C), to the **Carolina,** where the eerie owner says he will loan travelers a hammock and a place to hang it for 20 córdobas a night. The waves at Pochomil can get gargantuan, and it's advisable not to venture too far out.

In Masachapa, just around the bend in the coast, the waves are much milder, and consequently fishermen have decided to settle down here. The row of fishing boats along the beach puts the final touch on this pretty little postcard of a town. Lodgings in Masachapa are a little more rustic. The only hotel on the beach is the **Hotel Summer,** which tries to pawn off little rooms at 70 córdobas a pop. Cheaper lodging can be found elsewhere in the town. At pristine **Montelimar,** however, affordable accommodations are completely out of the question; look, but don't touch.

NICARAGUA

WEST OF MANAGUA

■■■ LEÓN

León is the second largest town in the largest Central American country, yet it seems to be stuck in time. As the din from 19 churches' bells heralds the rising sun, and as eager plants and blooming flowers raise their thirsty heads from the town's many courtyards, it's not hard to picture life before electricity, when a courtyard fire was the only way to illuminate a house. Meanwhile, mangy horses still pull cars full of produce and human passengers through the streets. With each hour, the town feels more and more like a big, baking adobe oven, and the voices of schoolchildren echo over high earthen walls, through the rippling, melting air.

Considering its many incarnations, it's no wonder that León has had a hard time placing itself in history. The first León, now known as León Viejo, was founded on the shore of Lake Xolotlán in 1524 by Hernández de Córdoba. After this city was destroyed by an earthquake in 1610, León was rebuilt 32km to the west. Though poorer than Granada, the new León soon became a cultural and intellectual stronghold; the heady atmosphere fueled the imagination of its favorite son Rubén Darío, born in 1867, whose poetry launched the modernist movement in Latin America (see Nicaragua, Arts, page 265). León was capital of Nicaragua for over 300 years.

Through it all, though, one trait has persisted; as the bumper stickers still proclaim, León is *"orgullosamente liberal"*: liberal and proud of it. To say that León is Nicaragua's most liberal metropolis is a little like saying that the Vatican is Italy's most Catholic city. Leftist León has a tradition of incessantly squabbling with conser-

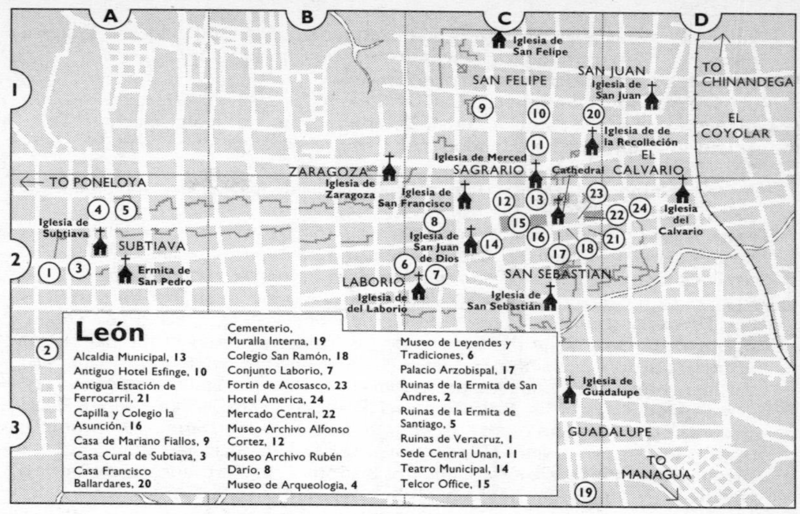

vative Granada, and along with Estelí, León was one of only two cities carried by the FSLN in the elections of 1990. The Universidad Nacional Autónoma de Nicaragua (UNAN), founded in 1812 as the country's first university, sharpens León's politics to a radical edge. Students roam the city from March to December, painting the town red with some of Nicaragua's best murals and graffiti.

ORIENTATION

If you've spent any time in Managua, León is a navigational cakewalk. The **bus terminal** lies just east of town, three long blocks past the train tracks. Express buses from Managua, however, sometimes stop at a gas station a few blocks southeast of the terminal, or even in the **Mercado Central,** just east of the cathedral. Either way, you can walk to the center of town (often a hot and dusty trek, but very manageable), or take a taxi for about five córdobas. Another of León's markets is on the eastern edge of town, five blocks north and four blocks east of the cathedral, just behind the **Iglesia de San Juan** and its adjacent park. León's center is the **Parque Jerez.** In the middle of the newly remounted plaza, atop a fountain guarded by four *leones* (lions), stands an amusingly diminutive statue of General Jerez, a 19th-century liberal political figure. The plaza is usually referred to as the **Parque Central.**

Brace for good news: León's streets are named! East-west streets are *calles;* **Calle Central Rubén Darío** fronts the north side of the Parque Central. From here, numbered streets ascend north (1a Calle Norte, 2a Calle Norte, etc.) and south. North-south streets are *avenidas.* (**Avenida Central** would run right between the Parque Central and the cathedral, except that the *avenida* is discontinued for a block at this point.) This naming won't help all that much, though; most *leones,* when asked for directions or addresses, stick to the standard Nicaraguan method. Thus, the Museo Archivo Rubén Darío is *cuatro cuadras abajo del TELCOR* (4 blocks down from the TELCOR office). Some useful landmarks for this purpose: **La Iglesia de la Recollectio** is 3 blocks north of the cathedral's northeast corner. **Esquina de los Bancos** is 1 block south of that. **Iglesia de la Merced** is 1 block north of the Parque Central.

PRACTICAL INFORMATION

Tourist Office: Inturismo (tel. 36-82), 3 blocks north of the Parque on Avenida Central, then ½ block east. Doesn't look like much, but they can answer your questions. Also ask about the **guía del centro historico,** which has a good map and descriptions of all the nearby architecture. A handy local guide (including a less-handy map) distributed. Open Mon.-Fri. 8am-1pm and 2-5pm.

Police: (tel. 115), on Carretera Chinandega.

Post Office and Telephones: TELCOR (tel. 56-78, 29-25, 20-47; fax 57-00), on the west side of the Parque Central. **Telephones** operate daily 7am-9pm. **Telegrams** and **faxes** daily 8am-noon and 2-5pm. Post office open Mon.-Sat. 7am-7pm. **Telephone code:** 0311.

Western Union: (tel. 24-26), 100m east of Esquina de los Bancos. Open Mon.-Fri. 8am-12:30pm and 2-5pm, Sat. 8am-noon.

Travel Agency: Viajes Mundiales (tel. 59-20, 69-20), 50m north of Iglesia de la Recolección. Open Mon.-Fri. 8am-12:30pm and 2-5:30pm, Sat. 8am-12:30pm.

Currency Exchange: Banco Nicaragüense de Industria y Comercios (tel. 50-51), across the street from La Iglesia de la Recolección. Cash, but not traveler's checks, exchanged Mon.-Fri. 8:30am-12:30pm and 1:30-4pm, Sat. 8:30am-noon. **Banpro** (tel. 34-45), on the Esquina de los Bancos ("corner of the banks," or financial district). Exchanges cash Mon.-Fri. 8:30am-4pm, Sat. 8:30-11:45am. Also try the *coyotes* (easily found on the Esquina de los Bancos) and the supermarkets.

Buses: 3 blocks east of the Railroad tracks on the main street 50m north of Hotel Avenida. To **Managua** (every 20min., 4:30am-6:20pm, 2 hrs., 10 córdobas; express microbuses 1¼ hrs., 12 córdobas); to **Estelí** (5:30am and 3pm, 3 hrs., 13 córdobas); to **Matagalpa** (4:30am and 2:45pm, 3 hrs., 10 córdobas); to **San Isidro** (every 30min., 4:30am-5pm, 2½ hrs., 9.5 córdobas); to **Chinandega** (every 15min., 4:30am-6pm, 1 hr., 3.5 córdobas); and to **La Paz Centro** (every 50min., 6am-5:40pm, 50min., 3.75 córdobas). From San Isidro, buses run to Estelí, Matagalpa, Managua, and Chinandega.

City Buses: A few *rutas* ply León's streets. There is a particularly useful east-west bus (Rte. 101) that runs between El Terminal de Buses (bus stop) and El Mercadito, west of town, where buses depart for the beach (see Near León, page 281). These are often *camionetas* (little pickup trucks with benches in the back), and usually cost 1 córdoba. These buses also cost 1 córdoba.

Supermarket: El Extra (tel. 59-13), in Plaza Metropolitana, 25m east of the Esquina de los Bancos. Open daily 8am-8pm.

Library: Biblioteca Pública Maria Eugenia (tel. 56-09), above the Colegio La Asunción on the south of the Parque Central. A soothing place to work or read if you don't mind the noise of the school children below. The windows offer a rare view of León from on high. Open Mon.-Fri. 8-11:45am and 2-4:45pm.

Red Cross: (tel. 26-27) 24-hr. ambulance service.

Pharmacy: Farmacia Meg-24 (tel. 67-75), across from the fire station, ½ block north of the northwest corner of the cathedral. Open daily 7:30am-10pm.

AMNLAE: (tel. 45-25), 2 blocks west and ½ block south of the Estatua de la Madre (Statue of the Mother). Offices include a clinic, a classroom, legal services, and a library on women's health and issues. Open Mon.-Fri. 8am-noon and 2-5pm.

ACCOMMODATIONS

León's got it all, from old colonial lodgings near the center of town to less luxurious and cheaper places a small hike away. For the most part, prices shrink as the distance from the cathedral grows. The hotels listed immediately below are those budget options to be found at varying distances to the north of town.

Hotel Avenida (tel. 20-68), ½ block south of road that leads east to the bus station (across from the Esso gas station). About 5 blocks north and 3 blocks east of the center of town. A gem. Mattresses thick enough to cushion a tender princess against the wooden slats below. Rooms and bathrooms are well-scrubbed and equipped with fans. Self-service laundry complete with *mucho* clothesline space. Food and drink sold. Solid locks. Singles 30 córdobas, with bath 40 córdobas; doubles with bath 70 córdobas; triples with bath 100 córdobas.

Hotel Telica (tel. 22-36), by the railroad tracks, 2½ blocks north of the street leading to the bus terminal. Simple, sometimes gloomy rooms may depress, but the price is sure to please. Communal showers need a good cleaning and the toilet has no seat. Doubles and triples have private baths. Cold drinks sold. 20 córdobas per person.

Hotel Primavera, 10 blocks north of the Parque Central, 1½ blocks west of the train tracks. For those carefully counting córdobas, this is the place. Primavera is far from the center of town though, and the neighborhood used to be questionable; women traveling alone might want to steer clear, but things are thought to have gotten much better. Singles with yucky showers only 25 córdobas. Small singles 15 córdobas; doubles 50 córdobas. Fans 10 córdobas extra.

Hotel Colonial (tel. 22-79), in the middle of León, 2½ blocks north of the northwest corner of Parque Central. Anyone can play domineering colonist in this fixed-up colonial mansion: just lounge in your rocking chair by the courtyard and stare contentedly at the 5m-ceilings above. Simple, tidy rooms upstairs all have fans. Both bedrooms and bathrooms are segregated by sex; however, couples can choose to be roomed in either section. Also has a restaurant and huge color TV. Singles 55 córdobas; doubles 100 córdobas, with A/C 180 córdobas.

FOOD

Like any self-respecting ultra-liberal university town, León has its fair share of artsy cafés and chi-chi restaurants. Better though, head to the **street buffet** a block-and-a-half east of the southeast corner of the cathedral. Sample huge portions of rice, chicken with potatoes in tomato sauce, *enchiladas,* salad, or fried potato cakes, all served up on a banana leaf—carry the food with you for just 10 to 15 córdobas (open from sundown until late in the evening).

Casa Vieja, across from the west side of the Casa de Cultura, 2 blocks west, 1½ blocks north of the Parque Central. A hip local spot notable for its tasty food and fair prices. So trendy you might have trouble finding a table on weekend nights. Fries, burgers, *licuados,* cheese sandwiches. Open Thurs.-Tues. 5-10pm.

El Rincón Azul (tel. 47-79), on Calle Central Rubén Darío, west of the Parque Central, diagonal from Parque Rubén Darío. As funky as it gets in Nicaragua—finger paintings, hand-prints, screwdrivers, pliers, and drawings all adorn the walls. A great place to grab a snack or a cool drink. A variety of hamburgers 7-10 córdobas. Guzzle a small pitcher of fresh-squeezed (5 córdobas). Open daily 3-11pm.

Restaurant Las Ruinas (tel. 47-67), on Calle Central Rubén Darío, 1 block west of the Parque Central. Tweaking the nose of a major superpower, the restaurant was called "Las Ruinas de Bagdad 17/12/90." A large Hofbraühaus hall serving fish filet (25 córdobas), filet mignon (40 córdobas), half a chicken in wine sauce (35 córdobas). Open daily 10am-1am; 10-córdoba cover at night (see Sights, below).

El Sosteo Café (tel. 53-27), a small sidewalk café right in the middle of León, on the Parque Central's north side. Great place to come any time of day to eat, drink, and watch the park's passersby. Serves breakfast, lunch, and dinner at slightly higher than average prices due to its prime location. Open daily 7am-midnight.

Cafetín Intimo (tel. 21-18), in the Casa de la Cultura (see Sights, below). A cozy, artsy joint that draws together a warm and friendly crowd. Art exhibits, a fountain, and a courtyard add a chic touch. *Comida corriente* is a steal at 8 córdobas, including drink. Open Mon.-Sat. 10am-10pm, Sun. only in the evening.

SIGHTS

The **Museo Archivo Rubén Darío** (tel. 23-88) on Calle Central Rubén Darío two blocks west of Parque Rubén Darío, is the shrine to the country's favorite poet. Some of the creepier exhibits include the poet's death mask and photographs of him on his death-bed (entitled "Rubén Darío in Agony"). The museum also boasts a collection of his manuscripts, first editions, and a series of Darío caricatures by various political cartoonists of the day. With permission, you can read the books in the archive (admission is free; open Tues.-Sat. 9am-noon and 2-5pm, Sun. 9am-noon).

One block east and a block-and-a-half north of the museum is the **Centro Popular de Cultura** (tel. 21-16). This was once the plush home of a Somoza crony (you can tell by the abandoned swimming pool); when he fled the country, the Sandinistas turned the house into a community center rife with political art. So it goes. Check out the long display of two dozen posters that tell the life story of Sandino, from lowly laborer exploited by foreign interests to prestigious leader of a revolutionary movement. The center offers classes in music, painting, woodworking, Spanish, and English. Ask about upcoming performances, presentations, and *noches festivos.* Alternatively, just stroll about, digging the artwork, the clack of typewriters, and the strains of radical folk-music being played on the guitar (open daily 9am-7pm).

León's **cathedral,** on the Parque Central, is the largest in Central America. It's a mammoth, mosque-like structure, a vast expanse of white paint that reflects and intensifies the blinding afternoon sun. Rubén Darío is buried beside the altar, and the paintings of the **Stations of the Cross** are quite famous. The cathedral has recently undergone a restoration, and though some locals complain about the poor quality of the paint used on the exterior, the inside of the cathedral is quite a sight. High, painted ceilings soar above a tremendous altar (open Fri.-Wed. 7am-noon and 4-7pm, Thurs. 7am-7pm). León has many other churches, and together they conspire to give the city a pleasantly beatific feel. Nearly every one of them is worth a peek inside, especially **El Calvario, Iglesia de la Recolleción,** and **La Merced.**

The **Mausaleo de Héroes y Mártires** commemorates the victims of the Revolución on the northeast corner of the Parque Central. (Those on the winning side, anyway.) Across the street, U.S. citizens shouldn't take it personally to see Sandino using Uncle's Sam's head as a footrest. Also, check out the murals by the **basketball court,** half a block north of the northwest corner of the plaza—expansive, pro-Sandinista works depicting socialists building schools and tearing down rightist regimes.

Over on the west end of town, the large and sprawling **Barrio Subtiava** contains a few points of interest, as well as the market from which buses leave to the nearby beach of Poneloya. The **Iglesia de Subtiava** is the oldest standing church in León and is famed across the land for its colonial altar. Local children also use the large open area on the side of the church to play an interesting Nicaraguan version of the playground game **Butts Up.** The oldest non-standing church in León is also found in Subtiava; it's better known as **Las Ruinas de Veracruz.** Originally built in the 16th century, the church was thrashed asunder by a volcano in 1835. It's still fun to roam around through the bits and pieces the volcano left behind. To get to Subtiava you can either walk about 10 blocks west of Parque Central, or take a taxi, or get on any bus marked for Route #101. The church is one block south of Calle Rubén Darío and the ruins are two blocks west of the church on the left. You have to enter a family's yard to get to the ruins, so ask their permission before crossing, lest you earn their dog's tornado-like wrath.

ENTERTAINMENT

The Parque Central and Mercado Central, as well as other nearby areas, are well-lit at night and patrolled by *vigilantes* (watchmen, and not what you think), hired by the *alcaldía* (mayoral district) to keep public areas safe at night. The Parque Central plays the roles of playground, meeting spot for friends, and scoping scene for randy youngsters on the prowl (especially on Saturday and Sunday nights). **El Túnel del Tiempo** is a bar/restaurant/disco outside of town at the *salida a Chinandega* (the exit to Chinandega), in a big white building. The crowd is young and rather affluent. When in disco mode, the club charges a variable cover. Getting there by taxi costs you five córdobas; the fare doubles at night. **Las Ruinas** (see Food, above) turns into a disco every night, and usually stages live acts Friday, Saturday, and Sunday. The cover is 10 córdobas, and the dancing floor is cool, thanks to the club's open-air design. Students from the university often hold parties at the **Club Universitaria,** half a block east of La Iglesia de la Recolección. Look for these parties when UNAN is in session (March-December); they're usually announced by raucous crowds of students circumnavigating the Parque Central in the back of blaring pick-ups.

The **basketball court** (see Sights) also serves as an informal center of nightlife. Across the street is a pool hall, **Lezama,** where a game costs 1.5 córdobas (open daily 10am-11pm). **El Alamo,** a bar, slouches on the nearby street corner. As in most of Latin America, the right dress for a night on the town is casual, but snazzy.

■ NEAR LEÓN

Two pleasant Pacific beaches, **Poneloya** and **Las Peñitas,** within easy reach of León, to its west and southwest. Expect crowds on hot summer weekends (December through May) and during *Semana Santa;* otherwise, the beach should be relatively empty. Catch a bus to these beaches at El Mercadito, on the western outskirts of León. Bus #101 serves the Mercadito from the Mercado Central, the Mercado behind San Juan church, and from the bus station. The ride, halfway in a bus and halfway in a *camioneta,* takes you up and over the hilly farmland that separates León from the Pacific. As you crest each hill, keep your eyes open for a great view of the farmland, the volcanoes of San Cristóbal, and their neighbors to the north (30min.; 3 córdobas). Buses leave every hour from 4am to 7pm. The bus first stops in Poneloya, which is farther north, and then goes back to Las Peñitas. The "beaches" are actually one long beach, parceled out by a big rocky outcropping called **La Peña del Tigre.** Houses are perched along its ridge, so walk around to get from one beach to the other. The beach is steep and the waves are fierce, so if you swim, be careful, and try to swim in the company of others, preferably locals. A walk along the beach offers safer and substantial rewards. Though a row of empty vacation houses are the beach's only decoration *per se,* watching the waves crash and the volcanic sands glitter is scenery enough. Walking far enough along the beach in either direction brings you to scattered inlets, which fill at high tide and empty with the ebb. Beyond these the beach is virtually deserted.

If it's geothermal activity and not beach recreation you seek, look no further than 25km west of León on the road to San Isidro to **Los Hervideros de San Jacinto,** a small field full of vigorously boiling pits of muddy water and holes spewing sulfuric steam. An underground stream supplies the water, heated personally by Baalzebub and his minions below. To get there take any bus bound for San Isidro (see Practical Information, Buses, page 278) and ask to be let off in **San Jacinto,** where the *hervideros* (bubbling springs) are. Follow the small road down the hill and take the first right. Go about five blocks until you see the archway on your left. Through the arch sprawl the seething *hervideros,* as well as a precariously positioned baseball field. Once through, a cloud of eager *niños* materializes, each able to show you where to step safely, thereby sparing you the pain of being boiled alive. Another geothermal plant is slated for construction at a nearby site, something similar to the one that already exists on the slopes of Volcán Momotombo (see Near Managua, page 275).

■■■ CHINANDEGA

Chinandega is appreciated around the country (and the world) not for the admirable work-ethic of its resident farmers, nor for the massive quantity of quality cotton that's churned out from the nearby regions each year, nor even for its blessed proximity to beautiful beaches and towering **Volcán San Cristóbal,** Nicaragua's tallest at 1745m. No, what earns this town praise from León to London and from Managua to Moscow is the unspeakably smooth, bewilderingly rich, mind-bendingly delicious **Flor de Caña** rum, thousands of gallons of which are produced annually just outside the town limits. Remarkably, though, the smallish city has a life beyond the heavenly concoction. Located in one of the hottest, driest parts of the country, Chinandega is the capital of the department of the same name, which is Nicaragua's northernmost region, making it ideal for travelers bound for local outdoor sites or as a stop on the way to the northern border with Honduras at Somotillo.

Orientation Buses arriving from León or Managua stop southwest of town at **Mercado Bisne** (*Bisne* as in "Business"—this place was the center of Chinandega's black market during the years of the embargo). From here, the Parque Central, (which lies a bit west of all the action), is six blocks north and eight blocks west. The walk is definitely manageable, but if you can't take the heat, get out of the kitchen, and while you're at it, take a taxi or one of the *camionetas* that runs from Mercado Bisne to Mercado Central, four blocks west of the Parque Central. **El Mercadito** lies one block north of the northeast corner of the Parque Central.

Practical Information Surprisingly, Chinandega has an **Inturismo office,** one block south and 1½ blocks east of the Mercado Central, though it's hard to predict when and whether it's open. **Tours Viajes Sol** (tel. 27-95), one block east and ½ block south of the southeast corner of the Parque Central, is a travel agency and a **Western Union** office (open Mon.-Fri. 8am-1pm and 2-5pm, Sat. 8am-noon). The **police station** (tel. 34-56, emergency tel. 115) faces the west side of the park.

Chinandega has a number of banks to change your dollars, but none for your traveler's checks. **Banco Nacional de Desarollo** (tel. 44-56) is one block east of the southeast corner of the Parque Central (open Mon.-Fri. 8am-4pm and Sat. 8:30-11am). **Banco Nicaragüense** (tel. 41-69, 41-03) is 1 block farther east (open Mon.-Fri. 8:30am-12:30pm and 1:30-4pm, Sat. 8:30am-noon). *Coyotes* also prowl half the streets around the banks and markets, and some of them are willing to change checks. **Buses** depart from Mercado Bisne to **León** (every 30min., 1¼ hrs., 3.50 córdobas); to **Managua** (2 hrs., 14 córdobas); and to the nearby port town of **Corinto** (45min., 2 or 3 córdobas). Buses for towns to the north of Chinandega (including **Somotillo** and the **Honduran border**), and also taxis and *camionetas* to **El Viejo,** leave from the Mercadito, one block north of Parque Central. **Pharmacies** abound in Chinandega. **Santa María** (tel. 27-58), four blocks east of the Parque Central, is located kitty-corner to the southwest corner of the market (open Mon.-Sat. 8:30am-8pm). **Hospital Mauricio Abdalah** (tel. 33-67, 34-66) is the gray building at the southwest of the Parque Central, south of the police station. **Red Cross** offers 24-hour ambulance service (tel. 31-32). The **TELCOR** office (tel. 39-05; fax 30-00) is located just north of the Parque Central's northwest corner. **Telephone** services offered daily from 7am-8:45pm. **Telephone code:** 0341. **Mail** and **fax** services offered Mon.-Fri. 8am-noon and 2-5pm, Sat. 8am-1pm.

Accommodations Good places to stay are few but not quite far between in Chinandega. **Hotel Chinandega** (1½ blocks south of the southwest corner of Central Market) is your best bet for simple rooms, at 30 córdobas per person. Shared showers and toilets are a little scary, but certainly bearable. A more opulent option is the **Hotel Glomar,** located one block south of Central Market. Respectable singles on the second floor (without baths) are a whopping 83 córdobas. If you really want to blow your wad, go to the **Hotel Consiqüina,** one block east and a half block south of Parque Central. The big, cushy lounge has a TV, and all rooms have A/C and private bath. Singles US$23 and doubles US$27 (ouch!). It is said, that there are cheaper *hospedajes* in Chinandega, but if you find one, be sure it's not a *hospedeje y bar;* that's where the wild things are—the wild things are all hookers.

Food Relative to its accommodations options, Chinandega has food in spades. Importantly, the town's water is chlorinated, and should be potable (though vaguely reminiscent of swim-lessons at the YMCA). Water's to be had from any of the numerous snack shops scattered around town, as well as in one of the burg's fancier restaurants, assuming that you've long since had your fill of Coca-Cola. Otherwise, you might want to grab some ripe, juicy fruits from the produce section of one of the markets. **El Kiosko,** the creatively named snack shop in the corpus of the Parque Central (southwest corner), is a great place to slurp down a delicious *refresco natural* or to have a beer (they have Heineken and American imports). They also serve a decent *comida corriente* lunch (10-12 córdobas). If the Parque is too public for you, **La Hacienda** (½ block east of the north side of the Parque Central) is tucked away in its own private garden. Tasteful bamboo and red tile architecture enclose this peaceful dining area. Chicken dishes ring in at 30 córdobas, while the bell-ringing beef costs 40 córdobas. Home to a small bar and dance floor (open 11:30am-10pm on quiet nights and until 1am if it's a party night). One last option is **El Hungaro,** a restaurant run by a locally stranded Hungarian national. Take the street that runs one block east of TELCOR north until you cross the bridge. Take the first right turn, up a dirt road, and El Hungaro is 200m on your left. Good, cheap food awaits those who survive the 1-hr. wait. Have a beer or two while the owner cranks American music through the bar.

Sights The steeples of several modest churches spice up the city skyline and evoke Chinandega's colonial past. The **Santa Ana** church borders the Parque Central on its north side. The façade of **El Calvario** and the greenery of its ensconcing park are visible when looking east from Santa Ana's entrance. The **Parque de las Rosas,** right beside the TELCOR office, is a quaint, flowery, and punnily named little park dedicated to the mother of Rubén Darío, Rosa Sarmiento, herself a native of Chinandega. For an impressive view of El Calvario's towers, caught dramatically against the backdrop of the giant Volcán San Cristóbal, trudge up to the third floor of the mayor's office (*alcaldía*), a half block south of the Mercado Central.

And if **Volcán San Cristóbal** makes a good backdrop, it makes a better vantage point. Those adventurous enough to climb Nicaragua's tallest volcano will be able to find reputable private guides in Chinandega, with whom they may scale the harrowing heights in relative security. Another option for outdoor hoots is accessible from the Mercadito, where you can catch buses to various remote beaches along the Pacific coast. A local favorite is the stretch of shoreline known as **Jíquilillo**.

Entertainment To thrill its cotton-pickin' populace, Chinandega has a few movie theaters up its sleeve. Just south of the TELCOR office, **El Pelón** has been of special visual interest ever since it lost part of its roof during a fire. Consequently, filmgoers can watch their movies under the stars, in open air. Chinandega also has its own version of a roller coaster, located just east of the Parque Central's north side by the basketball courts. At night people gather near the Parque Central, where trucks called *pelones* ("baldies," like the theater), *camiones* stripped of their roofs, all congregate in the basketball courts to gather their bedloads of passengers. Locals pay one córdoba to cruise the city in these makeshift convertibles, blaring Central American pop-favorites up and down the streets. Why not join the fun?

SOUTH OF MANAGUA

■■■ MASAYA

A young (and randy) Rubén Darío once paid a visit to the town of Masaya, and afterwards dubbed it "Ciudad de las Las Flores." He didn't choose this title for any botanical preferences, but rather because he was impressed by the town's abundance of beautiful women. While some may still be drawn to Masaya for its ladyfolk, the city is better known for its *artesanías.* Over 65% of Nicaragua's artisan-made products are said to hail from here, including some of the highest quality hammocks in the world, fine ceramics of all kinds, superb woodwork, paintings, jewelry, hats, leather goods, and more, all of which can be bought for bargain prices at Masaya's bustling **Mercado Nuevo.**

There's definitely something romantic about Masaya, though. Just take a stroll through the delightful streets: colorful churches rise beside shady plazas, the *malecón,* or dike, at the western edge of town offers an impressive view of sprawling Laguna de Masaya below, and towering Volcán Masaya dominates the horizon. Locals use the dike for hanging out, or more often, for making out; it might be fun to try one or the other, if only to fit in.

PRACTICAL INFORMATION

All of Masaya's main thoroughfares meet **Parque 17 de Octubre. Av. Zelaya** comprises its eastern border. Many buses arrive and depart from the **Mercado Nuevo,** five blocks east of the park on Calle Ernesto Fernandez, just past the bridge.

Inturismo (tel. 29-36), at the *entrada a Masaya,* a 15min. walk north of the Parque 17 de Octubre, claims to have information on Masaya, but it's slim pickins; they distribute no brochures or pamphlets, but can answer questions. Open Mon.-Fri. 8am-noon and 2-5pm. Another source of touristy information is the proprietor of the **Hotel Regis** (see Accommodations, below).

Police: (tel. 42-22) 1 block east and 1 block north of the park's northeast corner.

Currency Exchange: Banco Nacional de Desarollo (tel. 27-41, 27-42), 1 block east on the street just north of the park's northeast corner. Changes cash and traveler's checks for US$1 for every US$100 changed. Open Mon.-Fri. 8:30am-4pm, Sat. 8:30am-noon. **Banco Nicaragüense de Industria y Comercios** (tel. 20-21), 1 block east of the southeast corner of the Parque 17 de Octubre, changes dollars but not traveler's checks. Open Mon.-Fri. 8:30am-12:30pm and 1:30-4pm, Sat. 8:30am-noon.

Post office and telephones: the **TELCOR** office, on the west side of the park, has **telephone** and **telegram** services. Open daily 7am-9:30pm. The **post office** is in the same building as the TELCOR office, and it has **fax** service (fax 27-47). Open Mon.-Fri. 7am-noon and 1-5pm, Sat. 7am-noon. **Telephone code:** 052.

Buses to **Managua** depart from the north side of the closed and crumbling Mercado Viejo, on Calle San Miguel, 2 blocks east of the park (every 20min., beginning at 4am, 1 hr., 3 córdobas). Buses to **Granada** depart from the lot on Calle San Miguel, east of the Mercado Nuevo (every 30min., 2 córdobas). The bus to **Carazo** departs less frequently from the same spot, as does the bus to **Catarina, Niquinohomo,** and **San Marcos.**

Supermercado Loretto (tel. 45-35), next to the TELCOR office, sells good bottled water. Open Mon.-Sat. 8am-7:30pm, Sun. 8am-1pm.

Laundry: Not a mirage: **Dry Cleaning "Masaya"** washes clothes cheaply. They come back folded, lookin' sharp, and smellin' sweet. Two blocks south of Banco Nicaragüense. Next-day service available. Open Mon.-Sat. 8am-noon and 2-7pm.

Pharmacy: Farmacia Masaya (tel. 27-80), ½ block east of the park's southeast corner, is large and well stocked. Open Mon.-Fri. 8am-7:30pm and Sat. 8am-5pm.

Hospital Rafael Padilla (tel. 27-78), 5 blocks west of the park's northwest corner.

AMNLAE: Casa de la Mujer Sylvia Marlene Ramirez (tel. 21-38), half a block north of the park, specializes in internal medicine, acupuncture, and women's health. Open Mon.-Fri. 9am-noon and 2-6pm, Sat. 9am-noon.

Red Cross: (tel. 21-31), 1 block south of the park, on the street that bisects it.

NICARAGUA

ACCOMMODATIONS

Perhaps because of its proximity to Managua, Masaya has proportionately few places to stay. Unfortunately, the ones that do exist are a little on the pricey side, and the really cheap *hospedajes* are just a bit too cheap.

Hotel Regis (tel. 23-00), 3½ blocks north of the park on Av. Zelaya, is a wonderful place to spend the night. **Señor Francisco Castillo,** who manages the hotel with his charming wife, is a walking history text, a human warehouse stocked full of regional information. Constant mopping and sweeping make this place impeccably clean. Communal bathrooms are neat, and all doors are securely locked. The price of a room includes a fan, a roll of toilet paper, and free luggage storage for daytrippers. The couple also serves an enormous, delicious breakfast every morning for 15 córdobas. Curfew 10pm, check-out 10am. 40 córdobas per person.

Hotel Mone Carlo, 5 blocks north of the park on Av. Zelaya, is a nice, homey, and modern place flooded with lounging area, self-serve laundry facilities, adjacent restaurant, and a Masayan hammock to test before you buy your own. Sparkly rooms share a modern bathroom. Singles 50 córdobas; doubles 70 córdobas, with air-conditioning and private bath 100 córdobas.

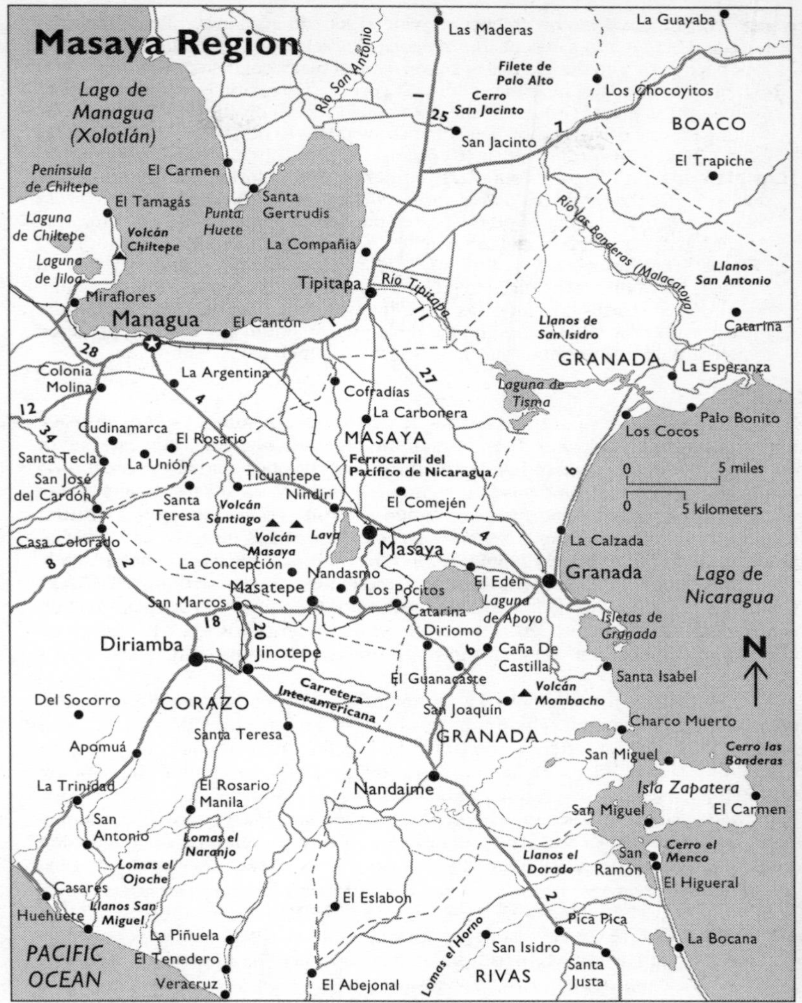

Hospedaje Rex is not marked by a sign, but can be identified as the bright yellow building across from the southwest corner of the park, south of La Iglesia San Jerónimo. Most rooms are squeezed into a rickety, attic-like space, but the rooms that are tucked into an *actual* thatchwork attic space are very sunny. The bathrooms could use a little elbow grease. 15 córdobas per person.

FOOD

The restaurant scene in Masaya leaves something to be desired (like, say, good restaurants), but the prospects are by no means hopeless. Conspicuously absent is a place for breakfast, although the small *sodas* in the park sometimes open early to cure the early-morning munchies.

Restaurante Che-Gris (tel. 59-42), ½ block south and ½ block east of Hotel Regis, has a high-ceilinged dining room, a garden, a patio in back, and a cow skull hanging over the bar. Dine on chicken in wine sauce (40 córdobas), filet mignon, or tongue. There is also a decent *comida corriente* served for 20 córdobas. Come to kick back with a coldie: bottles of *cerveza* are actually encrusted with ice.

Restaurante Sandalo, near the southwest corner of the park, is an enormous and fairly popular place. Groove to the Nicaraguan top-40 on the dance floor while waiting for one of many chop sueys and chow meins to be had for 28-32 córdobas each. Chicken 28 córdobas, fish 30 córdobas. Open daily 11:30am-10pm.

Los Manolos, on the park's southeast corner, is airy, colorful, and serves up the regular stuff at good prices. *Filete* and *carne asada* 25 córdobas, and a *comida corriente* with a number of off-the-beaten-track options (like *canelonis*) for only 13 córdobas. Hamburgers and sandwiches, 5 córdobas. Open daily 8am-10pm.

El Filete Steakhouse (tel. 47-00), a few kilometers down the highway toward Managua in Nindirí, is the place to go for a high-priced, high-quality steak (around 60 córdobas). Locals consider this to be the best restaurant in town. Eat on the garden patio or in the air-conditioned dining room, but in any case, be prepared to pay through the nose for your food and drink. Open daily 11am-11pm.

SIGHTS

Small stone sculptures complement the famed Masaya hammocks, woven mats, baseball bats, and handpainted ceramics of the **Mercado Nuevo,** at the east end of town. For a veritable orgy of hand-crafted delights, wander among the local *artesanías* who concentrate in the western end of the market. As always, quality of artisanship varies; look around first, and when the time comes, *bargain* (without haggling excessively). Various workshops sell their goods directly, and most of these can be found in **Barrio Monimbó,** to the south of town, which has a largely indigenous population. Another source for handicrafts is the showroom at **CECAPI** (Centro de Capacitación de la Pequeña Industria y Artesanías), in a squat building five blocks west of Parque Central, near the *malecón.* Prices at CECAPI tend to be higher, but its mood is lower-key, and the showroom is a great way to see what's out there.

If you're looking for a hammock, you might try **Ramiro Suazo y Familia,** one block east of the stadium. The family has been in the business for 45 years, and many international importers come to the Suazos for the hammocks they fashion behind their house. Prices are higher than you'll find anywhere in the surrounding market, but these are some serious hammocks.

Masaya's *alcaldía* houses the **Gallery of Heroes and Martyrs,** which exhibits masks worn by some of the first Sandinista guerillas, photographs of the rebelling forces—as well as the actual materials they used to construct clandestine bombs.

Diamonds in the rough

Nicaragua is one of the few Latin American countries where soccer is not the foremost sport. Here, it's baseball, and it wins by a good country mile. *Madres* are also well-loved, but apple pie is still waiting to catch on, and the ole U.S. of A. is very far indeed from winning itself any popularity contests. Although their country hasn't generated any U.S. major-leaguers yet, Nicaraguans have tapped into the heroics of another Latin American, Roberto Clemente, whose name lives on in Masaya's stadium. The famed Puerto Rican outfielder died in a plane on his way to deliver aid for earthquake victims in Nicaragua.

Nicaraguan kids have developed an uncanny ability to shape baseball fields out of whatever space they find themselves in. From streetcorners to crowded playgrounds, they can play ball with only two bases or as many as five, and they certainly don't need a bat, ball, or gloves, or at least not the official kind. Any old stick usually makes do as a bat, and shampoo bottles? Well, that's as good a ball as any; it doesn't fly quite the same, but you don't need gloves, and after a while the players get used to the peculiar flight of the bottle. Those brands with conditioner are reputed to help with knuckleballs, and watch out for sliders if the bottle contained moisturizers.

The Alcaldía is a two-story building on the west side of Calle Real San Jerónimo, 2½ blocks south of La Iglesia San Jerónimo (open Mon.-Fri. 8:30-11:30am and 1-4pm).

La Iglesia de la Asunción, in the Parque 17 de Octubre, was erected in 1833. Once inside, look up in order to see the high, wooden, flower-painted ceiling (perhaps another tribute to the beauty of the *masayanas?*). On the southern side of the park, a small plaque commemorates the 1856 defeat of the craven William Walker. Also, be sure to check out the **malecón,** or jetty, six blocks west of the park's southwest corner, if you haven't already happened to see it on your way about town.

■ NEAR MASAYA

Parque Nacional Volcán Masaya is home to a pair of volcanoes. Pocked by five craters, one of the seething mountains (Santiago) constantly belches gaseous fumes from its center, where a pool of lava can be seen glowing from one of the park's chief lookouts. The park itself is easily accessible from either Masaya or Managua. Perhaps apocryphal is the story about how Somoza would drop undesirables into the volcano from a helicopter: you make the call. The entrance to the volcano is along the *carreterra,* about 4km northwest of Masaya and towards Managua; most Managua-Masaya buses can drop you off. There's a small museum 2km from the entrance gate, and from there, it's another (steep) 5km to the top. The walk is tough but manageable. It's also very feasible to catch a ride with one of the frequently passing tourists, especially on weekends. If you're there when the park opens at 9am you can sometimes get a ride with park rangers all the way to the top; taking the same trip by taxi would be expensive.

Once there, enjoy the view: the splendid Laguna Masaya lies below, the city beyond. Far away you can see the **Cruz de Bobadilla,** which the Spaniards placed high atop the volcano in the 16th century. They thought the volcano was the *Boca del Infierno* (the proverbial "mouth of hell") and placed the cross there to keep the devil in his place. The cross has a terrific vantage of the countryside all around, but to see the lava you have to hike (or drive) around to the other side of the crater. From there you can hear the rumbling of the volcano and peer straight into the glowing fluid below. *Let's Go* does not recommend descending into the jaws of Hades. From the other side of the crater, a trail leads 150 yards to the "Bat Cave" (Cueva de Murcielagos, but probably not *that* Bat Cave). It was formed by lava that was forced up and out through the crater. If you want to explore it, bring a flashlight (gate open Tues.-Sun. 8am-5pm; admission 5 córdobas).

The small town **Nindirí** sits on the same road, between Masaya and the volcano, where a small but interesting archaeological museum displays artifacts retrieved from the outlying area, most of them former implements of field-plowing farmers. The **Museo Tenderi,** located one block west of the town's park, houses *ollos* (large burial pots), fine ceramics, a few *incensarios,* and some rusty Spanish muskets. Among the museum's more eye-catching displays is a map of all the Earth's volcanoes, information about all of the volcanoes in Nicaragua, and an artificial lava tunnel that you can walk through (and feel like you're being re-birthed).

The bus from Masaya to Carazo (which leaves the market every 20min.) serves four neat towns on its way. The village of **Catarina** has an absolutely spectacular lookout, about 15min. down the road from Masaya's city limits. The bus drops you off at a 3-way intersection where one road leads to Rivas, another to Jinotepe, and the last back to Masaya. From here, walk about 10 minutes straight through the tiny town, past the church, to arrive at the **Mirador de Catarina.** A windy bluff overlooks a picture of beautiful **Laguna de Apoyo, Lago de Nicaragua,** the city of Granada in miniature on the isthmus between the two, and **Volcán Mombacho** rising to the right. **Bar Marina,** perched atop the lookout, serves rather cheap food, considering its awesome setting: steak 35 córdobas, chicken 30 córdobas, and for the adventurous and ecologically insensitive, *huevo paslama* (turtle egg) 20 córdobas (open 7am-10pm). From the lookout, it's also possible to hike down to the Laguna where you can enjoy a swim in the crystal blue water (about 45min. each way). From Catarina, it's only about a 10 minute walk down the road to Rivas before you reach **San Juan del Oriente,** where numerous homes and cooperatives sell locally produced wares. A fascinating place to visit is the **Escuela de Ceramicá,** whence hails much of the native handiwork. Even though the ceramics are made here, the selection is not that much better than at the market in Masaya. A few miles from the intersection by Catarina, on the way toward Jinotepe, you'll see **Niquinohomo** ("valley of the warriors"), birthplace and boyhood home of Augusto Cesar Sandino. Sandino's home used to be a museum, but now it's a library (open Mon.-Sat. until 5pm). Niquinohomo is only about a 20-minute walk from the intersection at Catarina. If you don't feel like walking, the bus to Carazo passes by here too.

Hop aboard the same bus again to reach **San Marcos,** where a branch campus of the University of Mobile, Alabama does its best not to look too incongruous (see Alternatives to Tourism, page 259).

■■■ GRANADA

Granada's strategic location on the western shore of Lago de Nicaragua has shaped much of its history. Francisco Hernández de Córdoba founded the city in 1524, and though the Spanish soon exhausted the region's supply of gold, Granada continued to prosper as a trading center, taking advantage of its proximity to the Pacific coast and its easy access to the Caribbean via the Río San Juan. Granada soon became the country's conservative stronghold, and a rivalry with liberal León ensued.

Because of its wealth and its gateway onto the Caribbean, the city was repeatedly attacked by English and French pirates during the 17th century. After the country gained independence from Spain, Granada saw much fighting in the guise of civil war against neighboring León. Later, in the 1850s, William Walker captured the city and ruled Nicaragua from here for two years, until he was ousted. Before his retreat he set fire to the entire city. This destroyed or damaged many of the colonial buildings, most of which have since then been rebuilt. Today's Granada is as colonial a city as you'll find in Nicaragua: big, two-story homes line wide boulevards; tall palm trees shade the Parque Central.

A breeze from the lake takes the edge off the toaster-oven heat, and the most enjoyable pastime is simply walking, either within the city itself or along the lake shore. You might glimpse a colonial church set against the cloud-covered peak of Volcán Mombacho, which rises to the south of the city. Granada's historic value is more atmospheric than tangible; it has to do with all those who've kicked its cobblestones: pirates, colonists, revolutionaries, and a few tourists to boot.

ORIENTATION

Buses from Managua release passengers in the west part of town, six blocks west and two blocks north of the **Parque Central.** Buses from Masaya pull into a small lot two blocks west and two blocks south of the Parque Central. Buses from Rivas stop at a gas station one block west and four blocks south of the Parque Central. Granada's main north-south street, **Calle Atravesado,** runs one block west of the Parque Central. **Calle Real** borders the south of the park and runs west, past three pretty, painted churches. **La Calzada** spins off the eastern side of the park by the cathedral, and runs 1.5km east to the lake and pier. Almost all of the hotels listed are on La Calzada. If you're coming from Managua, bear in mind that "al lago" is no longer north, it's now east.

PRACTICAL INFORMATION

Tourist Office: As always, tourist information is provided by **Inturismo** (tel. 33-13) on the western side of the park next to the plush Hotel Alhambra (open Mon.-Fri. 8am-noon and 2-5pm). They get a lot of traffic here, so they're especially experienced and able to make good of your questions. Their colorful brochure is virtually useless, but their photocopied maps are worthwhile.

Police: (tel. 29-29).

Currency Exchange and Western Union: Banco Nacional de Desarrollo (tel. 28-11) west of the park on Atravesada, changes cash. Open Mon.-Fri. 8:30am-12:30pm and 1:30-4pm. **Banco Nicaragüense de Industria y Commercios** (tel. 27-21), west of the park and in front of the Teatro Gonzalez, changes cash and provides **Western Union** service. Open Mon.-Fri. 8:30am-12:30pm and 1:30-4pm, Sat. 8:30am-noon. The *coyotes* in Granada change traveler's checks as well, but at inferior rates. **Banco de America Central** (tel. 33-52) changes traveler's checks for a charge of 7 córdobas a check, or at a 6% commission charge if you want dollars. Open Mon.-Fri. 8am-4:30pm, Sat. 8am-1pm.

Telephone service is provided by **TELCOR,** in an unmarked light blue building across from the northeast corner of the park (tel. 20-90). Open daily 7am-10pm. **Fax and postal service** from the same building (fax 27-76). Open for mail Mon.-Fri. 8am-noon and 1-5pm, Sat. 8am-noon. **Telephone Code:** 055.

Buses to **Managua** leave from the station 6 blocks west and 2 blocks north of the Parque Central (every 20min., 5am-7pm, 1 hr., 6 córdobas). Buses to **Masaya** leave from a small lot 2 blocks west and 2 blocks south of the Parque Central (every 20min., 5am-7pm, 20min., 2 córdobas). From the gas station, 1 block west and 4 blocks south of the Parque Central, buses go to **Rivas** (every hr., 1½ hrs., 5 córdobas). You can also get to Rivas by taking a bus to **Nandaime,** and then catching another bus from there to Rivas. From Rivas, buses run to **San Juan del Sur, San Jorge** (where ferries leave for Isla de Ometepe), and to the Costa Rican border at **Peñas Blancas.**

Boats to **San Carlos** (on the southeast tip of the lake) and to **Isla de Ometepe** leave from the pier at the end of La Cazalda (Mon. and Thurs. at 2:30 and 3:30pm, 11.5 córdobas; to San Carlos is 17.5 córdobas). Express boats to San Carlos leave on Mon., Wed., and Thurs. at 9am (75 córdobas). On Fri., Sat., and Sun., an express leaves at 8am and stops on Isla de Ometepe before reaching San Carlos (Ometepe 38 córdobas; San Carlos 75 córdobas). On Sat. and Sun. at 10am and 1:30pm, an express leaves from Ometepe (38 córdobas).

Bicycle Rental: Repuestos Bonilla on La Calzada, 1½ blocks east of the Parque Central. Mountain bikes for 7 córdobas per hr., 40 córdobas for the day.

Market: Supermercado Lacayo (tel. 21-56) is 2 blocks west of the park. Open Mon.-Fri. 8:15am-12:30pm and 2-7:30pm, Sat. 8am-7:30pm, Sun. 8:30am-1pm.

AMNLAE provides women's services at **Casa de la Mujer Claudia Chamorro** (tel. 20-96), on La Calzada, 1 block east of the cathedral. Open Mon.-Fri. 8am-noon and 2-6pm.

Pharmacy: Farmacia el Rosario (tel. 29-44) is on Calle Atravesado, 1 block west of the park. Open Mon.-Sat. 8am-8pm, Sun. 8am-1pm.

Hospital (27-19 or 22-09), just south of the Managua bus stop, 1 block north and 6 west of the Parque Central.

Red Cross (tel. 27-11) is 6 blocks east down La Calzada toward the lake, across from the Hotel Granada.

ACCOMMODATIONS

Hospedaje Cabrera (tel. 27-81), on La Calzada, 2½ blocks east of the Parque Central, is distinguished by its clean rooms with fans, a scraggly garden, a noisy parrot, drooping clotheslines, and friendly proprietors. Rocking chairs and cable TV in the lounge serve as relaxatives. The large communal bathroom is graciously equipped with toilet paper (!) and a toilet seat. Whites whiter at the self-service laundry area. 15-córdoba breakfasts, snacks available during the rest of the day. 25 córdobas per person; 20 córdobas per person for groups of three or four.

Hospedaje Vargas (tel. 28-97), across the street from the Cabrera, and very similar to it, may amount to just a shade less; it too boasts a garden and courtyard, rocking chairs, TV, and laundry service—but no food. 20 córdobas per person.

Hospedaje Esfinge, across from the bustling market on Atravesado, 3 blocks south of the Parque Central, is housed in a big, run-down colonial building. Rooms have real beds with real mattresses, but not real walls. Rooms are separated by 3m-high partitions that zig and zag beneath an even higher roof. Friendly management, ping-pong table, cable TV, and clean bathrooms. 25 córdobas per person.

Hospedaje Central (tel. 59-00), on La Calzada, 1½ blocks east of the park. Offers a few rooms around a scrubby garden in the back of a family home; all of them are clean, and some are large enough to house a small band of rebels. Good locks make the doors relatively secure. All rooms have fans. 18 córdobas per person.

Hotel Granada (tel. 29-74; fax 41-28), on La Calzada across from La Iglesia Guadalupe and a few blocks west of the lake, is both sprawling *and* white-tiled. Rooms come with private bathrooms and A/C, and the price is good if you share a big room. Laundry service and a TV in the lounge keep you happy. Singles 150 córdobas; doubles 207 córdobas, with 2 beds, for 2 or 3 people, 230 córdobas. Rooms for up to 3 or 4 people 300 córdobas per person. Add 15% tax.

FOOD

Most of the fanciest places in town are in the Centro Turístico on the lakeside, east of town. The very cheapest food in town can be found at the *comedores* in and around the market, three blocks south of the Parque Central. Below are a few places that fall somewhere in between.

Restaurante Lejano Oriente (tel. 54-63), 1 block west of the park's northwest corner, serves up an impressive variety of chop sueys, chow meins, and rice dishes (rice with chicken, with shrimp, or *a la Valenciana*) for 20-35 córdobas. Normal *nica* standbys available at fair prices. Open daily 11:30am-9pm.

Cafetín Amigo, on Calzada next door to Hospedaje Central, in the Hospedaje district, is a small, simple place with cheap food where they treat you like a true amigo. *Comida corriente* of beef, chicken, or pork, 13 córdobas, fish 14 córdobas. Cheap breakfasts, too. Open daily 9am-10:30pm.

Cafetín Soya Nica (45-98), on the northwest corner of the park, has a few tables out front that offer a nice view of the park. Serves meaty meals, as well as non-meaty, cheese-and soy-based meals for 12-20 córdobas. Open daily 9am-10pm.

La Mariscada, ½ block west of the park's northwest corner, specializes in seafood but serves just about every other typical dish, at good prices. Breakfasts 10-15 córdobas, *comida corriente* 14-16 córdobas (with a drink), and shrimp 30 córdobas. Open daily 7am-10pm.

El Condo ice cream shop is the classy place on Calle Atrevesado, 1 block west of the park. Excellent malts, milkshakes, ice creams, and *refrescos naturales.* Open Mon.-Thurs. 11am-8pm, Fri.-Sun. 11am-9pm.

SIGHTS

On the west side of Parque Central stand the **Palacio de Cultura Joaquín Pasos,** the upscale **Hotel Alhambra,** and next door, the useful (and maybe not so attractive) **Oficina de Turismo.** The Palacio de Cultura, a large Neoclassical building, used to be the gathering place for Granada's Social Club. Now it houses various workshops, classes, art exhibitions, and a library. The flamboyant mural and the garden in the back contribute to the palpable grandeur of the place. On the south side of the park is the **palacio municipal,** which is now the seat of Granada's *alcaldía.* Another large Neoclassical structure, Granada's **cathedral,** graces the park's east side.

Plazuela de los Leones is the miniature rectangular plaza adjacent to the Parque Central at its northeast corner, near the TELCOR building and next door to the Casa de los Leones (even in Granada...). The time-worn **Fundación de los Tres Mundos** building, once a house, was burned to the ground in the blaze sparked by William Walker but has been rebuilt recently with funds from Austria, Germany, and Switzerland (the "Tres Mundos"). The building has art exhibits, workshops, and other cultural events (open daily 8am-6pm).

One block north and one block east of the Parque Central's northeast corner is the old **Iglesia y Convento San Francisco,** founded during Granada's first years and rebuilt after William Walker's attack. The convent has been converted into a museum; the chief attraction is a collection of 28 pre-Columbian statues found on the Lago de Nicaragua's Isla Zapatera (since turned into a national park). The statues, all 800-1000 years old, depict bizarre figures of humans, animals, and weird lycanthrope-permutations thereof. The museum is undergoing renovations, but is still open daily 9am-6pm (10 córdobas). The next best colonial churches in Granada are the **Iglesia de la Merced,** the **Iglesia de Xalteva,** and **Maria Auxiladora.**

The path that leads east from the cathedral down **La Calzada** also makes a nice walk. Locals fish (and dive) off the pier at the end of the road in the late afternoon, and from there you can try your hand at shark-sighting and not much more. Walk south of the pier along the lake shore to come to a tourist park lined with restaurants. Beyond the park and about half an hour from the pier lies **Puerto Asese,** where you can hire a *lancha* to see one of Granada's main tourist attractions, the small group of 368 populated lake islands (*isletas*) off Granada's shore. The *lanchas* charge 120 córdobas for a one-hour tour, which is cheap, considering that the boats can fit up to 20 people to split the cost. Boats leave most frequently on Sundays.

■■■ RIVAS

Rivas lies two hours south of Granada and only 45km north of the Costa Rican border at Peñas Blancas. The parts of town most often frequented by tourists are the bus stop and the pier a few kilometers out from **San Jorge,** where boats leave for Ometepe. The town is of interest to the traveler primarily as a focal point for bus and boat routes to points elsewhere, but it does have some history to its name. The best remaining evidence of its colonial period can be seen in a well-preserved church that lies six blocks toward the downtown area from the *carretera.*

PRACTICAL INFORMATION

Buses leave Rivas for Peñas Blancas (8, 9:30, 10:30, 11am, 12:20, 2:30, 3:30pm, 1 hr., 4 córdobas); for Managua (every 30min., 4am-5pm, 10 córdobas); for San Juan del Sur (every 45min., 6:45am-late afternoon, 4 córdobas), Granada (every 1½ hrs., 6:10am-3:30pm, 6 córdobas), and for San Jorge (every 30min., 10min., 1.5 córdobas). All leave from the bus stop just before the entrance to the main bus station-market area. **Taxis** also leave frequently from the market for San Jorge (just 4km away), and there are typically a few locals hanging out there, waiting for a taxi and willing to split the fare; expect to pay as little as three córdobas. **Boats** depart from San Jorge bound for Moyogalpa, on Isla de Ometepe (Mon.-Sat. at 11am, noon, 3pm, and 5pm, Sun. at 11am, 3pm, and 5pm, one-way fare 7 córdobas). If you really can't wait to get there, there's also an **express** (leaves daily 10am and 6pm, 45min., 17 córdobas).

The **police station** (tel. 33-3-35) is three blocks north of the market. The **TELCOR** office (tel. 33-4-72; fax 33-5-63), 1½ blocks west and a half block north of the bank, provides **telephone, telegram, fax,** and **postal** services (open Mon.-Fri. 8am-5pm, Sat. 8am-noon). The **telephone code** is 046. To exchange cash (U.S. dollars only) or traveler's checks for no commission or charge, head to **Banco Nacional de Desarrollo** (tel. 33-4-11), four blocks south of the market-bus station (open Mon.-Fri. 8:30am-4pm, Sat. 8:30-11:30am). **Farmacia La Salud** (tel. 33-3-05), 3½ blocks north of the market, is open daily 8am-8pm. The **Red Cross** (tel. 33-4-15) lies two blocks south and five blocks west of the bus lot.

If you need to spend the night in Rivas, a convenient option is the **Hospedaje Lidia,** 6½ blocks west and two blocks south of the market-bus station, and two blocks west of the Red Cross. It has no sign, so ask around. Rooms are clean and tidy, like the rest of the place (doors locked at 10pm; 30 córdobas per person). The restaurant fills daily with locals longing for Lidia's lunchtime cooking

BORDER CROSSING TO COSTA RICA

Sapoa is the Nicaraguan town on the Costa Rican border 37km south of Rivas, and Peñas Blancas is its neighboring town on the Costa Rican side, 4km south. Peñas Blancas is 80km north of Liberia, Costa Rica.

To reach Sapoa, you can take a bus from Rivas (last bus leaves at 3:30pm daily, 30min., 5 córdobas) or Managua from early in the morning until early afternoon. Get to the border before 4pm, or else the border will be closed.

From the bus depot, walk to the clump of administrative buildings and find the window where they check your passport and charge the five córdoba exit fee (regardless of nationality). This is where you'll have problems if you've overstayed your 30 day limit. Nearby, a bank changes córdobas to dollars, but not to Costa Rican colones. The money changers outside will change to colones directly, but their rates may be sketchy.

From here, board a bus to the Costa Rican immigration office 4km away (5 córdobas). The last bus leaves at 4pm. Taxis are also available. From there, pass your passport along for a stamp (and pay 75 colones). Buses for Liberia leave at 7:30, 9:30, 10:30am, 12:30, 2:30, 3:30, and 5pm. Some of these continue on to San José.

■■■ SAN JUAN DEL SUR

The beach town of San Juan del Sur was once home to more than halcyon beach-freaks. Set on the Pacific Coast just 30km west over the hills from Rivas, the town thrived and throbbed during the U.S. gold rush as the port from which Cornelius Vanderbilt's transport company embarked for California; in those days, Nicaragua was the quickest thoroughfare for travel between Atlantic and Pacific. While occasional boats still make their way through, most of the transport in San Juan these days materializes when someone decides to carry their towel down to the beach.

And a nice beach it is. San Juan del Sur is popular with both Nicaraguans and the frame-pack set for good reason: the town sits in a cove, along a flat, easy, comma-shaped beach, sheltered by enticing waters to the west, and by huge, cinematic rock outcroppings to the north and the south. Restaurants and beach houses line most of the beach, but less-populated sands await nearby. Most of the waves are only big enough for boogie boards, although a few surfers can usually be found during high tide at the north end of the beach.

Practical Information San Juan del Sur is set on a hill and is only a few blocks deep. At the northern end of the beach, a "river" (your toenails might get thoroughly soaked while crossing) meets the Pacific. At the southern end of the beach, a long pier tends to the light boat traffic. Two buildings south of the TELCOR office is the closest thing to a **police station** (tel. 82-3-82). To make **phone** calls or send **telegrams,** visit the **TELCOR office** (tel. 82-2-61, 82-2-62), a pastel-colored building at the southern end of the beach, below the red-and-white radio tower (open for telephone service daily 7am-10pm; open for telegrams, postal service, and **fax** Mon.-Fri. 8am-noon and 2-5pm). The **telephone code** is 046. Seek medical attention, and ye shall find it at **Servicios Médicos Communales,** near the TELCOR office.

Accommodations Moskitos inhabit the Caribbean coast, but the Pacific side is full of mosquitoes; bring or buy repellent and coils, and bust out that net. For clean, new rooms, check out **Hospedaje Elizabeth** (tel. 82-2-70), across the street from the bus stop. Elizabeth does her best to take wanderers under her gentle wing. Her pet monkey's shenanigans entertain for hours. Fans buffer buzzing bands of bugs. Communal bathrooms are clean, but seats are non-existent and you'll have to squat your way to hygiene. Buy delicious breakfasts here (15 córdobas) as well as snacks for the beach (lock-out 11pm; 30 córdobas per person, 90 for a double with private bath). **Surf Casa 28,** a half block north of the street that runs from the bus stop to the beach and one block before the beach, is nothing too fancy, but it's pretty popular. Rooms are pretty big and the bathroom is kept clean. The beds are just cots with foam pads, but somehow manage to be comfy. Rooms have ceiling fans, and management provides mosquito coils for a fee (25 córdobas per person). Where the street from the bus stop meets the beach stands **Hotel Estrella,** a two-story wooden building and the most visible hotel in town, it's bright green shutters, doors, and balconies contrasting with the field of whitewash beyond. The walls don't reach all the way to the ceiling, but the communal facilities are decent. The breezy restaurant has high ceilings (25 córdobas per diner). The **Hospedaje Buen Gusto** is across the street. The walls meet the ceilings and the communal facilities are cleaner, but it's a bit pricier (40 córdobas per person). The adjacent restaurant serves food in the fancy *sala* downstairs, and also upstairs at the deck. A step up in price is **Casa International Joxi** (tel. and fax 82-3-48), a half block away from the beach on the same street. Rooms have private bathrooms and A/C (Singles 110 córdobas, doubles 165 córdobas, triples 220 córdobas. One room has beds for 50 córdobas per person without A/C and with a shared bath.) Washing machines and dryers in the hotel charge 15 córdobas per load. The small adjoining café has a limited menu, but their fresh orange juice will perk you up in the morning. **Hotel Berlovento** (tel. 82-2-98), up on the hill east of town, has a great view, but it's far from the beach and the center of action. Rooms have A/C and private bathrooms (singles 173 córdobas, doubles 207 córdobas; roll in a cot for the young 'uns).

Food Excellent fresh fish can be had in just about any restaurant here; it's justified to choose an eatery solely based on its view of the sunset. The restaurants along the beach are the most expensive because of their great views. Case in point: **El Timón** and **Restaurante Las Brisas Marinas** serve comparably high-quality food at comparably boosted prices. Fish platters include rice, fries, and salad (35-45 córdobas). For cheaper fare, try **La Soya,** one block north of the bus stop street, one block back from the beach. *Comida corriente* of fish, chicken, and beef 15 córdobas. In addition, a number of people sell food from grills set up outside their front door. For a great breakfast, try **Elizabeth's Soda** at Hospedaje Elizabeth for 15 córdobas. On the north end of the beach luxuriates **Restaurante Lago Azul,** which boasts a diverse menu and excellent presentation—the soups are especially pretty. Sit at open-air tables under a shading roof and sink your teeth into filet mignon (42 córdobas), clams, burgers, and fish are also options (open daily 9am-10pm).

Sights Go swimming. The north end of the beach is the cleanest, has the biggest waves, and is the least crowded. Casa International Joxi rents body boards for 25 córdobas per day and organizes sailing trips for groups of seven or more. For unspoiled beaches, head south along the road toward the town of **Ostional.** After a couple of km, there's a sign for *Balneario Remanso,* an unpopulated beach with larger waves than at San Juan del Sur. The beach is 3km down this road. Playa del Coco, Playa del Tamarindo, La Flor, and the nearest beach, Playa Sucia (what's in a name?) all offer good swimming and decent snorkeling. 5km south of town, dip your hands in the grand sands of Playa Marselles.

LAGO DE NICARAGUA

Fed by over 40 rivers, streams, and brooks, Lago de Nicaragua is the largest lake in Central America and the tenth-largest freshwater lake in the world. According to popular belief, the sharks that inhabit the lake are a vestige of the days when Lago de Nicaragua was part of the Pacific Ocean. In fact, the seldom-seen creatures are Caribbean bowl sharks that have swum up the Río San Juan, which runs from the sea to the lake along the Costa Rican border. Hundreds of islands peek out from the surface of the lake; there are over 300 *isletas* just offshore from Granada. Easily accessible by *lancha,* some of the *isletas* are populated, and all are notable for their wildlife and for the pre-Conquest petroglyphs that stud their surfaces. An 18th-century Spanish fort named **San Pablo** still stands on one of the *isletas.* Another, **Isla Zapatera,** is thought to have been sacred to the indigenous tribes because of the large number of statues found here, which are now on display in Granada (see Granada introduction, page 288). Some structures can still be found on the island, which has since been named a national park. **Isla de Ometepe,** four hours by boat from Granada, is one of Nicaragua's most photogenic spots, formed by two enormous volcanoes rising out of the lake. Farther to the south, off from San Carlos, the **Archipiélago de Solentiname** is renowned for its beauty and for artists' communities that produce woodcrafts and minimalist paintings.

Boat travel on Lago de Nicaragua is easy, cheap, and pretty damn fun. Several times a week, two boats travel from Granada to **San Carlos,** a sleepy town on the Lago's southeast shore, then back again, sometimes stopping on Isla de Ometepe.

From San Carlos it's possible to cross the border into Costa Rica, or to take a trip down the 190km Río San Juan past an old Spanish fort and through tropical wilderness to the coastal Caribbean town of San Juan de Norte.

■■■ ISLA DE OMETEPE

Islands are, of course, something else entirely. Some people are preternaturally drawn to them. Even if you aren't one of those people, don't leave Nicaragua without seeing Isla de Ometepe. Ancient petroglyphs, friendly people, and great fish dinners aside, the sheer natural beauty of the island is cause enough for a visit. Isla de Ometepe was formed an eternity ago by **Volcán Concepción** (1610m), which is still active, and by **Volcán Madera** (1394m), which is quite extinct, having last erupted 2600 years ago. Before the 19th century, the island was split in two by a strip of water which indigenous islanders used as a transportation canal. An 1804 eruption of Concepción filled this gap, creating a single island shaped like two joined circles. The name means (roughly) "two" (*Ome-*) "peaks" (*tepe*).

A relatively well-maintained road circumnavigates the Concepción (northwest) side of the island, while a much poorer road makes it halfway around the Madera (southeast) side. The wide green belt surrounding both volcanoes consists of rich soil and supports banana, tobacco, cotton, and citrus farms. Haul out your boots and start walking, either to some of the virgin primary forest that shrouds the island, or by some of the many petroglyphs on the island, which were carved by island inhabitants approximately 800 years before the arrival of the Spanish. Some of the best and most easily accessible examples lie between the towns of **Balgue** and **Magdalena,** on the Madera side of the island just southeast of the land bridge connecting the two "volcanoes."

The quickest **ferry** to Isla de Ometepe (1 hour) is from San Jorge (4km from Rivas) to Moyogalpa, on the western side of the island (several times daily). Boats also travel from Altagracia to Granada and San Carlos several times a week.

MOYOGALPA

Situated on the island's western coast, Moyogalpa is the second-largest town on Isla de Ometepe but has the most developed tourist facilities. Moyogalpa means "place of mosquitoes"; there are worse misnomers, so bring your preferred method of mosquito protection. The **police station** is a block and a half south and three blocks east of the pier, on the same street as the TELCOR office (open 24 hrs.). **Banco Nacional de Desarrollo,** four blocks east of the pier, exchanges U.S. dollars only (open Mon.-Fri. 8:30am-12:30pm and 1:30-4pm, Sat. 8:30-11:30am). Hotel Ometepelt (see below) will change traveler's checks, but at sorry rates. For **telephone, telegram,** and **postal** service, head to the **TELCOR** office (tel. 33-213 or 33-370), in its brand-spankin'-new wooden building (open Mon.-Sat. 8am-noon and 2-6pm). The **express boats** to Moyogalpa from San Jorge depart at 10am and 6pm (17 córdobas, 45min.), and other boats leave at 11am, noon, 3pm, and 5pm (1 hr., 7 córdobas). Sundays there are no expresses, and the normal 3pm boat does not run. **Buses** to Altagracia, about 18km around the island, depart every 1½ hours or so (5 córdobas, 50min.). The road passes between the two volcanoes and provides some excellent views. Buses often wait to take passengers from arriving boats, and boats often do the same for buses. A *carretera* circumnavigates the Concepción side of the island, starting a few blocks east (uphill) of the pier. Moyogalpa's **hospital** is 700m south of the church on the highway (open daily 8am-5pm, **emergencies** 24 hrs.). Dr. Fernando Martinez has a private practice one block south of the church on the *carretera* (open Mon.-Fri. 7am-1pm).

Pleasantry is the word of the day at **Hotelito Aly** (tel. 94-1-96), three blocks uphill from the pier to the left, where clean and comfy rooms are set around a shady restaurant patio with an abundance of big, droopy tropical leaves. A couple of hammocks hang here, and big, tasty (though often too salty) plates of food are served in the restaurant (25 córdobas per person). **Hotel el Puerto,** just to the right as you leave the pier, has rippin' rooms and a patio restaurant overlooking the water (singles 30 córdobas; doubles 40 córdobas, with air-conditioning 100 córdobas). **Pensión Jade,** 4½ blocks uphill from the pier, is the cheapest place in town, and is equipped with sufficient but inferior rooms, but its padded cots are perfectly comfortable (15 córdobas per person, meals 15 córdobas as well). The hotels are the only reliable place to find dinner in Moyogalpa, but they're consistently good.

ALTAGRACIA

Altagracia (pop. 8000), on the northeast coast of the Concepción side of the island and about 1½km inland, is the island's biggest town. If the hustle and bustle of the place gets to you, then you've gone insane; there's very little to do here. For goodness' sake, *pigs* root around in the town park. Altagracia is the most convenient base from which to explore the island's sights; it's near the road that leads to the Madera side of the island and is also near the beginning of the trail up Volcán Concepción.

Buses to **Balgue,** on the Madera side of Ometepe, depart from the Parque Central (every hour or every 1½ hrs., from 4am-4pm; 30min; 4 córdobas). This bus passes by **Playa Santo Domingo,** the biggest beach on the island. Buses also leave for Moyogalpa (every 1-1½ hrs., 4am-5pm, 50min, 5 córdobas). Regular **boats** run from Altagracia to Granada (Tues. and Fri. 10am and 10pm, Sun. 10am, 4 hrs., 11.5 córdobas) and to San Carlos (Mon., Thurs. at 7pm, 8 hrs.). There is also a more expensive **express boat** that goes to both Granada and to San Carlos on Sat. and Sun. The pier is about a 15-minute walk from town. **Farmacia San Diego,** half a block west of the park's southwest corner is open Mon.-Sat. 8am-noon and 1-5:30pm. **TELCOR, telephones** and **mail service** are all half a block west of the park's northwest corner (open Mon.-Sat. 8am-noon and 2-6pm).

The **church** is on the south side of the Parque Central, behind some pre-Columbian statues that were found on the island in pretty good shape. On the northwest corner of the park is the town **museum** stocked with photos of the island and its main sights, some pre-Columbian artifacts, and displays on the history and folklore of the island. The museum is associated with the Ecotour office and can provide **tourist information** and arrange for guides to all parts of the island.

If there is a center of ecotourism in Nicaragua, it may just be **Hospedaje Castillo,** a half block north of the *carretera* and one block west of the park. Señor Castillo is an authority on the **petroglyphs** (see Sights Around the Island), and with luck, you may share his *hospedaje* with knowledgeable grad students collecting data for heavy theses in tropical ecology. The rooms are spare and clean, and the food is good (20 córdobas per person). Whether or not you're staying here, feel free to drop by for a meal or a chat with Señor Castillo, who can suggest any number of beautiful trips or hikes around the island, and can put you in touch with a guide to the petroglyphs or to either of the volcanoes. Expect to pay roughly 25 córdobas for 4 hours around the petroglyphs, and about 90 córdobas for a tour of either volcano. **Hotel/Bar Restaurante Central** (tel. 60-72) has nicer rooms and grounds than the Castillo, but lacks the knowledgeable host. It's less popular with travelers, perhaps for this reason. The garden is astonishingly beautiful and well-kept, complete with a pond, a little gazebo, and cabañas for the romantic types. (20 córdobas per person, 30 for private bath, and 100 for cabaña that sleeps 2 people. Entrees 30-35 córdobas, *comida corriente,* breakfasts 15 córdobas.) For a lip-smackin', penny-pinchin' home-cooked meal, try the **Restaurant Plaza Bar,** a block and a half north from the Parque Central, on the right as you walk north. Grilled marinated chicken with rice, bread, salad, cheese, and cold drink costs 10 córdobas. For a fantastic chocolate shake and a piece of cake, beeline for the *soda* at the center of the Parque Central.

SIGHTS AROUND THE ISLAND

The biggest and most popular **beach** on Isla Ometepe is Santo Domingo, which lies on the isthmus between the two volcanoes. It can be easily reached on any bus traveling from one side of the island to the other. There is a fairly-priced **hotel** on the beach, with hammocks in which to lounge slothfully.

Most of the **petroglyphs** on the island lie between the towns of Balgue and Magdalena, on the Madera side of the island. These are simple etchings carved into the rocks between the 11th and 13th centuries AD by indigenous inhabitants of the island. Many of the designs contain spirals and circles, but their significance is not known. You can try to find them yourself by asking around or you can get a guide from **Ecotour** (in Moyogalpa or at the museum in Altagracia) or from Señor Castillo. Ecotour also provides guides to the waterfall **Salto de San Ramón,** and to the **Charro Verde** lagoon (see gray box, below). You can probably find these sights on your own just by asking around.The real challenges on the island are the volcanoes.

Gills for the Guilty

Should you find yourself gazing longingly into the *verde* depths of the enchanted Charro Verde, be warned: legend has it that a magical community lives under the lagoon. No one seems to know how the creatures of the green lagoon spend their days—in fact, it is widely believed that if you, or any other landlubbing humans, ever happen to swim in the lagoon, its denizens will transmogrify your body into that of a fish. This might make travel around the rest of Lago de Nicaragua more convenient, but could have serious repercussions later on, should you get netted by Nicaraguan fishermen, for instance.

CLIMBING THE VOLCANOES

Volcano-climbing is the quintessential I'm-roughing-it-in-Nicaragua activity. Be careful, however. Although both volcanoes on Isla de Ometepe are considered relatively crime-free, roaming around in deserted areas is always risky, and rockslides are a problem in some areas. If you plan on making it to the top, you'll need boots, a full water bottle, and, if it's the rainy season (May-Oct.), a waterproof layer and a desire to get muddy. Long pants protect against prickly plants and biting bugs. Wise hikers hire out the services of **Ecotour** or hire a guide through Señor Castillo.

Volcán Madera

Reaching Madera's summit requires an early start; you'll want to be on the first bus to Balgue (5:20am from Altagracia). Recruit friends to split the price of a guide, if you haven't done so already. The bus stops beside a scruffy baseball field. Cross the field, then make your way through the derelict banana plantation. Continue straight along the path through the banana plantation for 10-15 minutes. After crossing through numerous barbed-wire fences, exit the banana plantation and follow as it curves left up a small, gently sloping hill through a **cow pasture.** Ten minutes after passing the banana plantation, look for a large wooden building on the hill to your right. This is a cooperative, and residents here will be willing to guide you up the volcano for about 80 córdobas. About 10 minutes up the trail you'll pass a small tent-abode, the last building that you'll see on this hike. For the first 30 minutes or so, the trail leads through banana, coffee, and cacao plantations. A lone petroglyph carved into a black rock stands to the left of the trail; here the vegetation begins.

At the volcano's lower altitudes, the vegetation qualifies as tropical dry forest (do not, however, take this to mean that you will stay dry). As you ascend higher, you'll enter tropical rainforest, where the trail is densely foliated. After a few hours the trail turns east (left) and wraps around the volcano, approaching the crater peak (*el cerro*) from the south. The last kilometer is tough going, and requires balance and two hands. The descent is a bit quicker, but will be difficult if the trail is very muddy.

Keep your eyes peeled for the many petroglyphs scattered throughout the forest and watch out for wildlife. The rare turquoise-brown Mot-Mot, Nicaragua's national bird, has a vibrant blue crown and a long rocket-flame tail. Much more common, but still fun to spot, is the Uracca (white-throated magpie-jay), a large, blue, black-crowned bird. You'll also likely hear the odd, groaning roar of the howler monkey and the distinctive bark of white-faced monkeys. The white-faced monkeys are the easier to spot—more common and less camouflaged. You may also have the distinct pleasure of seeing *agouti,* strange rodents that approach the size of small dogs.

Volcán Concepción

The taller of the two volcanoes, standing 1610m high, Concepción is said to have the most perfectly conical shape of all the volcanoes in Central America. It's also the less-frequently climbed of the two on Ometepe. Because it's still active, the terrain near the top consists primarily of loose rocks and sand, which makes climbing quite difficult. Rockslides pose a perpetual hazard. It is sometimes impossible to reach the actual crater, but you can always come close. The ascent begins in Altagracia, and it is highly recommended that you take a guide from there.

This side of the island receives much less rainfall than the Madera side, so there are fewer plants and animals, but this dearth allows for better visual access to the land in and around the volcano, as there is less foliage and less cloud cover to obstruct the many available views. If you come across a particularly cool vista, stop and enjoy it with a cup of water in hand.

NORTH OF MANAGUA

■■■ ESTELÍ

Estelí (pop. 100,000), the capital of the department of the same name, lies 150km north of Managua and roughly the same distance from the Honduran border on the Interamerican highway. A liberal stronghold, Estelí saw extremely heavy fighting during the Revolution; the city's recent history is proud and painful. The town's **Gallery of Heroes and Martyrs** is a solemn and powerful reminder of its recent past. During the 1980s, collective farms in the region swarmed with "work brigades" of international volunteers husbanding livestock, pressing cheese, and planting and harvesting cotton, tobacco, and vegetables. Even after the Sandinistas' fall, foreign volunteers still frequent Estelí, where some of them sharpen their Spanish skills at one of the town's few language schools. In July of 1993, violence broke out between rebellious *contras* frustrated with the government and former Sandinistas.

Problems aside, Estelí is an amicable and thriving agricultural town with a few noteworthy sights. The green, surrounding hills and low, ephemeral clouds that occasionally breeze through the sky bring a gentle cool that makes Estelí a refreshing change from the pounding heat and turmoil of cities like Managua and León.

ORIENTATION

There is only one main street in Estelí, and navigation inevitably entails going up and down it, over and over and over. **Av. Bolívar** runs north-south along the whole length of Estelí's blocks. The bus terminal is at the south end of town, one block west of Bolívar and 13 blocks south of the plaza. Six blocks north of the plaza, the city ends at the river. **Calle Perú** runs east-west one block south of the plaza. The Inter-American Highway runs along the east edge of town, six blocks east of Bolívar.

PRACTICAL INFORMATION

Tourist Office: Inturismo (tel. 32-6-51), six blocks south of the plaza, ½ block east of Bolívar, on the street just north of the hospital. The office distributes a moderately informative pamphlet containing the straight dope on Estelí and other smaller towns in the department. No maps available, but the staff can answer most questions. Open Mon.-Fri. 8am-noon and 2-5pm.

Police: (tel. 32-6-15), southeast of town, near the *carretera.*

Post Office and Telephones: TELCOR (tel. 33-3-00), one block south and one block east of the plaza. **Telephone** service 7am-9:30pm. The **post office** next door has mail and **fax** services (fax 322–40). Open Mon.-Sat. 7am-9pm. **Telephone code:** 071.

Travel Agencies: El Tisey (tel. 32-6-55), located right next to the Hotel Mesón and owned by the same people; one block north of the northeast corner of park. Cashes traveler's checks (when they're not out of money). Open Mon.-Fri. 8am-noon and 2-5pm, Sat. 8am-noon. **Agencia de Viajes Nicaragua** (tel. 320-18) is one block south and ½ block west of the Parque Central. Open Mon.-Fri. 8am-noon and 2-5:30pm, Sat. 8am-1pm.

Currency Exchange: Banco Nicaragüense de Industria y Comercios (tel. 32-2-65), 1 block south and 1 block west of the Parque Central, on the southeast corner of the Esquina de Bancos. Changes cash Mon.-Fri. 8:30am-12:30pm and 1:30-4pm, Sat. 8:30am-noon. **Hotel Mesón,** 1 block north of the northeast corner of the plaza, changes traveler's checks.

Regional Buses: Buses leave from the terminal at the south end of town. To Matagalpa (every 30min., 2 hrs., 6 córdobas); to Managua (every hr., 3:30am-early afternoon, 3 hrs., 10 córdobas); to Ocotal and to Somoto (every 30min.). Buses to the border at Las Manos can be caught at Ocotal, and for the border at Espino from Somoto. To reach León, take a Matagalpa bus and get off at San Isidro (1 hr., 4 córdobas), where they leave for León every 30min. (2.5 hrs., 9.5 córdobas).

City Buses: Run north-south, one street west of Bolívar, from Barrio Rosario to El Instituto Nacional, including a stop at the bus terminal (1 córdoba).

Supermarket: Super Económico (tel. 32-4-05), on Bolívar, 3 blocks south of the Parque Central. Open daily 7:30am-9pm.

Library: Biblioteca Pública Dr. Samuel Meza, 1 block south of the Esquina de Bancos. Open daily 8am-noon and 2-5pm.

AMNLAE: Casa de la Mujer Mercedes Rosales (tel. 32-6-96), on the Pan-American Highway, opposite the Shell station. Counseling and medical attention for women. Open Mon.-Sat. 8am-noon.

Red Cross: (tel. 32-3-30), 2 blocks east and 1 block south of the hospital.

Pharmacy: Farmacia Estelí (tel. 22-5-31), on Bolívar at Calle Perú. Open Mon.-Sat. 8am-1pm and 2-7pm. There is also a natural pharmacy in town, **La Farmacia Popular,** on Bolívar, 5½ blocks south of the plaza, grows its herbs organically on a *finca* outside of town. Open Mon.-Fri. 8am-noon and 2-5:30pm, Sat. 8am-noon.

Hospital: (tel. 32-4-39, 32-4-33), 7 blocks south of the plaza on Bolívar.

NICARAGUA

ACCOMMODATIONS

Estelí sees its fair share of travelers, and a good number of hotels and *hospedajes* have sprung up as a result. The following span the range from *muy barato* all the way up to *extra-moderno.* Take your pick.

Hotel Nicarao (tel. 32-4-90), on Bolívar, 1½ blocks south of the plaza. The large open-air courtyard walled by colorful murals, thick with tropical vegetation, and blessed with ample seating makes this the place to be. Friendly staff serves zippy food at reasonable prices. No laundry facilities, but the staff will clean your dirties for cheap. The door closes early at night; knock to be let back in. Singles 35 córdobas, with bath 45 córdobas; doubles 60 córdobas, with bath 70 córdobas.

Hospedaje San Francisco, on Bolívar, a few blocks north of the bus station, on the east side of the street. Intricate paint job on the walls and the latest in virtual wallpaper actually give the place a homey feel. Tall, skinny rooms are clean, bunk-beds make good use of vertical space. Room 7 is the secret hiding place of the

real Mona Lisa. The locks are solid. Self-service laundry area. Front door locks at 11pm. Singles 20 córdobas, doubles 30 córdobas.

Hospedaje Chepito, on Bolívar, just south of Hospedaje San Francisco and a few blocks north of the bus station. Clean, plain quarters surround a very small cement courtyard that doubles as clothesline space. Self-service laundry area. Just about the *cheap-ito*-est place in town. Singles 20 córdobas, doubles 30 córdobas.

Hotel Mesón (tel. 32-6-55), 1 block north of the northeast corner of the plaza. Aims at an aristocratic air, and comes pretty close. Simple, clean rooms ringed around a jungly garden. Ceiling fans are cool; hot water is hot. Adjoining restaurant roasts up delicious eats, and the hotel's travel agency cashes traveler's checks in spades. Rooms for 1-4 people, 70, 85, 100, and 130 córdobas respectively.

Hotel Moderno, 2½ blocks south of eastern edge of the cathedral. "Modern" is right; huge ceiling fans and fancy baths with hot water. Dignified lounge and restaurant as well. Modern prices to match: singles US$15; doubles US$20.

FOOD

A good number of *comedores* and *cafetines* can be found up and down Bolívar. All of them are fairly comparable, but a few places in town deserve special note.

China Garden, on the west side of the Parque Central. Not a garden, and the only Chinese fare consists of a pretty *faux* platter of chop suey. Its corrugated half-dome architecture suggests that the place was built of used drainage pipe. But the food draws throngs, rightfully. Shrimp 35 córdobas, *hamburguesas* 6 córdobas. Try the delicious coconut *flan* for dessert. Open Fri.-Wed. 11am-9:30pm.

El Recanto (tel. 32-5-78), two blocks south and ½ block west of the park. A friendly place with a few truly bizarre pieces of original, amateur art hung on its walls. Large selection of *refrescos naturales.* Try the awesome *enchiladas a la mexicana* (baked, not fried—a real treat!). Open daily 7:30am-6pm.

El Porchecito (tel. 32-7-84), on southern Bolívar, near Hospedajes San Francisco and Chepito, opposite the *parque enfantil.* Cheery restaurant sees the main drag from its little porch. Its name proves that you can append *-cito* to any word and make it sound cute. Tacos 15 córdobas. Fantastic juices 3 córdobas. Sandwiches and vegetarian dishes. Open daily 11am-10pm.

Hotel Mesón Restaurant (tel. 32-6-55), in the Hotel Mesón 1 block north of northeast corner of plaza. Swank. Polish your Tevas: this place is decked out with tablecloths and real cloth napkins. Pepper-and peanut-steaks, barbecue pork, seafood. *Comida corriente* 15 córdobas. Entrees 30-60 córdobas. Open daily 7am-10pm.

Cafetín Las Brasas, ½ block west of the plaza's northwest corner. Look for the green dragon outside. Curious Latino-Asian decor, replete with funky umbrella lampshades and an intimate bamboo back room. Fried rice 29 córdobas, sweet-and-sour pork 28 córdobas, various *brochetas* (skewered meat) 11-29 córdobas.

SIGHTS AND ENTERTAINMENT

The **Galería de Héroes y Mártires,** half a block south of the cathedral, effectively commemorates Estelí's revolutionary *callidos* (fallen ones). The abstract mural along the outside wall is superb (open daily and run by the Families of the Fallen Ones, who request donations). For another graphic reminder of the violence that transpired here, visit the large **bomb fragment** and accompanying monument, three blocks west of the red Firestone outlet on Bolívar.

The **Casa de la Cultura Leonel Rugama Rugama, Poeto y Revolucionario** (tel. 33-0-21) is just down the block from the Gallery of Heroes and Martyrs. The local youths have covered the walls with cartoons and propaganda that proffer opinions on health care, unemployment, and the environment. Classes in guitar, painting, drama, and dance are held here, and on Saturday nights the Casa hosts performances and exhibitions by local artists. The reception area sells some interesting books, pamphlets, and artwork (open Mon.-Fri. 8am-noon and 2-5pm, Sat. 8am-noon). On the south side of the plaza, in front of the Centro Recreativo, are the **boulders** from the archaeological dig at Las Pintadas, which bear prehistoric carvings of animals, birds, and human figures.

The **Centro Recreativo** (tel. 32-0-10), on the plaza's south side, is open every night of the week save Mondays, and there's always something going on. Saturday and Sunday evenings, studs don their studs for disco time (10 córdobas entrance fee, 25 córdobas if the music is live). Other nights people come here to play and watch games of basketball and volleyball. All are welcome, and there's usually a small crowd. Shoot some cut-throat at the **pool hall** on the west side of Bolívar, 2½ blocks south of the plaza.

■ NEAR ESTELÍ

Seven kilometers south of Estelí, **El Salto de Estanzuola** crashes and thunders like a 45m high waterfall is supposed to. Getting there requires a trip into the meandering hills and gorgeous countryside south of Estelí. *Camionetas* leave from the bus station at a leisurely and sporadic rate; just ask for the *camioneta para ir al Salto* (4 córdobas). After winding through the hills on a dirt road, get dropped off at the beginning of an even smaller dirt road with a gate across it. Follow this road; in less than 10 minutes it turns into a trail opening up into a small clearing beneath a huge cliff, over the top of which crashes the massive waterfall. The pool below, often muddied by the churning force of the current, is still good to swim in.

The direct hike between the Salto and Estelí is also perfectly negotiable, and beautiful to boot. Walk south along the main highway, about 10 minutes' distance past the police check-point; to your right, a dirt road branches off from the highway. Follow this road for about 5km, then ask for directions to the *Salto.* Take little of value, since locals sometimes follow *gringos* to the falls to relieve them of their cash.

The town of **Condega,** 30 minutes to the northeast of Estelí, makes for a nice day-trip as well. All buses destined for Somoto and Ocotal stop in Condega, so it's very easy to reach. The town's main attraction is the **Museo Arqueologico Julio C. Salgado,** the only official museum in the entire department of Estelí, and a very impressive one at that. A wide sample of intricately decorated pre-Columbian ceramics comprises the majority of the collection. The prize possessions of the museum, however, are its few **Incensarios Indígenas**—large, menacing, and funky-looking ceramic boxes, each of which is covered entirely by spikes on its exterior. The insides have been fashioned by the local tribes to serve as incense burners. In the same building as the museum lives the **Casa de la Cultura** of Condega, where local children undertake apprenticeships in leatherworking and luthiery. Their products (leather vests, bags, and belts, as well as fine guitars for 650-700 córdobas) are for sale on the premises. Visitors are welcome to wander around and peek in on the different workshops. Another reason to come to Condega is provided by its **public swimming pool,** on the Inter-American highway just to the west of the town. It looks quite luxurious, except for the fact that there is no water; the pool was closed in the summer of '95, but ask around to see if it's opened again.

For a tasty meal or a nice place to relax with a *refresco* in Condega, head to the **Bar and Restaurant Linda Vista,** a few yards north of the point to the south of the town where Condega's main street becomes the highway. The restaurant, a five-minute walk from the plaza, sits on a hill overlooking the surrounding countryside. A hot box *comida corriente*-to-chow costs 15 córdobas.

A 40-minute walk north of Condega lies the town of **Ducuale Grande,** famous for firing off fine ceramics into the rest of the world. Buses passing through Condega on the way to Somoto and/or Ocotal from Estelí can drop you off at a point along the highway where the road to Ducuale branches off to the west; walk the road for 15 minutes. Ducuale pottery is exported to the States and to Europe, most of it in the form of pitchers, covered bowls, and a few figurines; the selection varies seasonally. When you reach the town, ask for the *Taller Comunal.* All pottery here is quite cheap, the most expensive item (a small ceramic drum) sells for about 80 córdobas. Small bowls, plates, and earrings cost 10-20 córdobas. Samples are also on display in Estelí at the Tourist Office, or at the place across the street from the Hotel Mesón where they are sold. The museum in Condega also sells Ducuale pottery.

■■■ MATAGALPA

Lofty mountains and low clouds enshroud Matagalpa, a small, drowsy city on the eastern slopes of Nicaragua's central mountain range. This is coffee country, settled in the 19th century by small waves of Western European immigrants. The Europeans in Matagalpa these days are mostly volunteer workers or tourists, but the caffeinated concoction's industry still booms. Matagalpa's more recent history is heavily tainted by its affiliations with the Sandinista cause; Matagalpa was an FSLN stronghold during the revolution against the Somoza regime. In fact, Matagalpa's favorite son is the Revolutionary leader Carlos Fonseca, whose house is now a museum. *"Carlos vive,"* assures a sign in the park, *"porque su obra es inmortal"* ("Carlos lives because his work is immortal.")

The cool, moist climate and mountainous terrain of Matagalpa make this region one of Nicaragua's most visually arresting. The nearby **Selva Negra** (Black Forest) is actually very green. The encroaching vegetation and array of exotic animals makes hiking a thrill. On the other hand, if your boots aren't made for walkin', you don't even have to stand up to enjoy the spectacular views from the bus that winds to and from Matagalpa proper. Though Matagalpa may be a town of few archetypal tourist sights, it's easy to be wooed by the city's moderate climate and utterly insouciant atmosphere.

ORIENTATION AND PRACTICAL INFORMATION

Matagalpa sits on the east bank of the **Río Grande Matagalpa,** which is as narrow here as its namesake, but which widens to become one of Nicaragua's largest rivers before spilling out into the Caribbean. **Parque Rubén Darío** lies at the south end of town, five blocks east and two blocks north of the bus terminal. **Avenida José Benito Escobar,** often called "Calle de Commercios," abuts the west side of the Parque Rubén Darío and then runs north for another seven blocks to meet the *parque catedral.* **Avenida Central,** also known as Avenida de los Bancos, spins off the southeast corner of the *parque catedral* and runs roughly parallel with Benito Escobar, passing Parque Rubén Darío two blocks to the east.

Tourist Office: Inturismo, in the Centro Commercial Catalina, on Av. de los Bancos, three blocks south of the cathedral. The office has nothing to offer in the way of guides, maps, or brochures, but the staff speaks English and is happy to answer questions and offer advice. The women who work here lived in the States during the war. Open Mon.-Fri. 8am-12pm and 2-5pm.

Post Office and Telephones: the post office and **fax** services are located a few steps east of Calle de Commercios, 1 block south of the *parque cathedral* (fax 22-0-04). Open Mon.-Fri. 8am-noon and 1:30-5:30pm, Sat. 8am-noon. The **telephone office** stands 1 block east of the cathedral (tel. 23-6-56). Open daily 7am-10pm. **Telephone Code:** 061.

Currency Exchange: Banco Nacional de Desarollo (tel. 22-00-01), on Av. de los Bancos, 4 blocks south of the cathedral, under a beautiful sprawling tree. Changes cash and traveler's checks. Open Mon.-Fri. 8:30am-4pm, Sat. 8:30-11:30am. **Banpro** (tel. 23-5-42), on the southeast corner of the parque cathedral, changes cash and traveler's checks. Open Mon.-Fri. 8:30am-4pm, Sat. 8:30am-11:45am.

Western Union: At Banco Nicaragüense (tel. 33-6-93), just north of Banco Nacional de Desarollo. Open Mon.-Fri. 8:30am-4pm, Sat. 8:30am-noon.

Buses: 2 blocks south and 5 blocks west of the Parque Rubén Darío. To **Managua** (every 1½ hrs., first bus leaves at 6am, 3 hrs., 10 córdobas); to **Estelí** (every 30min., 2 hrs., 6 córdobas), to **Jinotega** (every 40min., 1½ hrs., last bus leaves at 6:20pm, 45min., 6 córdobas); to **Managua** (every 30min., 2½ hrs., 10 córdobas), and to **San Isidro** (every hr., 1 hr., 4 córdobas). Buses stop at **San Isidro** (1 hr., 4 córdobas) and buses leave San Isidro for **León** (every 30min., 2½ hrs., 9.5 córdobas). Buses bound for **Río Blanco** leave the Cotran de Guanaca, in the north of town, every 1½ hr. These buses stop 1½ hrs. into their trip at **Muy Muy** (12 córdobas, for the Matagalpa-Muy Muy leg). Buses to **Boaco** can be caught at Muy Muy (every 2 hrs., 1½ more hrs., 12 more córdobas). See Boaco, under Buses, page 305, for alternate routes and more details.

Library: 1 block west of Calle de Commercio, 4½ blocks south of the cathedral.

Pharmacy: Farmacia Blandon (tel. 23-0-80), on Calle de Commercio, 1½ blocks north of the Parque Rubén Darío. Dr. Armando J. Parajóa speaks English and consults 24-hrs., in case of emergency. Knock on the door if you come after hours.

Supermarket: La Fe (tel. 22-4-68), 1½ blocks north and 1 block west of the Parque Rubén Darío. Well-stocked, but you'll have to check your bags and guns at the door (seriously). Open Mon.-Sat. 8am-7:30pm, Sun. 8am-noon.

Police: (tel. 23-5-11, 23-8-70, 22-3-82), on the south side of the *parque catedral* in the triple-blue shaded building.

Red Cross: (tel. 22-0-59), 2 blocks west of the police station, just over the river.

Hospital: (tel. 22-0-81, 22-0-82) right next to Red Cross, with a big garden in front.

Travel Agency: (tel. 22-5-20) **Viajos America,** between Calle de Commercios and Avenida de los Bancos, 2 blocks south of the *parque cathedral.* Open Mon.-Fri. 8am-noon and 2-5pm.

ACCOMMODATIONS

Matagalpa offers up a nice spread of hotels and *hospedajes.* Be forewarned, however, that despite the fact that Matagalpa is situated on the banks of a river in one of the wettest regions of the country, water runs only sporadically; most establishments keep tanks and a bucket on hand for toilet-flushing and showers.

Hospedaje Plaza (tel. 22-3-80), on the south side of the Parque Rubén Darío. Clean rooms *sans* baths, over a green house. A few extra córdobas will get you a room in the courtyard. Bring your own toilet paper, unless your arse has an affinity for newsprint. Check out the planter in Room 20: plastic flowers, real dirt. 20 córdobas per person, 25 córdobas for rooms at the back with bathrooms.

Hotel Matagalpa (tel. 23-8-34), 1½ blocks east of the northeast corner of Parque Darío. Immaculate establishment with friendly management and a playful pooch. Lounge for TV watching, and adjoining restaurant serves decent food. Upstairs rooms nestled amid the fruit trees are breezy and have a pretty view. Singles 35 córdobas, 45 córdobas with bath; doubles 60 córdobas, 80 with bath.

Hotel Ideal (tel. 22-4-83, 23-3-13), 2 blocks north and 1 block west of the cathedral. The ritziest digs in Matagalpa, but only ideal if you're in the mood to blow a bundle. Big, comfortable rooms with ceiling fans and *agua purificada*. Nice restaurant too. Downstairs rooms for 1 or 2 people 100 córdobas, with bath 120 córdobas. Luxurious doubles and triples upstairs 140 córdobas.

Hotel Bermudez (tel. 23-4-39), 2 blocks east of Parque Rubén Darío. Small rooms, queen-sized porch. Courtyard with self-service laundry facilities. Breakfast is served, Jeeves. 20 córdobas a person, with or without private bath.

FOOD

Restaurant Jin Shan (tel. 23-0-24), between Avenida de los Bancos and Calle de Commercio, 1 block south of Parque Cathedral. Classic Chinese restaurant get-up, complete with lacquered fans and paper lamps. The food is distinctive though, in that it resembles Chinese food. Fried rice is nice. Chow mein, fit to reign. Sweet and sour pork, you eat with a fork. All dishes come in regular or *pequeño* servings. Regular dishes 35-45, *pequeño* 20-30. Open daily 11am-10pm.

Comedor San Martín, ½ block east of Calle de Commercio and 1 block north of Parque Rubén Darío. A favorite with the locals; step in and pretend you're a regular. Great, simple fare in a down-home atmosphere, but order your coffee *sin azucar,* or it will arrive as syrup. A good breakfast. *Comida corriente* 13 córdobas. Open Mon.-Sat. 6:30am-9:30pm, Sun. 7am-noon.

Cafetín El Colonial, on the north side of Parque Rubén Darío. By day, your basic *soda;* by night, a sizzlin' grill with a you-point-they-cook-it buffet. *Carne asada, ensalada, gallo pinto, plátanos,* all for 10 córdobas. Open daily 9am-midnight.

La Cusona (tel. 33-9-01), on Calle de Commercios, 2½ blocks south of the *parque cathedral.* This place cooks one mean chicken. And they cook it nice. Outdoor dining area in the back. Fried chicken and french fries 14 córdobas (+50 to your cholesterol count). Open 10am-11pm daily.

Restaurant Ideal (tel. 22-4-83, 23-3-13), in Hotel Ideal. Pleasant outdoor dining, at breezy tables under a roof. Sneak here to nurse a cold one and watch satellite TV from the States. Chicken in wine sauce 35 córdobas. *Bistec* 35 córdobas. Lobster 70 córdobas. Soups. Open Mon.-Sat. 6am-midnight, Sun. 6am-8pm.

SIGHTS AND ENTERTAINMENT

The **Museo y Casa Carlos Fonseca** is a must-see. Grainy black-and-white photographs trace the life of a revolutionary. The few artifacts on display (Fonseca's typewriter, his eyeglasses, his gun) were carefully selected to convey his socialist fervor. The museum also sells a slim biography of Fonseca for 10 córdobas (open Mon.-Fri. 8am-1pm). The local FSLN headquarters also has a small memorial to fallen revolutionaries. The office is on Av. Central, a few blocks south of the *parque catedral* (open Mon.-Sat. 8am-5pm). The **Casa de Cultura** is located next to the library. Fine examples of Nicaragua's **ceramica negra** can also be found in Matagalpa. This shiny, black kiln-work comes in all shapes and sizes, at prices that are startlingly cheap for handmade goods. The **Tienda de Ceramica Negra** (tel. 22-4-64), 2 blocks north of Parque Rubén Darío, between Avenida de los Bancos and Calle Commercios, is open Mon.-Sat. 8am-5:30pm, and sells some semi-cool gifts and souvenirs.

Matagalpa, like most festive-hearted Nicaraguan towns, gets to hopping on the weekends (Fri., Sat., and Sun. nights). One disco, **AutiFaz,** is located in the restaurant Rogal Bar, one block east of the bus station, in the south of town. Another, the

Familiar, is located near the *salida a Managua.* Both charge a cover of US$1-2. There are also a few cinemas, but they seem to be on their last legs.

Matagalpa also celebrates several saints' days with fiestas that include bullfights and plenty of rum-drinking. The two biggest celebrations fall on **Sept. 24th,** in honor of La Virgen de Mercedes (Matagalpa's patron saint), and on **July 26th,** in honor of the apostle Santiago.

■ NEAR MATAGALPA

The **Selva Negra** (Black Forest) is a coffee plantation, forest reserve, and hotel/restaurant all in one. In the 1890s, a group of about 30 German immigrants came to the mountains of northern Nicaragua to get themselves some elbow room and to try their hand at the coffee-growing business. The main coffee plantation at today's Selva Negra was founded at its current site by one of these original German immigrants. The settlers named their new homes after their old ones in Germany, and thus the coffee plantation at Selva Negra was named Hammonla. In high European pomp and splendor, the settlers used to get together for tea every Sunday. To this day, the Selva Negra hosts reunions of the German descendants in the area. In 1976, the **Hotel and Restaurant Selva Negra** was established by Eddie and Mausy Kühl, direct descendants for the original German immigrants. Mausy and Eddie can entertain you for hours with fascinating stories of the adventures and misadventures of their grandparents and great-grandparents, the fearless German settlers.

Meanwhile, the coffee production continues. Using ecologically-sound techniques, the farm produces high-quality coffee and then exports it to Europe and the U.S. The refuse from the coffee-refining process gets composted, and the resulting methane gas is used in the restaurant's kitchen. All of the electricity used by the farm is produced by a small turbine that spins at the base of the reservoir.

The hotel itself is composed of numerous *cabañas* that rent out for US$75 to US$150 a night and can sleep up to 6 people. (Scattered across the pastoral grounds, some *cabañas* even have kitchens). The more economical option is the **youth hostel,** run by the same people, which costs only US$10 a night. However, due to low demand, the hostel has no beds, and so if you request the advertised hostel rate, you may wind up with a *cabaña* to yourself. Many of these have porches that afford a fantastic shoreline view of a secluded pond (the best one is apartment "Dio").

The restaurant and administration are housed in a large Teutonic-looking building, perched on the shore of the aforementioned beautiful pond. The restaurant's menu is quite expensive, but cup of excellent Selva Negra coffee on the deck that overlooks the pond is cheap enough, and worth every centavo. A delicious buffet is served to Nicaragua's elite every Sunday, from 12:30-4:30pm (70 córdobas).

As if all this weren't enough to merit a visit, note that a large percentage of the Selva Negra estate is virgin forest that the owners have cordoned off and allowed to stay pure. The vegetation is laced with a number of trails for excellent hiking. As you walk through the cool moist jungle, the only audible sounds are the blunt calls of randy frogs, chirpy birds, and the occasional roar of a resident howler monkey. Early morning birdwatchers can hope to catch more than worms; the forest is inhabited by hummingbirds, vibrant toucans, woodpeckers, and even the mythical quetzal. The trails pass beneath the 150m canopy of dense foliage, around fallen and moss-covered trees, and over small jungle brooks. Take a hike, man; relax and forget about whatever frustrations life in urban Nicaragua has brought you.

To get there, take any bus bound for the Jinotega and ask to be let off at Selva Negra (about 35min. away). The road to Selva Negra is marked at its entrance by a rusted and mangled *tanquita* (little army tank). The first kilometer down this road is lined with evergreen trees, which then give way to the swaying, dark green leaves of coffee plants. When you reach the entrance to Selva Negra proper, you must pay a 20 córdoba entrance fee, which can be used towards payment for lodging and food. The restaurant, hotel, and reception area are up the hill and surrounded by cages of monkeys, parrots, turkeys, and rabbits.

EAST OF MANAGUA

■■■ BOACO

Like a rough gem set in Nicaragua's central mountains, Boaco is best known for its expansive cattle ranches, or better yet, its cattle ranchers. Hold on to your hats in Boaco, pardner, as cowboys ride the streets dressed to the nines in their riding boots, spurs, and *sombreros,* cattle switches at their sides. The most popular watering holes in town always have a few horses parked out front. Residents of Boaco overflow with cowboy pride and a patriotic spirit for their little mountain town, which just celebrated its centennial birthday in March 1995, and in which poverty only very rarely rears its ugly head. Many believe the town is blessed by its patron saint, the Apostle Santiago, whose saint's day is celebrated every year with a week-long fiesta culminating on July 25th. Legend has it that when the Sandinistas were camped outside Boaco, preparing to enter the city, Santiago himself conjured up the sounds of an enemy army approaching and scared the Sandinistas away. The FSLN forces never entered Boaco again.

Orientation and Practical Information The city's hilly contour contributes to its charm. The oldest and most prestigious area of Boaco is its **ciudad alta** (high city), built atop a hill, with beautiful vistas of the green mountains and **ciudad baja** below. The **bus station** lies at the south end of town, the ciudad alta lies at the north, and the *ciudad baja* fills the valley between the two. The street just west of the bus station and marketplace is Boaco's main street, heading downhill to the north, wending its way through the *ciudad bajo,* and then ascending a steep slope to emerge at the **Parque Central** in the *ciudad alto.*

Boaco once had a tourist office, but no longer. Cash, but not traveler's checks, can be exchanged at either of the two **banks,** located one block east and one block north of the Parque Central. **Police** (tel. 05-45-74, 05-45-64). **Banco Nacional de Desarollo** (tel. 05-42-10) is open Mon.-Fri. 8am-4:30pm, Sat. 8-11:30am. **Banco Nicaragüense** (tel. 05-42-63) is open Mon.-Fri. 8:30am-4pm, Sat. 8:30am-noon. **TELCOR** (phone, mail, fax), is located on the south side of the Parque Central. **Telephone service** (tel. 05-44-90) open 7am-9pm daily. **Telephone code:** 054. **Mail** and **fax** services (fax. 05-42-66) are open Mon.-Fri. 8am-noon and 1:30-5:30pm, Sat. 8am-noon. **Buses** leave from Boaco's bus station, in the south of town, for Managua (every 45min., 2 hrs., 9 córdobas) and Río Blanco. Exit Managua buses at San Benito in order to catch buses en route from Managua to Estelí, to San Isidro, and to Matagalpa. Alternatively, you can travel between Boaco and Matagalpa using back roads, which are unpaved and bumpy, but also unpopulated and beautiful. To do this, take a bus bound for Río Blanco, from Boaco, and disembark at Muy Muy (1½ hrs., 12 córdobas). Then catch a bus traveling from Río Blanco, through Muy Muy, and bound for Matagalpa (every 1½ hrs., 1½ hrs., 12 córdobas). The same schedules, prices, and times apply for the trip from Matagalpa to Boaco. To catch a bus for either Juigalpa or Rama, take any bus bound for Managua and get off after about 20 minutes at the *enpalme de Boaco* (intersection of Boaco; 5 córdoba). The **Farmacia Romero** (tel. 05-42-59), located just west of the Parque Central's northwest corner, meets your pharmaceutical needs. **Supermercado Hit** is located on the Parque Central's south side, open Mon.-Sat. 8am-8pm, Sun. 8am-1pm. **Hospital Niebrowsky** (tel. 05-43-01, 05-43-02) can be reached by following the sign from the bus station. **Red Cross:** (tel. 05-42-00).

Accommodations and Food **Hotel Sobalvarro** (tel. 05-45-15), on the Parque Central's south side, is the only hotel in the *ciudad alto.* Neat and comfy rooms share baths. The view from the patio out back will knock your socks off, but the cawing parrots in the courtyard may ruin the transcendent moment. The Sobalvarro is recognized as the best bet in town (singles 50 córdobas, doubles 80 córdobas). At **Hotel Boaco** the rooms aren't too shabby, either, and they do offer mediocre private baths—but no toilet seats, and you're certainly missing the Sobaluarro's view. The Boaco is conveniently located near the bus station, but far from the *ciudad alto (*singles 30 córdobas, doubles 50 córdobas). **Pension Montiel** is a final budget option, a half block east of the main street, just before the ascent into the high city. Rooms are cramped, the facilities rustic. Choose your toilet seat from one of the two on the wall. 20 córdobas per person.

La Cueva, just east of the south side of the Parque Central, is a nice place to scarf down some tasty *ranchero* vittles. Two levels of tables overlook the *ciudad baja.* Chicken 25 córdobas, shrimp 45 córdobas, *boacano* beef dishes 40-45 córdobas. Check the jake cowhide menus you can pet. Open Tues.-Wed. 11am-10pm, Thurs.-Sun. 11am-2am with a 5-córdoba cover charge after 7pm, when the place becomes a disco. **El Alpino,** (tel. 05-42-70) a half block north of the banks, has a wide selection of tasty hamburgers (9-16 córdobas) and even a chicken burger (10 córdobas). 18-córdoba breakfast includes coffee. Boaco *is* the cattle-country capital, and El Alpino cooks up its beef in every which way (38-48 córdobas). Air-conditioned side room operative on hot days (open daily 8am-9pm). **Restaurante Internacional,** a half block west of the Parque Central, offers a cheap *comida corriente.* Look for the obnoxious Old Milwaukee neon sign. The **kiosko** in the Parque Central is a nice place to buy a snack or a drink.

Sights and Entertainment More than anything, just soak up the view. One great place to do this is the **cemetery** in the south of town, a half block north of the bus station. (Open Mon.-Fri. 8am-noon and 1-5pm, Sat. 8am-noon and 2-5pm, Sun. 9am-noon and 2-4pm.) The cemetery covers a small hill with its motley and charming array of crosses, angels, and saints. A couple of other modest sights are the product of the centenary celebration Boaco recently enjoyed. The **Paseo de los Ballantes** is an ornate staircase which leads up from the *ciudad bajo* to the *ciudad alto,* one block east of the cathedral. On the southeast corner of the cathedral beckons a very small park dedicated to the present mayor of Boaco, Dr. Armando Incer, whose house on the north side of the park doubles as a **museum,** showcasing pre-Columbian totem-figures and an immense display of old riflery. For a centerpiece: Boaco's Mannekin-Pis, a small statue of a mischievous boy peeing. Word has it that the hottest place in town on weekend nights is **La Cueva** (see Food, above). Or, shoot a rack at **Billares Julia,** located at the base of the big hill on the main street.

■■■ JUIGALPA

Just about halfway between Managua and Rama, Juigalpa is much more than just a pit stop. The small town is the capital of the department of Chontales, and the region, along with Boaco to the northwest, produces most of Nicaragua's beef. Chonteleños are known throughout Nicaragua for their cattle-driving ways.

The town itself is far from stagnant. The **Parque Central** has recently undergone a substantial facelift: artistic mosaics which surround the park depict the landscape and daily activities of life in Chontales. Additions to the park include a rather unrealistic but thoughtful monument to the shoeshine boys that wander practically every Nicaraguan town. Meanwhile, potential for exploratory options abounds, including the **archaeological museum,** which is Nicaragua's best, and its **zoo,** which houses lions, baboons, and a lonely chimpanzee, all alongside native Nicaraguan species.

Juigalpa is only about 115m above sea level, but its location atop a small mesa provides impressive views of the surrounding range of peaks. The Parque Palo-Solo, at the east of town, presents a 180° panorama of the Cordillera de Amerrisque, the mountains directly east of Juigalpa. A stop-over in Juigalpa en route to the Atlantic Coast provides a good way to break up the long trip east.

Orientation and Practical Information Buses drop passengers off in the bus station/market area, just two blocks east of the Parque Central. Everything of interest, except the zoo, lies within a few blocks of the park. The local tourist office, the **Ministerio de Turismo** (tel. 23-07), one block south and a half block west of the banks on the park's southwest corner, distributes a slightly informative pamphlet about all of Chontales (open Mon-Fri. 8am-noon and 1:30-5pm). The travel agency **Viajes Universo,** one block south and 2½ blocks east of the Parque Central, is actually a woman's private home, but she may be able to help you out. The **police** station (tel. 29-45, 27-27) is 200m north of the *Escuela Normal.* **Banco Nacional de Desarollo** (tel. 28-26) changes cash and traveler's checks for no fee (open Mon.-Fri. 8:30am-12:30pm and 1:30-4pm, Sat. 8:30-11:30am). **Banco Nicaragüense** (tel. 24-85) changes only cash, but contains the **Western Union** office (open the same hours Banco Nacional, above). The **TELCOR** office (tel. 22-28) is located 3 blocks north of the park's northwest corner. **Telephone code:** 081.

Buses all leave from the market: to Managua (every 30min., 2½ hrs., 12 córdobas); to Estelí and to Matagalpa (get off the Managua bus at San Benito); to Boaco (get off Managua bus at the intersection); to Rama (starting at 4am, every 30min., 4½ hrs., 18 córdobas). The tour from Rama to Bluefields leaves on Tues., Thurs., Sat., Sun. at 10:30am; you should take the 5:30am bus from Juigalpa to Rama to catch the tour, or even an earlier one, just to be sure. The pharmacy **Botica Juigalpa** (tel. 25-32) two blocks east of the Parque Central, is well-stocked (open daily 8am-12:30pm and 2-7pm). The **Supermercado Chontal** (tel. 29-85) lies one block south and a half block east of the Parque Central's southwest corner. Both the **hospital** (tel.23-30) and **Red Cross** (tel. 22-33) are located at the *salida a Rama.*

Accommodations and Food The **Hotel Imperial** is one block west of the bus station and one block east of the Parque Central. Big, bare rooms all have fans. Its biggest advantage over the local competition: running water (singles 30 córdobas, doubles 50 córdobas). **Hospedaje Angelita** (tel. 24-08), located just west of the Parque Central's northwest corner, is a friendly, clean, family-run place. Lounge with the family in rocking chairs. Rooms in the already-breezy upstairs have fans and mosquito nets (20 córdobas per person). **Hospedaje Resbalon,** a half block south of the Parque Central's southeast corner, boasts clean enough rooms, but those with fans cost 40 córdobas for each transient tenant (singles without fan 20 córdobas).

Palo-Solo (tel. 2735), located five blocks east of the Parque Central, is the best place in town for food, drinks, or even just to sit. Panoramic views of the mountains tantalize the eye, while food delights the mouth (open daily noon-10pm, later on weekends). The **Pollo Amerrisque** serves up tasty food, but without the view—it's correspondingly cheaper, and located two blocks east and a half block south of the Parque Central's northeast corner. The restaurant is popular despite its tacky, American cheese-colored interior. Two pieces of finger-lickin' fried chicken, salad, rice, and bread 16 córdobas. The succulent *plancha* (steak; 30 córdobas) is brought to your table still sizzling (open daily 10am-10pm). **Soda Arco-Iris,** in the Parque Central (northwest corner), has an open-air patio right in the park for people-watching and comfortable dining. Typical soda fare: hamburgers and sandwiches 8 córdobas, tacos 16 córdobas, *comida corriente* 20 córdobas, and big glasses of *refresco natural* 3 córdobas. Breakfast is served, too (open daily 7am-9pm).

Sights For a town of its size, Juigalpa is near to bursting with things to see. First and foremost is the **Museo Arqueológico Gregorio Aquilar Barea,** which is well worth the 2-córdoba entrance fee. The museum boasts Nicaragua's largest collection of pre-Columbian statues; a lion's share of the figurines are of *chontaleño* origin, and the majority are thought to date from 800-1200 AD. Inside, a large collection of ceramics spans the entire gamut of recorded pre-Columbian pottery production, from 500 BC to 1500 AD. The collection is still being inventoried, so no explanatory labels exist as of yet, but the archaeologists that are usually on hand are often more than happy to share their extensive knowledge of the collection; just ask. The museum is 3 blocks east of the park's north end (open Mon.-Fri. 8am-noon and 2-4:30pm, Sat.-Sun. 8am-3pm).

In addition, Juigalpa is the home of one of Nicaragua's finest zoos, the **Jardín Zoológico,** seven blocks south, one block east, and then another half block south of the southwest corner of the Parque Central. The cages are haphazardly scattered about the zoo's muddy grounds, and many of the cages are unlabeled, so you have to guess what animal you're looking at. Four fearsome lions are kept here in a few skimpy, minimum-security cages (don't get too close!). Native jaguars and pumas are also kept here, along with local and imported primates and several species of small, furry animals gathered in a cage and grooving with a stick. Lonely as some of the animals look, the visit can depress as well as impress (open daily 8am-6pm).

Palo-Solo means "lone oak," and look, there it is. Head five blocks east of the Park's north side. The place has a romantic air about it, as it was christened long ago by lovers who came here to enjoy the view (hmm). Their tradition lives on.

■■■ RAMA

Rama, mama, is a relaxed little hamlet at the end of the only (allegedly) paved road connecting the rest of Nicaragua with the Atlantic Coast. The Río Síquia and the Río Rama run together at Rama, and because the rivers conspire to form the wide, east-flowing Río Escondido, the town enjoys unparalleled access to Nicaragua's most important Caribbean port, Bluefields. Spending a night in Rama is a fine way to break up the long trek from Managua to the Atlantic Coast, as the town is more conveniently located than Juigalpa, 4½ hours by bus to the west.

Practical Information Rama's **police** station (tel. 26) is one block north and four blocks east of the market and bus stop. **TELCOR** is one long block east of the bus stop. At present, no international phone service is available, but the situation is slated to be fixed by December 1995. Local **telephone** service is available daily from 7am-9pm, and **postal** service from Mon.-Fri. 8am-noon and 2-5pm, Sat. 8am-noon. The **Banco Nacional de Desarollo,** the only bank in town, is to be found one long block east of the church, and is worth your time only as a landmark, since it doesn't change either dollars or traveler's checks. **Christina's Store,** a half block north of the bank on the west side of the street (has no sign), provides helpful currency exchange info. **Buses** enter Rama from the north and empty their loads beside the market. Two blocks south of the market lies the **park,** where you'll find the tall modern **church,** which is very appealing in a concrete sort of way. **Buses** depart for Managua (every 30min., from 5-7am, with a slightly later one leaving at 9am). They also make their way to Juigalpa (every 30min., from 4am-2pm, 4½ hrs., 18 córdobas). The sluggish "Expresso" **boats** leave Rama for Bluefields from the dock one block west of the market (Tues., Thurs., Sat., and Sun. at 11am; 5 hrs.; 35 córdobas). On Mon., Wed., and Fri., a *panga* (small motorboat) leaves Rama at 8am. It is much faster than the express, taking only two hours, but it is also much more costly (100 córdobas per passenger, offering discounts for especially large groups). The town **pharmacy** has no sign either, but it is identifiably located in the garish brown and yellow house two houses north of Christina's place. Open daily 8am-1pm and 2-7pm, but outside these hours just knock on the door and someone can help you. The **Red Cross** (tel. 19) is one block north and two blocks east of the market. The **hospital** is 6km north of town on the highway.

Accommodations and Food Rama's all fall in the bleak genre, i.e. plain small rooms with a bed and shared shower or bath. **Hotel Johanna,** a half block south of the bank, is a bigger place with cleaner-looking beds. Rooms have fans and windows, and the showers and toilets here are the best of Rama's lot. Pin-up posters may offend. Rooms on the south are farthest from the noisy bar below. Restaurant/bar downstairs (*comida corriente* 18 córdobas, hamburgers 7 córdobas, and tacos 7 córdobas). **Hospedaje Central,** just west of the TELCOR office, is a family-run place with very clean rooms, each of them equipped with a fan. Clean pit toilets and bucket-style showers (25 córdobas per person). **Hospedaje Jiménez** is a spankin' new place, not yet running as of the summer of '95. Simple upstairs rooms, but beds, fans, and mosquito nets should all be next-to-new. It's the creamy green house just south of the market on the same street as the dock (20 córdobas per person).

Food in Rama is nothing special, only what you need to tide you over. **Hotel Johanna** has a restaurant (see above), as do other hotels. **Los Vindes,** a half block south of the market, serves enormous steaks for 35 córdobas, as well as has cable-TV, to get you caught up on The Jetsons. Shrimp 40 córdobas, chicken in wine sauce 35 córdobas (open daily 7am-10pm). There's also a *soda* in the park, where you can chill with a *refresco* or a snack. In the face of the dearth of recreational activities available, a good number of bars have sprung up to help pass the citizenry's time. There is also a popular pool hall just west of the bank.

THE ATLANTIC COAST

Nicaragua's Atlantic coast is unlike the rest of the country. The region is part of a larger geographical area known as **La Mosquitia** (see Honduras, page 254) a vast and sparsely populated expanse of rainforest, plains, and coastland extending the length of Nicaragua's east coast up around the northern coastline of Honduras, and home to some 70,000 Miskitos, a majority of the area's remaining *indígenas.* Other aboriginals, in lesser numbers, include the Sumos, the Ramas, and the Garifunas. In the south, most of the inhabitants speak English and are of West Indian descent.

Today, Nicaragua's Atlantic Coast remains distinct from the rest of the country. Politically, it is semi-autonomous. Culturally, it is almost a separate entity. Most Atlantic-coasters identify more strongly with their West Indian heritage or their indigenous community than they do with Managua. Sandinista policies meant to unify and develop the country included the institution of mandatory military service and the declaration of Spanish as Nicaragua's national language. To many residents of the Eastern Coast, these changes smacked of forced cultural assimilation. Some even preferred the reign of Somoza, who at least left them alone. For this reason, the Atlantic Coast is sometimes called the failure of the 1980s.

The Atlantic Coast has a great deal to offer the traveler: a colorful Caribbean atmosphere; beautiful, remote communities; and a number of wonderfully lazy beaches, and the opportunity to simply and truly explore. However, travel here is tricky, as there are almost no roads. Unless you fly (small planes serve Bluefields, Puerto Cabezas, Islas de Maíz, and a few towns in Honduras), getting from one place to another involves a great deal of waiting around for a boat that may or may not show up, and when it does, may or may not agree to take you where you want to go. You'll have to remain very flexible; still, therein lies much of the adventure.

GETTING AROUND THE ATLANTIC COAST

Between Managua and Bluefields you can either: 1) do the "Expresso" (ha ha) boat-bus combination; 2) take a Vargas/Peña bus (see above); or 3) arrive in Rama by bus independently, at any time and then take a *panga,* either the scheduled ones on Mon., Wed., and Fri. mornings, or by hiring your own.

The Expresso chugs between Rama and Bluefields on Tues., Thurs., Sat., and Sun. The crowded boat leaves Bluefields for Rama at 5am, and leaves Rama for Bluefields again at 11am (5 hours, 35 córdobas either way). A bus leaves Mercado Ivan Montenegro in Managua at about 2am to connect with the Expresso that trundles between Rama and Bluefields, on the days that it runs. This bus returns to Managua after the Expresso arrives in Rama, thereby providing a way for people to travel directly between Managua and Bluefields.

The company **Transportes Vargas/Peña** travels from Managua to Bluefields daily, leaving Mercado Ivan Montenegro at 11pm, leaving Rama by *panga* at 6am, and arriving in Bluefields at 10am. The return trip leaves Bluefields at 6am by *panga,* leaves Rama at 9am, and arrives in Managua at 3:30pm. Either trip costs 110 córdobas. For further information, contact the Vargas/Peña office in Bluefields (tel. 739), located on the main pier.

A third option is to take a *panga,* the big outboard launches. *Pangas* leave on Mon., Wed., and Fri. at irregularly scheduled times, but aside from these you have to hire your own. At two hours, the *panga* trip is much faster than the Expresso, makes for a very nice way to see the river (unless it rains), and also allows you to arrive in Bluefields ahead of the crowds. Every now and then, a *panga* and its passengers are robbed at gunpoint, but rarely does this banditry escalate to violence.

The Río Escondido voyage is thoroughly enjoyable. The thick forest along the banks is interrupted every now and then by small wooden huts. You'll also see a few small banana plantations; they were hurt badly by Hurricane Joan in 1988, but most of them have recovered. Farther downriver, Joan's damage is still evident; the forest here is low, with only a few spindly trunks squatting where there once stood a high canopy. Many ships line the river's banks, quietly fading into rusty anonymity. Some were victims of the hurricane, others of bankruptcy. Note, especially, the twisted iron and irony of the once-gleaming, now rotting Hope, named for Somoza's wife.

To get to the Caribbean coast by plane, check **La Costeña,** the company that carries the most flights out of Bluefields. The same planes fly from Bluefields to the Corn Islands and then on to Managua (Mon.-Sat. at 7:30am, 10:30am, and 3:30pm, Sun. at 8:30am and 3pm). One way prices: 265 córdobas for Bluefields-Corn Islands, 335 córdobas for Bluefields-Managua, 420 córdobas for Corn Islands-Managua. Round-trip fares make each leg a little cheaper, but not much. The carrier **Nica** flies the same route at the same prices on Mon., Wed., Fri., and Sun. at 8:30am and 2:30pm, and on Tues., Thurs., and Sat. at 12:30pm.

■■■ BLUEFIELDS

Bluefields is a vibrant zephyr of a Caribbean town. Named after Blauvelt, the Dutch pirate who founded the town in the 1600s, it is easy to imagine how Bluefields Bay would have made the perfect Pirate Cove of lore. The Bluefields of today is a *paella* of a city; the population is primarily creole and *mestizo,* but a good number of other indigenous groups, such as Miskito, Rama, and Garifuna, have been thrown in to spice up the mix. Its different folk speak English (with a sonorous West Indian lilt), Spanish, Miskito, and several other indigenous languages. The town convulses with music, much of it streaming out from the dance halls and clubs, to flood the streets with Reggae, Merengue, Salsa, or Bon Jovi.

Bluefields is Nicaragua's most important Caribbean port. All of the neighboring communities inland, along the coast, and from islands offshore all come to Bluefields for supplies and to sell and export their bananas, oranges, shrimp, lobster, and other edibles. The town plays a central role in the life of Nicaragua's remote and exotic Atlantic Coast region, and makes the best place from which to explore it.

ORIENTATION AND PRACTICAL INFORMATION

In Bluefields, the Caribbean Sea is always to the east. **Calle Central** runs north-south along the water. At the north end of this avenue, just north of the tall, red-roofed Moravian church, wades the town's main pier, where boats arrive and depart for everywhere but El Bluff. Three main streets run east-west; from north to south, they are **Avenida Reyes, Calle Cabezas,** and **Avenida Aberdeen.** Avenida Aberdeen in the south is the only one that extends east past Calle Central, where you can find a market and another pier where boats leave for El Bluff. A big, scruffy park lies on Aberdeen, one block south and three blocks west of the pier.

Tourist office: Bluefield's **Ministerio de Turismo** office is located in the airport. They can be of help in planning trips from Bluefields to the numerous senses-shattering places nearby. Open Mon.-Fri. 8am-noon and 2-5pm. Another place to get information on Bluefields and places nearby is from the **URACCAN** house, 3 blocks north of the Moravian church. Ask for Miss Carol.

Police: (tel. 447, 448), a few blocks north of the Moravian church on Calle Central.

Post office and telephones: The **TELCOR** office is three blocks west of the red-roofed Moravian church, on the park. Telephones open daily 8am-9pm. *Correo* open Mon.-Fri. 8am-noon and 1-5pm, Sat. 8am-1pm. **Telephone code:** 082.

Currency Exchange: Banco Nacional de Desrollo (tel. 261, 792), across from the Moravian church, will exchange U.S. dollars and will also exchange traveler's checks, but at a service charge of US$3 for up to 3 checks, and US$1 per check after that. Open Mon.-Fri. 8:30am-12:30pm and 1:30-4pm, Sat. 8:30am-noon.

Boats: Departures to the **Corn Islands** leave Bluefield's main pier 3 times a week and cost 40 córdobas. The **Lynx** leaves Wed. at 8:30am, and other boats leave Fri. and Sun. mornings at 10am. For more information, contact the Lynx office (tel. 558) on the south side of the Bluefields pier.

Pharmacy: Godoy Farmacia (tel. 471), on Calle Cabezas, ½ block west of Calle Central, is open Mon.-Sat. 8am-9pm, Sun. 9am-3pm.

Red Cross: (tel. 582), south of town down Calle Patterson (1 block west of Calle Central). The hospital is 2km southwest of town.

ACCOMMODATIONS

If you're on the Expresso from Rama, waste no time in finding a place to stay in Bluefields. There's often a rush on the town's hotels, which are most often already full of people who've come to town on business trips.

Hotel Hollywood (tel. 282), overlooking the water 2½ blocks south of the Moravian church, has 12 green and white, clean and breezy, wide and wooden rooms and a veranda, and a restaurant downstairs, armed with cool and clammy air-conditioning. Singles 40 córdobas; doubles 55 córdobas, with 2 beds 65 córdobas.

Mini Hotel-Cafetín Central (tel. 362), ½ block west of Calle Central on Calle Cabezas, can't seem to settle on a career. Clean, simple rooms with fans, and the facilities are pretty spotless—Cafetín in front is a great place to eat, with prices as low as you please. Grow up, Mini. Rooms 30 córdobas per person.

Hotel Manda Mans (tel. 429), a sparkling place next door to Claudia's, has a spiffy lounge and restaurant area downstairs. Its 3 single rooms with shared bath go for 40 córdobas, 50 córdobas per double. The rest of the rooms are mondo to the max: 170 córdobas yields private bath and cable TV.

Hotel Cueto, the cream-and-brown-colored building across from the Hotel Hollywood, will do in a pinch; the place may look scary on the outside, but the rooms are reasonably clean and each has a private bath. 50 córdobas per room.

FOOD AND ENTERTAINMENT

Mini Hotel Cafetín Central (see Accommodations, above) is one of the most popular places to eat in the whole town, and with good reason. It's the little extra touches that make dining here a treat: the designer beer mugs, the cable TV, and that high-tech lightboard that advertises the extensive menu. In addition to fish, chicken, and beef dishes, all 25 córdobas a piece (cheap for Bluefields), they serve snack foods and milkshakes. Open daily 8am-10pm.

Cafetín "Pesca-Frita," at the intersection of Calle Central and Avenida Aberdeen, is a gusty place, with an army of fans fighting to keep you cool. The green streamers and the waitresses' outfits give the *cafetín* a strangely Irish feel. *Comida corriente* 20 córdobas. Open daily 10am-10pm.

China Nica, ½ block west of Calle Central on Avenida Reyes, serves ample portions of peculiar yet tasty Nica-Chinese stir-fry concoctions. You might try their Sopa de Wang Tang, or Wang Tang's "pajaritos" fritos. Let's say that again, together: *Wang Tang's pajaritos fritos.* Everything is cheap, 20 córdobas a plate.

Restaurant Hollywood presents a somewhat more upscale option, just below the eponymous Hotel. The restaurant is air-conditioned and serves pretty good food at moderate prices (e.g. sea bass at 25 córdobas).

Bluefields hops. The music emanating from the clubs may loosen your teeth, but it'll keep you dancing. On the other hand, women may feel unsafe walking home alone at night. There is a raging, unmarked **reggae club** in a tumble-down building on the north side of the park 5-córdoba cover, if any. **Lego-Lego** is a bigger club, a winding 10-minute walk north of town; follow the music (cover 5 córdobas). **Bacchus,** just south of the park, is more upscale and plays salsa, merengue, and disco, all of it yours for the night, once you've paid the hefty cover charge. **El Flotante** is thought to be the fanciest of the clubs. It overlooks the water south of town, on the road to the airport. If you'd rather see someone else move, catch a good game of basketball in the gymnasium of the **Colegio Morava,** across from the Moravian church.

GETTING TO OTHER ATLANTIC COAST DESTINATIONS

As inconvenient as it might be to reach, Bluefields is practically the only point of access to Nicaragua's entire Atlantic Coast region, due to the area's extreme isolation and its thoroughly underdeveloped status. Travel along the coast may well provide you with some of the most difficult, adventurous, and rewarding travel experiences to be had. Remote lagoons, rivers, beaches, and islands speckled with indigenous communities are all out there, just waiting to be stumbled across.

Getting there can pose a problem, however. Some of the more prominent destinations offer regularly scheduled transportation to and from Bluefields and if none of these options fit your plans, you can always try to catch a ride on a passing boat.

All the area's boat traffic goes through **El Bluff,** Bluefields's off-shore port. From Bluefields, a *panga* to El Bluff costs 10 córdobas. These boats leave every 30min. or so from the pier in the south of town, by the market at the east end of Avenida Aberdeen. The trip takes about 10 minutes. In El Bluff, you can try to catch a ride to just about any point on the Atlantic Coast with a passing *pescadero* or *langostero.* It shouldn't be too hard to catch a lift to prominent destinations such as the Corn Islands or Puerto Cabezas; in general, the more obscure your intended destination, the poorer your chances of actually finding a ride, and the greater your chances of spending a day on the dock, watching metal rust, only to return to Bluefields in the evening. There's just no good way to know.

■ NEAR BLUEFIELDS

NICARAGUA

Far north of Bluefields, near the Honduran border, **Puerto Cabezas** is the Atlantic Coast's other main port. Its population is larger than Bluefields', making it the largest city for many, many miles along the northern Atlantic Coast. From here it's possible to explore this region's northern reaches. Fishing and cargo boats on the Atlantic Coast often stop in Puerto Cabezas, so it should not be hard to find a Cabezas-bound ride from Bluefields, El Bluff, or the Corn Islands. **La Costeña** also flies to Puerto Cabezas from Bluefields (Mon., Wed., and Fri., at 12:30pm; 380 córdobas, one way).

Laguna de Perlas, or "Pearl Lagoon" is a small community on the southern edge of a very large lagoon, 80km north of Bluefields. There are no oysters, but plenty of pure, pearly beauty to be seen. A trip here is also one of the best ways to get a look at authentic Atlantic Coast culture. Boats leave this small community for even smaller communities around the lagoon, and then to the 18 pearl cayes off the coast. **Transportes Vargas/Peñas** in Bluefields (see Bluefields, Practical Information, page 310) is blessed by boats that leave for Laguna de Perlas daily at 9am. It should also be possible to find a ride on another boat, or to hire your own *panga,* if you have enough fellow passengers. The trip takes one hour.

Rama Caye is a small island community about 20 minutes away from Bluefields, by boat. Its denizens are the descendents of the Rama Indians. It is said that there are only twelve people still alive who speak the Rama language. These days, the community is struggling to keep stray elements of its culture alive. You may want to check it out, before it's too late—you might even meet their legendary **Chief Rufino.**

■■■ THE CORN ISLANDS

The two Corn Islands, or *Islas del Maíz,* 65km off the Atlantic Coast, offer the chance to curl your toes in the sands of a relatively unsullied Caribbean isle; as of yet, the islands sport no resorts, fancy restaurants, dive shops, or other tourist facilities of any kind. A couple of "hotels" have been built to accommodate the islands' occasional visitors, but places to stay on the island are essentially extra rooms slapped along side a family's home. If you're looking for sparsely populated beaches of white sand and crystal blue water, or just want to see what life on a virtually untouristed Caribbean island is like, here you go.

Orientation and Practical Information The larger of the two islands is approximately 21km-square, with a predominantly Creole and Miskito population of 6000. The airstrip cuts across the island from north to south; most places can be accessed by walking its length. **Briggs Bay,** just to the west of the airstrip, is where most action takes place. The La Costeña and Nica offices are in the first building left of the airstrip.The **police** office is a block or so past Lydia's Restaurant. The **TELCOR** office and **bank** are located in the same building near the south end of the airstrip. TELCOR is open for **phone** calls 8am-8pm daily. The bank is open Mon.-Fri. 8-noon and 2-4pm. **Boats** return to Bluefields on Sun., Tues., and Thurs. See Bluefields "Practical Information" (page 310) or "Getting There" (page 312) sections for more information on travel to and from the Corn Islands. For travel from the Corn Islands to other destinations, try asking around the main pier, just south of the airstrip. There is a **pharmacy** on the road from the airport in to Briggs Bay. The **hospital** is still being built.

Accommodations and Food The cheapest and best place to stay is **Casa Blanca,** 100m or so down the left branch of the road leading from the airport. Simple, clean rooms in a family home have mosquito nets and fans, as well as a fresh porch (singles 50 córdobas, doubles 75). The next cheapest is **Morgan's,** on the road from the airport, with rooms and facilities all brand-new and clean. Singles 80 córdobas; doubles 120 córdobas. The main drawback here is the disco next door, which blares music until all hours; try to get a room on the opposite side of the building. **Hotel Panorama,** on the north side of the island, just west of the north end of the airstrip, up the road past Lydia's restaurant, offers big rooms with private bath and fan. There's not really a panorama, though (singles 120 córdobas, doubles 180 córdobas). Ask around, because other options are in the process of being built.

Of the restaurants clustered in Briggs Bay, notice **La Rotunda** on the left, a couple of buildings down the road, which serves up a cheap and simple breakfast for 15 córdobas. Other restaurants of note include **Lydia's Fisher's Caves Restaurant,** 100m or so up the right branch of the road from the airport. Fish 30 córdobas, shrimp 40 córdobas, lobster 50 córdobas. Eat while pondering the ships floating quietly before the white sand beaches and palm trees in the distance. **Dos Millas** is the other (relatively!) fancy restaurant in town, on the island's north side, just about 1km east of the north end of the airstrip. Same food, the same prices, a different view. Watch the waves gently breaking on the off-shore coral reef, all posed before the silhouette of the little Corn Island in the distance.

Sights City planners left no room for doubt when they named **Picnic Beach,** east of the south end of the airstrip, which also happens to be the nicest beach on the island. If you walk all its length, the shore becomes rocky. A one-hour hike along this deserted shore brings you to another, unnamed beach that's completely deserted and practically as nice as Picnic Beach, and with bigger waves. Another possibility is a hike to the top of **Mt. Pleasant,** the highest point on the island.

And if life on the larger Corn Island is too modern, you can always visit **the small island,** just a few miles away. Private boats leave for the small island frequently, from the pier near Lydia's restaurant. The small island has no electricity, though there are a few generators. No cars either, only paths for horses and people. There's really not much of anything, except pristine vegetation and coral, which unlike the main island's was not badly damaged by Hurricane Joan in 1988.

COSTA RICA

This is nature at its sexiest. Well-endowed with dripping cloud forests, red-hot volcanoes, and lush, luscious flora, Costa Rica seduces even the most fanatic of urbanites. A brief jaunt through any of the country's spectacular national parks releases childhood fantasies of storybook jungles and wild beasts with freakish forms and names. Adventure never tapers even outside the tapir-filled parks; driving from place to place may mean risking bodily integrity on potholed roads under merciless torrential rainfalls. Costa Rica has become by far the most touristed country in Central America partially because of its political and economic stability, but more importantly, because it is the perfectly exotic tropical paradise wrapped into one tight little area. Manageable and magnificent, Costa Rica also leads Central America in its vehement policy toward enlightened preservation. Visitors to the country face comparatively few challenges, and so easily lose themselves between the Babel of parrots and coatimundi and the voluptuous scent of countless drooping orchids.

Far too many ecotourists to Costa Rica dart right for jungle-enshrouded isolation, ignoring what is perhaps the nation's finest asset: the people. Ticos, as they call themselves and everything else Costa Rican, are justifiably proud of their country's strong democracy and excellent social security system. More than 28 percent of the national budget is invested in education, and the literacy rate soars over 90 percent. Most striking about the Costa Rican people, however, is their unconditional friendliness; to *hacer amistades* (make friends) is almost always a *tico*'s top priority.

Costa Rica boasts 24 national parks and biological reserves, which together comprise a total of 15 percent of the country's territory; most reserves are open to the public and are directly accessible from San José, the national capital. In other words, don't plan on staying for a day or two. The boom in ecotourism over the last few decades has encouraged investors (and the government) to make the often-trod tourist path as wide and smooth as possible, but still be prepared for the occasional logistical hardship. While undeniably more westernized than those of other countries in the region, Costa Rica's economy is still developing, and the same general precautions should be taken here as anywhere else in Central America. (See Essentials chapter for further information.)

COSTA RICA

ESSENTIALS

■■■ WHEN TO GO

CLIMATE

There are three types of climate in Costa Rica: wet and tropical on the Caribbean side (with high temperatures of 24-32°C/75-90°F and torrential rains); tropical with a dry season on the Península Nicoya and the Central Valley; and temperate in the higher regions of the country (with temperatures of 18-22°C/ 65-72°F). The winter rainy season (*invierno*) lasts from May to December, and chances are that if you are in Costa Rica, you *will* need rain gear.

FESTIVALS AND HOLIDAYS

Don't plan on taking care of bureaucratic or bank matters during national holidays, which include **January 1** (New Year's Day), **March 19** (Saint Joseph's Day), **March or April** (Holy Week), **April 11** (Juan Santamaría's Day), **May 1** (Labor Day), **June 29** (Saint Peter's Day), **July 25** (Guanacaste Annexation Day), **August 2** (Virgen de los Angeles), **August 15** (Mother's Day), **September 15** (Independence Day), **October**

12 (Día de la Raza), **December 8** (Immaculate Conception), **December 25** (Christmas). **Semana Santa** (Holy Week) is one big party along beaches: in 1996, **April 1-7.**

■■■ FEED YOUR HEAD

For publications and travel organizations of general interest, see Central America: Reading Up, page 1.

GOVERNMENT AGENCIES

Embassies of Costa Rica: U.S., 2114 S. St. NW, Washington, DC 20008 (tel. (202) 234-2945). **Canada,** 135 York St. No. 208, Ottawa, Ontario K1N 5T4 (tel. (613) 562-2852; fax 562-2582). **U.K.,** 14 Lancaster Gate, London W2 3LH (tel. (44) 171-706-8844; fax 706-8655).

Consulate of Costa Rica: 2112 S. St. NW, Washington, D.C. 20008 (tel. (202) 328-6628), or contact the embassy for the address of the consulate nearest you.

Costa Rica Expeditions, apdo. 6941-1000, Av. 3, Calle Central, San José (tel. (506) 257-0766, 222-0332; fax 257-1665), 1 block east of the San José post office (see San José: Practical Information, page 328), or write them in the U.S. at Dept. 235, Box 25216, Miami, FL 33102-5216. They organize jungle tours to Tortuguero National Park (US$199 for 1 day and night; US$265 for 3 days, 2 nights), as well as 1-day tropical forest adventures (US$79), white-water rafting (US$69-89), and volcano tours (US$28). English spoken. Open daily 8am-7pm.

Costa Rica Sun Tours, P.O. Box 1195-1250, Escazú (tel. (506) 255-3418, 255-3518; fax 255-4410). Full-service ecotourism recommended by the Audubon Society of Costa Rica. Custom itineraries for nature, birding, and educational and adventure tours, including cycling and rafting trips. They also own two lodges in Arenal National Park. 2-4-day packages US$165-495, including transportation, lodgings, meals, bilingual guides, and park fees.

Green Tortoise Adventure Travel, 494 Broadway, San Francisco, CA 94133 (tel. (800) 227-4766, (415) 956-7500; fax 956-4900). Their cheap-and-funky 14-day tour visits beaches, rainforests, volcanoes, and hotsprings. US$349 doesn't include airfare, but another US$101 gets you in the food fund.

Interviajes, S.A. P.O. Box 296, Heredia 3000 (tel. (506) 260-7676; fax 260-7740). Offers "super saver" day-long natural history tours to Poás Volcano National Park, Tortuguero, Monteverde, and other sights. US$50 includes fees, guides, and car, and lunch. Bring your lunch and save US$5.

Journey Latin America, 14-16 Devonshire Road, Chiswick, London W4 2HD, U.K. (tel. (44-181) 747-8315; fax 742-1312). 16-day tours include white-water rafting, Poás Volcano, Monteverde, Tortuguero, and Limón. Small-group rates start at £1500 (includes meals, accommodations, and airfare from London). 2-person custom trips (with shared twin beds) average £1,560 per person.

Jungle Trails per los Caminos de la Selva, Apdo. 2413, San José 1000 (tel. (506) 255-3486; fax 255-2782). Specializes in nature tours and conservation programs. Bird-watching and botany trips, as well as custom itineraries. Invites visitors to meet with subsistence farmers to better understand the motivations and circumstances behind deforestation. Tours 1-15 days. Portion of fee is donated to reforestation groups.

Preferred Adventures Ltd., 1 W. Water St., #300, St. Paul, MN 55107 (tel. (800) 840-8687, (612) 222-8131; fax 222-4221). Soft adventure and nature tours in Costa Rica. Birding, rainforest study, river rafting, mountain biking, and fishing. Average fee of US$150 per person per day includes accommodations, most meals, transport, guides, and park fees. Student prices US$75-100 per person per day. Low airfares with ground transportation from most major U.S. airports.

The Mountaineers Books, 1011 SW Klickitat Way, Seattle, WA 98134 (tel. (800) 553-4453; fax (206) 223-6306). Publishes *Costa Rica's National Parks and Preserves: A Visitor's Guide* (US$16.95), with park descriptions, trails, and maps.

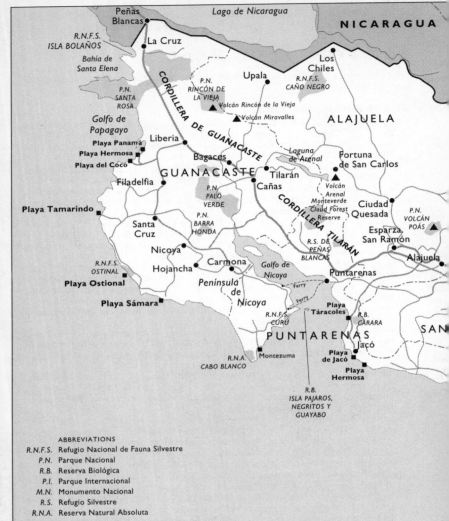

Lago de Nicaragua
NICARAGUA
Peñas Blancas
R.N.F.S. ISLA BOLAÑOS
La Cruz
Bahía de Santa Elena
P.N. SANTA ROSA
CORDILLERA DE GUANACASTE
P.N. RINCÓN DE LA VIEJA
Volcán Rincón de la Vieja
Volcán Miravalles
Upala
Los Chiles
R.N.F.S. CAÑO NEGRO
ALAJUELA
Golfo de Papagayo
Playa Panamá
Playa Hermosa
Playa del Coco
Liberia
Bagaces
Laguna de Arenal
Fortuna de San Carlos
Tilarán
GUANACASTE
Cañas
Volcán Arenal
Filadelfia
P.N. PALO VERDE
Monteverde Cloud Forest Reserve
CORDILLERA TILARÁN
Ciudad Quesada
P.N. VOLCÁN POÁS
Playa Tamarindo
P.N. BARRA HONDA
Santa Cruz
Esparza
San Ramón
Nicoya
R.S. DE PEÑAS BLANCAS
Alajuela
R.N.F.S. OSTINAL
Hojancha
Carmona
Golfo de Nicoya
Puntarenas
Playa Ostional
Península de Nicoya
Ferry
Ferry
Playa Sámara
R.N.F.S. CURU
Playa Táracoles
R.B. CARARA
PUNTARENAS
SAN
Jacó
Playa de Jacó
Montezuma
R.N.A. CABO BLANCO
Playa Hermosa
R.B. ISLA PAJAROS, NEGRITOS Y GUAYABO
OCÉANO PACÍF

ABBREVIATIONS

R.N.F.S.	Refugio Nacional de Fauna Silvestre
P.N.	Parque Nacional
R.B.	Reserva Biológica
P.I.	Parque Internacional
M.N.	Monumento Nacional
R.S.	Refugio Silvestre
R.N.A.	Reserva Natural Absoluta

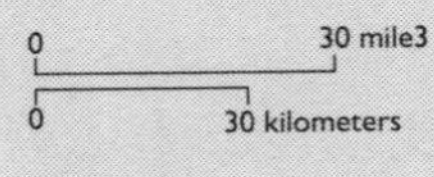

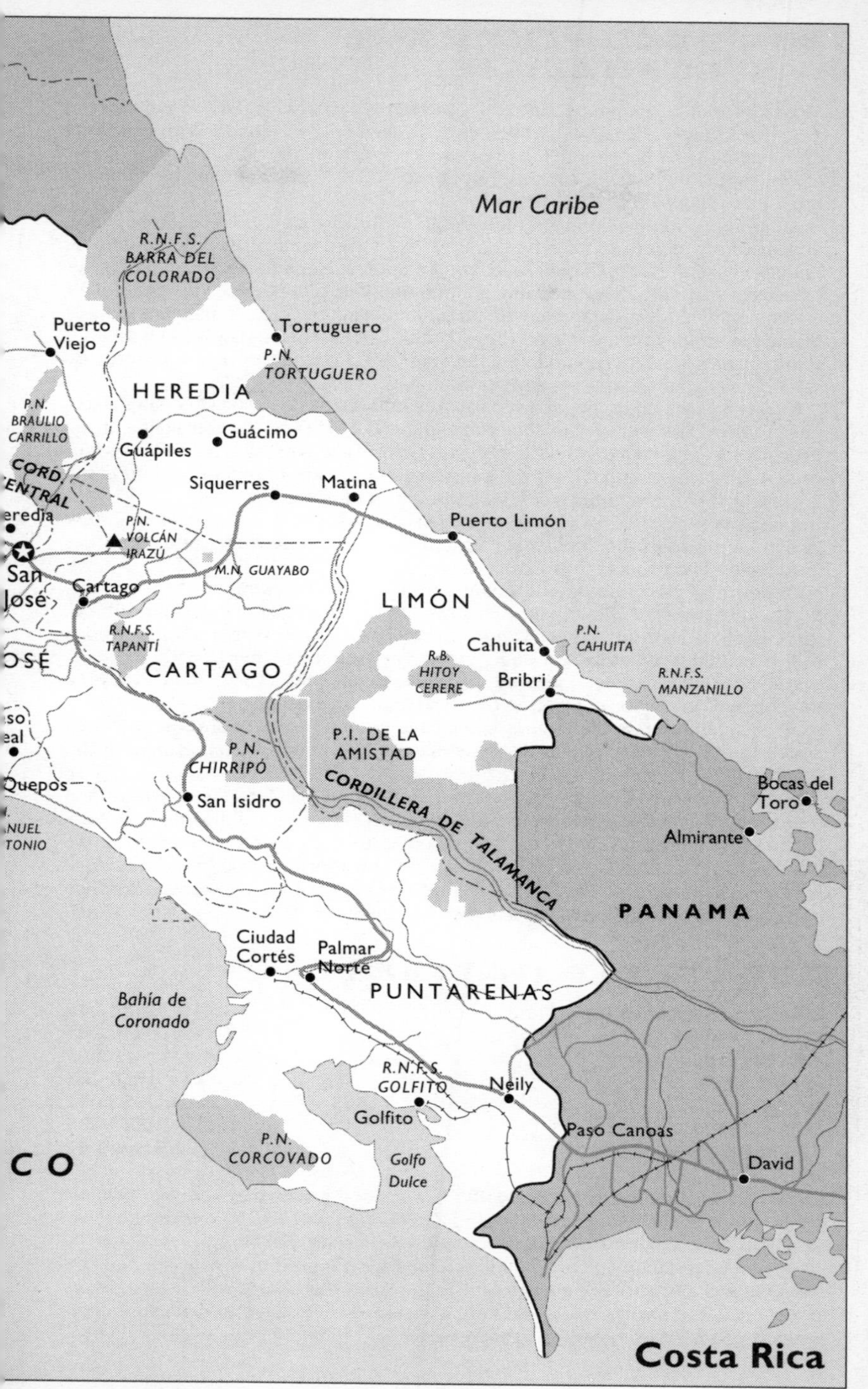

Mar Caribe
R.N.F.S.
BARRA DEL
COLORADO
Puerto
Viejo
Tortuguero
P.N.
TORTUGUERO
HEREDIA
P.N.
BRAULIO
CARRILLO
Guápiles
Guácimo
CORD.
ENTRAL
Siquerres
Matina
eredia
P.N.
VOLCÁN
IRAZÚ
Puerto Limón
San
José
Cartago
M.N. GUAYABO
LIMÓN
R.N.F.S.
TAPANTÍ
Cahuita
P.N.
CAHUITA
OSÉ
CARTAGO
R.B.
HITOY
CERERE
Bribri
R.N.F.S.
MANZANILLO
P.I. DE LA
AMISTAD
P.N.
CHIRRIPÓ
Quepos
San Isidro
CORDILLERA DE TALAMANCA
Bocas del
Toro
Almirante
PANAMA
Ciudad
Cortés
Palmar
Norte
PUNTARENAS
Bahía de
Coronado
R.N.F.S.
GOLFITO
Neily
Golfito
Paso Canoas
P.N.
CORCOVADO
Golfo
Dulce
David
CO
Costa Rica

■■■ DOCUMENTS AND FORMALITIES

Most visitors, not including U.S. and Canadian citizens, must have a **passport** to enter the country. Canadian and U.S. citizens need only an original birth certificate and a valid photo ID, although a passport is strongly recommended and probably easier, especially if you're carrying traveler's checks. Visitors arriving by plane are required to show a round-trip ticket.

All visitors entering Costa Rica must obtain a **tourist card** (*tarjeta de turismo*), available from airlines serving the country. You'll need your plane ticket and US$2. For citizens of the **U.S., Canada,** and the **U.K.,** tourist cards are valid for 90 days; for citizens of **Australia, New Zealand,** and the **Republic of Ireland,** cards are valid for 30 days only. Cards may be renewed for up to 90 days by going to the Dirección de Migración in San José (see Once There: Useful Organizations, page 322) with your return plane ticket, two photographs, an original birth certificate, and a passport. Be sure to carry your tourist card and passport at all times.

If you stay even a day beyond your allotment, leaving Costa Rica becomes a serious problem. You will have to obtain an exit visa (US$15) and pay a small fine. If you overstay for longer than 30 days, you will be charged an additional US$20-30 for each subsequent month. To get the exit visa you will have to provide a court certificate, which will cost you about US$0.50 and a lot of hassle.

A **visa** is not required for citizens of the U.S., Canada, the U.K., Australia, and New Zealand. Citizens of the Republic of Ireland and most western European countries must have a visa to enter Costa Rica.

Duties on goods entering and leaving Costa Rica can be extremely high. In addition to your personal effects, you are allowed to bring in 500g of tobacco products, three liters of alcohol, a mere 2kg of candy, and US$100 worth of other goods duty-free. You must wait six months before bringing in another US$100 worth of goods duty-free. There is an **airport departure tax** of US$7 (¢517). When crossing the border, you may be charged an **overland departure tax** of ¢75.

All **animals** entering the country must have permits. Owners of (domesticated) dogs and cats may obtain permits by contacting the Zoonosis Department of the Ministry of Health (tel. 223-0333, ext. 331; fax 255-2594).

The **Dirección de Transporte Automotor,** Av. 18, Calle 7, San José, will grant a temporary **driving permit** to a visitor over age 21 with a valid foreign driver's license. If you plan to drive in Costa Rica longer than 90 days, you must qualify to stay beyond the expiration of your tourist card and apply for a Costa Rican driver's license. Applicants must have a valid foreign license and a valid passport; the office of motor vehicles will determine whether you are medically fit.

■■■ MONEY MATTERS

US$1 = 185 colones (¢)	**¢1 = US$0.005**
CDN$1 = ¢136	**¢1 = CDN$0.007**
UK£1 = ¢288	**¢1 = UK£0.003**
IR£1 = ¢293	**¢1 = IR£0.003**
AUS$1 = ¢137	**¢1 = AUS$0.007**
NZ$1 = ¢121	**¢1 = NZ$0.008**
SARand 1 = ¢51	**¢ 1 = SARand 0.02**

The Costa Rican currency is the **colón** (¢). Printed prices may use two periods where other countries use a comma and a period (e.g., ¢1.234.56 means one thousand two hundred thirty-four colones and fifty-six hundredths).

All hotels, restaurants, bars, and nightclubs are required by law to add an 11% **sales tax** and a 10% **service charge** to all bills; usually this charge will be included in prices cited, but not always. In addition, it is customary to leave an extra tip for particularly good service (perhaps an additional 5%).

The **Thomas Cook MasterCard** office is at Agencia de Viajes Intertur, S.A., Edificio Irma, Primer Piso, Avenida Central, Calles 31/33, San José (tel. 253-7503).

■■■ HEALTH AND SAFETY

Life expectancy in Costa Rica is an impressive 74-plus years, a testimony to the quality of the universal medical care provided to all citizens, which includes disability, maternity, and old-age pension. Drinking water in major hotels and restaurants in the capital is purified. Outside San José, water should be boiled before drinking, or go with the bottled stuff.

Like most Central American countries, Costa Rica is home to lots of nasty diseases. The 1991 earthquake damaged the infrastructure of the Puerto Limón area, and the slow pace of reconstruction has resulted in poor sanitary conditions (look for the occasional vulture feeding on garbage) and a heightened risk of associated diseases. **Malaria** is a hazard in all areas of Costa Rica except Cartago and San José provinces. **Cholera** has also cropped up recently in Costa Rica, although the risk is smaller than in Guatemala and Mexico. **Typhoid fever** is common in Central America; a vaccine is recommended for those who plan to stay in rural areas. **Hepatitis A** is also a risk in rural provinces. Thousands of cases of **dengue fever** have been reported in the last few years, so take extra precautions against mosquitoes.

As the number of visitors to Costa Rica increases, so does the frequency of crimes against tourists. Incidents ranging from pick-pocketing to armed muggings have been on the rise in San José, at beaches, in banks, at the airport, and at national parks and other attractions. Don't flash wads of cash or bars of gold, and watch out for counterfeit money; contrary to what you may be told, Costa Rican currency does *not* look like Monopoly money.

As in many parts of Latin America, women are subject to more attention than might be expected or desired—it's hard for women to walk outdoors without hearing catcalls. Unfortunately, inappropriate overtures cannot always be deflected with a firm *lo siento, no me interesa* ("I'm sorry but I'm not interested"). It might be best to ignore whistles, since even acknowledging the catcaller can encourage his behavior. On the other hand, *mi amor* is frequently used by both women and men as a term of endearment, much like the British "love." A shopkeeper will sometimes innocently address a woman customer as *mi reina* ("my queen"); in this context, the term means simply, "May I help you."

■■■ ALTERNATIVES TO TOURISM

Costa Rica's tropical reserves and environmental hyper-consciousness make it an ideal destination for ecologically-minded travelers. Contact conservation groups for information on **volunteer** and **internship** positions relating to the environment. For teaching opportunities, contact **WorldTeach,** Harvard Institute for International Development, 1 Eliot St., Cambridge, MA 02138 (tel. (800) 4-TEACH-0). In Costa Rica: Centro Colón Apdo. 498, 1007 San José, Costa Rica (tel. 222-2073). Volunteers teach English and environmental education throughout Costa Rica. A one-year commitment is required. Participation fees are about US$3750 and include language and teacher training, travel costs, housing, and health insurance. Volunteers receive a stipend as well. Those interested in **Spanish language study** will find plenty of opportunities in the San José area; many programs offer language instruction in conjunction with environmental or cultural studies.

VOLUNTEER

Asociación Preservacionista de Flora y Fauna Silvestre (APREFLOFAS), P.O. Box 917-2150, Moravia, San José (tel. and fax (506) 240-6087). A nonprofit, volunteer organization that works to guard Costa Rica's natural resources from illegal and destructive exploitation. Promotes reforestation projects. They have a wealth of information on ecotourism in Costa Rica's national parks.

Association of Volunteers for Service in Protected Areas (ASVO), Apdo. 10104, San José. Volunteers work with park guards in the mountainous and coastal parks of Costa Rica. US$500/month includes food and lodging.

Centro de Derecho Ambiental y de los Recursos Naturales (CEDARENA), Apdo. 134-2050, San Pedro, Costa Rica (tel. (506) 224-8239, 225-1019; fax 225-5111). A nonprofit, nonpartisan association specializing in environmental law research. Their mission is to incorporate environmental concerns into legislation. Projects include land tenure/use reform, forest conservation, and marine resources management.

Genesis II Cloudforest and Reforestation Project, Apdo. 655, Cartago (please include 3 international reply coupons). Volunteers work 6 hrs. per day for 20 out of 28 days, planting trees and maintaining and constructing trails. Volunteers should be over 21 years of age. US$150 per week includes food and lodging.

Sea Turtle Restoration Project, 300 Broadway, Suite 28, San Francisco, CA 94133 (tel. (800) 859-7283; fax (415) 788-7324). Volunteers participate in important Ridley sea turtle research alongside biologists and environmentalists. Summer, fall, and winter expeditions. US$1175-1225 includes food, lodging, and in-country transportation.

Volunteers for Peace, 43 Tiffany Rd, Belmont, VT 05730 (tel. (802) 259-2759; fax 259-2922). A non-profit organization that has been coordinating workcamps around the world since 1981. Volunteer conservation work available in Costa Rica during June, July, and August. Volunteers must be fluent in Spanish and willing to make a commitment of at least 1 month. US$475/month, US$400 each additional month.

STUDY

American Institute for Foreign Study, College Division, 102 Greenwich Ave., Greenwich, CT 06830 (tel. (800) 727-2437; for high school students, (800) 888-2247). Organizes year, semester, quarter, and summer programs for high school and college study in Costa Rica. Open to adults. Minority and merit scholarships available.

Costa Rican Language Academy, Apdo. 336-2070, Av. Central, Calles 25/27, San José (tel. (506) 221-1624, 233-8914; fax 233-8670). Language and cultural study custom tailored for individual students. Homestays and weekend excursions plus lessons in Latin dance, Costa Rican cooking, Spanish music, and conversation. Monthly programs US$750-1100.

Council Voluntary Services Department, 205 E. 42nd St., New York, NY 10017 (tel. (212) 661-1414, ext. 1139). Offers two-to four-week environmental or community service projects in Costa Rica. Participants must be at least 18 years of age. US$165 placement fee.

Institute for Central American Studies (ICAS), Apdo. 1524-2050, San Pedro (tel. (506) 234-7682; fax 224-8910). Hosts journalism and Latin American studies internships (minimum of 6 months). Arranges paid English instruction positions for interns. Their language and study arm, the Mesoamerica Language Institute, offers a 1-day, 6-hr. course in Survival Spanish for Tourists with tips on travel and local customs (US$60 includes lunch). Conversation-oriented regular program gives 20 hrs. of instruction per week. Classes average 3-4 students (US$115 per week, homestays US$210 per week).

Instituto Centroamericano de Asuntos Internacionales (ICAI), in San José. Offers 2-4-week total immersion language programs. 4 hrs. of instruction per day, 5 days per week, plus excursions. 4 weeks with accommodations, 2 meals per day, and all activities US$962-1298. For information, contact Language Studies Enrollment Center, 13948 Hemlock Dr., Penn Valley, CA 95946 (tel. (916) 432-7690; fax 432-7615).

Intercultura of Costa Rica, P.O Box 3006, Peoria, IL 61612-3006 (tel. (800) 552-2051; fax (309) 673-5537). Four hours a day (or more) of levelled Spanish-learning fun, accompanied by a homestay and lessons about Costa Rican culture. 2 weeks US$685. One-on-one tutorials available. College credit available.

Monteverde Institute, Apdo.69-5655, Monteverde de Puntarenas (tel. (506) 645-5053; fax 645-5219). A nonprofit group offering short courses in tropical ecology and conservation for students, teachers, and other adult groups. Field trips, lectures, Spanish language, and Costa Rican culture study. Longer 8-10 week programs accredited by CIEE and the University of California Education Abroad Program.

Universidad de Costa Rica, Oficina de Asuntos Internacionales y Cooperación Externa, Ciudad Universitaria Rodrigo Facio, San Pedro, San José (tel. (506) 253-5323, ext. 5080; fax 225-5822). Offers 1-month intensive and regular semester language programs to students and professionals. Students proficient in Spanish may enroll in regular university programs. Many U.S. universities coordinate direct enrollment; see their listings here.

University at Albany—SUNY, Office of International Programs, Library 84, 1400 Washington Ave., Albany, NY 12222 (tel. (518) 442-3525; fax 442-3338). Arranges direct enrollment at the Universidad de Costa Rica after intensive 3-week pre-session. Must have completed 5 semesters of college-level Spanish or equivalent. Courses in natural sciences, social sciences, Spanish linguistics, and Spanish literature. Semester about US$7000 (US$4540 for New York State residents). Full-year programs available. Prices include documents, room and board, books, fees, insurance, and tuition.

University of Kansas, Office of Study Abroad, 203-F Lippincott Hall, Lawrence, KS 66045-1731 (tel. (913) 864-3742; fax 864-5040). Has arranged direct enrollment in the Universidad de Costa Rica since 1960. Initial 4-week language and cultural orientation, plus excursions. For sophomores and higher; 16 hrs. college-level Spanish with B average required. Semester about US$4500, full year about US$7000 (prices roughly 13% lower for KU students). Prices include orientation, room and board, tuition, activities, insurance, and documents. Environment-oriented students might like the new "Tropical Studies in Golfito" program.

■■■ KEEPING IN TOUCH

Mail service to and from Costa Rica is quite reliable. Airmail letters to the U.S. take about seven to 10 days each way (¢40 for postcards, ¢45 for airmail). Airmail to Europe may require a bit more time, but not much (¢50 for postcards, ¢55 for airmail). Steep customs duties (up to 100% of value) can be charged for anything larger than a letter, so bulky mailings can be expensive. If you do plan to receive packages, remind the sender to mark the contents and value clearly on the outside. Mail can be received general delivery through the *lista de correos;* address envelopes as follows:

R.W. Erik CHARLSON (name)
a/c Lista de Correos
4417 (postal code) Fortuna (city), Costa Rica
CENTRAL AMERICA

The use of postal codes is not essential.

Costa Rica has one of the best and most extensive **telephone** systems in Latin America and the Caribbean area. Phones function with coins of ¢5, ¢10, and ¢20 denominations. Calls from hotels cost about 30% more than calls from other phones. There are no long-distance area codes; for any call made within Costa Rica you need only dial the seven-digit phone number. In 1994, each six-digit phone number was converted to a seven-digit number in a systematic but complicated fashion. By now, most have converted, but pick up a phone number conversion table when you enter the country; it will help you convert any old number to a new one, just in case a listed number doesn't work. Dial 113 to obtain the telephone numbers of residents and business throughout Costa Rica. **Emergency service** in the greater San José metropolitan area is available by dialing 911; otherwise try 122. Contact the **police** by dialing 117 (or 127 in rural areas), and call the **fire department** at 118. **International collect** and **credit card** calls are made by dialing 116 first, or by dialing the USA direct operator at 114 (AT&T), 162 (MCI), or 163 (Sprint). To place a call to the U.S., dial 124 plus the U.S. area code and the number you wish to reach. The **country code** for Costa Rica is 506. Costa Rica operates on Central Standard time, but daylight-savings time is not observed.

■■■ GETTING THERE

Costa Rica's national airline is **LACSA,** 630 5th Ave., #246, New York, NY 10111-0334 (tel. (212) 245-6370). Other carriers serving San José's **Juan Santamaría Airport** include **American, British Airways, Mexicana, TWA, Continental, United,** and others. The preferred **border crossing** for travelers arriving from or going to Panama is at Paso Canoas (page 405), while those headed up into Nicaragua (or coming south from there) should go through Peñas Blancas (see page 384 for more information).

■■■ ONCE THERE

USEFUL ORGANIZATIONS AND PUBLICATIONS

For a list of **embassies** and **consulates,** see San José: Practical Information (page 328).

Dirección de Migración (tel. 220-0355), on the Antopista General Cañas Hwy. (the road to the airport in San José). Take the red bus to Alajuela from Av. 2, Calles 12/14 or at Calle 10/12 and tell the driver to drop you off at *La Oficina de Migración.* The place to go for permission to stay beyond the 30-or 90-day limit or to obtain costly exit visas if you overstay.

InfoTur, P.O. Box 10628-1000, San José (tel. 223-4481; fax 223-4476). A government information agency; can answer most tourist concerns and make reservations for all national and international tours, flights, hotels, etc. English spoken. Open Mon.-Fri. 8:30am-5:30pm, Sat. 9am-3pm.

Instituto Costarricense de Turismo (ICT), Apdo. 777-1000, on the Pl. de la Cultura, Avs. Central/2, Calle 5, San José (tel. (506) 223-1733; fax 223-5107). The national tourist bureau, with additional offices at the San José airport and at the northern and southern border crossings. Free maps available. Publishes a comprehensive listing of tour companies and lodgings.

OTEC Tours, Avs. 1/3, Calle 3, San José (tel. 222-0866). Offers discounts for students, youths, and teachers. Can arrange train tickets, youth hostels, language courses, and exchange programs, in addition to providing traditional travel services. Clients may be able to pay on a weekly basis, or on credit, for their airline tickets. Friendly staff speaks English.

TRANSPORTATION

The national airline **LACSA,** Apdo. 1531-1000, Av. 5, Calle 1, San José (tel. 231-0033, (800) 225-2272), makes reservations for flights to major points around Central America and beyond (open Mon.-Fri. 9am-5pm, Sat.-Sun. 9am-noon). **SANSA,** P.O. Box 999, 1007 Centro Colón, San José, at Av. Central/1, Calle 24 (tel. 233-0397; fax 233-0397), sends flights to Tamarindo (US$50 one way) and other destinations throughout Costa Rica, including Golfito, Palmar Sur, Nosara, Samara, and Quepos. **Travelair** (tel. 220-3054; fax 220-0413), handles domestic flights from San José to tourist areas, including daily flights to Tamarindo (US$136 round-trip), Quepos (US$72 round-trip), and Tambor (US$98 round-trip, US$62 one way).

The national rail line, **INCOFER,** runs **trains** throughout the Central Valley, one route runs between Heredia and San Pedro (¢50 one way), the other between San José and Cartago (¢60 one way). Tickets can be purchased at the Atlantic or Pacific Train Stations (see San José: Practical Information: Trains, page 328). The **bus** system is labyrinthine. In most large cities, each destination is served by a different company, and each company has its own bus terminal in a different part of town. Just about every reasonable road in Costa Rica has bus service, since private automobiles are relatively rare.

If you're traveling by **car,** you'll have a good network of highways at your disposal. Watch out, however, for the suggestively named **Cerro de la Muerte** (Hill of Death) section of the **Cartago-San Isidro** highway, plagued by frequent sink holes and thick fog. The road from San José to Puntarenas—narrow, twisty, and full of heavy trucks—is also dangerous. A seat belt must be used by the driver and any front seat passenger, and a safety helmet is required when driving a motorcycle. The speed limit on the Interamerican Highway is 90km per hour driving north from San José but 80km per hour driving south. Its minimum speed limit is 40km per hour. Other roads have limits ranging from 40km per hour to 60km per hour.

Tourists report that hitchhiking is generally safe, but *Let's Go* does not recommend it. Most Costa Ricans would pick up a hitcher, but few outside San José own cars. Between some smaller villages in the rural provinces, it is not uncommon to wait for a couple of hours before a single car passes. Costa Ricans themselves don't hitchhike much except in cases of emergency or dire need.

ADDRESSES

Even medium-sized cities in Costa Rica often have no formal system of street addresses. To the dismay of new arrivals, tourists must rely on dead reckoning by reference to landmarks well-known only to locals. Buildings are not numbered. Sometimes their locations are specified by a certain number of *metros,* north, south, east, or west from a particular point. *Metros* here refers to portions of city blocks, not meters; *100 metros al norte del Parque Rey Eduardo* indicates a building one block north of Parque Rey Eduardo. *Let's Go* uses blocks in its directions. Other times, addresses are referred to by the closest intersection: *Av. 1, Calle 2* indicates the building at or near the corner of Avenida 1 and Calle 2. In still another variation, addresses list the street the building is on and the *two* closest cross streets: *Av. 1, Calles 2/3* indicates the building on Avenida 1 between Calles 2 and 3.

ACCOMMODATIONS

The budget hotels of Costa Rica will most likely never appear in the pages of *Better Homes and Gardens,* but they're a frugal traveler's dream. You can spend less than US$7 a night at some places. Amenities are few in the sub-US$8 range (rooms are often merely cardboard partitions and hot water is not guaranteed), but a relatively painless step up to the US$11-16 zone can get you a furnished room with private bath and access to laundry service and cable TV.

Costa Rica is home to 12 of the more than 6000 official youth hostels worldwide which display the **HI** logo (a blue triangle) alongside the symbol of the national organization. Hostels are low-cost overnight accommodations, usually with separate quarters for males and females. For more information, or to get a **Hostelling International Guide,** write to them at 733 15th Street NW, Suite 840, Washington, DC 20005. Hostel cards are available from Council Travel and STA (see page 23), and from the hostelling organization of your own country.

COSTA RICA: AN INTRODUCTION

■■■ HISTORY

Only a fraction of the histories of Central America directly pertain to Costa Rica. After all, history is written of war and disgruntlement, in Central America of coups and insurgencies; in Costa Rica such strife is in exceptionally short supply. No news has translated into good news for the country and its inhabitants, from the time of its colonization almost continuously up until the present day, and in Central America's war-torn neighborhood good news is news indeed. That this tiny country near the middle of the troubled isthmus ever happened to weave its way through several bloody centuries into a position of graceful (if relative) prosperity is perplexing.

The origin of the land's name remains something of a mystery to this day, but it is clear from his journals that Columbus's first contact with native people was happy and peaceful. Columbus first reached the land on his fourth trip to the New World, arriving in 1502, and he stayed for only a few weeks to repair ships before moving on to more established colonial sites. During that brief time, he established friendly relations with the indigenous population, who were not seriously disturbed until the Spanish Empire's founding of the present day center of **Cartago,** in the country's central highlands. But Costa Rica's aboriginal inhabitants were relatively few, and as a result the system of slavery familiar to other colonies never got off the ground; after the decimation that the tribes suffered in the face of European diseases, they were too rare and scattered for it to be worth the *conquistadores'* while to subjugate them en masse. **Indígenas** comprise less than one percent of the country's population of three million and currently live on reservations, and **Black Caribs** concentrated in and around Puerto Limón comprise only about three percent of the population. Because of the homogeneity of the population (almost the whole country is of European descent), the established socioeconomic structures common to the rest of Latin America—poor *indígenas*, middle-class mestizos and rich *criollos*—never fully developed in Costa Rica.

Costa Rica's other saving grace was an ironic dearth of **precious metals.** Coupled with the province's distance from the colonial political centers of Mexico and Guatemala, this paucity ensured a great deal of unofficial independence for Costa Rica's first settlers. Taxation was nearly fruitless for the governing captaincy general in Guatemala, and so the subsistence economy that grew out of the region's tobacco and cacao farming generally was left in the hands of the farmers themselves. Costa Rica has always been able to keep its affairs directed internally, to a much greater degree than almost any other developing economic body in Central America.

On the heels of its neighbors, Costa Rica eventually entered the world of European mercantilism and Panamerican federations, but even then its involvement was limited. As with nearly all the isthmus's colonies, it achieved its independence from Spain by way of a confederation with the brief Mexican Empire, in 1821. As a member of the splinter **United Provinces of Central America,** Costa Rica was one of the first states to strike out on its own, leaving that interim union in 1838. At the same time, as with the other developing states, it shifted to that most exportable of crops: coffee. Within a decade, Great Britain was heavily invested in the Costa Rican coffee market, but as the arable land had already been divvied up on a small and equitable scale, increased cash from overseas only served to strengthen the distribution of power. When the Guanacaste province of Nicaragua seceded and sought union with bordering Costa Rica, it forecast a host of territorial disputes that arrived uninvited at the doorstep of a nation otherwise inclined toward isolation.

Costa Rica began to modernize rapidly under the heavy-handed leadership of the **General Tomás "Tommy" Guardia,** who brought in a base for future economic progress at the cost of civil liberties and a sizeable trade deficit over the course of his 1870-1882 reign. A new constitution was drafted in 1871, and the crop base was expanded from the coffee-core of thirty-years time to a more stable constellation of coffee, sugar, and bananas. This expansion in turn demanded improvements in the infrastructure; Guardia oversaw the construction of new roads and railroads for the transportation of the new crops between interior and coasts, as well as new schools and municipal buildings. Instrumental to the construction of the first Cartago-Atlantic line was the *norteamericano* entrepreneur **Minor Keith,** who represented the banana interest that eventually became the United Fruit Company, known as *El Pulpo* or "the Octopus" in Latin America, and as "Dole" in the USA. Economic and technological innovation had a marked impact on social and religious life: the Roman Catholic Church was all but extinguished during this period of reform, and at the same time, public secular education became compulsory and literacy reached levels previously unattained in the Spanish colonies. In 1890, Costa Rica conducted the first legitimate and large-scale election in Central American history.

Costa Rica's entrance into the twentieth-century was without a doubt one of the least graceful periods of its development. Guanacaste's annexation to the north and canal-related disputes with Panama to the south produced an extremely volatile situation in Costa Rican politics; on the southern front, U.S. intervention on Panama's behalf left in its wake a diplomatic mess that took decades to heal. Within this atmosphere of external strife, Costa Rica experienced its only modern flirtation with autocracy, when the congressionally appointed "victor" of the 1913 elections, **Alfredo González,** was usurped in a popular revolt led by the reactionary **General Federico Tinoco.** Despite its origins, Tinoco's stint was unpopular and brief, shortened unnaturally by constant threat of U.S. intervention against him.

The decades following Tinoco's ouster were characteristically smooth and prosperous for Costa Rica, and the role that the U.S. played against Tinoco's regime restored its popularity among *ticos.* The nation's democratic and educational structures flourished, even as a dependence on trade with foreign economies became more obvious. The only severe upheaval to alter its progress occurred in 1948, when communist insurgents banded together to prevent the successful presidential candidate from taking office. **José Figueres,** a wealthy coffee farmer and a socialist himself, marshalled regiments of the disorganized national army to suppress the revolt. In reaction, the Costa Rican legislature undertook its most drastic and internationally famous of measures: it dismantled the nation's entire military—to this day there is no such thing as the Costa Rican army, but instead only a Civil Guard, a (perhaps paramilitary) police force of 7000 members. Figueres, in turn, became a national hero, and in 1953, was himself elected to the office he had fought to defend. Once in office, he imposed many of the leftist reforms that had motivated the uprising in the first place. He nationalized banks and utilities, and set up the machinery that eventually broke United Fruit's stranglehold on the Costa Rican economy. Figueres's son is the president of Costa Rica today.

Since the dissipation of the military in 1948, Costa Rica has enjoyed virtually unblemished peace, relative political stability, and economic straits enviable by Third World standards. Figueres remained in the presidency for a period of twenty years, during which time his party, the **PLN,** came to dominate politics in the Legislative Assembly. As a result of Costa Rica's run-in with the globe-trotting filibuster and Wall Street financier **Robert Vesco,** the PLN fell out of power for a few years in the late 70s, but it has claimed the presidency and a majority of the national legislative seats for most of the period since its inception. (Vesco was finally arrested, after twenty-five years on the lam in the Caribbean, in May 1995; see William Walker, in Nicaragua, page 265!) Most non-financial problems faced by the little country in this half of the century have been due to civil strife in other Central American nations, especially in El Salvador and in Nicaragua.

It's been estimated that as many as 500,000 Salvadoran and Nicaraguan refugees have poured across Costa Rica's northern border since the late 1970s, when the first of this terrible twosome's civil wars began displacing and scaring away combatant and non-combatant alike, driving them to seek sanctuary in this peaceful country, by the truckload. This overflow has caused numerous internal problems for Costa Rica, as unemployment lines burgeon beyond any natural limits and tensions mount between otherwise hospitable *ticos* and their uninvited guests, as well as diplomatic strain between the overwhelmed governments. Former president **Oscar Arias Sánchez** made the best kind of international news when he authored a successful peace plan, negotiating a sustained cease-fire program for Costa Rica's neighbors and laying the groundwork for a unified Central American parliament. He won the Nobel Peace Prize and the envy of international statesmen far and wide. Though stagflation runs rampant, and the nation's businessmen are not without their anxieties, Costa Rica continues to enjoy a prolonged day in the sun, relatively speaking, as commercial gain due to the ecotourism boom of the past few years propels its economy beyond the pale of other Central American fiscal environments.

■■■ THE ARTS

Prior to the 20th century, Costa Rican **literature** drew primarily from folk tales and colloquial expression in a movement known as "costumbrism." Led by Joaquín García Monge's works *El Moto* and *Las Hijas del Campo,* the nation's working people were represented by one of their own, although the country never nurtured indigenous literature. Still, despite the strength of this movement, Costa Rican literature first came into full bloom in 1900, when it became associated with denunciation of the status quo. José Marín Cañas' *Infierno Verde,* a depiction of the Chaco War between Paraguay and Bolivia, bolstered developing anti-imperialist sentiment in its experimentation with darker and revolutionary themes. Similarly, Oreamuni's *La Ruta de su Evasión* confronts the tensions between parents and children and those stemming from Latin American machismo. A focus on bitter realities eventually took shape in the theater and in poetry, which pushes forward still today in a mature harmony between fiction and fact. Playwrights Alberto Cañas and Daniel Gallegos accompanied the so-called Circle of Costa Rican Poets in an attempt to unite the nation's thinkers against the sociopolitical cruelties of the age. Well-read *ticos* tend to regard two of their living authors above all others: Fabian Dobles, winner of the Premio Nacional, Costa Rica's highest distinction for artistic and intellectual achievement, and Carlos Salazar Herrera, painter, poet, professor, and the author of *Tres Cuentos de Angustias y Paisajes.*

■■■ MEDIA

The rule of thumb in Costa Rican popular culture, especially with teenagers, is a simple conditional: if it is *norteamericano,* then it is cool. Turn on a TV or a radio anywhere and thrill to the sight of U.S. sitcoms translated into Spanish, including The Simpsons, Scooby Doo, The Fresh Prince of Bel Air (called *Principe del Rap*), and of course, Baywatch. Similarly, the Costa Ricans are big fans of U.S. musical cheese, and the sappiest songs get translated into Spanish in a short time. Reggae is especially popular along the Caribbean coast, and traditional salsa and merengue music while harder to find on the radio, is often played in nightclubs.

In Spanish, *La Nación* and *La República* each represent the alternative views of the two main political parties in Costa Rica. In English, the *Tico Times* and *Costa Rica Today* offer an extensive summary of cultural events, hotels, restaurants, and current events. The *Tico Times'* publication *Exploring Costa Rica* is an invaluable guide to the country's tourist attractions and cities.

■■■ FOOD AND DRINK

Just like the people, the dining in Costa Rica tends to be causal and welcoming. Small local diners, called **sodas** by the *ticos,* are fixtures everywhere, from tiny coastal villages to downtown San José. *Sodas* are a budget traveler's best friend, selling homemade Costa Rican *típico* food at inexpensive prices. While *sodas* are small, laid-back, and usually family-owned, *restaurantes* are larger and generally a little more formal and expensive. But the traditional staples can be found anywhere, and although the names may sound unfamiliar, the actual food probably isn't anything new to the Latin Americanized. Costa Ricans frequent plentiful *sodas* for **empanadas** (turnovers) and **batidos** (fruit shakes). Costa Rica grows and roasts some of the best coffee in the world, and the numerous **panaderías** (bakeries) are good spots to enjoy a spur-of-the-moment coffee break. A common breakfast is **gallo pinto** (which translates, strangely, into "painted rooster"), but it's really nothing more than that good ole rice-and-beans mix, often served with eggs or meat. Fruits available range from the omnipresent pineapple and banana to the expected blackberry and strawberry to the truly exotic mango, papaya, tamarindo, and guanaba. The most traditional dinner is called a **casado,** which isn't a fixed entree, but is rather a mix of different items, usually a salad, some type of meat, beans, and either French fries or fried plantains, called *plátanos* or *patacones*. *Casado* literally means "married," and the meal got this name because wives traditionally served it to their husbands. On the Atlantic coast, where there is a strong Caribbean influence, everything from *gallo pinto* to chicken to a meat-and-vegetable stew called **rondon** (from the Carib-English "run-down," *nothing* like roadkill) can be found cooked in coconut milk. A popular way to wash it all down is with a *batido,* a fresh fruit shake which can be made with water (turning out like fruit juice—so watch out for water quality) or milk (more like a regular milkshake). Of course, anyone who's not a fan of Imperial, the ubiquitous native beer with the tell-tale eagle on the bottle, is liable to be chased out of the country. The local hard liquor is **guaro,** a clear moonshine which tastes godawful on its own, but manages to mix pretty nicely with just about anything.

■■■ RECENT NEWS

As is frequent in Costa Rica and envied in the rest of Central America, the past year has seen little in the way of calamity on the level that would merit international attention. Nonetheless, the tiny nation's governing body and fiscal health have not gone unplagued by ravages familiar to developing economies. President Figueres' regime has become dangerously unpopular in the light of current financial policy failures and looming deadlocks in the legislature.

A symptom of these woes has been a reshuffling of the presidential cabinet, including the delegation of overall economic responsibility to Rebeca Grynspan. Rumors have it that this change and a few others presage a massive overhaul within the PLN (Figueres's party, dominant in Costa Rica and left-of-center). Most *ticos'* gripes with the current state of affairs link variously with the PLN's fiscal policy, but these concerns pull in different directions: many citizens are dismayed by the state of health care, education, and the poor, but a whopping 44% cite increases in the cost of living as the most severe problem. The division in interests precipitates a situation familiar to U.S. politicos; in a nutshell, PLN and the opposition, PUSC, both observe a need to cut public spending, but PLN sees increased efficiency in the bureaucracy as the appropriate means to reduction while PUSC, far less committed to Costa Rica's remarkable implementation of the welfare state, wants to ensure reduced spending by cutting programs outright. The conflict comes to a head in ongoing (summer of 1995) debates on tax reform. *Norteamericanos* traveling in the area may want to know that the U.S. Congress, led by Sen. Jesse Helms, has recently made it impossible for Costa Rica to receive U.S. aid as a penalty for disregarding U.S. standards for compensating businesses inconvenienced or requisitioned by the Costa Rican government.

San José

Blame it on money and its reliable sidekick, industrialization, but San José is *not* the Costa Rica most tourists see in their travel brochures. The car exhaust suffocates, the blaring horns deafen, and the omnipresent fast-food joints remind travelers far too much of home. Growth and sprawl intimidate the moist serenity of the rainforests surrounding the city, and the cross-cultural diversity reaches electric extremes.

Ringed by mountain ranges and perched 1182 meters (3800 feet) above sea level, San José was first settled in 1736. The city was the sleepy center of tobacco production after being colonized by the Spanish in 1736, and only moved into the spotlight of Costa Rican political and economic life in the 19th century. In 1823, the capital was moved from Cartago to San José, and the city became a focal point for the growing Costa Rican coffee economy. Since the 1950s, San José has grown rapidly in both area and population; it is now an important transportation hub and home to two major universities and a great many industrial (if not botanical) plants.

Today, the city has 308,000 residents, and one-third of all Costa Ricans call the San José province their home. As usual, first-time visitors are hit hardest by the contrasts, of street vendors shouting the names of obscure fruits next to ever-ubiquitous and never-unfamiliar McDonald's. Billboards preach marital fidelity, while the opposite side shows seductive women drinking Coke.

While history and circumstance have vaulted San José into the political, social, and economic center of Costa Rican life, some things never change. The summer heat is grueling: from May to August, San Jose swelters and sweats. Respite, however, comes like clockwork every afternoon, when the skies shake, rain pummels the city, and water literally pours from every wall, refreshing *ticos* and tourists alike.

■■■ ORIENTATION

San José's streets form a regular grid. *Calles* run north-south and *avenidas* east-west. Odd-numbered *calles* are east of **Calle Central,** while even-numbered ones fall to its west. Similarly, odd-numbered *avenidas* run to the north of **Avenida Central,** and even-numbered ones to the south. Therefore, an address like "Av. 3, Calle 3" is in the northeast part of town. However, many streets are not marked and some addresses and directions are given with respect to major landmarks. For example, if an address says *"200 metros al sur del Teatro Nacional"* (200 meters from the National Theater), first find the National Theater and then walk two blocks south of it. *Metros* refers to city blocks, not to actual meters; *100 metros* is one block, *150 metros* is one-and-a-half blocks, etc. If the address is given as Avs. 3/5, Calle 2, it means the building is on Calle 2 between Avenidas 3 and 5. Because the city is relatively small, walking is an easy way to get around in San José; the complicated intra-city bus system, keyed as it is to the landmark system, can be somewhat difficult to use. It should not, however, intimidate.

■■■ PRACTICAL INFORMATION

Tourist Office: Instituto Costarricense de Turismo (ICT), Avs. Central/2, Calle 5 (tel. 222-1090), on the Plaza de la Cultura, down the wide staircase and to the left of the Gold Museum. Exceptionally helpful information on sights, bus schedules, and hotels. Excellent (and free) country and city maps. English spoken. Wheelchair accessible. Open Mon.-Fri. 9am-5pm, Sat. 9am-1pm. **Airport branch** (tel. 242-1820), directly behind customs and before the exit of the building. Services similar to those provided at the main office. Open daily 8am-9pm.

Embassies and Consulates: U.S., Rohmuser, Carretera Pavas (tel. 220-3939, after hours and weekends 220-3127), in front of Centro Comercial. Open Mon.-Fri. 8am-4:30pm. **Canada,** in Sabana Sur, Oficentro Ejecutivo building #5 (tel. 296-4149). **U.K.,** Po. Colón, Calles 38/40, Edificio Colón, 11th floor (tel. 221-5566). Open Mon.-Fri. 8:30am-noon and 1-2:30pm. **Australia** has no embassy, but has official representatives at Calle 33, Avs. 5/7 (tel. 224-1152), in Barrio Escalante. Open Mon.-Fri. 8am-1pm. **Guatemala,** 50m east, 100m north, 50m east of the Pizza Hut in the Plaza del Sol. Open Mon.-Fri. 9am-noon. **Mexico,** Av. 7, Calles 11/13 (tel. 233-8874). Open Mon.-Fri. 8:30am-noon and 3-4pm. **Panama,** Calle 38, Avs. 5/7 (tel. 257-3241). Open Mon.-Fri. 8am-noon. **Nicaragua,** Barrio la California, Av. Central, Calle 27 (tel. 222-2373), across from Pizza Hut. Open Mon.-Fri. 8:30am-noon. **El Salvador,** Los Yoses, Av. 10, Calle 35 (tel. 225-3861). Open Mon.-Fri. 9am-1pm. **Honduras,** Zapote (tel. 234-9502), 250m east, 200m north, 100 east of Itan. Open Mon.-Fri. 9am-2pm. **Belize** (tel. 234-9969), 400m east, 100m south of Iglesa Santa Teresita. Open Mon.-Fri. 9am-noon and 2-4pm.

Police: 911 or 117. Ministerio de Seguridad Pública (tel. 227-4866), 150m east of the Centro Comercial de Sur.

Currency Exchange: Banco Nacional, Avs. 1/3, Calles 2/4 (tel. 223-2166), and **Banco de Costa Rica,** Avs. Central/2, Calles 4/6 (tel 255-1100), generally have

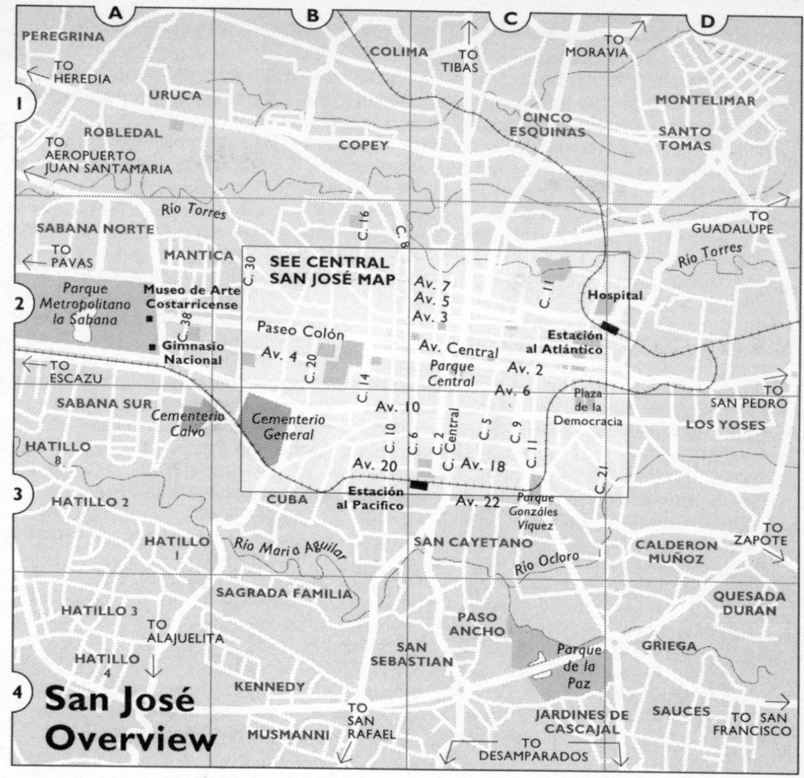

long lines; each charges commission on traveler's checks (about 0.75% if changing to colones, 2% if changing to dollars). **Casa de Cambio GAB-International,** Av. 2, Calles 1/3 (tel. 223-7221), to the left of the Gran Hotel Costa Rica, has long hours and good rates. Open. Mon.-Sat. 8am-5pm.

American Express: Av. 3/5, Calle Central (tel. 223-3644), inside Banco San José. Cash advances for card holders in dollars or colones only. English spoken. Open Mon.-Fri. 8:15am-4pm.

Post Office: Calle 2, Avs. 1/3 (tel. 223-9766, 223-9079), in the large green building. There are no street mailboxes in San José, so all mail must be dropped off here. *Lista de correos.* Mon.-Fri. 8am-5pm, Sat. 8am-noon. **Postal code:** 1000.

Telephone: Radiográfica, Calles Central/ 2, Av. 5 (tel. 287-0087). Just pick up one of their many phones to make a free collect call. Also has direct AT&T and Sprint service. Open Mon.-Fri. 8am-10pm, Sat.-Sun. 8am-8pm.

Telegram: Radiográfica, (see Telephones). US$0.40 per word to U.S., US$0.67 per word to Europe. **Fax** and **telex** also available. Open Mon.-Fri. 8am-10pm, Sat.-Sun. 8am-8pm. Service also available at the **post office** (see above, tel. 223-9766, ext. 239). Open Mon.-Sat. 7am-6pm.

Fax: Radiográfica (see Telephones). ¢342 per page to the U.S. Open Mon.-Fri. 8am-10om, Sat.-Sun. 8am-8pm. **Post office** (see above: tel. 223-9766, ext. 239), US$2.50 per page to U.S. or current equivalent in colones. Open Mon.-Sat. 7am-6pm.

Airport: Juan Santa María International Airport (tel. 441-0704), about 15km northwest of San José on the highway to Alajuela. Departure tax US$7 (¢517). **Taxis** to and from the airport run ¢2000 (tel. 235-5847, 224-6969, 235-9966). Red

buses from Alajuela run every 5min. between the airport and the San José bus terminal at Av. 2, Calles 12/14 (¢70).

Trains: Atlantic Train Station, Av. 3, Calles 19/23. Trains from the suburb of San Pedro to Heredia, Mon.-Fri. at 5:45am, and 5:15pm (14km, 45min). Return from Heredia to San Pedro, Mon.-Fri. at 6:30am, 1, and 6pm. ¢50 each way.

Buses: No central terminal, as each destination served by a different carrier. Consult the tourist office for a list of companies and destinations. **Transportes Mepe,** Avs. 9/11, Calle Central (tel. 257-8129), serves Sixaola, (daily at 6am, 1:30, 3:30pm, ¢980); Cahuita (Mon.-Fri. 6am, 1:30, and 3:30pm, Sat.-Sun. 8:30am and 3:40pm, ¢565); and Puerto Viejo (Mon.-Fri. 10am, 3:40pm, Sat.-Sun. at 8:30am, 10am, and 3:30pm, 4 hrs., ¢635). **Autotransportes Caribeños,** Av. 3, Calles 19/21 (tel. 226-6629), across the street form the train station, has direct and indirect buses to Limón (every 30min. from 6:15am-8pm, ¢505). Other carriers offer frequent service to Alajuela (see Airport), to Ciudad Quesada (a.k.a. San Carlos, every hr., 5am-7:30pm) from the Coca-Cola bus station at Avs. 1/3, Calle 16; to Fortuna and Volcán Arenal (6:15, 8:40, and 11:30am), from the Coca-Cola bus station; to Quepos and Manuel Antonio National Park (6am, noon, and 6pm); from the Coca-Cola bus station, to Jacó (daily at 7:15am and 3:30pm) from the Coca-Cola bus station; to Liberia (7, 9, 11:30am, 1, 3, 4, 6, and 8pm) from Avs. 3/5, Calle 14; to Nicoya (6, 8, 10am, noon, 1, 2:30, 3, and 5pm) from Avs. 3/5, Calle 14; to Puntarenas (every 30min., 6am-7pm) from Av. 10/12, Calle 16; to Cartago (every 10min., 2 hrs.) from Av. 18, Calle 5; to Heredia (every 10min. from 5am-10pm) from Avs. 7/9, Calle 1; and to Limón (every 30min., 6:15am-8pm, 2½ hrs., ¢505), from Av. 3, Calles 19/21. MUSOC buses (tel. 222-2422) leave for San Isidro de el General from Calle 16, Av. 1 (hourly 5:30am-5pm; ¢540).

Taxis: Coopetico Taxi Co. (tel. 221-2552). **Coopetaxi Taxi Co.** (tel. 235-9966). ¢100 for the first km, ¢60 each additional km. Most routes within San José run ¢160-280. Fare to the airport is ¢2500. 20% surcharge after 10pm.

Car Rental: Complete list of rental offices available at the tourist office. **Budget,** Po. Colón, Calle 30 (tel. 223-3284). Open daily 7am-5:30pm. US$35 per day, including insurance, taxes, and free mileage. Must be 21. Those under 25 pay extra US$8 for insurance. To rent a Range Rover, try **Rent-A-Rover S.A.** (tel. and fax 533-3037, or 225-3948 to hear a recorded message). Free delivery in San José.

Market: Central Market framed by Avs. Central and 1, Calles 6 and 8. Open daily until 6pm. A labyrinth of cheap grub and souvenirs, especially leather bags and sandals. Tourists should be careful here and guard their possessions carefully. **AM-AutoMercado,** Av. 3, Calle 3 (tel. 233-5511). Supermarket. Mon.-Sat. 8:15am-7:30pm.

Laundromat: Laundromats are in a galaxy far, far away from central San José. Drycleaning is more commonly available, and most places will give special rates for bundles of clothes, by the kilogram. **Sixapla,** Av. 2, Calles 7/9 (tel. 221-2111), and many other locations throughout the city. Wash, iron, and fold laundry, ¢475 per kg. Ready in 48 hrs. **American Dry Cleaning,** Avs. 10/12, Calle Central (tel. 222-6247). Wash only (¢450 per kg). Next-day service. Hotels have laundry service; some allow you to use one of their machines to do a load and lessen costs (see Toruma Youth Hostel (HI) under Accommodations, below).

English Bookstore: Book Traders, Av. 1, Calles 5/7 (tel. 255-0508). Trade in your old books or buy used ones at 50% of the printed cover price. Everything from classics to trashy romance novels. Small French and German selection also. Mon.-Sat. 9am-6pm, Sun. 10am-5pm. **Librería Lehmann,** Av. Central, Calles 1/3 (tel 223-1212). Books, travel guides, maps, and major North American publications. Open Mon.-Fri. 8am-6:30pm, Sat. 9am-5pm.

Pharmacies: Fischel, Av. 3, Calle 2 (tel. 223-0909), near the center of town. Open Mon.-Sat. 8am-7pm. Huge selection of medicines and toiletries. Sun. deliveries only. **Clínica Bíblica,** Av. 14, Calles Central/1 (tel. 257-5252). Open 24 hrs.

Hospital: Hospital San Juan de Dios, Paseo Colón, Calles 14/18 (tel. 257-6282). Large white building where Av. Central turns into Paseo Colón, after Calle 14. Emergency service 24 hrs. Doctor consultations free, but no English spoken. **Hospital Clínica Bíblica,** Av. 14, Calle 1 (tel. 257-5252). English Spoken. Doctor consultation ¢3000-¢5000. Emergency service 24 hrs. (tel. 257-0466).

Central San José

A B C D E F G
1 2 3 4

TO LA SABANA & MUSEO DE ARTE COSTARRICENSE

PASO DE LA VACA
COCA COLA
AMON
OTOYA
CARMEN
MERCED
SANTA LUCIA
SAN BOSCO
BOLÍVAR
SOLEDAD
BELLAVISTA

Río Torres

Parque Zoológico Simón Bolívar
Hospital Calderón Guardia
Atlantic Train Station
Asamblea Legislativa
National Library
Parque Nacional
TO LA UNIVERSIDAD DE COSTA RICA
Museo Nacional
Plaza de la Democracia
Museo de Jade
Parque España
Serpentario
Parque Morazán
Museo de Oro
Teatro Nacional
Catedral Metropolitana
Parque Central
Banco National
Post Office
Mercado Central
Coca Cola Bus Station
Hospital San Juan de Dios
Hospital Nacional de Niños
Hospital Cervantes
Jewish Synagogue
Paseo Colón
Juan Santa Maria
Pacific Train Station

Avenida 11, Avenida 9, Avenida 7, Avenida 5, Avenida 3, Avenida 1, Avenida Central, Avenida 2, Avenida 4, Avenida 6, Avenida 8, Avenida 10, Avenida 12, Avenida 14, Avenida 16, Avenida 18, Avenida 20

Calle 28, Calle 26, Calle 24, Calle 22, Calle 20, Calle 18, Calle 16, Calle 14, Calle 12, Calle 10, Calle 8, Calle 6, Calle 4, Calle 2, Calle Central, Calle 1, Calle 3, Calle 5, Calle 7, Calle 9, Calle 11, Calle 13, Calle 15, Calle 17, Calle 19, Calle 21

1 5 9

N

0 200 yards
0 200 meters

COSTA RICA

Red Cross: Av. 6, Calle 16 (tel. 128, 233-7033). No English spoken.
Emergency: tel. 911 or 117.

■■■ ACCOMMODATIONS

Budget accommodations in San José are evenly dispersed throughout the city. Since prices are similar from neighborhood to neighborhood, it's worth avoiding the northeast part of the city, where streets and rooms tend to be somewhat dirtier and less safe. To a certain extent, the cost of a room in San José varies inversely with the amount of street noise that filters in through the windows.

Toruma Youth Hostel (HI), Av. Central, Calles 31/33 (tel. and fax 224-4085). Take the San Pedro bus (¢25) from the Teatro Nacional, a huge white Neoclassical building draped in exotic greenery. Single-sex rooms and bathrooms. Bunks—equipped with a light, small fan, shelves, and a lock—are more like cupboards for up to 6 to a suite. Early birds may be able to snag a more spacious quad for the same price (US$12/bed, HI members and ISIC holders US$9). Singles and doubles available (US$26, HI members and ISIC holders US$23). Still, Toruma luxuriates in collectivist amenities—a spacious lobby with sofas and cable TV, spotless communal facilities with hot water, free breakfasts included, even its own tourist information center. Free storage available. Laundry ¢350/5 pieces, self-service free, but BYO-Soap. Reception daily 7am-10pm; check-ins after 10pm need passports.

Pensión Otoya, Avs. 5/7, Calle Central (tel. 221-3925). Shoddy exterior, but soothing, well-lit lobby and sunny, plant-lined, brick walls provide a welcome respite from the hectic city outside. The huge TV room and friendly owners warm the heart. Singles and doubles are moderately sized, but the two triples are gigantic. Well-maintained communal or private bathrooms available. Key to the front door allows 24-hr. access. Storage facilities, TV room, communal kitchen with refrigerator, and self-serve laundry. Singles ¢1280, ¢1575 with bath; doubles ¢1975, ¢2650 with bath; triples ¢2430, ¢2724 with bath. Prices change constantly.

Hotel Rialto, Av. 5, Calle 2, 3rd Floor (tel. 221-7456). The surrounding neighborhood drowns in traffic, but Rialto offers sanctuary in its dark, wood-paneled lobby and halls. Rooms even have windows: a San José budget rarity. Single-sex communal bathrooms aren't pristine, but hot water flows 24 hrs. 24-hr. Laundry facilities, incoming phone calls. Singles ¢700; doubles ¢1100, ¢1300 with bath.

Hotel Boston, Av. 8, Calle Central/2 (tel. 221-0563), next to Hotel Berlin. The proper Bostonian even smells like PineSol, and the rooms' mint-green walls are freshly painted. Puritanical prices are slightly higher but well worth it—rooms are spacious and bright, and all have TV and private bathroom facilities. Hot water 24 hrs. Laundry service available. Open 24 hrs. Reservations recommended. Singles ¢1850, doubles ¢3000, triples ¢3600, quads ¢4020.

Casa Ridgway, Av. 6, Calle 15 (tel. and fax 233-8168), in the short, dead-end street between Avs. 6 and 8. The Ridgway shares its bright yellow building with the "Friends' Peace Center," and peace is what you'll find at this hotel/hostel. Quiet hrs. 10pm-7am. Wood floors and lush indoor garden with couches and a small, multilingual library. Kitchen, fridge, laundry (by machine ¢350, by hand ¢50), communal bathrooms and showers make Casa Ridgway well worth the search. Singles ¢1400, private singles ¢1750; doubles 2500; triples ¢2800; quads ¢5440.

Tica Linda, Av. 2, Calles 5/7 (tel. 233-0528; fax 506-257-2272). A backpacker's favorite, and a great place to get travel hints from veterans. Marked only by a tiny sign on the door, next to Bar Esmerald. The rooms may not be the best in town, but all come equipped with locks (windows less secure). 24-hr. hot water in one of the two communal bathrooms. Reception desk closes at 11pm, so night revelers should get a key (deposit ¢200). Singles ¢850, shared with 2 or more strangers ¢680; doubles ¢1700; triples ¢2040.

■■■ FOOD

Seafood dishes, black beans, and rice are San José's staples. Unfortunately, Western pop culture has left its mark, and now fast food joints of McDonald's style and caliber stand sentry over nearly every downtown street. Prices are good everywhere, but the cheapest grub is found in the eateries of the **central market,** where authentic *tico* meals like a *chuleta* (pork chop) with rice and salad go for only ¢300.

Cuartel de la Boca del Monte, Av. 1, Calles 2/3 (tel. 221-0327). One of the liveliest spots in town. Crowded, especially Mon. and Wed. nights, when live music blares. Bands play near the bar with the amazing 152-cocktail menu; ¢750 cover after 9pm. House specialty is the *lomito cuartel* (ham, cheese and tomato, ¢825). For those with a greasophobia, baked chicken is available. Open Mon.-Fri. 11:30am-2pm and 6pm-2am, Sat.-Sun. 6pm-2am.

Restaurant Vishnu, Av. 1, Calles 1/3 (tel. 222-2549). Two other locations: Av. 4, Calle 1, and Calle 14, Avs. Central/1. Fresh fruit, big paintings of jungle scenes, and the azure, four-armed Preserver of Worlds encourage a lively and amiable atmosphere. Vegetarian menu popular with budget travelers as well as locals. Chow down on *integral* sandwiches (¢225), fruit with yogurt and granola (¢200), and *jugos* (fruit juices, ¢110). Open Mon.-Sat. 7am-9pm, Sun. 9am-7:30pm.

Spoon, Av. Central, Calles 5/7 (tel. 221-6702). Red-brick paneling, woven-grass chairs, quiet Latin American pop music, eerily hip name, and delicious desserts make this café irresistible. Always busy around lunchtime (sandwiches around ¢300) the real reasons to come are the Kahlua-involving pastries (¢305), including *Kalúa con nuez* (with nuts), *chocofresa* (chocolate strawberry), and *caramelo con crema Chantilly.* Coffee or tea ¢91-105. Open daily 9:30am-9pm.

Restaurant Shakti, Av. 8, Calle 13 (tel. 222-9096). A haven for die-hard vegetarians. Vegetables everywhere, even growing under the glass table-tops. Completely vegetarian menu includes *chalupa* (beans, cheese, and soya, ¢350), spaghetti with mushrooms, raisins, and cheese (¢450), and *"energético,"* yogurt with honey, fruit, granola, and pollen (¢175). Sells packaged grains and vitamins. Open Mon.-Fri. 10am-6pm, Sat. 10am-3pm.

Pollo Campesino, Av. 2, Calle 7 (tel. 222-1170). Sure, you can order beef, pork, or shrimp, but which? The house specialty, *pollo al la leña,* makes for a healthy change from the commonly fried poultry of many other grubberies, a *pollo entero* is enormous and comes with a choice of side orders (¢1100) and can be ordered in half-(¢600) or quarter-sized (¢300) portions. Open daily 10am-midnight.

Soda Nini, Av. 3, Calles 2/4 (tel. 233-7771), across from the post office. Remember your middle school cafeteria? The self-serve lines and hard, nailed-down chairs and tables have all been recreated at Soda Nini, an inexpensive *soda* by day, a *discoteca* and bar by night. *Ensalada mixta* ¢155, *arroz cantones* ¢130. Popular with local fans of cheap eats. Open daily 10:30am-11pm.

Restaurant Omni, Av. 1. Calles 3/5 (tel. 221-2-3218). Thought that Chinese-food craving couldn't be satisfied in San José? In a mellow, roofed courtyard set back from the street, Omni fries up their rice with the best of Beijing. Chop suey ¢520, won ton soup ¢550, fried rice ¢500. You should be pleasantly haunted by MSG-flashbacks in years to come. Open daily 9:30am-midnight.

■■■ SIGHTS

The stunning **Teatro Nacional** (National Theater), Av. 2, Calles 3/5 (tel. 221-1329), is almost unbelievably extravagant, graced throughout with ornately sculpted gold banisters and high ceiling frescos. Its Renaissance façade is anointed with Italian sculptor Pitro Bulgarelli's personifications of Dance, Music, and Fame. The theater's lavish interior space is flanked by marble columns filed along its vestibules, an ornate Paris Opéra-inspired grand staircase, and bright overhead reliefs painted by Bespasiano Bignami, who was later commissioned to work on the Moscow Opera House. Concerts are held in the grand auditorium, which consists of an orchestra pit surrounded by three tiers of balconies. Seating in the main area is neither sloped nor staggered; those stuck behind the likes of Carmen Miranda or Shaquille O'Neil suffer accordingly. For official receptions and conferences, the floor of the pit can be raised and the auditorium used as a great ballroom. Construction of the teatro was begun in 1890. In January of that year, an opera company led by the renowned Adelina Patti was performing in Guatemala; the company was unable to perform in San José because the city lacked an "appropriate" facility. Snubbed by the snobs, a group of merchants and coffee barons wrote to acting president Durán. Arguing that "a Capital with a culture such as ours cannot be deprived of a center of this kind," and knowing full well that the national budget couldn't be made to fund such a venture, the merchants and barons pledged to donate five cents for every 25 pounds of coffee they exported. The rest, as they say, is history. The teatro was inaugurated in 1897 and declared a national monument in 1965. Over the years, thousands of Costa Ricans have seen performances at the theater. However, not as many have come as some would have liked: the novelist Marín Cañas once claimed in jest that the teatro nacional was the largest in the world. After all, he argued, "so far, nobody has been able to fill it." (Open Mon.-Sat. 9am-5pm. Admission ¢400.)

Appearances can be deceiving: of the roughly three dozen museums in the greater San José area, the **Museo Nacional,** Avs. Central/2, Calle 17 (tel. 257-1433), may well have the best collection, but it languishes behind what is undoubtedly the worst façade. The museum is housed in a fading yellow fortress that cries out for some serious plastic surgery. Inside, however, the museum boasts expertly maintained collections of pre-Hispanic art, as well as exhibits on Costa Rican history, colonial life, archaeology, and geology. One of the most impressive displays features *metates,* three-legged funeral offerings made of hardened lava. The nightmarish "flying panel" *metates* are elaborately decorated with anthropomorphic animal figures holding decapitated heads. The museum also enjoys an incredible view of San José, as seen from the dried-grass gazebo in its sprawling bamboo-and-palm garden—guaranteed to knit up unraveled nerves. The gift shop is also strictly for looking; the faux-gold jewelry and indigenous pottery go for outrageous prices (open Tues.-Sun. 8:30am-5pm; admission ¢200, students free with ID).

The **Museo del Oro,** in the Plaza de la Cultura, Avs. Central/2, Calle 5 (tel. 223-0528), across from the tourist office, houses a magnificent collection of pre-Hispanic artifacts, including 2300 pieces of jewelry, armor plates, and figures used for religious devotion and spiritual healing. Shamans used these animal figurines to communicate with spirits; the many serpents and alligator heads symbolize fertility via association with their aquatic origins, as ought to be intuitively clear to anyone interested in pursuing a career in shamanism. Especially cool: the miniature gold animals of Exhibit 42 and the lip rings in the adjacent case. Signs label the displays in Spanish and English and give a detailed history of the state of metallurgy in 400 BC, including diagrams that describe different types of casting to visitors with spare time and gold ore on their hands (open Tues.-Sun. 10am-4:30pm; admission ¢750, students ¢150 with ID).

Several temporary art and sculpture exhibits share a building with the Museo del Oro, including the **Numismatic Museum,** whose displays of coins and currencies feature a token of almost everything from the first Spanish colonial coin to the modern day colón. A large collection of jade, along with ceramic and gold exhibits, resides in the (three guesses) **Museo de Jade,** Av. 7, Calles 9/13 (tel. 223-5800), on the 11th floor of the INS building on the north side of Plaza de España. The carved figures of green, white, pink, and black jade seem to glow incandescently in their lighted display cases. Included among the more practical artifacts are some long, tubular jade beads that were used as brassieres by the wives of indigenous chieftains; watch out, WonderBra (open Mon.-Fri. 8am-5pm; free). The **Museo de Arte Costarricense,** Calle 42, Po. Colón (tel. 222-7155), in the Sabana Metropolitan Park, exhibits the works of native Costa Rican artists from 1950 to the present. On the second floor is the Gold Room, famous for the four gold bas-reliefs by French artist Louis Feron depicting the history of Costa Rica (open Tues.-Sun. 10am-5pm; admission ¢300, Sun. free; students with ID free).

An unusual exhibit of subtle charms is the **Serpentarium,** Av. 1, Calles 9/11 (tel. 255-4210), a collection of serpents and other reptiles as well as tarantulas and amphibians, all of them native to Costa Rica. Amidst slimy creepers and slick slitherers you'll find the legendary poison arrow frogs, those media darlings that peer out from every hackneyed book cover and postcard in the country. The vicious glances from the mini-crocodiles are enough to keep even the bravest from touching the glass. Paragraphs printed in English and Spanish describe the behaviors and natural habitat of each animal (open daily 9am-6pm; admission ¢500). Pathetically small, the **Simón Bolívar Zoo** (veer right on the twisted Av. 11 past Calle 7, in the northeast part of town) is nonetheless diverting; birds, monkeys, turtles, and even a lion and a tiger do their best to frolic—but it's hard in such cramped and almost unsanitary conditions. The museum casts a shadow of doubt over Costa Rica's dedication to wildlife (open Mon.-Fri. 8am-3:30pm, Sat.-Sun. 9am-4pm; admission ¢200).

Parque de España, enclosed by Avs. 3 and 5 and Calles 11 and 13, is a great place to walk, talk, or simply be quiet. The long-hanging limbs of its broad trees create a refuge for city-weary couples. It's one of the few places in town where you can actually hear the birds singing and feel the wind on your face *without* choking on car exhaust. The park is joined by **Parque Morazán,** Avs. 3/5, Calles 5/9, blanketed in thick grass (protected by armed guards), orchid-laden benches, and an enormous gazebo. Beware of the early afternoon, though—the park is overrun with the noise of running children when the *escuela* across the street grants its daily furlough.

Parque Nacional, Avs. 1/3, Calles 15/19, is the closest you'll see in San José to a real rainforest. The trees along the perimeter of the park form a fortress against the belligerent city streets, and the statue of national hero Juan Santamaría stands guard to make sure none of its picnickers are disturbed. Adjacent to the park are the **Legislative Building** and the **National Library.**

■■■ ENTERTAINMENT

San José will not disappoint restless travelers who feel compelled to shake their booties in every capital of the world. **Salsa 54,** Avs. 1/3, Calle 3 (tel. 223-3814), is a disco bonanza. Separate dance floors play love songs, 60s hits from the U.S., and—by far the most popular—the eponymous *salsa.* Only the most daring *gringos* join the salsa masters under the colorful disco lights of the center state; the rest simply try to blend in on the dark dance floor (open daily 8pm-2am; cover Tues.-Sat. ¢350, Sun. ¢300, Mon., when the live band plays, ¢500; women free Wed. nights). **La Esmeralda,** Av. 2, Calles 5/7 (tel. 221-0530), next door to Tica Linda, is reminiscent of a real dance hall, featuring guitar music 8-9pm and Latin American favorites from the *mariachi* band until the wee hours. They serve a lunch buffet including a main dish, salad, and a refreshment from 11:30am-2pm (¢400-¢500). Dinners ¢500-¢3000, beers ¢180, but there's a ¢500 minimum per person after 11pm. For ¢1000, crooners will sing your favorite ditty (open Mon.-Sat. 11am-5am) The epicenter of Costa Rica's disco universe is **Centro Comercial el Pueblo,** an adobe maze of giftshops, bars, and dance clubs. **El Tango Bar** is a retro-style joint where the pianist pounds out the Argentine tangos of his glorious youth (open Mon.-Sat. 9pm-3am; no cover; drinks start at ¢180). **The Plaza Disco Club** (tel. 222-5143), located at the entrance of the Centro Comercial el Pueblo, plays more standard pop music and is often filled to the brim with teenagers on weekend nights (open Mon.-Sat. 7pm-4am. Fri.-Sat. cover ¢600, Sun.-Thurs. no cover but a ¢450 minimum bar tab.) Other popular discos located in the Centro Comercial el Pueblo include **Coco Loco** (tel. 222-8782), a smaller dance floor and an older crowd (open Mon.-Sat. 6pm-1am; happy hour 6pm; cover Fri.-Sat. ¢800, less on weeknights); and **El Infinito** (tel. 223-2195), heavy with fluorescent palm trees, a waterfall in one of the dance rooms, and other such kitsch. One of two dance rooms is intended strictly for the college-age crowd and features American favorites only, while the other blasts more traditional salsa beats, and plenty of bars and rooms for cozying span the distance between (cover Sun-Thurs.

¢300, Fri.-Sat. ¢500, includes first drink). **Discoteque Tonite** (tel. 223-0833), a gay disco, is located on Avs. Central/1, Calle 7.

For those who aren't up for a night on the town, there are a number of movie theatres that show fairly recent U.S. releases. And your Spanish skills don't need to be in their prime—most flicks are shown in English, with Spanish subtitles. In the center of downtown, **Cine Rey,** Av. 4, Calles Central/2 (tel. 221-0041), shows flicks daily at 4, 6:30, and 8:45pm (¢350). **Cine California,** Av.1, Calle 23 (tel. 221-4738), also shows 3-6-month-old U.S. releases daily at 4pm, 6:45pm, and 9:10pm (¢350). **Cine Magaly,** Av. Cent./2, Calle 23, is slightly more expensive, but shows current U.S. hits daily, at 4, 6:30, and 9pm (¢450).

■ NEAR SAN JOSÉ

VOLCÁN POÁS

Northwest of San José lies **Parque Nacional Poás,** a vast cloud forest laced with indígena trails shaded and moist with mosses, palms, orchids, and bromeliads (like pineapples). Poás makes a good daytrip for anyone tired of San José's dirt and noise, but unfortunately, it is the most visited park in the country, and thus it is increasingly difficult to see the allegedly numerous birds and mammals living there. Occasional shrill cries belie the presence of the quetzal, the bird sacred to the Maya. It is best to visit the park in the early morning, before clouds and tourists cramp your style. The park's highlight is the steam-belching crater of the emunctory **Volcán Poás** (2700m above sea level), a 10-minute walk from the parking lot through a tunnel of ferns and gnarled, moss-covered trees. Bright green fumaroles—bubbling vents in the earth's crust—pock the bottom of the 1.5km-wide, 300-meter deep hole. In a 1910 eruption, the volcano produced a cloud of ash 8km high, and it still occasionally emits a geyser-like plume. The volcano suddenly ran out of steam between 1953 and 1955, and since 1981 it has simply released acidic gases, causing significant damage to cattle, coffee crops, and strawberry fields. Nothing is real, or so it seems from the vista from the park, where the boiling fumaroles can often be seen erupting, but it's never a given that activity will be visible. For a more sure-fire spectacular view than the bubbling pits and capricious crater, follow the trail for a 10-minute hike to Laguna Botos, a flawless 450-meter wide, sparkling blue lake—the kind of place you suspect exists only in postcards.

The visitor's center is equipped with a museum, souvenir shop, a video about the national parks, bathrooms, and a small coffee shop (open daily 8am-3:30pm; entrance to the museum is free and its signs are mostly in Spanish; entrance to the park ¢2400). On Sundays, buses run directly but slowly to the park from San José, leaving from the Parque de la Merced, at Avs. 2/4, Calle 12, at 8:30am and returning at 3:30pm (round trip ¢700). The bus stops at the Parque Central in Alajuela at 9am, and at the **Restaurante El Poás** about 20 minutes before arriving at the park, where you can pick up a delicious *batido* (¢125) or have a dialogical conversation with a talking parrot. English spoken (but not by the bird). There is no direct transportation to the park on weekdays. Buses do, however, run to **Poasito,** a small village 10km from the park. You can also a taxi to the park from **Poás,** a town 25km away from it, which costs about ¢900 each way.

VOLCÁN IRAZÚ

Parque Nacional Irazú, 54km east of San José, is an ideal destination for those who want to escape San José but who aren't up for a jaunt to Poás. Even the drive up to **Volcán Irazú,** which at an elevation of 3432m is the tallest volcano in Costa Rica, provides an amazing view of the farmland and the prodigious vegetation of the Central Valley. The volcano, however, seems positively unearthly—much more like the set for a sci-fi movie, with its bleak, moonlike craters, all covered in black ash. The volcano last erupted on March 9, 1963 (the same day John F. Kennedy arrived in Costa Rica for a presidential visit), when it coughed up "cold" lava (mud) and caused the evacuation of 200 villagers from the nearby town of Fatima. The massive

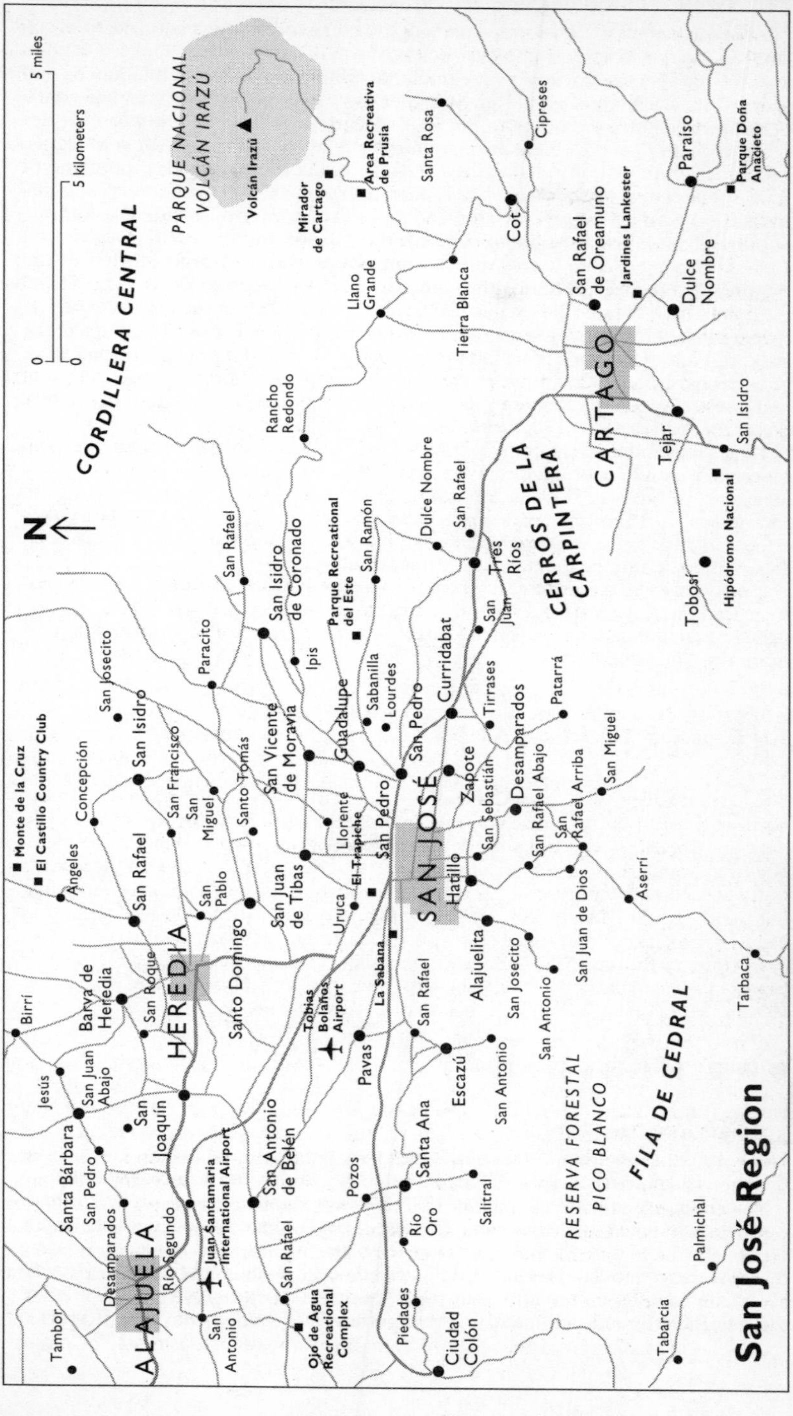

San José Region

blast of earth and ash transformed parts of the green forest into a gray, dusty wasteland, and so the area remains. Nevertheless, the park surrounding the volcano hosts a variety of species: coyotes prey on a large rabbit population, while juncos and sparrow hawks flit through the air. At higher elevations, harsh environmental conditions favor life-forms common to the South American Andes; the few avian species hardy enough to survive here are hummingbirds, which hibernate on cold nights, and squat, hunched on red-flowered bushes during the day. Today, only one of Irazú's four craters, *cráter principal*, is perceptibly active. 100 meters deep, this crater is filled with yellow-green water, and looks like an enormous witch's cauldron. Supposedly, it is also possible to see both the Atlantic and the Pacific Oceans and Lago de Nicaragua from Irazú's summit, but clouds usually obstruct all views without prejudice, especially during the rainy season. In fact, most of the volcano's highest points are off-limits; the established trail only circles half of the *cráter principal.* Arrive early, before the fog sets in, and dress warmly. There is a small cafeteria in the park, run out of the back of an old green truck. Coffee and tea cost ¢100 and sandwiches cost around ¢200, but the menu is quite limited. Offering a wider selection and portlier prices, the **Restaurante Linda Vista** is located about a third of the way down the road (coffee ¢150, *tortilla de queso* ¢225).

To get Volcán Irazú, catch the yellow school bus across the street from the **Gran Hotel de Costa Rica** in San José, next to the Plaza de Cultura, at 8am on Saturdays and Sundays. The bus also stops in from of the Cartago ruins at 8:30am. It leaves Irazú promptly at 12:15pm and arrives back in San José around 3pm. The round-trip costs ¢760 and park rangers charge another ¢2400 to enter the park. The park is open 8am-3:30pm. Camping in Irazú Park is not permitted.

It might also be easier to reach parts of **Parque Nacional Braulio Carrillo** (see Near Heredia, page 341) from San José than from Heredia. A Coop Limon bus (tel. 223-7811) to the park leaves San José every half hour from 5:30am-7pm and departs from Avs. 7/9, Calle 12.

THE CENTRAL VALLEY

The Central Valley, or **Meseta Central,** is a high and vast region cordoned off to the north and south by the great volcanic mountain ranges that divide Costa Rica in two; the **Cordillera Central** and the **Cordillera de Talamanca.** Many of the volcanoes that bound the horizon on all sides are still active, and have caused the valley's residents heartache more than once in the history of its post-Columbian civilization, but their ash have also blessed these temperate plains with fertile soil enough to feed several nations. And so it's no surprise to hear that almost two-thirds of all *ticos* have come to find their livelihoods in this valley, and that four of Costa Rica's five largest cities mark its center. Almost every trip to the country begins and ends in the Meseta Central, if not in San José then in one of its outlying neighbors.

■■■ HEREDIA

Perched atop rolling hills 11km north of San José, Heredia (pop. 30,000) is a laid-back, mid-sized university town, swelling full of local pride. Since its founding in the 1570s, Heredia has seemed a bit out of step with the rest of the nation. Throughout the colonial era, Heredia lagged behind Cartago in wealth and stature. After Mexico won its independence from Spain in 1821, Heredia's residents campaigned to have Costa Rica annexed to Mexico—but the rest of the country disagreed. Costa Ricans chose Heredia as their capital briefly in the 1830s, but soon reconsidered, sending the government to San José instead. Once home to small tobacco farms, Heredia eventually jumped on the coffee-growing bandwagon; today coffee and cattle are the town's livelihood, and many residents commute to work in San José. Heredia is

a neat, well-kept city, cooler and cleaner than the capital, its pride reflected in the exquisitely tidy Parque Central and Mercado Municipal.

Orientation and Practical Information Leaving the station, the bus from Heredia to San José passes a stadium to its left and takes a sharp left onto Av. 6 before passing **Parque Central,** the center of action in Heredia and a good place to disembark. Three blocks south and one block west of the park is another useful point for orientation, the **Mercado Municipal.** Heredia's streets are arranged in a grid aligned with the four points of the compass. *Calles* run north-south; *avenidas* run east-west. An air-tight logic prevails: Parque Central is bordered by Avenida Central and Calle Central.

The **police** patiently await your call (tel. 237-0438). A central police station can also be called (tel. 237-0438), but it's easiest just to dial the special number for **emergencies** (tel. 117). Exchange traveler's checks at the **Banco Nacional,** Avs. 2/4, Calle 2 (tel. 261-0403), at a 0.75% commission for the change to colones (open Mon.-Fri. 8:30-3:45pm). The **post office,** Av. Central, Calle 2 (tel. 260-0461; fax 260-6767), is across the street from the northeast corner of the Parque Central, and has *lista de correos.* Those with something pressing to communicate can send a **telegram** or a **fax** from the post office. Telegrams cost US$0.50 per word to the U.S., US$0.75 per word to Europe; faxes go for US$2.50 per page to the U.S., US$3.50 per page to Europe (open Mon.-Fri. 7:30am-5:30pm; Sat. 8am-noon). **Pay phones** cluster gregariously on the north side and southwest corner of the Parque Central. **Buses** from Heredia to San José depart from Avs. 7/8, Calle 1 (¢58). **Taxis** wait on Av. 2 between Calles Central and 2, to the south of Parque Central, and on the east side of the central market on Calle 2. The **Mercado Municipal,** bordered by Calles 2 and 4 and by Avs. 6 and 10, satisfies most basic nutritional needs (open Mon.-Sat. 6am-6pm, Sun. 7am-noon). Non-urgent medical difficulties can be handled at **Farmacia Benini,** Avs. 4/6, Calle 2 (tel. 237-0371; open Mon.-Sat. 8am-1pm and 3-7pm), but more urgent matters should be handled by the **Red Cross** (tel. 237-1115).

Accommodations Finding a cheap room in Heredia is as easy as getting wet during the rainy season. **Hotel El Parqueto,** Avs. 6/8, Calle 4 (tel. 338-2882), is inexpensive and friendly to boot. There is no hot water, and the plaster walls are sprinkled with a little graffiti, but this family-run hotel is pleasant and relatively secure—rooms are girded by sturdy deadbolts. The communal toilet has lost its seat, but comes with plenty of reading material. There's an 11:30pm curfew Mon.-Fri.; respect it: a family lives here (¢750 per person, cash only). **Hotel El Verano,** Avs. 6/8, Calle 4 (tel. 237-1616), just a few steps north of Hotel El Parque, had a color-blind decorator, but the rooms are grime-free; there is 24-hr. access, and the two collective bathrooms were recently upgraded to a semi-rugged state (but there's still no hot water. ¢1000 per person.) If you have some money you're just a-dyin' to spend, ramble on to **Hotel Ramble,** Av. 8, Calles 10/12 (tel. 238-3829; fax 237-0803), a very clean private home, though the green awning outside and the astro-turf lining the stairs lend the place a country-club feel. Shoot a birdie, then enjoy spotless white walls, desks in each room, and the standard private bath with elbow-room. TV can be brought in on request (singles US$25, doubles US$30).

Food Gastronomic options in Heredia favor the rough-and-ready. Any of the fruit and vegetable stands or *sodas* that crowd the **Mercado Municipal** can quench simple cravings at the drop of a *sombrero.* Alternatively, the **Super Canasta Basica,** Av. 10, Calles 2/4 (tel. 237-1303), carries most everything (open Mon.-Fri. 8am-8pm, Sat. 7am-8pm, Sun. 8am-1pm). Even more daring supermarket shoppers should check out **Rayo Azul,** Avs. 4/6, Calle 6 (tel. 261-0006), featuring a deli, cosmetics counter, and a feast of free samples (open Mon.-Sat. 8am-9pm, Sun. 8am-7pm).

For real meals 'round the clock, there's always **Soda y Restaurante Cafetín,** Avs. 2/4, Calle 2 (tel. 260-4320). Inside, it's dark, clean, and cool—ideal for zoning out in front of the TV while sipping a cup of coffee (¢60). A chicken breast with fries and rice runs a mere ¢425, but don't eat the accompanying salad unless you've seen them rinse it in *agua purificada.* **Soda Caballo Blanco,** Av. 10, Calle 4 (tel. 237-0643), is located across from the southwest corner of the central market. If you've ever wanted to act in a spaghetti western, this is your chance; pull a Clint Eastwood through the chest-high swinging doors, or stage a showdown between the two opposing entrances. Cold drinks sell for ¢120; *casados* run ¢275 (open daily 6am-9pm). Or just take in some open air and open minds with university students at **Fresas,** Av. 1, Calle 7 (tel. 237-3915). The *batidos* (¢210) come in tall glasses and the fruit salad with ice cream (¢415) is large, assuring plenty of time for conversation under the red-and-white awning (open daily 8am-midnight).

Sights and Entertainment A cosmopolitan college town, Heredia retains the knowing air of San José while shedding the frenetic pace and urban grime of the capital. The immaculate **Parque Central,** Avs. Central/2, Calles Central/2, is perpetually crowded with chatting retirees and pigeons that swoon between its tall trees, monuments, statues, and benches. A massive fountain and a gazebo stand at the center of the park. Supremely collegiate plaques quote Cervantes to proclaim the importance of tranquil centers for thought.

The pleasantly ventilated **Iglesia de la Concepción,** Avs. Central/2, Calles Central/3, overlooks the east side of the park and relaxes with its doors propped open on western, northern, and southern sides—flocks of birds fly on cool breezes above worshippers' heads. Massive columns and rows of attentive pews face the church's gleaming altar, which will celebrate its 200th birthday in 1997. The adjacent **Jardines de la Immaculada,** gardens dedicated to the Virgin Mary, are tucked into the northeast corner of the park. Its rarer plants, like the Japanese cypress, are marked with a sign, while daisies and orchids grow in organized and perfect cultivation.

Housed in what was once the residence of Presidente Alfredo Gonzales Flores, the **Casa de la Cultura** (tel. 260-2588) stands on the northeast corner of the park. Local artists exhibit their works here on a rotating basis, and the main meeting room houses concerts and lectures. Even when the building is completely empty, the security guard is still eager to give tours (open daily 8am-10pm; admission free). The **Fortín de Heredia** waits nearby, a curious little fort built in 1824. Its tower is ringed by funnel-shaped slits designed to maximize defensive rifle range while minimizing the snipers' exposure to enemy bullets. Ask at the municipal building next door for entrance to the locked tower. Peer out through the slits and view Heredia through the eyes of a terrified soldier.

Five blocks east of the cathedral on Avenida Central is the **Universidad Nacional.** To the casual visitor, the university resembles a large garden interrupted by incidental classrooms—college on the veranda. A bookstore located in the center of campus sells books, T-shirts, and postcards (open Mon.-Fri. 8am-11:45am and 1-4:30pm). When you tire of pawing through sweatshirts and notepads emblazoned with the university logo, head to the **Cine Isabel,** Av. 2, Calles Central/2, just south of the Parque Central, which shows U.S. releases already relegated to video stores north of the Río Grande (shows Mon.-Fri. 8pm, Sat.-Sun. 3pm and 8pm; ¢225).

■ NEAR HEREDIA

PARQUE NACIONAL BRAULIO CARRILLO

Named for Costa Rica's third president, P.N. Braulio Carrillo lies 19km north of San José. The enormous reserve encompasses a whopping 109,000 acres and is home to a phantasmagoric Noah's Ark of flora and fauna; more than 6000 species make their home here. Jaguars and puma compete for nimble deer while howler monkeys watch from arboreal bleachers. Hummingbirds, mountain robins, bare-necked umbrella birds, and the rare, revered quetzal share the park's moist airways. The ostoche, a nocturnal raccoon-like creature with a striped tail, haunts the park in its witching hours. The dense forest is equally diverse: cypress, bitterwood, camphor, mayo, and the Poás magnolia all hold their own against the dominant native fir. Some of the park's giant oaks pre-date the Spanish conquest. In the dry season, the park drips under a misty canopy of clouds; in the wet season, the mist turns to a constant stream of rain. A staggering 4.5m of rain falls on the forest each year—4.5m is taller than Neil Young on Patrick Ewing's shoulders. Vast expanses of the park are still unexplored, hundreds of its species still uncounted.

The cheapest way to see the park is by trekking up one of the many uphill hiking trails accessible form the Zurquí or Quebrada Gonzales stations, where the ¢2400 admission fee is paid. Ask the ranger which trails are safe, especially during the rainy season, when the paths can get slippery and muddy. From the paths, there are amazing vistas of the thick primary forest—tree ferns and palms, red-and-yellow epiphytes, and *sombrillas del pobre* (huge hand-shaped leaves—"umbrellas of the poor") that seem to extend without end. Buses leave from Avs. 7/9, Calle 12 in San José every 30min. (daily 5:30am-7pm), stopping at both stations. Wait on the highway for the return bus, which comes every 45min. during the same hours.

The financially blessed can get a spectacular, one-of-a-kind view of the park in an aerial tram ride (tel. 257-5961; fax 257-6053). Made out of a converted ski lift, the 2.6km tram takes adventurers into the forest's canopy, up to see everything that's out-of-reach during a normal jaunt through Braulio Carrillo. The most common sight is the prevalent *bota rama,* also called "broccoli tree" for its bushy tufts of leaves. Bright red flowers called "hot lips" pucker up, and *lianas* (wooly vines) twist around tree branches before tumbling into the tram's path. An English-speaking naturalist guide leads the 90-min. tram ride as well as short, interspersed hikes, pointing out the different varieties of butterflies, hummingbirds, and insects along the way. But lest you get too excited: the tour costs ¢8450 (US$47.50). If there's any way to spare the money, though, it's a great way to splurge. (Tram hours: Tues.-Sun. 6am-3:30pm, Mon. 9am-3:30pm. Reservations strongly recommended.)

VOLCÁN BARVA

Making an expedition from Heredia to **Volcán Barva,** which lies inside the southwestern quarter of the forest, is slightly more difficult. From Heredia, take the bus headed for San José de la Montaña, which departs from the south side of the Mercado Municipal (Mon.-Sat. 6:30, 11am, and 4:30pm, Sun. 11am and 4:30 pm, ¢70). Bite the bullet and get up at six to catch the earliest bus—there's a long hike ahead. Buses return to Heredia from San José de la Montaña at 7:30am, 1, and 5pm. Ride the bus as far as the driver will go, to a place called **Paso Llano** (about an hour), then begin the 6-km walk uphill from San José de la Montaña. The first half of the trail is paved, but the last three km traverse a rough, rocky, and eroded road. (Think twice about attempting this hike anytime between April and December, when the rainy season leaves the trail awash in mud.) After about two hours of steady hiking you'll reach the Volcán Barva **ranger station** (open daily 8am-4pm, entrance fee ¢2400). Although camping is prohibited elsewhere in the park, it's permitted in the vicinity of the Barva ranger station for a fee of ¢300 per person. Ask the ranger to show you where to camp, and notify the station when you leave. The facilities have space for 10 tents and provide access to clean water and toilets. If you plan to camp, bring a sleeping bag and warm clothing; it gets wet at night.

The initial 6km before even reaching the park is pleasant, though it comprises most of the walk. On one side, cows graze in bucolic pastures (some of the farmland here is owned by the family of ex-president and Nobel Peace Prize winner Oscar Arias Sánchez); on the other side, the tall, thin pine trees are reminiscent of the Swiss Alps. The path up to the park isn't tended, though, so watch out for mud and slippery rocks, as well as bellicose bulls whom trespassers might rile.

After the Barva ranger station, the scenery becomes familiar Costa Rican rain forest. An hour-long hike (2.85km) on a moss-lined path lies between the station and the first lagoon, **Laguna Barva.** The moss is everywhere, some of it brown and delicate like lace, some of it covering otherwise bare trees, making them look green and fuzzy. The trail leads up to the very edge of the lagoon, its banks circled with tiny, gummata-like pebbles of volcanic ash.

An acidic pool cupped in the crater of an extinct volcano, Laguna Barva is too caustic for fish, but its waters suit a menagerie of aquatic insects. A second lagoon, **Laguna Copey,** is another hour (5km) away. A fast hiker maintaining a strong, leg-burning pace can make it to Laguna Barva and back to San José de la Montaña in time to catch the 1pm bus back to Heredia. Other trails beginning near the Barva ranger station branch off in various directions; don't stray from the trails.

Although there are a couple of *sodas* on the way up, it's a good idea to bring food and water along. Also remember that since the volcano is 2.9km above sea level, it's likely to be very cold at some points; expect rain and wind year-round. Whether you plan a fast daytrip or a hard-core, overnight stay, bring appropriate clothing, keep the calories flowing, and stay hydrated.

■■■ ALAJUELA

Perhaps best-known today as a stop on the Interamerican Highway, Alajuela is a city with a heroic past. In 1821, Alajuela (known then as Villahermosa) lent strong and active support to the movement for independence from Spain; the city's reward for this painful commitment came in the next decade, when it served (briefly) as the nation's capital. When the notorious U.S. military adventurer William Walker spearheaded an invasion of Costa Rica in 1856 (see page 264), the hero of the defense was a soldier from Alajuela, Juan Santamaría, ever since a profligate namesake. These days, Alajuela has passed out of its rough-and-ready adolescence, settled into a comfortable middle age, and developed a fruity bouquet. Mature beyond repelling invaders, Alajuela now welcomes the battalions of tourists who use the city as a base for visiting nearby attractions. Only 3km from the Juan Santamaría Airport and 18km northwest of San José, Alajuela is a convenient first or last stop on a Costa Rican tour and a fine place to rest your head.

ORIENTATION AND PRACTICAL INFORMATION

The streets of Alajuela form a grid: *calles* run north-south while *avenidas* run east-west. Odd-numbered *calles* fall to the east of Calle Central, even-numbered ones to the west. Odd-numbered *avenidas* run to the north of Avenida Central; even-numbered ones to the south. Be forewarned, however: many street corners are not marked. Further warning: both Av. 9 and Calle 12 are called **Calle Ancha.**

Tourist Office: Instituto Costarricense de Turismo (ICT) Airport Branch (tel. 242-1820). There is no office in Alajuela proper; rely on the ICT's airport office. Open daily 8am-9pm.

Police: (tel. 117), or try the central station (tel. 441-6208).

Currency Exchange: Banco Nacional, Avs. Central/1, Calle 2 (tel. 441-0373). Exchanges traveler's checks. Open Mon.-Fri. 8:30am-3pm and 4-6pm.

Post Office: Av. 5, Calle 1 (tel. 441-8107), with an EMS Courier sign in front. *Lista de correos.* **Fax** and **telegram** service available. Open Mon.-Fri. 7:30am-5:30pm. **Postal code:** 4050.

Telephone: At the Parque Central, Avs. Central/1 and Calles Central/2. **Taxis: Cootaxa** (tel. 442-3030), and **Taxi Punto Azul** (tel. 442-5051).

Buses: During the day, buses leave for San José from the TUASA station (Avs. Central/1, Calle 8) every few minutes; in the middle of the night, expect to wait up to 1 hr. Buses typically stop at the airport on their way to San José, but check with the driver and simultaneously prevent long detours to Heredia and other nearby cities. Buses go to Sarchí (every 30min., 5am-10pm, 90min.), to the Finca de Mariposas in Guácima Abajo (daily at 6:20, 9, 11am, and 1pm; 40min.), and to Volcán Poás (from Parque Central, Sun. at 9am; 1 hr.).

Car Rental: Solid, Av. 1, Calles 5/7 (tel. 442-5042; fax 442-0144). Rentals start at US$42 per day for the first 2 days, 150km limit per day. For 3 days or more, US$37 per day and unlimited mileage. Insurance included. Must be 21 and have a major credit card. Open Mon.-Sat. 8am-6pm. **Manglar,** Av. 2, Calle 3 (tel. 442-1534). Prices start at ¢7000 (US$43) per day, including insurance and unlimited mileage. No minimum age to rent cars, but drivers under 21 must leave a US$660 deposit. Open Mon.-Fri. 7:30am-5:30pm, Sat. 7:30am-noon.

Pharmacy: Farmacia Chavarria, Av. Central, Calle 2 (tel. 441-1231), next to the Hotel Alejuela. Open Mon.-Sat. 8am-7pm.

Hospital: Av. 9 (Calle Ancha), Calles Central/1 (tel. 441-5011). No English spoken. **Red Cross:** (tel. 441-3939).

ACCOMMODATIONS

Most of the inexpensive hotels near the bus station charge either by the hour or by the night; local rumor has it that some of these hotels are places of ill-repute. There are, however, reasonable overnight options in other parts of the city.

Pensión Alajuela, Av. 9 ("Calle Ancha" strikes again), Calles Central/2 (tel. and fax 441-6251), across from the courthouse. Feeling hot? Enjoy hot sandwiches and hot water all day long. Alternatively, you can chill your head in the communal refrigerator, lounge on the outdoor patio, or peruse parts of the tidy indoor library. Cable TV in the lobby, which doubles as a a bar. Cantabrigian owner hasn't forgotten his English. Laundry ¢1100 per load. Guests have 24-hr. access. One room with bath is wheelchair-accessible. Singles or doubles with bath ¢3500, doubles without bath ¢3000, triples without bath ¢3500.

Hotel Alajuela, Avs. Central/1, Calle 2 (tel. 441-6595; fax 506-441-7912). A creatively named, newly renovated establishment. Comfortable rooms, complete with phone, overhead fan, and an amazingly clean private bathroom. Laundry service available 8am-5pm (US$8). Guests have 24-hr. access. Wheelchair-accessible. Some of the rooms even have balconies. Alas, all of these luxuries must come at a stiff price—singles US$36, doubles US$40, triples US$43. Maybe a splurge for night just off the plane, though.

FOOD

Marisquería la Sirenita, Av. Central, Calles Central/1 (tel. 441-9681), across from the Parque Central. The name of this family restaurant means "the Little Mermaid," and Ariel's smiling face greets diners on the sign outside. A fish tank, shells decorating the walls, and a few plastic lobsters snared in a huge net on the ceiling quickly reveal the nefarious plans that this place has for her. *Arroz marinera* ¢500, lobster in garlic and butter (enough for 2) ¢2100. Open daily 9am-10pm.

La Tacarena, Av. 7, Calle 2 (tel. 441-2662). A pizza joint/tropical Caribbean cabin, from the bamboo-corduroy walls and seashell wind chimes to the sweltering heat that persists in spite of the ceiling fans. Large pizza ¢900, choice of toppings includes salami, ham, chicken, and a vegetarian mix. Open daily 10:30am-11pm.

Soda Puppy, Av. 4, Calles 4/6 (no tel.). Small (four seats at a counter) and friendly—you know, like a puppy. Ignore the shack-like exterior and come in to chow down on some incredibly inexpensive grub or chat it up with the talkative owner, who named the place after his exotically named dog. *Torte carne* ¢80, *empanadas* ¢80, cake ¢70, *refrescos* ¢60. Open Mon.-Sat. 7:30am-7pm.

Ital Pan, Av. Central, Calles 4/6 (tel. 441-6139). A convenient bakery, perfect for a quick bite to eat, heaven for sweet teeth. *Cachos de mantequilla* (similar to eclairs) ¢70, peach and strawberry *tortas* ¢150. Open daily 6am-9:30pm.

Tikal, Av. Central, Calle 6 (tel. 442-6261). A grocery store well-stocked with fresh fruits and vegetables, deli items, and a variety of household items. Special section devoted to macrobiotic products (like granola). Open daily 8am-8:30pm.

SIGHTS

Alajuela has little in the way of traditional sights. The **mercado** (Avs. Central/1, Calles 4/6) smells just a little too much like a barn, and is surprisingly quiet compared to the central markets of most towns; this is probably due to the pleasant fact that it is composed mostly of fruit and vegetable stands, meat shops, and spice stores for the locals, rather than of souvenir stands. The **Parque Central** (Avs. Central/1, Calle Central/2) is crowded with shady mango trees and stone benches set around the perimeters of raised grassy islands. A small fountain adorns the center of the park, but more eye-catching is the huge white dome-like structure on the east side, surrounded by a moat and used for outdoor concerts. On the west side of the park stands an immense marble Neoclassical church, its twin towers rising in perfect symmetry over Corinthian columns at its entrance. Those starved for a more touristy experience might try the humble **Museo Histórico Cultural Santamaría,** Avs. 3, Calles Central/2 (tel. 441-4775), filled with historical mementos like medals and swords from the *Campaña Nacional* of 1856-57, in which local heroes followed Santamaría to defeat the American invader William Walker, thereby assuring independence for Costa Rica (open Tues.-Sun. 10am-6pm; admission is free).

■ NEAR ALAJUELA

The small village of **Sarchí,** about 30km from San José, is famous for its beautifully painted ox-carts, wooden wheelbarrow-like structures intricately designed with bright colors. To witness the birth of these masterpieces-on-wheels, visit the **Fábrica de Carretas Joaquín Chaverrí** (tel. 445-4412; fax 445-4111), at the entrance to the village, where they've been cranking out ox-carts and many other wooden handicrafts and pieces of furniture since 1903. Ask for 67-year-old Carlos Chaverrí, who has dedicated himself to the art since he was seven years old and loves to tell the story of the carts, which used to transport bananas and coffee from Limón to San José. Every several years there is a parade of ox carts, from which the single best among hundreds is chosen (open daily 7am-5pm). Just a few meters uphill is the **Plaza de la Artesanía** (tel. 445-4271 for the information center), a breeding ground for tourists with its 30 souvenir shops, all filled with wooden hand-painted knick-knacks. A full-sized ox-cart runs about ¢40,000, but for those lacking money or space, the pocket-sized version goes for ¢380. There are also a number of reasonably priced restaurants and cafeterias in the complex, including an ice cream stand mysteriously named after *los pitufos* (the Smurfs). The Plaza is open Mon.-Fri. 8am-6pm, Sat. 8am-6:30pm, Sun. 9am-6:30pm. To get to Sarchí directly, catch a bus from Alajuela, Av. Central/1, Calle 8 (daily every 30min., from 5am-10pm, 90min., ¢85), or catch the bus to Grecia from the Coca-Cola station in San José (about every 40min. Mon.-Sat. 6am-10pm, 1 hr., ¢95) and then catch one of the constantly running local buses to Sarchí (15min., ¢35).

Although **Parque Nacional Poás** (see above, page 336) is actually closer to Alajuela than to San José, it's much easier to reach from the capital. If you insist on making the trip from Alajuela, first catch a bus to San Pedro de Poás; from there, take a cab. Expect to pay about ¢2700 for the cab.

Fly on, Little Wing

Southwest of Alajuela in La Guácima lies the renowned **Finca de Mariposas** (tel. and fax 448-0115), a spectacular stomping ground for our fuzzy, airborne friends. The four-acre farm at La Guácima has become Latin America's oldest exporter of butterflies, selling over 70 different species all over the world. A covered garden filled with exotic ferns, bright flowers, and even a small waterfall, is left open to visitors year-round, and the butterflies glide overhead, flittering just overhead, even landing on the arms and shoulders of some of the visitors who lose themselves to the surreal experience. Come early during the day if it's the rainy season; the roof is just a screen and the water causes the insects to hide. Dry conditions also make it easier to hike along the dirt paths of the 700 square-meter outdoor garden, which includes a couple of banana patches, an area supporting medicinal plants like aloe, and a bee garden, where pollen-filled flowers attract hundreds of the buzzing insects. Admission runs ¢1240 (US$7), which includes a tour of the nursery, where an English-speaking guide explains the butterfly's life-cycle and shows specimen larvae, pupae, and chrysalises in cultivation. There is also a 30-minute video, available in four languages (open daily 9am-5pm, with tours starting every hour until 3pm).

To reach the farm from Alajuela, take the "La Guácima Abajo" bus from the corner of Av. 2, Calle 8, which departs at 6:20, 9, 11am, and 1pm. Tell the driver to stop at *la finca de mariposas.* Buses returning to Alajuela pass the farm at 9:45, 11:45am, 1:45, 3:45, and 5:45pm. Buses leave less frequently from San José, departing from Av. 1, Calles 20/22 (Mon.-Sat. at 11am and 2pm, 1 hr., ¢75—it's the bus going to San Antonio de Belén), and returning at 3:15pm.

■■■ CARTAGO

Cartago (pop. 90,000), lying 22km southeast of San José in the Cartago Valley, is a city defined by a few simple twists of fate. Founded in 1563, Cartago was the capital of the nation until 1823, when Costa Ricans realized the city was doomed to perpetual misfortune and moved the government elsewhere. Perennial disasters—both natural and human—have repeatedly destroyed the city. Without a Hannibal to defend it, pirates pillaged Cartago throughout the 17th century, and a string of violent earthquakes reduced all buildings to rubble. Today, no old buildings survive—the colonial-looking structures you see are all later imitations—but the romantic stone ruins of a demolished cathedral still stand proudly in the city's center. But good luck also blesses Cartago—the city is best known for **La Basílica de Nuestra Señora de los Angeles,** where a miracle graced the *cartageños* in 1635, and thousands of Costa Ricans still come to pray every August in order to try their luck against the lightning-never-strikes-twice principle. Visitors come to town to see the nearby botanical gardens and hot springs, but don't count on passing a pleasant night here—you may stop into a strange hotel, with the neon burnin' bright, but pretty soon you're likely to feel that emptiness inside—good budget accommodations are notably absent in Cartago.

Orientation Unlike most major towns in the Central Valley, iconoclastic Cartago does *not* have either a Avenida Central or an Calle Central. Instead, an Av. 1 and a Calle 1 form the two perpendicular axes of the city's street grid. Otherwise, Cartago follows the model of other mid-sized towns; *calles* run north-south, with even *calles* to the east and odds to the west. *Avenidas* run east-west, with evens to the north and odds to the south. At the city center, where Av. 1 and Calle 1 intersect, **Parque Central** encompasses the Ruinas, the cathedral destroyed by an earthquake.

Practical Information The **police** can be dialed free from any public phone (tel. 117). Traveler's checks magically become colónes (minus a 0.75% commission) at the **Banco Nacional,** Av. 2, Calle 3 (tel. 551-9350; open for exchange Mon.-Fri. 8:30am-3pm). **Banco Popular,** Av. 1, Calles 2/4 (tel. 551-8445), has 24-hr. **ATM** machines but does not exchange traveler's checks (open Mon.-Fri. 8:30am-8pm). The **post office** stands at Avs. 6/8, Calle 1 (tel. 552-4595). **Fax** service is available for ¢445 per page to the U.S., and telegrams cost ¢79 per word overseas (open Mon.-Fri. 7:30am-5pm). The **postal code** is 7050. The **bus station** at Av. 4, Calle 2, sends a bus every 10 minutes to San José (45min., ¢70). To catch a bus to Orosi, head to the bus station at Av. 1, Calle 4. Buses to Lankester Gardens are labeled "Paraíso" and depart from the south side of Parque Central. **Taxis** loiter throughout the city and wait by the phones with baited breath (tel. 551-9191, 551-0247). Snag some petrol at the **gas station,** Av. 2, Calle 4, under the big "Castrol" sign. The **public library,** Av. 2, Calle 3, is diagonally across from the Banco Nacional (open Mon.-Fri. noon-7pm, Sat. 9am-2pm.) The **Mercado Central,** Avs. 4/6, Calles 1/5, bustles with commerce seven days a week. **Farmacia Central** (tel. 551-0698) is on Av. 1, Calle 2 (open Mon.-Sat. 8am-8pm). **Hospital Max Peralta Jiménez** is at Avs. 5/7, Calles 1/3 (tel. 551-2806). No English spoken. To contact the **Red Cross,** just call (tel. 551-0421).

Accommodations and Food Don't plan to spend the night in Cartago. If by some fluke you find yourself stranded in town in the middle of the night, your options are severely limited. Most hotels in town are not places where a god-fearing family would want to pass the night. More respectable but pricier rooms at the **Los Angeles Lodge,** Av. 4, Calles 14/16 (tel. 551-09-54), next to the basilica, include complimentary breakfasts and private bathrooms with hot water. The Lodge can also arrange tours to the Orosi and Ujarras Valleys, Volcán Irazú, Lankester Garden, and other nearby attractions.

Food in Cartago is basic. The **central market,** bounded by Avs. 4 and 6 and Calles 1 and 5, is the place for fresh fruit, vegetables, and bread. For packaged foods, head to **Supermercado Rayo Azul,** Av. 4, Calle 6 (tel. 551-0000; open daily 8am-8pm). The prototypical Costa Rican *soda* is **Soda Pollo Brumoso,** Av. 2, Calle 10 (tel. 551-9090)—quick, no-frills *comida típica* (traditional food). No tables here—just stand and eat at the counter. Half-chickens ¢450, half-liters of cold beverages ¢100, and half-cups of coffee ¢25 (open daily 8am-4pm). Down the street is **Integro Sui,** Av. 2, Calles 10/12 (tel. 551-0003), a vegetarian *soda* with only enough space to squeeze in two tables and call it cozy, though the owner might bring over fresh roses to brighten things up. Pasta with salad, bread, and a drink goes for a mere ¢400, and fruit salad for ¢275 (open Mon.-Fri. 9:15am-3pm and 6:30-9pm, Sat. 9:15am-5pm). **Restaurant AutoServicio 88,** Av. 4, Calle 1 (tel. 551-6004), is an inexpensive self-serve buffet joint serving everything from mashed potatoes to stir-fry. On the way in, note the phony plastic entrees displayed in glass cases—fortunately, real dishes here taste better than their plastic *Doppelgängers* look. Fill up on beans and rice, with a cold coke to top it off, for just ¢245.

Sights and Entertainment In Cartago the main attraction is **La Basílica de Nuestra Señora de los Angeles,** bordered by Avs. 2 and 4 and Calles 14 and 18. Per-

haps the most famous place of worship in Costa Rica, the cathedral is a sacred destination for the hundreds of *ticos* who make the annual pilgrimage from San José every August 2, many of whom walk the whole 22km from the capital to Cartago. According to believers, a small dark statue of the Virgin Mary was found by a *mestizo* peasant girl on that site on August 2, 1635. When the statue was removed, the dark-skinned Virgin appeared in the flesh, right on the spot. The vision was interpreted as a divine directive to end racial segregation in the city and the original cathedral was erected on the site. Destroyed by an earthquake in 1926, the basilica was rebuilt as a Byzantine wooden shell, illuminated by delicate stained-glass windows. The cathedral's interior is crammed full with cabinets containing myriad offerings to the Virgin—medallions, notes, a set of bongo drums, a baseball, a piece of burnt wood salvaged from a house fire, a cycling jersey, and dozens of small metal trinkets, each molded into the shape of a body part believed to be healed by the Virgin. At the northeast corner of the basilica, a flight of stairs leads down to *la cripta de la piedra* (the Crypt of the Stone), where a statue of La Negrita holding the infant Jesus in her arms is perched atop the boulder where she was supposedly first sighted. In a ritualistic healing gesture, pilgrims rub the stone under the Virgin and then rub their heads, arms, and feet.

A church of a different sort stands smack in the center of town at Avs. 1/2, Calle 2/4. The crumbling walls of the **Parque Ruinas** were once part of a short-lived cathedral. Built in 1575, the cathedral was dedicated to Apostle Santiago, the patron saint of Spain, and there it stood until it was wrecked by an earthquake in 1841. While the cathedral was reconstructed, it was destroyed by another quake in 1910. Today, the grounds surrounding the ruins are a public park and a testament to the victory of creeping, vegetable entropy over ephemeral human vanities. Trees have now grown taller than the old cathedral walls themselves, leaves sprout from cracks in the crumbling stones, and orphaned chunks of the church now serve as modest benches. Inside the park hides a lovely garden surrounded by tall, ruined walls and containing a pair of ponds. The garden itself is now closed to the public, but curious visitors can peer in through gates and barred windows.

■ NEAR CARTAGO

Jardín Botánico Lankester

Jardín Botánico Lankester is 6km east of Cartago, near the village of Paraíso. An internationally famous garden dedicated to the preservation of tropical flora, Jardín Lankester was founded in the 1950s by Charles H. Lankester, a British naturalist, and is currently maintained by the University of Costa Rica. The garden is home to a remarkable variety of epiphytes, parasitical plants that leech off of other vegetation, as well as an incredible 800 species of orchids—a good fraction of the 1400 species of orchids found in Costa Rica. But this isn't any old typical flower garden—it's a maze of prolific growth lifted carefully from the country's 12 different microclimates. Tossed all together all pell-mell, the hodge-podge of plants make for quite a visual mishmash—rinky-dink palms with leaves fanning out willy-nilly next to towers of bamboo bent under their own weight, just a few feet away from the of moss-covered riff-raff that dangles purple-flowered vines down across the zig-zagging trail—and that's no flim-flam. Crossing over a log bridge into the tropical rainforest area, which receives over a meter of rain each year, is especially breath-taking. The sign at the entrance says that a self-tour should take about an hour, but it's almost too easy to lose oneself and take twice as long. To get to the Jardín Lankester from Cartago, catch a bus destined for Paraíso from the south side of the Parque Ruinas (daily every 30min. from 4:30am-10:30pm; 15min.; ¢30), and tell the driver you want to get off at the garden. From the drop-off point in front of Restaurante Casa Vieja, take a brief hike down a well-marked gravel road (open daily 8:30am-3:30pm; self-guided tours are allowed to begin every 30min; admission ¢500).

Orosi

The small village of Orosi, 15km south of Cartago, functioned peacefully as a communal society during most of the colonial 16th century, long before Marx ever dreamed of such a thing. Today, it is best known for its aging **adobe church,** set in the middle of a small valley cultivated for coffee. Built by Franciscan missionaries in 1743, the thick-walled white adobe structure is surrounded by flowers and palm trees and humbly stands back behind the main road. Enough years of hot sun and torrential rain have made its red roof tiles fragile and rusty, and weathered its elderly church bells into a graceful green patina. Inside, wooden columns rise from the brick floor to the roof and paintings of a crucified Christ droop from the adobe walls. The intricately carved wooden altar at the front of the church is painted gold and adorned with a few forlorn plastic flowers. There are a number of superstitions connected with the church—that a headless man was seen climbing the bell tower, that there is a tunnel leading from the inside of the building to the nearby mountains, that incurable ills can somehow be remedied there. Adjoining the church, the **Museo de Arte Religioso,** a collection of Christian relics from the 1699-1766, earns its keep by wooden sculptures of Jesus and Mary from Guatemala, paintings by known Mexican artists, manuscripts, priest's robes, and an old wood-and-leather bed from the church's convent days (open daily 9am-noon and 1-5pm; ¢150).

A pleasant 2km walk through rolling hills and coffee plantations leads to **Los Patitos** (tel. 553-3070), the mineral baths which are Orosi's other claim to fame. Soothing water is pumped through a kilometer-long pipe from a hot springs to Los Patitos; at the source, the water is a hot, hot, hot 60°C (140°F) but cools to a mere 50°C (122°F) by the time it bubbles out of the pipe into the pool. For that sauna sensation, sit in the hot springs until your brain bursts, next induce cardiac arrest by jumping into the adjacent cold-water pool, then fortify your hopes of recovery at the restaurant nearby. Usually, though, the water continues to lose temperature in the pool (a lukewarm 35°C, not much different from a tub of bathwater). (Pools open Tues.-Sun. 8am-4pm.; admission ¢200; remember a bathing suit and towel.)

To get to Orosi from Cartago, take the bus waiting on the southeast corner of the ruins in the Parque Central (Mon.-Fri. every 90min, Sat.-Sun. every hour from 6am-10pm; 30min.; ¢53).

■■■ TURRIALBA

With the construction of the Guápiles highway 10 years ago, Turrialba lost its chance to become a major tourist hub. Now traffic on the way to the Atlantic coast can drive through Braulio Carrillo Park in a fraction of the time that a detour through Turrialba would entail, and shortly, even rail service to the city will be disconnected. Although it cost the town economic depression, it enabled Turrialba to maintain that old-time, small town, close-knit feel. Things don't move too fast or get too hectic around here; after all, what are you missing when you're surrounded by coffee, bananas, and sugarcane? Turrialba's charm comes from the fact that it is so *tranquilo;* a local once tempted to move to San José claims that the town's "spiritual energy" is what kept her here. Not only the mood, but also the rivers, pull people into Turrialba, and without the benefit of a strong undertow. The nearby Río Reventazón nets barrels of white-water rafters and kayakers yearly. Turrialba is also close enough to centers of important agricultural production and to Costa Rica's most important archaeological site that it still gets a taste of the commercial traffic that had distinguished its previous generations.

Orientation and Practical Information Like so many other Costa Rican cities, Turrialba's *calles* run north-south (actually, more like northwest-southeast), and its *avenidas* run east-west. Even-numbered *calles* run to the west of Calle Central, and odd ones to the east. Even-numbered *avenidas* run to the north of Av. Central, and odd ones are to the south. As a variation on the theme, the Parque Central is not bordered by the central roads; instead it is bordered by Calles Central/1 and Avs. 4/6. Street numbers, however, are practically useless, as very few streets are marked. More useful are a handful of landmarks, like the Parque Central and adjacent white church tower and the old train station in the southeast part of the town.

Traveler's checks can be exchanged for a 0.75% commission at the **Banco Nacional,** Av. Central, Calles 1/3 (tel. 556-0132; open Mon.-Fri. 8:30am-3:45pm). **Telephones** can be found at the southeast corner and on the south side of the Parque. The **post office,** Av. 8, Calle Central (tel. 556-0427) can **fax** and **telegram** (open Mon.-Fri. 7:30am-5:30pm). The **postal code** is 7150. There are two **bus stations**—one at Av. 4, Calle Central/2, serving San José and Siquirres every hour, the other at Avs. Central/2, Calles Central/2 for local routes, including the bus to Monumento Nacional Guayabo. **Taxis** can be found near the bus stations or the Parque Central, or call **Taxi Turrialba** (tel. 556-1844). The **Farmacia la Salud,** Calle Central, Avs. 2/4 (tel. 566-0239), is open Mon.-Sat. 7:30am-6:30pm. The **hospital** can be reached by phone (tel. 556-1133), or call the local **Red Cross** (tel. 556-0191).

Accommodations and Food Although Turrialba isn't a place where many tourists decide to hit the sack, there are nevertheless a couple of decent, inexpensive places to lay one's head for the night. **Pensión Chelita,** Avs. Central/2, Calle 4 (tel. 556-0214), is an apartment-style complex. Its spacious rooms come equipped with a fan and TV, and the bathrooms are also roomy, well-cleaned, and hot-watered. Rooms on the top floor have balconies, but no private bath (singles ¢1200, ¢1500 with bath; doubles ¢1800, ¢2000 with bath). The heart of **Hotel Interamericano** (tel. 556-0142), on Av. 1 along the train tracks, a family-owned joint, is in its lobby. Doubling as a restaurant, this downstairs room is cool and spacious, with dogs and birds to liven things up, as well as a TV and a jukebox booming Latin favorites. The rooms, however, are hot and box-like, but the walls, sheets, and bathrooms are spotless. Singles ¢1000, ¢2100 with bath; doubles ¢1800, ¢2100 with bath.

Bar Restaurante La Giralda, diagonally across from the gas station (tel. 556-1089), takes its authentic *a la leña* (a type of wood-fire roasting) cooking seriously, with a brick oven and huge rotisserie wheel in the window. Half a chicken, cooked *la leña* (of course), with fries, a salad, and tortillas runs a mere ¢390 (open Wed.-Mon. 11am-10pm). If the poster of a bikini-clad woman and the graffiti outside proclaiming "*No Gringos*" don't chase tourists away from **Pizza Julian** (tel. 556-1165), Av. 6, Calles Central/1, across from the north side of the Parque Central, they'll find uniquely themed pizzas like the "Mexicana," with jalapeños, ground beef, and onions. Large pizza ¢800-¢990 (open Mon.-Fri. 5-10pm, Sat. 3-11pm, Sun. 2-10pm). **Almacen Lorenzo Quirós** (tel. 566-0090), Av. 6, Calle Central, across from the northwest side of the Parque Central, has a fully-stocked supermarket (open Mon.-Thurs. 7:30am-12:30pm and 2-7pm, Fri.-Sat. 7:30am-7pm).

Sights and Entertainment Turrialba's **Parque Central,** Avs. 4-6, Calles Central/1, is a shining exemplar of the small town park. Emblazoned trash cans wear signs that preach against the evils of drug abuse, the gazebo in the middle of the quiet, grassy recreational area is dedicated to a local music teacher, and on the most Norman-Rockwellian of Costa Rican days, an aging band of mariachi players will haul out its instruments for a free concert. There's even a min-greenhouse with ferns and aloe plants growing inside, its walls woven of cyclone-wire fencing of thick enough a gauge to allow small birds to fly in and out of the structure at will. **Cine Norma,** Avs. Central/2, Calle 1, shows U.S. films that have been circulating in the States for 6-12 months (daily at 7:30pm; ¢300).

Turrialba is also the proud home of the Centro Agronómico Tropical de Investigación, or **CATIE** (tel. 556-6431), one of the largest tropical research centers in the world, with the largest English-language agricultural library in Latin America. Maybe that doesn't sound so thrilling, but any nature lover get a kick out of the 27,500-acre facilities, which include a number of orchards and greenhouses, as well as walking trails and a bird-friendly lake. Just call CATIE in advance to arrange a guided tour, or come without a reservation to enjoy the view. It's a pleasant four km stroll east through coffee plantations, or you may be able to snag the right bus out of Turrialba.

■■■ GUAYABO NATIONAL MONUMENT

Located 19km northeast of Turrialba, **Guayabo National Monument** is considered Costa Rica's most important archaeological site. Though it doesn't stand so tall when measured against the likes of Tikal or Copán, Guayabo's still worth a daytrip, as the only place in Costa Rica where the interaction between the natural habitat and the indigenous culture can be seen firsthand.

As there are no officially guided tours, it's definitely worth shelling out the cash for a self-guided tour pamphlet (just ¢50). From there it's almost too easy; simply follow the well-cleared path, which should take close to an hour (1200m), if you stop at each of the numbered signs to read about a different point of interest listed in the pamphlet. The pride of Guayabo, however, is the actual excavation site of the city of Guayabo, which was inhabited between 1000-1400 AD by a tribe centered around their *cacique,* or religious and political leader. From a lookout point along the trail, the remains of the city can be seen. From a lookout point, it just looks like a bunch of grassy mounds, but after following the trail down into the site itself, the *calzadas* (riprap roads), circular stone bases for buildings, bridges, and aqueducts finally become visible. Visitors are only allowed to roam within a small restricted area along the guided trail. It's possible to **camp** in the National Park (¢300), where you'll find a toilet, cold shower, and barbecue pits (park admission: ¢2400.)

Getting to Guayabo isn't too hard, but leaving is a real pain. From the local bus terminal in Turrialba, buses leave Mon.-Sat. at 11am (so if you're coming in from San José, be sure to catch the 9am direct bus to Turrialba), Sun. at 9am (1 hr.; ¢100), and drops its load smack at the ranger station at the entrance to the monument. But from at this point, problems develop. On weekdays and Saturday, the bus leaves Guayabo around 12:40pm and doesn't return again that day; 12:40pm does not leave enough time to see the monument. On Sun., the bus doesn't return until 5pm, long after the park closes. So the only thing left to do is to walk the 4km downhill from the National Monument to the main road, there to catch a 4pm bus from there to Turrialba. Unfortunately, this turns a one hour jaunt in the monument into an all-day excursion, but the only quicker option is to hitch back to Turrialba. Travelers say it's generally pretty safe and easy, and most people are headed to Turrialba anyway, but still, we at *Let's Go* don't recommend it.

Another option is to spend the night at **La Calzada,** a lodge located 400m downhill from the monument (tel. 556-0465; fax 556-0427; all rooms ¢2500). Or stop at the **restaurant** here before that long trek downhill—sit down on the converted front porch to devour a fruit plate (¢375) or *arroz con pollo* (¢475), among other things, or a soda (¢110).

THE PACIFIC COAST

The most Costa Rican of Costa Rica, the extended, beachside paradise of the central Pacific Coast is jam-packed with perennial traveler's favorites. In recent years, the biggest crowds have migrated south from the regional center of Puntarenas to the hip, young, and rad environs of small Jacó. Azure waves pound against hundreds of miles of rocky coastline and brilliant white-sand beaches. If you can find the space, this is an especially great place to pitch camp and make further expeditions up and down the Pacific side of this pacific country; its centrality may crowd many of its better-known beaches and the famous national parks, but it also ensures that you're never more than a daytrip away from whatever other *tico* towns and attractions your whimsy may lead you to. The **Monteverde Cloud Forest,** for instance, the most spectacular and widely renowned of Costa Rica's otherworldly rainforests, hides in the verdant northeast corner of the Puntarenas province.

■■■ PUNTARENAS

Puntarenas (pop. 86,000), the fading capital of the eponymous province, provides access to the beaches closest to San José, only 90 minutes away. Although the peninsula (the name translates literally to "sandy point") was once the busiest Costa Rican port on the Pacific coast, much of Puntarenas' economic vigor has been sapped by the newly constructed port of **Caldera,** 25km to the south. Half abandoned, the city has descended into a tragic decrepitude. Still, beaches and plentiful seafood manage to compensate tourist for other aspects of the surrounding area. *La chucheca,* a species of shellfish driven close to extinction, reigns over the culinary landscape. Other shellfish specialties include *la almeja* and *el mejillón.*

Ferries arrive on the north side, where Av. 3 is packed with services, shops, and cheap restaurants. **Paseo de las Turistas** encompasses the southern side of the peninsula and is home to most of the hotels and discos popular with *gringos.* But Puntarenas has clearly seen better, if not cleaner days; after a look at the polluted beach, most tourists board the ferry for someplace where they can actually swim.

ORIENTATION AND PRACTICAL INFORMATION

Calles run north-south; *avenidas* run east-west. Odd-numbered *calles* lie to the west of Calle Central; even ones are to its east. Odd-numbered *avenidas* can be found north of Avenida Central; even ones to the south. Avenida 4, at the southern end of the peninsula, is known as **Paseo de los Turistas** between Calles 3-15.

Tourist Office: Cámara Puntarense de Turismo (CAPUT) (tel. 661-1985), is not quite, yet. The first in a series of offices and shops across the street from the INS and on the north side of the museum. **Phone** and **fax** services. English spoken. Open Mon.-Fri. 9am-5pm, Sat. 9am-noon.
Police: (tel. 117), 1 block north of Banco de Costa Rica. Open 24 hrs.
Currency Exchange: Banco de Costa Rica, Av. 2, Calle 5 (tel. 661-0444). Open Mon.-Fri. 9am-3pm. **Banco Nacional,** Av. 3, Calle 1 (tel. 661-0033), a few blocks west of the market. Open Mon.-Fri. 9am-3pm.
Post Office: (tel. 661-0440), ½ block north of the church and just a few meters north of Surtidor la Lapa. *Lista de correos,* **telegrams,** and **fax.** Open Mon.-Fri. 8am-5:30pm, Sat. 8am-noon. **Postal code:** 5400.
Buses: (tel. 661-2158). Buses to and from Puntarenas are usually coordinated with the ferries. Departures to **San José** leave from Calle 2, Paseo de los Turistas (Av. 4), (daily every 30min. from 6am-7pm, 2 hrs., ¢405). Other buses leave from Calle 4, Av. 2: to **Liberia** (daily 5, 7, 9:30am, 3, and 5pm, 2½ hrs., ¢250), to **Cañas, Tilarán,** and **Volcán Arenal** (11:30am and 4:15pm, 3 hrs., ¢250), to **Jacó** (daily 5am, 11am, and 2pm, 2 hrs., ¢285), to **Quepos** (via **Jacó**—daily 5am, 11am, 2pm, 3½ hrs., ¢530), to **Santa Verde** and **Monteverde** (daily 2:15pm), and to **Barranca** (every hr., 20min., ¢30). Buses depart for **Orotina** leave from Super Mercado Pali at Avs. 1/3, Calle 5, across from Farmacia Andrea (4, 6, 9am, and 4:30pm, 1 hr., ¢100).
Taxis: Try **Coopetico** (tel. 663-2020) or **Coopepuntarenas** (tel. 663-1625). Herds of cabs congregate near the market, at Av. 3, Calle 2.
Ferries: Departing daily for **Playa Naranjo** (tel. 661-1069) from the dock in the northwest end of the peninsula (Calle 31, behind Av. 3), at 3:30, 7, 10:50am, 2:50, and 7pm (1 hr.; ¢280). To get to the dock, take the bus (¢30) to Barrio Carmen from Av. 1, Calle 2, in front of Chung Wah Restaurant, and get off at its last stop. Otherwise, grab a cab (¢170). Since the dock is about 3km from the San José bus stop, this is wise for anyone heavily encumbered or pressed for time. Ferries return to Puntarenas at 5:10am, 8:50am, 12:50, 5, and 9pm. ¢250 per person, children ¢120, cars ¢1500, four-wheel drive vehicles ¢1800, motorcycles and bicycles ¢450. Departures for **Paquera** (tel. 661-1444, ext. 118) leave from the northeast side of the peninsula, from behind the market at 6:15, 11am, and 3pm (90min., ¢220). Ferries return to Puntarenas at 8:15am, 12:30pm, and 5pm. Ticket booth in the blue-and-white building behind the market.
Laundromat: Lavandería Puntarenas (tel. 663-0171). Opens at 2pm.
Pharmacy: Botica Central, Avs. Central/1, Calle Central (tel. 661-0361), 1½ blocks south of Banco Nacional. Open Mon.-Sun. 7:30am-10pm.
Hospital: tel. 663-0033.
Red Cross: (tel. 661-0184), 2½ blocks west of the church. Open 24 hrs.

ACCOMMODATIONS

Though budget hotels and *pensiones* abound, their quality has declined. Fans are of the essence. Camping on the beach is not very sanitary, nor is it recommended.

Hotel Ayi Con, Avs. 1/3, Calle 2 (tel. 661-0164, 661-1477). The budget hotel of choice in these parts. Some rooms have fans, others are blessed with A/C. Either way you'll feel nice 'n fresh, hopefully enough to forget the lack of natural light. Private-bath-less rooms are a little more cramped, but the communal bathrooms are large (and have toilet seats). TV in lobby. Check-out 2pm. ¢975 per person, ¢1350 with bath, ¢1645 with bath and A/C.

Hotel Helen, Avs. Central/2, Calle 2 (tel. 661-2159). Clean rooms and decent communal facilities, but the toilet-seat thief has struck again. Some rooms have little wooden partitions called "private baths." No hot water, but the owner reassures that the showers are "naturally warm." 24-hr. access with key. Check-out noon. Traveler's checks accepted. ¢800 per person, ¢1000 with bath.

Hotel Río, Av. 3, Calles Central/2 (tel. 661-0331 or 661-0938), down an alley in a good, Jimmy-Buffet sort of way. Communal baths are OK, but the sage traveler follows a strict dress code for showering—nude, with sandals. Rooms without bath secured only by a slide-bolt latch. Storage available in lockers. Singles like shoeboxes ¢600, ¢1100 with bath; doubles ¢1000, ¢2000 with bath.

FOOD

For a welcome relief from the pricey establishments along the Paseo de los Turistas, try the cheap *sodas* in and around the market.

Soda Adita, in the market. An inexpensive, busy place to eat, with enough Spanish flying around that you'll probably feel more like a *gringo* than usual. Close to the Paquera ferry dock—good for a quick snack before the boat leaves. Rice with chicken ¢220, cheese sandwich ¢145. Open daily 6am-5pm.

Soda la Amistad, Av. 1, Calles Central/1 (tel. 661-2011). True to its name, this simple, cozy *soda* is friendly and welcoming, with fake flowers and bright pink tablecloths brightening up the interior. Sandwiches ¢150, *gallo pinto* ¢200. Open Mon.-Sat. 6am-9pm, Sun. 6am-noon.

Queen's, a few doors west of the tourism office. Indoor and outdoor seating in a pleasant, shaded area. For one peaceful meal, the rest of Puntarenas seems to disappear. *Gallo pinto* with meat ¢300, juice ¢80. Open Mon.-Sat. 7:30am-5pm.

Restaurant Club de Playa San Isidro, on the beach behind Cabinas San Isidro, 7km inland. Ocean breeze, big *palapa,* and tropical music make a meal on the beach especially dreamy. Fish filet in garlic sauce ¢450, pasta ¢300. Open Wed.-Mon. 9am-10pm.

SIGHTS AND ENTERTAINMENT

Aside from swimming—which isn't always a good idea, due to pollution in the area—there's not much to do here for most of the year. Puntarenas's modest **Casa de la Cultura,** Avs. Central/2 and Calles 5/7 (tel. 661-1493), houses the **Museo Histórico Marino de la Ciudad de Puntarenas,** displaying historical artifacts of the town's seafaring culture (open Mon.-Sat. 9am-noon and 1-5pm; admission ¢100). Experts on Iberian architecture will note that the peninsula's **church,** Calles 5/7, Avs. Central/1, is constructed in the Portuguese fashion, in the middle of the city park, rather than nestled *behind* the park, as is the less symmetrical Spanish style. **Playa de Doña Ana,** 14km from Puntarenas and 2km from Caldera, is a well-maintained beach with swimmable waters. Amenities include toilets, showers, and a restaurant (open daily 8am-4pm; admission ¢75). Another option is the beach behind Cabinas de San Isidro, 7km from Puntarenas; take any of the buses to

Hail Marys—Puntarenas-style

If you can swing it, come to Puntarenas during **La Fiesta a la Virgen del Mar** (July 9-16); the city self-ignites with concerts and dances on the beach for an entire week before the locally sacred holiday. The Fiesta commemorates the miraculous rescue of Don Meregildo, a *puntarense* big-shot from around the turn of the century. Meregildo and his crew would set sail every January, to return to the docks of Puntarenas loaded down with pearls, shells, and bushels of foreign *monedas* just in time for *Semana Santa*—when they would then unleash their new-found wealth to fund a big bash for the town. In 1913, however, a big storm caused the perennially debauched crew to lose control of their boat. Don Meregildo experienced an abrupt loss of chutzpah, knelt down on the deck, and prayed to the Virgin, promising a huge celebration in her honor, should his boat be returned safely to Puntarenas; in other words, he swore to continue his plundering, partying ways. When the ship limped into port, Don Meregildo threw an extravagant *fiesta* in the Virgin's name, hence the traditional, annual *fiesta.* Every summer, boats of all sizes gather along the shoreline and pass a statue of the Virgin from vessel to vessel.

Esparza, Miramar, Barranca, or El Roble (¢20). And there's always the **municipal pool** at the western tip of the peninsula (take a Barrio Carmen bus, ¢15). It offers clean water, showers, bathrooms, and a small refreshments kiosk. (open Tues.-Sun. 9am-4:30pm; admission ¢150, children ¢100).

When foot traffic in the park and plaza dies down to a patter, try the disco at **Hotel Oasis del Pacífico,** on the Paseo de los Turistas, where a disco ball shines its thousand glittering eyes down upon the dance floor and endless bar (open Mon.-Fri. 8pm-2am, Sat.-Sun. 1pm-1am; cover ¢100). For a mellower evening drop by **Cine Central,** on the southwest corner behind the church, which shows mostly U.S. films at 7:30pm and 10pm (¢200).

Most of the time, however, enjoying yourself in Puntarenas involves leaving the city. For a pretty penny or two, boats whisk tourists away to nearby islands, fishing sites, and national parks. Tours to nearby **Tortuga Island,** a protected forest, can be arranged through **Fantasia Tours** (tel. 222-0791). Boats touring Tortuga leave Puntarenas at 9am and cost US$65, including lunch. **Taximar** (tel. 661-1143) offers tours of San Lucas, an old island prison, for ¢5000-7000. Boats meet passengers on the north side of Playa Cocal..

■ NEAR PUNTARENAS: CARARA BIOLOGICAL RESERVE

Though Puntarenas province is home to numerous national parks and wildlife refuges, many are more accessible from San José than from Puntarenas city. The park most easily reached from Puntarenas is the **Carara Biological Reserve,** 57km southeast of Puntarenas on the road to Quepos. The reserve is particularly fascinating to biologists because it encompasses an "ecotone," a region where the wet tropical jungle of the south meets the dry forest of the north. In turn, these conditions give rise to a remarkable diversity of species, many of them endangered. *Carara* means "crocodile" in one of the area's indigenous languages, and sure enough, the threatened crocodile finds haven here in the muddy waters and silt-covered banks of the Tárcoles River. The crocodiles themselves are an amazing sight: surprisingly flat, with meaty-looking striped tails, they resemble enormous logs crawling across the mud on tiny, shriveled legs. Carara is one of the best places in Costa Rica to spot scarlet macaws; look up into dead trees for potential nesting sites. Macaws share the forest with white-faced monkeys, vibrant blue *Morpho* butterflies, poison dart frogs, and *fer-de-lance*—literally, "spearheads," large and extremely venomous pit vipers. Flora include rare purpleheart trees, water hyacinths buoyed by skirts of floating roots, and kapok ("silk cotton") trees which release a downy fluff that was used to stuff sleeping bags during World War II. The reserve was originally home to a fiercely independent indigenous community. When, in the 1560s, Juan Vasquez de Coronado came to conquer the area, the famed indigenous leader Garabito disappeared into the jungle, evading capture for years and by a clever ruse rescuing his imprisoned wife from the Spaniards' camp. Centuries later, the land itself was barely rescued from a proposed government development plan in the late 1970s.

To get to the Carara Reserve, take the 5am bus from Puntarenas toward Quepos. Coming from Puntarenas, you'll find the entrance of the reserve 4km after you cross the river (look for crocodiles as you bump over the river—it may be your only chance). Only a short, one-km trail stretches away from this entrance. A longer (5-km) and more interesting trail straight into the heart of the forest starts 2km before the official entrance, when you approach from Quepos. Look for a gate with a small black sign in yellow lettering. Both trails are well marked, once you find them, and not especially strenuous—engrossing yourself in the sounds of the jungle will not leave your legs feeling crampy. Ask at the ranger station to find out where camping is permitted (¢250 per tent), and give their toilets a go while you're at it; they're the last you'll see for a while (park open Tues.-Sun. 7am-4pm; admission free).

Other national parks accessible from Puntarenas are **Curú Wildlife Refuge,** 4km north of Paquera, and **Cabo Blanco Nature Reserve,** 11km southwest of Montezuma. For both, take the ferry to Paquera and then the appropriate buses.

■■■ JACÓ

Practically everyone can find a niche and a party to their liking at Jacó. Since it's one of the closest beaches to San José (100km, 2½ hrs. by bus), Jacó is an easy weekend and vacation spot for city-shackled *ticos,* who share the sands with truckloads full of tourists. Surfers come here and to nearby Playas Hermosa and Herradura for the killer year-round waves, and a startling number of ex-pat Canadians have decided to make Jacó their home. At night, they all hold court at the discos, bars, and casinos, giving Jacó its reputation as the party beach of Costa Rica. Jacó's sudden popularity has made it like an awkward teenager: a few years ago the town was hardly developed; now new hotels are popping up in uncontrollable spurts, and the weary-looking beach doesn't seem to know how to deal with the break-out. But no matter how grimy the sand may be, the waves still roll, the sunsets are still spectacular, and the beer still flows like there's no tomorrow.

Orientation and Practical Information It's pretty hard to get lost in Jacó. There's one main street through town where all the traffic courses, side roads leading to the beach every 100m or so. The eternally-under-construction bridge in the center of town makes a convenient landmark in a pinch.

For any and all sorts of information, head over to the **ICT office** (tel. 643-3000), in the center of town, 150m east of the bridge. They've got all the facts on tours, hotels, car rentals, and restaurants in the area, and they sell stamps and maps. They also have **public phones,** and for ¢100 can make connections for international calls (open Mon.-Sat. 8am-5pm). **The Budget Traveler** (tel. 643-3509) has an office at El Tabacón. Dial tel. 117 to reach the **police. Banco de Costa Rica** (tel. 643-3334, 643-3695), at the Plaza Jacó, 700m west of the bridge, exchanges cash and traveler's checks. **Casa de Cambio** (tel. 643-3640), across the street from the Red Cross, does the same for no commission (open Tues.-Fri. 8am-8pm, Sat. 8am-2pm). The **post office** (tel. 643-3479), with **fax** and **telegram,** is way out on the east side of town, near Hotel Jacó Fiesta (open Mon.-Fri. 8am-4pm). The **postal code** for Jacó is 4023. The **bus stop** is in the center of town, next to the Rayo Azul supermarket. **Buses** to San José leave daily at 5am and 3pm (2½ hrs.). The Puntarenas-Quepos bus passes through Jacó en route to both destinations. To Puntarenas, the bus passes through at about 6am, noon, and 3pm, but often arrives late (2 hrs., ¢285). To Quepos and Manuel Antonio, it passes through at 7am, 1, and 4pm (1½ hrs., ¢250). The bus to Orotina leaves at 5:30, 7, 9am, noon, 2, 4, and 5pm. Call for **taxis** (tel. 643-3290, 643-3030), or just look for one waiting near the bus stop. Car rental is available at **Ada Rent-a-Car** (tel. 664-3207), across the street and just west of the ICT office. Automobiles and motorcycles are available for US$35 per day, including insurance and free mileage. To rent a car, you must be 21 years old, have a valid credit card, and leave a US$75 deposit (open daily 8am-6pm). **Moped rental** is available at Toby's Rental (tel. 441-0642), on the west side of the bridge, just west of Restaurante Emily, for just US$6 the first hour, US$2.95 each additional hour, or US$25 first day, US$13 per additional day. **Supermercado Rayo Azul** (tel. 643-3025), in the center of town across the street from Cabinas el Recreo, is a well-stocked supermarket (open Mon.-Fri. 8am-6pm, Sat. 8am-9pm, Sun. 8am-6pm). Clean those dirty dishes at the **Lavandería,** next to the ICT office. One load washed, dried, and folded takes two hours and costs ¢500 (open Mon.-Sat. 9am-noon and 1-6pm). **Farmacia Jacó** (tel. 643-3205), 50m west of Camping el Hicaco, can take care of all pharmaceutical needs (open Mon.-Sat. 8am-9pm, Sun. 9am-5pm). There is no hospital anywhere in town, but the **Clínica de Jacó** (tel. 643-3238), on the east side of town, near Hotel Jacó Fiesta, deals with other medical problems; English spoken. **Red Cross** (tel. 643-3090, within Jacó (tel. 128) is 50m east of Camping el Hicaco.

Accommodations Jacó doesn't cater to budget travelers. It's a popular resort for both *ticos* and tourists; so hotel owners milk guests for all it's worth. Good luck finding affordable lodging in the high season; it helps to be in a group. **Aparthotel los Ranchos** (tel. 643-3070), down towards the beach on the first side street east of the bridge, is among the best options around for groups of three or more. Large, apartment-style quads have kitchens, or private split-level bungalows sleep six to seven. All rooms come with safe, private bathroom, hot water, a night watchman on duty; laundry service is available (triples US$25, quads with kitchen US$35, bungalow with kitchen (fits six or seven) US$50). Surfers receive an automatic discount. Call ahead to make reservations—this place is often full, even in the low season. **Chuck's Rooms and Boards** (tel. 643-3328), 300m west of the bridge; turn toward the beach at Jacó Bell. Chuck, a gnarly Floridian surfer, offers the only true budget accommodation in town. All the guests bond quickly, hanging out on the front porch and raving about the day's waves. Simple rooms with three beds go for US$8 per person year-round, and Chuck offers "bro deal" discounts to rad, long-term guests. **Cabinas Emily** (tel. 643-3328), 200m west of the bridge, behind Restaurante Emily. Owned by Chuck's mother-in-law (see Chuck's, above), these cabinas are nothing to write home about, but they're about as good as it gets within its price range. Ceiling fans keep the place cool and the beds are comfy. Private bath, but the shower is no more than an overhead faucet (doubles ¢2000, triples and quads ¢3000). **Camping el Hicaco** (tel. 643-3004), across the street from the Red Cross, is by far the cheapest option around. Since no camping is permitted anywhere on the beach, you can feel thankful to set up tent in the owner's patchy backyard. Picnic tables, showers, toilets, and laundry basins available. An exorbitant ¢400 per person.

Food Fine diners may complain about Jacó's dearth of fine top-notch cuisine, but restaurants along the main road serve fine budget travelers just fine, thank you.

The Garden Café (tel. 643-3404), 100m west of the bridge, is a bit costly but you won't have to eat again for a week—the large dinner entrees all come with all-you-can-eat salad, garlic bread, vegetables, and mashed potatoes. Excellent breakfasts and lunches are also served on the outdoor patio. Small submarine sandwiches ¢400; vegetarian Oriental stir-fry with fried rice ¢800, baby snook filet ¢1800 (open daily 6:30am-10pm). **Killer Munchies** (tel. 643-3406), just east of the Garden Café. Whoever dreamed up the toppings on these pizzas was a creative genius, and anything ordered is likely to be Killer, even if you're only hungry on life. All pizzas are cooked in a wooden stove, as you watch. Both the whole-wheat vegetarian (small ¢850, large ¢1600) and the Southern barbequed chicken (small ¢900, large ¢1700) are delightful (open Mon. and Wed.-Fri. 5:30pm-9pm, Sat.-Sun. noon-9pm). **Restaurante Emily** (tel. 643-3328), 200m west of the bridge, is a casual, inexpensive place to dine the *tico* way; Emily doesn't even try to brown-nose the surfers, but just delivers friendly service and tasty food at low prices (*gallo pinto* with eggs ¢350, soup of the day ¢350, fruit plate ¢400). **Chatty Cathy's Family Kitchen** (tel. 643-3479), on the east side of town next to Restaurant Sen Ly. Cathy's a warm, welcoming Canadian (and a big fan of the Tasmanian Devil and the Canadian Neil Young) who will tell her life story to whoever's ready to listen. Her breakfasts and baked goods are mouth-watering, from chewy chocolate-chip cookies (¢70) to fresh blueberry muffins (¢250) to heavenly cinnamon buns (¢275; open Tues.-Sat. 6am-2pm).

Sights and Entertainment It would be a crime to spend a Jacó day inside. Surfers come from far and wide to ride the waves, many citing **La Roca Loca,** a rocky peninsula to the south, as their favorite spot in town. Chuck of Chuck's (see Accommodations, above) rents good fiberglass boards for US$15 per day, and also does board repairs. **Fun Rentals** (tel. 643-3242), next door to the ICT, also rents boogie boards for ¢275 an hour, but when there are gorgeous beaches to either side of Jacó, riding a bike there is breezy; opt for one of Fun Rentals' 18-speed mountain **bikes,** loaned for US$2 an hour, US$11 a day, US$36 a week; or their single-rider **mopeds,** for US$10 an hour, US$30 a day US$100 a week. Credit card deposit required (open daily 8am-5:30pm, last rental is at 5pm). **Casa de los Cuadraciclos** (tel. 643-3035), just southeast of the bridge, rents out funky, pedal-powered go-carts, called "quadricycles" for ¢400. Or enjoy it all from the top of a **horse.** Go to Chatty Cathy's to ask about renting horses for ¢800 per rider. **Jacó Beach Horseback Riding Tours** (tel. 643-3248), across from Supermarket Rayo Azul, organizes expeditions of trails in the area (open daily 9am-noon and 3-6:30pm).

Nightlife ...is serious business around these parts. Going to the disco is not simply a weekend activity, any more than going to the bathroom is, and anyone who falls down just when the crowds finally empty out of one of these places is a goner. The largest and most popular dancing spot in Jacó is **Discotheque la Central,** 4 blocks southeast of the bridge, down a side street towards the beach. (Open Sun.-Thurs. 8pm-1am, Fri.-Sat. 8pm-2am, despite what the sign outside says. Cover ¢400-500, depending on the season.) A block away shimmers the smaller and no less-crowded **Disco los Tucanes** (open daily 8pm-1am; free). After the discos close, everyone stumbles over to **Pancho Villa's,** on the main road between the two discos, for some late-night grub. For a mellower evening of drinking and chatting, head over to **Bar el Zarpe,** in Plaza Jacó on the northwest side of town, where charismatic *bocas* (appetizers), like *ceviche de plátano* (nachos in a plantain dip), go for ¢100 each. Folks lucky enough to come on the right night simply tilt their throats back and let the bar pour down its special mix of pineapple juice and *guaro* (Costa Rican for "Everclear"), until they can't drink no more (open daily 4pm-midnight). Another late-night fave is the **Copacabana** (tel. 643-3131). Turn at Jacó Bell; it's down past Chuck's, all the way by the beach. Owned by Canadian sports fans who own the only 8m-wide satellite dish in town, ESPN is its station *de*-every-*jour,* the music is always cranking, and drinks always flow freely from the swim-up bar; live music on weekends during the high season.

■ NEAR JACÓ: PLAYA HERMOSA

Don't even think about confusing this idyll with the upscale beach on Península Nicoya of the same name. *This* Playa Hermosa is strictly for surfers, many of whom would be upset to see their favorite spot listed in a travel guide. Look down the secluded black-sand beach and see picture-perfect wave after wave roll onto the shore. Behind the beach, the extent of development is a few grass-roofed hotels and restaurants. Most of Playa Hermosa's surfers come for the day, but group accommodations are available. Rates are cheaper here than in Jacó, but unless you've an affinity for goats and cows, there's no comparing the two towns' nightlives.

Vista Hermosa (tel. 643-3422) has huge, apartment-style suites for groups of two, four, and eight people. All rooms have a kitchen, dining room tables, and immaculate private bathrooms. All this and more, including the owners' pleasant company, and all for only US$10 per person, less if the group is bigger. At **Cabinas las Olas** (tel. 643-3687), live out that childhood fantasy of ruling the perfect clubhouse. Wooden ladders outside grant access to the second floors of these doll-housy private bungalows. On the bottom floor, there's a kitchen, refrigerator, and bathroom with hot water; upstairs are the beds and fans. Rooms for two US$26, for three US$30, for four US$40, for five or six US$45. Make reservations. The **Restaurante Ola Bonita** (tel. 643-3422), adjacent to the Vista Hermosa, serves its patrons on an indoor porch graced by enough sweeping ocean views that it's like being outside. Look for the big gazebo with a dried palm-leaf roof just behind the beach, then look behind it. Vegetarian spaghetti ¢535, grilled chicken ¢600 (open daily 9am-9pm).

Playa Hermosa is only about 5km south of Jacó and there are several ways to get between the two. **Walking** takes about one hour, but the beach won't take you directly; you have to walk along the main highway. Rent a **bike** in Jacó and make the trip in 20 minutes. It's a somewhat arduous ride up the hill, but the return leg makes for smooth sailing. Or spare the sweat and catch a bus to Quepos, asking to be dropped off here. Buses to Quepos pass through Jacó daily at 7am, 1pm, and 4pm.

■■■ QUEPOS

Way back when, Quepos (7km north of Manuel Antonio) used to be a booming banana port and fishing town. Nowadays, all that's left of those times is a decrepit dock and a couple of private sportfishing boats. Quepos is trying to regain its prosperity by taking advantage of its serendipitous proximity to the popular **Manuel Antonio National Park.** In the way of impediment, the dingy streets of Quepos are none too comely, its beach no good for swimming, and drugs and crime are a growing bane. Still, hotels are generally nicer and cheaper than those in Manuel Antonio, and it's easy to grab a bus over to the park. Quepos also tries to lure tourists with its ever-expanding nightlife, which includes many bars, a disco, and a casino.

Orientation and Practical Information Quepos fits into that neat grid pattern; *calles* running north-south and *avenidas* running east-west. Odd-numbered *calles* fall to the east Calle Centra, and the one even-numbered *calle* to its west. Odd-numbered *avenidas* fall to the north of Avenida Central, the even ones to the south, and **Av. Central bis.** and **Av. 2 bis** to the north of their namesakes. Calle Central and Avenida Central don't meet up anywhere special; the bus stop and Central market are at Calle Central/1, Avs. Central/Central bis.

La Buena Nota (tel. 777-0345; fax 777-1002), just before the bridge, is a good place to go for all sorts of general information about the area (open Mon.-Sat. 8am-4:30pm). Exchange cash or traveler's checks at **Banco de Costa Rica,** Av. 2 bis, Calle Central (tel. 777-0285; open Mon.-Fri. 9am-3pm). There are **public phones** on the east side of the bus terminal. The **post office** (tel. 777-1471) is way down Av. Central, at the soccer field. There's a *lista de correos* there, as well as **fax** and **telegram** service (open Mon.-Fri. 7:30am-5:30pm). **Postal code:** 6350. The **bus station** is right next to the central market, at Avs. Central/Central bis, Calles Central/1. Direct **buses** leave daily for **San José** (6am, noon, and 5pm; 3½ hrs.; ¢870); others stop along the way (5, 8am, 2, 4pm on a 5-hr. route with stops). Buses leave for Puntarenas at 4:30am, 10:30am, and 3pm, stopping in Jacó on the way. Buses to San Isidro and Dominical depart at 5am and 1:30pm (3½ hrs.). The local shuttle between Manuel Antonio and Quepos runs often (thirteen a day, each way, 20min., ¢50), leaving the park from its main entrance. **Taxis** wait on the street in front of the bus station, or call **Coopetico Quepos** (tel. 777-0425) or **Taxis Unidos** (tel. 777-1837). Car rental is available at **Elegante Rent-a-Car** (tel. 777-0115), on Calle 2, north of Av. 1, next to La Buena Nota (open Mon.-Fri. 7:30am-noon and 1:30-5:30pm, Sat. 7:30am-noon). There's even a pharmacy open every day: **Farmacia Botica Quepos,** Av. 2 bis, Calle 2 (tel. 777-0038; open Mon.-Sat. 7am-7pm, Sun. 7am-2pm). Call the **Red Cross** (tel. 777-0116). The **hospital** is all the way down Calle 2, towards Manuel Antonio (tel. 777-1397).

Accommodations and Food Rooms and private bath are clean and simple at **Mar y Luna,** Av. Central bis., Calles Central/2 (tel. 777-0394), but it's the atmosphere that makes this place. Alvaro, the owner, is friendly even for a *tico,* and a short stay here can win you a pal for life. Refrigerator privileges, and a TV in lobby (¢1000 per person). Across the street, the recently built **Hotel Melissa,** Av. Central bis., Calles Central/2 (tel. 777-0025), has spotless white walls, immaculate sheets, and private bath, but no hot water. Rooms facing the street are brighter, but a bit noisy. TV in lobby, refrigerator privileges. ¢1130 per person.

Restaurante y Bar Marquesa, Avs. Central bis./1, Calle 2 (tel. 777-0004), has amazingly low prices, tasty food, and good service. Beware, though; they charge that pesky 20% service tax. *Gallo pinto* with eggs ¢175, *refresco natural* ¢70, whole fish ¢450 (open Mon.-Sat. 6am-10pm, Sun. 6am-4pm.) **Pizza Gabriel's,** Av. Central bis., Calle Central (tel. 777-1085). Some will swear that this is the best pizza they've ever tasted, but apparently not enough; it's not usually very crowded. Pies range in size from *pequeño* (1 person) to *super grande* (6 people). Large pizza (feeds 3) with everything on it ¢1200 (open daily 7am-11pm). **George's American**

Bar and Grill, Av. 2 bis., Calle Central, is the place for homesick *gringos* to go to stew over some familiar food in a Cheersy setting. But not all the waitstaff will know your name, or even your language, though George is a genuine *norteamericano*. BLT ¢545, bacon cheeseburger ¢745, cheese omelette with homefries and toast ¢545 (open daily 8am-11pm; happy hour, with ¢100 beers and free *bocas*, 5-7pm).

Entertainment and Nightlife Nobody in Quepos expects the tourists to stick around during the day—that's what the Manuel Antonio beaches and national park are for (see below). There are a few sportfishing and river-rafting agencies offering daytrips, but they generally cost ten times the price of a Budget Fun-filled day. **Ríos Locos,** Av. Central bis., Calles Central/2 (tel. 777-1647), offers a day of white-water rafting, kayaking, and an "eco-río-psycho tour" on the Río Savegre or Río Naranjo for US$65.

But where Quepos really tries, and where it really shines, is in its nightlife department, charged with the formidable task of luring everyone back into town after dusk. **Discotheque Arco Iris,** across the bridge at the north end of Calle 2, is a popular place for young ticos and tourists alike to shake their booties to incessant reggae until after the sun goes down (open daily 7pm-2am; ¢300 cover charge on Sat.). A beautiful place to pass the early evening is the garden setting of the bar **La Boca Nueva,** at the north end of Calle 2, just before the bridge. Every evening around 6pm, pairs of green parrots fly into the treetops to play and, ahem, do a little more than just dance the merengue. La Boca also serves short, tasty shots of a bright blue secret brew called a pitufo ("smurf", ¢75; open daily 4-11pm). Diehard crap-shooters who don't deign disco crowds daring enough may prefer the ritzy **Casino Kamuk,** Av. Central, Calles Central/2 (tel. 777-0379), which is always more than happy to milk every last colón out of its gamblers, while prodding them on with free drinks and, to be safe, a free taxi ride home (open daily 8pm-3am). The **Pub Kamuk,** Av. Central, Calle 2, is a mellow spot to listen to live music and contemplate how to get back home after losing all your money at the casino next door (open daily 10pm-3am).

■■■ MANUEL ANTONIO NATIONAL PARK

At **Manuel Antonio National Park,** warm, jade-green waves lap at the edges of lush, tropical forests. Popular with both nationals and foreigners, Costa Rica's smallest national park can seem more like a human zoo than a secluded preserve. The park's white-faced monkeys have been photographed and fed into a pigeon-like state of chubby dependence. However, if you diligently search out a special spot you will be rewarded with a generous stretch of sand all to yourself and your furry or feathered companions. Despite the crowds of humans, spectacular and rare life-forms still manage to subsist in Manuel Antonio. Brown pelicans plumb the watery depths while sea turtles lay eggs in the sands. Tyrant hawk-eagles reign over brown boobies. Three-toed anteaters and two-toed sloths collaborate on counting to ten. Fifty-nine species of bats share the park with howler monkeys, gray foxes, iguanas, crabs, and ctenosaurs (not dinosaurs but iguana-like creatures).

Manuel Antonio is most renowned for its four spectacular beaches. The first, **Playa Espadilla,** actually lies outside the national park and is popular with surfers, swimmers, and sunbathers who want to skip out on the park's admission fee. Enter the park just past Cabinas Manuel Antonio and the adjacent short stretch of sand. Cross the stream, enter the forest, and you'll come upon the park ranger's booth (admission ¢2400; open daily 7am-4pm). The second beach, **Playa Espadilla Sur,** extends south from the park's entrance. Its perfect white sand and radiant blue waters are breath-taking, even when packed to capacity with tourists (which is practically a given on weekends and during the entire high season). That tree-covered peninsula ahead is **Punta Catedral,** which used to be an island. One hundred thousand years of sediment deposits created a *tómbolo,* or natural bridge, connecting the point to the mainland. A circular hike around the perimeter of the peninsula takes about 30 minutes. On the other side of Punta Catedral lies the third beach, **Playa Blanca** (a.k.a. **Playa Manuel Antonio**), another popular tourist spot, thanks largely to its proximity to the picnic area, bathrooms, showers, and clean running water. In fact, the only way to escape the crowds and enjoy the luminous turquoise waters in peace is to make the 20-minute hike to the fourth and least-accessible beach, **Playa Puerto Escondido.** The walk, which involves a bit of rock-climbing, can only be made during low tide, so head back before the water rises. Along the path to Puerto Escondido, there is a break in the road, with another trail leading to the **Mirador.** The walk to the Mirador kindly requires a 45-minute hike through jungle paths filled with lazy blue butterflies and hanging vines. Camping is not permitted anywhere in the park or on the beaches.

ACCOMMODATIONS AND FOOD

Staying in nearby Quepos (7km north) is cheaper than in Manuel Antonio, but not quite as convenient and definitely not as scenic. However, a few bargains can be found in Manuel Antonio. To find **Cabinas Irarosa** (tel. 777-1089) for instance, walk 50m beyond Costa Linda, past the Coca-Cola sign. Clean-floored private baths abound, though the tiles above shoulder level have seen better days (singles ¢1500, doubles ¢2400, larger rooms ¢1300 per person). To reach **Albergue y Travotel Costa Linda** (tel. 777-0304), go east up the road, past the Soda Marlyn and over the slight incline; it's on the left. Some of the doors' locks look flimsy, but the rooms and the communal bathroom are clean, and the staff is helpful and amiable. Storage space, language classes, and even boomerang lessons are available (singles ¢900, dorm-like rooms with bath and kitchen ¢1200 per person). **Hotel Manuel Antonio** (tel. 777-1237) has snagged that prime location just before the entrance to the park. Rooms are all passable, but they leave groups in a dilemma: singles are clean and comfortable, with a fan and a sink, but singles share an outhouse and shower with the campers (singles ¢1500, doubles ¢2500, triples ¢3000). No camping is permitted in the park or on the beach, but Hotel Manuel Antonio allows campers to pitch tent in their backyard for ¢300 per person, including toilets and showers.

Most restaurants in Manuel Antonio offer authentic dishes in a simple setting. Popular for its excellent and hearty dishes is **Soda Marlyn** (tel. 777-1134), a road's-width up from the beach. Surfers come here to refuel and trade stories in fluent Spanglish; anecdotes are typically preceded by a near-missed high-five and an enthusiastic *"Sí,* man, *sí. Buenos*! Best wave!" Chow down on rice with chicken (¢495), *casado* with fish or chicken (¢475), or sandwiches (open daily 7am-10pm.) Farther north up the beach waits the **Restaurante Mar y Sombra** (tel. 777-0591, 777-0510), where you can wave-watch from a shady beach-side table roofed by interlocking branches and palm leaves, all the while gulping down spaghetti with sausage (¢450), T-bone steak (¢1500), and beer (¢150). Lather up with bug repellent before dinner (open daily 7:30am-11pm).

ENTERTAINMENT

There's no lack of sun-soaking activities outside the national park. During the high season, the **Fun in the Sun** beach rental folks loan boogie boards (¢300 per hr., ¢1200 per day), snorkel equipment (¢300 per hr., ¢1200 per day), surfboards (¢500 per hr., ¢1500 per day) and big beach umbrellas (¢1500 per day). During the rest of the year, go to **Howard** by Soda la Perla, on the main road near Soda Marlyn, who charges slightly higher rates but rents during the low season too. Boogie boards ¢350 per hour, ¢1200 per day; snorkel equipment ¢1200 per day. The Manuel Antonio area is also a beautiful place for horseback riding. **Hotel Mariposa** (tel. 777-0355), on the main road about halfway between Quepos and Manuel Antonio, rents horses for ¢1500 per hour. **Marlboro Stables,** about 300m north of Restaurant Mar y Sombra, is reputed to offer better rates.

■■■ MONTEVERDE RESERVE

The **Reserva Biológica Bosque Nuboso Monteverde,** 184km northwest of San José and due north of Puntarenas, encompasses 27,400 acres and is one of Costa Rica's most famous environmental preserves. The area was settled in 1951 by 44 Alabama Quakers, some of whom had served jail time as conscientious objectors to U.S. military activities. Seeking private peace in Costa Rica, a nation with no armed forces, the Quakers established a community of farms in the northwest. The vast tract of land they set aside as a wildlife refuge was christened the Monteverde Cloud Forest Reserve in 1972; a privately owned forest, it is administered by the all-volunteer **Monteverde Conservation League.** Bordering the Monteverde Reserve is the **Bosque Eterno de los Niños** (Children's Rainforest), purchased for preservation in 1987 by a group of concerned Swedish elementary-school children, and expanded and maintained by charitable contributions from all over the world. The Children's Rainforest is not open to the public, however, except for the **Bajo del Tigre trail** on the Pacific slope (open daily 7:30am-4:30pm; admission ¢600, ¢300 for students with ID). Guided tours are available; call 645-5003 or fax 645-5004.

Together, the preserves are home to more than 600 species of animals—two-thirds of which are birds—and over 2500 species of plants. Evergreens draped with mosses, ferns, and clinging orchids populate its cool, wet slopes; "elfin" forests of stubby, wizened trees grow at higher elevations. The Monteverde Reserve's most famous residents are its rare golden toads, members of a species not found anywhere else in the world. Unfortunately, these unique creatures have not been spotted in the reserve for more than a decade, and are feared to be extinct. A more common but still elusive resident of the reserve is the queztal, a vibrantly colored bird worshipped by the Maya. Jaguars, opossums, howler and spider monkeys, foxes, armadillos, and mountain lions haunt the forest. Its diverse collection of birds includes falcons, parrots, hummingbirds, egrets, owls, woodpeckers, and toucans.

Admission to the Cloud Forest Reserve is ¢1440, ¢720 for students with ID. A **visitor's center** (tel. 645-5122) at the entrance to the park provides information and sells generic doo-dads (open daily 7am-noon and 1-4pm). Three-hour guided tours in English begin at 8:30am (US$15)—sign up at the hummingbird gallery near the entrance. Night hikes start at 7:15pm (US$12; tel. 645-5118, 645-5311). If you choose to spend the night at the reserve, the visitor's station will provide you with a bed, access to communal showers, and three square meals for US$20. Inside the reserve itself, a few lodges with bunks and kitchens provide a free night's stay for hard-core backpackers. Bring a sleeping bag and food, and get a map at the ranger's station; the hike to the shelters may be wet and muddy.

GETTING THERE

To reach the Monteverde Reserve from San José (see San José, Practical Information, page 328), take the bus that departs from Avs. 9/11, Calle 14, daily at 6:30am and 2:30pm (3½ hrs., ¢905). A more comfortable option for travel between San José and Monteverde is to take the microbus from **Tico Explorers, S.A.** (tel. 645-5051), which leaves from the Toruma Youth Hostel (US$12). A daily public bus also leaves from Tilarán at 7am (3 hrs.). From Liberia, take a bus to San José (or any bus traveling along the Interamerican Highway) and ask to be let off at Lagarto, a tiny town 35km from Monteverde. Wave down the San José bus as it passes by, around 7:30am and then again at 3:30pm. Once off the main highway, the bus to Monteverde begins its 35-km ascent along the walls of deep, emerald valleys. There are no guard-rails along the road, so enjoy the spectacular, unobstructed views of forests and farmland in the valleys below. The bus passes through the town of **Santa Elena** 3km before it reaches the village of Monteverde. The bus back to San José from Santa Elena doesn't leave until either 6:30am the next morning (Mon.-Thurs.) or 3:30pm the next afternoon (Fri. and Sun.). A bus to Tilarán departs daily at 7am (3 hrs., ¢250). All buses leave Santa Elena from the stop in front of Restaurante Daykiri.

From Santa Elena, the reserve is either a moderately long walk or an expensive taxi ride (¢1000) away.

PRACTICAL INFORMATION

Santa Elena is a good place to run errands and take care of little chores. The **police station** (tel. 645-5166), next to the post office, opens at 7am. **Banco Nacional** (tel. 645-5027), at the end of the main street, changes traveler's checks (open Mon.-Fri. 8:30am-3:45pm). The **post office** (tel. 645-5042), atop the first hill you crest on entering Santa Elena, has **telegram** and **fax** services (open Mon.-Fri. 7:30am-5:30pm) The **postal code** is 5655. Restaurante Daykiri has **public telephones. Market la Esperanza** (tel. 645-5068), across from the post office, provides alimentary staples and toiletries (open daily 6:30am-8pm) Call for a **taxi** (tel. 645-5148). The **bus stop** is across the street from Restaurante Daykiri (see Getting There, above). Buy San José tickets in advance from the Marza Transporte ticket office there (tel. 645-5159 in Santa Elena; 222-3854 in San José; open Mon.-Fri. 6am-noon and 1-4pm, Sat.-Sun. 6am-noon and 1-3pm). **Chunches** (tel. 645-5147), on the main road toward Monteverde, has a **laundromat** (¢350 wash, ¢350 dry, ¢100 soap) and a **bookstore** with English-language novels and U.S. publications (open Mon.-Sat. 9am-6pm).

ACCOMMODATIONS AND FOOD

Lodging is available both in the village of Monteverde and in Santa Elena. There is a bigger selection of budget hotels in Santa Elena, but the walk to the preserve is nearly 6km. Most accommodations are family-run and serve homemade meals for an additional charge. In **Monteverde,** soothe your bones at **Pensión Manakin** (tel. 645-5080). Mario and Yolanda Villegas and their young children welcome guests to small but comfortable rooms, some with private bath. Yolanda and her daughter cook delicious breakfasts (US$3) and dinners (rooms US$7 per person, with bath US$18 per person). Another option in Monteverde is sleeping in or just outside the reserve (see above). In Santa Elena roosts **Pensión el Tucán** (tel. 645-5017), which teems with young backpackers. Rooms are comfortable, with nice wood walls and clean private and communal bathrooms with hot water. Breakfast (¢350) and dinner (¢500) available from a good-sized menu (rooms ¢1000 per person, ¢1500 with bath). **Hotel Albergue Santa Elena** (tel. 645-5051), besides being a tourist information center and an IYHF-affiliated hostel, has surprisingly cozy, well-built, and tastefully furnished rooms. Private bathrooms are large and spotless; shared bathrooms are a little more run-down (US$15 per person with bath, US$10 in low season; US$10 per person without bath; US$5 in low season). **Pensión el Colibri** is about as cheap as it comes in the Monteverde area, and although the rooms would make a decent display case for a hummingbird taxidermist, they're actually quite cozy. The family who owns it puts the "accommodate" back into Accommodations. Ask for an upstairs room, with new redwood floors. Shared bathroom has hot water and fuzzy, plush rugs. Meals available (¢600 per person, ¢500 in low season).

Most of the family-run hotels serve homemade meals to their guests, so restaurant selection is sparse. **Stella's Bakery,** across from CASEM in Monteverde, should not be missed, though—her rich chocolate brownies (¢125) and other mouth-watering pastries are famous throughout Costa Rica and make the trip to Monteverde worthwhile on their own (open daily 6am-5pm). Coming down from the Monteverde Reserve, the first restaurant is the vegetarian **Hira Rosa,** with all-natural cuisine on the tables and all-natural art on the walls. **Johnny's Pizzeria** (tel. 645-5066), down the hill toward Santa Elena, has good calzones and even better pizza. Cheese pizza, small ¢545, large ¢1240; vegetarian calzones, small ¢670, large ¢1510; fettuccine alfredo ¢850 (open daily 1:30-9pm).

SIGHTS

Although the Cloud Forest Reserve is Monteverde's most famous attraction, it's by far not the only thing to see or do here. In fact, there are so many interesting little excursions here that a short trip to Monteverde can turn into nearly a week-long stay (especially during the wet season, when it usually rains half the day).

The **Santa Elena Reserve,** located 5km from the town of Santa Elena, was created in 1989 to relieve some of the burden of excessive tourism from Monteverde's slooping shoulders. Home to some of the same species of flora and fauna as the Monteverde Reserve, this is a cheaper alternative, and it won't leave you feeling like a packed sardine. Points within the Santa Elena Reserve reach the highest altitudes in the area (some of them over 1700m), providing magnificent lookout points. The walk here and back is a hike in itself, so some may want to take a taxi (reserve open daily 7am-5pm; admission US$5. The **Ecological Farm** has a couple of well-maintained trails running through primary and secondary cloud forest. Every so often there's a waterfall, one of the rolling Monteverde hills with the gulf of Nicoya in the background. Most trails take around two hours or less to traverse. Several species of small, furry animals live here, including coatimundi (weird, snouted, cat-sized humanoid things). Sadly, it's rumored that some guides leave food out on the trail so that their guests might have a more exciting tour (open daily 7am-4pm; admission US$5 or ¢900, students with ID ¢350).

And if your best attempts to catch them in the wild just don't seem to be cutting it, the **Monteverde Butterfly Garden** (or Jardín de las Mariposas) and the **Santa Elena Serpentarium** (tel. 645-5238) are safe bets. There are small glass cages and boxes in the Butterfly Garden's gallery in which various insects are caged and mounted, like the enormous, ferocious-looking rhinoceros beetle. The rear of the building is divided into three indoor gardens, each representing a different microclimate and a colorful medley of 35-40 indigenous butterflies. An informative tour is included in the admission fee (open daily 9:30am-4pm; admission US$5 or ¢900). Herpetophiles will want to head over to the Serpentarium, a recently opened attraction, to visit a large collection of their slithery, venomous and non-venomous friends (open daily 9am-5pm; admission US$3). Just before the entrance to the Monteverde Reserve, there's a house on the left with a strange buzzing sound resonating from its midst: welcome to the **Hummingbird Gallery and Rainforest Slide Shows.** That patio, where a bunch of feeders are set up, is host to hundreds of hummingbirds, darting in every direction overhead. The different species in attendance depend on the season, but the brilliant, green-crowned and stripe-tailed hummingbirds are common year-round. Daily slide shows are shown inside at 3:15pm and 4:30pm daily. Slide shows cost US$3 or ¢500 per person.

Less on the jungly side, see the **Monteverde Cheese Factory** (tel. 645-5029). It's up the street from CASEM and Stella's bakery; look for the metallic cow on the sign in front. A local Quaker innovation, the cheese factory offers tours during the high season at 7:30am and 1:30pm. Otherwise, visitors can watch the mesmerizing churning process through the glass walls of the observation room while monching on samples (open Mon.-Sat. 7:30am-4pm, Sun. 7:30am-12:30pm). With endless acres of gorgeous scenery, it's no wonder that **horseback riding** has caught on so well in Monteverde. **Meg's Stables** (tel. 645-5052), next to Stella's Bakery, also provides a guide and access to private trails for US$10 an hour. Many hotels just rent out the horses and are considerably cheaper; Hotel Villa Verde charges US$25 for four hours and Pensión el Colibri, Pensión el Sueño, and Pensión el Tucán all charge US$7 per hour (see Accommodations, above, for hours). Founded in 1982 to provide job opportunities for women taking care of families at home, **CASEM** (tel. 645-5050; fax 645-5006) now includes 140 artisans who sell their handmade crafts at the store (across the street from Stella's Bakery). Carved wood and hand-painted items prevail, and many artists use their designs to depict local animals from the reserve, such as the quetzal and the golden toad (open Mon.-Sat. 8am-5pm). The **Monteverde Music Festival,** hosted by the Hotel Fonda Vela (tel. 645-5125), is a month-long annual celebration, with everything from classical music to big bands. The festival runs from around Jan. 2 to Feb. 14. Music begins nightly at 5pm, and shuttle service from Santa Elena leaves at 4:20pm. Hotel Fonda Vela also hosts concerts during the year, like the International Festival of Music, a two-week celebration of classical music in early August (performances at 5pm, US$11; call for reservations).

...through the trees, with the greatest of ease

Not for the faint-hearted, **Canopy Tours** (tel. 645-5243) takes spendthrift daredevils 14m up the center of a hollow strangler fig tree to trapeze between platforms at the tops of the rainforest itself. Not only is it the closest most people will ever come to feeling like Tarzan or Jane, but it also provides a one-of-a-kind view of the upper growth, or canopy, of the forest. Don't worry—everyone is strapped and harnessed tightly, and the guides know what they're doing. The cost is a little high for a couple of 10-second rushes, but the company claims it's the only tour of its kind in the world. Proceeds help to conserve and reforest Costa Rica. (Office open daily 7am-9pm. Tours leave daily at 7:30am, 10:30am, and 2pm. US$40, students with ID US$30. Transport to and from hotel US$6.)

PENÍNSULA NICOYA

From the highland heart of Costa Rica's cattle industry, to some of the most popular beaches in Central America, more different lands and lives crowd the Nicoya Peninsula than you can shake a surfboard at, and far more than you could hope to visit on one trip. The majority of Península Nicoya lies within the boundaries of the province of Guanacaste (see page 373). The inland region bears almost no resemblance to any other part of the country, and none whatsoever to any image on a Costa Rican postcard you're ever likely to see; rugged cowpokes amble through dusty streets high on *gaucho* heels. Meanwhile, all along the northern coast, the beaches of the Península Nicoya are magnificently empty—their pristine beauty has not yet been exploited by Costa Rica's soaring tourism industry. Every silver lining has a cloud, however, and underdevelopment has made transportation in the region very difficult. Traveling down the Pacific coast is impossible; getting between two beaches most often requires backtracking to Liberia or Nicoya. But by the time you've reached the southern tip at Playa Tamarindo and Montezuma, you're at some of the most popular and *gringo*fied sites in Central America.

■■■ NICOYA

In the place of tropical beaches and lush rainforest, Nicoya looks more like the set for an old Western—stony-faced cattle-types squint out at the horizon from under their wide-brim cowboy hats and stage an annual rodeo every July to celebrate Annexation Day, the date of Guanacaste's integration with Costa Rica proper. The locals even have a different ethnic background from standard, homogeneous *tico* stock; there's a large Chinese population, and others trace their roots back to the indigenous Chorotega. The town is even named after an Indian leader—Chief Nicoya ruled when the first Spaniards arrived here in 1523. Today, Nicoya fills an important role in the cattle industry and serves as the commercial and political center of the peninsula, while serving as a valuable transportation hub for travelers.

PRACTICAL INFORMATION

Tourist Information: Paco Gordenber, a local who knows just about everything about the region, runs an information center out of **Bar el Molino** (tel. 685-5001), 250m north of the hospital.

Police: (tel. 117), or call the judicial office, **OIJ** (tel. 685-5328).

Currency Exchange: Banco Nacional de Costa Rica (tel. 685-5366), on the main road heading north. Open Mon.-Fri. 8:30am-3:45pm.

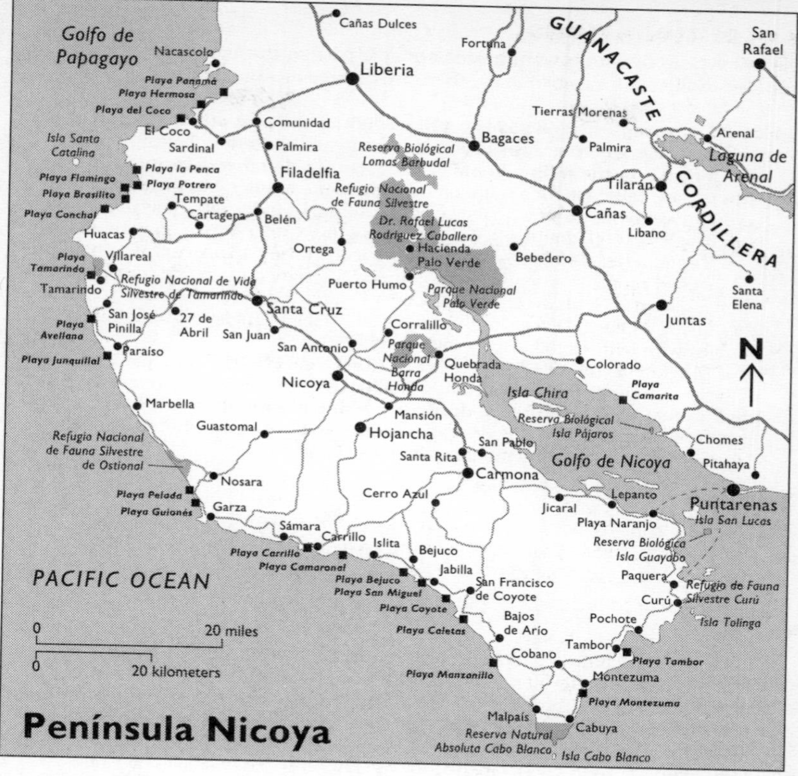

Post Office: (tel. 686-6402), across from the southwest corner of the *parque central* (open Mon.-Fri. 7:30am-5:30pm). **Postal code:** 5200. Also the place to **fax** and to send **telegrams.**

Buses: The main bus stop, serving the **Empresa Alfaro** line (tel. 685-5032), is at the southeast corner of town. Buses leave for San José daily (5, 5:30, 7, 9:30am, noon, 2:30, and 5:20pm; 6 hrs.; ¢780). Buses also go to Playa Naranjo daily (5:15am and 1pm; 2 hrs.; ¢250) and to Playa Sámara during the low season (Mon.-Fri. 3pm; 1½ hrs.; ¢210). The other bus stop, east of the main street and across from Hotel las Tinajas, serves **Transportes la Pampa** (tel. 685-0111), which sends buses daily to Liberia (every hr.; 2½ hrs.; ¢205) via Santa Cruz (40min.; ¢60) and Filadelfia.

Taxis: Many line up on the east side of the *parque central,* or call **Coopetico Nicoya** (tel. 685-6226). Nicoya cabs don't have meters, so check to see the driver's *lista de precios* (list of prices) to avoid getting ripped off.

Telephones: All around the *parque central,* west of the main road.

Pharmacy: Farmacia Nicoyana (tel. 685-5138), on the main road, 50m north of Café Daniela. Open Mon.-Sat. 8am-6pm.

Public Health Clinic: (tel. 685-5021), on the south side of the *parque central.* Open Mon.-Thurs. 7am-3:30pm, Fri. 7am-3pm.

Hospital: Hospital de la Anexión (tel. 685-5021), 400m north of Banco Nacional de Costa Rica. Some English spoken. Open 24 hrs.

Red Cross: tel. 685-5458.

ACCOMMODATIONS

Nicoya is geared more toward businesspeople passing through mid-week than to travelers. Still, that isn't a bad thing; there are definite deals to be had.

Hotel Chorotega (tel. 685-5245), 150m south of the post office. Chorotega is a friendly place where groups of locals can always be found chatting outside or watching TV in the lobby. Rooms are decent-sized and well-maintained, most with private bath. Ask for a room on the patio—it's sunnier, but the talking parrot could drive anyone batty with its daylight routine. Laundry service available. With bath: singles ¢1000, doubles ¢1600, triples ¢2400. ¢500 per person without bath.

Hotel Venecia (tel. 685-5325), on the north side of the *parque central.* The furniture-packed rooms surround a large courtyard designed expressly for communal lounging; replete with rocking chairs, tables, and a garden in the back, this space begs guests to linger. Everything is impeccably clean. Singles without bath ¢650, doubles with bath ¢2200, triples with bath ¢2500.

Hotel Elegancia (tel. 685-5159), next to Hotel Venecia. The only place in town with the unique distinction of having a tailor shop in the lobby. Rooms have that outdoor feel—after all, they're decorated with patio furniture and have clotheslines running across them. Beds are a minimal (some are cots), but bathrooms are decent. ¢800 per person with bath, doubles ¢1300.

FOOD

There aren't as many typical *sodas* here as in most towns. Nicoya has a large Chinese population, and so Chinese restaurants have popped up on every streetcorner. Everything here is pretty simple—don't expect the meal of a lifetime.

Café Daniela (tel. 686-6148), 1 block east of the *parque central.* Nicoya's token coffee shop, Daniela serves up tasty pastries (¢70-120) and *comida típica.* A relaxed and friendly atmosphere; service can be unpredictable, though. *Casados* ¢450, ice cream and fruit salad ¢290. Open Mon.-Sat. 8am-9pm, Sun. 5-10pm.

Restaurant Teyet 1 block southeast of the *parque central,* across from Hotel Yenny. Chinese food the locals all swear by, even though it may not be exactly what you're used to, portions are heaping and delicious. Chop suey in sauce ¢480, won ton soup ¢550. Open Mon.-Fri. 11am-11pm, Sat.-Sun. 11am-1am.

Soda Colonial Across from the southeast corner of the *parque central.* With old friends chatting their heads off, tidy gingham tablecloths, and *telenovelas* (soap operas) on the TV, the kind of place every small town still needs—except for the *telenovelas.* The food here is the cheapest around. Super taco with fries ¢250, chicken *casado* ¢350 half-order. Open Mon.-Sat. 6am-9pm, Sun. 6am-2pm.

■ BARRA HONDA NATIONAL PARK

When one imagines spending a day in a Costa Rican national park, plumbing a limestone cavern 70m underground doesn't jump to mind. Despite the fact that **Barra Honda** is one of the least visited parks (it's not very accessible and equipment costs are high) doesn't mean that it doesn't rank with the most spectacular of the volcanoes and rainforests. Avid spelunkers flock to the 2300-hectare park, a hillside riddled with a maze of 42 caves, some of them more than 220m deep. Only 19 caverns have been explored, and just one, **Terciopelo Cave,** is open to the public.

From the ranger station, it's a one and a half-hour hike up to Terciopelo, through a dry tropical forest alive with scarlet macaws and New World monkeys. Locals are also releasing endangered white-tailed deer back into the region. An uphill detour of about 30min. from the cave leads to the breath-taking **Mirador,** a panorama of the farmland and hills of the peninsula and even the yawning Gulf of Nicoya.

Simply entering the cave is enough to get the old adrenals a-pumpin'. The only way to get down is by scaling a free-hanging, six-inch wide steel-rope ladder (but don't worry—nobody's allowed down without the aid of three guides and a harness). At the bottom is an amazing cavern of limestone splendor—the result of a geologic upheaval of 60-70 million-year old coral reefs. Forests of stalagmites and stalactites peak and poke everywhere, and intricate folds in the walls gleam with a cold and delicate light and feel almost like porcelain. Every so often, a sightless toad or salamander darts through a shadowy crevice. A park ranger (Spanish-speaking only) leads the way through narrow passageways deep into the cave's bottom, flashlight in hand. Surprisingly, these gigantic caverns were only discovered by locals within this century—until then, they had been kept Ancient Chorotega Secret.

Unfortunately, the costs of a day of spelunking can really add up. There are no buses directly to the park—the closest bus from Nicoya stops at **Santa Ana,** 3km away. And its schedule isn't exactly convenient either; it leaves Nicoya daily at 12:30pm and returns at 7:30am. A better bet is to take a four-wheel drive taxi, which takes about 30min. and costs ¢1500 each way. Arrange a time to be picked up with the taxi driver. Then comes that pesky ¢2400 admission fee to the park (only ¢900 if you buy it the day before; park open daily 8am-4pm). Anyone can walk the path to the Mirador unguided, but to enter the cave you need to rent climbing equipment (¢1500 per person) and also to hire three guides per group of one to eight novitiates. (Rates vary within the group range: ¢7000 total for 1-2 people, ¢8000 for 3-5, and ¢8500 for 6-8.) The guides usually leave from the restaurant around 8am, but it's best to call for reservations (tel. 685-5580) the day before. Horses can also be rented from the same people for ¢400 per hour. Again, call at least one day in advance.

A group of 26 families runs the park autonomously as a part of the Las Delicias complex, a project intended to stimulate both the local economy and the ecology. They recently built a small hotel at the entrance to the park, **Apartamentos las Grutas,** three spacious eight-person cabins with private bath that charge ¢1500 per person. **Camping** is allowed in a small grassy area for ¢500 per person per night, and bathrooms are located at the side of the **restaurant,** which serves *gallo pinto* with eggs and coffee (¢400), and *casados* (¢550; open daily 6am-6pm). For any information about the park or about Proyecto las Delicias, call tel. 685-5580.

■■■ PLAYA TAMARINDO

Watch out for hordes of marauding *gringos* at Playa Tamarindo, on the western shore of the Península Nicoya; chances are nil that you will have to watch for long. Although it's not nearly as crowded as other, smaller Pacific coast beaches like Manuel Antonio and Jacó, it's still the most touristed spot on the peninsula; there's something for everyone here. The scenery, sunbathing, swimming, snorkeling, and surfing isn't the best around, but there aren't many other places that combine so much to do during the day *and* a raging nightlife. Witness the benefits of mass-production in the tourist-joy industry. Besides various discos and bars, visitors can also go to nearby Playa Grande to watch leatherback turtles lay their eggs, or go for a night swim to see the motion-sensitive phosphorescent bacteria in the water.

Practical Information **Banco Nacional** (tel. 654-4016), on the main road, changes cash and traveler's checks. There is no **post office** in Tamarindo; mail goes through **The Palm Shop** (tel. and fax 654-4223), on the main road, has **faxes** (open Mon.-Sat. 9am-1pm). **Pay phones** are located in the cul-de-sac at the end of the main road and in front of Johan's Bakery. The town's only supermarket, **Supermercado el Pelícano,** up the first street off the main road, tends to be overpriced, and so many visitors tote their own food from Santa Cruz (open Mon.-Sat. 8am-5pm). The locals of Tamarindo must feel invincible; they have no hospital, doctor, or police. It's not possible to call a **taxi,** but there are two in town—one waits in front of Cabinas Marielos on the main road, the other in the cul-de-sac, alongside the **bus stop.**

A direct bus to Tamarindo from San José, provided by **Tralapa Co.** (tel. 221-7202), leaves from Av. 3, Calle 20, daily at 4pm, returning to San José again at 6am (6 hrs.; ¢820). The only way to get to Tamarindo from the Península Nicoya is by way of Santa Cruz, a town 29km to the east. Buses leave from Nicoya to Santa Cruz daily (every hr., 40min., ¢60). After getting off in Santa Cruz, walk a few blocks to the Tralapa terminal (ask for directions), where a bus picks up passengers headed to

Tamarindo (daily at 10:35am, 1½ hrs., ¢200). Return buses to Santa Cruz leave Tamarindo daily at 6:30am, 9am, and noon. **Program Pura Natural** (tel. 233-9709; fax 223-9200) has faster, more comfortable microbuses which depart for Liberia (daily at 1:30pm, US$10), Fortuna (US$35), Puntarenas (US$20), and San José (US$25).

Accommodations and Food Most of the hotels and restaurants are expensive; judging by the crowded beach, this doesn't stop many people from coming. Campers have it best here: **Tito's Camping,** on the beach, 200m past the end of the main road, has a night guard to boost security. Most frequently frequented by surfers, Tito's charges ¢350 per person per night, and rents tents for an extra ¢250. Homemade *casados* and fresh juice (¢500) are available at the restaurant here. For roof-covered sleeping here, your surest bet is the **Hotel Dolly,** on the main road. Even though the rooms are fashioned of grim concrete, are not quite insect-free, and exhibit a tendency to flood when it rains too hard, the hotel is still secure a good deal (¢1000 per person, ¢2000 per person with bath).

Food also tends to be priced egregiously here, but a little searching will turn up a few more affordable places. **Johan's Bakery,** on the main road, sells a wide selection of tasty, pricey homemade goodies. Sometimes Johan himself even shows up. Croissants ¢130, chocolate eclaires ¢160, pizza slices ¢200 (open daily 6am-8pm). A local favorite is **El Almendro,** a.k.a. **Fish Shack,** at the end of the main road. It started off as a rest stop on a fisherman's road, but pretty soon everyone who heard about the delicious and inexpensive red snapper wanted to eat here. Get a large dinner—gut-pleasing fish, rice, beans, and plátanos (¢600; open daily until 9pm).

Sights and Entertainment During the day, there's no lack of things to do; everything from snorkeling to horseback riding to simply lounging on the sand under a makeshift parasol. **Tamarindo Tours and Rentals** (tel. 654-4078), on the main road, has the cheapest rental prices and a huge selection of stuff, including beach chairs (¢500 per day), boogie boards (¢800 per day), and bikes (¢1000 per day), as well as a variety of horseback riding, fishing, and boat trips (open daily 8am-6pm). **Iguana Surf** (tel. and fax 654-4019) has a good selection of high-quality kayaks (US$35 per day), surfboards (US$10 per half-day), and snorkeling gear (US$5 per half-day). They also offer personal surfing lessons (US$15 per hr.) and guided kayaking, sailing, and snorkeling tours (US$25-45; open daily 8am-6pm). **Hotel Captain Suiza** (tel. 680-0853), 400m down the beach past the end of the main road, rents **horses** (US$20 for the first hour, US$10 each additional hour). **Surfers** head north to the Tamarindo estuary or to **Playa Grande,** a flat beach content with its decent waves. Playa Grande recently became part of **Las Baulas National Park,** as it is the nesting site for the leatherback turtle (or *baula*). These aquatic reptiles can get longer than 1.5m and heavier than 900lbs.; they lay most of their eggs in the winter.

For a livelier night scene, check out **Zullymar,** near the end of the main road, a food-by-weekday-disco-by-weekend joint that blasts Latin and *norteamericano* dance music under colorful lights. Or head over to **Cantina las Olas,** a bar run by some *gringos,* home to the only pool table in town (open Wed.-Mon. 6pm-1am).

■■■ PLAYA SÁMARA

Samsara is the Buddhic name for the world of suffering that precedes nirvanic eternity and Playa *Sámara,* 29km south of Nicoya, proves once again, with resounding force, just what an incredible difference one letter and a simple accent can make. This place may as well be Nirvana itself—and you don't even need to die to get there. Virtually undiscovered by *gringos,* Sámara's calm, clear, shallow waters and seemingly endless white-sand shore are one national treasure the *ticos* have kept to themselves. It's a popular vacation spot for locals; ex-President and Nobel Prize laureate Oscar Arias Sánchez even has a beach house here. Sámara is the perfect place for simple pleasures—taking a romantic stroll down a mile-long strip of sand, basking in the sun in solitude, snorkeling off the rocks of a tree-covered island to the east. Not everything is quite so tropical, though; witness the nearby farmland and the loitering horses and cows, to be seen from most roadsides. The pastoral tranquility of Sámara is in jeopardy, though; Cangrejal, the northern end of the beach, foreshadows a darker future for this coastal idyll, as it is gradually cleared, flattened, and developed to make way for a large-scale resort. Hurry.

Practical Information The **police** station is right across the street from the bus stop (tel. 117). **Public telephones** can be found at the **post office,** which is next door to the police station and has a *lista de correos* and **telegram** service. The **postal code** is 5235. **Buses** stop on the main road to the beach, in front of Cabinas Comedor Arenas. Buses leave daily for San José (4am, 6 hrs.), and for Nicoya (6:30am, 3pm; 1½ hrs.; ¢210). Call for a **taxi** (tel. 686-6776, 685-5634). **Pulpería Mileth,** at the end of the main road to the beach, is an all-purpose general store that quenches basic needs with groceries, sunscreen, and their ilk (open daily 7am-noon and 1-8pm.) The closest hospital or pharmacy is in Nicoya, as is the only available **Red Cross** (tel. 685-5458).

Accommodations and Food Cabinas Arenas, on the main road to the beach, has floors are bare cement, but that's not enough to kill the hominess of the wood ceiling and quilted beds, and its private bathrooms stay spotless (¢2000 per person). Next door, **Cabinas Magaly** is a bit grimier and more cramped, with private bathrooms that could stand to be a little cleaner. The doors look tough with their strong deadbolt locks, though (¢1500 per person in high season, ¢1000 in low). **Hotel Playa Sámara** (tel. 685-5055), at the far end of the soccer field, is also rather cramped and dingy, and gets routinely deafened by the downstairs disco on weekends. The view falls short of the ocean, instead landing squarely in the soccer field below (¢1500 per person in high season, ¢1000 in low). Of course, there's always **Camping Cocos** (no tel.), if you just turn left on the beach and walk 250m. Pitch tent in a private backyard only 100m from the water, amid palm trees and a stunning view of the waves. The communal bathroom facilities, however, leave much to be desired, viz. toilet seats and a real shower nozzle. It's also hard to take seriously the cleanliness of a place that has a *Coopere con el aseo* (roughly, "Keep the place clean") graffito on its bathroom door. (¢400 per person per night.)

The small *sodas* are your best bet for dining; their food's just as good as anywhere else, and at about half the price. The two women who run **Soda Restaurante Yure** definitely know what they're doing—they've been cooking up this kind of *tico* fare for their family for years. *Arroz con pollo* ¢300 by the half-order, *casados* ¢500. (Open Mon.-Sat. 6am-8pm.) **Soda el Jicaro,** run by Alba, has picnic benches right next to the soccer field and gets a bit more business. It also serves traditional Costa Rican food, i.e. *casados* (¢400), as well as hamburgers (¢250) and sandwiches (¢150-200; open daily 7am-9pm.

■■■ MONTEZUMA

Montezuma has gained a reputation as an irreproachably hippie and tie-dyed colony of vegans, and that's not entirely incorrect. Some travelers might be put off by the fact that there's more English than Spanish to hear on the streets, but as a kind, green buddy explains, it's a "community of international harmony." And it's not much of a challenge to live the pleasant life in a place like this. A jewel of a spot, carefully set in the southern tip of the Península Nicoya, Montezuma's rocky coast is interspersed with choice swimming beaches. While the area lacks the endless sand of other beaches, it compensates with spectacular aesthetic pleasures—powerful waves smashing into the shore, warm emerald-green water, and foaming surf that cascades over jagged black rock. Needless to say, Montezuma has a way of sedating even the most frazzled traveler. For those who simply can't sit still, the surrounding area is ideal for hiking and nature-watching. Montezuma is a scant 11km from the original Costa Rican nature reserve, **Cabo Blanco.** The park's expansive green forest—and the monkeys, pumas, and armadillos that thrive in it—are protected by a great many regulations. As if diverse fauna weren't enough, **Río Lajas,** 1-km hike from town, sprouts three playful waterfalls, each filling a pool fit for swimming, diving, or sedate appreciation.

Getting There The best way to reach Montezuma is to catch a **ferry** departing from the dock behind the market in Puntarenas. Departures are at 6:15am, 11am, and 3pm (6:15am, 11am, and 3pm; 1½ hrs.; ¢220). Be sure to board the ferry bound for Paquera, *not* Playa Naranjo, because there is no way to get directly from Playa Naranjo to Paquera, except by way of a ¢4000 taxi. Once the boat arrives in Paquera, there will be a "Turismo" **bus** waiting to take visitors to Montezuma. Buses leave Puerto Paquera at approximately 7:30am, 12:30am, and 4:30pm (2 hrs., ¢400). The bus passes through Paquera and Cóbano before reaching Montezuma.

If you are coming from other beaches on the Península Nicoya, take one of the buses headed for San José, get off at Barranca, and change there to Puntarenas, where you can catch the 6am, 11am, or 3pm ferry to Paquera. It may seem longer on the map, but it's infinitely faster than any route down the Península—even with the best of planning and the best of luck, you still can't get past Playa Naranjo without a transfer or three; if you plan on busing this way, you'll want to bus to Playa Naranjo from Nicoya (leaves daily at 5:15am and 1pm, 2 hrs., ¢250) and then ferry from Playa Naranjo to Puntarenas (daily at 5am, 8:50am, 12:50, 5, and 9pm, 1 hr., ¢280), and then ferry from Puntarenas to points beyond (see Puntarenas, Practical Information)—the whole trip could take a good eight hours. The road between Playa Naranjo and Paquera is extremely tough and there are no buses or cars that attempt it. If you are hopelessly masochistic and just *must* go overland, you'll have to rely on one or more of the 15-ton trucks, which will take you across the 27km stretch in 2½-3 hours. *Let's Go* does not recommend hitchhiking.

Buses bound for Puerto Paquera leave Montezuma three times daily (5:30am, 10am, and 2pm, ¢400). The bus will connect with a ferry heading back to Puntarenas (8am, 12:30pm, and 5pm).

Practical Information Forty-one kilometers west of **Paquera** and 7km south of **Cóbano,** Montezuma consists almost entirely of *pensiones* and *cabinas*. Local people and tourists alike are very ecologically conscious and development has been generally unobtrusive. **Tourist information** is available at **Monte Aventuras** (tel. 642-0025), on a little hill at the entrance to town, diagonally across from Cabinas el Tucán and Hotel la Aurora. In keeping with Montezuma's hip reputation, the office can provide information on yoga classes, as well as times and prices of guided tours around the area and an ultra-complete bus-and-ferry schedule for the entire Península Nicoya. **Fax** service and **public phones** are also available. *Se habla inglés.* (Open Mon.-Sat. 8am-noon and 4-8pm from Dec.-April and July-Aug, Mon.-Sat. 4-8pm from May-June and Sept.-Nov.) Or try the tourist shop next to Hotel Montezuma, **Ecological Fund Tienda** (tel. 642-0058), where some English is spoken. It also serves as a **post office,** selling everything from stamps to condoms (open Mon.-Sat. 8am-8pm, Sun. hours vary.) The **market,** a small and slightly overpriced *pulpería,* **Abastecedor Montezuma,** 1½ blocks east of Hotel Montezuma (open daily 6am-9pm). **Librería a Topsy,** 100m west of the police station, at the top of the hill next to the soccer field, unrelated to the coroner, sells new and used books in English and Spanish, or lends them out for ¢100.

All other services are located in **Cóbano;** buses leave for Cóbano from in front of the Hotel Montezuma daily at 5:30am, 10am, and 2pm. Its **police** station (tel. 117), next door to the post office, is available 'round the clock to deal with emergencies, but not to speak English. Cóbano's **Banco Nacional** (tel. 642-0210, ext. 210), in the center of town, changes traveler's checks (open Mon.-Fri. 8:30am-3pm.) The **post office,** three blocks from the center on the road to Paquera, posts a *lista de correos* and sends **telegrams** (open Mon.-Fri. 9am-noon and 2:30-5pm, Sat. 9am-noon.) The

public phone (tel. 661-0566) is half a block toward Paquera (open daily 7am-noon and 1-8pm.) Medical aid is available at the **Clínica de Cóbano** (open daily 7am-5pm).

Accommodations Hotel prices vary in and around Montezuma; depending on your degree of savvy, you can either sleep cheap or lose your shirt. Hot water is absent from budget lodgings (and pretty unnecessary anyway). The strong ocean breeze makes fans redundant, though a set of mechanized blades will help keep bugs away. **Camping** on the beach is free and popular, and relatively safe (though it's never a good idea to leave bags unguarded), but there are no communal facilities are available. Some camping supplies are routinely available at the market. The rustic **Pensión Arenas,** just west of Chico's Bar on the beach, is an amazing hotel that makes a splendiferous scene of the sea through encircling ranks of palms and sand. Were Papa Hemingway to have come to Montezuma, his nose would have led him here; earnest imitators can lounge in the hammock. Rooms are tidy and freshly painted, beds are comfy, bathrooms are communal but clean (singles ¢750, ¢1000 in high season). **Pensión Jenny,** 50m down the road to Cabo Blanco and another 50m up the hill north of the soccer field, is a great deal; set in a big old blue-and-white wooden house, the rooms receive lots of light and fresh air through the large, barn-like windows, and there's an ocean view from the balcony. Bathrooms are communal bathrooms. ¢600 per person. **Casa el Tucán** (tel. 661-1122, ext. 284), across from the tourist information booth, offers shiny wood paneling and floors in cute-as-a-button bungalows. Tragically, all of its rooms' potential ocean views are obscured by treetops. Rooms have fans and share communal bath facilities, and guests can explore that communal feeling by bonding on the porch's rocking chairs. Singles ¢1000, doubles ¢1700. **Hotel Moctezuma** (tel. 642-0058, ext. 258) is next to the pizza shop in "downtown" Montezuma. Rooms include fans and some have private baths; back rooms enjoy ocean views. Less fortunate guests are sent to the overflow housing across the street, which has little going for it save the cool prints on the walls. Books and laundry service available. The staff also arranges tours. Some wheelchair-accessible rooms. Singles ¢1000, ¢2000 with bath, doubles ¢1700, ¢2900 with bath. ¢500 for each additional person.

Food Find vegetarian and health-conscious cuisine at **El Sano Banano** (tel. 642-0272, ext. 272), halfway up the hill between Monte Aventuras and Hotel Moctezuma. Your purchase helps support the Montezuma Ecological Fund and prices are jacked accordingly. Daily specials range from ¢550-850, and even the simplest dishes are uncannily delicious. The menu includes fruit shakes, frozen yogurt, and other natural foods served in a comfortable open-air environment. Come early for dinner—they show a movie every day at 7:30pm (free with ¢300 minimum order), and the place gets packed (open daily 7am-9:30pm). At **Restaurante El Parque,** in front of Pensión Arenas, ocean breezes sigh across wooden tables shaded by thatched roofs. Waves roll right up to the feet of patrons munching chicken *casados* with mashed potatoes (¢550) or spaghetti gorgonzola (¢700). They also serve a wild selection of floofy fruit smoothies with names like Morning Zen and The Forbidden Drink (¢180-220). (Open daily 7am-9:30pm.) **Restaurante Montezuma** (tel. 642-0058), next to Hotel Montezuma, is a popular spot along the beach to grab a reasonably priced bite to eat. The monstrous Super Sandwich Montezuma costs ¢850, but it's huge enough to feed at least two, as is the paella (¢950), served fresh every Thursday. The scenic upstairs terrace is open for dinner from 6-10pm, and after hours the place hosts a happening bar scene. (Open Tues.-Sun. 8am-10pm.)

Sights And Entertainment The **beaches** of Montezuma are ideal for relaxed contemplation. Walking east you'll find sand stretches and a few clear spots where you can jump in the water and race enormous waves, but beware of the rocky bottom. The Ecological Fund Tienda rents boogie boards for ¢700 per day. If you walk west toward Cabo Blanco, you will pass a *palapa* (a thatched-roof hut) and a small bridge; immediately after this point the bridge to the waterfalls (*cataratas,* or cataracts) begins. Follow the riverbed for 15 minutes and the largest waterfall of the three looms before you. Some of the water is good for swimming; locals say that the basin is deep enough for diving from the surrounding rocks. Across from the waterfall, a steep and slippery trail leads up to the other two waterfalls, but it's probably best to find a *tico*-in-the-know to show you the way.

Horseback riding is a terrific way to see this gorgeous area. Go to the white wooden information kiosk across the street from the Ecological Fund Tienda to ask about rentals (but be warned—it's rumored that they only recommend their friends). Luis Angel, who can be found by the *panadería,* and Armando Castro Cerdas, who usually hangs out at El Sano Banano, both rent horses for around US$25 per day. Armando also leads tours of the Cabo Blanco Nature Reserve for ¢3500, but he's a bit of a character and perhaps a bit too much of one to walk around with for an entire and enjoyable day.

Begin the evening by catching a flick at the **Tucán Movie House,** in the Sano Banano Restaurant. The day's featured title is chalked onto a blackboard at the restaurant. Gain admission either by forking over ¢300 or by purchasing ¢300 worth of food or drink (but this rule isn't always very stringently enforced). The show begins at 7:30pm—unless the power goes out. The place fills up quickly, so come early for a decent seat, especially if it's a subtitled U.S. movie.

Chico's Bar (tel. 642-0258), 25m north of Hotel Moctezuma, is where everyone goes at night for want of anything else to do. Watch the population of Montezuma quadruple as the reggae beat the people out of the woodwork. Chico's also serves food, at fairly inflated prices. Once Chico's gets old, stagger over to **Bar Montezuma,** on the other side of the hotel, where the restaurant dwells by day. It's basically the same thing, but the crowd is more up for drinking than for dancing. On the weekends, the **Kaliolin Disco,** 1km up the hill towards Cóbano, pumps out the dancy faves. Its floor is fairly small, so walk out back to the beach for some fresh air, or to get cozy with special someone. The crowd is mostly young and *tico,* but they're more than happy to do anything they can to help the *gringas* have a good time. (Open Wed.-Sat. 11pm-3am, ¢500 cover on weekends. Free transportation from in front of the Hotel Montezuma on Sat. starting at 11:30pm.)

■ NEAR MONTEZUMA: CABO BLANCO BIOLOGICAL RESERVE

A dirt road runs 10km from Montezuma to the **Reserva Natural Absoluta Cabo Blanco.** At the southernmost tip of the peninsula, the reserve covers some 2900 acres of land that used to be completely cleared away for fields and cattle; amazingly, this forest is a product of only 30 years of regeneration.

Founded in 1963 through the efforts of the Swiss pioneer Niel Olaf Wessberg, this protected tract became the cornerstone of the extensive Costa Rican reserve system. Its unusual mix of evergreens and moist tropical forest and has provided an environment of particular interest to tropical zoologists. Toucans, parakeets, pelicans, howler and white-faced monkeys, armadillos, pumas, boas, and iguanas have all been observed within its bounds. Particularly interesting are the rare or endangered species that inhabit the unusual forest: the brocket deer, the crested guan (a large tropical forest bird resembling a turkey), and the jaguarundi (a slender, short-legged wildcat) have all found a haven in Cabo Blanco. A beautiful, 4.5-km nature trail leads through the heart of the forest to several kilometers of rocky coastline and sandy beaches. Shortly before its end, the trail splits, its right branch (Balsitas) running to a group of small waterfalls which are accessible only in the dry season. For the return trip, it is sometimes possible to walk along the beach; otherwise, just follow your footsteps back. Ask about it at the **ranger station** at the entrance to the reserve, where there's also a tidal schedule (permission aside, the high tides do a good job of washing away footprints.) The ranger station provides bathrooms and drinking water and there are two potable streams along the trail (open Wed.-Sun. 8am-4pm; admission ¢2400, but only ¢900 if you buy it that day). Bug repellent and drinking water are absolutely essential for the five-hour round-trip hike through the hot and humid forest. Sandals do not an advisable means of locomotion make, as there are vicious ants along the trail and the path gets rather muddy during the rainy season. To get to the reserve, catch one of the **taxi-vans** which depart at 9am from the Moctezuma Hotel in Montezuma; vans return at 4pm (round-trip ¢800). Monte Aventuras offers a good deal—transportation and a ticket to the park for ¢2400.

If you want to spend more than an afternoon at the reserve, lodging is available in **Ancla de Oro** in **Cabuya,** a tiny village 2km from the reserve. Nature-lovers can sleep in thatched-roof cabins hoisted high above ground for ¢600 a night. Or go to **Sunshine,** where singles with refrigerators go for ¢1000.

GUANACASTE

Arid plains and dripping forests rub elbows in Guanacaste, Costa Rica's most geographically peculiar department. To the south, the region is green and wet, and the Monteverde Cloud Forest Reserve boasts a mind-boggling diversity of tropical species. During the dry season and moving north and west, the ground becomes parched and chokingly dry. This half of Guanacaste seems out of place in the tropics—it's African savannah minus the cheetahs. During the wet season, the plains bloom in full force, resulting in a vast sea of green providing remarkable contrast to the spectacular strips of blue ocean in Parque Nacional Santa Rosa. Dotted with cattle ranches, Guanacaste still retains the independent spirit of its youthful days: the department remained a self-governing state until 1824, when it finally opted to join Costa Rica. To celebrate the decision, Annexation Day, July 25, is widely celebrated with a daring combination of large quantities of alcohol and a few disgruntled bulls. Costa Ricans and travelers alike have reason to celebrate the glory of the department, which includes (among many other things) most of Nicoya Peninsula, the sweeping wetlands of Palo Verde, the caves of Barra Honda, the jet-set Playas del Coco and Hermosa, and part of Lago Arenal.

■■■ FORTUNA

According to local legend, the little town of Fortuna got its name from the flotsam and jetsam that would float down the nearby river during floods—*indígena* cups, tools, and relics were scooped up by villagers as signs of good "fortune." Luck doesn't seem to have run out yet for this modest community of 5000, as it's situated only a few kilometers east of the spectacular Volcán Arenal and the relaxing hot springs of Tabacón. Faced with a huge influx of visitors trying to get in on the action, Fortuna is scrambling to build new hotels and has lost some of its small-town feel; fortunately, it's not the town that counts, but rather the potential for wild adventures in the natural playground nearby, which includes the lava-spewing volcano, crashing waterfalls and river rapids, gentle pools for swimming, mazes of caves, and halcyon Lago Arenal.

Orientation and Practical Information Fortuna is 33km northwest of Ciudad Quesada (San Carlos) and can be reached by bus from San José, Tilarán, or Arenal. The east-west road leading into Fortuna serves as the main street; most businesses line this thoroughfare. Immediately south is Fortuna's big soccer field, which serves as the town's center; the church respectfully faces the field's west side.

Todo el mundo has opened a **tour company** in Fortuna. All companies organize tours to nearby attractions (see Near Fortuna, below). In general, you're more likely to get professional treatment from the hotels and tour companies than from the guys who approach you on the street, but they may offer a cheaper price. Whatever you do, look around before committing. The **police** (tel. 117), are a block and a half east of the soccer on the main drag. The main door is open 7:30am-9pm; ask at the window after hours.Exchange currency or traveler's checks at the **Banco Nacional** (tel. 479-9022) in the northeast corner of the soccer field (open Mon.-Fri. 8:30am-3:45pm). The **post office** (tel. 479-9178), next to the police station, posts a *Lista de Correos* and has a **fax** service (open Mon.-Fri. 7:30-11:30am and 1:30-5:30pm, Sat. 7:30-11:30am). The **postal code** is 4417. There is a **public phone** (tel. 479-9199) at Sunset Tours, just north of the soccer field's northeast corner, as well as on the main drag and elsewhere.

Buses arrive and depart next to Restaurant El Jardín, one block east of the soccer field. Buses from Fortuna travel direct to San José (12:40, 2:45pm; 4½ hrs.; ¢350). San José can also be reached easily from Ciudad Quesada (also called San Carlos; 5 buses in the morning, 1½ hrs., ¢170). Buses also go to Tilarán (3 hrs.) via Arenal (8am and 4pm, 2 hrs., ¢250). Rent **bikes** from **Repuestos y Accesorios Fortuna,** facing the gas station one block east of the soccer field (¢200 per hr., ¢1400 for the day. Open Mon.-Sat. 7am-5pm.) The **pharmacy** (tel. 479-1721) is a block and a half north of Restaurant El Jardín (open Mon.-Sat. 7am-7pm). The **medical clinic** (tel. 479-9142) is a block and a half north of the pharmacy; some English spoken (open Mon.-Thurs. 7am-4pm, Fri. 7am-3pm).

Accommodations and Food It's easy to end up paying a lot of money for a hotel room in Fortuna; look hard, though, and you'll find some comfortable mid-to low-range options. **Hotel La Central** (tel. 479-9045; fax 479-9004), stands on main street facing the soccer field. Rooms are basic, but airy and clean, like the communal bathrooms. Gawk at passers-by through big windows in some rooms; one quad has private bath. Prices are often negotiable (¢700 per person). The hotel also organizes **tours** to the volcano and hot springs (¢1000 per person), the caverns (¢3500), and Caño Negro (¢4500); all tours include lunch. **Hotel Fortuna** (tel. 479-9197), conveniently located near the bus stop, has the cheapest rooms in town. Luckily, there's no flotsam in these bathrooms, and rooms aren't fancy, but are adequate. There's a deck upstairs and a restaurant downstairs. Laundry service, and various good tours to the volcano and waterfalls (doubles ¢1000, ¢1500 with bath). **Cabinas Charlie** is a super-friendly, quiet, family-run alternative. Cheap rooms are spotless and have fans and new mattresses. Their java is some of the most excellent in town (singles ¢600; prices go up in the high season).

For a tasty burger (¢800), head to **Restaurante Rancho la Cascada** (tel. 479-9145), under the massive thatched roof across from the northeast corner of the soccer field. Breakfasts are in the ¢250-350 range; lunches and dinners are reasonably priced. Try the excellent fruit juices with milk (¢100; open daily 6am-10:30pm). At **Restaurante Central** (tel. 479-9004), beneath Hotel Central, the chairs are padded and large wooden tables groan under the weight of traditional dishes. Relive your childhood with a banana split (¢220). Chicken *cordon bleu* ¢95; the plate of the day (¢350 with drink) is cheap enough to order it two times over (open 6am-11pm). **Restaurante Jardín** (tel. 479-9072), across from the gas station on the main street, is a popular place for whiling away the hours. Enjoy spaghetti (¢800), *lomito relleño* (¢900), ice cream, and beer as you watch ridiculous soaps on TV. Plate of the day (¢275) doesn't come with a drink, but ask for free garlic bread (open daily 6:30am-11pm). For amazing breakfasts and some of the best vegetarian food around, try **Restaurante Vegetariano El Lirio y la Luna,** on the main drag just west of the park. Granola, yogurt, omelettes (¢80-100), and pancakes loaded with fruit (¢200; open daily 7am-7pm, but come too early or too late and you may not get served). This is also the haunting grounds of Gabino, the only guide who takes people to Volcán Arenal, for those who lust to be showered with lava and molten rock.

■ NEAR FORTUNA

RÍO AND CATARATA FORTUNA

The Río Fortuna is a moderate-sized river that passes Fortuna a few km to the south. Below one of the river's bridges, there's a perfect little swimming hole, complete with a vine swing and a cool little **waterfall.**

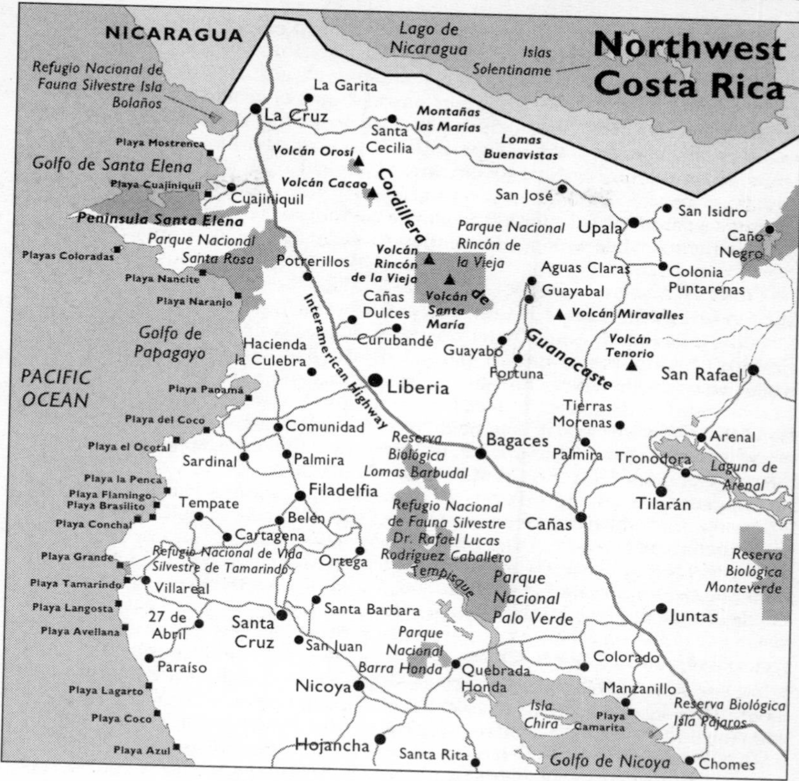

To reach the river, follow signs to the waterfall posted near the south side of the church (it's the road to San Ramón). About 2km from Fortuna, the road crosses the river. About 50m before you reach the bridge, the dirt road to the waterfall branches off to the right. The rest of the walk boasts several sublime views; look for the waterfall on the left. Thanks to knotty roots along the trail, you can hike the steep and narrow trail that leads to the bottom of the falls. While the pool right under the falls is dangerous for swimming, farther to the left there are a few calmer spots for cooling off. It takes about one or two hours to reach the falls on foot, and it can be very muddy. Taxis can take most of the way until the road gets too steep (about ¢400). Tours on horseback are available; Hotel Fortuna has them for ¢1500. The trip would also make a fun bike ride.

VOLCÁN ARENAL

If you've ever wanted to pay a visit to Satan, make a pilgrimage to Volcán Arenal. By day, the gigantic cone spouts smoke and roars with the din of falling rocks. By night, red-hot lava bursts from the top and trickles down the sides of the volcano's black walls. With good reason, the town of Fortuna is built on the side where lava doesn't flow, so there's only access on the eastern side. Unfortunately, the summit is often obscured by thick cloud cover, especially in the rainy season. The volcano has been active since 1968, when an earthquake triggered an enormous eruption which killed several dozen people. Since then, the volcano has exploded several times daily, occasionally falling silent like a sullen child. Climbing the volcano is dangerous and strongly discouraged. Ambitious but naïve tourists have been injured or killed;

it's best to observe the volcano from afar; if you insist on going, take a tour with Gabino (see Restaurante El Lirio y la Luna in Food, above).

Every night, groups of tourists venture out to the volcano in hopes that something dramatic will happen. To see your own personal hunk of oozing lava, catch one of the many volcano/hot springs tours that leave Fortuna every night. Hotel Central has a schoolbus that leaves at 6pm (¢1000), and Hotel Fortuna has a bus at 7pm (¢500). These go by the observation station at the National Park, then stop by the hot springs on the way home. Another option is simply to take a taxi for ¢1000 per carload to where the volcano and lava are visible, just not as close, to actually watch the volcanic puffing while soaking in style in some steaming...

HOT SPRINGS

The **hot springs** of **Tabacón,** 10km west of Fortuna on the road to the volcano, are actually a river of hot water. There, you can submerge your troubles and sore muscles in a labyrinth of hot springs, pools, and waterfalls amidst well-kept gardens while you watch the Volcán Arenal ooze its magical orange juices. One way to reach Tabacón is by catching a bus headed for Tilarán (see Fortuna: Practical Information). Some travelers resort to soliciting rides. Tabacón Resort unfortunately occupies the prime real estate here; it has a restaurant, gardens, and fancy swimming pools, but they charge about US$10 to get in (discounts for students or after 6pm). If you're feeling deeply decadent, opt for a full-hour massage (about ¢2500). (Open daily 10am-10pm.) A cheaper place to enter is at **Río Tabacón,** across the street and down the hill. Here, you can find a comfy spot right in the river, or macerate in the shallow pools for only ¢400 (open 10am-10pm). You can skip the entrance fee altogether by using any of the several unattended springs along the road. The bus driver can drop you off at one of these springs if you ask.

CAVERNAS DE VENADO

While one river bubbles into hot springs, another is responsible for forging the tortuous network of caves in the town of Venado, northwest of Fortuna. The caves are open to visitors every day, and the property owners rent flashlights (¢150), helmets (¢50), and boots (¢100). Admission to get in is ¢300. Each group receives a guide for the price, and it's a damn good thing, too. The labyrinth of caverns extends two km underground through eight rooms and contains several waterfalls, freaky mineral formations, and—Holy Venado, Batman!—lots of bats. If you take the tour, be prepared to get down and dirty. To remember what it was like to be birthed, ask the guide to take you through the narrow and aptly named **Baño.** Much of the hike is actually along the underground river, so bring good river shoes or rent boots at the entrance. If you appreciate the guide's services, it's good form to give a tip.

Many tour companies go to the caves, but if you can get to the town of Venado, there's no need for a tour. From Fortuna, take the road east for 7km until you reach El Tanque (Ciudad Quesada buses pass here). From there, Venado is about 15km northwest up the road. Buses pass frequently, and some say it works to hitchhike.

LAGUNA DE ARENAL

Hydroelectric dams have created **Laguna de Arenal;** tourists have turned the lake into a fishing, boating, and windsurfing playground. For information on **fishing tours** in Laguna de Arenal, contact the tourist office or **Agencia Aventuras Arenal** in Fortuna (tel. 479-9133). Tours with all equipment provided cost US$25 per hour, with a minimum of four hours. You might also call or stop by the well-outfitted Hotel Aurora in the town of Arenal. For windsurfing, you're better off heading to the resorts outside of Tilarán.

■■■ ARENAL

And you thought Fortuna was a small town. The village of Arenal is miniscule to the extreme, but still attracts a good number of travelers set on exploring Lago Arenal and the surroundings. Fortuna is better located for hopping off to most places, but Arenal is central to the lake's shore and is a great place to get information.

The entire village is centered around the loop formed by the road, which encloses the church and soccer field. This loop is connected to the highway by Arenal's 100m main street. **Centro de Informacion Turistica** (tel. 694-4132; fax 694-4025), where the main street splits to the town loop, is *the* place to get tourist information in Arenal, or to get kayak rentals, or take Spanish lessons, or.... Owner Stephanie is German, but she speaks English and Spanish, too; her tours of the area range from US$20-80. The tour to **Volcán Tenorio** is not available from Fortuna, so snag it here. The **police** are nearby, on the right coming from the highway.The **bus** lets off half way up this street, in front of Restaurante Lajas. Buses go to Tilaran (six a day, 1 hr., ¢110) and to Fortuna (8am and 1:30pm, 2 hrs., ¢220). **Banco Nacional** (tel. 694-4122) changes traveler's checks and gives cash advances on Visa cards (open Mon.-Fri. 8:30am-3:45pm). The **post office,** also a **telegram office,** is on the right coming from the highway, next to the police (open Mon.-Fri. 7:30-11:30am and 1:30-5:30pm, Sat. 7-11am).

The few **hotels** and **restaurants** that Arenal has are certainly adequate. **Cabinas Rodriguez** (tel. 664-4237) is a family-run place and is the cheapest in town. Rooms are pretty small, but are clean and have fans (¢750 per person, ¢1000 with private bath). Next door is the fancy **Aurora Inn** (tel. 694-4245; fax. 694-4245), which has modern rooms with fan, private bath, and beautiful hard wood floors. You can watch volcanic fireworks from the deck on clear nights (singles US$30, doubles US$35). The Inn is one of the best outfitted places on Lake Arenal for fishing. A guide, a boat, all equipment, and sack lunches for the day cost US$60, split by however many can fit on the boat. **Hotel Restaurante Lajas,** on main street where the bus lets off, is satisfactory in its own right. Rooms are clean, the deck out back has a nice view, and the restaurant lets fly with zippy food. Pancake breakfast ¢350 (¢900 per person, ¢1100 with private bath). Lake View Arenal serves food, including meat and rice dishes (¢500) with a view next to Aurora on the lake side of the town loop (open daily 8am-9pm). Stephanie's also serves *leckeres deutsches essen; guten appetit!* (Open Mon.-Sat. 9am-9pm.)

■■■ TILARÁN

An oasis of newly plumbed and painted structures amidst hilly fields and cattle ranches, Tilarán (pop. about 10,000) is a good base for exploring Lake Arenal and the surrounding sights—although Fortuna serves the same purpose and provides more amenities. Tidy Tilarán doesn't particularly cater to tourists, but it is a convenient stopover in the complex web of bus connections from Fortuna to the Pacific coast. While relaxing and waiting for the bus in the immense city park, suck in plenty of the town's fresh, cool air, the likes of which are rare elsewhere in the department. Air also brings a large contingent of wind-surfers to Tilarán, who try to catch air while taking advantage of the lake's fast, windy air.

Tilarán's streets have no names and its buildings have no numbers—the thoroughfares are just anonymous paved surfaces. You'll be forced to grope around using the sun, the stars, or a compass. If you accidentally dropped your astrolabe into the bright green fumaroles of Arenal Volcano, the Catholic church serves as a crude but effective substitute—Tilarán's most sacred structure sits east of the park.

Practical Information For information on fishing trips or waterskiing excursions to Lake Arenal, try **Cabinas Mary,** on the park's south side. **Banco Nacional** (tel. 695-5028), across from the southwest corner of the park, changes traveler's checks and gives cash advances on Visa cards (open Mon.-Fri. 8:30am-3:45pm).

Tilarán's **post office** (tel. 695-5387) is one block north and one-and-a-half blocks east of the park's northeast corner. **Telegrams** and **faxes** can be sent from the post office (open Mon.-Fri. 7:30am-5:30pm). For free collect phone calls, try **Agencia ICE** (tel. 695-5166), on the second floor of the Edificio Municipal, half a block west of the plaza and next to the bus station (open Mon.-Fri. 8am-3:30pm). **Pay phones** are located on the west and south sides of the park.

The **bus station,** across from the park's northwest corner, serves San José (7am, 7:45am, 2pm, and 4:55pm, 3½ hrs., ¢385), Puntarenas (6am and 1pm), Ciudad Quesada/San Carlos (7am and 12:30pm), which passes Fortuna and Arenal along the way. Roll to Guatuso (noon), Arenal (10am and 4:30pm, 3 hrs., ¢250), and Cañas (six a day; to Monteverde at 12:30pm only). Buses go from Cañas to Liberia all day long. For **medical assistance,** call the **Red Cross** (tel. 695-5256; **emergency** tel. 128), one block east of Banco de Costa Rica (open 24 hrs). **Farmacia Tilarán** (tel. 695-5064) is on the south side of the park next to Restaurant Mary (open Mon.-Sat. 7am-8:30pm, Sun. 7am-2pm). Though they speak no English, the **police** (tel. 695-5001), half a block west of the bus station, answer the phone 24 hours a day.

Accommodations and Food **Cabinas Mary** (tel. 695-5479), in the southeast corner of the plaza, makes you pay dearly for the wall-to-wall carpeting upstairs; still, the staff is merry and the rooms are clean. Hot water and laundry services are available (singles ¢1300, with bath ¢2300; doubles with bath ¢3000). **Hotel Yasmine** (tel. 695-5043), on the west side of the park, feels like a hospital and achieves a level of cleanliness approaching sterility. Heck, you could whip out your scalpel and do surgery here. There's a TV in the lobby, too, with Cinemax in English (singles ¢905). **Cabinas Lago Lindo** (tel. 695-5555) is next to Hotel El Sueño and one block north of the bus station. The lobby looks like a 70s-era hair parlor, but it's clean as a whistle (singles ¢798; doubles ¢1360, with bath ¢2150; triples ¢2945).

If your stomach starts to fuss while you're waiting for a bus, there's really not much need to venture far. Simply summon up the lark, head to the west side of the park, to **Soda Stephanie y Familiar.** Rice and meat dishes go for ¢350, soup for ¢200 (open Mon.-Sat. 6am-5pm). **Restaurant Mary** (tel. 695-5891) is on the south side of the park, below Cabinas Mary. (Coincidence? Conspiracy? You decide.) Enjoy the almost-fancy atmosphere while you sample the extensive menu, including spaghetti (¢750), fried chicken (¢550), and sea bass in tomato sauce (¢895). Breakfasts are in the ¢500 range.

■■■ CAÑAS

Cañas is a small, sweltering town in the middle of the extensive ranch and farmland of Guanacaste. Don't worry if you don't see more of the town than the bus station; tourists usually only pass through here en route between the Pacific and Lago and Volcán Arenal. The town has excellent access to Parque Nacional Palo Verde, but so does the more hospitable town of Liberia. If you're looking for a river tour in or near Palo Verde, there are a couple of outfitters near Cañas that can help you out. Contact **Safari Corobici** (tel. 669-0544), four km north of Cañas on the Interamerican Highway, or **Lata Tours** in Bebedero, about 25km west of Cañas, accessible by bus.

The unmarked **tourist office** (tel. 669-1515) is located on the southwest corner of the stadium, which is two blocks north and one block west of the park on the highway. They provide useful information, but still can't tell you anything interesting about Cañas (open Mon.-Fri. 8am-noon and 1-4pm, Sat. 8am-noon). **Banco Nacional** (tel. 669-1144) is on the northeast corner of the park (open Mon.-Fri. 8:30am-3:45pm). **Phone calls** can be made from pay phones on the south of the park or from ICE (tel. 669-0028), 1 block south of the southeast corner of the park (open Mon.-Fri. 8am-3:30pm). The **post office** (tel. 669-0117; fax 669-0309) sits one block north and one block west of the park (open Mon.-Fri. 7:30am-5:30pm). The Cañas **bus station** is 4 blocks north of the park, and a couple of blocks east of the Interamerican Highway. **Buses** run to San José (Tues.-Thurs., Sat. six a day, Mondays seven a day, Fri. and Sun. at 5:15pm). To Tilarán (6, 9, 10:30am, noon, 1:45, 3:30, and 5:30pm; 45min.; ¢65). To Liberia (seven a day), to Puntarenas (seven a day), to Upala (five a day), to Bebedero (six a day). **Farmacia Actio** (tel. 669-0028) is on the south of the park (open Mon.-Sat. 8am-8pm, Sun. 8am-noon). **Pali Supermarket** is two blocks north of the northwest of the park (open daily 8:30am-7pm).

Hotels in Cañas are either cheap-and-it-shows or swish-swank-and-costly. In the budget range is **Hotel Guillen,** on the south side of the plaza. It's got the basics, and that's about all it has. Two out of three toilets have seats; try your luck. All rooms have tiny fans, though (¢600 per person, ¢800 for a room off the balcony overlooking the park). The **Gran Hotel** is nothing grand. Located a half block north of the northwest of the park, it's similar to Guillen in most respects, including price (¢700 per person). The ritz places in town are **Hotel Cañas** and **Nuevo Hotel Cañas.** The old one (tel. 669-0039) is a block north of the park's northwest corner, and offers singles for around ¢2000, doubles for around ¢3150.

Cañas has a few good places to **eat.** For general cuisine, there's **Hotel Cañas** (see above), where breakfast runs ¢400-500, meat plates about ¢800, and brobdingnagian portion of fried rice goes for a mere ¢600. **Buona Pizza** serves good pizza. Green and red table cloths, parmesan shakers, and big glasses of *refrescos* evoke Little Italy in the summer time. Small (plenty for one person) pizza (¢475-650), large ¢1400-1750. They serve other things, too (open Tues.-Sun. noon-10pm). If it's Chinese you crave, look to the restaurants on the north of the park's west side. Servings are generally large and cheap; chop suey, whoop-de-wooey; kung pao, holy cow.

■ PARQUE NACIONAL PALO VERDE

Palo Verde National Park is one of the most important wetland conservation areas not only in Costa Rica, but in all of Central America. Situated on the northwest corner of the Gulf of Nicoya, the park is bordered on the west by the wide, brown **Río Tempisque** and on the east by the **Río Bebedero.** Due to poor drainage, the area is subject to seasonal floods which create a wide diversity of habitats, including lowland mangroves, murky everglades, and rolling forests among limestone hills.

Some of the highlights of the park include four rocky **miradores,** or lookout points, from the tops of limestone hills; climb to these for spectacular views of the park and Río Tempisque slowly snaking its way to the Nicoya Gulf. **Mirador Guayacan** can be accessed from the Palo Verde Ranger Station. The view from the top is a satisfying reward for the half-hour hike through the sweat-inducing, bug-infested forest below. Aside from numerous nasty mosquitoes, you may run into monkeys, coatimundi, deer, and various bird life. Signs are few and far between and trails are not well marked, so it's often necessary to rely on divine intervention and inspiration to reach your destination.

The trail to **Mirador La Roca** trail starts about 1 km east of the biological station, which lies between **Puesto Palo Verde** and the turnoff from the park entrance. It takes only about 15min. to hike the trail, and the view isn't quite as good as from Guayacan (above). Two *miradores* can also be accessed from **Puesto Catalina** in the east of the park. For a closer look at the Laguna Palo Verde, around which the park is centered, visit the birdwatching tower near the biological station; approach quietly and you may catch an alligator or two sunning nearby.

Another possibility is a boat ride to **Bird Island** (Isla de Pajaros), which lies in the Río Tempisque on the edge of the park. **Chalalo,** a park ranger who lives at the Puesto Palo Verde, takes people on a trip reportedly costing ¢4000-8000. Try contacting the **Tempisque Conservation Area** (tel. 671-1290) in Bagaces for more info.

The park has two ranger stations where camping is permitted (Puesto Palo Verde and Puesto Cataline). From the park entrance, a road leads 6km into the park and then splits. One road leads west 9km to Puesto Catalina. None of these roads is paved, so they can get quite nasty during the rainy season. A semi-useful map of the park with bilingual information is sold for ¢200 at the park entrance, which is reached via a 28-km dirt road rom the town of **Bagaces,** about 25km from both Cañas and Liberia on the Interamerican Highway.

■■■ LIBERIA

A rough-and-ready working-class town, Liberia personifies the independent spirit of Guanacaste, the arid, self-reliant cattle-ranching region of which it is the capital. The area around Liberia is usually dry and desolate, but fortunately, Pacific beaches offer a tempting antidote to Liberia's oppressive heat, luring windsurfers and beach bums to their cool waters. Liberia is a pleasant enough town with plenty of services available, which makes it a good base from which to explore the beaches and national parks of Guanacaste, including the **Rincón de la Vieja, Guanacaste,** and **Santa Rosa National Parks,** which contain thermal springs, waterfalls, beautiful nature walks, and volcanoes. It's also just a little over an hour south of the Nicaraguan border, making it a convenient stop for those heading north.

ORIENTATION AND PRACTICAL INFORMATION

The city is built on a regular grid, but the well-organized streets have no names and addresses are given with respect to major landmarks and **Parque Central.** The most important of these landmarks are the **church** on the east side of the Parque Central, **La Gobernación** (the government palace) on its southeast corner, and **Banco de Costa Rica** on the park's northeast corner. The bus station is 4 blocks west and 3 blocks north of the park, and the Interamerican highway runs north-south about 6 blocks west of the *parque central.*

Tourist Office: (tel. 666-1606), 3 blocks south and 1 block east of the park's southeast corner; follow the signs from the south side of the plaza. Competent, English-speaking staff can answer most questions. Open Mon.-Sat. 8am-noon and 1pm-4pm.

Currency Exchange: Banco Nacional (tel. 666-0996), 3 blocks west of Parque Central's southwest corner. Open Mon.-Fri. 8:30am-3:45pm. **Banco de Costa Rica** (tel. 666-0148), on the northeast corner of the park. Open Mon.-Fri. 9am-3pm.

Post Office: (tel. 666-0359 or 666-1649), 3 blocks west and 1 block north of the *parque.* **Telegraph, fax,** and *Lista de Correos.* Open Mon.-Fri. 7:30am-5:30pm. **Postal Code:** 5000.

Telephones: encircling Parque Central, and at **ICE** (tel. 666-0166), 4 blocks east and 25m north of the park. Open Mon.-Fri. 8am-3:30pm. Another ICE office, 2 blocks west and 50 meters south of the park's southwest corner, has telephone and **fax** services (tel. 666-2255; fax 666-2019). Open Mon.-Fri. 7:30am-5pm and Sat. 8am-noon.

Supermarket Marillo y Castrillo: ½ block north of the park's northeast corner. Open daily 7am-8pm.

Buses: leave about 5 blocks northwest of Parque Central, opposite the market. To Playa del Coco (six a day, 40min., ¢120); to Playa Hermosa and Playa Panama (11:30am and 7pm, 1 hr., ¢120); to Puntarenas (5am, 8:30am, 10am, 11:15am, and 3:15pm); to San José (6am, 6:30am, 9am, 12:15pm, 5pm); to Peñas Blancas via La Cruz (8 a day, 75min., 200 colones); to Cañas Dulces (6am and noon, 4:30pm); to Bagaces and Canas (5:45am, 1:30, 4:30pm); and to Filadelfia, Santa Cruz, and Nicoya (hourly 5am-8pm).

Car Rental: Aventura Rent-a-Car (tel. 666-2349), in Hotel Bramadero, on the Interamerican Highway 6 blocks west of the park, rents 4-wheel drive vehicles to those over 21yrs old for US$69 per day including insurance and unlimited miles. 15% discount for 3 days and 25% for 5 days or more. Open Mon.-Fri. 8am-noon and 1pm-5pm, Sun. 8am-1pm. **Sol Rent-A-Car** (tel. 666-2222), across the highway, rents cars (3 days US$120, 5 days US$190), 4-wheel drive vehicles (3 days US$168, 5 days US$270), and minivans (3 days US$141, 5 days US$225), insurance and mileage included. Open Mon.-Fri. 8am-5:30pm, Sat.-Sun. 8am-5pm.

Luggage Storage: Nacascolo Tours (tel. 666-0450), 1½ blocks east of La Gobernación, holds bags for US$1/bag per day. Open Mon.-Fri. 8am-7pm, Sat. 8am-noon.

Market: 4 blocks west and 3 north of Parque Central, across from the central bus station. Open daily 8am-6pm.

Laundry: La Batea (tel. 666-2330), 1 block south and 1 1/2 blocks west of the park. Charges by the item: t-shirts ¢80, shorts ¢60, shirts ¢90, and pants ¢100. Prices go down for bigger loads. Open Mon.-Sat. 7am-1pm and 2pm-6pm. **Hotel Liberia** also has a washing machine. ¢500 for 1/2 load, ¢1000 for a full load.

Pharmacy: Farmacia Liberia (tel. 666-0747), 2 1/2 blocks east of the park's northeast corner. Open Mon.-Sat. 8am-8pm, Sun 8am-noon. **Farmacia Santa Margarita** (tel. 666-1665), 1 block north of the church's northeast corner. Open Mon.-Sat. 8am-8pm, Sun. 8am-noon.

Emergency: Contact the **Red Cross** (tel. 666-0994), 2 blocks east of La Escuela Enseñanza Especial.

Police: (tel. 117), in a large white building at the northwest corner of the Parque Central.

ACCOMMODATIONS AND FOOD

Liberia has a pretty good selection of budget accommodations due to all the tourists and business folk passing through. **Jade Tour** (tel. 666-1258), three blocks west of the park's northwest corner, arranges homestays with local families; bed and breakfasts run about ¢1000 a night. **Hotel Liberia** (tel. 666-0161), half a block south of the church, is the most amicable option; the cabins in the back are wondrous; the beds are large and comfy, and communal facilities are well-maintained. Washing machines, open-air design, a hammock, and delicious breakfasts (¢400) make guests even happier (¢1000 per person, with private bath ¢1500). **Hotel Guanacaste** (tel. 666-0085; fax 666-2287), 5 blocks west of the park's northwest corner (3 blocks south of the bus station). Clean and modern rooms surround a small garden and attached restaurant. Rooms and facilities are spiffy, but can be expensive (singles ¢2644, doubles ¢3526). Hostelling International members can get a bunk bed in a not-always-private room for ¢1000 per person. **Pensión Margarita** (tel. 666-0468), two blocks east of the northeast corner of the church, in a creaky building; gaps between walls, ceiling, and floor suggest the use of non-Euclidean geometry in the construction. Rooms are clean, but irregularly bulging mattresses make you take some lumps while sleeping (¢1000 per person).

Liberia has plenty o' good little restaurants and *sodas*. **Pizza Pronto**, two blocks south and one east of Parque Central, proffers a cheezy Italian remedy for those rice-and-beans blues. The smoky odor of adobe-baked pizzas floats through the classy wooden interior, right onto the neat map tables; watch yourself watching yourself. Medium Supreme serves 2, ¢1000. Pasta ¢800 (open daily noon-10pm). **Jardín de Azucar**, one block north of the northeast corner of the park, offers cafeteria buffet fare for cheap, including some vegetarian dishes. The heavily laden "plate of the day" comes with a drink (¢375). **Cuatro Mares** dillydallies 2 blocks east of the park's southeast corner. True to the Chinese food restaurant genre, the large menu boasts huge servings of cheap food (chop sueys ¢500, rice dishes ¢500; open 11am-11pm daily). **La Tortuga**, two blocks south of the southwest corner of the park, is a nice little bar and restaurant with garden dining. Beer on tap is served with a *boca,* little plate of scrumptious appetizers for free. A large pitcher goes for ¢1100, a small is ¢800 (open Tues.-Fri. 2pm-midnight, Sat. noon-midnight, and Sun. 11am-midnight). **Pop's** ice cream, next door to Las Tinajas, has yummy shakes and ice cream (¢160) to lick as you stroll about the park (open daily 10am-10pm).

SIGHTS AND ENTERTAINMENT

Traditional sightseeing within the Liberia city limits comes down to two museums. **Museo del Sabanero,** joined to the tourist office, is a single hallway with an exhibit depicting the daily routines of early farmers in the region (open Mon.-Sat. 8am-4pm; free) **Museo de Arte Religioso,** located in Iglesia Hermita, five blocks east of the church, is run by an elderly woman who lives around the corner, so hours vary (free). Nighttime diversions also come in pairs: **Discoteque Kuru,** across from the gas station (open daily 8pm-5am, or sometimes earlier, depending on the size of the crowd. Admission ¢500. Women get in free Thurs.). Or if you're in the mood for a movie, look no further than one block north of the park's northeast corner, where you'll find **Teatro Olimpia**. Stale movies are shown daily at 8pm.

■ NEAR LIBERIA

It goes to reason that there's nothing to do in Liberia proper; who would possibly seek entertainment in town when boundless opportunities await nearby? Well, not quite boundless; to find out more about nearby Santa Rosa, Guanacaste, and Rincón de la Vieja National Parks, contact the main administrative office for the **Guanacaste Conservation Area,** located in the Santa Rosa National Park (tel. 695-5598), 7km down a paved road from the entrance to the park, which lies on the Interamerican Highway 32km north of Liberia. (Buses between Liberia and Penas stop here, but from the entrance to the administration, you must walk or hitchhike. Let's Go doesn't recommend hitchhiking, but hitchers say it's pretty easy here.) For other info, call the toll-free National Park Services (tel. 192).

SANTA ROSA NATIONAL PARK

Santa Rosa is one of the few Costa Rican national parks which is important for its historical significance as well as for its ecology and natural beauty. It was here that Costa Rican forces under the command of President Juan Rafael Mora Porras defeated troops sent south from Nicaragua by the American filibuster **William Walker** (see page 264); the alacritous battle of Mar. 20, 1856 lasted only 14 minutes. At the time, Walker was already in control of Nicaragua and was attempting to take over Costa Rica. He was soon forced out of Nicaragua as well, and when he returned to Central America a little while later, again with hopes of conquering the whole region, he was captured and killed in Honduras.

The *hacienda* where the battle took place has been converted into a museum, the **Casona de Santa Rosa,** which presents the history of the battle, of Costa Rican daily life through the ages, and info on the ecology of the park. The Casona is located near the buildings 7km from the park's entrance, on the CA-1.

The ecology of the park is primarily dry tropical forest, which is home to 115 species of mammals, 250 species of birds, and 100 species of amphibians and reptiles. Perhaps the most beautiful parts of this park are the isolated expanses of sandy beaches which serve as nesting sites for 3 different species of sea turtle, including the endangered **Olive Ridley turtle.** Unfortunately, the beaches can only be accessed by a 12km dirt road that leaves from the administrative area. The road is often impassable during the wet season, so you should count on walking. About halfway to the beach, a couple of trails branch off the road to *miradores* (scenic lookouts), both of which lie about 1km from the road. The first, **Sendero Los Patos,** branches to the right, as does the second, **Mirador Valle Naranjo,** about 1 km later.

The second half of the road descends into a valley full of majestic trees and more exotic animals; you might see (or hear) howler monkeys, whitefaced monkeys, or white-tailed deer. Three km before the beach, the road forks and the left branch leads to **Estero Real** (an estuary where additional campsites are located). Soon thereafter, the land turns swampy, the air tainted with sale. The main **campsites** are nestled in a grassy, low forest running along the beach. The sites have running water, grills, and picnic tables. All campsites cost ¢300 a person a night; the entrance fee for foreigners is ¢2400 colones if you buy it at the park entrance, or ¢1600 if you buy it a day ahead of time in San José or at another National Park Service office. If you're looking for more than just a stroll on the beach, **Sendero Carbona** skirts the shore a ways inland, past **Laguna El Limbo** where crocodiles live.

The park entrance is 32km north of Liberia on the Interamerican Highway and can be reached on Liberia-Peñas Blancas buses. The 7km from there to the Casona and administrative buildings must be walked or hitched. Lodging is available at the administrative buildings for US$19.50 US a night. Meals are about US$4.45 each. September and October are the best times to catch turtles laying eggs on the beach.

GUANACASTE NATIONAL PARK

Santa Rosa continues on the other side of the Interamerican Highway, but goes under an alias: Guanacaste National Park. Like its namesake department, Guanacaste has a diverse ecology, including a rain forest, tropical wet forest, tropical dry forest, and cloud forest; the environment is similar to that of Santa Rosa at lower altitudes, but it changes along with elevation heading up the summits of **Volcán Orosi** (1487meters) and **Volcán Cacao** (1659 meters).

The park is exploited more by researchers than by tourists, so tourist facilities are not as well developed as in other parks. Guanacaste has three biological stations, each of which can provide lodging and access to different areas of the park. Lodging at the stations costs US$19.50 per person. Camping is also permitted near the stations for ¢300 per person per night.

Cacao Biological Station can be reached from the town of **Potrerillos**, 25km north of Liberia on the Interamerican Highway. From here you must go nine km to Quebrada Grande, then 15 km more to Gongora. From Gongora to the station, proceed on foot or by horse. The station has no electricity, and visitors must bring their own food. Trails lead from this station to another station (at Maritzo) and also to the top of the volcano. **Maritzo Biological Station** can be reached by an 18km stretch of unpaved road that starts from Cuajiniquil intersection on the Interamerican highway 8km north of the entrance to Santa Rosa. The station here does have electricity and food service is available if requested in advance. Rain forest, tropical dry forest, and transitional forest are all found near this station. **Pitilla Biological Station** can be reached from the town of Santa Cecilia 22km north of the entrance to Santa Rosa National Park. Pitilla is 7km south of this town by dirt road. It has no electricity or food service. For more info on the park and/or to make arrangements, contact the Guanacaste Conservation Area Office in Santa Rosa National Park (tel. 695-5598).

RINCÓN DE LA VIEJA NATIONAL PARK

Admittedly, the most outstanding feature in Rincón de la Vieja Park is the active **volcano** of the same name, whose towering 1898 meters are all the more intimidations combined with fume-belching and lava-spewing. Before going straight for the glowing goo, however, take a little time to explore the park's out-of-the-crater wonders. The lower altitudes abound with sulfuric lagoons, boiling mud pits, *volcanitos*, and thermal waters to bathe in. In addition, the park encompasses a large natural watershed system of 32 rivers and numerous small streams, which the park's hiking trails criss-cross at several points, sometimes over crashing, picture-book waterfalls, elsewhere over safe, placid swimming pools. The trails also wind from site to site through dense, wet forests teeming with white-faced, howler, and spider monkeys, coatimundi, and hundreds of species of birds, insects, and reptiles.

The only problem is getting to the park. It lies only 25km to the northwest of Liberia, but unfortunately no public transportation covers this distance. One dirt road leads from Liberia's Barrio La Victoria to the Santa Maria sector of the park. Another dirt road leads from 5km north of Liberia on the Interamerican Highway, heading 20 km west of the Las Pailas sector of the park. There are several ways to reach the park if you don't have a car. Park rangers' and other vehicles travel these roads fairly frequently and you could try to catch a ride. (Let's Go does not recommend hitchhiking.) **Hotel Guanacaste** in Liberia takes groups of 4 or more to the park, leaving at 7am and returning at 4pm for ¢1000 each way per person. Alternatively, you can hire one of the 4-wheel drive taxis in Liberia which charge about ¢4000 each way. A last option is to renting a bike in Liberia (see Liberia, Practical Information, page 380). Getting there is mostly uphill and quite hellish, but getting back to Liberia is a breeze.

The campsite in the **Las Pailas** sector, 100 meters from the entrance post, is right on the banks of a refreshingly beautiful river, good for swimming and whatever else. A shameless and plump coatimundi frequents the campsite in search of succulent bits of charity from campers. The park asks that you not feed the animals. An approximately 4km **loop trail,** east of the campsite, passes a small waterfall (only in the rainy season), a sulfuric lagoon, a *volcancito,* and the boiling mud pits. Trails to the west of the campsite lead to the park's biggest waterfalls, **Cataratas Escondidas** (4.3km) and **Catarata La Cangreja** (5.1km). The trail to the crater of Rincón de la Vieja leaves from the Las Pailas Sector, as well. It is 7.7km to the top; allow an entire day for the round-trip journey.

The **Santa Maria** sector is 8km east of Las Pailas, used to be a cattle ranch; a large part of it is currently being reforested. This sector also has a **campsite**, 1 km west of which (toward Las Pailas) tumbles the waterfall of the **Bosque Encantada;** 2.75km west of the campsite (6km east of Las Pailas) are the **aguas termales** (hot springs), which supposedly have therapeutic powers. The trails through the thick, monkey-filled forest are well-marked. Entrance to the park costs ¢2400 the day of visit, ¢1600 bought in advance at another park or at a National Park Services office.

A few km from the park beckon a number of mountain lodges offering meals, lodging, and horseback riding tours of the park. **Hacienda Guachipelin** is located on the road from the Interamerican Highway to Las Pailas, 5km before the park (tel. 442-2864 during office hours). The lodge charges US$14 for a single and US$32 for a double, but has student discount rates for beds in a bunk house (¢1000). There are also student rates for meals. Normal price for the bunkhouse is US$9. Horses rent for US$12 for a half day, US$18 for full day. Other lodges with similar rates and services are the **Albergue Buena Vista** (tel. 373-5000) and the **Rincón de la Vieja Lodge** (tel. 695-5553). Contact the tourist office in Liberia for more information.

BORDER CROSSING TO NICARAGUA

Liberia is only an hour away the border at Peñas Blancas; **buses** leave at 5:30, 8:30, 9, 11am, noon, 2, 6, and 8pm (1 hr., ¢200). Be sure to arrive early in the afternoon since Nicaraguan immigration closes at 4pm.

At Costa Rican **immigration,** show your passport and pay ¢75 exit fee. Money changers here can change dollars or colones to córdobas. From there, buses go to the Nicaraguan immigration office, 4km to the north (5 córdobas). Taxis may be available as well. Once there, you must pay a US$2 entry fee (only in US dollars), then move on to pay US$5 for a tourist card. Last but not least comes the baggage inspection in customs. Nicaraguan boys hang around to guide you through this complex process for a few córdobas. There is a bank on the Nicaraguan side that changes dollars to cordobas, and money changers outside can change colones too (but be careful, they like to rip off tourists). Buses run from here to Rivas 37km to the north. If you're going to San Juan del Sur get off at La Virgen and head to San Juan from there.

■■■ PLAYA HERMOSA

This beach's name speaks for itself. Having successfully resisted pressure from wealthy investors who endeavor to turn the beach into a tourist trap, Playa Hermosa is everything Playa del Coco might once have been: tranquil, clean, pristine. The beach's blissful sands remain relatively secluded, and you may wind up completely by yourself, on a lucky day during the low season. The water is generally gentle, but keep an eye out for riptides. When the tides are just right, waves pound the shore powerfully and the surfing here can get heavy-duty.

Playa Hermosa's **post office** (i.e. place to drop off mail) is located at Aqua Sports (tel. 670-0450, see above). A **pay phone** can be found at the Bar Rancho de Nando, 200m up the main road, past Agua Sports. An extremely modest **grocery store** is located in the same building as Aqua Sports. Expect cookies, canned tuna, and overpriced pop; don't expect bottled water (open daily 8am-10pm). Getting between

Playa Hermosa, other local beaches, and the big cities is difficult, but not impossible. A **bus** bound for Playa Hermosa (and Playa Panamá, just to the north) leaves San José from Avs. 5/7, Calle 12 (3:20pm, 5 hrs.). The bus back to San José leaves Playa Panamá at 5am and passes Hermosa shortly thereafter. This is the only direct bus to San José, so arrive at the main road early in order to flag it down. Buses from Liberia depart for the two beaches daily at 7:30, 11:30am, 3:30, and 5:45pm. The bus from Playa Panamá headed back to Liberia comes along the same road (at 6, 10am, 4, and 5pm; 1 hr.; ¢120). Playa Hermosa is 10km north of Playa del Coco on a paved road, and then a kilometer's walk (or taxi ride) west, down a dirt road. Locals are working to connect the two beaches by a road.

There are only two hotels in town that are even remotely affordable for budget travelers. The first, **Cabinas Playa Hermosa** (tel. and fax 670-0136), is on the high end of the price spectrum, but it delivers. Rooms are spacious, irreproachably clean, and equipped with closets, mirrors, fans, and—though it's doubtful anyone will need it—hot water. With shady trees and a beautiful view of the ocean, its outside garden area is perfect for reading and relaxing. (Singles US$25, doubles US$40, triples US$50, quads US$60, quints US$70. Prices reduced US$10-20 in the low season.) A cheaper but less glamorous option exists in **Cabinas Vallejos,** the faded yellow *cabinas* behind the restaurant next door, each of them a sparse and sanitary quad with a shared bathroom. (¢2000 per person).

Food is not cheap here. But the *restaurant* in Cabinas Playa Hermosa provides a cool respite from the heat and glare of the beach. Besides admiring the hotel's garden, lucky diners are also amused by watching the circus of animals that loiters about the tables—parrots, iguanas, and a squadron of lovely toads. Beware of the monkeys; they've been know to jump right onto the table and steal the food out from under gaping human jaws, in turn prompting the managers to hurl rocks in their direction. Gorge on grilled red snapper ¢1100, and shish kebab ¢900, fine view of the ocean included (open daily 7-10am, noon-3pm, and 6-10pm.) Next door to the cabinas of the same name skulks the tiny **RestauranteVallejos** (tel. 670-0402); the two aren't related. There's no cheaper restaurant in town. Whole fish ¢800, *arroz con pollo* ¢750, steak ¢700 (open daily 7am-6pm). There's also a tiny and comfortable restaurant *within* Cabinas Vallejos, with a limited menu of *gallo pinto* (¢400) for breakfast and *casados* (¢500) the rest of the day (open daily 6am-9pm).

The only diversion from tranquil lounging awaits at **Aqua Sports** (tel. 670-0353; fax 670-0439), which rents snorkeling equipment (US$5 per ½ day), boogie boards (¢150 per hr.), and plenty of other water toys. They also have boat trips to nearby beaches, leaving in the morning and returning at the end of the day (¢5000-8000 total, can fit up to 6 people). The boats and windsurfers are rented out from June to November only, when winds are low (office open daily 8am-5:30pm). **Southern Exposures Expeditions** (tel. 670-0458) provides boat trips to Witch's Rock, a surfer's haven with perfect, tubular waves off Santa Rosa National Park, as well as tours with multilingual private guides to various national parks (US$55-85).

■■■ PLAYA DEL COCO

Playa del Coco, only 37km west of **Liberia,** is the most easily accessible and—surprise—the most touristed beach on the peninsula. Many Costa Rican families spend their vacations here, and the beach sports several busy restaurants and numerous anchored boats. For all first impressions are worth, though, Coco projects a rather disagreeable one. The orange-and-yellow cluster of benches that marks the center of town is a tacky eyesore, the dock is rickety and decrepit, and loud bubble-gum pop blares from a beachside discotheque at all hours of the day and night. But beyond the less-than-utopic exterior lies a long stretch of clean (if not crowded) white sand beach and calm water for swimming or snorkeling. Solitudinous succor, however, is also not one of Coco's strong suits. You won't be alone. If you are looking for nightlife, on the other hand, there's plenty. Head to **Discoteque CocoMar** (tel. 670-0358) on the beach, right next to Cabinas Coco, where the music is pumped out nightly from 8pm to 2am (cover ¢300-400, depending on the night).

Practical Information and Accommodations The **police** (tel. 117, 670-0418) are next to the bus stop, in the same building as the post office but around on its back side (open 24 hrs.) There are no **banks** in Playa del Coco, but cash and traveler's checks can be exchanged in the **Casino de Coco Restaurant** (tel. 670-0292) next to the disco (open daily 8am-2am) or at the **Luperón supermarket** (tel. 670-0150), on the west end of the soccer field (open Mon.-Sat. 7am-8pm, Sun. 7am-noon). The **post office** (tel. and fax 670-0418), next to the bus stop, posts a *lista de correos* and provides **fax** and **telegram** service (open Mon.-Fri. 8am-noon and 1-4:30pm). The **bus stop** is located at the end of the main road, in front of the post office, by the ugly orange benches. **Buses** for Playa del Coco leave San José daily at 10am from Avs. 1/3, Calle 14, and return to San José from Coco daily at 9:15am (5 hrs., ¢560). Coco-bound buses leave Liberia at 5:30, 8:15am, 12:30, 2, 4:30, and 6:15pm, and return from Playa del Coco at 5:30am, 2, 3, and 6pm (1 hr., ¢140). Buses from Sardinal depart at 11am daily and return from Coco at noon. Buses depart from Playa del Coco for San José (9:15am), Liberia (7am, 2pm, 3pm, and 6pm), and Filadelfía (11:30am and 4:30pm).

Lodging in Playa del Coco is expensive, but compared to the other pricey beaches in the area, Coco may seem like a budget paradise. The best deal can be found at **Cabinas Catarino** (tel. 670-0156), on the main road into town about 100m from the bus stop—look for the small blue sign. The rooms are simpletons, but they're pretty spacious and have a private bath, along with kitchen privileges and laundry service. Catarino, the owner, is quite a card-player. (¢1000 per person). For double the colones, and nearly double your pleasure, well-maintained rooms with fans and private baths can be had at **Cabinas Luna Tica** (tel. 670-0127; fax 670-0246), one block to the left of Hotel Tica Luna Anexo (its newer, more expensive sister). Laundry service is available, check-out at 2pm. (Singles ¢2245, doubles ¢2775, triples ¢3570, quads ¢4485. Rooms with air-conditioning cost even more.) **Camping** sites can be found at the well-lit **Guardaropa y Camper Afor** (follow the big signs near the soccer field). Campers have access to showers and toilets, and a locker for storing bags is included. It's even possible for beach-bathers to rent a locker just for one day. The communal bathrooms are scum-slicked (i.e. bring sandals for the showers), but the owner swears he's about to renovate. There are also cabins available for groups of 7-12, with a kitchenette and private bathroom (¢900-1300; camping ¢500 per person. One-day locker rental for non-campers ¢300.)

Food and Entertainment A slew of *sodas* cluster near the bus stop. On the main road, **Soda Restaurante, Teresita, Marisquería el Paraíso, Soda el Almendro,** and **Restaurante Oasis** (across the street) all serve inexpensive, typical Costa Rican food. For something different, head over to **San Francisco Treats,** on the main road, for a taste of sunny California. The vegetarian lasagna (¢800) and black bean chili with smoked chicken (¢525) are delicious, but it's the amazing brownie sundae topped with ice cream (¢500) that brings in the crowds (open Sun.-Tues. and Thurs. 11am-10pm). **Mariscos la Guajira** (tel. 670-0107), on the beach behind Restaurante Papagayo, sets its tables on an open porch facing the ocean, and dangles an intimidating collection of large shark jaws behind the bar. Steak and onions ¢700, shrimp salad ¢1300 (open daily 10am-10pm) For a good attempt at the fine-dining effect, try **Restaurante Cocos** (tel. 670-0113), across the street from the post office. Grilled fish goes for ¢900, and a lobster will set you back ¢3500 (open daily 11am-11pm). Don't overlook the tiny but lively **Bohio Yacht Club** (tel. 670-0047) next door. They've got cheap Mexican food (enchiladas ¢350, tacos ¢300), as well as nine types of pizza. Free chips and salsa during the 4-6pm happy hour, and as the sign in the window says, there's a karaoke nightly, "God willing." (Open Mon.-Fri. 3pm-1am, Sat.-Sun. 10am-2am.) To satisfy those disco-induced hunger pains, check out **Casino de Coco,** next to the discotheque (tel. 670-0292). Despite the spurious name, there's not actually a casino here, though employees are quite adept with money and perfectly happy to exchange cash and traveler's checks. The dining room is large and has an open view of the ocean (Spaghetti ¢450, fish ¢450-1300; open daily 8am-2am). **Soda Coco Mar** is just a little food stand by the disco—not much selection, but good for a greasy snack. Eat outside, though—the few patrons at the scuzzy-looking tables behind the counter subject themselves to cheesy American reruns on TV. Hot dog ¢150, fries ¢150 (open daily 9am-2am).

Besides the discotheque (which the entire town revolves around), Coco's next big attraction to offer are the **water sports. Rich Coast Diving** (tel. 670-0176), about 300m up the main road, rents snorkeling gear (mask and snorkel US$3 per day, fins US$2 per day, wetsuits US$7 per day), and scuba gear (US$25 per day, US$6/air fill). They also offer open-water scuba certification (US$295) and day-(US$40) and night-(US$45) scuba diving trips (open daily 8am-5pm). Across the street, **Diving Safaris** (tel. and fax 670-0012), has snorkeling, surfing, and fishing trips, and **Mario Vargas Expeditions** (tel. 670-0351) has daily dives leaving from 9am-1:30pm (open daily 8am-6pm).

CARIBBEAN LOWLANDS

The boggy coastal lowlands that line Costa Rica's eastern shore with the Caribbean Sea articulate a drastic contrast to the more stereotypically *tico* land and culture of the Pacific seaboard. Physically, the lowlands support none of the volcanoes, jagged peninsulas, or cool cloud forests that best characterize the parkland west of the Central Valley. Instead, get prepared for a relatively deserted Caribbean beachscape, replete with constant (daily, at least) precipitation, unbroken sandy beaches, inland tidal marshes, and muggier than muggy weather. You're not in California anymore. The local populace's constitution is also quick to demonstrate the difference that a few hours' bus trip can make; the diverse ethnic and cultural makeup of the region's cities and maritime villages is reflected in their cuisine and their language, as well in their faces. Limón, or Puerto Limón, Costa Rica's premier but decaying Atlantic port city, serves as a crossroads for tourists traveling to points of ecological and recreational interest north and south, like the **Tortuguero** breeding grounds, the national park at **Cahuita,** or the placid beach community of **Puerto Viejo de Talamanca.**

■■■ LIMÓN

Limón is the largest city on the Atlantic coast and is a vital port for the entire country, yet it's continuously given the shaft in the larger public's eye. Due partly to racism toward the city's mainly Afro-Caribbean population, as well as to inflated rumors about rampant crime and drug abuse, many *ticos* unjustly denounce Limón as a hopeless slum. True, this place sees grimmer action than most other areas of the peaceful and tourist-oriented nation, but it's not the spawning pit of evil that it's commonly made out to be. Poverty runs deep in Limón, due in large part to Costa Rica's 1991 earthquake, which hit this province the hardest. Afterward, the government turned Limón an unduly cold shoulder, and denied the city sufficient federal money to rebuild. Four years later, there are still burgeoning ranks of abandoned buildings, all slouching in shambles, and the tap water is not yet safe to drink. Clearly, Limón is not the darling scenic village designed exclusively for Mlle. Tourist's pleasure. Most travelers stop here just long enough to change buses or occasionally to spend the night, as Limón is the transportational hub between the Caribbean coast and the rest of the country. But a few beautiful sights, like the view from Parque Vargas or the *malecón* (the seaside boardwalk), show that Limón didn't and doesn't need to be the Compton of Costa Rica. Once a year, partiers flock in from all over for the **Día de la Raza** (Columbus Day) celebration on October 12, a festive carnival of music, dancing, and drinking spilling out into the streets for a week. If you happen to be in town, just grab a tambourine and jump into the flood of merrymakers; odds are, it will parade through the city until dawn.

Orientation and Practical Information Although Limón does have a system of *avenidas* and *calles,* they're hardly ever used, and finding street signs is nearly impossible. Ask a local on the street which *calle* he's on, and odds are he won't know. For those who insist on doing things the hard way though, the intersection of Avenida 1 and Calle 1 is in the southeast corner of town and at the southwest corner of Parque Vargas. From there, the east-west *avenidas* increase by ones as you head north, and the north-south *calles* increase by ones going west. But invaluably more useful is knowledge of a few local landmarks—the **Mercado Municipal** in the center of town (Avs. 2/3, Calles 3/4) is the major one; **Parque Vargas,** in the southeast corner of town, is another.

The **police,** as always, can be reached by dialing tel. 117, or go directly to the Organismo de Investigación Judicial, the **OIJ** (tel. 758-1865), a sort of Costa Rican FBI, in the Corte Suprema building, 100m east and 100m north of the market. Alternatively, if you've passed Go and you've a fistful of dollars and nowhere to spend them, check out **Banco Nacional** (tel. 758-0094), which sits across the street from the south side of the market (open Mon.-Fri. 8:30am-3:45pm). The **post office** (tel. 758-1543), southwest of the market, has a *lista de correos* (Mon.-Fri. 7:30-11am and 1:30-5:30pm), as well as **fax** and **telegram** service (open Mon.-Fri. 7:30am-5:30pm). The **bus stop** for San José is 100m east, 50m south of the market (daily, every hour on the hour from 5am-7pm; 2½ hrs.; ¢510). The bus stop to Cahuita and Puerto Viejo is located 100m north, 50m west of the market (buses leave daily at 5, 10am, 1, and 4pm; 1 hr., ¢135 to Cahuita; 1½ hrs., ¢200 to Puerto Viejo). Buses run to Moín, the departure point for Tortugero, from a stop 50m west and 50m north of the corner of the Cahuita/Puerto Viejo stop (buses leave daily every hour on the hour from 6am-10pm, 20min., ¢28). **Taxis** are easier to catch than mosquito bites, stopping most frequently at that **Mercado Municipal** which has been popping up so much. Full of bustling fruit stands, it sprawls 300m west of the beach. **Farmacia Buenos Aires** (tel. 798-4430), 25m east of the Banco Nacional, is open Mon.-Sat. 7am-7pm. **Hospital Tony Facio** (tel. 758-2222), is a bit of a walk away, about 300m north along the *malecón.* **Red Cross** awaits patiently at tel. 758-0125.

Accommodations and Food Spending the night in Limón isn't pleasant. Actually, nothing in Limón is very pleasant after dark; it's usually a good idea to clear out of here before nightfall. Stay away from the ultra-cheap places (under ¢1200)—you get what you pay for, and these generally aren't so safe. But don't fret, there are some decent, secure, and inexpensive accommodations to be found.

The **Park Hotel** (tel. 758-3476), along the *malecón,* 200m east of the mercado is the best, if extra cash becomes available. Not only do the suites have amazing ocean views, but they've also got private bathrooms with hot water (!) as well as a fan (of inestimable importance on the Caribbean coast), freshly washed sheets and towels, and plenty of toilet paper. The rooms are rather boring and the bathrooms have seen cleaner days, but the windows make it worth the going ("Moderate" singles ¢2100, doubles ¢3234, triples ¢3800.) Though it doesn't have a view (except for serious students of Limón's street culture), **Hotel Tete** (tel. 758-1122; fax 758-0707), southeast of the *mercado,* across the street from the post office, has just about everything else it needs to keep guests comfortable. There's a sort of lounge on the breezy balcony with couches, the daily paper, and a big color TV; just inside the lobby there's also a coffee maker and a water cooler. Rooms are spacious enough to fit a desk, luggage rack, ceiling fan, phone, double bed with comforter, and very green private bathroom (singles ¢1800, doubles ¢2500; add ¢400 for air-conditioning). The truly tight-budgeted travelers will probably flock to **Hotel Palace** (tel. 758-3419), 100m east, and 50m south of the northeast end of the *mercado,* where bright pink walls are the first to tip you off that this is not the planet's premier *château du chic.* It wouldn't kill the staff to be a bit friendlier, the mattresses

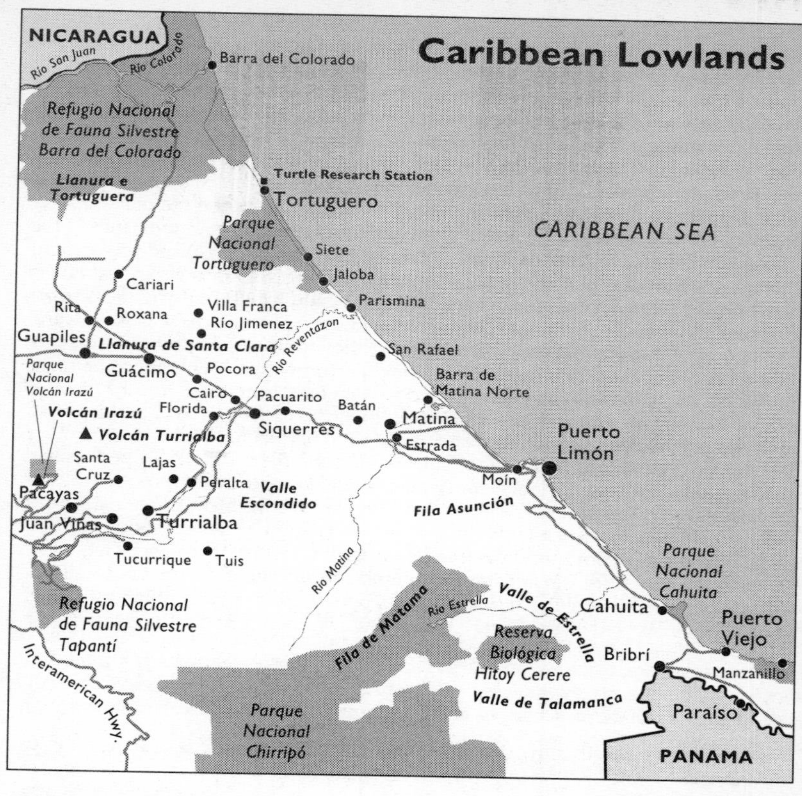

sag pitifully, and the communal cold-water bathroom smells just as raunchy as it looks. On the bright side, rooms are secure and there's a hanging garden over the open patio (singles ¢1150, doubles ¢1850).

Grub in Limón is like standard San José fare with a Caribbean twist. *Gallo pinto* and *casados* still reign supreme, but fresh seafood also finds its way onto most menus. Remember, though, it's the big city; to find real down-home Caribbean cooking, look to smaller towns down the coast. **Soda Mares** (tel. 758-1347), across the street from the south side of the *mercado*, tries really, really hard to seem beachy, stuffing itself with assorted tropical kitsch, potted palm trees, plastic-lobster-studded fishing nets, and a sailor's wheel. The seafood is great, but a little pricey. *Ceviche de pulpo,* surges with various denizens of the undersea, octopus taking center stage (¢950; open daily 6am-10pm). Don't be turned away by the run-down exterior of **Restaurante Doña Toda,** on the east side of the *mercado*—the inside's simple but comfy as can be and prices are low. Enjoy plastic chairs and paisley tablecloths while spending a measly ¢400 on a full meal of *casado,* or ¢2200 for a sandwich. Diners daring and dastardly will ask about the *aleta de tortuga* (turtle fin) dinner (¢500; open daily 7am-7pm). Drop by **Soda Bar Restaurante Kings** (tel. 798-4614), on Calle Central, 50m north of the northeast corner of the *mercado,* for a quick bite while waiting for the Cahuita/Puerto Viejo bus. It's a dark, simple café with a big bar area in the back, or eat burgers (¢180-270; open daily 10am-10pm).

Sights and Entertainment It's important to find something worthwhile in your trip to Limón. Be careful while walking through the **Mercado Municipal** (Avs. 2/3, Calles 3/4). Even though it may seem calmer and more organized than most central *mercados,* it's venerable territory for pickpockets. The Caribbean influence is quite apparent here, where vendors proudly display fresh coconuts, bananas, fish, and lobster. To get to **Parque Vargas,** in the southeast corner of town, just look up and walk toward the towering coconut palms. It's also a plethora of wildlife—hummingbirds darting from flower to flower, the occasional sloth bumbling around in the treetops, young tykes playing tag. Right along the ocean, it's possible on a clear day to see the island of Uvita, 1km away, where Columbus landed on his fourth and final journey to the New World; Limón is full of pride for the famous explorer (they've either forgiven or forgotten their subsequent treatment at the hands of the European *conquistadores*). Come around Columbus Day (Oct. 12) and you're in for a chaotic whirlwind of festivities. If another ocean view sounds good, just take a stroll down the *malecón,* a coast-hugging promenade which starts by the *parque* on the south side of town and makes a relaxing walk as it wends its way northward. But be smart and think a little before taking the stroll—it's not safe to be alone around dawn or dusk, and no sane, unarmed person would ever want to be there after dark, alone or not. The young crowd looking for waves, rays, or just a place to chill usually heads over to **Playa Bonita,** 4km northwest of Limón, a beach with a split personality. On one side, the water is calm and perfect for wading; on the other side, the waves start to build up, so surfers and swimmers can live in perfect harmony, and later relax with a beer and a never-ending reggae beat for backdrop, as it emanates from a nearby bar. To get to Playa Bonita, take the Moín bus and get off at one of the first stops (just ask the driver), or take a taxi, which costs about ¢400.

At night, Limón's hot spot is the **Bar Acuarius** (tel. 750-1010), a dance club in the Hotel Acon, across the street from the Mïnpik and the supermarket. It's a a dim-lit and simple place where the reggae rhythms pound, and where a number of older men come to sit and stare. Cover charge ¢200, women free on Thursdays (open Tues.-Sun. 8pm-3am).

■■■ TORTUGUERO

Nobody knows exactly how they do it, but every year hundreds of female turtles return from points very far and very wide to the familiar beaches of **Tortuguero National Park,** 83km northwest of Limón, to lay their eggs. Native indigenous peoples thought the turtles were guided by nearby Tortuguero Mountain; scientists believe the chemical qualities of the sand and sea may leave some kind of imprinting. However they do it, the turtles swim thousands of miles from all throughout the Atlantic ocean to get to this spot. The most famous turtles are the *tortugas verdes* that nest from the end of June through September. Contemporaries of the dinosaurs, the green turtles have been around for over 100 million years, and only now are they being forced to take a long hard look in the face of extinction, thanks to modern man, and in particular to the artificial oceanic jetsam that suffocates their nests and to the poachers who steal their eggs. Plastic bags are often responsible for asphyxiating the endangered reptiles, who mistake them for edible jellyfish. To our credit, Dr. Archie Carr founded the Caribbean Conservation Corporation in 1956 to help bring the sea turtles into the international limelight, and in 1970 the Costa Rican government declared this 35-km long strip of land and sea a national park.

More so than almost any other place, it's hard to imagine Tortuguero accurately without actually seeing it. Disneyland must've modeled their Jungle Boat cruise after it, the chief difference being that here the sounds of the howler monkeys in the treetops, the rainbow-beaked toucans coasting overhead, and the leathery caimans stealthily gliding through the water are all real. And there are no African hippos. In Tortuguero National Park, wildlife peeks around every twist of the canals; you just have to keep your eyes and ears open and your mouth shut.

Getting There Cheaply? Try hitching a ride on a leatherback's shell, because anything else is going to cost colossal colones. There are two ways to go about trekking to Tortuguero—either invest in one of the prepackaged tours which includes hotel and transportation, or be adventurous and travel independently. Shopping around for a good packaged deal is a smart idea—it's definitely a less nerve-wracking way to travel, and could actually be much cheaper than doing it yourself. **Tortuguero Expeditions** in San José, Av. Central/Calle 11, Office 34 (tel. 222-2175), in the white building at the corner, offers a two-night trip including transportation, hotel room, and guided tour, starting at US$55.

Alternatively, you might go for the self-sufficient, adventurous option of doing it all yourself, which is likely to cost around US$70. Not exactly a sight for sore budget traveler eyes, but the few boat pilots have a real stranglehold on the market, and gasoline is expensive for them in the first place. The *lanchas,* here flat-bottomed six-person boats covered by canopies, leaves from the port of Moín from the northwest corner, 50m west of the Cahuita/Puerto Viejo bus stop (daily every hour from 6am-10pm; 20min.; ¢28). When the huge Del Monte and Dole banana boats come into view, that's Moín. Walk downhill towards the water, to the small dock behind Restaurante Papa Manuel, where *lancha* pilots are usually waiting to make their killing. A round-trip boat ride usually costs around US$50. Single travelers are sometimes quoted prices as high as US$120; hook up with some people and kvetch just a little and the price could drop as low as US$45 each. *Lanchas* usually leave early in the morning, and it's possible to stay in Moín instead of Limón, at the **Hotel Moín Caribe** (tel. 758-2436), up the road from the docks, where ¢1500 buys a comfortable night's sleep with a double bed, private bathroom, and color TV on request.

The ride to Tortuguero is a scenic two-hour journey down an artificial canal—that is, unless the *lancha* gets stuck in tangled masses of water hyacinth, in which case your travel time could double. Try to find a loquacious pilot; this ride can be almost as interesting as a tour of the National Park itself, as you tool past legions of monkeys, turtles, baby crocs, and bright-plumed birds along the canal's banks. Passengers are dropped off in Tortuguero Village, a light sprinkling of houses, inexpensive hotels, and small *sodas* at the north end of the park.

Practical Information Other places may call themselves villages, but Tortuguero Village is *small.* Bring bottled water from the mainland, as the price for it here is hiked beyond belief. A flashlight is also a must, especially during rainy season, as the power tends to go out during storms. It's almost pointless to try to give directions, as there are no streets here (just makeshift dirt paths), and buildings are scattered about. Just ask a local for directions—this place is small enough that any visitor staying more than a day's time will know its buildings like his or her own knuckles. Some useful landmarks are the **kiosk** in the center of town that dishes out info about the park and the **soccer field.** The national park is on the south side of the village.

The best place to go for information is **The Jungle Shop** (tel. 710-6716; fax 233-2243; beeper 233-3333, #631), just northwest of the kiosk, where Antionette Gutiérrez, an American, and her *tico* husband Elvin sell souvenirs and give invaluable aid and advice. Call before arriving and they'll arrange a tour with local guides. (open daily 9am-6pm). Another good place to go is **Souvenir Paraíso Tropical** (tel. 710-0323), 100m north of The Jungle Shop, where they speak English. These are the only two places in the village with private phones.

There are no **banks** in Tortuguero Village, but The Jungle Shop and Paraíso Tropical can exchange traveler's checks. **Mail** can be sent using the Cortel service near Paraíso Tropical. There are **public telephones** at Miss Junie's, along the main path toward the north side of town, and at Pulpería Jorge, in the center of town. For any problems requiring a **doctor,** or the **police,** go to the central headquarters of the park service, the Administración de Tortuguero, at the south end of town. In case of a serious **medical emergency,** a doctor in Limón can be called from The Jungle Shop or Paraíso Tropical.

Accommodations and Food All the ritzy, expensive hotels are across the canal; in Tortuguero Village the lodging is strictly budget. The best value in town is actually in a new and as yet unnamed establishment—look for the white building with a green roof and an awning made of palm fronds; just south of the soccer field. The rooms are pretty spacious and have three beds, and the private bathrooms are big, with modern showers. Plus, the owner is really nice—she even brings candles to each room when the electricity goes out (¢1000 per person). **Cabinas Mery Scar,** 200m south of the kiosk, has very basic, box-like rooms and a primitive communal bathroom—but at least it's clean. It's a family-run establishment, so please be quiet and let the kids get some sleep in the 10pm-8am quiet hours, and don't be surprised if breakfast is waiting on the table when you wake up (¢1000 per person). If money is an object and also the *only* object, head over to **Cabinas Sabina,** 100m east of the kiosk. But beware—don't expect the warmest of welcomes, and you may have to share the room with some unexpected creepy-crawly roommates (¢750 per person with collective bath). **Brisas del Mar,** north of the kiosk, is a good deal but only for big groups. A no-frills, four-bed room, and use of the cold water communal outhouses costs a flat ¢2400; get some friends to share it and then do some computing—it may well work out to be the cheapest option in town.

There's really no such thing as a typical **restaurant** in Tortuguero Village. Most of them are run by women who spend the day taking care of the children and cleaning the house—but if people decide that they'd like to eat on her converted front porch, she's happy to cook for them, in exchange for a dash of cash, of course. Often, it's necessary to give a few hours' notice before a big meal—after all, someone has to go out and catch the fish. A quick, easy place to stop is **El Tucán Soda and Restaurante,** just northwest of the kiosk. It's got you covered for every meal—from a *gallo pinto* breakfast with eggs, cheese, and ham (¢500) to a whole fish dinner with potatoes and a salad (¢850; open daily 6am-8 or 10pm, depending on customer-turnout). For some sweet homemade Caribbean cooking and an absolutely sweet lady, head over to **Miss Junie's,** 200m north of The Jungle Shop. She'll cook whatever's caught that day, but give her a few hours' notice so she can have the meal ready exactly when her guests want it. Fresh fish ¢800 (open daily 7am-9pm, or longer if there's sufficient demand). "Dear Visitor Welcome" greets the sign outside **Restaurante la Macha** (tel. 710-6716), just east of the Pulpería Jorge, and indeed it is welcoming, with open windows all the way around and little garden inside. The only stand-offish gesture is that they charge ¢25 to use the bathroom. *Gallo Pinto* with eggs (¢375), *casado* with chicken or steak (¢500), fried fish (¢800; open daily 7:30am-9pm).

Sights and Entertainment Before going out on a nocturnal run to see the turtles, check out the Caribbean Conservation Corporation's **museum** at the **Natural History Visitor Center.** They show a 15-min. video about the history of the region, the park, and the sea turtles first, and then open up a number of exhibits about all the area's flora and fauna (open Tues.-Sun. 1-6pm; admission ¢200).

Now that you're good and educated, it's time for the biggest event around here—the nightly *desbove,* the laying of the turtles' eggs. The female turtle makes her way up the sand, constantly pausing to look for danger, until she finds the perfect spot. Then she uses her rear flippers to dig a one-foot deep body pit with a cavity for the eggs. After laying about 110 of her leathery eggs, she fills in the hole with sand and returns to sea, the entire process taking about one hour. Don't try to watch the *desbove* unguided, because the beaches are dangerous at night and most people who don't know what they're doing are prone to scare the turtles away. The national park takes people out on a two-hour sighting for US$5; buy tickets at the information kiosk at 5:30pm. However, this expedition leaves at 8pm, and it's best to look for the turtles as late as possible. Most local guides charge about the same price as the park and will go at any time; ask around. When you go, wear good walking shoes and dark clothing, and don't bring a flashlight or a camera with a flash—bright lights blind the turtles and they won't be able to make it back to the sea. Just follow the guide's movements and try not to make any extra noise, because if a turtle is disturbed before she starts laying her eggs, she'll abandon her spot and go back to the water. Different types of turtles are around throughout the year, but the popular *tortuga verde* only nests from June through September.

The portion of the park that can be seen without a guide or a boat is limited. The park's ranger station is at the south end of the village; two hiking trails start from there (open daily 8am-4pm; admission ¢2400). **Sendero El Gavilan** is 2km long, and **Sendero Gavilan Tucán** is 4km—quiet hikers may be able to spot monkeys, toucans, and those tiny red poison dart frogs. But hiring a guide is much more informative and, if you find the right one, much more fun. **Mr. Dama's** tours are a blast—start off in a canoe, then enter a jungle path that Dama cleared away himself, complete with a wild swing made from a vine and a piece of wood. Dama's lived here all his life and knows just about every species of plant, animal, bird, and insect (at least by their local names)—he'll probably even let you handle a few, including the poison dart frog. (*Let's Go* does not recommend playing with venomous animals, but Mr. Dama does seem to know what he's doing.) Look for Dama's place near Cabinas Mery Scar. (¢500 per person per hour. Tours usually last 4 hrs. Does not include admission fee to the park.)

Other guides, however, can provide a flora and fauna-filled day without ever entering the national park (thus evading the dread entrance fee). The same biological thrills and chills can be had from the **Caño Palma biological station** and its surrounding canals, and admission there is free. If you make it to Caño Palma, look for Canadian scientific officer Pat Opay—he's a great source of information.

■■■ PUERTO VIEJO DE TALAMANCA

Don't move too fast in the cozy beach village of Puerto Viejo—it might scare the locals. Puerto Viejo's all about unwinding and forgetting life's worries for a while; in fact, there's a growing population of Europeans and *norteamericanos* who have encountered such terrific success in these exotic endeavors as to have made permanent and unanticipated homes out of their vacation getaways. Blond Californian surfers meet dreadlocked Caribbefarians on the glistening black beaches; it's such a small place that after a day or two, they're likely to be old friends. The locals are very concerned about preserving the environment and promoting local tourism (goals that go hand in hand here, in a rare and Platonic confluence of prudence and morality), so don't expect any resorts to pop up here any time soon. The living here is simple and slow, and you've brought too much ambition if you're armed with any plans beyond catching the perfect wave or the perfect tan.

Practical Information The first place to take your questions should be the **ATEC** (Talamanca Association for Ecotourism and Conservation) office in the center of town. Their grass-roots organization was founded in order to promote local tourism while preserving the region's heritage and ecology. Mauricio Salazar, the president, often guides wilderness tours of the area. The staff of ATEC can give information about local hotels, restaurants, rental stores, as well as seasonal tours (open Mon.-Fri. 7:30am-noon and 1-8pm, Sat.-Sun. 8am-noon and 1-5pm).

There aren't any **banks** in Puerto Viejo, but **Pulpería Girasol,** just north of the center road in the middle of town, exchanges money and traveler's checks at no commission (open daily 9am-9pm). ATEC serves as a **post office,** sells stamps, and has a *lista de correos.* **Faxes** can also be sent from there. The three **public phones** each charge ¢100 per minute: at ATEC (7am-9pm), Hotel Maritza (just east of the bus stop inside town; 8am-10pm), and Pulpería Manuel León (down the street from Hotel Maritza, past the center road; 6am-8pm). There's only one **taxi** in town—approaching from the bridge, make the second right; the sign says "Charlie's Taxi Service," but everyone knows him as Bull, and if Bull's red minivan isn't parked outside, it's likely to be pulling in soon. Various other truck owners, like Spence of Cabinas Spence, are willing to give rides, but they're likely to charge more. **Laundry** can be done at Girasol or the Old Harbor's Fresco Shop (turn left just after crossing the bridge) for ¢750 per load. There is no **pharmacy** in Puerto Viejo, but Pulpería Manuel León's got the basics, like aspirin and Alka-Seltzer (open daily 7am-8pm).

When the bridge at the entrance to town in traversable condition, the **bus stop** is by the abandoned barge, 50m west of the Hotel Maritza. Otherwise, it's just outside of town, in front of the bridge. Direct buses to San José leave daily (6:30am, 9:30am, and 4:30pm; 4 hrs.; ¢635). Buses to Cahuita and Limón leave daily (6am, 8:15am, 1, 4, 5, and 5:15pm; 30min., ¢100 to Cahuita; 1½ hrs., ¢235 to Limón). Buses for Bribri and Sixaola leave daily (6:20, 9:20, 11:20am (Bribri only), 5:20pm, and 7:15pm).

Accommodations The **Jacaranda Cabinas** (from the center road, follow the signs to The Garden), in the middle of town, weren't named after a tropical flower for nothing. Some people would probably pay admission to see the incredible collection of birds of paradise, orchids, lilies, and hyacinths here—and many more are glad to be served at The Garden restaurant, which occupies the same plot. Small touches make this place heavenly, from the hanging wicker lanterns in the patio area to the bamboo ceilings. Even the communal bathroom seems quaint. Singles ¢1500, doubles ¢2000, triples ¢2400. At **Cabinas Casa Verde** (from Restaurante el Parquecito, walk 100m away from the center road and turn left), the house isn't actually green, but its gardens look well greenthumbed-through. The sign rightfully proclaims, "Peace and quiet in the heart of Puerto Viejo"—even close to the center of town, its wooden gate is all it takes to achieve pacific seclusion. Each room has its own front porch with hammocks and lounge chairs, the perfect place to just kick back and hide from the world for a while. Communal bathrooms, but a sink in each room. Laundry service available (spacious singles US$10, dinosaur doubles US$15). A favorite among surfers and tight-budget travelers, **Hotel Puerto Viejo,** between Restaurante el Parquecito and the soccer field, is for rugged types. Their doubles have dumpy cots or makeshift bunk palettes, and the wooden walls look fit to collapse. The dirt-cheap singles downstairs are called "the dungeon," and aptly so. But people keep flocking back—maybe it's the friendly Californian owner and his Hawaiian dad, or maybe it's the Mexican restaurant downstairs (singles ¢800, doubles ¢2000). Another popular place for surfers is the beachfront The adventurous will want to head toward the **camping area,** outside of town, about 50m past Salsa Brava. For only ¢300, Miss Iris (known affectionately by regulars as Mama-San) will rent out a tarp-covered camping space, and if you don't have a tent, she'll give you a hammock for free (but you're on your own to battle the mosquitoes). There's even an outdoor kitchen with pots, pans, and a wood-burning stove, as well as refrigerator access (well, maybe not *that* adventurous). Some people stay for months at a time, forming their own little community. Iris locks campers' bags up in her house at night, but be careful; it's still not so safe outside, even during the day.

Food Locals often actually claim that there's nowhere to eat in Puerto Viejo. They're either just being modest, or they have incredibly high standards. Although many an Italian restaurant has laid claim to the title, **Coral,** off the center road in the middle of town, just may have the best pizza in Costa Rica (¢540-¢945, depending on toppings). They also have excellent whole-wheat buttermilk pancakes (¢375) and divine key lime pie (¢250; open Tues.-Sun. 7am-noon and 5:30-9:30pm). **Old Harbor's Fresco Shop,** between the bridge and the bus stop on the road along the beach, full of healthy treats like fresh-squeezed orange (¢150) and carrot juices (¢200), granola with yogurt and fruit (¢400), and homemade banana bread (¢150). Vegetarian options, as well as seafood and grill specials, can also be found at **The Garden,** which you can find by following signs off the center road in the middle of town. A self-proclaimed Carib-Asian delight, it features original creations like *roti* with Madras curry, a wheat-and-potato flatbread filled with vegetables and cooked in a curry sauce (¢1095). Unfortunately, it's often closed during the off-season. Of course, good old down-home Caribbean cooking never comes in short supply here either. Most places serve out on a converted front porch and have a simple, easy-to-remember two-item menu: jerk chicken and fish cooked *a la caribe,* with a sauce made from coconut oil. The prices are usually about the same also—¢500-600 for the chicken, ¢700-1000 for the fish, depending on its size. **Soda Tamara,** across the street from ATEC, right in the center of town, is another popular spot, offering *patacones* (fried green plantains: *very* Southern) to accompany meals for ¢100 extra and delicious homemade desserts, like buttercake and brownies, for ¢90 (open Wed.-Mon. 7:30am-9pm).

Sights and Entertainment Most surfers head straight over to **La Salsa Brava,** the surf-hole extraordinaire to the east of the village. Unfortunately, there's nowhere to rent surfboards in town, so it's strictly BYO-board. The waves over here are a little too strong for swimmers, but look for **Annu** (a septualingual Swiss-Indian) in front of Restaurante el Parquecito—he rents boogie boards or snorkeling equipment for ¢1500 per day. Many of the hotels and shops in the area rent **bikes;** Old Harbor's Fresco Shop charges ¢800 for five hours, ¢1400 for an entire day. **Tortuguero Tours** (fax 798-4244), 50m north of Restaurante el Parquecito, rents bikes for ¢1000 per day and horses for US$7 per hour without a guide, US$45-75 for two to four riders to spend three hours with one guide. They also arrange tours: to Tortuguero, for two days and one night including hotel, guide, and transportation (¢9500), or for just one day (US$50); to Mazanillo and Punta Mona for five hours, including lunch and transportation (US$40 each for two people, US$30 for three, US$25 for four); or just three hours' trail-hiking with a guide in the nearby hills (US$15). Liberated women and men should ask about the Woman Jungle Trips, a one-day trip to Manzanillo guided by a female, at the Old Harbor's Fresco Shop (2-3 people pay US$30 each, four to six people US$25 each).

Laid-back as Puerto Viejo may be, the locals don't go to sleep when the sun goes down. Many head over to **Johnny's Place,** next to the Pulpería Manuel León, a Chinese restaurant by day and a raging disco by night. All types of music get air-time here, from salsa to reggae and back again. Another disco cooks it up at **Stanford's Restaurant Caribe,** over by Salsa Brava (open Mon., Wed.-Fri. 7pm-midnight, Sat.-Sun. 7pm-1am).

■ NEAR PUERTO VIEJO

PUNTA UVA

If Puerto Viejo begins to seem too crowded or the surfers' mating cries too loud, no need to fuss. That sublimely secluded beach with the perfect waves lies somewhere down the coast. Moving southeast, the closest beach to Puerto Viejo is **Playa Cocles,** 2km down the shore, which reputedly offers the best surfing on the Caribbean coast. Next in line is **Playa Chiquita,** 4km farther down. Another 7km along the road lie the gorgeous white sand beaches of **Punta Uva.** The warm water is perfect for swimming and the small waves that break close to shore are ideal for body surfing. Best of all, it's usually empty, and so solipsistic seekers of personal pan-paradises ought to rejoice. Palm and mango trees line the shore only 150m from the water's edge, trailing purple-flowered vines that creep along the ground for a few meters closer—and then…just the pristine smoothness of unbroken beach. Wheehooo! Look to the east to see the actual "grape point" for which this place is named—a small peninsula juts off the shoreline, exposing a natural tunnel, like a little window to the ocean on the other side. Nobody has to think too much about Desolation Row, between the windows of the sea, where lovely mermaids flow. Everyone visiting Punta Uva stays in **Selvin's Cabinas** (look for the sign off the road). Though the doubles are pretty spartan, the cold-water communal bathrooms are downstairs, and the walls are so paper-thin you'll pray there's not a snorer next door, still Selvin and his family are great, and the 50m path to the beach is just a few steps away. Additionally, there's a good restaurant open during the weekends. Doubles ¢1500. For hungry weekday guests, **Naturales** is right across the street, with an astonishing three-story view to offer. The food couldn't be fresher, but beware—the menu deceptively puts the prices in dollars, not colones, so a meal can be rather expensive. Shrimp in garlic sauce US$7.50, i.e. ¢950 (open Fri.-Wed. 2-10pm.)

MANZANILLO

The village of **Manzanillo** is another 5½km southeast. Also blessed with a spectacular beach, Manzanillo is best distinguished by its trailhead that opens onto the dense jungle path that trots from village, down the beach, all the way to Panama. This long stretch of land is part of the **Gandoca-Manzanillo Wildlife Reserve,** based in the town of Gandoca, 9km away. The main purpose of this refuge is to protect the *baulas* (leatherback turtles) that lay their eggs in the sand of Gandoca's beach.

There's only one place to go in the village of Manzanillo, and that's Maxi's. Set back from the beach a little, **Restaurant Maxi** serves delicious fresh seafood from a lovely, ocean-looking upstairs porch. The catch of the day costs ¢600-800, depending on its size, lobster ¢2000. That green building behind the restaurant is **Cabinas Maxi,** pretty basic digs, with rugged bathrooms and mattresses on the floor doing their best bed-impressions (doubles ¢1500).

From Maxi's, start following the dark dirt trail between the restaurant and the beach. Walk a few hundred meters, passing a soccer field, until you reach a small lagoon. To the right there's a wooden bridge leading to a house—Willie Barton, who guides jungle tours for ¢2000 an hour, lives there. Keep on keepin' on, cross a small stream, and see the trail begin amid a forest of coconut-laden palms that extends up to the horizon. The path is really nothing more than a series of small, unmaintained clearings between the trees; even in the dry season, it's often necessary to climb over branches and rocks to stay on track, and during the wet season mud-swimming may be your only option. Wear sturdy shoes and insect repellent, and bring bottled water. It's a bad idea to try this hike shortly after rainfall, as it can be easy to lose the trail amid the undergrowth. After about 10 minutes' walk, the trail climbs uphill and culminates in an excellent lookout or camping spot—a cliff that leans out into the water, a modest but defiant precipice. The trail continues on another 2km to **Punta Mona,** another impressive vantage. Most people end their walk here, but it is possible to continue on another two hours to the Gandoca ranger station, or another three hours to the Panamanian border.

Ordinarily, buses run from Puerto Viejo to Manzanillo, leaving daily at 7am and 4pm, passing through Punta Uva and the other beaches. Due to the poor condition of the roads and bridges however, that bus hadn't run in years as of summer 1995, and no one knew when it might start running again. Ask about it at the ATEC office in Puerto Viejo. Otherwise, your only options are walking, biking, hitching a ride, or taking a taxi (which will cost ¢1000-1500 from Puerto Viejo to Manzanillo). The walk along the beach is gorgeous and peaceful, about one hour to Punta Uva, and another 80 minutes to Manzanillo.

■■■ CAHUITA

Silhouettes of palm trees on the white sand against a stunning pink-and-orange sunset. Clear, warm, turquoise eaves lapping up on a black sand beach. Dark howler monkeys playing in the treetops of a coastal rainforest, crying out their jarring and unearthly rhapsodies. Such are the sights of Cahuita, 48km southeast of Limón, destination of nature-lovers, Rastafari, and laid-back beach bums of all shapes and sizes. Most come for **Cahuita National Park,** southeast of the village, home to the best coral reef on Costa Rica's Caribbean coast, as well as a pristine white-sand beach and a jungle trail. But the other side of the village is no slouch—there, sun-worshippers can find a black-sand paradise.

Not all of Cahuita is so idyllic. The village itself is rather grimy, and has gotten increasingly unsafe in recent years. Theft is a constant danger, and it has gotten practically impossible to walk down the street at night without garnering solicitations for something or other illicit. (It is rumored that many of the dealers here are in cahoots with the police; as soon as they make their sale, the cops move in to nab the buyer.) As usual, women shouldn't walk alone at night. But relax your grip on that can of mace; a vast majority of Cahuita's visitors report no problems of any sort.

Practical Information There are no banks in Cahuita, but **Cahuita Tours and Rentals** (tel. 758-1515, ext. 232, 758-0652; fax 758-0652), 200m northwest from the bus stop and away from the park, will exchange dollars and traveler's checks—for a ridiculously high rate of commission. It doubles (more kindly) as an excellent source of information about Cahuita in general, and it's staff speaks good English (open daily 7am-noon and 1:30-7pm). The **post office** can be reached by continuing past Cahuita Tours towards the black beach and turning right (open Mon.-Fri. 8am-noon and 1-5pm). The **postal code** is 7302. **Faxes** can be sent from Cahuita Tours and Rentals (see above). There are **public telephones** at Cahuita Tours, Hotel Cahuita (200m toward the park, from the bus stop), and Soda Uvita (100m short of the park, from the bus stop). The **bus stop** is in the center of town, across the street from Salon Vaz. Buses head to San José (daily at 7am, 9:30am, and 4:30pm; 4 hrs.; ¢650), to Limón (5, 8, 10am, 3, and 7pm, but are often late; 1 hr.; ¢135), and to Puerto Viejo (6, 9, 11am, 1, and 5pm; 30min.; ¢100). You can do **laundry** at Cabinas Palmer (tel. 758-1515, ext. 243), 50m northeast of the bus stop, toward the ocean, ¢10 each for socks and underwear, ¢50 for larger items. Return to Cahuita Tours with your **rental** needs: they loan bicycles out for ¢1000 per day, as well as snorkeling gear (see Sights, below), and arrange four-hour **tours** of beaches and indigenous communities by Jeep (ask for prices) and glass-bottomed boat rides for US$20.

Accommodations and Food **Cabinas Vaz** (tel. 758-1575, ext. 218), 150m southeast of the bus stop, has large, clean rooms. They even leave fresh soap and toilet paper for each new patron to use in the private bathrooms, some of which have hot water (singles ¢2000, doubles ¢2500, triples ¢3000). The scenery at **Cabinas Sol y Mar,** 200m southeast of the bus stop, near the entrance to the national park (tel. 758-1515, ext. 237), is more extreme: the rooms hide behind a ramshackle yard hung with laundry, but its spacious rooms are graced with exquisitely carved wooden headboards and a mahogany dresser set. Plus, the immaculate private bathrooms actually have hot water! A breakfast-only restaurant (from 7:30am-noon) sees globe-trotting Nintendo fans face the *tico* masters (singles ¢1500, doubles ¢2500, triples ¢3500). **See-Side Cabinas,** from the bus stop walk towards the ocean and turn right at the beach, run by Nan-Nan and his girlfriend Vanessa, can't be beat location-wise. Just don't spend too much time in the rooms, or you'll end up fending off roaches or scraps of falling stucco. All rooms with private bath and cold water; try to bargain (doubles ¢2000, triples ¢2500, quads ¢3000). **Hotel National Park** (tel. 758-1515, ext. 244) is at a prime location—right on the white sand beach, at the entrance to the national park. It's a new place—in fact, so new that as of June 1995, guests were living on the second floor while the third floor was still being built. There are definite benefits to staying in such a new hotel; the showers in the private bathrooms (with hot water) are clean, newly tiled, and roomy, and the towels are still fluffy (doubles ¢2500, triples ¢3500).

Any hungry traveler's first stop should be at **Miss Edith's:** walk 100m from the bus stop toward the beach, make the first left, and continue 300m to the end of the road. It's almost as much of a landmark as the National Park, and rightfully so—the Caribbean-style food is absolutely delicious. Feast on incredible vegetarian yuca vegetable soup (¢375), fish in coconut milk (¢980), or her special *rondon* stew (¢970-1880)—but let her know your wishes at least four hours in advance (open Mon.-Sat. 7am-noon, 3-6pm, and 7-10pm). **El Cactus** (tel. 758-1515, ext. 276), toward the black beach on a side road before looking for the sign, has a European feel—it's an Italian joint run by a Brit, with some delicious food. Many different individual pizzas for around ¢650, pastas around ¢850. Mouth-watering crepes with chocolate and banana or rum and lemon for ¢350—all of it excellent. Live music on the weekends during high season (open Tues.-Sun. 4-11pm). **Soda Sedentario,** diagonally across from Salon, Vaz, is the perfect place for a quick, natural snack. Tropical breakfast with juice, fruit salad and yogurt, toast with marmalade, and coffee or tea (¢400), mixed salad (¢300), and a fruit stand (open daily 7am-5pm).

Sights Even though most of the park is not even terrestrial, the coastal rainforest is the most accessible area of the park. A 7-km trail leads from Cahuita Village into the park, around the peninsular **Punta Cahuita,** and to the **Puerto Vargas station** at the other end. Everyone's wallet gets a break here; generally admission is not charged when entering from the Cahuita side, nor are there official park hours. Walk ½km away from town on the beach behind Hotel National Park until you see the path jutting out through the trees, just past a small lagoon. The walk along the trail is wonderfully disconcerting. Look to the left and there's the rolling waves of the Caribbean drumming against a secluded white-sand beach. Look to the right and the picture has totally changed—now there's a swampy forest thick with red mangroves and towering coconut-bearing palms. The treetops of Cahuita are some of the best places in the country to spot monkeys; loud shrieks from the howler monkeys are the surest sign that they're nearby. Just look for a rustling in the trees and you're likely to spot one. At sunrise and sunset, the playful primates often come down from their perches to frolic on the beach, so come early to try to catch them. The half-hour walk itself is flat and not strenuous, but it's a good idea to bring bottled water and insect repellent.

Looking down on the trail can be rewarding. Orange hermit crabs, some as big as baseballs, scurry across the path alongside white ghost crabs. Observe the backs of those brightly striped lizards carefully—if there are spines running down to the trail it's an iguana; if not, then it's probably a Jesus Christ lizard (so named for of its ability to walk on water, and not for any physical resemblance). The medicinal *sangrillo* tree's trunk has thick folds bunching up and protruding so as to make the tree to look as if it were resting on a wrinkled pyramidal base. The "bloodwood" is named for its crimson sap. Delicate blue porter weed, with its tiny, butterfly-attracting flowers lines the sides of the trail, together with rows of tough, leathery ferns.

But Cahuita's real claim to fame can't be seen from the hiking path, as it lies about 100m off-shore, in its spectacular coral reef. In the past few years, the reef has been shrinking, due in part to the accumulation of eroded soil from banana plantations, and in part to the 1991 earthquake. These influences have made it nearly impossible for snorkelers to find good reef sites on their own—there's too much dead coral floating in the water for casual expeditions to get very far—and so it's better to ask a park ranger at the Puerto Vargas station exactly where in relation to Punta Cahuita the sea life is most visible and abundant, or else to hire a local fisherman (ask for Robert) or a guide from Cahuita Tours to go out in a boat. Cahuita Tours and Rentals rents snorkel equipment (see Practical Information, above) for ¢1000 per day, but scuba divers ought to bring their own equipment. Detritus notwithstanding, once you find the right spot around Punta Cahuita and it's amazing. Elkhorn and brain corals line the ocean floor (and yes, it does look like noggin-innards). Look, but don't touch—too much handling kills the coral. Fish of all shapes, sizes, and colors of the rainbow make their home in Cahuita's reef, including queen angelfish, French angelfish, rock beauty, blue parrotfish, and even the great barracuda.

Camping is permitted near the Puerto Vargas side of the park. Each of the 48 camping sites is removed some from the hiking path and includes room to park a car, as well as a picnic table and a personal ocean vista. Latrines are spaced out, and there are showers, sinks, and toilets at the Puerto Vargas ranger station.

SOUTHWEST COSTA RICA

Costa Rica has been so heavily barraged with tourists seeking untouched nature that presumably it's all been touched by now. On the contrary, the southern part of

Costa Rica, from San Isidro de El General and Parque Nacional Chirripó to Peninsula de Osa around Golfo Dulce, offers the kind of "come and get me if you dare" attractions that brought travelers to Central America in the first place. The going's a bit rougher than elsewhere in the country (buses aren't occasionally late here; they frequently *don't come*), but you're more likely to interact directly with the nation's people, while praising the size of their forests' anteaters and sloths. If derring-do doesn't do it, the region has its share of beckoning beaches, which are ideal and idyllic places to snag a snooze before dashing off into Panama.

■■■ SAN ISIDRO DE EL GENERAL

The modern city of San Isidro provides links to the real world for the residents of several nearby farming villages; for travelers, the city serves as a springboard for the unreal worlds of Parque Nacional Chirripó, the main entrance to which stands in nearby San Girardo. Don't bounce away too hastily, though; unlike San José, San Isidro has retained almost all of its small-town charm, a trait which hasn't been lost on the many U.S. citizens who've come to retire here. Relax over beer and *criollas* with them and local farmers at Hotel Chirripó; just watch yourself on Sundays during the soccer season, when a win brings a nearly riotous bombardment of happy, firecracker-laden fans through the streets.

ORIENTATION AND PRACTICAL INFORMATION

San Isidro is numerically gridded along *calles* and *avenidas,* but few streets are actually marked. Fortunately, the warm residents of San Isidro are more than happy to direct tourists around the city. The **cathedral** is adjacent to **Parque Central,** at the intersections of Av. Central and Calle Central. Most services are nearby. The police station is about 10km outside of San Isidro, near Río San Isidro.

Currency Exchange: Banco Nacional del Costa Rica, (tel. 771-32-89), on Av. 1 and Calle Central, changes currency, traveler's checks, and gives cash advances on Visa. Open Mon.-Fri. 8:30am-4pm.

Post Office, (tel. 771-0348; fax 771-3060), on Av. 4 and Calle 3, offers public **faxes, telegrams,** *lista de correos,* and public bathrooms. Open Mon.-Fri. 7am-5:30pm. **Parte-Tica** (right next door) sells envelopes, postcards, greeting cards, and paper. Open Mon.-Fri. 8-11am and 2-5:30pm.

Telephones: Public phones are clustered on Parque Central.

Farmacia San Isidro (tel. 771-1467), on Calle Central near Parque Central. Well-stocked, minimal English spoken. Open Mon.-Sun. 7am-8pm.

Clínica Dental, Av. 3 on Calle Central (tel. 771-0985). Get your wisdom teeth pulled by Dr. Matamoros. Open Mon.-Fri. 9am-1pm and 3-7pm.

Buses: the 5am bus to San Girardo and P.N. Chirripó leaves from the Parque Central/Pollo Delji stop, at 2pm from the main terminal at Av. 6 and Calle Central (1½ hrs., ¢130). To San José go MUSOC buses from Av. 3, Calle 2 (¢540). Buses to Puerto Jimenez leave from Av. Central, Calle 3 next to the gas station (5:30am, noon; 5 hrs.).

Taxis: A taxi to San Girardo runs approximately ¢2000-2500 (tel. from San Girardo, 771-1161).

Public Transportation: The two buses that operate from San Isidro to neighboring towns are commonly known as the "big bus" and the "small bus." The van-like bus (¢45) takes less time (15min.) than the larger, multi-colored buses (30min., ¢25). Buses run daily 5:30am-10:30pm.

Car rental: National Car Rental, (tel. 771-1037), at Av. 2 and Calle 1. Must be 21 years. A basic, "Class A" car costs US$38 plus US$13 tax. Valid passport required. Major credit cards accepted. Open Mon.-Sat. 8am-6pm, Sun. 8am-4pm.

Travel Agency. Agencia de Viajes Colón, S.A. (tel. 771-1772), located on the second floor of Edicifio de Gonzalez on Calle Central and Av. Interamericana. Mon.-Fri. 8am-noon and 2-6pm, Sat. 8am-2pm. Very friendly service.

ACCOMMODATIONS

Hotel Chirripó (tel. 771-05-29), Av. 2 at Calle 1. Located in the heart of San Isidro. Rooms are immaculate, as are shared bathrooms. The patioed café in back provides extra safety. A popular point for travelers to congregate. 24 hr. reception (singles with bathroom ¢1420).

Hotel Jardín (tel. 771-03-49), Av. 2 at Calle Central. The reception desk is a laundry table in the washroom out back, but somehow the hotel retains dignity. You could even live in the ultra-clean tiled bathrooms, but don't bother; the rooms are very well-kept, as well (singles ¢1200, doubles ¢1400, triples ¢2000).

Hotel Lala (tel. 771-0191), on Calle Central at Av. Interamericana. Bauhaus design in design and in price. Well-kept quarters are furnished with requisite desk-look-alike slab of wood, mattress, and optional private bath. Public bath equipped with 1 toilet, 1 sink, 1 shower (singles ¢500; doubles with bath ¢970).

Hotel Balboa (tel. 771-7676), Av. 1 and Calle 2, welcoming lobby with regular clientele watching TV, reading the paper, and gaily whooping it up. Rooms surround the lobby and are adequately equipped with queen-sized beds, chair, desk. No fans, so it's a bit of a human greenhouse. Public bathrooms only (singles ¢400, doubles ¢800, triples ¢1300).

FOOD

There are *sodas* on every corner; each has its own pack of regulars. For fruits and vegetables, check out the weekly Farmer's Market, held Friday mornings from 8am-2pm. The **market** takes up Av. 6.

Pizzeria El Tenedor (tel. 771-08-81), Av. 1 and Calle Central. Small, medium, large pizzas with the works. Large pizza goes for ¢1000. Wind up belly-up on the bar while the DJ j-j-jams the tunes (with anchovies). Open daily 2pm-10pm.

Pollos Delji (tel. 771-5747), Av. 2 at Calle Central. Hang with the teeny-boppers at San Isidro's own version of the Peach Pit. Regress with checkered tiles and 2 pieces of chicken, a *papita,* and a Coke (¢450); it's enough for two!

Bakery, Av. 2, Calle Central. Uncommercialized, fresh-smelling temptations. Chomp into a *Campesino,* a volcano-like, foot-log loaf with tomato sauce (¢115), San Maria bread for ¢70 load. Cake, cookies, and a fruit-filled swiss cheese bar (¢50).

Soda José, Av. 2 at the Interamerican Highway. Costa Rican staples like *chicarrones, criollas,* and *comidas especial.* Get a hearty plateful of grub (¢100-350).

■ NEAR SAN ISIDRO

SAN GIRARDO

One km from the bus stop, the tiny town San Girardo seems to think its pretty big; fewer than 1000 inhabitants enjoy a multi-purpose recreational facility, the site of frequent discos, classes for adults, and of course, all-popular soccer games. The people are very down to earth, and are always ready for questions about a Chirripó, a park they consider their own. To call anybody in San Girardo, call the town's only phone (tel. 771-0433)

You can stay the night in **Cabinas Descanso,** the first lodging on the road into town. The hotel has been frequented by many a foreign tourists, most of whom left behind their business cards. It's not surprising; the **restaurant** hang-out is charming, complete with a foosball table, a wall of trophies and medals won by park ranger and hotel co-owner Francisco, and some darn fine food (rice with a choice of fish, chicken, or steak ¢500). The **rooms** are small but clean, and have clean communal bath; sleeping bags rented for ¢1000. Reserve ahead of time in the summer (Singles without bath ¢600, with bath ¢1000; doubles ¢1200; bed in a dorm room ¢500). **Hotel Roca Dura,** near the public phone, the farthest cabinas on the road, is as convoluted as the Swiss Family Robinson Treehouse. Climb Mt. Chirripó, or gawk at the abstract depiction on the huge boulder out front. The rooms are small, but the views are worth the stay. The lobby is a patio overlooking an unbelievable valley

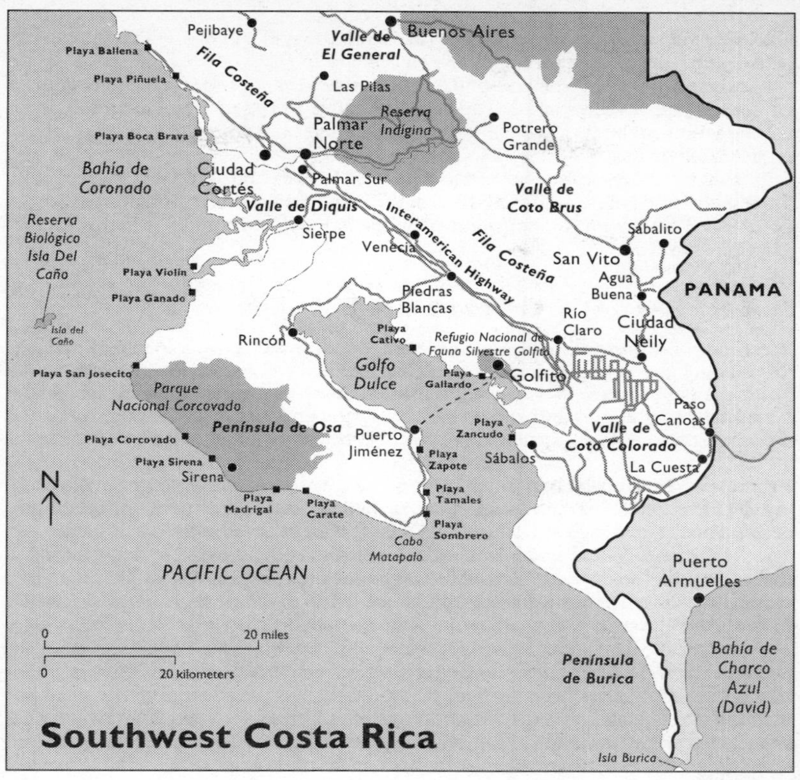

(singles ¢500, with bath ¢1000; doubles ¢1000; quads with bath ¢400 per person. Dorm rooms also available, but reserve in the high-season.)

PARQUE NACIONAL CHIRRIPÓ

After being bombarded with the roaring cascades of Río del Pacífico, the cooing of countless birds, and the mooing of grazing cows, even the most jaded cynics wax poetic about P.N. Chirripó, home to the highest peak in Costa Rica (3820m). The aftermath of the devastating forest fire of 1992 manifests itself only in the park's adamancy against camping and smoking outdoors, which is how the fire originated. For more information before your hike, stop in at the **tourist office,** which is clearly marked, 50ft. from the bus stop in San Girardo. They provide clear advice on recommended trails, maps, equipment, and safety tips, including the "Manual de Ingreso." Plus they'll hit you up for the non-Tico ¢2400 admission fee. Francisco, the park ranger, rents out horses during the spring and summer seasons from ¢400 per hour.

To take it all in, the park ranger recommends three days at Chirripó. The climb to Mount Chirripó, takes eight hours from the San Girardo base at the tourist office. Plan ahead accordingly. There are two main trails, one leading to Mt. Chirripó and the other leading to the **Crestones,** a rock-climber's fantasy. The trail to Mt. Chirripó is tame—wide, cemented, clearly-marked, and frequently traveled by tourists. No guides are required for the trail and the ranger considers it safe for solo hikers, women, and novices. On the way to the peak, hikers can stop to drink and fill up on potable water near Cerro Urán; bring plenty of water anyway. About 8km into the hike, the **Refugio Llano Bonito** provides food and shelter for those dividing their hike over intervals. Other *refugios* lie 12km into the trail and 6 km from the peak. Hire a guide to take the other path, which is new.

Reservations should be made with **SPN-Mirenem** (tel. 771-3155), the park council, for lodging at the *refugios.* The only alternative to the cabins is **camping,** but tenting is only at the end of the Río Tierra, and then only with a group of 15 people for a fee of ¢300.

Be aware that during the winter season, the trail to Mt. Chirripó can get very cold, the temperature falling as low as -10°C at the peak. Additionally, though hikers are considered safe from human night prowlers, jaguars and other beasties roam Chirripó after dark.

■■■ PUERTO JIMÉNEZ

Everybody knows everybody else in Jiménez, which was built by gold-miners earlier this century as a center of trade and exchange. Gold still exists here, actually, and hotels pander to travelers with the fever, offering gold-panning tours along the Osa Peninsula. More importantly, Jiménez sits near the entrance for P.N. Corcovado, a well-preserved rainforest which draws the majority of the peninsula's tourists.

Practical Information What can ambitiously be called the town's commercial center is actually a small strip of the main road, one that is neither paved nor even named. The **police** station (tel. 735-51-14) is right before the soccer field and across the street.Two **mercados** provide necessary produce, and a boutique across the street offers shampoo, lotion, etc. **Telephones** stand ready for public use near Cantina Catalina. The **post office** (tel. and fax 735-5141), near the *soda* and across from the field, has **fax, telegrams,** and a *lista de correos* (open Mon.-Fri. 7:30-11:30am and 1:30-5:30pm.) **Banco Nacional de Costa Rica** (tel. 735-5020; fax 735-5006) exchanges dollars and traveller's checks and gives cash advances on Visa. The **bus** to San Isidro leaves from the Soda de Frutera, across the street from the Judicial Building (9am, 3pm; 4-4½ hrs.; ¢680). The other option is to take a **ferry** (¢500) from Golfito at the port, which can take 1½-3 hours, depending on the captain's particular mood. Ferries leave Jiménez at 6am and depart from Golfito at 11:30am. more ferry stuff: Accurate and efficient service to Golfito, leaving at 6am and returning to Jiménez at 11:30am. Information for chartered **planes** can be found at either the Puerto Jiménez (tel. 735-5178; fax 735-5112) or Golfito office (tel. 775-15-15) of Captain Alvaro Ramirez, Jr. (8min., ¢12,000). The Golfito office is at the airport on the far end of the soccer field. Planes also travel to the entrance to P.N. Corcovado in **Sireno** (17min.) as well as to Neily.

Accommodations and Food There are several reasonably priced places to stay in Jiménez. **Cabinas Marinas** (tel. 735-50-07; fax 735-60-45), near the **Sansa** office on the opposite end of the street from the soccer field, is the only place in Jiménez offering treats from back home. The lobby has a color TV, comfy couches, and each of the six rooms has a private bath, fan, and ample space to sprawl. They store luggage, yes they do, they store luggage, how 'bout you? Reserve ahead; breakfast included (singles ¢1000, doubles ¢1800, triples ¢1400). On the opposite end of the field meows **Cabinas Katty** (tel. 735-52-04). (Make a right at the basketball courts), Katty lacks amenities (and is out of the way), but offers guests spacious rooms, electric outlets, fans, and a restaurant right upstairs (doubles and triples ¢1000). Right next-door is **Pensión Quintero,** the best barn you'd ever want to stay in. Don't be deterred by the dark halls and rustic ambience; it's by far the cheapest place around. Prices aren't set, so haggle with the manager for a room with electricity, fan, and a lightbulb for ¢700-1000.

In the immediate town, there are only *sodas* and *cantinas.* **Soda Johana** (tel. 735-61-08) in the heart of town, whips up large meals of rice and a choice of chicken, beef, or fish for ¢400 (open daily 8am-noon and 1-7pm). Other *sodas* around town are similarly priced. **Agua Luna,** off the pier, 300m to the right after the soccer field, is a tropical *tiki* bar with tiled bathrooms, serving up sea-salt laden wonders like shrimp with rice (¢600). Count the sides in the door (we found eight), play foosball and billiards, or play chess while U.S. music blares.

■ NEAR PUERTO JIMÉNEZ

Sprawling along pretty much the entire western coast of Osa Peninsula, and home to sloths, monkeys, anteaters, and almost 400 species of birds (including the magnificent scarlet macaw and harpy eagle), **Corcovado National Park** continues to do what it was meant to do: deter natural destruction through industry and gold-mining. The park is only 21 years old, but feels enough like the Garden of Eden to eradicate all notions of time from visitors' overwhelmed minds. Best of all, it's not hard to access once you're in Puerto Jiménez: a taxi *collectivo* passes through the city and onto Carate, the nearest stop to the park's entrance, at 6am and 2pm. The road is bumpy and the ride a long one, approximately 45 minutes, so don't bring your own car here unless it's in tip-top shape.

Either buy tickets at the main park station at Puerto Jiménez, near the bank (¢1600 per day), or at the station entrance in Corcovado, where the price is hiked up to ¢2400 per day. Make reservations for food and lodging at the station (tel. 735-5306). Cars have to stop in Carate, and visitors have to follow a beach to the **ranger station** 3km away; the walk takes 30-40 minutes. To **Sireno,** the site of the deepest jungles and trails, requires another 16km-walk, day-long walk. The **ranger station,** where you turn in your tickets, offers little in terms of maps, guides, and tour information, but is the nearest medical clinic in the vicinity. In addition, the station offers campsites (no camping on the beach) for ¢300 per day. The rangers are very friendly. An expert chef at the station offers food at expert chef prices (breakfast ¢700, lunch ¢1000, dinner ¢2700).

About 20km from Puerto Jiménez to the south, **La Tierra de Milagros** (Land of Miracles) awaits travelers who want to pay something back to nature. Founded in 1990 by disgruntled *norteamericanos,* the commune was created to support a reforestation project on the peninsula while providing volunteers with the chance to work hands on toward meeting ecotourism's goals. A monthly fee provides for accommodations, and volunteers are asked to work on the project while at the commune. Take a taxi from Puerto Jiménez for about ¢1700.

■■■ GOLFITO

Golfito poorly hides its economic hardships. Abandoned by the United Fruit Company and its promised investments, Golfito's blocks are mostly a sprawl of sad ghost stores, waning memories of something almost grand. In places, though, hope lives on; an indulgent yacht-travelling population makes Golfito the last stop on a coastal tour from Alaska, and between their parties and purchases in the duty-free zone on the edge of town, happy cash-flow may once again help the city to burgeon. Residents portray the city's resilience perfectly; friendly to tourists and ambitious about the future, they bring character to a city that could easily be passed over on the way to Panama. Hang out on nearby **Cacao** and **Zancudo** beaches, hang ten on the waves, or head to a hangar for a flight over to Puerto Jiménez and P.N. Corcovado.

Practical Information **Banco Nacional de Costa Rica,** right next to Supermercado El Imperio, exchanges dollars and gives cash advances on Visa (open Mon.-Fri. 8:30am-3:45pm). The **post office,** off the main road near the cemetery, has a **fax, telegrams,** and a *lista de correos* (open Mon.-Fri. 7:30-11:30am and 1:30-5:30pm). **Buses** drive from near the bank to San José (6, 10am, 1pm, 6 hrs., ¢1000). Buses from the bus station at the center of town near the launch serve Neily (¢140), Río Claro (¢80), and Paso Canoas (every 1½ hrs., 2 hrs., ¢180). **Public buses** (*urbanas*) around Golfito cost ¢30. A **ferry** runs to Golfito at 6am. **Laundry** is right across from

Restaurante Eurekita (open Mon.-Sat. 8:30am-12:30pm and 1-5pm). Dress wounds at the **hospital,** at the edge of town near the *depósito* (**ambulance** tel. 775-03-97).

Accommodationsand Food The hotels in the **Zona Americana** (the center of town) are twice as expensive as the harder-to-find cabinas only a few km away, toward the depósito. Take a ¢30 bus ride down the street for affordable and pleasant stays. **Hotel Uno** (tel. 778-00-61), right near the launch and Neily bus terminal, is the only inexpensive hotel in Zona Americana. The 21 rooms are decent and central to the dock and bus terminals. As a super-special bonus-treat, the restaurant downstairs has affordable, filling meals (singles ¢400, doubles ¢800, triples ¢1200). Near the Depósito is **Cabinas Navarrette** (tel. 775-0197). Rooms are small, but cheaper than many hotels in the city. The quiet surroundings are a plus. Only four rooms are available, so reservations are recommended (¢600 per person). **Cabinas Aisilio** is 400 meters from the Depósito. Don't look at the boxes they call rooms, the distant location, or the less-than-welcoming reception. Just admire all the colones left in your pocket after the night (¢300 per person). For classier, more expensive accommodations, leave your heart in **Cabinas San Francisco** (tel. 775-0635), across from San José TRACOPA bus terminal. The Moralez family who lives upstairs should have its own half-hour family sitcom. The warm faces and jubilant laughter of the Moralez family upstairs warms the soul. Pleasant rooms have zany tiles, clean bathrooms, and fans. Don't get dizzy and throw up on the spiral staircase.

Across from the post office toward the cemetery is **Restaurante La Eurekita.** Here, the weary and laid-back nurse exotic ice-cream dishes and gelatin-cocktail ice-cream boats (¢350), or, in the *soda* in the other corner of the patio, they grab the grub that gluts Golfito's guts. To impress the stranger you met on the bus, visit **Samoa Del Sur** (tel. 775-0233) in the Centro Turisto, near the launch two blocks toward the Depósito. The lush and alluring restaurant-bar offers over-priced meals, but the prices for drinks are average, and they come with billiards, darts, a big-screen TV, and a beautiful view of the adjacent Golfito Peninsula. Another option is **Palenque Los Bruncas,** near the center of town towards Depósito. An open patio overlooking the peninsula, a boisterous crowd, and a black-eyed dog (which looks more like a startlingly ugly pig) welcome the swinging and hip to swing their hips.

Sights and Entertainment For a change of pace from Golfito, stop by the **Golfito Nature Reserves,** which lie along the main road opposite the sea. With little more to do around town, a day-long hike to observe exotic plants (not animals) may be worth it. There are two timid trails through the reserves; one entrance lies 150m from the Samoa del Sur and the other is off the main road close to the supermarket and bank. Then, if you're really bored and feeling loaded, **Depósito Libre** (Duty-free) offers 52 stores of cheap stuff from electronics to perfumes to liquor to shoes and clothes. Stock up on gallons of cologne to mask that odor problem. The Urbana bus from the center of town takes visitors there as a regular stop; the walk is long, passing several residential neighborhoods along the way. As an annoyance, **entrance tickets** into the grounds are free, but must be obtained a day in advance. Pick up tickets at the **Depósito** (Mon. 1-8pm, Tues.-Sat. 8am-8pm).

■ NEAR GOLFITO

There's next to nothing of note in **Neily;** a video-rental store is the biggest building in town. Still, many buses pass through here, and it's close enough to the border to be practical for an overnight before heading into Panama. Patrol officers wander the streets twirling their batons, most buildings are run-down, and even the sodas are less than welcoming, so relish the bus terminal for what it's worth.

Banco de Costa Rica has a branch next to the Chevron station. Neily has a **post office** around the block from the bus terminal. The **hospital** is just outside the city. **Buses** to the border at Paso Canoas run throughout the day beginning at 5am. To San José, they leave at 4:30, 5, 8:30, 11:30am, and 3:30pm. A direct bus leaves at

1:45. Buses to San Isidro leave at 7am, 10am, 1pm, and 3pm. Buses depart bound for Golfito every hour.

Hotel Nohelia, around the corner from Parque Central, has collective bathrooms (singles ¢400, doubles ¢800). **Hotel Villa,** near Tienda El Tiburón, is similarly simple: communal bathrooms, but some rooms have fans (singles ¢500). **Cabinas Elviro** (tel. 783-3057) has fans across the board (singles ¢500, with bath ¢1200; doubles ¢850). For a grumbly stomach during layovers, **Restaurant El Rancho,** across from the gas station, serves *típico* fare in decent atmosphere at a reasonable price.

Paso Canoas is more than the location of immigration offices at the Panamanian and Costa Rican borders; the dwarfish town also has one mighty big flea market, a great place to buy some last second *tico* souvenirs before jammin' on to Panama. The city makes no claim to be a tourist spot, and the town's hotels are there mainly to facilitate hapless travelers who get their feet stuck in bureaucratic mud. **Change currency** at Banco Panama, right next to the Panamanian immigration office on the border. There's a **post office** (tel. 771-6592) in the back of the Costa Rican immigration office. In the town proper, there's a **pharmacy** (tel. 771-6542; fax 771-6544), in Almacén Wong Chung, across from Mister Pan.

If you're stuck in Paso Canoas on the Costa Rican side of the border, try **Hotel Del Sur.** It's vaguely reminiscent of a dog's cage, but padlocks on the doors keep the clean rooms safe (singles ¢500). **Hotel Palace Sur** (tel. 732-2015), two doors down, has all the basics but not much more. All rooms have fans and either private or communal bathrooms (singles ¢545, doubles ¢1500). There are several *sodas* in Paso Canoas. **Bar Disco Malibu** is the grandest dance hall in the city, and is a great place to vent those border woes. **Soda Panelia del Sur,** on the border, is a charming alternative to the booth-and-stool joints, serving breads, pastries, and coffee.

BORDER CROSSING INTO PANAMA

Obtain all necessary visas required for entry into Panama before arriving at the border (see Panama: Documents and Formalities, page 408, for more information). The process required for entry at Paso Canoas is two-fold: first, visit the Costa Rican Immigration office at the border for your exit stamp. Then, on the Panamanian side, get your stamp, visa, or tourist card. Keep a carbon copy of the form you're required to fill out. For more information, call the **Departamento de Migración** at 771-6502. From the border, daily buses run to David (every 15min., 1 hr., US$1.50) and stop at points along the Interamerican Highway. Snag a bus to Panama City in David.

PANAMA

As a bridge between oceans and a link between continents, Panama has seen more than its share of passers-through. For some reason, though, the country has never been much of a popular destination for budget travelers; perhaps because of its scarred reputation because of "Operation Just Cause" (the United States' invasion of Panama), or simply the country's higher prices (relative to other parts of Central America), Panama tends to attract more jet-setting bankers and businesspeople. In reality, the political situation is relatively stable, the prices aren't that high (most museums charge US$0.25 admission), yet nearly every path through the country's lush and wildly diverse natural settings has gone untraversed and unsullied. IPAT, the national board of tourism, offers the bizarre statistic that Panama has 1,398 tourist attractions, most of which are of the waterfalls and wilderness parks variety. Backpack through for a month and you're bound to meet no more than ten other travelers; take the opportunity to discover beautiful places with rhythmic names like Chiriquí, Boquete, Chitré, and Penonome, towns that pulse with a vibrance that could only be produced by the cultural meshings of one of the world's true melting pots. The *molas* (patched quilts) for which the Kuna Indians are renowned are full of lively, multi-layered patterns, resulting from a frenzied conglomeration of images, shapes, and colors in an organized whole; no creation could better represent a cross-section of the Panamanian people.

The dollars pumped into Panama's economy through the canal have clearly had an effect on the country: roads tend to be better paved than elsewhere in Central America, buses run on schedule, and English is much more widely spoken. On the other hand, Panama refreshes some travelers precisely because it *is* less rustic; pristine Caribbean shores are still within a few hours' drive of a thriving modern metropolis, but it's a drive not hindered by logistical frustrations. Historically, though, the constant foreign presence in Panama has enhanced, rather than exorcised, Panamanian cultural traditions. There remains among the people a zesty, rough-and-tumble spirit inherited from the Latin tradition and the country's several indigenous peoples, including the Kuna, Guayamí, and Choco Indians. The dichotomy between new and old is striking; a few miles beyond the cluttered banks and paved roads of Santiago, for example, classrooms full of young girls end their Fridays at school by mowing their lawns, vigorously slashing away with machetes no bigger than their own arms. Perhaps to protect what is familiar to them, Panamanians have started to welcome ecotourism, a phenomenon widely viewed as a means of preserving the environment as well as attracting tourists' cash. In the end, Panama might not have quite as much to offer as other destinations, but it'd be wise to stop to enjoy—and not just cross—that bridge when you come to it.

ESSENTIALS

■■■ WHEN TO GO

CLIMATE

The weather in Panama varies wildly from one coast to the other, mostly in terms of how much rain falls. The Caribbean coast can receive up to 140 inches of rain each year, while the Pacific side averages a "mere" 60 inches annually. Moreover, the rainy season (from May to December) actually only applies to the southern side, since the Caribbean receives rain year-round. Be prepared for waves of flesh-melting

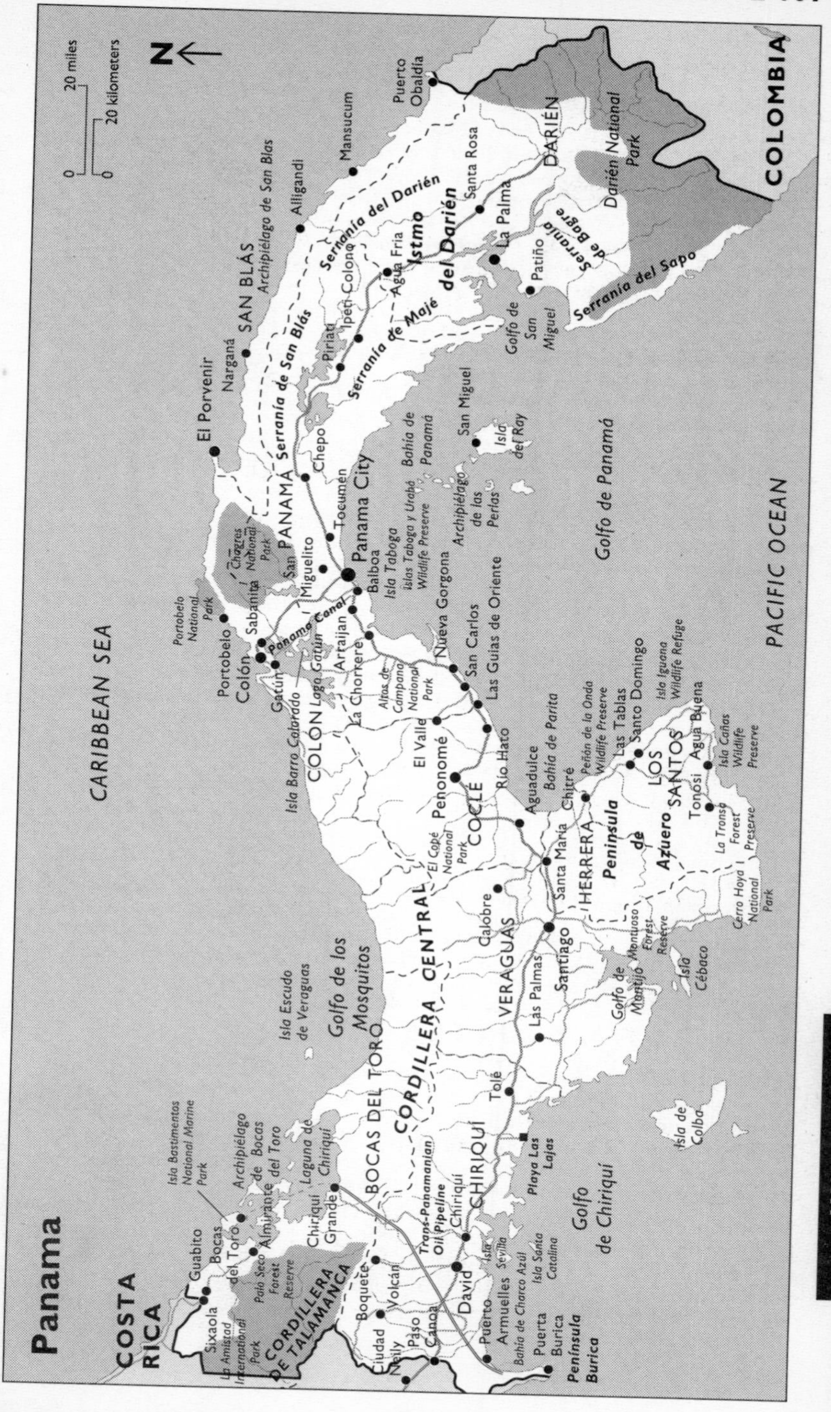

Panama

CARIBBEAN SEA
PACIFIC OCEAN
0 20 miles
0 20 kilometers
N
COSTA RICA
COLOMBIA
Guabito
Sixaola
Bocas del Toro
Isla Bastimentos National Marine Park
Archipiélago de Bocas del Toro
La Amistad International Park
Palo Seco Forest Reserve
Almirante
CORDILLERA DE TALAMANCA
Chiriquí Grande
Laguna de Chiriquí
Isla Escudo de Veraguas
Golfo de los Mosquitos
Boquete
Ciudad Neily
Volcán
Paso Canoa
BOCAS DEL TORO
CORDILLERA CENTRAL
Trans-Panamanian Oil Pipeline
David
Chiriquí
CHIRIQUÍ
Puerto Armuelles
Isla Sevilla
Bahía de Charco Azúl
Puerta Burica
Isla Santa Catalina
Playa Las Lajas
Península Burica
Golfo de Chiriquí
Tolé
VERAGUAS
Calobre
Las Palmas
Santiago
Santa María
HERRERA
Isla de Colba
Golfo de Montijo
Montuoso Forest Reserve
Isla Cébaco
Península de Azuero
Cerro Hoya National Park
La Tronsa Forest Preserve
Tonosí
Agua Buena
Isla Cañas Wildlife Preserve
LOS SANTOS
Las Tablas
Santo Domingo
Isla Iguana Wildlife Refuge
Chitré
Peñón de la Onda Wildlife Preserve
Aguadulce
Bahía de Parita
Río Hato
COCLÉ
El Copé National Park
Penonomé
El Valle
Altos de Campana National Park
Nueva Gorgona
San Carlos
Las Guias de Oriente
La Chorrere
Arraijan
COLON
Lago Gatún
Isla Barro Colorado
Gatún
Colón
Portobelo
Portobelo National Park
Sabanita
Panama Canal
Chagres National Park
San Miguelito
PANAMÁ
Balboa
Isla Taboga
Islas Taboga y Urabá Wildlife Preserve
Panama City
Tocumen
Chepo
Bahía de Panamá
Archipiélago de las Perlas
San Miguel
Isla del Ray
Golfo de Panamá
El Porvenir
Narganá
SAN BLÁS
Archipiélago de San Blas
Serranía de San Blás
Alligandi
Mansucum
Serranía del Darién
Piriati
Ipeti Colono
Serranía de Majé
Agua Fria
Istmo del Darién
Santa Rosa
La Palma
Puerto Obaldía
Golfo de San Miguel
Patiño
Serranía de Bagre
DARIÉN
Serranía del Sapo
Darién National Park

heat and humidity at any time throughout the year; temperatures rarely drop below 80°F, except in the highland areas.

FESTIVALS AND HOLIDAYS

Check with tourist officials to find out where and when local festivals take place. The whole country flocks to **Chitré** and **Las Tablas** around Semana Santa; to be a part of that party, reserve a room weeks in advance. Other national holidays include **January 1** (New Year's Day), **January 9** (Martyr's Day), **February** (Carnival), **March or April** (Good Friday), **May 1** (Labor Day), **November 3** (Independence from Colombia), **November 4** (Flag Day), **November 10** (First Call for Independence from Spain), **November 28** (Emancipation Day), **December 8** (Mother's Day), and **December 25** (Christmas Day).

■■■ FEED YOUR HEAD

For publications and travel organizations of general interest, see Central America: Feed Your Head, page 1.

Embassy of Panama, U.S. 2862 McGill Terrace NW, Washington D.C., 20008 (tel. (202)-483-1407; fax (202)-483-8413). **Canada** 130 Albert St. #300, Ottawa, Ontario K1P 5G4 (tel. (613) 236-7177; fax 236-5775). **U.K.** 40 Hertford St., London W1Y TTG (tel. (44) 171-409-2255; fax 493-4499).

Consulate of Panama, 1212 Ave. of the Americas, 10th Floor, New York, NY 10036 (tel. (212) 840-2450; fax (212) 840-2469). Open 9am-2pm. Provides visa information and assistance, and offers tourist information for walk-ins only. There are other consulates in Miami, 444 Brickell Ave., Miami, FL, 33133 (tel. 371-7031), and in Houston, San Francisco, New Orleans, and Tampa.

Instituto Panameño de Turismo (IPAT), P.O. Box 4421, Panama 5, Republic of Panama (tel. 226-7000; fax 226-3483). For a **brochure** about Panama sent from the United States, call (800) PANAMA-7, or 726-2627. The institute also provides the numbers of several Spanish language schools in Panama City.

Asociación Panameña de Agencias de Viajes y Turismo (APAVIT), Apdo. 55-1000, Paitilla, Panamá 3, República de Panamá (tel. 264-3029; fax 264-1570). Provides numbers and addresses of tour groups and other tourist information.

ANCON, Calle Alberto Navarro in El Cangrejo in Panama City, Apdo. 1387, Zona 1, Panamá (tel. 64-8100; fax 64-1836). A private organization offering volunteer opportunities in reforestation projects, cleaning up the beaches, etc. Volunteers need to buy an I.D. for $5. Open weekdays 8am-2pm, Sat. 9am-1pm.

Smithsonian Tropical Research Institute (tel. 227-6021), in Panama City, takes volunteers to work on biological field labs on both the San Blas Islands and Isla Barro Colorado.

■■■ DOCUMENTS AND FORMALITIES

Citizens of the United States, Australia, Canada, and Ireland need a valid **passport,** return ticket, and tourist card to travel in Panama. Citizens of Panama need no tourist card. A **tourist card** ($5-10) can be acquired in the airport when arriving or at the border; however, because tourist cards are occasionally unavailable at the border, getting a pre-arranged tourist card is advised. A stamped visa allows travelers to stay for 30 days, with extensions possible for up to 60 additional days. A **pre-arranged visa** is necessary for citizens of South Africa and Israel; this can take anywhere from 1-20 days to arrange and may cost from $10-40; apply well in advance. References may be demanded; consult the consulate for more information. When the time comes to get an **extension** on your visa, you may be asked to produce a letter stating the reason for your extension, an application, proof of a return flight, two passport photos, and some cash.

Travelers coming into Panama may bring three bottles of liquor and one carton of cigarettes or one pound of tobacco. A departure tax of $20 may be required upon leaving. **Children** (under 18) need to have written authority from both parents to enter Panama.

■■■ MONEY MATTERS

CURRENCY AND EXCHANGE

US$1 = $1.00	**$1 = US$1.00**
CDN$1 = $0.74	**$1 = CDN$1.36**
UK£1 = $1.55	**$1 = UK£0.64**
IRL£1 = $1.58	**$1 = IRL£0.63**
AUS£1 = $0.74	**$1 = AUS$1.36**
NZ£1 = $0.66	**$1 = NZ$1.53**
SARand = $0.27	**$1 = SARand 3.66**

The Panamanian currency, the **Balboa** ($), is directly linked to the U.S. dollar—no, wait, the currency *is* the U.S. dollar, just with a new name. The only difference between the currencies is that different pictures adorn the coins; studly, long-haired Spaniards replace rigid, dead U.S. founders. A mongo-sized fifty cent piece is also used regularly. **ATMs** are virtually unheard of in the interior, except in larger cities like David and Santiago. Money machines are everywhere in Panama City, however. There are **Western Union** offices throughout the country, even in some small villages. Few businesses accept traveler's checks as direct payment, but many banks are willing to exchange American Express checks in particular. Except at border crossings, black market currency trading is not the common phenomenon it is elsewhere in Central America. Visa and Mastercard are more easy to use at businesses than other cards, although most hotels and restaurants still demand cash. **Thomas Cook MasterCard** has an office in Panama City: contact Agencias Giscome (tel. 640-111; fax: 638-706). **Banco del Istmo** regularly provides cash advances on credit cards; there's a two dollar service charge per $100. **Tipping** is not usually expected, but is well-appreciated. At more touristed locations, it is standard to offer up a 10-15% tip. The minimum age for gambling is 18 years.

■■■ SAFETY

The explosion of an airplane flying between Colón and Panama City has led authorities to beef up security on domestic flights, and bus hijackings have been known to occur between Panama City and Colón. Travelers heading through the Darién Gap should beware of robberies and kidnappings. Panama City and Colón are particularly popular haunting grounds for criminals, but watch out for muggers, robbers, and pick-pockets throughout the country. As usual, keep all jewelry out of sight, especially those grapefruit-sized diamonds and pearls. All travelers should carry identification, preferably a passport, on them at all times.

Women traveling alone should expect to receive numerous catcalls when traveling in Panama, both in Spanish and English. A self-defense class is never a bad idea, and the strong infusion of *machismo* in some Panamanian men might lead to greater persistence of unwanted attention than elsewhere. Women are less welcome (and safe) in many casinos and bars, and should use discretion in such places.

■■■ HEALTH

See Central America: Health (page 11) for more specific information about disease prevention and control in Panama.

If arriving in Panama from an infected area, be ready to show vaccination certificates for **yellow fever** and **small pox.** If you're planning to travel to eastern Panama (including Archipelago San Blás), mefloquine should be taken against malaria; chloroquine is effective in other parts of the country, where a non-resistant strain prevails in rural areas. **Cholera** has recently hit the country, as has **typhoid fever.** Also take precautions against other region-wide diseases such as **hepatitis, rabies, traveler's diarrhea,** etc.

Despite what locals tell you, most **water** in small towns should be considered unsafe. Water is safer in big cities, but be aware of the sanitary conditions of the establishment whose tap you're using. Purified water is always safer than tap water.

■■■ GETTING THERE

See Central America: Getting There, page 23, for more information on getting to Panama from outside Central America.

Several **airlines** service Panama City's Tocumen International Airport from Europe and North America, including Aviateca, British Airways, Continental, and United. Miami and Houston are common hub cities for flights from the United States. In the summer of 1995, flights from New York City to Panama City cost about $500.

Drivers arriving in Panama with a car can drive up to 90 days with their own driver's license. Drivers will have to pay a vehicle permit fee $4.20 at the **Registro de Propiedad** at the border; the car must be inspected and the documents thoroughly checked. The suggested **border crossings** into Panama from Costa Rica are at Paso Canoas, along the Interamerican highway, and at Sixaola, in the northwest section of Panama. See Costa Rica, Paso Canoas, page 405, for more information.

■■■ ONCE THERE

TRANSPORTATION

To drive into Panama with a **car,** bring proof of ownership along with your visa and passport. Insurance is recommended. Roads are in relatively good condition, but mechanics are few and far between, as are good, safe parking places.

Airplanes moving between cities are small, single-engine wonders. Reservations are usually not taken more than two days in advance for flights within Panama. National airlines flying between major cities (Panama City, Santiago, David) and resort towns (Bocas del Toro, San Blas, etc.) include **Aeroperlas** (tel. 269-4555), **ALAS** (tel. 264-6448), **AeroTaxi** (tel. 264-8644), **Transpasa** (tel. 226-0932), and **Parsa** (tel. 226-3803).

Buses in Panama are the major means of transportation for budget travelers, and are the only means of getting to remote locations in the interior. Bus quality ranges from pick-up truck "limousines" to veritable party buses with merengue blasted by the occasional blasted driver. Many buses between cities aren't converted school buses, but rather mini-vans with cushioned seats and air-conditioning. Usually, a bus's destination is written on the front of the vehicle. Ask around for terminals; many buses linger around a town's central park or major gas station. Pay when getting off, but confirm the fare before getting on.

If you stick your thumb out along a Panamanian road, people are more likely to wonder what kind of dance you're doing than to stop to pick you up; hitchhiking just never caught on here. In some cases, hitchers say it's worth a try, but as always, use extreme caution. *Let's Go* doesn't recommend roadside jigs *or* hitchhiking.

ACCOMMODATIONS

Hotels in Panama are more expensive than elsewhere in Central America, but outside of resortified areas there are usually plenty of cheap places to stay. Expect to pay $5-30 for a night's stay. Usually, even the dingiest looking hotels are safe, honestly run, and populated by traveling workers. In some places, relatively luxurious rooms (with queen-sized beds, private bathtubs, and TV) go for about $20. The larger the town, the more you should pay attention to safety when considering a hotel. There are so few travelers in the country that camping hasn't caught on (and so isn't regulated), but always ask permission before pitching a tent.

KEEPING IN TOUCH

Mail from Panama takes about two weeks to get to the United States, although occasionally a letter slips through and makes it in a few days. Rates average about $0.40 for a normal size letter to the U.S. To receive mail in Panama, note that "Lista de Correos" is *not the* phrase of choice; instead, use "Entrega General." and also remember to write República de Panamá and not just Panamá, since Panama City is often referred to as just Panamá. Address letters as follows:

Marco PASCHOTTA (or the name of the addressee)
Entrega General
David (city), Chiriquí (Province)
República de Panamá
Centroamerica

Telephones are reasonably reliable in Panama; public phones can be capricious, so the best bet is to hunt down an established hotel or an office of INTEL, the national telephone office, for calling cards. INTEL is expected to privatize soon, however, and so may change many of its policies. AT&T works better than MCI at this time, though either can be used with enough effort. Dial 108 from public phones for **MCI** service, 109 for **AT&T.** 102 is the number to call for **information.** Without a card, calls are possible if you offer to pay for costs or call collect; dial 106 to make a **collect call.** As an alternative, fax machines are ubiquitous in the country; check in post offices, banks, and hotels to send or receive a fax. Panama's **telephone code** is 507.

PANAMA: AN INTRODUCTION

■■■ HISTORY

Panama's fate has traditionally been linked to other nations' interest in the isthmus' status as a bridge between Central America and South America, and between the Atlantic and Pacific Oceans; as a result, the nation has been mired in a centuries-old identity crisis. By some counts not even part of Central America (as the nation was not part of the United Provinces of Central America during the 19th century), its geographical value as a passageway between the Atlantic and the Pacific has encouraged foreign involvement in the nation's affairs for the last five hundred years. Modern Panamanians feel secure knowing they are protected by other, more powerful nations, but at the same time resent the consequential ambivalence that characterizes their identity as a nation and a culture.

The Pre-Columbian period is perhaps the only part of Panama's history that can be said to be entirely its own. The indigenous **Kuna, Guaymí,** and **Choco Indians** that inhabited the isthmus first saw their land fall into foreign hands in 1501, when the Spanish explorers **Rodrigo de Bastidas** and **Vasco Núñez de Balboa** stumbled upon Panama's Atlantic coast and quickly suppressed the natives. After hearing tales of a vast sea to the south, Balboa became the first European to cross the bridge of Panama, and in 1513 he boldly claimed for Spain the Pacific Ocean and all the land it touched. The first colonists capitalized on Balboa's "discovery," using settlements on the Pacific coast near modern day Panama City (called Panamá, or "abundance of fish") as a launching point for domination of the South American Incas, whose riches the Spanish transported away on the **Camino Real** (the king's highway), a stone path between the Atlantic and Pacific coasts. Portobelo, the town on the Atlantic side of the road, flourished along with the Spanish mercantile economy.

Although repeated attacks by **Henry Morgan** and other English raiders weakened the cities throughout the 17th century, causing the Spanish to re-route many of their trade paths and move Panama City, continued foreign trade provided prosperity and comfort to Panama, which did not join its Central American neighbors to the north in revolting against Spain. Only the revocation of foreign trade rights sparked resentment, and by 1843 Panama had seceded to become a state within the **United Nation of Gran Colombia.**

During the next century, Panama's course was dictated more and more by other nations' quests to make a bigger and better path from sea to shining sea. The United States fostered dreams of creating its own "Camino Real" in the form of a transcontinental railroad. Between the signing of a treaty which granted the U.S. free transit across the isthmus in 1846 and the completion of the railroad in 1855, Panama's politics were turbulent; twenty governors were inaugurated and then rejected. Meanwhile, the glitter of gold in California compelled thousands of Americans to cross through Panama, and the economy surged. The completed railroad prompted plans for the construction of a canal, the rights to which were originally granted to the French in 1848 **Ferdinand de Lesseps,** a French diplomat who had already proved his "canal can-do" at Suez, was chosen to engineer the project, but malaria and repeated landslides caused his trans-American canal to fail. The United States bought up the French stake, but was unable to acquire the Canal Strip from Colombia. With the help of U.S. naval forces, grumbling public resentment toward Colombia resulted in a revolutionary junta, which declared the independence of the "Republic of Panama" in 1903. The U.S. acquired the necessary land in 1904, and the canal was completed just 10 years later. Along with control of the waterway, Panama's new constitution granted the U.S. intervention rights, which were exercised several times during periods of unrest in the next few decades.

Panama has gained increasingly more independence and control over the canal throughout the century, but the United States is still heavily active in Panamanian affairs. The **Hull-Alfaro Treaty** of 1936 forced the U.S. to abandon their intervention rights, and increased the fees paid for the Canal Zone, but by 1958 U.S. control was still disturbing enough a presence to provoke student riots against both the Panamanian and U.S. governments. The riots were quickly squelched, and within 15 years a series of failed elections led to a revision of the constitution; **Colonel Torrijos Herrera** emerged as the virtual dictator of Panama. A benevolent despot (and notorious party-lover), Torrijos splurged on expanding the country's public works, despite a steadily growing debt. He developed housing for the poor, raised wages, and sponsored a program intended to expand nationalism and develop Panamanians' pride in their country. To encourage such sentiment, he signed a treaty with U.S. President Carter that guaranteed total Panamanian control over the canal by the year 2000. A mysterious plane crash ended Torrijos' life, and opened the door to a new political crisis; leadership passed between various men, and control of the National Guard ended up in the hands of **General Manuel Noriega,** Torrijos' head of intelligence.

Noriega became involved in governmental affairs early in his life; while still a pimply student at a military academy in Peru, the American Defense Intelligence Agency had paid him $20 a week to spy on his fellow students. After helping to hone his skills, the U.S. hired Noriega as a C.I.A. operative and contact with the Nicaraguan Contras, and he eventually became head of Panamanian intelligence

Upon his seizure of control of the National Guard in 1983, Noriega quickly granted himself dictatorial power by controlling the press, creating military brute squads, and managing Panama's drug traffic together with Colombian drug cartels. In 1984, the General allowed an election; the popular **Arnulfo Arias** seemed a clear winner, but Ardito Barlett, Noriega's candidate, "magically" emerged victorious and became Noriega's newest puppet president. In 1988, Noriega was indicted in the U.S. on drug trafficking charges, and as **President Ronald Reagan** tightened sanctions on Panama, Noriega closed his grip on power in Panama, nullifying yet another presidential election which his candidate had lost; Noriega had the winning candidate beaten to a pulp on national television.

No sooner did Noriega declare himself president than word started to spread that Panama was at war with the U.S. After the killing of an unarmed U.S. Marine officer, **President George Bush** acted quickly, ordering 24,000 troops to Panama to remove Noriega by force. As the Panamanian General was cavorting with his favorite prostitute, U.S. paratroopers silently floated down into Panama City. Noriega fled into the Papal Nuncio, where American soldiers assailed him with a bizarre form of psychological torture; they blared "Voodoo Chile," "I Fought the Law and the Law Won," and other rock tunes in order to flush him out. A few days later, Noriega (who claims not to have heard the music), surrendered and was flown to Florida to await trial for drug charges. In 1992, he was found guilty on eight charges of conspiracy to manufacture and distribute cocaine, and was sentenced to 40 years imprisonment.

With the stated goals of "liberating" Panama from Noriega's tyranny, protecting American lives, and bringing Noriega to justice, **"Operation Just Cause"** was criticized internationally as bullying and self-interested foreign policy. Estimates of the number of civilian deaths caused by U.S. explosive shells ranged between 200 and 4,000, and the newly installed government of **Guillermo Endara** has faced high rates of poverty, unemployment, and crime since the invasion. Still, Panamanians were generally supportive of U.S. action during the invasion, (though many later demanded reparation for civilian lives lost). A public referendum rejected more than 50 proposed reforms by the president, and opposition groups demanded the drafting of a new constitution. Endara has been more successful at engaging Panama in Central American affairs, establishing the country's membership in the Central American Parliament in 1993 and committing Panama to economic integration in the Central American Common Market, but he was nonetheless voted out of office, replaced by **Ernesto Pérez Balladares.** Still, Panama's problem of occluded identity lives on, as Panamanians feel helpless in their continuing role as "little buddy" to the United States.

■■■ THE ARTS

Panama's position as bridge between continents and oceans has opened it to artistic influences from all sides. The chants of indigenous peoples continue to thrive for their lyrical melodies, but also for their magical potency; reportedly, a hunter once paid $15 to a musician to teach him a song that supposedly attracted turtles. The most well-known Panamanian dance is the licentious **tamborito,** which is accented by hand claps, rhythms played out on three drums, and men fanning women with their hats. Also characteristic of the country's music is the **Mejorana,** played on two guitars and accompanied by a square dance, and the **Punto,** which is more uptempo. The most popular music in Panama is undoubtedly merengue, which blares in buses and from every radio station. For more solemn, intimate moments, Panamanians turn to Mr. Adult Contemporary himself, Kenny G, whose smooth effluvia shapes ambience in wherever you go. It's not clear if Panamanians like the music, or if they just like Mr. G for his hair.

Panama's distance from the cultural centers of Guatemala and Columbia left it's literature underdeveloped until this century, when the Canal became the central focus of many authors' works. Prior to then, poetry, such as that of **José María Alemán** and **Darío Herrera,** was the main outlet for romantic and modernist thought. Since the building of the Canal, foreign nations' role in Panamanian affairs and the turmoil of the lives of those living along the Canal have become the dominant theme of works by authors like **Renato Ozores** and **Carlos Francisco Changmarín.**

Don't worry about not finding traditional Panamanian arts and crafts; nearly every town has a **Mercado Artesanal,** a market packed with baskets, ceramics, and clothing native to the area and to all of Panama. Shelf after shelf of vases and pots adorned with bold, geometric patterns fill the markets in Western and Central Panama, many of the products following the traditional folk-art of the Guaymí Indians. More predominant in the east are the intricately patterned clothes of the Kuna tribes indigenous to the San Blas Islands. (See That's-a Mola, page 441, for more information). Some artisans have taken wicker-work to new extremes, making helicopters, airplanes, and cars along with countless baskets.

■■■ FOOD AND DRINK

With two expanses of oceans and a lot of green in between, it's not surprising that Panama brims with ambrosia. The coasts abound with luscious tropical treats like drip-down-the-edge-of-your-chin mangos and freshly harvested lobsters, while in the hills of the interior hearty, savory stews and scrumptious oranges are all the rage. (Don't be put off by the oranges' color; it's not blight, just raw goodness.) The national dish is *sancocho,* a stew made with chicken, corn, potatoes, and onions.

Quality, price, and safety are variable according to where you sit, what you expect to pay, and how much you eat. In pretty much every town, there are little *sodas* offering pork and chicken standards for $1-2. Red meat is everywhere, but vegetarians and travelers keeping kosher can almost always count on a town's fruit stand for sweet (cost next to) nothings.

■■■ MEDIA

Panama has three main television stations, each offering its own news, prime time programming, and highly addictive soap operas. A great way to make instant friends at the local hotel or grocery store is to ask how Lupe could possibly escape her father's torment and marry the priest. Similarly entertaining is "Cocina al Minuto," a cooking show on daily at 8:30am, where the motherly chef cooks up alluring meringues with merengue spice.

Most Panamanians stay informed through *La Prensa*, *Crítica, La República,* and other dailies as sources of straight news; *El Siglo* spoons out more tabloidish news. All three publications are sold on the street and in hotels for pennies.

■■■ THIS YEAR'S NEWS

President Ernesto Pérez Balladares, member of the Partido Revolucionario Democrático (PRD), took office in January of 1995, and is already thinking about his re-election, which isn't allowed by the country's constitution. The opposition party, the Coordinadora Democrática Nacional (CDN), lacks leadership, especially following the pardon received by Panama City's mayor, Omayra Correa, for using public money to fund her campaign. The third party, led by Salsa master and famed singer Rubén Blades, doesn't seem to want to take a stance on anything. Other than their own elections, the most pressing concern for Panama's leaders is how to deal with the Canal, which the U.S. is scheduled to hand over at the end of the decade. The Canal Zone is estimated to be worth about $80 billion, and Panama currently lacks the organization needed to administer the waterway. Another issue is just how much cleaning up the U.S. should do before leaving, and whether they are responsible for the toxic wastes buried beneath its military bases. Before bailing, though, the United States is urging whatever reforms it can, including the re-institution of a military police squad to hinder corruption and drug trafficking in Panama. Currently, Panama has no military force.

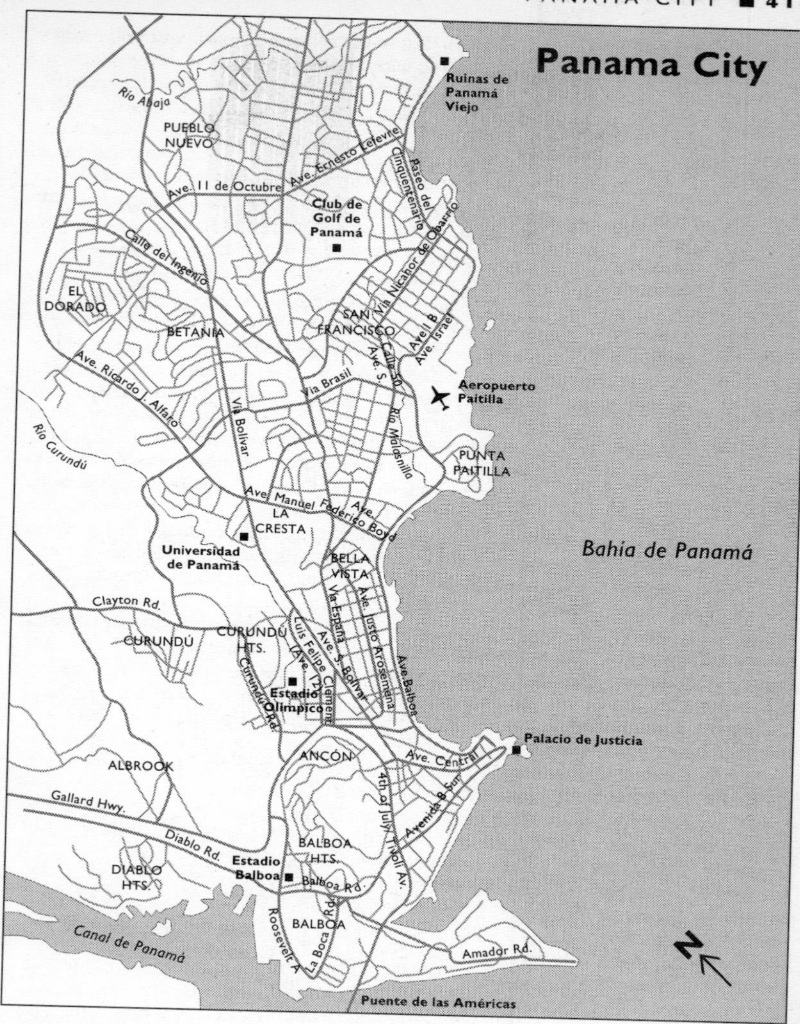

Panama City

Nowhere else are a city's buses as much a microcosmic representation of the flare and tastes of the place itself than in Panama City. Covered front-fender to tailpipe with frenzied and freakish air-brushed depictions of Rambo, Batman, and Jesus Christ, the psychedelic mobile murals zoom around corners as Panamanians of Chinese, Jewish, Kuna, and Spanish descent try to cut through blaring honks with cries of "Parada!" As residents of the desperately pumping heart of the world's crossroads, the 800,000 inhabitants of Ciudád de Panamá have known and will always know what it is to be on a collision-course with postmodernity.

Frustrated by having to live with reeking, infertile swamps and rank, virile pirates, residents of Panamá Viejo decided in 1673 to leave their settlement and move 10km to the west to a rocky peninsula. With water flowing in from El Chorrillo, a mountain stream to the north, citizens rejoiced, despite the waning trans-isthmian trade upon which they had previously depended. Razing fires in the 18th century bode poorly for Panama City, but the construction of the inter-oceanic railway and the California gold rush in the mid 19th century resurrected the flailing city. By the beginning of this century, plans for a water passage were complete, and when the first ship passed through the canal's Miraflores Locks in 1914, the city's fate was sealed. Panama is scheduled to take the canal from the U.S. at the end of the decade, but regardless of ownership, the canal will invariably continue to inject Panama City with snippets of the world as it has done since its construction.

■■■ ORIENTATION AND SAFETY

Panama City's sprawl along **Panama Bay** begins on the western side at the Canal, which is lined with U.S. Air Force bases near the spanning **Bridge of the Americas.** The upper-crust (and heavily U.S. inhabited) neighborhoods of **Balboa, Albrook, Ancón,** and **Curundú** all lie in this western portion. Many hotels, services, and attractions are clustered on **San Felipe,** the small, jutting peninsula in the west (sometimes called Casco Viejo; not to be confused with **Amador,** which is still farther west). **Avenida A** comes into San Felipe from the west, whereas **Avenida Central,** one of the city's major thoroughfares, leads into San Felipe from the east. Av. Central branches off at various points to other major avenues, including the coastal road, **Av. Balboa** (Av. 6 Sur), and **Vía Simón Bolívar** to the north. Farther east, Av. Central becomes **Vía España,** the heart of the business and banking district. Av. Central roughly divides the north and south neighborhoods in the center of the city, including **Calidonia, La Exposicion, Bella Vista,** and **La Cresta.** Still to the east roost the neighborhoods **El Cangrejo** and **San Francisco.** Located north of Vía España, El Cangrejo includes Albert Einstein Plaza, Vía Argentina, and Vía Brasil. The eastern end of the city is **Panamá Viejo**, the cite of the city's beginnings.

Streets are laid out in a grid in **La Exposición,** between Calidonia and Bella Vista, and in various other parts of town, but elsewhere, roads twist and turn. Av. Central marks the dividing street for addresses along east-west running streets, with Av. 1 Nte. one block north and Av. 1 Sur to the south. North-south running calles are also labelled in their relation to **Calle 1,** on the west side of town. Numbered streets often have (obsolete) names, so learning both in a hurry can be very helpful. Use landmarks like **Plaza 5 de Mayo,** near Av. 3 Sur and Av. Central.

The **Bella Vista** and **El Cangrejo** neighborhoods are generally considered safe, Calidonia and El Chorillo less so. Sort of in-between, Bella Vista and El Cangrejo offer several interesting sights and provide a fair scope of life in the city. Bella Vista is a middle class quiet suburb with *villas* interspersed with high-rise apartments; El Congrejo is upper middle-class, located north of Via España, and includes **Albert Einstein Plaza, Vía Brasil,** and the city's main restaurant district line **Vía Argentina.**

Calidonia has a warped, split personality. One half teems with squalid markets, lurking ruffians, and dens of prostitution; the other half, a few blocks away, is a major medical district with labs and specialized institutions sprawled among the streets bordering Bella Vista. In this section, streets are considered safe both day and night, though they're situated in a humdrum part of the city. In between Yucksville and Tonsiltown languish administrative and government buildings.

Panama City Center

Cathedral, **3**
U.K. Embassy, **17**
Hospital de La Caja de Seguro Social, **13**
Hospital Santa Fe, **14**
Iglesia del Carmen, **12**
Museo Afro-Antillano (Afro-West Indian Museum), **10**
Museo de Historia de Panamá, **4**
Museo del Hombre Panameño, **9**
Museum of Natural Sciences, **11**
National Institute of Culture/ National Theater, **1**
Palacio Presidencial, **8**
Plaza de La Independencia, **2**
Plaza Ghandi, **6**
Post Office, **5**
Red Cross Hospital, **7**
U.S. Embassy, **16**
Universidad de Panamá, **15**

Cerro Ancón
Estadio Juan D. Arosemena
CURUNDÚ
PEREIL
LA CRESTA
LA EXPOSICION
CALIDONIA
BELLA VISTA
EL MARAÑON
SANTA ANA
Cementerio Amador
Corregimiento Ancón
Corregimiento Santa Ana
SAN FELIPE (Casco Vieja)
Bahía de Panamá
Monumento a Balboa
Parque
TO VIA ESPAÑA
Ave. 4a Norte
Ave. 3a Norte (Luis F. Clement)
Ave. Gorgas
Calle Manzanillo
Via Simón Bolívar
Ave. 1a Norte
Ave. Martin Sosa
Ave. Jose de Fabrega
Ave. Manuel J Hurtado
Ave. Juan A. Duque
Avenida Central
Calle Herrick
Calle K
Calle J
Calle I
Calle H
Calle E
Calle C
Calle B
Calle Estudiante
Ave. Peru
Ave. Cuba (Ave 2a Sur)
Ave. Justo Arosemena
Ave. Mejico
Avenida Balboa
Ave. Chile (Ave. 5a Sur)
Ave. 3a Sur
Ave. 4 Sur
Ave. 4a Sur
Ave. 5a Sur
Ave. 5 Sur
Ave. Federico Boyd
Calle 23 Este
Calle 25 Este
Calle 27 Este
Calle 29 Este
Calle 31 Este
Calle 33 Este
Calle 35 Este
Calle 37 Este
Calle 39 Este
Calle 41 Este
Calle 43 Este
Calle 45 Este
C. 17 Este
Calle 11 Este
Calle 9a Este
Calle 8a Este
Calle 4a Este
Calle 3a Este
Ave. A
Ave. B
Ave. Sur
Calle 19 Oeste
Calle 18 Oeste
Calle 17 Oeste
Calle 15 Oeste
Calle 13 Oeste
Calle Colon
Ave. Eloy Alfaro
Ave. Pablo Arosemena

PANAMA

San Felipe is frenetic and slightly run-down, but nevertheless sprouts beautiful historical buildings and panoramic ocean views. The whole area radiates colorful pastels, the result of restoration efforts. The neighborhood's citizens represent a clean cross section of your average Panamanian José. The **Mercado Público** and other markets on Av. Central and Plaza 5 de Mayo represent the city's bustle to the extreme. Women walking through the area should expect raunchy catcalls. Nearby **El Chorrillo** is less crowded and less safe. This neighborhood's main attractions are the **Mercado de Artesanías** and the main **bus terminal** serving several major cities.

Ritzy condos shield some of Panama City's richest in **Punta Paitilla,** a neighborhood that's only 15 years old and looks it. Of most interest to travelers here is probably the attractive and moderately priced plaza near the freeway entrance. Punta Paitilla is also home to a number of kosher markets and restaurants (even a supermarket called **Superkosher**). Coco Mar and San Francisco are generally pleasant neighborhoods, filled predominantly with gorgeous and posh villas, including Manuel Noriega's former residence, **Rancho Solola.** The stretch to the east of Coco Mar marks a continuum of dilapidation, culminating in the crumbling ruins of Panamá Viejo; the area around the tourist site is notorious for crime, and is said to be dangerous to travelers.

■■■ PRACTICAL INFORMATION

Tourist Office: IPAT has its national central office at the **Atlapa Convention Center,** Via Israel, San Francisco, P.O. Box 4421, Zona 5 (tel. 226-7000, 226-3483). IPAT provides information on every province and island in the country, including lists of hotels, phone numbers, immigration requirements, medication, and prices. The staff speaks excellent English.

Police: San Felipe, Santa Ana (tel. 223-8620); **San Francisco, Paitilla, Bella Vista** (tel. 226-5692); **Balboa** (tel. 252-6503).

Post Office: There are offices throughout Panama City. The **San Felipe** office, near the Palacio Municipal in San Felipe, is the main office (open Mon.-Fri. 7am-5pm). Letters sent to *Entrega General* in Panama City should be sent to Zona 1, Vía Espana to be received at this address.

Telephones: INTEL has an office has a few offices throughout the city: Try the one at Calle 51 B and Vía España for phoning, **fax,** and **telegram** service. Open daily 7am-11:30pm.

Telegrams: Available at the post office, along with **fax** service.

Embassies: United States, on Av. Balboa and Calle 40, Apdo. Postal 6959 Zona 5 (tel. 227-1777; fax 227-1964); **Canada,** on Calle MM Icaza, Edificio Aeroperú, 5th floor (tel. 264-7014); **United Kingdom,** Calle 53, Edificio Swissbank, 4th floor (tel. 269-0866); **Costa Rica,** Edificio Grobman, Piso 6, Calle Manuel M. Icaza 12 (tel. 264-9266; fax 223-1134); **El Salvador,** Via España 124 (tel. 223-3020); **Guatemala,** Edificio Versailles, Av. Frederico Boyd, Calle 48 (tel. 269-3406; fax 223-1922); **Honduras,** Oficina Comercial, Edificio Galeria Central, Piso 2, Av. 7 A Central (tel. 225-8200; fax 262-2319); **Israel,** Calle Manuel M. Icaza 12 (tel. 263-1594; fax 264-2706); **Nicaragua,** Av. J. San Martin 31 (tel. 223-0981). **Colombia,** Edificio Grobman, Piso 6, Calle Manuel M. Icaza 12 (tel. 264-9266; fax 223-1134).

Immigration, Calle 29, Av. 2 Sur in Calidonia. Visa extensions and exit stamps. Come as early in the day in possible, since it gets horrendously crowded. For **passport photos,** run across the street.

Banks: Willing, helpful banks are located all over the city, particularly around Vía España. Many have ATM machines, and almost all exchange traveler's checks.

Many are affiliated with international banks. **Bank of America,** Av. José de la Cruz Herrera, Calle 53 Este, doesn't charge a commission.

American Express: (tel. 264-2444), Calle 50 at Av. Nicanor de Obarrio, Av. Balboa on the 9th floor. Cardmembers' services offered. Open Mon.-Fri. 8:30am-4pm.

Western Union (tel. 269-1055); Vía España, Edificio Multicredit Bank. Open daily 8am-4pm.

Airport: Tocumen International Airport (tel. 238-4322) serves the city and the country. From there, several airlines fly to the rest of the world, including **American** (tel. 269-6022); **Continental** (tel. 263-9177); **COPA** (tel. 227-5000); **TACA** (269-6066); **United** (tel. 269-8555); and domestic carrier **Aeroperlas** (tel. 269-4555), which serves David, Bocas del Toro, Chitré, Santiago, and Colón, and beyond. **Paitilla Airport** (tel. 226-7959), closer to the city, is a departure point for domestic flights with **Chitreana** (tel. 226-3069; flights to Chitré); **Aerotaxi** (tel. 264-8644; flights to San Blas), and others. **ANSA** (tel. 226-7891), **Aerotaxi** (tel. 264-8644), and **Transpasa** (tel. 226-0843) fly to San Blas; prices are similar across the board. Planes usually leave from Paitilla Airport within minutes of each other (between 6-6:30am). Buy your ticket as early as 5am on the day of the flight.

Buses: To **David** (along the Interamerican Highway) depart from Av. Balboa and Calle 17 Este (hourly, 7am-7pm, 6hrs, $15). These buses also stop in **Penenomé** (1 hr., $3) and **Santiago** (3 hrs., $7). Express buses to **Colón** depart from Av. Central and Calle 26 Oeste, near Plaza 5 de Mayo (every 30min. 5:30am-7pm, 2 hrs., $2). The main bus terminal for other buses is in Santa Ana (El Chorrillo), near the Mercado Artesanía. The bus to **San José, Costa Rica** leaves from the front of Hotel Ideal, on Calle 17 (18 hrs., $25 one-way). An express to Colón stops in Calidonia (1-2 hrs., $2). To **Portobelo,** either take the express to Colón from Calidonia, or head to **Sabanitas** from the main terminal (3 hrs.).

Taxis: From one point on Vía España to another $1. Other fares range from $1-5.

Public buses: A steady stream of ultra-colorful city buses runs along Vía España and throughout the city. They're noisy, so shout to get off. Fare $0.15.

Car rentals: Passport and driver's license are usually required for rental, and some places say you have to be 25. **International Car Rental,** at Calle 55, E.A.Morales, El Congrejo (tel. 264-4540; fax 263-3405), charges $20.90 for a Toyota Corrola. Rent for a week, get one day free. There's another office at the airport. **Budget Rent-a-car** (tel. 263-8777; fax 263-7721); prices change frequently. Open daily.

Supermarket: Rey Supermercado is all over the place, even on Vía España, across from Figali's Dept. Store, or on Plaza Amador, Calle B at Calle 16 Oeste. They've got it all, even a pharmacy.

Laundry: Lavamatico Katty (tel. 223-3644), El Cangrejo, down the street from Manolo's Restaurant. Open Mon.-Sat. 7am-7pm, Sun. 8am-3pm. Self-serve wash $1.75, dry $1.30. Bring your own detergent.

Pharmacy: Farmacía Arrocha (tel. 238-4503, 238-4505), throughout the city and across from El Panamá hotel on Vía España and Calle 49 A Este. A fully stocked pharmacy catering to every possible 3am urge, with sphygmomanometers, sticker books, even Monopoly. Credit cards accepted. Open 24 hrs.

Firefighters: 103

Red Cross: 228-2187

Hospital: Hospital del Niño (tel. 225-1546; emergency: 225-3677), Calle 34, 1-81; **Hospital Clínica America** (tel. 229-1627; emergency 229-1627).

■■■ ACCOMMODATIONS

San Felipe is definitely the place to crash for spartan living at little cost. Bella Vista has its share of semi-luxurious and affordable hotels, but relative to Casco Viejo is far removed the city's hubbub and hoopla. The majority of Calidonia's hotels tend to be popular among sticky-thrill seekers, and the few above-satisfactory hotels available in the medical district fall in the $15-25 range. The hotels listed below are all large, and should have at least a room or two available upon demand.

Hotel Central (tel. 262-8044), on Calle 5 in the heart of San Felipe, near the main post office and the Plaza de la Independencia. A grand hotel dating back to 1919, with 46 room capacity, private and communal baths, and fans everywhere. Relive past glory for only $7 per person without private bath, $8 with private bath.

Hotel Colonial (tel. 262-3858), near Plaza Bolívar on Calle 4. Big, blue, and white, the building's pretty hard to miss; rooms were created for both large groups and singles/doubles. 39 rooms. $6.60 per person, $9.90 with private bath.

Hotel Foyo (tel. 262-8023), Avenida A and Calle 6. Pick one of 39 rooms for a safe haven from the noisy outdoors. All rooms have fans. Reception open 24 hrs. Singles $6, $11 with private bath.

Pensión Panamá (tel. 262-8053), across from the Foyo, isn't exactly a welcoming place, with prison-cell bars separating guests from staff workers, but the 25 rooms with either 2 separate beds or 1 matrimonial all have communal baths, so it's not hard to get to know your fellow inmates and talk about how darn little you're paying. Singles $4, doubles $6.

■■■ FOOD

Panama City is the heart of international cuisine in Central America and you might as well throw conscience to the wind and pack your guts with every type of food imaginable, from Argentine to Indian to Chinese and Swiss. Oh, and there's some good Panamanian food, too. The **market** near Plaza 5 de Mayo abounds with fruit, vegetables, and heaping plates of hot goodies that won't dent your wallet. Restaurants dot the city on every side, but the main strip for fantabulous dining is **Vía Argentina,** where many places are snooty and overpriced, but which is also home to affordable and mind-twistingly sapid plates o' joy. Seafood is almost never a letdown, though fish often runs as high as $7-10 a plate. For cheap, greasy *típico* fare, wander around San Felipe and stop in any one of the similar restaurants.

Café Ejecutivo (tel. 264-3333), Calle 51 Bella Vista (one street from Vía España, near Hotel Ejecutivo). Live the good life with the affordable breakfast menu. Tantalizing *Crepes Frances Enrollado* with marmalade goes for $2.50. Soothing, laid-back atmosphere smacks of elegance. Open 24 hrs.

Mando's Cafetería, in back of Hotel El Panamá, off Vía España near Calle 49 Oeste. Breakfast is a bit pricey (Spanish eggs for $3.10), but lunches and dinners are more reasonable. The outdoor patio and busy street-side location provide entertainment for a super meal. Sausage sandwich $2.50, hamburger with eggs $2.40, octopus with garlic sauce $4.50. Open daily 6am-1am.

Sorrento Pizza (tel. 269-0010), near the Continental Grande Hotel, across Vía España from Vía Argentina. If pictures of the pope visiting the restaurant aren't pacifying enough, the subdued music and reasonable prices most certainly should be. Most entrees run about $4. Pizza with clams $3.

Niko's Café, close to Ciné Aries, just south of Vía España on Calle 51 B Este. Beautiful customers enhance the otherwise dull decor, especially since mirrors on every wall indulge narcissists to no end. Fair people paying fair prices for fair fare. Arroz con pollo $2.50, fish $4. Gyros and sandwiches available, too. Open 24 hrs.

A Mangiare (tel. 223-3151), Vía España up from the Ciné. Italian food priced as if it were imported directly from Sicily, but this is *specialized* cuisine. Pizza with chicken $3. Pasta and fish available, *a mangiare.*

Bon Profit (tel. 263-9667), Vía Argentina, Edificio Baleares. The wine's on the table, and the menu has a cover page, but believe it or not, it's possible to have a full, affordable meal here. Kiddie menu! Yea, kiddie menu! Wines are expensive, so kill three birds with one stone and get the chicken in white wine with onions $5.50, or frolic in filet of flat fish $6.50.

Candies Bazaar, near the Fotokira sign, Vía Argentina. Chocolate tums. Chocolate crayons. Rum chocolate. Chocolate bandaids. Tongue splashers. Spin-poppers. Kosher frozen dairy sweets. Goodies are rather expensive, but so are chocolate fetishes. Open Mon.-Fri. 7am-5pm, Sun. 8am-2pm.

■■■ SIGHTS

Head to Casco Viejo to get the most bang for your walking-tour buck; the old city-center is packed with striking memorials to politicians, heroes, and the heavens above. A good place to begin is on Av. A and Calle 3, at the **Church and Convent of Santo Domingo,** which dates back to 1673. The church's vast arch, **Arco Chato,** is famous for its mortar construction and lack of internal supports; Panamanian leaders used the arch's survival as proof that the country was earthquake-free, an important argument in the battle with Nicaragua to acquire rights to the trans-isthmian canal. Nearby, the **Museo de Arte Colonial Religioso** contains archaeological artifacts, relics, and sculptures, from the country's colonial past.

Walk farther south to the end of Av. Central and follow **Paseo Las Bóvedas,** the path overlooking the Pacific. Encompassing the peninsula's tip, the area was used way back when, as a defense barrier against encroaching pirates and escaped prisoners from nearby island penal colonies. Now it functions as a make-out hideaway for teenagers and, on weekends, as a gathering place for families. Las Bóvedas refers to the vaults around the area; listen for the echo of prisoners from centuries past before partaking of the vaults' modern incarnation as shops and galleries. Attractive **Plaza Francia,** at the peninsula's tip, was engineered by Leonardo de Villanueva Meyer, and was built in honor of the ground-laying efforts of thousands of Frenchmen who died trying to build the canal in the late 19th century. At the end of the path, the stage floor entertains chamber orchestras playing to hushed crowds on summer evenings. **Club de Clases Distropas,** at the end of the path, marks the remains of Noriega's heyday; the building was once a thriving social club filled with generals and lieutenants, socialites, and celebrities wooed by the former dictator. The four decrepit, graffiti-littered walls now house ghosts of the dictator's debauched past, serving as living testament to the public's disdain for Noriega's jet-setting lifestyle. Just near the club is **Iglesia San José,** a monument to Incan architecture built before the Republic of Panama was even conceived.

Follow the path back to Av. A and cut west to Av. Central; one block east on Calle San Francisco lolls the **Teatro Nacional,** representing the Neoclassical architecture popular at the turn of the century. Speak with the administrators to be let in; then sink into one of the heavenly red velvet balcony chairs overlooking the grand theater, while staring up at the ceiling's hovering cherubim for a little distraction.

Once outside again, the tower of **Cathedral San Francisco** soars nearby. A block away, **Parque Simón Bolívar** features a monument honoring the liberator himself. Would-be world leader pretend that he is, Bolívar's ankle was graced by some vandal with an R.E.M. tattoo. Across the street is the Instituto Nacional de Cultura's **Museo de la Nacionalidad,** which features furniture, paintings, and historical documents illustrating Panama's past (open Tues.-Sat. 9:30am-12:30pm and 1:30-4pm, Sunday 9am-noon; adults $0.25, *niños* $0.10).

Cutting back to Av. Central and heading inland a few blocks brings you to serene **Plaza Cathedral,** which coincidentally rests before the big **cathedral.** Erected in 1798 with white-washed, mother-of-pearl twin-towers and domes, the cathedral is the most famous in the city. Also on the plaza stands the **Correos,** the main post office, which isn't just for mail anymore; the 120-year-old structure is historically significant as the first post office built in Panama, starting up in its current role in 1916. Looking at **Palacio Municipal,** on Parque Central next to the post office, you wouldn't guess this is mostly just a big administrative building. In 1903, the palacio was the site of the signing of the Act of Independence, which liberated Panama from Colombia.

Along Av. Alfaro (on the seafront) between Calles 3 and 4 stands the **Palacio Presidencial,** also called the "Palace of the Herons" because of the long-necked birds which hover around the entrance. Representative of Spanish-Moorish architecture, the building is, in fact, still home to El Prez, so entrance is generally not permitted. Instead, gawk at the beautiful **murals** by Roberto Lewis. Looking for the salt of the earth? There's plenty of it at the **mercado público,** off Av. Central on the water, San

Felipe's biggest collection of fruit, fish, and meat kiosks (open daily 4am-8pm). Beyond that, the other **markets** on Av. Central offer mega-cheap clothing (shirts for $5, shoes for $1); merchants buy stuff here and sell it elsewhere for a profit.

Most of the city's other tourist attractions lie off Vía España near Bella Vista. Walking that way from San Felipe along Vía España, stop for a rest at the **Plaza 5 de Mayo,** which was erected in honor of the corps of firemen who heroically battled the flames of an exploded gunpowder storage warehouse back in 1914. Nearby, **El Mercado de Buhonerías y Artesanías** (tel. 262-9333), on Calle 3 de Noviembre, has an extensive range of ceramics, fake flowers, dragon heads, and percussion instruments (open daily 7am-7pm). Afterwards, if memorial statues still hold allure, continue up Vía España and head north on Vía Argentina a block or two; on the right is **Albert Einstein Plaza,** featuring a massive bronze statue of the genius Pisces, himself. The statue's behemoth cranium makes the piece seem nearly life-like.

Otherwise, **shop** until you drop at one or two or fifty of Panama City's unique stores; where else in the world can you find a Jewish kippa adorned with a *mola* from the Kuna Indians for less than $5? Indeed, **Flory Saltzman's Artesanía** (tel. 223-6963) offers many marvelous, multi-colored molas, either on their own, or sewn together into quilts and beautiful wall hangings. Flory undeniably knows her stuff, and she's as close to the source as it gets (without actually going to the Kuna themselves). Similarly representative of the city's odd-ball hodge-podge is **Sol de la India** (tel. 269-1903; fax 263-8029), which sells both run-of-the-mill Panamanian souvenirs and truly impressive imports from India and neighboring countries, including some high-grade waterpipes (open Mon.-Sat. 9am-7pm, Sun. 10am-6pm). Right next to Cine Aries sits **Slendertone** (tel. 269-7319); if the electrodes connected to plastic buttocks in the front window don't entice you enough, go in and ask to view the video demonstration. **Bella Panamá** (tel. 261-9742), across from the Continental Grand Hotel, has an excellent souvenir shop with Cuban cigars and Panamá Beer dominoes (open Mon.-Sat. 8:30am-7pm). And pretty much the whole city seems to be proud of the new **mall** on Vía España, near the bridge over the street, which consists of three-stories of boutiques with aggressive employees. **Figali's,** an upscale department store, keeps the whole place afloat.

■■■ ENTERTAINMENT

La Accedemia Italiano features **El Teatro en Círculo** (tel. and fax 223-4874), at Calle 47, a running program of Italian plays and operas. Call for prices and current shows. **Guitar** performances are held every Sunday in **Santuario Nacional,** near Hong Kong Bank, which itself is a solid church inside and out. In February of each year, IPAT sponsors a theater festival; folklore is presented in dramatic form at Panamá Viejo. Call IPAT for more info. **Movie theaters** include **Cines Aries** (tel. 269-1632), just off Vía España on Calle 52 Este, with 7 screens (flicks fly between 3-11pm). Check papers for listings for theaters such as **Cine Plaza** (tel. 269-4928), Vía España, in the plaza with Banco del Istmo. Artsier films are shown in the **Cine Universidad,** on the campus of Universidad Nacional behind gothic-style Iglesia Carmen.

Hit a Hard Eight, snake-eyes, or box-cars at one of the city's many **casinos,** in Hotel El Panamá on Vía España west of Calle 49 B Oeste. Try your hand at slot machines, poker, blackjack, and the rest; unlike casinos elsewhere in the country, this casino is family-oriented during the day (open daily 9:30am-5pm and midnight-6:30am).

For **nightlife,** San Felipe has more than its share of bars and poolhalls, but the area is considered unsafe after dark; instead, head up to the neighborhood of El Cangrejo off Vía España has numerous discos and bars. Just off Calle 52 Este and Vía España lies **Discoteca Bacchus** (near Cine Arias): remember de Medici's Song of Bacchus: "Be happy today, for tomorrow is unsure." What's sure is that you won't have a hangover after imbibing the two drinks that come with the $7 cover. Also on Vía Argentina and Vía España is **La Zingara.** Shake, rattle, and roll a few blocks away on Calle 49 Este, north of Vía España, at **My Place** and **Daiquiri.**

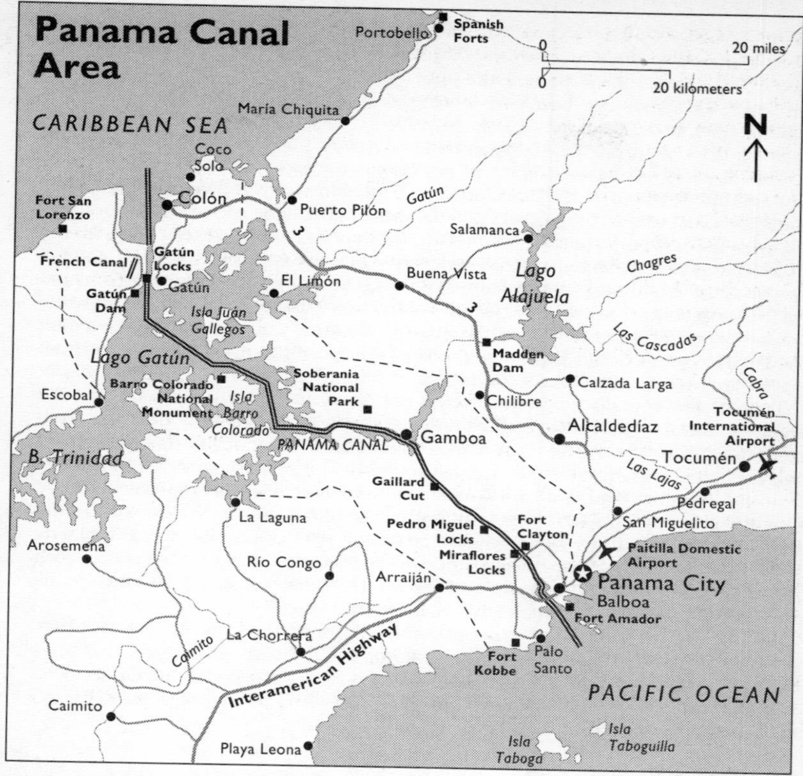

NEAR PANAMA CITY

PANAMA CANAL

The fifty mile stretch of water connecting the Atlantic and Pacific oceans is believed by many to be not only the country's single must-see attraction, but also one of the world's greatest engineering feats. Standing at the edge of the awesome **Gatún Locks,** one of several points along the canal where ships are required to shift water levels, claims of such magnitude seem well-deserved. The Canal's construction left a giant notch not only in Panama's geography, but in world history, marking triumph following several centuries of failure, a re-shaping of Panama's importance as a nation, and the tightening of the United States' grip on Central American affairs. (See Panama: History, page 411, for more on the canal's role in Panamanian history).

Serving as go-between was nothing new to Panama when the canal was finally completed on August 15, 1914. The novelty in the canal, the fruit of the labor of **John Stevens, Col. George Goethals,** and thousands of laborers from around the world, was that it was a direct water route, a way for cargo ships to avoid the tiresome and lengthy trip around the southern tip of South America. **Charles I** of Spain had tried to find a way through in 1534, and the canal-savvy Frenchman **Ferdinand de Lesseps,** mastermind behind the Suez Canal, drained his bank account before managing to dredge the banks of the canal. When the **Hay-Bunau-Varilla treaty** of 1903 granted sovereignty of a "Canal Zone" to the U.S., all that remained for the U.S. to simplify its trade with Asia were a man, a plan, a canal: Panama. **President Roosevelt** provided the capital to back the enterprise, and together with the crucial efforts of **Col. WIlliam Gorgas,** who launched an aggressive campaign to prevent disease among workers, it took only 10 years for the Canal to be completed. While the U.S has directed the Canal ever since, Panama has gradually gained control throughout the century. Thanks to a treaty signed in 1977, the United States will transfer the Canal to Panama on Dec. 31, 1999.

Since 1914, more than 700,000 ships have passed through the Canal's intricate system of locks, taking an average of nine hours for each trip. Any vessel passing through the canal pays a fee based on its weight; Panamax-sized vessels, the largest ships the canal can accommodate, pay thousands of dollars, and even the few people who have swum through have had to fork over a few cents each. The majority of the ships passing through service trade between the East Coast of the U.S. and the Far East; the canal saves these ships about 3,000 miles. Ships coming from the Pacific drop about 85 feet in the Gatun Locks (after passing through the sprawling **Gatun Lake**) to reach the level of the Atlantic. **Gaillard Cut,** the narrow stretch on the Pacific side of Gatun Lake, was the site of most of the blasting and accidental deaths incurred for the Canal's completion.

Tourists not actually cruising through the canal on a boat or ship congregate along the locks to watch the engineering marvels in effect. To view the canal from land, ride a bus to any American Armed Forces base (Howard, Kodman, Clayton) and check out the American bridge that serves as the primary entrance to the city from the interior (**Bridge of the Americas**). **Contractor's Hill** overlooks Gaillard Cut, and is another popular observation site. The Miraflores Locks, just west of the city, are open daily form 9am-5pm; catch a bus headed for Gamboa from Plaza 5 de Mayo. It's also possible to visit the office of the Panama Canal Commission, which provides quality tourist brochures and maps of the canal (tel. 252-2122; open Mon.-Sat. 7:15am-4:15pm). For general information, call 264-0714.

Taking a tour through the canal is highly recommended, mostly for the spicy information and first-hand views that accompany the trip. Several tour agencies make the trip: **Argo Tours** (tel. 228-4348) heads to Isla Taboga via the Canal, as do **Servitur** (tel. 264-3014) and **Reisa Tours** (tel. 225-4721). Prices range from $10-30 to check out all the locks.

PANAMÁ VIEJO

Explorer **Pedrarias Dávila** was skilled at finding continents, not founding cities, and so it's not surprising that his choice of location for Panama City in 1519 was doomed to fail; the area around his settlement seethed with stinky, slimy mangrove swamps, and out of olfactory odium (and repeated sackings by British pirate Henry Morgan), the city was moved 10km west to modern day Panama City in 1673. However, Panamá Viejo (as the old site was thereafter called) managed in its day to flourish as the Pacific terminus of Spain's **Camino Real.** A vast network of trade fairs enabled the Spanish to trade and carry goods from South America through to the Caribbean at Nombre de Dios; some of those traded "goods" were African slaves, many of whom escaped and proceeded to terrorize the trade passage. Assaulted by pirates on all sides, city leaders wised up, deciding that to transplant the whole darn place would be the best means of escape.

Getting older every second, today's Panamá Viejo offers an intriguing peek into the urban design of a 16th century city. A fort, several convents, a hospital, and other structures still stand, the crumbling stones bolstered by stucco and ongoing restoration efforts. Most impressive is the towering **catedral,** whose height alone probably caused a few non-Christians to convert. The few walls and the 50 ft. buttress still remaining are extraordinary, the bare altar still facing the buds of tiers sprouting from the fertile ground.

A trip to Panamá Viejo from Panama City takes about half a day. Capture the contrast in colors between the brown and gray, hundred year-old bricks and the plush green grass. **Getting there** is cheap: buses from Plaza 5 de Mayo ($0.15) take you to the cathedral; the pick up for returning buses is at the gas station at the end of the ruins. There are only a few restaurants around the ruins, and all are overpriced, catering to wealthier tourists. Taking along a picnic is a better idea, though there are *sodas* near the gas station.

Panama Viejo's **Artesanías Nacionales,** stuck at the end of the highway, consists of several mini-shops chock full of souvenirs from different regions of the country. The goods are reasonably priced, but try to bargain (open Tues.-Sun. 9am-6pm).

ISLA TABOGA

Uninhabited, Isla Taboga, about 20km from Panama City off the shore, would be paradise on earth; the beaches are big and beautiful, monolithic boulders around the shore push any hiker to new heights, and a smooth breeze combined with buttery sun set the mood for bliss. As it stands, though, the island is far too crowded; two boats carry approximately 200 people to Taboga each day, and along with the island's bikini-clad permanent (or seasonal) residents, opportunities for isolation are about as secure as the tiers of wobbly houses stacked against the island's rocks. Still, in the off-season (on an off-day), it's easier to remove yourself from today and imagine the past centuries of flower blossoms, pirate lore, and Spanish settlement that led tourists to come here to begin with.

The island itself has few amenities; there is but one main road. The **Centro de Salud** (tel. 250-2094), left of the dock, is easy to spot, and has a general **pharmacy,** as well as a **doctor** who comes in on Monday and Thursday.

Try not to overnight it if you can help it, as rooms are very expensive at the **Hotel Taboga** (tel. 250-2122), near the dock to the right. Still, the hotel rents out other treats: beach chairs ($3), hammocks ($3), pedal boats ($7 per hour), and other games help to make the day complete. Other, cheaper rooms are available at **Hotel Chu** (tel. 250-2035 on Taboga; tel. 263-6933 in Panama City), off the main road left of the dock (pleasant and festive rooms run for $19 per person, doubles $24). To get to Isla Taboga from Panama City, take a taxi to **Muelle Balboa** ($1.90), buy a boat ticket at the dock with **Argotours** (tel. 228-4348), and hop aboard (Mon.-Fri. 8:30am, 3pm; Sat.-Sun. 8:30, 11:30am, 4pm; $7 round trip). The IPAT office on the port can provide informative reads for the trip.

NORTH OF PANAMA CITY

■■■ PORTOBELO

Portobelo, Portobelo. Let the name dribble off your tongue a few times for a taste of just how smooth and mellow things are in this minuscule coastal town. Even the refreshing breeze that pulls through the streets doesn't motivate the heat-lulled residents to move much, and as a visitor, it's easy to forget that the port was once crucial in Spain's efforts to defend Panama from pillaging and plundering pirates; ruins of forts are still accessible just a short distance from town. The long, scenic drive to Portobelo past Lago Gatún is delightfully scenic in its own right, a view shared annually by the thousands of purple-clad Panamanians who come to the town's church in October to view the sacred and powerful Black Christ statue near the altar.

Portobelo has no accommodations and few services, and so is best experienced as a daytrip from the capital. There are two **ruins** of Spanish defense sites along the Portobelo coast and one atop a steep (but climbable) mountain. Along the coast, cages of cannonballs near massive cannons stand ready to fire over the barricades down below, and the watch tower still stands erect and ready for action. The chilling coastal breeze and dead silence of the area makes the fort seem a bit *too* prepped, as if pirates were expected to attack sometime very soon.

The huge church near the last defense site houses the much-worshipped, miracle-working **Black Christ.** On the way back to Portobelo from Panama City, **Playa Maria Chiquita** and **Playa Langosta** demand attention. The beaches' proximity to some reefs make them ideal for scuba diving and snorkeling. **Scuba Portobelo** stands out among the three local dive shops because it offers cabins for overnight stays and trips to Isla Mamay, a major scuba/snorkeling island (one night stay during the week $30 per person, on the weekend $50). Make reservations for weekend stays; one-tank dives go for $20. **Jet ski** rental is also available. Contact **Scuba Panamá** in Panama City (261-4084) for more information.

Go, Man, Go!

Regardless of the Freudian implications, the easiest way to eat a mango is to pluck an end with your fingernail, peel it like a banana, and suck away. But for hygiene's sake, consider a fancier option: cut along both sides of the seed, leaving you with two pieces and a seed with some fruit around the edges. Next, peel the skin around the seed and chomp away. Then take your two bowl-shaped pieces and cut down into the fruit, creating a grid in the pulp. Turn the skin inside-out and scrape out the pieces. Diced mango! Alternatively, cut the fruit into strips, shove them into your mouth, and use your teeth to scrape off the pulp. The one vital rule of mango-eating: with all the peeling, slicing, sucking, and dicing, never, ever wear a white shirt.

SOBERANÍA NATIONAL PARK

Twenty five km along the canal toward Gamboa (on the Canal's east side) breathes Soberanía National Park, a large rainforest of more than 22,000 hectares set aside for city-folk to dabble in nature when mega-markets and behemoth banks start to get overbearing. Several trails through the park thread through dense, green foliage, and a number of bird and mammal species call humid Soberanía home. For a brochure filled with tips, info., and trail information, contact the park office in Panama City (tel. 256-6370).

ISLA BARRO COLORADO

Less accessible to tourists, but a better place to enjoy nature at its purest, Isla Barro Colorado is a man-made island created as an ecological research and reserve area. The **Smithsonian Tropical Research Institute** runs the island, and is adamant about their intentions: nature first, tourists second. That means that of the 40sq.km of greenery, visitors are only allowed to follow a 2.5km trail and return home at the end of the day. It also means that only a small number of tourists are allowed to visit the island each year, and then only on Saturdays and Sundays. If you plan to visit Barro Colorado, make reservations well in advance (i.e. five months ahead of time), or prepare to do some serious talking. Sometimes, last-minute cancellations make it possible for others to join tours on shorter notice. Only two boat companies, the Smithsonian and **Ecotours,** provide transport to the island because of the institute's stringency about using electric boats to preserve the waters. Despite the hassle of getting there, Barro Colorado is said to be worth every bit of the effort. To get more information and to make reservations, call the Smithsonian Tropical Research Institute (tel. 227-6022; fax 262-6084) or contact Ecotours (tel. 236-3076; fax 236-3550).

WEST OF PANAMA CITY

■■■ EL VALLE

Upon stumbling into El Valle, famed river explorer Anton Martín must have wondered about those mushrooms he had eaten the night before. Situated 27km north of San Carlos and the Interamerican Highway, El Valle is truly a surprise-filled wonderland: luscious oranges swing pendulously near trees with square trunks, golden frogs jump and croak in gushing waterfalls, and beyond cave walls filled with cryptic, doodled ancient petroglyphs sleeps *La India Dormida,* the giant, anthropomorphic silhouette of the mountains in the distance. Though El Valle is small, the village packs more than its share of touristic punch, and is a popular destination for foreign and Panamanian visitors alike.

Practical Information There are no street signs in El Valle and, with the exception of the center of town, few landmarks, so put on your asking cap. Questions about square trees are enthusiastically welcomed at the tiny **IPAT** office, next door to the **Mercado.** The closest bank is over an hour away, but **traveler's checks** are exchanged at the mini-market near the **Mercado El Valle.** There are two public **telephones** inside the mercado. A zippy way to get around town is with one of the four **taxi** drivers (tel. 983-6148). Sr. Alfredo Sanchez, Taxi #2T-118, speaks excellent English, and he knows the town like the back of his taxi. For **medical assistance,** contact the **Centro de Salud,** down the street from the mercado (doc's in da' house Mon.-Fri 9am-3pm; fend for yourself on weekends).

Accommodations and Food Valle's hotel owners know their town is popular, and many hike their hotel prices to rude heights. The best bet is to camp out near the waterfalls—or anywhere else. Just ask around in town and make sure the weather is ok. **Cabañas Las Mozas** (tel. 983-7071), near the primary school, has but five rooms, and all have private baths ($35 covers 1 or 2 people). **Hotel Greco** (tel. 983-6149) has more rooms, and again, all have private bath. Call early for reservations in the busy season (doubles $19.50, triples $23). **Motel Niña Delia** (tel. 983-7110), at the entrance of El Valle, has a pleasant patio with hammocks and comfortable chairs. Mostly used by visiting carpenters and construction workers, it still maintains high prices ($15 with communal bathroom, $20 with private bath). The restaurant serves meals throughout the day. **Pensión Rana Dorada** (tel. 983-6181) has four clean rooms, all with private bathrooms ($30 per person). Most of the few **restaurants** in Valle are attached to *cabañas* and hotels. The restaurant attached to Cabañas Las Mozas has tiny tables and woven leather chairs, which provide comfort for diners in the small outdoor *soda.* **Cafe La Ranchita,** right next door, is a Gilligan-esque hut with hand-made wooden furniture filling a subterranean outdoor dining room; the two arcade games were a stroke of the professor's genius.

Sights For a good 10 seconds of fun, look off into the distance at the outlying mountains that surround the valley. Look closely, and you'll see that they aren't mountains at all, but actually a giant, sleeping Indian; keep it down, lest you wake *La India Dormida.* Legend has it that an indígena maiden, **Flor del Aire,** fell in love with a conquering Spaniard; her prior lover killed himself out of desperation, and the girl, disgraced and tormented, wandered into the hills to die, lying down on her back to stare forever at the skies above. Less like a soap opera, but more time-consuming a distraction is **El Nispero,** the local nursery and zoo, which exotic crabs, "titi" monkeys, and Mandarin ducks all call home. At least take a peek at the zaftig and indigenous *ranas doradas* (golden frogs; $1 admission). The town's gorgeous twin waterfalls, **El Macho** and **Las Moras,** are located on the road to the town of La Mesa, about 500m from the Doña Chabela bridge. Set in the midst of serene countryside, the pools at the base of the falls are prime for swimming. The weekly **Sunday Arts Fair** takes place in the **Mercado El Valle** (7am-3pm). Artisans from miles around swarm in by foot from their secluded mountain farms, carrying their crafts on *chorillos;* many make their whole living solely on what they sell at the market. Sculpted pots, intricately weaved chairs, and even wicker helicopters are all available for tourist perusal and consumption. The fair ends so early in the day because the families have to head back into the hills before dark. After checking out the avant-garde of the artisan scene, explore the origins of art in the nearby town of **La Pintada,** where you can gawk at giant rock adorned with semi-intelligible, but very funky **petroglyphs.** At the end of the day, indulge in hours of comforting maceration in the **hot springs** near the Anton river, which percolates medicinal, arthritis-curing waters from the volcanic crust below ($0.25 admission).

■■■ PENONOMÉ

Claustrophobes beware: a few days in tiny Penonomé might drive you batty, providing all the more reason to explore the surrounding region's villages and the beautiful beaches that skulk just a half hour away. Still, with a little imagination (and strong interest in the region's arts and handicrafts), otherwise bland Penonomé spreads its little arms in a gesture of warm welcome.

Send a postcard to Grandma at the **post office,** in the municipal building (tel. 997-9666); use the **telegram** service if she's the impatient type (open Mon.-Fri. 7am-6pm, Sat. 7am-5pm). **Buses** stop frequently, as Penonomé is a stop for buses running between Panama City and David. **Farmacia Arco Iris** (tel. 997-8155), next to the massive indoor fruit **market,** accepts major credit cards for over the counter and prescription drugs (open Mon.-Sat. 7:30am-7:30pm, Sun. 7:30am-noon). **Clínica Penonomé/Farmacia Nazareno** (tel. 997-9451), on Av. Hector C. Bermudez, has an **emergency** ambulance available 24 hrs. The **hospital** (tel. 997-9386) seduces the ill from next to the Artesanía market at the Interamerican Highway.

It's clear why families choose to stay at **Hotel Dos Continentes** (tel. 997-9326), on Av. Juan D. Arosemana, given its 40 clean rooms, restaurant, and established feel (singles with fan and private bath $10.90, with A/C $16, doubles with air $26). **Pensión Los Pinos,** across from Artesenal, doesn't exactly put out the welcome mat, but rooms are decent and have fans and private bath (singles $11.50, doubles $13.50).

It's not hard to miss **Mercado Artesenal** (tel. 97-9011), down the road from Hotel Dos Continentes, past Av. Juan D. Arosemana on the Interamerican Highway. Cause of the great sucking sound heard all over town, this place vacuums in tourists better than the mightiest of Hoovers (even Herbert). Many items are overpriced, but most of the handicrafts are affordable and quite attractive. The people in the adjacent office offer insight into the crafts and the personalities behind the scenes. Originally a government-run enterprise intended to spur tourism in the area, the market helps to raise money for indigenous artisans, an unconditionally worthy cause. Follicularly challenged travelers might head off to **Artesanía de Sombreros,** near the Shell station, to cover that scurfy scalp with one of the hats, hats, and more hats hanging from the walls; the type of *sombrero* sold is unique to this region. Just beyond stands **Iglesia San Juan Bautista,** an elegant church. **Mercado Publico,** in the center of town (and impossible to miss), is a monolithic fruit market. Tap into the town's grapevine while picking up vines of berries and sumptuous avocados. To get to the **Museo Arqueologico,** in San Antonio, take a bus toward Aguadulce and tell the driver to stop at San Antonio. Slather your skin with sun-oil and sand at one of three pristine beaches nearby—**Playa Juan Hombrón, Playa Farallón,** and **Playa Santa Clara,** all of which are about 20-30 minutes away.

■■■ CHITRÉ

With verve and vim and nerve and whim inspired by Panama City, without the girth, but down to earth, Chitré's got stuff more gritty. It feels small-town, but don't you frown, this city loves to party; 'round Easter time the mood is prime for dancing and Bacardi. But never fear, there's more than beer: the culture here is rich; those partisans of artisans can count on more than kitsch. The folklore's hot—a bore it's not—and locals love to chuckle, to share their zest for customs' best, like weavings and belt buckles. **Herrera's** prime to share your time, **Los Santos** merits visits; the **biotopo** suits your hopes so much you'll want to kiss it. In other words, to watch cool birds, or just to be inspired, head to Chitré to spend a day and stay until you're tired.

Practical Information IPAT (tel. 996-4331), near Hotel Hong Kong on the way to Los Santos in the Edificio de Comercio e Industria, is extremely helpful to tourists. The almost constant festivals around these parts are not widely advertised, and moreover, the beaches are hard to get to without a little prior research. Speak with Carlos Villareal, the office's extraordinarily knowledgeable and enthusiastic director. Not Stewart Copeland, but other **police** should be called for dire situations (tel. 996-4333). Several **banks** around the center of town wait to change traveler's checks. The **post office** (tel. 996-4974) is intimately attached to the **Intel** building (open Mon.-Fri. 8am-6pm). **Telegram** service is available, but alas, no fax. **Supermercado Machetuzo,** in the center of town, has everything from electrical supplies to pharmaceuticals to sugar cereals to cheesecake to… **Buses** to small beaches and cities can be reached from throughout town, especially near the cathedral. Buses to Las Tablas leave regularly during the day (30-45min., $1.35); to Panama City (10 a day, $6). **Farmacia El Vigia** (tel. 996-2311), near Banco del Istmo, is well-stocked (open 8am-8pm). Have boils lanced at the **hospital** (tel. 996-4444, 996-4410).

Accommodations and Food The easiest way to remedy ferocious post-party hangovers is to drink some water and find a fluffy bed in which to writhe and moan during the day after. **Hotel El Prado** (tel. 996-4620), on Av. Herrera, fits the bill with clean, big bedrooms with TV, private bath, and air-conditioning. The 2nd story lobby is *schön* to the max. (singles $9.50, $14.70 with air conditioning, doubles $15, $20 with air conditioning). For cheaper sleeps, **Pensión Azuero,** near the cathedral, isn't a bad place if you're staying a short while, but it's a bit out of the way. Rooms cost $6 and are worth $6. Rooms in **Hotel Santa Rita** (tel. 996-4610), Av. Herrera, are decently clean and cleanly decent; rooms have private bath (singles $7.70, doubles $13). When hunger hits, explore the streets around the cathedral. **Manolo,** by the Machetazo monster department store, serves regional specialties and vegetarian delights (veggie pizza $3).

■ NEAR CHITRÉ

Other than for its overwhelming proclivity to throw *fiestas* at every turn, Chitré is actually less renowned among travelers than are other nearby beaches, parks, and villages in the province of Herrera. Many of the nearby locales are lilliputian, and because all of them can be reached by buses from Chitré, it may prove convenient to make Chitré the base for day-long excursions.

BEACHES AND ISLANDS

There are many beaches along the coast of the Los Santos province, but if building sand-castles and body surfing are your main priorities, Las Tablas, an hour or so closer to the shore, is actually the place to be (see below). Ask around; every beach but Playa Venado is serviced by a bus from Las Tablas (most are 2-2½ hrs. away). The *playa* closest to Chitré is **Monagre,** near Los Santos. Other recommended beaches include **Playa Arenal,** near **Padasi,** which has access to **Isla Iguana,** a treasure trove of exotic birds and plants. Particularly interesting to divers, the reefs around the Isla Iguana have been the site of an extensive effort to help coral grow, and already extant coral heads provide fodder to morays and even elusive white sharks. Padasi is also is the departure point for two daily buses to other beaches, including **Playa Venado, Punta Mala,** and **Biotopo Isla Cañas,** another biological reserve which is otherwise accessible by a daily 8am ferry departing from the town of Parita. **Punta Mala** is the residential center closest to all of these beaches, so come here to get to tinier, less popular beaches by taxi.

PARQUE NACIONAL SARIGUA

Modern folks aren't the first humans ever to tread on the dry soil of Parque Nacional Sarigua; Pre-Columbian habitation of the area dates back thousands of years. But somehow, the secluded desert park manages to evoke a feeling of utter isolation and first-time exploration. A short hike yields spectacular views not of lush forest, but of vast expanses of red-brown earth. Mangroves are among the most thrilling flora here, but frolicking pelicans, sonarcas, and butterflies liven up the potential for communing with nature. To get to Sarigua from Chitré, take one of the infrequent buses to the nearest town, **Puerto Limón,** near Los Santos. It's only a 15-20min. drive from Los Santos (which is only 15min. from Chitré). Once there, walk the dirt road for about 30min. until you get to the ranger station (tel. 974-4343; admission is free).

LOS SANTOS AND LA ARENA

Stroll down Av. Nacional away from Chitré, or hop on a quick bus to get to the little village of **Los Santos,** which is roused yearly from deep slumber by thousands of eager *fiesta*-seekers from throughout the country. The city's other draw is **El Museo de la Nacionalidad,** which is mysteriously enshrouded in a blurry haze during festivals, but at other (sober) times, the museum features artifacts from Panama's history. Particularly interesting are the original letters of the man responsible for liberating the nation from Spain, Simón Bolívar. An accompanying 7-foot statue of a well-endowed woman heralding her freedom symbolizes Bolívar's actions (open Tues.-Sat. 9am-12:30pm and 1:30-4pm, Sun. 9am-noon; adults $0.25, children $0.10). Keep walking, and note the old residential homes on the outskirts of the city; they're over 80 years old, and most still use outhouses. Intricately woven roofs hold the houses together; wooden branches support the structures, and are occasionally stapled with a wire or two for the luxury of electricity.

The minute village of **La Arena** is famous for producing some of the finest ceramics in Panama. Stores line the main highway heading in from Chitré, only 10min. away by car or bus. Very likely, the guy who sells you the vase or pot made it himself. The prices are affordable, and the people don't take to bargaining. Ask around town for Balzibar, who is particularly gifted.

LAS TABLAS

As yet another frisky teenage couple scurries by after making out in the park, as one more parakeet hovers around your shoulder, zip-a-dee-do-da-like, and as one last elegant woman glides by in a fantastically embroidered dress, there's no escaping the conclusion that you're in **Las Tablas.** For some reason, throngs of tourists from all over Panama come to this little town during Semana Santa (travelers should make reservations *well* in advance), but at other times, uproarious romping and revelry give way to soft smiles and deep traditions, exhibited by prayers of devotion at the gold-leafed altar of the **Iglesia de Santa Librada,** and by continued acceptance of the local dress (the *pollera*) and numerous local dances (see gray box, below).

The center of town (where the hotels are) is 1km north of the bus stop (at the Shell station) along the main road. The road runs straight into Parque Central. There's a **post office,** one block right of the *supermercado,* across from *seguro social.* Send letters (Mon.-Fri. 7am-6pm, Sat. 7am-5pm) or **telegrams** (Mon.-Fri. 7am-10pm, Sat. 7am-10pm, Sun. 8am-10pm). The **supermarket,** one block north of the Shell station, is loaded with candy bars and other goodies. **Buses** to Panama City and to nearby beaches (and beach towns) congregate at the Shell station near the supermarket ($6.50 to Panama City). Also go to Chitré (30min., $1.30) or Playa Venado each day (2-2½ hrs.). **Farmacia Neña** (tel. 994-7744) squats up the street from the supermarket. There's a **lavandería** across from the high school. Get your stomach pumped 24 hrs. at the **Hospital,** across the street from the Shell station.

Head to **Casa de Artesania,** down from the Shell Station on the main road, for *polleras,* ceramics, rich leather, and even painted coconut shells. On Sundays, peek into the back of **Escuela Presidente Porras,** 2-3 blocks from Parque Central, to see groups of children learning the *pollera* dance, particularly around festival time.

It's not unwise to get a **hotel** room with A/C, since Las Tablas often swelters at night. All ten rooms in **Hotel Piamonte** (tel. 994-6372) are safe, clean, pretty, have air-conditioning and private baths, and house up to three people. The adjacent restaurant serves up piping hot breakfasts for $2 (singles $14, doubles $21, triples $24).

Hotel Zafiro (tel. 994-8200), across from Banco del Istmo near the park, proffers small rooms with no fans, but oh, are those rooms clean and those baths private! (Singles $14, doubles $26.) **Hotel Mariela** (tel. 994-6473), across from Hotel Piamonte, offers six dirty, cheap rooms with rickety doors and communal baths, but the price is right ($4 per person).

So the kids they dance and shake their bones

The annual *Fiesta de Santa Librada,* held around July 20, sways hand in hand with the *Fiesta de la Pollera,* which celebrates the glory of the region's traditional dress (which can easily be measured by the number of tourist brochure pictures in which the dress is worn). But while any traveler with the yen can don a pollera for a few balboas, only a special elite have the know-how to trip the light fantastic, Herrera-style. Indeed, the region's traditional dances are a fantastic trip for the crowds who gather to watch; each shimmy is linked to a folk tale, so for the full scoop, buy a wise local a beer for informative sideline narration. In *La Dansa de Toros,* for example, a single man plays the part of the bull (actually swinging around a paper-maché bull's head), while other "matadors" intimidate the bull with red handkerchiefs. That is, until the bull goes mad, taking his vengeance on the audience. In *La dansa de Guapos,* several men dress up outlandishly as women before swinging around their stuffed their bras to the tight rhythms of a local folk song. Last (but by no means least) comes the spooky *Dansa de los Diablos,* in which little boys dressed up as scary munchkin skeletons march around and scream to wake the dead.

■■■ SANTIAGO

Word on the street is that Santiago is an incorrigibly boring city, especially considering its stature as capital of the Veraguas province. While it may have few of the attractions tourists are used to, Santiago deserves recognition for its exceptionally personable citizens. Don't expect to be left alone in this town; perhaps because they see so few tourists, bankworkers, uniformed school children, and random passers-by can't act fast enough to toss out a friendly "good day" or buy foreigners a drink at the bar. Santiago's other bonus is its location between Panama City and David, making the city a good spot for a layover. And lo and behold! Hotels situated right on the Interamerican Highway facilitate just this feature.

Orientation and Practical Information The center of Santiago houses the stores, banks, and the majority of the population, and the stretch along the *Interamericana* hosts buses and nicer hotels. There are hotels in both locations, designed for either the "Wow, Santiago, I've had crazy dreams about this place" travelers, or the "Darnit, I'm stuck for the night, what's the name of this city again?" types. Avenida Central serves as focal point for the city center, and major businesses extend outward from this major thoroughfare for a few blocks.

Banco General, on Av. Central near the cathedral, changes traveler's checks and cash (open Mon.-Fri. 8am-3pm, Sat. 9am-noon). **Banco del Istmo** has one of the region's rare ATM machines. **Buses** stop frequently, as Santiago is a stopover between Panama City and David. **Farmacia La Placita** (tel. 998-4465) vegetates next to the cathedral (open daily 8am-7pm). Keep up with pen-pals at the **post office** (tel. 998-4293), on Calle 8.

Accommodations and Food In the city center, **Hotel Santiago** (tel. 998-4824), near the church at the end of Calle 6, has been age-mellowed like a classy, refined wine. Take a whiff of the lobby's sweet bouquet, and let the taste dance along the tastebuds. The air-conditioned, telephoned rooms are large enough to bowl in. All rooms have private bathrooms and fans. Traveler's checks accepted; pay a buck more for a TV (singles $7.70; doubles $11, with A/C $14). **Hotel Gran**

David (tel. 998-4510, 998-2622), right next to the Santiago-Panama bus terminal, near the Interamerican Highway, boasts refreshingly affordable rooms, given the gracious staff, beautiful rooms with private bath, and the connected restaurant and bar with pool tables. Rooms with A/C also have other fancy stuff, like telephones and TVs. The clientele are all business (singles $8.80, with A/C $13.30 per person). Make reservations for the busy season. **Hotel Pana-China** (tel. 998-5977), in the center of town, across from the fruit stand and Cesar Store, is roomy, clean, and reasonably priced, for the necessities. Choose air-conditioning or fan. Some rooms have private baths; the communal bathrooms are clean. Lump up to 4 people in a room ($8 per person, $9.50 with private bath, $10.50 with A/C and private bath).

Find all the elegant **restaurants** in the hotels. Otherwise, there's a huge fruit stand on Calle 6, Av. Central for all your veggie needs, a bundle of great-smelling **bakeries** loaf nearby, and there are mom-and-pop places serving cheap, *típico* meals all around town.

Sights and Entertainment Walk around Santiago and see some really big churches. Get a bit out of Santiago and see big churches *and* a whole lot more.

On the crossroads of the Interamericana and Av. Central, a sign points to **La Iglesia San Francisco,** 18km away. If admiring architecture and really tall buttresses sounds like a fun day trip, this is where to go. Buses travel there all day. Ask the father to show you around; he's happy to entertain questions. A bit farther along stands **Iglesia Atalaya,** which is connected to a *colegio.*

If you want to trek out beyond Santiago proper, the tiny town of **Calabre** offers some **hot springs** to help to ease bus-trip induced aches, pains, and muscle-tension. Even farther beyond, in the town of Natá, stands the **Altar de Oro Museo Arqueologico,** an extensive archaeological museum specializing in artifacts made out of silver? No. Gypsum? No. It's gold. The town and museum can be reached by hopping on an east-bound bus to either Chitré or Panama City; buses pass on the main highway heading east, so just flag them down with a wave. Tell the driver to drop you off as close to Natá as possible. It's a good idea to start off in the morning so there's enough time to explore the museum before closing.

CHIRIQUÍ AND BOCAS DEL TORO

The westernmost provinces in Panama, Chiriquí and Bocas del Toro are just far enough from Panama City to have kept out the jet-setters and commercialized, stylized tourism more common in the east. Chiriquí feels more like the Central America budget travelers come for, and its sensual rainforests and skyscraping volcanoes don't disappoint. The indigenous Guaymí know a good thing when they see it, having inhabited the region since pre-Columbian times. With the regional capital David as a springboard, a few hours drive to the north leads to charming coffee-growing villages, from which Volcán Barú can be suitably explored.

North of Chiriquí, Bocas del Toro sings a different siren song, offering not rugged thrills but alluring Caribbean islands and beaches. British and French pirates used to stop in the archipelago to repair their ships, and different Guaymí tribes inhabited the region between Volcán Barú and the Costa Rican border, land today set aside for massive **Parque Nacional La Amistad.** An earthquake in 1992 disrupted many services in the region, but most of the damage has been fixed.

■■■ DAVID

Granted, David *is* the third largest city in Panama, and it *does* deserve some credit as capital of the entire Chiriquí province, and the city *might* be home to more than 120,000 people, but as much as the town boasts impressive titles, it just doesn't feel all that big. Scattered banks, semi-menacing *supermercados,* and some governmen-

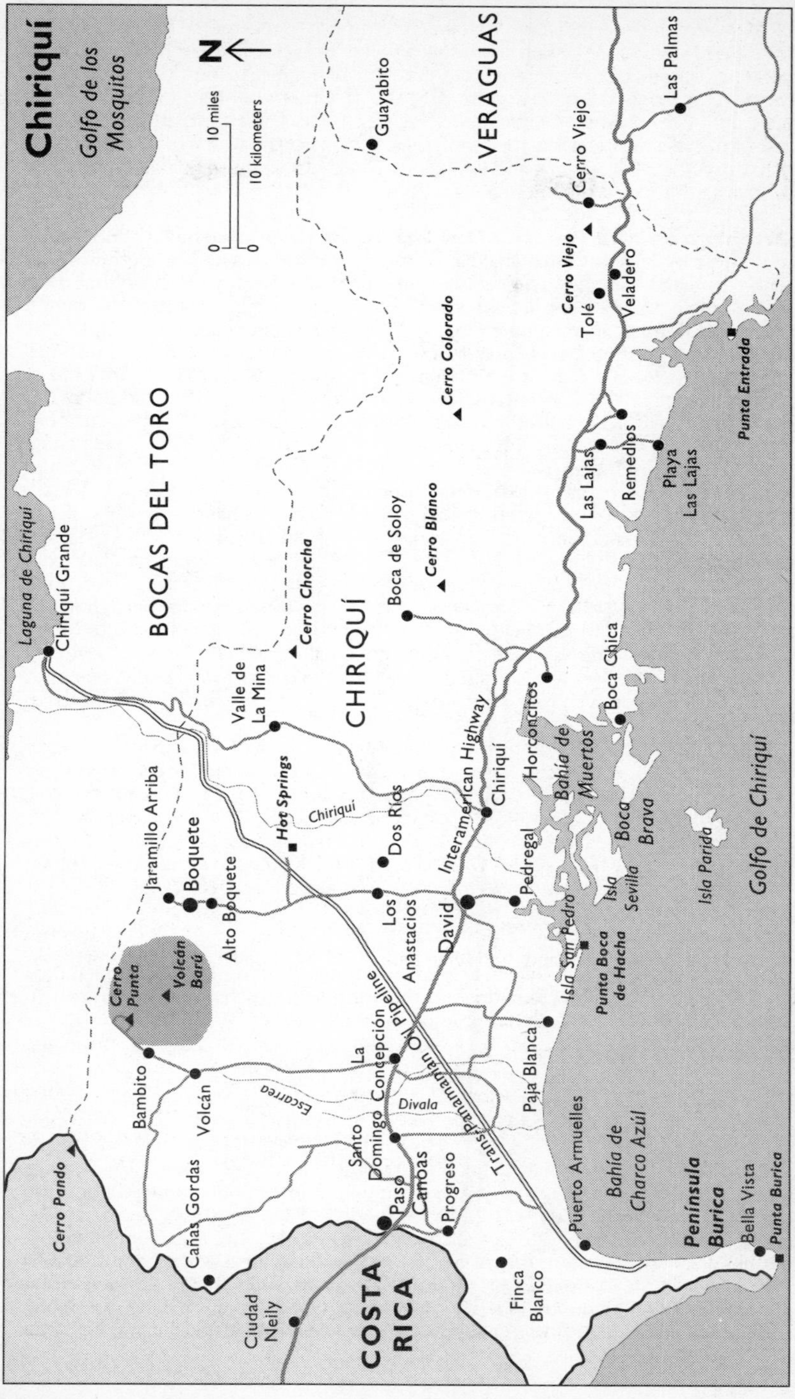

Chiriquí

Golfo de los Mosquitos

0 — 10 miles
0 — 10 kilometers

N

BOCAS DEL TORO

VERAGUAS

CHIRIQUÍ

COSTA RICA

Laguna de Chiriquí
Chiriquí Grande
Guayabito
Cerro Viejo
Las Palmas
Veladero
Tolé
Cerro Colorado
Punta Entrada
Las Lajas
Remedios
Playa Las Lajas
Cerro Blanco
Boca de Soloy
Cerro Chorcha
Valle de La Mina
Boca Chica
Horconcitos
Interamerican Highway
Chiriquí
Bahía de Muertos
Boca Brava
Isla Parida
Golfo de Chiriquí
Isla Sevilla
Pedregal
Dos Ríos
Hot Springs
Jaramillo Arriba
Boquete
Alto Boquete
Los Anastacios
David
Isla San Pedro
Punta Boca de Hacha
Cerro Punta
Volcán Barú
Oil Pipeline
Transpanamanian
La Concepción
Paja Blanca
Bambito
Volcán
Escarrea
Divala
Santo Domingo
Puerto Armuelles
Bahía de Charco Azúl
Península Burica
Bella Vista
Punta Burica
Cerro Pando
Cañas Gordas
Paso Canoas
Progreso
Ciudad Neily
Finca Blanco

PANAMA

tal plazas are the only indicators that this "metropolis" is the central artery to the coffee-infused veins of the region, a bustling ambience quickly negated by the clucking, cackling roosters that run through the streets at all hours. The only time David truly rocks out is for its yearly festival in early March. Otherwise, David retains friendliness and charm beyond its size, and serves as an ideal base for exploration of the rest of the region's wonders, or simply as a pitstop on the way west to Costa Rica. (See Costa Rica: Documents and Formalities, page 318, and Paso Canoas, page 405, for more information on entering Costa Rica).

Orientation and Practical Information David is laid out in a grid, cut off to the east by busy Avenida Obaldía. North-south running Avenidas are numbered with Oeste and Este designations, starting on either side of Avenida Central. East-west running calles are designated with the ABCs, increasing to the north and south from Calle Central. Spend a little time, and the whole system becomes simple. The central plaza **(Parque Cervantes)** sprawls between Av. Bolívar and Av. 3 de Noviembre (3 blocks east of Av. Central) and Calles A and B Norte. The **tourist office,** ITAP (tel. and fax 775-4120), sits across from Parque Central on the 2nd floor. The very helpful staff helps with the basics of the area—safety issues, prices, customs, directions, etc. Call for any information about buses or other questions plaguing your life. Pick up the English version of the Focus Panama booklet, which includes maps of the country and David. **Bancomer,** across from Parque Central, doesn't give dollars for Visa cards, but does other bankish stuff, like change traveler's checks (open Mon.-Fri. 8am-1pm, Sat. 9am-noon). **Banco del Istmo** (tel. 775-3131), Av. Centenario, Calle A Norte, near the bus terminal, magically extracts dollars from your Visa account and changes American Express checks. There's a mighty **post office** (fax. and tel. 775-4136) across from the Toyota showroom, one block north of Parque Cervantes, for mail madness, as well as **fax** and **telegram** services (open Mon.-Fri. 7am-5:30pm, Sat. 7am-4:30pm). Make calls at **INTEL,** at Av. 2 Este and Calle C Norte. The **immigration office** (tel. 775-4515), near Fábrica de Paraguas, is the place to get your visa renewed or extended. Ask for Paz y Salvo (open Mon.-Fri. 8am-3pm).

David is the hub for all destinations to the highlands of Chiriquí; trips to smaller cities are frequent and cheap. Buses to the Costa Rican border at **Paso Canoas** leave not from the terminal, but from near Parque Central ($1.50). The **Tracopa** bus (tel. 775-0585) to San José, Costa Rica departs from Av. 5 Este, Calle A Sur (daily at 8am, 12:30pm; $12.50 one way). All other buses depart from a large and efficient **bus terminal** at the edge of town on Av. Obaldia at Av. Cincuentenario (2 blocks east of Av. Central). Buses run regularly to Volcán ($2); to Boquete ($1); to Río Sereno ($4); to Chiriquí Grande (Tues.-Sun., noon or 1pm, $6); and to Almirante (7pm, $4), whence floateth ferries for Chiriquí Grande. Other buses (tel. 775-8444) also run regularly to Santiago ($6) and then on to Panama City (11 daily, $13). **Urbana buses,** the line running around the city, charges $0.20 per ride. A trip in a **taxi** to anywhere in the city costs about $1.00.

Accommodations One of the hottest cities in Panama, David demands that visitors consider air-conditioning when picking a hotel. Fans only tend to push the hot air in your face. **Pensión Mi Casita,** across from Hotel Nacional, can be your *casita,* too, if you dig basic rooms with private bath and air conditioning. Five rooms are available (singles $5, doubles $7). **Hotel Iris** (tel. 775-2251), across from Parque Cervantes, isn't architecturally admirable, but the convenient location has benefits galore; bite into other frills, too, like air conditioning and telephones. Rooms are clean and adequate (singles $15, doubles $20, triples $24). **Pensión Canton** (tel 774-4044), near Restaurante Yau on Calle Central, Av. 5 Nte., has no air-conditioning, but has a snazzy restaurant downstairs, as well as communal bath and public telephone (singles $5.50, doubles $7, triples $15 with air-conditioning). **Pensión María Jilma** (tel. 775-4733), on Av. 3 Oeste, Calle 6 Sur, is cheap; rooms have private baths and fans ($8 for one person, $9 for two people). **Hotel Madrid** (tel. and fax. 775-

2051), next to the bus station, sits in a great location for overnighters. All rooms come with private bath, air conditioning, and zoomy buses below (one person, $12.50, two people $18). And finally, to live the life of luxury, **Hotel Occidental** (tel. 775-4068) is right in the shopping plaza, Av. 4 Este at Calle B Norte. Overlooking Parque Central, it's a luxurious hotel in the heart of David, enclosed in cool and safe proximity to designer boutiques. An elevator carries guests to one of 60 rooms, all of which have private bath, air conditioning, TV, and a telephone. Balconies on each hallway hover over the of the city, making David look like a sprawling, fiery ant farm (with a little imagination). Laundry service available (one person $16.50, doubles $19, triples $25, quads $30, quints $35).

Food Most of the chow-joints around David dish out exclusively *típico* fare, but for some reason, Chinese restaurants abound. The area around Parque Cervantes is particularly saturated with inexpensive *sodas.* **Soda Jardin Oriental,** next door to Cine Plaza on Calle B and Av. 2 Este, might be just a *soda,* but it's a *soda* in a magnificent Oriental hall with high ceilings and a cool atmosphere to while away the afternoon hours ($2-3 for a main meal). **Restaurante Yau** (and bakery) offers six squishy, steaming French rolls for $0.25. **Restaurante El Oasis,** on Calle Central, near McPato, swings throughout the night, and everybody knows your name. Enjoy the evening sky and the mild Panamanian *cerveza* in the open patio or at the bar, which is a refreshing step above the machismo-dominated bars around the corner.

Sights and Entertainment **Museo de Historia y Arte José de Obaldía,** on 7 Av. Est. and Calle B Norte, Apt. A-57 (tel. 775-7839), apart from having a hell of a name, displays archaeological artifacts, colonial religious materials, and historical documents all relating to José de Obaldía, founder of the Chiriquí province. Some parts of the small museum feel like the stuffy living room of some wacko history teacher, but some offer interesting insights into the region's past, particularly into the daily life of Obaldía's family, who lived in the house.

There are a number of glass-walled, heavily guarded department **stores** and boutiques around the center of town, but unless you've got the Gold Card handy for pricey foreign brands, these stores aren't worth a visit. If shopping strikes you as drab anyway, spare yourself the misery and split, and instead roll over to the 10 lane **bowling alley** (tel. 775-2221), in the Hotel Nacional on Calle Central (open Tues.-Sat. 4-11pm). **Cine Plaza** (tel. 775-4041), on Calle B Norte and Av. 2 Este, shows a mere one movie per day, between 7-9pm or from 9-11pm. U.S.-made movies are about six months stale, but are shown in English with Spanish subtitles; *Tales from the Crypt* flicks are particularly popular. The theater is huge, seating roughly 350 people ($2 for adults, $1 for the kiddies). Crap out at David's **casino,** in the Hotel Nacional (open nightly until 11pm).

■■■ BOQUETE

Cool, clean air and august mountain scenery overshadow Boquete's fading, crumbling stores and restaurants, making the city an attractive alternative to sweltering David and its immediate *campo* surroundings. The area's allure has not been lost on daytrippers from David, who arrive with giddy gusto to ride horses, watch birds, stare at cool trees, or just groove with nature. While the nearby roaring rivers are visually stunning, their wrath is fierce during the rainy season, when the city falls prey to heavy flooding (and subsequent landslides), which sometimes block hiking trails into the mountains. Still, even if they have to trudge through muddy slop, most travelers come to this part of Chiriquí to explore the mountains, especially nearby **Volcán Barú,** the tallest volcano in the country. Looming over Boquete at 10,000 ft, Barú poses a challenge to those who want to climb it, but gently welcomes less ambitious hikers. Even if hiking doesn't sound appealing, a peeling is at least in order for the scrumptious, drool-in-your-lap navel oranges, harvested in Boquete between November and February.

Practical Information Boquete's **police** (tel. 770-1222) roost one block south of the post office. **Banco Nacional de Panamá,** across from the Delta gas station on the south edge of town (tel. 770-1328), trades money but won't give cash on Visa. The **post office,** across from Parque Central, also has a **telegram** and **fax** service (open Mon-Fri. 7am-6pm). **Buses** leave for David around the Parque Central (every ½ hr; 1 hr., $1.20). For medical emergencies, call the **hospital** (tel. 770-1356) or get to **Centro Médico San Juan Bautista,** near the Romero Bridge (tel. 770-1881), which has a 24-hr. emergency room.

Accommodations and food Sleep isn't usually difficult to come by in Boquete, especially in **Pensión Marilos** (tel. 770-1380), which pandiculates on the south end of town; follow the "Hotel Rebequet" sign. One of the nicest *pensiónes* in the area, the home-style, English-speaking management and beckoning lobby are as comforting as mom's chicken soup on a rainy day. Come here to find out about hiking trails. Five bedrooms all have private baths. There's also a kitchen with laundry facilities available for communal use. Still to come: a game room! Traveler's checks accepted (singles $9.90, doubles $15.40; after that, $2 per person to share). **Pensión Virginia** (tel. 720-1270), across from Parque Central, is a mighty hotel; the unobtrusive rooms are more than adequate, and all have private baths with hot water (singles $12.50, doubles $22.50, triples $27.50). **Hotel Rebequet** (720-1365), on the south edge of town across from Pensión Marilos, is the place for a splurge. The large lobby has a pool table, and rooms have private bath with hot water, refrigerators, and color TVs; every room faces the impeccably gardened outdoor patio. Ask about the guided tours to and around Volcán Baru (ask for José Gonzales). A common kitchen and dining room are available (singles and doubles $20).

Squeeze the oranges for all they're worth, then head off to one of Boquete's many restaurants. **Merendero El Oasis** (tel. 770-1337) is nestled across the bridge, and is worth the crossing; the patio's situated right near Boquete's uproarious river, and every table offers a spectacular view of surrounding landscape. Some items are a bit pricy, but this is tasty *típico* (Mon.-Fri. 6pm-midnight, Sat.-Sun. 8pm-midnight). **Restaurante Salvatore** (tel. 770-1857), down the street from the Clínica, dishes out New York Pizza in a berserk New York atmosphere, or as close as you can get in the highlands of Panama. The patio at **Restaurante Lourdes** (tel. 770-1031), on the main road across from Parque Central, is perched above the street, and so offers keen views of the mountains. Sink your teeth into a steak dinner for $1.50.

■ NEAR BOQUETE

VOLCÁN BARÚ

Massive and verdant **Volcán Barú** no longer oozes lava, but, together with five meters of yearly rainfall, still manages to pump the fire of life into the surrounding national park and beyond. The various levels of foliage springing out of the fertile volcanic soil support not only the dozens of villages in the area, but also countless animals, including tapirs and jaguars, and breathe vigor into those travelers who come to wander and climb.

For those wishing to climb Volcán Baru by **car,** there is an entrance in Boquete with a trail frequently used by 4x4s. A possibility for hikers is to find someone who's driving in and then get dropped off at the park gate, which lies about 6 hrs. from the summit. Walking from town up to the summit might be too much for one day. Except for those who like to be able to say they've been to the top of Panama, many travelers find it's not necessary to go the top, which offers a wide panoramic view, but which is cluttered by huge telecommunications towers and repairmen trying to get even higher. Because of the heavy rains, asking for permission before hiking is strongly recommended between May and November. Some hikers follow a rough trail between **Cerro Punta** (see Near Volcán, below) and Boquete, some 24km apart along the circuitous path; hire a guide if you're intending to do this. The nature watching's great and there are cabins for crashing over night, but the trail isn't always easy to find. **PILA,** the **ranger station** for Volcán Baru park and other nearby parks (tel. 771-2171 in Cerro Punta), has a staff of English-speaking volunteers to help answer questions and provide guides to the park. Camping is allowed on the volcano, but dress warmly; temperatures drop to near 40° at night.

For the days before or after meandering through Volcán Baru, there's a **gazebo** across the bridge from Boquete, which is ideal for a happy little picnic. The forests nearby provide sweet hiking, though clear trails are few and far between. For hiking in other parts, take a $0.25 taxi to **Los Naranjos,** a tiny town north of Boquete, and hike the wide, paved roads 5km through the countryside past plantations and friendly villagers.

HATO DEL VOLCÁN AND NEARBY VILLAGES

Paths cut through Volcán Barú and lead to an entrance on the other side near the town of Hato del Volcán (or Volcán), another deliciously enervating coffee-producing town. Ask at one of the hotels for directions to the entrance to the park if you're starting off here. Volcán has a **Banco del Istmo,** near the center of town, which changes money and gives cash advances on Visa (open Mon.-Fri. 8am-3:30pm, Sat. 9am-noon), and there's a **post office** (tel. 771-4222), next to Ferremax store, open Mon.-Fri. 7am-6pm. If you need some ointment for blisters after hiking through, there's **Farmacía Don Bosco** (tel. and fax 771-4317), near the center of town, which accepts credit cards. For more severe emergencies, contact the **hospital** (tel. 771-4283) or the **police** (tel. 771-4231).

None of the *pensiones* and *cabinas* is particularly budget-oriented; the cheapest runs at $15 per person. Camping along the outskirts of the national park is permitted; bring your own gear. In town, **Cabinas Señorial** (tel. 771-4239), the first hotel on the way into town on the road, charges $15 per person for up to 2 people. Private baths have hot water, but rooms have no fans. Otherwise, **Cabinas Reinas** (tel. 771-4338) are the next cabinas into town after Señorial; follow the signs and turn right at the crossroads. Each cabin has its own kitchen and dining table, private bath, hot water, refrigerator, and spacious room to boot. Bring a large group to cut costs. Traveler's checks are accepted ($15 per person for groups of three). **Hotel California** (tel. 771-4272) squats past the bank, left at the sign. Rooms have no fans, but they do have private baths and hot water, for that sweet summer sweat ($16 for 1 or 2 people, $20 for 3 people).

Everyone in town, from teething babies to the local grease monkeys, hangs out at the Panadería/DulcerEa in the hub of town. Dripping ice cream or biting into luscious, baked loaves is a great excuse for tapping into the town gossip or just asking for directions. **Reina Restaurante** (tel. 771-4640) awaits on the south end of town, near the primary school. The huge sign advertising "Rose's Restaurant," which points directly to this building, must have been the focus of some bitter wrangling, but the bickering hasn't made the grub worse or costlier. Panamanian fare costs around $3 per plate; get stuffed on *arroz con pollo* for $1.50 (open daily 6am-9pm).

The surrounding, smaller **villages** are also worth exploring, if only for the heavenly aroma of coffee that intoxicates the streets. Several coffee plantations are located about 8km from the center of town; the hike and a tour of the plantations' operations make an entertaining (and energizing) daytrip. Hotels offer tours, but these are often overpriced, and with a bit of creativity and flexibility, the ambitious (or caffeine-hooked) can easily whip up a tour of their own and avoid getting ripped off. Or imbibe the city's own java in one of the city's own cafés, Hemmingwaying it as the laid back locals move through the sedate streets. Don't plan on switching to de-caf during April, when the crazy **Feria de Flores y Café** shakes the otherwise placid towns. Make reservations in advance.

11km away from Volcán is **Cerro Punta,** yet another village and prime starting point for exploration of the volcano. Cerro Punta also has its fair share of plantations and farms of perennial flowers in addition to strawberry and coffee plantations paint the mountains with vibrant colors. Ask the ranger station in Cerro Punta for more information. Nearby, and encompassing thousands of acres in both Panama and

Costa Rica, **Parque Internacional La Amistad** is a unique for its transcendence of international boundaries, a symbolic gesture of friendship. Part of the second-largest park in Panama, the forest contains seven "life zones," and has an extensive system of trails for birding and exploration. In the park, **Los Quetzales Cloud Forest Retreat** (tel. 232-6568) provides accommodations, either cabins or rooms, including full kitchens, hot water baths, and romantic lantern lighting. From Los Quetzales, bilingual speaking guides are available at extra cost (cabins $90 for up to 4 people; rooms $25 per person).

For recreation of a different sort, **El Valle,** a small town off of Volcán (go north of the town and look for the sign), is blessed with three placid **lagoons** nestled in lush greenery. Camping and fishing are allowed at the lagoons. On the way, 25min. from the police station in Volcán, stands a large sign for the piping hot springs, where climbers can soak their bunions in the medicinal waters before camping.

CHIRIQUÍ GRANDE

If it weren't for the bone-jellifying aura of the ultimately paradisical Archipelago de Bocas del Toro off the coast, some travelers might actually want to spend some time in Chiriquí Grande. There are enough transport vehicles along the buzzing port to move the whole darn place across the ocean, and enough clothing vendors on the street to dress all of Europe to the nines. Buses drive directly from David to Chiriquí Grande, so it's a natural stopover before chugging on to paradise. **Banco Nacional de Panamá** (tel. 757-9711), across from the Texaco station, exchanges traveler's checks (open Mon.-Fri. 8am-3pm, Sat. 9am-noon). E.T. phoned home, and you can too from the **public telephone,** to the right of the arrival/departure stop of the Almirante/Chiriquí Grande **ferry** (Tues.-Sun. 1:30pm., 40min., $8); from there, catch a boat to Bocas del Toro. **Farmacia Luz,** across from Billares, next to Pensión Sinquiem, has drugs (open daily 8am-9pm).

Pensión Siquiem (tel. 757-9303), near Parque Central off the main road, sits away from the town's chaotic commercial core. All 10 rooms have fans and are thoroughly locked, pleasant, and humble. Some have private bathrooms (singles $7, doubles $9, triples $9). **Casa de Empeño,** next to the dock, offers small, basic, and cheap rooms (singles $5.50, doubles $9, triples $11). There are several similarly designed patio restaurants that offer *típico* food as well as a cool source of shade from the afternoon sun.

■■■ BOCAS DEL TORO

Chuck that watch off the ferry, and get ready and rearin' for some real relaxation. There's actually a lot to do in Bocas, really: breathe, slice open a mango, take a nap, stare at the cool trees.... The most ambitious visitors to Bocas actually manage to work a few day trips into their itineraries, especially to the shell-strewn beaches of **Zapatilla Island** or **Hospital Point,** where bodacious snorkeling and swimming are only a slothful step or two away. The islands of **Bastimentos** and **Zapatilla** offer less in the way of self-indulgence, having been laid out for ecotourism. The English-speaking island natives are as mellow as they get; don't even think about haggling on prices, just go with the flow, dude.

Practical Information For **tourist information,** check out the **Mangrove Roots Shop,** on the left side of the main road. The manager is exceptionally enthusiastic and helpful. There's a **post office** (tel. 757-9273) in the main municipal building, across from the *parque central* (open 7am-6pm). **Banco Nacional de Panamá** (757-9230), one block north of Parque Central to the right (open Mon.-Fri. 8am-3pm, Sat. 9am-2pm), changes traveler's checks but offers no cash advances on Visa cards. **Ferries** leave Bocas del Toro for Almirante Sunday (7:30am, 3, 4:30pm); Mon. (6, 6:30, 7:30am, 3, 4:30pm); Tues. and Thurs. (7:30am, noon, 3pm); Wednesday (8am, 3pm); Friday (6:30am, 5pm); Saturday (6:30am, 4:30pm). The **hospital** (tel.

778-9201) is just a ferry ride away. A doctor makes daily visits to the island, however, so just ask around.

Accommodations and Food **Hotel Las Brisas** (tel. 778-9248; fax 778-9247), at the end of the main road, waddles right on the dock, with an attractive patio deck for watching the sunrise. Rooms are quaint, and all have private bathrooms and fans. Make reservations ahead of time. Families are particularly welcome ($8.80 per person, $13.50 for two). **Pensión Las Delicias** (757-9318), the second hotel on the main road on the left side, was made especially for groups. The restaurant on the first floor prepares meals for package deals. Manual laundry facilities available (1 person $10.10, 2 people $14, 3 people $18, $19 per person with meals. **Hotel Bahia** (tel. 778-9626), the first hotel visible from arrival at the Almirante ferry, has an established air about it, and is the only hotel offering air-conditioning in some rooms (referred to as VIP rooms, thank you very much). All rooms have private bath (one person pays $13.20, doubles $16.50, triples $18, quads $22).

Restaurante Chicho, on the main road, serves cheap continental breakfast—coffee, cinnamon rolls, eggs, ham/bacon, and juice, all for $1.50. Panamanian stick-to-your-stomach rice and beans are available, too. Tourists huddle around candlelit tables, sharing stories and showing off scars around hearty pizzas at **Restaurante Pomodoro,** upstairs from the Mangrove Roots shop.

Sights and Entertainment A union of self-made **tour guides** takes tourists to a string of islands along the Bocas del Toro archipelago for approximately 4 hrs. The fee can't be avoided, as there is no other way to get to these islands than with a private boat. The cheapest tours are $8.50, 4 person minimum; the most expensive is $12.50. Tours feature **ecological observations,** snorkeling, swimming, diving, fishing, and suntanning. Hospital Point Island and **Mangrove Point** are both tranquil and filled with mango trees, exotic insects, and plenty of lush greenery. **Bird Island** has a whole lot of you-know-whats, and was specially designed for the ornithologically-inclined. Isla Bastimentos has the **Parque Nacional Bastimentos,** a preserved and relatively unexplored sanctuary for a vast array of fauna and flora.

For diving and snorkeling, make safety a priority; make sure instructors are certified, and don't disrupt the creatures of the sea. The Mangrove Roots Shop (on the main road of Bocas island) offers snorkeling rental gear and a diving instruction operation called **Turtle Divers** (tel. 757-9594); speak with Angel Gonzales Díaz (open daily 9am-noon, 2-6pm, and 7:30-10pm). The **Bocas Dive Shop,** opposite the Pensión Las Delicias (tel. 778-9541) also rents out scuba gear (open daily 8am-5pm). For other kicks, **Hotel Las Brisas,** at the very end of the main road, rents out bikes ($1.50 per hour) and kayaks.

Drinking starts early in the morning at **Timorogo Disco Bar,** and builds in a crescendo throughout the day to rollicking laughter and lunacy by the evening. Merengue seeps from the restaurant's every orifice. Come to arm wrestle or listen to tales about the size of the fish the locals caught that afternoon. For other nightlife, dig your feet into the sands on the main island, where beers are served nightly until at least 11pm.

■■■ ALMIRANTE

With only the waning remnants of a flourishing port industry to mark its place on the map, Almirante longs for days gone by. Like the isthmus it sits on, Almirante suffers eternally because nobody wants to stay here, but exploits its position as an optimal bridge for zipping off to Bocas del Toro or moving on to Costa Rica.

Gotta' problem? Contact the **police** (tel. 104). **Banco Nacional de Panamá,** across from Hotel Hong Kong, acts bankish (Mon.-Fri. 8am-3pm, Sat. 8am-noon). There's a **post office,** down the block from the bank, and in case of health crises, call the **hospital** (tel. 778-3745). Arrive early to get a seat on the **train** running to **Changuinola** twice daily (7:30am and 12:30pm). **Ferries** to Bocas del Toro leave throughout the week (Sun. 7am, 2, 4pm; Mon. at 5, 6, 7am, 2, 4pm; Tues. and Thurs. 7, 8am, 2pm; Wed. 7:30am, 2pm; Fri. 5:30am, 4pm; Sat. 5:30am and 4pm). **Buses** to Changuinola leave Almirante every 15min. Get the ticket at the terminal before getting on.

Accommodations are not easy to find in Almirante; it's best to ask someone for directions. **Hotel Hong Kong** (tel. 778-3363) has 17 adequately sized and furnished rooms with private baths, and it's one of the safer places in town. Plus, there's a restaurant and private baths ($11 for a double). **Pensión Colón,** up the street from the Hotel Hong Kong, proffers small and basic rooms with communal bathrooms. Don't count on luxury, just remember what it costs ($5 per person). **Pensión San Francisco** (tel. 758-3779), near the bus station, rests in a (bus)tling part of town, with nine modest rooms. $11 for one person, $15 for private bath and air conditioner.

The nearby town of **Changuinola,** 30min. from Almirante on the way to the Costa Rican border, has a **bank,** or at least one that gives cash advances on Visa cards. Changuinola thrives on traveling merchants and the nearby banana plantations, including a branch of the Chiquita processing plant, which is identifiable as the hulking space-craft on the outskirts of the city. Other banana plantations surrounding the city are open to visitors. Buses from Changuinola proceed on to the **border crossing to Costa Rica;** look for buses marked Las Tablas, or Sixaola. The border is open 8am-4pm daily; remember to set your watch back upon coming through. From Sixaola, regular buses run to San José, Costa Rica. See Costa Rica: Documents and Formalities, page 318, for more information.

EAST OF PANAMA CITY

■■■ SAN BLAS ARCHIPELAGO

Only a fraction of the 365 baby islands comprising the island chain of San Blas are inhabited, and the rest are left by themselves to soak in Robinson-Crusoe-meets-the-Blue-Lagoon-type tropical nirvana. Both because of the undefiled surroundings and the interesting culture of the islands' natives, the **Kuna** tribe, Panamanians are resoundingly proud of the islands, and eagerly push travelers in San Blas' direction. But perhaps because of inconvenience or expense, neither gluttonous resort tourists nor roaming backpackers have yet found themselves a rut along these sands, and a majority of the *gringo* visitors are anthropologists or field biologists.

San Blas' perpetual and indigenous residents, the Kuna are famous for their *mola* artwork (see gray box, below), their intricately designed clothes, and their all-encompassing sense of communal living. Each tribal subgroup inhabits a separate island, and their tribal customs are intriguing. When Kuna girls turn fourteen, they go through a sacred puberty ritual in which the whole tribe comes together for four days and drinks rum from dawn to dusk. Meanwhile, the young girl waits longingly in an isolated hut until her Kuna elderwoman approaches her on the last day to cut her hair and adorn her with clothes and jewelry. Observe with respectful distance, and avoid taking photographs.

Activity among the Kuna begins at daybreak and shuts down with the wailing generator at 10pm. In the darkness, the only audible sounds are the roar of the waves and the plaintive, pious prayers of a village elder (*Saila*) calling to the gods for the safe birth of a pregnant villager. Still, even without phones, no one could claim the islanders don't have their priorities straight: beer is available from every store at any time, and together with a hammock and some shade, it's not hard to forget who and where you are. If that's still not enough oblivion for one day, some of the nearby uninhabited islands can actually be rented out for a day or two from the Kunas. Most hotels offer tours to other islands for free.

Tourists arrive on the island of **Porvenir. Hotels** are quick to take guests to the airport when you step off the plane. **Hotel San Blas,** on Nalunega Island, has 17 rooms and huts, with guests living directly among the Kunas and receiving three meals a day. Rooms are very basic and utterly tranquil ($25 per day). Planes leave the island daily in the morning, so staying at least one night is required.

That's-a mola!

You'll definitely know the Kuna when you see them. Although the men demonstrate an inexplicable preference for neckties, Kuna women stand out for their gold nose rings and facial markings, usually a black line painted along the nose to the forehead. Most of the time they go topless, but below their waists don blouses adorned with beautiful, hand-stitched, rectangular panels of cloth known as "*molas.*" *Molas* are comprised of several layers, and can take months to complete; as proof of the adornment's status as "art," rather than folk-craft, many Kuna refuse to use modern sewing machines to facilitate their labor, instead cherishing the effort required to complete a single piece. Despite the increasing numbers of molas depicting contemporary political and pop-cultural icons (like those dedicated to Operation Just Cause or Beavis and Butthead), most *molas* still represent Kuna religious icons, such as water demons, medicine men, or ducks. Purchasing a mola in San Blas might be expensive, but it's the best way to ensure the piece's authenticity.

EASTERN PANAMA: DARIÉN

The largest province in Panama is also the least developed and most sparsely populated; getting into Darién as a tourist is not easy, and getting through to Colombia is next to impossible. Enveloped by thick jungle, the Choco, Kuna, and other *indígenas* have managed to successfully inhabit the area for years, but roads are in poor condition and pose many dangers to travelers. For those who make it to Darién, the rewards are bountiful; the Choco Indians, divided into the linguistically distinct **Embera** and **Wounaan** tribes, live a lifestyle completely foreign even to other Panamanian tribes, adorning their faces with colorful pigment (jagua) and even hunting with blowguns and poison darts along the mighty Tuira River. **Parque Nacional Darién** is one of the largest parks in Central America, with 579,000 hectares teeming with exotic species of plants and animals. The road linking Central to South America may soon be completed; prior work was hindered by lawsuits filed by environmental groups and concern about the drug trade and foot-and-mouth disease. Until the action goes through, crossing to Colombia is only possible with a tricky combination of river boat trips and walking.

Before undertaking any venture into Darién, inform yourself about road conditions, health and safety issues, and whatever other logistical problems might arise. The region is accessible by air, land, and sea, though air and land travel are recommended. Contact IPAT in Panama City for the names of tour leaders to Darién; several companies make trips to **Yaviza, El Real, La Palma,** and **El Real de Santa Maria,** the gateway to P.N. Darién. The Interamerican highway only goes as far as Yaviza; **buses** leaving from the main bus terminal in Panama City stop in various villages, going all the way to Yaviza only during the dry season (8-12 hrs., $15). From Yaviza, overland passage is possible, but not easy by any means. Travel during the dry season (Nov.-May), prepare the proper visas required for entry into Colombia prior to leaving, and bring along at least one guide, preferably a reputable, experienced native. Guerrilla activity in the Darién Gap has thwarted the passage of travelers in the past. Food, water, and gas are not available along most stretches of the jungle, and so an adequate supply must be carried. Do not undertake the venture without extensive additional research.

YUCATÁN PENINSULA

Too engrossed in hunting for slaves to watch where he was going, Hernández de Córdoba mistakenly ran aground here in 1517. When the freshly disembarked sailors asked the locals where they were, the Mayans, naturally not understanding Spanish, replied something to the effect of "We haven't a clue what you're talking about." Unfamiliar with the Mayan language, Córdoba only caught the last few syllables of their reply, *"Tectetán,"* and erroneously dubbed the region Yucatán before shoving off again. This encounter established a paradigm that would hold throughout Yucatán's history; misunderstood and continually molested by outsiders, it would never be fully conquered. Today the peninsula's culture remains essentially Mayan, but foreign influence fights on. Maya is still the first language of most of the inhabitants, *indígena* religions persist (often with a Catholic veneer), and fishing, farming, and hammock-making out-produce big industry and commerce. Burgeoning tourism, however, is threatening the traditional *yucateco* way of life.

Travelers to Central America who venture into the Yucatán most often cross the border to explore the magnificent ruins along **La Ruta Maya** (The Mayan Route) that stretches from Campeche, on the peninsula's western coast, to Tulum, on the eastern edge. Aside from its impressive Mayan legacy, the Yucatán offers visitors both a glimpse of Mexico's colonial grandeur and a series of sumptuous beaches along the glorious *costa torquesa,* the Yucatán's Caribbean coast.

■■■ EMBASSIES

Embassy of Mexico, 1911 Penn. Ave. NW, Washington, DC 20006 (tel. (202) 728-1600); **U.K.,** 42 Hertford St., Mayfair, London W1 (tel. (0171) 495-4024); **Canada,** 45 O'Connor St. #1500, Ottawa, Ont. K1P 1A4 (tel. (613) 233-8988).

■■■ MONEY MATTERS

US$1 = 6.24 pesos
CDN$1 = 4.59 pesos
UK£1 = 9.61 pesos

1 peso = US$0.16
1 peso= CDN$0.22
1 peso = UK£0.10

■■■ TOURIST CARDS

All visitors to Mexico must carry a **tourist card** (FMT, Spanish for *folleto de migración turística*) in addition to a passport. If you're crossing Mexico *en route* to Guatemala or Belize, ask for a **transmigrant form,** which allows you to remain in Mexico for up to 30 days; you'll need a passport or current photo ID, a Guatemalan or Belizean visa, and proof of sufficient funds for your trip. Many people get their cards when they cross the border or when they check in for their flight into Mexico. Try to get a card that will be valid longer than your projected stay, since getting an extension on a 90-day FMT is a hassle. If you need an extension, visit an office of the **Delegación de Servicios Migratorios** weeks before your FMT expires. While in Mexico, you are required to carry your FMT at all times. **Visas** are not necessary for U.S., Canadian, or British citizens unless they will be in Mexico for more than six months. Holders of European Community passports need only their **permanent resident cards ("green cards").** Australians and New Zealanders do need visas, regardless of the length of stay. Inquire at a consulate.

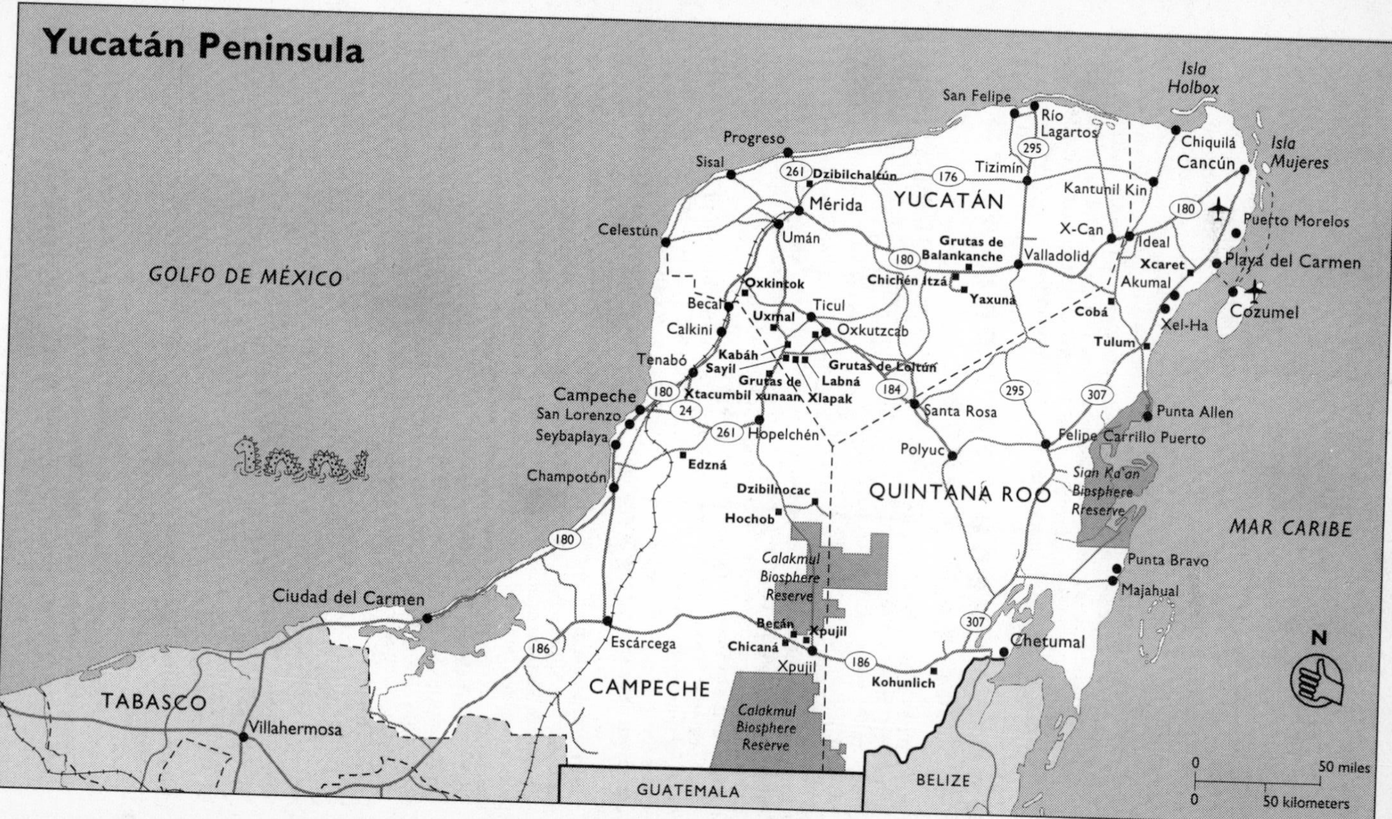

Yucatán Peninsula
GOLFO DE MÉXICO
MAR CARIBE
YUCATÁN
QUINTANA ROO
CAMPECHE
TABASCO
BELIZE
GUATEMALA
Isla Holbox
Isla Mujeres
Chiquilá
Cancún
Puerto Morelos
Playa del Carmen
Cozumel
Xcaret
Akumal
Xel-Ha
Tulum
Cobá
Punta Allen
Felipe Carrillo Puerto
Sian Ka'an Biosphere Reserve
Punta Bravo
Majahual
Chetumal
Kohunlich
Xpujil
Becán
Chicaná
Calakmul Biosphere Reserve
Escárcega
Ideal
X-Can
Valladolid
Kantunil Kin
Río Lagartos
San Felipe
Tizimín
Grutas de Balankanche
Yaxuna
Chichén Itzá
Santa Rosa
Polyuc
Oxkutzcab
Grutas de Loltún
Ticul
Labná
Xlapak
Grutas de Xtacumbil xunaan
Kabáh
Sayil
Uxmal
Oxkintok
Dzibilchaltún
Mérida
Umán
Progreso
Sisal
Celestún
Becal
Calkini
Hopelchén
Dzibilnocac
Hochob
Edzná
Tenabó
Campeche
San Lorenzo
Seybaplaya
Champotón
Ciudad del Carmen
Villahermosa
N
0
50 miles
0
50 kilometers
180
295
307
176
184
261
24
186

■■■ KEEPING IN TOUCH

Mexican mail service can be slow, but it is more or less dependable. Airmail often reaches the U.S. in as few as six days, but can just as easily take a month or more. It takes even longer to Europe and other destinations. Postage for letters costs about three pesos, or two pesos for *tarjetas postales* (postcards). You can have letters sent to you in Mexico through **Lista de Correos** (see page 31).

Calling abroad from Mexico is extremely expensive. Call collect if you can; using a U.S. operator to call collect or with a calling card will let you pay U.S. rates (around US$5-6 per min.). **LADATEL** phones, increasingly prevalent, take coins or LADATEL phone cards. International calls using these phones are cheaper and involve less waiting than any of the alternatives. LADATEL **phone cards,** available at Teléfonos Mexicanos offices and various stores, eliminate the need for coins. Dial 95-800-462-4240 from LADATEL phones to reach an **AT&T USADirect** operator; dial 95-800-674-7000 from LADATEL phones to reach an **MCI WorldPhone** operator.

■■■ CAMPECHE TO MÉRIDA: THE MAYAN ROUTE

Often called **La Ruta Maya,** the long route between Campeche and Mérida (254km on Rte. 261) traverses the Puuc Hills, an area that was home to about 22,000 people during the Classic period of Mayan civilization (4th-10th centuries).

Uxmal, Kabah, the Grutas de Xtacumbilxunaan, and Dzibilnocac can be reached by **public bus** (the first three from either Campeche or Mérida, the last from Campeche only). First-class buses take the short route. Be sure to board a bus that follows the long route (*vía larga*), and ask the driver to let you off close to the sites. The return trip can be tricky. Find out in advance when buses or *combis* will pass the site, and wave your arms wildly to flag down a ride.

To guarantee a return ride, rent a car or go on an organized tour. In Campeche, the state tourist office can refer you to guides who will take you on a private tour to any of these sites. From Mérida, the cheapest way to see the sites is to take the special Autotransportes del Sur "Ruta Puuc" bus that leaves daily at 8am. The bus stops for two hours at Uxmal and about 40 minutes at Kabah, Sayil, Xlapak, and Labná and returns to Mérida at around 3:30pm. Even though it doesn't include admission to the ruins, the 31-peso bus fare is one serious bargain (see Mérida, Practical Information: Bus Stations on page 449). The state tourist office in Mérida has information on tours organized by travel agencies—most offer daytrips to Uxmal and Kabah and to Chichén Itzá (see Mérida, Practical Information: Travel Agencies on page 448). At most sites hotels and restaurants are scarce. The sole exception is Uxmal. Those who cannot afford the rates there have two options: base yourself in Mérida, or take advantage of the cheap accommodations in **Ticul,** 28km away off Rte. 261.

Edzná is the closest ruin to Campeche. Dzibilnocac and Hochob lie 88km south of the highway at Hopelchén, which itself is 41km east of Campeche. A few hundred yards north of the Campeche-Mérida state border, the Sayil-Oxkutzcab road veers east. Sayil (5km from the crossroads), Xlapak (10km), and Labná (14km) lie along the road before it ends at the Grutas de Loltún (30km). This road is paved, but the paths are often muddy. Continuing north on the highway after the turnoff to Sayil, Kabah is 5km further; 23km past Kabah lies Uxmal.

■ TICUL

A bustling provincial town off the Campeche-Mérida highway, Ticul (pop. 40,000) is a convenient and inexpensive base from which to explore the Ruta Puuc sites.

Orientation and Practical Information Ticul's streets form a grid with the main drag, **Calle 23,** passing east-west through the center. Even-numbered streets run north-south. Most commercial activity transpires between the *zócalo* (Calle 24) and Calle 30, four blocks to the west.

Police headquarters (tel. 2-00-10 or -11) are on the northeast corner of the *zócalo* on Calle 23 (open 24 hrs.). Ticul's **post office** (tel. 2-00-40) is on the *zócalo* (open Mon.-Fri. 8am-2:30pm). **Postal Code:** 97860. **Banco del Atlántico,** Calle 23 #195, off the *zócalo,* changes U.S. dollars and traveler's checks (open Mon.-Fri. 9am-2pm). Make **calls** from the long-distance *caseta,* Calle 23 #210 (tel. 2-00-00), between Calles 26 and 28 (open 8:30am-10pm). **Telephone Code:** 997.

Combis gather at Parque de la Madre, Calle 23 between Calles 28 and 30, collecting passengers for Oxkutzcab and Muna (3 pesos each). *Combis* for Santa Elena (3 pesos) leave from Calle 24 on the *zócalo.* From Muna, 6 **buses** run daily to Campeche (20 pesos) via Uxmal and Kabah. Hourly buses head north to Mérida (7 pesos). **Farmacia San Jose,** Calle 23 #214-J (tel. 2-03-93), is between Calles 28 and 30 (open 8am-1pm and 4-10pm). Dr. Sanabria can be reached at the same number for 24-hr. **medical assistance,** though no one in the pharmacy speaks English.

Accommodations and Sights Ticul has several hotels and good restaurants. **Hotel San Miguel** (tel. 2-63-82), on Calle 28 opposite Parque de la Madre, offers small, clean rooms with fans and basic bathrooms. (singles 25 pesos; doubles 32 pesos, with two beds 38 pesos). **Hotel Sierra Sosa** (tel. 2-00-08), on Calle 24, off the *zócalo,* has saggy beds and fans (singles 40 pesos; doubles 55 pesos; triples with TV 50 pesos).

While Uxmal and Kabah are fairly accessible given some luck with *combi* transfers, the absence of traffic on the Sayil-Oxkutzcab road will leave travelers frustrated and stranded. To reach the **ruins** around Uxmal, take a Mérida-bound bus from the Ticul bus station (tel. 2-01-62), on Calle 24 behind the main church to Muna (every ½hr., 3 pesos). *Combis* for Muna leave from Parque de la Madre, Calle 23 between Calles 28 and 30. From Muna, board a southbound bus or *combi* for Uxmal, Kabah, or other sites. Alternatively, you can reach the ruins by catching a *combi* in the *zócalo* to Santa Elena (30min., about 3 pesos). Change *combis* at Santa Elena for Uxmal (16km towards Mérida) or Kabah (south towards Campeche). *Combis* are most plentiful in the morning.

To reach the **Grutas de Loltún**, snag a *combi* to Oxkutzcab at Parque de la Madre; you'll be let off at the intersection of Calles 23 and 26 (15min., about 3 pesos). *Combis* leave for Loltún from the lot across from Oxkutzcab's market "20 de Noviembre." Tell the driver to let you off at the *grutas* (10min., about 3 pesos). Because the road is crowded with *combis,* it's easier to reach the Grutas than Uxmal or Kabah.

■ UXMAL

The largest site along the Ruta Puuc, Uxmal (oosh-MAL) is as wondrous as you've heard. The combination of proud pyramids, finely sculpted reliefs, and immense masks here is simply without peer. Though many of the sculptures originally unearthed at Uxmal have been lost to museums and thieves, the city's architecture maintains today the grandeur that drew 25,000 people to the site at its height.

Practical Information **Autotransportes del Sur (ATS)** sends six buses a day from Mérida to Uxmal (1½ hrs., 10.50 pesos). If you're willing to make a long day of it, several Ruta Puuc ruins can be explored in one day from Mérida (see Mérida, Practical Information: Travel Agencies and Car Rental on page 448). A frugal option is the ATS "Ruta Puuc" bus, which visits Uxmal, Kabah, Sayil, Xlapak, and Labná all in one day (31 pesos; see Mérida, Practical Information: Bus Stations on page 449). The last bus to Mérida passes at 8pm.

Accommodations Uxmal's accommodations are expensive. Consider staying 30min. away in Ticul, where rooms cost half as much. In Uxmal, the cheapest option is **Rancho Uxmal** (tel. 47-80-21), 4km north of the ruins on Rte. 261. From the highway near Uxmal, you can reach Rancho Uxmal by hopping aboard a passing bus or *combi* (about 2 pesos). Concrete-floored rooms feature two double-beds and toilet-seat-less bathrooms. The pool is usually in service during peak season (singles 100 pesos, 20 pesos per additional person). Four concrete platforms beneath *palapas* are available for tent-pitching or hammock-slinging (15 pesos per person, including the use of communal toilets and showers; hammock rental 10 pesos).

Sights The 40m-tall near-pyramid visible upon entering Uxmal is the **Temple of the Magician.** The pyramid was built by a dwarf-magician who, it is claimed, hatched from a witch's egg and grew to maturity in the space of a single year. The legend of the dwarf-magician's birth struck terror into the heart of the governing lord of Uxmal, who challenged him to a contest of building skills. The dwarf's pyramid, built overnight, easily outclassed the governor's Great Pyramid, still visible to the right of the Governor's Palace. Grasping at straws, the spiteful ruler complained that the base of the dwarf's pyramid was neither square nor rectangular but was actually elliptical. Having undermined the legitimacy of the dwarf-magician's triumph, the governor proposed that he and his adversary compete to see who could break a *cocoyol* (a small, hard-shelled fruit) on their heads. The dwarf-magician, in whose skull a turtle shell had been placed, easily cracked open the *cocoyol.* The governor crushed his unaltered skull trying to match the dwarf fruit for fruit.

The elegant south-facing arch leads to the **ballcourt.** Note the glyphs on the rings through which well-padded players tried to knock a hardened rubber ball. Emerging from the ballcourt, head right along a narrow path to the **Cemetery Group,** a small, leafy plaza bounded by a small pyramid to the north and a temple to the west. Stones that once formed platforms bear haunting reliefs of skulls and crossbones.

Returning to the ballcourt, head south to the well-restored **Great Pyramid,** built by the governor in his contest with the dwarf-magician. To the west, the pyramid looks down on the jagged face of the Palomar, behind which lie the jungle-shrouded remains of the **Chenes Temple.**

The **House of Turtles** and the **Palace of the Governor** top a man-made escarpment east of the Great Pyramid. The two-story House is on the northwest corner of the escarpment and is adorned along its upper frieze with a series of sculpted turtles. (Symbolizing rain, turtles were venerated by the Maya.) Over 100m long and built on three landscaped terraces, the palace is typical of Puuc style. The eastern frieze is covered by 20,000 decorations, which together form 103 masks of Chac.

From the Palace of the Governor, try to spot the overgrown, pyramidal **House of the Old Woman,** which lies to the east. About 400m south of the house is the **Temple of the Phalli.** Phallic sculptures hang from the cornices of this ruined building and spurt rain runoff from the roof. (Site open daily 8am-5pm. Admission 23 pesos, free Sun. Parking 8am-5pm, 4 pesos.)

■ KABAH

Once the second largest city in the northern Yucatán, Kabah was built with the blood and sweat of many slaves. The most elaborate of Kabah's structures is the **Codz Pop Temple** ("rolled mat" in Mayan), which was named for the odd shape of the rain god Chac's nose. The temple's broad façade displays nearly 300 masks of Chac, each comprised of 30 carved pieces. The elaborate Chenes style of the temple is unique to the Codz Pop—its neighbors to the east, **El Palacio** (a 25m pyramid) and **Las Columnas,** were executed in plainer fashion. The site is thought to have served as a court where justices settled disputes with the aid of the gods.

Across the highway, a dirt road leads in three directions. An unrestored group of temples lies to the right, the nearly camouflaged West Group is to the left, and a beautifully sculpted arch resides directly ahead. The arch marks the beginning of the *sacbé* (paved, elevated road) which ended in a twin arch at Uxmal. The perfect alignment of the archway with the north-south line is testimony to Mayan astronomical knowledge (open daily 8am-5pm; admission 10 pesos, free Sun. and holidays).

Getting There: Bisected by Rte. 261 on its way from Campeche to Mérida, Kabah lies 23km southeast of Uxmal. Because of its location on the Campeche-Mérida highway (*vía ruinas*), Kabah can be easily reached by any second class bus running between the two capitals. Buses will stop at Kabah only if a passenger notifies the driver beforehand or if the driver sees a person gesticulating on the shoulder of the highway. To make things easy, hop on an ATS "Ruta Puuc" bus (see Mérida, Practical Information: Bus Stations on page 449). Since almost all the tourists who come to Kabah have cars, many hitchers find rides.

■ SAYIL

The **Palace of Sayil,** "Place of Red Ants," is an architectural standout among the region's ruins. Between its three terraced levels, the building's 50 rooms exhibit unparalleled ornamental diversity. Walls are carved with slender columns; the second-story frieze depicts the descending serpent-god's body; and elegant chambers open onto pleasant porticos, each graced by bulging columns. Behind the palace sits a *chultún* (plastered catch basin) that ancients used to collect rainwater.

The path continues past the palace to **El Mirador** (the lookout), a lofty temple with grandiose columns. Left of El Mirador, the path leads deeper into the jungle, where the **Estela del Falo** (Stela of the Phallus) will make even sexually liberated visitors blush (site open daily 8am-5pm; admission 10 pesos, free Sun. and holidays).

Getting There: The only public transportation to Sayil is the Autotransportes del Sur "Ruta Puuc" bus (31 pesos), which leaves Mérida daily at 8am and also stops at several other ruins (see Mérida, Practical Information: Bus Stations on page 449). Buses do run, however, from Mérida to Kabah, 10km away on the main highway (see Kabah). Hitching from Kabah to Sayil is not unheard of.

■ LABNÁ

Labná's buildings were constructed towards the end of the late-Classic period (600-900 CE), when the Puuc cities were connected by a *sacbé* (white road). Today, a short reconstructed section of the *sacbé* runs between Labná's two most impressive sights: the palace and the stone arch. When the Yucatán flooded, the raised *sacbé* allowed the Mayans to pass from one city to another. To weather parched conditions, however, the Maya constructed huge *chultunes* (catch basins), many of which are found at Labná. The *chultunes* collected both water (up to 8000 gallons in each) and the bodies of peasants who couldn't afford to be buried.

Labná's **palace** is on the northern side of the site, to your left as you enter. While the construction of this building occupied the Maya for several centuries, the edifice was never actually completed. Labná's palace is reminiscent of the one at Sayil insofar as both boast an exceptionally ornate second-floor façade.

Labná is famed for its picturesque **stone arch,** 3m wide and 6m high. Its western façade is intricately decorated in a trellis pattern, while the eastern side remains more bland. Archaeologists believe that the arch served as a ceremonial point of entry for victorious warriors returning from the battlefield.

Beyond the arch, on the unrestored base of a pyramid, stands the **observatory,** also known as **El Mirador** (the lookout). Its façade rises over the box-like structure and bears sculptures attached by tenons or dowels. The terracing around the temple contained many *chultunes* (open daily 8am-5pm; admission 10 pesos, free Sun.).

Getting There: The final stop on the "Ruta Puuc" bus, Labná lies 42km east of Uxmal, and 4km beyond Xlapak (see Mérida, Bus Stations on page 449).

■ GRUTAS DE LOLTÚN

The Grutas de Loltún are 58km east of Uxmal on the Sayil-Oxkutzcab road. Below a dense jungle of mahogany and *ceiba,* 1.5km of enormous caverns wind through the rock. Important caverns include the **Room of the 37 Inscriptions,** which includes many still-visible markings, and the **Na Cab** (House of the Bees), where you can see the *ka'ob* (grindstones) left by the Maya. Ancient inhabitants broke off the stalactite tips in the **Gallery of Fallen Rocks** to use as spears and arrows. In the **Gallery of the Five Chultunes,** a sculpted jaguar head drips water into cisterns while a huge warrior and eagle look on. The **Cathedral** is a palatial room that once hosted Mayan feasts and assemblies. Several caves contain partially hollow stalactites and columns—thump one with the heel of your hand and listen to the soft booming sound reverberate throughout the cave system. Archaeologists speculate that the Maya used these formations as a musical means of underground communication.

Entrance to Loltún is allowed only at 9:30, 11am, 12:30, 2, and 3pm, when a guide leads a tour through the caves. Guides speak Spanish and mangled English. (Admission 17 pesos, 7 pesos Sun.). **Getting There:** To get to Loltún, catch a bus as far as Muna or Ticul, hop in a *combi* headed for Oxkutzcab, and then pray for deliverance for that last leg of the journey. A pick-up truck in Oxkutzcab's *zócalo* may be willing to make the trip, though it will cost you at least 20 pesos.

■■■ MÉRIDA

Built atop the ruins of the Mayan capital of T'ho, modern Mérida is haunted by pre-Hispanic history—the stones of the city's fortress-like cathedral even bear traces of the Mayan temples from which they were stripped. The Maya called this site "place of the fifth point," to indicate that it was the center of the universe, the spot between the four points of north, south, east, and west. Today, Mérida (pop. 1.5 million) isn't the center of the universe, but it's certainly the center of Yucatán—it's the state's capital and key commercial center.

ORIENTATION

Rte. 180 rushes over from Cancún (322km) and Valladolid (168km) to the east, becoming **Calle 65,** which passes through the busiest part of town one block south of the *zócalo.* Those approaching on Rte. 180 from Campeche, 153km to the southwest, end up on **Avenida Itzáes** (also called **Avenida de la Paz**), which runs north-south, or on Calle 81, which feeds into the north-south Calle 70. Both intersect Calle 59, the best route to the center of town, running east to a point one block north of the *zócalo.* **Paseo Montejo** begins at Calle 47, running north as Rte. 261. The *zócalo* fills one city block, bordered by Calle 61 to the north, Calle 62 to the west, Calle 63 to the south, and Calle 60 to the east. To reach the *zócalo* from the **second-class bus terminal,** head east to Calle 62, walk three blocks, and turn left (north); the *zócalo* is three blocks ahead. From the **train station,** take a taxi (10 pesos), catch the "Seguro Social" bus, or walk six blocks west on Calle 55 and three blocks south on Calle 60. **Taxis** do not roam the streets soliciting riders. You must call for one or have your hotel or restaurant call for you. There are stands along Paseo de Montejo, at the airport, and at the *zócalo.* Expect to pay at least 10-15 pesos for a trip within the *centro.* Taxi-*colectivos* charge only 1.25 pesos for any destination in the city; dropoffs are on a first-come, first-serve basis.

PRACTICAL INFORMATION

Tourist Information: Central Office (tel. 24-92-90), in the Teatro Peón Contreras, on Calle 60 between Calles 57 and 59. Additional offices at the airport (tel. 46-13-00) and at the second-class bus station. All offices open daily 8am-8pm.

Police: (tel. 25-25-55 or 25-73-98), on Av. Reforma (Calle 72) between Calles 39 and 41. Catch the "Reforma" bus. Some English spoken.

Telephones: It's impossible to place collect calls to the U.S. from most Mérida *casetas.* **Tel World,** Calle 60 #486-A (tel. and fax 24-76-00), between Calles 55 and 57. Open daily 7am-10pm. **Telephone Code:** 99.

Travel Agencies: Yucatán Trails, Calle 62 #482 (tel. 28-25-82, 24-hr. urgent tel. 25-75-94; fax 24-19-28), between Calles 57 and 59. Canadian owner Denis Lafoy is a genial source of information on Mérida and the Yucatán. Good, all-inclusive deals on daytrips to Ruta Puuc sites (transport, guide, lunch, and entrance fee included). Prices vary. Open Mon.-Fri. 8am-2pm and 4-7pm, Sat. 8am-1pm. **Travel Club,** Calle 59 #501 (tel. 25-75-94), on the second floor, just west of Calle 60. Super-low off-peak VW Beetle rentals (110 pesos, 160 pesos during peak season) include insurance and 300km free. Open daily 8am-8pm.

Consulates: U.S., Montejo 453 (tel. 25-50-11), at Av. Colón. Open Mon.-Fri. 7am-1pm. **U.K.,** Calle 58 #498 (tel. 28-61-52), at Calle 53. Open Mon.-Fri. 9am-1pm.

Currency Exchange: Bánamex (tel. 24-10-11 or 24-11-32), in Casa de Montejo on the *zócalo.* 24-hr. Cirrus, MC, and Visa **ATM**. Open Mon.-Fri. 9am-5pm.

American Express: Paseo de Montejo 494, office #106 (tel. 28-42-22 or 28-43-73; fax 28-42-57), between Calles 43 and 45. English spoken. Open Mon.-Fri. 9am-2pm and 4-6pm, Sat. 9am-1pm. Money exchange desk closes 1hr. early.

Main Post Office: (tel. 24-35-90), on Calle 65 between Calles 56 and 56A, 3 blocks southeast of the *zócalo* in the Palacio Federal. *Lista de Correos.* Open Mon.-Fri. 7am-7pm, for stamps only Sat. 9am-1pm. **Postal Code:** 79000.

Airport: On Rte. 180, 7km southwest of the city. **Aeroméxico,** Paseo Montejo 460 (tel. 27-95-66 or 27-90-00), between Calles 35 and 37, and at the airport (tel. 46-14-00). **Mexicana,** Calle 58 #500 (tel. 24-67-54), and at the airport (tel. 46-13-32). Access to most cities in Mexico, with limited international destinations.

Bus Stations: Most bus lines operate out of the main second class terminal, **Unión de Camioneros,** Calle 69 #544, between Calles 68 and 70, three blocks west and three blocks south of the *zócalo.* **Autotransportes del Oriente (ADO)** (tel. 23-22-87), sends buses to Cancún (every hr., 4:30am-midnight, 6 hrs., 41 pesos) and Chichén Itzá (every hr., 5am-8pm, 2 hrs., 16 pesos). From the same terminal, **Autotransportes del Sur (ATS)** goes further afield to Campeche (every hr., 3 hrs., 25 pesos), Escárcega (5 per day, 5½ hrs., 44 pesos), and Uxmal (6 per day, 1½ hrs., 10.50 pesos). **Autotransportes Peninsulares** (tel. 24-90-55) sends a 6:30pm bus to Ticul (10 pesos) plus two cheap, slow buses to Chetumal (8 hrs., 52.50 pesos). From the **first-class terminal** around the corner on Calle 70 between 69 and 71, **ATS** provides a special **Ruta Puuc bus** (8am, 31 pesos, admission to sites not included) which visits the archaeological sites of Uxmal, Kabah, Sayil, Xlapak, and Labná, returning around 3:30pm. **ADO** has first-class buses to Campeche (every ½hr., 2½ hrs., 31 pesos). The **Expreso de Oriente** station on Calle 50 between Calles 65 and 67, sends hourly buses at 15min. past the hour during the day to Cancún (6-6½ hrs., 41 pesos), via Pisté/Chichén Itzá (2½ hrs., 16 pesos), and Valladolid (3 hrs., 20.50 pesos). **Autobuses del Noreste** station is on the corner of Calles 50 and 67. **Autobuses de Occidente,** on Calle 71 between Calles 64 and 66, go to Celestún (12 per day, 2 hrs.). **Autoprogreso** buses shuttle between Mérida and Progreso (every 10min., 5am-10pm, 45min., 4.50 pesos), leaving from the station on Calle 62 between Calles 65 and 67. *Combis* leave the Parque de San Juan for Ticul (1½ hrs., 10 pesos) every 20 min. or so.

Red Cross: Calle 68 #533 (tel. 24-77-74), between Calles 65 and 67. 24-hr. emergency and ambulance services (tel. 24-67-64). Some English spoken.

Pharmacy: Farmacia Canto, Calle 60 #513 (tel. 28-50-27), between Calles 63 and 65. Open 24 hrs.

Hospital: Centro Médico de las Américas, Calle 54 #365 (tel. 26-21-11 or 26-26-19), at Calle 33A. 24-hr. service, including ambulance. English spoken.

ACCOMMODATIONS AND FOOD

You came to the Yucatán to see ruins? You'll see some—in Mérida's aging hotels. These fading dinosaurs are unique accommodations, though, and many enclose courtyards with sun-bleached frescoes, gurgling fountains, and towering palms. The cheapest food in town fills the **market** that stretches south from Calle 65, two blocks east of the *zócalo.* For more substantial nourishment, head to the market's second level off Calle 56 at Calle 67.

Hotel Trinidad Galería, Calle 60 #456 (tel. 23-24-63; fax 24-23-19), at Calle 51. Sprawling complex of assorted rooms houses an art gallery and a pool out back. Friendly, helpful staff. Parking available. Check-out 1pm. Rooms start at 45 pesos for a single, 55 pesos for a double. For bigger rooms you'll pay about 30 pesos more. The room with A/C goes for 100 pesos.

Casa Bowen, Calle 66 #521-B (tel. 24-07-28 or 28-61-09), between Calles 65 and 67, halfway between the main bus station and the *zócalo.* A colonial mansion—mingle with assorted international guests. Large rooms and attractive bedspreads. Check-out 1pm. Double-bed singles 45 pesos. Doubles 50 pesos, with two beds 55 pesos. Rooms with kitchenette and fridge 65 pesos, with A/C 90 pesos.

SIGHTS AND ENTERTAINMENT

The *zócalo* is busiest of all on Sundays, when street vendors cram in dozens of stalls, Yucatecan folk dancers perform in front of the Palacio Municipal, and half the city comes out to people-watch. The twin towers of the yellow **cathedral** loom over the eastern side of the *zócalo.* The sturdy stone blocks from which the cathedral was built were stolen from the Mayan temples of T'ho. Built in the austere Herrericano style, the cathedral features rose-colored arched domes and a giant blistering Christ, the second largest crucifix in the world (supposedly open daily 6am-6pm). On the northern edge of the *zócalo* stands the **Palacio de Gobierno.** Inside, gigantic murals narrate the history of the peninsula (open daily 8am-10pm). Concerts and classes in *jarana,* the Yucatecan colonial dance, take place under the balcony of the **Palacio Municipal,** across the *zócalo* from the cathedral (open Mon.-Sat. 8am-8pm).

On the southern side of the *zócalo,* the **Casa de Montejo,** the oldest colonial structure in Mérida, was constructed in 1549 by order of city founder Francisco de Montejo. The building now houses a Bánamex branch (open Mon.-Fri. 9am-5pm).

Mérida's most impressive museum, the **Museo de Antropología,** is housed in a magnificent Italian Renaissance-style building on the corner of Paseo Montejo and Calle 43. Archaeological finds on display illustrate the *indígena* history of the Yucatán. The shop downstairs sells comprehensive English-language guidebooks for much less than the price charged at the ruins themselves (museum and shop open Mon.-Sat. 8am-8pm, Sun. 8am-2pm; admission 14 pesos, free Sun.).

■■■ CHICHÉN ITZÁ

Chichén Itzá's reputation as prize cultural attraction of the Yucatán is well-deserved. The design and orientation of **El Castillo,** breathtaking from the bottom and harrowing from the top, attests to an incredible level of astronomical understanding. On the walls of the expansive ballcourt, beneath the still-intact rings which were once goals, grisly carvings depict the fate of the ancient game's players. The thousand columns stand wistfully in faultless symmetry, stripped bare of their thatched roofing by the forces of time. You can't claim to have seen Yucatán without a visit to Chichén Itzá—don't miss it for the world.

ORIENTATION

The town of **Pisté** flanks the highway 2.5km west of the ruins and provides travelers with basic accommodations and services. Consider spending the night in Pisté. This allows you to experience the light and sound show the night before (see Sights) and to visit the ruins early the next morning, before the buses from Cancún arrive.

Getting to the ruins is easy. Many **buses** leave Mérida for Chichén Itzá (hourly from 5am-8pm, 2 hrs., 10 pesos) and first-class buses cruise in from Cancún (8:45am and 2:30pm, 3 hrs., 32 pesos). From Pisté, flag down any east-bound bus (2-3 pesos) which roll through town approximately every ½hr. A vigorous, supplicatory wave to the driver is a good idea. Or catch a taxi (10 pesos) to hit the site at eight in the morning (when it first opens). To head back to Pisté or another destinations after a day at the ruins, hang out in the bus parking lot until one heading in the right direction swings by. Alternatively, take a taxi to the Pisté bus station (see below).

PRACTICAL INFORMATION

Services at Chichén Itzá are located in the large stone edifice at the site's western entrance. Across from the ticket counter is a small **information booth.** The long-distance **telephone** (tel. 6-27-24) is right around the corner from the ticket counter, but it won't let you make international collect calls. **Telephone Code:** 985. The *caseta* stores luggage for free (open daily 8am-5pm). A gift shop changes U.S. dollars at a fair rate. Parking (4 pesos) is available at the site, from 8am-5pm and ½hr. before each light and sound show. Pisté manages to provide a few additional services. A single **police** officer sits at a desk in the *comisario* on the eastern side of the *zócalo.* The **post office** is in a small gray building near the *zócalo* across from Abarrotes "El Alba" (open Mon.-Fri. 8:30am-3pm). **Centro Telefónico** (tel. 1-00-89; fax 1-00-88), across from the bus station, charges about 11 pesos per min. for calls to most parts of the U.S. Collect calls 10.45 pesos. As the town has no bank, the gift shop at the ruins probably offers a better exchange rate than establishments in town. **Buses** leave from Pisté's bus station (tel. 1-00-52), near the Stardust Inn on the eastern side of town. Buses depart for Mérida (about every 1½ hrs., 6am-9pm, 1½ hrs., 15 pesos). **Clínica Promesa,** Calle 14 #50 (tel. 6-31-98, ext. 198), in the blue-green building past the *zócalo* and 100m off Rte. 180, is open 24 hrs. for medical emergencies. **Farmacia Isis,** Calle 15 #53, lies a short way past the *zócalo* towards the ruins (open daily 7:30am-9:30pm).

ACCOMMODATIONS AND FOOD

The budget options are in Pisté—these *posadas* are nothing to write home about, but your early-morning attack on the ruins is only a 3-minute taxi ride away. You can pitch a tent in the **RV trailer park** right next to the bus station. The park is administered by the Stardust Inn (tel. 1-01-22), on the other side of the bus station. The Mayan Empire may well rise again on the profits from Chichén Itzá's restaurants. The following listings are located on Calle 15, Pisté's main drag.

Posada Olalde, to the left of Calle 15 (Rte. 180), two blocks down the unmarked dirt road directly across the street from the Carrousel Restaurant. Huge pastel rooms with ceiling fans and private bathrooms. Singles 50 pesos. Doubles 70 pesos. Triples 90 pesos. During high season, extra people can string up hammocks for 10 pesos per person. Traveler's checks accepted.

El Carrousel (tel. 1-00-78), in central Pisté. Ever-popular with an international crowd, this restaurant serves a wide selection of regional food at reasonable prices. 4 chicken tacos 10 pesos. Open daily 7am-10:30pm.

SIGHTS

As the Mayan name Chichén Itzá ("Mouth of the Well") implies, the area's earliest inhabitants were drawn here by two nearby freshwater *cenotes.* Much of what is known about these sedentary people is based on the pottery shards recovered by archaeologists. Later periods in Chichén Itzá's history are illuminated by the *Chilam Balam,* one of the few pre-Hispanic Mayan texts to survive the early missionaries' book-burnings. The *Chilam Balam* describes the construction of many buildings visible today, focusing on the period between 500 and 800 CE.

Chichén was mysteriously abandoned at its height in the 7th century CE, and for the next 300 years it remained a crumbling ghost town. Sometime before 1000 CE, the Toltec tribes of Tula, in what is now Hidalgo state, infiltrated the Yucatán and overcame peaceful Mayan settlements, bringing with them the cult of the plumed serpent Quetzalcóatl (here known as Kukulcán). The Toltecs fortified Chichén and, in the wake of regional imperialism, it became the most important city on the peninsula. Chichén's buildings bear the stamp of Toltec influence, and the images of plumed serpents, warriors, jaguars, and eagles are trademark Toltec images. As the Toltecs glorified human sacrifice, the *chac-mool* was the preeminent altar. In 1461, Chichén Itzá was again abandoned, this time because of war. Today, the relentless flow of the curious ensures that Chichén Itzá will never again stand in solitude.

The Ruins

Pause in the **visitor's complex** at the entrance to Chichén Itzá for an overview of the site. On the terrace, a scale model artfully shrinks the ruins and lays them at your feet. A small **museum** recaps the history of Chichén Itzá and displays a sampling of sculptures and objects removed from the sacred *cenote.* The notice board outside the **auditorium** announces screenings of documentary videos about the ruins in Spanish and in English (museum and auditorium open daily 10am-5pm; free).

If you are mainly interested in the architectural significance of the ruins, hiring a guide at the entrance is unnecessary. If you carry a guidebook and read the explanatory captions (in English) on plaques at each major structure, you can appreciate the ruins inexpensively and at a more leisurely pace. Free maps are available around the corner from the ticket counter, at the telephone *caseta* desk.

The entire site of Chichén Itzá is open daily from 8am-5pm (admission 21 pesos, free Sun. and for kids 13 and under). From the main parking lot and visitor's center, the first group of ruins is up the gravel path and to the left.

The first sight to meet your eyes is **El Castillo,** Chichén's hallmark. This pyramid, built in honor of Kukulcán, rises in perfect symmetry from the neatly cropped lawn, culminating in a temple supported by pillars in the form of serpents. El Castillo stands as tangible evidence of the astronomical enlightenment of the ancient Maya: the 91 steps on each of the four faces, plus the upper platform, total 365 (the number of days in the non-leap year); the 52 panels on the nine terraced levels equal the number of years in a Mayan calendar cycle; and each face of the nine terraces is divided by a staircase, yielding 18 sections representing the 18 Mayan months.

But that's not all: El Castillo's axes are specifically aligned to produce a biannual optical illusion. At sunrise during the semi-annual equinox, the rounded terraces cast a serpentine shadow on the side of the northern staircase. The sculpted serpent head at the bottom of the staircase completes the illusion. In March, the serpent appears to be sliding down the stairs, while in September the motion is reversed. A light-and-shadow lunar serpent-god, identical to that of the equinoxes, creeps up and down the pyramid at the dawn of the full moon following each equinox.

Nestled within El Castillo is an early Toltec temple, the inner chamber of which can be entered through a door at the bottom of the north staircase, behind the serpent's ears. A set of narrow, slippery steps ascends to a ceremonial chamber with a grimacing *chac-mool* sacrificial altar and a rust-red, jaguar-faced throne encrusted with jade stones and flint fangs (open daily 11am-3pm and 4-5pm; free).

West of El Castillo, or to the left of the entrance, lies the **ballcourt.** The enormous "I"-shaped playing field is bounded by two high, parallel walls with a temple at each end. Though this is the largest ballcourt in Mesoamerica, good acoustics make it seem smaller than it is. The court also produces an amazing side-to-side echo, which repeats seven times. (Reminds you of long-distance calls from Mexico, no?) The game played here was called *pok-ta-pok.* Players kept the *chicle* ball in constant motion, trying to score by knocking it through stone rings still visible high up on the long walls. Though little more is known about the game (guides tell all sorts of fantastic tales), it appears that one or more players sometimes met their glorious ends here. The famous reliefs at the base of the walls depict two competitors, the one having just decapitated the other. The plumes issuing from the neck of the less fortunate player turn into snakes, representing the soul's passage to the afterlife.

A short distance from the ballcourt toward the grassy open area is the **Tzompantli,** Aztec for "Platform of the Skulls." When the Spaniards conquered the Aztecs, they were shocked by the ritualized human sacrifice they found and horrified by the racks in Tenochtitlán designed to display the skulls of the sacrificed. Chichén's Toltec-designed Tzompantli served a similar macabre purpose. Today, eerie rows of skulls in bas-relief decorate the low platform's walls.

Next to the Tzompantli stands the **Platform of Jaguars and Eagles,** named after the military orders who took the names of these animals and who were charged with obtaining prisoners for human sacrifice. To either side of the serpent heads on the balustrades, reliefs of jaguars and eagles clutch human hearts. East of the platform is the **Temple of Venus,** where a serpent holds a human head in its mouth.

The dirt path leading directly north from El Castillo, over the ancient Mayan roadway, links the ceremonial plaza with Chichén Itzá's most important religious center, the **Sacred Cenote,** 300m away. The roughly circular sink-hole, perhaps 60m across, induced vertigo in the victims perched on the platform before their 25m plunge into the murky depths. The rain-god Chac supposedly dwelt beneath the water's surface and needed frequent gifts to grant good rains. Remains recovered by divers suggest that children and young men were the victims of choice.

The Temple of the Warriors marks the end of Chichén's restored monuments and the beginning of an overgrown area extending southeast of El Castillo. This corner houses the **Palace of the Sculptured Columns,** the back of which hides a few masks of Chac. The rest of the quadrangle is comprised of the **Southeastern Colonnade,** the **market** and its courtyard, and the expansive **Western Colonnade.**

A dirt path on the south side of El Castillo leads to the less photogenic **South Group.** Beyond the cafeteria and bathrooms, the first pyramid on the right is the **Ossuary,** or **High Priest's Grave,** its distinctive serpent heads mimicking El Castillo. A natural cave extends from within the pyramid 15m down into the earth. The bones found in this cavern are thought to be those of an ancient high priest.

Past the Ossuary, the road forks, presenting two different routes to the second set of ruins in the South Group, often missed by tourists but well worth the visit. The most interesting structure in this group is the **Observatory,** the large circular building on the left-hand side. This ancient planetarium consists of two rectangular platforms with large west-facing staircases and two circular towers. Because of the tower's interior spiral staircase (not open to the public), this structure is often called **El Caracol** ("the Great Conch"). The slits in the dome of the Observatory could be aligned with the important celestial bodies and cardinal directions. Notice the small red handprints on the wall of the building just as you come up the stairs; these were supposedly the hands of the sun god Itzamná. Walking south from El Caracol, toward the Nunnery at the other end of the clearing, you will pass a tiny, ruined sauna and then the **Temple of the Sculptured Wall Panels** behind it. Though difficult to decipher, the panels on the exterior walls contain emblems of Toltec warriors—jaguars, eagles, and serpents—in three rows.

The largest structure in this part of Chichén is the misnamed **Nunnery,** on the south side of the quadrangle. Although it was probably a royal palace to the Maya who built it, its stone rooms reminded Spaniards of a European convent. Above the entrance on the eastern side of the building, you can still see Mayan hieroglyphs. Also on the eastern side, a smaller annex built at an angle is visible. The annex's sculpted masks of Chac and lattice motif are in the Chenes style, usually found only in northeastern Campeche, as at Edzná. Diagonally across from the nunnery and annex is the religious center, its upper walls encrusted with intricate masks of the hook-nosed Chac. Beginning about 1km south of the Nunnery, and spreading out southwest of the main site, **Chichén Viejo** is a collection of unrestored minor ruins.

The overgrown **Cenote Xtoloc** (Shtoh-LOC) hides in a dip behind the South Group ticket office. To reach it from the office, take the first left 20m into the site. The *cenote* is in the hollow, beyond the small, ruined temple of Xtolob, the lizard god. There is no path down the steep slope through the undergrowth, and swimming is prohibited because of the dangerous underwater currents. In counterpart to the holy waters of the Sacred Cenote, this pool at one time provided all of Chichén with secular drinking water. Following **sacbé No. 5,** which becomes a narrow, winding trail, takes you to the back of the observatory.

■■■ CANCÚN

Drunk on the success of Puerto Vallarta and Acapulco, Mexican entrepreneurs began a sweeping search in the late 60s to locate the perfect geographic location to give birth to their enormous ambitions. Cancún (pop. 300,000), blessed with miles of magnificent white beaches bordering steel-blue water, was chosen—with the backing of the Mexican government—as the site for this new tourist nirvana. The government's choice was aesthetically and logistically ideal: connected to the mainland by two bridges, each spanning less than 100 yards, the L-shaped island provides 360° water access and close proximity to the Mayan ruins of Quintana Roo and Yucatán. Cancún's attractions are obvious. Here, in the middle of the *norteamericano* winter, you can parasail and scuba dive, snack at McDonald's, and slam tequila at rowdy Tex-Mex bars—all the while speakin' English and spendin' greenbacks. The beach at the **Sheraton Hotel** is one of the safest and most pleasant in Cancún.

ORIENTATION

Cancún has two sections: **Ciudad Cancún,** center of shopping and services, and **Isla Cancún,** home of the **Zona Hotelera** and the pure white beaches. The cheapest way to reach either section from the airport is to hop into an official *colectivo,* one of the distinctive white jeeps that shuttle new arrivals to their hotels. (30 pesos.) Alternatively, a taxi runs 50 pesos. In Ciudad Cancún, the main drag, **Avenida Tulum** parallels **Yaxchilán** (Yash-chee-YAN), four blocks over. These streets form a rough parallelogram with **Cobá** and **Uxmal.** From the bus station, Tulum and *el centro* stretch to the right of the white monument in the center of the traffic circle.

PRACTICAL INFORMATION

Tourist Offices: Av. Tulum 26 (tel. 84-80-73 or 84-06-72), and other booths all over town. More helpful is the staff of **Cancún Tips** (tel. 84-40-44 or 84-44-43), at Pl. Caracol in the Hotel Zone and at the airport. The firm publishes an English-language magazine (*Cancún Tips*) with invaluable maps and practical information. It also provides discounts at various restaurants and clubs. Try and snag one for free at the airport. English spoken at all offices.

Police: (tel. 84-19-13), next to City Hall on Tulum.

Post Office: Av. Xel-Ha at Sun Yax Chén (tel. 84-15-24). From Tulum, cut through any side street to Yaxchilán and head up Sun Yax Chén. The post office is 4 blocks farther. Mon.-Fri. 8am-7pm, Sat. 9am-1pm. **Postal Code:** 77500.

Telephones: LADATELs dot the *centro.* **Telephone Code:** 98.

Consulates: U.S., Av. Náder 40 at Uxmal (tel. 84-24-11). Open Mon.-Fri. 9am-2pm and 3-5:30pm. **Canada,** Av. Tulum 200 in Pl. México (tel. 84-37-16). Open Mon.-Fri. 10am-2pm. For emergencies outside of office hours, call the Canadian Embassy in Mexico City (tel. 915-724-7900). **United Kingdom,** in the Hotel Royal Caribbean (tel. 85-11-66, ext. 462). Open Mon.-Fri. 9am-5pm.

Currency Exchange: Of all the banks along Av. Tulum, **Bancomer,** Av. Tulum 20, gives the best rate. Open for exchange Mon.-Fri. 9am-1:30pm. Both **Bánamex** and **Banco Serfín** give cash advances on Visa/MC and have Cirrus **ATMs.**

American Express: On Tulum at Cobá (tel. 84-54-41), next to Hotel América. Open Mon.-Fri. 9am-6pm, Sat. 9am-1pm.

International Airport: (tel. 86-00-49), on Rte. 307 just south of the city. *Colectivos* 30 pesos, taxis 50 pesos (fixed rates to town; buy a ticket at the desk beforehand).

Bus Station: On Uxmal, at Tulum (tel. 84-13-78). You can stow your luggage here for 3-5 pesos for 24 hrs. There are a number of different bus lines at this difficult-to-navigate station, including **ADO, Caribe, Interplaya,** and **Expreso de Oriente. ADO** provides first-class service to Chichén Itzá (8:45am and 2:30pm, 3 hrs., 32 pesos). **Expreso de Oriente** provides the most efficient first-class service to Mérida (every hr. 6am-7pm, 10pm, and midnight-2am, 4 hrs., 58 pesos).

Ferries: To Isla Mujeres, take a bus or a van marked "Pto. Juárez" to the two ferry depots north of town (Punta Sam for car ferries, Puerto Juárez for passenger ferries). Ferries (5 pesos or 10 pesos, depending on the boat) shuttle across 15 times from 6am-8:30pm. Ferries to Cozumel (20 or 25 pesos) leave regularly from Playa del Carmen, south of Cancún, accessible by bus from the terminal in town.

Pharmacy: Farmacia Paris, Yaxchilán 32 (tel. 84-01-64), at Calle Rosas. 24 hrs.

Medical Services: For an ambulance call **Total Assist** at Claveles 5 near Av. Tulum (tel. 84-40-92 or 84-81-16). English spoken.

ACCOMMODATIONS AND FOOD

Budget travelers either stay at the **CREA Youth Hostel** or avoid the *Zona Hotelera* altogether. You can pitch a tent cheaply at the CREA. Most hotels accept credit cards and during high season phone reservations are a good idea. In the *Zona Hotelera,* "cheap" and "restaurant" are mutually exclusive. You can nevertheless dine well and inexpensively at the many joints along Avs. Cobá, Tulum and Yaxchilán.

CREA Youth Hostel (HI), Paseo Kukulcán, Km. 2.5, (tel. 83-13-37). 100 single-sex dorm rooms with four bunk beds apiece. Personal lockers provided; lock your valuables when showering. Bathrooms lack amenities and hot water. Maximum stay is 15 days. Lockers, sheets, towels provided. 30 pesos per person, plus a 30-peso deposit. No ID required. No curfew. Check-out 1pm.

Hotel Coral, Sun Yax Chén (Sun-yash-CHEN) 30 (tel. 84-20-97). Heading west from Av. Yaxchilán, the hotel is two blocks down on the left. Spacious rooms; ancient air conditioners get the job done. Hot water. Courtyard with pool. Check-out 1:30pm. Singles 50 pesos, 25 pesos for each additional person.

100% Natural, Sun Yax Chén 6 (tel. 84-36-17), at Yaxchilán. Not to be confused with the smaller juice shop on Yaxchilán, its beamed, leafy porch and lush garden will sooth sun-dazed spirits. Steer clear of the expensive dishes and sample the fruits and vegetables in all their forms. Wheelchair access. Open daily 7am-11pm.

■■■ TULUM

On the eastern edge of the age-old Etaib (Black Bees) jungle lies Tulum, the walled Mayan "City of the Dawn." Although the ruins here are less extensive than those at Uxmal and Chichén Itzá, their backdrop is stunning: Tulum's graying temples and nearly intact watchtowers rise above white sand pummeled by the steely-blue Caribbean Sea and tall, wind-bent palm trees.

Orientation and Practical Information Tulum (pop. about 10,000) is the southernmost link in the chain of tourist attractions on the Caribbean coast of Quintana Roo. Although few people live here, Tulum sprawls out over three separate areas: **el crucero** (the crossroads), the beach **cabañas,** and **Pueblo Tulum.** Arriving in Tulum from Cancún on Rte. 307, buses first stop at *el crucero,* a few kilometers before the town and the intersection with Rte. 180 to Mérida. Here, a couple of restaurants, hotels, and minimarts huddle together 800m west of the ruins. The access road turns south at the ruins, leading to food and lodging at *cabañas* 2km down the road. Pueblo Tulum, 4km south of *el crucero,* offers a handful of roadside restaurants, more minimarts, and some services.

The few services available in Pueblo Tulum are along Rte. 307, which serves as the tiny town's main street. There is no tourist office, though a few stands at the ruins can provide sketchy **maps.** Those desperate to **exchange money** can do so at the *crucero* or next to the bus office in Pueblo Tulum. The **police** (tel. 1-20-55), are in the Delegación Municipal, on the left side of Rte. 307 (after the baseball diamond) if coming from the north, two blocks past the post office (open 24 hrs.). The **post office** is a few hundred meters into town on the left side of Rte. 307 as you pass through from the north. (Open Mon.-Fri. 9am-1pm and 3-6pm). **Postal Code:** 77780. Make calls from the **Caseta de Tulum** (tel. and fax 1-20-01 or -02), on the right side of Rte. 307 just as you enter town from the north. Ask for directions to "GOPI." **Telephone Code:** 987. The **bus station** is opposite the Hotel Maya. **ADO** leaves for Chetumal (5 per day, 3 hrs., 39.50 pesos), Escárcega (8am, 8 hrs., 70 pesos), and Villahermosa (4:30pm, 11 hrs., 110 pesos). **ATS** runs every 45min. to Playa del Carmen (1hr., 9 pesos) and Cancún (2 hrs., 18 pesos). **Expreso de Oriente** leaves at 6, 11am, 1, and 6pm to Cobá (45min., 5.50 pesos), Valladolid (2½ hrs., 22 pesos), Chichén Itzá (3½ hrs., 26.50 pesos) and Mérida (5-6 hrs., 40.50 pesos). Buses heading north to Playa del Carmen will stop on request at destinations along the way. **Taxis** are available at *el crucero,* in Pueblo Tulum, along Rte. 307, and at various *cabañas.* Unless you're in a group, taxis are way costly. **Super Farmacia** (tel. 1-20-52), rests on the left of Rte. 307 just past the post office (open daily 8am-9pm).

Accommodations and Sights Tulum offers two kinds of lodging: hotels at the *crucero* or in town, or beachside *cabañas.* Clustered along the beach 1km from the ruins, the campgrounds and *cabañas* allow you to meet international travelers and escape the conventional tourism just a short distance away. A taxi to the *cabañas* from town is 20 pesos. Theft has become a problem at some *cabañas.* Industrious thieves will burrow through the sand and into your *cabaña* (remember, in many cases they have sand floors) if they want your valuables bad enough. **Don Armando Cabañas** (tel. 45-46-03), is on the left side of the paved road 1km south of the ruins. With a cheap restaurant, solid walls, a hammock or cement bed, mosquito netting, decent communal showers, and doors with locks, who could ask for more? (Well, maybe flush toilets.) Security guards patrol the premises. (*Cabaña* with 1 bed and 1 hammock for 1 or 2 people 50 pesos. 2-bed *cabañas* 60 pesos. *Cabañas grandes* 70 pesos. Deposit 25 pesos. Camp or hang a hammock for 10 pesos per person.)

Tulum's ruins lie a brisk 8-minute walk east of Rte. 307 from the *crucero.* Your first glimpse of Tulum will be of the still-impressive **wall** which once shielded the city from the aggression of neighboring Mayan city-states.

Just inside and to the left of the west gate stand the remains of platforms which once supported huts. Behind these platforms are the **House of the Halach Uinik** (the House of the Ruler), characterized by a traditional Mayan four-column entrance, the **House of the Columns,** and the **Temple of the Frescoes,** a stellar example of post-Classical Mayan architecture. Well-preserved 600-year-old murals inside the temple depict deities intertwined with serpents. Masks of Itzamná, the Mayan creator, occupy the northwest and southwest corners of the building.

As with many Mayan structures, four of Tulum's temples were built along astronomical guidelines so that the inner chambers of each are illuminated naturally during one of the two equinoxes or solstices. The classic Mayan practice of cutting stones to exactly the right dimensions, fitting them together without mortar, and polishing their surfaces was abandoned here.

El Castillo, the most prominent structure in Tulum, looms behind the smaller buildings and over the rocky seaside cliff. Serving as a pyramid and temple, it commands a view of the entire walled city. It also served as a lighthouse, allowing returning fishermen to find the only gap in the barrier reef just offshore. In front of the temple is the sacrificial stone where the Maya held battle ceremonies.

To the right of El Castillo on the same plaza is the **Temple of the Initial Series.** The temple bears a date that corresponded to the beginning of the Mayan religious calendar in the year 761 CE. The **Temple of the Descending God,** with a fading relief of a feathered, armed deity diving from the sky, stands on the other side of El Castillo's plaza. Perched on its own precipice on the other side of the beach, the **Temple of the Winds** was acoustically designed to act as a storm-warning system. Surely enough, before Hurricane Gilbert struck in 1988, the temple's airways dutifully whistled their alarm (site open daily 8am-5pm; admission 16 pesos, free Sun.).

Offshore, you can see the waves mysteriously breaking on Tulum's **barrier reef,** the largest in the Americas; it runs the full length of the Yucatán peninsula, including Belize. Although the water here is not as clear as at nearby and overrated Xel-Ha, the fish are just as plentiful. To enjoy them, you can rent scuba and snorkeling equipment from the **dive shop** (open daily 8am-3:30pm) at Cabañas Santa Fe.

■■■ CHETUMAL

Home to more people than all of Belize just minutes to the south, Chetumal (pop. 200,000) sits on the Caribbean coast in Quintana Roo's southeastern corner. No beaches or hidden ruins are to be found in Chetumal—just deteriorating brick streets and busy shoppers scoping the forest of duty-free shops. Otherwise, the town serves mainly as a stopover between the Yucatán and Tikal or Belize.

ORIENTATION AND PRACTICAL INFORMATION

The pointlessly large **bus terminal** at Av. de los Insurgentes and Av. Belice is Chetumal's ground transportation hub. **Autotransportes del Caribe, Batty's, Dorada, ADO, Maya de Oro,** and **Cristóbal Colón** all serve the terminal, although Batty's bus service and **Venus,** with connections to Belize, also run from the Mercado Nuevo four blocks away on Calzada Veracruz and Segundo Circuito.

Chetumal's thriving shopping district lines **Avenida de los Héroes,** starting at Av. Efrain Aguilar at the city's market and extending 1km south to the bay. This compact commercial area encompasses most of Chetumal's hotels and restaurants. At the southern terminus of Héroes lies **Boulevard Bahía,** a wide avenue flanked by statues and small plazas that follows the bay for several kilometers.

Tourist Office: An **information booth** on Héroes at Aguilar. Staffers provide maps of the city. Open Mon.-Sat. 8am-1pm and 5-9pm, though unreliably.

Post Office: P. E. Calles 2A (tel. 2-25-78), six blocks south and one block east of the Mercado. Open Mon.-Fri. 8am-7pm, Sat. 9am-1pm. **Postal Code:** 77000.

Telephones: Public phones in Chetumal take either the rare 1 peso coins, credit cards, or **LADATEL** phone cards, which can be purchased at Hotel Tulum on Héroes at Aguilar. **Telephone Code:** 983.

Consulates: Guatemala, Chapultepec 354 (tel. 2-85-85), at Cecilio Chi. Will happily help you with your Guatemalan jaunt. For a 90-day tourist visa you'll need your passport and a photocopy of it (fee US$5). For a 30-day free tourist visa, you'll need your passport plus photocopy and you'll also have to prove you have sufficient funds for your trip. Open Mon.-Fri. 9am-5pm. **Belize** (tel. 2-28-71), west of Héroes on Obregón, next to Bancomer. Open Mon.-Fri. 9am-2pm and 5-8pm.

Currency Exchange: Bánamex, Juárez 51 (tel. 2-47-13), at Obregón, eight blocks south and one block west of the Mercado. Open Mon.-Fri. 9am-2pm. Cirrus ATM.

Bus Stations: At Insurgentes and Belice (tel. 2-78-86). **ADO** (tel. 2-06-39) offers first-class service to Cancún (9 per day, 6 hrs., 55 pesos). **Dorada** (tel. 7-13-57) serves Mérida (7:30am, 1:30, 5, and 11:30pm, 8 hrs., 66 pesos). **Batty's Bus** runs to Belize City (10:45am, 2:15, 3:15, and 5:15pm, 4 hrs., 30 pesos). Batty's buses also leave from the Mercado Lázaro Cárdenas (also called Mercado Nuevo) at Calzada Veracruz and Segundo Circuito. Take a taxi (5 pesos) or a bus going to Mercado Nuevo (0.80 pesos) from the *mercado* (9 per day, 4 hrs., 35 pesos).

Market: Aguilar at Héroes. Open daily 6am-3pm.

Red Cross: Chapultepec at Independencia (tel. 2-05-71), a block south and 2 blocks west of the bus station, in the back of Hospital Civil Morelos. Open 24 hrs.

Pharmacies: Farmacia Canto, Av. Héroes 99 (tel. 2-04-83), is conveniently located at the northern end of the market. Open daily 7am-11pm.

ACCOMMODATIONS

While Chetumal's hotels fail to astound, they at least provide a convenient location and inexpensive lodging. For the most part, budget accommodations cluster along or just off Heroés, south of the market. Facilities are spartan.

CREA Youth Hostel (HI), Heróica Escuela Naval at Calzada Veracruz (tel. 2-34-65), at the eastern terminus of Obregón. Clean, modern, single-sex rooms with 2 bunkbeds each. Check-out noon. Lawn for camping (6 pesos). Bed with sheets, towel, and locker 12.50 pesos. Deposit 20 pesos. 25% off with Plan Joven, 10% with IYH. Front desk manned 7am-11pm but you can arrange to return later.

Hotel Brasilia, Aguilar 186 (tel. 2-09-64), at Héroes, across from the market. Spacious rooms upstairs enjoy a strong breeze from noisy fans. Lobby is as clean as it gets for the price. Private baths with hot water. Check-out noon. Friendly management will store packs. Singles 27 pesos. Doubles 40 pesos. Triples 52 pesos. To make reservations, wire money in advance.

APPENDICES

GLOSSARY

abarrote	a corner grocery store
abanico	fan
abono de ahorro de transporte	money-saving transit pass available in some cities
aduana	customs
aire acondicionado	A/C
albergue (juvenil)	youth hostel
alcaldía	mayoral district or headquarters
almuerzo	lunch, midday meal
amigo/a	friend
antojitos	literally "little cravings," appetizers
avenida	avenue
azufral	mineral spring
bahía	bay
balneario	spa or resort on the water
baño	bathroom
barato/a	cheap
borracho	drunk
barrio	neighborhood
bocas	appetizers, at a bar
cabina	a class of transportation ticket, with which you get your own room and bed
calle	street
cambio	change
camino	path or track
camioneta	small, pickup sized truck
campamento	campground
campesino/a	person from a rural area
cantera	water-holding vessel
cantina	drinking establishment, usually male dominated
caro/a	expensive
carretera	highway
carro	car, or sometimes a train car
casa de cambio	currency exchange establishment
casado/a	married
caseta de larga distancia	long distance phone booth
catarata	waterfall
cena	dinner, a light meal usually served after 8pm.
cenote	natural well
centro	city center
cerca	close by
cerveza	beer
ceviche	fish marinated in lemon juice, herbs and vegetables
coche	car
colectivo	municipal transit bus
colonia	neighborhood in a large city
combi	municipal transit bus
comida corrida	multi-course *á la carte* meal

consulado	consulate
cruda	hangover
cruz roja	Red Cross
cuadra	street block
cuarto con dos camas	a room with two beds; **con una cama:** with one bed
desayuno	breakfast
descompuesto	broken, out of order
embajada	embassy
emergencia	emergency
farmacia	pharmacy
feria	a fair
ferrocarriles	trains
finca	a plantation-like agricultural enterprise
ganga	bargain
guarache	sandal
herbido/a	boiled
hospicio	hospice
kilo	kilogram
ladrón	thief
larga distancia	long distance
lavandería	laundromat
lejos	far
Lista de Correos	the general delivery system in most of Central America
litera	bunkbed
malecón	pier or seaside thoroughfare
maneje despacio	drive slowly
menú del día	fixed daily meal often offered for a bargain price
mercado	market
micro	a municipal transit bus
mordida	literally "little bite," bribe
oficina de turismo	office of tourism
panadería	bakery
parque de trailer	trailer and RV park
parroquia	parish
peligroso/a	dangerous
pesero	a municipal transit bus
piropo	jibe, verbal wolf-whistle
Quitos	diminutive of Marcos
reloj	watch, clock
remolque	RV or camper
ropa	clothes
sala	room
salida	exit
seguro/a	a lock, the adj. safe
semana	week
Semana Santa	Holy Week
SIDA	the Spanish acronym for AIDS
soda	a small food establishment in Costa Rica
solo carril	one-lane road or bridge
taquería/taquetería	a taco stand or vendor
tienda	store
tipo de cambio	exchange rate
torre	tower
virrey/virreina	viceroy

■■■ NOTES ABOUT LANGUAGE

Even if you speak no Spanish, a few basics will help you along. Any attempts at Spanish are appreciated and encouraged, and you'll find that many people in larger cites understand some English. You are likely to hear *indígena* languages as well as Spanish. Those who already know peninsular Spanish will find that many common nouns and expressions are different in Mexico.

Pronunciation is straightforward. Vowels are always pronounced the same way: a ("ah" in father); e ("eh" in escapade); i ("ee" in eat); o ("oh" oat); u ("oo" in boot); y, by itself, is pronounced like i. Most consonants are the same as English. Important exceptions are: j, pronounced like the English "h" in "hello"; ll, pronounced like the English "y" in "yes"; ñ, which is pronounced like the "gn" in "cognac"; rr, the trilled "r"; h is always silent; x has a bewildering variety of pronunciations.

Let's Go provides approximations for particularly tough town names. Stress in Spanish words falls on the second to last syllable, except for words ending in "r," "l" and "z," in which it falls on the last syllable. All exceptions to these rules require a written accent on the stressed syllable.

■■■ USEFUL PHRASES

No hablo español.	no AHB-loh eh-spahn-YOHL	"I don't speak Spanish."
¿Habla Usted inglés?	AHB-la oo-STED een-GLEHS?	"Do you speak English?"
¿Puede Usted ayudarme?	POOEH-deh oos-TED a-yoo-DAR-meh?	"Can you help me?"
¿Cuánto cuesta un cuarto para x personas?	KWAHN-toh KWEH-sta oon KWAHR-toh PAH-rah x PEHR-soh-nahs	"How much does a room for x person(s) cost?"
¿Dónde hay un hotel, restaurant?	DOHN-deh aie oon oh-TEL, res-taw-RAN?	"Where is there a hotel, restaurant?"
¿Dónde está el hotel x?	DOHN-deh es-TAH el oh-TEL x?	"Where is the hotel x?"

¿Puedo ver un cuarto?	"May I see a room?"
¿El cuarto tiene agua caliente, baño privado, un abanico?	"Does the room have hot water, a private bathroom, a fan?"
¿A qué hora sale el autobús a Chichicastenango?	"At what time does the bus to Chichicastenango leave?"
Hola.	"Hello."
Yo me llamo...	"My name is ..."
¿Cómo se llama Usted?	"What is your name?"
Mucho gusto conocerlo/la.	"Pleased to meet you."
¿Qué hora es?	"What time is it?"

Learn the vocabulary of courtesy as well; you'll be treated more kindly if you can be polite to those around you:

Con permiso	con pehr-MEE-so	"Excuse me", an important phrase, used more frequently than its English counterpart, whether on a crowded bus or to excuse yourself from someone's company.
¿Qué pasa?	keh PAH-sah	"What's up?"
Por favor	pohr fah-VOHR	"please"
Gracias	GRAH-seeahs	"thank you."
De nada	deh NAH-dah	"You're welcome" ("It's nothing").

Learn the numbers, if only to bargain and to reassure yourself that you're on the right bus. 1: *uno;* 2: *dos*; 3: *tres;* 4: *cuatro;* 5: *cinco;* 6: *seis;* 7: *siete;* 8: *ocho;* 9: *nueve;* 10: *diez;* 11: *once;* 12: *doce;* 13: *trece;* 14: *catorce;* 15: *quince;* 16: *dieciséis;* 17-19: *dieci*-plus the units; 20: *veinte;* 21: *veintiuno;* 30: *treinta;* 31, 32, etc.: *treinta y*-plus the units; 40; *cuarenta;* 50: *cincuenta;* 60: *sesenta;* 70: *setenta;* 80: *ochenta;* 90: *noventa;* 100: *cien;* 101, 102, etc: *ciento-* plus units; 1000: *mil;* 2000, 3000, etc.: units plus *mil.*

No offense is meant if you are called a *gringo/a* (GREEN-goh/gah). You may offend, however, if you call yourself an *americano/a*; as part of the Americas, Central and South Americans resent monopolization of the term by the U.S. Instead, refer to yourself as a *norteamericano/a*. *Güero/a* (GWEH-roh/rah, light-haired or light-skinned person) and *moreno/a* (moor-REH-noh/nah, dark-skinned person) are common forms of address among strangers in the streets. The most appropriate term for the descendants of the Maya and other groups—Native Americans, indigenous peoples, aboriginal peoples, *indígenas*—varies from country to country and person to person. *Let's Go* uses *indígena* (in-DEE-heh-nah) or indigenous; the only term that is guaranteed to be universally *offensive* is *indio*.

For those uniquely Central American situations (?), learn some basic phrases:

¡Déjame (en paz)!	"Leave me (alone)!"
¡Ayúdame!	"Help me!"
Es la hora de llamar a casa.	"It's time to call home."
Me gustaría una copa de...	"I'd like a cup of..."
Sólo hay 50 córdobas en mi cartera.	"There are only 50 córdobas in my wallet."
Me niego a sentarme encima del autobús con los pollos.	"I refuse to sit on top of the bus with the chickens."
Disfruto de mirar fijamente los árboles padres.	"I enjoy staring at cool trees."
El jugo de mango se chorrea por mi barbilla.	"The mango juice is running down my chin."

■■■ RECALIBRATION

WEIGHTS AND MEASURES

The metric system is used almost universally throughout Central America, with the exception that U.S. gallons are used to measure gasoline. Although you may encounter miscellaneous other terms for weight (including *libra*, or pound) and distance (such as the Honduran *vara*, about .8 meters), someone should be able to convert back to meters upon request.

TIME DIFFERENCE

Belize, El Salvador, Honduras, and Costa Rica are all six hours behind Greenwich Mean Time (in other words, they keepU.S. Central Time). Panama is five hours behind GMT (the same as U.S. Eastern Standard Time). Nicaragua and Guatemala both have loose versions of daylight savings, so the countries are either 5 or 6 hrs behind GMT, depending on the season. The rest of Central America does not have "daylight savings," so add an hour for this part of the year.

ELECTRICAL CURRENT

110 volts, the same as the U.S., is standard voltage in Central America. Ask first, though, as some places might have alarm-clock-melting 220 volt outlets. If you're planning to rely heavily on electricity, bring ample adapters, and converters, including one for converting three prongs to two. Many hotel rooms won't have outlets, or will have only one (which is taken by the fan).

INDEX

H

I

J

K

L

M

N